Social Psychology

FOURTH CANADIAN EDITION

Elliot Aronson
University of California, Santa Cruz

Timothy D. Wilson
University of Virginia

Robin M. Akert
Wellesley College

Beverley Fehr
University of Winnipeg

Pearson Canada
Toronto

Library and Archives Canada Cataloguing in Publication

Social psychology / Elliot Aronson . . . [et al.].—4th Canadian ed.
ISBN 978-0-13-603954-9
1. Social psychology—Textbooks. I. Aronson, Elliot
HM1033.S62 2010   302   C2009-900021-0

ISBN-13: 978-0-13-6039549
ISBN-10: 0-13-6039545

Vice-President, Editorial Director: Gary Bennett
Editor-in-Chief and Acquisitions Editor: Ky Pruesse
Executive Marketing Manager: Judith Allen
Developmental Editor: Joel Gladstone
Production Editors: Tara Tovell, Mary Ann Blair
Copy Editor: Lu Cormier
Proofreader: Tara Tovell
Production Coordinator: Janis Raisen
Compositor: Macmillan Publishing Solutions
Photo and Permissions Research: Christina Beamish
Art Director: Julia Hall
Cover and Interior Design: Miguel Acevedo
Cover Image: Getty/UpperCut Images

4 5   13 12 11

Printed and bound in United States.

To my grandchildren, Jacob, Jason, Ruth, Eliana, Natalie, Rachel, and Leo Aronson. My hope is that your wonderful capacity for empathy and compassion will help make the world a better place.

—E.A.

To my family, Deirdre Smith, and Christopher and Leigh Wilson

—T.D.W.

To my mentor, colleague, and friend, Dane Archer

—R.M.A.

To my sister, Lois Weston

—B.F.

Brief Contents

Contents

CHAPTER 4   **Social Perception: How We Come to Understand Other People   88**

CHAPTER 9   **Interpersonal Attraction: From First Impressions to Close Relationships 264**

CHAPTER 10   Prosocial Behaviour: Why Do People Help?   304

CHAPTER 11   Aggression: Why We Hurt Other People   **334**

CHAPTER 12   Prejudice: Causes and Cures   370

SOCIAL PSYCHOLOGY IN ACTION 2   Social Psychology and Health   434

SOCIAL PSYCHOLOGY IN ACTION 3   Social Psychology and the Law   466

Preface

When we began writing this book, our overriding goal was to capture the excitement of social psychology. We have been pleased to hear, in many kind letters and e-mail messages from professors and students, that we succeeded. One of our favourites was from a student who said that the book was so interesting that she always saved it for last, to reward herself for finishing her other work. With this student—and, we hope, with others—we succeeded in making our book an enjoyable, fascinating story, not a dry report of facts and figures.

The excitement of social psychology is transmitted when students understand the whole context of the field: how theories inspire research, why research is performed as it is, how further research triggers yet new avenues of study. We have tried to convey our own fascination with the research process in a down-to-earth, meaningful way and have presented the results of the scientific process in terms of the everyday experience of the reader. However, we did not want to "water down" our presentation of the field. In a world where human behaviour can be endlessly surprising and where research results can be quite counterintuitive, students need a firm foundation on which to build their understanding of this challenging discipline.

Our goal in *Social Psychology*, Fourth Canadian Edition, is to capture the excitement of social psychology for students in Canada by presenting the field in a Canadian context. In the novel *Tamarind Mem* (1996), Indo-Canadian writer Anita Rau Badami tells the story of two young girls growing up in India whose parents sought to enhance their status by emulating British ways. To keep abreast of British fashion and hair styles, their mother faithfully subscribed to an expensive British magazine. One of the daughters, Kamini, recalls that the magazine also contained a children's story that usually focused on the sandwich and ginger beer picnics of two young British girls, Nora and Tilly. Kamini comments, "I liked Nora and Tilly but wished that they had different names—Gauri and Geetha, perhaps, or Mini and Bani" (p. 24).

This quotation captures the sentiment of your Canadian author, Beverley Fehr, who taught social psychology for years using the U.S. edition of this text. Although her students always enjoyed the book, she felt that they would have been happier if the news stories, historical examples, and statistics reflected their Canadian experience. In short, she was convinced that social psychology would come alive for students in Canada when they discovered the relevance of social psychological theories and concepts to the society in which they live.

A word on the organization of this text: We have seen a lot of syllabi from social psychology courses and spoken with many colleagues who teach the course, and have been impressed by the many different ways in which the course can be taught. To accommodate the diverse ways in which instructors may choose to present topics, we have tried to create a sensible, yet flexible, organization.

Each chapter of *Social Psychology*, Fourth Canadian Edition, is self-contained in terms of topics and concepts. Consequently, instructors can assign the chapters in any order they please; concepts are always explained in clear terms so that students won't need to have read earlier chapters in order to grasp the meanings of later ones. Further, the three Social Psychology in Action modules at the end of the text may be integrated into the course at several points, or assigned at the end. However you choose to arrange your course, we are confident that this text presents a rigorous, scientific approach to social psychology in a way that is sure to engage and fascinate students in Canada. Here's why:

A Storytelling Approach

Social psychology is full of good stories, such as how the actions of Justice Peck—a 14-year-old resident of Prince George who saved a woman and her children from their burning house—can be explained, how the Holocaust inspired investigations into obedience to authority, and how reactions to the marriage of the Crown Prince of Japan to Masako Owada, a career diplomat, illustrate cultural differences in the self-concept. By placing research in a real-world context, we make the material more familiar, understandable, and memorable.

Opening Vignettes

Each chapter begins with a real-life vignette that epitomizes the concepts to come. We refer to this event at several points in the chapter to illustrate to students the relevance of the material they are learning. Examples of the opening vignettes include excerpts from Canadian author Eva Tihanyi's short story on how her Hungarian-born grandmother shaped her sense of self (Chapter 5, Self-Knowledge and the Need to Maintain Self-Esteem); the actions of Trent Fenwick, a 37-year-old resident of Kelowna, British Columbia, who donated one of his kidneys to help a Chicago man whom he had never met (Chapter 10, Prosocial Behaviour); and the case of a Vancouver man, Thomas Sophonow, who was wrongfully convicted of murder based on faulty eyewitness testimony, and endured three trials and four years in prison as a result (Social Psychology in Action 3, Social Psychology and the Law). To illustrate more specifically the way in which the opening vignettes are tied to social psychological principles, here are a few examples in more detail:

- Chapter 6, Attitudes and Attitude Change, begins with the intriguing story of the Solar Temple Cult. The leader of the cult, Luc Jouret, believed that the world was about to be destroyed by fire and that the only salvation was for followers to take a "death voyage" by ritualized suicide to the star Sirius, where they would be reborn. Jouret set up headquarters in villages in Quebec and Switzerland. The people in Quebec who joined the cult were mainly respected professionals, including the mayor of Richelieu and his wife, people in upper management positions with Hydro-Québec, a civil servant, and a journalist. In 1994, 53 people, including the mayor of Richelieu and his wife, died in fires set in buildings owned by the cult. In all, 74 deaths linked to this cult have been documented.

  Why would respected, intelligent people willingly hand over their wealth and material possessions to this charismatic leader? How could they reach the point of handing over their very lives—and in some cases, even those of their children? Cognitive dissonance theory provides insight into what would otherwise seem utterly incomprehensible human behaviour. By the end of this chapter, students will see that these behaviours are not unfathomable, but rather are an extreme manifestation of a basic human tendency—the need to justify our actions.

- In Chapter 9, Interpersonal Attraction, we draw students in by describing an incredible "love at first sight" experience in which Bradley Bird, a Winnipeg newspaper writer, fell in love with a woman from Georgia (near Russia) on a bus to Istanbul, Turkey. Despite their difficulty communicating in English, within hours, they were intensely in love. They began to make plans for Nina to come to Canada. When Nina mentioned in a letter that Bradley would need to travel to the Canadian Embassy in Turkey to plead her case, he dropped everything, including a teaching position that he had just secured, and booked himself a flight to Turkey and two tickets back to Canada. It turned out that Nina had decided to return to her husband. Bradley Bird had never known there was a husband. Although one might have expected him to become extremely bitter, Bradley maintains that he will always be thankful to Nina for giving him the happiest hours of his adult life.

  This vignette serves to raise two key questions that are addressed in Chapter 9: What exactly is love? And why are people so motivated to seek it—so motivated that they might even rearrange their lives after a chance meeting with a stranger?

- Chapter 12, Prejudice, begins by introducing Mary Young, director of the Aboriginal Student Services Centre at the University of Winnipeg. Mary was raised in Bloodvein First Nation, an Ojibway community in northern Manitoba. Growing up, she thought of herself as Anishinabe and was comfortable with that identity. It wasn't until she moved to Winnipeg, at the age of 14, with the dream of being the first person from her community to graduate from high school, that she discovered that she was perceived as "Indian." Moreover, she quickly learned that being labelled as an Indian made her the target of racism and prejudice. Mary had never expected to feel embarrassed about her cultural heritage and identity. However, hearing comments such as "the only good Indian is a dead Indian" filled her with shame and resentment that she was Native. Mary's story serves to illustrate prejudice against groups such as Canada's Native people and provides a heart-wrenching glimpse into the effects of prejudice and discrimination on their targets.

"Mini" Stories in Each Chapter

Our storytelling approach is not limited to these opening vignettes. There are several "mini" stories woven into each chapter that illustrate specific concepts and make the material come alive. They each follow a similar format: First, we describe an example of a real-life phenomenon that is designed to pique students' interest. These stories are taken from current events (mainly Canadian), literature, and our own lives. Second, we describe an experiment that attempts to explain the phenomenon. This experiment is typically described in some detail, because we believe that students should not only learn the major theories in social psychology but also understand and appreciate the methods used to test those theories. We often invite the students to pretend that they were participants in the experiment, to give them a better feel for what it was like and what was found. Here are a few examples of our mini stories (by thumbing through the book, you will come across many others):

- In Chapter 1, Introduction to Social Psychology, when discussing basic human motives, we explain how the need to feel good about ourselves can conflict with the need to be accurate. We illustrate the phenomenon of self-justification by referring to Prime Minister Stephen Harper's failure to accept responsibility for the Chuck Cadman affair, despite reports that an offer of life insurance had been made to the dying man in exchange for Cadman's vote on an issue that could have brought down the government.

- In Chapter 3, Social Cognition, we introduce the idea of schemas and discuss research showing that people will distort evidence to make it schema-consistent. We illustrate this point with a humorous anecdote from Pamela Wallin about an experience she had covering a G-7 summit hosted by Canada. CTV had managed to secure interviews with the (then) British prime minister and the West German chancellor. Ms. Wallin excitedly asked viewers to stay tuned for interviews with Margaret Thatcher and Helmut Shit. She was mortified at her mispronunciation of his name and left the studio, fully expecting that her broadcasting career was over. To her amazement, the people she ran into commented that they thought for a moment that she had mispronounced the chancellor's name, but then realized that they hadn't had their coffee yet, or the vacuum cleaner was running, and so on. . . . In short, it was so inconsistent with Canadians' schemas that Pamela Wallin would make such a slip of the tongue on the air that they disbelieved their ears and concluded that she really had said "Schmidt."

- In Chapter 7, Conformity, we discuss the classic Milgram experiment and show striking parallels between the results of that laboratory experiment and the real-world behaviour of U.S. soldiers in charge of the Abu Ghraib prison in Iraq.

- In Chapter 8, Group Processes, when introducing the concept of deindividuation, we offer classic examples such as the My Lai massacre in Vietnam and lynch mobs in the southern United States. However, we also bring this concept closer to home by describing the brutal attack on a Toronto teen, Matti Baranovski, who was approached in a park by a group of youths wearing balaclavas, bandannas, and ski goggles to conceal their identities. The injuries that resulted from this attack were so severe that Baranovski later died in hospital.

Social Psychological Methods: Another Good Story

It might seem that a storytelling approach would obscure the scientific basis of social psychology. Quite to the contrary, we believe that part of what makes the story so interesting is explaining to students how to test hypotheses

scientifically. In recent years, the trend has been for textbooks to include only short sections on research methodology and to provide only brief descriptions of the findings of individual studies. In this book, we integrate the science and methodology of the field into our story in a variety of ways.

Separate Chapter on Methodology

Unlike virtually all other texts, we devote an entire chapter to methodology (Chapter 2). "But wait," you might say, "How can you maintain students' interest and attention with an entire chapter on such dry material?" The answer is by integrating this material into our storytelling approach. Even the "dry" topic of methodology can be brought alive by telling it like a story. We set the stage by describing examples of pressing, real-world problems related to violence and aggression. For example, we open the chapter with the story of Virginie Larivière, a 13-year-old girl who was convinced that violent television programming was to blame for the brutal sexual assault and murder of her younger sister. The national publicity she garnered resulted in an investigation into the effects of violent television programming by the Standing Committee on Communications and Culture (1993). The committee interviewed people such as the chair of the CRTC and film and broadcasting executives. Their conclusion? There is little, if any, evidence that exposure to violent television programming produces violent behaviour. We contrast this report with one published by the Department of Canadian Heritage (1995) in which a social psychologist (Wendy Josephson) was commissioned to answer this question, based on an analysis of scientific studies. Her conclusion? Television violence does increase aggressive behaviour, particularly among children who are predisposed toward aggression. This example serves to illustrate the value of the scientific method in answering questions with important societal implications.

We then use actual research studies on this topic (as well as the related topic of why bystanders don't intervene to help victims of violence, as illustrated by the Kitty Genovese murder) to illustrate the three major scientific methods (observational research, correlational research, and experimental research). Rather than a dry recitation of methodological principles, the scientific method unfolds like a story with a "hook" (What are the causes of real-world aggression?) and a moral (Such interesting, real-world questions can be addressed scientifically.). We have been pleased by the reactions to this chapter in previous editions.

Detailed Descriptions of Individual Studies

We describe prototypical studies in more detail than most texts. We discuss how a study was set up, what the research participants perceived and did, how the research design derives from theoretical issues, and how the findings offer support for the initial hypotheses. As we mentioned earlier, we often ask the reader to pretend that he or she is a participant, in order to understand the study from the participants' point of view. Whenever pertinent, we've also included anecdotal information about how a study was done or came to be; these brief stories allow the reader to see the hitherto hidden world of creating research. See, for example, the description of Aronson's jigsaw puzzle technique in Chapter 12, Prejudice (pp. 411–413).

Emphasis on Classic, Modern, and Canadian Research

As you will see from flipping through the book, we include a large number of data figures detailing the results of individual experiments. The field of social psychology is expanding rapidly, and exciting new work is being done in all sub-areas of the discipline. The vast majority of the 290 new Canadian references in this edition were published in the 2000s. In addition to that, more than 300 new references from the U.S. sixth edition, upon which this fourth Canadian edition is based, were incorporated. Thus, the book includes thorough coverage of up-to-date, cutting-edge research in Canada and in the field as a whole.

In emphasizing what is new, many texts have a tendency to ignore what is old. We have striven to strike a balance between current, up-to-date research findings and classic research in social psychology. Some older studies deserve their status as classics (e.g., early work in dissonance, conformity, and attribution) and are important cornerstones of the discipline. For example, unlike several current texts, we present detailed descriptions of the Festinger and Carlsmith (1959) dissonance study (Chapter 6, Attitudes and Attitude Change), the LaPiere (1934) study on attitude–behaviour inconsistency (Chapter 6), and the Asch (1956) conformity studies (Chapter 7, Conformity). To illustrate to students how research on the classics has been updated, we follow a discussion of the classics with modern approaches to these same topics, such as research conducted at the University of Waterloo on the process of dissonance reduction in different cultures (Hoshino-Browne, Zanna, Spencer, Zanna, Kityama, & Lackenbauer, 2005, in Chapter 6). We also place the issue of attitude–behaviour inconsistency in a modern context by including a section on the implications of attitude–behaviour inconsistency for safe sex (Chapter 6). In this section, we describe studies conducted at the University of Waterloo and Queen's University (MacDonald & Martineau, 2002) and at Queen's University and York University (Hynie, MacDonald, & Marques, 2006), among others, that provide insight into why people report positive attitudes toward condoms, yet fail to use them. In Chapter 7, we follow Milgram's classic obedience studies with recent research conducted at the University of British Columbia, identifying conditions under which people do not obey authority figures (Conway & Schaller, 2005). This way, students see the continuity and depth of the field, rather than viewing it only as a mass of studies published in the past few years.

As these examples illustrate, the inclusion of Canadian research is not gratuitous. We highlight how current Canadian research builds on classic contributions to social psychology (Canadian and non-Canadian alike) and showcase the role of Canadian research in moving the field forward. Perhaps most importantly, this coverage does not come at the expense of omitting other important classic and modern contributions made by non-Canadian researchers.

A Canadian Context

Canadian research and cultural examples are integrated throughout the text to provide a familiar context and comfortable learning environment for Canadian students. Here is just a partial listing of the rich Canadian content you will find woven into every chapter of *Social Psychology*, Fourth Canadian Edition:

Chapter 1, Introduction: Opening vignette contains stories taken from across the country that act as springboards for the social psychological investigation: Altruism is introduced with accounts of the great lengths to which Canadians went to provide assistance following the December 2004 tsunami disaster in Asia. One example is the story of Greg Baytalan, a 46-year-old Kelowna man who cut short his vacation in Australia to fly to Thailand and assist in the gruesome task of transporting bodies to a morgue. The story of Jean-François Caudron and his university hockey team's hazing rituals exemplifies suffering and self-justification, and the tragic story of the Order of the Solar Temple cult points to a later discussion of our need to justify our actions. The example of the David Milgaard–Larry Fisher case illustrates what can go wrong in the legal process; the story of Dee Brasseur shows a woman forced to retire from the military because of continual sexual harassment, yet still defending the institution. In a discussion of basic human motives, the chapter presents research on the lengths that people go to in order to reduce the terror associated with the realization of mortality. Research presented includes a University of British Columbia study showing that when people are reminded of their mortality (e.g., by writing about what it will feel like to die) they report stronger beliefs in God and other supernatural agents (Norenzayan & Hansen, 2006). Similarly, at York University, recent research has shown that mortality salience causes some people to hold political and other personal beliefs with greater zeal (McGregor, Gaillot, Vasquez, & Nash, 2007).

The issue of whether fear appeals are persuasive in getting people to change their behaviour is also introduced, including recent research in which the effects of warning messages on cigarette packages in Canada, the United Kingdom, Australia and the United States were compared. It was concluded that Canada's large, graphic warnings were the most effective (Hammond, Fong, Borland, Cummings, McNeill, & Driezen, 2007).

Chapter 2, Methodology: Opening vignette discusses Virginie Larivière, a 13-year-old Quebec girl who became an activist against violence on television after the murder of her younger sister, prompting a government committee to publish a report on the effects of TV violence, in contrast to another government report that reached the opposite conclusion. Research includes studies out of York University by Debra Pepler and Wendy Craig (Queen's University) and colleagues, which demonstrate methods of observing bullying in school playgrounds and how the product of these observations has resulted in bullying interventions (Atlas & Pepler, 1998; Craig & Pepler, 1997; Pepler et al., 2004; Smith, Pepler, & Rigby, 2004); studies conducted at the University of Manitoba (Morry & Staska, 2001; Nowatzki & Morry, in press) and at York University (Spizter, Henderson, & Zivian, 1999) on ideal male and female body images; and research with French-Canadian university students showing that the correlation between having positive attitudes toward condoms and actually using them is disturbingly low (Hébert et al., 1989). The story of "Tillie the Rainmaker" shows the difference between correlation and causation. There is an expanded section on cross-cultural research, which includes a discussion of the pitfalls of applying research methods developed in one culture to another culture. For example, University of British Columbia researchers recently discovered that people of East Asian heritage are more likely to endorse the mid-points of scales whereas people of European Canadian heritage are more likely to endorse the end-points (i.e., make more extreme ratings; Hamamura , Heine, & Paulhus, 2007). The chapter ends with a table presenting the Canadian Psychological Association's ethical principles in the conduct of research.

Chapter 3, Social Cognition: Opening vignette focuses on the story of Kevin Chappell, an Ottawa man who is unable to perceive objects due to a brain injury. This story illustrates the usefulness of schemas in navigating through the physical and social world and how difficult it would be to function without them. The chapter also contains a Brandon University study on memory for schema-consistent information. Specifically, Corenblum (2003) found that both Euro-Canadian and Native Canadian children were more likely to remember positive behaviours performed by a white child than by a Native child. A section on stereotypes (schemas) about race and weapons includes a study by researchers at the University

of British Columbia showing that the negative stereotype of blacks—particularly traits relevant to danger (e.g., crime)—came to mind more quickly for participants who were seated in a dark room than for participants who were seated in a brightly lit room (Schaller, Park, & Mueller, 2003). The chapter also discusses numerous Canadian studies on counter-factual thinking (e.g., White & Lehman, 2005, at the University of British Columbia; Mandel & Dhami, 2005, at Defense Research and Development Canada and at City University in the United Kingdom; Miller & McFarland, 1986, at Simon Fraser University; Roese & Olson, 1997, at the University of Western Ontario).

Chapter 4, Social Perception: Studies conducted at the Université de Québec à Montréal show that we automatically mimic other people's facial expressions, such as happiness, sadness, disgust, and sadness (Bourgeois & Hess, 2008; Hess & Blairy, 2001). The possibility that mirror neurons are involved in the capacity to experience others' emotions is discussed. The story of Nadia Hama, the B.C. woman who was suspected of dropping her baby off of the Capilano suspension bridge, demonstrates attributions. Numerous Canadian studies show how the fundamental attribution error can lead to blaming victims for their plight (Mantler, Schellenberg, & Page, 2003; Menec & Perry, 1998,at the University of Windsor and the University of Manitoba; Rotenberg, 1998, Lakehead University; Lawson, 2003, using a sample of university employees and physicians across Canada; Perrott, Miller, & Delaney, 1997; Perrott & Webber, 1996, at Mount Saint Vincent University; Kristiansen & Giulietti, 1990, at Carleton University; Hafer, 2000a, 2000b, 2002, at Brock University), and a Connections box features victim blaming in the Canadian legal system, with references to the Honourable Madame Justice L'Heureux-Dubé (2001) and Kwong-leung Tang (2000). Other research includes numerous Canadian studies on unrealistic optimism in romantic relationships (e.g., Gagné & Lydon, 2001, Gagné, Lydon, & Bartz, 2003, at McGill University; MacDonald & Ross, 1999, at the University of Waterloo; Murray & Holmes, 1997, at the University of Waterloo); a cross-cultural study of Canadian and Japanese students by Heine and Lehman (1995) showing that unrealistic optimism may not be a universal phenomenon; and several Canadian studies on just world beliefs (Callan, Ellard, & Nicol, 2006, University of Calgary; Hafer, 2000b, 2002; Hafer & Bègue, 2005, Brock University).

Chapter 5, Self-Knowledge and the Need to Maintain Self-Esteem: The Try It! box "A Measure of Self-Concept Clarity" is based on a scale developed by Campbell, Trapnell, Heine, Katz, Lavallee, and Lehman (1996) at the University of British Columbia. Research includes cross-cultural studies on cultural differences in self-conceptions (Anthony, Holmes, & Wood, 2007, University of Waterloo; David Watkins, University of Hong Kong; John Adair, University of Manitoba; and researchers from many other countries, including Watkins, Adair et al., 1998 and Watkins, Akande et al., 1998) a study by University of British Columbia researchers on alleviating the discomfort of aversive self-awareness (Moskalenko & Heine, 2003); and numerous Canadian studies on intrinsic and extrinsic motivation in a variety of domains (Bailis & Segall, 2004; Knee, Lonsbary, Canevello, & Patrick, 2005; Pelletier, Fortier, Vallerand, & Brière, 1996; Vallerand & Ratelle, 2002; Green-Demers, Pelletier, Stewart, & Gushue, 1998; Losier and Koestner, 1999; Koestner & Losier, 2002). Studies by Baldwin and Holmes (1987) and Baldwin, Carell, and Lopez (1990) at the University of Waterloo show how priming significant relationships affects one's momentary sense of self; and studies by Lockwood and Kunda (1997, 1999, 2000; Lockwood, 2002; Lockwood, Sadler, Fyman, & Tuck, 2004; Pinkus, Lockwood, Schimmack, & Fornier, 2008) at the University of Toronto and the University of Waterloo examine the effects of social comparison on the self. The chapter also includes studies by Wilson and Ross (2000, 2001, Ross & Wilson, 2002), at Wilfrid Laurier University and the University of Waterloo, on people's appraisals of earlier and current selves. This chapter also includes numerous studies by Heine and colleagues (Heine, 2001, 2003; Heine & Hamamura, 2007; Heine & Renshaw, 2002; Heine, Kitayama, & Lehman, 2001; Heine, Takata, & Lehman, 2000; White & Lehman, 2005b; Ross, Heine, Wilson, & Sugimori, 2005) on self-enhancement in Canadian and Asian students, as well as University of Waterloo research on activation of bicultural selves among Chinese-Canadian students (Ross, Xun, & Wilson, 2002).

Chapter 6, Attitudes and Attitude Change: Research includes numerous studies on attitudes by Haddock and Zanna at the University of Waterloo and Esses at the University of Western Ontario (Esses, Haddock, & Zanna, 1993; Haddock, Zanna, & Esses, 1993; Haddock & Zanna, 1994, 1998; Haddock, Zanna, & Esses, 1994); research by Bell and Esses (2002) and Newby-Clark, McGregor, and Zanna (2002) on attitudinal ambivalence; and a study by Hafer, Reynolds, and Obertynski (1996) on whether people are swayed by peripheral cues when issues are described using complicated, jargon-laden language. A section on the theory of planned behaviour as applied to condom use highlights many Canadian contributions (e.g., Hynie, MacDonald, & Marques, 2006; MacDonald, Fong, Zanna, & Martineau, 2000; MacDonald & Martineau, 2002; Maticka-Tyndale, Herold, & Mewhinney, 2001). Additional research includes a study by researchers at Concordia University and McGill University on fear and attitude change (Conway & Dubé, 2002); research out of the University of Waterloo on using subliminal messages to change attitudes (Strahan, Spencer,

& Zanna, 2002); a study by Bernard, Maio, and Olson (2003) on resisting persuasion attempts; the example of the Somalia scandal used to illustrate how people use dissonance to justify cruel actions toward others; a new section describing recent research on product placement, showing that people are persuaded by strategically placed products in movies and television shows; and research on cognitive dissonance and culture (Heine & Lehman, 1997a; Hoshino-Browne, Zanna, Spencer, Zanna, Kitayama, & Lackenbauer, 2005).

Chapter 7, Conformity: Opening vignette on the need to conform features the story of the vicious beating and murder of B.C. teenager Reena Virk. Research includes a study by Vorauer and Miller (1997) at the University of Manitoba on conformity by students exposed to other students' negative or positive self-evaluations; recent research on Vancouver's "toxic bus" case (May 2004) suggesting that the mysterious symptoms experienced by people on the bus that day constitute a modern-day case of mass psychogenic illness; a figure and studies out of the University of Waterloo (Griffin & Buehler, 1993; Buehler & Griffin, 1994) on construal processes following the decision to conform or dissent; the case of a Canadian soldier who complained publicly about an out-of-date Anthrax vaccine he was given during the Gulf War, and who was consequently silenced and assigned menial tasks as punishment for his nonconformity; a University of Toronto study on the reluctance to express minority opinions (Bassili, 2003); recent research using fMRI technology to provide biological evidence of the discomfort of nonconformity (Berns, Chappelow, Zink, Pagnoni, Martin-Skurski, & Richards, 2005); and a study out of the University of British Columbia by Campbell and Fairey (1989) suggesting that the effects of group size depend on the kind of social influence that is operating. The chapter also includes Guimond's (1999) study of informational versus social influence among Canadian military college students and a University of Western Ontario study on heightened conformity in response to ridicule (Janes & Olson, 2000). The conformity pressures experienced by bicultural minority students are explored in a study conducted at the University of Toronto by Tafarodi, Kang, and Milne (2002). There is a new Connections section on how conformity influences the songs that people download from internet sites. The chapter ends with recent work by Canadian researchers focusing on those who refuse to obey in obedience studies and the factors that underlie disobedience (Conway & Schaller, 2005; Packer, 2008).

Chapter 8, Group Processes: Opening vignette on faulty group decision making tells the story of allegedly unsafe vaccines given to Canadian military personnel. A study by Cooper, Gallupe, Pollard, and Cadsby (1998) at Queen's University looks at anonymity and idea generation. The example of the murder of Toronto teen Matti

Baranovski, in which some of his assailants wore disguises, illustrates deindividuation. Other research includes a study by James Cameron (1999) at Mount Allison University suggesting that the groups to which we belong play an important role in defining who we expect to be in the future; and recent research showing that even high performing individuals do better when working on problems in groups versus alone (Laughlin, Hatch, Silver & Boh, 2006). The chapter also contains research on personality correlates of leadership by Suedfeld and colleagues at the University of British Columbia (Suedfeld, Conway, & Eichorn, 2001) and by Bradley, Nicol, Charbonneau, and Meyer (2002). The Meech Lake Accord failure, and more recently, then U.S. President George W. Bush's decision to invade Iraq in 2003 are used as examples of groupthink. The chapter also includes research by Vorauer and Claude (1998) on negotiations, showing that the assumption that our goals are obvious to everyone is not necessarily warranted, and a recent meta analysis showing that electronic discussions lead to less trust and cooperation than face-to-face negotiations (Stuhlmacher & Citera, 2005). Recent research on cultural differences in cooperation also is presented (Wong & Hong, 2005).

Chapter 9, Interpersonal Attraction: This chapter begins with a University of Calgary study on the risks associated with intimate relationships (Boon & Pasveer, 1999) and highlights a new section on the development of relationships online and research conducted at various Canadian universities on how ordinary people define love (Button & Collier, 1991; Fehr, 1988, 2006; Fehr & Russell, 1991). The attachment theory perspective on close relationships is discussed, including studies on attachment and relationship satisfaction (Keelan, Dion, & Dion, 1994, at the University of Toronto), coping strategies (Lussier, Sabourin, & Turgeon, 1997), interpersonal expectations (Baldwin, Fehr, Keedian, Siedel, & Thomson, 1993), conflict (Campbell, Simpson, Boldry, & Kashy, 2005), and reactions to breakups (Sprecher, Felmlee, Metts, Fehr, & Vanni, 1998). The chapter also addresses the conceptualization of avoidant attachment by Bartholomew (1990) and Bartholomew and Horowitz (1991); research by Baldwin and Fehr and colleagues on the instability of attachment styles and a reconceptualization of attachment styles as schemas (Baldwin & Fehr, 1995; Baldwin, Fehr, Keedian, Seidel, & Thomson, 1993; Baldwin, Keedian, & Fehr, 1996); as well as recent research on general versus relationship-specific attachment (Fraley, 2002; Pierce & Lydon, 2001; Ross & Spinner, 2001; Simpson, Rholes, Campbell, & Wilson, 2003). The chapter features extensive research out of McGill University on commitment processes by Lydon and colleagues, focusing on the role of adversity in maintaining relationships (Lydon, 1999; Lydon, Fitzsimons, & Naidoo, 2003; Lydon, Menzies-Tolman, Burton, & Bell, 2008; Lydon & Zanna, 1990); research by Murray and Holmes and colleagues at the

University of Waterloo (Murray & Holmes, 1993, 1997, 1999; Murray, Holmes, Bellavia, Griffin, & Dolderman, 2002; Murray, Holmes, & Griffin, 1996a, 1996b; Murray, Holmes, Dolderman, & Griffin, 2000), and by Gagné and Lydon (2003; McGill University) on the role of positive illusions in romantic relationships; and a new section featuring recent research on boredom in relationships (Harasymchuk, 2008; Harasymchuk & Fehr, 2007, 2008).

Chapter 10, Prosocial Behaviour: Opening vignette of a Winnipeg man who was viciously attacked when he intervened to protect a woman who was being harassed by a panhandler while bystanders did nothing introduces the concepts of altruism and bystander non-intervention. Recent research focuses on the relation between helping and feeling part of a community (Oishi, Rothman, Snyder, Su, Zehm, Hertel, Gonzalez, & Sherman, 2007; Twenge, Baumeister, DeWall, Clarocco, & Bartles, 2007). Research includes Roberts and Strayer's (1996) study conducted with children in British Columbia, finding that empathy is related to helping even among children as young as five; Pancer and Pratt's (1999) research on volunteering among Canadian youth; and a study by James McDonald and Stuart McKelvie (1992) at Bishop's University on embarrassment and prosocial behaviour. Recent research looks at helping in communal versus exchange relationships (Clark & Monin, 2006; LeMay, Clark & Feeney, 2007); Brown and Moore's (2000) evolutionary analysis of prosocial behaviour; and research on cultural differences in altruism (Fu, Lee, Cameron, & Xu, 2001; Lee, Cameron, Xu, Fu, & Board, 1997; McCrae, Yik, Trapnell, Bond, & Paulhus, 1997).

Chapter 11, Aggression: This chapter features a number of studies by Pihl and colleagues at McGill University on alcohol and aggression (Hoaken & Pihl, 2000; Pihl & Hoaken, 2002; Pihl & Peterson, 1995; Pihl, Young, Harden, Plotnick, Chamberlain, & Ervin, 1995). Research on the culture of honour includes studies by Graham and colleagues on alcohol and aggression in various Ontario bars (Graham & Wells, 2001a, 2001b; Graham, West & Wells, 2000; Wells, Graham & West, 2000) as well as recent research on baseball players being more likely to be hit by pitchers from the U.S. south (Timmerman, 2007). The chapter also features studies on relative deprivation (with students at McGill University, Wright, Taylor, & Moghaddam, 1990; and with Canadian policewomen, Tougas, Rinfret, Beaton, and De la Sablonniére, 2005); a study by Van Oostrum and Horvath (1997) on aggression and the attribution of hostile intentions; research by Josephson (1987) finding that violent television programming increases aggression among those who are predisposed toward aggression; and research on gender differences in physical aggression, including a new table featuring research on gender differences in violence against dating partners conducted in 16 countries, including Canada (Straus, 2004); and University of Manitoba research by Neil Malamuth and James Check (1981) on the effects of watching sexual violence in movies on men's attitudes toward violence against women. The chapter features recent research on the relation between social exclusion and aggression (Twenge, Baumeister, Tice, & Stucke, 2001; Baumeister, DeWall, Ciarocco, & Twenge, 2005), including a study showing that people are motivated to form new social bonds after experiences of social exclusion (Maner, DeWall, Baumeister, & Schaller, 2007).

Chapter 12, Prejudice: The Try It! exercise "Multiculturalism: Is It Working?" examines Canada's multiculturalism policy in light of research by Osbeck, Moghaddam, and Perreault (1997). Research includes numerous studies out of Brandon University by Corenblum and colleagues on white Canadians' attitudes toward Native Canadians, and vice-versa (Corenblum & Annis, 1993; Corenblum, Annis, & Young, 1996; Corenblum & Stephan, 2001); and studies by Esses at the University of Western Ontario and Zanna at the University of Waterloo and their colleagues on emotions, cognitions, and behaviour as predictors of prejudice toward stigmatized groups (Esses & Dovidio, 2002; Esses & Zanna, 1995; Esses, Haddock, & Zanna, 1993; Esses, Dovidio, Jackson, & Armstrong, 2001; Esses, Wagner, & Wolf, 2006; Haddock, Zanna, & Esses, 1993, 1994; see also University of Manitoba study by Mohipp & Morry, 2004). The chapter also includes research by Peter Grant (1992, 1993) showing that discrimination against out-groups is more likely when a person's sense of social identity is threatened; research on how prejudice can be reduced by manipulating social identity (e.g., reminding people of the superordinate groups to which they belong; Esses, Wagner, & Wolf, 2006; Levin, Prosser, Evans, & Reicher, 2005; Wohl & Branscombe, 2005; Van Bavel & Cunningham, 2007); research conducted by Mark Schaller at the University of British Columbia on the origins of stereotype content (Schaller & Conway, 1999, 2001, 2005; Schaller & O'Brien, 1992; Schaller, Conway, & Tanchuk, 2002); research by Lisa Sinclair and colleagues on the selective activation of stereotypes as a function of self-enhancement goals (Sinclair & Kunda, 1999; Livingston & Sinclair, 2008); a series of studies on meta-stereotypes conducted at the University of Manitoba by Vorauer and colleagues (Vorauer, 2003; Vorauer & Kumhyr, 2001; Vorauer & Turpie, 2004; Vorauer, Main, & O'Connell, 1998; Vorauer, Hunter, Main, & Roy, 2000) showing that our attitudes toward out-groups are determined, in part, by the stereotype we believe they hold of us; extensive research by Altemeyer at the University of Manitoba (1981, 1988, 1996, 2001) on right-wing authoritarianism and prejudice; and recent research conducted at the University of Manitoba on "choking" under the pressure of interacting with members of stigmatized groups (Vorauer, 2005; Vorauer & Sakamoto, 2006). The effects of prejudice on its targets are also examined, including recent Canadian

research on stereotype threat (e.g., Davies, Spencer, & Claude, 2005; Davies, Spencer, Quinn, & Gerhardsteine, 2002; Davies, Spencer, & Steele, 2005; Dar-Nimrod & Heine, 2006; Steele & Ambady, 2006), as well as research on self-blaming attributions for discrimination by Ruggiero and Taylor (1995, 1997), Dion (2001), Dion and Kawakami (1996), Taylor, Wright, Moghaddam, and Lalonde (1990), Foster and Matheson (1999), Foster and Tsarfati (2005), Quinn, Roese, Pennington, and Olson (1999), and Hodson & Esses (2002). The chapter ends with research by Simon Fraser University social psychologist Steve Wright and colleagues, demonstrating the value of cross-group friendships in reducing prejudice and discrimination (Brody, Wright, Aron, McLaughlin-Volpe, 2009; McLaughlin-Volpe, Aron, Wright, & Reis, 2000; Wright, Brody & Aron, 2005; Wright & Van Der Zande, 1999; Wright, Aron, McLaughlin, & Ropp, 1997).

Social Psychology in Action 1, Social Psychology and the Environment: The module opens with the negative environmental and health consequences of Alberta's tar sands (Nikiforuk, 2008), as well as other research on the effects of toxic waste sites on well-being, including Nova Scotia's tar ponds (O'Leary & Covell, 2002) and landfill sites in Ontario (Wakefield & Elliott, 2000). The module includes a new section reviewing the experimental method and showing how it can be used to evaluate the effectiveness of psychological interventions. Research on sustaining the environment is presented, including studies on predictors of recycling in various Ontario communities (Pelletier, Dion, Tuson, & Green-Demers, 1999; Scott, 1999); McKenzie-Mohr, Nemiroff, Beers, and Desmarais's (1995) study showing that B.C. residents' environmental and cost-saving concerns predicted the use of energy-saving devices such as compact fluorescent bulbs and programmable thermostats; and studies on recycling in Edmonton (Wall, 1995) and communities in the Greater Toronto Area (Scott, 1999). The findings of a 1991 Statistics Canada survey on the environment (Berger, 1997) demonstrate that people are much more likely to participate in proenvironmental programs if they are made convenient. Research is presented on another strategy for promoting environmentally sustainable behaviours—namely, the use of descriptive and injunctive norms. For example, recent research by Cialdini and colleagues shows that descriptive norms can be used to encourage hotel patrons to re-use their towels (Goldstein, Cialdini, & Griskevicius (2008).

Social Psychology in Action 2, Social Psychology and Health: Opening vignette looks at Manitoba senior Elvira Toews, who manages to maintain an optimistic outlook on life despite daunting personal tragedies. Research includes a study on the benefits of perceived control and rape victims (Regehr, Cadell, & Jansen, 1999); studies on coping with traumatic events such as the Holocaust (Sigal & Weinfeld, 2001) or the residential school experiences of First Nations people (Hanson & Hampton,

2000); longitudinal research by the Canadian Aging Research Network on the benefits of perceived control and aging (Chipperfield, Perry, & Menec, 1999; Menec, Chipperfiled, & Perry, 1999; Menec & Chipperfield, 1997), as well as new research on perceived control and academic achievement (Perry, 2003; Perry, Hladkyj, Pekrun, & Pelletier, 2001); Allison, Dwyer, and Makin's (1999) study of Toronto high-school students on exercise and self-efficacy; and recent Canadian studies on strategies for increasing self-efficacy (Koestner, Horberg, Gaudreau, Powers, Dio, Bryan, 2006; Vasquez & Buehler, 2007). The module also includes research on gender difference in stress and social support-seeking (Day & Livingstone, 2003; Matud, 2004; Tamres, Janicki, & Helgeson, 2002) as well as research on the effectiveness of social support in dealing with stress (Lefrançois, Leclerc, Hamel, & Gaulin, 2000; Marin, Holtzman, DeLongis, & Robinson, 2007; Stewart, Craig, MacPherson, & Alexander, 2001; Yum & Schenck-Hamlin, 2005). The module ends with research on strategies for coaxing people into performing health-enhancing behaviours (e.g., using cognitive dissonance, message framing).

Social Psychology in Action 3, Social Psychology and the Law: Opening vignette on Thomas Sophonow's wrongful conviction for the murder of a Winnipeg teen forms a running thread through the entire module, illustrating the psychological concepts involved in wrongful conviction. The many hazards of relying on eyewitness testimony are documented, including studies by Yarmey et al. (1996) and Tollestrup et al. (1994), finding that the longer the time that elapses between seeing a suspect and being asked to identify the person from a lineup, the greater is the likelihood of error; research conducted at York University (Schuller & Paglia, 1999) and at Simon Fraser University (Rose & Ogloff, 2001) on jurors' understanding of judges' instructions; and recent Canadian studies on the detection of deception (Cullen & Bradley, 2004), including a study finding that Canadian federal parole officers are no better at detecting deception than university students (Porter, Woodworth, & Birt, 2000). Researchers at Dalhousie University and at Grant MacEwan College have taken a first step in trying to disentangle truthful versus fabricated reports of traumatic experiences (Porter, Peace, & Emmett, 2007). The module also includes research on own-race bias (the tendency to recognize members of one's own race more accurately than members of other races; Meissner & Brigham, 2001b; Sangrigoli, Argenti, Ventureyra, & Sehonen, 2005), including a Brandon University study by Corenblum and Meissner (2006) showing that this bias emerges at an early age. Various perspectives (from judges, lawyers, and psychologists) are presented on the debate over the value of expert testimony in the courtroom (Peters, 2001; Saunders, 2001; Yarmey, 2001a). The module describes programs that social psychologists are developing to instruct jurors and judges on the

pitfalls of relying on eyewitness testimony and suggestions for how best to question witnesses to a crime (Cynkar, 2007). There is a new section on interrogation techniques and how they can elicit false confessions.

Integrated Coverage of Culture and Gender

To understand behaviour in a social context, we must consider such influences as culture and gender. Rather than adding a chapter on these important topics, we discuss them in every chapter, as they apply to the topic at hand. In many places, we discuss the wonderful diversity of humankind, by presenting research on the differences between people of different cultures, races, or genders. We also discuss the commonalities people share, by illustrating the applicability of many phenomena across cultures, races, and genders. Here are examples:

- Chapter 1, Introduction: The issue of universality versus the cultural relativity of social psychological principles is introduced.

- Chapter 2, Methodology: The issue of how to generalize the results of studies across different types of people is discussed in the section on external validity. In addition, we discuss issues involved in conducting cross-cultural research.

- Chapter 3, Social Cognition: The chapter touches on the issue of gender differences and achievement (e.g., girls' math performance), raising the question of whether these differences are due to the expectations about gender held by teachers and parents. There is also a section on the cultural determinants of schemas that discusses classic work by Bartlett.

- Chapter 4, Social Perception: This chapter includes a good deal of material on culture and gender, with a discussion of controversy over the universality of facial expressions of emotion; cultural differences in other channels of nonverbal communication, such as eye contact, gaze, and personal space; cultural variation in implicit personality theories; and cultural differences in attribution processes. The chapter also includes a new section on gender and nonverbal communication and, in the section on attributions, examines how the gender of the victim influences victim-blaming attributions.

- Chapter 5, Self-Knowledge and the Need to Maintain Self-Esteem: A major focus of this chapter is cultural differences in self-conceptions and self-evaluations, featuring research by Heine, Lehman, Markus, Kitayama, and others. There is also a section on gender differences in the definition of the self. These lines of inquiry are integrated in research by Adair,

Watkins, and colleagues that examines gender differences in the definition of the self in different cultures.

■ Chapter 6, Attitudes and Attitude Change: This chapter includes a section on culture and the basis of attitudes. We also present research on effectiveness of different kinds of advertisements (e.g., in Korea and the United States in Han & Shavitt, 1994). In the context of a discussion of the effects of advertising, we consider ways in which the media can transmit cultural stereotypes about race and gender. When discussing cognitive dissonance theory, we describe many studies on cultural differences in cognitive dissonance and dissonance reduction, including a recent study by Hoshino-Browne and colleagues (2005) showing that people from Asian cultures experience dissonance only when making decisions for a close other, whereas Canadians experience dissonance only when making decisions for the self. We also include a section on cultural differences in dissonance and self-affirmation.

■ Chapter 7, Conformity: This chapter includes a discussion of the role of normative social influence in creating and maintaining cultural standards of beauty. We also discuss gender and cultural differences in conformity and a meta analysis by Bond and Smith (1996) comparing conformity on the Asch line task in 17 countries.

■ Chapter 8, Group Processes: We discuss research on gender and culture at several points in this chapter, including gender and cultural differences in social loafing and in leadership styles. In addition, we discuss social roles and gender and include a student exercise in which students are asked to deliberately violate a gender role and keep a journal of people's responses to them.

■ Chapter 9, Interpersonal Attraction: The role of culture comes up at several points in this chapter, including sections on cultural standards of beauty and comparisons between Canada, the United States, and Korea in the "what is beautiful is good" stereotype (Wheeler & Kim, 1997). We also discuss cultural and gender differences in the effects of physical attractiveness on liking, conceptions of love, and reactions to the dissolution of relationships.

■ Chapter 10, Prosocial Behaviour: In this chapter we include a section on gender differences in prosocial behaviour and a section on cultural differences in prosocial behaviour (e.g., comparisons between Canada and Asian countries; McCrae et al., 1998; Lee et al., 1997).

■ Chapter 11, Aggression: There is a major section in this chapter on cultural differences in aggression, including a discussion of differences in homicide rates in different countries. We also discuss research on gender differences in aggression and the effects of

violent pornography on violence against women. A Try It! student exercise focuses on gender differences in spousal violence.

■ Chapter 12, Prejudice: Issues about in-groups and out-groups and ways of reducing prejudice are central to this chapter. For example, we present research on stereotype threat, including U.S. and Canadian studies on achievement in minority groups and in men versus women. We also discuss research by Sinclair and Kunda (1999, 2000) on motivational factors underlying the activation of racial and gender stereotypes. In addition, a Try It! exercise prompts students to evaluate Canada's multiculturalism policy in light of social psychological findings.

■ Social Psychology in Action modules on Environment, Health, and Law: These modules include numerous discussions relevant to culture and gender. For example, in the health module, we discuss research on cultural differences in the Type A personality as well as gender and cultural differences in social support. And in the law module, we compare crime rates in countries (and states) that use capital punishment with crime rates in regions that do not invoke the death penalty.

The Social Psychology of Terrorism

The fear of terrorism has intensified significantly in people's lives since the attacks on the World Trade Center in New York on September 11, 2001, so we have added new coverage of the social psychology of terrorism. We use recent examples of terrorism (e.g., the World Trade Center attacks, the London subway bombings) to illustrate social psychological concepts such as the automatic activation of stereotypes.

We also present empirical research on terrorism in several places in this book. For example, when discussing the empathy–altruism hypothesis (Chapter 10, Prosocial Behaviour), we describe a study by Piferi and colleagues (2006) showing that people who were high in empathy reported providing more help (e.g., donating money, giving blood) both immediately after September 11 and one year later, compared with those who were low in empathy. In the section on social categorization (Chapter 12, Prejudice), we cite a study by Dumont, Yzerbyt, Wigboldus, and Gordjin (2003) showing that one week after the New York terrorist attacks, Europeans felt more fearful, but also were more willing to extend help, if their identity as Westerners (i.e., Americans would be considered part of the in-group) was made salient rather than their identity as Europeans (i.e., Americans would be considered part of the out-group). In the Social Psychology in Action module on health, we present research on psychological and physical problems experienced by people affected by the terrorist attacks of September 11, 2001 (Lampert, Baron, McPherson, & Lee, 2002; Schlenger, Caddell, Ebert, Jordan, Rourke, Wilson et al., 2002; Silver, Holman, McIntosh, Poulin, & Gil-Rivas, 2002). We also examine the role of resilience in helping Americans cope with the September 11 attacks (Fredrickson, Waugh, & Tugade, 2003), including recent research showing that people are able to "bounce back" fairly quickly from traumatic events such as terrorist attacks (Bonanno, 2004, 2005; Tucker, Pfefferbaum, Doughty, Jones, Jordan, & Nixon, 2002). We also present recent research on the role of social support (i.e., talking with others) in coping with terrorist attacks (Yum & Schenck-Hamlin, 2005). This material illustrates how social psychological research addresses pressing, current real-world issues.

The Evolutionary Approach

In recent years, social psychologists have become increasingly interested in an evolutionary perspective on many aspects of social behaviour. Once again, our approach is to integrate this perspective into those parts of chapters where it is relevant, rather than devote a separate chapter to this topic. We present what we believe is a balanced approach, discussing evolutionary psychology as well as alternatives to it. Here are examples of places in which we discuss the evolutionary approach:

- Chapter 1, Introduction: We introduce the evolutionary perspective in this chapter. We also recommend Crawford and Kreb's (1998) *Handbook of Evolutionary Psychology* in the reading list as a resource for students who wish to learn more about this theory.

- Chapter 4, Social Perception: We discuss the controversy over whether some facial expressions are universal, including Darwin's view that they are.

- Chapter 8, Group Processes: We discuss whether we have inherited the need to belong from our evolutionary past.

- Chapter 9, Interpersonal Attraction: We present the evolutionary perspective on gender differences in romantic attraction and on why people fall in love. A new Connections section presents recent research conducted from an evolutionary perspective, showing that women can tell whether a man is interested in casual sex or a long-term relationship simply by looking at his face (Boothroyd, Jones, Burt, DeBruine, & Perrett, 2008).

- Chapter 10, Prosocial Behaviour: Evolutionary psychology is presented as one of the major theories of

why humans engage in prosocial behaviour. We present evidence for and against this perspective and contrast it to other approaches, such as social exchange theory.

- Chapter 11, Aggression: We include a section on whether aggression is inborn or learned, including a discussion of an evolutionary explanation of aggressive behaviour.

- Chapter 12, Prejudice: We touch on the issue of whether there might be an evolutionary basis for prejudice.

Social Psychology: The Applied Side

One of the best ways to capture students' interest is to point out the real-world significance of the material they are studying. From the vignette that opens each chapter and runs throughout it to the discussions of historical events, current affairs, and our own lives that are embedded in the story line, the narrative is highlighted by real, familiar examples. Applications are an integral part of social psychology, however, and deserve their own treatment. In addition to an integrated coverage of applied topics in the body of the text, we include additional coverage in three ways.

Connections

Special sections called Connections highlight issues that are particularly relevant to interesting and important problems in everyday life. For example, Chapter 4, Social Perception, includes a Connections section on victim blaming in the Canadian legal system. We also include a new Connections section examining the accuracy of portraying emotions over the internet versus face to face. In Chapter 6, Attitudes and Attitude Change, the use of counter-attitudinal advocacy to solve social problems such as racism or the spread of AIDS is considered. As mentioned above, in Chapter 9, Interpersonal Attraction, we present new research showing that people's faces reveal whether they are interested in casual sex or a long-term relationship. In Chapter 12, Prejudice, we look at whether social categorization affects a person's reaction to terrorism. We believe that students will appreciate these links to important social issues.

Try It! Student Exercises

In each chapter, we feature a series of Try It! exercises, in which students are invited to apply the concepts they are learning to their everyday life. These exercises include detailed instructions about how to attempt to replicate actual social psychological experiments, such as

Milgram's (1963) lost letter technique in Chapter 10, Prosocial Behaviour, and Reno and colleagues' (1993) study on norms and littering in Social Psychology in Action 1, Social Psychology and the Environment. Other Try It! exercises reproduce self-report scales and invite the students to fill them out to see where they stand on these measures. Examples include Campbell and colleagues' (1996) measure of self-concept clarity in Chapter 5, Self-Knowledge and the Need to Maintain Self-Esteem; the Passionate Love Scale in Chapter 9, Interpersonal Attraction; and a stress scale specifically tailored to students in Social Psychology in Action 2, Social Psychology and Health. Still others are quizzes that illustrate social psychological concepts, such as a Reasoning Quiz in Chapter 3, Social Cognition, that illustrates judgmental heuristics; or demonstrations that explain how to use a particular concept in a student's everyday life. The format of, and the time frame required for, each of these exercises varies. You might want to flip through the book to look at other examples in more detail.

Try It! exercises are not only in the text itself, but built into the online resources as well. Students will find a new Try It! exercise for each chapter in MyPsychLab. You can use Try It! exercises as class activities or as homework.

We believe that the Try It! exercises will generate a lot of interest in learning social psychological concepts by making them more memorable and engaging.

MyPsychLab Resources

At the end of each chapter, a MyPsychLab feature directs students to specific online resources—such as video clips and simulations—that broaden and deepen the coverage of specific topics.

Social Psychology in Action Modules

You will note from the Detailed Contents that there are three modules devoted to applied topics in social psychology: one on the environment, one on health, and one on law. Each has the pre-title of Social Psychology in Action. You might wonder why these modules have a different name and numbering system than the other chapters. The reason is that they are designed to be free-floating units that can be assigned at virtually any point in the text. Although we do occasionally refer to earlier chapters in these modules, they are designed to be independent units that could fit into many different points of a course in social psychology.

In talking with many professors who teach social psychology, we have been struck by how differently they present applied material. Some prefer to assign these modules at the end of the course, after they have covered the major concepts, theories, and research findings. Others prefer to integrate the applied modules with the more theoretical material when relevant. Our applied units are designed to be used in either way.

Supplements to the Text

A really good textbook should become part of the classroom experience, supporting and augmenting the professor's vision for his or her class. *Social Psychology,* Fourth Canadian Edition, offers a number of supplements that will enrich both the professor's presentation of social psychology and the student's understanding of it.

Student Supplements

PEARSON mypsychlab Supplied with every new copy of *Social Psychology,* Fourth Canadian Edition, MyPsychLab provides students with access to a wealth of resources, including

- diagnostic tests that assess your understanding of the text
- a custom study program that creates a personalized study plan using the ebook and based on your diagnostic test results
- a media-enriched ebook, loaded with animations, videos, and additional resources
- Live!Psych Experiments and Simulations

For example, Chapter 2 has a simulation on unconscious stereotyping that includes a test of students' own assumptions. Chapter 7 contains a video about an updated look at Stanley Milgram's obedience study, and Chapter 8 features Philip Zimbardo speaking about the Stanford prison experiment. In Chapter 9, students can test their responses on the passionate love scale. In the module on health, they can work through a Live!Psych simulation on stress and health.

MyPsychLab includes access to Research Navigator, Pearson's fully searchable online collection of academic and popular journals.

Get started with the personal access code provided with your new copy of the text. Personal access codes for MyPsychLab can also be purchased separately at www.mypsychlab.com.

Instructor Supplements

Instructor's Resource CD-ROM (ISBN 978-0-13-609439-5). This CD-ROM gathers the following instructor resources in one handy package. Some of these resources are also available for downloading from a password-protected section of our online catalogue at www.pearsoned.ca/highered, and in the instructor view of MyPsychLab. See your Pearson Education Canada sales representative for details.

- **Instructor's Resource Manual.** Includes lecture ideas, teaching tips, suggested readings, chapter outlines, student projects and research assignments, Try It! exercises, critical thinking topics and discussion questions, and a media resource guide.

- **Test Item File.** Each question in this 2000-question test bank is referenced to the corresponding text page number, topic, and skill level. The test bank is available both as a Test Item File in Microsoft Word format and in MyTest format (see below).

- **PowerPoint Presentations.** These presentations cover the key concepts in each chapter.

- **Image Library.** Figures and tables from the text are provided in electronic format.

Pearson MyTest. MyTest from Pearson Education Canada is a powerful assessment generation program that helps instructors easily create and print quizzes, tests, and exams, as well as homework or practice handouts. Questions and tests can all be authored online, allowing instructors ultimate flexibility and the ability to efficiently manage assessments at any time, from anywhere. MyTest for *Social Psychology*, Fourth Canadian Edition includes approximately 2000 questions. These questions are also available in Microsoft Word format on the Instructor's Resource CD-ROM (see Test Item File, above).

CourseSmart. CourseSmart is a web platform that allows instructors and students to access textbooks online anytime from anywhere. With thousands of titles across hundreds of courses, CourseSmart helps instructors choose the best textbook for their class and give their students a new option for buying the assigned textbook as a lower cost eTextbook. For more information, visit www.coursesmart.com.

Technology Specialists. Pearson's Technology Specialists work with faculty and campus course designers to ensure that Pearson technology products, assessment tools, and online course materials are tailored to meet your specific needs. This highly qualified team is dedicated to helping schools take full advantage of a wide range of educational resources, by assisting in the integration of a variety of instructional materials and media formats. Your local Pearson Education sales representative can provide you with more details on this service program.

Acknowledgments

Elliot Aronson is delighted to acknowledge the general contributions of his best friend (who also happens to be his wife), Vera Aronson. Vera, as usual, provided a great deal of inspiration for his ideas and acted as the sounding board for and supportive critic of many of his semi-formed notions, helping to mould them into more sensible analyses. He would also like to thank his son, Joshua Aronson, a brilliant young social psychologist in his own right, for the many stimulating conversations that contributed mightily to the final version of this book.

Tim Wilson would like to thank his graduate mentor, Richard E. Nisbett, who nurtured his interest in the field and showed him the continuity between social psychological research and everyday life. He thanks his parents, Elizabeth and Geoffrey Wilson, for their overall support. Most of all, he thanks his wife, Deirdre Smith, and his children, Christopher and Leigh, for their love, patience, and understanding, even when the hour was late and the computer was still on.

Robin Akert would like to thank her students and colleagues at Wellesley College for their support and encouragement. In particular, she is beholden to Professor Jonathan Cheek and Professor Patricia Berman, Allison Bibbins Ward, and Linda DuFresne for their advice, feedback, and sense of humour. She also wishes to thank her students in social psychology. Their intelligence, perspicacity, dedication, and joie de vivre are her continuing sources of energy and motivation for this book. She is deeply grateful to her family, Michaela and Wayne Akert, and Linda and Jerry Wuichet; their inexhaustible enthusiasm and boundless support have sustained her on this project as on all the ones before it. Finally, no words can express her gratitude and indebtedness to Dane Archer, mentor, colleague, and friend, who opened the world of social psychology to her and who has been her guide ever since.

Beverley Fehr would like to thank her colleagues at the University of Winnipeg and her social psychology colleagues at the University of Manitoba for their enthusiasm and support throughout this project. She is indebted to Lisa Sinclair, Wendy Josephson, and Marian Morry and Cheryl Harasymchuk for their emotional and practical support. Beverley would also like to express gratitude to her capable, highly skilled research assistants, David Kille and Maia Kredenster. On a more personal note, Beverley's dear friends Lydia Friesen Rempel and Lorrie Brubacher provided the unfailing emotional support and good cheer that have sustained her through many a project over the years. Beverley's sister Lois has been a constant source of support and encouragement in her life. Beverley would also like to thank her husband, Marvin Giesbrecht, for his generosity and kindness in doing "more than his share" of domestic chores and the more mundane aspects of child care so that she could focus on writing this book. Beverley's children, Genevieve and Everett, provided much-needed comic relief after long hours of writing. Their smiles, hugs, and antics were an invaluable source of joy and energy. Finally, Beverley would like to thank the staff at Bread and Circuses Café, where much of her writing was done, for their warmth, friendliness, and the countless refills of coffee.

No book can be written and published without the help of a great many people working with the authors behind the scenes, and this book is no exception. Beverley would like to thank the people at Pearson Education Canada who worked with her on this text. She would like to express appreciation to Joel Gladstone and Suzanne Schaan, developmental editor and supervising developmental editor, for their competence, patience, support, and understanding throughout this project. Beverley would also like to thank editor-in-chief Ky Pruesse for his encouragement, warmth, and contagious enthusiasm, and copy editor Lu Cormier and production editor/proofreader Tara Tovell for their expertise, conscientiousness, and patience in dealing with an author who struggled to meet deadlines because of her passion for including "just one more" Canadian study.

Finally, we would like to thank the many colleagues who read one or more chapters of previous editions of the book. Reviewers of this fourth Canadian edition included the following:

Susan Boon, University of Calgary
David Bourgeois, St. Mary's University
Loraine Lavallee, University of Northern British Columbia
Christine Lomore, St. Francis Xavier University
Tom Murphy, University of Western Ontario
Lisa Sinclair, University of Winnipeg
Christine Werk, University of Lethbridge

Thank you for inviting us into your classroom. We welcome your suggestions, and we would be delighted to hear your comments about this book.

Elliot Aronson: elliot@cats.ucsc.edu
Tim Wilson: tdw@virginia.edu
Robin Akert: rakert@wellesley.edu
Beverley Fehr: bfehr@uwinnipeg.ca

About the Authors

Elliot Aronson

When I was a kid, we were the only Jewish family in a virulently anti-Semitic neighbourhood. I had to go to Hebrew school every day, late in the afternoon. Being the only youngster in my neighbourhood going to Hebrew school made me an easy target for some of the older neighbourhood toughs. On my way home from Hebrew school, after dark, I was frequently waylaid and roughed up by roving gangs shouting anti-Semitic epithets.

I have a vivid memory of sitting on a curb after one of these beatings, nursing a bloody nose or a split lip, feeling very sorry for myself and wondering how these kids could hate me so much when they didn't even know me. I thought about whether those kids were taught to hate Jews or whether, somehow, they were born that way. I wondered if their hatred could be changed—if they got to know me better, would they hate me less? I speculated about my own character. What would I have done if the shoe were on the other foot—that is, if I were bigger and stronger than they, would I be capable of beating them up for no good reason?

I didn't realize it at the time, of course, but eventually I discovered that these were profound questions. And some 30 years later, as an experimental social psychologist, I had the great good fortune to be in a position to answer some of those questions and to invent techniques to reduce the kind of prejudice that had claimed me as a victim.

Elliot Aronson is one of the most renowned social psychologists in the world. In 2002 he was chosen as one of the 100 most eminent psychologists of the twentieth century. He is currently Professor Emeritus at the University of California at Santa Cruz and Distinguished Visiting Professor at Stanford University.

Dr. Aronson is the only person in the 110-year history of the American Psychological Association to have received all three of its major awards: for distinguished writing, distinguished teaching, and distinguished research. Many other professional societies have honoured his research and teaching as well. These include the American Association for the Advancement of Science, which gave him its highest honour, the Distinguished Scientific Research award; the American Council for the Advancement and Support of Education, which named him Professor of the Year of 1989; and the Society for the Psychological Study of Social Issues, which awarded him the Gordon Allport prize for his contributions to the reduction of prejudice among racial and ethnic groups. In 1992, he was named a Fellow of the American Academy of Arts and Sciences. He has served as president of the Western Psychological Association as well as president of the Society of Personality and Social Psychology.

Tim Wilson

One day, when I was eight, a couple of older kids rode up on their bikes to share some big news: They had discovered an abandoned house down a country road. "It's really neat," they said. "We broke a window and nobody cared!" My friend and I hopped onto our bikes to investigate. We had no trouble finding the house—there it was, sitting off by itself, with a big, jagged hole in a first-floor window. We got off of our bikes and looked around. My friend found a baseball-sized rock lying on the ground and threw a perfect strike through another first-floor window. There was something exhilarating about the smash-and-tingle of shattering glass, especially when we knew there was nothing wrong with what we were doing. After all, the house was abandoned, wasn't it? We broke nearly every window in the house and then climbed through one of the first-floor windows to look around.

It was then that we realized something was terribly wrong. The house certainly did not look abandoned. There were pictures on the wall, nice furniture, books in shelves. We went home feeling frightened and confused. We soon learned that the house was the residence of an elderly couple who were away on vacation. Eventually my parents discovered what we had done and paid a substantial sum to repair the windows. For years, I pondered this incident: Why did I do such a terrible thing? Was I a bad kid? I didn't think so, and neither did my parents. How, then, could a good kid do such a bad thing? Even though the neighbourhood kids said the house was abandoned, why couldn't my friend and I see the clear signs that someone lived there?

How crucial was it that my friend was there and threw the first rock? Though I didn't know it at the time, these reflections touched on several classic social psychological issues, such as whether only bad people do bad things, whether the social situation can be powerful enough to make good people do bad things, and the way in which our expectations about an event can make it difficult to see it as it really is. Fortunately, my career as a vandal ended with this one incident. It did, however, mark the beginning of my fascination with basic questions about how people understand themselves and the social world—questions I continue to investigate to this day.

Tim Wilson did his undergraduate work at Williams College and Hampshire College and received his Ph.D. from the University of Michigan. Currently Sherrell J. Aston Professor of Psychology at the University of Virginia, he has published numerous articles in the areas of introspection, attitude change, self-knowledge, and affective forecasting, as well as the recent book Strangers to Ourselves: Discovering the Adaptive Unconscious. *His research has received the support of the National Science Foundation and the National Institute for Mental Health. He has been associate editor of the Journal of Personality and Social Psychology and a member of the Social and Groups Processes Review Committee at the National Institute of Mental Health. He has been elected twice to the Executive Board of the Society for Experimental Social Psychology and is a fellow in the American Psychological Society. Wilson has taught the Introduction to Social Psychology course at the University of Virginia for more than 20 years. He was recently awarded an All University Outstanding Teaching Award.*

Robin Akert

One fall day, when I was about 16, I was walking with a friend along the shore of the San Francisco Bay. Deep in conversation, I glanced over my shoulder and saw a sailboat capsize. I pointed it out to my friend, who took only a perfunctory interest and went on talking. However, I kept watching as we walked, and I realized that the two sailors were in the water, clinging to the capsized boat. Again I said something to my friend, who replied, "Oh, they'll get it upright, don't worry."

But I was worried. Was this an emergency? My friend didn't think so. And I was no sailor; I knew nothing about boats. But I kept thinking, "That water is really cold. They can't stay in that water too long." I remember feeling very confused and unsure. What should I do? Should I do anything? Did they really need help?

We were near a restaurant with a big window overlooking the bay, and I decided to go in and see if anyone had done anything about the boat. Lots of people were watching but not doing anything. This confused me too.

Very meekly, I asked the bartender to call for some kind of help. He just shrugged. I went back to the window and watched the two small figures in the water. Why was everyone so unconcerned? Was I crazy?

Years later, I reflected on how hard it was for me to do what I did next: I demanded that the bartender let me use his phone. In those days before "911," it was lucky that I knew there was a Coast Guard station on the bay, and I asked the operator for the number. I was relieved to hear the Guardsman take my message very seriously.

It had been an emergency. I watched as the Coast Guard cutter sped across the bay and pulled the two sailors out of the water. Maybe I saved their lives that day. What really stuck with me over the years was how other people behaved and how it made me feel. The other bystanders seemed unconcerned and did nothing to help. Their reactions made me doubt myself and made it harder for me to decide to take action. When I later studied social psychology in college, I realized that on the shore of the San Francisco Bay that day, I had experienced the "bystander effect" fully: The presence of other, apparently unconcerned bystanders had made it difficult for me to decide if the situation was an emergency and whether it was my responsibility to help.

Robin Akert graduated summa cum laude from the University of California at Santa Cruz, where she majored in psychology and sociology. She received her Ph.D. in experimental social psychology from Princeton University. She is currently a professor of psychology at Wellesley College, where she was awarded the Pinanski Prize for Excellence in Teaching early in her career. She publishes primarily in the area of nonverbal communication and recently received the AAUW American Fellowship in support of her research. She has taught the social psychology course at Wellesley College every semester for over 20 years.

Beverley Fehr

I suspect that many social psychologists, like me, didn't start out with the intention of becoming social psychologists. I was attending university as a music major, taking psychology courses for interest. I enjoyed them, but kept experiencing a vague sense of disappointment—each course wasn't quite what I had thought psychology would be about. When I enrolled in a social psychology course that was offered one summer, I was delighted to have finally found a course that captured what I had been looking for. One day, as part of a class exercise, our professor handed out copies of Rubin's (1970) love and liking scale for us to complete with reference to a romantic partner and a friend. (This scale is still widely used in close relationships research today.) I was dating someone at the time about whom I cared deeply, although I had a feeling that he was not a particularly good choice as a long-term partner. I was astonished, when we scored the scale, that the love score for this person was extremely high, but the liking score was distressingly low! Quite aside from the personal implications of this result, I was utterly fascinated that social psychologists could use the scientific method to gain insight into issues that are highly relevant to people's everyday lives. This, and other experiences in that class, prompted me to reconsider my career choice and I ended up changing my major to psychology. I suspect that this experience may also have played a role in my eventual decision to become a social psychologist who studies close relationships.

Beverley Fehr graduated with a B.A. (Hons.) from the University of Winnipeg where she was awarded the Gold Medal for the highest standing in psychology. She received her M.A. (under the guidance of Jim Russell) and her Ph.D. (under the guidance of Dan Perlman) from the University of British Columbia. Her doctoral thesis on lay people's conceptions of love and commitment won the Iowa/International Network for the Study of Personal Relationships Dissertation Prize. She has published numerous articles and book chapters on the topics of emotion and close relationships. Her book Friendship Processes *(1996) was awarded the 1997 Outstanding Academic Book Award by* Choice: Current Reviews for Academic Libraries. *Beverley's research is supported by grants from the Social Sciences and Humanities Research Council of Canada and the Fetzer Institute. She is past president of the International Association for Relationships Research, has served as associate editor of the* Journal of Personality and Social Psychology, *and is a fellow of the Canadian Psychological Assocation.*

Social Psychology

1

Introduction to Social Psychology

The task of the psychologist is to try to understand and predict human behaviour. Different kinds of psychologists go about this in different ways, and in this book we will attempt to show you how social psychologists do it. Let's begin with a few examples of human behaviour. Some of these might seem important; others might seem trivial; one or two might seem frightening. To a social psychologist, all of them are interesting. Our hope is that by the time you finish reading this book you will find all of these examples as fascinating as we do. As you read, try to think about how you would explain why each event unfolded as it did.

- "Canadians amaze with their giving"; "Canadians open their wallets in record numbers." Headlines such as these were a daily occurrence in Canadian newspapers, as story after story documented the extent to which Canadians were moved to assist the victims of the December 2004 tsunami disaster in Asia. Assistance included benefit concerts, school bake sales, fundraising drives at sports events, and extended hours at the offices of relief organizations such as the Red Cross so that all of the donations could be accommodated. There were stories of families travelling long distances over icy roads so that their children could donate the contents of their piggy banks in the office of a relief organization. Two polls released on January 14, 2005, reported that more than 50 percent of Canadians had donated money toward the tsunami relief effort—an unprecedented level of giving. Bruce Anderson, CEO of Decima Research, which conducted one of these polls, commented that "it's undoubtedly a reflection of our value system as a nation that so many people have felt moved to take action in response to this crisis" (Dugas, 2005). One such person is Greg Baytalan, a 46-year-old health inspector from Kelowna, British Columbia. Baytalan was enjoying a vacation in Australia when he heard news of the tsunami and felt compelled to help. He flew to Thailand and helped with the gruesome task of unloading recovered bodies and carrying them to a morgue. This is an experience that Baytalan believes he will never be able to erase from his memory: in his words, "It was beyond horror" (Cheadle, 2005).

What would make a person such as Greg Baytalan give up his vacation to reach out to help complete strangers in a faraway country, especially when doing so came at such an enormous cost? Why did so many Canadians open their hearts and their wallets to help the tsunami victims?

- You are in a coffee shop with your friends. You happen to notice the December 19, 2007, issue of *Maclean's* magazine in the café's newspaper stand. One of the headlines reads, "Why Santa Claus can't get into the U.S." The article details the obstacles facing those who want to cross the border, including the new requirement that Canadians must have a passport to enter the United States. You are about to express your belief that given the war on terrorism, people should be prepared to comply with additional security measures. Compared with the devastating events of September 11, 2001, you feel that having to apply for a passport and being subjected to long lineups and searches at the border is a small price to pay. Just as you are opening your mouth to speak, your friend Maria says, "All of this heightened security is ridiculous. There's no way we should be letting the Americans dictate what happens at the border." Steve chimes in, "You're absolutely right. The U.S. is Canada's major trade partner and these new restrictions are killing our economy." As he flips through the magazine article, he points out that the cost of post-9/11 border delays amounts to approximately $14 billion per year. "I agree that the Americans are going way overboard," says Emily, "and it's not just trade that's affected. Tourism is going down the tubes, too." All eyes turn to you.

    What would you say? Would you state your own opinion or conform to your friends' unanimous attitude? Would it surprise you to learn that when placed in a similar situation most university students would go along with the majority opinion rather than appear odd or out of step?

- On the cover of the March 6, 2000, issue of *Maclean's*, a headline reads, "A barbaric rite of passage: hazing in university athletics." The article begins with the story of Jean-François Caudron from St-Hubert, Quebec, the recipient of a hockey scholarship from the University of Vermont. As a rookie, he was subjected to a hazing that involved shaving his pubic hair, painting his toenails, and drinking warm beer until he vomited.

Based on his experiences on Canadian hockey teams, Jean-François knew there was no escaping rookie night: "You knew about this night and you were nervous. You feel pressure that you have to do it." One might expect that Jean-François would have nothing but bad memories about his hazing experiences. However, he describes it this way: "[O]nce it was over, I was so happy. I really felt part of the team" (O'Hara, 2000).

Why would Jean-François feel so happy to be part of a team that inflicted pain, embarrassment, and humiliation on him?

- In the mid-1980s, residents of Quebec were introduced to the Order of the Solar Temple—a cult founded by Luc Jouret and his partner Joseph Di Mambro. Prominent citizens, including the highly respected mayor of Richelieu and his wife, joined the cult. They were taught that the only redemption from their sins was to experience death by fire, which would transport them to the star Sirius, where they would be reborn. Suicides were to take place during the spring or autumn equinox. The cult attracted worldwide attention in October 1994 when 53 cult members, including the mayor of Richelieu and his wife, died in a combined mass murder-suicide. An elaborate system of explosives set fire to the buildings they inhabited in Quebec and Switzerland. Nearly a year later, another 16 cult members, including several children, died in a remote village in France. So far, at least 74 members of this cult have died.

How can people agree to kill themselves and their own children? Were they crazy? Were they under some kind of hypnotic spell? How would you explain it?

We now have presented several questions about human social behaviour—questions we find fascinating. Why do people sometimes go to great lengths to help complete strangers, as Greg Baytalan did when he gave up his vacation to help carry the bodies of tsunami victims to a morgue? When people disagree on issues such as the need for heightened security measures, why are they likely to go along with the majority rather than voice their true opinion? Why did Jean-François Caudron like being part of hockey teams that forced him to endure barbaric hazing rituals? And how could large numbers of people be induced to kill their own children and themselves in Quebec, Switzerland, and France? In this chapter, we will consider what these examples have in common and why they are of interest to us. We will also put forth some reasonable explanations based upon social psychological research.

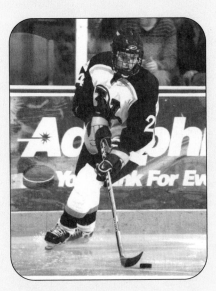

▲ Jean-François Caudron was subjected to severe initiations as a rookie, but remembers his teammates with fondness.

What Is Social Psychology?

At the heart of social psychology is the phenomenon of social influence: Everyone is influenced by other people. When we think of social influence, the kinds of examples that readily come to mind are direct attempts at persuasion, whereby one person deliberately tries to change another person's behaviour. This is what happens in an advertising campaign when creative individuals employ sophisticated techniques to persuade us to buy a particular brand of toothpaste, or during an election campaign when similar techniques are used to get us to vote for a particular political candidate. Direct attempts at persuasion also occur when our friends try to get us to do something we don't really want to do ("Come on, have another beer—everyone else is in") or when the schoolyard bully uses force or threats to get smaller kids to part with their lunch money or completed homework.

These attempts at direct social influence form a major part of social psychology, and will be discussed in our chapters on conformity, attitudes, and group processes. To the social psychologist, however, social influence is broader than attempts by one person to change another person's behaviour. For one thing, social influence extends beyond behaviour—it includes our thoughts and feelings, as well as our overt acts. In addition, social influence takes on many forms other than deliberate attempts at persuasion. We are often influenced merely by the presence of other people. Moreover, even when we are not in the physical presence of other people, we are still influenced by them. Thus, in a sense, we carry our mothers, fathers, friends, and teachers around with us, as we attempt to make decisions that would make them proud of us.

On a more subtle level, each of us is immersed in a social and cultural context. Social psychologists are interested in studying how and why our thoughts, feelings, and behaviours are shaped by the entire social environment. Taking all these factors into account, we can define **social psychology** as the scientific study of the way in which people's thoughts, feelings, and behaviours are influenced by the real or imagined presence of other people (Allport, 1985).

The Power of Social Interpretation

Other disciplines, such as anthropology and sociology, are also interested in how people are influenced by their social environment. Social psychology is distinct, however, primarily because it is concerned not so much with social situations in any objective sense, but rather with how people are influenced by their interpretation, or **construal**, of their social environment. To understand how people are influenced by their social world, social psychologists believe, it is more important to understand how they perceive, comprehend, and interpret the social world than it is to understand the objective properties of the social world itself (Lewin, 1943).

In a murder trial, for example, the prosecution may present evidence such as DNA tests that it believes will have a decisive impact on the verdict. But no matter how powerful the evidence might be, the final verdict will always hinge on precisely how each member of the jury construes that evidence—and these construals may rest on a variety of events and perceptions that may or may not bear objective relevance to the matter. Such construal processes can produce very different outcomes. In the O. J. Simpson trial in the United States, even though objective evidence concerning DNA and hair and fibre samples was presented, the jury decided that Simpson was not guilty of murdering his ex-wife and her friend. In contrast, in the case of Larry Fisher—who was tried for the murder of Gail Miller after David Milgaard was finally exonerated—the same kind of objective evidence (results of DNA tests) led to a first-degree murder conviction, even though the defence tried to persuade the jury that the DNA evidence proved only that he had sexually assaulted Gail Miller, not that he was her killer.

social psychology

the scientific study of the way in which people's thoughts, feelings, and behaviours are influenced by the real or imagined presence of other people

construal

the way in which people perceive, comprehend, and interpret the social world

Another distinctive feature of social psychology is that it is an experimentally based science that tests its assumptions, guesses, and ideas about human social behaviour empirically and systematically, rather than relying on folk wisdom, common sense, the opinions and insights of philosophers, novelists, political pundits, grandmothers, and others wise in the ways of human beings. As you will see, doing systematic experiments in social psychology presents a great many challenges, primarily because we are attempting to predict the behaviour of highly sophisticated organisms in a variety of complex situations. As scientists, our goal is to find objective answers to a wide array of important questions: What are the factors that cause aggression? How might people reduce prejudice? What causes two people to like or love each other? Why do certain kinds of political advertisements work better than others? The specific ways in which social psychologists conduct experiments to meet these challenges will be illustrated throughout this book and discussed in detail in Chapter 2.

We will spend most of this introductory chapter expanding on the issues raised in the section above: what social psychology is and how it is distinct from other, related disciplines. A good place to begin is with what social psychology is not.

Some Alternative Ways of Understanding Social Influence

Let's take another look at the examples at the beginning of this chapter. Why did people behave the way they did? One way to answer this question might simply be to ask them. For example, we could ask Jean-François Caudron why he was so happy to be part of a hockey team that inflicted pain on him or ask followers of Luc Jouret why they joined the cult. The problem with this approach is that people are not always aware of the origins of their own responses (Nisbett & Wilson, 1977a). It is unlikely that Caudron knows why the hazing he experienced made him feel part of the team, or that the members of the Solar Temple know why they got pulled into a cult.

Folk Wisdom Journalists, social critics, and novelists have many interesting things to say about these situations. Such commentary is generally referred to as *folk wisdom* or *common sense*. A great deal can be learned about social behaviour from journalists, social critics, and novelists—and in this book we quote from all of these. There is, however, at least one problem with full reliance on such sources: More often than not, they disagree with one another, and there is no easy way of determining which of them is correct. Consider what folk wisdom has to say about the factors that influence how much we like other people. On the one hand, we know that "birds of a feather flock together," and with a little effort, each of us could come up with many examples in which we liked and hung around with people who shared our backgrounds and interests. But on the other hand, folk wisdom *also* tells us that "opposites attract," and if we tried, we could come up with examples in which people with backgrounds and interests different from our own did attract us. Which is correct? Similarly, are we to believe that "out of sight is out of mind" or that "absence makes the heart grow fonder"; that "haste makes waste" or that "he who hesitates is lost"?

There is no shortage of folk theories for events such as the Solar Temple tragedy. When cult members kill themselves and their children at the request of their leader, explanations range from the view that the leader must have employed hypnotism and drugs to weaken the resistance of his followers, to suspicion that the people who were attracted to his cult must have been disturbed, self-destructive individuals in the first place. Such speculations, because they underestimate the power of the situation, are almost certainly incorrect—or at the very least oversimplified. Indeed, what is most striking about members of the Solar Temple cult is that they tended to be highly respected, well-functioning members of society—including a mayor, a journalist, a civil servant, and a sales manager.

▲ While attorneys do their best to convince a jury, in the end, the verdict will depend on how the individual jurors construe the evidence. In the case of Larry Fisher, pictured here, the jury was shown DNA evidence proving that Fisher sexually assaulted Gail Miller, and decided that he must have murdered her as well.

Unfortunately, because so-called common sense frequently turns out to be wrong or oversimplified, people tend not to learn from previous incidents. The Solar Temple was probably the first mass suicide involving Canadians, but certainly not the first or the last event of this kind. In 1978, nearly 800 members of a California-based religious cult died in Jonestown, Guyana, when they drank a deadly mixture of Kool-Aid and cyanide in response to a command from their leader, the Reverend Jim Jones. Subsequent doomsday cults capitalized on fears that the millennium would bring about the end of the world, and managed to persuade their followers to take their lives and those of their children. A particularly chilling example is the Ugandan Movement for the Restoration of the Ten Commandments of God. One of that cult's beliefs is that childhood is sinful. The leaders managed to persuade parents that handing over their children to die was the only way to prevent them from falling into the hands of Satan. On March 17, 2000, hundreds of people, many of whom were children, were led into a sealed chapel that was set on fire (Associated Press, 2000). Hundreds of other cult members and their children died in other ways. While it is difficult to determine the exact number of casualties, most reports suggest that between 800 and 1000 people perished, placing this cult on the same horrific scale as the California-based Jonestown cult (Wasswa, 2002).

Still more recently, in April 2008, more than 400 children—one of them Canadian—were seized by Child Protective Services authorities in Texas. There are allegations that young girls, and perhaps some boys, were beaten, starved, and forced to have sex with much older men. The charismatic leader of the Yearning for Zion Mormon sect, Warren Jeffs, and four others were indicted on charges of felony sexual assault of a child. Another man was charged with failing to report child abuse (Roberts, 2008, July 22). Although all of the children were returned in June, a new hearing was scheduled to try to take six girls and two boys back into protective custody (Roberts, 2008, August 5). Jeffs claimed that God told him to marry at least three young virgins, and preferably many more. Jeffs also maintained that "spiritual marriages" of girls as young as age 13 to men in their forties and fifties should be arranged. According to news outlets, Jeffs also "reassigned" wives and children to other men in the sect.

▶ Charismatic leaders are able to persuade people to willingly hand over their children to be mistreated and sexually abused. Warren Jeffs, leader of the Yearning for Zion Morman sect, continues to receive support from his followers, despite having been indicted on grounds of sexual assault.

It is difficult for most people to grasp just how powerful a cult can be in affecting the hearts and minds of relatively normal people. Accordingly, the general population is eager to find someone to blame. Often people blame the victims themselves, accusing them of stupidity or of suffering from mental illness. Fixing blame may make us feel better by resolving our confusion, but it is no substitute for understanding the complexities of the situations that produced those events.

We social psychologists address many of the same questions that ordinary people ask about the world around them, but we attempt to look at these questions scientifically. One of the tasks of the social psychologist is to make educated guesses (called *hypotheses*; see Chapter 2) about the specific situations under which one outcome or the other would occur. Just as a physicist performs experiments to test hypotheses about the nature of the physical world, the social psychologist performs experiments to test hypotheses about the nature of the social world. This is an enormous challenge because the world is a complicated place. Let us return for a moment to our earlier discussion about the kinds of people we like, and the relationship between absence and liking. Almost certainly, there are some conditions under which birds of a feather *do* flock together and other conditions under which opposites *do* attract; similarly, there are some conditions under which absence *does* make the heart grow fonder and others under which out of sight *does* mean out of mind. Each of these can be true. If you really want to understand human behaviour, however, knowing that these situations can be true is not sufficient. One of the tasks of the social psychologist is to design experiments sophisticated enough to demonstrate the specific situations under which one or the other applies. This enriches our understanding of human nature and allows us to make accurate predictions once we know the key aspects of the prevailing situation. In Chapter 2, we will discuss in more detail the scientific methods that social psychologists use.

Social Psychology Compared with Sociology

Social psychology's focus on social behaviour is shared by several other disciplines in the social sciences, most notably sociology. Both disciplines are concerned with the influence of social and societal factors on human behaviour. There are important differences, however. One such difference is the level of analysis. Social psychology is a branch of psychology and, as such, is rooted in an interest in individual human beings, with an emphasis on the psychological processes going on in their hearts and minds. *For the social psychologist, the level of analysis is the individual in the context of a social situation.* To understand why people intentionally hurt one another, for example, the social psychologist focuses on the specific psychological processes that trigger aggression in specific situations. To what extent is aggression preceded by a state of frustration? Is frustration necessary? If people are feeling frustrated, under what conditions will they vent their frustration with an overt, aggressive act? What factors might preclude an aggressive response by a frustrated individual? Aside from frustration, what other factors might cause aggression? We will address these questions in Chapter 11.

Sociology is more concerned with broad societal factors that influence events in a given society. Thus, the focus is on such topics as social class, social structure, and social institutions. It goes without saying that because society is made up of collections of people, some overlap is bound to exist between the domains of sociology and social psychology. The major difference is this: Sociology, rather than focusing on the psychology of the individual, tends toward a more macro focus—that of society at large. Sociologists, like social psychologists, are interested in aggressive behaviour, but sociologists are more likely to be concerned with why a particular society produces different levels and types of aggression in its members. Sociologists might ask, for example, why the murder rate in the United States is so much higher than in Canada. Within Canada, why is the murder rate higher in some social classes than in others? How do changes in society relate to changes in aggressive behaviour?

The difference between social psychology and sociology in level of analysis reflects another difference between the disciplines—namely, what they are trying to explain. *The goal of social psychology is to identify universal properties of human nature that make everyone susceptible to social influence, regardless of social class or culture.* The laws governing the relationship between frustration and aggression, for example, are hypothesized to be true of most people in most places—not just members of one social class, age group, or race. Social psychology is a young science that, until recently, had developed mostly in North America; therefore, many of its findings have not yet been tested in other cultures to see if they are indeed universal. However, cross-cultural research is increasing, and as it continues to grow, we are learning more about the extent to which these laws are universal. This type of cultural expansion is extremely valuable because it sharpens theories, either by demonstrating their universality or by leading us to discover additional variables, the incorporation of which will ultimately help us make more accurate predictions of human social behaviour. We will encounter many examples of such cross-cultural research in subsequent chapters.

Social Psychology Compared with Personality Psychology

Like social psychology, some other areas of psychology focus on studying individuals and the reasons they do what they do. Paramount among these is personality psychology. Let's discuss how social psychology and personality psychology differ in their approach and concerns.

If you are like most people, when you read the examples presented at the beginning of this chapter and began to think about how those events might have come about, your first thoughts were about the strengths, weaknesses, flaws, and quirks of the personality of the individuals involved. When people behave in interesting or unusual ways, it is natural to try to pinpoint what aspects of their personality led them to respond as they did. Most of us explain these kinds of behaviours in terms of the personalities of the people involved. What might these be? Some people are leaders and others are followers; some people are bold and others are timid; some people are public-spirited and others are selfish.

When trying to find explanations of social behaviour, personality psychologists generally focus their attention on **individual differences**—the aspects of an individual's personality that make him or her different from other individuals. To explain why the people in the Solar Temple cult ended their own lives and those of their children, for example, it seems natural to point to their personalities. Perhaps they were all "conformist types" or weak-willed; maybe they were even psychotic. An understanding of personality psychology increases our understanding of human behaviour. But social psychologists are convinced that explaining behaviour primarily in terms of personality factors ignores a critical part of the story: the powerful role played by social influence. Remember that it was not just a handful of people who died in a ski resort in Quebec and in two villages in Switzerland. It is thought that, in all, 74 people lost their lives to the Solar Temple cult. In the Jonestown tragedy in northern Guyana, 800 Americans took their own lives, and in the Ugandan cult, at least that many—many of whom were children—perished. More than 400 children from the Texas polygamy sect were removed by authorities because of allegations of rape and sexual exploitation, while their mothers continued to deny that there was wrongdoing. While it is conceivable that all of these people were psychotic, that explanation is highly improbable. If we want a deeper, richer, more thorough explanation of these tragic events, we need to understand what kind of power and influence the charismatic leaders of these cults possess, the nature of the impact of living in a

individual differences

the aspects of people's personalities that make them different from other people

TABLE 1.1

Social psychology compared with related disciplines

Sociology	Social Psychology	Personality Psychology
Provides general laws and theories about societies, not individuals.	Studies the psychological processes people have in common with one another that make them susceptible to social influence.	Studies the characteristics that make individuals unique and different from one another.

closed society cut off from other points of view, and myriad other factors that might have contributed to the abuse, and ultimately, the deaths.

These two different approaches can be illustrated with an everyday example. Suppose you stop at a roadside restaurant for a cup of coffee and a piece of pie. The waitress comes to take your order, but you are having a hard time deciding which kind of pie you want. While you are hesitating, she impatiently taps her pen against her order book, rolls her eyes toward the ceiling, scowls at you, and finally snaps, "Hey, I haven't got all day, you know!"

What do you conclude about this event? When faced with such a situation, most people would conclude that the waitress is a nasty or unpleasant person; consequently, they would be reluctant to enter that particular restaurant again—especially when that nasty person was on duty. That would certainly be understandable. However, suppose we were to tell you that the waitress is a single parent and was kept awake all night by the moaning of her youngest child, who has a painful terminal illness; that her car broke down on her way to work and she has no idea where she will find the money to have it repaired; that when she finally arrived at the restaurant, she learned that her co-worker was too drunk to work, requiring her to cover twice the usual number of tables; and that the short-order cook kept screaming at her because she was not picking up the orders fast enough to please him? Given all this information, you might revise your judgment and conclude that she is not necessarily a nasty person—just an ordinary person under enormous stress.

The key fact remains that when trying to account for a person's behaviour in a complex situation, the overwhelming majority of people will jump to the conclusion that the behaviour was caused by the personality of the individual involved rather than consider the influence of the situation. And this fact—that we often fail to take the situation into account—is important to a social psychologist, for it has a profound impact on how human beings relate to one another.

In sum, social psychology is located somewhere between its closest intellectual cousins, sociology and personality psychology (see Table 1.1). Social psychology shares with sociology an interest in situational and societal influences on behaviour, but focuses more on the psychological makeup of individuals that renders them susceptible to social influence. Social psychology shares with personality psychology an emphasis on the psychology of the individual, but rather than focusing on what makes people different from one another, it emphasizes the psychological processes shared by most people that make them susceptible to social influence.

The Power of Social Influence

When trying to convince people that their behaviour is greatly influenced by the social environment, the social psychologist is up against a formidable barrier: the inclination we all have for explaining people's behaviour in terms of their personalities (e.g., the case of the waitress discussed above). This barrier is

Try it!

▶ Social Situations and Behaviour

1. Think about one of your friends or acquaintances whom you regard as a shy person. For a moment, try not to think about that person as "shy," but rather as someone who has difficulty relating to people in some situations but not in others.

2. Make a list of the social situations that you think are most likely to bring out your friend's "shy" behaviour.

3. Make a list of the social situations that might bring forth more outgoing behaviour on his or her part. (For example, if someone showed a real interest in one of your friend's favourite hobbies or topics of conversation, it might bring out behaviour that could be classified as charming or vivacious.)

4. Try to create a social environment in which this would be accomplished. Pay close attention to the effect it has on your friend's behaviour.

---

fundamental attribution error

the tendency to overestimate the extent to which people's behaviour stems from internal, dispositional factors and to underestimate the role of situational factors

known as the **fundamental attribution error**—the tendency to explain people's behaviour in terms of personality traits, thereby underestimating the power of social influence. While reading this book, try to suspend judgment for a short time and consider the possibility that to understand why people do what they do, it is important to look closely at the nature of the social situation. The accompanying Try It! exercise may help you do just that.

Underestimating the Power of Social Influence

When we underestimate the power of social influence, we experience a feeling of false security. For example, when trying to explain why people do repugnant or bizarre things—such as the members of the Solar Temple cult taking their own lives or killing their own children—it is tempting, and in a strange way comforting, to write off the victims as flawed human beings. Doing so helps the rest of us believe that it could never happen to us. However, by failing to appreciate fully the power of the situation, we tend to oversimplify complex situations; oversimplification decreases our understanding of the causes of a great deal of human behaviour. Among other things, this oversimplification can lead us to blame the victim in situations where the individual was overpowered by social forces too difficult for most of us to resist—as in the Solar Temple tragedy.

> The head monkey at Paris puts on a traveller's cap, and all the monkeys in America do the same.
>
> —Henry David Thoreau, philosopher (1817–1862)

Here is an example of the kind of oversimplification we are talking about: Imagine a situation in which people are playing a two-person game wherein each player must choose one of two strategies. They can play competitively, where they try to win as much money as possible and ensure that their partner loses as much as possible, or they can play cooperatively, where they try to ensure that both they and their partner win some money. We will discuss the details of this game ("The Prisoner's Dilemma") in Chapter 8. For now, it is important to note that there are only two basic strategies people can use when playing the game—competitive or cooperative. Now think about some of your friends. How do you think they would play this game?

Few people find this question hard to answer; most people have a sense of the relative competitiveness of their friends. "Well," you might say, "I am certain that my friend Sam, who is a cutthroat business major, would play this game more competitively than my friend Richard, who is a really caring, loving

CONNECTIONS

The Fundamental Attribution Error: When We Blame the Victims of Violence

The tendency to explain others' behaviour as stemming from internal rather than situational factors can lead to tragic consequences, including a tendency to blame victims for their plight. Even if people are made aware of the situational factors responsible for the plight of disadvantaged members of society (e.g., inadequate nutrition, disrupted family life), they may still see such individuals as responsible for their misfortune. This tendency extends even to victims of violence. For example, women who are sexually assaulted are often seen as having somehow "caused" the attack (Morry & Winkler, 2001; Harrison & Abrishami, 2004), and battered wives are often seen as responsible for their abusive husbands' behaviour (Summers & Feldman, 1984).

Research conducted at Carleton University (Kristiansen & Giulietti, 1990) and at Mount Saint Vincent University (Perrott, Miller, & Delaney, 1997) has shown that people justify blaming victims of violence by assuming that the person must have done something to provoke the attack. The role that perceived provocation plays in judgments of blame was examined in a study by Kristiansen and Giulietti (1990). They asked participants to read the following scenario:

> Mrs. X explained that as she was late coming home from work, she was preparing leftovers. Upon hearing this, Mr. X got upset and angry. He argued that as she has a family to attend to, Mrs. X should ensure that she gets home on time.

Some participants received the provocation version of this scenario. For these participants, the scenario went on to read:

> Mrs. X then became upset. She began to yell at Mr. X, and as her anger heightened, she began to shout various obscenities at him, calling him a "nagging bastard."

All participants then read the same ending:

> Mrs. X then went into the kitchen to prepare dinner. Mr. X followed her. He grabbed her by the arm and slapped her, knocking her to the floor, and kicked her several times. He subsequently left the house.

In this study, participants who received the provocation information assigned more blame to the victim than those who did not receive this information. This tendency to see other people as responsible for their plight can result in tragic consequences, such as seeing the victims of abuse and violence as responsible for their suffering.

person." That is, people think of their friends' personalities and answer accordingly. They usually do not think much about the nature of the social situation when making their predictions.

But how accurate are such predictions? Should the social situation be considered? To find out, Lee Ross and Steven Samuels (1993) conducted the following experiment. First, they chose a group of students at Stanford University who were considered by the resident assistants in their dorm to be either especially cooperative or especially competitive. The researchers did this by describing the game to the resident assistants and asking them to think of students in their dormitories who would be most likely to adopt the competitive or cooperative strategy. As expected, the resident assistants had no trouble thinking of students who fit each category.

Next, Ross and Samuels invited these students to play the game in a psychology experiment. There was one added twist. The researchers varied a seemingly minor aspect of the social situation—namely, what the game was called: They

▶ Suppose these students were asked to play a game for money. Would they play cooperatively or competitively? Do you think their personalities or the situation will be most likely to influence them?

told half the participants that it was the "Wall Street Game" and half that it was the "Community Game." Everything else about the game was identical. Thus, because people who were judged as either competitive or cooperative played the game under one of two names, the experiment resulted in four conditions.

Again, most of us go through life assuming that what really counts is an individual's personality—not something as trivial as what a game is called. Some people seem competitive by nature and would relish the opportunity to go head to head with a fellow student. Others seem much more cooperative and would achieve the most satisfaction by ensuring that no one lost too much money and no one's feelings were hurt. Right? Not so fast! As seen in Figure 1.1, even as trivial an aspect of the situation as the name of the game made a tremendous difference in how people behaved. When it was called the Wall Street Game, only one-third of the people responded cooperatively, whereas when it was called the Community Game, approximately two-thirds of the people responded cooperatively. The name of the game conveyed strong social norms about what kind of behaviour was appropriate in this situation. In Chapter 7, we will see that social norms shape people's behaviour in powerful ways.

FIGURE 1.1

What influences how cooperative people will be—their personalities or the nature of the social situation?

In this situation, the student's personality made no measurable difference in the student's behaviour. The students who were labelled "competitive" (by the resident assistants in their dormitories) were no more likely to adopt the competitive strategy than those labelled "cooperative." However, the name of the game—whether it was called the Wall Street Game or the Community Game—did make a tremendous difference. Such seemingly minor aspects of the social situation can have powerful effects on people's behaviour, overwhelming the differences in their personalities.

(Adapted from Ross & Samuels, 1993)

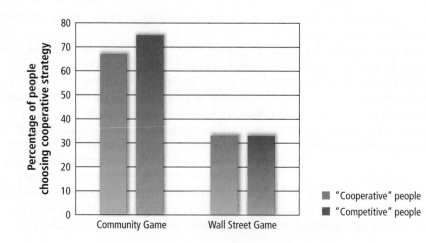

This is not to say that personality differences do not exist or are unimportant. They do exist and frequently are of great importance. But we have learned that social and environmental situations are so powerful that they have dramatic effects on almost everyone. That is the domain of the social psychologist.

The Subjectivity of the Social Situation

We have argued that the social situation often has profound effects on human behaviour. But what exactly do we mean by the social situation? One strategy for defining it would be to specify the objective properties of the situation, such as how rewarding it is to people, and then to document the behaviours that follow from these objective properties.

This was the approach taken by **behaviourism**, a school of psychology maintaining that to understand human behaviour one need only consider the reinforcing properties of the environment—that is, how positive and negative events in the environment are associated with specific behaviours. For example, dogs come when they are called because they have learned that compliance is followed by positive reinforcement (e.g., food or fondling); children memorize their multiplication tables more quickly if you praise them, smile at them, and give them a gold star following correct answers. Psychologists in this tradition, such as John Watson (1924) and B. F. Skinner (1938), suggested that all behaviour could be understood by examining the rewards and punishments in the organism's environment, and that there was no need to study such subjective states as thinking and feeling. Thus, to understand why Greg Baytalan cut short his vacation to help transport the bodies of tsunami victims to a morgue, a behaviourist would analyze the situation to see what specific objective factors were promoting helpful actions. What were the objective rewards and punishments implicit in taking a specific course of action? What were the rewards and punishments implicit in doing nothing?

Behaviourists chose not to deal with issues such as cognition, thinking, and feeling, because they considered these concepts too vague and mentalistic, and not sufficiently anchored to observable behaviour. Elegant in its simplicity, the behaviourist approach can account for a great deal of behaviour. But because behaviourism does not deal with cognition, thinking, and feeling—phenomena vital to the human social experience—this approach has proven inadequate for a complete understanding of the social world. We have learned that social behaviour cannot be fully understood by confining our observations to the physical properties of a situation. Instead, it is important to look at the situation from the viewpoint of the people in it, to see how they construe the world around them (Griffin & Ross, 1991; Ross & Nisbett, 1991). For example, if a person approaches you, slaps you on the back, and asks you how you are feeling, is that rewarding or not? On the surface, it might seem like a reward, but it is, in actuality, a complex situation that depends on your thoughts and feelings. You might construe the meaning differently, depending on whether the question is asked by a close friend of yours who is deeply concerned that you might be working too hard, a casual acquaintance simply passing the time of day, or an automobile salesperson intending to sell you a used car—even if the questions are worded the same and asked in the same tone of voice. In responding to the salesperson's question, it is unlikely that you will begin a detailed description of the pains you've been having in your kidney—something you might do in response to your closest friend's inquiry.

This emphasis on construal, the way people interpret the social situation, has its roots in an approach called Gestalt psychology. Initially proposed as a theory of how people perceive the physical word, **Gestalt psychology** holds that we should study the subjective way in which an object appears in people's minds (the gestalt, or whole), rather than the way in which the objective physical

behaviourism

a school of psychology maintaining that to understand human behaviour one need only consider the reinforcing properties of the environment—that is, how positive and negative events in the environment are associated with specific behaviours

Gestalt psychology

a school of psychology stressing the importance of studying the subjective way in which an object appears in people's minds, rather than the objective physical attributes of the object

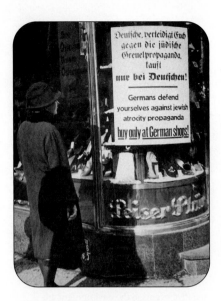

▲ In the 1930s, a woman reads a government-sponsored storefront sign urging the German people to boycott Jewish businesses. This was an early step that eventually led to the Holocaust.

▲ Kurt Lewin—"If an individual sits in a room trusting that the ceiling will not come down, should only his 'subjective probability' be taken into account for predicting behaviour or should we also consider the 'objective probability' of the ceiling's coming down as determined by engineers? To my mind, only the first has to be taken into account" (1943).

(Archives of the History of American Psychology, The University of Akron)

attributes of the object combine. One way to try to understand how people perceive a painting, for example, would be to break it down into its individual elements—such as the exact amounts of primary colours applied to the different parts of the canvas, the types of brush strokes used to apply the colours, and the different geometric shapes they form—and to attempt to determine how these elements are combined by the perceiver to form an overall image of the painting. According to Gestalt psychologists, however, it is impossible to understand the way in which an object is perceived simply by studying these building blocks of perception. The whole is different from the sum of its parts. One must focus on the phenomenology of the perceiver—that is, on how an object appears to people—instead of on the individual elements of the objective stimulus.

The Gestalt approach was formulated in Germany in the first part of the twentieth century by Kurt Koffka, Wolfgang Kohler, and Max Wertheimer, and their students and colleagues. Among these was Kurt Lewin, generally considered to be the founding father of modern experimental social psychology. As a young German-Jewish professor, Lewin directly experienced the anti-Semitism rampant in Nazi Germany. This experience had a major impact on his thinking, and once in the United States, he helped shape social psychology and directed it toward a deep interest in the exploration of causes and cures of prejudice and ethnic stereotyping.

As a theorist, Lewin took the bold step of applying Gestalt principles beyond the perception of objects to social perception—how people perceive other people and their motives, intentions, and behaviours. Lewin was the first scientist to fully realize the importance of taking the perspective of the people in any social situation to see how they construe (e.g., perceive, interpret, distort) this social environment. Social psychologists soon began to focus on the importance of considering subjective situations (how they are construed by people). These early social psychologists and their key statements are presented below.

Such construals can be rather simple, as in the example of the question "How are you feeling?" discussed earlier. Other construals might appear simple but are, in reality, remarkably complex. Suppose, for example, that Maria gives Shawn a kiss on the cheek at the end of their first date. How will Shawn respond to the kiss? We would say that it depends on how he construes the situation. Does he interpret it as a first step—a sign of awakening romantic interest on Maria's part? Or does he see it as an aloof, sisterly expression—a signal that Maria wants to be friends but nothing more? Or does he see it as a sign that Maria is interested in him but wants things to go slow in their developing relationship?

Were Shawn to misconstrue the situation, he might commit a serious blunder; he might turn his back on what could have been the love of his life—or he might express passion inappropriately. In either case, we believe that the best strategy for understanding Shawn's reaction would be to find a way to determine his construal of Maria's behaviour, rather than to dissect the objective nature of the kiss itself (e.g., its length, degree of pressure). But how are these construals formed? Stay tuned.

Where Construals Come From: Basic Human Motives

How will Shawn determine why Maria kissed him? If it is true that subjective and not objective situations influence people, then we need to understand how people arrive at their subjective impressions of the world. What are people trying to accomplish when they interpret the social world? Again, we could address this question from the perspective of people's personalities. What is it about Shawn, including his upbringing, family background, and unique experiences, that makes him view the world the way he does? As we have discussed, such a focus on individual differences in people's personality, while valuable, misses what is usually of far greater importance: the effects of the social situation on people. To understand these effects, we need to understand the fundamental laws of human nature, common to all, that explain why people construe the social world the way they do.

We human beings are complex organisms; at a given moment, myriad intersecting motives underlie our thoughts and behaviours. Over the years, social psychologists have found that two of these motives are of primary importance: *the need to be accurate* and *the need to feel good about ourselves*.

As we go through life, there are times when each of these motives pulls us in the same direction. Often, however, we find ourselves in situations where these two motives tug us in opposite directions—where to perceive the world accurately requires us to face up to the fact that we have behaved foolishly or immorally.

Leon Festinger, one of social psychology's most innovative theorists, was quick to realize that it is precisely when these two motives tug an individual in opposite directions that we can gain our most valuable insights into the workings of the human heart and mind. An example will clarify. On May 19, 2005, the Liberal Party needed the support of Chuck Cadman, a member of Parliament sitting as an Independent, on a budget amendment vote in order to stay in power. The Conservative Party, led by Stephen Harper, needed Cadman's vote to force an election. At the time, Cadman was critically ill with cancer. His wife, Dona, later claimed that the Conservatives had offered her dying husband a $1 million life insurance policy two days before the crucial vote. The so-called Cadman affair came to light in 2008. One of the revelations was a recording of an interview with Stephen Harper in July 2005, conducted by Vancouver journalist Tom Zytaruk shortly after Cadman's death. In the interview, Harper said that he was aware that representatives of the Conservative Party had engaged in discussions with Cadman, but maintained that the financial offer "was only to replace financial considerations he might lose due to an election" (Harper, as quoted in "Opposition MPs Grill PM," 2008). Members of the opposition challenged this statement, pointing out that the dying Cadman would not have been able to run in an election. Tom Flanagan, former chief adviser to Stephen Harper, admitted that he and others tried to persuade Cadman to rejoin the Conservative caucus, despite the fact that Cadman was seriously ill. (Cadman sat as a Conservative before becoming an Independent member of Parliament). The last of these discussions took place merely hours before the critical vote. In reflecting on these events, Flanagan comments that "this last desperate try with Cadman shows how we were all caught up in the attempt to force an election. . . . It's an excellent example of how the passions of politics lead to decisions that later make you scratch your head" (Flanagan, as quoted in Geddes, 2008).

Did Stephen Harper similarly admit that the behaviour of the Conservatives was out of line in this case? Not a chance. When the Cadman affair was brought to light, Harper, who by then was Canada's prime minister, defended the actions of the Conservatives and categorically denied that any deal had been offered to Cadman in the form of life insurance for his widow. Moreover, he launched a lawsuit against the Liberal Party for claiming that he knew of an offer to bribe Cadman to change his vote. On September 17, 2008, Harper's lawsuit was postponed until after the October 14, 2008, election. Lawyers for the Liberal Party accused Harper's legal team of deliberately delaying the proceedings, lest some unpleasant facts come to light that could jeopardize the election.

It will be some time before the truth of the Cadman affair will be fully known—if ever, given that the key witness is no longer living. What is clear is that Harper's response to this situation has been self-justification. Sometimes the need for self-justification can fly in the face of the need to be accurate. This is how many Canadians construe the Chuck Cadman affair. According to an Ipsos-Reid

▲ Fritz Heider—"Generally, a person reacts to what he thinks the other person is perceiving, feeling, and thinking, in addition to what the other person may be doing" (1958).

(Archives of the History of American Psychology, The University of Akron)

▲ Leon Festinger—"The way I have always thought about it is that if the empirical world looks complicated, if people seem to react in bewilderingly different ways to similar forces, and if I cannot see the operation of universal underlying dynamics, then that is my fault. I have asked the wrong questions; I have, at a theoretical level, sliced up the world incorrectly. The underlying dynamics are there, and I have to find the theoretical apparatus that will enable me to reveal these uniformities."

poll conducted in March 2008, 44 percent of respondents believe that the Conservatives did make an offer to Chuck Cadman, and nearly one-third believe that Steven Harper is not telling the truth (Russell, 2008).

The Self-Esteem Approach: The Need to Feel Good about Ourselves

Most people have a strong need to maintain reasonably high **self-esteem**—that is, to see themselves as good, competent, and decent (Aronson, 1992; Aronson, 1998; Baumeister, 1993; Kunda, 1990; Tavris & Aronson, 2007). The reason people view the world the way they do can often be traced to this underlying need to maintain a favourable image of themselves. Given the choice between distorting the world in order to feel good about themselves and representing the world accurately, people often take the first option.

Justifying Past Behaviour   Suppose a couple gets divorced after 10 years of a marriage made difficult by the husband's irrational jealousy. Suppose the husband blames the breakup of his marriage on the fact that his ex-wife was not sufficiently responsive or attentive to his needs, rather than admitting the truth: that his jealousy and overpossessiveness drove her away. His interpretation serves some purpose, in that it makes him feel better about himself; it is very difficult to own up to major deficiencies in ourselves, even when the cost is seeing the world inaccurately. The consequence of this distortion, of course, is that it decreases the probability that the individual will learn from experience; that is, in his next relationship, the husband is likely to run into the same problems.

We do not mean to imply that people totally distort reality, denying the existence of all information that reflects badly on them; such extreme behaviour is rare outside of mental institutions. Yet it is often possible for normal people like us to put a slightly different spin on the existing facts, one that shows us in the best light. Consider Roger—everybody knows someone like Roger. He's the guy whose shoes are almost always untied and who frequently has coffee stains on the front of his shirt or mustard stains around his lips. Most observers might consider Roger to be a slob, but Roger might see himself as casual and noncompulsive. The fact that people distort their interpretation of reality so that they feel better about themselves is not surprising, even to the most casual observer of human behaviour. The ways in which this motive operates, however, are often startling—and shed a great deal of light on behaviour that would otherwise be mystifying.

Suffering and Self-Justification   Let's go back to one of our early scenarios: the case of Jean-François Caudron. Why did Jean-François feel happy to be a part of hockey teams that made him endure rookie-night hazings? Perhaps his teammates were usually such a great bunch of guys that he was able to overlook their behaviour on rookie night. That is quite possible. But a far more compelling possibility involves the hazing itself. Specifically, we would contend, a major factor that increased Jean-François's liking for his teammates was, in fact, the unpleasant hazing ritual he experienced. That sounds a little strange. Why would something so unpleasant cause Jean-François to like his team? Doesn't it seem obvious that people like things that are associated with rewards rather than punishments? Not necessarily.

Here's how it works. If Jean-François goes through a hazing in order to be accepted by a team of mean-spirited players who do nasty things to one another, he will feel like a fool: "Why did I go through all that pain and embarrassment in order to be accepted by a bunch of jerks? Only a moron would do a thing like that." To avoid feeling like a fool, he will try to justify his decision to undergo the hazing by seeing his team in the best possible light.

But what about situations in which people experience severe hazings—more severe than having their toenails painted and being forced to drink warm beer until they vomit? Surely, under these conditions people wouldn't decide that

---

self-esteem

people's evaluations of their own self-worth—that is, the extent to which they view themselves as good, competent, and decent

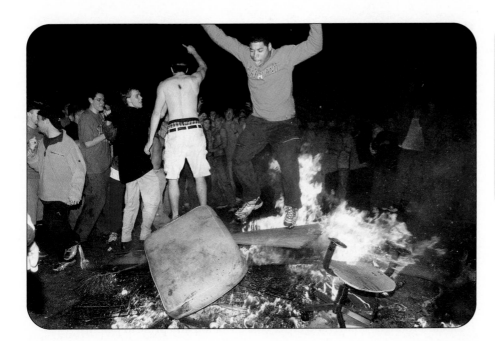

◄ Our desire to maintain self-esteem can have surprising consequences. Social psychological research demonstrates that when people submit to a painful or embarrassing initiation in order to join a group, they need to justify the experience to avoid feeling foolish. One way they do that is to decide that the initiation was worth it because the group is so wonderful. While a sports or military hazing may be silly or dangerous, at the same time, it does build cohesiveness.

they really want to belong to the group, would they? As it turns out, they often do. Consider the case of Dee Brasseur, one of Canada's first female military pilots. Her applications to fly with the elite all-male Snowbirds jet team were repeatedly turned down because of her gender. She also endured harassment, assault, and even rape during her 21-year career in the military. "Battle fatigue" caused by years of gender discrimination eventually forced her to retire. How does Dee Brasseur sum up her feelings toward the military? "I still love it. . . . I would recommend it to anybody, despite what occurred" (Branswell, 1998).

While an unmotivated observer might consider these costs of belonging to a group to be high, people such as Jean-François Caudron and Dee Brasseur who have experienced them are motivated to see the experiences differently. Jean-François Caudron, like many athletes, considers hazing a small price to pay for the sense of team solidarity that it creates. And Dee Brasseur remains fiercely loyal to the military.

Does this sound unbelievable? Are people actually more attracted to groups that subject them to pain and abuse? As far-fetched as it may sound, a series of well-controlled laboratory experiments conducted in the 1950s and 1960s demonstrated conclusively that the more unpleasant the procedure the participants underwent to get into a group, the more they liked the group (Aronson & Mills, 1959; Gerard & Mathewson, 1966). This phenomenon will be discussed more thoroughly in Chapter 6. The important points to remember here are that

- human beings are motivated to maintain a positive picture of themselves, in part by justifying their past behaviour, and that

- under certain specific conditions, this leads them to do things that at first glance might seem surprising or paradoxical—for example, they may prefer people and things for whom they have suffered over people and things they associate with pleasure.

Again, we want to emphasize that the results of this research tradition should not be taken to mean that behaviourist theories are dead wrong; those theories explain some behaviour very well (e.g., see our discussion in Chapter 9 of the research on social exchange theory). In our view, however, behaviourist approaches are inadequate to account for a huge subset of important attitudes and behaviours. This will become much clearer as you read on; in future chapters, we will try to specify the precise conditions under which one or the other set of principles is more likely to apply.

The Social Cognition Approach: The Need to Be Accurate

As we've seen, even when people are bending the facts to cast themselves in as favourable a light as they can, they do not completely distort reality. It would not be very adaptive to live in a fantasy world, believing, for example, that the car speeding toward you as you step off the curb is really a mirage, or that your future spouse will be Keira Knightley or Kanye West. In fact, human beings are quite skilled at thinking, contemplating, and deducing. One of the hallmarks of being human is the ability to reason. As a species, human beings have developed truly amazing logical and computational abilities. In our lifetimes, we have witnessed such extraordinary cognitive achievements as the invention and development of computers, the exploration of outer space, and the conquering of many human diseases.

Moreover, on a more common—but perhaps more important—level, it is impossible to observe the cognitive development of a child without being awestruck. Just think of the vast gains in knowledge and reasoning that occur in the first few years of life. In a relatively short time, we see a child transform from a squirming, helpless newborn, who seems to do little but eat, cry, and sleep, into a sophisticated, garrulous four-year-old, who can utter complex sentences, hatch diabolic plots to frustrate a younger sibling, and evoke consternation and pride in parents.

social cognition

how people think about themselves and the social world; more specifically, how people select, interpret, remember, and use social information

Social Cognition Given the amazing cognitive abilities of our species, it makes sense that social psychologists, when formulating theories of social behaviour, would take into consideration the way in which human beings think about the world. We call this the cognitive approach to social psychology, or **social cognition** (Fiske & Taylor, 1991; Kunda, 1999; Nisbett & Ross, 1980). Researchers who attempt to understand social behaviour from the perspective of social cognition begin with the assumption that people try to view the world as accurately as possible. Accordingly, human beings are viewed by researchers as amateur sleuths who are doing their best to understand and predict their social world.

But this is by no means as easy or as straightforward as it may seem. We human beings frequently run into problems because we almost never know all the facts we need to in order to make the most accurate judgment of a given situation. Whether it is a relatively simple decision, such as which breakfast cereal is the best combination of nutrition and tastiness, or a slightly more complex decision, such as our desire to buy the best car we can for under $1800, or a much more complex decision, such as choosing a marriage partner who will make us deliriously happy for the rest of our lives, it is almost never easy to gather all the relevant facts in advance. Moreover, we make countless decisions every day; even if there were a way to gather all the facts for each decision, we simply lack the time and the stamina to do so.

Does this sound a bit overblown? Aren't most decisions fairly easy? Let's take a closer look. We will begin by asking you a simple question: Which breakfast cereal is better for you, Lucky Charms or 100% Natural from Quaker? If you are like most of our students, you answered, "100% Natural from Quaker." After all, Lucky Charms is a kid's cereal, full of sugar and cute little marshmallows. There is even a picture of a leprechaun on the box, for goodness' sake. And 100% Natural has a picture of raw wheat on the box, the box is the colour of natural wheat—and doesn't *natural* mean "good for you"? If that is the way you reasoned, you have, understandably, fallen into a common cognitive trap—you have generalized from the cover to the product. A careful reading of the ingredients in small print on the packages will inform you that although Lucky Charms has a bit more sugar in it than 100% Natural, the latter contains far more fat—so much so that the respected journal *Consumer Reports* has judged it to be less healthful than Lucky Charms. Things are not always as they appear; thus, coming up with an accurate picture of the social world is not always easy.

Expectations about the Social World   To add to the difficulty, sometimes our expectations about the social world get in the way of our accurate perception of it. Our expectations can even change the nature of the social world. Imagine, for example, that you are an elementary school teacher dedicated to improving the lives of your students as best you can. You are aware at the beginning of the academic year of how each student performed on standardized intelligence tests. Early in your career, you were pretty sure, but not *entirely* sure, that these tests could gauge each child's true potential. But after several years of teaching, you have gradually become certain that these tests are accurate. Why the change? Almost without fail, you have come to see that the kids who got high scores on these tests are the ones who did the best in your classroom, and the kids who got low scores performed poorly in class.

This scenario doesn't sound all that surprising, except for one key fact: You might be wrong about the validity of the intelligence tests. It might be that the tests weren't very accurate but that you unintentionally treated the kids with high scores and the kids with low scores differently, making it seem as if the tests were accurate. This is exactly what Robert Rosenthal and Lenore Jacobson (1968) found in their investigation of a phenomenon called the *self-fulfilling prophecy.* They first entered elementary school classrooms and administered a test. They then informed each teacher that according to the test, a few specific students were bloomers—that is, they were about to take off and perform extremely well. In actuality, the test showed no such thing; the children labelled as bloomers were chosen by drawing names out of a hat and thus were no different, on average, from any of the other kids. Lo and behold, on returning to the classroom at the end of the school year, Rosenthal and Jacobson found that the bloomers were performing extremely well. The mere fact that the teachers were led to expect these students to do well caused a reliable improvement in their performance. This striking phenomenon is no fluke; it has been replicated a number of times in a wide variety of schools (Rosenthal, 1995).

How did it come about? While this outcome seems almost magical, it is embedded in an important aspect of human nature. If you were one of those teachers and were led to expect two or three specific students to perform well, you would be more likely to treat those students in special ways—such as paying more attention to them, listening to them with more respect, calling on them more frequently, encouraging them, and trying to teach them more difficult material. This in turn would almost certainly make these students feel happier, more respected, more motivated, and smarter, and *voilà*—a self-fulfilling prophecy. Thus, even when we are trying to perceive the social world as accurately as possible, we can go wrong in many ways, ending up with the wrong impressions. We will explain why—and the conditions under which social perception is accurate—in Chapters 3 and 4.

Other Motives: Ensuring Our Survival and Coping with Mortality

We want to reiterate what we stated earlier: The two major sources of construals we have emphasized here—the need to maintain a positive view of ourselves (the self-esteem approach) and the need to view the world accurately (the social cognition approach)—are the most important of our social motives. But they are certainly not the only motives influencing people's thoughts and behaviours. As noted earlier, we human beings are complex organisms, and under various conditions, a variety of motives influence what we think, feel, and do. Biological drives such as hunger and thirst, of course, can be powerful motivators, especially under circumstances of extreme deprivation. At a more psychological level, we can be motivated by fear or by the promise of love, favours, and other rewards involving social exchange. These motives will be discussed at length in Chapters 9 and 10. Finally, at a fundamental level, human behaviour is motivated by the need to survive. Not only do we need to survive, but we also need to cope with the fear that is produced by the realization that we are mortal beings. We discuss these motives next.

Ensuring Our Survival   Both humans and non-humans are motivated to survive. This is a central tenet of evolutionary psychology, a theory that is receiving increasing prominence in social psychology. **Evolutionary psychology** is a theoretical branch of psychology that attempts to explain social behaviour in terms of genetic factors that evolved over time according to the principles of natural selection (Buss, 1994, 1996a; Buss & Kenrick, 1998; Simpson & Kenrick, 1997; Wright, 1994). The theory of evolution was originally articulated by Charles Darwin, and the key idea underlying it is natural selection, the assumption that characteristics that help an organism survive will be passed on to its offspring. The application of this idea to human behaviour has generated considerable controversy. The theory has generally been interpreted to mean that human behaviour is driven by biology alone and therefore that the environment has little or no effect. However, current evolutionary theorists take the perspective that biological influences on human behaviour are, in fact, responsive to the environment (Buss & Kenrick, 1998; Crawford & Krebs, 1998). As we will discuss later, evolutionary explanations have been offered for a variety of human social behaviours, including situations under which people select dating and mating partners (Chapter 9), people offer help to others (Chapter 10), and when people aggress against one another (Chapter 11).

Terror Management Theory   Although both humans and non-humans have a need to survive, only human beings possess the awareness that one day they will die. According to **terror management theory**, this realization produces fear—actually terror—in people and they will go to great lengths to reduce these negative feelings (Greenberg, Pyszczynski, & Solomon, 1986; Solomon, Greenberg, & Pyszczynski, 1991; Wisman & Goldenberg, 2005; see Greenberg, Solomon, & Pyszczynski, 1997, for a review). An extensive program of research has shown that reminding people of their mortality (i.e., that they will die one day) sets in motion a variety of coping responses intended to reduce this fear. These responses frequently involve boosting one's self-esteem, usually by clinging to the standards and values of one's culture. For example, in one study, participants who were interviewed about their attitudes toward various local charities in front of a funeral home (intended to remind them that one day they would die) expressed more positive attitudes toward various local charities than those who were interviewed in a more neutral location (Jonas, Schimel, Greenberg, & Pyszczynski, 2002). In a follow-up study, these researchers found that participants who were reminded of their mortality actually donated more money to a charity than those who were not. University of British Columbia researchers have shown that when people are reminded of their mortality (e.g., by writing about what it will feel like to die) they report stronger beliefs in God and other supernatural agents (Norenzayan & Hansen, 2006). Similarly, at York University, recent research has shown that mortality salience causes some people to hold political and other personal beliefs with greater zeal (McGregor, Gailliot, Vasquez, & Nash, 2007).

Schimel and colleagues have demonstrated that the converse is also true—namely, that when people's worldviews are threatened, thoughts of death are more accessible. In a series of studies conducted at the University of Alberta, students who were highly invested in Canadian culture were exposed to a website that either attacked Canadian values (e.g., hockey, poutine, healthcare) or Australian values (e.g., Australian-style football, kangaroos). Participants whose own worldviews were threatened (i.e., the attack on Canadian values) subsequently reported more death-related thoughts than participants in the Australia condition (Schimel, Hayes, Williams, & Jahrig, 2007). The researchers concluded that cultural worldviews shield us from thoughts of death, and when these worldviews are threatened, thoughts of death are more likely to come to mind.

---

evolutionary psychology

the attempt to explain social behaviour in terms of genetic factors that evolved over time according to the principles of natural selection

terror management theory

the realization that we are going to die produces fear, and people will go to great lengths to reduce this feeling

Social Psychology and Social Problems

To recapitulate, social psychology can be defined as the scientific study of social influence. Social influence can best be understood by focusing on the major roots of human behaviour. It might have occurred to you to ask why we want to understand social influence in the first place. Who cares? And what difference does it make whether a behaviour has its roots in the desire to be accurate, the desire to bolster our self-esteem, or the desire to survive and pass on our genes?

There are several answers. The most basic is simple: We are curious. Social psychologists are fascinated by human social behaviour and want to understand it on the deepest possible level. In a sense, all of us are social psychologists. We all live in a social environment, and we are all more than mildly curious about such issues as how we become influenced, how we influence others, and why we fall in love with some people, dislike others, and are indifferent to still others.

Many social psychologists have another reason for studying the causes of social behaviour: to contribute to the solution of social problems. From the very beginning of our young science, social psychologists have been keenly interested in such social problems as the reduction of hostility and prejudice, and the increase of altruism and generosity. Contemporary social psychologists have continued this tradition and have broadened the issues of concern to include endeavours such as inducing people to conserve natural resources such as water and energy (Dickerson, Thibodeau, Aronson, & Miller, 1992), educating people to practise safer sex in order to reduce the spread of AIDS (Aronson, 1997a, 1998; Stone, Aronson, Crain, Winslow, & Fried, 1994), understanding the relationship between viewing violence on television and violent behaviour (Eron, Huesmann, Lefkowitz, & Walder, 1996; Josephson, 1987), developing effective negotiation strategies for the reduction of international conflict (Kelman, 1997), and helping people adjust to life changes such as the entry to college or the death of a loved one (Harris, 1986).

The ability to understand and explain complex and dysfunctional social behaviour brings with it the challenge to change it. For example, given the health risks associated with smoking, there has been increased pressure on governments to persuade people to stop smoking. In 2000, Canadian cigarette packages began to display the largest, most graphic warning images and messages anywhere in the world. The federal government's intent was to frighten people into stopping (or not starting) smoking. As you have probably seen, the images include pictures of a cancerous mouth, of premature infants with warnings to pregnant women not to smoke (because of the link between smoking and sudden infant death syndrome), and of brain fragments with a warning that smoking leads to increased risk of strokes. This seems consistent with common sense. If you want people to do something they aren't inclined to do, why not scare the daylights out of them?

This is certainly not a stupid idea. Researchers at the University of Waterloo recently compared the effects of warning messages on cigarette packages in Canada, the United Kingdom, Australia and the United States and concluded that Canada's large, graphic warnings were the most effective (Hammond et al., 2007). As we shall see in subsequent chapters, there are many dysfunctional acts (e.g., cigarette smoking, drunk driving) for which the induction of fear can and does motivate people to take rational, appropriate action to preserve their health (Petty, 1995). However, based on years of systematic research on persuasion, social psychologists have realized that this approach is not effective in all situations. For example, the fear-inducing approach has been applied in the case of AIDS, where it does not produce the desired effect of persuading people to practise safer sex. Rather, the research evidence suggests that most people do not want to be thinking about dying or contracting a painful illness while they are

Would you trade the rest of your life for two minutes* of ecstasy?

If you don't abstain, use a condom.
* ACTUAL TIMES MAY VARY

ABSTINENCE REMAINS AN OPTION.

Continental PIR
COMMUNICATIONS

Photo © Rod Newbery / Photo Search Ltd.

Funding for this publication was provided by Health Canada in partnership with Alberta Health and the Canadian Public Health Association. For more copies: Canadian HIV/AIDS Clearinghouse, Canadian Public Health Association, 400-1565 Carling Avenue, Ottawa, ON, K1Z 8R1, Tel: 613-725-3434, Fax: 613-725-9826, E-mail: aidsstat@cpha.ca, Internet: www.cpha.ca

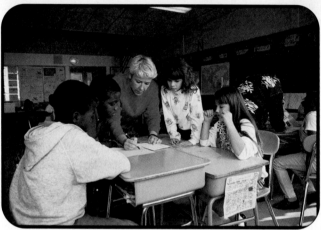

▲ Among the many kinds of relevant issues social psychologists investigate are the following: (a) Does watching violence on television produce violent behaviour in children? (b) Does cooperation reduce prejudice? (c) Does fear motivate people to change dangerous sexual practices?

getting ready to have sex. Such thoughts can interfere, to say the least, with the romance of the occasion. Moreover, most people do not enjoy using condoms because they feel that interrupting the sexual act destroys the mood. As demonstrated in a study with French-Canadian university students, people who feel that condoms are inconvenient are less likely to use them (Hébert, Bernard, deMan, & Farrar, 1989). Given these considerations, when people have been exposed to frightening messages, instead of engaging in rational problem-solving behaviour, most tend to reduce that fear by engaging in denial; for example, in research conducted at various universities in Ontario, students expressed beliefs such as, "It can't happen to me," "Surely none of my friends have AIDS," and "This person I've just met doesn't seem like the type who would sleep around" (MacDonald, Zanna, & Fong, 1996; Maticka-Tyndale, Herold, & Mewhinney, 1998).

The astute reader will see that the process of denial stems not from the desire to be accurate but from the desire to maintain self-esteem. That is, if people can succeed in convincing themselves that their sexual partners could not possibly have AIDS, then they can continue to engage in unprotected sex while maintaining a reasonably positive picture of themselves as rational individuals. By understanding the conditions under which self-esteem maintenance prevails, social psychologists have been able to contribute important insights into AIDS education and prevention, as we will discuss (Aronson, 1997a; Aronson, Fried, & Stone, 1991; Stone et al., 1994).

Throughout this book, we will examine many similar examples of the applications of social psychology. Likewise, we will discuss some of the underlying human motives and characteristics of the social situations that produce significant social behaviours, with the assumption that if we are interested in changing our own or other people's behaviour, we must first know something about these fundamental causes. Although most of the studies discussed are concerned with such fundamental causes, in the process, they also address critical social problems, including the effects of mass media on attitudes and behaviour (Chapter 6), violence and aggression (Chapter 11), and prejudice (Chapter 12). For the benefit of the interested reader, we have also included three separate modules that apply social psychology to contemporary issues involving the environment, health, and law. Your instructor may assign them at any time during the semester, or may decide not to assign them at all, leaving that decision to your own curiosity.

SUMMARY

People are constantly being influenced by others. **Social psychology** is defined as the scientific study of the way in which people's thoughts, feelings, and behaviours are influenced by the real or imagined presence of other people. Social influence is often powerful, usually outweighing and frequently overwhelming **individual differences** in people's personalities as determinants of behaviour. As a result, we must try to avoid making the **fundamental attribution error**—the tendency to explain our own and others' behaviour entirely in terms of personality traits, thereby underestimating the power of social influence.

To appreciate the power of social influence, we must understand how people form **construals** of their social environment. This is a departure from **behaviourism**, a school of thought maintaining that in order to understand behaviour, we need only to consider whether the properties of the environment in which the individual is situated are positive or negative. Social psychologists argue that we are not computer-like organisms who respond directly and mechanically to environmental stimuli; rather, we are complex human beings who perceive, think about, and sometimes distort information from our environment. Social psychology's emphasis on the way in which people construe the social world has its roots in the tradition of **Gestalt psychology**.

A person's construals of the world derive primarily from two fundamental motives: the desire to maintain **self-esteem**

and the desire to form an accurate picture of oneself and the social world (the **social cognition** approach). Accordingly, to understand how we are influenced by our social environments, we must understand the processes by which we do the perceiving, thinking, and distorting.

Human behaviour also is motivated by a very basic need: the need for survival—of oneself and one's offspring. This **evolutionary** perspective has been used to explain various social psychological phenomena, including mate selection, prosocial (helping) behaviour, and aggression. According to **terror management theory**, the awareness that we are mortal sets in motion a number of anxiety-reducing mechanisms.

Social psychological insights have been applied to a variety of practical problems in contemporary society such as prejudice reduction, the curbing of violence, and persuading people to live healthier lives.

We also discussed an important point about social psychology: that it is an empirical science. Social psychologists attempt to find answers to key questions about social influence by designing and conducting research, rather than by relying on common sense or the wisdom of the ages. In Chapter 2, we will discuss the scientific methods that social psychologists use when conducting such research.

Along with a dynamic, electronic version of this text, MyPsychLab offers a wealth of resources to deepen your understanding and test your recall of the material in this chapter—including video and audio clips, simulations and activities, self-assessments, practice tests, and other study materials. The following specific resources are available for this chapter:

 Fundamental Attribution Error

 Introduction to Social Psychology

The Power of the Situation: Phil Zimbardo

To access MyPsychLab, please visit www.mypsychlab.com (Student Access Code required—packaged with this book).

2

Methodology:

How Social Psychologists Do Research

In 1993, the parliamentary Standing Committee on Communications and Culture published a report on the effects of television violence titled "Television Violence: Fraying Our Social Fabric." This report was triggered, at least in part, by a petition initiated by 13-year-old Virginie Larivière, whose 11-year-old sister had been robbed, sexually assaulted, and murdered. Virginie Larivière was convinced that television violence was responsible for her sister's death. She and her family gathered more than 1.3 million signatures from Canadians across the country. The petition called for a boycott of violent television programming and for federal government legislation to reduce the violent content of television programming. The 11 members of Parliament who served on the Standing Committee interviewed the chair of the Canadian Radio-television and Telecommunications Commission, professors, executives from the Canadian Association of Broadcasters, and the president of the Canadian Film and Television Production Association. Based on these interviews and various reports, the committee decided there was not enough evidence to support the conclusion that violence on television contributes to violent behaviour: "Many factors contribute to violence in society and the part played by television violence can only be estimated and amounts to an unknown fraction." As a result, the committee recommended against legislating a reduction in violent content in television programming, preferring industry self-regulation and public education instead.

The question of whether television violence produces violent behaviour is an extremely important one, particularly in light of allegations—such as those made by Virginie Larivière—that violence on television plays a role in brutal, deadly assaults on innocent people. However, as the Standing Committee on Communications and Culture discovered, different experts have different opinions, making it difficult to draw firm conclusions. How can one decide who is right? Is this a case where majority opinion rules, or is there a more scientific way to determine the answers?

Consider, now, a 1995 report commissioned by the federal Department of Canadian Heritage to address the same question. This report, titled "Television Violence: A Review of the Effects on Children of Different Ages," was prepared by social psychologist Wendy Josephson, who analyzed the results of hundreds of scientific studies. Her conclusion was that television violence does increase aggressive behaviour—at least among children predisposed toward aggression. She pointed out that "although the group especially at risk might be a minority of viewers, they are likely to be the majority of aggressors." Josephson's conclusion, based on a careful analysis of scientific evidence, was quite different from the conclusion reached by the Standing Committee on Communications and Culture, which relied on reports and interviews with individuals—many of whom were from the television industry. In this chapter, we will examine the kinds of research methods that allow us to scientifically answer important questions about the causes of violence.

Social Psychology: An Empirical Science

> *I love games. I think I could be very happy being a chess player or dealing with some other kinds of games. But I grew up in the Depression. It didn't seem one could survive on chess, and science is also a game. You have very strict ground rules in science, and your ideas have to check out with the empirical world. That's very tough and also very fascinating.*
>
> —Leon Festinger, 1977

A fundamental principle of social psychology is that many social problems, such as the causes of and reactions to violence, can be studied scientifically (Aronson, Wilson, & Brewer, 1998; Reis & Judd, 2000). Before we discuss how social psychological research is done, we begin with a warning: The results of some of the experiments you encounter will seem obvious, because the topic of social psychology is something with which we are all intimately familiar—social behaviour and social influence. Note that this separates social psychology from other sciences. When you read about an experiment in particle physics, it is unlikely that the results will connect with your personal experiences and have a ring of familiarity. We don't know about you, but none of your authors has ever thought, "Wow! That experiment on quarks was just like what happened to me while I was waiting for the bus yesterday," or "My grandmother always told me to watch out for quarks, positrons, and antimatter." When reading about the results of a study on helping behaviour or aggression, however, it is quite common to think, "Aw, come on, I could have predicted that. That's the same thing that happened to me last Friday."

The thing to remember is that when we study human behaviour, the results may appear to have been predictable—in retrospect. Indeed, there is a well-known human tendency called the *hindsight bias*, whereby people exaggerate how much they could have predicted an outcome *after* knowing that it occurred (Bradfield & Wells, 2005; Fischhoff, Gonzalez, Lerner, & Small, 2005; Guilbault, Bryant, Brockway, & Posavac, 2004). Hindsight is 20/20, as the saying goes. This phenomenon was illustrated in a study by Roese and Olson (1996). They asked students at the University of Western Ontario to read a story, based on World War I events, about a young British soldier who devised a plan to save a small village that was about to be invaded. In one condition, participants were told that the soldier managed to convince others in the military to accept his plan and the village was saved. When asked how predictable this outcome was, they felt it was obvious all along that the village would be saved. In another condition, participants were told that the soldier's plan was rejected and the village was destroyed. When asked how predictable this outcome was, these participants thought it was obvious that the village would be destroyed! As this study shows, the opposite finding of an experiment might seem just as obvious as the results that actually were obtained. The trick is to predict what will happen in an experiment *before* you know how it turns out.

To find out for yourself what we mean when we say not all findings that may seem obvious can actually be predicted in advance, take the accompanying Try It! quiz. Each answer is based on well-established social psychological research. In our experience as teachers, we have found that few of our students get all the answers correct. Findings that seem obvious in retrospect may not be easy to predict in advance.

Social psychology is an empirical science with a well-developed set of methods to answer questions about social behaviour, such as the ones about violence with which we began this chapter. These methods are of three types: the *observational method*, the *correlational method*, and the *experimental method*. Any of these methods can be used to explore a specific research question; each is a powerful tool in some ways and a weak tool in others. Part of the creativity in conducting social psychological research involves choosing the right method, maximizing its strengths, and minimizing its weaknesses.

Try it!

▶ Social Psychology Quiz

Take a moment to answer the questions below, each of which is based on social psychological research. While the correct answers may seem obvious in retrospect, many are hard to guess in advance.

1. Suppose an authority figure asks university students to administer near-lethal electric shocks to another student who has not harmed them in any way. What percentage of these students will agree to do it?

2. If you give children a reward for doing something they already enjoy doing, they will subsequently like that activity (a) more, (b) the same, or (c) less.

3. Who do you think would be happiest with their choice of a consumer product, such as an art poster? (a) People who spend several minutes thinking about why they like or dislike each poster. (b) People who choose a poster without analyzing the reasons for their feelings.

4. Repeated exposure to a stimulus, such as a person, a song, or a painting, will make you like it (a) more, (b) the same, or (c) less.

5. You ask an acquaintance to do you a favour—for example, to lend you $10—and he or she agrees. As a result of doing you this favour, the person will probably like you (a) more, (b) the same, or (c) less.

6. When making a complex decision, is it best to (a) decide right away without further thought, (b) think carefully about the different options, or (c) find something to distract you for a while, then make up your mind?

7. In Canada and the United States, female university students tend not to do as well as male students on math tests. Under which of the following circumstances will women do as well as men? (a) They are told that there are no gender differences on a test. (b) They are told that women tend to do better on a difficult math test, because under these circumstances, they rise to the challenge. (c) They are told that men outperform women under almost all circumstances.

8. Which statement about the effects of advertising is most true? (a) Subliminal messages implanted in advertisements are more effective than normal, everyday advertising. (b) Normal, everyday advertising, such as television ads for painkillers or laundry detergents, are more effective than subliminal messages implanted in ads. (c) Both kinds of advertising are equally effective. (d) Neither type of advertising is effective.

9. In public settings, (a) women touch men more, (b) men touch women more, or (c) there is no difference—men and women touch each other equally.

10. Which things in their past do people regret most? (a) Actions they performed that they wish they had not. (b) Actions they did not perform that they wish they had. (c) It depends on how long ago the events occurred.

See page 54 for answers.

In this chapter, we will discuss these methods in detail. We, the authors of this book, are not primarily textbook writers—we are social scientists who have done a great deal of research in social psychology. As such, we will try to provide you with an understanding of both the joy and the difficulty of doing research. The joy comes in unravelling the clues about the causes of interesting and important social behaviours, just as a sleuth gradually unmasks the culprit in a mystery. Each of us finds it exhilarating that we have the tools to provide definitive answers to questions that philosophers have debated for centuries. At the same time, as seasoned researchers we have learned to temper this exhilaration with a heavy dose of humility, for the practical and ethical constraints involved in creating and conducting social psychological research are formidable.

Formulating Hypotheses and Theories

There is lore in science that brilliant insights come all of a sudden, as when Archimedes shouted, "Eureka! I have found it!" when the solution to a problem flashed into his mind. While such insights do sometimes occur suddenly, science is a cumulative process, and researchers typically generate hypotheses from previous theories and research. We define a **theory** as an organized set of principles that can be used to explain observed phenomena.

theory
an organized set of principles that can be used to explain observed phenomena

Many studies stem from a researcher's dissatisfaction with existing theories and explanations. After reading other people's work, a researcher might believe that he or she has a better way of explaining people's behaviour (e.g., why they fail to help in an emergency). Social psychologists, like scientists in other disciplines, engage in a continual process of theory refinement. They develop a theory, test specific hypotheses derived from that theory, and based on the results, revise the theory and formulate new hypotheses. We define a **hypothesis** as a testable statement or idea about the relationship between two or more variables.

hypothesis
a testable statement or idea about the relationship between two or more variables

Theory is not the only way to derive a new hypothesis in social psychology. Researchers often observe a phenomenon in everyday life that they find curious and interesting. They then construct a theory about why this phenomenon

▶ Kitty Genovese was attacked in this area in full view of her neighbours. Why didn't anyone call the police?

TABLE 2.1

A summary of research methods

Method	Questions Answered
1. Observational/Archival	Description: What is the nature of the phenomenon?
2. Correlational	Description: What is the relation between variable X and variable Y?
3. Experimental	Causality: Is variable X a cause of variable Y?

occurred and design a study to see if they are right. Consider the murder of Kitty Genovese. Genovese was attacked while walking to her car and brutally murdered in the alley of an apartment complex. The attack lasted 45 minutes. No fewer than 38 of the apartment residents admitted later that they had rushed to their windows after hearing Genovese's screams for help. However, not one of these bystanders attempted in any way to help her—none of them even telephoned the police.

As you might imagine, the Kitty Genovese murder received a great deal of publicity. Reporters, commentators, and pundits of all kinds came forward with their personal theories about why the bystanders had done nothing. Most people blamed her neighbours' failure to intervene on the apathy, indifference, and callousness that big-city life breeds. Two social psychologists who taught at universities in New York, however, had a different idea. Bibb Latané and John Darley got to talking one day about the Genovese murder. Here is how Latané describes it: "One evening after [a] downtown cocktail party, John Darley . . . came back with me to my 12th Street apartment for a drink. Our common complaint was the distressing tendency of acquaintances, on finding that we called ourselves social psychologists, to ask why New Yorkers were so apathetic" (Latané, 1987, p. 78). Instead of focusing on "what was wrong with New Yorkers," Latané and Darley thought it would be more interesting and more important to examine the social situation in which Genovese's neighbours found themselves: "We came up with the insight that perhaps what made the Genovese case so fascinating was itself what made it happen—namely, that not just one or two, but 38 people had watched and done nothing" (Latané, 1987, p. 78).

The researchers had the hunch that, paradoxically, the more people who witness an emergency, the less likely it is that any given individual will intervene. Genovese's neighbours might have assumed that someone else had called the police, a phenomenon Latané and Darley (1968) referred to as the *diffusion of responsibility*. Perhaps the bystanders would have been more likely to help had each thought he or she alone was witnessing the murder.

Once a researcher has a hypothesis, whether it comes from a theory, previous research, or an observation of everyday life, how can he or she tell if it is true? In science, idle speculation will not do; the researcher must collect data to test his or her hypothesis. Let's look at how the observational method, the correlational method, and the experimental method are used to explore research hypotheses such as Latané and Darley's. These methods are summarized in Table 2.1.

The Observational Method

There is a lot to be learned by being an astute observer of human behaviour. If the goal is to describe what a particular group of people or type of behaviour is like, the **observational method** is very useful. This is the technique whereby a researcher observes people and systematically records measurements of their

observational method

the technique whereby a researcher observes people and systematically records measurements of their behaviour

behaviour. This method varies according to the degree to which the observer actively participates in the scene. At one extreme, the observer neither participates nor intervenes in any way; instead, the observer is unobtrusive and tries to blend in with the scenery as much as possible. For example, Debra Pepler at York University and Wendy Craig at Queen's University have developed a particularly unobtrusive method for observing bullying behaviour in school settings (Atlas & Pepler, 1998; Craig & Pepler, 1997; Pepler & Craig, 1995; Pepler, Craig, O'Connell, Atlas, & Charach, 2004). The children wear waist pouches containing small microphones, while a hidden video camera films their interactions. Thus, children can freely roam over relatively large areas (e.g., school playgrounds) while having their behaviour recorded. This combination of audio and visual technology allows the researchers to observe overt physical acts of aggression, as well as more subtle forms of bullying, such as indirect aggression and verbal threats or insults. (Subtle forms of bullying are especially difficult to detect when researchers rely on more traditional methods, such as standing outside a playground fence and making check marks whenever they notice particular behaviours.)

The waist-pouch microphone technology also addresses an age-old problem in observational research—namely, that people change their behaviour when they are being observed. Bullies, for example, tend not to engage in bullying when adults are around (Craig & Pepler, 1997; Pepler et al., 2004). Therefore, an advantage of using unobtrusive measures, such as Pepler and Craig's, is that researchers can observe spontaneous, naturally occurring behaviour.

In all observational research—regardless of whether observers are on the spot or later analyze video- or audiotapes—it is important for the researchers to clearly define the behaviours of interest. For example, in Pepler and Craig's research an episode is classified as bullying only if there is a power imbalance between the individuals involved, if there is intent to harm on the part of the person doing the bullying, and if the victim shows distress (Atlas & Pepler, 1998; Craig & Pepler, 1997; Pepler et al., 2004). Note that the importance of clearly defining the behaviours of interest applies to all psychological research, not just to observational studies. The term **operational definition** refers to the precise specification of how variables are measured or manipulated. Recall, for example, that a power imbalance is one of the criteria that Pepler and colleagues use to define bullying. Are you able to come up with an operational definition of this variable that would be useful in the context of observing playground interactions? Pepler and Craig operationally defined a power imbalance as a discrepancy in terms of height and weight between the children involved. In other words, in situations involving aggression on the playground, the researchers assume that a bigger child is likely to be in a position of power relative to a smaller child.

If, on the other hand, the researchers were interested in observing bullying in a corporate boardroom, they presumably would specify a different operational definition of power imbalance—perhaps the discrepancy between the individuals' status in the corporation (e.g., vice-president versus manager).

Some situations, by their nature, require researchers to interact with the people being observed but to try not to alter the situation in any way. The method by which researchers attempt to understand a group or culture by observing it from the inside without imposing any preconceived notions they might have is known as **ethnography**. The goal is to understand the richness and complexity of the group by observing it in action. Ethnography is the chief method of cultural anthropology, the study of human cultures and societies. As social psychology broadens its focus by studying social behaviour in different cultures, ethnography is increasingly being used to describe different cultures and generate hypotheses about psychological principles (Fine & Elsbach, 2000; Hodson, 2004; Uzzel, 2000).

operational definition

the precise specification of how variables are measured or manipulated

ethnography

the method by which researchers attempt to understand a group or culture by observing it from the inside without imposing any preconceived notions they might have

CONNECTIONS

Using Observational Research to Develop Anti-Bullying Programs

Observational research can be used to address important social problems. For example, Debra Pepler and colleagues' research on bullying has led to the development of an anti-bullying intervention program that has been used in schools across Canada (Pepler et al., 1994; Pepler et al., 2004). This program, modelled after a successful intervention program developed in Norway and Sweden (Olweus, 1996, 1997; 2004), educates children, teachers, administrators, and parents about the problem of bullying. Children are taught how to respond when they are the victims of bullying and how to intervene when they observe incidents of bullying. Teachers are trained to be vigilant for instances of bullying and to make swift interventions. This program has met with mixed success. The good news is that the incidence of bullying observed on the playground declines. The bad news is that schools and teachers vary tremendously in terms of the support for, and resources dedicated to, such programs. Moreover, there is little evidence that peers are more likely to intervene in bullying situations, despite the fact that peer intervention generally stops bullying. This latter point is critical because, according to Pepler, "Research indicates that when students intervene, in 57 per cent of the cases the bullying stops within 10 seconds . . . so we really need to empower our children to know what to do in bullying situations" (Pepler, as quoted in "Don't Stand By . . . Stand Up," 2006). This has been the focus of more recent interventions, which are aimed at encouraging bystanders to speak up— to tell a teacher, parent, guidance counselor, or others until the situation is addressed. In some programs, children watch films of bullying incidents and participate in role-modelling exercises in which they rehearse how and when to intervene (Rigby & Johnson, 2006–2007). It is encouraging that research on the dynamics of bullying is leading to the development of anti-bullying programs all over the world (see Smith, Pepler, Rigby, 2004).

Consider this example from the early years of social psychological research. In the 1950s, a group of people in the U.S. Midwest predicted that the world would come to an end in a violent cataclysm on a specific date. They also announced that they would be rescued in time by a spaceship that would land in their leader's backyard. Assuming that the end of the world was not imminent, Leon Festinger and his colleagues thought it would be interesting to observe this group closely and chronicle how they reacted when their beliefs and prophecy were disconfirmed (Festinger, Riecken, & Schachter, 1956). However, unlike the case of observing children at play, the researchers couldn't stand on the other side of the fence and unobtrusively observe the subtleties of the group members' behaviour. (Even if Pepler and colleagues' technology had been available, it is doubtful that cult members would have agreed to be video- and audiotaped.) To monitor the hour-to-hour conversations of this group, the social psychologists found it necessary to join the group and pretend that they too believed the world was about to end. (In case you are wondering what happened when the world didn't actually end—the cult members still clung to their beliefs and assumed that a spaceship would eventually come to rescue them. Many became even more committed to the belief system and renewed their efforts to convert others. The cult members needed to assure themselves that the spaceship rescue would still take place, so visitors to the group were often perceived as coming to them from outer space to deliver messages.)

But, you might be wondering, how can we be sure that the observers are presenting an accurate portrayal of social behaviour? In observational research— whether observing children's behaviour on a playground or the behaviour of members of doomsday cults—it is important to establish **interjudge reliability**,

interjudge reliability

the level of agreement between two or more people who independently observe and code a set of data; by showing that two or more judges independently come up with the same observations, researchers ensure that the observations are not the subjective impressions of one individual which is the level of agreement between two or more people who independently observe and code a set of data. By showing that two or more judges independently come up with the same observations, researchers ensure that the observations are not the subjective impressions of one individual.

Archival Analysis

archival analysis

a form of the observational method, whereby the researcher examines the accumulated documents, or archives, of a culture (e.g., diaries, novels, magazines, and newspapers)

Another form of the observational method is **archival analysis**, whereby the researcher examines the accumulated documents, or archives, of a culture (Mullen, Rozell, & Johnson, 2001; Simonton, 1999). Diaries, novels, suicide notes, popular music lyrics, television shows, movies, magazine and newspaper articles, and advertising, for example, all tell us a great deal about how a society views itself. Much like our earlier example, specific, well-defined categories are created and then applied to the archival source. Archival analysis is a powerful form of observational research because it allows a unique look at the values and interests of a culture. (If you want to try your hand at archival analysis, see the accompanying Try It! exercise.)

For example, recently Eric Patton at Saint Joseph's University, Philadelphia, and Gary Johns at Concordia University in Montreal analyzed portrayals of women's absenteeism in the workplace by examining the content of articles published in the *New York Times* over the last 100 years (Patton & Johns, 2007). Although there was some variation across time, women generally were portrayed as missing work because of familial and domestic obligations. Moreover, their absenteeism was viewed negatively. The authors suggest that this portrait of women's absenteeism serves to perpetuate gender stereotypes and may lead to discrimination in the workplace.

To give another example, Pettijohn and Jungeberg (2004) analyzed *Playboy* magazine's "Playmates of the year" published between 1960 and 2000 to examine whether there is a relation between social and economic conditions and what is considered an ideal body type for women. They found that when times are tough, more mature-looking body types (older, taller, heavier) are favoured; in times of prosperity, younger, smaller, more "babyish" looking women are preferred. Similarly, researchers at York University have used archival analysis to examine the relation between body ideals (as portrayed in magazines such as *Playboy* and *Playgirl*) and the body sizes of average young women and men (Spitzer, Henderson, & Zivian, 1999). It turns out that the body sizes of *Playboy* models and beauty pageant winners have decreased over time to the point where, currently, nearly 100 percent of these women are underweight according to Health Canada's guidelines. The researchers comment that "clearly the North American ideal for female beauty as portrayed in the media is at a weight deemed to be dangerous by Canadian and World Health officials" (p. 559). Interestingly, the body mass index of North American women actually has increased in the past four decades (somewhat more so for American than Canadian women). Thus, the average woman's body is now further from the cultural ideal than it was 40 years ago.

The recent deaths of high-profile anorexic models, such as Brazilian model Ana Carolina Reston, who weighed only 40 kilograms (88 pounds), have shocked some governments into taking action aimed at changing the cultural ideal of thinness. In April 2008, the French government introduced a law that would make it a crime to promote excessive thinness in the fashion industry, not only in shows but also on websites, in magazines, and in advertisements. In Spain, fashion-show organizers have banned models with a body mass index under 18 (starvation level) from fashion runways. So far, Canada has decided not to follow suit (Agrell, 2008).

LOUIS VUITTON

As for men's bodies, Spitzer and colleagues found that the body sizes of *Playgirl* centrefolds and average young men have both increased over time. However, as a look around your classroom probably will verify, the average guy doesn't look like a *Playgirl* centrefold. The reason is that the bodies of *Playgirl* centrefolds have increased dramatically in muscle, not fat, whereas for average men, increases have tended to occur in the other direction.

Findings such as these lead us inexorably to some disturbing questions: Does the ideal of thinness for women contribute to body dissatisfaction and destructive behaviours such as bulimia or excessive exercise that could ultimately end in death? Does the muscular ideal for men contribute to dangerous behaviours such as anabolic steroid use? To answer such questions, researchers must use research methods such as the correlational method and the experimental method. These methods will be discussed next.

▲ Archival studies have found that women and men are portrayed differently in advertisements. What are the differences in the way the men and woman are portrayed in these photos? To learn more about these differences, do the Try It! on this page.

Try it!

▶ Archival Analysis: Body Image and the Media

Try doing your own archival analysis to see how the ideal body types for women and men are portrayed in the media. Choose three or four magazines that differ in their topic and audience: for example, a "women's" beauty magazine such as *Glamour*, a "men's" magazine such as *GQ*, and a fitness magazine such as *Shape* or *Muscle and Fitness*. For each magazine, open the pages randomly until you find a photograph of a woman's or a man's body. Repeat this so you look at two or three such photographs in each magazine.

- What is the ideal body type for women portrayed in these magazines? What is the ideal body type for men portrayed in these magazines? In answering these questions, note the following:

  (a) the ideal weight portrayed
  (b) the ideal muscle-versus-fat ratio
  (c) other characteristics (e.g., width of shoulders relative to waist, size of bust/chest).

- Does the ideal body type portrayed in the magazines seem attainable for each gender? Are the ideals that are portrayed healthy?

According to research conducted at the University of Manitoba and the University of Winnipeg (Morry & Staska, 2001; Nowatzki & Morry, in press), internalizing the body ideals portrayed in the media can be harmful to your health. The researchers found that women who frequently read beauty magazines were more likely to accept the societal ideal of thinness for females. Internalization of this ideal was associated with greater body dissatisfaction and with higher incidence of eating disorders. And what about men? Men who frequently read fitness magazines were more likely to internalize the muscular ideal, which in turn was associated with body dissatisfaction, disordered eating behaviours, and steroid use. The bottom line, regardless of your sex, is to beware of too readily accepting the ideals portrayed in the media—it could be dangerous to your physical and emotional health.

The Correlational Method

Social scientists usually want to do more than document social behaviour—they want to understand relations between variables and to be able to predict when different kinds of social behaviour will occur; for example, is there a relation between the amount of violence children see on television and their aggressiveness? To answer such questions, researchers frequently use a different approach: the correlational method.

The **correlational method** is the technique whereby two variables are systematically measured and the relation between them—how much you can predict one from the other—is assessed. For example, using the correlational method, researchers might be interested in testing the relation between children's aggressive behaviour and how much violent television they watch. They also might observe children on the playground, but here the goal is to assess the relation, or correlation, between the children's aggressiveness and other factors, such as television viewing habits, that the researchers also measure.

Researchers look at such relations by calculating the **correlation coefficient**, which is a statistic that assesses how well you can predict one variable based on another; for example, how well you can predict people's weight from their height. A positive correlation means that increases in the value of one variable are associated with increases in the value of the other variable. Height and weight are positively correlated; the taller people are, the more they tend to weigh. A negative correlation means that *increases* in the value of one variable are associated with *decreases* in the value of the other. We might expect, for example, that as the number of classes a student skips goes up, the student's mark in the course will go down—the more classes cut, the lower the grade. It is also possible, of course, for two variables to be completely uncorrelated, so that a researcher cannot predict one variable from the other. Knowing someone's shoe size will not allow you to predict how many books that person owns.

Correlation coefficients are expressed as numbers that can range from -1.00 to $+1.00$. A correlation of 1.00 means that two variables are perfectly correlated in a positive direction; thus, by knowing people's standing on one variable, the researcher can predict exactly where they stand on the other variable. In everyday life, of course, perfect correlations are rare; for example, one study found that the correlation between height and weight was $+0.47$ in a sample of men aged 18 to 24 (Freedman et al., 1991). This means that, on average, the taller people were heavier than the shorter people, but there were exceptions. A correlation of -1.00 means that two variables are perfectly correlated in a negative direction. Thus, a correlation of -0.47 would tell you that, on average, students who skip classes get lower grades, but, once again, there are exceptions. Finally, a correlation of zero means that two variables are not correlated. It may surprise you that the correlation between having positive attitudes toward condom use and actually using them is disturbingly close to zero: $+0.23$ in a sample of French-Canadian university students (Hébert et al., 1989). Thus, if you know that someone has positive attitudes toward using condoms, this information will not allow you to make a very accurate prediction about whether the person actually will use one the next time he or she has sex.

Surveys   The correlational method is often used in **surveys**, research in which a representative sample of people are asked questions about their attitudes or behaviour. Surveys are a convenient way to measure people's attitudes; for example, people can be telephoned and asked which candidate they will support in an upcoming election or how they feel about a variety of social issues. Researchers often apply the correlational method to survey results, to predict how people's responses to one question predict their other responses. Political scientists, for

correlational method

the technique whereby researchers systematically measure two or more variables and assess the relation between them (i.e., how much one can be predicted from the other)

correlation coefficient

a statistical technique that assesses how well you can predict one variable based on another (e.g., how well you can predict people's weight from their height)

surveys

research in which a representative sample of people are asked questions about their attitudes or behaviour example, might be interested in whether people's attitudes toward a specific issue, such as gun control, predict how they will vote. Psychologists often use surveys to help understand social behaviour and attitudes—for example, by seeing whether the amount of pornography men say they read is correlated with their attitudes toward women.

Surveys have a number of advantages, one of which is that they allow researchers to judge the relationship between variables that are often difficult to observe, such as how often people engage in safer sex. For example, Herold and Mewhinney (1993) wanted to know whether people who had positive attitudes toward the use of condoms would be more likely to engage in safer sex. To answer this question, they asked women and men in various singles bars in southern Ontario to complete a survey that assessed their agreement with attitude statements such as, "If I were to have sex with someone I just met, I would be uncomfortable suggesting to my partner that we use a condom." Respondents also were asked about the frequency with which they actually used condoms. (As discussed on the previous page, the correlation between positive attitudes toward condoms and the frequency of using them was surprisingly low.)

Another advantage of surveys is the ability to sample representative segments of the population. Answers to a survey are useful only if they reflect the responses of people in general—not just the sample of people actually tested. Survey researchers go to great lengths to ensure that the people they sample are typical. They select samples that are representative of the population on a number of characteristics important to a given research question (e.g., age, educational background, religion, gender, income level). They also make sure to use a **random selection** of people from the population at large, which is a way of ensuring that a sample of people is representative. As long as the sample is selected randomly, it can be assumed that the responses are a reasonable match to those of the population as a whole. (Random selection also is important when researchers conduct experiments—which we discuss later.)

There are some famous cases whereby people tried to generalize from samples that were not randomly selected—to their peril. In the fall of 1936, a weekly magazine in the United States called *The Literary Digest* conducted a large survey asking readers whom they planned to vote for in the upcoming presidential election. The magazine obtained the names and addresses of its sample from telephone directories and automobile registration lists. The results of its survey of 2 million people indicated that the Republican candidate, Alf Landon, would win by a landslide. There never was a President Landon; instead, Franklin Delano Roosevelt won every state but two. What went wrong with *The Literary Digest*'s poll? In the depths of the Great Depression, many people could not afford telephones or cars. Those who could afford these items were, by definition, doing well financially, were frequently Republican, and overwhelmingly favoured Alf Landon. However, the majority of the voters were poor—and overwhelmingly supported the Democratic candidate, Roosevelt. By using a list of names that excluded the less affluent members of the population, *The Literary Digest* created a nonrepresentative sample. *The Literary Digest* never recovered from this methodological disaster and went out of business shortly after publishing its poll.

Another potential problem with survey data is the accuracy of the responses. Straightforward questions—regarding what people think about an issue or what they typically do—are relatively easy to answer. For example, in plebiscites held in 2002 and 2008, residents of Brandon, Manitoba, were asked a question about a hotly contested issue: "Do you favour the establishment of a casino in the city of Brandon?" This kind of straightforward question tends to produce straightforward answers. More than half of voters (56 percent in 2002; 57 percent in 2008) responded "No." As a result, no casino was built. However, in social psychological research, participants are generally not asked a single question with a yes or no answer. Extensive research by Norbert Schwarz and colleagues (Schwarz, 1999;

random selection

a way of ensuring that a sample of people is representative of a population, by giving everyone in the population an equal chance of being selected for the sample

▶ The importance of random selection in surveys. In 1936, a U.S. magazine, *The Literary Digest*, conducted one of the first political polls. It randomly selected names from telephone directories and automobile registration lists, and asked people for whom they planned to vote in the presidential election: Alf Landon or Franklin Roosevelt. As seen here, the poll indicated that Landon would win by a landslide. He didn't; Roosevelt carried virtually every state in the union. What went wrong with this poll?

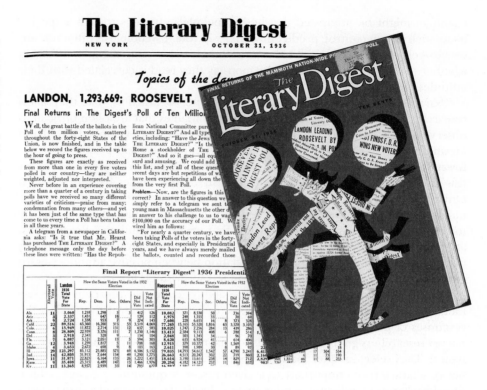

Sudman, Bradburn, & Schwarz, 1996) has shown that even seemingly trivial factors such as the response scale that participants are given or the order in which questions are asked can make a difference. For example, in one study, German university students were asked how much TV they watch. Participants in the low-frequency condition were provided with a response scale that ranged from "up to ½ hour" to "more than 2½ hours." Participants in the high-frequency condition were asked the same question, but were provided with a response scale ranging from "up to 2½ hours" to "more than 4½ hours." Did the rating scale affect the students' answers? Yes, it did. Only 16.2 percent of participants reported watching TV for more than two and a half hours per day when they answered the question on the low-frequency scale. In contrast, more than twice as many participants (37.5 percent) reported watching TV for more than two and a half hours per day when they were given the high-frequency scale (Schwarz et al., 1985). One might think that it would be easy to answer a "factual" question such as how much TV you watch in a day. However, as this study demonstrated, the way in which the question is asked can influence our answers.

Needless to say, as the question becomes more complex, it is even more challenging to elicit accurate answers. Asking respondents to predict how they might behave in some hypothetical situation or to explain why they behaved as they did in the past is an invitation to inaccuracy (Schuman & Kalton, 1985; Schwarz, 1999; Schwarz, Groves, & Schuman, 1998). Often people simply don't know the answer—but they think they do. Dick Nisbett and Tim Wilson (1977a) demonstrated this phenomenon of "telling more than you can know" in a number of studies in which people often made inaccurate reports about why they responded the way they did. Their reports about the causes of their responses pertained more to their theories and beliefs about what should have influenced them than to what actually influenced them. (We discuss these studies at greater length in Chapter 5.)

In summary, correlational techniques are ideal for answering questions about whether two variables are related—and, if so, what is the strength of that relation? Many important questions about human social behaviour can be answered using the correlational method, such as whether people's level of compassion is related to how much money they donate toward famine relief, whether the amount of time spent reading beauty magazines is associated with the acceptance of the body ideal of thinness, and whether attitudes toward condom use are related to the frequency with which condoms are actually used. We will see many more examples of the usefulness of the correlational method throughout this book.

Limits of the Correlational Method: Correlation Does Not Equal Causation   The major short-coming of the correlational method is that it tells us only that two variables are related, whereas the goal of the social psychologist is to identify the causes of social behaviour. We want to be able to say that A causes B, not just that A is related to, or correlated with, B.

If a researcher finds that there is a correlation between two variables, it means that there are three possible causal relations between these variables. For example, researchers have found a correlation between the amount of violent television children watch and how aggressive they are (Eron, 1982). One explanation of this correlation is that watching TV violence causes kids to become more violent. It is equally probable, however, that the reverse is true: that kids who are aggressive to begin with are more likely to watch violent television. Or there might be no causal relation between these two variables; instead, both television watching and violent behaviour could be caused by a third variable, such as having neglectful parents who do not pay much attention to their kids. (Experimental evidence does support one of these causal relationships; we will discuss which one in Chapter 11.) When we use the correlational method, it is wrong to jump to the conclusion that one variable is causing the other to occur. *Correlation does not prove causation.*

Unfortunately, one of the most common methodological errors in the social sciences is for a researcher to forget this adage. Drawing causal conclusions from correlational data also frequently occurs in everyday life. Consider, for example, a column in the *Winnipeg Free Press* featuring Tillie the Rainmaker. It all began in 1986 when Tillie took a trip to Sacramento, California. As soon as she stepped off the plane, the skies poured with rain, ending a six-week drought. Until then, Tillie had seen herself as an average Jewish grandmother. But at that moment, she realized that she had special powers. Tillie claims to have ended many droughts and extinguished major forest fires since then. Winnipeg rabbi Alan Green is a strong supporter of Tillie and her work. "I can't prove scientifically that there is cause-and-effect," says Green. But he does believe that such things are possible. Besides, he says, "It's a freely offered gift. . . . There can be no harm" (Reynolds, 2000, p. D3).

◄ Tillie Goren believes that she has the ability to end droughts because on several occasions when she has visited a drought-stricken area, it has started to rain. Is this a case of correlation or causation?

In a letter to the editor the next week, a psychology professor suggested that a more likely explanation for Tillie's special powers is that she and her rabbi inferred causality from correlational events (Double deception, 2000). In some cases, this might be quite harmless, as Rabbi Green points out. However, it is not sound scientific practice, and the consequences can be quite serious, as demonstrated by a study of birth control methods and sexually transmitted diseases (STDs) in women (Rosenberg et al., 1992). These researchers examined the records of women who had visited a clinic for STDs, noting which method of birth control they used and whether they had STDs. Surprisingly, the researchers found that women who relied on condoms had significantly more STDs than women who used diaphragms or contraceptive sponges. This result was widely reported in the popular press, along with the conclusion that the use of diaphragms and sponges caused a lower incidence of disease. Some reporters urged women whose partners used condoms to switch to other methods.

Can you see the problem with this conclusion? The fact that the incidence of disease was correlated with the type of contraception women used is open to a number of causal interpretations. Perhaps the women who used sponges and diaphragms had sex with fewer partners. (In fact, condom users were more likely to have had sex with multiple partners in the previous month.) Perhaps the partners of women who relied on condoms were more likely to have STDs than the partners of women who used sponges and diaphragms. There is simply no way of knowing. Thus, the conclusion that the use of diaphragms and sponges offers protection against STDs cannot be drawn from this correlational study. (In fact, condoms are still considered to be one of the best forms of protection from STDs.)

Other examples of the difficulty of inferring causality from correlational studies are shown in the accompanying Try It! box.

Try it!

▶ Correlation Does Not Equal Causation

It can be difficult to remember that when two variables are correlated, it doesn't necessarily mean that one caused the other; correlation does *not* allow us to make causal inferences. For each of the following examples, think about why the correlation was found. Even if it seems obvious which variable was causing the other, are there alternative explanations?

Correlation Does Not Equal Causation Quiz

1. Recently, a politician extolled the virtues of the Boy and Girl Scouts organizations. In his salute to the Scouts, the politician mentioned that few teenagers convicted of street crimes had been members of the Scouts. In other words, he was positing a negative correlation between activity in Scouting and frequency of criminal behaviour. Why might this be?

2. A recent study reported that the more milk children drank, the more weight they gained. One researcher concluded that children who need to control their weight should not drink much milk. Is this a valid conclusion?

3. A recent study of soldiers stationed on army bases found that the number of tattoos a soldier had is correlated positively with his becoming involved in a motorcycle accident. Why?

4. Recently, it was reported that a correlation exists between people's tendency to eat breakfast in the morning and how long they live, such that people who skip breakfast die younger. Does eating Cheerios lead to a long life?

5. A recent study found that adolescents who are religious are less likely to commit crimes and more likely to wear seat belts than adolescents who are not religious. Does religion make people more likely to obey the law?

6. A research study found that having a pet in childhood is correlated with a reduced likelihood of becoming a juvenile delinquent in adolescence. Why is this?

7. A recent survey found that people who watch public television have more sex than people who do not. "Who would have thought," the researchers reported, "that National Geographic specials or Ken Burns' history of baseball could get people in the mood?" How would you explain this correlation?

See pages 54 and 55 for answers.

The Experimental Method: Answering Causal Questions

experimental method

the method in which the researcher randomly assigns participants to different conditions and ensures that these conditions are identical except for the independent variable (the one thought to have a causal effect on people's responses)

The only way to determine causal relations is with the **experimental method**. Here, the researcher systematically orchestrates the event so that people experience it in one way (e.g., they witness an emergency along with other bystanders) or another way (e.g., they witness the same emergency but are the sole bystander). The experimental method is the method of choice in most social psychological research, because it allows the experimenter to make causal inferences. The observational method is extremely useful in helping us describe social behaviour; the correlational method is extremely useful in helping us understand what aspects of social behaviour are related. However, only a properly executed experiment allows us to make cause-and-effect statements. For this reason, the experimental method is the crown jewel of social psychological research design.

The experimental method always involves direct intervention on the part of the researcher. Let's return for a moment to Latané and Darley's hypothesis, discussed earlier, that the more people who witness an emergency the less likely it is that any given individual will intervene. By carefully changing only one aspect of the situation (e.g., group size), they could test whether this aspect is the cause of the behaviour in question (e.g., whether people help in an emergency). Sound simple? Actually, it isn't. Staging an experiment to test Latané and Darley's hypothesis involves severe practical and ethical difficulties. What kind of emergency should be used? Ideally (from a scientific perspective), it should be as true to the Genovese case as possible. Accordingly, you would want to stage a murder that passersby could witness. In one condition, you could stage the murder so that only a few onlookers were present; in another condition, you could stage it so that a great many onlookers were present.

Obviously, no scientist in his or her right mind would stage a murder for unsuspecting bystanders. But how can we arrange a realistic situation that is upsetting enough to be similar to the Genovese case without it being too upsetting? In addition, how can we ensure that each bystander experiences the same emergency except for the variable whose effect we want to test—in this case, the number of bystanders?

Let's see how Latané and Darley (1968) dealt with these problems. Imagine you were a participant in their experiment. You arrive at the scheduled time and find yourself in a long corridor with doors to several small cubicles. An experimenter greets you and takes you into one of the cubicles, mentioning that five other students, seated in the other cubicles, will be participating with you. The experimenter leaves after giving you a pair of headphones with an attached microphone. You put on the headphones, and soon you hear the experimenter explaining to everyone that he is interested in learning about the kinds of personal problems that college students experience. To ensure that people will discuss their problems openly, he explains, each participant will remain anonymous; each will stay in his or her separate room and communicate with the others only via the intercom system. Further, the experimenter says, he will not be listening to the discussion, so that people will feel freer to be open and honest. Finally, the experimenter asks that participants take turns presenting their problems, each speaking for two minutes, after which each person will comment on what the others said. To make sure this procedure is followed, he says, only one person's microphone will be turned on at a time.

> ❝ Theory is a good thing, but a good experiment lasts forever. ❞
> —Pyotr Leonidovich Kapitsa, Nobel physicist
> (1894–1984)

The group discussion then begins. You listen as the first participant admits that he has found it difficult to adjust to college. With some embarrassment, he mentions that he sometimes has seizures, especially when under stress. When his two minutes are up, you hear the other four participants discuss their problems, after which it is your turn. When you have finished, it is the first person's turn to speak again. To your astonishment, after he makes a few further comments, he seems to begin to experience a seizure:

> I—er—um—I think I—I need—er—if—if could—er—er—somebody er—er—er—er—er—er—er—give me a little—er—give me a little help here because—er—I—er—I'm—er—er—h—h—having a—a—a real problem—er—right now and I—er—if somebody could help me out it would—it would—er—er s—s—sure be—sure be good . . . because—er— there—er—er—a cause I—er—I—uh—I've got a—a one of the—er— sei—er—er—things coming on and—and—and I could really—er—use some help so if somebody would—er—give me a little h—help—uh— er—er—er—er—c—could somebody—er—er—help—er—uh—uh—uh (choking sounds) . . . I'm gonna die—er—er—I'm . . . gonna die—er— help—er—er—seizure—er (chokes, then quiet). (Darley & Latané, 1968, p. 379)

What would you have done in this situation? If you were like most of the participants in the actual study, you would have remained in your cubicle, listening to your fellow student having a seizure, and done nothing about it. Does this surprise you? Latané and Darley kept track of the number of people who left their cubicle to find the victim or the experimenter before the end of the victim's seizure. Only 31 percent of the participants sought help in this way. Fully 69 percent of the students remained in their cubicles and did nothing—just as Kitty Genovese's neighbours failed to offer her assistance in any way.

Does this finding prove that the failure to help was because of the number of people who witnessed the seizure? How do we know that it wasn't because of some other factor? Here is the major advantage of the experimental method. We know because Latané and Darley included two other conditions in their experiment. In these conditions, the procedure was identical to that described above, with one crucial difference: The size of the discussion group was smaller, meaning that fewer people were witnesses to the seizure. In one condition, the participants were told that there were three other people in the discussion group aside from themselves (the victim plus two others). In another condition, participants were told that there was only one other person in their discussion group (namely, the victim). In this latter condition, each participant believed that he or she was the only one who could hear the seizure. Did the size of the discussion group make a difference? As you'll see in a moment, it did.

Independent and Dependent Variables

The number of people witnessing the emergency in the Latané and Darley study was the **independent variable**, which is the variable a researcher changes or varies to see if it has an effect on some other variable. The **dependent variable** is the variable a researcher measures to see if it is influenced by the independent variable; the researcher hypothesizes that the dependent variable will be influenced by the level of the independent variable. That is, the dependent variable is hypothesized to depend on the independent variable (see Figure 2.1). Latané and Darley found that their independent variable—the number of bystanders—did have an effect on the dependent variable—whether they tried to help. When the participants believed that four other people were witnesses to the seizure, only 31 percent offered assistance. When the participants believed that only two other people were aware of the seizure, the amount of helping behaviour increased to 62 percent of the participants. When the participants believed that they were the only person listening to the seizure, nearly everyone helped (85 percent of the participants). Thus, Latané and Darley were successful in identifying one important determinant of whether people help—the number of bystanders who are present.

independent variable

the variable a researcher changes or varies to see if it has an effect on some other variable

dependent variable

the variable a researcher measures to see if it is influenced by the independent variable; the researcher hypothesizes that the dependent variable will depend on the level of the independent variable

Independent Variable	Dependent Variable
The variable that is hypothesized to influence the dependent variable. Participants are treated identically except for this variable.	The response that is hypothesized to depend on the independent variable. All participants are measured on this variable.

Example: Darley and Latané (1968)	
The number of bystanders	**How many participants helped?**
Participant　+　Victim	85%
Participant　+　Victim　+　Two others	62%
Participant　+　Victim　+　Four others	31%

FIGURE 2.1

Independent and dependent variables in experimental research

These results indicate that the number of bystanders strongly influences the rate of helping, but it does not mean that the size of the group is the only cause of people's decision to help. After all, when there were four bystanders, a third of the participants still helped; conversely, when participants thought they were the only witness, some of them failed to help. Obviously, other factors influence helping behaviour—such as the bystanders' personalities and their prior experience with emergencies. Nonetheless, Latané and Darley succeeded in identifying one important determinant of whether people help: the number of bystanders present.

Internal Validity in Experiments

How can we be sure that the differences in help across conditions in the Latané and Darley (1968) seizure study were a result of the different numbers of bystanders who witnessed the emergency? Could this effect have been caused by some other aspect of the situation? Again, this is the beauty of the experimental method. We can be sure of the causal connection between the number of bystanders and helping because Latané and Darley made sure that everything about the situation was the same in the different conditions *except* the independent variable: the number of bystanders. Keeping everything the same but the independent variable is referred to as *internal validity*. Latané and Darley were careful to maintain high internal validity by ensuring that everyone witnessed the same emergency. They prerecorded the supposed other participants and the victim, and played their voices over the intercom system.

The astute reader will have noticed, however, that there was a key difference between the conditions of the Latané and Darley experiment other than the number of bystanders: Different people participated in the different conditions. Maybe the observed differences in helping were a result of characteristics of the participants instead of the independent variable. The people in the sole-witness condition might have differed in any number of ways from their counterparts in the other conditions, making them more likely to help. Maybe they were more likely to have had loving parents, to know something about epilepsy, or to have experience helping in emergencies. Were any of these possibilities true, it would be difficult to conclude that it was the number of bystanders, rather than something about the participants' backgrounds, that led to differences in helping.

Fortunately, there is a technique that allows experimenters to minimize differences among participants as the cause of the results: **random assignment to condition**. This is the process whereby all participants have an equal chance of taking part in any condition of an experiment; through random assignment, researchers can be relatively certain that differences in the participants' personalities or backgrounds are distributed evenly across conditions. Because Latané and Darley's participants were randomly assigned to the conditions of their experiment, it is very unlikely that the ones who knew the most about

random assignment to condition

the process whereby all participants have an equal chance of taking part in any condition of an experiment; through random assignment, researchers can be relatively certain that differences in the participants' personalities or backgrounds are distributed evenly across conditions

probability level (*p*-value)

a number, calculated with statistical techniques, that tells researchers how likely it is that the results of their experiment occurred by chance and not because of the independent variable(s); the convention in science, including social psychology, is to consider results significant if the probability level is less than 5 in 100 that the results might be attributable to chance factors and not the independent variables studied

PRO

internal validity

ensuring that nothing other than the independent variable can affect the dependent variable; this is accomplished by controlling all extraneous variables and by randomly assigning people to different experimental conditions

epilepsy all ended up in one condition. Knowledge about epilepsy should be randomly (i.e., roughly evenly) dispersed across the three experimental conditions. This powerful technique is the most important part of the experimental method.

However, even with random assignment there is always the (very small) possibility that different characteristics of people did not distribute themselves evenly across conditions. For example, if we randomly divide a group of 40 people into two groups, it is possible that more of those who know the most about epilepsy will by chance end up in one group than in the other—just as it is possible to get more heads than tails when you flip a coin 40 times. This is a possibility we take seriously in experimental science. The analyses of our data come with a **probability level (*p*-value)**, which is a number, calculated with statistical techniques, that tells researchers how likely it is that the results of their experiment occurred by chance and not because of the independent variable. The convention in science, including social psychology, is to consider results significant if the probability level is less than five in 100 that the results might be attributable to chance factors, and not the independent variables studied. For example, if we flipped a coin 40 times and got 40 heads, we would probably assume that this was very unlikely to have occurred by chance and that there was something wrong with the coin. (We might check the other side to ensure that it wasn't one of those trick coins with heads on both sides!) Similarly, if the results in two conditions of an experiment differ significantly from what we would expect by chance, we assume that the difference was caused by the independent variable (e.g., the number of bystanders present during the emergency). The *p*-value tells us how confident we can be that the difference was attributable to chance rather than to the independent variable.

To summarize, the key to a good experiment is to maintain high **internal validity**, which we can now define as making sure that the independent variable, and *only* the independent variable, influences the dependent variable. This is accomplished by controlling all extraneous variables (other variables that could conceivably affect the independent variable) and by randomly assigning people to different experimental conditions (Campbell & Stanley, 1967). We should note that random assignment is also extremely important in experiments that include a control group—a group of participants who do not receive the researchers' intervention. Let's say that you wanted to test whether wearing a nicotine patch actually helps people quit smoking. You select a group of people who want to quit smoking. You give them the patch, then you contact them two weeks later and ask how many cigarettes a day they are smoking. Let's say that your participants now report an average of four cigarettes a day. Was your intervention effective? The only way to know would be to include a control group—a comparison group that does not receive the treatment condition—in this case, a group of participants who do not get the patch. (Note that the experimental group and the control group must be identical in every way—except in terms of the treatment itself, which only the experimental group receives.) If people in your control group are still smoking two packs a day after two weeks, you could be more confident that your intervention made a difference. Note that in this kind of experiment, you want these two groups to be as identical as possible (e.g., both groups consisting of people who want to quit smoking), so that you can be more confident that your results are due to your intervention, and not some other difference between the groups, such as the desire to quit.

When internal validity is high, the experimenter is in a position to judge whether the independent variable causes the dependent variable (in your experiment, whether the patch caused the lower rate of smoking). This is the hallmark of the experimental method that sets it apart from the observational and correlational methods. Only the experimental method can answer causal questions.

External Validity in Experiments

For all of the advantages of the experimental method, there are some drawbacks. By virtue of gaining enough control over the situation so as to randomly assign people to conditions and rule out the effects of extraneous variables, the situation can become somewhat artificial and distant from real life. For example, one could argue that Latané and Darley strayed far from the original inspiration for their study, the Kitty Genovese murder. What does witnessing a seizure while participating in a laboratory experiment in a college building have to do with a brutal murder in New York? How often in everyday life does anyone have discussions with other people through an intercom system? Did the fact that the participants knew they were in a psychology experiment influence their behaviour?

These are important questions that concern **external validity**, which is the extent to which the results of a study can be generalized to other situations and other people. Note that two kinds of generalizability are at issue:

(a) the extent to which we can generalize from the situation constructed by an experimenter to real-life situations (generalizability across *situations*), and

(b) the extent to which we can generalize from the people who participated in the experiment to people in general (generalizability across *people*).

Generalizability across Situations   Research in social psychology is sometimes criticized for being conducted in artificial situations, such as psychology experiments at a university, that cannot be generalized to real life. To address this problem, social psychologists attempt to increase the generalizability of their results by making their studies as realistic as possible. However, it is important to note that there are different ways in which an experiment can be realistic. By one definition—the similarity of an experimental situation to events that occur frequently in everyday life—it is clear that many experiments are decidedly unreal. In many experiments, people are placed in situations they would rarely, if ever, encounter in everyday life, such as occurred in Latané and Darley's group discussion of personal problems over an intercom system. We can refer to the extent to which an experiment is similar to real-life situations as the experiment's **mundane realism** (Aronson & Carlsmith, 1968).

It is more important to ensure that a study is high in **psychological realism**— how similar the psychological processes triggered in an experiment are to psychological processes that occur in everyday life (Aronson, Wilson, & Brewer, 1998). Even though Latané and Darley staged an emergency that in significant ways was unlike ones encountered in everyday life, was it psychologically similar

external validity

the extent to which the results of a study can be generalized to other situations and to other people

mundane realism

the extent to which an experiment is similar to real-life situations

psychological realism

the extent to which the psychological processes triggered in an experiment are similar to psychological processes that occur in everyday life; psychological realism can be high in an experiment, even if mundane realism is low

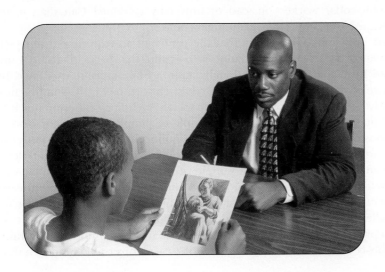

◄A good deal of social psychological research takes place in laboratory settings. How do social psychologists generalize from the findings of these studies to life outside the laboratory?

to real-life emergencies? Were the same psychological processes triggered? Did the participants have the same types of perceptions and thoughts, make the same types of decisions, and choose the same types of behaviours that they would have in a real-life situation? If so, then the study is high in psychological realism and the results are generalizable to everyday life.

Psychological realism is heightened if people find themselves engrossed in a real event. To accomplish this, it is often necessary to tell the participants a **cover story**—a false description of the study's purpose. You might have wondered why Latané and Darley told people that the purpose of the experiment was to study the personal problems of college students. It certainly would have been simpler to tell participants, "Look, we are interested in how people react to emergencies, so at some point during the study we are going to stage an accident, and then we'll see how you respond." We think you will agree, however, that such a procedure would be very low in psychological realism. In everyday life, no one knows when emergencies are going to occur and people do not have time to plan responses to them. Consequently, the kinds of psychological processes triggered would differ widely from those of a real emergency, reducing the psychological realism of the study.

Further, as discussed earlier, people don't always know why they do what they do, or even what they will do until it happens. Therefore, describing an experimental situation to participants and then asking them to respond normally will produce responses that are, at best, suspect. For example, after describing the Latané and Darley seizure experiment to our students, we usually ask them to predict how they would respond, just as we asked you earlier. Invariably, most of our students think they would have helped the victim, even when they know that in the condition where the group size was six, most people did not help. Unfortunately, we cannot depend on people's predictions about what they would do in a hypothetical situation; we can only find out what people will really do when we construct a situation that triggers the same psychological processes as occur in the real world.

Generalizability across People   Recall that social psychologists study the way in which people in general are susceptible to social influence. Latané and Darley's experiment documented an interesting, unexpected example of social influence, whereby the mere knowledge that others were present reduced the likelihood that people helped. But what have we learned about people in general? The participants in their study were 52 male and female students at New York University who received course credit for participating. Would the study have turned out the same if a different population had been used? Would the number of bystanders have influenced helping behaviour had the participants been middle-aged blue-collar workers instead of university students? Canadian instead of American? Nova Scotians instead of New Yorkers?

The only way to be certain that the results of an experiment represent the behaviour of a particular population is to ensure that participants are randomly selected from that population. Ideally, samples in experiments should be randomly selected, just as they are in surveys. Unfortunately, it is impractical and expensive to select random samples for social psychology experiments. It is difficult enough to convince a random sample of people to agree to answer a few questions over the telephone as part of a political poll, and such polls can cost thousands of dollars to conduct. Imagine the difficulty Latané and Darley would have had convincing a random sample of Americans to board a plane to New York to take part in their study, not to mention the cost of such an endeavour.

Of course, concerns about practicality and expense are not good excuses for poor science. Many researchers address this problem by studying basic psychological processes that make people susceptible to social influence, assuming that these processes are so fundamental that they are universally shared. In that case,

---

cover story

a description of the purpose of a study given to participants that is different from its true purpose; cover stories are used to maintain psychological realism participants for social psychology experiments don't really have to come from every corner of the earth. Of course, as we shall discuss in this textbook, some social psychological processes do vary in different cultures and in those cases, diverse samples of people have to be studied. The question then is, how can researchers tell whether the processes they are studying are universal?

Replications   Suppose a researcher claims that her study is high in psychological realism—that it has thus captured psychological functioning as it occurs in everyday life—and that it doesn't matter that only Introductory Psychology students at one university participated because these psychological processes are universal. Should we take her word for it?

Not necessarily. The ultimate test of an experiment's external validity is **replication**—conducting the study over again, generally with different subject populations or in different settings. Sometimes researchers will also use different methods, to see if they still get the same results. Do we think that Latané and Darley found the results they did only because their participants knew they were in a psychology experiment? If so, we should try to replicate their study in an experiment conducted outside the laboratory. Do we think that their results are limited to only certain kinds of emergencies? Then we should try to replicate the results with a different emergency. Do we think that only New Yorkers would be so unhelpful? Then we should try to replicate the study with participants from different parts of the United States and in different countries. Only with such replications can we be certain about how generalizable the results are.

When many studies of one problem are conducted, the results can vary. Several studies might find an effect of the number of bystanders on helping behaviour, for example, whereas a few do not. How can one make sense out of this? Does the number of bystanders make a difference or not? Fortunately, there is a statistical technique called **meta analysis** that averages the results of two or more studies to see if the effect of an independent variable is reliable. Earlier, we discussed p-levels, which tell us the probability that the findings of one study are attributable to chance or to the independent variable. A meta analysis essentially does the same thing, except that it averages across the results of many different studies. If, say, an independent variable is found to have an effect in only one of 20 studies, the meta analysis will tell us that that one study was probably an exception and that, on average, the independent variable is not influencing the dependent variable. If an independent variable is having an effect in most of the studies, the meta analysis is likely to tell us that, on average, it does influence the dependent variable.

Most of the findings we will discuss in this book have been replicated in a number of different settings, with different populations, thereby demonstrating that they are reliable phenomena that are not limited to the laboratory or to Introductory Psychology students. For example, Latané and Darley's original findings have been replicated numerous times. Increasing the number of bystanders has been found to inhibit helping behaviour with many kinds of people, including children, university students, and future ministers (Darley & Batson, 1973; Latané & Nida, 1981); in Israel (Schwartz & Gottlieb, 1976); in small towns and large cities in the U.S. (Latané & Dabbs, 1975); in a variety of settings, such as psychology laboratories, city streets, and subway trains (Harrison & Wells, 1991; Latané & Darley, 1970; Piliavin & Piliavin, 1972; Piliavin et al., 1981); and with a variety of types of emergencies, such as seizures, potential fires, fights, and accidents (Latané & Darley, 1968; Shotland & Straw, 1976; Staub, 1974), as well as with less serious events, such as having a flat tire (Hurley & Allen, 1974). In addition, many of these replications have been conducted in real-life settings (e.g., on a subway train) where people could not possibly have known that an experiment was being conducted. We will frequently point out similar replications of the major findings we discuss in this book.

replication

repeating a study, generally with different subject populations, or in different settings, or using different methods

meta analysis

a statistical technique that averages the results of two or more studies to see if the effect of an independent variable is reliable

Cross-Cultural Research

As we have just discussed, while universal patterns of social behaviour likely exist, it is also the case that many important psychological processes are shaped by the culture in which a person grows up. For example, Charles Darwin (1872) argued that there is a basic set of human emotions (e.g., anger, happiness) that are expressed and understood throughout the world. As we discuss in Chapter 4, a lively controversy has arisen as to whether Darwin was right (Russell, 1994; Russell & Fehr, 1987). However, it is generally accepted that there are some similarities in the facial expression of emotions across cultures, even in remote cultures (Ekman, 1994; Elfebein & Ambady, 2003).

To find out how culturally dependent a psychological process is, social psychologists conduct **cross-cultural research**. Some findings in social psychology are culture-dependent, as we will point out at many points throughout this book (Heine, 2008; Heine & Buchtel, in press; Fiske, Kitayama, Markus, & Nisbett, 1998; Moghaddam, Taylor, & Wright, 1993; Nisbett, 2003; Norenzayan & Heine, 2005). In Chapter 5, for example, we discuss research showing that there are cultural differences in the very way people define themselves. Many Western (i.e., European and North American) cultures tend to emphasize individualism and independence, whereas many Eastern (i.e., Asian) cultures emphasize collectivism and interdependence (Heine, 2003; Heine & Hamamura, 2007; Markus & Kitayama, 1991; Triandis, 1989).

Conducting cross-cultural research is not a simple matter of travelling to another culture, translating materials into the local language, and replicating a study there (Heine, Buchtel, & Norenzayan, 2008; Heine, Lehman, Peng, & Greenholtz, 2002; van de Vijver & Leung, 1997). Researchers always have to guard against imposing viewpoints and definitions learned from their own culture onto another culture with which they are unfamiliar. They also have to be sure that their independent and dependent variables are understood in the same way in different cultures (Bond, 1988; Lonner & Berry, 1986). University of British Columbia researchers recently discovered that there are even cultural differences in how people rate items on questionnaires (Hamamura, Heine, & Paulhus, 2007). These researchers found, for example, that people of East Asian heritage were more likely to endorse the mid-points of scales whereas people of European-Canadian heritage were more likely to endorse the end-points (i.e., make more

cross-cultural research

research conducted with members of different cultures, to see whether the psychological processes of interest are present across cultures or whether they are specific to the culture in which people were raised

▶ Some basic psychological processes are universal, whereas others are shaped by the culture in which one lives. Are people's self-concepts shaped by cultural rules of how people must present themselves, such as the requirement by the Taliban in Afghanistan that women cover themselves from head to toe? Are people's ideas about their relationships to their family and social groups influenced by cultural practices, such as cradling one's child while at work, as this woman from Indonesia is doing? Cross-cultural research is challenging, but necessary to explore how culture influences the basic ways in which people think about and interact with others.

extreme ratings). Thus, a researcher might erroneously conclude that two cultures are very different because members of those cultures responded so differently to a questionnaire, when, in reality, the two cultures might actually be quite similar in terms of the construct in question. Most cross-cultural researchers are sensitive to these issues, and as more and more cross-cultural research is conducted carefully, we will be able to determine which social psychological processes are universal and which are culture-bound.

The Basic Dilemma of the Social Psychologist

When we conduct experiments in psychology, there is almost always a trade-off between internal and external validity—that is, between

(a) having enough control over the situation to ensure that no extraneous variables are influencing the results and to randomly assign people to conditions, and

(b) ensuring that the results can be generalized to everyday life.

One of the best ways to increase external validity is by conducting **field experiments**. In a field experiment, people's behaviour is studied outside the laboratory, in its natural setting. A field experiment is identical in design to a laboratory experiment (e.g., the researcher controls the occurrence of an independent variable to see what effect it has on the dependent variable), except that it is conducted in a real-life setting. The participants in a field experiment are unaware that the events they experience are in fact an experiment. The external validity of such an experiment is high because it is taking place in the real world, with real people who are more diverse than a typical university student sample.

Many such field studies have been conducted in social psychology. For example, Latané and Darley (1970) tested their hypothesis about group size and bystander intervention in a convenience store outside New York City. Two "robbers"—with the full knowledge and permission of the cashier and manager of the store—waited until there were either one or two other customers at the checkout counter. Then they asked the cashier to name the most expensive beer the store carried. The cashier answered the question and then said he would have to check in the back to see how much of that brand was in stock. While the cashier was gone, the robbers picked up a case of beer in the front of the store, declared, "They'll never miss this," put the beer in their car, and drove off.

Because the robbers were rather burly fellows, no one attempted to intervene directly to stop the theft. But when the cashier returned, how many people would help by telling him that a theft had just occurred? The number of bystanders had the same inhibiting effect on helping behaviour as in the laboratory seizure study. Significantly fewer people reported the theft when there was another witness/customer in the store than when they were alone.

Real life can best be captured by doing a field experiment such as Latané and Darley's (1970) beer theft study, but it is difficult to control all extraneous variables in such studies. For example, the astute reader will have noticed that Latané and Darley's study was unlike laboratory experiments in an important respect: People could not be randomly assigned to the alone or in-pairs conditions. If this were the only study Latané and Darley had performed, we could not be certain whether the kinds of people who prefer to shop alone, compared with the kinds of people who prefer to shop with a friend, differ in ways that might influence helping behaviour. By randomly assigning people to conditions in their laboratory studies, Latané and Darley were able to rule out such alternative explanations.

The trade-off between internal and external validity has been referred to as the basic dilemma of the social psychologist (Aronson & Carlsmith, 1968). The challenge is to devise a study that maximizes both. Wendy Josephson's (1987)

field experiments

experiments conducted in natural settings, rather than in the laboratory study on the relation between television violence and aggressive behaviour is an example of one that rose to this challenge and elegantly captured both internal validity and external validity. In this study, boys in grades 2 and 3 from 13 schools in Winnipeg watched either a violent or a nonviolent television show. Internal validity was achieved by controlling the television show the participants watched. For example, Josephson ensured that the violent and nonviolent shows were equivalent in terms of excitement, liking, and physiological arousal. This level of control ensured that any differences in subsequent behaviour between the two groups were because of differences in violent content, rather than other variables that might be associated with violent programming, such as excitement. Internal validity was further enhanced by random assignment of participants to either the violent or the nonviolent condition. External validity was maximized by having the participants play floor hockey in their school gymnasium (an activity typical for boys this age) after they had finished viewing the television segment. (As you will see in Chapter 11, in social psychological research, aggression is often assessed in terms of the severity of electric shocks administered to another research participant—a procedure that may be high in internal validity, but that certainly lacks external validity.)

In Josephson's (1987) study, observers recorded instances of aggression after the boys had viewed the television shows. The observers were unaware whether the boys had seen the violent or the nonviolent show. This procedure is known as keeping observers "blind" to the experimenter's hypothesis. To make the observation as natural as possible, participants were told that the observers would be doing "play by plays" just the way they do in "real" hockey games. The observers spoke into microphones, noted the number on a child's jersey, and recorded the kind of aggression that occurred. (One of the observers was Wendy Josephson's mother, who apparently had to swallow hard before recounting some of the instances of verbal aggression!) The results of this study indicated that exposure to violent programming did, in fact, increase aggression—but only among boys who were predisposed toward aggression.

Generally, both internal and external validity are not captured in a single experiment. Most social psychologists opt first for internal validity, conducting laboratory experiments in which people are randomly assigned to different conditions and all extraneous variables are controlled; here, there is little ambiguity about which variable is causing which result. Other social psychologists prefer external validity to control, conducting most of their research in field studies. And many social psychologists do both. Taken together, both types of studies meet the requirements of the perfect experiment. Through replication, researchers can study a given research question with maximal internal and external validity.

Basic versus Applied Research

You might have wondered how people decide which specific topic to study. Why would a social psychologist decide to study helping behaviour, or the effects of violent television on aggression? Is he or she simply curious? Or does the social psychologist have a specific purpose in mind, such as trying to reduce violence?

In general, we can distinguish between two types of research, each having a different purpose. The goal in **basic research** is to find the best answer as to why people behave the way they do, purely for reasons of intellectual curiosity. The researchers aren't directly trying to solve a specific social or psychological problem. In contrast, the goal in **applied research** is to solve a particular social problem; building a theory of behaviour is usually secondary to solving the specific problem, such as alleviating racism, reducing violence, or stemming the spread of AIDS.

basic research

studies that are designed to find the best answer as to why people behave the way they do and that are conducted purely for reasons of intellectual curiosity

applied research

studies designed specifically to solve a particular social problem; building a theory of behaviour is usually secondary to solving the specific problem

In social psychology, the distinction between basic and applied research is fuzzy. Even though researchers may label themselves as either basic or applied scientists, it is clear that the endeavours of one group are not independent of those of the other group. There are countless examples of advances in basic science that at the time had no known applied value but later proved to be the key to solving a significant social or medical problem. As we discuss later in this book, for instance, basic research with dogs, rats, and fish on the effects of feeling in control of one's environment has led to the development of techniques to improve the health of elderly nursing home residents (Langer & Rodin, 1976; Schulz, 1976; Seligman, 1975). Similarly, research on attribution has been used to help new students cope with the transition to university or college (Wilson & Linville, 1982, 1985).

> *There is nothing so practical as a good theory.*
>
> —Kurt Lewin, 1951

Most social psychologists would agree that in order to solve a specific social problem, it is vital to have a good understanding of the psychological processes responsible for it. Kurt Lewin (1951), one of the founders of social psychology, coined a phrase that has become a motto for the field: "There is nothing so practical as a good theory." He meant that to solve such difficult social problems as violence or racial prejudice, one must first understand the underlying psychological dynamics of human nature and social interaction. Even when the goal is to discover the psychological processes underlying social behaviour, the findings often have clear applied implications, as you'll see. We also include three Social Psychology in Action units at the end of the book that discuss how social psychology has been applied to important social problems.

Ethical Issues in Social Psychology

As you read this chapter, did it bother you to learn that researchers sometimes mislead people about the true purpose of their study, or that in Latané and Darley's seizure study, people were put in a situation that might have been upsetting? This study illustrates that in their quest to create realistic, engaging situations, social psychologists frequently face an ethical dilemma. On the one hand, for obvious scientific reasons, we want our experiments to resemble the real world as much as possible and to be as sound and well controlled as we can make them. On the other hand, we want to treat our participants respectfully and avoid causing them undue and unnecessary stress, discomfort, or unpleasantness. These two goals often conflict as the researcher goes about the business of creating and conducting experiments.

Researchers are concerned about the health and welfare of the individuals participating in their experiments. Researchers are also in the process of discovering important information about human social behaviour—such as bystander intervention, prejudice, conformity, aggression, and obedience to authority. Many of these discoveries are bound to be of benefit to society. Indeed, given the fact that social psychologists have developed powerful tools to investigate such issues scientifically, many scholars feel it would be immoral not to conduct these experiments. However, in order to gain insight into such critical issues, researchers must create vivid events that are involving for the participants. Some of these events, by their nature, are likely to produce a degree of discomfort for the participants. Thus, what is required for good science and what is required for ethical science can be contradictory. The dilemma cannot be resolved by making pious claims that no participant ever experiences any kind of discomfort in an experiment, or by insisting that all is fair in science and forging blindly ahead. Clearly, the problem calls for a middle ground.

The dilemma would be less problematic if researchers could obtain **informed consent** from their participants prior to participation. Informed consent is the

informed consent

the procedure whereby researchers explain the nature of the experiment to participants before it begins, and obtain their consent to participate procedure whereby the researcher explains the nature of the experiment to participants before it begins and asks for their agreement to participate. If the participants are made fully aware of the kinds of experiences they are about to undergo and state that they are willing to participate, the ethical dilemma is resolved. In many social psychology experiments, this sort of description is feasible—and where it is feasible, it is done. But sometimes it is impossible. Suppose Latané and Darley (1970) had told their participants that a seizure was about to be staged, that it wouldn't be a real emergency, and that the hypothesis stated they should offer help. As we explained earlier, such a procedure would be bad science. In this kind of experiment, it's essential that the participant experience contrived events as if they were real; this is called a deception experiment. **Deception** in social psychological research involves misleading participants about the true purpose of a study or the events that transpire. (Note that not all research in social psychology involves deception.)

Guidelines for Ethical Research

To ensure that the dignity and safety of research participants are protected, the Canadian Psychological Association has published a set of ethical principles that apply to psychology research and clinical practice conducted in Canada; these guidelines are summarized in Figure 2.2. In addition, there is a set of ethics guidelines, the Tri-Council Policy Statement, that governs research conducted at Canadian universities. All psychology research is reviewed by a Research Ethics Board to ensure that the strict guidelines of the Tri-Council Policy are met. Any aspect of the experimental procedure that this board judges to be stressful or upsetting must be changed or eliminated before the study can be conducted.

In all research studies, participants must be told that they can withdraw at any time, for any reason, without fear of consequences for doing so. They must also be assured of the anonymity and confidentiality of their responses. When deception is used, a post-experimental interview, called the debriefing session, is crucial and must occur. **Debriefing** is the process of explaining to the participants, at the end of the experiment, the purpose of the study and what exactly transpired. If any participants experienced discomfort, the researchers attempt to undo and alleviate it. The debriefing session also provides an opportunity to inform the participants about the goals and purpose of the research, thereby serving an important educational function. Regardless of whether deception was used in the experiment, the best researchers question their participants carefully after the experiment and listen to what they say. (For a detailed description of how debriefing interviews should be conducted, see Aronson, Ellsworth, Carlsmith, & Gonzalez, 1990.)

deception

the procedure whereby participants are misled about the true purpose of a study or the events that will actually transpire

debriefing

the process of explaining to the participants, at the end of the experiment, the purpose of the study and exactly what transpired

FIGURE 2.2

Procedures for the protection of participants in psychological research

(Adapted from Canadian code of ethics for psychologists [Canadian Psychological Association, 1991] and Ethical principles of psychologists in the conduct of research [American Psychological Association, 1992])

Ethical Principles of Psychologists in the Conduct of Research

1. Respect for dignity of persons. The central ethical principle underlying psychological research is respect for human dignity. This principle forms the foundation for the other principles that follow.
2. Informed consent. As much as possible, the researcher should describe the procedures to participants before they take part in a study, and document their agreement to take part in the study as it was described to them.
3. Minimizing harm. Psychologists must take steps to avoid harming their research participants.
4. Freedom to withdraw. Participants must be informed that they are free to withdraw from a study at any point, and that there will be no negative consequences for doing so.
5. Privacy and confidentiality. All information obtained from individual participants must be held in strict confidence.
6. Use of deception. Deception may be used only if there are no other viable means of testing a hypothesis, and only if a Research Ethics Board rules that it does not put participants at undue risk. After the study, participants must be provided with a full description and explanation of all procedures, in a post-experimental interview called the debriefing.

In our experience, virtually all participants understand and appreciate the need for deception, as long as the time is taken in the post-experimental debriefing session to go over the purpose of the research and to explain why alternative procedures could not be used. Studies that have investigated the impact of participating in deception studies have consistently found that people do not object to the kinds of mild discomfort and deceptions typically used in social psychological research (e.g., Christensen, 1988; Finney, 1987; Gerdes, 1979). For example, in a study at the University of Manitoba, attitudes toward deception research were assessed in 1970 and again, 20 years later, in 1990 (Sharpe, Adair, & Roese, 1992). At each time period, there was no evidence that students who had participated in deception studies felt negatively about their experience. In fact, participants who had been deceived were more likely to agree with arguments in favour of deception research than were those who had not experienced deception. And, importantly, those who had experienced deception did not show greater distrust of psychologists. Some studies have even found that people who participated in deception experiments said they had learned more and enjoyed the experiments more than did those who participated in nondeception experiments (Smith & Richardson, 1983). Similarly, Latané and Darley (1970) reported that during their debriefing the participants said that the deception was necessary and that they were willing to participate in similar studies in the future—even though they had experienced some stress and conflict during the study.

We do not mean to imply that all deception is beneficial. Nonetheless, if mild deception is used and time is spent after the study discussing the deception with participants and explaining why it was necessary, the evidence shows that people will not be harmed.

SUMMARY

The goal of social psychology is to answer questions about social behaviour scientifically. The **hypotheses** that social psychologists test come from many sources. Sometimes, researchers are inspired by previous studies and **theories**; they have a different explanation that they want to test. At other times, researchers come up with hypotheses from their own personal observations of social events, such as the Kitty Genovese murder in the early 1960s.

The principal research designs used are **observational, correlational**, and **experimental methods**. Each has its strengths and weaknesses and is appropriate for certain research questions. Each method allows the researcher to make a different type of statement about his or her findings. Regardless of the method used, it is important for researchers to provide an **operational definition** for their variables, meaning a precise specification of how variables are measured or manipulated.

Observational methods vary in terms of how visible the researcher is. In some cases, the researcher is unobtrusive; in other cases, the researcher interacts with the people being observed (this is known as **ethnography**). In **archival analysis**, the researcher examines the accumulated documents or archives of a culture. When conducting observational research it is necessary to establish **interjudge reliability**, which is the level of agreement between two or more people who independently observe and code a set of data.

The **correlational method** allows the researcher to determine if two or more variables are related—that is, whether one can be predicted from the other. **Survey** research is one kind of correlational research. The **correlation coefficient** is a statistical technique that reveals the extent to which one variable can be predicted from another. Correlations are often calculated from survey data, in which there is **random** selection of a sample from a larger population. This ensures that the responses of the sample are representative of those of the population. The major drawback of the correlational method is that it cannot determine causality. It is not possible to determine from a correlation whether A causes B, B causes A, or some other variable causes both A and B.

The **experimental method** is the preferred design in social psychology; it alone allows the researcher to infer the presence of causality. In experiments, researchers vary the level of an **independent variable**, which is the one hypothesized to have a causal effect on behaviour. The **dependent variable** is the measured variable hypothesized to be caused or influenced by the independent variable. The researcher ensures that participants are treated identically except for the independent variable, and randomly assigns people to the experimental conditions. **Random assignment to condition**, the hallmark of true experimental design, minimizes the possibility that different types of people are unevenly distributed across conditions. A **probability level** (*p*-value) is calculated, telling the researcher how likely it is that the results are attributable to chance versus attributable to the independent variable.

Experiments are designed to be as high as possible in **internal validity** (ensuring that nothing other than the independent variable is influencing the results) and in **external validity** (ensuring that the results can be generalized across people and situations). **Mundane realism** reflects the extent to which the experimental setting is similar to real-life settings. **Psychological realism** reflects the

extent to which the experiment involves psychological responses like those occurring in real life. The best test of external validity is **replication**—repeating the experiment in different settings with different people, to see if the results are the same. A statistical technique called **meta analysis** allows researchers to see how reliable the effects of an independent variable are over many replications.

Experiments can be conducted in the laboratory or in the field; **field experiments** are those conducted in natural settings and therefore are high in external validity. Many social psychologists conduct **cross-cultural research**, which is research conducted with members of different cultures to see whether psychological principles are universal or specific to the culture in which people were raised. Researchers engage in both **basic research** and **applied research**. While the line between these is often blurred, basic research aims to gain understanding of human social behaviour, without trying specifically to solve a particular problem, whereas applied research aims to solve a specific problem, often one with social policy implications.

A major concern in social psychological research is the ethical treatment of participants. Canadian researchers carefully follow the Canadian Psychological Association's guidelines, which specify procedures such as obtaining **informed consent**, the participant's right to leave the study at any time, ensured anonymity and confidentiality, and **debriefing** following an experiment, particularly if **deception** (involving a **cover story** about the supposed purpose of the study or the independent or dependent variables) has been used.

Scoring the Try It! Exercises

▶ Page 29

1. In studies conducted by Stanley Milgram (1974), up to 65 percent of participants administered what they thought were near-lethal shocks to another subject. (In fact, no real shocks were administered.)

2. (c) Rewarding people for doing something they enjoy will typically make them like that activity less in the future (e.g., Lepper, 1995, 1996; Lepper, Greene, & Nisbett, 1973).

3. (b) Wilson et al. (1993) found that people who did not analyze their feelings were the most satisfied with their choice of posters when contacted a few weeks later.

4. (a) Under most circumstances, repeated exposure increases liking for a stimulus (Zajonc, 1968).

5. (a) More (Jecker & Landy, 1969).

6. (c) Research by Dijksterhuis and Nordgren (2006) found that people who were distracted made the best choices, possibly because distraction allowed them to consider the problem unconsciously.

7. (a) Research in Canada (Walsh, Hickey, & Duffy, 1999) and in the United States (Spencer, Steele, & Quinn, 1997; Steele, 1997) has found that when women think there are sex differences on a test, they do worse because of stereotype

threat—the fear that they might confirm a negative stereotype about their gender. When women are told that there are no gender differences in performance on the test, they do as well as men.

8. (b) There is no evidence that subliminal messages in advertising have any effect, whereas there is substantial evidence that normal, everyday advertising is quite effective (Chaiken, Wood, & Eagly, 1996; Merikle, 1988; Weir, 1984; Wilson, Houston, & Meyers, 1998).

9. (b) Men touch women more than vice versa (Henley, 1977).

10. (c) In the short run, people regret acts of commission (things they did that they wish they hadn't) more than acts of omission (things they didn't do that they wish they had). In the long run, however, the opposite is true (Gilovich & Medvec, 1995; Gilovich, Medvec, & Chen, 1995).

▶ Page 40

1. The politician ignored possible third variables that could cause both Scouts membership and crime, such as socioeconomic class. Traditionally, Scouting has been most popular in small towns and suburbs among middle-class youngsters; it has never been very attractive or even available to youths growing up in densely populated, urban, high-crime areas.

2. Not necessarily, because milk drinking may have little to do with weight gain. Children who drink a lot of milk might be more likely to eat cookies or other high-calorie foods.

3. Did tattoos cause motorcycle accidents? Or, for that matter, did motorcycle accidents cause tattoos? The researchers suggested that a third (unmeasured) variable was in fact the cause of both: A tendency to take risks and to be involved in flamboyant personal displays led to tattooing one's body and to driving a motorcycle recklessly.

4. Not necessarily. People who do not eat breakfast might differ from people who do in any number of ways that influence longevity—for example, in how obese they are, in how hard-driving and high-strung they are, or even in how late they sleep in the morning.

5. It is possible that religion makes people more likely to obey the law. It is equally possible, however, that some other variable increases the likelihood that people will be religious and follow the rules—such as having parents who are religious.

6. Families who can afford or are willing to have a pet might differ in any number of ways from families who neither can afford nor are willing to have one. For example, families that own pets might experience less financial stress, be less likely to move frequently, or be more nurturant and loving. Any one of these factors could reduce the likelihood that an adolescent will get into trouble.

7. It is possible that watching public television makes people want to have more sex. It is equally possible, however, that some third variable, such as health or education, influences both television preferences and sexual behaviour. It is even possible that having sex makes people want to watch more public television. Based on the correlation the researchers reported, there is no way of telling which of these explanations is true.

Along with a dynamic, electronic version of this text, MyPsychLab offers a wealth of resources to deepen your understanding and test your recall of the material in this chapter—including video and audio clips, simulations and activities, self-assessments, practice tests, and other study materials. The following specific resources are available for this chapter:

 Correlations Do Not Show Causation

 Distinguishing Independent and Dependent Variables

 Research Methods

To access MyPsychLab, please visit www.mypsychlab.com (Student Access Code required—packaged with this book).

Social Cognition:

How We Think about the Social World

Kevin Chappell was on his way to the top. It was 1988 and the 29-year-old man with an IQ of 147 had just been accepted to medical school, had graduated at the top of his class from Trent University, and was working on a master's degree. He was also an avid soccer player and had played lead guitar in a rock and roll band. On January 30, 1988, he decided to go for a run after a hard day of studying. It was a dark, rainy evening, and as he crossed a street, he was hit by a car. From that moment, Chappell's life was changed immeasurably. He sustained severe brain damage, leaving him unable to recognize things. He could see objects but didn't know what they were—a condition known as visual agnosia. There are very few people in the world with visual agnosia—so, not surprisingly, Chappell's condition attracted the attention of neuropsychologists.

Psychologist Gordon Winocur, a specialist in memory at Trent University, met Chappell just after he had been diagnosed with visual agnosia. Chappell didn't touch the cup of coffee that Dr. Winocur had served him, which wasn't unusual for someone with this diagnosis. Why would you pick up a cup of coffee if you don't recognize what it is? One day, however, Chappell happened to run into Winocur and greeted him by name. Winocur was stunned. How could someone who didn't recognize objects know who he was?

It became apparent that Chappell does recognize one thing: faces. He doesn't recognize arms, legs, or feet. He doesn't recognize faces that are upside down or sideways, but he does recognize faces that are upright. This ability probably makes him unique in the world. Winocur teamed up with two neuropsychologists, Morris Moscovitch from the University of Toronto and Marlene Behrmann from Carnegie Mellon University in Pittsburgh, to formally study Kevin Chappell. Their findings were published in the science journal *Nature*, in 1992 (Behrmann, Winocur, & Moscovitch, 1992). In follow-up research, it was shown that Kevin Chappell's ability to recognize faces extends to photographs of faces, caricatures, and cartoon faces. He can even recognize faces made up of objects—although he isn't able to recognize the objects (Gauthier, Behrmann, & Tarr, 1999; Moscovitch, Winocur, & Behrmann, 1997).

▲ Because of a brain injury, Kevin Chappell, shown here standing between his two sons, lives in a world of unidentifiable objects.

social cognition

how people think about themselves and the social world; more specifically, how people select, interpret, remember, and use social information to make judgments and decisions

In order to recognize an object, we have to be able to perceive its parts, synthesize them, and match them to the representation of that object stored in our brain. Dr. Moscovitch comments that "Kevin seems to be fine at identifying the bits and pieces. . . . It's his ability to integrate the information rapidly and then match it to the internal representation that seems to be impaired" (Scott, 2002).

A writer interviewing Chappell, then age 44, shows him a pair of sunglasses. "It's brown with bits of silver and two horns," Chappell says. But what is it? Chappell has no idea. "I don't know what I see," he replies, "I have to guess" (Scott, 2002). It is hard to imagine what Kevin Chappell's world must be like. When we enter a classroom, for example, we do not see a bunch of objects that have platforms parallel to the floor connected to four legs with another flat surface at a right angle that we then mentally assemble to figure out what they are. Instead of having to pause and think, "Let's see. Oh, yes, those are chairs," we quickly, unconsciously, and effortlessly categorize the objects as chairs. The fact that we do this automatically allows us to use our conscious mind for other, more important purposes ("What's going to be on the quiz today?" or "Should I strike up a conversation with that cute guy in the third row?") Similarly, when we encounter people we know, the process of recognizing them requires little effort on our part, thereby allowing us to focus on our interaction with them.

In this chapter we will explore **social cognition**, which is the way people think about themselves and the social world—how they select, interpret, remember, and use social information to make judgments and decisions. Not only are we able to recognize chairs and other physical objects without any apparent effort, but we are also able to make complex judgments about people at lightning speed. Of course, we also occasionally make mistakes, and sometimes these mistakes are costly. In this chapter you will see how sophisticated we are as social thinkers, as well as the kinds of mistakes we are prone to make.

> *It is the mind which creates the world about us, and even though we stand side by side in the same meadow, my eyes will never see what is beheld by yours.*
>
> —*George Gissing,* The Private Papers of Henry Ryecroft, *1903*

To understand how people think about the social world and how accurate their impressions are likely to be, one needs to distinguish between two different kinds of social cognition. One kind of thought is quick and automatic—as when we effortlessly classify an object as a chair. Other times, we pause and think about ourselves and our environment, and carefully contemplate what is going on around us. You may have spent hours deliberating over important decisions in your life, such as where to go to university or college, what to choose as your major, and whether to break up with your boyfriend or girlfriend. This is the second kind of social cognition—*controlled thinking*, which is more effortful and deliberate.

Often, the automatic and controlled modes of social cognition work very well together. Think of a plane that can fly on automatic pilot, that monitors hundreds of complex systems and adjusts instantly to changes in atmospheric conditions. The autopilot does just fine most of the time, though occasionally it is important for the human pilot to take over and fly the plane manually. Humans, too, have an "automatic pilot" that monitors their environment, draws conclusions, and directs their behaviour. But people can also "override" this automatic type of thinking and analyze a situation slowly and deliberately. We will begin by examining the nature of automatic thinking.

On Automatic Pilot: Low-Effort Thinking

People typically size up a new situation very quickly: They figure out who is there, what is happening, and what might happen next. Often these quick conclusions are correct. When you attended your first university class, for example, you probably made quick assumptions about who people were (the person standing at the lectern was the professor) and how to behave. We doubt that you confused the class with a birthday party. And you probably reached these conclusions without even being aware that you were doing so.

Imagine a different approach. Every time you encounter a new situation, you stop and think about it slowly and deliberately, like Rodin's statue *The Thinker*. When you are introduced to someone new, you have to excuse yourself for fifteen minutes while you analyze what you have learned and how much you like the person. When you drive down an unfamiliar road, you have to pull over and analyze its twists and turns before knowing how to proceed. Sounds exhausting, doesn't it? Instead, we form impressions of people quickly and effortlessly, and navigate new roads without much conscious analysis of what we are doing. We see an object with two dark lenses attached to curved arms and immediately know that those are sunglasses. We do these things by engaging in an automatic analysis of our environments, based on our past experiences and knowledge of the world. **Automatic thinking** is thought that is nonconscious, unintentional, involuntary, and effortless. While different kinds of automatic thinking meet these criteria to varying degrees (Bargh, 2007; Bargh & Ferguson, 2000; Wegner & Bargh, 1998), for our purposes we can define automaticity as thinking that satisfies all or most of these criteria.

People as Everyday Theorists: Automatic Thinking with Schemas

Automatic thinking helps us understand new situations by relating them to our prior experiences. When we meet someone new, we don't start from scratch to figure out what he or she is like; we categorize the person as "an engineering student" or "like my cousin Helen." The same goes for places, objects, and situations. When we walk into a fast-food restaurant we've never visited, we know, without thinking, not to wait at a table for a waiter and a menu. We know that we have to go to the counter to order because our mental "script" automatically tells us that this is what we do in fast-food restaurants, and we assume that this one is no different.

More formally, people use **schemas**, which are mental structures that organize our knowledge about the social world. These mental structures influence the information we notice, think about, and remember (Bartlett, 1932; Janicik & Larrick, 2005; Markus, 1977). The term *schema* is very general; it encompasses our knowledge about many things—other people, ourselves, social roles (e.g., what a

▲ Rodin's famous sculpture, *The Thinker*, mimics controlled thinking, where people sit down and consider something slowly and deliberately. Even when we do not know it, however, we are engaging in automatic thinking, which is nonconscious, unintentional, involuntary, and effortless.

automatic thinking

thinking that is nonconscious, unintentional, involuntary, and effortless

schemas

mental structures people use to organize their knowledge about the social world around themes or subjects and that influence the information people notice, think about, and remember librarian or an engineer is like), and specific events (e.g., what usually happens when people eat a meal in a restaurant). In each case, our schemas contain our basic knowledge and impressions that we use to organize what we know about the social world and interpret new situations.

Schemas also influence the way in which we process information. For example, there is evidence that information relevant to a particular schema is processed more quickly than information unrelated to it. To illustrate this phenomenon, Gardner, MacIntyre, and Lalonde (1995) asked English-speaking students living in Quebec to rate the characteristics of various groups (e.g., English Canadians, French Canadians, males, females). Participants were faster when rating the stereotypical characteristics of each group than when rating its nonstereotypical characteristics; for example, when the target group was males, characteristics such as *rugged, impatient,* and *talkative* were rated more quickly than characteristics such as *irreligious, artistic,* and *impolite.*

We also tend to "fill in the blanks" with schema-consistent information (Lenton & Bryan, 2005). In a study by Kunda, Sinclair, and Griffin (1997), students at the University of Waterloo were told that Michael was either a salesperson or an actor, and that his friends described him as very extroverted. They were then asked, "What kinds of behaviours do you suppose they have in mind when they describe him this way?" The researchers found that when told that Michael was a salesperson, participants generated pushy descriptions (e.g., loud speaking, monopolizes conversations), whereas when Michael was described as an actor, they generated descriptions such as "life of the party" and "not afraid of the spotlight." In another study by these researchers, participants read about John the lawyer versus John the construction worker, and were asked to generate examples of aggressive behaviour that John might perform. John the lawyer was seen as more likely to argue, whereas John the construction worker was seen as more likely to punch and fight (Kunda, Sinclair, & Griffin, 1997). In other words, given a label, we fill in the blanks with all kinds of schema-consistent information. As we discuss next, this tendency to "fill in the blanks" allows for more efficient information processing, but it also can have tragic consequences.

Stereotypes about Race and Weapons   When applied to members of a social group such as gender or race, schemas are commonly referred to as *stereotypes,* which we will discuss in detail in Chapter 12. For now, we point out that the stereotypes can be applied rapidly and automatically when we encounter other people. For example, researchers recently have conducted experiments to test whether people's stereotypes about African Americans can influence their perception of whether a person is holding a weapon (Payne, Shimizu, & Jacoby, 2005). In one study, non-black college students saw pairs of pictures in rapid succession on a computer screen (Payne, 2001). The first picture was always of a face, whereas the second picture depicted either a tool or a gun. Participants were told to pay attention only to the second picture and to press one key as rapidly and as accurately as they could if it was a tool and another key if it was a gun. In fact, they had only half a second to identify the picture and press a key.

It just so happened that half of the faces in the first picture were of whites and half were of blacks. The question was, did the race of the face influence people's perception of whether they saw a gun or a tool in the second picture? Indeed it did; people were significantly more likely to misidentify a tool as a gun when it was preceded by a black face than when it was preceded by a white face.

In another study, people performed a task that mirrored the kind of dilemma that police officers encounter in real life (Correll, Park, Judd, & Wittenbrink, 2002). Non-black participants played a video game in which they saw photographs of young men in realistic settings, such as in a park, at a train station, and on a city sidewalk. Half of the men were African American, and half were white. And half of the men in each group were holding a handgun and half were holding a

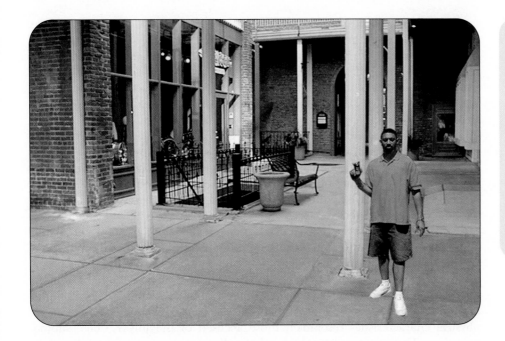

In a study by Correll et al. (2002), people played a video game in which they saw photographs of men who were holding a handgun or nonthreatening objects such as cellphones, like the picture shown here. Half of the men were black and half were white. Participants were instructed to press a button labelled "shoot" if the man had a gun and a button labelled "don't shoot" if he did not. Similar to a situation for a real police officer, they had very little time to make up their minds (just over half a second). The most common mistake people made was to "shoot" a black man who was not holding a gun, like the man in this picture.

nonthreatening object such as a cellphone, wallet, or camera. Participants were instructed to press a button labelled "shoot" if the man in the picture had a gun and a button labelled "don't shoot" if he did not. Like a real police officer, they had very little time to make up their minds (just over half a second). Participants won or lost points on each round of the game, modelled after the risks and benefits faced by officers in real life. Participants earned 5 points for not shooting someone who did not have a gun and 10 points for shooting someone who did have a gun. They lost 20 points if they shot someone who was not holding a gun and lost 40 points if they failed to shoot someone who was holding a gun (which, in real life, would be the most life-threatening situation for a police officer).

The results? Participants were especially likely to pull the trigger when the person in a picture was black, whether or not he was holding a gun. This "shooter bias" meant that people made relatively few errors when a black person was in fact holding a gun but also that they made the most errors, shooting an unarmed person, when a black person was not holding a gun (see Figure 3.1). When the men in the picture were white, participants made about the same number of errors whether the men were armed or unarmed. Sadly, these effects are not limited to the laboratory. In 1999, police officers in the Bronx mistakenly thought that Amadou Diallo, a black man, was reaching for a gun when he was simply reaching for his wallet. Police fired a total of 41 shots at Diallo, killing him instantly.

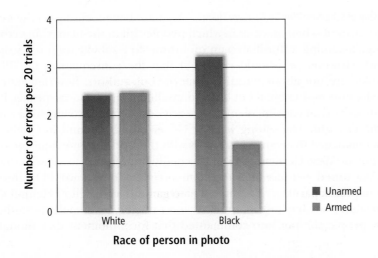

FIGURE 3.1

Errors made in "shooting" people in video game

Participants played a video game in which they were supposed to "shoot" a man if he was holding a gun and withhold fire if he was not. People were influenced by the race of the men in the pictures. As seen in the figure, people were prone to make mistakes by "shooting" black men who were unarmed.
(Adapted from Correll et al., 2002)

In other research, it was found that when a crime object, such as a gun, was displayed on a computer screen, white university students and police officers were quicker to identify black faces (also presented on a computer screen) than white faces (Eberhardt et al., 2004). Similarly, researchers at the University of British Columbia found that the negative stereotype of blacks—particularly traits relevant to danger (e.g., crime)—came to mind more quickly for participants who were seated in a dark room, compared with participants who were seated in a brightly lit room (Schaller, Park, & Mueller, 2003). This tendency was particularly pronounced among those who regard the world as a dangerous place.

In all these studies, people had to respond so quickly that they had little time to control their responses or think about what they were doing. The errors they made were the result of automatic thinking that probably is rooted in the pervasive stereotypes in North American culture about black people and violence.

Obviously, the effects we have been discussing are not limited to stereotypes about black people and violence. In the summer of 2005, news headlines focused on the police shooting of Jean Charles de Menezes, a 27-year-old Brazilian man living in London, England. De Menezes was shot five times in the head at close range as he approached a subway station. Members of Britain's Muslim community expressed alarm and concern that police were targeting men whose race or physical characteristics resembled those accused of the July 7, 2005, subway bombings. The response from the head of police was that tragic mistakes such as this occur because officers are forced to make "incredibly difficult fast-time decisions in life-threatening situations" (Frankel, 2005).

Closer to home, on January 31, 2005, Winnipeg police officers were searching for suspects in a home invasion. Eighteen-year-old Matthew Dumas was in the vicinity, although he was not a suspect. However, police officers noticed that he was concealing a metal object up his sleeve. The object turned out to be a screwdriver. He was ordered to drop it, and when he refused, one of the officers fired two shots at him. Dumas died shortly afterward. At an inquest held in June 2008, Morris Swan Shannacappo, grand chief of the Southern Chiefs Organization, pointed to similar shootings of aboriginal men. "We know Matthew was racially profiled. If he had not been aboriginal, he would not have been stopped" (Rollason, 2008).

We should keep in mind that stereotypes, such as the Bronx police officers' assumptions about Amadou Diallo, the British police officers' assumptions about Jean Charles de Menezes, and the Winnipeg police officers' assumptions about Matthew Dumas—based on their race—are a special case of a more general phenomenon: people's organization of the world into schemas (Kunda, 1999). In addition to schemas about classes of people, for example, we have schemas about specific individuals (e.g., what Aunt Jane is like), social roles (e.g., how mothers are supposed to behave), or how people act in specific situations (e.g., at a party or in a restaurant). We now turn to properties of schemas more generally.

The Function of Schemas: Why Do We Have Them?   We have been focusing on the negative consequences of schemas, cases in which people "fill in the blanks" in erroneous ways (e.g., assuming a Brazilian man on his way to a subway train is a suspected terrorist). However, we should point out that the consequences of "filling in the blanks" are not always harmful. One of your authors, Beverley Fehr, once attended a fundraising breakfast for a counselling centre. Guest speaker Pamela Wallin described an early incident that nearly cost her her broadcasting career—or so she thought. The setting was the G-7 economic summit in Quebec, and CTV had managed to arrange interviews with the British prime minister and the chancellor of West Germany. Wallin excitedly announced to viewers that they should stay tuned, because after the commercial break they would be interviewing then prime minister Margaret Thatcher and chancellor Helmut "Shit." Convinced that she had just committed career suicide, Wallin left the studio. The first few people she ran into commented that for a moment they thought she had mispronounced Chancellor Schmidt's name but then realized that the vacuum cleaner had been on, or that they hadn't had their morning coffee yet, or . . . In short, the fact that Pamela Wallin said "shit" on television was so inconsistent with people's schemas of her that they convinced themselves they must have heard wrong—that she really must have said "Schmidt."

If schemas can sometimes make us misperceive the world, why do we have them? Schemas are typically very useful for helping us organize and make sense of the world and to fill in the gaps of our knowledge. Think back, for a moment, to our opening story about Kevin Chappell, a man who lives in a world of unidentifiable objects. What would it be like to have no schemas about the social world? What if everything you encountered was inexplicable, confusing, and unlike anything else you'd ever known? Tragically, this is what happens to people who suffer from a neurological disorder called Korsakov's syndrome. People who suffer from Korsakov's syndrome also have difficulty forming schemas, just as Kevin Chappell does because of his visual agnosia. This can be so unsettling—even terrifying—that some people with Korsakov's syndrome go to great lengths to try to impose meaning on their experiences. The neurologist Oliver Sacks gives the following description of a Korsakov patient named Mr. Thompson:

> He remembered nothing for more than a few seconds. He was continually disoriented. Abysses of amnesia continually opened beneath him, but he would bridge them, nimbly, by fluent confabulations and fictions of all kinds. For him they were not fictions, but how he suddenly saw, or interpreted, the world. Its radical flux and incoherence could not be tolerated, acknowledged, for an instant—there was, instead, this strange, delirious, quasi-coherence, as Mr. Thompson, with his ceaseless, unconscious, quick-fire inventions, continually improvised a world around him . . . *for such a patient must literally make himself (and his world) up every moment.* (Sacks, 1987; emphasis in original)

In short, it is so important to us to have continuity, to relate new experiences to our past schemas, that people who lose this ability invent schemas where none exist.

Schemas are particularly important when we encounter information that can be interpreted in a number of ways, because they help us reduce ambiguity. Consider a classic study by Harold Kelley (1950), in which students in different sections of an economics class were told that a guest lecturer would be filling in that day. In order to create a schema about what the guest lecturer would be like, Kelley told the students that the economics department was interested in how

▲ People who know him consider him to be a rather cold person, industrious, critical, practical, and determined.

▲ People who know him consider him to be a very warm person, industrious, critical, practical, and determined.

different classes reacted to different instructors and that the students would receive a brief biographical note about the instructor before he arrived. The note contained information about the instructor's age, background, and teaching experience. It also gave one of two descriptions of his personality. One version said, "People who know him consider him to be a rather cold person, industrious, critical, practical, and determined." The other version was identical, except that the phrase "a rather cold person" was replaced with "a very warm person." The students were randomly given one of these personality descriptions.

The guest lecturer then conducted a class discussion for 20 minutes, after which the students rated their impressions of him. How humorous was he? How sociable? How considerate? Given that there was some ambiguity in this situation—after all, the students had seen the instructor for only a brief time—Kelley hypothesized that they would use the schema provided by the biographical note to fill in the blanks. This is exactly what happened. The students who expected the instructor to be warm gave him significantly higher ratings than did the students who expected him to be cold, even though all of the students had observed the same teacher behaving in the same way. Students who expected the instructor to be warm were also more likely to ask him questions and to participate in the class discussion.

> *I know that often I would not see a thing unless I thought of it first.*
>
> —Norman Maclean, A River Runs through It, 1976

It is important to note that there is nothing wrong with what Kelley's students did. As long as people have reason to believe their schemas are accurate, it is perfectly reasonable to use them to resolve ambiguity. If a suspicious-looking character approaches you in a dark alley and says, "Take out your wallet," your schema about such encounters tells you the person wants to steal your money, not admire pictures of your family. This schema helps you avert a serious, and perhaps deadly, misunderstanding. The danger comes when we automatically apply schemas that are not accurate, such as assuming that a black person reaching into his pocket is about to produce a gun.

Schemas as Memory Guides Schemas also tend to influence what we remember. There is considerable evidence that people are more likely to remember information that is consistent with their schemas (Fiske & Taylor, 1991; Kunda, 1999; Lenton & Bryan, 2005). For example, Barry Corenblum (2003) found that students attending schools in Brandon, Manitoba, were more likely to remember positive behaviours performed by a white child than a Native child and negative behaviours performed by a Native child rather than a white child. Sadly, both European-Canadian and Native-Canadian children showed these memory effects, suggesting a commonly held schema of white children as better than Native children.

> *It is a capital mistake to theorize before you have all the evidence. It biases the judgment.*
>
> —Sherlock Holmes (Sir Arthur Conan Doyle), 1898

It will probably not surprise you that memory errors also tend to be consistent with people's schemas. For example, participants in a study by Linda Carli (1999) read a story about a woman named Barbara and her relationship with a man named Jack. After dating for a while, Barbara and Jack went to a ski lodge for a weekend getaway. In one condition, the story ended with Jack proposing to Barbara; in the other condition, the story ended with Jack raping Barbara. Two weeks later, participants took a memory test in which they read several facts about Jack and Barbara, and judged whether these facts had appeared in the story. In the marriage-proposal condition, people were likely to misremember details that were consistent with a proposal schema, such as "Jack wanted Barbara to meet his parents" and "Jack gave Barbara a dozen roses." Neither of these details had been in the story, but people in the proposal condition tended to think they were. Similarly, people in the rape condition were likely to misremember details that were consistent with a sexual assault schema, such as "Jack liked to drink" and "Jack was unpopular with women."

The fact that people filled in the blanks in their memory with schema-consistent details suggests that schemas become stronger and more resistant to

CONNECTIONS

Reconstructing the Movies: Schemas Affect What You Remember

We don't remember exactly what occurred in a given setting as if our minds were a film camera recording precise images and sounds. Instead, we remember some information that was there—particularly information our schemas lead us to notice and pay attention to—and we remember other information that was never there but that we have unknowingly added later (Darley & Akert, 1993; Markus & Zajonc, 1985). If you ask people what is the most famous line of dialogue in the classic Humphrey Bogart and Ingrid Bergman movie, *Casablanca*, they will probably say, "Play it again, Sam." Similarly, if you ask them what is one of the most famous lines from the 1966–69 *Star Trek* television series, they will probably say, "Beam me up, Scotty." Here is a piece of trivia that might surprise you: Both of these lines of dialogue are reconstructions—the characters in the movie and the television series never said them.

change over time. We will explore the implications of this fact for changing prejudiced attitudes and stereotypes in Chapter 12.

Which Schemas Are Applied? Accessibility and Priming   The social world is full of ambiguous information that is open to interpretation. Imagine for example that while you are riding on a city bus, a man gets on and sits beside you. He mutters incoherently to himself, stares at everyone on the bus, and repeatedly rubs his face with one hand. How would you make sense of his behaviour? You have several schemas you could use. What dictates your choice? Your impression of the man on the bus can be affected by **accessibility**, the extent to which schemas and concepts are at the forefront of our minds and therefore are likely to be used when we are making judgments about the social world (Higgins, 1996; Sanna & Schwarz, 2004; Todorov & Bargh, 2002; Wyer & Srull, 1989).

Schemas can be accessible for three reasons: First, some schemas are chronically accessible due to past experience (Chen & Andersen, 1999; Dijksterhuis & van Knippengerg, 1996; Higgins & Brendl, 1995; Rudman & Borgida, 1995). This means that these schemas are constantly active and ready to use to interpret ambiguous situations. For example, if there is a history of alcoholism in your family, traits describing an alcoholic are likely to be chronically accessible to you, increasing the likelihood that these traits will come to mind when you are thinking about the behaviour of the man on the bus. If someone you know suffers from mental illness, however, then thoughts about how mentally ill people

accessibility

the extent to which schemas and concepts are at the forefront of people's minds and are therefore likely to be used when making judgments about the social world

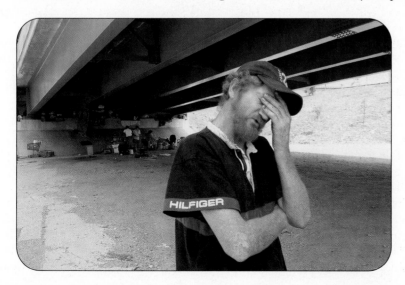

◄ Is this man an alcoholic or just down on his luck? Our judgments about other people can be influenced by schemas that are accessible in our memories. If you had just been talking to a friend about a relative who had an alcohol problem, you might be more likely to think that this man has an alcohol problem as well, because alcoholism is accessible in your memory.

behave are more likely to be accessible than are thoughts about alcoholics, leading you to interpret the man's behaviour very differently.

Second, schemas can become accessible because they are related to a current goal. The concept of mental illness might not be chronically accessible to you, but if you are studying for a test in your abnormal psychology class and need to learn about different kinds of mental disorders, this concept might be temporarily accessible. As a consequence, you might be likely to notice the man on the bus and interpret his behaviour as a sign of a mental disorder—at least until your test is over and you no longer have the goal to learn about mental illness (Forster, Liberman, & Higgins, 2005; Kuhl, 1983; Martin & Tesser, 1996).

Third, schemas can become temporarily accessible because of our recent experiences (Bargh, 1996; Higgins & Bargh, 1987; Oishi, Schimmack, & Colcombe, 2003; Stapel & Koomen, 2000). This means that a particular schema or trait is not always accessible but happens to be primed by something people have been thinking about or doing before encountering an event. Suppose, for example, that right before the man on the bus sat down, you were reading Ken Kesey's *One Flew over the Cuckoo's Nest*, a novel about patients in a mental hospital. Given that thoughts about mental patients are at the forefront of your mind, you would probably assume that the man's strange behaviour was attributable to mental illness. If, on the other hand, thoughts about alcoholism were fresh in your mind—for example, you had just looked out the window and seen a person leaning against a building drinking a bottle of wine—you would probably assume that the man on the bus had had a few too many drinks (see Figure 3.2). These are examples of **priming**, the process by which recent experiences increase the

priming

the process by which recent experiences increase the accessibility of a schema, trait, or concept

FIGURE 3.2

How we interpret an ambiguous situation: The role of accessibility and priming

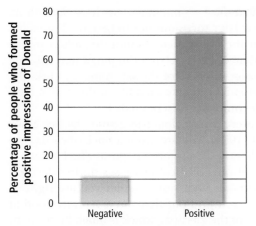

Words memorized in the first study

Description of Donald

Donald spent a great deal of time in his search of what he liked to call excitement. He had already climbed Mt. McKinley, shot the Colorado rapids in a kayak, driven in a demolition derby, and piloted a jet-powered boat—without knowing very much about boats. He had risked injury, and even death, a number of times. Now he was in search of new excitement. He was thinking, perhaps, he would do some skydiving or maybe cross the Atlantic in a sailboat. By the way he acted, one could readily guess that Donald was well aware of his ability to do many things well. Other than business engagements, Donald's contacts with people were limited. He felt he didn't really need to rely on anyone. Once Donald made up his mind to do something it was as good as done no matter how long it might take or how difficult the going might be. Only rarely did he change his mind—even when it might well have been better if he had.

FIGURE 3.3

Priming and accessibility

People read the paragraph about Donald and formed an impression of him. In a prior study, some people had memorized words that could be used to interpret Donald in a positive way (e.g., adventurous, self-confident), while others had memorized words that could be used to interpret Donald in a negative way (e.g., reckless, conceited). As seen in the graph, those who had memorized the positive words formed a much more positive impression of Donald than did those who had memorized the negative words.

(Adapted from Higgins, Rholes, & Jones, 1977)

accessibility of a schema, trait, or concept, making it more likely that you will use this information to interpret a new event—such as the behaviour of the man on the bus—even though this new event is completely unrelated to the one that originally primed the schema, trait, or concept.

Tory Higgins, Stephen Rholes, and Carl Jones (1977) illustrated this priming effect in the following experiment. Research participants were told they would take part in two unrelated studies. The first was a perception study, in which they would be asked to identify different colours while at the same time memorizing a list of words. The second was a reading comprehension study, in which they would be asked to read a paragraph about someone named Donald and then give their impressions of him. This paragraph is shown in Figure 3.3. Take a moment to read it. What do you think of Donald?

You might have noticed that many of Donald's actions are ambiguous, interpretable in either a positive or a negative manner. Take the fact that he piloted a boat without knowing much about it and wants to sail across the Atlantic Ocean. It is possible to put a positive spin on these acts, and decide that Donald has an admirable sense of adventure. It's just as easy, however, to put a negative spin on these acts, and assume that Donald is a rather reckless and foolhardy individual.

How did the participants interpret Donald's behaviour? Higgins, Rholes, and Jones (1977) found, as expected, that it depended on whether positive or negative traits were primed and accessible. In the first study, the researchers divided people into two groups and gave them different words to memorize. People who had first memorized the words *adventurous*, *self-confident*, *independent*, and *persistent* later formed positive impressions of Donald, viewing him as a likeable man who enjoyed new challenges. People who had first memorized *reckless*, *conceited*, *aloof*, and *stubborn* later formed negative impressions of Donald, viewing him as a stuck-up person who took needlessly dangerous chances.

But it was not memorizing just any positive or negative words that influenced people's impressions of Donald. In other conditions, research participants memorized words that were also positive or negative, such as *neat* or *disrespectful*. However, these traits did not influence their impressions of Donald because the words did not apply to Donald's behaviour. Thoughts, then, have to be both accessible and *applicable* before they will act as primes, exerting an influence on our impressions of the social world.

Priming is a good example of automatic thinking because it occurs quickly, unintentionally, and unconsciously. When judging others, people are usually not aware that they are applying concepts or schemas that they just happened to be thinking about earlier.

The Persistence of Schemas After They Are Discredited Sometimes, we hear something about an issue or another person that later turns out not to be true. For example, a jury might hear something in the courtroom about a defendant that is false or labelled as inadmissible evidence. Even though the judge may instruct the jurors to disregard that information, because of the way schemas work, the jurors' beliefs can persist. Indeed, schemas can take on a life of their own, even after the evidence for them has been completely discredited.

Imagine, for example, that you were a participant in a study by Lee Ross, Mark Lepper, and Michael Hubbard (1975). You are given a stack of cards containing both real and fictitious suicide notes. Your job is to guess which ones are real, supposedly to study the effects of physiological processes during decision making. After each guess, the experimenter tells you whether you are right or wrong. As the experiment progresses, you find out that you are pretty good at this task. In fact, you guess right on 24 of the 25 cards, which is much better than the average performance of 16 correct.

At this point, the experimenter tells you that the study is over and explains that it was actually concerned with the effects of success and failure on physiological responses. You learn that the feedback you received was bogus; that is, you had been randomly assigned to a condition in which the experimenter said you were correct on 24 of the cards, regardless of how well you actually did. The experimenter then gives you a final questionnaire, which asks you how many answers you think you really got correct and how many times you think you would guess correctly on a second, equally difficult test with new cards. What would you say? Now pretend you were in the other condition of the study. Here everything is identical, except you are told that you got only 10 of the 25 answers correct, which is much worse than average. How would you respond to the questionnaire after you found out the feedback was bogus?

Depending on which condition you were in, you would have formed a schema that you were either very good or very poor at the task. What happens when the evidence for this schema is discredited? Ross, Lepper, and Hubbard (1975) went to some pains to ensure that the participants realized the feedback had been randomly determined and had nothing to do with their actual performance. Even though the participants believed this, those who had received the "success" feedback still thought they had gotten more of the items correct and would do better on a second test than did people who had received the "failure" feedback. In addition, when asked how they would do on a new test, success participants said they would do better than failure participants did (see Figure 3.4).

This result is called the **perseverance effect** because people's beliefs persisted even after the original evidence was discredited. When people received the

perseverance effect

the finding that people's beliefs about themselves and the social world persist even after the evidence supporting these beliefs is discredited

FIGURE 3.4

The perseverance effect

People were told they had done very well (i.e., given "success" feedback) or very poorly (i.e., given "failure" feedback) on a test of their social sensitivity. They were then told that the feedback was bogus and had nothing to do with their actual performance. People's impressions that they were good or poor at the task persevered, even after learning that the feedback was bogus.

(Adapted from Ross, Lepper, & Hubbard, 1975)

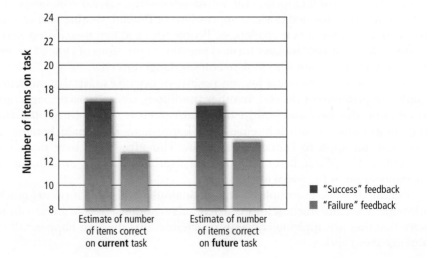

feedback, they explained to themselves why they were doing so well or so poorly, bringing to mind evidence from their past that was consistent with their performance (e.g., "I am really very perceptive. After all, last week I was the only one who realized that Jennifer was depressed" or "Well, I'm not so good at this stuff; my friends always say I'm the last to know"). Even after learning that the feedback was false, these thoughts were still fresh in people's minds, making them think they were particularly good or poor at the task (Anderson, 1995; Anderson & Lindsay, 1998; Davies, 1997; Sherman & Kim, 2002).

Making Our Schemas Come True: The Self-Fulfilling Prophecy   We have seen that when people encounter new evidence or have old evidence discredited, they tend not to revise their schemas as much as we might expect. People are not always passive recipients of information, however—they often act on their schemas, and in doing so, can change the extent to which these schemas are supported or contradicted. In fact, people can inadvertently make their schemas come true by the way they treat others. This is called a **self-fulfilling prophecy**, and it occurs when we have an expectation about what another person is like that influences how we act toward that person, which in turn, causes that person to behave consistently with our expectations. In other words, our expectations come true. Figure 3.5 illustrates this self-perpetuating cycle of self-fulfilling prophecy.

In what has become one of the most famous studies in social psychology, Robert Rosenthal and Lenore Jacobson (1968) examined whether teachers' expectations for students can have self-fulfilling effects. They administered an IQ test to all students in an elementary school and told the teachers that some of the

self-fulfilling prophecy

the case whereby people (a) have an expectation about what another person is like, which (b) influences how they act toward that person, which (c) causes that person to behave consistently with their original expectations

FIGURE 3.5

The self-fulfilling prophecy: A sad cycle in four acts

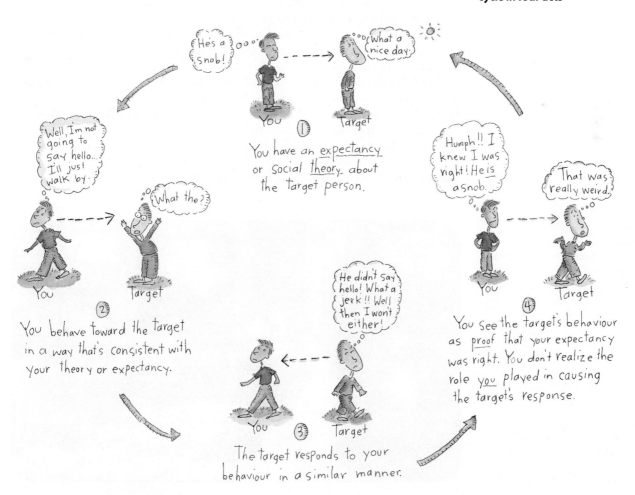

The self-fulfilling prophecy. Percentage of first and second graders who improved on an IQ test over the course of the school year

Those whom the teachers expected to do well actually improved more than did the other students.

(Adapted from Rosenthal & Jacobson, 1968)

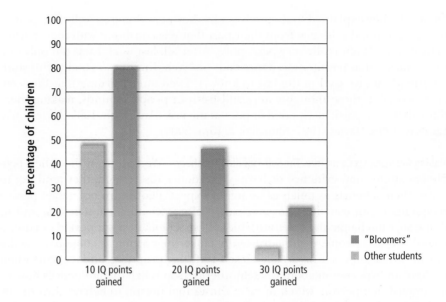

"Bloomers"
Other students

> *Prophecy is the most gratuitous form of error.*
>
> —George Eliot (Mary Ann Evans Cross), 1871

students had scored so well that they were sure to "bloom" academically in the upcoming year. In fact, the students identified as "bloomers" were chosen randomly by the researchers. As we discussed in Chapter 2, the use of random assignment means that, on average, the students designated as bloomers were no smarter or more likely to bloom than any of the other kids. The only way in which these students differed from their peers was in the minds of the teachers. (Neither the students nor their parents were told anything about the results of the test.)

After creating the expectation in the teachers' minds that some of the kids would do especially well, Rosenthal and Jacobson waited to see what would happen. They observed the classroom dynamics periodically over the school year, and at the end of the year they tested all of the children again with an actual IQ test. Did the prophecy come true? Indeed it did—the students in each class who had been labelled as bloomers showed significantly higher gains in their IQ scores than did the other students (see Figure 3.6). The teachers' expectations had become reality. Rosenthal and Jacobson's findings have since been replicated in a number of experimental and correlational studies (Babad, 1993; Blank, 1993; Maddon, Guyll, Spoth, & Willard, 2004; Smith, Jussim, & Eccles, 1999).

▶ Teachers can unintentionally make their expectations about their students come true by treating some students differently from others.

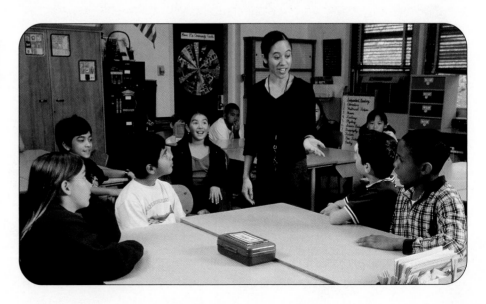

Try it!

▶ Avoiding Self-Fulfilling Prophecies

Examine some of your own schemas and expectations about social groups, especially groups you don't particularly like. These might be members of a particular race or ethnic group, of a rival university, of a political party, or people with a particular sexual orientation. Why don't you like members of this group? "Well," you might think, "one reason is that whenever I interact with francophones (substitute anglophones, North Americans, Jews, Muslims, gays, or members of any other social group), they seem cold and unfriendly." And you might be right. Perhaps they do respond to you in a cold and unfriendly fashion. Not, however, because they are this way by nature but because they are responding to the way you have treated them.

Try this exercise to counteract the self-fulfilling prophecy. Find someone who is a member of a group you dislike and strike up a conversation. For example, sit next to this person in one of your classes or approach him or her at a party. Try to imagine that this individual is the friendliest, kindest, sweetest person you have ever met. Be as warm and charming as you can be. Don't go overboard—if, after never having spoken to this person before, you suddenly act like Mr./Ms. Congeniality, you might arouse suspicion. The trick is to act as if you expect him or her to be pleasant and friendly.

Observe this person's reactions. Are you surprised by how pleasantly he or she responded to you? People you thought were inherently cold and unfriendly will probably behave in a warm and friendly manner themselves, in response to the way you have treated them. If this doesn't work on your first encounter with the person, try it again on one or two occasions. In all likelihood, you will find that friendliness really does breed friendliness.

Did the teachers in the Rosenthal and Jacobson (1968) study callously decide to give more encouragement and attention to the bloomers? Not at all. Most teachers are dedicated and try not to treat some students in a more advantageous manner than others. Far from being a conscious, deliberate act, the self-fulfilling prophecy is instead an example of automatic thinking (Chen & Bargh, 1997). Interestingly, the teachers in the Rosenthal and Jacobson (1968) study reported that they spent slightly less time with the students who were labelled as bloomers. In subsequent studies, however, teachers have been found to treat bloomers (i.e., the students they expect to do better) differently in four general ways: (1) They create a warmer emotional climate for bloomers, giving them more personal attention, encouragement, and support; (2) they give bloomers more material to learn and material that is more difficult; (3) they give bloomers more and better feedback on their work; and (4) they give bloomers more opportunities to respond in class and give them longer to respond (Brophy, 1983; Jussim, 1986; Rosenthal, 1994; Snyder, 1984).

A distressing implication of the fact that self-fulfilling prophecy occurs automatically is that our schemas may be quite resistant to change. Suppose a teacher has the schema that boys possess innate ability that makes them superior in math to girls. "But Mr. Jones," we might say, "how can you hold such a belief? There are plenty of girls who do very well in math." Mr. Jones would probably be unconvinced because he would have data to support his schema. "In my classes over the years," he might reply, "nearly three times as many boys as girls have excelled at math." His error lies not in his characterization of the evidence but in his failure to realize his role in producing it. Robert Merton referred to this process as a "reign of error," whereby people can "cite the actual course of events as proof that [they were] right from the very beginning" (1948). See the accompanying Try It! for a way to overcome your own self-fulfilling prophecies.

Cultural Determinants of Schemas   Have you ever met someone from another culture and been amazed at what he or she noticed and remembered about your country?

If so, it may have been because the person was applying different schemas to what he or she saw. One of the authors (Beverley Fehr) supervised an honours student from China in 2008, when the Tim Hortons Brier Curling Championship was taking place in Winnipeg. The student decided that she should experience Canadian culture and went to watch a game. She reported back that it was very amusing to see people paying so much money to watch "a couple of guys mopping the floor." The student also decided to attend a Manitoba Moose game because she had picked up that hockey was important to the Canadian identity. That event also proved mystifying—and amusing—to her. She later commented on how "cute" it was that large men, who looked even bigger with all of their padding, would be put in tiny, little "punishment boxes."

Clearly, an important source of our schemas is the culture in which we grow up. In fact, schemas are a very important way in which cultures exert their influence—namely, by instilling mental structures that influence the very way we understand and interpret the world. In Chapter 5, we will see that across cultures there are fundamental differences in people's schemas about themselves and the social world, with some interesting consequences. For now, we point out that the schemas our culture teaches us have a large influence on what we notice and remember about the world. One researcher, for example, interviewed a Scottish settler and a local Bantu herdsman in Swaziland, a small country in southeast Africa (Bartlett, 1932). Both men had been present at a complicated cattle transaction that had transpired a year earlier. The Scottish man had little memory about the details of the transaction; he had to consult his records to remember how many cattle were bought and sold and for how much. The Bantu man, when asked, promptly recited from memory every detail of the transaction, including from whom each ox and cow had been bought, the colour of each ox and cow, and the price of each transaction. The Bantu people's memory for cattle is so good that they do not bother to brand them; if a cow happens to wander away and get mixed up with a neighbour's herd, the owner simply goes over and takes it back—having no trouble distinguishing his cow from dozens of others.

It is not the case that the Bantu simply have better memories overall. Each of us has a superb memory, in the areas that are important to us, areas for which we thus have well-developed schemas. Cattle are a central part of the Bantu economy and culture, and as a result, the Bantu have well-developed schemas about cattle. To a person who grew up in a different culture, one cow might look like

▶ The Bantu have an excellent memory for their cattle, possibly because they have much better schemas for cattle than people in other cultures do.

any other; this person undoubtedly has well-developed schemas about things that are quite foreign to the Bantu, such as transactions on the Toronto Stock Exchange, foreign movies, or, for that matter, why people would pay big bucks to watch someone "mop the floor."

To summarize, we have seen that the amount of information we face every day is so vast that we have to reduce it to a manageable size. In addition, much of this information is ambiguous or difficult to decipher. One way we deal with this "blooming, buzzing, confusion," in William James's words (1890), is to rely on schemas, which help us reduce the amount of information we need to take in and help us interpret ambiguous information. These schemas are applied quickly, effortlessly, and unintentionally; in short, they are one form of automatic thinking. Another form of automatic thinking is to apply specific rules and shortcuts when thinking about the social world. These shortcuts are, for the most part, extremely useful, but as we will see, they too can sometimes lead to erroneous inferences about the world.

Mental Strategies and Shortcuts: Heuristics

Think back to your decision of where to apply to university. How did you narrow down your list from the schools you considered to the ones to which you actually applied? One strategy would be to investigate thoroughly each of the more than 70 universities in Canada as well as all of the community colleges. You could read every catalogue from cover to cover, visit every campus, and interview as many faculty members, deans, and students as you could find. Getting tired yet? Such a strategy would, of course, be prohibitively time consuming and costly. Instead of considering every university and college, most high school students narrow down their choice to a small number of options and find out what they can about these schools.

This example is like many decisions and judgments we make in everyday life. When deciding which job to accept, what car to purchase, or whom to marry, we usually do not conduct a thorough search of every option ("Okay, it's time for me to get married; I think I'll consult the census lists of unmarried adults in my city and begin my interviews tomorrow"). Instead, we use mental strategies and shortcuts that make the decision easier, allowing us to get on with our lives without turning every decision into a major research project. These shortcuts do not always lead to the best decision. For example, if you had exhaustively studied every college and university in Canada, maybe you would have found one that you liked better than the one you attend now. Mental shortcuts are efficient, however, and usually lead to good decisions in a reasonable amount of time (Gigerenzer, 2000; Gilovich & Griffin, 2002; Griffin & Kahneman, 2003; Nisbett & Ross, 1980).

What shortcuts do people use? One, as already discussed, is to use schemas to understand new situations. Rather than starting from scratch when examining our options, we often apply previous knowledge and schemas. We have many schemas, about everything from colleges and universities (e.g., what community colleges are like versus what universities are like) to other people. When making specific kinds of judgments and decisions, however, we do not always have a ready-made schema to apply. At other times, there are too many schemas that could apply, and it is not clear which one to use. What do we do?

At times like these, people often use mental shortcuts called **judgmental heuristics**. The word *heuristics* comes from the Greek word meaning "to discover"; in the field of social cognition, heuristic refers to the mental shortcuts people use to make judgments quickly and efficiently. Before discussing these heuristics, we should note that they do not guarantee people will make accurate inferences about the world. In fact, we will document many mental errors in this chapter. However, keep in mind that people use heuristics for a reason: Most of the time, they are highly functional and serve us well.

judgmental heuristics

mental shortcuts people use to make judgments quickly and efficiently

How Easily Does It Come to Mind? The Availability Heuristic   Suppose you are sitting in a restaurant with several friends one night, when it becomes clear that the waiter made a mistake with one of the orders. Your friend Michael ordered the veggie burger with onion rings but instead got the veggie burger with fries. "Oh, well," he says, "I'll just eat the fries." This starts a discussion of whether he should have sent back his order, and some of your friends accuse Michael of being unassertive. He turns to you and asks, "Do you think I'm an unassertive person?" How would you answer this question?

One way, as we have seen, would be to call on a ready-made schema that provides the answer. If you know Michael well and have already formed a picture of how assertive he is, you can recite your answer easily and quickly: "Don't worry, Michael, if I ever need a used-car salesman, you'd be the first person I'd call." Suppose, though, that you've never really thought about how assertive Michael is and have to think about your answer. In such a situation, you might rely on how easily different examples come to mind. If it is easy to think of times when Michael acted assertively (e.g., that time he stopped someone from butting in line in front of him at the movies), you will conclude that Michael is a pretty assertive guy. If it is easier to think of times when Michael acted unassertively (e.g., that time he let a phone solicitor talk him into buying an expensive long-distance calling plan), you will conclude that he is pretty unassertive.

This mental shortcut is called the **availability heuristic**, which is basing a judgment on the ease with which you can bring something to mind (Oppenheimer, 2004; Rothman & Hardin, 1997; Schwarz & Vaughn, 2002). The first studies demonstrating the availability heuristic were conducted by Tversky and Kahneman (1973) at the Hebrew University of Jerusalem. (Daniel Kahneman, who took a position at the University of British Columbia from 1978 to 1986, won the Nobel Prize in Economics in 2002 for his research on the psychology of decision making. In 2007, he received the highest honour bestowed by the American Psychological Association, the Award for Outstanding Lifetime Contributions to Psychology.) In one of their studies, participants were presented with the names of famous and non-famous people. When asked to recall the names, participants were more likely to remember the famous ones, even though there were fewer famous than non-famous names on the list. Presumably, the famous names were more available in memory. When other participants were asked to estimate the number of male and female names, they gave higher estimates for the gender that was famous. For example, if a list contained the names of 19 famous women and 20 non-famous men, participants believed there had been a greater number of women's names than men's on the list. Tversky and Kahneman's findings have been replicated in research conducted in other countries, including Canada (McKelvie, 1995, 1997).

There are many situations in which the availability heuristic is a good strategy. If you can easily bring to mind several times when Michael stood up for his rights, he probably is an assertive person; if you can easily bring to mind several times when he was timid or meek, he probably is not an assertive person. The trouble with the availability heuristic is that sometimes what is easiest to bring to mind is not typical of the overall picture, leading to faulty conclusions. When physicians are diagnosing diseases, for example, it might seem a relatively straightforward matter for them to observe people's symptoms and figure out what disease, if any, they have. Sometimes, though, medical symptoms are quite ambiguous and might be a sign of several different disorders. Do doctors use the availability heuristic, whereby they are more likely to consider diagnoses that come to mind easily? Several studies of medical diagnoses suggest that the answer is yes (Eraker & Politser, 1988; Fox, 1980; Travis, Phillippi, & Tonn, 1989; Weber et al., 1993).

Consider Dr. Robert Marion's diagnosis of Nicole, a bright, sweet, nine-year-old patient. Nicole was normal in every way, except that once or twice a year she

availability heuristic

a mental shortcut whereby people base a judgment on the ease with which they can bring something to mind

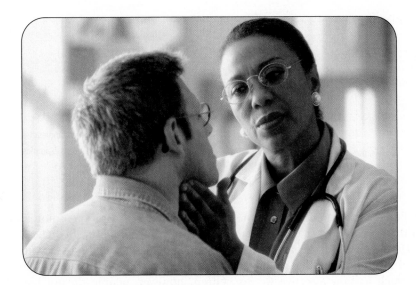

◄ Physicians have been found to use the availability heuristic when making diagnoses. Their diagnoses are influenced by how easily they can bring to mind different diseases.

had strange, neurological attacks, characterized by disorientation, insomnia, slurred words, and strange mewing sounds. Nicole had been hospitalized three times, had seen more than a dozen specialists, and had undergone many diagnostic tests, including CT scans, brain-wave tests, and virtually every blood test there is. The doctors were stumped; they could not figure out what was wrong with her. Within minutes of seeing her, however, Dr. Marion correctly diagnosed her problem as a rare, inherited blood disorder called acute intermittent porphyria (AIP). The blood chemistry of people with this disorder often gets out of sync, causing a variety of neurological symptoms. It can be controlled with a careful diet and by avoiding certain medications.

How did Dr. Marion diagnose Nicole's disorder so quickly, when so many other doctors failed to do so? Dr. Marion had just finished writing a book on the genetic diseases of historical figures, including a chapter on George III of England, who—you guessed it—suffered from AIP. "I didn't make the diagnosis because I'm a brilliant diagnostician or because I'm a sensitive listener," reports Dr. Marion. "I succeeded where others failed because [Nicole] and I happened to run into each other in exactly the right place, at exactly the right time" (Marion, 1995). In other words, Dr. Marion used the availability heuristic. AIP happened to be available in his memory, making the diagnosis easy. Though this was a happy outcome of the use of the availability heuristic, it is easy to see how it can go wrong.

Take the case of Dr. Harrison Alter, an emergency-room physician working on a Navajo reservation in Tuba City, Arizona (Groopman, 2007). Over a three-week period, Dr. Alter had seen dozens of people with viral pneumonia. One day, Blanche Begaye (not her real name), a woman in her sixties, appeared in the emergency room. She was breathing very rapidly and had a fever. She had taken aspirin, but her condition had only gotten worse. Her lungs sounded fine and a chest X-ray did not show signs of pneumonia. Her white cell blood count was not elevated (which would be expected if she had pneumonia), although an analysis of her blood electrolytes showed that her blood was slightly acidic. Dr. Alter's diagnosis was that Begaye was in the early stages of pneumonia. He admitted Begaye, ordered an IV, and placed her in the care of an internist. Shortly thereafter, the internist took Dr. Alters aside and said, "That's not a case of viral pneumonia. She has aspirin toxicity." (Groopman, 2007). Dr. Alter immediately knew that the internist was right: "She was an absolutely classic case—the rapid breathing, the shift in blood electrolytes—and I missed it." (Groopman, 2007). Dr. Alter's misdiagnosis illustrates the downside of using the availability heuristic.

Availability and assertiveness

People who were asked to think of 6 times they behaved assertively found it easy to do so and therefore concluded that they were pretty assertive people. People who were asked to think of 12 times they behaved assertively found it difficult to think of so many examples and therefore concluded that they were not very assertive people (see the left side of the graph). Similar results were found among people asked to think of either 6 or 12 times they behaved unassertively (see the right side of the graph). These results show that people often base their judgments on availability, or how easily they can bring information to mind.

(Adapted from Schwarz et al., 1991)

The fact that he had recently seen so many patients with viral pneumonia meant that this was the first diagnosis that came to mind when he saw Blanche Begaye.

Do people use the availability heuristic to make judgments about themselves? It might seem that we have well-developed ideas about our own personalities, such as how assertive we are. Often, however, people do not have firm schemas about their own traits (Kunda et al., 1993; Markus, 1977) and therefore might make judgments about themselves based on how easily they can recall examples of their own behaviour. To see if this is the case, Norbert Schwarz and his colleagues (1991) performed a clever experiment in which they altered how easy it was for people to bring to mind examples of their own past behaviours. In one condition, they asked people to think of six times they had acted assertively. Most people found this to be pretty easy; examples came to mind quickly. In another condition, the researchers asked people to think of 12 times they had acted assertively. This was much more difficult; people had to try hard to think of this many examples. All participants were then asked to rate how assertive they thought they really were.

The question was, did people use the availability heuristic (the ease with which they could bring examples to mind) to infer how assertive they were? As seen on the left side of Figure 3.7, they did. People who were asked to think of 6 examples rated themselves as relatively assertive, because it was easy to think of 6 examples ("Hey, this is easy—I guess I'm a pretty assertive person"). It might surprise you to learn that people asked to think of 12 examples rated themselves as relatively unassertive, because it was difficult to think of 12 examples ("Hmm, this is hard—I must not be a very assertive person"). Other people were asked to think of either 6 or 12 times they had acted *un*assertively, and similar results were found—those asked to think of six examples rated themselves as more unassertive than those who were asked to think of 12 examples (see the right side of Figure 3.7; Schwarz, Bless, Strack, Klumpp, Rittenhauer-Schtaka, & Simmons, 1991). In short, people use the availability heuristic—the ease with which they can bring examples to mind—when making judgments about themselves and other people.

How Similar Is A to B? The Representativeness Heuristic   Suppose, for example, that you attend a university in Alberta. One day you meet a student named Lyne standing in line for one of the food outlets on campus. Lyne is fashionably dressed, orders a café au lait and a croissant, and from the way she pronounces *croissant*, it's apparent she speaks French. Which province do you think Lyne is from? Because Lyne seems similar to many people's stereotype of a Quebecer, you might guess Quebec, or at least seriously entertain this possibility. If so, you would be using the **representativeness heuristic**, which is a mental shortcut whereby people classify something according to how similar it is to a typical case—such as how similar Lyne is to your conception of a typical Quebecer (Gilovich & Savitsky, 2002; Kahneman & Frederick, 2002; Kahneman & Tversky, 1973; Tversky & Kahneman, 1974). We rely on the representativeness heuristic when deciding whether

representativeness heuristic

a mental shortcut whereby people classify something according to how similar it is to a typical case people (or objects) belong to a particular category. Is she Jewish? Is he gay? Is our host a right-wing conservative? In making these judgments, we assess whether the person matches our image of the typical member of that category. If so, we conclude that the person is a member of the category.

Categorizing things according to representativeness is often a perfectly reasonable thing to do. If you did not use the representativeness heuristic, how else would you decide where Lyne comes from? Should you just randomly choose a province? Actually, there is another source of information you might use. If you knew nothing about Lyne, it would be wise to guess that she was from Alberta, because at Alberta universities there are more in-province than out-of-province students. If you guessed Alberta, you would be using what is called **base rate information**, or information about the relative frequency of members of different categories in the population (e.g., the percentage of students at Alberta universities who are from Alberta).

What do people do when they have both base rate information (e.g., knowing that there are more students from Alberta than from Quebec at a university) and contradictory information about the person in question (e.g., encountering Lyne, who dresses fashionably and speaks French)? Kahneman and Tversky (1973) found that people do not use base rate information sufficiently, paying most attention to how representative the information about the specific person is of the general category (e.g., Quebecers). While this is not a bad strategy if the information about the person is reliable, it can get you into trouble when the information is flimsy. Returning to our example of Lyne, given that the base rate of students from Quebec attending universities in Alberta is low, you would need to have very good evidence that Lyne was from Quebec before ignoring the base rate and guessing that she is one of the few exceptions. And given that it is not unusual to find people from Alberta who dress well, speak French, and enjoy café au lait and croissants, you would, in this instance, be wise to use the base rate. How do heuristics influence your thinking? Take the accompanying Try It! quiz to find out.

base rate information

information about the frequency of members of different categories in the population

Try it!

▶ Reasoning Quiz

Answer each of the following questions:

1. Consider the letter *r* in the English language. Do you think that this letter occurs more often as the first letter of words (e.g., rope) or more often as the third letter of words (e.g., park)?

   (a) more often as the first letter

   (b) more often as the third letter

   (c) about equally often as the first and third letter

2. Which of these do you think causes more fatalities in Canada?

   (a) accidental death

   (b) death from strokes

   (c) each causes about the same number of deaths

3. Suppose you flipped a fair coin six times. Which sequence is more likely to occur? (H = heads, T = tails)

   (a) H T T H T H

   (b) H H H T T T

   (c) both sequences are equally likely

4. After observing the sequence T T T T T, what is the probability that the next coin flip will be heads?

   (a) less than 0.5

   (b) 0.5

   (c) greater than 0.5

See page 87 for the answers.

The Pervasiveness of Automatic Thinking

Part of the definition of automatic thinking is that it occurs unconsciously. Although it might seem magical that we can think without being aware that we are thinking, social psychologists are increasingly reaching the conclusion that we can do just that (Bargh, 2007; Hassin, Uleman, & Bargh, 2005; Wilson, 2002). If we had to rely on slow, conscious thinking alone we would be in a pickle because we often need to make very fast decisions about what is happening around us, what to pay attention to, and which of our goals to pursue. We would be left scratching our heads while the world whizzed by. As we have seen, these fast, unconscious processes can sometimes lead to tragic errors. Most of the time, however, unconscious thinking is critical to navigating our way through the world.

Have you ever been chatting with someone at a party and suddenly realized that someone across the room mentioned your name? The only way this could happen is if, while you were engaged in conversation, you were unconsciously monitoring the other conversations to see if something important came up (such as your name). This *cocktail party phenomenon* has been demonstrated in several experiments (Harris & Pashler, 2004; Moray, 1959).

Unconscious thinking may also be involved when we have competing goals and are not sure which one to act on. Suppose, for example, that you are taking a difficult course in which the professor grades on a curve, guaranteeing that only a few people will get A's. A classmate you don't know very well tells you he is having difficulty with some of the material and asks whether you can have coffee and go over your notes for the class. On the one hand you want to be helpful, satisfying your goal of being a caring, compassionate person. On the other hand you want to satisfy your goal of doing well in the class and are hesitant to hurt your chances by raising someone else's grade. Which goal do you act on? You could mull this over for a while, consciously weighing your options. However, often it is our nonconscious mind that chooses the goal for us in such situations, basing the decision in part on which goal has been recently activated or primed. For example, John Bargh and his colleagues (2001) asked students to play a game in which they had to choose to cooperate or be competitive with another student. Just prior to playing the game, they completed a task (supposedly for another professor) in which they had to make sentences out of a list of words. In one condition, many of the words had to do with cooperation, such as "helpful," "fair," and "share." In the control condition, the words were unrelated to cooperation or competition, such as "salad" and "umbrella." (It is important in this kind of study that participants do not realize that there is a connection between the sentence-making task and the cooperation game.) It turns out that the people who made sentences out of words having to do with cooperation were significantly more likely to cooperate in the game with the other student than were students in the control condition. The words were sufficient to prime the goal of being cooperative unconsciously, without people knowing that they had made such a choice at all (Bargh, Gollwitzer, Lee-Chai, Barndollar, & Trötschel, 2001).

There is even evidence that our unconscious minds can do better at some tasks than our conscious minds. Suppose you were shopping for an apartment, and after looking at several places you narrowed your choice to four possibilities. You have a great deal of information about each apartment, including its location, cost, size, whether it has free internet access, and so on. Each one has pros and cons, making it difficult to decide which apartment to rent. How should you go about making up your mind? Given the importance of this decision, most of us would spend a lot of time thinking about it, consciously analyzing the alternatives to determine what our best option is. Surely, you might think, this

> *Outside consciousness there rolls a vast tide of life which is perhaps more important to us than the little isle of our thoughts which lies within our ken.*
>
> —E. S. Dallas

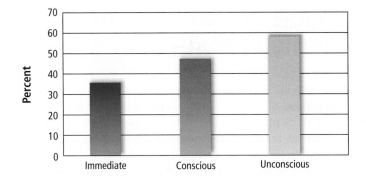

FIGURE 3.8
The power of unconscious thinking
After receiving a great deal of information about four apartments, participants chose one immediately (immediate condition), or thought about the apartments consciously for three minutes (conscious condition), or were distracted for three minutes, allowing their unconscious to work unimpeded (unconscious condition). People in the latter condition were most likely to pick the apartment that had the most positive qualities and the fewest negative qualities.
(Adapted from Dijksternhuis, 2004)

would be better than *avoiding* conscious thought about the apartments, by, say, spending several minutes memorizing words for a vocabulary test in your Spanish class and then choosing one of the apartments.

As absurd as this last approach might sound, research by Dijksterhuis (2004) suggests that it might actually produce the best choice. He gave people a lot of information about four apartments in a short amount of time, which made it difficult for them to determine right away that one of the apartments was, in fact, superior to the others (that is, which one had the highest ratio of good to bad attributes). He then randomly assigned people to one of three conditions. In the *immediate choice* condition, he asked people to choose the apartment they thought was the best right away. In the *conscious thought* condition, he asked people to think carefully about the apartments for three minutes and then choose the best one. In the *unconscious thought* condition, he gave people a distracting task for three minutes so that they could not think about the apartments consciously, with the assumption that they would continue to think about the apartments unconsciously.

Who was most likely to choose the best apartment? As seen in Figure 3.8, it was people in the unconscious thought condition. Because people in this condition could not consciously think about the apartments, something else must have happened that produced the best choice. In subsequent research, it was found that when people were distracted they were still working on the task unconsciously, organizing the information in a way that made the best choice more apparent to them (Dijksterhuis & Nordgren, 2005).

Research on unconscious thought is in its infancy, and we would not yet recommend that you find something to distract you whenever you are faced with an important choice. It is becoming clearer, however, that automatic, nonconscious thinking is far more pervasive than previously thought, and that this kind of thinking can lead to good decisions.

At this point, you might be wondering why we have spent so much time on the automatic, nonconscious type of social cognition. Didn't we say earlier that there are two modes of thinking—automatic and controlled? Isn't it possible to think about the social world slowly, carefully, and deliberately, such as when someone takes time to sit down and really think a problem through? Indeed it is. We've spent so much time on automatic thinking, however, because it is so pervasive and dominates much of people's mental lives. Just as modern jetliners fly mostly on automatic pilot, so do people rely a great deal on automatic thinking to get through their days. However, just as an airline pilot can take control of the plane when trouble occurs, controlled thinking takes over and influences our behaviour when unusual events occur—sometimes for better, sometimes for worse.

Controlled Social Cognition: High-Effort Thinking

Racial profiling—official action toward people based on their race, ethnicity, or national origin instead of their behaviour—has received a great deal of attention since the events of September 11, 2001. Because the terrorists who flew the planes into the World Trade Center towers, a field in Pennsylvania, and the Pentagon were of Middle Eastern descent, some people feel that anyone who looks as if he or she might be of a similar background should receive special scrutiny when flying on commercial airlines. On the New Year's Eve after the attacks, Michael Dasrath and Edgardo Cureg boarded a Continental Airlines flight from New Jersey to Tampa. Dasrath was a U.S. citizen who was born in South America, and Cureg was a U.S. resident from the Philippines. Both had successfully passed through extensive security checks. Dasrath, seated in first class, was removed from the plane when a woman complained that he made her uncomfortable. Cureg was also removed from the flight, allegedly because he made other passengers nervous. Neither man posed a threat but, because they had brown skin, they were singled out and refused service. Both have sued the airlines for violating their civil rights ("Judge Rules," 2002).

These examples of racial profiling bear some similarities to the tragedy of Jean Charles de Menezes, the Brazilian man gunned down by London police, as discussed earlier. In these cases, innocent people were suspected of a crime because of the colour of their skin. In other respects, however, the examples are quite different. In de Menezes' case, the police had very little time to react— seconds or less—as he approached a subway station. More than likely, the police officers' automatic thinking took over. In the case of the men removed from the airplane, however, the airline officials presumably had ample time to think about and consider their actions. Racial prejudice can thus be the result of automatic thinking or of conscious, deliberative thinking—an issue we will take up in detail in Chapter 12. For now, we use this example to illustrate the more conscious, controlled type of social cognition.

▶Racial profiling is official action toward people based on their race, ethnicity, or national origin instead of their behaviour. Since the tragic events of September 11, 2001, caused by terrorists of Middle Eastern descent, some innocent people who look as if they might be of Middle Eastern descent have not been allowed on airplanes.

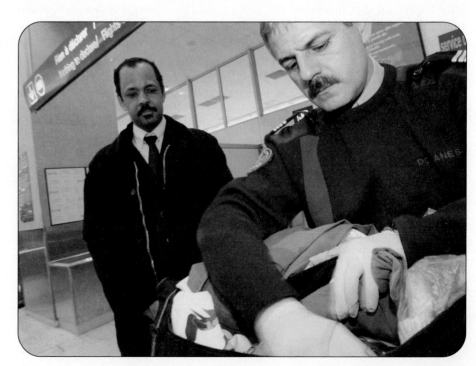

Controlled thinking is defined as thinking that is conscious, intentional, voluntary, and effortful. People can usually turn on or turn off this type of thinking at will and are fully aware of what they are thinking. Further, this kind of thinking is effortful in the sense that it requires mental energy. People have the capacity to think in a conscious, controlled way about only one thing at a time; they cannot be thinking about what they will eat for lunch today at the same time they are thinking through a complex math problem. Automatic thinking, in contrast, can occur in the background with no conscious effort at all.

controlled thinking

thinking that is conscious, intentional, voluntary, and effortful

Thinking about What Might Have Been: Counterfactual Reasoning

When do people go off automatic pilot and think about things more slowly and consciously? One circumstance is when they experience a negative event that was a "close call," such as failing a test by just a point or two. Under these conditions, people engage in **counterfactual thinking**—mentally changing some aspect of the past as a way of imagining what might have been (Kahneman & Miller, 1986; Kahneman & Tversky, 1982; Markman, Gavanski, Sherman, & McMullen, 1995; Roese, 1997; Roese & Olson, 1997; Sanna, Carter, & Small, 2006). "If only I hadn't fallen asleep while studying the night before the test," you might think, "I would have gotten a better grade," or "If only I had worked up the courage to ask Michelle, she might be going out with me instead of my best friend." If you had mustered up the courage to ask out Michelle and the two of you were now head over heels in love, chances are you probably wouldn't be spending much time agonizing over how the outcome could have been different.

counterfactual thinking

mentally changing some aspect of the past as a way of imagining what might have been

There is considerable evidence that we are most likely to engage in counterfactual thinking when we "just missed" avoiding a negative event. For example, missing a plane by five minutes causes more counterfactual thinking ("If only I had driven a little faster," "If only I hadn't stopped to pick up a coffee") and more regret than missing a plane by half an hour (Kahneman & Miller, 1986; Miller, Turnbull, & McFarland, 1990). Similarly, if you sold a winning lottery ticket to your sister one hour before the draw, you would experience more regret than if you had sold the ticket two weeks before the draw (Miller & Taylor, 2002). As you might expect, people also feel greater sympathy for others in near-miss situations. To demonstrate this, Miller and McFarland (1986) had students at Simon Fraser University read a scenario in which a man attempted to walk to safety after his plane crashed in an isolated northern area. Those who were told that the man perished 0.4 kilometres from the nearest town awarded greater compensation to his family than did those who were told that he died 120 kilometres from the nearest town.

The use of hypothetical scenarios such as these is common in counterfactual research. In addition to the scenarios we have discussed, students at the University of British Columbia have been asked to imagine a man taking an unusual route home and having an accident (Kahneman & Tversky, 1982; Mandel & Lehman, 1996). Students at the University of Western Ontario have been asked to imagine a man catching or missing a flight out of Pearson Airport in Toronto (Roese & Olson, 1996), getting a good or poor grade on a project with a classmate (Roese & Olson, 1993), or going on a blind date that ends in disaster (Roese & Olson, 1995). The researchers then assess whether the participants engage in counterfactual thinking, the emotions they would experience in that situation, and so on. However, it is important to note that the effects that we have been discussing are not limited to people's reactions to hypothetical scenarios (Branscombe et al., 1996; Davis & Lehman, 1995). Indeed, as Davis, Lehman, Wortman, Silver, and Thompson (1995) have demonstrated, counterfactual thoughts have a great impact on people's emotional reactions to actual events. These researchers interviewed people who had experienced the trauma of losing a spouse or child in a car accident or the death of an infant from sudden infant death syndrome. They discovered that thoughts such as, "If only I had done something differently, my spouse [child] would still be alive" were common. In fact, for half of the participants, these kinds of thoughts persisted four to seven years later. Sadly, the more they engaged in such counterfactual thinking, the greater their distress. Similar findings were obtained when Davis and colleagues (1996) interviewed spinal cord injury victims. As expected, the more these people imagined ways in which the tragedy could have been averted, by mentally "undoing" the circumstances preceding it, the more distress they reported.

Counterfactual reasoning can also lead to some paradoxical effects on emotions. For example, who do you think would be happier: an Olympic athlete who won a silver medal (came in second) or an Olympic athlete who won a bronze medal (came in third)? Though you might think that the athlete who performed better (the silver medal winner) would be happier, that is not what Victoria Medvec, Scott Madey, and Tom Gilovich (1995) predicted. They reasoned that the silver medal winner should feel worse, because he or she could more easily imagine having won the event and would therefore engage in more counterfactual reasoning. To see if they were right, they analyzed videos of the 1992 Olympics. Both immediately after their event and while athletes received their medals, silver medal winners appeared less happy than bronze medal winners. Analyses of media interviews with the athletes confirmed that the thoughts of silver medallists were focused on "I almost won . . ." whereas bronze medallists focused on "At least I did this well. . . ." Subsequent research has confirmed these findings (e.g., Medvec, Madey, & Gilovich, 2002) and shown that silver medalists are particularly unhappy if they expected to get gold, whereas bronze medalists are particularly happy if they did not expect to win a medal at all (McGraw, Mellers, & Tetlock, 2005).

▼Who do you think would be happier: the silver or bronze medallist in an athletic competition? Research by Medvec, Madey, and Gilovich (1995) suggests that bronze medallists are happier because it is harder for them to engage in counterfactual reasoning—imagining ways in which they could have won the event. This certainly seems to have been true for Canada's Tracy Cameron (*left*), shown here after she and her partner won the bronze medal in lightweight double sculls rowing in the 2008 Summer Olympics. By contrast, Kelly Bechard (*right*), whose team placed second in the 2008 Women's Ice Hockey World Championships, hangs her head after losing the gold to the American team.

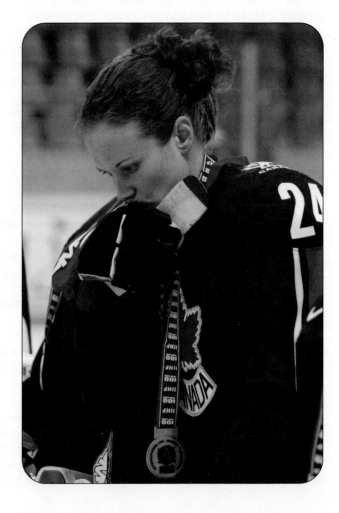

Earlier we described controlled thinking as conscious, intentional, voluntary, and effortful, but different kinds of controlled thought meet these requirements to different degrees. Counterfactual reasoning is clearly conscious and effortful; we know we are obsessing about the past, and this kind of thinking can take up so much mental energy that we cannot think about anything else. It is not, however, always intentional or voluntary. Even when we want to stop dwelling on the past and move on to something else, it can be difficult to turn off the "if only" thinking that characterizes counterfactual reasoning. This is not so good if counterfactual thinking results in rumination, whereby people repetitively focus on negative things in their lives. Rumination has been found to be a contributor to depression (Lyubomirsky, Caldwell, & Nolen-Hoeksema, 1993). Thus, it is not advisable to ruminate constantly about a bad test grade to the point where you can't think about anything else.

Counterfactual thinking actually can be useful, however, if it focuses people's attention on ways that they can cope better in the future. Research conducted at the University of Western Ontario (Roese, 1994; Roese & Olson, 1997) and at the University of British Columbia (Mandel & Lehman, 1996) shows that counterfactual thinking involves thinking not only about why an event occurred, but also about how various outcomes could have been avoided. This latter aspect can have beneficial effects. For example, in one study, Roese (1994) asked students at the University of Western Ontario to think of an exam they had written in the past year on which they had performed very poorly. Some participants were then asked to "list some specific actions that, in retrospect, could have been taken to have improved your exam score." These students subsequently expressed greater intentions to perform success-enhancing behaviours in the future (e.g., studying), and in fact, actually worked harder to improve their performance compared with students who were asked to focus actions that could have made the outcome even worse. Research conducted at the University of British Columbia has produced similar findings (Nasco & Marsh, 1999; Roese & Olson, 1997). Moving beyond academic settings, researchers at Defence Research and Development Canada and at City University in the United Kingdom asked prisoners to generate counterfactuals (e.g., "I probably wouldn't have been convicted, if only I had . . .") or, in the control condition, to report on the facts of their case (Mandel & Dhami, 2005). The results suggested that generating counterfactuals might be beneficial in helping offenders not to re-offend.

Finally, researchers at the University of British Columbia recently demonstrated that people generate more counterfactuals when asked to focus on *self-improvement* (writing down ways they could learn or be improved by negative situations such as being in a car accident or experiencing a relationship breakup) than when asked to focus on *self-enhancement* (what they could do to make themselves "feel better" in such situations; White & Lehman, 2005). Thus, counterfactual thinking can be useful when it motivates us to take steps to prevent similar outcomes from occurring in the future.

Thought Suppression and Ironic Processing

Instead of ruminating about something, we might simply do our best not to think about it. How successful are we at **thought suppression**—the attempt to avoid thinking about something we would just as soon forget, such as a lost love, an unpleasant encounter with one's boss, or a delectable piece of cheesecake in the refrigerator? That depends on the interaction of two processes, one relatively automatic and the other relatively controlled (Wegner, 1992, 1994; Wegner, Wenzlaff & Kozak, 2004). The automatic part of the system, called the *monitoring process*, searches for evidence that the unwanted thought is about to intrude on consciousness. Once the unwanted thought is detected, the more controlled part of the system, called the *operating process*, comes into play. This is the effortful,

thought suppression

the attempt to avoid thinking about something a person would prefer to forget conscious attempt to distract oneself by finding something else to think about. These two processes operate in tandem, like two parents conspiring to keep their kids away from junk food outlets at a mall. One parent's job, akin to the monitoring process, is to keep a watch out for the food joints and let the other one know when they are in the vicinity ("McDonald's alert!"). The other parent's job, akin to the operating process, is to divert the kids' attention away from the fast-food places ("Hey, kids, look at the giant picture of SpongeBob in that store window!"). This system works pretty well as long as each process (parent) does its job—one ever alert for the topic we want to avoid and the other diverting our attention from this topic.

What happens, though, when the controlled operating process is unable to do its job because the person is tired or preoccupied? The monitoring process continues to find instances of the unwanted thought, which then intrude on consciousness unchecked by the controlled process. A state of hyperaccessibility results, in which the unwanted thought occurs with high frequency. If the parent who is supposed to distract the children falls down on the job, for example, the kids will become even more aware that fast-food joints are in the vicinity because they will keep hearing the monitoring parent point them out (Renaud & McConnell, 2002; Wenzlaff & Bates, 2000).

The irony is that when we are trying our hardest not to think about something (e.g., you are on guard not to think about jokes about short people because your height-challenged boss is standing next to you), those thoughts are especially likely to pop into our minds. When we are tired or preoccupied—that is, under *cognitive load*—it is even more likely that these thoughts will spill out unchecked.

Before leaving this topic, we should note that there can be an emotional and physical cost to thought suppression. In one study, medical school students wrote about a personal topic once a day for three days (Petrie, Booth, & Pennebaker, 1998). After each writing episode, some participants were asked to suppress all thoughts about what they had just written for five minutes. These participants showed a significant decrease in immune system functioning compared with those who did not suppress their thoughts. In another study, women who had had an abortion were asked how much they had tried to suppress thoughts about the abortion (Major & Gramzow, 1999). The more the women reported that they tried not to think about the abortion, the greater their reported psychological distress. As you will see in the second Social Psychology in Action module, "Social Psychology and Health," it is generally better to open up about your problems by writing about or discussing them than to try to suppress your thoughts about the problems.

A Portrayal of Social Thinking

By now we have seen two rather different modes of social cognition: one that is effortless, involuntary, unintentional, and unconscious (automatic thinking) and another that is more effortful, voluntary, intentional and conscious (controlled thinking). We have also discussed that both kinds of thinking can lead to consequential errors. Matthew Dumas' death may have been the result of an automatic assumption made by the Winnipeg police officer who shot him, based on his race. Other kinds of racial prejudice, such as racial profiling, can be the result of more controlled thinking. So how good a thinker is the typical human being anyway? How can we reconcile the fact that human beings have amazing cognitive abilities that have resulted in dazzling cultural and intellectual achievements but at the same time humans are prone to making consequential mental errors like the ones documented in this chapter?

One way of addressing this question is to ask which kind of thinking—automatic or controlled—is more important in human functioning. The answer to this question has engendered a lively debate among social psychologists. It is fair to say that there has been an increasing appreciation of the role of automatic thinking in human thought; more and more research has shown that people operate on automatic pilot when thinking about the social world. Some researchers have gone so far as to argue that the role of conscious, controlled thinking actually may be quite limited in human functioning (Bargh, 2007; Bargh & Chartrand, 1999; Wegner, 2002, 2004; Wilson, 2002). Others have argued that although it can be difficult, it is possible to gain conscious control over unwanted automatic responses, such as prejudiced ones (Devine, 1989b; Devine & Monteith, 1999; Fiske, 1989a). Debate over these fundamental issues, such as the role of consciousness in human functioning, is likely to generate a good deal of research in the next several years.

What is clear is that despite the troubles they can cause, both kinds of thinking are extremely useful. It would be difficult to live without the ability to process information about the social world automatically and make quick assumptions about our environment; we would be like a primitive, extremely slow computer, chugging away constantly as we tried to understand what was happening around us. And it is clearly to our advantage to be able to switch to controlled mode, where we can think about ourselves and our social world more slowly and carefully.

The following portrait of the social thinker is emerging: People are very sophisticated social thinkers who have amazing cognitive abilities. No one has yet been able to construct a computer that comes close to matching the power of the human brain. But there is plenty of room for improvement. The shortcomings of social thinking we have documented can be tragic, as demonstrated by the examples of racial prejudice in this chapter (Gilovich, 1991; Nisbett & Ross, 1980; Quattrone, 1982; Slusher & Anderson, 1989). Tim Wilson and colleagues have gone so far as to use the term *mental contamination* to describe the kinds of biases that are pervasive in everyday life (Wilson & Brekke, 1994; Wilson, Centerbar, & Brekke, 2002). Perhaps the best metaphor of human thinking is that people are "flawed scientists"—brilliant thinkers who are attempting to discover the nature of the social world in a logical manner but do not do so perfectly. People are often blind to truths that don't fit their schemas and sometimes treat others in ways that make their schemas come true—something that good scientists would never do.

Improving Human Thinking

One purpose of controlled thinking is to provide checks and balances for automatic thinking. Thus, when trouble occurs, controlled thinking may "kick in." How successful are people at correcting their mistakes? Can they be taught to do better?

One approach is to make people a little more humble about their reasoning abilities. Often we have greater confidence in our judgments than we should (Blanton, Pelham, De Hart, & Carvallo, 2001; Buehler, Griffin, & Ross, 2002; Vallone, Griffin, & Ross, 1990). For example, research conducted in Canada and Britain has shown that if people are able to answer a few difficult questions correctly, they tend to overestimate just how much general knowledge they have (Griffin & Buehler, 1999). Anyone trying to improve human inference is thus up against an **overconfidence barrier** (Metcalfe, 1998). Many people seem to think that their reasoning processes are just fine the way they are; hence, there is no need for remedial action. One approach, then, might be to address this overconfidence directly, getting people to consider the possibility that they might be wrong. This tack was taken by Lord, Lepper, and Preston (1984), who found that when people were asked to consider the opposite point of view to their own, they realized there were other ways to construe the world than their own way; consequently, they made fewer errors in their judgments (Anderson, Lepper, & Ross, 1980; Hirt, Kardes, & Markman, 2004; Mussweiler, Strack, & Pfeiffer, 2000).

overconfidence barrier
the barrier that results when people have too much confidence in the accuracy of their judgments; people's judgments are usually not as correct as they think they are

❝ *The greatest of all faults, I should say, is to become conscious of none.* ❞
—*Thomas Carlyle, essayist (1795–1881)*

Another approach is to directly teach people some basic statistical and methodological principles about how to reason correctly, with the hope that they will apply these principles in their everyday lives. Many of these principles are already taught in courses in statistics and research design, such as the idea that if you want to generalize from a sample of information (e.g., a group of welfare mothers) to a population (e.g., all welfare mothers), you must have a large, unbiased sample. Do people who take such courses apply these principles in their everyday lives? Are they less likely to make the kinds of mistakes we have discussed in this chapter? A number of studies have provided encouraging answers to these questions, showing that people's reasoning processes can be improved by university statistics courses, graduate training in research design, and even brief one-time lessons (Fong, Krantz, & Nisbett, 1986; Malloy, 2001; Nisbett, Krantz, Jepson, & Kunda, 1983; Nisbett, Fong, Lehman, & Cheng, 1987; Schaller, Asp, Rosell, & Heim, 1996). Thus, there is reason to be cautiously optimistic—cautiously because a study conducted at Concordia University found that training in statistics and research methods does not guarantee the transfer of these concepts to everyday life. Specifically, Mill, Gray, and Mandel (1994) found that in order to improve reasoning abilities, it was necessary to introduce tutorial sessions that focused explicitly on the application of course material to reasoning in everyday contexts (e.g., evaluating claims made by politicians, choosing between competing products).

In summary, there is reason to be hopeful about people's ability to overcome the kinds of mistakes we have documented in this chapter. And you don't have to go to graduate school to do it. Sometimes it helps simply to consider the opposite, as participants in the Lord and colleagues (1984) study did. Beyond this, formal training in statistics helps, at both the graduate and undergraduate levels—especially if your instructor illustrates how these principles apply in real-life situations. So, if you were dreading taking a university statistics course, take heart: It might not only satisfy a requirement for your major but improve your reasoning as well!

> *The sign of a first-rate intelligence is the ability to hold two opposed ideas at the same time.*
>
> —F. Scott Fitzgerald (1896–1940)

> *Modest doubt is called the beacon of the wise.*
>
> —William Shakespeare, Troilus and Cressida, 1601

SUMMARY

Social cognition is the study of how people select, interpret, and use information to make judgments and decisions. One kind of social cognition involves **automatic thinking**, thinking that is nonconscious, unintentional, involuntary, and effortless. For example, people automatically use **schemas**, cognitive structures that organize information around themes or subjects. Schemas have a powerful effect on what information we notice, think about, and remember. While schemas are typically quite useful, they have a down side. Schemas about other people can lead to automatic stereotyping. For example, some studies have found that people automatically associate black people with weapons.

One determinant of the schema that people apply in a given situation is **accessibility**, the extent to which a schema is at the forefront of the mind and therefore is likely to be used when making judgments about the social world. Schemas can become accessible through **priming**, the process by which recent experiences increase the likelihood that a particular schema, trait, or concept will be brought to mind.

Relying on schemas is adaptive and functional up to a point, but people can be overzealous. For example, sometimes we persevere in our beliefs even when they're disproved, as shown in research on the **perseverance effect**.

Finally, schemas also affect our behaviour—we act on the basis of our schemas. The most fascinating example of this is the **self-fulfilling prophecy**, wherein our schemas come true when we unconsciously treat others in such a way that they begin to act consistently with our schemas.

In addition to schemas, we use **judgmental heuristics** to help us deal with the large amount of social information with which we are faced. Heuristics are rules of thumb people follow to make judgments quickly and efficiently. The **availability heuristic**, the ease with which we can think of something, has a strong effect on how we view the world. The **representativeness heuristic** helps us decide how similar one thing is to another; we use it to classify people or situations on the basis of their similarity to a typical case. We also have a tendency to ignore **base rate information**—the prior probability that something or someone belongs in that classification. Although these heuristics are useful, they can also lead to incorrect conclusions.

A second kind of social cognition is **controlled thinking**—thinking that is conscious, intentional, voluntary, and effortful. People can usually turn on or turn off this type of thinking at will and are fully aware of what they are thinking. Further, this kind of thinking is effortful in the sense that it requires mental energy. People have the capacity to think in a conscious, controlled way about only one thing at a time.

One example of controlled thinking is **counterfactual thinking**—thinking about what might have been. This kind of thinking can influence people's emotional reactions to events and can serve a preparative function for the future.

When people are unmotivated or preoccupied, however, controlled thinking is difficult to do. In such cases, people are more likely to accept false information and to have difficulty engaging in **thought suppression**—the attempt to avoid thinking about something they are trying to forget.

The issue of whether people are good thinkers has been the subject of considerable debate. Perhaps the best metaphor of the social thinker is that people are like flawed scientists—brilliant thinkers who often blind themselves to truths that don't fit their theories and who sometimes treat others in ways that make those theories come true.

While people generally use strategies effectively, there is room for improvement in social thinking. For one thing, people are up against an **overconfidence barrier**, whereby they are too confident in the accuracy of their judgments. Fortunately, recent research has indicated that some of the shortcomings of human reasoning can be improved, particularly by training in statistics.

Scoring the Try It! Exercises

▶ **Page 77**

1. The correct answer is (b), the third letter. Tversky and Kahneman (1974) found that most people thought that the answer was (a), the first letter. Why do people make this mistake? Because, say Tversky and Kahneman, they find it easier to think of examples of words that begin with *R*. By using the availability heuristic, they assume that the ease with which they can bring examples to mind means that such words are more common.

2. The correct answer is (b). According to Statistics Canada information, deaths resulting from cerebrovascular disease (stroke is a major component) are nearly twice as likely as accidental deaths (14 626 cases versus 8986 cases in 2004; Canada, 2007). Slovic, Fischhoff, and Lichtenstein (1976) found that most people think that (a) is correct (accidental deaths). Why do people make this error? Again, it's the availability heuristic. Accidental deaths are more likely to be reported by the media; consequently, people find it easier to bring to mind examples of such deaths than they do deaths from strokes.

3. The correct answer is (c). Both outcomes are equally likely, given that the outcomes of coin flips are random events.

Tversky and Kahneman (1974) argue that due to the representativeness heuristic, people expect a sequence of random events to "look" random. That is, they expect events to be representative of their conception of randomness. Thus, many people choose H T T H T H, because this sequence is more representative of people's idea of randomness than H H H T T T. In fact, the chance that either sequence will occur is 1 out of 2^6 times, or 1 in 64. As another illustration of this point, if you were to buy a lottery ticket with four numbers, would you rather have the number 6957 or 1111? Many people prefer the former number, because it seems more "random" and therefore more likely to be picked. In fact, both numbers have a 1 in 1000 chance of being picked.

4. The correct answer is (b). Many people choose (c) because they think that after five tails in a row, heads is more likely "to even things out." This is called the gambler's fallacy, which is the belief that prior random events (e.g., five tails in a row) have an influence on subsequent random events. Assuming that the coin is fair, prior tosses have no influence on future ones. Tversky and Kahneman (1974) suggest that the gambler's fallacy derives in part from the representativeness heuristic. Five tails and one head seems more representative of a chance outcome than do six tails in a row.

PEARSON
mypsychlab

Along with a dynamic, electronic version of this text, MyPsychLab offers a wealth of resources to deepen your understanding and test your recall of the material in this chapter—including video and audio clips, simulations and activities, self-assessments, practice tests, and other study materials. The following specific resources are available for this chapter:

 Schemas

 Unconscious Stereotyping

 Social Cognition

To access MyPsychLab, please visit www.mypsychlab.com (Student Access Code required—packaged with this book).

Social Perception:

How We Come to Understand Other People

A s you have no doubt noticed, other people are not easy to figure out. Why are they the way they are? Why do they do what they do? The frequency and urgency with which we pose these questions are demonstrated in this touching story, sent in by a reader to the *New York Times*:

> After ending an office romance, a female friend of mine threw a bag full of her former paramour's love letters, cards, and poems into an outside dumpster. The following day he called and wanted to know why she would throw out his letters. She was stunned. He explained that a homeless person going through the garbage read the correspondence and called the number found on a piece of stationery. The homeless man was curious as to why two people who seemed so in love could now be apart. "I would have called you sooner," the man told the former boyfriend, "but this was the first quarter I was given today." (DeMarco, 1994)

The homeless man was down on his luck—no home, no money, reduced to rifling through garbage cans—and yet that endless fascination with the human condition still asserted itself. He needed to know why the couple broke up. He even spent his only quarter to find out.

We all have a fundamental fascination with explaining other people's behaviour. But the reasons why others behave as they do are usually hidden from us. All we have to go on is observable behaviour: what people do, what they say, their facial expressions, gestures, and tone of voice. Unfortunately, we can't read other people's minds; we can't know, truly and completely, who they are and what they mean. Instead, we rely on our impressions and theories, putting them together as well as we can, hoping they will lead to reasonably accurate and useful conclusions.

Our desire to understand people is so fundamental that it carries over into our hobbies and recreational lives. We go to movies, read novels, watch soap operas, and "people-watch" at airports because thinking about the behaviour of even strangers and fictional characters fascinates us. This basic aspect of human cognition has been exploited brilliantly by "reality TV" programmers, who cast television shows with real people instead of actors, and place them in unusual or difficult situations. This relatively new genre of television has proved a powerhouse. Since the original version of *Survivor*, shot in 2000, reality shows have crowded the top 10 list of most-watched shows every year. Why are these shows so popular? Because we enjoy figuring people out. We do it all day long, as a necessary part of social survival, and then we go home, turn on the television, and do it for fun and entertainment. Take, for example, two popular reality shows that are particularly interesting from a social psychological perspective: *Survivor* and *American Idol* (and its Canadian counterpart, *Canadian Idol*). In *Survivor*, the contestants scheme, lie, and form secret alliances as, one by one, they vote their fellow contestants off the show in hope of being the last survivor and collecting the reward of $1 million. In a typical segment, we see one contestant form an alliance with another and then turn around and betray that person without blinking an eye. When are the contestants lying and when are they telling the truth? And what are they really like as people—are they deceitful, manipulative opportunists or are they just playing the game?

In *American Idol* and *Canadian Idol*, we watch an array of contestants compete to be named the favourite singer and winner of a lucrative recording contract. The compelling aspects of the show are threefold: The contestants are very much "real people," with a variety of backgrounds; their talent varies, so much so that the early episodes of the show present people who truly can't sing (but naively think they can); and the judges can be very critical and even cruel in their feedback. In short, an emotional train wreck is put into motion, wherein some contestants will be embarrassed and maligned, and will dissolve into tears on camera. Clearly, viewers enjoy watching this real-life emotional spectacle and competition; *American Idol* has become the most popular show on U.S. television since it first debuted in 2002. And viewers play a critical role in the process—they vote someone off the show each week. In the 2008 *American Idol* finale, a record number of votes—estimates range from 63 million to more than 66 million—were cast to decide which of the two finalists would win. More Americans voted in the *Idol* finale than had voted in any election for a U.S. president. Viewers so enjoy making these decisions that many websites (including online betting sites) have spontaneously arisen to allow them to communicate with each other about the show (Arthur, 2006).

Why do we care? Why do we expend so much time and energy observing and trying to explain the behaviour of others? Because doing so helps us understand and predict our social world (Heider, 1958; Kelley, 1967).

In this chapter, we discuss **social perception**—the study of how we form impressions of other people and make inferences about them. One important source of information that we use is nonverbal behaviour, such as facial expressions, body movements, and tone of voice.

social perception

the study of how we form impressions of and make inferences about other people

Nonverbal Behaviour

What do we know about people when we first meet them? We know what we can see and hear, and even though we know we should not judge a book by its cover, this kind of easily observable information is critical to our first impressions. For example, physical characteristics such as attractiveness influence the way we judge others (Hatfield & Sprecher, 1986a). We also pay a great deal of attention to what people say. After all, our most noteworthy accomplishment as a species is the development of verbal language. But people's words are only part of the story. We communicate volumes without words (Ambady & Rosenthal, 1992, 1993; DePaulo & Friedman, 1998; Gifford, 1991, 1994). **Nonverbal communication** refers to how people communicate, intentionally or unintentionally, without words. Facial expressions, tone of voice, gestures, body position and movement, the use of touch, and eye gaze are the most frequently used and most revealing channels of nonverbal communication (Henley, 1977; Knapp & Hall, 2006).

Interestingly, our ability to read nonverbal cues is not limited to members of our species. Researchers at the Université du Québec à Montréal photographed cats expressing different emotions (e.g., fear was produced by running a vacuum cleaner; Thibault, Bourgeois, & Hess, 2006). It turned out that people were remarkably accurate at identifying the cats' emotions. We are not the only species that can read nonverbal communication. For example, dogs are adept at reading not only "dog nonverbals" but human nonverbals as well, and even outperform chimpanzees when it comes to understanding human nonverbal cues (Hare & Tomasello, 2005). Nonetheless, human nonverbal communication is particularly eloquent and sophisticated. In other research conducted at the Université du Québec à Montréal using facial electromyography (recording the movements of facial muscles), it has been shown that we automatically mimic other people's facial expressions, such as happiness, sadness, and disgust (Hess & Blairy, 2001). These mimicry effects are especially pronounced when we like the other person or consider him or her to be a member of our group (Bourgeois & Hess, 2008). The researchers suggest that our tendency to mimic other people's facial expressions may reflect empathy—the capacity to feel what someone else is feeling. This capacity may even be hardwired into our brains. Recent research in neuroscience has found that humans (and our close relatives, primates) have a special kind of brain cell called *mirror neurons*. These neurons respond when we perform an action *and* when we see someone else perform the same action (Gallese, Fadiga, Fogassi & Rizzolatti, 1996). For example, when we see someone crying, these mirror neurons fire automatically and involuntarily, just as if we were crying ourselves. Bruno Wicker and his colleagues (2003) investigated the role of mirror neurons in the emotion of disgust. They used functional magnetic-resonating imaging (fMRI) to look at the pattern of brain cells firing in research participants as they performed two different tasks: smelling obnoxious, gross odours, and watching a film of an actor wrinkling his face with a disgusted look. The researchers found that feeling disgusted oneself (from smelling something gross) and observing someone else's facial expression of disgust activated the same region of a participant's brain (Wicker, Keysers, Plailly, Royet, Gallese, & Rizzolatti, 2003). Thus, one way that we are able to connect with each other emotionally is through the activation of these mirror neurons. At least some of the time, as researcher Vittorio Gallese put it, "We don't have to *think* about what other people are . . . feeling, we simply *know*"—in short, we feel it too (Winerman, 2005, p. 50).

Nonverbal cues serve many functions in communication. They help people express their emotions, their attitudes, and their personality. For example, you

nonverbal communication

the way in which people communicate, intentionally or unintentionally, without words; nonverbal cues include facial expressions, tone of voice, gestures, body position and movement, the use of touch, and eye gaze express "I'm angry" by narrowing your eyes, lowering your eyebrows, staring intently, and setting your mouth in a thin, straight line. You convey the attitude "I like you" with smiles and extended eye contact. And you convey the personality trait of being an extravert with broad gestures and frequent changes in voice pitch and inflection (Knapp & Hall, 2006).

Some nonverbal cues repeat or complement the spoken message, as when you smile while saying, "I'm so happy for you!" Others actually contradict the spoken words. Communicating sarcasm is the classic example of verbal-nonverbal contradiction. Think about how you'd say, "I'm so happy for you" sarcastically. (You could use your tone of voice, stressing the word *so* with an ironic twist, or you could roll your eyes as you speak, a sign of sarcasm in our culture.) Nonverbal cues can also substitute for a verbal message. Hand gestures, such as flashing the "okay" sign (forming a circle with the thumb and forefinger and the rest of the fingers curve above the circle) or drawing a finger across your throat, convey clear messages without any words at all (Ekman, 1965).

Nonverbal forms of communication have typically been studied individually, in their separate "channels" (e.g., eye gaze or gestures), even though in everyday life nonverbal cues of many kinds occur all at the same time in a dazzling orchestration of information (Archer & Akert, 1980, 1984). Let's focus on a few of these channels.

> *An eye can threaten like a loaded and leveled gun, or can insult like hissing or kicking; or, in its altered mood, by beams of kindness, it can make the heart dance with joy.*
>
> —Ralph Waldo Emerson, The Conduct of Life, 1860

Facial Expressions of Emotion

The crown jewel of nonverbal communication is the facial expressions channel. This aspect of communication has the longest history of research, beginning with Charles Darwin's (1872) book *The Expression of the Emotions in Man and Animals*. Its primacy is attributable to the exquisite communicativeness of the human face (Kappas, 1997; McHugo & Smith, 1996; Wehrle et al., 2000). Look at the accompanying photographs; you can probably figure out the meaning of these expressions with very little effort.

Darwin's research on facial expressions has had a major impact on the field in many areas. We will focus on his belief that the primary emotions conveyed by the face are universal—the idea that all human beings everywhere **encode** or express these emotions in the same way, and all human beings can **decode** or interpret them with equal accuracy. Darwin's (1872) interest in evolution led him to believe that nonverbal forms of communication were "species-specific" and not "culture-specific." He maintained that facial expressions were vestiges of once-useful physiological reactions—for example, if early hominids ate something that tasted terrible, they would have wrinkled their noses in displeasure (from the bad smell) and expelled the food from their mouths. Note that the photograph showing the disgusted expression demonstrates this sort of reaction. Such facial expressions then acquired evolutionary significance; being able to communicate such emotional states (e.g., the feeling of disgust, not for food but for another person or a situation) had survival value for the developing species (Hansen & Hansen, 1988; Izard, 1994; McArthur & Baron, 1983). Was Darwin right? Are facial expressions of emotion universal?

According to Paul Ekman and Walter Friesen, the answer is yes, at least for six major emotions: anger, happiness, surprise, fear, disgust, and sadness (Ekman & Friesen, 1986). To demonstrate that the facial expressions of these emotions are universal, Ekman and Friesen (1971) travelled to New Guinea, where they studied the decoding ability of the South Fore, a preliterate society that had had little contact with Western civilization. They told the Fore people brief stories with emotional content and then showed them photographs of

encode

to express or emit nonverbal behaviour, such as smiling or patting someone on the back

decode

to interpret the meaning of the nonverbal behaviour other people express, such as deciding that a pat on the back was an expression of condescension and not kindness

▲ These photographs depict facial expressions of the six major emotions. Can you guess the emotion expressed on each face?

ANSWERS: *(clockwise, beginning with upper-left photo):* anger, fear, disgust, sadness, surprise, and happiness.

American men and women expressing the six emotions. The Fore participants' job was to match the facial expressions of emotion to the stories. The researchers concluded that the Fore people were almost as accurate as American research participants had been. They then asked the Fore people to demonstrate, while being photographed, facial expressions that would match the stories they were told. When these photographs were shown to American research participants, they were also decoded quite accurately. Based on these and other data, it is generally accepted that the ability to interpret these six emotions is universal—part of being human, and not a product of people's cultural experience (Biehl et al., 1997; Ekman, 1993, 1994; Ekman et al., 1987; Elfenbein & Ambady, 2002; Izard, 1994).

Subsequently, other emotions have been added to this list of basic emotions. These additions tend to be emotions that are involved in social interaction (and, therefore, probably occurred later in evolution)—namely, contempt (Haidt & Keltner, 1999; Matsumoto & Ekman, 2004; see the photo on page 94), pride, embarrassment, anxiety, shame, and guilt (Ekman, O'Sullivan, & Matsumoto, 1991; Harrigan & O'Connell, 1996; Keltner & Shiota, 2003; Tracy & Robins, 2006, 2007). We note that much research on emotion continues to focus on the original six basic emotions identified by Ekman and colleagues.

> *When the eyes say one thing, and the tongue another, a practiced man relies on the language of the first.*
>
> —Ralph Waldo Emerson, The Conduct of Life, 1860

Are Facial Expressions of Emotion Universal? Not all emotion theorists have agreed with Ekman's conclusion that there are six (or more) universal facial expressions. As we shall see, there are some thorny issues involved in drawing conclusions about universality. One issue concerns the level of accuracy that participants must achieve in order to conclude that a given facial expression is being perceived in the same way across cultures. For example, when Ekman and Friesen (1975)

▲ Recent research suggests that "contempt" may be a universally recognized expression.

showed photographs of their six basic emotions to participants in the United States, Brazil, Chile, Argentina, Japan, and New Guinea, at least 82 percent of participants in each culture labelled their happiness facial expression as such. However, these percentages were substantially lower for some of the other emotions. For example, the fear expression was identified by only 54 percent of participants in both Argentina and New Guinea, and less than half (44 percent) of the New Guinea participants recognized the disgust expression.

According to Russell, Suzuki, and Ishida (1993), there is even less agreement when participants are asked to name the emotion shown in a face, rather than to select emotion terms from a list in which the number of emotion terms matches the number of faces (a common procedure in Ekman and Friesen's studies). Russell and colleagues approached adults in various public places in Canada, Greece, and Japan, and showed them photographs of the six basic facial expressions of emotions, plus contempt. Once again, the facial expression of happiness was identified by the majority of respondents in each country, whereas recognition rates for the other emotions were much lower. For example, only 14 percent of Japanese participants generated fear-related words for the fear expression. The contempt photograph was not labelled as such by participants in any of the cultures. Similar findings have been obtained in studies with Canadian, Chinese, Japanese, Indian, and Belgian participants (Hess & Blairy, 2001; Hess, Philippot, & Blairy, 1998; Mandal, Bryden, & Bulman-Fleming, 1996; Yik, Meng, & Russell, 1998; Yik & Russell, 1999). If the perception of certain basic emotions is universal, people in all cultures should be able to identify these emotions with relative ease. This does not appear to be the case. The accompanying Try It! encourages you to come up with your own answer to the question of how many basic facial expressions of emotion exist.

The claim of universality also suggests that basic facial expressions of emotion should be easily identified regardless of the context in which they are perceived. This also does not appear to be the case. In a series of studies conducted at the University of British Columbia (UBC), James Russell and Beverley Fehr (1987) found that the judgment of a given facial expression depended on what other faces were presented. If, for example, participants were exposed to a happy face and then a neutral face, the neutral face was perceived as sad. If a sad face was encountered first, the neutral face appeared happy. Most important, these effects were not limited to neutral faces. An angry face was perceived as sad, for example, when participants were first exposed to an expression such as disgust. Similar context effects have been examined in recent research conducted at the University of Toronto and at the Hebrew University of Jerusalem. Aviezer and colleagues found that the context (e.g., a disgust face in a fear context) influenced which parts of the face people fixated on (e.g., eyes versus mouth) in trying to decode the emotion being expressed (Aviezer, Hassin, Ryan, Grady, Susskind, Anderson, Moscovitch, & Bentin, 2008). The situation a person is in also can influence the emotion read from a face. Consider, for example, the facial expression of the man in the middle of the top row on page 93. Most people perceive this face as showing fear. Do you agree? Carroll and Russell (1996) found that UBC students who were told that the man had just experienced an extremely frustrating situation thought he was expressing anger. One final note on this topic: People in Asian cultures are more influenced by the context when interpreting the facial expression of emotion than are Westerners. For example, University of Alberta researcher Takahiko Masuda and colleagues found that the facial expressions of people in the background influenced the intensity of emotion that Japanese participants perceived in a target individual's face. This is consistent with the cultural emphasis on the group rather than the individual. North American participants are less influenced by the context—they focus primarily on the target individual's face, consistent with that culture's individualistic ethos (Masuda, Ellsworth, Mequita, Leu, Tanida, & Van de Veerdonk, 2008; Wang,

▶ How Many Universal Facial Expressions of Emotion Are There?

How many universal facial expressions of emotion are there? Come up with your own answer the next time you are with a group of friends. You can take turns posing facial expressions of emotion while the others in the group try to guess the emotion that is being conveyed. Here are some emotions you may wish to focus on:

1. **Happiness, sadness, anger, fear, disgust, surprise** These are the six facial expressions originally identified as universal by Ekman and Friesen (1975). If these are basic, universal facial expressions, it should be relatively easy for the people doing the posing to show those emotions on their faces. It should also be easy for the rest of the group to identify the emotion being displayed.

2. **Contempt** This is an emotion that Paul Ekman has more recently added to the list of universal facial expressions. Is contempt easily conveyed via facial expression? Was it easily recognized?

3. **Embarrassment** Research by Dacher Keltner (1995; Keltner & Shiota, 2003) suggests that embarrassment has a distinctive facial expression—the person turns his or her head away, looks down and to the side, and smiles with pressed lips. Is this how embarrassment looked when it was posed in your group? Should it be considered a universal facial expression?

4. **Heroism, humour/amusement, love, peace, wonder** Are these emotions easily conveyed via facial expression? According to an analysis of ancient Hindu writings, these emotions—along with anger, disgust, fear, sadness, and shame/embarrassment—may be universal (Hejmadi, Davidson, & Rozin, 2000). When participants in India and the United States were presented with videotaped expressions of these emotions (conveyed via facial expression and body movement), they were quite accurate at identifying them.

5. **Pride** Recently, psychologists have suggested that pride should be added to the list of universal emotions (Tracy & Robins, 2007).

So, exactly how many universal facial expressions of emotion are there? Which emotions should be included in that set? If you and your friends disagree, take heart—emotion researchers aren't quite sure either.

Masuda, Ishii, 2008). Thus, context effects, such as the presence of other facial expressions or the social situation in which an emotion is expressed, can have powerful influences on the perception of emotion. Such findings challenge the idea of universality of facial expressions of emotion and have generated lively debate among researchers (e.g., Ekman & O'Sullivan, 1988; Russell, 1994; Russell & Fehr, 1988).

Why Is Decoding Sometimes Inaccurate? Emotion theorists do agree, however, on some other factors that limit the accuracy with which facial expressions are decoded. First, people frequently display **affect blends** (Ekman & Friesen, 1975), wherein one part of their face is registering one emotion and another part is registering a different emotion. Take a look at the photographs on the next page and see if you can tell which two emotions are being expressed in each face. In the bottom photograph, we see a blend of anger (the eye and eyebrow region) and disgust (the nose and mouth region). (It may help to cover half the photograph with your hand to see each emotion clearly.) This is the sort of expression you might display if a person told you something that was both horrible and inappropriate—you'd be disgusted with the content and angry that the person had told you.

Second, at times, people try to appear less emotional than they are so that no one will know how they really feel. For example, if someone says something mean to you, you may hide your hurt feelings, allowing nothing to show on your face. By suppressing your emotional response, you are not giving your tormentor the satisfaction of knowing he or she has upset you. Psychologists have studied what happens when people suppress their negative facial expressions. Their results tell an interesting cautionary tale (Gross, 1998; Gross & Levenson, 1993,

affect blend

a facial expression in which one part of the face is registering one emotion and another part of the face is registering a different emotion

▲ Often people express more than one emotion at the same time. Can you tell which emotions these people are expressing? The answers are printed below.

(Adapted from Ekman & Friesen, 1975)

ANSWERS: The man is expressing a blend of anger and disgust. The woman is expressing a blend of surprise and happiness.

display rules

culturally determined rules about which nonverbal behaviours are appropriate to display

1997; Richards & Gross, 1999). For example, in one study, research participants who were told to suppress their emotions while discussing an upsetting topic with a stranger experienced an increase in blood pressure, reported more negative emotions, and felt less rapport with their conversational partner than participants who did not engage in suppression (Butler, Egloff, Wilhelm, Smith, Erickson, & Gross, 2003). A third reason that decoding facial expressions can be difficult has to do with culture. We turn to this topic next.

Culture and Nonverbal Communication

For decades, Paul Ekman and his colleagues have studied the influence of culture on the display of emotions (Ekman & Davidson, 1994; Ekman & Friesen, 1969). They have concluded that **display rules** are particular to each culture and dictate what kind of emotional expression people are supposed to show. For example, North American cultural norms discourage emotional displays in men, such as grief or crying, but allow the facial display of such emotions in women. Thus, when Canadian novelist Robertson Davies portrays a funeral scene in *Murther and Walking Spirits* (1991) with the phrase, "they sat in rows of weeping men and grim-faced women," he is fully aware that this description runs contrary to cultural norms, and adds an explanation: "For in our day there has been a reversal which makes it perfectly all right for a man to give way to feeling, whereas women must show no such weakness." So far, the reversal about which Davies speaks appears to exist only in fiction. Women are still much more likely than men to express emotion by crying (Fehr & Baldwin, 1996).

In Japan, traditional cultural rules dictate that women should not exhibit a wide, uninhibited smile (Ramsey, 1981). Japanese women will generally hide their wide smiles behind their hands, while Western women are allowed—indeed, encouraged—to smile broadly and frequently (Henley, 1977; La France, Hecht & Paluck, 2003).

In collectivist cultures, the expression of strong negative emotions is discouraged because to do so can disrupt group harmony. Thus, in Japan, people tend to cover up negative facial expressions with smiles and laughter and to display fewer facial expressions in general (Aune & Aune, 1996; Gudykunst, Ting-Toomey, & Nishida, 1996; Leathers, 1997). In India, also a collectivist country, expressions of fear and anger are not very distinct, making it difficult for both Canadians and Indians to identify them (Mandal, Bryden, & Bulman-Fleming, 1996). Indians also judge fear and anger as more unpleasant than do Canadians. The researchers suggest that because of collectivist cultural norms, Indians probably have less experience displaying these emotions and perceive them as more aversive when expressed.

There are, of course, other channels of nonverbal communication. These nonverbal cues are shaped by culture as well. Eye contact and eye gaze are particularly powerful nonverbal cues. In North America, most people become suspicious when a person doesn't "look us in the eye" while speaking, and they find talking to someone who is wearing dark sunglasses quite disconcerting. However, as you can see in Figure 4.1, in other parts of the world, direct eye gaze is considered invasive or disrespectful.

Cultures also vary greatly in what is considered normative use of personal space (Hall, 1969). For example, in countries such as Canada and the United States, most people like to have a bubble of open space, at least 0.5 metres in radius, surrounding them; in comparison, in some other cultures, strangers will think nothing of standing right next to each other, to the point of touching (see Figure 4.1). Differences in personal space can lead to misunderstandings when people of different cultures interact. For example, when Neil Malamuth was at the University of Manitoba, he helped organize a student exchange program in which North American students travelled to Israel. On one occasion, he

Eye contact and gaze

In North America, direct eye contact is valued; a person who won't "look you in the eye" is perceived as being evasive or even lying. However, in other cultures, direct eye contact is considered disrespectful, especially with superiors; for example, in Nigeria, Puerto Rico, and Thailand, children are taught not to make direct contact with their teachers and other adults. Many aboriginal people in North America use minimal eye contact as well. Japanese use far less direct contact than North Americans. In contrast, Arabs use a great deal of eye contact, with a gaze that would be considered piercing by people from some other cultures.

Personal space and touching

Societies vary in whether they are high-contact cultures (where people stand close to each other and touch frequently), or low-contact cultures (where people maintain more interpersonal space and touch less often). High-contact cultures include Middle Eastern, South American, and southern European countries. Low-contact cultures include North American and Asian countries, Pakistan, and most North American aboriginal cultures. Cultures also differ in how appropriate they consider same-sex touching among friends. For example, in Korea and Egypt, men and women hold hands, link arms, or walk hip to hip with their same-sex friends, and these nonverbal behaviours carry no sexual connotation. In North America, such behaviour is much less common, particularly between male friends.

Hand and head gestures

The "okay" sign: In North America, this sign means "okay"; in Japan, this gesture means "money"; in France, it means "zero"; in Mexico, it means "sex"; and in Ethiopia, it means "homosexuality." Finally, in some South American countries (e.g., Brazil), it is an obscene gesture, carrying the same meaning as the North American "flipping the bird" or "giving the finger."

The thumbs-up gesture: In North America, this sign means "okay." Several European countries have a similar meaning for this gesture; for example, in France, it means "excellent!" In Japan, this gesture means "boyfriend," while in Iran and Sardinia, it is an obscene gesture.

The "hand-purse" gesture: This gesture, which has no clear meaning in North America, is formed by straightening the fingers and thumb, and bringing them together so the tips touch, pointing upward. In Italy, it means "What are you trying to say?"; in Spain, it means "good"; in Tunisia, it means "slow down"; and in Malta, it means "You may seem good but you are really bad."

Nodding the head: In North America, nodding one's head up and down means "Yes" and shaking it from side to side means "No." In some parts of Africa and India, the opposite is true: nodding up and down means "No" and shaking from side to side means "Yes." In Korea, shaking one's head from side to side means "I don't know" (which, in North America, is communicated by a shrug of the shoulders). Finally, a Bulgarian indicates disagreement by throwing the head back and then returning it upright—which is frequently mistaken by North Americans as meaning agreement.

FIGURE 4.1

Cultural differences in nonverbal communication

organized a dance so the students from the two countries could get to know one another. Because of cultural differences in personal space, there were some unintended consequences:

> The scripted behaviour for an Israeli female in slow dances is generally not to have direct bodily contact with her dancing partner unless she is intimately involved with him. North American scripts, as you know, frequently prescribe body contact in such dances even when no intimacy is involved or desired. The consequence of the different cultural scripts was that the Israeli males thought that the North American women with whom they danced desired immediate sexual intimacy. The North American males dancing with Israeli partners, on the other hand, seemed very uncomfortable in being kept at a physical distance and later reported that they had been thinking that the Israelis must have found something about them highly offensive. (Malamuth, 1983)

Gestures of the hands and arms are also a fascinating means of communication. We are adept at understanding certain gestures, such as the "okay" sign (see Figure 4.1) and "giving someone the finger" (also known as the "up yours" gesture; Wolfgang & Wolofsky, 1991), in which one bends all the fingers down at the first knuckle except the longest, middle finger. Gestures such as these, for which there are clear, well-understood definitions, are called **emblems** (Archer, 1997; Ekman & Friesen, 1975). The important point about emblems is that they, too, are not universal; each culture has devised its own emblems. For example, Wolfgang and Wolofsky (1991) photographed actors displaying 23 different Canadian emblems. They asked Canadians and students from Asian, Latin, and Mediterranean countries to identify them. Overall, identification rates were high because even the participants from other countries already had some exposure to Canadian emblems. However, Canadians showed the highest rate of correct identification (97 percent). Thus, when the late prime minister Pierre Trudeau gave protesters "the finger," it was a clear communicative sign that protesters and the media at the time had no difficulty interpreting. In some parts of Europe, however, one would have to make a quick gesture with a cupped hand under one's chin to convey the same message.

In conclusion, many forms of nonverbal behaviour are specific to a given culture. A gesture that has meaning in one culture may not mean anything in

emblems

nonverbal gestures that have well-understood definitions within a given culture; they usually have direct verbal translations, such as the "okay" sign

CONNECTIONS

The Email Dilemma: Communicating without Nonverbal Cues

There you are, working at 4:00 in the morning on your psychology paper, which is due the next afternoon. You have a question and decide to email your professor, figuring there may be a chance he'll respond the next morning. You add a little joke about "waiting until the last minute" to do your paper, when in fact the complexity of your question should indicate that you've been working on it for days. Next morning, a blistering email arrives from your professor, criticizing you for not taking the assignment seriously. Oh dear. Your professor didn't get that you were joking.

Scenarios like this demonstrate the dilemma of email communication: Words go out, but there are no nonverbal cues to give them additional meaning. Humour, sarcasm, sadness, and other emotions are stripped away and your words stand alone, potentially open to misinterpretation. Sometimes we try to clarify our words by inserting *emoticons*, like this one: ☺. Although there are many emoticons in existence, they can be inappropriate if your message is a formal one, and they are often hard to interpret. For example, what does "%-(" or ";~/" mean? ("I'm confused" and "I'm unsure," respectively; Kruger, Epley, Parker & Ng, 2005).

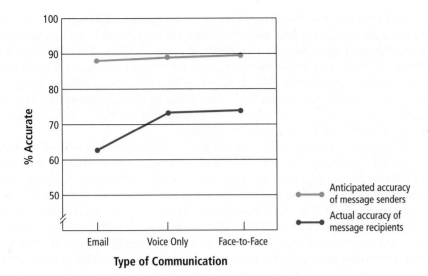

Do email writers realize to a sufficient extent that the loss of nonverbal cues can be a problem? Research by Justin Kruger and his colleagues (2005) suggests no. They conducted a study where college students were given a number of topics about which to communicate (e.g., "dorm life," "dating"), which were matched to one of four emotions: sarcasm, sadness, anger, or seriousness. Their job was to construct a statement on the topic that successfully conveyed the associated emotion. They communicated their statements in one of three ways: face-to-face to another person; to another person but using their voice only; or via an email. Finally, participants communicated their messages to either a stranger or a close friend.

Before they delivered their statements, participants were asked to what extent they thought they had successfully communicated the emotion in their message. As you can see in Figure 4.2, this "anticipated accuracy" is very high. Participants were very confident of their communicative abilities—regardless of the mode of interaction, they felt they'd done it accurately almost 90 percent of the time. Next, the message recipients were asked to indicate what emotion was in the message—the "actual accuracy." As Figure 4.2 shows, recipients were significantly less likely to get the emotional meaning if the message was communicated via email. To make these results even more worrisome, participants' friends did no better at decoding the correct emotion than did complete strangers! Thus, email writers were overconfident about their ability to communicate emotion with words alone—they thought they had communicated clearly, but in fact, they had not (Kruger et al., 2005).

The moral of the story: Relying on words alone, as occurs in email, means using an impoverished medium of communication. Be careful. Be very, very careful when you email. You can easily be misunderstood, and those misunderstandings (as we'll see throughout this chapter) can have serious effects on your interactions with others. And remember too that you are very likely to think your meaning is clear to the recipient of an email, when in fact, it may be clear only to *you*.

another. Moreover, the same nonverbal behaviour can exist in two cultures, but have very different meanings in each. Such nonverbal differences can lead to misunderstanding when people from different societies interact.

Gender and Nonverbal Communication

Who is better at decoding nonverbal cues—men or women? And who is better at encoding nonverbal information? Many studies show that women are better at both decoding and encoding (Hall, 1979, 1984; Rosenthal & De Paulo, 1979).

As with most rules, however, there is an exception: Although women are more accurate in interpreting nonverbal cues when a person is telling the truth, men are better at detecting lies (De Paulo, Epstein, & Wyer, 1993; Rosenthal & De Paulo, 1979). Given that women are generally superior decoders, why do they lose their advantage when faced with deceit? It may be because women are more polite than men. While women have the ability to decode nonverbal cues of lying, they tend to turn off this skill in the face of deception, in polite deference to the speaker (Rosenthal & De Paulo, 1979).

This interpretation fits nicely with a theory of sex differences offered by Alice Eagly (1987). According to Eagly's **social role theory**, most societies have a division of labour based on gender, whereby men work in jobs outside the home, and women work within the home. This division of labour has two important consequences. First, gender-role expectations arise. Members of the society expect men and women to have certain attributes that are consistent with their role. Consequently, women are expected to be more nurturing, friendly, expressive, and sensitive than men because of their primary role as caregivers to children and elderly family members (Eagly & Karau, 2002). Second, men and women develop different sets of skills and attitudes, based on their experiences in their gender roles (Barrett, Lane, Sechrest, & Schwartz, 2000). Finally, because women are less powerful in many societies and less likely to occupy roles of higher status, it is more important for women to learn to be accommodating and polite than it is for men (Deaux & Major, 1987; Henley, 1977). According to Eagly (1987), gender-role expectations and sex-typed skills combine to produce sex differences in social behaviour, such as the differences in nonverbal behaviour just discussed.

One way to test this theory would be to examine sex differences in cultures that have different gender-role expectations and sex-typed skills. If women are more polite in reading nonverbal cues because of the social roles they occupy in society, then this tendency to be polite should be especially strong in cultures where women are most oppressed. This is exactly what Judith Hall (1979) found in her cross-cultural study of nonverbal behaviour. First, she classified 11 countries as to the level of oppression of women, based on such statistics as the number of women who go to college and the prevalence of women's groups in each country. She then examined how likely women in each country were to show the "politeness pattern" when reading other people's nonverbal behaviours—that is, to focus on nonverbal cues that convey what people want others to see and to ignore nonverbal cues that "leak" people's true feelings. Sure enough, the tendency of women to be nonverbally polite in this manner was especially strong in those cultures where women are most oppressed.

To summarize, you can learn quite a lot about people from their nonverbal behaviour, including their attitudes, emotions, and personality traits. Nonverbal behaviour offers many bits of information—"data" that we then use to construct our overall impressions or theories about others. But nonverbal cues are just the beginning of social perception. We turn now to the cognitive processes people use when forming impressions of others.

Implicit Personality Theories: Filling in the Blanks

As we saw in Chapter 3, when people are unsure about the nature of the social world, they use their schemas to fill in the gaps (Fiske & Taylor, 1991; Kunda, 1999). An excellent example of the use of schemas is the way in which people form impressions of other people. If you know that someone is kind, you use a type of schema called an **implicit personality theory** to determine what other

---

social role theory

the theory that sex differences in social behaviour derive from society's division of labour between the sexes; this division leads to differences in gender-role expectations and sex-typed skills, both of which are responsible for differences in men's and women's social behaviour

implicit personality theory

a type of schema people use to group various kinds of personality traits together; for example, many people believe that if someone is kind, he or she is generous as well qualities the person has. You might assume for example, that this person is also generous; similarly, you assume that a stingy person is also irritable. These theories consist of people's ideas about what kinds of personality traits go together (Asch, 1946; Schneider, 1973; Sedikides & Anderson, 1994; Sherman & Klein, 1994; Werth & Foerster, 2002).

Implicit personality theories serve the same function as does any schema. You can extrapolate from a small to a much larger amount of information (Fiske & Taylor, 1991; Markus & Zajonc, 1985). In this case, you can use just a few observations of a person as a starting point, and then, using your schema, create a much fuller understanding of what that person is like (Kim & Rosenberg, 1980). This way, you can form impressions quickly, without having to spend weeks with people to figure out what they are like.

However, this efficiency can come at some cost and in some cases could even be fatal. How could our implicit personality theories cost us our lives? A team of researchers in the United States and Canada found that university students relied on implicit personality theories to determine whether they should use condoms (Williams, Kimble, Covell, Weiss, Newton, Fisher, & Fisher, 1992). If they knew their partner and liked their partner, participants assumed that he or she couldn't possibly be HIV positive. If participants didn't know their partner, they relied on superficial characteristics, such as the person's age, the way he or she dressed, or even whether the person was from a large city versus a small town. For example, if a potential sexual partner didn't dress provocatively or wasn't from a large city, participants assumed that a condom wasn't necessary. The researchers concluded that young people are placing themselves at considerable risk by relying on such implicit personality theories, because these variables are not accurate indicators of whether a sexual partner actually has HIV or AIDS. Similar findings have been obtained in more recent studies conducted by a team of researchers from universities across Canada (Knäuper, Kornik, Atkinson, Guberman, & Aydin, 2005).

> *Others are to us like the "characters" in fiction, external and incorrigible; the surprises they give us turn out in the end to have been predictable—unexpected variations on the theme of being themselves.*
>
> —Mary McCarthy, novelist and essayist, 1912–89

Culture and Implicit Personality Theories

Implicit personality theories are strongly tied to culture. Like other beliefs, they are passed from generation to generation in a society. One culture's implicit personality theory might be very different from another culture's (Anderson, 1995; Chui, Morris, Hong & Menon, 2000). For example, a strong implicit personality theory in our culture involves physical attractiveness. We presume that "what is beautiful is good"—that people with physical beauty will also have a whole host of other wonderful qualities (Dion, Berscheid, & Walster, 1972; Eagly et al., 1991; Jackson, Hunter, & Hodge, 1995). Consistent with this belief, when Dion and Dion (1987) showed visitors to the Ontario Science Centre photographs of attractive and unattractive individuals, more positive qualities (e.g., kind, considerate, sincere) were attributed to the attractive individuals. Participants also predicted that attractive individuals would experience more successes in life.

Dion, Pak, and Dion (1990) wondered whether physical attractiveness stereotyping might be less likely to occur in collectivist cultures (e.g., China) where social judgments are more likely to be based on group-related attributes (e.g., family, position in a social group) than on characteristics of the individual. Indeed, they found that Chinese students at the University of Toronto who were highly involved in Toronto's Chinese community—and therefore, probably more collectivist—were less likely to assume that an attractive person possessed desirable personality traits compared with students who were not as involved in the Chinese community.

Cultural variation in implicit personality theories was also demonstrated in an intriguing study by Hoffman, Lau, and Johnson (1986). They noted that different cultures have different ideas about personality types. In Western cultures, there is a kind of person who has an artistic personality: a person who is creative, intense, and temperamental, and who has an unconventional lifestyle. The Chinese, however, do not have a schema or implicit personality theory for an artistic type. Conversely, in China there are categories of personality that do not exist in Western cultures; for example, a *shi gú* person is someone who is worldly, devoted to family, socially skillful, and somewhat reserved. Hoffman and colleagues hypothesized that these culturally specific implicit personality theories would influence the way people form impressions of others. To test this hypothesis, they wrote stories, in English and Chinese, describing a person behaving like an artistic type or a *shi gú* type, without using those labels. They gave the stories written in English to a group of unilingual English speakers and to a group of Chinese-English bilingual participants. They gave the stories written in Chinese to another group of Chinese-English bilingual participants. The task for participants was to write down their impressions of the characters in the stories. The researchers then examined whether the participants listed traits that were not used in the stories but fit the artistic or *shi gú* personality type. In other words, they looked at whether participants used their implicit personality theories to "fill in the blanks." For example, the term *unreliable* was not mentioned in the "artistic personality type" story but is consistent with that implicit personality theory.

As seen in Figure 4.3, when the unilingual English speakers read about the characters, they formed an impression that was more consistent with the artistic type than with the *shi gú* type. This was also the case for the Chinese-English bilingual participants who read the descriptions in English. However, Chinese-English bilingual participants who read the descriptions in Chinese showed the opposite pattern of results. Their impression of the character was more consistent with the *shi gú* type than with the artistic type because the Chinese language provides a convenient label or implicit personality theory for this kind of person.

These results are consistent with a well-known argument by Benjamin Whorf (1956) that the language people speak influences the way they think about the world. Characters described identically were perceived differently by the bilingual research participants, depending on the language—and therefore the implicit personality theory—used. Consequently, one's culture and one's language produce widely shared implicit personality theories, and these theories can influence the kinds of inferences people make about each other.

▶Implicit personality theories differ from culture to culture. Westerners assume that there is an artistic type of person: someone who is creative, intense, temperamental, and unconventional—for example, poet/songwriter Leonard Cohen *(left)*. The Chinese have no such implicit personality theory. They have a category of *shi gú* person—someone who is worldly, devoted to family, socially skillful, and somewhat reserved *(right)*. Westerners do not have this implicit personality theory.

The artistic type (a Western implicit personality theory)

The *shi gú* type (a Chinese implicit personality theory)

Causal Attribution: Answering the "Why" Question

We have seen that when we observe other people, we make guesses about their personalities, such as how friendly or outgoing they are, often based on their nonverbal behaviour. And once we get this far, we use our implicit personality theories to fill in the blanks. If a person is friendly, she must be sincere as well. Or, more disturbingly, if a person is likeable, he or she must not have AIDS.

However, nonverbal behaviour and implicit personality theories are not fail-safe indicators of what a person is really thinking or feeling. If you meet an acquaintance and she says, "It's great to see you!" does she really mean it? Perhaps she is acting more thrilled than she really feels, out of politeness. Perhaps she is outright lying. The point is that even though nonverbal communication is sometimes easy to decode and implicit personality theories can streamline the way we form impressions, there is still substantial ambiguity as to what a person's behaviour really means. Why did that acquaintance behave as she did? To answer this "why" question, we use our immediate observations to form more elegant and complex inferences about what people really are like and what motivates them to act as they do. How we go about answering these questions is the focus of **attribution theory**, the study of how we infer the causes of other people's behaviour.

The Nature of the Attributional Process

Fritz Heider is frequently referred to as the father of attribution theory. His influential book defined the field of social perception, and his legacy is still very much evident in current research (Gilbert, 1998a; Ross, 1998). Heider (1958) discussed what he called "naive" or "common sense" psychology. In his view, people are like amateur scientists, trying to understand other people's behaviour by piecing together information until they arrive at a reasonable explanation or cause. Heider was intrigued by what seemed reasonable to people and how they arrived at their conclusions.

FIGURE 4.3

Implicit personality theories: How our culture and language shape our impressions of other people

People formed impressions of characters in stories that were consistent with the implicit personality theory contained in their language. For example, when Chinese-English bilinguals read stories about people in English, they were likely to form impressions consistent with a Western implicit theory, the artistic personality. When Chinese-English bilingual participants read the same stories in Chinese, they were likely to form impressions consistent with a Chinese implicit theory, the *shi gú* personality.

(Adapted from Hoffman, Lau, & Johnson, 1986)

" In the beginning was not the word, not the deed, not the silly serpent. In the beginning was why? Why did she pluck the apple? Was she bored? Was she inquisitive? Was she paid? Did Adam put her up to it? If not, who did? "

—*John le Carré*, The Russia House, *1989*

attribution theory

a description of the way in which people explain the causes of their own and other people's behaviour

▶According to Fritz Heider (1958), we tend to see the causes of a person's behaviour as internal. So when a man asks us for money, we will most likely at first assume that he is at fault for being poor—perhaps lazy or drug-addicted. If you knew the person's situation—that perhaps he has lost his job due to a plant closing or has a spouse whose medical bills have bankrupted them—you might come up with a different, external attribution.

internal attribution

the inference that a person is behaving in a certain way because of something about him or her, such as his or her attitude, character, or personality

external attribution

the inference that a person is behaving a certain way because of something about the situation he or she is in; the assumption is that most people would respond the same way in that situation

One of Heider's (1958) most valuable contributions is a simple dichotomy: When trying to decide why people behave as they do—for example, why a father just yelled at his young daughter—we can make one of two attributions. One option is to make an **internal attribution**, deciding that the cause of the father's behaviour was something about him—his disposition, personality, attitudes, or character—an explanation that assigns the causes of his behaviour internally. For example, we might decide that the father has poor parenting skills and disciplines his child in inappropriate ways. Alternatively, we might make an **external attribution**, deciding that something about the situation, not he personality or attitudes, caused the behaviour. If we conclude that he yelled because his daughter had just stepped into the street without looking, we would be making an external attribution for his behaviour. (See the accompanying Try It! exercise.)

Another of Heider's (1958) important contributions was his observation that people generally prefer internal attributions over external ones. Although

Try it!

▶ Listen as People Make Attributions

Forming attributions is a major part of daily life. (Note, for example, the Rhona Raskin column in Figure 4.10 on page 113.) You can watch the attribution process in action, too. All it takes is a group of friends and an interesting topic to discuss. Perhaps your friends are discussing another person whom everybody knows. As they talk, pay very close attention to what they say. They will be trying to figure out why the person being discussed did what he or she did, or said what he or she said. In other words, they will be making attributions. Your job is to try to keep track of their comments and label the attributional strategies they are using.

In particular, do they make internal attributions, about a person's character or personality, or do they make situational attributions,

about all of the other events and variables that make up a person's life? Do your friends seem to prefer one type of attribution over the other? If their interpretation is dispositional (internal), what happens when you suggest another possible interpretation, one that is situational (external)? Do they agree or disagree with you? What kinds of information do they offer as "proof" that their attribution is right?

Observing people when they are making attributions in real conversations will show you just how common and powerful this type of thinking is when people are trying to understand one another.

either type of attribution is always possible, Heider noted that we tend to see the causes of a person's behaviour as residing in that person. We are perceptually focused on *people*—they are who we notice—while the *situation*, which is often hard to see and hard to describe, can be overlooked (Bargh, 1994; Carlston & Skowronski, 1994; Gilbert, 1998b; Jones, 1979, 1990; Jones & Davis, 1965).

The Covariation Model: Internal versus External Attributions

The first, essential step in the process of social perception is determining how people decide whether to make an internal or an external attribution. Harold Kelley's (1967, 1973) major contribution to attribution theory was the idea that we notice and think about more than one piece of information when we form an impression of another person. For example, let's say that you ask your friend to lend you her car, and she says no. Naturally, you wonder why. In formulating an answer, Kelley's theory, called the **covariation model**, states that you will examine multiple instances of behaviour, occurring at different times and in different situations. Has your friend refused to lend you her car in the past? Does she lend it to other people? Does she normally lend you other possessions of hers?

Kelley, like Heider before him, assumed that when we are in the process of forming an attribution, we gather information, or data, that will help us reach a judgment. The data we use, according to Kelley, are how a person's behaviour "covaries" or changes across time, place, different actors, and different targets of the behaviour. By discovering covariation in people's behaviour (e.g., your friend refuses to lend you her car; she agrees to lend it to others), you are able to reach a judgment about what caused their behaviour.

When we are forming an attribution, what kinds of information do we examine for covariation? Kelley (1967, 1972, 1973) identified three key types of information: *consensus*, *distinctiveness*, and *consistency*. Let's describe these types of information through an example. You are working at your part-time job in a clothing store and you observe your boss yelling at another employee, Hannah, telling her in no uncertain terms that she's an idiot. Without any conscious effort on your part, you pose the attributional question: "Why is the boss yelling at Hannah and being so critical—is it something about the boss, or is it something about the situation that surrounds and affects him?"

Now let's look at how Kelley's model of covariation assessment answers this question. **Consensus information** refers to how other people behave toward the same stimulus—in this case, Hannah. Do other people at work also yell at Hannah and criticize her? **Distinctiveness information** refers to how the actor (the person whose behaviour we are trying to explain) responds to other stimuli. Does the boss yell at and demean other employees in the store? **Consistency information** refers to the frequency with which the observed behaviour between the same actor and the same stimulus occurs across time and circumstances. Does the boss yell at and criticize Hannah regularly and frequently, whether the store is busy with customers or empty?

According to Kelley's theory, when these three sources of information combine into one of two distinct patterns, a clear attribution can be made. People are most likely to make an *internal attribution*—deciding the behaviour was a result of something about the boss—when the consensus and distinctiveness of the act are low, but consistency is high (see Figure 4.4 on the next page). We would be pretty confident that the boss yelled at Hannah because he is a mean and vindictive person if we knew that no one else yells at Hannah, that the boss yells at other employees, and that the boss yells at Hannah every chance he gets. People are likely to make an *external attribution* (in this case, about Hannah) if consensus, distinctiveness, and consistency are all high. Finally, when consistency is low, we cannot make a clear internal or external attribution and so resort to a special kind of external or *situational attribution*,

covariation model
a theory stating that in order to form an attribution about what caused a person's behaviour, we systematically note the pattern between the presence (or absence) of possible causal factors and whether or not the behaviour occurs

consensus information
information about the extent to which other people behave the same way as the actor does toward the same stimulus

distinctiveness information
information about the extent to which one particular actor behaves in the same way to different stimuli

consistency information
information about the extent to which the behaviour between one actor and one stimulus is the same across time and circumstances

FIGURE 4.4

The covariation model

Why did the boss yell at his employee, Hannah? To decide whether a behaviour was caused by internal (or dispositional) factors, or external (or situational) factors, people use consensus, distinctiveness, and consistency information.

Why did the boss yell at his employee, Hannah?

People are likely to make an *internal attribution*—it was something about the boss—if they see this behaviour as	*low* in consensus: the boss is the only person working in the store who yells at Hannah	*low* in distinctiveness: the boss yells at all the employees	*high* in consistency: the boss yells at Hannah almost every time he sees her
People are likely to make an *external attribution*—it was something about Hannah—if they see this behaviour as	*high* in consensus: all of the employees yell at Hannah, too	*high* in distinctiveness: the boss doesn't yell at any of the other employees	*high* in consistency: the boss yells at Hannah almost every time he sees her
People are likely to think it was something peculiar about the particular circumstances in which the boss yelled at Hannah if they see this behaviour as	*low or high* in consensus	*low or high* in distinctiveness	*low* in consistency: this is the first time that the boss has yelled at Hannah

one that assumes something unusual or peculiar is going on in these circumstances—for example, the boss just received very upsetting news and lost his temper with the first person he saw.

The covariation model assumes that people make causal attributions in a rational, logical way. People observe the clues, such as the distinctiveness of the act, and then draw a logical inference about why the person did what he or she did. Several studies have confirmed that people often do make attributions the way that Kelley's (1967) model says they should (Gilbert, 1998b; Hewstone & Jaspars, 1987; White, 2002)—with two exceptions. First, studies have shown that people don't use consensus information as much as Kelley's theory predicted; they rely more on consistency and distinctiveness information when forming attributions (McArthur, 1972; Wright, Luus, & Christie, 1990). Second, people don't always have the relevant information they need on all three of Kelley's dimensions; for example, you may not have consistency information because this is the first time you have ever asked your friend to borrow her car. In these situations, research has shown that people proceed with the attribution process using the information they do have, and if necessary, making inferences about the "missing data" (Fiedler, Walther, & Nickel, 1999; Kelley, 1973).

To summarize, the covariation model portrays people as master detectives, deducing the causes of behaviour as systematically and logically as Sherlock Holmes would. However, as we saw in Chapter 3, sometimes people aren't that accurate or rational when forming judgments about others. Sometimes they distort information to satisfy their need for high self-esteem (see Chapter 5). Attributions also can be biased or distorted when people use mental shortcuts (see Chapter 3). In the next section, we will discuss some specific errors or biases that plague the attribution process. One shortcut is very common, at least in Western cultures: assuming that people do what they do because of the kind of people they are, not because of the situation they are in.

The Correspondence Bias: People as Personality Psychologists

On September 22, 1999, Nadia Hama made newspaper headlines when her 18-month-old daughter Kaya fell 47 metres from the Capilano Suspension Bridge in North Vancouver, British Columbia. People in the media and on the street were quick to blame Hama, accusing her of deliberately throwing Kaya off the bridge. These accusations mounted as it came to light that her daughter had Down syndrome and that Hama had looked into placing her for adoption. In short, Hama was portrayed as a bad mother who intentionally tried to kill her child. Other people agreed that Nadia Hama may have tried to kill her child, but pointed to situational factors in explaining her behaviour. They focused on the extremely high levels of stress in her life—raising a handicapped child, being embroiled in an ugly divorce and not receiving child-care payments from her estranged husband. Not surprisingly, Hama explained her behaviour as situationally caused—maintaining that baby Kaya's fall was accidental.

Whether we make internal or external attributions for someone's behaviour can have serious consequences. In Nadia Hama's case, those who made internal attributions concluded that she was a cold-hearted murderer; in contrast, those who made external attributions felt compassion, sympathy, and pity. Quite a difference! Perhaps even more important, the fate of Hama rested on the attributions made for baby Kaya's fall. Ultimately, police and Crown prosecutors did not find sufficient evidence to charge her with either attempted murder or criminal negligence causing bodily harm (D'Angelo, 2000).

Other research has shown that when people are convicted of committing crimes, attributions play a role in the severity of sentencing. Linda Coates (1997) recorded the kinds of attributions made by judges in transcripts of 70 cases of sexual assault in British Columbia. The kind of attributions made had important implications for sentencing: If the assault was seen as the result of a decision to be violent or due to the offender's violent nature, the sentence was harsher than if situational or external attributions were made (e.g., the assault was attributed to stress or negative mood).

The pervasive, fundamental theory or schema most of us have about human behaviour is that people do what they do because of the kind of people they are, not because of the situation they are in. Thus, in Nadia Hama's case, people's first impulse was to attribute her behaviour to being a bad mother and cold-hearted murderer. When thinking this way, we are more like personality psychologists, who see behaviour as stemming from internal dispositions and traits, than social psychologists, who focus on the impact of social situations on behaviour. This tendency to infer that people's behaviour corresponds to or matches their dispositions and personality has been called the **correspondence bias** (Fiske & Taylor, 1991; Gilbert & Malone, 1995; Jones, 1979, 1990). The correspondence bias is so pervasive that many social psychologists call it the **fundamental attribution error** (Heider, 1958; Jones, 1990; Ross, 1977; Ross & Nisbett, 1991).

There have been many empirical demonstrations of the tendency to see people's behaviour as a reflection of their dispositions and beliefs, rather than as influenced by the situation (Gawronski, 2003; Jones, 1979, 1990; Miller, Ashton, & Mishal, 1990; Riggs & Gumbrecht, 2005). In a classic demonstration of this effect, Edward Jones and Victor Harris (1967) asked university students to read a fellow student's essay that either supported or opposed Fidel Castro's rule in Cuba, and then to guess how the author of the essay really felt about Castro. In one condition, the researchers told the students that the author freely chose which position to take in the essay, thereby making it easy to guess how he or she really felt. If the author chose to write in favour of Castro, then clearly he or she must indeed be sympathetic to Castro. In another condition, however, the students learned that the author did not have any choice about which position to take—he or she had been assigned the position as a participant in a debate.

correspondence bias

the tendency to infer that people's behaviour corresponds to or matches their disposition (personality)

fundamental attribution error

the tendency to overestimate the extent to which people's behaviour is attributable to internal, dispositional factors, and to underestimate the role of situational factors

FIGURE 4.5

The fundamental attribution error

Even when people knew that the author's choice of an essay topic was externally caused (i.e., in the no-choice condition), they assumed that what he or she wrote reflected how he or she really felt about Castro. That is, they made an internal attribution for the author's behaviour.

(Adapted from Jones & Harris, 1967)

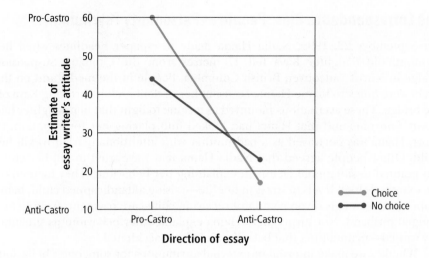

Logically, if we know someone could not choose the topic, we should not assume the writer believes what he or she wrote. Yet the participants in this study, and in dozens of others like it, assumed that the author really believed what he or she wrote, even when they knew he or she could not choose which position to take. As seen in Figure 4.5, people moderated their guesses a little bit—there was not as much difference in people's estimates of the author's attitude in the pro-Castro and anti-Castro conditions—but they still assumed that the content of the essay reflected the author's true feelings.

Why is the correspondence bias—the tendency to explain behaviour in terms of people's dispositions—often called the fundamental attribution error? It is not always wrong to make an internal attribution; clearly, people frequently do what they do because of the kind of people they are. However, there is ample evidence that social situations can have a strong impact on behaviour—indeed, the major lesson of social psychology is that these influences can be extremely powerful. The point of the fundamental attribution error is that people tend to underestimate these influences when explaining other people's behaviour. Even when a situational constraint on behaviour is obvious, as in the Jones and Harris (1967) experiment, people persist in making internal attributions (Lord, Scott, Pugh, & Desforges, 1997; Newman, 1996; Ross, 1977; Ross, Amabile, & Steinmetz, 1977; Ross & Nisbett, 1991).

The Role of Perceptual Salience in the Fundamental Attribution Error Why do we fall prey to the fundamental attribution error? One reason is that when we try to explain someone's behaviour, our focus of attention is usually on the person, not on the surrounding situation (Heider, 1958; Jones & Nisbett, 1972). In fact, the situational causes of another person's behaviour are practically invisible to us (Gilbert, 1998b; Gilbert & Malone, 1995). If we don't know what happened to a person earlier in the day (e.g., she received an *F* on her midterm), we can't use that situational information to help us understand her current behaviour. Even when we know her situation, we still don't know how she interprets it—for example, the *F* may not have upset her because she's planning to drop the course anyway. If we don't know the meaning of the situation for her, we can't accurately judge its effects on her behaviour.

What information does that leave us? People, not the situation, have **perceptual salience** for us—people are what our eyes and ears notice. And what we notice seems to be the reasonable and logical cause of the observed behaviour (Heider, 1958). Several studies have confirmed the importance of perceptual salience, including a particularly elegant one by Shelley Taylor and Susan Fiske (1975). In this study, two male students engaged in a "get acquainted"

perceptual salience

information that is the focus of people's attention; people tend to overestimate the causal role of perceptually salient information

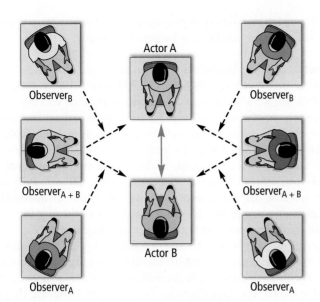

FIGURE 4.6

Manipulating perceptual salience

This is the seating arrangement for two actors and the six research participants in the Taylor and Fiske study. Participants rated each actor's impact on the conversation. The researchers found that people rated the actor they could see most clearly as having the largest role in the conversation.

(Adapted from Taylor & Fiske, 1975)

conversation. (They were actually both accomplices of the experimenters and were following a script during their conversation.) At each session, six actual research participants also took part. They sat in assigned seats, surrounding the two conversationalists (see Figure 4.6). Two of them sat on each side of the actors; they had a clear, profile view of both individuals. Two observers sat behind each actor; they could see the back of one actor's head but the face of the other. Thus, who was visually salient—that is, who the participants could see the best—was cleverly manipulated in this study.

After the conversation, the research participants were asked questions about the two men—for example, who had taken the lead in the conversation, and who had chosen the topics to be discussed? As you can see in Figure 4.7, the person they thought had the most impact on the conversation was the one they could see best. Even though all the observers heard the same conversation, those who were facing actor A thought *he* had taken the lead and chosen the topics, whereas those who were facing actor B thought *he* had taken the lead and chosen the topics. In comparison, those who could see both students equally well thought both were equally influential. Perceptual salience, or our visual point of view, helps explain why the fundamental attribution error is so widespread. We focus our attention more on people than on the surrounding situation because the situation

> ❝ *Be not swept off your feet by the vividness of the impression, but say, 'Impression, wait for me a little. Let me see what you are and what you represent.'* ❞
>
> —*Epictetus*, Discourses, AD 101

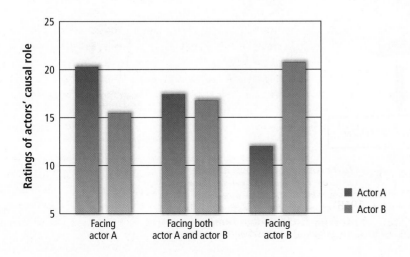

FIGURE 4.7

The effects of perceptual salience

These are the ratings of each actor's causal role in the conversation. People thought that the actor they could see the best had the most impact on the conversation.

(Adapted from Taylor & Fiske, 1975)

is so hard to see or know; we underestimate or even forget about the influence of the situation when we are explaining human behaviour.

two-step process of attribution

analyzing another person's behaviour first by making an automatic internal attribution and only then thinking about possible situational reasons for the behaviour, after which one may adjust the original internal attribution

The Two-Step Process of Making Attributions We go through a **two-step process** when we make attributions (Gilbert, 1989, 1991, 1993; Krull, 1993). First, we make an internal attribution; we assume that a person's behaviour was due to something about that person. In the second step, we attempt to adjust this attribution by considering the situation the person was in. But we often don't make enough of an adjustment in this second step. Indeed, when we are distracted or preoccupied, we often skip the second step, making an extreme internal attribution (Gilbert & Hixon, 1991; Gilbert & Osborne, 1989; Gilbert, Pelham, & Krull, 1988). Why? Because the first step (making the internal attribution) occurs quickly and spontaneously, whereas the second step (adjusting for the situation) requires more effort and conscious attention (see Figure 4.8).

We will engage in this second step of attributional processing if we consciously slow down and think carefully before reaching a judgment, if we are motivated to reach as accurate a judgment as possible, or if we are suspicious about the behaviour of the target person, for example, believing that he or she is lying or has ulterior motives (Burger, 1991; Fein, 1996; Hilton, Fein, & Miller, 1993; Webster, 1993).

Consequences of the Fundamental Attribution Error Even if people are made aware of the situational factors responsible for the plight of disadvantaged members of our society (e.g., inadequate nutrition, disrupted family life), they may still see these individuals as responsible for their misfortune. Guimond and Dubé (1989), for example, found that Anglophone students viewed Francophones themselves, rather than situational factors, as responsible for their lower economic status in Quebec.

FIGURE 4.8

The two-step process of attribution

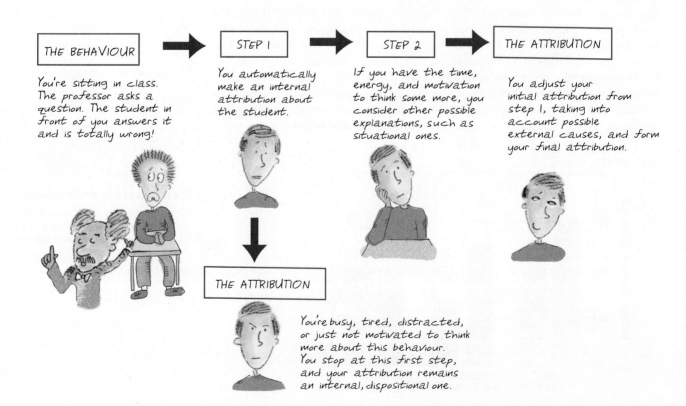

THE TWO-STEP PROCESS OF ATTRIBUTION

THE BEHAVIOUR

You're sitting in class. The professor asks a question. The student in front of you answers it and is totally wrong!

STEP 1

You automatically make an internal attribution about the student.

STEP 2

If you have the time, energy, and motivation to think some more, you consider other possible explanations, such as situational ones.

THE ATTRIBUTION

You adjust your initial attribution from step 1, taking into account possible external causes, and form your final attribution.

THE ATTRIBUTION

You're busy, tired, distracted, or just not motivated to think more about this behaviour. You stop at this first step, and your attribution remains an internal, dispositional one.

Another way in which the fundamental attribution error leads to victim blaming is when people decide that victims could have exercised control over the situation but didn't. Research conducted at the University of Windsor and the University of Manitoba has shown that people who attribute serious illnesses (e.g., HIV, heart disease, lung cancer) to controllable factors are more likely to blame victims for their illness (Mantler, Schellenberg, & Page, 2003; Menec & Perry, 1998). Similarly, Lawson (2003) found that women who gave birth to a disabled child were blamed more when prenatal diagnostic testing had been available to them, compared with mothers for whom this test had not been available. This held true for both a large sample of university employees and a group of Canadian doctors. Other research has shown that people are more prejudiced toward overweight people if they are seen as personally responsible for being fat (Crandall, D'Anello, Sakalli, Lazarus, Wieczorkowska, & Feather, 2001). Finally, in research conducted at Lakehead University, Rotenberg (1998) found that students were less accepting of a lonely student if they attributed his or her loneliness to controllable factors. Thus, the consequences of our tendency to explain other people's behaviour in dispositional terms can lead to tragic consequences, including a tendency to blame those who are victimized or stigmatized for their plight.

Culture and the Fundamental Attribution Error   For decades, it was taken for granted that the fundamental attribution error was universal: People everywhere, it was thought, applied this cognitive shortcut when forming attributions (Norenzayan, Choi, & Nisbett, 1999). However, it turns out that the fundamental attribution error is most likely to occur in North American and other Western cultures that emphasize individual freedom and autonomy (Dix, 1993; Rholes, Newman, & Ruble, 1990). In contrast, collectivist (often Asian) cultures emphasize group membership, interdependence, and conformity to group norms (Fletcher & Ward, 1988; Markus & Kitayama, 1991; Newman, 1991; Triandis, 1990; Zebrowitz-McArthur, 1988). These cultural values suggest that people would be socialized to take situational factors into account. In a classic study, Joan Miller (1984) asked people of two cultures—Hindus living in India and Americans living in the United States—to think of various examples of behaviours performed by their friends, and to explain why those behaviours occurred. Consistent with what we've said so far, the U.S. participants preferred dispositional explanations for the behaviours; they were more likely to say that the causes of their friends' behaviours were the kinds of people they are, rather than the situation or context in which the behaviours occurred. In contrast, Hindu participants preferred situational explanations for their friends' behaviours (Miller, 1984).

The cultural explanation of the fundamental attribution error received further support in a clever study that compared newspaper articles in Chinese- and English-language newspapers. Michael Morris and Kaiping Peng (1994) targeted two similar crimes, both mass murders, one committed by a Chinese graduate student in Iowa, the other committed by a white postal worker in Michigan. The researchers coded all of the news articles about the two crimes that appeared in the *New York Times* and the *World Journal*, a Chinese-language U.S. newspaper. As you can see in Figure 4.9 on the next page, journalists writing in English made significantly more dispositional attributions about both mass murderers than did journalists writing in Chinese. For example, English-language reporters described one murderer as a "darkly disturbed man" with a "sinister edge" to his personality. Chinese-language reporters, when describing the same murderer, emphasized more situational causes, such as "not getting along with his adviser" and his "isolation from the Chinese community."

Finally, in a more recent study, Chiu, Morris, Hong, and Menon (2000) asked members of the public in the United States and Hong Kong to read a scenario about patients who got sick because a pharmacy worker made an error while mixing medicines. As expected, Americans made more dispositional

The role of culture in the fundamental attribution error

Newspaper articles about two murderers, appearing in English- and Chinese-language newspapers, were coded for the types of attributions made. Journalists writing in English made significantly more dispositional attributions about both the Chinese and the Anglo-American murderer than did journalists writing in Chinese.

(Adapted from Morris & Peng, 1994)

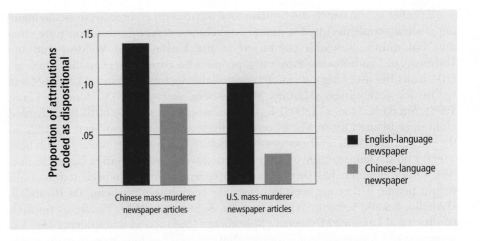

attributions (assigning responsibility to the worker), whereas the Chinese were more likely to assign responsibility to the clinic (e.g., poor management, incompetent training of workers). This cultural difference was even more pronounced in a follow-up laboratory study when some participants answered the questions while performing another task. Presumably under these conditions, participants engaged in automatic processing (see Chapter 3), with the result that U.S. participants were especially likely to blame the worker and Chinese participants were especially likely to blame the clinic.

Thus, people in Western cultures appear to be more like personality psychologists, viewing behaviour in dispositional terms. When making attributions about others, the initial, automatic, and effortless attribution tends to be dispositional. Only if they are motivated to think more deeply will Westerners come up with situational explanations (Lee, Hallahan, & Herzog, 1996; Webster, 1993). In contrast, people in Asian (collectivist) cultures seem to be more like social psychologists, viewing behaviour in situational terms (Heine & Buchtel, in press). Their initial, automatic, and effortless attribution tends to be situational; only if they are motivated to engage in more cognitive work will they come up with possible dispositional attributions (Lee, Hallahan, & Herzog, 1996; Krull, 1993).

The Actor/Observer Difference

An interesting twist on the fundamental attribution error is that it does not apply across the board. Whereas we tend to attribute other people's behaviour to internal causes, we look beyond ourselves, to the situation, to explain our own behaviour. Thus, if we see a woman yelling at her child in a grocery store, we are quick to make the attribution that she's a mean, bad parent. The woman, however, would probably explain her behaviour in more situational terms, such as sleep deprivation or the stress she's under since she lost her job. This difference in attributions is called the **actor/observer difference** (Hansen, Kimble, & Biers, 2001; Jones & Nisbett, 1972; Robins, Spranca, & Mendelsohn, 1996). The letter to Rhona Raskin (see Figure 4.10) is an interesting demonstration of the actor/observer difference. The writer focuses on the external forces affecting her life and shaping her behaviour. Raskin, however, will have none of it. She makes a strong, internal attribution, declaring that the woman herself, not the situation, is the cause of her problems.

There have been countless demonstrations of the actor/observer difference. For example, University of British Columbia social psychologist Peter Suedfeld (2003) examined the attributions made by survivors of the Holocaust (i.e., their explanations for why they survived). Participants in the control group—Jews who had been safe from Nazi persecution—were asked to explain why some Jews

actor/observer difference

the tendency to see other people's behaviour as dispositionally caused, while focusing more on the role of situational factors when explaining one's own behaviour

Dear Rhona:

I get harassing phone calls throughout the day from a woman whose boyfriend I know. Honestly, I was just friends with this guy, but since all this pestering started we've become sexually involved. I am not looking to steal him away from her—it's just great sex! It seems to work for him too. I suspect that he's never been the faithful type to begin with. I've asked her to stop bothering me but to no avail. Is this all destined to blow up into ugliness for me?

HARASSED

Dear H:

Your pleasure centre is wired to danger. It's my only explanation for a woman who'd even CONSIDER continuing to boink a guy who is so thoughtless that he not only cheats on his girlfriend, but also leaves a trail of crumbs to his co-conspirator. You act as though the girlfriend's behaviour is beyond belief. Really, it's yours that needs investigation. Yes, she is stalking you and there are restraining orders that can be put in place, but imagine all the effort that will take. And how predictably catty--two women fighting over a man. Oh right, you only care for the sensational part while the girlfriend wants the whole package. Go meditate on the concept of karma. Yours needs an overhaul.

FIGURE 4.10

Actor/observer differences in attribution

The advice column letter and its response depict actor/observer differences in attribution. Schoeneman and Rubanowitz (1985) examined letters to the "Ann Landers" and "Dear Abby" advice columns and found strong evidence for actor/observer differences. Letter writers tended to attribute their problems to external factors, whereas the advice columnists tended to make dispositional attributions to the letter writers. Similarly, in this column, the writer attributes her problems to the behaviour of the girlfriend of the man with whom she has become sexually involved, rather than to her own behaviour. Rhona Raskin, on the other hand, puts the blame squarely on the letter writer's shoulders and tells her to shape up.

survived the Holocaust. Survivors were most likely to make situational attributions, reporting that they had survived because of the help and support of other people, or because of luck, fate, or help from God. In contrast, those in the control group (who were explaining the behaviour of the survivors) were more likely to mention internal factors, such as the survivors' determination and persistence. Also in line with the actor/observer difference, there is evidence that people perceive more consistency in the attitudes of other people than in their own attitudes, as demonstrated in a series of studies conducted at Memorial University (Grant, Button, Hannah, & Ross, 2003).

> *Resemblances are the shadows of differences. Different people see different similarities and similar differences.*
>
> —*Vladimir Nabokov, Pale Fire, 1962*

Perceptual Salience Revisited   Why, at times, do the attributions made by actors and observers diverge so sharply? One reason is our old friend perceptual salience (Jones & Nisbett, 1972). As mentioned earlier, we notice other people's behaviour more than their situation. When it comes to ourselves, we notice our own situation more than our own behaviour. None of us is so egotistical or self-centred that we walk through life constantly holding up a full-length mirror in order to observe ourselves. We are looking outward; perceptually salient to us are other people, objects, and the events that unfold. As a result, when the actor and the observer think about what caused a given behaviour, they are swayed by the information that is most salient and noticeable to them: the actor for the observer, and the situation for the actor (Malle & Knobe, 1997; Nisbett & Ross, 1980; Ross & Nisbett, 1991).

The Role of Information Availability in the Actor/Observer Difference   The actor/observer difference occurs for another reason as well. Actors have more information about themselves than observers do. Actors know how they've behaved over the years; they know what happened to them that morning. Thus, they are far more aware than observers are of both the similarities and the differences in their behaviour across time and across situations (Greenwald & Banaji, 1989; Jones & Nisbett, 1972; Krueger, Ham, & Linford, 1996; Malle & Knobe, 1997). In Kelley's (1967) terms, actors have far more consistency and distinctiveness information about themselves than observers do. For example, if you are quiet and sit alone at a party, an observer is likely to make a dispositional attribution about you ("Gee, that person is quite an introvert"). In fact, you may know that this is not how you usually behave at a party. Maybe you are just feeling tired or depressed by some recent bad news. It is not surprising, then, that actors' self-attributions usually reflect situational factors, because they know more about how their behaviour varies from one situation to the next than do most observers, who see them in limited contexts.

Finally, we should note that social psychologists have also examined the link between culture and the actor/observer difference (Van Boven, White, Kamanda, & Gilovich, 2003). For example, Incheol Choi and Richard Nisbett (1998) examined the actor/observer difference among U.S. and Korean research participants. These groups did not differ in the attributions they made to themselves—the "actors." They both made situational attributions for their behaviour. They differed only in the attributions they formed about another person, and in a way we've seen already in this discussion of cultural differences: U.S. participants were more likely to think that the other person's behaviour derived from his or her disposition (the fundamental attribution error), whereas Korean participants were more likely to think that the other person's behaviour was caused by the situation.

So far, our discussion of the mental shortcuts people use when making attributions has covered the role of perceptual salience and information availability. But what about a person's needs, desires, hopes, and fears—do these more emotional factors also create biases in our attributions? Are you motivated to see the world in certain ways because these views make you feel better, both about yourself and life in general? The answer is yes. The shortcuts discussed next have a motivational basis; they are attributions that protect our self-esteem and our belief that the world is a safe and just place.

Self-Serving Attributions

Imagine that Alison goes to her chemistry class one day with some apprehension because she will find out how she did on the midterm. When the professor returns her exam, Alison sees that she has received an A. What will Alison think is the reason for her great grade? It probably will come as no surprise that people tend to take personal credit for their successes but blame their failures on external events that were beyond their control. Therefore, Alison is likely to think that her success was due to the fact that she's good at chemistry and just plain smart.

How can we explain this departure from the typical actor/observer pattern of attributions? The answer is that when people's self-esteem is threatened, they often make **self-serving attributions**. Simply put, these attributions refer to our tendency to take credit for our successes (by making internal attributions) but to blame others or the situation (by making external attributions) for our failures. Many studies have shown that people make internal attributions when they do well on a task but make external attributions when they do poorly (McAllister, 1996; Miller & Ross, 1975; Pronin, Lin & Ross, 2002; Robins & Beer, 2001).

A particularly interesting arena for studying self-serving attributions is professional sports. When explaining their victories, athletes and coaches point overwhelmingly to aspects of their own teams or players (Sherman & Kim, 2005). In fact, in an analysis of professional athletes' and coaches' explanations for their teams' wins and losses, it was found that 80 percent of the attributions for wins were to internal factors. Losses were more likely to be attributed to external factors (Lau & Russell, 1980). Consider, for example, a headline that appeared in the sports section of the August 15, 2008, *National Post:* "Humidity wears down Dancevic." Frank Dancevic, from Niagara Falls, Ontario, competed in his first Olympics in men's tennis in Beijing. He won the first set in a match

---

self-serving attributions

explanations for one's successes that credit internal, dispositional factors and explanations for one's failures that blame external, situational factors against ninth-seeded Stanislas Wawrinka, but lost the next two. This is how he explained his loss: "The humidity started getting to me as the match went on in the second set and it started sapping away at my body." He also pointed to the smog and pollution in Beijing: "I feel like my lungs are burning from the pollution and smog. . . . It's a huge factor" (Dancevic, as quoted in Arthur, 2008). In other words, Frank Dancevic made self-serving attributions—blaming the loss on external factors, rather than on himself.

We should note that there are some exceptions. For example, experienced athletes are less likely to make self-serving attributions than are less experienced ones. Experienced athletes realize that losses sometimes are their fault and that wins are not always because of them (Roesch & Amirkhan, 1997). Consider the attributions made by Susan Nattress, an Olympic athlete from Edmonton. Beijing was the sixth Olympics for this very experienced trap shooter. How did she explain her disappointing 11th place finish? By placing the blame squarely on her own shoulders: "I moved my eyes instead of letting the bird go and then moving my eyes. It's trying too hard. I was excited, so I moved before I really saw it" (Nattress, as quoted in Hall, 2008). You can explore self-serving attributions by sports figures in the accompanying Try It! exercise.

The self-serving bias has a number of important implications that extend well beyond the world of sports. For example, it leads people to believe that their actions are rational and defensible, but that the actions of others are unreasonable and unjustified. This phenomenon was demonstrated by Sande, Goethals, Ferrari, and Worth (1989), who found that U.S. students attributed positive motives to the United States for both positive actions (e.g., saving whales trapped in ice) and negative actions (e.g., building more nuclear-powered submarines). However, these same actions were attributed to negative, self-serving motives if participants were told the actions had been performed by the former Soviet Union. Apparently one participant remarked that the only reason Soviets would save trapped whales was to slaughter and eat them later; another participant assumed that the whales must have been blocking Soviet shipping lanes! Canadian students tended to attribute similar motives to U.S. and Soviet actions.

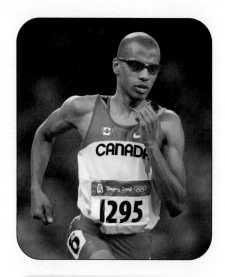

▲ After the first heat of the men's 800-metre race at the Beijing Olympics, it wasn't clear whether Gary Reed, from Kamloops, B.C., would qualify for the finals. How did this experienced athlete explain his disappointing performance? "I made stupid mistakes"? "I made mental errors"? "I ran a bad race"? He did ultimately qualify, and finished in fourth place.

Try it!

▶ Self-Serving Attributions in the Sports Pages

Do athletes and coaches tend to take credit for their wins but make excuses for their losses? Find out for yourself the next time you read the sports section of the newspaper or watch television interviews after a game. Analyze the sports figures' comments to see what kinds of attributions they make about the cause of their performance. Is the pattern a self-serving one? For example, after a win, does the athlete make such internal attributions as, "We won because of excellent teamwork; our defensive line really held today" or "My serve was totally on"? After a loss, does the athlete make such external attributions as, "All the injuries we've had this season have really hurt us" or "That line judge made every call against me"?

According to the research, these self-serving attributions should occur more often than the opposite pattern where, for example, a winner says, "We won because the other team played so badly it was like they were dead" (external), or where a loser says, "I played terribly today. I stank" (internal).

Finally, think about why people make self-serving attributions. If, for example, a famous athlete such as Sidney Crosby attributes his team's loss to factors outside himself, do you think he is protecting his self-esteem (i.e., trying to look good in front of others) or making the most logical attribution he can, given his experience (i.e., he's so talented, most team losses really aren't his fault)?

Self-serving biases also tend to creep in whenever we work on tasks with others (Sande, Ellard, & Ross, 1986; Shestowsky, Wegener, & Fabrigar, 1998; Zanna & Sande, 1987). For example, in a classic study conducted at the University of Waterloo, Ross and Sicoly (1979) found that students working on a group project had very good memories when asked to recall their contributions to the project. However, their memories were considerably poorer when asked to recall the contributions of the other group members. As you may have observed, this tendency extends even to our closest relationships. In another study, Ross and Sicoly (1979) asked married couples living in student housing at the University of Waterloo to indicate the extent to which each spouse assumed responsibility for 20 different activities (e.g., cooking, deciding how money should be spent, resolving conflicts). Each person tended to overestimate his or her contribution, such that when the husband's and wife's estimates of responsibility were added, the total was greater than 100 percent!

Finally, research suggests that, like the other attributional biases we have discussed, the self-serving bias has a strong cultural component as well. For example, traditional Chinese culture values modesty and harmony with others. As a result, Chinese students are expected to attribute their successes to other people—such as their parents or teachers—or to other aspects of the situation—such as the quality of their school—rather than to themselves (Bond, 1996; Leung, 1996). Indeed, in several experiments, researchers have found that Chinese participants take less credit for their successes and more blame for their failures than do American participants (Anderson, 1999; Lee & Seligman, 1997; Oishi, Wyer, & Colcombe, 2000). In Chapter 5, we will discuss related research showing that Asian students tend not to believe success feedback but readily accept failure feedback, whereas Canadian students show just the opposite tendency.

Defensive Attributions People also alter their attributions to deal with other kinds of threats to their self-esteem. One of the hardest things to understand in life is the occurrence of tragic events, such as sexual assaults, terminal diseases, and fatal accidents. Even when they happen to strangers we have never met, they can be upsetting. They remind us that if such tragedies can happen to someone else, they can happen to us. One way we deal with this is by making **defensive attributions**, which are explanations for behaviour that defend us from feelings of vulnerability and mortality.

One form of defensive attribution is **unrealistic optimism**, wherein people believe that good things are *more* likely to happen to them than to others, and bad things are *less* likely to happen to them than to others (Harris, 1996; Heine & Lehman, 1995; Klein, 1996; Regan, Snyder, & Kassin, 1995; Weinstein & Klein, 1996). Suppose we asked you to estimate how likely it is that each of the following will happen to you, compared with how likely it is that they will happen to other students at your college or university: owning your own home, liking your postgraduate job, living past age 80, having a drinking problem, getting divorced, and being unable to have children. When Neil Weinstein (1980) asked students these and similar questions, he found that people were too optimistic. Virtually everyone thought that the good things were more likely to happen to them than to their peers and that the bad things were less likely to happen to them than to their peers.

Unrealistic optimism seems to pervade all aspects of people's lives, including women's attitudes about getting breast cancer and men's attitudes about getting prostate cancer (Clarke et al., 2000), heroin users' attitudes about the risk of overdosing (McGregor, Darke, Ali, & Christie, 1998), gamblers' attitudes about winning the lottery (Rogers, 1998), motorcyclists' attitudes about having a serious accident (Rutter, Quine, & Albery, 1998), and bungee jumpers' attitudes

defensive attributions

explanations for behaviour that avoid feelings of vulnerability and mortality

unrealistic optimism

a form of defensive attribution wherein people think that good things are more likely to happen to them than to their peers and that bad things are less likely to happen to them than to their peers about the risk of injury (Middleton, Harris, & Surman, 1996). We seem to cling to the belief that bad things are more likely to happen to others than to us.

According to research conducted at the University of Waterloo, unrealistic optimism abounds when it comes to people's romantic relationships. For example, Murray and Holmes (1997) found that both dating and married couples claimed that they were unlikely to encounter the kinds of difficulties and conflicts that affect most relationships. They also believed that should problems arise, they were better equipped to deal with them than the average couple. When forecasting the fate of their relationship, these couples believed that their relationship had a brighter future than most.

Similarly, MacDonald and Ross (1999) found that University of Waterloo students who were in dating relationships expected that their relationship would last longer than that of the typical first-year student. In an interesting twist, they also asked each participant's parents and dormitory roommates how long they thought the participant's relationship would last. These "outsiders" were less optimistic about the longevity of these relationships than were the participants themselves. Who was right? To answer this question, the researchers contacted the participants over the next year to see whether their relationships were still intact. It turned out that the participants' parents and roommates were better at predicting how long these relationships would last than were the unrealistically optimistic participants. Apparently, when judging the likelihood of their relationship surviving, the participants tended to focus only on its positive aspects, whereas parents and roommates were more likely to take negative information into account. This more balanced approach resulted in more accurate predictions. Thus, if you are in a dating relationship and are wondering whether it will last, your best bet is to ask your friend or your mother!

Research conducted at McGill University shows that we are most likely to show this kind of unrealistic optimism when we have decided that we want a relationship to continue and are focusing on achieving that goal (Gagné & Lydon, 2001). In contrast, if we are in the process of assessing the pros and cons of staying in a relationship, we tend to be in a more realistic frame of mind. And this greater realism enables us to make more accurate forecasts about the chances of the relationship surviving (Gagné, Lydon, & Bartz, 2003).

Finally, on a much sadder note, battered women have also been found to be unrealistically optimistic about the personal risks they run when they return to live with their abusive partners. They estimate that their own risk is significantly lower than the risk of most battered women—even when the facts of their situation would suggest otherwise (Martin et al., 2000). Thus, although unrealistic optimism may help us feel better in the short term, in the long term it can be a potentially fatal attribution error.

Before leaving this topic, we note that like many of the other attributional biases we have been discussing, unrealistic optimism also may be a Western phenomenon. In a study by Heine and Lehman (1995), students at the University of British Columbia showed classic unrealistic optimism. They assumed that negative events (e.g., contracting AIDS, becoming an alcoholic) were less likely to happen to them than the "average" UBC student, and that positive events were more likely to happen to them. However, when students at Nagasaki University in Japan were asked to make the same judgments, the opposite was true: Japanese students believed that bad things were more likely to happen to them and good things were less likely to happen to them than to the average student at their university.

Belief in a Just World   Another form of defensive attributions is to believe that bad things happen only to bad people—or at least, only to people who make stupid

belief in a just world

a form of defensive attribution wherein people assume that bad things happen to bad people and that good things happen to good people

mistakes or poor choices. Therefore, bad things won't happen to us because we won't be that stupid or careless. Melvin Lerner (1980; Lerner & Simmons, 1966), formerly at the University of Waterloo, has called this the **belief in a just world**—the assumption that people get what they deserve and deserve what they get. By using this attributional bias, the perceiver does not have to acknowledge that there is a certain randomness in life—that an accident or a criminal or unemployment may be just around the corner for an innocent person. Indeed, in an ingenious set of experiments, Carolyn Hafer (2000a) at Brock University demonstrated that the more people's belief in a just world was threatened by hearing about an attack on an innocent person, the more likely they were to derogate the victim's character and to distance themselves from the victim. Presumably, by doing so they were able to convince themselves that bad things happen only to bad people—and since they themselves are good, surely no misfortune will befall them. A recent review of 66 experiments that have been conducted since the 1980 review published by Lerner confirms that there is solid research evidence that people engage in this kind of defensive attribution (Hafer & Bègue, 2005). One development in this work has been to explore the functions of just-world beliefs. According to Hafer (2000b, 2002), such beliefs motivate us to invest in our future. The idea is that we will not be very motivated to plan ahead and make long-term investments if we believe that the world is an unfair, unjust place. To test this idea, Hafer (2000b) asked Brock University students to write an essay about their plans after graduation; other students were asked to write about their current university courses and activities. Later, all students saw a video of a young woman named Sarah who was seeing a counsellor because she had recently contracted a sexually transmitted disease. In the "innocent victim" version of the videotape, Sarah said that she and her partner had used a condom but it had broken during sex. In the "not innocent" version, Sarah admitted that no condom had been used. Who was most likely to blame Sarah for contracting the disease, even when she was portrayed as an innocent victim? You guessed it—the students who earlier had been asked to focus on their long-term goals and plans. Presumably, these participants most needed to be reassured that their long-term investments would be rewarded according to principles of fairness and justice. By blaming Sarah for her fate, they were able to maintain this belief.

Finally, recent research conducted at the University of Calgary shows that people are so motivated to maintain the belief that the world is a just place that they will engage in irrational thinking in order to preserve this belief (Callan, Ellard, & Nicol, 2006). In one of these studies, participants were told that a man was seriously injured when he was hit by a car. Some participants were also told that the man was having an affair. Others (in a control condition) were not given this information. Participants who were told the man was having an affair were more likely to think that he deserved to be in the accident than those in the control group. Thus, even though the two events were completely unrelated, participants linked them in order to preserve their belief that the world is a just place. Does this sound far-fetched? Consider the horrific stabbing and beheading of Tim McLean—a passenger riding a Greyhound bus that was travelling from Winnipeg to Edmonton on August 2, 2008. The murder was clearly unprovoked. In fact, McLean was sleeping when he was first attacked. How does one preserve a belief in a just world in the face of such a shocking, tragic event? According to one religious group in Kansas, God sent a man to behead McLean as punishment for Canada's liberal stance on homosexuality, abortion, and adultery. Members of this group planned to attend McLean's funeral in order to convey this message (Gackle, 2008). This example shows that there seems to be no limit to the lengths that people will go to in order to assure themselves that the world is a just place where people get what they deserve.

Consequences of Just-World Beliefs Suppose a female student on your campus was the victim of a date rape by a male fellow student. How do you think you and your friends would react? Would you wonder if she'd done something to trigger the sexual assault? Was she acting suggestively earlier in the evening? Had she invited the man into her room? Research by Elaine Walster ((Hatfield), 1966) and others has focused on such attributions (e.g., Burger, 1981; Lerner & Miller, 1978; Stormo, Lang, & Stritzke, 1997). In several experiments, it has been found that the victims of crimes or accidents are often seen as causing their fate. For example, people tend to believe that rape victims are to blame for the sexual assault (Bell, Kuriloff, & Lottes, 1994; Burt, 1980; Lambert & Raichle, 2000). Those who believe in rape myths (e.g., women falsely report rape to get attention) are especially likely to engage in victim blaming, as shown by research conducted at the University of Manitoba (Morry & Winkler, 2001).

Similarly, battered wives are frequently seen as responsible for their abusive husbands' behaviour (Summers & Feldman, 1984). According to research conducted at Carleton University (Kristiansen & Giulietti, 1990) and at Mount Saint Vincent University (Perrott, Miller, & Delaney, 1997), women are especially likely to be blamed for domestic assaults if they are seen as having done something to provoke their partner (see Connections on page 13 in Chapter 1).

CONNECTIONS

Attributional Biases: Present in the Courtroom?

Sadly, the tendency to blame victims extends to the courtroom. Consider, for example, the 1998 case of *R. v. Ewanchuk*. The complainant in this case was a 17-year-old woman who was raped by a man while he was interviewing her for a job. The man was 45-year-old Steve Ewanchuk, a contractor with a history of convictions for rape and aggravated sexual assault. At the time of this incident, he was under a court order not to hire any females under the age of 18. The young woman testified in the Alberta Court of Queen's Bench that she did not consent to Ewanchuk's advances and in fact felt very afraid during their encounter. The trial judge, however, held her responsible for not having communicated her fear and ruled that consent had been implied. As a result, Ewanchuk was acquitted. The case then went to the Alberta Court of Appeal. One of the appeal judges commented that Ewanchuk's actions were "far less criminal than hormonal" and suggested that the 17-year-old should have taken actions to stop him by using "a well-chosen expletive, a slap in the face, or, if necessary, a well-directed knee" (*R. v. Ewanchuk*, 1998). Once again, Ewanchuk was acquitted. This decision was finally overturned by the Supreme Court of Canada in 1999, which ruled that there is no such thing as implied consent. One of the Supreme Court judges, Madam Justice L'Heureux-Dubé, wrote, "This case is not about consent, since none was given. It is about myths and stereotyping." These myths include the belief that a woman could resist a sexual attack if she really wanted to, that women deserve to be raped because of the way they dress, and so on. Despite the Supreme Court's ruling, concerns remain that women who are the victims of sexual assault will be further victimized by rape myths and by victim blaming when they appear in the courtroom (L'Heureux-Dubé, 2001; Tang, 2000).

(*Note:* On November 8, 2005, Steve Ewanchuk was convicted of repeatedly sexually assaulting an eight-year old girl. The Crown attempted to have him labelled as a dangerous offender, which would have kept him behind bars indefinitely. However, on January 26, 2007, an Edmonton judge rejected the dangerous offender label, choosing instead to declare Steve Ewanchuk a long-term offender—meaning that he will be supervised in the community for 10 years after serving the term for his most recent conviction.)

We should point out that it is not only female victims of violence who are blamed. Perrott and Webber (1996) presented students at Mount Saint Vincent University with scenarios in which a man or a woman was attacked. Overall, there was greater blaming of female victims than of male victims. However, male victims were not exempt from blame. Moreover, different attributions were made for the assault, depending on the victim's gender. Female victims were blamed for being "too trusting" and for not having anticipated the assault. Male victims, on the other hand, were blamed for not having been able to fight off the attackers. Perrott and Webber found the extent of victim blaming disturbing, especially given most of their participants were female students attending a university that has a strong women's issues focus.

To end on a more positive note, you may be less vulnerable to making these kinds of attributions simply because you are taking this course! Guimond and Palmer (1996) studied the attributions of social science and commerce students at an Ontario university over a three-year period. The two groups of students made similar attributions for poverty and unemployment in their first year of university. However, by their third year, commerce students were more likely to make dispositional attributions—blaming the poor for their poverty and the unemployed for their unemployment, whereas social science students were more likely to make situational attributions. Similar results were obtained in a subsequent study comparing the attributions of social science and engineering students in a Canadian Armed Forces college (Guimond, 1999).

How Accurate Are Our Attributions and Impressions?

When we make attributions, our goal is to be able to understand other people and predict what they will do. It is obviously to our advantage to make attributions that are as accurate as possible. But how accurate are we? The answer in a nutshell is that under many circumstances, we are not very accurate, especially compared with how accurate we *think* we are. For example, research has found that first impressions—the quick, attributional snapshots we form when we first meet someone—are not very accurate (DePaulo, Kenny, Hoover, Webb, & Oliver, 1987; Funder & Colvin, 1988). However, our impressions of others do become more accurate the more we get to know them (Wegener & Petty, 1995). At the University of British Columbia, Delroy Paulhus and his colleagues (Paulhus & Bruce, 1992; Paulhus & Reynolds, 1995) had students complete a variety of standard personality questionnaires. They then interacted in groups on a weekly basis for a seven-week period. Each group consisted of between five and seven students who had not previously known one another. After weeks 1, 4, and 7, the group members rated one another's personalities. As shown in Figure 4.11, the correlation between students' self-ratings and the group members' ratings of them increased over time, suggesting that people's perceptions of one another were becoming more accurate. Note that the accuracy of the group members' perceptions was far from perfect. (Recall from Chapter 2 that a perfect correlation is 1.00.) But it did increase significantly with increased acquaintance. Similar findings were obtained in more recent research assessing acquaintanceship among roommates at Queen's University (Starzyk, Holden, Fabrigar, & MacDonald, 2006). It is also the case that as we get to know someone and observe them in a wider variety of situations, our impressions become more specific and finely nuanced. Moreover, these more specific traits become

FIGURE 4.11

Accuracy of impressions of other people

As we get to know people, our impressions of them correspond more closely to how they view themselves. In a study by Paulhus and Bruce (1992), students' impressions of one another became more accurate over time.

organized into a coherent whole. Thus, our impressions become more complex and sophisticated, rather than having only a general impression of the person, as demonstrated by UBC researcher Jeremy Biesanz and colleagues (Biesanz, West, & Millevoi, 2007).

Thus, the evidence suggests that our impressions of others do become more accurate as we get to know them. However, it is also apparent that there is plenty of room for improvement. Sometimes our impressions of other people—even those we know well—are just plain wrong. Why might that be?

The first culprit is our familiar friend, the fundamental attribution error. People are too ready to attribute others' actions to their personalities rather than to the situations. For example, suppose you meet Andrea at a party and she is acting in an outgoing, sociable manner. If you are like most people, you will conclude that Andrea is outgoing and sociable, rather than taking into consideration that you are meeting her in a situation where most people act sociably—a fun party. We don't mean to imply that people are always wrong when making dispositional attributions, but when they overlook situational causes of another person's behaviour they are likely to end up with faulty impressions.

To improve the accuracy of your impressions, remember that the fundamental attribution error, the actor/observer difference, and defensive attributions exist, and try to counteract these biases. Before deciding that another person is shy, for example, ask yourself whether the situation that he or she is in might account for the seeming shyness. Even if a person actually is shy, try to resist the tendency to draw inferences about his or her other qualities based on your implicit personality theories. For example, UBC researchers Paulhus and Morgan (1997) found that if someone was shy, people also tended to assume that the person was unintelligent—an assumption that simply was not true. To reduce defensive attributions, it can be helpful to give our self-esteem a boost (e.g., via self-affirmation; see Chapter 6) so that we are less likely to feel threatened when we fail or when bad things happen (Sherman & Kim, 2005).

Let's cut to the chase. Yes, we are quite accurate perceivers of other people. We do very well most of the time. We are adept at reading and interpreting nonverbal forms of communication; in fact, most of us are actually better at this than we realize (Ambady, Bernieri, & Richeson, 2000; Archer & Akert, 1980). We become more accurate at perceiving others as we get to know them better, and since most of our truly important social interactions involve people we know well, this is good news. In short, we are capable of making both blindingly accurate assessments of people and horrific attributional mistakes.

SUMMARY

Social perception is the study of how people form impressions and make inferences about other people. People constantly form such impressions because doing so helps them understand and predict their social worlds.

One source of information people use is the nonverbal behaviour of others. **Nonverbal communication** is used to **encode** or express emotion, convey attitudes, communicate personality traits, and facilitate and regulate verbal speech. Many studies show that people can accurately **decode** subtle nonverbal cues, although there is debate surrounding the claim that six basic facial expressions of emotion are perceived accurately around the world. One reason that perception of emotion can be inaccurate is that the context in which a face is perceived can influence the emotion attributed to it. Also, sometimes facial expressions are **affect blends**, in which one part of the face registers one emotion and another part of the face registers another. In addition, facial expressions vary according to culturally determined **display rules**. These rules dictate which expressions are appropriate to display. **Emblems**—nonverbal gestures that have specific meanings—are also culturally determined.

Often it is difficult to tell how someone feels, or what kind of person he or she is, solely from his or her nonverbal behaviour. As a result, we go beyond the information given in people's behaviour, making inferences about their feelings, traits, and motives. One way we do this is to rely on an **implicit personality theory** to fill in the blanks. Such a theory is composed of our general notions about which personality traits go together in one person. While the use of implicit personality theories allows us to form impressions of others efficiently, there can be some serious consequences when, for example, people decide that because a potential sexual partner is likeable, he or she does not have AIDS.

According to **attribution theory**, we try to determine why people do what they do, in order to uncover the feelings and traits that are behind their actions. The **covariation model**, a theory of attribution, focuses on observations of behaviour across time, place, different actors, and different targets of the behaviour, and examines how the perceiver chooses either an **internal** or an **external attribution**. We make such choices by using **consensus**, **distinctiveness**, and **consistency** information.

People also use various mental shortcuts when making attributions. One common shortcut is the **correspondence bias**, the tendency to believe that behaviour corresponds to disposition. This bias can lead to the **fundamental attribution error**, which is

the tendency to overestimate the extent to which people do what they do because of internal, dispositional factors. According to the **two-step process of attribution**, the initial, automatic attribution about another person's behaviour tends to be dispositional, but it can be corrected at the second step with conscious and effortful thinking, bringing to mind possible situational explanations. A reason for this automatic attribution to dispositional factors is that a person's behaviour often has greater **perceptual salience** than the surrounding situation. The fundamental attribution error can result in tragic consequences, such as blaming victims for their victimization and denying them the help they need.

The **actor/observer difference** is a qualification of the fundamental attribution error: We are more likely to commit this error when explaining other people's behaviour than when explaining our own behaviour. The actor/observer effect occurs because perceptual saliency and information availability differ for the actor and the observer.

People's attributions are also influenced by their personal needs. **Self-serving attributions** occur when people make internal attributions for their successes and external attributions for their failures.

Defensive attributions help people avoid feelings of mortality. One type of defensive attribution is **unrealistic optimism** about the future, whereby we think that good things are more likely to happen to us than to other people, and that bad things are less likely to happen to us than to others. Another type of defensive attribution is the **belief in a just world**, whereby we believe that bad things happen to bad people and good things happen to good people. Like the fundamental attribution error, defensive attributions also can lead to blaming victims for their plight in order to preserve a sense of the world as a just place.

Culture plays an important role in the formation of attributions. People from collectivist cultures are more aware of situational explanations of behaviour and therefore are less likely to make the fundamental attribution error and less likely to show the actor/observer effect than members of individualist cultures. People from collectivist cultures are also less likely to fall prey to self-serving biases and unrealistic optimism than are people in individualistic cultures.

Not surprisingly, the more we get to know someone, the more accurate we are. Moreover, our impressions of other people become more complex and sophisticated as we observe them in a wide variety of settings.

Along with a dynamic, electronic version of this text, MyPsychLab offers a wealth of resources to deepen your understanding and test your recall of the material in this chapter—including video and audio clips, simulations and activities, self-assessments, practice tests, and other study materials. The following specific resources are available for this chapter:

 Fundamental Attribution Error

 Internal & External Attributions

 Social Perception

To access MyPsychLab, please visit www.mypsychlab.com (Student Access Code required—packaged with this book).

5

Self-Knowledge and the Need to Maintain Self-Esteem

"Who I Am Because of Who She Was" is the title of a memoir by Canadian writer Eva Tihanyi. In the story, Tihanyi reflects on the role her Hungarian-born grandmother played in shaping her sense of self. Eva Tihanyi was raised by her grandmother for much of her life and dedicated one of her books to her with these words: "My grandmother, Elizabeth Kalán Tihanyi, without whom I would not have become who I am." Exactly who is Eva Tihanyi? This is how she answers the question: "Who I am is a dogma-hating feminist who insists on thinking for herself; a wife who has maintained her own idea of what it is to be a wife; a mother who loves her son unconditionally but has not sacrificed her own self to do so; a teacher who believes that a classroom is an exciting forum rather than a jail; a writer for whom writing is not just an act of putting words on paper but also a way of viewing the world" (Tihanyi, 1999, p. 102).

If you were asked to answer the question, "Who am I?" what responses would you give? Would they be similar to or different from those of Eva Tihanyi? How did you become who you are? Were there particular people who were influential in developing your sense of self?

More generally, what is the nature of the self, and how do people discover it? As we will discuss, the process by which people come to know themselves, and how they evaluate this knowledge, is a fascinating one. These are the questions to which we now turn.

◄ Eva Tihanyi (age six) and her grandmother, Elizabeth Kalán Tihanyi, at the Budapest airport in 1962. Eva is about to board the plane that brings her to Canada to be reunited with her parents.

The Nature of the Self

Who are you? How did you come to be this person you call "myself"? One of the founders of psychology, William James (1842–1910), described the basic duality of our perception of self. First, the self is composed of one's thoughts and beliefs about oneself, or what James (1890) called the "known" or more simply the "me." Second, the self is also the active processor of information, the "knower" or the "I." In modern terms, we refer to the "known" aspect of the self as the **self-concept**, which is the contents of the self (our knowledge about who we are), and to the "knower" aspect as **self-awareness**, which is the act of thinking about ourselves. These two aspects of the self combine to create a coherent sense of identity. Your self is both a book—full of fascinating contents collected over time—and the reader of that book—who at any moment can access a specific chapter or add a new one. In this chapter, we will focus on these aspects of the self: the nature of the self-concept and how people come to know themselves through self-awareness. In the last part of the chapter, we will focus on self-esteem: whether we evaluate our self positively or negatively.

A good place to begin is with the question of whether humans are the only species with a sense of self. Some fascinating studies suggest that we are not alone in this regard. Gallup (1977; Gallup & Suarez, 1986) placed a mirror in an animal's cage until the animal became familiar with it. The animal was then briefly anaesthetized and an odourless red dye was painted on its brow or ear (called the "rouge test"). What happens when the animal wakes up and looks in the mirror? Chimpanzees and orangutans immediately touch the area of their heads that contains the red spot. Dolphins also have shown signs of recognizing themselves in mirrors (Emery & Clayton, 2005; Reiss & Marino, 2001). These studies indicate that chimps and orangutans, and possibly dolphins, have a rudimentary self-concept. They realize that the image in the mirror is them and not another animal, and recognize that they look different from the way they looked before (Gallup, Anderson, & Shillito, 2002; Kennan, Gallup, & Falk, 2003).

What about humans? Researchers have used a variation of the rouge test with humans and found that self-recognition develops at around two years of age (Courage, Edison, & Howe, 2004; Lewis & Ramsay, 2004). As we grow older, this self-concept, of course, becomes more complex. Psychologists have studied how people's self-concept changes from childhood to adulthood by asking people of different ages to answer a simple question: "Who am I?" Typically, a child's self-concept is concrete, with references to clear-cut, easily observable characteristics

self-concept

the contents of the self; that is, our knowledge about who we are

self-awareness

the act of thinking about ourselves

▶ Researchers have examined whether species other than humans have a self-concept by seeing whether they recognize that an image in a mirror is themselves and not another member of their species. The same procedure has been used with humans, revealing that people develop a self-concept at about the age of two.

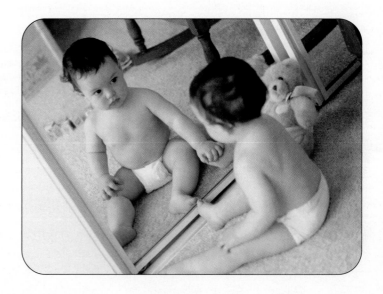

such as age, sex, neighbourhood, and hobbies. For example, a nine-year-old answered the question, "Who am I?" this way: "I have brown eyes. I have brown hair. I have brown eyebrows. . . . I'm a boy. I have an uncle that is almost seven feet tall" (Montemayor & Eisen, 1977). As we mature, we place less emphasis on physical characteristics and more emphasis on our psychological states (e.g., our thoughts and feelings), our traits or characteristics, and considerations of how other people judge us (Hart & Damon, 1986; Montemayor & Eisen, 1977; Sande, Goethals, & Radloff, 1988). Thus, we might define ourselves as an extrovert, a cautious person, a spiritual person, an only child, a worrier, someone who is not very interested in politics, and so on.

Research conducted by Jennifer Campbell at the University of British Columbia suggests that some of us have a clearer sense of self than others. Self-concept clarity is defined as the extent to which knowledge about the self is stable, and clearly and consistently defined (Campbell, 1990; Campbell, Trapnell, Heine, Katz, Lavallee, & Lehman, 1996). Self-concept clarity has important cognitive and emotional implications (Campbell & Fehr, 1990; Campbell, Assanand, & Di Paula, 2000). For example, people who are low in self-concept clarity are more likely to be neurotic and have low self-esteem, and are less likely to be aware of their internal states. They also engage in chronic self-analysis and rumination—an involuntary, negative form of self-focus associated with threat or uncertainty (e.g., "Sometimes it's hard for me to shut off thoughts about myself"). People low in self-concept clarity are less likely to engage in positive forms of self-focus such as reflection (e.g., "I love exploring my 'inner self'"; Campbell et al., 1996). Thus, not having a clear, confident sense of who you are can have negative effects on your thoughts and emotions. To find out where you stand in terms of self-concept clarity, see the Try It! on the next page.

Functions of the Self

We have seen that people develop a self-concept at an early age and that people differ in terms of self-concept clarity. But why do humans have self-concepts in the first place? Researchers have found that the self serves both an organizational function and an executive function (Baumeister, 1998; Graziano, Jensen-Campbell, & Finch, 1997; Leary & Tangney, 2003).

Organizational Function of the Self   As we saw in Chapter 3, schemas help us organize what we know about the social world; schemas also influence the information we notice, think about, and remember. Similarly, we have **self-schemas**—mental structures that help us to organize our knowledge about ourselves (Markus, 1977; Oyserman, Kemmelmeir, Fryberg, Brosh, & Hart-Johnson, 2003; Shadel, Cervone, Niaura, & Abrams, 2004; von Hippel, Hawkins, & Schooler, 2001).

> **self-schemas**
> mental structures that people use to organize their knowledge about themselves and that influence what they notice, think about, and remember about themselves

Suppose that over the course of a day, Sarah and Caitlin play volleyball together and watch an old movie on television. How will they organize, remember, and think about these experiences? It depends on their self-schemas. Say that Sarah plays a lot of sports and that athleticism is an important part of her self-schema. She is likely to think about and remember the volleyball game more than the movie. Caitlin, on the other hand, has performed in several plays and loves to act. Because acting is more likely to be part of Caitlin's self-schema, she will think about and remember the movie more than the volleyball game. Self-schemas also act as lenses through which people view others. Suppose that Sarah and Caitlin meet Sam, a talented athlete and actor. Sarah is more likely to notice and remember his athletic skills, whereas Caitlin is more likely to notice and remember his acting talents (Showers & Zeigler-Hill, 2003).

Having a rich set of self-schemas can be advantageous. Try this experiment out on your friends. Divide your friends into two groups, and read them a list of 20 adjectives, such as "warm," "colourful," "quiet," and "soft." Ask one group to

Try it!

▶ A Measure of Self-Concept Clarity[†]

		strongly disagree				strongly agree
1. My beliefs about myself often conflict with one another.*		1	2	3	4	5
2. One day I might have one opinion of myself and on another day I might have a different opinion.*		1	2	3	4	5
3. I spend a lot of time wondering about what kind of person I really am.*		1	2	3	4	5
4. Sometimes I feel that I am not really the person that I appear to be.*		1	2	3	4	5
5. When I think about the kind of person I have been in the past, I'm not sure what I was really like.*		1	2	3	4	5
6. I seldom experience conflict between the different aspects of my personality.		1	2	3	4	5
7. Sometimes I think I know other people better than I know myself.*		1	2	3	4	5
8. My beliefs about myself seem to change very frequently.*		1	2	3	4	5
9. If I were asked to describe my personality, my description might end up being different from one day to another day.*		1	2	3	4	5
10. Even if I wanted to, I don't think I could tell someone what I'm really like.*		1	2	3	4	5
11. In general, I have a clear sense of who I am and what I am.		1	2	3	4	5
12. It is often hard for me to make up my mind about things because I don't really know what I want.*		1	2	3	4	5

[†]This Self-Concept Clarity Scale was developed by Campbell, Trapnell, Heine, Katz, Lavallee, & Lehman (1996) to measure the extent to which people have a stable, clear, and consistently defined sense of self. The items with asterisks (*) are reverse-scored. To find out how you score on this scale, first reverse your answers to the items with asterisks. If you answered 5, change it to a 1; if you answered 4, change it to a 2, and so on. Then sum your ratings on all 12 questions. The higher your score, the more clearly defined your sense of self is. Among Canadian students, average scores on this scale range from 38 to 43. The researchers expected that in less individualist cultures, such as Japan, scores would be lower on this scale. Indeed, when University of British Columbia students completed the Self-Concept Clarity Scale, the average score was 40; when students in Japan completed the scale, the average score was 35.

(Adapted from Campbell et al., 1996. Copyright 1996 by the American Psychological Association. Reprinted with permission.)

self-reference effect

the tendency for people to remember information better if they relate it to themselves

think about how much each adjective describes themselves, and ask the other group to think about how much it describes someone else. Then ask both groups to write down as many of the words as they can remember. More than likely you will find a **self-reference effect**, which is the tendency for people to remember information better if they relate it to themselves (Markus, 1977; Kihlstrom, Beer, & Klein, 2003; Symons & Johnson, 1997). Integrating information with our self-schemas helps us organize it better and connect it to other information about ourselves, which makes us more likely to remember it later.

Of course, as we learned in Chapter 3, our schemas can also bias memory processes. At the University of Waterloo, Ziva Kunda and her colleagues (Kunda, Fong, Sanitioso, & Reber, 1993; Sanitioso, Kunda, & Fong, 1990) found that the desire to see ourselves in a positive light can influence which of our past actions we are most likely to remember. For example, in one of their studies, participants were told that research shows that the trait of introversion is associated with professional success; others were told that extroversion is associated with success. All participants were then asked to list behaviours they had performed that were relevant to the dimension of introversion/extroversion. Those who were led to believe that introversion was associated with success were more likely to remember introverted, rather than extroverted, behaviours they had performed. The opposite was true for those who were led to believe that extroversion was associated with success (Sanitioso, Kunda, & Fong, 1990). According to the researchers, when people are motivated to see themselves as possessing a desired quality or trait, they conduct a selective memory search for examples of past behaviours consistent with that trait. This body of evidence then allows them to draw the "rational" conclusion that the desirable trait is part of their self-schemas.

Self-Regulation: The Executive Function   The self also serves an executive function, regulating people's behaviour, choices, and plans for the future, much like the chief executive officer of a corporation (Baumeister & Vohs, 2003; Carver & Scheier, 1998; Higgins, 1989, 2005; Leary, 2004). We appear to be the only species that can imagine events that have not yet occurred and engage in long-term planning, and it is the self that does this planning and exerts control over our actions (Gilbert, 2006). Regulating our behaviour and choices in optimal ways, of course, can be easier said than done, as anyone who has been on a diet or tried to quit smoking knows. An interesting question, then, is how the self engages in self-regulation. When we face a difficult choice ("Should I go to the party or study for my midterm?"), what determines how successful we will be at exerting self-control?

We discuss these questions in relation to health-related behaviours (e.g., trying to quit smoking) in Module 2. For now, we will briefly mention an intriguing theory of self-control called the *self-regulatory resource model*. According to this model, self-control is a limited resource, like a muscle that gets tired with frequent use but then rebounds in strength (Baumeister & Hetherington, 1996; Schmeichel & Baumeister, 2004; Vohs, Baumeister, & Ciarocco, 2005). The idea is that people have a limited amount of energy to devote to self-control and that spending it on one task limits the amount that can be spent on another task, just as going for a 10 kilometre run makes it difficult to then immediately play a game of basketball.

This idea has been tested by having participants exert self-control on one task and then assessing whether this reduces their ability to exert control on a subsequent, completely unrelated task. In one study, for example, people who were instructed to suppress a thought (don't think about a white bear) were worse at trying to regulate their emotions on a second task (try not to laugh while watching a comedy film), compared with people who did not first have to suppress their thoughts (Muraven, Tice, & Baumeister, 1998). Although the tasks were quite different, the researchers suggested that the first task depleted the resource people use to control their behaviours and feelings, making it difficult to engage in a subsequent act of self-control. More recent research has shown that if people are asked to make a very positive impression on another person (a task that presumably requires some effort), they subsequently show more depletion (e.g., lowered persistence on tasks, more likely to "blurt" things out) compared with when they are told to act neutral (Vohs et al., 2005).

These findings help explain why we often fail at self-control when we are under stress. Former smokers, for example, are more likely to take up smoking again when experiencing life's slings and arrows. Dealing with stress depletes the "self resource," such that there is less to spend in other areas. Similarly, efforts at self-control are more likely to fail at night, when the self resource has been depleted by a day of making choices and resisting temptations; dieters are more likely to break their diets at night, and bulimics are more likely to engage in binge eating at night (Baumeister, Muraven, & Tice, 2000). People are best at self-control when they are well rested and not too stressed out.

Cultural Differences in Defining the Self

In June 1993, Masako Owada, a 29-year-old Japanese woman, married Crown Prince Naruhito of Japan. Masako was a very bright career diplomat in the foreign ministry, educated at Harvard and Oxford. She spoke five languages and

▲ People had very different reactions to Masako Owada's decision to give up her promising career to marry Crown Prince Naruhito of Japan—due in part to cultural differences in the importance of independence versus interdependence.

was on the fast track to a prestigious diplomatic career. Her decision to marry the prince surprised some observers because it meant she would have to give up her career. Indeed, she gave up any semblance of an independent life, becoming subservient to the prince and the rest of the royal family and spending much of her time participating in rigid royal ceremonies. Her primary role was to produce a male heir to the royal throne.

How do you feel about Masako's decision to marry the prince? Your answer may say something about the nature of your self-concept and the culture in which you grew up. As mentioned in Chapter 4, in many Western cultures, people have an **independent view of the self**, which is defining oneself in terms of one's own internal thoughts, feelings, and actions, and not in terms of the thoughts, feelings, and actions of others (Heine et al., 1999; Kitayama & Markus, 1994; Kitayama & Uchida, 2005; Markus & Kitayama, 1991, 2001; Triandis, 1995). Westerners learn to define themselves as quite separate from other people and to value independence and uniqueness. Thus, many Western observers were mystified by Masako's decision to marry the crown prince. Some assumed she was coerced into the marriage by a backward, sexist society that did not properly value her worth as an individual with an independent life of her own.

In contrast, many Asian and other collectivist cultures have an **interdependent view of the self**, which is defining oneself in terms of one's relationships to other people and recognizing that one's behaviour is often determined by the thoughts, feelings, and actions of others. Connectedness and interdependence between people is valued, whereas independence and uniqueness are frowned on. For example, people from Asian cultures are more likely to see themselves in terms of communal qualities such as being kind, accepting, and loyal, whereas Canadians are more likely to see themselves in terms of individual characteristics such as having an exciting personality and being physically attractive, interesting, and so on (Anthony, Holmes, & Wood, 2007). Similarly, when asked to complete sentences beginning with "I am . . . ," people from Asian cultures are more likely to refer to social groups, such as one's family or religious group, than are people from Western cultures (Bochner, 1994; Triandis, 1989). Thus, to many Japanese and other Asians, Masako Owada's decision to give up her career was not at all surprising: It was a positive, natural consequence of her view of herself as connected and obligated to others, such as her family and the royal family. What is viewed as positive and normal behaviour by one culture might be viewed very differently by another.

We do not mean to imply that every member of a Western culture has an independent view of the self and that every member of an Asian culture has an interdependent view of the self. Within cultures there are differences in the self-concept, and these differences are likely to increase as contact between cultures increases. It is interesting to note, for example, that Masako's decision to marry the prince was unpopular among at least some young Japanese women, who felt that her choice was not a positive sign of interdependence but a betrayal of the feminist cause in Japan (Sanger, 1993). Women in Japan are joining the workforce in record numbers, and more women are postponing or forgoing marriage in favour of careers (Faiola, 2004). And the restricted life in the Imperial Household seems to have taken its toll on Princess Masako. In 2004 she stopped making public appearances, and the press office for the royal family announced that she was receiving therapy for depression (Onishi, 2004).

Consider again Jennifer Campbell's notion of self-concept clarity. It might already have occurred to you that self-concept clarity is probably a Western phenomenon, given that it is based on a premise that the self is a stable configuration of internal traits that govern behaviour across situations. The sense of self might be less clear in cultures in which the self is perceived as interdependent

independent view of the self

defining oneself in terms of one's own internal thoughts, feelings, and actions, and not in terms of the thoughts, feelings, and actions of other people

interdependent view of the self

defining oneself in terms of one's relationships to other people; recognizing that one's behaviour is often determined by the thoughts, feelings, and actions of others

❝*The squeaky wheel gets the grease.*❞

—North American proverb

❝*The nail that stands out gets pounded down.*❞

—Japanese proverb

(that is, based on relationships with others). To find out, Campbell and her colleagues (1996) administered the Self-Concept Clarity Scale to Canadian and Japanese students. (See the Try It! on page 128.) Japanese participants did, in fact, have lower self-concept clarity than Canadian participants. Moreover, self-concept clarity was not as strongly linked to self-esteem for the Japanese participants as it was for the Canadian participants (Campbell et al., 1996).

In summary, the difference between an independent and an interdependent sense of self is real and has interesting consequences for communication between different cultures. Indeed, differences in the sense of self are so fundamental that it is difficult for people with independent selves to appreciate what it is like to have an interdependent self, and vice versa. Western readers might find it difficult to appreciate the Asian sense of interdependence; similarly, many Japanese find it difficult to comprehend that North Americans could possibly know who they are, separate from the social groups to which they belong.

Gender Differences in Defining the Self

There is a stereotype that when women get together, they talk about interpersonal problems and relationships, whereas when men get together, they talk about sports or politics—anything but their feelings. Research suggests that there is some truth to the stereotype (Fehr, 1996) and that it reflects a difference in women's and men's self-concepts (Baumeister & Sommer, 1997; Cross, Bacon, & Morris, 2000; Cross & Madson, 1997; Gabriel & Gardner, 1999, 2004). Specifically, women's self-concepts reflect more *relational* interdependence, meaning that they focus more on their close relationships, such as how they feel about their romantic partner, a friend, or their child (Brewer & Gardner, 1996). In recent research conducted at the University of Waterloo, for example, women rated relational traits (e.g., warm, affectionate, loving) as more self-descriptive than did men (Anthony et al., 2007; see also Guimond, Chatard, Martinot, Crisp, & Redersdorff, 2006). This gender difference also has been found in research conducted by David Watkins (University of Hong Kong), John Adair (University of Manitoba), and researchers from many other countries (Watkins, Adair et al., 1998; Watkins, Akande et al., 1998). These researchers administered the sentence completion test ("I am . . .") to thousands of participants in as many as 15 different cultures. In these studies, women were found to hold a more relational view of the self—but only in individualist cultures (e.g., Canada, white South Africa, New Zealand). In collectivist cultures that emphasize interdependence (e.g., China, Ethiopia, black South Africa), women and men were equally likely to hold a relational view of the self.

This is not to say that men in individualist cultures are completely lacking in interdependence. Quite the contrary. According to research by Cross and Madson, interdependence is part of men's conception of self, but it is not the kind of relational interdependence shown by women. Rather, men tend to define themselves in terms of social groups, such as the sports teams to which they belong (Cross, Bacon, & Morris, 2000; Cross & Madson, 1997; Gabriel & Gardner, 1999). This is known as *collective* interdependence (Gabriel & Gardner, 1999). To see how much your self-concept is based on a sense of relational interdependence, answer the questions in the Try It! on the next page.

When interpreting gender differences such as these, it is important to keep in mind the bigger picture. Even though women and men differ in their self-conceptions, overall, the psychological differences between women and men are far fewer than the similarities (Deaux & LaFrance, 1998; Fehr & Broughton, 2001).

To summarize, the self-concept serves basic adaptive functions common to all cultures, but culture and gender also play a role in how people define themselves. But how do people learn who they are in the first place? How did you

Try it!

▶ A Measure of Relational Interdependence†

Instructions: Indicate the extent to which you agree or disagree with each of these statements.

		strongly disagree						strongly agree
1.	My close relationships are an important reflection of who I am.	1	2	3	4	5	6	7
2.	When I feel close to someone, it often feels to me like that person is an important part of who I am.	1	2	3	4	5	6	7
3.	I usually feel a strong sense of pride when someone close to me has an important accomplishment.	1	2	3	4	5	6	7
4.	I think one of the most important parts of who I am can be captured by looking at my close friends and understanding who they are.	1	2	3	4	5	6	7
5.	When I think of myself, I often think of my close friends or family also.	1	2	3	4	5	6	7
6.	If a person hurts someone close to me, I feel personally hurt as well.	1	2	3	4	5	6	7
7.	In general, my close relationships are an important part of my self-image.	1	2	3	4	5	6	7
8.	Overall, my close relationships have very little to do with how I feel about myself.	1	2	3	4	5	6	7
9.	My close relationships are unimportant to my sense of what kind of person I am.	1	2	3	4	5	6	7
10.	My sense of pride comes from knowing who I have as close friends.	1	2	3	4	5	6	7
11.	When I establish a close friendship with someone, I usually develop a strong sense of identification with that person.	1	2	3	4	5	6	7

†To compute your score, first reverse the rating you gave to questions 8 and 9. That is, if you circled a 1, change it to a 7; if you circled a 2, change it to a 6; if you circled a 7, change it to a 1; and so on. Then total your answers to the 11 questions. High scores reflect more of a tendency to define yourself in terms of relational interdependence. Cross, Bacon, and Morris (2000) found that women tend to score higher than men; in eight samples of university students, women averaged 57.2 and men averaged 53.4.

(Adapted from Cross, Bacon, & Morris, 2000)

discover those things that make you uniquely *you?* We will now discuss how people gain self-knowledge.

> *There is one thing, and only one in the whole universe which we know more about than we could learn from external observation. That one thing is [ourselves]. We have, so to speak, inside information; we are in the know.*
>
> —C. S. Lewis, 1960

introspection

the process whereby people look inward and examine their own thoughts, feelings, and motives

Knowing Ourselves through Introspection

When we told you we were going to describe the sources of information you use to construct a self-concept, you may have thought, "Good grief! I don't need a social psychology textbook to tell me that! It's not exactly a surprise; I just think about myself. No big deal." In other words, you rely on **introspection**—you look inward and examine the "inside information" that you, and you alone, have about your thoughts, feelings, and motives, just as the quotation by C. S. Lewis suggests. And indeed, you do find some answers when you introspect. But there are two interesting things about introspection. First, people do not rely on this source of information as often as you might think—surprisingly, people spend very little time thinking about themselves. According to one study, only 8 percent of thoughts are about the self; most of the time, people are thinking about work, chores, and time

(Csikszentmihalyi & Figurski, 1982). Second, even when people do introspect, the reasons for theirfeelings and behaviour can be hidden from conscious awareness (Wilson, 2002). As Nietzsche observed, much of the self may be unknown. In short, self-scrutiny isn't all it's cracked up to be. If this was your only source of knowledge about yourself, you would be in trouble.

Focusing on the Self: Self-Awareness Theory

As just discussed, we do not focus on ourselves very often. However, when we do stop to think about ourselves, what happens? What are the consequences of turning the spotlight of consciousness on ourselves, instead of focusing our attention on the world around us? Research suggests that when we are feeling self-aware (e.g., because people are watching us, we are seeing ourselves on videotape, or we are staring at ourselves in a mirror), we tend to assume that we also are more transparent to others—not just to ourselves. In a series of studies conducted at the University of Manitoba and the University of Waterloo, Vorauer and colleagues (Vorauer & Ross, 1999; Vorauer, 2001) found that when people were made to feel self-aware, they tended to assume that another person also would have this heightened access to their traits. This tendency was particularly pronounced among those high in collectivism—that is, those who are high in interdependence and see their self as merged with that of other group members (Vorauer & Cameron, 2002). The assumption that others had access to their inner thoughts and feelings was incorrect, however. Outside observers did not discern the traits of self-aware participants any more accurately than the traits of participants who had not been made self-aware. Thus, when we are focused on our self, we have a tendency to erroneously assume that others also share this awareness. Nevertheless, as we discuss next, the mere fact that we have focused on our self has some interesting and important effects.

According to **self-awareness theory**, when we focus our attention on ourselves, we evaluate and compare our current behaviour against our internal standards and values (Carver, 2003; Duval & Silvia, 2002; Duval & Wicklund, 1972; Phillips & Silvia, 2005). In short, we become self-conscious, in the sense that we

> "We are unknown, we knowers, ourselves to ourselves; this has its own good reason. We have never searched for ourselves—how should it then come to pass, that we should ever find ourselves?"
> —Friedrich Nietzsche, 1918

> "I swear to you . . . that to be overly conscious is a sickness, a real, thorough sickness."
> —Fyodor Dostoevsky, Notes from Underground, 1864

self-awareness theory
the idea that when people focus their attention on themselves, they evaluate and compare their behaviour with their internal standards and values

"Steer clear of that group. They're all terribly self-aware."

◄The people on the couch look awfully smug; they must like what they see when they are self-aware.

become objective, judgmental observers of ourselves. Let's say that you feel that you should quit smoking, and one day you catch an image of yourself in a store window smoking a cigarette. How do you think you would feel?

Seeing yourself will make you aware of the disparity between your behaviour and your internal standards. If you can change your behaviour to match your internal guidelines (e.g., quit smoking), you will do so. If you feel you can't change your behaviour, then being in a state of self-awareness will be very uncomfortable because you will be confronted with disagreeable feedback about yourself.

This dissatisfaction with ourselves can be painful. As a result, we take steps to alleviate the discomfort of unpleasant realizations about the self. Figure 5.1 illustrates this process—how self-awareness makes us conscious of our internal standards and directs our subsequent behaviour.

Consider, for example, a study by Sophia Moskalenko and Steven Heine (2003). These researchers told some participants that they had done very poorly on a task that reflected their level of intelligence. Others were told that they had done well. Moskalenko and Heine reasoned that the participants who were given the failure feedback would be highly motivated to escape self-awareness and therefore would be most likely to pay attention to a video that was on in the room. And that is exactly what happened.

Sometimes people go even further in their attempt to escape the self. Roy Baumeister (1991) has pointed out that such diverse activities as alcohol abuse, binge eating, sexual masochism, and suicide have one thing in common: All are effective ways of turning the internal spotlight away from oneself. Getting drunk, for example, is one way of avoiding negative thoughts about oneself (at least temporarily). Suicide, of course, is the ultimate way of ending self-scrutiny. The fact that people regularly engage in harmful behaviours is an indication of how aversive self-focus can be (Hull, 1981; Hull & Young, 1983; Hull, Young, & Jouriles, 1986).

> *I have often wished I had time to cultivate modesty. . . . But I am too busy thinking about myself.*
>
> —*Dame Edith Sitwell (1887–1964)*

FIGURE 5.1

Self-awareness theory: The consequences of self-focused attention

When people focus on themselves, they compare their behaviour with their internal standards.

(Adapted from Carver & Scheier, 1981)

We hasten to add that self-awareness does not inevitably have negative effects. Self-focus can also be a way of keeping you out of trouble, by reminding you of your sense of right and wrong. For example, several studies have found that when people are self-aware (e.g., in front of a mirror), they are more likely to follow their moral standards, such as avoiding the temptation to cheat on a test (Beaman, Klentz, Diener, & Svanum, 1979; Diener & Wallbom, 1976; Gibbons, 1978). According to Baumeister (1991), people sometimes escape self-awareness through more positive means, such as through religious expression and spirituality. It is also important to point out that self-focus is not always unpleasant. If you have just experienced a major success, focusing on yourself can be quite enjoyable because it highlights your positive accomplishments (Greenberg & Musham, 1981; Silvia & Abele, 2002).

Thus, self-awareness can have negative or positive effects. And in those cases where self-awareness feels aversive, those bad feelings can be alleviated in either a constructive or a destructive manner.

Judging Why We Feel the Way We Do: Telling More than We Can Know

Even when we are self-aware and introspect to our heart's content, it can be difficult to know *why* we feel the way we do. As we saw in Chapter 3, many of our basic mental processes occur outside of awareness (Kihlstrom, 1987; Mandler, 1975; Neisser, 1976). This is not to say that we are thinkers without a clue—we are aware of the final result of our thought processes (e.g., deciding that we are in love); however, we are often unaware of the cognitive processing that led to the result. It's as if the magician pulled a rabbit out of a hat: You see the rabbit, but you don't know how it got there. How do we deal with this rabbit problem?

Even though we often don't know why we feel a certain way, it seems we are always able to come up with an explanation. Richard Nisbett and Tim Wilson referred to this phenomenon as "telling more than we know" because people's explanations of their feelings and behaviour often go beyond what they can reasonably know (Nisbett & Ross, 1980; Nisbett & Wilson, 1977a; Wilson, 1985, 1994, 2002; Wilson & Stone, 1985). For example, in one study, university students were asked to keep journals of their moods every day for five weeks (Wilson, Laser, & Stone, 1982). The students also kept track of things that might affect their daily moods, such as the weather and how much they had slept the night before. At the end of the five weeks, the students estimated how much their mood was related to these other variables. Wilson and colleagues found that in many cases, people were wrong about what predicted their mood; for example, most people believed that the amount of sleep they got predicted how good a mood they were in the next day, when in fact this wasn't true—amount of sleep was unrelated to people's moods.

In a conceptually similar study, McFarlane, Martin, and Williams (1988) had students at the University of British Columbia keep track of their moods every day for a 70-day period. Later, the students were asked to recall what their moods had been. These researchers found that participants "remembered" more positive moods on weekends and "bluer Mondays" than they actually experienced. Interestingly, women also reported having been in worse moods during their premenstrual and menstrual phases than was the case. (In fact, during the menstrual phase of their cycle, female participants were actually in an especially pleasant mood!)

What participants in these studies relied on, at least in part, were their **causal theories**. People have many theories about what influences their feelings and behaviour, and often use these theories to help them explain why they feel the way they do (e.g., "I am in a bad mood—I bet it's because I got only four hours of sleep last night, or because it's Monday, or because it's that 'time of the month'").

causal theories

theories about the causes of one's own feelings and behaviours; typically, we learn such theories from our culture (e.g., "absence makes the heart grow fonder")

We learn many of these theories from the culture in which we grow up. The only problem, as discussed in Chapter 3, is that our schemas and theories are not always correct and thus can lead to incorrect judgments about the causes of our actions.

Consider this example of causal theories in action from the researchers who have studied them. One night, Dick Nisbett and Tim Wilson were meeting in an office at the University of Michigan. They were trying to think of ways to test the hypothesis that people rely on causal theories when trying to uncover the reasons for their feelings, judgments, and actions. Brilliant insights were not forthcoming, and the researchers were frustrated by their lack of progress. Then they realized that a source of their frustration (or so they thought) was the annoying whine of a vacuum cleaner that a custodial worker was operating right outside their office. This realization led them to wonder whether distracting background noises are more bothersome than people think. Maybe this was an example of the very kind of situation they were looking for—one that would influence people's judgments but would be overlooked when people explained their behaviour.

After shutting the door, Nisbett and Wilson (1977a) designed a study to test this possibility. They showed participants a documentary in the presence of an annoying noise. About a minute into the film, a "construction worker" (actually, Dick Nisbett) turned on a power saw right outside the door to the room and ran the saw intermittently until Tim Wilson, the experimenter, went to the door and asked him to please stop sawing until the film was over. At the end of the film, the participants rated how much they enjoyed it. The experimenter then asked them whether the hallway noise had influenced their evaluations. To see if the noise really did have an effect, there was a control condition in which other participants viewed the film without any distracting noise. The hypothesis was that the noise would lower people's evaluation of the film but that people would not realize the noise was responsible for the negative evaluation.

Does this seem like a reasonable hypothesis? It did to the researchers, but as it happened, they were completely wrong. The participants who watched the film with the annoying background noise did not like it any less than did those who saw the film without the distracting noise (in fact, they liked it slightly more). However, when the participants were asked how much the noise had influenced their ratings, most people reported that it had lowered their ratings of the film. Thus, even though the noise had no detectable effect on people's feelings about the film, it influenced their explanations for their feelings.

In a further study, Nisbett and Wilson (1977a) asked people in a shopping mall to evaluate the quality of items of clothing, such as pantyhose. Much to the surprise of the researchers, the position of the items on the display table had a large effect on people's preferences. The more to the right an item was, the more people liked it. The researchers knew that it was the position that was influencing people's judgments because in fact all of the pairs of pantyhose were identical. However, the participants were completely in the dark about this effect of position on their judgments. Instead, they generated other causal theories for their choices. Thus, introspecting about our past actions and our current thoughts does not always yield the right answer about why we feel the way we do.

Knowing Ourselves by Observing Our Own Behaviour

Suppose that a friend asks you how much you like classical music. You hesitate because you never listened to classical music when you were growing up, but lately you have found yourself listening to symphonies on the radio every now and then. "Well, I don't know," you reply. "I guess I like some kinds of classical music. Just yesterday, I listened to a Beethoven symphony on the radio while I was commuting to work." In giving this response, you used an important source of self-knowledge: observations of one's own behaviour.

Self-perception theory argues that when our attitudes and feelings are uncertain or ambiguous, we infer these states by observing our behaviour and the situation in which it occurs (Bem, 1972). Let's consider each part of this theory. First, we infer our inner feelings from our behaviour only when we are not sure how we feel. If you've always known that you are a classical music lover, then you do not need to observe your behaviour to figure this out (Andersen, 1984; Andersen & Ross, 1984). However, if you aren't sure how much you like classical music, you are especially likely to use your behaviour as a guide to how you feel. This effect was demonstrated by Chaiken and Baldwin (1981) with University of Toronto students. First, the researchers assessed whether the participants had well-defined attitudes toward protecting the environment. Then they asked participants to check off which behaviours from a list of pro- or anti-environmental actions they had performed (e.g., "I frequently leave on lights in rooms I'm not using") as a way of reminding them of their past behaviour. The researchers hypothesized that being reminded of their past behaviour would influence only the participants whose attitudes were more uncertain. Indeed, participants with less clearly defined environmental attitudes were strongly affected by these behavioural cues; those who were reminded of their pro-environmental behaviour subsequently reported that they held pro-environmental attitudes, whereas those who were reminded of their anti-environmental behaviour later reported more negative environmental attitudes. In contrast, being reminded of their past behaviour had little effect on the participants who already had clear attitudes on this issue.

Self-perception theory also claims that people evaluate whether their behaviour really reflects how they feel or whether the situation they are in made them act that way. If you freely choose to listen to the classical music station—no one makes you do it—you are especially likely to conclude that you listen to that station because you love classical music. If it is your roommate and not you who always tunes in to the classical station, you are unlikely to conclude that you listen to classical music because you love it.

Intrinsic versus Extrinsic Motivation

An interesting implication of self-perception theory is that if people are given rewards for engaging in certain activities, they may conclude that they actually don't enjoy that activity, but rather that they are just doing it for the reward. Let's say you love to play the piano. You spend many hours happily practising, simply enjoying the act of making music and the feeling that you are getting better. We would say that your interest in playing the piano stems from **intrinsic motivation**, which is the desire to engage in an activity because you enjoy it or find it interesting, not because of **extrinsic motivation**—external rewards or pressures (Deci & Ryan, 1985, 2002; Harackiewicz & Elliot, 1993, 1998; Harackiewicz, Durik, & Barron, 2005; Lepper, Corpus, & Iyengar, 2005; Ryan & Deci, 2000; Sansone & Harackiewicz, 1996).

Whether our behaviour is motivated by intrinsic versus extrinsic factors has a number of far-reaching effects (Koestner & Losier, 2002; Losier & Koestner, 1999; Vallerand, 1997; Vallerand & Ratelle, 2002). For example, Robert Vallerand and his colleagues found that intrinsic motivation was positively correlated with persistence (over a two-year period) among competitive swimmers (Pelletier, Fortier, Vallerand, & Briere, 1996) and with maintaining interest in repetitive figure skating tasks, as demonstrated with competitive figure skaters from clubs in the Ottawa–Carleton area (Green-Demers, Pelletier, Stewart, & Gushue, 1998). Similarly, Bailis and Segall (2004) found that intrinsic motivation was correlated

self-perception theory

the theory that when our attitudes and feelings are uncertain or ambiguous, we infer these states by observing our behaviour and the situation in which it occurs

❝ *I've always written poems.... I never know what I think until I read it in one of my poems.* ❞

—Virginia Hamilton Adair, 1913–1996

intrinsic motivation

the desire to engage in an activity because we enjoy it or find it interesting, not because of external rewards or pressures

extrinsic motivation

the desire to engage in an activity because of external rewards or pressures, not because we enjoy the task or find it interesting with continuing one's membership (over a two-year period) in a Winnipeg wellness centre. In the domain of academics, intrinsic motivation has been correlated with positive language learning outcomes (e.g., feeling competent speaking French in a sample of French immersion students; Noels, Clément, & Pelletier, 1999), and with remaining in school rather than dropping out, as has been shown in several studies with French-Canadian high school students (Koestner & Losier, 2002; Vallerand, Fortier, & Guay, 1997; see also Guay, Mageau, & Vallerand, 2003). Intrinsic motivation is also associated with actively seeking information about environmental issues (e.g., nuclear waste, pesticides in food) and engaging in pro-environmental behaviours (e.g., recycling, conserving resources, purchasing environmentally friendly products), as demonstrated in several studies of Ontario residents (Pelletier, 2002; Séguin, Pelletier, & Hunsley, 1999).

Finally, intrinsic motivation is also linked with a number of relationship benefits. For example, relationship partners who are motivated to be in the relationship for its own sake, rather than to receive external benefits or rewards, are more likely to view relationship problems as "challenges" rather than "hassles" (Blais, Sabourin, Boucher & Vallerand, 1990), engage in more constructive conflict resolution (Knee, Lonsbary, Canevello, & Patrick, 2005), and report greater relationship satisfaction (Blais et al., 1990).

The Overjustification Effect Return, for a moment, to our earlier example of the joy you experienced while playing the piano. Now let's say your parents get the brilliant idea of rewarding you with money for playing the piano. They figure that this will make you practise even harder. After all, rewards work, don't they? However, your parents have now added an extrinsic reason for you to play the piano. Unfortunately, extrinsic rewards can undermine intrinsic motivation. Whereas before you played the piano because you loved it, now you're playing it so that you'll get the reward. What was once play is now work. The sad outcome is that replacing intrinsic motivation with extrinsic motivation makes people lose interest in the activity they initially enjoyed. This result is called the **overjustification effect**, whereby people view their behaviour as caused by compelling extrinsic reasons (e.g., a reward), making them underestimate the extent to which their behaviour was caused by intrinsic reasons (e.g., their enjoyment of the activity; Deci, Koestner, & Ryan, 1999a, 1999b; Deci & Ryan, 1985; Harackiewicz, 1979; Lepper, 1995; Lepper, Keavney, & Drake, 1996; Ryan & Deci, 1996).

Preserving Intrinsic Interest Does society's reward system wreak havoc with intrinsic motivation? Fortunately, there are conditions under which overjustification effects don't come into play. Rewards will undermine interest only if interest was high initially (Calder & Staw, 1975; Tang & Hall, 1995). If a child has no interest in reading, then getting him or her to read by offering free pizzas is not a bad idea, because there is no initial interest to undermine.

Also, the type of reward makes a difference. So far, we have discussed **task-contingent rewards**, meaning that people get them only for doing a task, regardless of how well they do it. Sometimes **performance-contingent rewards** are used,

overjustification effect

the case whereby people view their behaviour as caused by compelling extrinsic reasons, making them underestimate the extent to which their behaviour was caused by intrinsic reasons

task-contingent rewards

rewards that are given for performing a task, regardless of how well the task is done

performance-contingent rewards

rewards that are based on how well we perform a task

▶ Making children read for external reasons can lead to an overjustification effect, whereby they infer that they have no intrinsic interest in reading.

whereby the reward depends on how well people perform the task. For example, grades are performance-contingent because you get a high reward (an A) only if you do well. This type of reward is less likely to decrease interest in a task—and may even increase interest—because it conveys the message that you are good at the task (Deci & Ryan, 1985). Thus, rather than giving kids a reward for playing math games regardless of how well they do (i.e., a task-contingent reward), it is better to reward them for doing well in math. Even performance-contingent rewards must be used with care because they too can backfire. Although people like the positive feedback these rewards convey, they do not like the apprehension caused by being evaluated (Harackiewicz, 1989; Harackiewicz, Manderlink, & Sansone, 1984). The trick is to convey positive feedback without making people feel nervous and apprehensive about being evaluated.

Knowing Ourselves through Social Interaction

People are not solitary seekers of self-knowledge, but social beings who often see themselves through the eyes of other people. James (1890) stressed the importance of social relationships in people's definition of self, noting that they can have different "selves" that develop in response to different social situations. For example, the self that you present to your friends is probably different than the self you present when interacting with your social psychology professor. Not only is it true that we present ourselves differently to different people, but it is also the case that other people shape how we view ourselves. It's as if other people reflect their image of us back for us to see.

Seeing Ourselves through the Eyes of Others: The Looking-Glass Self

The idea that we see ourselves through the eyes of other people—either present or imagined—and incorporate their views into our self-concept is called the **looking-glass self** (Cooley, 1902; Mead, 1934). Mark Baldwin and his colleagues have explored this idea in an ingenious set of experiments (Baldwin, 1992; Baldwin & Meunier, 1999; Baldwin & Sinclair, 1996; Baldwin et al., 2003). Imagine you were a participant in one of their studies. Think of an older member of your family. Try to form a vivid picture of this person in your mind. Imagine that this person is sitting beside you. Focus on the colour of the person's eyes or hair, and then focus on the sound of the person's voice. Imagine talking to this person.

Now imagine reading a story about a woman who engages in sexually permissive behaviour. How much do you think you would enjoy the story? Not very much, according to Baldwin and Holmes (1987). They found that female students at the University of Waterloo who had previously imagined older family members rated a *Cosmopolitan* magazine story about a women's permissive sexual behaviour as less enjoyable than women who had imagined their (presumably more permissive) university friends. In another study (Baldwin, Carrell, & Lopez, 1990), graduate students at the University of Michigan were asked to evaluate their recent research ideas. For some of the students, an evaluative authority figure was primed by subliminal exposure (flashing a slide so quickly that the participants weren't consciously aware of what had been shown) to the scowling face of their program director. Other students were exposed to an approving figure—the warm, friendly face of a postdoctoral student (John Ellard, now a social psychology professor at the University of Calgary). Students who were exposed to the scowling face of their program director subsequently evaluated

looking-glass self

the idea that we see ourselves through the eyes of other people and incorporate their views into our self-concept

▲ The looking-glass self. In one study (Baldwin, Carrell, & Lopez, 1990), students were subliminally exposed either to a photo of the chair of their department, scowling, or to a photo of a postdoctoral student, smiling. Those exposed to their scowling chair subsequently rated their own research more negatively than did those exposed to the friendly postdoctoral student. In another study (Baldwin et al., 1990), participants were subliminally exposed either to a picture of a scowling man unknown to them, or to a picture of Pope John Paul II, altered to look particularly disapproving. Practising Catholic women rated themselves more negatively after reading a sexually permissive passage when they had been exposed to the picture of the disapproving pope.

their research ideas more negatively than did those exposed to the friendly face of the postdoctoral student.

In the final study in this series, Baldwin and colleagues (1990) primed a sense of self as a Catholic among Catholic women at the University of Waterloo through subliminal exposure to a picture of then Pope John Paul II looking disapproving. Other participants were exposed to the scowling face of a man who was unfamiliar to them—and therefore should not have had implications for their sense of self. All participants then read a sexually permissive passage. As expected, women exposed to the disapproving countenance of the pope rated themselves more negatively than did women exposed to the disapproving face of an unfamiliar man. However, this effect was obtained only for women who defined themselves as practising Catholics. Presumably for these women, the pope was an especially relevant internal audience.

Who we are, then, is determined, at least in part, by the internal audience we have in mind. If we are reminded of a significant person in our lives who seems critical or disapproving, we will tend to see ourselves as possessing negative traits (e.g., immoral or incompetent). On the other hand, if we happen to have a supportive, approving internal audience in mind, we are more likely to view ourselves as having positive characteristics.

Knowing Ourselves by Comparing Ourselves with Others

We also come to know ourselves through comparison with other people (Brown, 1990; Collins, 1996; Kruglanski & Mayseless, 1990; McFarland & Miller, 1994; Suls, Martin, & Wheeler, 2000; Wood, 1996). Suppose, for example, we gave you a test that measured your social sensitivity, or how aware you are of other people's problems. The test involves reading excerpts from autobiographies and guessing the nature of each author's personal problems, if any. After you've taken the test, we tell you that you achieved a score of 35. What have you learned about yourself? Not much, because you don't know what a score of 35 means. Suppose we told you that the test is scored on a scale from 0 to 50. Now what have you learned? A little more than you knew before perhaps, but this is still pretty uninformative if you don't know how other people did on the test. If we told you that everyone else in your class scored between 0 and 20, you would probably say, "Wow—I really am a sensitive person!" On the other hand, you might feel differently if we told you that everyone else scored between 45 and 50.

This example illustrates Leon Festinger's (1954) **social comparison theory**, which holds that people learn about their own abilities and attitudes by comparing themselves with other people. The theory revolves around two important questions: When do you engage in social comparison? With whom do you choose to compare yourself?

The answer to the first question is that you socially compare when there is no objective standard for you to measure yourself against and when you experience some uncertainty about yourself in a particular area (Suls & Fletcher, 1983; Suls & Miller, 1977). That is, when you're not sure how well you're doing or exactly what you're feeling, you'll observe other people and compare yourself with them.

As to the second question—with whom do people compare themselves?—not surprisingly, people find it most informative to compare themselves with others who are similar to them on the attribute or dimension in question (Goethals & Darley, 1977; Miller, 1982; Wheeler, Koestner, & Driver, 1982; Zanna, Goethals, & Hill, 1975). For example, if you are wondering about your artistic ability, it will not be very informative to compare yourself with Picasso—one of the great artists of the twentieth century. It also will not be that informative to compare your artistic endeavours with the finger painting and scribbles of your four-year-old sister. It is better to compare yourself with the other people in your drawing class, if your goal is to assess your own abilities.

social comparison theory

the idea that we learn about our own abilities and attitudes by comparing ourselves with other people

The Need to Feel Good about Ourselves

As we have discussed, people are motivated to understand themselves. It is also the case that people need to feel good about themselves. We now turn to the topic of self-evaluation.

Social Comparison Revisited

Constructing an accurate image of ourselves is only one reason that we engage in social comparison. We also use social comparison to boost our egos. Is it important to you to believe that you are a fabulous artist-in-the-making? Then compare yourself with your little sister—you have her beat! This use of **downward social comparison**—comparing yourself with people who are worse than you on a particular trait or ability—is a self-protective, self-enhancing strategy (Aspinwall & Taylor, 1993; Buunk, Oldersma, & de Dreu, 2001; Davison, Pennebaker, & Dickerson, 2000). Indeed, research shows that if you compare yourself with people who are less smart, less talented, or sicker than you are, you'll feel very good about yourself. For example, Joanne Wood, Shelley Taylor, and Rosemary Lichtman (1985) found evidence of downward comparison in interviews with cancer patients. The vast majority of patients spontaneously compared themselves with other cancer patients who were more ill than they were, presumably as a way of making themselves feel more optimistic about the course of their own condition. Wood and her colleagues also examined spontaneous social comparisons in everyday life by having students at the University of Waterloo keep track of times when they compared themselves with another person over a three-week period (Wood, Michela, & Giordano, 2000). An analysis of these diaries confirmed that people were most likely to spontaneously engage in downward social comparisons when they wanted to feel better about themselves.

In an interesting twist on this issue, Anne Wilson at Wilfrid Laurier University and Michael Ross at the University of Waterloo suggested that we might even be able to get a self-esteem boost by comparing our current performance with

downward social comparison

the process whereby we compare ourselves with people who are worse than we are on a particular trait or ability our own past performance (Ross & Wilson, 2002; Wilson & Ross, 2000, 2001; see also Redersdorff & Guimond, 2006). We are still using downward social comparison, but in this case, the target of comparison is a "past" self instead of another person. For example, in one of their studies, a participant mentioned that her "university student" self was more outgoing and sociable than her former shy, reserved "high school student" self. In related research, Cameron, Ross, and Holmes (2002) showed that if we are forced to think about a time when we behaved badly in a relationship, we will bend over backwards to show how much we and our relationships have improved since then. In other words, when we are reminded of a negative "past" self, we restore our self-esteem by focusing on how much better our current self is.

It is important to point out that downward comparison does not inevitably result in increased self-esteem. According to Penelope Lockwood (2002), comparing ourselves with someone who is worse off will make us feel good only if we don't feel vulnerable to that person's negative outcomes. In one of her studies, first-year students at the University of Toronto who were doing well academically read about the experiences of another first-year student who was struggling. In this situation, students showed the usual self-enhancement effect of downward social comparison. They could feel good about the fact that they, themselves, were not experiencing academic difficulties. Quite the opposite occurred, however, when participants were presented with a situation that could, in fact, happen to them. This time, first-year students read about a recent graduate who did well in university at the outset but then declined in academic performance over his four years at the University of Toronto. After he graduated, he could only find work in fast-food restaurants. In this case, downward social comparison had a negative effect. Those who were asked to imagine experiencing a similar fate felt worse about themselves than students in a control group (who wrote about a typical day in their lives). Thus, comparing ourselves with someone who is worse off can make us feel better about ourselves—but only if we are confident that the other person's fate cannot befall us.

How do we feel if we instead compare ourselves with someone who is better than we are—thereby engaging in **upward social comparison**? According to Lockwood and Kunda (1997, 1999, 2000), the answer is, "It depends." You might feel better or worse, depending on the sense of self that is activated (brought to mind) at the time. Imagine that you were a participant in one of their studies. Think of a peak academic experience that made you especially proud. If you are like the math, biology, and computer science students at the University of Waterloo who participated in this study, you would have no trouble coming up with an answer. Now imagine reading an article in your campus newspaper that describes a student, of the same gender as you, who has had a stellar academic career. This person has won all kinds of awards, and university officials are raving about how truly outstanding this student is. How do you feel now? If you suddenly don't feel so good, you are not alone. Lockwood and Kunda found that when participants' "best" self had been activated, it was depressing for them to be exposed to a "superstar." They tended not to feel very good about themselves, and their motivation to study hard took a dive.

What if, instead of describing your "best" self, you focused on your "usual" self? Other participants in this study did just that—they were simply asked to describe what they had done the day before. For these participants, reading about the superstar student was inspiring. They imagined that they, too, could achieve greatness, and as a result they felt very good about themselves—even better than participants who focused on their usual self but did not read about the superstar. (These results are shown in Figure 5.2.)

The importance of attainability—the feeling that we, too, can achieve another person's success—was examined in a series of studies by Mills, Polivy, Herman, and

> " There is little satisfaction in the contemplation of heaven for oneself if one cannot simultaneously contemplate the horrors of hell for others. "
>
> —P. D. James, The Children of Men, 1992

upward social comparison

the process whereby we compare ourselves with people who are better than we are on a particular trait or ability

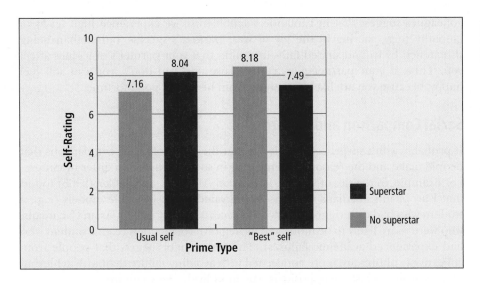

FIGURE 5.2

Effects of upward social comparison on self-enhancement

People who focused on their usual self evaluated themselves more positively following exposure to a "superstar" than did people who were not exposed to a superstar. However, people who focused on their "best" self evaluated themselves more negatively following exposure to a superstar than did those who were not exposed to a superstar (Lockwood & Kunda, 1999).

Tiggemann (2002). In one of their studies, female students at the University of Toronto at Mississauga who were dieting were shown magazine advertisements featuring very thin women. Before seeing the ads, some participants were given an article that made thinness seem attainable. The article, titled "New Hope for the Slimward Bound," argued that dieting is effective and that people should not give up. Other participants were given an article titled "Fat Chance: The Truth about Dieting," which was intended to make thinness seem unattainable by arguing that diets rarely work and that body weight is genetically determined. As predicted, women for whom slimness was made attainable were inspired by exposure to the thin model in the ads and subsequently felt better about themselves than did women for whom slimness was portrayed as difficult to achieve.

Thus, when we focus on our actual or usual self, exposure to outstanding others inspires us to generate higher hopes and aspirations for ourselves than we would have if we hadn't been exposed to the superstar. However, if we happen to be focusing on our best or ideal self, it can be discouraging to realize that someone else has already surpassed our highest hopes and dreams.

In sum, the kinds of social comparisons we engage in depend on the nature of our goals (Lockwood, Sadler, Fyman, & Tuck, 2004). If we want to feel good, we can engage in downward comparison and compare ourselves with our past selves or to those who are less fortunate. Doing so will make us look better by comparison—as long as we're convinced that we are not vulnerable to the same misfortunes. Upward social comparisons generally make us feel bad—it is threatening to our self-esteem to be outperformed by others, unless we feel that it is possible for us to achieve the superstars' level of performance. In that case, upward social comparison can have positive effects and motivate us to pursue our dreams.

Before leaving this topic, we should make one final point. The research we have been discussing focuses on comparisons with others whom we may not even know (e.g., reading about another student who has done well). Recent research shows that social comparison has very different effects when the person we are comparing ourselves with is our romantic partner (Pinkus, Lockwood, Schimmack, & Fournier, in press). When our romantic partner is the comparison target, we actually feel better after engaging in upward social comparisons (focusing on domains in which your partner outperforms you) than in downward social comparisons (focusing on areas in which you perform better than your partner). Why might this be the case? Pinkus and

▼ This man has engaged in too much upward social comparison.

"Of course you're going to be depressed if you keep comparing yourself with successful people."

colleagues suggest that in romantic relationships, we experience high levels of empathy (e.g., sharing in the joy of your partner's success, rather than being threatened by it) and shared fate—meaning that your partner's outcomes affect you. Thus, if your partner gets a hefty raise and you don't, you can still feel happy, because you are likely to benefit from his or her good fortune.

Social Comparison and Culture

It probably won't surprise you to learn that the kinds of social comparisons that people make and the reasons for engaging in social comparison differ by culture. For example, in a series of studies, Lockwood, Marshall, and Sadler (2005) found that European Canadians were more motivated by positive role models (e.g., a student who had experienced academic success) compared with Asian Canadians, who were more likely to be motivated by negative role models (e.g., a student who had experienced academic failures). The researchers suggest that people from collectivist cultures are more concerned with avoiding failure than with achieving success, whereas just the opposite is true in individualistic cultures.

Recent research also shows that people from collectivist cultures seek self-improvement to a greater extent than do those from individualist cultures, and this, too, affects the kind of social comparison information that is sought. For example, White and Lehman (2005b) found that Asian Canadians were more likely than European Canadians to choose to compare their performance with that of someone who did better than they did on a task (upward social comparison), rather than comparing themselves with a person who did worse than they did (downward social comparison). In other words, unlike European Canadians, Asian Canadians did not capitalize on an opportunity to get a self-esteem boost

CONNECTIONS

Promoting Social Good through Social Comparison

We can boost our self-esteem by comparing our performance with that of others. If others are doing more poorly than we are, that can make us feel better about ourselves (downward social comparison). If others are doing better than we are, that can motivate us to try harder to improve our own performance (upward social comparison). Might this basic human tendency to compare our performance with that of others be used to promote social good? Consider a study conducted by Frans Siero to try to get people to conserve energy in the workplace (Siero et al., 1996). At one unit of a factory in the Netherlands, the employees were urged to engage in energy-saving behaviours. For example, announcements were placed in the company magazine asking people to close windows during cold weather and to turn off lights when leaving a room. In addition, the employees got weekly feedback on their behaviour: graphs were posted that showed how much they had improved their energy-saving behaviours, such as how often they had turned off the lights. This intervention resulted in modest improvement. For example, by the end of the program, the number of times people left the lights on had decreased by 27 percent.

Another unit of the factory took part in an identical program, with one difference. In addition to receiving weekly feedback on their own energy-saving actions, they received feedback about how the other unit was doing. The researchers hypothesized that this social comparison information would motivate people to do better than their colleagues in the other unit. They were right. By the end of the program, the number of times people left lights on had decreased by 61 percent. Clearly, engaging people's competitive spirit had a large impact on their behaviour. Thus, our desire to perform well relative to those around us can not only give our self-esteem a boost but also be good for the environment!

but, rather, used social comparison information to identify areas for self-improvement. Earlier we also discussed research showing that people enhance their self-esteem by viewing their current self more positively than their past self. Research has shown that Japanese people are less likely to engage in this kind of self-enhancement than are Canadians (Ross, Heine, Wilson, & Sugimori, 2005).

Self-Discrepancy Theory

The work of E. Tory Higgins and his colleagues (Higgins, 1987, 1989, 1996, 1999; Higgins, Klein, & Strauman, 1987) is concerned with understanding how violations of personal standards influence how people feel about themselves. In particular, these researchers have taken a close look at the nature of the emotional distress that occurs when we perceive ourselves as not measuring up to our ideals and standards. **Self-discrepancy theory** posits that we become distressed when our sense of who we truly are—our actual self—is discrepant from our personal standards or desired self-conceptions. For Higgins and his colleagues, these standards are reflected most clearly in the beliefs we hold about the type of person we aspire to be—our "ideal" self—and the type of person we believe we should be—our "ought" self. Comparing our actual self with our ideal and ought-to-be selves provides us with an important means of self-evaluation.

self-discrepancy theory

the theory that we become distressed when our sense of who we truly are—our actual self—is discrepant from our personal standards or desired self-conceptions

What happens when we become aware that we have failed to measure up to our own standards? Consider the predicament of Sarah, a first-year university student who has always had very high academic standards. In terms of self-discrepancy theory, academic competence is a central component of her ideal self. In her first semester at a competitive, prestigious university, however, Sarah has discovered that A's are now much harder to come by. As a matter of fact, in her Introductory Chemistry course—a prerequisite for her major—she barely managed to earn a C. Given this scenario, how is Sarah likely to experience this discrepancy between her ideal and actual selves?

To begin with, we might imagine that the threat to her self-concept as a high achiever would almost certainly generate fairly strong levels of emotional discomfort—for example, disappointment in herself and perhaps an unaccustomed sense of uncertainty regarding her abilities. Self-discrepancy research supports this view. In a series of studies, Higgins and his colleagues (Higgins, 1989; Higgins, Bond, Klein, & Strauman, 1986) have found that when people are made mindful of a discrepancy between their actual and ideal selves, they tend to experience a pattern of feelings involving dejection, sadness, dissatisfaction, and other depression-related emotions.

On the other hand, what if Sarah had encountered a self-discrepancy involving her "ought" self—that is, not the ideal self she aspired to but the "should-be" self she felt obligated to uphold? Imagine that being a top-notch student was not enormously significant to Sarah. Instead, suppose that her parents had always held this standard as highly important, and that Sarah, out of respect for them, tried to achieve academic excellence. How then would Sarah experience this discrepancy between her actual and "ought" selves, in the face of a mediocre performance in her first semester at university? Research by Higgins and his colleagues indicates that, in this case, Sarah would be likely to experience fear, worry, tension, and other anxiety-related emotions.

More recent research shows that discrepancies between our ideal and "ought" selves are especially likely to produce negative emotion when we are feeling self-aware (e.g., sitting in front of a mirror while contemplating who we are, who we should be, and who we would ideally like to be; Phillips & Silvia, 2005).

How do people cope with the negative feelings generated by either of these forms of self-discrepancy? According to the theory, self-discrepancies not only produce emotional discomfort but also provoke strivings to minimize the gap between the actual and the ideal, or the actual and "ought," selves. Thus, Sarah,

▲ Self-discrepancy theory posits that we are distressed when our sense of who we truly are does not match our desired self-conception. For this high-achieving student, finding out she's done poorly on a test would generate strong levels of emotional discomfort.

who is coping with her lacklustre performance in chemistry, might convince herself that the grading was unfair or that her chemistry instructor was totally inept, or might in some other way interpret her mediocre performance in the most positive light possible. Of course, justifying her actions in order to maintain self-esteem—while a self-protective strategy in the short run—might not be the most adaptive approach Sarah could adopt. Rather, she would undoubtedly benefit far more from reassessing her situation—concluding perhaps that maintaining her high academic standards might require greater effort than she had been accustomed to exerting in the past when her courses were less challenging.

Finally, we should note that more recent research by Higgins and colleagues (Higgins, 1997, 1998; Semin, Higgins, de Montes, Estourget, & Valencia, 2005) shows that when we are focusing on our ideals, we tend to be *promotion-oriented*—meaning that we are motivated to achieve our goals and attain positive outcomes. In contrast, when we are in "ought" mode, we tend to be *prevention-oriented*—meaning that we channel our energy into avoiding negative outcomes and experiences.

Self-Discrepancies and Culture In cultures that emphasize interdependence, self-criticism is valued because group members are expected to continually strive to improve themselves in order to function harmoniously with others (Heine et al., 1999). Heine and Lehman (1999) reasoned that this emphasis on self-criticism might lead people in Asian cultures to experience larger discrepancies between their ideal and actual self than people in Western cultures. Indeed, in research conducted at the University of British Columbia and at Ritsumeikan University in Kyoto, Japan, they found that Japanese students viewed their actual self as falling short of their ideal self—particularly on traits they regarded as important—to a greater extent than did the Canadian students. Interestingly, discrepancies between the actual and ideal selves were not as depressing for Japanese students as they were for Canadian students. Heine and Lehman suggest that the Japanese participants may have been accustomed to thinking of their inadequacies as areas for improvement and therefore found it less upsetting that they weren't measuring up to their ideals.

Self-Evaluation: Biased or Accurate?

So far we have been operating on the assumption that people—at least in individualistic cultures—have a need to feel good about themselves. One way of feeling good about ourselves is to distort or exaggerate our positive qualities. We could even convince ourselves that we are better than most other people. Such positive illusions could certainly bolster self-esteem. On the other hand, probably most of us don't want to live in a fantasy world in which we are fooling ourselves about the kind of person we are. In fact, we might even want other people to "tell it like it is" so that we develop an accurate picture of who we are. Consequently, it seems we are caught between wanting to view ourselves in the most positive possible light and wanting an accurate assessment of what we are really like. Given these conflicting motives, do our self-evaluations tend to show a positivity bias, or do they tend to be accurate? Let's examine the evidence for each side of this issue.

Self-Enhancement: Wanting to Feel Good about Ourselves, Regardless of the Facts

Take a moment to answer the following questions: How attractive are you compared with the average student (of your gender) at your university? How adaptive are you compared with the average student? How well are you able to get along with others compared with the average student?

Chances are you see yourself as better than the average student with regard to at least some of these qualities, or perhaps even all of them. One way of boosting our self-esteem is to hold unrealistically positive views of ourselves, a tendency known as **self-enhancement**. "Well," you might be thinking, "in my case, it really isn't unrealistic to have a positive view of myself—I really am a great person." We don't doubt that you *are* a great person. The problem, however, is that most people have a tendency to think this way, and it really isn't possible for everyone to be better than most people, is it? This is why self-enhancement is defined as an unrealistically positive view of oneself.

Research confirms that we really do paint quite a flattering picture of ourselves. For example, when Heine and Lehman (1999) asked students at the University of British Columbia the kinds of questions with which we began this section, they found that participants tended to view themselves as better than the average student. In research along the same lines, Jennifer Campbell (1986) found that students at the University of British Columbia showed a false uniqueness effect—they believed that many other students shared their weaknesses, but that they were unique in their strengths. Similarly, researchers at Simon Fraser University have found that people tend to rate themselves as happier, more intelligent, more ethical, and even as having stronger emotional reactions than those around them (McFarland & Miller, 1990; Miller & McFarland, 1987). Does engaging in this kind of unrealistic thinking actually make us feel better about ourselves? Apparently so. Research conducted at the University of British Columbia by Del Paulhus and colleagues has found that the more we distort reality to paint a flattering picture of ourselves, the higher our self-esteem (Paulhus, 1998; Yik, Bond, & Paulhus, 1998).

There is also evidence that having a positive view of ourselves may help us cope with adversity. In a fascinating study, Bonanno and colleagues examined the relation between self-enhancement and psychosocial adjustment following the terrorist attacks on the World Trade Center in New York on September 11, 2001 (Bonanno, Rennicke, & Dekel, 2005). These researchers recruited people who had worked in or near the World Trade Center and therefore were directly affected by the attacks. Eighteen months later, those who were high in self-enhancement showed greater resilience than those who were low. Specifically, self-enhancers reported better coping, more positive affect, less depression, and less post-traumatic stress than those who did not hold unrealistically positive views of the self. The downside was that friends and relatives of self-enhancers tended not to share these optimistic perceptions. In other words, even though self-enhancers perceived themselves as coping well, close friends and family members did not necessarily agree. In fact, there was a tendency for close others to perceive self-enhancers as decreasing in adjustment since the attacks.

Self-Enhancement and Culture   As we have seen, self-enhancement is largely a phenomenon of individualistic cultures. Unrealistically positive self views are not common in collectivist, interdependent cultures. In fact, in Asian cultures, the tendency is to hold a negative view of oneself—a phenomenon known as *self-effacement* (Heine et al., 1999; Heine, 2001, 2003). This tendency is established at a relatively young age. For example, Kwok (1995) found that grade 4 students in Hong Kong rated themselves lower in scholastic competence, athletic competence, physical appearance, and overall self-worth than did grade 4 students in Canada. Interestingly, this was the case even though the Chinese students performed better than the Canadian children on standardized math tests. Similarly, Japanese university students see themselves as worse than their peers, whereas Canadian students view themselves as superior to their peers. Self-effacement is particularly pronounced among Japanese students after they are given failure

self-enhancement

an unrealistically positive view of oneself

feedback. In contrast, failure feedback does nothing to tarnish the positive self-view of Canadians (Heine, Kitayama, & Lehman, 2001; for related findings, see Endo, Heine, & Lehman, 2000; Heine & Renshaw, 2002).

In conceptually related research, students working on group projects at the University of British Columbia and at the Chinese University of Hong Kong were asked to rate one another's personality traits (Yik, Bond, & Paulhus, 1998). Canadian students showed classic self-enhancement—they rated themselves more positively than the other group members rated them. Just the opposite was found for Chinese students—they rated themselves more negatively than their peers rated them. Given findings such as these, it is perhaps not surprising that Asian university students score lower on measures of self-esteem than do Canadian students (Campbell et al., 1996; Endo, Heine, & Lehman, 2000; Heine & Lehman, 1997b; Sato & Cameron, 1999).

Might people evaluate themselves differently depending on the cultural identity that is activated? To find out, Ross, Xun, and Wilson (2002) asked Chinese-born students who had lived in Canada for an average of seven years to complete a questionnaire on various aspects of the self. The questionnaire was written in either Chinese or English. Participants who answered in Chinese described themselves in more collectivist terms, were more self-effacing, and scored lower on a self-esteem measure than the participants who completed the questionnaire in English. In fact, the responses of Chinese participants who answered in English were more similar to those of a comparison group of Canadian-born students than they were to Chinese participants responding in Chinese. In short, the language used primed different senses of self—the Chinese language brought to mind the participants' collectivist, self-effacing self, whereas the English language activated their individualistic, self-enhancing self.

Before leaving this topic, we consider one final question: Might people in Asian countries in fact secretly engage in self-enhancement but not feel comfortable openly bragging about themselves on questionnaires? To find out, Heine, Takata, and Lehman (2000) designed a study in which they measured self-enhancement in a subtle way—namely, by examining whether students believed or accepted certain kinds of feedback. In this research, students at the University of British Columbia and at Nara University in Japan took a computerized mathematical judgment test. Later, participants were asked who had performed better on the test—they or the average student at their university? In order to answer this question, they were given (false) information on how they had performed on each trial and how the average student had performed. Participants were told that they could keep viewing trials until they had enough information to answer the question. Participants in the success condition were given higher scores than the average student on most trials; for participants in the failure condition, the average student's scores generally were higher. The critical question was how many of these trials participants would want to view before making a decision about whether they had performed better than the average student. As shown on the left side of Figure 5.3, in Canada, participants in the failure condition tended to view more trials than participants in the success condition. In other words, Canadians found it hard to believe that they had done worse than the average student and therefore needed ample "proof" that that was the case. However, if the feedback indicated that they had outperformed the average student, they did not need to see many trials to be convinced. Here, Canadians showed self-enhancement. In Japan, participants showed exactly the opposite pattern. They did not have to see many trials in which they had been outperformed before concluding that the average student had performed better than they had (see the right side of Figure 5.3). However, when it came to concluding that they had performed better than the average student, they needed plenty of proof—Japanese participants in the success condition viewed the greatest number of trials. These results are consistent with self-effacement.

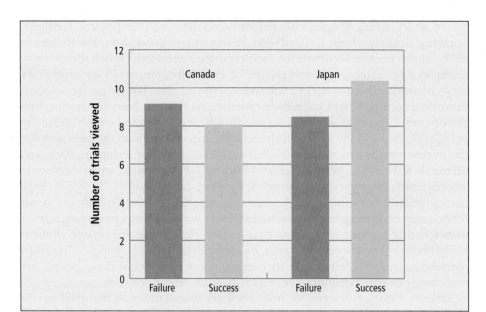

FIGURE 5.3
Cultural differences in self-enhancement

When Canadian participants received feedback that they had performed worse than the average student, they needed greater "proof" that this had been the case than when they received feedback that they had performed better than the average student. Japanese students found it easy to believe that they had performed poorly but hard to believe that they had performed well.

(Based on Heine, Takata, & Lehman, 2000)

Based on these and other findings, Heine and colleagues have reached the conclusion that when it comes to self-enhancement, people from Eastern cultures simply don't do it! A meta analysis of 81 studies examining self-enhancement among North Americans and East Asians supports this conclusion (Heine, 2003; Heine & Hamamura, 2007).

Self-Verification: Wanting to Know the Truth about Ourselves

So far we have focused on research showing that, at least in North America, people tend to be highly motivated to feel good about themselves, to the point where they will happily distort reality in order to maintain a positive self-concept. According to William Swann and his colleagues, people also are motivated to know the truth about themselves—even if the truth hurts (Giesler, Josephs, & Swann, 1996; Swann, 1990, 1996; Swann & Hill, 1982; Swann & Pelham, 1988; Swann & Schroeder, 1995). Swann calls this **self-verification theory**, suggesting that people have a need to seek confirmation of their self-concept whether the self-concept is positive or negative. In some circumstances, this tendency can conflict with the desire to uphold a favourable view of oneself.

Consider, for example, Patrick, who has always thought of himself as a lousy writer with poor verbal skills. One day he is working on a term paper with a friend, who remarks that she thinks his paper is skillfully crafted, beautifully written, and superbly articulate. How will Patrick feel? He should feel pleased and gratified, we might predict, because the friend's praise gives Patrick's self-esteem a boost. On the other hand, Patrick's friend has given him feedback that challenges his long-standing view of himself as a poor writer, and he might be motivated to maintain this negative view. Why? For two reasons. First, it can be unsettling and confusing to have our views of ourselves "disconfirmed"; if we changed our self-concept every time we encountered someone with a different opinion of us, it would be impossible to maintain a coherent sense of self. Second, self-verification theory holds that it can be uncomfortable to interact with people who view us differently from the way we view ourselves. People who don't know us might have unrealistic expectations, and it would be embarrassing to have them discover that we are not as smart or as artistic or as creative as they think we are. Better to let them know our faults at the outset.

self-verification theory

a theory suggesting that people have a need to seek confirmation of their self-concept, whether the self-concept is positive or negative; in some circumstances, this tendency can conflict with the desire to uphold a favourable view of oneself

In short, when people with negative self-views receive positive feedback, opposing needs go head to head—the desire to feel good about themselves by believing the positive feedback (i.e., self-enhancement needs) versus the desire to maintain a consistent, coherent picture of themselves and avoid the embarrassment of being found out (i.e., self-verification needs). Which needs win out? According to Swann and colleagues, whether we want to have accurate, rather than positive, feedback depends on two things: the dimension on which we are being evaluated and the nature of the relationship we have with the person doing the evaluating (Swann, Bosson, & Pelham, 2002; see Katz & Joiner, 2002, and Sciangula & Morry, in press, for related findings). For example, when it comes to a quality such as physical attractiveness, we want dating partners to give us high marks—regardless of the facts. However, we want the truth when it comes to our other qualities. If the person assessing our looks is a friend or a roommate, rather than a dating partner, it's honesty that counts. Similarly, if our artistic ability is being evaluated by our art instructor, or our athletic ability is being evaluated by our teammates, we prefer positivity over accuracy. However, if these people are evaluating our other qualities, the self-verification motive wins out.

Before leaving this topic, we note a few additional limits on the need to self-verify. First, people generally strive to uphold their negative self-beliefs only when they are highly certain of those beliefs (Maracek & Mettee, 1972; Swann & Ely, 1984; Swann & Pelham, 1988). To return to our earlier example, if Patrick had been less thoroughly convinced of his poor talents as a writer, he almost certainly would have been more receptive to his friend's praise. Second, if the consequences of being improperly evaluated are not too great—for example, if our contact with these individuals is rare so that it is unlikely they will discover we are not who we appear to be—then even people with negative views prefer positive feedback (Aronson, 1992). Finally, if people feel there is nothing they can do to improve their abilities, they generally prefer positive feedback to accurate feedback. Why remind ourselves that we are terrible if there is nothing we can do about it? If, however, people feel that a negative self-attribute can be changed with a little work, they prefer accurate feedback because this information can help them figure out what they need to do to get better (Steele, Spencer, & Josephs, 1992).

SUMMARY

In this chapter, we have explored how people come to know and evaluate themselves. The **self-concept** refers to the contents of the self—namely one's knowledge of one's own thoughts, beliefs, and personality traits. People differ in the extent to which their sense of self is clearly defined. Those who are high in self-concept clarity are more likely to have high self-esteem.

The self-concept serves an organizational function and an executive function. People organize information about themselves into **self-schemas**, which are knowledge structures about the self that help people understand, explain, and predict their own behaviour. One advantage of self-schemas is that people can remember information better if they relate it to themselves. This is known as the **self-reference effect.** The self also serves to regulate people's behaviour, choices, and plans for the future. Research on the self-regulatory resource model suggests that we have a limited amount of energy to devote to exercising self-control. Self-control is more difficult when we are depleted (e.g., feeling stressed or sleep-deprived).

There are interesting cross-cultural and gender differences in the self-concept. In many Western cultures, people have an **independent view of the self**, whereby they define themselves mainly in terms of their own thoughts, feelings, and actions. In many Eastern cultures, people have an **interdependent view of the self**, whereby they define themselves primarily in terms of their relationships with other people. In North America, women define themselves more in relation to other people and close intimate relationships than do men; this kind of interdependence is known as *relational* interdependence. North American men also show interdependence, but it takes a different form from that in women; specifically, men tend to focus on the groups to which they belong—a kind of interdependence known as *collective* interdependence.

There are three basic ways in which we come to know ourselves: through (1) **introspection**, (2) observations of our own behaviour, and (3) social interaction. **Self-awareness** refers to the act of thinking about ourselves. Research on **self-awareness theory** has found that introspection can be unpleasant because it focuses our attention on how we fall short of our internal standards. When this occurs, we may distract ourselves from these unpleasant feelings (e.g., by watching television). A benefit of self-focus is that it can make us more aware of our feelings and traits. Thinking about why we feel the way we do, however, is more difficult. Many studies show that people's judgments about the reasons for their feelings and actions are often incorrect, in part because people rely on **causal theories** when explaining their behaviour.

Self-perception theory holds that we come to know ourselves through observations of our own behaviour, just as an outsider would. This occurs in particular when our internal states are unclear and there appears to be no external reason for our behaviour. One interesting application of self-perception theory is the **overjustification effect**, which is the discounting of our **intrinsic motivation** for a task, as a result of inferring that we are engaging in the task because of **extrinsic motivation**. That is, rewards and other kinds of external influences can undermine our intrinsic interest; an activity we once liked seems like work instead of play. The kinds of rewards that are given also make a difference. **Task-contingent rewards** are given for doing a task, regardless of how well it is one. **Performance-contingent rewards** are based on how well people perform the task. Generally, performance-contingent rewards are less likely to undermine intrinsic motivation because they convey the message that you are good at the task.

Another way we come to know ourselves is through social interaction. According to the **looking-glass self**, our sense of who we are is based on others' perceptions of us. These perceptions become internalized and can influence our sense of self at any given time. We also know ourselves through comparison with others. **Social comparison theory** states that we will compare ourselves with others when we are unsure of our standing on some attribute and there is no objective criterion we can use. Typically, we choose to compare ourselves with similar others, for this is most diagnostic.

We also engage in social comparison to satisfy another basic human need: the need to maintain self-esteem. **Downward social comparison**, comparing ourselves with those who are inferior on the relevant attribute, can make us feel better about ourselves—as long as we are confident that we are not vulnerable to their plight. **Upward social comparison**, comparing ourselves with those who are superior on the relevant attribute, can make us feel better about ourselves if we are focusing on our actual (usual) self, but it can make us feel worse about ourselves if we are focusing on our best or ideal self.

According to **self-discrepancy theory**, we will feel bad about ourselves when our actual self falls short of the self we feel we should be (our "ought" self) or the self we would like to be (our "ideal" self). Discrepancies between our actual and ideal selves produce feelings of dejection and depression, whereas discrepancies between our actual self and our "ought" self produce feelings of anxiety.

Research on **self-enhancement** suggests that the need to feel good about ourselves is so strong that we tend to hold unrealistically positive views of ourselves. In contrast, **self-verification theory** holds that we want accurate information about what we are like—even if it is not flattering. Generally, people opt for self-enhancement rather than self-verification. Finally, it is important to realize that self-enhancement is limited to individualistic (Western) cultures. In collectivist (Eastern) cultures, people are more likely to be self-critical, a phenomenon known as *self-effacement*.

PEARSON
mypsychlab

Along with a dynamic, electronic version of this text, MyPsychLab offers a wealth of resources to deepen your understanding and test your recall of the material in this chapter—including video and audio clips, simulations and activities, self-assessments, practice tests, and other study materials. The following specific resources are available for this chapter:

 Schemas

 Multiple Selves

 Cultural Psychology: Kaiping Peng

To access MyPsychLab, please visit www.mypsychlab.com (Student Access Code required—packaged with this book).

Attitudes and Attitude Change:

Influencing Thoughts, Feelings, and Behaviour

March, 1997. Quebec police were stunned when they learned that five people had committed suicide in Saint-Casimir, a village west of Quebec City. The people who died were members of the Solar Temple cult (discussed in Chapter 1). The cult was led by Luc Jouret and his right-hand man, Joseph Di Mambro. Those who joined the Solar Temple cult were mainly wealthy professionals, including the mayor of Richelieu, Quebec, and his wife, people in upper management positions at Hydro-Québec, a journalist, and a civil servant. Jouret was a charismatic spiritual leader with formidable powers of persuasion. A cult member interviewed by *Maclean's* reported, "He asked all of us to empty our bank accounts" (Laver, 1994). She and her husband sold their property in Switzerland and handed over the proceeds—$300 000—to Jouret. Others followed suit. Most disturbing of all, Jouret convinced cult members that the world was about to be destroyed by fire and that the only salvation was to take a "death voyage" by ritualized suicide to the star Sirius, where they would be reborn.

The cult attracted worldwide attention in October 1994, when buildings used by Jouret and his followers in a small village in Switzerland, and a chalet owned by Di Mambro in Morin Heights, Quebec, erupted in flames. Swiss firefighters discovered a chapel in which 22 cult members, cloaked in ceremonial robes, lay in a circle, with their faces looking up at a Christ-like figure resembling Jouret. In Morin Heights, police found the bodies of cult members clad in ceremonial robes and wearing red and gold medallions inscribed with the initials *T. S.* (Temple Solaire). At the end of the day, the death toll was 53 people, including several children. It is believed that both Jouret and Di Mambro died in the Swiss fires. So did the mayor of Richelieu, Quebec, and his wife (Laver, 1994).

Sadly, the 1994 deaths did not put an end to the cult. Some of the remaining followers continued to take death voyages. However, by 1997, Quebec police believed that the Solar Temple had finally run its course.

▲ Luc Jouret, leader of the Order of the Solar Temple cult, died in the 1994 mass murder–suicide along with 52 other cult members

Apparently that was not the case. Five suicides in Saint-Casimir brought the total to 74 deaths in Canada and Europe over a five-year period.

How could intelligent, rational people be persuaded to hand over their money and even their lives to a charismatic leader? As we shall discuss in this chapter, people can be swayed by appeals to their fears, hopes, and desires. We will also show that once people change their attitudes, a powerful process of self-justification sets in. People feel a strong need to justify their decisions, and in the process of doing so, become even more committed to their decision. But first, what exactly is an attitude, and how is it changed? These questions, which are some of the oldest in social psychology, are the subject of this chapter.

The Nature and Origin of Attitudes

attitude

an evaluation of a person, object, or idea

Most social psychologists define an **attitude** as an evaluation of a person, object, or idea (Ajzen, 2001; Eagly & Chaiken, 1998; Fazio, 2000; Olson & Zanna, 1993; Petty, Cacioppo, Strathman, & Priester, 2005). Attitudes are evaluative in that they consist of a positive or negative reaction to something. Sometimes people actually experience ambivalence, or "mixed feelings," toward someone or something. For example, research conducted at the University of Waterloo has shown that some people have ambivalent attitudes toward feminists—they see feminists in both positive and negative terms (MacDonald & Zanna, 1998)—and toward issues such as capital punishment and abortion (Newby-Clark, McGregor, & Zanna, 2002). According to research conducted at the University of Western Ontario, some of us have ambivalent attitudes toward Canada's Native peoples (Bell & Esses, 1997, 2002) and toward Asian immigrants to Canada (Maio, Bell, & Esses, 1996). Our point is that people are not neutral observers of the world but constant evaluators of what they see. It would be very odd to hear someone say, "My feelings toward anchovies, snakes, chocolate cake, and my roommate are completely neutral." We can elaborate further on our definition of an attitude by stating more precisely what we mean by an "evaluation." An attitude is made up of three components:

- an *affective* component, consisting of emotional reactions toward the attitude object (e.g., another person or a social issue)
- a *cognitive* component, consisting of thoughts and beliefs about the attitude object, and
- a *behavioural* component, consisting of actions or observable behaviour toward the attitude object.

Consider your attitude toward a particular model of car, such as a Toyota Prius. What is your affective reaction when you see the car? Perhaps it triggers feelings of pleasure or excitement. If you are a Canadian autoworker examining a new foreign-made model, you may feel anger or resentment. What is your cognitive reaction? What beliefs do you hold about the car's attributes? Perhaps you admire the hybrid engine in the Prius that makes it one of the most fuel-efficient cars you can buy. And what about your behavioural reaction? Do you go to the dealership to test-drive the car and actually buy one? These components combine to form your overall attitude toward the Prius.

Where Do Attitudes Come From?

Social psychologists have focused primarily on the way that attitudes are created by people's affective, cognitive, and behavioural experiences. One important finding is that not all attitudes are created equally. Although attitudes have affective, cognitive, and behavioural components, any given attitude can be based more on one type of experience than another (Zanna & Rempel, 1988).

Affectively Based Attitudes An attitude based more on emotions and feelings than on an objective appraisal of pluses and minuses is called an **affectively based attitude** (Breckler & Wiggins, 1989; Zanna & Rempel, 1988). Sometimes we simply like a certain brand of car, regardless of whether it gets good gas consumption or whether it has enough cupholders. Occasionally we even feel very positive about something—such as another person—in spite of having negative beliefs. An example is falling in love with someone despite knowing that the person has a history of infidelity. As a guide to which attitudes are likely to be affectively based, consider the topics that etiquette manuals suggest should not be discussed at a dinner party: politics, sex, and religion. People seem to vote more with their hearts than their minds—for example, basing their decision to vote for a political candidate on how they feel about the person or the party, rather than on a well-reasoned evaluation of the policies (Abelson et al., 1982; Granberg & Brown, 1989). The nephew of one of the authors (Beverley Fehr) learned this first hand when he was campaigning for a political candidate in Calgary. One of the questions he asked when he knocked on people's doors was whether they were happy with the Conservative candidate currently serving in that riding. A frequent response in this Conservative stronghold was, "Yes. I think he's doing a great job." The member of Parliament in that riding was actually a woman!

Where do affectively based attitudes come from? One source is people's values, such as their religious and moral beliefs. Attitudes about such issues as abortion, the death penalty, and premarital sex are often based on one's value system (Hodson & Olson, 2005; Murray, Haddock, & Zanna, 1996; Schwartz, 1992; Smith, Bruner, & White, 1956). For example, in a study conducted at the University of Western Ontario, Maio and Olson (1995) varied the message on posters soliciting donations for cancer research. In the value-expressive condition, the poster read, "Save people's lives, help researchers find a cure for cancer and *help others live*"; in the non-value condition, the message ended with "and *protect your future.*" For participants in the value-expressive condition (help others live), there was a positive correlation between altruistic values and having favourable attitudes toward donating to cancer research. In contrast, in the non-values condition (protect your future), there was no relation between altruistic values and attitudes toward donating money.

Affectively based attitudes have certain key features in common:

(a) they do not result from a rational examination of the issues;

(b) they are not governed by logic (e.g., persuasive arguments about the issues seldom change an affectively based attitude); and

(c) they are often linked to people's values, so that trying to change them challenges those values (Katz, 1960; Smith, Bruner, & White, 1956).

> **affectively based attitude**
>
> an attitude based primarily on people's emotions and feelings about the attitude object

> ❝ *We never desire passionately what we desire through reason alone.* ❞
>
> —François de la Rochefoucauld, Maxims, 1665

> ❝ *That is the way we are made; we don't reason; where we feel, we just feel.* ❞
>
> —Mark Twain, A Connecticut Yankee in King Arthur's Court, 1889

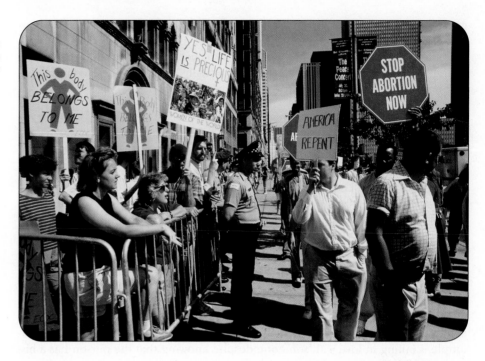

▶ Attitudes toward abortion, the death penalty, and premarital sex are examples of affectively based attitudes that are likely to be based on people's value systems.

cognitively based attitude

an attitude based primarily on a person's beliefs about the properties of an attitude object

behaviourally based attitude

an attitude based primarily on observations of how one behaves toward an attitude object

❝ *How can I know what I think till I see what I say?* ❞

—*Graham Wallas,* The Art of Thought, *1926*

Cognitively Based Attitudes   Sometimes our attitudes are based primarily on the relevant facts, such as the objective merits of an automobile. How many kilometres per litre of gas does it get? Does it have air conditioning? To the extent that a person's evaluation is based primarily on beliefs about the properties of an attitude object, it is a **cognitively based attitude**. The purpose of this kind of attitude is to classify the pluses and minuses of an object so we can quickly tell whether it is worth our while to have anything to do with it (Katz, 1960; Murray, Haddock, & Zanna, 1996; Smith, Bruner, & White, 1956). Consider your attitude toward a utilitarian object such as a vacuum cleaner. Your attitude is likely to be based on your beliefs about the objective merits of particular brands, such as how well they vacuum up dirt and how much they cost—not on how sexy they make you feel! How can we tell if an attitude is more affectively or cognitively based? See the accompanying Try It! for one way of measuring the bases of people's attitudes.

Behaviourally Based Attitudes   A **behaviourally based attitude** stems from people's observations of how they behave toward an attitude object. This may seem a little odd—how do we know how to behave if we don't already know how we feel? According to Daryl Bem's (1972) *self-perception theory* (discussed in Chapter 5), under certain circumstances people don't know how they feel until they see how they behave. Suppose, for example, that you asked a friend how much she enjoys exercising. If she replies, "Well, I guess I like it, because I always seem to be going for a run or heading over to the gym to work out," we would say she has a behaviourally based attitude. Her attitude is based more on an observation of her own behaviour than on her cognition or affect.

Comparing Affective, Cognitive, and Behavioural Bases of Attitudes   As we have been discussing, not all attitudes are created in the same way. Geoffrey Haddock, Mark Zanna, and Victoria Esses have conducted a series of studies, mostly with University of Waterloo students, to determine which attitudes are most likely to be based on affective, cognitive, or behavioural experiences (Esses, Haddock, & Zanna, 1993; Haddock & Zanna, 1994, 1998; Haddock, Zanna, & Esses, 1993, 1994). It turns out that when attitudes are negative toward particular groups, they are often

▶ Affective and Cognitive Bases of Attitudes

Fill out this questionnaire to see how psychologists measure the affective and cognitive components of attitudes.

1. Record the number on each scale that best describes your feelings toward snakes:

hateful	–3	–2	–1	0	1	2	3	loving
sad	–3	–2	–1	0	1	2	3	delighted
annoyed	–3	–2	–1	0	1	2	3	happy
tense	–3	–2	–1	0	1	2	3	calm
bored	–3	–2	–1	0	1	2	3	excited
angry	–3	–2	–1	0	1	2	3	relaxed
disgusted	–3	–2	–1	0	1	2	3	accepting
sorrowful	–3	–2	–1	0	1	2	3	joyful

2. Record the number on each scale that best describes the traits or characteristics of snakes:

useless	–3	–2	–1	0	1	2	3	useful
foolish	–3	–2	–1	0	1	2	3	wise
unsafe	–3	–2	–1	0	1	2	3	safe
harmful	–3	–2	–1	0	1	2	3	beneficial
worthless	–3	–2	–1	0	1	2	3	valuable
imperfect	–3	–2	–1	0	1	2	3	perfect
unhealthy	–3	–2	–1	0	1	2	3	wholesome

Once you have answered these questions, sum all your responses to Question 1, and all your responses to Question 2. These scales were developed by Crites, Fabrigar, and Petty (1994) to measure the affective and cognitive components of attitudes. Question 1 measures the affective component of your attitude toward snakes; you were asked to rate your feelings about them. Question 2 measures the cognitive component of attitudes; you were asked to rate your beliefs about the characteristics of snakes. Most people's attitudes toward snakes are more affectively than cognitively based. If this was true of you, your total score for Question 1 should depart more from zero (in a negative direction, for most people) than your total score for Question 2.

Now, substitute "vacuum cleaners" for "snakes" for questions 1 and 2, and mark the scales again. Most people's attitudes toward a utilitarian object such as a vacuum cleaner are more cognitively than affectively based. If this was true of you, your total score for Question 2 should depart more from zero than your total score for Question 1.

cognitively based. More specifically, these researchers found that people's negative attitudes toward homosexuals and Pakistanis were based on a kind of cognition that they called symbolic beliefs—namely, beliefs that these groups threaten their value system (Esses, Haddock, & Zanna, 1993; Haddock, Zanna, & Esses, 1993). Attitudes toward other social groups that were studied (English Canadians, French Canadians, and Native Canadians) were more positive; these attitudes were more likely to be based on affect—how the participants felt about these groups (Haddock, Zanna, & Esses, 1993). Haddock and Zanna (1998) also found that attitudes toward social issues such as capital punishment were more likely to be based on how people felt about the issue (affect), rather than on their thoughts about it (cognition). Thus, when it comes to our attitudes concerning different social groups, it appears that if we dislike the group, our attitudes are likely to have a cognitive basis—specifically, the belief that the group threatens our value system. Attitudes toward groups that we like are apt to be based on our feelings toward that group (i.e., affect). In short, different attitudes have different bases.

Explicit versus Implicit Attitudes

explicit attitudes

attitudes that we consciously endorse and can easily report

implicit attitudes

attitudes that are involuntary, uncontrollable, and at times unconscious

Once an attitude develops, it can exist at two levels. **Explicit attitudes** are ones we consciously endorse and can easily report; they are what we think of as our evaluations when someone asks us a question such as "What is your opinion on imposing carbon taxes?" or "What is your opinion on imposing carbon taxes, compared with that of other students at your university or college?" (Olson, Goffin, & Haynes, 2007). People can also have **implicit attitudes**, which are involuntary, uncontrollable, and at times unconscious evaluations (Bassili & Brown, 2005; Fazio & Olson, 2003; Greenwald & Banaji, 1995; Wilson, Lindsey, & Schooler, 2000).

Consider Sam, a white, middle-class university student who genuinely believes that all races are equal and who abhors any kind of racial bias. This is Sam's explicit attitude, in the sense that it is his conscious evaluation of members of other races that governs how he chooses to act. For instance, consistent with his explicit attitude, Sam recently signed a petition in favour of affirmative action policies at his university. However, Sam has grown up in a culture in which there are many negative stereotypes about minority groups, and it is possible that some of these negative ideas have seeped into him in ways of which he is not fully aware (Devine, 1989a). When he is around people from Pakistan, for example, perhaps some negative feelings are triggered automatically and unintentionally. If so, he has a negative implicit attitude toward Pakistanis, which is likely to influence behaviours he is not monitoring or controlling, such as how nervous he acts around them (Dovidio, Kawakami, & Gaertner, 2002).

We will discuss such automatic prejudice in Chapter 12 (see also our discussion of automatic thinking in Chapter 3). For now, we point out that people can have explicit and implicit attitudes toward virtually anything, not just other races. For example, students can believe explicitly that they hate math but have a more positive attitude at an implicit level (Hofmann, Gawronski, Gschwendner, Le, & Schmitt, 2005; Nosek, Banaji, & Greenwald, 2002; Rudman, 2004). How do we know? A variety of techniques have been developed to measure people's implicit attitudes, some of which we discussed in Chapter 3. One of the most popular is the Implicit Association Test, or IAT (Gawronski & Bodenhausen, 2005; Greenwald, McGhee, & Schwartz, 1998; Greenwald & Nosek, 2001), in which people categorize words or pictures on a computer. (Rather than going into detail about how this test works, we encourage you to visit a website where you can take the test yourself and read more about how it is constructed: https://implicit.harvard.edu/implicit.)

▶People can have explicit and implicit attitudes toward the same subject. Explicit attitudes are those we consciously endorse and can easily report; implicit attitudes are involuntary, uncontrollable, and at times, unconscious. Social psychologists have been especially interested in people's explicit and implicit attitudes toward members of other races.

Research on implicit attitudes is in its infancy, and psychologists are actively investigating their origins, how to measure them, and their relation to explicit attitudes. The focus in the remainder of this chapter will be on how explicit attitudes change and their relation to behaviour. We will return to a discussion of implicit attitudes in Chapter 12 as they apply to stereotyping and prejudice.

When Will Attitudes Predict Behaviour?

It might seem that once we know someone's attitudes, it would be easy to predict their behaviour. Knowing, for example, that someone holds positive attitudes toward a politician should enable you to predict whether that person will vote for that politician in the next election. Right? Actually, the relation between attitudes and behaviour is not nearly so straightforward as one might expect.

In the early 1930s, Richard LaPiere (1934) embarked on a sightseeing trip across the United States with a young Chinese couple. Because prejudice against Asians was commonplace among Americans at that time, he was apprehensive about how his Chinese friends would be treated. At each hotel, campground, and restaurant they entered, LaPiere worried that his friends would confront anti-Asian prejudice and that they would be refused service. Much to his surprise, of the 251 establishments he and his friends visited, only one refused to serve them.

After his trip, LaPiere wrote a letter to each establishment that he and his friends had visited, asking if it would serve a Chinese visitor. Of the many establishments who replied, only one said it would. More than 90 percent said they definitely would not (the rest said they were unde-cided). People's attitudes—as expressed in their response to LaPiere's written inquiry—were in stark contrast to their actual behaviour toward LaPiere's Chinese friends.

LaPiere's study was not, of course, a controlled experiment. As he acknowledged, there are several possible reasons why his results did not show consistency between people's attitudes and behaviour. For example, he had no way of knowing whether the proprietors who answered his letter were the same people who had served him and his friends. Further, people's attitudes could have changed in the months that passed between the time they served the Chinese couple and the time they received the letter. Nonetheless, the lack of correspondence between people's attitudes and what they actually did was so striking that we might question the assumption that behaviour routinely follows from attitudes. Indeed, when Allan Wicker (1969) reviewed dozens of more methodologically sound studies, he reached the same conclusion: People's atti-tudes are poor predictors of their behaviour.

> *If actions are to yield all the results they are capable of, there must be a certain consistency between them and one's intentions.*
>
> —François de la Rochefoucauld,
> Maxims, 1665

How can this be? Does a person's attitude toward Asians or political candidates really tell us nothing about how he or she will behave? How can we reconcile LaPiere's findings—and other studies like it—with the fact that many times behaviour and attitudes *are* consistent? Stay tuned for the answer.

The Theory of Planned Behaviour

In subsequent research, social psychologists have discovered that attitudes can ac-tually predict behaviours quite well—but only under certain conditions (DeBono & Snyder, 1995; Fazio, 1990; Zanna & Fazio, 1982). What are these conditions? According to the **theory of planned behaviour** (Ajzen & Fishbein, 1980, 2005; Ajzen & Sexton, 1999; Fishbein & Ajzen, 1975), the best predictor of people's behaviour is their intention (i.e., whether they intend to perform the behaviour

theory of planned behaviour

a theory that the best predictors of a person's planned, deliberate behaviours are the person's attitudes toward specific behaviours, subjective norms, and perceived behavioural control

FIGURE 6.1

The theory of planned behaviour

According to this theory, the best predictors of people's behaviours are their behavioural intentions. The best predictors of their intentions are their attitudes toward the specific behaviour, their subjective norms, and their perceived control of the behaviour.

(Adapted from Ajzen & Fishbein, 1980)

in question), which is in turn determined by three things: their attitudes toward the specific behaviour, their subjective norms, and their perceived behavioural control (see Figure 6.1). Let's consider each of these in turn.

Specific Attitudes The theory of planned behaviour holds that only *specific attitudes* toward the behaviour in question can be expected to predict that behaviour. In one study, researchers asked a sample of married women about their attitudes toward birth control pills, ranging from the general (the women's attitude toward birth control) to the specific (their attitude toward using birth control pills during the next two years; see Table 6.1). Two years later, the women were asked whether they had used birth control pills at any time since the last interview. As Table 6.1 shows, the women's general attitude toward birth control did not predict their use of birth control at all. This general attitude did not take into account other factors that could have influenced their decision, such as concern about the long-term effects of the pill and their attitudes toward other forms of birth control. The more specific the question was about the act of using birth control pills, the better this attitude predicted their actual behaviour (Davidson & Jaccard, 1979).

This study helps explain why LaPiere (1934) found such inconsistency between people's attitudes and behaviours. His question to the proprietors—whether they would serve "members of the Chinese race"—was very general. Had he asked a much more specific question—such as whether they would serve an educated, well-dressed, well-to-do Chinese couple accompanied by a white

TABLE 6.1

Specific attitudes are better predictors of behaviour*

Different groups of women were asked about their attitudes toward birth control. The more specific the question, the better it predicted their actual use of birth control. If a correlation is close to 0, it means that there is no relationship between the two variables. The closer the correlation is to 1, the stronger the relationship between attitudes and behaviour.

Attitude Measure	Attitude Behaviour Correlation
Attitude toward birth control	0.08
Attitude toward birth control pills	0.32
Attitude toward using birth control pills	0.53
Attitude toward using birth control pills during the next two years	0.57

* If a correlation is close to 0, it means that there is no relationship between the two variables. The closer the correlation is to 1, the stronger the relationship between attitudes and behaviour.

(Adapted from Davidson & Jaccard, 1979)

American professor—the proprietors might have given an answer that was more in line with their behaviour.

Subjective Norms   In addition to measuring attitudes toward the behaviour, we also need to measure people's subjective norms—their beliefs about how the people they care about will view the behaviour in question (see Figure 6.1). To predict someone's intentions, it can be as important to know these beliefs as to know his or her attitudes. For example, suppose we want to predict whether Kristen intends to go to a heavy metal concert. We happen to know that she can't stand heavy metal music. Based on her negative attitude, we would probably say she won't go. Suppose, however, that we also know that Kristen's best friend, Malcolm, really wants her to go. Knowing this subjective norm—her belief about how a close friend views her behaviour—we might make a different prediction.

Perceived Behavioural Control   Finally, as seen in Figure 6.1, people's intentions are influenced by perceived behavioural control, which is the ease with which people believe they can perform the behaviour. If people think it is difficult to perform the behaviour, such as sticking to a gruelling exercise regimen, they will not form a strong intention to do so. If people think it is easy to perform the behaviour, such as remembering to buy milk on the way home from work, they are more likely to form a strong intention to do so.

There is considerable research support for the idea that asking people about these determinants of their intentions—attitudes toward specific behaviours, subjective norms, and perceived behavioural control—increases the ability to predict their behaviour. Most of this research has focused on behaviours related to health and exercise, such as smoking among Quebec high school students (Hill et al., 1997); exercise among Alberta women and men receiving treatment for cancer (Courneya & Friedenreich, 1997, 1999); exercise, maintaining a low-fat diet, and smoking among Quebec men (Nguyen, Beland, Otis, & Potvin, 1996); and participation in exercise classes for the elderly offered at the University of Western Ontario (Estabrooks & Carron, 1999). To give one last example, Mummery and Wankel (1999) used the theory of planned behaviour to predict whether a cycle of intensive training would be completed by 116 competitive swimmers (aged 11 to 18 years) from swimming clubs throughout Canada. Consistent with the theory, swimmers who had positive attitudes toward the training cycle, who believed that important people in their life wanted them to complete it, and who believed that they were capable of doing so were most likely to report that they intended to complete the upcoming cycle of training. Importantly, swimmers with these intentions also were the most likely to actually complete their training.

Below, we will focus on how the theory of planned behaviour applies to an important social issue—namely, persuading people to engage in safer sex.

The Theory of Planned Behaviour: Implications for Safer Sex

There is one area in which people's attitudes are often inconsistent with their behaviour, even though the consequences can be fatal. The inconsistency takes the form of having positive attitudes toward using condoms, expressing intentions to use condoms, but then failing to actually use them in sexual encounters (Hynie & Lydon, 1996). For example, in one study, nearly 100 percent of the patrons of various dating bars in southern Ontario agreed with statements such as "If I were to have sex with someone I just met, I would have no objections if my partner suggested that we use a condom" (Herold & Mewhinney, 1993). However, these favourable attitudes toward condom use did not translate into safer sex practices. Only 56 percent of the people at the bar who engaged in casual sex had used a condom in their most recent sexual encounter. Even more frightening, a mere 29 percent of the women and men who had engaged in casual sex in the past year reported that they always used a condom.

▲ If people fear a negative reaction, they are less likely to raise the issue of condom use with a potential sexual partner.

Why would people with positive attitudes toward condom use risk their lives by not using them? Perhaps the theory of planned behaviour can provide some clues. As you'll recall, according to this theory, attitudes are not the only predictor of behaviour. Subjective norms, perceived behavioural control, and behavioural intentions also play a role. Can these variables help us understand why people so often fail to use condoms, despite having positive attitudes toward condom use? Let's take a look at some studies.

Subjective Norms People's beliefs about how others view the behaviour in question are an important determinant of their behaviour. In one study, it was found that 65 percent of the students at a high school in Nova Scotia believed that their sexually active friends use condoms (Richardson, Beazley, Delaney & Langille, 1997). Such beliefs should promote condom use. Indeed, there is evidence that whether university students use condoms depends on the norms for sexual behaviour that operate among their friends (Winslow, Franzini, & Hwang, 1992). For example, researchers at York University and Queen's University found that social norms (the belief that others in one's social group think that using condoms is important) predicted intentions to use condoms. Importantly, subjective norms also predicted actual condom use, as reported in a follow-up study six weeks later (Hynie, MacDonald, & Marques, 2006). Of course, social norms may vary, depending on the situation. For example, students from various universities in eastern Ontario on "break loose" vacations in Daytona Beach, Florida, report that it is more acceptable to have casual sex while on such vacations than while at home (Maticka-Tyndale, Herold, & Mewhinney, 1998, 2001; Mewhinney, Herold, & Maticka-Tyndale, 1995). Unfortunately, the norm of permissive sexuality that evolves in such settings is accompanied by a low rate of condom use (Eiser & Ford, 1995).

Our beliefs about how our sexual partner feels about condom use is another example of a subjective norm. If we anticipate a negative reaction from our partner, we are less likely to use condoms. Several studies conducted in Montreal have shown that women, in particular, anticipate a negative reaction from their partner if they provide condoms (Hynie & Lydon, 1995; Maticka-Tyndale, 1992).

Perceived Behavioural Control If people think it is difficult to perform a behaviour, they will not form strong intentions to do so. At first glance, using condoms might seem like an easy thing to do. However, that is actually not the case. A study conducted with sexually active students at the University of British Columbia found that those who were embarrassed about buying condoms bought them less often than did those who were not embarrassed (Dahl, Gorn, & Weinberg, 1998). Further, in a series of studies conducted at McGill University, it was found that people can feel awkward about bringing up the topic of condoms during a sexual encounter (Hynie et al., 1998; Hynie & Lydon, 1996). Thus, the more difficult you find it to perform behaviours such as buying condoms or bringing up the topic with your partner, the less likely you are to actually use them.

Behavioural Intentions The importance of intentions in predicting condom use has been demonstrated in studies of the Latin American community in Montreal, the English-speaking Caribbean community in Toronto, and the South Asian community in Vancouver (Godin, Maticka-Tyndale, Adrien, Manson-Singer, Willams, & Cappon, 1996), as well as in a survey of first-year university students across Canada (Hawa, Munro, & Doherty-Poirier, 1998). What factors might affect people's intentions to use condoms? Researchers at the University of Waterloo and at Queen's University (MacDonald & Martineau, 2002; MacDonald et al., 2000; MacDonald, Zanna, & Fong, 1996) have found that there are a number of answers to this question. One factor is your mood. In a study conducted with female university students, MacDonald and Martineau (2002) found that participants who were in a bad mood were more likely to report intentions to engage in sexual intercourse without a condom than those who were in a good mood. Women who were low in self-esteem were especially likely to intend to engage in unprotected sex when they were in a bad mood. The researchers suggest that people with low self-esteem who are experiencing negative mood may be especially worried about the threat of rejection and therefore may be less likely to insist on condom use.

MacDonald and colleagues also have found that for both women and men, alcohol intoxication is associated with lower intentions to use condoms—even among those who have positive attitudes toward condom use (MacDonald, Zanna, & Fong, 1996; MacDonald et al., 2000). The researchers explain that when people are intoxicated, their ability to process information is impaired, such that they are able to focus only on the most immediate aspects of the situation (e.g., short-term pleasure) rather than on the long-term consequences of their actions. These findings are alarming, given that alcohol is present in many of the settings in which people are likely to encounter cues that promote casual sex (e.g., bars, parties, vacations; Maticka-Tyndale, Herold, & Mewhinney, 1998, 2001).

In summary, even the most positive of attitudes toward condom use do not guarantee that people will practise safer sex. The theory of planned behaviour suggests that other variables must be taken into account as well, including subjective norms, perceived behavioural control, and behavioural intentions.

Attitude Change

As we have seen, attitudes do not necessarily translate into behaviour. However, this fact does not stop people from trying to change our attitudes, hoping our behaviour will follow. Advertisers, for example, assume that changing people's attitudes toward products will result in increased sales, and politicians assume that positive feelings toward a candidate will result in a vote for that candidate on election day. But what is the best way to change people's attitudes? As you'll see next, this is a question that has fascinated social psychologists for decades. Here are some of their answers.

Persuasive Communications and Attitude Change

Suppose the Canadian Cancer Society has given you a five-figure budget to come up with an anti-smoking campaign that could be used nationwide. You have many decisions ahead of you. Should you pack your public service announcement with facts and figures? Or should you take a more emotional approach in your message, including frightening visual images of diseased lungs? Should you hire a famous movie star to deliver your message, or a Nobel Prize–winning medical researcher? Should you take a friendly tone and acknowledge that it is hard to quit smoking, or should you take a hard line and tell smokers to (as the Nike ads put it) "just do it"? You can see the point—it's not easy to figure out how to construct a truly **persuasive communication**, one that advocates a particular side of an issue.

Fortunately, social psychologists have conducted many studies on what makes a persuasive communication effective, beginning with Carl Hovland and his colleagues (Hovland, Janis, & Kelley, 1953). These researchers conducted experiments on the conditions under which people are most likely to be influenced by persuasive communications. In essence, they studied "who says what to whom," looking at the *source of the communication* (e.g., how expert or attractive the speaker is); the *communication itself* (e.g., the quality of the arguments; whether the speaker presents both sides of the issue); and the *nature of the audience* (e.g., which kinds of appeals work with hostile versus friendly audiences).

persuasive communication

communication (e.g., a speech or television advertisement) advocating a particular side of an issue

❝ *Of the modes of persuasion furnished by the spoken word, there are three kinds. The first kind depends on the personal character of the speaker; the second on putting the audience into a certain frame of mind; the third on the proof, or apparent proof, provided by the words of the speech itself.* ❞

—*Aristotle*, Rhetoric, 350 BC

FIGURE 6.2
The Yale Attitude Change Approach

The Yale Attitude Change Approach

The effectiveness of persuasive communications depends on who says what to whom.

Who: The Source of the Communication

- Credible speakers (e.g., those with obvious expertise) persuade people more than speakers lacking in credibility (Hovland & Weiss, 1951; Jain & Posavac, 2000).
- Attractive speakers (whether due to physical or personality attributes) persuade people more than unattractive speakers do (Eagly & Chaiken, 1975; Petty, Wegener, & Fabrigar, 1997).

What: The Nature of the Communication

- People are more persuaded by messages that do not seem to be designed to influence them (Petty & Cacioppo, 1986; Walster & Festinger, 1962).
- Is it best to present a one-sided communication (one that presents only arguments favoring your position) or a two-sided communication (one that presents arguments for and against your position)? In general, two-sided messages work better, if you are sure to refute the arguments on the other side (Crowley & Hoyer, 1994; Igou & Bless, 2003; Lumsdaine & Janis, 1953).
- Is it best to give your speech before or after someone arguing for the other side?

If the speeches are to be given back to back and there will be a delay before people have to make up their minds, it is best to go first. Under these conditions, there is likely to be a *primacy effect,* wherein people are more influenced by what they hear first. If there is a delay between the speeches and people will make up their minds right after hearing the second one, it is best to go last. Under these conditions, there is likely to be a *recency effect,* wherein people remember the second speech better than the first one (Haugtvedt & Wegener, 1994; Miller & Campbell, 1959).

To Whom: The Nature of the Audience

- An audience that is distracted during the persuasive communication will often be persuaded more than one that is not (Festinger & Maccoby, 1964; Albarracin & Wyer, 2001).
- People low in intelligence tend to be more influenceable than people high in intelligence, and people with moderate self-esteem tend to be more influenceable than people with low or high self-esteem (Rhodes & Wood, 1992).
- People are particularly susceptible to attitude change during the impressionable ages of 18 to 25. Beyond those ages, people's attitudes are more stable and resistant to change (Krosnick & Alwin, 1989; Sears, 1981).

Yale Attitude Change Approach

the study of the conditions under which people are most likely to change their attitudes in response to persuasive messages; researchers in this tradition focus on "who said what to whom"—that is, on the source of the communication, the nature of the communication, and the nature of the audience

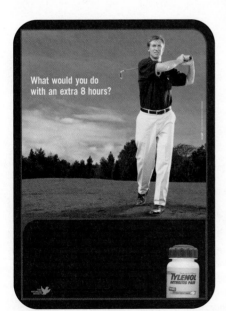

What would you do with an extra 8 hours?

TYLENOL

▲To sell a product, it is effective to have a credible, trustworthy celebrity, such as Wayne Gretzky, provide an endorsement.

Because these researchers were at Yale University, this approach to the study of persuasive communications is known as the **Yale Attitude Change Approach**.

This approach has yielded a great deal of useful information on how people change their attitudes in response to persuasive communications. Some of this information is summarized in Figure 6.2. Regarding the source of the communication, for example, research has shown that speakers who are credible, trustworthy, attractive, or likeable are more persuasive than those who are not. In a study on the effects of speaker credibility, students at the University of Waterloo listened to a tape-recorded speech in which it was argued that vigorous exercise is actually harmful (Ross, McFarland, Conway & Zanna, 1983). Participants in the credible condition were told that the speaker was Dr. James Rundle, a world authority on the effects of exercise; those in the non-credible condition were told that the speech was delivered by a local representative of the Fat Is Beautiful organization. As you might expect, participants were more influenced by the message when it was attributed to a credible source. More recent research conducted at the University of Alberta shows that people are more likely to not only remember arguments from a credible source, but also to change their behaviour accordingly (Jones, Sinclair, & Courneya, 2003).

Research inspired by the Yale Attitude Change approach has been important in identifying the determinants of effective persuasion. However, it has not been clear which aspects of persuasive communications are most important—that is, when one factor should be emphasized over another. For example, let's return to that job you have with the Canadian Cancer Society—it wants to see your ad next month! If you were to read the many Yale Attitude Change studies, you would find much useful information about who should say what to whom in order to construct a persuasive communication. However, you might also find yourself saying, "Gee, there's an awful lot of information here, and I'm not sure where I should place the most emphasis. Should I worry most about who delivers the ads? Or should I worry more about the content of the message itself?"

The Central and Peripheral Routes to Persuasion Some well-known attitude researchers have asked the same questions: When is it best to stress factors central to the communication—such as the strength of the arguments—and when is it best to stress factors peripheral to the logic of the arguments—such as the credibility or attractiveness of the person delivering the speech? An answer is provided by two influential theories of persuasive communication: Shelly Chaiken's **heuristic-systematic persuasion model** (Chaiken, 1987; Chaiken, Liberman, & Eagly, 1989; Chaiken, Wood, & Eagly, 1996; Chen & Chaiken, 1999), and Richard Petty and John Cacioppo's **elaboration likelihood model** (Petty & Cacioppo, 1986; Petty & Wegener, 1999; Petty, Cacioppo, Strathman, & Priester, 2005). These theories specify when people will be influenced by what the speech says (i.e., the logic of the arguments) and when they will be influenced by more superficial characteristics (e.g., who gives the speech or how long it is).

Both theories state that under certain conditions, people are motivated to pay attention to the facts in a communication, and so will be most persuaded when these facts are logically compelling. That is, sometimes people elaborate on what they hear, carefully thinking about and processing the content of the communication. Chaiken (1980) calls this *systematic processing*; Petty and Cacioppo (1986) call this the *central route to persuasion*. Under other conditions, people are not motivated to pay attention to the facts; instead they notice only the surface characteristics of the message, such as how long it is and who is delivering it (Martin, Hewstone, & Martin, 2003). The logic of the arguments does not have much persuasive power in this case because people are not paying close attention to what the communicator is saying. Instead, they are persuaded if the message is long, or if the communicator is attractive or an expert. Chaiken (1980) calls this *heuristic processing* and Petty and Cacioppo (1986) call this the *peripheral route to persuasion*, because people are swayed by things peripheral to the message itself.

What are the conditions under which people take the central versus the peripheral route to persuasion? The key, according to Petty, Cacioppo, and Chaiken, is whether people have the motivation and ability to pay attention to the facts. If people are truly interested in the topic and motivated to pay close attention to the arguments, they are more likely to take the central route. Similarly, if people have the ability to pay attention—for example, if nothing is distracting them—they will also take the central route (see Figure 6.3). If people are bored, tired, or otherwise not able to concentrate, they will tend to take the peripheral route. For example, in research conducted at Brock University, Hafer, Reynolds, and Obertynski (1996) found that people were more likely to take the central route when the message was presented in clear, comprehensible language; they relied on the peripheral route when arguments were presented using complicated, jargon-laden language.

Now that you know a persuasive communication can change people's attitudes in either of two ways—via the central or the peripheral route—you may be wondering what difference it makes. As long as people change their attitudes, should any of us care how they got to that point? If we are interested in creating long-lasting attitude change, we should care a lot. People who base their attitudes on a careful analysis of the arguments are more likely to maintain this attitude over time, are more likely to behave consistently with this attitude, and are more resistant to counter-persuasion than people who base their attitudes on peripheral cues

heuristic-systematic model of persuasion

the theory that there are two ways in which persuasive communications can cause attitude change: people either process the merits of the arguments (known as *systematic processing*) or are swayed by factors that are peripheral to the message itself, such as, "Experts are always right" (known as *heuristic processing*)

elaboration likelihood model

the theory that there are two ways in which persuasive communications can cause attitude change: the *central route* occurs when people are motivated and have the ability to pay attention to the arguments in the communication, and the *peripheral route* occurs when people do not pay attention to the arguments but are instead swayed by surface characteristics (e.g., who gave the speech)

❝ *The ability to kill or capture a man is a relatively simple task compared with changing his mind.*❞

—*Richard Cohen, 1991*

FIGURE 6.3

The elaboration likelihood model

The elaboration likelihood model describes how people change their attitudes when they hear persuasive communications.

(Chaiken, 1980; Mackie, 1987; Martin, Hewstone, & Martin, 2003; Petty, Haugvedt, & Smith, 1995; Petty & Wegener, 1998). For example, Perlini and Ward (2000) attempted to increase knowledge of AIDS among high school students in Sault Ste. Marie by providing them with scripts describing characters who either had AIDS or were medical experts on AIDS. The purpose of these scripts was to create awareness of how AIDS can be prevented, how it is contracted, and so on. The participants then acted out these various scripts in a role play. Other participants received the same information, but it was delivered via a lecture or videotape. The researchers reasoned that the active participation required by the role-play exercise would invoke the central route to persuasion. And indeed four weeks later, the role-play participants showed more positive attitudes toward AIDS prevention than did participants in the other groups. Those in the role-play condition also showed the greatest improvement in knowledge of AIDS prevention.

Fear and Attitude Change

Now you know exactly how to construct your ad for the Canadian Cancer Society, right? Well, not quite. Before people will consider your carefully constructed arguments, you have to get their attention. If you are going to show your anti-smoking ad on television, for example, how can you be sure that people will watch your ad rather than head for the refrigerator? One way to get people's attention is to scare them. This type of persuasive message is called a **fear-arousing communication**. Public service ads often take this approach by trying to scare people into practising safer sex, wearing their seat belts, and staying away from drugs. As mentioned in Chapter 1, in 2000, the Canadian government began to place frightening images on cigarette packages—larger and more graphic than those used anywhere else in the world. In 2004, the European Union called for European governments to require that cigarette packages display graphic images similar to those instituted by Canada. There is evidence that such fear-arousing communications do produce fear (Dillard, Plotnick, Godbold, Freimuth, & Edgar, 1996) and that smokers—particularly those in Canada—view these messages as effective (Hammond et al., 2007).

fear-arousing communication

a persuasive message that attempts to change people's attitudes by arousing their fears

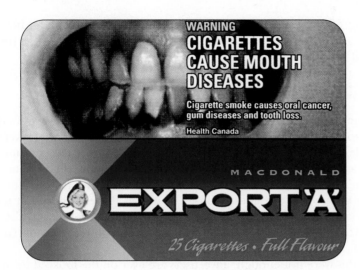

◀ Health Canada requires that all cigarette packs display pictures that warn about the dangers of smoking. Do you think this ad would scare people into quitting?

But does fear actually get people to change their attitudes? It depends on whether the fear influences people's ability and motivation to pay attention to and process the arguments in a message. If a moderate amount of fear is created and if people believe that listening to the message will teach them how to reduce this fear, they will be motivated to analyze the message carefully and will likely change their attitudes via the central route (Petty, 1995; Rogers, 1983). Consider a study by Leventhal, Watts, and Pagano (1967), who showed a group of smokers a graphic film depicting lung cancer and gave them pamphlets with specific instructions about how to quit smoking. These people reduced their smoking significantly more than did people who were shown only the film or only the pamphlet. Why? Seeing the film made people scared, and giving them the pamphlet reassured them that there was a way to reduce this fear—by following the instructions on how to quit. Seeing only the pamphlet didn't work very well, because there wasn't the fear to motivate people to read it carefully. Seeing only the film didn't work very well either, because people were likely to tune out a message that raised fear but did not give information about how to reduce it. This may explain why some attempts to frighten people into changing their attitudes and behaviour have not been very successful; they succeed in scaring people but do not provide specific recommendations for them to follow (Becker & Josephs, 1988; DeJong & Winsten, 1989; Job, 1988; Soames, 1988). When specific recommendations are offered, people will be more likely to accept them, particularly if they are feeling vulnerable and worried that they are at risk for experiencing the feared event (Das, de Wit, & Stroebe, 2003; De Hoog, Stroebe, & de Wit, 2005).

It is important, though, for fear-arousing appeals not to be so strong that people feel extremely threatened. If people are scared to death, they will become defensive, deny the importance of the threat, and be unable to think rationally about the issue (Janis & Feshbach, 1953; Jepson & Chaiken, 1990; Liberman & Chaiken, 1992). According to researchers at Concordia University and McGill University, humour can be an effective tool for reducing distress among people who find fear messages especially threatening. In a series of studies, Conway and Dubé (2002) showed that among those who were most threatened by fear messages, the use of humour resulted in greater attitude change and intentions to enact the desired behaviours (e.g., using sunscreen to avoid skin cancer and using condoms to avoid AIDS) than did nonhumorous messages.

So, if you have decided to arouse people's fear in your ad for the Canadian Cancer Society, keep these points in mind. First, try to create enough fear to motivate people to pay attention to your arguments, but not so much fear that people will tune out or distort what you say. You may even want to throw in a bit of humour for the benefit of those who find fear-inducing messages especially distressing. Second, include some specific recommendations about how to stop smoking, so people will be reassured that paying close attention to your arguments will help them reduce their fear.

Advertising and Attitude Change

How many times, in a given day, does someone attempt to change your attitudes? Be sure to count every advertisement you see or hear, because advertising is nothing less than an attempt to change your attitude toward a consumer product, be it a brand of laundry detergent, a type of automobile, or a political candidate. Don't forget to include ads you get in the mail, calls from telemarketers, and signs you see on the sides of buses, as well as those ever-present television commercials. How many did you come up with? You might be surprised at the answer. According to some estimates, we encounter 300 to 400 advertisements per day (Pratkanis & Aronson, 1991).

As if this were not enough, advertisers are ever on the lookout for new ways of reaching consumers. Entire cable television channels are now devoted to pitching products, either through home shopping networks or infomercials designed to look like regular television programs, not to mention all of the ads posted on websites. Even in our most private moments, we are not immune from advertisements, as witnessed by the proliferation of advertisements placed in public washrooms—above the hand dryers and even on the inside doors of washroom stalls.

> ❝ *You can tell the ideals of a nation by its advertisements.* ❞
>
> —*George Norman Douglas,*
> South Wind, *1917*

A curious thing about advertising is that most people think it works on everyone but themselves (Wilson & Brekke, 1994). People make comments such as, "There's no harm in watching commercials. Some of them are fun and they don't influence me." Are they right? This is an important question for social psychologists because each of us is confronted with hundreds of attempts to change our attitudes every day in the form of advertisements. Do these ads really work or are companies wasting the billions of dollars a year they spend on advertising?

It turns out that people are influenced by advertising more than they think. There is substantial evidence indicating that advertising works—when a product is advertised, sales tend to increase (Lodish, Abraham, Kalmenson, Lievelsberger, Lubetkin, Richardson, & Stevens, 1995; Ryan, 1991; Wells, 1997).

Tailoring Advertisements to People's Attitudes Which types of ads work the best? It depends on the type of attitude we are trying to change. As we saw earlier, some attitudes are based more on beliefs about the attitude object (cognitively based attitudes), whereas others are based more on emotions and values (affectively based attitudes). Several studies have shown that it is best to fight fire with fire. If an attitude is cognitively based, try to change it with rational arguments; if it is affectively based, try to change it using emotion (Edwards, 1990; Edwards & von Hippel, 1995; Fabrigar & Petty, 1999; Shavitt, 1989; Snyder & DeBono, 1989). In one study, for example, Sharon Shavitt (1990) gave people advertisements for different kinds of consumer products. Some of the items were ones Shavitt called utilitarian products, such as air conditioners and coffee. People's attitudes toward such products tend to be based on an appraisal of the utilitarian aspects of the products (e.g., how energy-efficient an air conditioner is) and thus are cognitively based. The other items were ones Shavitt called social identity products, such as perfume and greeting cards. People's attitudes toward these types of products are based more on their values and concerns about their social identity and so are more affectively based.

As seen in Figure 6.4, people reacted most favourably to the ads that matched the type of attitude they had. If people's attitudes were cognitively based (e.g., toward air conditioners or coffee), the ads that focused on the utilitarian aspects

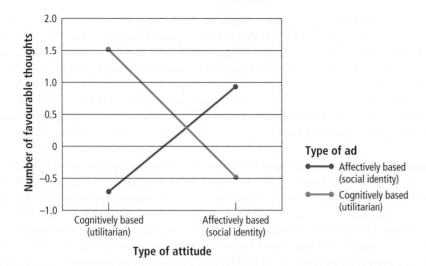

FIGURE 6.4
Effects of affective and cognitive information on affectively and cognitively based attitudes

When people had cognitively based attitudes (e.g., toward air conditioners and coffee), cognitively based advertisements that stressed the utilitarian aspects of the products worked best. When people had more affectively based attitudes (e.g., toward perfume and greeting cards), affectively based advertisements that stressed values and social identity worked best. (The higher the number, the more favourable the thoughts people listed about the products after reading the advertisements.)

(Adapted from Shavitt, 1990)

of these products were most successful. If people's attitudes were more affectively based (e.g., toward perfume or greeting cards), the ads that focused on values and social identity concerns were most successful. Thus, if you ever get a job in advertising, the moral is to know what type of attitude most people have toward your product, then tailor your advertising accordingly.

Cultural Differences in Advertising As we discussed in Chapter 5, there are differences in people's self-concept across cultures; Western cultures tend to stress independence and individualism, whereas many collectivist (e.g., Asian) cultures stress interdependence. Sang-pil Han and Sharon Shavitt (1994) reasoned that these differences in self-concept might also reflect differences in the kinds of attitudes people have toward consumer products. Perhaps advertisements that stress individuality and self-improvement might work better in Western cultures, whereas advertisements that stress one's social group might work better in Asian cultures. To test their hypothesis, Han and Shavitt (1994) created ads for the same product that stressed independence (e.g., an ad for shoes said, "It's easy when you have the right shoes") or interdependence (e.g., "The shoes for your family") and showed them to Americans and Koreans. Americans were persuaded most by the ads stressing independence; Koreans were persuaded most by the ads stressing interdependence. The researchers also analyzed actual magazine advertisements in the United States and Korea, and found that these ads were, in fact, different. American ads tended to emphasize individuality, self-improvement, and benefits of the product for the individual consumer, whereas Korean ads tended to emphasize the family, concerns about others, and benefits for one's social group.

Subliminal Advertising: A Form of Mind Control? We cannot leave the topic of advertising without discussing one of its most controversial topics: the use of **subliminal messages**—defined as words or pictures that while not consciously perceived, supposedly influence people's judgments, attitudes, and behaviour. A majority of the public believes that these messages can unknowingly shape attitudes and behaviour (Zanot, Pincus, & Lamp, 1983). Given the near-hysterical claims that have been made about subliminal advertising, it is important to discuss whether it really works.

In the late 1950s, James Vicary supposedly flashed the messages, "Drink Coca-Cola" and "Eat popcorn" during a movie and claimed that sales at the concession stand skyrocketed. Apparently, Vicary made up these claims (Weir, 1984). But that was not the last attempt at subliminal persuasion. Wilson Bryan Key (1973, 1989), who has written several best-selling books on hidden persuasion techniques, maintains that advertisers routinely implant sexual messages in

subliminal messages

words or pictures that are not consciously perceived but that supposedly influence people's judgments, attitudes, and behaviours

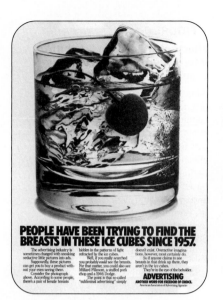

PEOPLE HAVE BEEN TRYING TO FIND THE BREASTS IN THESE ICE CUBES SINCE 1957.

The advertising industry is sometimes charged with sneaking seductive little pictures into ads.

Supposedly, these pictures can get you to buy a product without your even seeing them.

Consider the photograph above. According to some people, there's a pair of female breasts

hidden in the patterns of light refracted by the ice cubes.

Well, if you really searched you probably *could* see the breasts. For that matter, you could also see Millard Fillmore, a stuffed pork chop and a 1946 Dodge.

The point is that so-called "subliminal advertising" simply

doesn't exist. Overactive imaginations, however, most certainly do.

So if anyone claims to see breasts in that drink up there, they aren't in the ice cubes.

They're in the eye of the beholder.

ADVERTISING

ANOTHER WORD FOR FREEDOM OF CHOICE.

American Association of Advertising Agencies

▲ There is no scientific evidence that implanting sexual images in advertising boosts sales of the product. The public is very aware of the technique, however—so much so that some advertisers have begun to poke fun at subliminal messages, right in their ads.

print advertisements, such as the word *sex* in the ice cubes of an ad for gin, and male and female genitalia in everything from pats of butter to the icing in an ad for cake mix. In addition, there is a large market for audiotapes containing subliminal messages to help people lose weight, stop smoking, improve their study habits, raise their self-esteem, and even shave a few strokes off their golf scores. In 1990, sales of subliminal self-help tapes were estimated to be $50 million (Krajick, 1990). Are subliminal messages effective? Do they really make us more likely to buy consumer products, or help us to lose weight and stop smoking?

Debunking the Claims about Subliminal Advertising   Fortunately, many studies of subliminal perception have been conducted, allowing us to evaluate the sometimes outlandish claims that are being made. Simply stated, there is no evidence that the types of subliminal messages used in everyday life have any influence on people's behaviour. Hidden commands to eat popcorn do not cause us to line up at the concession stand and buy popcorn any more than we normally would do, and the subliminal commands on self-help tapes do not (unfortunately!) help us to quit smoking or lose a few pounds (Merikle, 1988; Moore, 1995; Pratkanis, 1992; Trappey, 1996). Consider, for example, a study that evaluated the effectiveness of subliminal self-help tapes (Greenwald, Spangenberg, Pratkanis, & Eskenazi, 1991). Half of the participants listened to tapes that, according to the manufacturer, contained subliminal messages designed to improve memory (e.g., "My ability to remember and recall is increasing daily"); the others listened to tapes that had subliminal messages designed to raise self-esteem (e.g., "I have high self-worth and high self-esteem"). Neither of the tapes had any effect on people's memory or self-esteem.

Interestingly, the participants in this study *thought* the subliminal tapes were working, even though they were not. The researchers were a little devious, in that they correctly informed half of the participants about which tape they listened to, but misinformed the others (i.e., half of the people who got the memory tape were told it was designed to improve their memories, whereas the other half were told it was designed to improve their self-esteem). Those who thought they had listened to the memory tape believed their memories had improved, even if they had really heard the self-esteem tape. And people who thought they had listened to the self-esteem tape believed their self-esteem had improved, even if they had heard the memory tape. This finding explains why subliminal tapes are such a lucrative business. Even though the tapes don't work, people believe that they do.

Evidence for Subliminal Influence in the Lab   We've seen that subliminal messages are ineffective when used in advertising. But there is some evidence for such effects in carefully controlled laboratory studies. Recall that in Chapter 5 we discussed research by Baldwin, Carrell, and Lopez (1990), who flashed slides of a scowling program director, a friendly postdoctoral student, or a disapproving-looking pope so quickly that they were not consciously perceived. Nevertheless, these images did have the predicted effects on participants' self-evaluations. Several other researchers have found similar effects of pictures or words flashed at subliminal levels (e.g., Bargh & Pietromonaco, 1982; Bornstein & Pittman, 1992; Dijksterhuis & Aarts, 2002; Dijksterhuis, Aarts, & Smith, 2005). However, all successful demonstrations of subliminal stimuli have been conducted under meticulous laboratory conditions that are difficult to reproduce in everyday life. Researchers have to ensure that the illumination of the room is just right, that people are seated just the right distance from a viewing screen, and that nothing else is occurring to distract them as the subliminal stimuli are flashed. Recent research conducted at the University of Waterloo shows that people also have to be motivated to accept the persuasive message (Strahan, Spencer, & Zanna, 2002). For example, in one of these studies, participants in the experimental condition were subliminally primed with words such as "dry" and "thirsty."

▶ Advertising and Mind Control

Here is an exercise on people's beliefs about the power of advertising that you can try on your friends. Ask 10 or so friends the following questions—preferably friends who have not had a course in social psychology! See how accurate their beliefs are about the effects of different kinds of advertising.

1. Do you think you are influenced by subliminal messages in advertising? (Define subliminal messages for your friends as words or pictures that are not consciously perceived but that supposedly influence people's judgments, attitudes, and behaviours.)

2. Do you think you are influenced by everyday advertisements that you perceive consciously, such as television ads for laundry detergent and painkillers?

3. Suppose you had a choice to listen to one of two speeches that argued against a position you believe in, such as whether marijuana should be legalized. In Speech A, a person presents several arguments against your position. In Speech B, all of the arguments are presented subliminally—you will not perceive anything consciously. Which speech would you rather listen to, A or B?

Tally results for each person in a table like the one below:

Question 1	Question 2	Question 3
Yes: _____	Yes: _____	Yes: _____
No: _____	No: _____	No: _____

Turn to page 189 to see if your results match those of scientific studies. Show off your knowledge to your friends. Ask them why they are more wary of subliminal messages than everyday advertising, when it is everyday advertising and not subliminal messages that changes people's minds. Why do you think people are most afraid of the kinds of ads that are least effective? What does this say about people's awareness of their own thought processes?

Participants in a control condition were subliminally exposed to neutral words. Later, those in the experimental group were more persuaded by an advertisement for "Superquencher" drinks than those in the control group. But even in the laboratory there is no evidence that subliminal messages can get people to act counter to their wishes, values, or personalities, making them march off to the supermarket to buy drinks when they're not thirsty or vote for candidates they despise.

Ironically, the hoopla surrounding subliminal messages has obscured a significant fact about advertising: Ads are more powerful when we can consciously perceive them. As we have discussed, there is ample evidence that the ads people encounter in everyday life and perceive consciously can have substantial effects on their behaviour—even though they do not contain subliminal messages. It is interesting that people fear subliminal advertising more than they do regular advertising, when regular advertising is so much more powerful (Wilson, Houston, & Meyers, 1998). (Test the power of advertising with your friends or fellow students with the accompanying Try It! exercise.)

Resisting Persuasive Messages

By now, you are no doubt getting nervous (and not just because the chapter hasn't ended yet!). With all of these clever methods to change your attitudes, are you ever safe from persuasive communications? Indeed you are, or at least you can be, if you use some strategies of your own. Here's how to ensure that all of those persuasive messages that bombard you don't turn you into a quivering mass of constantly changing opinion.

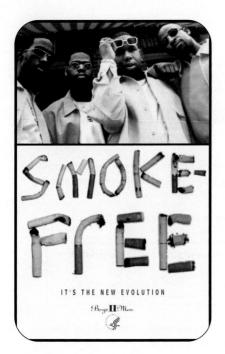

▲ Numerous programs designed to prevent smoking in adolescents have had some success. Many celebrities have lent their names and pictures to the effort, as in this ad featuring Boyz II Men.

attitude inoculation

the process of making people immune to attempts to change their attitudes by initially exposing them to small doses of the arguments against their position

The chief effect of talk on any subject is to strengthen one's own opinions and, in fact, one never knows exactly what he does believe until he is warmed into conviction by the heat of the attack and defense.

—Charles Dudley Warner,
Backlog Studies, 1873

Attitude Inoculation

One approach is to get people to consider the arguments for and against their attitude before someone attacks it. The more people have thought about pro and con arguments beforehand, the better they can ward off attempts to change their minds using logical arguments. William McGuire (1964) demonstrated this by using what he called **attitude inoculation**—the process of making people immune to attempts to change their attitudes by exposing them to "small doses" of arguments against their position. Having considered the arguments beforehand, people should be relatively immune to the effects of the communication—just as exposing them to a small amount of a virus can inoculate them against exposure to the full-blown viral disease. For example, in one study, McGuire (1964) "inoculated" people by giving them brief, weak arguments against beliefs that most members of a society accept uncritically, such as the idea that we should brush our teeth after every meal. Two days later, people came back and read a much stronger attack on the truism, one that contained a series of logical arguments about why brushing your teeth too frequently is a bad idea. The people who had been inoculated against these arguments were much less likely to change their attitudes compared to a control group who had not been. Why? Those inoculated with weak arguments had the opportunity to think about why these arguments were unfounded and were therefore in a better position to contradict the stronger attack they heard two days later. The control group, never having considered why people should or should not brush their teeth frequently, was particularly susceptible to the strong communication arguing that they should not.

The logic of McGuire's inoculation approach can be extended to real-world situations such as peer pressure. Consider Jake, a 13-year-old who is hanging out with some classmates, many of whom are smoking cigarettes. The classmates begin to make fun of Jake for not smoking and dare him to take a puff. Many 13-year-olds, faced with such pressure, would cave in. But suppose we immunized Jake to such social pressures by exposing him to mild versions of them and showing him ways to combat these pressures. We might have him role-play a situation where a friend calls him a wimp for not smoking a cigarette, and teach him to respond by saying, "I'd be more of a wimp if I smoked it just to impress you." Would this help him resist the more powerful pressures exerted by his classmates?

Several programs designed to prevent smoking in adolescents suggest that it would. For example, McAlister and his colleagues (1980) used a role-playing technique with seventh graders, very much like the one described above. The researchers found that these students were significantly less likely to smoke three years after the study, compared with a control group that had not participated in the program. This result is encouraging and has been replicated in similar programs designed to reduce smoking (Chassin, Presson, & Sherman, 1990; Falck & Craig, 1988; Killen, 1985).

Inoculation is also effective in resisting attacks on our attitudes. Bernard, Maio, and Olson (2003) had participants generate various kinds of arguments supporting the value of equality. A control group was not required to generate any arguments. Later, those who had formulated arguments were less likely to be persuaded by messages attacking the value of equality. Importantly, there is evidence that if people are able to resist an attack on their attitudes, they may actually come to hold those attitudes with greater certainty as a result (Tormala & Petty, 2002).

Being Alert to Product Placement

In an episode of the television show, *Desperate Housewives*, Gabrielle needs to find work while her husband is in prison. She lands a job at the local mall, where she promotes a new car model. Was it a coincidence that the car was a Buick LaCrosse? Apparently not; according to some reports, the show had an agreement with Buick to promote their cars by incorporating them into the script (Guthrie, 2005).

When an advertisement comes on during a TV show, people often decide to press the mute button on the remote control or get up to get a snack. To counteract this tendency to tune out, advertisers look for ways of displaying their wares during the show itself. With this technique, called **product placement**, companies pay the makers of a TV show or movie to incorporate their product into the script. In the movie *E.T.: The Extra-Terrestrial*, for example, Elliott left a trail of Reese's Pieces to draw out E.T., after which sales of the candy boomed. In a 1996 James Bond movie, Agent 007 abandoned his usual Aston Martin and drove a BMW Z3 roadster, reportedly in return for a $3 million fee from the BMW company. Consumers responded with $240 million in advance purchases of the car (York, 2001). Children can be especially vulnerable. One study, for example, found that the more often children in grades 5 to 8 had seen movies in which adults smoked cigarettes, the more positive were their attitudes toward smoking (Sargent, Dalton, Beach, Mott, Tickle, Ahrens, & Heatherton, 2002; Wakefield, Flay, & Nichter, 2003).

One reason product placement may be so successful is that people do not realize that someone is trying to influence their attitudes and behaviour. People's defenses are down; when we see E.T. eating Reese's Pieces or James Bond driving a BMW, we don't think about the fact that someone is trying to influence our attitudes and we don't generate counter-arguments (e.g., "Is the BMW really better than the Aston Martin that 007 used to drive?"). This leads to the question of whether forewarning people that someone is about to try to change their attitudes is an effective tool against product placement or persuasion more generally.

It turns out that it is. Several studies have found that warning people about an upcoming attempt to change their attitudes makes them less susceptible to that attempt. When people are forewarned, they analyze what they see and hear more carefully and as a result are likely to avoid attitude change. Without such warnings, people pay little attention to the persuasive attempts and tend to accept them at face value (Sagarin, Cialdini, Rice, & Serna, 2002; Wood & Quinn, 2003). So, before letting kids watch TV or sending them off to the movies, it is good to remind them that they are likely to encounter several attempts to change their attitudes.

product placement

strategically placed products in movies and television shows that are intended to persuade us

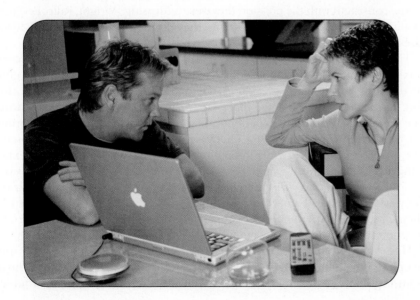

◄ Product placement, in which a commercial product is incorporated into the script of a movie or television show, has become common practice. In an episode of *24*, for example, agent Jack Bauer discusses strategies over his prominently displayed Macintosh PowerBook.

Changing Our Attitudes because of Our Behaviour: The Theory of Cognitive Dissonance

We have been focusing on persuasion—those times when other people attempt to change your attitudes. But there is another route to attitude change that might surprise you. Sometimes people change their attitudes not because another person is trying to get them to do so but, rather, because their own behaviour prompts them to do so. How does this happen? As we discuss next, this can happen when people behave in ways that contradict, or are inconsistent with, their attitudes. This realization produces discomfort. One way to alleviate the discomfort is for people to change their attitudes and bring them in line with their behaviour. Let's take a look at how this process works.

Leon Festinger was the first to investigate the precise workings of this powerful phenomenon, and elaborated his findings into what is arguably social psychology's most important and most provocative theory—the theory of cognitive dissonance (Festinger, 1957). **Cognitive dissonance i**s defined as the uncomfortable feeling we experience when our behaviour is at odds with our attitudes or when we hold attitudes that conflict with one another. Dissonance most often occurs whenever we do something that makes us feel stupid or immoral (Aronson, 1968, 1969, 1992, 1998; Aronson, Chase, Helmreich, & Ruhnke, 1974; Harmon-Jones & Mills, 1998; Thibodeau & Aronson, 1992). It always produces discomfort, and because discomfort is unpleasant, we are motivated to take steps to reduce it (Zanna & Cooper, 1974). How do we know this is the case? Is there any evidence that people who experience cognitive dissonance are in a state of discomfort or arousal? Take a moment to place yourself in the following situation.

If you are like most university students, the idea of taking a class at 6:30 a.m. isn't particularly inviting. Imagine, however, that you are asked to write an essay in favour of 6:30 a.m. classes and that your arguments might affect whether your university actually adopts such a policy. As you start writing, you begin to experience that uneasy feeling that you recognize as cognitive dissonance. You really do not want your classes to begin at 6:30 a.m.; yet, here you are, formulating compelling arguments for why such a policy should be implemented. This is just the situation in which some students at the University of Alberta found themselves, and most of them showed classic dissonance reduction—they changed their attitudes to become consistent with the position they were endorsing (Wright, Rule, Ferguson, McGuire, & Wells, 1992). In other words, they decided that the idea of 6:30 a.m. classes wasn't so bad after all.

That's not the whole story, however. Before writing the essay, some participants were given a drug—supposedly to improve memory—and were told either that the drug would have no side effects or that the drug would make them tense. The researchers expected that participants who were told the drug would make them tense would not experience dissonance because they would attribute their uneasy feelings to the drug ("Oh, right—I took a pill that's supposed to make me feel tense; that's why I'm feeling this way"). And if they weren't experiencing dissonance, there would be no need to change their attitudes, would there? Indeed, participants in this condition were most likely to retain their negative views toward 6:30 a.m. classes, despite writing an essay promoting such a policy. Thus, the experience of dissonance is unpleasant and uncomfortable, and as a result, we will take steps to alleviate the discomfort.

How can we reduce dissonance? As we saw in the Wright et al. (1992) study, one option is to attempt to justify our behaviour through changing one of the dissonant cognitions. Most often, this takes the form of changing our attitudes to

cognitive dissonance

a feeling of discomfort caused by the realization that one's behaviour is inconsistent with one's attitudes or that one holds two conflicting attitudes

FIGURE 6.5
How we reduce cognitive dissonance

bring them in line with our behaviour. There are other ways to reduce dissonance, as well. We could change our behaviour to bring it in line with the dissonant cognition. We could also attempt to justify our behaviour by adding new cognitions. These different ways of reducing dissonance are illustrated in Figure 6.5.

To illustrate, let's look at a behaviour that millions of people engage in several times a day—smoking cigarettes. Suppose you are a smoker. You are likely to experience dissonance because it is absurd to engage in behaviour that stands a good chance of producing a painful, early death. How can you reduce this dissonance? The most direct way is to change your behaviour—to give up smoking. Your behaviour would then be consistent with your knowledge of the link between smoking and cancer. While many people have succeeded in doing just that, it's not easy—many have tried to quit and failed. What do these people do? It would be wrong to assume that they simply swallow hard and prepare to die. They don't. Instead, they try to reduce their dissonance in a different way—namely, by convincing themselves that smoking isn't as bad as they thought.

Smokers can come up with pretty creative ways to justify their smoking. Some succeed in convincing themselves that the data linking cigarette smoking to cancer are inconclusive. Others will try to add new cognitions—for example, the erroneous belief that filters trap most of the harmful chemicals, thus reducing the threat of cancer. Some will add a cognition that allows them to focus on the vivid exception: "Look at old Sam Carouthers—he's 90 years old and he's been smoking a pack a day since he was 15. That proves it's not always bad for you." Still others will add the cognition that smoking is an extremely enjoyable activity, one for which it is worth risking cancer. Others even succeed in convincing themselves that, all things considered, smoking is worthwhile because it relaxes them, reduces nervous tension, and so on.

These justifications may sound silly to the nonsmoker. That is precisely our point. People experiencing dissonance will often go to extreme lengths to reduce it. We did not make up the examples of denial, distortion, and justification listed above; they are based on actual examples generated by people who have tried and failed to quit smoking. Similar justifications have been generated by people who try and fail to lose weight, who refuse to practise safer sex, or who receive bad news about their health (Aronson, 1997b; Croyle & Jemmott, 1990; Goleman, 1982; Kassarjian & Cohen, 1965; Leishman, 1988). To escape from dissonance, people will engage in quite extraordinary rationalizing.

▶ Once we have committed a lot of time or energy to a cause, it is nearly impossible to convince us that the cause is unworthy.

© Peanuts. Reprinted by permission of United Features Syndicate, Inc.

Decisions, Decisions, Decisions

In any decision, whether it is between two cars, two schools, or two potential lovers, the chosen alternative is seldom entirely positive, and the rejected alternative is seldom entirely negative. Let's pretend that you are trying to decide which of two attractive people to date: Chris, who is funny and playful, but a bit irresponsible; or Pat, who is interesting and smart, but not very spontaneous. You agonize over the decision but eventually decide to pursue a relationship with Pat. After you've made the decision, you will experience dissonance because, despite Pat's good qualities, you did choose to be with someone who is not very spontaneous. Dissonance also is created because you ended up turning down someone who is playful and fun. We call this **postdecision dissonance**.

Cognitive dissonance theory predicts that in order to feel better about the decision, you will do some mental work to try to reduce the dissonance. What kind of work? You would convince yourself that Pat really was the right person for you and that Chris actually would have been a lousy choice. An early experiment by Jack Brehm (1956) illustrates this phenomenon. Brehm posed as a representative of a consumer testing service and asked women to rate the attractiveness and desirability of several kinds of appliances, such as toasters and electric coffee makers. Each woman was told that as a reward for having participated in the survey she could have one of the appliances as a gift. She was given a choice between two of the products she had rated as being equally attractive. After she made her decision, her appliance was wrapped up and given to her. Twenty minutes later, each woman was asked to re-rate all of the products. Brehm found that after receiving the appliance of their choice, the women rated its attractiveness somewhat higher than they had done the first time. Not only that, but they drastically lowered their rating of the appliance they had decided to reject. In other words, following a decision, to reduce dissonance, we change the way we feel about the chosen and not chosen alternatives—cognitively spreading them apart in our own minds to make ourselves feel better about the choice we made.

postdecision dissonance

dissonance that is inevitably aroused after a person makes a decision; such dissonance is typically reduced by enhancing the attractiveness of the chosen alternative and devaluing the rejected alternatives

Much of the research conducted since Brehm's classic study has adopted this kind of methodology. Participants first evaluate a set of items; they then are given a choice between two items they found attractive; once they have made their choice, they again rate the items to see if their evaluations have changed. A consistent finding is that people rate the chosen item more positively, and the rejected item more negatively, than they did before making their decision (Gilbert & Ebert, 2002). In recent research conducted at the University of Western Ontario, it has been demonstrated that these effects occur even when people's evaluations are assessed at an implicit (unconscious) level (Gawronski, Bodenhausen, & Becker, 2007).

There is another variation on this methodology—namely, having participants choose between two *un*attractive alternatives. For example, in a study by Shultz, Léveillé, and Lepper (1999), children attending a day camp in Montreal rated the attractiveness of various posters. Some children were allowed to choose between two posters they had rated highly. Consistent with classic dissonance research, these children rated the poster they rejected more negatively than they had before. Other children had to choose between two posters that they didn't particularly like. These children also reduced dissonance—in this case, by increasing their liking for the poster they chose. Interestingly, dissonance reduction was greater when choosing between unattractive alternatives than when choosing between attractive alternatives. Thus, according to this research, if you are at a buffet dinner, trying to decide between the delectable strawberry shortcake and the scrumptious chocolate hazelnut torte, and you choose the torte, you will end up deciding that the strawberry shortcake didn't look so great after all. However, your thumbs-down rating of the strawberry shortcake will not be as emphatic as your thumbs-up rating on the limp, tasteless green beans if you chose them instead of the soggy, overcooked broccoli.

The Permanence of the Decision Decisions vary in terms of how permanent they are—that is, how difficult they are to revoke. It is a lot easier, for instance, to go back to a car dealership to exchange a defective new car for another one than to extricate yourself from an unhappy marriage. The more permanent and less revocable the decision, the greater the need to reduce dissonance.

An excellent place to investigate the significance of irrevocability is the racetrack. Experienced bettors typically spend a great deal of time poring over the "dope sheets," trying to decide which horse to put their money on. When they make a decision, they head for the betting windows. While they are standing in line, they have already made their decision but, we would hypothesize, because it is still revocable, they have no urge to reduce dissonance. However, once they get to the window and place their bet—even if it's for only $2—there is no turning back. Thirty seconds later, they cannot go back and tell the nice person behind the window that they have changed their mind. If irrevocability is an important factor, one would expect greater dissonance reduction among bettors a few minutes after placing the bet than a few minutes before placing the bet.

In a simple but clever experiment, Knox and Inkster (1968) intercepted people at the Exhibition Park Race Track in Vancouver who were on their way to place $2 bets and asked them how certain they were their horses would win. The investigators also intercepted other bettors just as they were leaving the $2 window, after having placed their bets, and asked them the same question. Almost invariably, people who had already placed their bets gave their horses a much better chance of winning than did those who had yet to place their bets. Since only a few minutes separated one group from another, nothing real had occurred to increase the probability of winning; the only thing that had changed was the finality of the decision—and thus the dissonance it produced.

The Decision to Behave Immorally Needless to say, life is made up of more than just decisions about cars, posters, appliances, and racehorses. Often our decisions

▶ Once an individual makes a final and irrevocable decision, he or she has a greater need to reduce dissonance. At the racetrack, for example, once bettors have placed their bet, their certainty is greater than it is immediately before they've placed it.

involve moral and ethical issues. When is it permissible to lie to a friend, and when is it not? When is an act stealing, and when is it borrowing? Resolving moral dilemmas is a particularly interesting area in which to study dissonance. Believe it or not, dissonance reduction following a difficult moral decision can cause people to behave either more *or less* ethically in the future—it can actually change their system of values.

Take the issue of cheating on an exam. Suppose you are a third-year university student taking the final exam in a chemistry course. You have always wanted to be a surgeon and you know that your admission to medical school depends heavily on how well you do in this course. The key question on the exam involves some material you know well, but you experience acute anxiety and draw a blank. You simply cannot think. You happen to be sitting behind the smartest person in the class and notice that she has just written down her answer to this question. You could easily read it if you chose to. Time is running out. What do you do? Your conscience tells you it's wrong to cheat—and yet if you don't cheat, you are certain to get a poor grade. And if you get a poor grade, there goes medical school.

Regardless of whether you decide to cheat or not, you are doomed to experience dissonance. If you cheat, your cognition that "I am a decent, moral person" is dissonant with your cognition that "I have just committed an immoral act." If you decide to resist temptation, your cognition that "I want to become a surgeon" is dissonant with your cognition that "I could have acted in a way that would have ensured a good grade and admission to medical school, but I chose not to. Wow, was that stupid!"

In this situation, some students decide to cheat; others decide not to. What happens to the students' attitudes about cheating after their decision? For students who decide to cheat, an efficient path of dissonance reduction would be to adopt a more lenient attitude toward cheating, convincing themselves that it is a victimless crime that doesn't hurt anybody, that everybody does it and so it's not really that bad. Students who manage to resist the temptation to cheat also could reduce dissonance by changing their attitude about the morality of the act—but this time in the opposite direction. That is, in order to justify giving up a good grade, they would have to convince themselves that it is dishonest and immoral to cheat and that only a despicable person would do such a thing.

The dissonance reduction that occurs for these students—regardless of whether they cheated or not—is not merely a rationalization of their behaviour but an actual change in their system of values; individuals faced with this kind of choice will undergo either a softening or a hardening of their attitudes toward cheating on exams, depending on whether they decided to cheat.

These speculations were put to the test by Judson Mills (1958) in an experiment he performed at an elementary school. Mills first measured the attitudes of sixth graders toward cheating. He then had them participate in a competitive exam, offering prizes to the winners. The situation was arranged so it was almost impossible to win without cheating. Moreover, Mills made it easy for the children to cheat on the exam and created the illusion that they could not be detected. Under these conditions, as one might expect, some of the students cheated and others did not. The next day, the sixth graders were again asked to indicate how they felt about cheating. Children who had cheated became more lenient toward cheating, and those who had resisted the temptation to cheat adopted a harsher attitude toward cheating.

The Justification of Effort

Suppose you expend a great deal of effort to get into a particular club, and it turns out to be a totally worthless organization, consisting of boring, pompous people engaged in trivial activities. You would feel pretty foolish, wouldn't you? This situation would produce a fair amount of dissonance; your cognition that you are a sensible, adept human being is dissonant with your cognition that you worked hard to get into a worthless club. How would you reduce this dissonance? You might start by finding a way to convince yourself that the club and the people in it are nicer, more interesting, and more worthwhile than they appeared to be at first glance. Activities and behaviours are open to a variety of interpretations; if people are motivated to see the best in people and things, they will tend to interpret these ambiguities in a positive manner. We call this the **justification of effort**—the tendency for individuals to increase their liking for something they have worked hard to attain.

In a classic experiment, Elliot Aronson and Judson Mills (1959) explored the link between effort and dissonance reduction. In their experiment, university students volunteered to join a group that would be meeting regularly to discuss various aspects of the psychology of sex. To be admitted to the group, they volunteered to go through a screening procedure. For one-third of the participants, the procedure was extremely demanding and unpleasant; for one-third it was only very mildly unpleasant; the final one-third was admitted to the group

justification of effort

the tendency for individuals to increase their liking for something they have worked hard to attain

◄ Going through a lot of effort to become a soldier will increase the recruit's feelings of cohesiveness and pride in the corps.

FIGURE 6.6

The tougher the initiation, the more we like the group

The more effort we put into gaining group membership, the more we like the group we have just joined.

(Adapted from Aronson & Mills, 1959)

without undergoing any screening procedure. Each participant was then allowed to listen in on a discussion being conducted by the members of the group they would be joining. The discussion was arranged so it was as dull and bombastic as possible. After the discussion was over, each participant was asked to rate it in terms of how much he or she liked it, how interesting it was, how intelligent the participants were, and so forth. The major findings are shown in Figure 6.6.

The results supported the predictions. Participants who underwent little or no effort to get into the group did not enjoy the discussion very much. They were able to see it for what it was—a dull and boring waste of time. Participants who went through a severe initiation, however, succeeded in convincing themselves that the same discussion, though not as scintillating as they had hoped, was dotted with interesting and provocative tidbits, and therefore, in the main, was a worthwhile experience. In short, they justified their effortful initiation process by interpreting all the ambiguous aspects of the group discussion in the most positive manner possible.

We want to be clear that we are not suggesting that most people enjoy effortful, unpleasant experiences—they do not. What we are asserting is that if a person agrees to go through a difficult or an unpleasant experience to attain some goal or object, that goal or object becomes more attractive. As we mentioned in Chapter 1, it is not unusual for people in the military or on sports teams to be subjected to barbaric, cruel hazing rituals. On the face of it, you might expect that the victims of hazings would despise those who made them suffer. However, by now you are probably in a better position to understand the reactions of people such as Dave Tremblay. When Dave Tremblay, a former Quebec Nordiques prospect, joined the Pickering Panthers of the Ontario Hockey Association, he was blindfolded, shaved, and forced to sit in a hot liniment that badly burned his genitals. A few years later, he was hazed again when he received a hockey scholarship from a U.S. university. That time, he was sick for days, suffering from alcohol poisoning. How does he remember the teammates who inflicted this cruelty on him? Remarkably, with fondness: "They came by and checked on us when it was over. . . . They didn't just beat the crap out of us and leave us" (O'Hara, 2000). If it weren't for cognitive dissonance theory, such a reaction would be difficult to understand!

The Psychology of Insufficient Justification

Imagine your best friend invites you to the first performance of a band that he has proudly put together. The vocalist is awful, the bass player shows little talent, and as it turns out, your friend should have kept up with his saxophone lessons.

Afterward, your friend excitedly asks you how you enjoyed the band. How do you respond? You hesitate. Chances are you go through something like the following thought process: "Jeremy seems so happy and excited. Why should I hurt his feelings and possibly ruin our friendship?" So you tell Jeremy that the band was great. Do you experience much dissonance? We doubt it. Your belief that it is important not to cause pain to people you like provides ample **external justification** for having told a harmless lie.

Counter-Attitudinal Advocacy What happens, on the other hand, if you say something you don't really believe and there isn't a good external justification for doing so? That is, what if Jeremy sincerely needed to know your opinion of the band because he was thinking of quitting school to devote his life to music? If you still tell him the band was great, you will experience dissonance. When you can't find external justification for your behaviour, you will attempt to find **internal justification**—that is, you will try to reduce dissonance by changing something about your attitudes or behaviour. How can you do this? You might begin looking for positive aspects of the band—some evidence of creativity or potential that might be realized with a little more practice or a few new talented band members. If you look hard enough, you will probably find something. Within a short time, your attitude toward the band will have moved in the direction of the statement you made—and that is how saying becomes believing. This phenomenon is referred to as **counter-attitudinal advocacy**, a process that occurs when a person states an opinion or attitude that runs counter to his or her private belief or attitude. When we do this with little external justification, we start to believe the lie we told.

This proposition was first tested in a groundbreaking experiment by Leon Festinger and J. Merrill Carlsmith (1959). In this experiment, university students were induced to spend an hour performing a series of excruciatingly boring and repetitive tasks. The experimenter then told them that the purpose of the study was to determine whether people would perform better if they had been told in advance that the tasks were interesting. They were each informed that they had been randomly assigned to the control condition—that is, they had not been told anything in advance. However, he explained, the next participant, a young woman who was just arriving in the anteroom, was going to be in the experimental condition. The experimenter said that he needed to convince her that the task was going to be interesting and enjoyable. Since it was much more convincing if a fellow student rather than the experimenter delivered this message, would the participant do so? With this request, the experimenter induced the participants to lie about the task to another student.

Half of the students were offered $20 for telling the lie (a large external justification), while the others were offered only $1 for telling the lie (a very small external justification). After the experiment was over, an interviewer asked the lie-tellers how much they had enjoyed the tasks they had performed earlier in the experiment. The results validated the hypothesis. Students who had been paid $20 for lying—that is, for saying that the tasks had been enjoyable—rated the activities as the dull and boring experiences they were. But those who were paid only $1 for saying that the task was enjoyable rated the task as significantly more enjoyable. In other words, people who had received an abundance of external justification for lying told the lie but didn't believe it, whereas those who told the lie without a great deal of external justification succeeded in convincing themselves that what they said was closer to the truth.

Insufficient Punishment If you really want to stop someone from behaving badly (e.g., trying to stop a bully from beating up little kids) you should dish out punishment—and make sure it is severe enough to have a deterrent effect. Right? Not so, according to dissonance theory. Dissonance theory would predict just the opposite. Give the bully mild punishment. Then, when the bully stops

▲ "How do I look?" your friend asks. Do you tell him the truth? Chances are you don't. Your concern about his feelings provides enough external justification for telling a white lie, so you experience little dissonance.

▲ How can we induce this child to give up playing with a violent toy?

insufficient punishment

the dissonance aroused when individuals lack sufficient external justification for having resisted a desired activity or object, usually resulting in individuals devaluing the forbidden activity or object

beating up little kids, dissonance is created. "I like beating up little kids, but I'm not doing it. Why?" He doesn't have a convincing answer to this question because the threat is so mild it doesn't produce a superabundance of justification. In short, this is **insufficient punishment**. This dissonance can be reduced by deciding "I guess I stopped because it's really not that much fun after all." In contrast, if this bully had received severe punishment, he or she would have ample external justification for having stopped ("I'm not beating up kids because I'll get kicked out of school if a teacher sees me"). In this case, the behaviour may decrease, but probably only when a teacher isn't around. In other words, true attitude change hasn't taken place.

These speculations were put to the test by Elliot Aronson and J. Merrill Carlsmith (1963) in an experiment with preschoolers. In this study, the experimenter first asked each child to rate the attractiveness of several toys. He then pointed to a toy that the child considered to be among the most attractive, and told the child that he or she was not allowed to play with it. Half of the children were threatened with mild punishment (the experimenter said he would be annoyed) if they disobeyed; the other half were threatened with severe punishment (the experimenter said he would be very angry, would take their toys away, and would never come back again). The experimenter then left the room for several minutes to provide the children the time and opportunity to play with the other toys and to resist the temptation of playing with the forbidden toy. None of the children played with the forbidden toy.

The experimenter then returned to the room and asked each child to rate how much he or she liked each of the toys. Initially, all the children had wanted to play with the forbidden toy, but during the temptation period, all of them had refrained from playing with it. Clearly, the children were experiencing dissonance. How did they respond? The children who had received a severe threat had ample justification for their restraint. They knew why they hadn't played with the toy and therefore they had no reason to change their attitude toward it. These children continued to rate the forbidden toy as highly desirable; indeed, some even found it more desirable than they had before the threat.

But what about the others? Without much external justification for avoiding the toy, the children in the mild threat condition needed an internal justification to reduce their dissonance. They succeeded in convincing themselves that the reason they hadn't played with the toy was that they didn't really like it. They rated the forbidden toy as less attractive than they had at the beginning of the experiment. Subsequent research showed that these effects are quite long lasting (Freedman, 1965). The implications for child rearing are fascinating. Parents who use punishment to encourage their children to adopt positive values should keep the punishment mild—barely enough to produce a change in behaviour—and then the values will follow.

The Aftermath of Good and Bad Deeds

Imagine that you realize that your actions have hurt another person. How would you react? Would you be especially kind to this person to make up for your transgression? Sadly, that is not what dissonance theory would predict. According to dissonance theory, when we hurt someone, we come to dislike or hate that person as a way of justifying our cruelty. This phenomenon was demonstrated in an early experiment performed by Keith Davis and Edward E. Jones (1960). Participants watched a young man (a confederate) being interviewed and then provided him with an analysis of his shortcomings as a human being. Specifically, the participants were told to tell the young man that they believed him to be a shallow, untrustworthy, boring person. The participants succeeded in convincing themselves that they didn't like the victim of their cruelty—after the fact. In short, after saying things they knew were certain to hurt him, they convinced

CONNECTIONS

Using Counter-Attitudinal Advocacy to Tackle Social Problems

Can research on counter-attitudinal advocacy be used to solve social problems? Would it be possible, for example, to get people to endorse a policy favouring a minority community and then see whether attitudes become more positive toward that community? Absolutely. In an important set of experiments, Mike Leippe and Donna Eisenstadt (1994, 1998) demonstrated that laboratory experiments on counter-attitudinal advocacy can be applied directly to important societal problems—in this case, race relations and racial prejudice. They induced white students at an American university to write a counter-attitudinal essay publicly endorsing a controversial proposal at their university—to double the funds available for academic scholarships for African-American students. Because the total funds were limited, this meant cutting by half the scholarship funds available to white students. As you might imagine, this was a highly dissonant situation. How might they reduce dissonance? The best way would be to convince themselves that they really believed deeply in that policy. Moreover, dissonance theory would predict that their general attitude toward African-American people would become more favourable and much more supportive. And that is exactly what Leippe and Eisenstadt found.

Counter-attitudinal advocacy has also been applied to another important societal issue: the prevention of the spread of AIDS. As we discussed earlier in this chapter, although college and university students are aware that AIDS is a serious problem, a surprisingly small percentage use condoms every time they have sex. Is there anything that can be done about this? Elliot Aronson and his colleagues (Aronson, Fried, & Stone, 1991; Stone et al., 1994) have had considerable success at convincing people to use condoms by employing a variation of the counter-attitudinal advocacy paradigm. They asked university students to compose a speech describing the dangers of AIDS and advocating the use of condoms every single time a person has sex. In one condition, the students merely composed the arguments. In another condition, the students composed the arguments and then recited them in front of a video camera, after being informed that the videotape would be played to an audience of high school students. In addition, half of the students in each condition were made mindful of their own failure to use condoms, by having them make a list of the circumstances in which they had found it particularly difficult, awkward, or impossible to use them.

Essentially, then, the participants in one condition—those who made a video for high school students after having been made mindful of their own failure to use condoms—were in a state of high dissonance. This was caused by their being made aware of their own hypocrisy; they were fully aware of the fact that they were preaching behaviour to high school students that they themselves were not practising. In order to remove the hypocrisy, they would need to start practising what they were preaching. And that is exactly what Aronson and his colleagues found. Later, when the students were given the opportunity to purchase condoms very cheaply, those in the hypocrisy condition were the most likely to buy them. A follow-up telephone interview several months after the experiment demonstrated that the effects were long lasting. People in the hypocrisy condition reported far greater use of condoms than did those in the control conditions.

themselves that he deserved it. They found him less attractive than they had prior to saying the hurtful things to him.

These effects can operate on quite a subtle level, as when we tell disparaging jokes about particular groups. Even though it may seem like harmless fun, we end up evaluating the group more negatively as a means of justifying our put-downs, as demonstrated in a program of research conducted at the University of Western Ontario (Hobden & Olson, 1994; Maio, Olson, & Bush, 1997). For example, participants who were asked to recite disparaging jokes about Newfoundlanders later reported more negative stereotypes of this group than those who recited nondisparaging jokes.

> " We do not love people so much for the good they have done us as for the good we have done them. "
>
> —Leo Tolstoy, 1869

▲ When defenceless civilians such as the elderly, women, and children are targets of military violence, the soldiers committing the violence will be inclined to derogate or dehumanize their victims to reduce their own dissonance. Here, Master Corporal Clayton Matchee of the Canadian Airborne Regiment smiles and points at Somali teenager Shidane Arone, whom members of the regiment tortured and beat to death in 1993. This photo, taken by one of the soldiers, shows the dehumanization of Somali people in the eyes of the soldiers.

Do people in real-world situations also use dissonance to justify cruel actions toward another human being? Sadly, the answer appears to be yes. In March 1993, Canadian soldiers from the elite Canadian Airborne Regiment on a peacekeeping mission in Somalia captured 16-year-old Shidane Arone trying to sneak into their compound. He was tied up, savagely beaten, and tortured to death. A court martial later learned that one of the soldiers beat Arone with a wooden riot baton, a metal pipe, and his feet and fists. Other soldiers joined in. According to newspaper reports, the young Somali boy's cries of "Canada, Canada, Canada" as he drifted in and out of consciousness could be heard across the compound. Canadians were shocked and deeply disturbed by this incident. Perhaps most shocking was that the soldiers posed for "trophy" photographs—in one photograph, soldiers posed beside the unconscious Somali boy; in another photograph, a soldier held the boy's head up by jamming a wooden baton into his bloody mouth; still others showed a soldier holding a gun to Arone's head. What was so chilling about these photographs was the broad smiles on the soldiers' faces. As James Travers, the editor of the *Ottawa Citizen*, commented, "They not only tortured, beat, and killed him, but were obviously playing when they did this" (Boadle, 1994). How could anyone gleefully torture and murder a 16-year-old boy? By deciding that he deserved it. It may seem absurd to suggest that Canadian peacekeepers could convince themselves that an unarmed, civilian boy deserved to be beaten to death for trying to enter their compound. However, as various inquiries into this tragedy revealed, some of the higher-ranking officers had issued orders to "abuse" any Somali intruders. While the soldiers who committed these atrocities were aware that it was illegal to torture or kill anyone they captured, the fact that some of their superiors advocated punishing intruders appears to have been all the justification they needed. In short, the soldiers may have convinced themselves that Arone deserved what he got.

Another way in which people reduce dissonance for having committed cruel acts is to derogate or dehumanize their victim. According to the report of the Somalia Commission of Inquiry, the Canadian soldiers referred to the Somali people as "gimmes," "smufties," and "nignogs" (Canada, 1997). Unfortunately, history keeps repeating itself. In 2005, Americans in charge of the Abu Ghraib prison near Baghdad tortured and killed Iraqi prisoners. The images of torture and humiliation bore a chilling resemblance to the photos of Shidane Arone. One of the striking similarities was the dehumanization of the victims—the prisoners were shown naked, with hoods over their faces, or crawling on all fours with leashes around their necks.

Ironically, success at dehumanizing the victim virtually guarantees a continuation or even an escalation of the cruelty. It becomes easier to hurt and kill "subhumans" than to hurt and kill fellow human beings. Thus, reducing dissonance in this way has sobering future consequences: it increases the likelihood that the atrocities people are willing to commit will become greater and greater through an endless chain of violence followed by self-justification (in the form of dehumanizing the victim), followed by greater violence and still more intense dehumanization. In this manner, unbelievable acts of human cruelty—such as the Nazi Final Solution that led to the murder of 6 million European Jews, the murders of 2 million Cambodians in Pol Pot's Killing Fields in the 1970s, and the massacre of 600 000 Tutsis in Rwanda in 1994—can occur. Unfortunately, such atrocities are not a thing of the past but are as recent as today's newspaper. (Many examples are provided in a fascinating, yet disturbing, book by Carol Tavris and Elliott Aronson (2007), titled *Mistakes Were Made (But Not by Me): Why We Justify Foolish Beliefs, Bad Decisions, and Hurtful Acts.*)

Dehumanization of victims is not limited to situations in which countries are embroiled in war, as demonstrated in recent research conducted with prison guards who carry out executions in the United States. How do execution guards respond when they kill another person as part of their job? Clearly, they need to reduce their cognitive dissonance. Taking a life is a supremely immoral act, so they will very much need to engage in self-justification in order to do it. Michael Osofsky, Albert Bandura, and Phillip Zimbardo (2005) studied guards on the execution teams of three southern state prisons, and compared them with their fellow guards who did not conduct executions. All of the guards responded anonymously to a questionnaire that asked them to rate their level of agreement with statements such as "Because of the nature of their crime, murderers have lost the right to live," and "Those who carry out state executions should not be criticized for following society's wishes."

The researchers found a highly significant difference in the attitudes of the two types of guards. The execution-team guards demonstrated much more "moral disengagement" from their work than did the other guards. The execution-team guards denied all personal responsibility for the executions. They strongly felt they were just following orders—in this case, those of a judge and jury. They also dehumanized the prisoners more than the regular prison guards, seeing them as lacking important human qualities. They perceived the prisoners as more of a threat to society, such that it was necessary that they be killed. All of these attitudes helped the execution guards reduce their qualms about the morality of what they did at work. As one guard put it, "I had a job to do, that's what we did. Our job was to execute this man and we were going to do it in a professional manner" (Osofsky, Bandura & Zimbardo, 2005; p. 386).

Avoiding the Rationalization Trap

The tendency to reduce dissonance by justifying our behaviour can lead us into an escalation of rationalizations that can be disastrous. We call this the **rationalization trap**—the potential for dissonance reduction to produce a succession of self-justifications that ultimately results in a chain of stupid or irrational actions. The irony, of course, is that to avoid thinking of ourselves as stupid or immoral, we set the stage to increase our acts of stupidity or immorality.

Is there a way that people can be persuaded not to rationalize their behaviour when they make mistakes? A clue as to how such behaviour might come about can be found in research on self-affirmation (Steele, 1988). **Self-affirmation theory** suggests that people will reduce the impact of a dissonance-arousing threat to their self-concept by focusing on and affirming their competence on some dimension unrelated to the threat.

Research by Claude Steele and his colleagues (Steele, 1988; see also Steele & Liu, 1981, and Aronson, Cohen, & Nail, 1998) shows how self-affirmation comes about. Suppose that immediately after Mary acted cruelly, but before she had an opportunity to derogate her victim, she was reminded of the fact that she had recently donated several units of blood to Canadian Blood Services or that she had recently received a high score on her physics exam. This self-affirmation would likely provide her with the ability to resist engaging in typical dissonance-reducing behaviour. In effect, Mary might be able to say, "It's true—I just did a cruel thing. But I am also capable of some really fine, intelligent, and generous behaviour." In a series of clever experiments, Steele and his colleagues demonstrated that if—prior to the onset of dissonance—you provide people with an opportunity for self-affirmation, they will generally grab it (Steele, 1988; Steele & Liu, 1981).

But can self-affirmation actually serve as a cognitive buffer, protecting a person from caving in to temptation and committing a cruel or immoral act? In an early experiment on cheating (Aronson & Mettee, 1968), university students were first given a personality test, and then given false feedback that was either positive (i.e., aimed at temporarily raising self-esteem) or negative (i.e., aimed at temporarily lowering self-esteem), or they received no information at all.

rationalization trap

the potential for dissonance reduction to produce a succession of self-justifications that ultimately result in a chain of stupid or immoral actions

self-affirmation theory

a theory suggesting that people will reduce the impact of a dissonance-arousing threat to their self-concept by focusing on and affirming their competence on some dimension unrelated to the threat

> " Both salvation and punishment for man lie in the fact that if he lives wrongly, he can befog himself so as not to see the misery of his position. "
>
> —Leo Tolstoy (1828–1910)

Immediately afterward, they played a game of cards in which, to win a large pot, they could easily cheat without getting caught. The results were striking. Students in the high self-esteem condition were able to resist the temptation to cheat to a far greater extent than were the students in the other conditions. In short, a temporary boost in self-esteem served to inoculate these students against cheating, because the anticipation of doing something immoral was more dissonant than it would otherwise have been. Thus, when they were put in a tempting situation, they were able to say to themselves, "Terrific people like me don't cheat." And they didn't (see also Spencer, Josephs, & Steele, 1993; Steele, Spencer, & Lynch, 1993).

Recent studies conducted by University of British Columbia researchers point to another promising approach for avoiding the rationalization trap (Aquino, Reed, Thau, & Freeman, 2007). In this research, participants were primed with moral identity words (e.g., "caring," "honest," "helpful") or in the control condition, with positive, but not moral, words (e.g., "happy," "open-minded"). Participants also were asked to write stories about themselves using these words. Later, they were exposed to pictures and newspaper articles about prisoner abuses in Abu Ghraib prison and at Guantanamo Bay. Those whose moral identity was made salient (that is, brought to the forefront of their minds) subsequently reported more negative emotions in response to these abuses than those in the control condition.

Thus, there is evidence that affirming people in some way (e.g., boosting their self-esteem) or reminding them of their morals may reverse the rationalization trap. We find these results encouraging.

Dissonance, Self-Affirmation, and Culture   According to Heine and Lehman (1997a), the experience of dissonance may be unique to cultures in which the self is defined as independent. If the focus in a culture is on the individual (as in North America), it becomes important for the individual to behave in ways that are consistent with his or her attitudes, because the person's behaviour is seen as diagnostic of what he or she is really like. On the other hand, if the self is defined in relation to others, as is the case in Asian cultures, behaviour is more likely to be tailored to the demands of the group. If an individual behaves in an attitude-inconsistent way, others are likely to invoke situational explanations. (You may recall from our discussion of the fundamental attribution error in Chapter 4 that people in Asian cultures do, in fact, make more situational attributions for others' behaviour than do those in Western cultures.) Based on this reasoning, Heine and Lehman hypothesized that people in Asian cultures should experience little dissonance when their attitudes and behaviours are inconsistent.

To test this idea, the researchers conducted a study in which students at the University of British Columbia and Japanese students visiting Vancouver signed up for a marketing research study. First, the researchers administered a bogus personality test. Then participants were asked to rate the desirability of 10 CDs. In the meantime, their personality tests supposedly had been scored. Some participants received positive personality feedback and others received negative feedback. (Participants in a control group did not receive any personality information.) Next, participants were given a choice between their fifth- and sixth-ranked CDs. After they made their selection, they were asked to again rate all 10.

Canadian participants in the control group showed classic dissonance reduction—they rated the chosen CD higher than they had previously and the rejected CD lower than they had previously. However, consistent with self-affirmation theory, those who received positive personality feedback did not engage in dissonance reduction. Because they had been reminded of what wonderful people they were, they did not feel a need to reduce dissonance by changing their ratings of the CDs. Those who received negative feedback were especially likely to engage in dissonance reduction.

And what about the Japanese participants? They did not show dissonance reduction in any of the conditions. Japanese students felt as badly as Canadian students did about the negative personality feedback and were more likely than the Canadian participants to believe that it was accurate. However, they did not reduce dissonance by changing their ratings of the CDs, even under these circumstances.

In an interesting twist, Hoshino-Browne and colleagues (2005) examined whether East Asians might experience dissonance when they have to make a decision that affects a member of their group. In this research, students at the University of Waterloo and at Kyoto University in Japan rated the 10 dishes they would prefer most at a new Chinese restaurant (the self condition), or rated the 10 dishes a close friend would prefer (the friend condition). Later, participants were shown coupons for the fifth- and sixth-ranked dishes and were told to select one. Those in the self condition were asked to once again rate their preferences for all of the dishes; those in the friend condition rated their friend's preferences. European-Canadian participants showed classic postdecision dissonance in the self condition—they now rated the dish for which they had chosen the coupon more positively and the "rejected" dish (i.e., the coupon for the dish they didn't select) more negatively than they had before. East Asian participants did not show this effect. However, in the friend condition, the results were opposite—here European Canadians did not show evidence of dissonance reduction, but Asian participants did. In other words, European Canadians tended to justify their decisions when they made choices for themselves, whereas East Asians tended to justify their decisions when they made choices for a close other (Hoshino-Browne, Zanna, Spencer, Zanna, Kitayama, & Lackenbauer, 2005).

In follow-up studies, the researchers examined the role of two different types of self-affirmation in reducing dissonance—either an independent self-affirmation (e.g., writing about a value that uniquely describes you) or an interdependent self-affirmation (writing about why a certain value is held by you and your family members). As you can probably guess, an independent self-affirmation diminished the need for dissonance reduction among European Canadians; an interdependent self-affirmation diminished the need for dissonance reduction among East Asians. Interestingly, both kinds of self-affirmation were effective for bicultural participants (i.e., East Asians living in Canada who strongly identified with both cultures). Hoshino-Browne and colleagues conclude that in order for self-affirmation to protect people from engaging in dissonance reduction, it is important to affirm a culturally valued trait.

To summarize, throughout this chapter, we've indicated that human beings generally have a need to see themselves as intelligent, sensible, and decent people who behave with integrity. Indeed, what triggers the attitude change and distortion that can take place in the process of dissonance reduction is precisely the need people have to maintain this picture of themselves.

The Solar Temple Revisited

At the beginning of this chapter, we raised a vital question regarding the followers of Luc Jouret and Joseph Di Mambro of the Solar Temple. How could intelligent people allow themselves to be led into what, to the overwhelming majority of us, is obviously senseless and tragic behaviour—resulting in mass suicide-murders? Needless to say, the situation is a complex one; there were many factors operating, including the charismatic, persuasive power of each of these leaders, the existence of a great deal of social support for the views of the group from other members of the group, and the relative isolation of each group from dissenting views, producing a closed system—a little like living in a room full of mirrors.

In addition to these factors, we are convinced that the single most powerful force was the existence of a great deal of cognitive dissonance. You know from reading this chapter that when individuals make an important decision and invest heavily in that decision in terms of time, effort, sacrifice, and commitment, the result is a strong need to justify those actions and that investment. The more they sacrifice and the harder they work, the greater the need to convince themselves that their views are correct; indeed, they may even begin to feel sorry for those who do not share their beliefs. The members of the Solar Temple cult sacrificed a great deal for their beliefs; they abandoned their friends and families, relinquished their money and possessions, and if they were female, subjected themselves to sexual exploitation. All of these sacrifices served to increase their commitment to the cult. Those of us who have studied the theory of cognitive dissonance were not surprised to learn that intelligent, respected, professional people could be persuaded that through death by fire, they could escape the imminent apocalypse on Earth and be reborn on the star Sirius. To begin to question these beliefs would have produced too much dissonance to bear. Although tragic and bizarre, the death voyages of the Solar Temple members are not unfathomable. They are simply an extreme manifestation of a process—cognitive dissonance—that we have seen in operation over and over again.

SUMMARY

An **attitude** is a person's enduring evaluation of a person, object, or idea. All attitudes have affective, cognitive, and behavioural components. An **affectively based attitude** is based more on people's emotions and feelings. A **cognitively based attitude** is based mostly on people's beliefs about the properties of the attitude object. A **behaviourally** based attitude is based on people's actions toward the attitude object. Attitudes vary in terms of whether they are more likely to be based on affect, cognition, or behaviour. **Explicit attitudes** are ones that people consciously endorse and can easily report, whereas **implicit attitudes** are involuntary, uncontrollable, and at times unconscious.

When do people behave in line with their attitudes? According to the **theory of planned behaviour**, the best predictors of people's behaviour are their intentions to perform the behaviour. Behavioural intentions, in turn, are best predicted by people's specific attitudes toward the behaviour in question, their **subjective norms** (their beliefs about how others view the behaviour in question), and perceived behavioural control—the belief that it is easy or difficult to perform the behaviour.

The theory of planned behaviour is useful in understanding an area in which people's attitudes and behaviour are often inconsistent—namely, practising safer sex. Although people tend to express positive attitudes toward using condoms, they frequently fail to do so. Why? One reason has to do with subjective norms: If people believe that their peers are not using condoms, or if they believe their partner would disapprove of condom use, they probably will not use them. Another reason is perceived behavioural control: If people find it embarrassing to buy condoms or to bring up the topic of condom use with their

partner, it is unlikely that they will use condoms. Finally, condoms also will not be used if people's intentions to use them are undermined (e.g., by excessive alcohol consumption).

In the next part of the chapter, we focused on attitude change. One way attitudes change is if people receive a **persuasive communication**. According to the **Yale Attitude Change Approach**, the persuasiveness of a communication depends on aspects of the communicator, or source of the message, aspects of the message itself (e.g., its content), and aspects of the audience. The **heuristic-systematic model of persuasion** and the **elaboration likelihood model** specify when people are persuaded more by the strength of the arguments in the communication and when they are persuaded more by surface characteristics, such as the attractiveness of the speaker. People will take the *central route to persuasion* (systematic processing) when they have both the ability and the motivation to pay close attention to the arguments. People will take the *peripheral route to persuasion* (heuristic processing) when they either do not want to or cannot pay close attention to the arguments. Under these conditions, they are persuaded by such peripheral cues as the attractiveness of the speaker or the length of the speech. Importantly, attitude change is longer lasting and more resistant to attack when it occurs via the central systematic route.

A common tactic for changing attitudes is the use of fear. **Fear-arousing communication** can cause lasting attitude change if a moderate amount of fear is aroused and if specific recommendations are provided for performing the desired behaviours. The effectiveness of persuasive communications also depends on the type of attitude people have. Appeals to emotion work best if the attitude is based on affect; appeals to utilitarian features work best if the attitude is based on cognition. Under controlled laboratory conditions, **subliminal messages** can have subtle effects on people's preferences, but there is no evidence that subliminal messages have been used successfully in real-world marketing campaigns.

It is possible to make people resistant to attacks on their attitudes. **Attitude inoculation** is the technique whereby people are exposed to small doses of arguments against their position, making it easier for them to refute these arguments when they hear them later. It is also important to be on the lookout for **product placement**—strategically placed products in movies and television shows that are intended to persuade us.

In the final part of the chapter, we discussed another powerful determinant of attitude change: our own behaviour. According to **cognitive dissonance theory**, people experience discomfort (dissonance) whenever they behave in ways inconsistent with their attitudes or when they hold two conflicting attitudes. There is evidence that dissonance is an uncomfortable state and that people are motivated to reduce it. People reduce dissonance by either justifying their past behaviour or changing their behaviour. The resulting change in attitude stems from a process of self-persuasion.

Dissonance inevitably occurs after important decisions (**postdecision dissonance**), because the thought that "I chose alternative X" is inconsistent with the thought that "I might have been a lot better off with alternative Y." People reduce this dissonance by increasing their liking for the chosen alternative and decreasing their liking for the negative alternative. Dissonance also occurs after people choose to exert a lot of effort to attain something boring or onerous. A **justification of effort** occurs, whereby people increase their liking for what they attained.

Another source of dissonance occurs when people commit foolish, immoral, or absurd acts for **insufficient punishment**. For example, when people say something against their attitudes (**counter-attitudinal advocacy**) for low **external justification**, they find an **internal justification** for their behaviour, coming to believe what they said. Similarly, if people avoid doing something desirable for insufficient punishment, they will come to believe that the activity wasn't really all that desirable after all.

Dissonance reduction can have sinister effects. If we find ourselves acting cruelly toward someone for insufficient justification, we will derogate the victim, assuming he or she must have deserved it. The problem with reducing dissonance in this way is that while it makes us feel better about ourselves, it can result in a **rationalization trap**, whereby we set the stage for acts of increasing stupidity or immorality. As suggested by **self-affirmation theory**, we can avoid this trap by reminding ourselves of our competencies in other areas. It is also useful to remind ourselves that we are good and decent people, so that we do not have to justify and rationalize every stupid or immoral act we perform.

Scoring the Try It! Exercises

▶ **Page 171**

1. Wilson, Gilbert, and Wheatley (1998) found that 80 percent of university students preferred not to receive a subliminal message because it might influence them in an undesirable way.

2. Wilson, Gilbert, and Wheatley (1998) found that only 28 percent of university students preferred not to receive a regular, everyday television ad because it might influence them in an undesirable way.

3. When Wilson, Houston, and Meyers (1998) asked university students to choose to listen to the type of speech they thought would influence them the least, 69 percent chose the regular speech and 31 percent chose the subliminal speech. Ironically, it was the regular speech that changed people's minds the most.

mypsychlab
PEARSON

Along with a dynamic, electronic version of this text, MyPsychLab offers a wealth of resources to deepen your understanding and test your recall of the material in this chapter—including video and audio clips, simulations and activities, self-assessments, practice tests, and other study materials. The following specific resources are available for this chapter:

 Elaboration Likelihood Model

 Cognitive Dissonance

 Attitude and Attitude Change

To access MyPsychLab, please visit www.mypsychlab.com (Student Access Code required—packaged with this book).

Conformity:
Influencing Others

The judgment brought down by Mr. Justice Macaulay on May 10, 1999, begins with the statement, "Reena Virk died on November 14, 1997, after a vicious beating" (*R. v. Warren Paul Glowatski*, 1999). The transcript of the trial documents the events that led to the tragic death of this 14-year-old girl. During an exchange with Reena Virk, a student at her school extinguished a lit cigarette on her forehead. Other friends of this student joined in and began beating Virk. One girl testified that she grabbed a lighter and tried to set Virk's hair on fire; others began punching and kicking Virk in the head and face. According to the pathologist's report, Virk's head injuries alone were severe enough to be life threatening. She also suffered massive internal injuries. The pathologist considered the force of these injuries to be comparable with crush injuries that would result from being run over by a car. The unconscious Virk was dragged by Kelly Ellard and Warren Glowatski to the Gorge waterway not far from downtown Victoria, where she was drowned. Apparently, Ellard smoked a cigarette as she stood with one foot on Virk's head, holding it under water.

Glowatski and eventually Ellard were charged with second-degree murder. Glowatski appealed his conviction, but it was upheld by the appeal court. Ellard was tried three times; her most recent trial resulted in a conviction on April 12, 2005. She appealed. The appeal court overturned Ellard's second-degree murder conviction in September 2008, and ordered a fourth trial (at the time of writing, the date had not been set). Six other girls involved in the beating were given sentences ranging from a 60-day conditional sentence to one year in jail.

▲ Reena Virk, a B.C. teenager, was savagely beaten by her schoolmates, and then drowned by two other teenagers. She died on November 14, 1997.

Canadians were horrified by Reena Virk's brutal death. How could ordinary high school students in Victoria, British Columbia, engage in such savage acts against a defenceless 14-year-old? Why did some students participate in the beatings, rather than attempt to stop this tragedy? Sadly, as we shall see, the need to conform to a group probably played a role in Reena Virk's murder. Under what conditions and for what reasons are we likely to fall under the influence of others? That is the key question to be addressed in this chapter.

Conformity: When and Why

conformity

a change in behaviour as a result of the real or imagined influence of other people

> **❝** Do as most do, and [people] will speak well of thee. **❞**
>
> —Thomas Fuller (1608–1661)

> **❝** It were not best that we should all think alike; it is difference of opinion that makes horse races. **❞**
>
> —Mark Twain (1835–1910)

Think for a moment about the word **conformity**, which we can define as a change in behaviour as a result of the real or imagined influence of others (Kiesler & Kiesler, 1969). Which of the two quotations on this page do you find more appealing? Which one best describes your immediate reaction to the word *conformity*?

We wouldn't be surprised if you preferred the Mark Twain quotation. North American culture stresses the importance of not conforming (Hofstede, 1986; Markus, Kitayama, & Heiman, 1996). This is part of being in an individualistic culture—one that emphasizes being independent, thinking for yourself, and standing up for yourself. We want to be perceived as people who make up our own minds—not as spineless, weak conformists; not as puppets, but players (Hornsey & Jetten, 2004, 2005). As a result, we may maintain the belief that our behaviour is not influenced by others, even when reality suggests otherwise. This phenomenon was illustrated in a program of research by Jacquie Vorauer and Dale Miller (1997). In one of their studies, students at the University of Manitoba were asked to rate how satisfied they felt with their intellectual abilities. Before making their ratings, they were allowed to see the same ratings supposedly given by another student. Were participants influenced by the other student's responses? Yes, they were. Specifically, if the other student provided a positive self-assessment, participants also evaluated themselves positively—more so than if the other student had provided a negative self-assessment. Most importantly, participants were not aware that they had been influenced by the other student's responses. In other words, we probably conform a lot more than we realize (or want to admit).

Indeed, people do conform—sometimes in extreme and surprising ways, as suggested by the deaths of 74 Solar Temple cult members (discussed in Chapter 6). But you might argue that is an unusual case—surely most people do not conform to this extent. We might convince ourselves that the followers of Luc Jouret and Joseph Di Mambro were disturbed people who were somehow predisposed to do what charismatic leaders told them to do. There is, however, another more chilling possibility. Maybe most of us would have acted the same way, had we been exposed to the same long-standing conformity pressures. Perhaps almost anyone would have conformed had he or she been put in these same extreme situations. If this statement is true, we should be able to find other situations in which people, put under strong social pressures, conform to surprising degrees. Unfortunately, we do not have to look very far to find such instances.

We opened this chapter with the deeply disturbing story of Reena Virk, who died at the hands of a group of high school students. Once one of the students began attacking Virk, others went along. In Chapter 6, we described the chilling story of Shidane Arone, who was tortured to death by Canadian peacekeepers in Somalia. In that situation as well, one soldier began beating the boy and others joined in. And, of course, the Holocaust in World War II provides countless horrific examples of conformity at its worst.

The examples we have seen so far are all cases of conformity with bad consequences: Human beings lost their lives as a result of people going along with others. However, conformity is not simply "good" or "bad" in and of itself. Rather than labelling conformity as "good" or "bad," the social psychologist is interested in *why* people conform. Knowing why and when people are influenced by others will help us understand whether a given act of conformity in their own life is wise or foolish. To return to the example of the Solar Temple cult, some members probably conformed because they did not know what to do in a confusing or unusual situation; the behaviour of the people around them served as a cue about how to respond, and so they decided to act in a similar manner. Other people probably conformed because they did not wish to be ridiculed or punished for being different from everybody else; they chose to act the way the group expected them to, so they wouldn't be rejected or disapproved of by group members. Let's see how each of these reasons for conforming operates.

Informational Social Influence: The Need to Know What's "Right"

One of the important things we get from interacting with other people is information. There are many situations in which we don't know what to do, or even know what is happening. Unfortunately, life, unlike our clothing, does not come with labels attached, telling us what is going on and how we should respond. Instead, the social world is frequently ambiguous and ill-defined. For example, how should you address your psychology professor—as Dr. Berman, Professor Berman, Ms. Berman, or Patricia? How should you vote on a proposal to increase your tuition to expand student services? Is the scream you just heard coming from a person joking with friends or from the victim of a mugging?

In these and many other everyday situations, we feel uncertain about what to think or how to act. We simply don't know enough to make a good or accurate choice. Fortunately, we have a powerful and useful source of knowledge available to us—the behaviour of other people. Asking others what they think or watching what they do helps us reach a definition of the situation (Kelley, 1955; Thomas, 1928). When we subsequently act like everyone else, we are conforming—but not because we are weak, spineless individuals with no self-reliance. Instead, the influence of other people leads us to conform because we see them as a source of information to guide our behaviour. This is called **informational social influence** (Cialdini, 1993, 2000; Cialdini & Goldstein, 2004; Deutsch & Gerard, 1955).

As an illustration of how other people can be a source of information, imagine you are a participant in a classic experiment by Muzafer Sherif (1936). In the first phase of the study, you are seated alone in a dark room and asked to focus your attention on a dot of light 5 metres away. The experimenter asks you to estimate in centimetres how far the light moves. You stare earnestly at the light and, yes, it moves a little. You say, "About 5 centimetres," though it is not easy to tell exactly. The light disappears and then comes back; you are asked to judge again. The light seems to move a little more, and you say, "10 centimetres." After several of these trials, the light seems to move about the same amount each time—about

informational social influence

conforming because we believe that others' interpretation of an ambiguous situation is more correct than ours and will help us choose an appropriate course of action

5 to 10 centimetres. Now, the interesting thing about this task is that the light was not actually moving at all. It looked as if it was moving because of a visual illusion called the *autokinetic effect.* If you stare at a bright light in a uniformly dark environment (e.g., a star on a dark night), the light will appear to waver. This occurs because you have no stable reference point to anchor the position of the light. The distance that the light appears to move varies from person to person but becomes consistent for each person over time. In Sherif's (1936) experiment, the participants all arrived at their own, stable estimates during the first phase of the study, but these estimates differed from person to person. Some people thought the light was moving only 2.5 centimetres or so, whereas others thought it was moving as much as 25 centimetres.

Sherif chose to use the autokinetic effect because he wanted a situation that would be ambiguous—where the correct definition of the situation would be unclear to his participants. In the second phase of the experiment, a few days later, the participants were paired with two other people, each of whom had had the same prior experience alone with the light. Now the situation became a truly social one, as all three made their judgments out loud. Remember, the autokinetic effect is experienced differently by different people; some see a lot of movement, some not much at all. After hearing their partners give judgments that were different from their own, what did people do? Over the course of several trials, people reached a common estimate, and each member of the group conformed to that estimate. These results indicate that people were using each other as a source of information, coming to believe that the group estimate was the correct one (see Figure 7.1).

An important feature of informational social influence is that it can lead to **private acceptance**, whereby people conform to the behaviour of others because they genuinely believe that these other people are correct. It might seem equally plausible that people publicly conformed to the group but privately maintained the belief that the light was moving only a small amount. For example, maybe someone privately believed that the light was moving 25 centimetres but announced that it had moved 7.5 centimetres (the group estimate) to avoid looking silly or foolish. This would be a case of **public compliance**, whereby a person conforms publicly without necessarily believing in what the group is saying or doing. Sherif cast doubt on this interpretation, however, by asking people to judge the lights once more by themselves, after participating in groups. Even though they no longer had to worry about looking silly in front of other participants, they continued to give the answer the group had given earlier. These results suggest that people were relying on each other to define reality and came to privately accept the group estimate.

> 'It's always best on these occasions to do what the mob do.' 'But suppose there are two mobs?' suggested Mr. Snodgrass. 'Shout with the largest,' replied Mr. Pickwick.
> —Charles Dickens, Pickwick Papers, 1836–1837

private acceptance

conforming to other people's behaviour out of a genuine belief that what they are doing or saying is right

public compliance

conforming to other people's behaviour publicly, without necessarily believing in what they are doing or saying

FIGURE 7.1

One group's judgments in Sherif's (1936) autokinetic studies

People estimated how far a point of light appeared to move in a dark room. When they saw the light by themselves, their estimates varied widely. When they were brought together in groups and heard other people announce their estimates, they conformed to the group's estimate of how much the light moved.

(Adapted from Sherif, 1936)

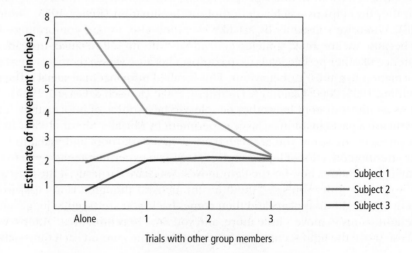

In everyday life, of course, we are rarely asked to judge how much a stationary light is moving. However, there are many common situations in which we rely on other people to help us define what is going on. Think about the first time you were at the symphony or at a jazz concert. You knew that you would applaud at some time—but exactly when? After a solo? Only at the end of a piece? What about standing ovations, or shouting for an encore? No doubt, you looked to others in the audience to help you learn the appropriate way of showing approval in each setting. Later research has shown that information conformity does, indeed, occur in real-life situations (Baron, Vandello, & Brunsman, 1996; Levine, Higgins, & Choi, 2000). It has also revealed another variable that affects informational social influence: how important it is to the individual to be accurate at the task. It may surprise you to learn that when participants are convinced that the task is important, they are *more* likely to conform to the group than participants who are led to believe the task is unimportant. In other words, when we are facing an important decision, we are even more likely to rely on other people for information and guidance. In short, informational social influence is pervasive in our day-to-day lives.

When Will People Conform to Informational Social Influence?

What kinds of situations are most likely to produce conformity because of informational social influence? We will discuss three: ambiguous situations, crises, and situations in which an expert is present.

When the Situation Is Ambiguous   You may have had the experience of hearing a fire alarm in a building. What did you do? If you are like most people, you turned to the people around you to see if the situation was an emergency. If other people seemed unconcerned and weren't making moves to leave the building, you probably decided that there wasn't a need to evacuate. On the other hand, if other people started rushing toward the emergency exit doors, your behaviour would probably be quite different. When you are unsure of the correct response, the appropriate behaviour, or the right idea, you will be most open to influence from others. Research shows that the more uncertain you are, the more you will rely on others (Baron, Vandello, & Brunsman, 1996; Tesser, Campbell, & Mickler, 1983; Walther, Bless, Strack, Rackstraw, Wagner, & Werth, 2002).

When Shidane Arone entered the compound of the Canadian peacekeepers in Somalia, the soldiers experienced considerable ambiguity about how to handle such a situation. One of the commanding officers had given an order that the soldiers should "abuse" intruders. During the court martial, the defence argued that the officer's instruction was that physical force could be used to capture intruders and that the term "abuse" did not imply that torture was acceptable. Regardless of what was intended, it seems that soldiers did not have a clear sense of what should be done if they caught someone entering their compound. More generally, reports of investigations of these events suggest that the peacekeepers had not been well prepared for their mission. As discussed later, investigations into the abuses of Iraqi prisoners at the hands of American soldiers similarly suggest that the soldiers were not given clear instructions on what should be done with detainees. In such situations, when ambiguity abounds, people are especially likely to be influenced by the actions of those around them. Tragically, as the Shidane Arone case illustrates, such actions can result in the loss of lives.

When the Situation Is a Crisis   When the situation is a crisis, we usually do not have time to stop and think about exactly which course of action we should take. We need to act and act now. If we feel scared and panicky, and are uncertain what to do, it is only natural for us to see how other people are responding—and to do likewise. Unfortunately, the people we imitate may also feel scared and panicky, and not behave rationally.

Consider what happened on Halloween night in 1938. Orson Welles, the gifted actor and future film director, and the Mercury Theatre broadcast a radio play based loosely on H. G. Wells's 1898 science fiction fantasy, *The War of the Worlds*. Remember that this was the era before television; radio was a source of entertainment, with music, comedy, and drama programs, and the only source for fast-breaking news. That night, Welles and his fellow actors put on a radio drama of a cataclysm—the invasion of Earth by hostile Martians—that was so realistic and effective that at least 1 million listeners in the United States became frightened, and several thousand were panic-stricken (Cantril, 1940). The result was a **contagion**—the rapid transmission of emotions or behaviour through a crowd, in this case, the listening audience. Why were so many Americans convinced that what they had heard was a real news report of an invasion by aliens? One reason is that the play parodied existing radio news shows very well, and many listeners missed the beginning of the broadcast, when it was clearly labelled as a play, because they had been listening to the nation's number-one-rated show, *Charlie McCarthy*, on another station. Another culprit, however, was informational social influence. Many people were listening with friends and family, and naturally turned to each other out of uncertainty to see whether they should believe what they had heard. Seeing looks of concern and worry on their loved ones' faces added to the panic people were beginning to feel. "We all kissed one another and felt we would all die," reported one listener (Cantril, 1940).

Closer to home, Luc Jouret, a leader of the Solar Temple cult, apparently was convinced that the world was coming to an end and managed to persuade his followers that this was true (see Chapter 6). Needless to say, this constituted a crisis for those who accepted this belief, and they turned to him for guidance. Sadly, they believed him when he said that death by fire was the correct course of action so they could be reborn on the star Sirius. Such instances of mind control, or brainwashing, can actually be extreme cases of informational social influence. When people believe that they are in a crisis situation, they are more likely to succumb to these forms of influence.

When Other People Are Experts Typically, the more expertise or knowledge a person has, the more valuable he or she will be as a guide in an ambiguous or crisis situation (Allison, 1992; Bickman, 1974; Cialdini & Trost, 1998). For example, a passenger who sees smoke coming out of an airplane engine will probably look

contagion

the rapid transmission of emotions or behaviour through a crowd

▶ The *New York Times* headlined the 1938 *War of the Worlds* incident. Partly because of informational social influence, many listeners believed that the fictional radio broadcast by Orson Welles and the Mercury Theatre players about an invasion by Martians was true.

Try it!

▶ Informational Social Influence and Emergencies

One of the most interesting examples of informational social influence in action is the behaviour of bystanders in emergencies. An emergency is by definition a crisis situation. In many respects, it is an ambiguous situation as well. Sometimes there are "experts" present, but sometimes there aren't. In an emergency, the bystander is thinking, "What's happening? Is help needed? What should I do? What's everybody else doing?"

As you'll recall from the story told by your author Robin Akert on page xxxiii, trying to decide if an emergency is really happening and if your help is really needed can be very difficult. Bystanders typically rely on informational social influence to help them figure out what to do. Other people's behaviour is a source of important information in an unusual situation; unfortunately, as in Akert's story, if other people are acting as if nothing is wrong, you could be misled by their behaviour and also interpret the situation as a non-emergency. In that case, informational social influence has backfired.

In order to explore informational social influence, gather some stories about people's reactions to emergencies when they were bystanders (not victims). Think about your own experiences and ask your friends to tell you about emergencies they have been in. As you recollect your own experience, or talk to your friends about their experiences, note how informational social influence played a role:

1. How did you (and your friends) decide that an emergency was really occurring? Did you glance at other passersby and watch their responses? Did you talk to other people to help you figure out what was going on?

2. Once you decided it was an emergency, how did you know what to do? Did you do what other people were doing? Did you show (or tell) them what to do?

3. Were there any experts present—people who knew more about the situation or how to offer assistance? Did you do what the experts told you to do? If you were in the role of expert (or were at least knowledgeable) at the scene of the emergency, did people follow your lead?

The issues raised by these questions are all examples of informational social influence in action.

around for the flight attendants to check their reaction; they have more expertise than the vacationer in the next seat. However, experts are not always reliable sources of information. Imagine the fear felt by the young man who was listening to Welles's broadcast of *The War of the Worlds* and called his local police department for an explanation—only to discover that the police also thought the events described on the radio were actually happening.

The role of experts in exerting informational social influence was examined in a study of students in a military college who were training to become Canadian Armed Forces officers. Serge Guimond (1999) found that students in the social sciences became more liberal in their views over their three years in college (e.g., became less blaming of the victims of poverty and unemployment), whereas engineering students became more conservative. Guimond concluded that the students' attitudes had changed as a result of informational social influence—in this case, the information they learned from their professors in these courses.

In the accompanying Try It!, you can explore how the informational social influence variables of ambiguity, crisis, and expertise have operated in your life and in your friends' lives.

When Informational Conformity Backfires

The War of the Worlds incident reminds us that using other people as a source of information can be dangerous. If other people are misinformed, we will adopt their mistakes and misinterpretations. Depending on others to help us reach a definition of the situation can sometimes lead to an inaccurate definition indeed. An example of extreme and misdirected informational social influence is **mass psychogenic illness** (Bartholomew & Wessely, 2002; Colligan,

mass psychogenic illness

the occurrence of similar physical symptoms in a group of people for which there is no known physical or medical cause

Pennebaker, & Murphy, 1982), the occurrence of similar physical symptoms in a group of people for which there is no known physical or medical cause.

Consider, for example, the "toxic bus" case. On May 25, 2004, as a man disembarked from a Vancouver bus, he made a comment to the driver to the effect that the driver was about to have a bad day. Shortly afterward, the driver began to feel nauseated and started vomiting. He checked if any of the other passengers were feeling ill. A passenger seated behind him reported having a headache and thought that there was a suspicious smell on the bus. Fearing that there had been a chemical attack, the driver placed a distress call. Other passengers began to feel sick, as did several of the paramedics who were called to the scene. Six passengers and three paramedics were taken to a Vancouver hospital. Some of them were vomiting. Others complained of a burning sensation in their eyes. Nineteen people, including the driver, passengers, emergency personnel, and journalists were quarantined. Vancouver Police began to search for the man who had made the mysterious comment. In early June of that year, Vancouver's chief medical health officer announced that the medical symptoms experienced by those involved were not consistent with chemical poisoning. Moreover, tests of the bus had not revealed the presence of toxic chemicals. He concluded that the symptoms were a case of mass psychogenic illness. The allegation that the medical symptoms were brought on by anxiety over a possible chemical attack outraged the paramedics who had become ill. The Vancouver Police took their side, stating that "you're talking about two very senior ambulance attendants and they're not going to have psychosomatic symptoms" (Crawford, 2004; "Chemical Probably Cause of Bus Mystery," as cited in Bartholomew & Wessely, 2007). The police arranged for additional experts to test the bus. These tests revealed the presence of methyl chloride. However, this did little to clarify matters. Given that methyl chloride is common in the environment, there was controversy over whether the levels found were sufficient to cause poisoning. Moreover, other "nontoxic" buses were not tested, so there was no way of knowing whether the toxic bus had higher levels of methyl chloride than other buses. Psychiatrists from Australia and Britain analyzed the "toxic bus" case and concluded that the medical symptoms experienced were attributable to mass psychogenic illness (Bartholomew & Wessely, 2007). According to these psychiatrists, in the post-9/11 world, people's fears of terrorist attacks—including the use of chemical or biological attacks—are heightened. They explained the symptoms experienced by those involved in the toxic bus incident as an anxiety reaction. Needless to say, this interpretation has been vehemently rejected by the ambulance attendants who became ill (Bartholomew & Wessely, 2007). Thus, although the controversy continues, the toxic bus case may be another example of informational conformity gone awry.

What is particularly interesting about modern cases of mass psychogenic illness (as well as other peculiar forms of informational conformity) is the powerful role that mass media play in their dissemination. Through television, radio, newspapers, magazines, the internet and email, information is spread quickly and efficiently to all segments of the population. Whereas in the Middle Ages it took 200 years for the "dancing manias" (a kind of psychogenic illness) to crisscross Europe (Sirois, 1982), it takes only minutes for most of the inhabitants of the planet to learn about an unusual event today. Luckily, the mass media also have the power to quickly squelch these uprisings of contagion by introducing more logical explanations for ambiguous events.

Resisting Informational Social Influence

Relying on others to help us define what is happening can be an excellent idea—or it can be a tragedy in the making. How can we tell when other people are a good source of information and when we should resist other people's definition of a situation? First, it is important to remember that it is possible to resist illegitimate or inaccurate informational social influence. Some Solar Temple cult members refused to take their own lives. Not every student on the scene participated in the fatal attack on Reena Virk. And not every soldier in the Canadian Airborne Regiment participated in the beating death of Shidane Arone. Similarly, during the *War of the Worlds* broadcast, not all listeners panicked (Cantril, 1940). Some engaged in rational problem solving: They checked other stations on the radio dial and discovered that no other station was broadcasting the same news. Instead of relying on others and being caught up in the contagion and mass panic, they searched for and found information on their own.

One reason that the decision about whether to conform is so important is that it influences how people define reality. If you decide to accept other people's definition of a situation, you will come to see the world as they do. If you decide to reject other people's definition of a situation, you will come to see the world differently from the way they do. This basic fact about how we define reality has been demonstrated in an interesting program of research conducted at the University of Waterloo (Buehler & Griffin, 1994; Griffin & Buehler, 1993).

> *Yes, we must, indeed, all hang together or, most assuredly, we shall all hang separately.*
>
> —Benjamin Franklin, at the signing of the Declaration of Independence, 1776

In one study, Roger Buehler and Dale Griffin (1994) asked students to read newspaper reports of a real, highly controversial incident in which an African-Canadian teenager driving a stolen car was shot and killed by white police officers. Many of the details of the situation were ambiguous, such as how much the youth had threatened the officers and how much the officers had feared for their lives. Buehler and Griffin first asked participants how they interpreted the situation. How fast was the victim's car going? Was the victim trying to ram the police car? Did he realize that his pursuers were the police? What were the police officers thinking and feeling? Each participant was then told that other participants believed that the police were 75 percent responsible and the victim was 25 percent responsible. After indicating whether they agreed with this assessment, the participants were told that their original responses had supposedly been lost in a computer crash and were again asked how they interpreted the situation. Here's the critical question: Did participants now interpret the situation differently, depending on whether they agreed with other people's assessments?

The first result of interest was that not everyone conformed to other people's views. As you might expect, those who did conform to the group's opinion started out with more police-blaming than those who did not. More importantly, people's decision about whether to conform influenced their definition of the situation. As shown in Figure 7.2 on the next page, people who agreed with the group that the police were mainly responsible changed their interpretations to be consistent with the group opinion—they now believed that the victim had not threatened the police and that police had not feared for their lives. What about the people who did not conform? Interestingly, they also changed their interpretations, but in the opposite direction—they now believed that the victim's car was about to ram the police and that the police were in fear for their lives. It is remarkable that once we have formed an opinion of a situation, we may interpret that same situation quite differently a mere 10 minutes later to bolster our decision to go along with, or deviate from, the majority opinion.

Decisions about whether to conform to informational influence, then, will affect not only people's behaviour but also their interpretation of reality (Bless, Strack, & Walther, 2001; Hoffman, Granhag, See, & Loftus, 2001). Thus, it is important to consider carefully whether other people's reactions to a situation are any more legitimate than your own. Ask yourself these questions:

- Do other people know more about what is going on than I do? Is there an expert handy, someone who should know more?

- Do the actions of other people or experts seem sensible? If I behave the way they do, will it go against my common sense, or against my internal moral compass—my sense of right and wrong?

FIGURE 7.2

Pre-decision and post-decision construals by conformity decision

People who conformed to the group's opinion that the police were to blame for the death of an African-Canadian teenager subsequently formed a more police-blaming interpretation of the event. Those who decided not to conform to the group (i.e., the dissenters) later reinterpreted the situation such that the police were seen as less blameworthy.

(Buehler & Griffin, 1994)

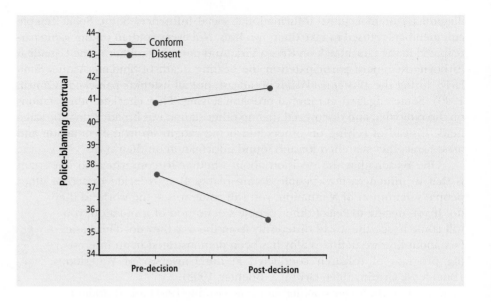

By knowing how informational social influence works in daily life, you are in a better position to know when it is useful and when it is not.

Normative Social Influence: The Need to Be Accepted

In the 1990s, in Rio de Janeiro, Brazil, teenage boys and girls engaged in a reckless game: They "surfed" on the tops of trains, standing with arms outstretched as the trains sped along. An average of 150 teenagers died each year from this activity, and 400 more were injured by falling off the trains or hitting the 3000-volt electric cable; despite these facts, the surfing continued (Arnett, 1995). More recently, in the United States and Australia, teenagers surfing speeding cars has

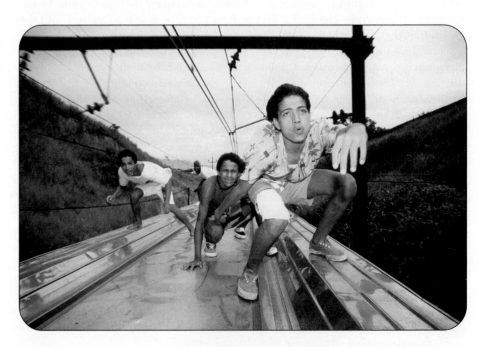

▶ The desire to be accepted and liked by others can lead to highly dangerous behaviour. Here, Brazilian teenagers "surf" on top of trains because it has become the popular thing to do in their peer group.

become a growing problem, resulting in severe injuries and deaths (Daniel & Nelson, 2004). In many Canadian cities, young partiers flock to all-night raves where they buy drugs such as ecstasy from strangers. Between 2:00 and 3:00 a.m., hospital emergency units have come to expect teens who are experiencing "bad trips" from having taken such drugs. A Toronto Public Health report (2000) documented that in the previous 2 years there were 13 ecstasy-related deaths in Ontario alone. Despite this, a Canada-wide survey of drug use among students in grades 7 to 12 categorizes ecstasy as a drug that increased in use during the 1990s and is currently at a "stable, but elevated" level of use (CAMH, 2003). A nation-wide survey found that 2.5% of university students had used ecstasy during the past year. That number doubled (5.4%) when non-university students of the same age were surveyed (Adlaf, Demers, & Gliksman, 2005). Why do these young people engage in such risky behaviour? Why does anyone follow the group's lead when the resulting behaviour is less than sensible and may even be dangerous? We doubt that these young people risk their lives as a result of informational conformity—it is difficult to argue that a participant at a rave would say, "Gee, I don't know what to do. A stranger wants to sell me drugs that might kill me. I guess it must be a good idea; I see other people doing it."

This example tells us that there is another reason why we conform, aside from the need for information. We also conform so we will be liked and accepted by other people. This is known as **normative social influence**. This type of conformity results in public compliance with the group's beliefs and behaviours but not necessarily in private acceptance (Cialdini, Kallgren, & Reno, 1991; Deutsch & Gerrard, 1955; Levine, 1999; Nail, McDonald & Levy, 2000). We human beings are by nature a social species. Few of us could live happily as hermits, never seeing or talking to another person. Through interactions with others, we receive emotional support, affection, and love, and we partake of enjoyable experiences. Given this fundamental human need for social companionship, it is not surprising that we often conform to be accepted by the group to which we belong. Groups have certain expectations about how the group members should behave, and members in good standing conform to these rules, or **social norms**. Members who do not are perceived as different, difficult, and eventually deviant. Deviant members can be ridiculed, punished, or even rejected by the other group members (Kruglanski & Webster, 1991; Levine, 1989; Miller & Anderson, 1979; Schachter, 1951). University of Western Ontario researchers Leslie Janes and James Olson (2000) conducted a series of studies on what they call "jeer pressure." Participants observed someone either ridiculing another person or engaging in self-ridicule. Those who observed someone else being ridiculed later showed the greatest conformity to their peers. Why might this be? According to Janes and Olson, groups use ridicule as a means of punishing group members who fail to comply with the group's norms. Thus, when we observe someone else being ridiculed, we will be especially likely to go along with the group in order to avoid being the next target.

Normative social influence is another reason why soldiers in Canada's Airborne Regiment participated in the torture and fatal beating of Shidane Arone, and why high school students in Victoria participated in the brutal beating and drowning of Reena Virk. In the case of Virk, fears of being rejected or punished by the group didn't end at the scene. Later, when giving statements to the police and testifying in court, some of the students lied because they were afraid of the consequences of "ratting" on their friends.

normative social influence

the influence of other people that leads us to conform in order to be liked and accepted by them; this type of conformity results in public compliance with but not necessarily with private acceptance of the group's beliefs and behaviours

social norms

the implicit or explicit rules a group has for the acceptable behaviours, values, and beliefs of its members

> "Customs do not concern themselves with right or wrong or reason. But they have to be obeyed; one reasons all around them until [one] is tired, but [one] must not transgress them, it is sternly forbidden."
>
> —Mark Twain (1835–1910)

Conformity and Social Approval: The Asch Line Judgment Studies

You probably don't find it too surprising that people sometimes conform in order to be liked and accepted by others. After all, if the group is important to us

The judgment task in Asch's line studies

In a study of normative social influence, participants judged which of the three comparison lines on the right was closest in length to the standard line on the left. The correct answer was obvious (as it is here). However, members of the group (actually confederates) said the wrong answer out loud. Now the participant is in a dilemma. Should he say the right answer and go against the whole group, or should he conform to their behaviour and give the obviously wrong answer?

(Adapted from Asch, 1956)

Standard line   Comparison lines

and it is a matter of wearing the right kind of clothing or using the right cool words, why not go along? But surely we won't conform when we are certain that the group's behaviour is wrong and the pressures are coming from a group that we don't care all that much about. Or will we?

To find out, Solomon Asch (1951, 1956) conducted a series of classic studies exploring the parameters of normative social influence. Asch initiated this program of research because he believed that there are limits to how much people will conform. Naturally, people conformed in the Sherif studies, he reasoned, given that the situation was highly ambiguous—trying to guess how much a light was moving. Asch believed, however, that when a situation was completely unambiguous, people would act like rational, objective problem solvers. When the group said or did something that contradicted an obvious truth, surely people would reject social pressures and decide for themselves what was going on.

To test his hypothesis, Asch conducted the following study. Had you been a participant, you would have been told that this was an experiment on perceptual judgment and that you would be taking part with seven other students. Here's the scenario: The experimenter shows everyone two cards, one with a single line, the other with three lines, labelled 1, 2, and 3. He asks each of you to announce aloud which of the three lines on the second card is closest in length to the line on the first card (see Figure 7.3). It is crystal clear that the correct answer is the second line. Not surprisingly, each participant says, "Line 2." Your turn comes next

▶ Participants in an Asch conformity study. The real participant is seated in the middle. He is surrounded by the experimenter's accomplices who have just given the wrong answer on the line task.

to last, and, of course, you say it's line 2 as well. The last participant concurs. The experimenter then presents a new set of cards and asks the group members to again make their judgments and announce them out loud. Again, the answer is obvious, and everyone gives the correct answer.

At this point, you are probably thinking to yourself, "What a boring experiment! How many times will we have to judge these silly lines? I wonder what's for dinner tonight." As your mind starts to wander, something surprising happens. The experimenter presents the third set of lines and again the answer is obvious—line 3 is clearly the closest in length to the target line. But the first participant announces that the correct answer is line 1! "Geez," you think, "this guy must be so bored that he fell asleep." The second person also announces that he, too, believes line 1 is the correct answer. The third, fourth, fifth, and sixth participants concur; then it is your turn to judge. By now, you are probably looking at the lines very closely to see if you missed something. But no, line 3 is clearly the correct answer. What will you do? Will you bravely blurt out, "Line 3," or will you go along with the group and give the obviously incorrect answer, "Line 1"?

As you can see, Asch set up a situation to see if people would conform even when the right answer was cut and dried. The other participants were actually accomplices of the experimenter, instructed to give the wrong answer on 12 of the 18 trials. Contrary to what Asch thought would happen, a surprising amount of conformity occurred: 76 percent of the participants conformed on at least one trial. On average, people conformed on about one-third of the 12 trials on which the accomplices gave the incorrect answer (see Figure 7.4).

Why did people conform so much of the time? One possibility is that people genuinely had a hard time with the task and therefore assumed that other people were better judges of the length of lines than they were. If so, this would be another case of informational social influence, as we saw in the Sherif study. This interpretation doesn't make much sense, however, because the correct answers were obvious—so much so that when people in a control group made the judgments by themselves, they were accurate more than 99 percent of the time. Instead, normative pressures came into play. Even though the other participants were strangers, the fear of being the lone dissenter was very strong, causing people to conform, at least occasionally. One participant had this to say about why he conformed: "Here was a group; they had a definite idea; my idea disagreed; I didn't want particularly to make a fool of myself. . . . I felt I was definitely right . . . [but] they might think I was peculiar" (Asch, 1955). These are classic normative reasons for conforming. People know that what they are doing

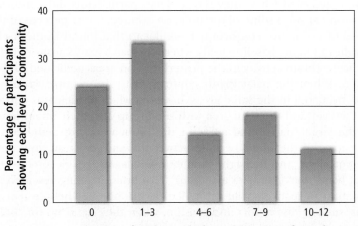

FIGURE 7.4

Results of the Asch line judgment study

Participants in the Asch line study showed a surprisingly high level of conformity, given how obvious it was that the group was wrong in its judgments: 76 percent of the participants conformed on at least one trial; only 24 percent of participants never conformed at all (see the bar labelled zero). Most participants conformed on one to three of the 12 trials when the group gave the wrong answer. However, a sizeable number of participants conformed to the group's response nearly every time it gave the wrong answer (see the two bars on the right).

(Adapted from Asch, 1957)

is wrong but go along anyway so as not to feel peculiar or look like a fool. These reasons illustrate an important fact about normative pressures: In contrast to informational social influence, normative pressures usually result in *public compliance without private acceptance*—that is, people go along with the group even if they do not believe in what they are doing or think it is wrong (Cialdini, Reno, & Kallgren, 1990; Cialdini & Trost, 1998; Deutsch & Gerard, 1955; Sorrels & Kelley, 1984).

What is especially surprising about Asch's results is that people were concerned about looking foolish in front of complete strangers. It is not as if the participants were in danger of being ostracized by a group that was important to them. Nor was there any risk of open punishment or disapproval for failing to conform, or of losing the esteem of people they really cared about, such as friends and family members. Yet decades worth of research indicates that conformity for normative reasons can occur simply because we do not want to risk social disapproval, even from complete strangers we will never see again (Crutchfield, 1955; Tanford & Penrod, 1984). As Moscovici (1985) comments, the Asch studies are "one of the most dramatic illustrations of conformity, of blindly going along with the group, even when the individual realizes that by doing so he turns his back on reality and truth."

In a variation of his study, Asch (1957) demonstrated the power of social disapproval in shaping a person's behaviour. The confederates gave the wrong answer 12 out of 18 times, as before, but this time the participants wrote their answers on a piece of paper, instead of saying them out loud. Thus, people did not have to worry about what the group thought of them, because the group would never find out what their answers were. Conformity dropped dramatically, occurring on an average of only 1.5 of the 12 trials.

Recent research by Gregory Berns and his colleagues has provided biological evidence for just how unpleasant and uncomfortable it is to resist normative social influence (Berns, Chappelow, Zink, Pagnoni, Martin-Skurski, & Richards, 2005). Berns and his research team used functional magnetic resonance imaging (fMRI) to examine the alterations in brain activity of research participants as they either normatively conformed to a group's judgment or maintained their independence and disagreed with the group. During the task, the participant completed one-third of the trials with no knowledge of the answers of the four other people, who they believed were also doing the task. On the remaining two-thirds of the trials, the participant saw the four group members' answers on a visual display. Half the time, the group had all chosen the wrong answers, and the other half of the time, they had all chosen the right answers.

Now, what did the participants do, and most importantly, what areas of their brains were activated when they did it? First, participants did conform to the group's wrong answers some of the time, on average, for 41 percent of the trials. (This level of normative conformity is similar to that found in the Asch [1951, 1956] studies.) On the baseline trials, where the participants answered alone, the fMRI indicated brain activity in the posterior brain areas dedicated to vision and perception. When the participants conformed to the group's wrong answers, activation occurred in the same areas; however, when participants chose to give the right answer and thus disagree with the group and their unanimous wrong answer, the visual/perceptual areas of the brain were not activated. Instead, different areas of the brain became active: the amygdala, an area devoted to negative emotions, and the right caudate nucleus, an area devoted to modulating social behaviour (Berns et al., 2005). This brain imaging research supports the idea that normative social influence occurs because people feel negative emotions, such as discomfort and tension, when they stand up for their beliefs and go against the group.

> *It isn't difficult to keep alive, friends—just don't make trouble—or if you must make trouble, make the sort of trouble that's expected.*
>
> —Common Man in Robert Bolt's A Man for All Seasons, 1966

CONNECTIONS

Have I Got a Song for You: Social Influence and Music Preferences

Popular music is a big part of students' lives. You're likely to download music, discovering bands before they make it big, and to share your musical finds with your friends. In fact, music likes and dislikes are one of the ways that young adults communicate who they are to their peers (Rentfrow & Gosling, 2006). But there's so much music and so little time. How do you learn about new bands? Do you think that other people's knowledge influences you? And once you've heard a new song, does knowing that it's popular (or unpopular) influence your liking for it? Salganik, Dobbs and Watts (2006) conducted an ingenious study to find out. They created an online music marketplace that attracted 14 341 participants. Their music site contained previously unknown songs from unknown bands (who had posted their own music). When participants entered the site, they were asked if they wanted to take part in a study about musical tastes. After agreeing, they were (unknown to them) randomly assigned to one of two conditions: the independent condition or the social influence condition.

Those in the independent condition saw a list of 48 songs. They could decide which ones to listen to. After listening, they were asked to rate the song. Finally, they were given the opportunity to download the song for free, if they wished. The social influence condition was exactly the same, with one difference. The same 48 songs were listed, but next to each song was the number of downloads it had received from others. Note that these were real download counts, as truly occurred when the other participants decided they wanted a song. The 48 songs were listed in descending order by their number of downloads, a measure of their current popularity. Thus, songs in the social influence condition contained information about others' opinions, while the same songs in the independent condition contained no such information.

How did the number of downloads a song received compare across the two conditions? In the social influence condition, some songs were downloaded much more frequently (and some, much less frequently) than were the same songs in the independent condition. In other words, in the social influence condition, the popular songs were more popular (and the unpopular ones were less popular) than in the independent condition. Clearly, people were paying attention to which songs others had downloaded, and their own opinions of the songs were influenced by how others had responded to them.

When faced with a list of 48 songs, participants in the independent condition were on their own. Should they listen to all of them, or just pick a few—but which ones? There was no way of knowing which were the ones worth listening to. In comparison, in the social influence condition, participants could use informational social influence. They could look at the download numbers and immediately sample just those songs that had the highest numbers, shortening their task and increasing the odds they'd find some good ones. Normative social influence was probably operating too. Knowing that others liked a certain song enough to download it in high numbers suggests that it's a "hip" song, perhaps soon to break out on the radio, and one wouldn't want to be left out of this cool group of people "in the know."

When Will People Conform to Normative Social Influence?

Although conformity is commonplace, we are not lemmings who always do what everyone else is doing. And we certainly do not agree on all issues, such as abortion, affirmative action, or same-sex marriages. One need only tune in to a radio talk show to appreciate how much people disagree on topics such as these. Exactly when are people most likely to conform to normative pressures? The answer to this question is provided by Bibb Latané's (1981) **social impact theory**. According to this theory, the likelihood that you will respond to social influence from other people depends on three variables:

(a) *Strength*: How important is the group to you?

(b) *Immediacy*: How close is the group to you in space and time during the influence attempt?

(c) *Number*: How many people are in the group?

social impact theory

the theory that conforming to social influence depends on the strength of the group, its immediacy, and the number of other people in the group

Social impact theory predicts that conformity will increase as strength and immediacy increase. Clearly, the more important a group is to us, and the more we are in its presence, the more likely we will be to conform to its normative pressures. Number, however, operates in a different manner. As the size of the group increases, each additional person has less of an influencing effect—going from 3 people to 4 makes more of a difference than going from 53 people to 54; in other words, when the group is small, adding another member will increase conformity pressure—but if a group is large, adding yet another voice to the chorus doesn't have much effect. Latané (1981) constructed a mathematical model that captures these hypothesized effects of strength, immediacy, and number, and has applied this formula to the results of many conformity studies. The formula has done a good job of predicting the actual amount of conformity that occurs (Bourgeois & Bowen, 2001; Latané, 1981; Latané & Bourgeois, 2001; Latané & L'Herrou, 1996). For example, gay men who lived in communities that were highly involved in AIDS-awareness activities (where strength, immediacy, and number would all be high) reported feeling more social pressure to avoid risky sexual behaviour and stronger intentions to do so than did men who lived in less involved communities (Fishbein et al., 1993). Similarly, as we mentioned in Chapter 6, whether people use condoms depends, at least in part, on the norms for sexual behaviour that operate in their group of friends. (The accompanying Try It! gives you a chance to observe and experience normative pressures in action.)

Social impact theory covers conformity to all kinds of social influence. For present purposes, let's see in more detail what it says about the conditions under which people will conform to normative social pressures.

Try it!

▶ Fashion: Normative Social Influence in Action

You can observe social impact theory in action by focusing on fashion—specifically, the clothes and accessories that you and your group of friends wear, as well as the "look" of other groups on campus. You can also observe what happens when you break those normative rules for fashion; for example, by dressing in a way that deviates from that of your group. When you are with a group of friends and acquaintances, note carefully how everyone is dressed. Pretend you are from another culture and not acquainted with the norms of this group; this will help you notice details you might otherwise overlook. For example, what kinds of pants, shoes, shirts, jewellery, and so on are worn by this group? Are there similarities in their haircuts? Can you discover their fashion "rules"?

Next, spend some time "people watching" on campus; specifically, observe what other groups of people are wearing. Can you discern different subgroups on your campus, defined by their style of dress? If so, there are different types of normative conformity operating on your campus; groups of friends are dressing according to the rules of their subgroup and not according to the rules of the campus as a whole.

Finally, if you are brave, break the fashion rules of your normative group. You can do this subtly or you can be very obvious!

(Do be sensible, however, and don't get yourself arrested!) For example, if you're male, you could wear a skirt around campus. That would definitely attract attention; you will be not conforming to normative influence in a very major way! If you're female, you'll have to get more creative to break the normative rules (since women's fashion includes pants, blazers, and other typically male clothing). You could wear a large, green garbage bag (with holes cut out for your head and arms) over your clothing. In either case, simply walk around campus as usual—as if you don't notice you are wearing anything strange. The interesting part will be how people react to you. What will your friends say? Will strangers stare at you?

Your group of friends, as well as the students at your school in general, may well have the qualities that social impact theory discusses—the group is important to you; the group size is more than three; and the group is unanimous—which is the case if your friends or your university or college has definite fashion norms. If you stop conforming to this normative social influence, the other group members will exert some kind of pressure on you, to try to get you to return to conformity.

FIGURE 7.5

Effects of group size on conformity

Asch varied the size of the unanimous majority and found that once the majority numbered four people, adding more people had little influence on conformity.

(Adapted from Asch, 1955)

When the Group Size Is Three or More   As you just saw, conformity increases as the number of people in the group increases—up to a point. Imagine you are a participant in Solomon Asch's study, where you judged the length of lines. If there are only you and one other participant, and the latter gives a blatantly wrong answer about the length of the lines, will you be less likely to cave in and conform to that person's response than if there are five other participants all giving the wrong answer? What if there are 15 people in the majority? Asch (1955) studied this question, and as you can see in Figure 7.5, conformity increases as the number of people in the group increases, but only up to a point.

Subsequent research has verified that although conformity pressures generally increase as the size of the majority increases (Bond & Smith, 1996), conformity pressures peak once the majority reaches about four or five in number (Gerard, Wilhelmy, & Conolley, 1968; McGuire, 1968; Rosenberg, 1961)—just as social impact theory suggests.

We should note that research conducted at the University of British Columbia by Campbell and Fairey (1989) suggests that the effects of group size depend on the kind of social influence that is operating. According to these researchers, in situations where the group is clearly wrong, conformity will be motivated by normative influence; the participants will conform in order to be accepted by the group. And in these situations, the size of the group matters. A participant may not feel much pressure to conform when the first person gives an incorrect response. However, conformity pressure will mount as each additional group member also gives the same incorrect response.

In contrast, in situations where the group is making a judgment that may be correct, participants will turn to the group as a source of information. Here, group size is less likely to matter. Once the first group member has given his or her response, it adds very little information if two, three, or four group members also provide the same response.

Thus, the size of a group is most likely to affect conformity under the conditions we have been discussing here—namely, when normative social influence is operating. And as we have seen, it does not take an extremely large group to create normative social influence.

When the Group Is Important   Another tenet of social impact theory is that the strength of the group—defined as how important the group is to us—makes a difference. Normative pressures are much stronger when they come from people whose friendship, love, and respect we cherish, because there is a large cost to losing this love and respect. Thus, groups to which we are highly attracted and with which we strongly identify will exert more normative influence on us than groups to which

> *Hain't we got all the fools in town on our side? And ain't that a big enough majority in any town?*
>
> —*Mark Twain,* The Adventures of Huckleberry Finn, *1884*

we have little or no attachment (Abrams et al., 1990; Hogg, 1992; Nowak, Szamrej, & Latané, 1990).

These processes were examined in fascinating study by Tafarodi, Kang, and Milne (2002). These researchers reasoned that members of bicultural visible minorities (e.g., people who are second-generation Canadians) might feel that they are not fully accepted as members of the majority group (i.e., European Canadians) because of their physical distinctiveness. As a result, such people might be especially motivated to conform to the majority in terms of dress, speech, or behaviour. This hypothesis was tested among Chinese women—who were either born in Canada or had come to Canada as young children—attending the University of Toronto. The women were asked to participate in a study on esthetic judgment and were told they would be required to rate how much they liked various pieces of art presented on a computer screen. The computer "happened" to display various sets of ratings of each painting, including those supposedly given by Chinese Canadians and by European Canadians. Half of the participants completed their ratings in view of a mirror (intended to remind them of their visible-minority appearance); the other half completed the ratings without a mirror. Tafarodi and colleagues hypothesized that the participants who were reminded of their distinctive appearance would be most likely to conform to the ratings of the majority (i.e., European Canadians). And that is exactly what happened. Thus, when we are attracted to a group and are reminded that we don't quite fit in, we are especially motivated to conform.

When the Group Is Unanimous   Normative social influence is most powerfully felt when everyone in the group says or believes the same thing—for example, when your group of friends all believe that *101 Dalmations* was the greatest movie ever made. Resisting such unanimous social influence is difficult or even impossible—unless you have an ally. If another person disagrees with the group—say, by nominating the first *Star Wars* movie as the best movie ever—this nonconformist behaviour will help you to buck the tide as well.

To test the importance of having an ally, Asch (1955) conducted another version of his conformity experiment. In this variation, he had six of the seven confederates give the wrong answer, whereas one confederate gave the right answer on every trial. Now, the participant was not alone. Having even one ally dramatically helped him or her resist normative pressures. People conformed on an average of only 6 percent of the trials in this study, compared with 32 percent in the version where all of the confederates gave the wrong answer. Several other studies have found that observing another person resist normative social influence emboldens the individual to do the same (Allen & Levine, 1969; Morris & Miller, 1975; Nemeth & Chiles, 1988).

This effect of allies produces some interesting anomalies in everyday life—people who hold unpopular beliefs are able to maintain them in the face of group pressure if they can convince at least a few others to agree with them. For example, since the seventeenth century, there have been proponents of the hollow earth theory—the idea that an unknown civilization resides at the centre of the earth. Now, American scientists and a Utah adventure guide, Steve Currey, claim to have pinpointed the exact location of the hole that leads to the earth's hollow core. Apparently it can be found in the Arctic Sea, just beyond Canada's Arctic Islands (Foot, 2007). In 2006, Steve Currey organized a North Pole inner earth expedition. People were invited to take the journey to the centre of the earth, at a mere cost of US$20 000. When Currey suddenly died of brain cancer, Brooks Agnew, a Kentucky-based physicist stepped in. He plans to make the journey to the centre of the earth sometime in 2009. Randy Freeman, a Yellowknife writer, warns that "besides heaps of throwaway cash, prospective cruisers should bring along enough gullibility to swallow an outlandish theory that, despite centuries of scorn, refuses to die" (Foot, 2007). Despite such

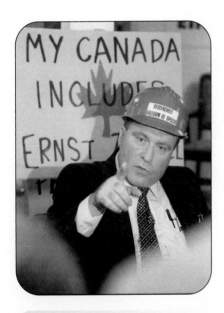

▲ If you can get a few allies to agree with you, it's easier to buck the majority and believe some rather strange things. Ernst Zundel, a German Holocaust denier who was deported from Canada to Germany in 2005 for propagating hate, tries through his books and website to get people to believe that the Holocaust never happened, despite the massive amount of documented evidence to the contrary. When he arrived in Germany, Zundel faced charges of inciting hatred, libel, and disparaging the dead. On February 15, 2007, he was convicted and sentenced to a five-year term in a German prison. Zundel continues to have followers all around the world.

criticism, Brooks Agnew is not deterred and has convinced a small band of believers to join him.

Gender Differences in Conformity   Is it the case that women and men differ in how readily they conform to social pressures? For many years, the prevailing wisdom has been to answer this question in the affirmative: Women are more conforming than men (Crutchfield, 1955). For decades, this finding was presented as a fact. More recently, researchers have taken an objective look at this question by conducting meta analyses. (Recall from Chapter 2 that a meta analysis is a statistical technique that allows you to combine the results across a large number of studies and come up with a meaningful statistical summary.) Alice Eagly and Linda Carli (1981), for example, performed a meta analysis of 145 studies on influenceability that included more than 21 000 participants. Consistent with previous literature, they found that, on average, men are less easily influenced than women. But the size of the difference is very small.

Not only are sex differences in influenceability small but they depend on the type of conformity pressures impinging on people. Gender differences are especially likely to be found in group-pressure situations, where an audience can directly observe how much you conform (e.g., the Asch study where answers were given in the presence of all participants). When faced with this kind of social pressure, women are more likely to conform than are men. In situations where conformity is private (e.g., the Asch study where participants answered privately), gender differences in influenceability virtually disappear. Eagly (1987) suggests that this pattern of results stems from the social roles men and women are taught in our society (see Chapter 4 for a discussion of social role theory). Women are taught to be more agreeable and supportive, whereas men are taught to be more independent in the face of direct social pressures. Further, Eagly points out that both women and men are more likely to exhibit such gender-consistent behaviours in public situations, where everyone can see how they respond (e.g., the Asch-type conformity study). But, once again, it is important to keep in mind that the size of these differences is small.

One other finding in this area is surprising and controversial. The gender of the researchers conducting conformity studies makes a difference, too. Eagly and Carli (1981) found that male researchers were more likely than female researchers to find that men conformed less than women. They suggest that researchers may be more likely to use experimental materials and situations that are familiar to their own gender. Male researchers, for example, may be more likely than female researchers to study how people conform to persuasive messages about sports. As we noted earlier, people are more likely to conform when confronted with an unfamiliar, ambiguous situation; thus, women may be more likely to conform in the unfamiliar situations designed by male experimenters.

A study by Sistrunk and McDavid (1971) speaks to this issue. These researchers constructed a questionnaire in which some topics were more familiar to men (e.g., mechanics), some were more familiar to women (e.g., fashion), and others were gender neutral. Interestingly, women conformed more than men on the masculine items, men conformed more than women on the feminine items, and women and men conformed equally on the gender-neutral items. The same pattern of findings was obtained in a similar study conducted with University of Saskatchewan students (Maupin & Fisher, 1989).

When the Group's Culture Is Collectivist   Is it the case that the society in which one is raised affects the frequency of normative social influence? Perhaps not surprisingly, the answer is yes. Rod Bond and Peter Smith (1996) conducted a meta analysis of 133 Asch line judgment studies in 17 countries. Participants in collectivist cultures showed higher rates of conformity on the line task than did participants in individualist cultures. In fact, in individualist cultures, including

▲ The extent to which conformity is valued varies across cultures. Hunting cultures that prize independence and assertiveness, like the Inuit, show low levels of conformity.

Canada (Lalancette & Standing, 1990), the rate of conformity in Asch-type studies has been declining. In contrast, in collectivist cultures, conformity is considered a valued trait—not a negative one, as in North America. Agreeing with others is not an act of submission or cowardice in collectivist cultures, but an act of tact and sensitivity (Smith & Bond, 1999; Hodges & Geyer, 2006). Because emphasis is on the group and not the individual, people in such cultures value normative social influence because it promotes harmony and supportive relationships in the group (Guisinger & Blatt, 1994; Kim et al., 1994; Markus, Kitayama, & Heiman, 1996). We want to underscore that this emphasis on one's group is critical—some researchers have found that when Japanese students participate in Asch-type studies where the others in the experiment are strangers, they conform even less than do North Americans (Frager, 1970; Williams & Sogon, 1984).

J. W. Berry (1967; Kim & Berry, 1993) explored the issue of conformity as a cultural value by comparing two cultures that had very different strategies for accumulating food. He hypothesized that societies that relied on hunting or fishing would value independence, assertiveness, and adventurousness in their members—traits that are needed to find and bring home food—whereas societies that were primarily agricultural would value cooperativeness, conformity, and acquiescence—traits that make close living and interdependent farming more successful. Berry compared the Inuit of Baffin Island in Canada, a hunting and fishing society, with the Temne of Sierra Leone, Africa, a farming society, on an Asch-type conformity task. The Temne showed a significant tendency to accept the suggestions of the group, while the Inuit almost completely disregarded them. One Temne put it this way: "When the Temne people choose a thing, we must all agree with the decision—this is what we call cooperation" (Berry, 1967, p. 417). In contrast, the few times the Inuit did conform to the group's wrong answer, they did so with "a quiet, knowing smile" (Berry, 1967, p. 417).

The Consequences of Resisting Normative Social Influence

One way to observe the power of normative social pressure is to see what happens when people resist it. If a person refuses to do as the group asks and thereby violates its norms, what happens? Think for a moment about the norms that operate in your group of friends. Some friends have an egalitarian norm for making group decisions. For example, when choosing a movie, such groups will ensure that everyone gets to state a preference; the choice is then discussed until agreement is reached. Think about what would happen if, in a group with this kind of norm, you stated at the outset that you wanted only to see the latest *Harry Potter* movie and weren't going with them otherwise. Your friends would be surprised by your behaviour; they would also be annoyed with you, or even angry. If you continued to disregard the friendship norms of the group by failing to conform to them, two things would happen. First, the group would try to bring you "back into the fold," chiefly through increased communication with you. Teasing comments and long discussions would ensue as your friends tried to figure out why you were acting so strangely and would try to get you to conform to their expectations (Garfinkle, 1967). If these discussions didn't work, your friends would most likely curtail communication with you (Festinger & Thibaut, 1951; Gerard, 1953). Now, in effect, you would be rejected (Abrams, Marques, Bown & Henson, 2000; Hornsey, Jetten, McAuliffe & Hogg, 2006; Milgram & Sabini, 1978).

Stanley Schachter (1951) demonstrated how the group responds to an individual who ignores their normative influence. He asked groups of university students to read and discuss a case history of "Johnny Rocco," a juvenile delinquent. Most of the students took a middle-of-the-road position about the case, believing that Rocco should receive a judicious mixture of love and discipline. Unbeknown to the participants, however, Schachter had planted an accomplice in the group, who was instructed

" Success or failure lies in conformity to the times. "
—*Niccolò Machiavelli*, The Prince, 1513

to disagree with the group's recommendations. He consistently argued that Rocco should receive the harshest amount of punishment, regardless of what the other group members argued.

How was the deviant treated? He received the most comments and questions from the real participants throughout the discussion, until near the end, when communication with him dropped sharply. The group had tried to convince the deviant to agree with them; when it appeared that wouldn't work, they ignored him. In addition, they punished the deviant. After the discussion, they were asked to nominate one group member who should be eliminated from further discussions if the size of the group had to be reduced. They nominated the deviant. They were also asked to assign group members to various tasks in future discussions. You guessed it—they assigned the unimportant or boring jobs, such as taking notes, to the deviant.

Are the findings of Schacter's 1951 study relevant today? Consider the case of Master Seaman Biden, a military police officer with 20 years of service in the Canadian Forces. He was injected with the anthrax vaccine during the 1991 Persian Gulf War and subsequently experienced medical problems. When he learned that the vaccine was out of date and that the Michigan manufacturer of the drug had been charged by the U.S. government for numerous health violations, he wrote a letter to his member of Parliament. Subsequently, Biden received a scathing letter from his commanding officer because members of the military are expected not to voice complaints publicly. He was ordered to stop talking to the media and was ostracized at work. He told an *Ottawa Citizen* reporter that he was assigned menial jobs that were usually done by junior privates: "He cleaned rifles while junior officers sat idle, sipping coffee" (Blanchfield, 2000). The parallels between Biden's experience and the way in which participants in Schacter's 1951 study treated a deviant group member are striking.

As we have seen, social groups are well versed in how to bring a nonconformist into line. According to John Bassili (2003), we are keenly aware of the negative consequences of expressing views that contradict those of the majority, which is why we are so reluctant to express minority opinions. He conducted a series of studies in which University of Toronto students were telephoned and asked about their attitudes on various issues (e.g., exams, hospitals). A computer recorded how long it took them to respond to each question. When participants believed their attitude was in a minority position, they took longer to give their response than when they believed their attitude was held by the majority of University of Toronto students. (You can find out what it's like to resist normative social influence in the Try It! on the next page.)

Overcoming Normative Social Influence

Can we find the courage to resist normative pressure? Fortunately, there are some strategies that work. First, simply be aware that social normative influence is operating. Is the presence of others causing you to change your behaviour from what you think is right? The second step of resistance is to take action. More specifically, try to find an ally. We know that having an ally helps us resist normative pressures. Thus, if you are in a situation where you don't want to go along with the crowd but you fear repercussions if you don't, try to find another person—or better yet, a group—who thinks the way you do.

Finally, it is important to remember that conforming to normative influence most of the time earns you the right to deviate occasionally without serious consequences. This interesting observation was made by Edwin Hollander (1958, 1960), who stated that conforming to a group over time earns you **idiosyncrasy credits,** much like putting money in the bank. Thus, your past conformity allows you, at some point in the future, to deviate from the group (or act idiosyncratically) without getting into too much trouble. If you refuse to drive your friends

▲ Krista Piche paid a high price for not conforming to the military code of silence after being sexually assaulted by a petty officer. She filed a complaint, despite being advised by a medical warrant officer not to do so. Military brass responded by forcing her to work alongside the man who had assaulted her and repeatedly denied her requests for a transfer. Even though a career with the military had been her lifelong dream, these consequences of nonconformity made her life so unbearable that she eventually left the military.

idiosyncrasy credits

the credits a person earns, over time, by conforming to a group's norms; if enough idiosyncrasy credits are earned, the person can, on occasion, behave deviantly without retribution from the group

Try it!

▶ Unveiling Normative Social Influence by Breaking the Rules

Every day, you talk to a lot of people—friends, professors, co-workers, and strangers. When you have a conversation (whether long or short), you follow certain interaction "rules" that operate in North American culture. These rules for conversation include nonverbal forms of behaviour that we consider normal as well as polite. For example, in conversation, we stand a certain distance from each other—not too far and not too close. About two-thirds of a metre to a metre is typical for Canadians. In addition, we maintain a high level of eye contact when we are listening to the other person; in comparison, when we're talking, we look away from the person more often.

You can find out how powerful these norms are by breaking them and noting how people respond to you; their response is normative social influence in action. For example, have a normal conversation with a friend and stand either too close (e.g., 30 centimetres) or too far away (e.g., 2 metres). Note how he or she responds. If you're too close, your friend will probably back away; if you continue to keep the distance small, he or she may seem uncomfortable and may

terminate your conversation sooner than usual. If you're too far away, your friend will probably come closer; if you back up, he or she may think you are in a strange mood. In either case, your friend's response will probably include some of the following: looking at you a lot, having a puzzled look on his or her face, acting uncomfortable or confused, talking less than normal, or ending the conversation.

You have acted in a non-normative way, and your conversational partner is, first, trying to figure out what is going on and, second, responding to get you to stop acting oddly. From this one brief exercise, you will get the idea of what would happen if you behaved "oddly" all the time—people would try to make you change. Then, if you persisted, they would probably start avoiding or ignoring you.

When you're done, please debrief your friend, telling him or her about the exercise, so that your behaviour is understood. Let your friend see what it's like to alter interpersonal distance by talking to you too close or too far away.

and yourself home because you've had a few drinks, for example, they may not become upset with you if you have followed their friendship norms in other areas in the past—you've earned the right to be different, to deviate from their normative rules in this area. Thus, resisting normative influence may not be as difficult or scary as you might think, especially if you have earned idiosyncrasy credits within a group.

Social Influence in Everyday Life

Social influence operates on many levels in our daily lives. For example, although few of us are slaves to fashion, we nonetheless tend to wear what is considered appropriate and stylish at a given time. The wide ties worn in the 1970s gave way to narrow ties in the 1980s. Similarly, women's hemlines dropped from mini to maxi and rose again in the 1990s. Social influence is at work whenever you notice a "look" shared by people in a certain group. No doubt, a few years from now current fashions will look dated and silly, and none of us will conform to them.

Fads are another fairly frivolous example of social influence. Certain activities or objects can suddenly become popular and sweep the country. In the late 1950s, every girl had to have a hula hoop or risk social ostracism. University students swallowed live goldfish in the 1930s, crammed as many people as possible into phone booths in the 1950s, and "streaked" (ran naked) at official gatherings in the 1970s.

Social Influence and Women's Body Image A more sinister form of social influence involves people's attempts to conform to cultural definitions of an attractive body. Though many, if not most, world societies consider plumpness in females attractive, Western culture—and particularly North American culture—currently values thinness in the female form (Fouts & Burggraf, 1999; Jackson, 1992; Lamb et al., 1993; Thompson & Heinberg, 1999; Weeden & Sabini, 2005).

▲ In 1969, hippie fashions in clothing and hairstyles were all the rage.

FIGURE 7.6

What is the "ideal" female body across cultures?

Researchers divided 54 cultures into groups, depending on the reliability of their food supply. They then determined what was considered to be the "ideal" female body in each culture. Heavy female bodies were considered most beautiful in cultures with an unreliable food supply. Furthermore, the moderate to heavy body range was preferred by the majority in all cultures except those with a very reliable food supply. Only in cultures where food was readily available was the slender body valued, and only in this type of culture did the majority prefer a body in the slender to moderate range.

(Adapted from Anderson et al., 1992)

For example, at Simon Fraser University, Judith Anderson and colleagues (1992) analyzed what people in 54 cultures considered to be the ideal female body. The researchers also assessed how reliable the food supply was in each culture. They hypothesized that in societies where food was frequently scarce, a heavy body would be considered the most beautiful—these would be women who had enough to eat and therefore would be healthy and fertile. As you can see in Figure 7.6, their hypothesis was supported. Heavy bodies for women were preferred over slender or moderate ones in cultures with unreliable food supplies. Furthermore, heavy to moderate bodies were preferred by the vast majority in all cultures. The exception was cultures with very reliable food supplies (such as the United States)—only in these cultures did the majority prefer moderate to slender female bodies (Anderson, Crawford, Nadeau, & Lindberg, 1992).

Have North Americans always considered thinness to be the ideal standard for the female body? Analyses of photographs of women in magazines such as *Ladies' Home Journal* and *Vogue* show a startling series of changes in the cultural definition of female bodily attractiveness during the twentieth century (Silverstein et al., 1986). At the turn of the twentieth century, an attractive woman was voluptuous and heavy; by the "flapper" period of the 1920s, the preferred look for women was rail-thin and flat-chested. The ideal body type changed again in the 1940s, when World War II "pinup girls," such as Betty Grable, exemplified a heavier standard. The curvaceous, heavier female body remained popular during the 1950s; witness, for example, Marilyn Monroe. However, the "swinging 1960s" fashion look, exemplified by the reed-thin British model Twiggy, introduced a very thin silhouette again. This extremely thin standard of feminine physical attractiveness continues to this day.

To give another example, the standards for physical attractiveness for Japanese women have also undergone changes in recent decades. Since World War II, the preferred look has taken on a Westernized element: long-legged, thin bodies, or what is called the *hattou shin* beauty (Mukai, Kambara, & Sasaki, 1998). This cultural shift has had an effect—Japanese women experience strong normative pressures to be thin (Mukai, 1996). In fact, Mukai and colleagues (1998) found that college-aged Japanese women were even more likely than American women to perceive themselves as being overweight. They also reported greater dissatisfaction with their bodies than American women did—despite the fact that the Japanese women were significantly thinner than the American women. In addition, it was found that participants' "need for social approval" was a significant predictor of eating disorders for

No woman can be too slim or too rich.

—Wallis Simpson, Duchess of Windsor
(1896–1986)

▶ Cultural standards for women's bodies change rapidly. Whereas today's female models and movie stars tend to be lean and muscle-toned, many female icons of the 1940s and 1950s, such as Marilyn Monroe, were curvaceous, heavier, and less muscular.

Japanese women but not for the American women. Japanese culture places a greater emphasis on conformity than U.S. culture; hence, the pressure to be thin operates with even more serious consequences for Japanese women (Mukai et al., 1998).

Informational social influence is the mechanism by which women learn what kind of body is considered to be attractive at a given time in their culture. Women learn what an attractive body is and how they compare from family, friends, and the media. For example, researchers have coded articles and advertisements in magazines aimed at teenage girls and adult women, as well as female characters on television shows (Cusumano & Thompson, 1997; Levine & Smolak, 1996; Nemeroff et al., 1995). The message is clear: To be considered an attractive female, one has to be thin. As we mentioned in Chapter 2, the ideal of thinness has been taken to such an extreme that the weights of beauty pageant contestants and *Playboy* models are considered "dangerous" by Canadian health and World Health Organization officials (Spitzer, Henderson, & Zivian, 1999). Moreover, the "ideals" are getting thinner at a time when average young women in Canada and the United States are getting heavier. Thus, women are getting a strong message that their bodies are not conforming to cultural standards of beauty. What are the consequences of this message? Research on body image indicates that women tend to perceive themselves as overweight and as heavier than they actually are (Cohn & Adler, 1992), and that this effect is heightened if they've just been exposed to media portrayals of thin women (Fredrickson et al., 1998; Lavine, Sweeney & Wagner, 1999).

Normative social influence explains women's attempts to create the ideal body through dieting and, more disturbingly, through eating disorders such as anorexia nervosa and bulimia (Gimlin, 1994; Jackson, 1993; Morry & Staska, 2001). As early as 1966, researchers found that 70 percent of high school girls surveyed were unhappy with their bodies and wanted to lose weight (Heunemann et al., 1966; Hill, Oliver, & Rogers, 1992). Currently, it is estimated that as many as 80 percent of girls want to be thinner. The sociocultural pressure for thinness operating on women is a potentially fatal form of normative social influence. It is estimated that 200 000 to 300 000 Canadian women aged 13 to 40 currently have anorexia nervosa, and that twice as many have bulimia. These illnesses are fatal for 10 to 15 percent of those affected (Support, Concern and Resources for Eating Disorders, 2002).

Social Influence and Men's Body Image What about cultural definitions of the attractive *male* body? Have those changed over time as well? Do men engage in conformity, too, trying to achieve the perfect body? Until

❝*You cannot make a man by standing a sheep on its hind-legs. By standing a flock of sheep in that position, you can make a crowd of men.*❞

—*Sir Max Beerbohm, Zuleika Dobson, 1911*

1964	1974	1994	1998
12.2"	15.2"	16.4"	26.8"
The original G. I. Joe from 1964 had relatively normal proportions.	A decade later, Joe was bulked up and given a "kungfu grip."	Gung-Ho, the ultimate marine, had a Marine Corps tattoo.	This incarnation is the aptly named G. I. Joe Extreme.

recently, there was very little research on these questions, but studies conducted in the past decade suggest that yes, cultural norms have changed, in that men are beginning to come under the same pressure to achieve the ideal body that women have experienced for decades (Cafri, Thompson, Ricciardelli, McCabe, Smolak, & Yesalis, 2005; Cafri & Thompson, 2004; Petrie et al., 1996). Specifically, the ideal body for males is much more muscular now than it was in the past. For example, Harrison Pope and colleagues (1999) analyzed boys' action figure toys, such as G. I. Joe dolls, by measuring their waists, chests, and biceps. The changes in G. I. Joe from 1964 to 1998 are startling, as you can see in the photographs from their research (Pope, Olivardia, Gruber & Borowiecki, 1999).

In another study, Pope and colleagues (2000) asked men in the United States, France, and Austria to alter a computer image of a male body in terms of fat and muscle until it reflected, first, their own bodies; second, the body they'd like to have; and finally, the body they thought women would find most attractive. The men were quite accurate in the depiction of their own bodies. However, men in all three countries chose an ideal body that had on average 12.5 kilograms more muscle than their own. This ideal standard was also the body they chose for what they thought women would find attractive. In fact, when women participants did the task, they chose a very normal, typical-looking male body as their ideal (Pope, Phillips, & Olivardia, 2000).

These data suggest that informational and normative social influence may be operating on men, as well as on women. Adolescent and young men are responding to this pressure by developing strategies to achieve the ideal "six-pack" body (McCabe & Ricciardelli, 2003a, 2003b; Ricciardelli & McCabe, 2003). As we mentioned in Chapter 2, men—especially those who read fitness magazines (which, of course, portray very muscular bodies)—are engaging in dangerous behaviour such as crash diets and use of risky substances such as anabolic steroids or ephedrine (Cafri et al., 2005; Morry & Staska, 2001; Spitzberg & Rhea, 1999).

▲Has the North American cultural ideal of the male body changed over time? Harrison Pope and colleagues (1999) measured the waist, chest, and biceps of the most popular action figure toys over three decades, including G. I. Joe dolls, pictured here. The researchers found that the toy figures had grown much more muscular over time, far exceeding the muscularity of even the largest human bodybuilders. The researchers suggest that such images of the male body may contribute to body image disorders in boys.

Minority Influence: When the Few Influence the Many

We shouldn't end our discussion of social influence by leaving the impression that the individual never has an effect on the group. As Serge Moscovici (1985, 1994) says, if groups really did succeed in silencing nonconformists, rejecting deviants, and persuading everyone to go along with the majority point of view,

minority influence

the case where a minority of group members influences the behaviour or beliefs of the majority

> ❝ *Never let anyone keep you contained, and never let anyone keep your voice silent.* ❞
>
> —*Adam Clayton Powell (1865–1953)*

then how could change ever be introduced into society? We would all be like robots, marching along with everyone else in monotonous synchrony, never able to adapt to changing reality.

Instead, Moscovici (1985, 1994) argues, the individual, or the minority of group members, can influence the behaviour or beliefs of the majority. This is called **minority influence**. How can a minority influence a majority? The key is consistency. People with minority views must express the same view over time, and different members of the minority must agree with each other. If a person in the minority wavers between two different viewpoints or if two individuals express different minority views, the majority will dismiss them as people who have peculiar and groundless opinions. If, however, the minority expresses a consistent unwavering view, the majority is likely to take notice and may even adopt the minority view (Moscovici & Nemeth, 1974).

In a meta analysis of nearly 100 studies, Wendy Wood and colleagues described how minority influence operates (Wood, Lundgren, Ouellette, Busceme, & Blackstone, 1994). People in the majority can cause other group members to conform through normative influence. People in the minority can rarely influence others through normative means—the majority has little concern for how the minority views them. In fact, majority group members may be loath to agree publicly with the minority; they don't want anyone to think they agree with the unusual or strange views of the minority. Minorities, therefore, exert their influence on the group via the other principal method—informational social influence. The minority introduces new, unexpected information to the group and causes the group to examine the issues more carefully. Such careful examination may cause the majority to realize that the minority view has merit, leading the group to adopt all or part of the minority's view. In short, majorities often cause public compliance because of normative social influence, whereas minorities can produce private acceptance because of informational social influence (De Dreu & De Vries, 2001; Levine, Moreland & Choi, 2001; Wood, Pool, Leck, & Purvis, 1996).

Compliance: Requests to Change Your Behaviour

We have discussed two main reasons why people conform: because other people serve as a useful source of information (informational social influence) and because of pressures to follow social norms (normative social influence). We will now look at how these reasons for conformity apply to some familiar situations in which you might be asked to do something you really do not want to do. Some of these situations are quite common, such as a salesperson pressuring you into subscribing to some magazines or a charity trying to get you to donate money to its cause. Others are less common but more frightening, such as an authority figure asking you to do something that is against your morals. When and why will people conform in these situations?

compliance

a change in behaviour in response to a direct request from another person

We will begin with the case of **compliance**—that is, a change in behaviour in response to a direct request from another person. We can hardly make it through a day without a request from someone asking us to do something we would rather not do, be it a letter from a charity asking for money, a telephone call (invariably during dinner) from someone selling time-share vacation property, or a friend wanting to borrow $25. Social psychologists have studied when and why people are likely to comply with these kinds of requests.

The Door-in-the-Face Technique

Suppose you have agreed to go door to door to ask people to donate money to the Canadian Heart Association. Here is a good way to get people to give. First, ask people to donate a large amount of money, with the full expectation that they will refuse. When someone answers the door, you might say, "Hello, I'm asking for donations to the Canadian Heart Association. Do you think you could donate $500?" Once people refuse, you immediately retreat to a more reasonable request: "Well, okay, but do you think you could donate $5?" This approach is called the **door-in-the-face technique**, because the first request is purposefully so large that people will want to slam the door shut. Several studies show that it works well in getting people to agree to the second, more reasonable request (Cialdini & Trost, 1998; Patch, Hoang, & Stahelski, 1997; Reeves et al., 1991; Wang, Brownstein, & Katzev, 1989).

Robert Cialdini and colleagues (1975) decided to see if they could get students to volunteer to chaperone problem adolescents on a two-hour trip to the zoo. When they approached students on a university campus, only 17 percent agreed to this request. In another condition, before asking people to go on the zoo trip, the experimenter made a very large request. The students were asked if they would be willing to work as unpaid counsellors at a juvenile detention centre. The experimenter went on to explain that the position would require two hours of their time per week and that they would have to make a commitment for a minimum of two years. Not surprisingly, no one agreed to such a large request. When students refused, the experimenter said, "Well, we also have another program you might be interested in," and went on to ask if they would chaperone the zoo trip. These students were three times more likely to agree to go on the zoo trip than were the students asked this smaller request alone, as shown on the left side of Figure 7.7 on page 219 (Cialdini, Vincent, Lewis, Catalan, Wheeler, & Darby, 1975).

The **reciprocity norm** says that if people do something nice for us, we should reciprocate by doing something nice for them (Cialdini & Trost, 1998; Cialdini, Green, & Rusch, 1992; Uehara, 1995; Whatley et al., 1999). Salespeople and charities capitalize on this tendency for people to follow the reciprocity norm mindlessly. They give us a small gift, such as greeting cards, personalized address labels, or free food to taste in the grocery store. Their plan is to make us feel obligated to reciprocate by buying their product or giving money to their cause (Church, 1993; James & Bolstein, 1992). To illustrate how strong the reciprocity norm is—and how mindlessly people follow it—one researcher chose some names at random out of the telephone book and sent each person a Christmas card, signed with his name (Kunz & Woolcott, 1976). Most people sent a card back to him, even though he was a complete stranger!

In the case of the door-in-the-face technique, the reciprocity norm is invoked when the person backs down from an extreme request to a smaller one. We feel as if the requester is doing us a favour by changing his or her position, trying to meet us halfway; because of the reciprocity norm, we then feel obligated to return the favour and appear reasonable, too.

One disadvantage of the door-in-the-face technique is that it is likely to be short-lived. Once people have agreed to the smaller request, they have met their obligation by meeting the requester halfway; therefore, they will not be more likely to agree to subsequent requests. Suppose, for example, that your goal is to get people to donate money to the Canadian Heart Association on a regular basis. Once you have retreated from your request for $500 to the more reasonable request for $5 and your neighbour has met you halfway by agreeing, his or her obligation is over. If you ask for another $5 next month, he or she may well feel exploited, thinking, "This person sure is pushy. You'd think I'd get a break after being so reasonable last time." So what should you do if you want long-term compliance? Stay tuned.

door-in-the-face technique

a technique to get people to comply with a request, whereby people are presented first with a large request, which they are expected to refuse, and then with a smaller, more reasonable request, to which it is hoped they will acquiesce

reciprocity norm

a social norm by which the receipt of something positive from another person requires you to reciprocate, or behave similarly, in response

The Foot-in-the-Door Technique

Put yourself in the following situation: You are participating in a study in order to fulfill your introductory psychology research requirement. At the end of the study, the experimenter asks if you would mind spending 5 or 10 minutes rating some materials for her next study. You agree to help her out. Then she makes another request. Would you volunteer to spend a few extra hours participating in research—over and above the hours required for your research requirement—so that some graduate students can complete their studies?

This is a situation in which University of Western Ontario students found themselves in research conducted by Gorassini and Olson (1995). They were participants in a study on the **foot-in-the-door technique**, a compliance technique in which people are presented first with a small request, to which they are expected to acquiesce, followed by a larger request, to which it is hoped they will also acquiesce. The expression *foot in the door* comes from salespeople who discovered that they were more likely to make a sale if they could get the customer to agree to an initial smaller request, such as letting them into the house to display their products. Thus, this technique is the opposite of the door-in-the-face method.

Does the foot-in-the door strategy work? According to the personal experience of one of your authors (Beverley Fehr), this technique is quite effective—even when used on a social psychologist who is familiar with it! Here is her story:

> I was a new assistant professor at the University of Winnipeg, teaching psychology courses for the first time. In October of that year, my department chair approached me and made a request. Would I agree to teach the social psychology class of a colleague who had become ill? It would involve only a class or two. . . . I was extremely busy preparing lectures for my own classes, but I reluctantly agreed. After all, it was only a class or two. . . . At the end of that week, my department chair made another request. Would I be kind enough to teach my colleague's class for another week while things got sorted out? Again, I reluctantly agreed. Before I knew it, I had taught the rest of the course, and in December I found myself making up the final exam and grading it!
>
> I am convinced that if my department chair had come to me at the outset and presented only the large request ("Would you teach someone else's class for the rest of the semester and compose the final exam and grade it?"), I would have explained that I already had more than a full schedule teaching my own classes for the first time and therefore, unfortunately, I would have to decline.

The effectiveness of the foot-in-the-door technique is not limited to the personal experience of your authors. In a classic study, Jonathan Freedman and Scott Fraser (1966) tested whether homeowners would agree to put up a large, obtrusive sign in their front yards that said "Drive Carefully." When someone came to their door and asked the homeowners to do this, only 17 percent agreed. But what if they had agreed earlier to a smaller request? The researchers first asked a different group of homeowners to sign a petition indicating that they were in favour of safe driving. Just about everyone agreed to this innocuous request. Two weeks later, a different individual approached these homeowners and asked them to put the sign in their front yard. Though the sign was just as big and obtrusive as the sign used in the control group, these homeowners were over three times more likely to agree to put it in their front yard (see the right side of Figure 7.7).

A recent meta analysis confirms the effectiveness of the foot-in-the-door technique (Burger, 1999). Interestingly, it works for a very different reason than does the door-in-the-face technique. Instead of invoking a reciprocity norm, it triggers a change in self-perception. By agreeing to the small request, people

foot-in-the-door technique

a technique to get people to comply with a request, whereby people are presented first with a small request, to which they are expected to acquiesce, followed by a larger request, to which it is hoped they will also acquiesce

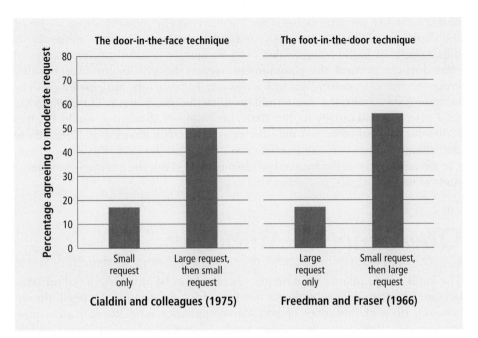

The door-in-the-face technique

The foot-in-the-door technique

Cialdini and colleagues (1975)

Freedman and Fraser (1966)

FIGURE 7.7

Two ways to increase compliance with a request

Both the door-in-the-face technique and the foot-in-the-door technique increase compliance to a moderate request. Which technique is likely to lead to the most long-term compliance, whereby people agree to repeated moderate requests? See the text for the answer.

(Adapted from Cialdini et al., 1975; Freedman & Fraser, 1966)

come to view themselves as the kind of person who helps others. Once this self-image is in place, it makes people more likely to agree to the second, larger request, even when it comes later. So, if you are collecting money for the Canadian Heart Association and want your neighbours to donate on a long-term basis, first ask them for a small amount, such as 50 cents or $1. If they agree, they will come to view themselves as the kind of people who give to this worthy cause, increasing the likelihood that future donations will be forthcoming (Burger, 1986; Cialdini, 1993; Cialdini, Trost, & Newsom, 1995; Dillard, 1991; Dolin & Booth-Butterfield, 1995). If you are trying to create long-term compliance, the foot-in-the door technique is a good way to go.

Lowballing

Another technique for inducing compliance is called **lowballing** (Cialdini et al., 1978; Weyant, 1996). Robert Cialdini, a distinguished social psychologist, temporarily joined the sales force of an automobile dealership to observe this technique closely. Here's how it works: You enter a car showroom, intent on buying a particular car. Having already priced it at several dealerships, you know that you can purchase it for about $22 000. You are approached by a personable, middle-aged man, who tells you that he can sell you one for $20 000. Excited by the bargain, you agree to the deal and at the salesperson's request write out a cheque for the down payment. Meanwhile, you rub your hands in glee, as you imagine yourself driving home in your shiny new bargain. Alas, 10 minutes later, the salesperson returns, looking forlorn. He tells you that in his zeal to give you a good deal, he made an error in calculation and the sales manager caught it. The price of the car actually comes to $22 499. You are disappointed. Moreover, you are pretty sure that you can get it a bit cheaper elsewhere.

The decision to buy is not irrevocable. Yet, research by Cialdini and colleagues (1978) suggests that far more people will go ahead with the deal than if the original asking price had been $22 499, even though the reason for purchasing the car from this particular dealer—the bargain price—no longer exists. Why?

There are at least three reasons that lowballing works. First, while the customer's decision to buy is certainly reversible, a commitment of sorts does exist—through the act of signing a cheque for a down payment. This creates the illusion

lowballing

an unscrupulous strategy whereby a salesperson induces a customer to agree to purchase a product at a very low cost, then subsequently raises the price; frequently, the customer will still make the purchase at the inflated price of irrevocability, even though—if the car buyer really thought about it—he or she would quickly realize that it is a nonbinding contract. However, in the razzle-dazzle world of high-pressure sales, even temporary illusion can have powerful consequences. Second, this commitment triggers the anticipation of an exciting event—in this case, driving out with a new car. To thwart the anticipated event by not going ahead with the deal would produce disappointment. Third, while the final price is substantially higher than the customer thought it would be, it is probably only slightly higher than the price at another dealership. Under these circumstances, the customer in effect says, "Oh, what the heck. I'm already here, I've already filled out the forms, I've already written out the cheque—why wait?" And off he or she goes, in a shiny, new car.

Obedience to Authority

The kinds of compliance we have just discussed can be annoying; a skillful sales-person, for example, can make us buy something we don't really need. Rarely, however, do such instances of everyday compliance have life-or-death consequences. Yet, unfortunately, another kind of social influence can be extremely serious and even tragic: **obedience**—conformity in response to the commands of an authority figure—to hurt or kill a fellow human being.

Consider the My Lai massacre during the Vietnam War. On the morning of March 16, 1968, a company of U.S. soldiers boarded helicopters that would take them to the village of My Lai. One of the helicopter pilots radioed that he saw Vietcong soldiers below. The troops jumped out of the helicopters with rifles firing. They soon realized that the pilot was wrong, that there were no enemy fighters. Instead, the soldiers found several villagers—women, children, and elderly men—cooking their breakfast over small fires. Inexplicably, the leader of the platoon, Lieutenant William Calley, ordered one of the soldiers to kill the villagers. Other soldiers began firing, and the carnage spread. The Americans rounded up and systematically murdered all the villagers of My Lai. They shoved women and children into a ravine and shot them; they threw hand grenades into huts of cowering villagers. Though no one knows the exact number of deaths, the estimates range from 450 to 500 people (Hersh, 1970).

Why did the soldiers obey Lieutenant Calley's order to kill the innocent villagers? We suspect that all of the reasons people conform combined to produce

obedience

conformity in response to the commands of an authority figure

▶Under strong social pressure, individuals will conform to the group, even when this means doing something immoral. During the Vietnam War, U.S. soldiers massacred several hundred Vietnamese civilians— old men, women, and children—in the village of My Lai. This award-winning photograph of some of the victims chilled North Americans. Why did the soldiers commit this atrocity? The social influence pressures of conformity and obedience can cause decent people to commit indecent acts.

this atrocity. The behaviour of the other soldiers made the killing seem like the right thing to do (*informational influence*); the soldiers wanted to avoid rejection and ridicule from their peers (*normative influence*); and the soldiers followed the social norm for obedience to authority too readily, without questioning or taking personal responsibility for what they were doing (i.e., mindless conformity). It was the power of these conformity pressures—not personality defects in the soldiers—that led to the tragedy. This makes the incident all the more frightening because it implies that similar incidents can occur with any group of soldiers if similar conformity pressures are present.

The twentieth century was marked by repeated atrocities and genocides—in Armenia, Germany, Ukraine, Rwanda, Cambodia, Bosnia, Afghanistan, to name just a few. One of the most important questions facing the world's inhabitants is, where does obedience end and personal responsibility begin? The philosopher Hannah Arendt (1965) argued that most participants in the Holocaust in World War II were not sadists or psychopaths who enjoyed the mass murder of innocent people but were ordinary citizens subjected to complex and powerful social pressures. She covered the trial of Adolf Eichmann, the Nazi official responsible for the transportation of Jews to the death camps, and concluded that he was not the monster that many people made him out to be; rather, he was a commonplace bureaucrat like any other bureaucrat, who did what he was told without questioning his orders (Miller, 1995).

Our point is not that the soldiers at My Lai, or Adolf Eichmann, or, closer to home, the Canadian peacekeepers who killed Shidane Arone in Somalia be excused for the crimes they committed. The point is that it is too easy to explain their behaviour as the acts of madmen. It is more fruitful—and indeed more frightening—to view their behaviour as the acts of ordinary people exposed to extraordinary social influence. But how do we know whether this interpretation is correct? How can we be sure that it was social influence and not the work of evil people that produced these atrocities?

The way to find out is to study social pressure in the laboratory under controlled conditions. We could take a sample of ordinary citizens, subject them to various kinds of social influence, and see to what extent they will conform and

◀Victims of the Holocaust in World War II at Nordhausen, April 1945. According to social psychologists, most of the German guards and citizens who participated in the Holocaust were not madmen but ordinary people exposed to extraordinary social influences.

▶ The shock generator used in the Milgram (1974) experiments (*left*). The learner (an accomplice of the experimenter) is strapped into the chair, and electrodes are attached to his arm (*right*).

obey. Can an experimenter influence ordinary people to commit immoral acts, such as inflicting severe pain on an innocent bystander? Stanley Milgram (1963, 1974, 1976) decided to find out, in what has become the most famous series of studies in social psychology.

Imagine you were a participant in one of Milgram's studies (1963, 1974). You answer an ad in the paper asking for participants in a study on memory and learning. When you arrive at the laboratory, you meet another participant, a 47-year-old, somewhat overweight, pleasant-looking fellow. The experimenter explains that one of you will play the role of a teacher and the other that of a learner. You draw a slip of paper out of a hat and discover that you will be the teacher. It turns out that your job is to teach the other participant a list of word pairs (e.g., "blue–box," "nice–day") and then test him on the list. The experimenter instructs you to deliver an electric shock to the learner whenever he makes a mistake, because the purpose of the study is to examine the effects of punishment on learning.

You watch as the other participant—the learner—is strapped into a chair in an adjacent room and electrodes are attached to his arm. You are seated in front of a shock generator whose 30 switches deliver varying levels of shock in 15-volt increments, from 15 to 450 volts. There are labels accompanying these switches, from "Slight Shock," to "Danger: Severe Shock," to an ominous "XXX" beside the highest levels (see the accompanying photos). The experimenter tells you that the first time the learner makes a mistake, you should give him a shock of 15 volts—the smallest amount—and then increase the amount by 15 volts for each subsequent mistake he makes. So you will know what the shocks feel like, the experimenter gives you a sample shock of 45 volts, which is rather painful.

You read the list of word pairs to the learner and then begin the testing phase. After announcing the first word of a pair, you give four possible answers; the learner responds by pressing one of four switches, which illuminates a light on the answer box in front of you. Everything begins smoothly, as the learner gets the first few answers right. Then he gets some wrong and, as instructed, you deliver a shock for each one, increasing the voltage as you have been instructed.

At this point, you are probably becoming concerned about the number and severity of the shocks you will have to give. When you get to the 75-volt level, the learner, whom you can hear over an intercom, emits a painful, "Ugh!" Perhaps you pause and ask the experimenter what you should do. "Please continue," he responds. As the learner continues to make mistakes, you deliver a few more shocks. The learner protests, shouting, "Ugh! That's all! Get me out of here!" You look at the experimenter with grave concern. He tells you, "It is absolutely essential that you continue" (see Figure 7.8).

What would you do? How many people do you think would continue to obey the experimenter and increase the level of shock until they had delivered the maximum amount—450 volts? When this question was posed to psychology majors at Yale University, they estimated that only about 1 percent of the population would go to this extreme. A sample of middle-class adults and a panel of psychiatrists

Learner's Protests

75 volts: Ugh!

90 volts: Ugh!

105 volts: Ugh! (louder)

120 volts: Ugh! Hey this really hurts.

135 volts: Ugh!!

150 volts: Ugh!!! Experimenter! That's all. Get me out of here. I told you I had heart trouble. My heart's starting to bother me now. Get me out of here, please. My heart's starting to bother me. I refuse to go on. Let me out.

165 volts: Ugh! Let me out! (shouting)

180 volts: Ugh! I can't stand the pain. Let me out of here! (shouting)

195 volts: Ugh! Let me out of here. Let me out of here. My heart's bothering me. Let me out of here! You have no right to keep me here! Let me out! Let me out of here! Let me out! Let me out of here! My heart's bothering me. Let me out! Let me out!

210 volts: Ugh! Experimenter! Get me out of here. I've had enough. I won't be in the experiment any more.

225 volts: Ugh!

240 volts: Ugh!

255 volts: Ugh! Get me out of here.

270 volts: Ugh! (Agonized scream) Let me out of here. Let me out of here. Let me out of here. Let me out. Do you hear? Let me out of here.

285 volts: Ugh! (Agonized scream)

300 volts: Ugh! (Agonized scream) I absolutely refuse to answer any more. Get me out of here. You can't hold me here. Get me out. Get me out of here.

315 volts: Ugh! (Intensely agonized scream) I told you I refuse to answer. I'm no longer part of this experiment.

330 volts: Ugh! (Intense and prolonged agonized scream) Let me out of here. Let me out of here. My heart's bothering me. Let me out, I tell you. (Hysterically) Let me out of here. Let me out of here. You have no right to hold me here. Let me out! Let me out! Let me out of here! Let me out!

Instructions Used by the Experimenter to Achieve Obedience

Prod 1: Please continue *or* Please go on.
Prod 2: The experiment requires that you continue.
Prod 3: It is absolutely essential that you continue.
Prod 4: You have no other choice; you must go on.

The prods were always made in sequence: Only if prod 1 had been unsuccessful could prod 2 be used. If the subject refused to obey the experimenter after prod 4, the experiment was terminated. The experimenter's tone of voice was at all times firm but not impolite. The sequence was begun anew on each occasion that the subject balked or showed reluctance to follow orders.

Special prods. If the subject asked whether the learner was likely to suffer permanent physical injury, the experimenter said, Although the shocks may be painful, there is no permanent tissue damage, so please go on. [Followed by prods 2, 3, and 4 if necessary.]

If the subject said that the learner did not want to go on, the experimenter replied, Whether the learner likes it or not, you must go on until he has learned all the word pairs correctly. So please go on. [Followed by prods 2, 3, and 4 if necessary.]

FIGURE 7.8

Transcripts of the learner's protests and the experimenter's prods to achieve obedience in Milgram's obedience study

(Adapted from Milgram, 1963, 1974)

When you think of the long and gloomy history of man, you will find more hideous crimes have been committed in the name of obedience than in the name of rebellion.

—C. P. Snow, "Either-Or"

made similar predictions. However, having read our discussion of conformity thus far, you are probably not as optimistic. Whereas no one would have believed that such travesties as the Holocaust in World War II or the My Lai massacre in Vietnam could have occurred, they did. Like the people who committed these horrific acts, most of Milgram's participants succumbed to the pressure of an authority figure. The average maximum amount of shock delivered was 360 volts—and 62.5 percent of the participants delivered the 450-volt shock, the maximum amount. A full 80 percent of the participants continued giving the shocks even after the learner, who earlier had mentioned that he had a heart condition, screamed, "Let me out of here! Let me out of here! My heart's bothering me. Let me out of here! . . . Get me out of here! I've had enough. I won't be in the experiment any more" (Milgram, 1974).

It is important to know that the learner was actually an accomplice of the experimenter and play-acted his role; he did not receive any actual shocks. (See the learner's script in Figure 7.8.) It is equally important to note that the study was very convincingly done, so that people believed they really were shocking the learner. Here is Milgram's description of one participant's response to the teacher role:

> I observed a mature and initially poised businessman enter the laboratory smiling and confident. Within 20 minutes he was reduced to a twitching, stuttering wreck, who was rapidly approaching a point of nervous collapse. He constantly pulled on his earlobe and twisted his hands. At one point he pushed his fist into his forehead and muttered, "Oh God, let's stop it." And yet he continued to respond to every word of the experimenter and obeyed to the end. (Milgram, 1963)

It seems particularly disturbing that in the Milgram studies, obedience occurred "across the board." Milgram's research participants ranged in age from their twenties to their fifties and included blue-collar, white-collar, and professional workers. Although most of his research participants were men, he obtained the same rate of obedience in the one study he conducted with female participants. More recently, Burger (in press) replicated Milgram's research (with many ethical precautions such as having a clinical psychologist present to intervene if a participant appeared to be distressed). Rates of obedience did not vary as a function of gender, age, ethnicity, or education. Also, the few personality variables that were examined (e.g., empathy) did not produce clear-cut findings. Thus, it appears that no one is immune from the pressure to obey authority (Blass, 2004).

It is also important to point out that although we might dismiss Milgram's findings as a vestige of an earlier time when people were more conforming, the rate of obedience in Burger's (in press) very recent research does not differ significantly from that obtained in the original Milgram studies. A recent review confirms that rates of obedience in Milgram-type studies have remained consistent over time (Blass, 2004).

Milgram's studies raise an important but disturbing question: Why did ordinary, decent people conform to the wishes of the experimenter, to the point where they, at least in their own minds, were inflicting great pain on another human being? Why were the students, middle-class adults, and psychiatrists so wrong in their predictions about what people would do? The reasons we have just discussed for why people conform combined in a dangerous way. Let's take a close look at how this worked in the Milgram experiments.

The Role of Normative Social Influence

First, it is clear that normative pressures made it difficult for people to refuse to continue. As we have seen, if someone really wants us to do something, it can be difficult to say no. This is particularly true when the person is in a position of authority over us. Milgram's participants probably believed that if they refused to continue, the experimenter would be disappointed, hurt, or maybe even angry—all of which put pressure on them to continue. It is important to note that this study, unlike the Asch study, was set up so the experimenter actively attempted to get people to conform, giving such stern commands as, "It is absolutely essential that you continue." When an authority figure is so insistent that we obey, it is difficult to say no (Blass, 2000, 2003; Hamilton, Sanders, & McKearney, 1995; Miller, 1986). Recent research conducted at the University of British Columbia has shown that obedience is highest in the presence of a directive authority figure. (Interestingly, if the authority figure is removed from the scene, there can be a backfiring effect such that people begin to behave contrary to what the authority figure has commanded them to do [Conway & Schaller, 2005].)

The fact that normative pressures were present in the Milgram experiments is clear from a variation of the study he conducted (1974). This time there were three teachers, two of whom were confederates of the experimenter. One confederate was instructed to read the list of word pairs; the other was instructed

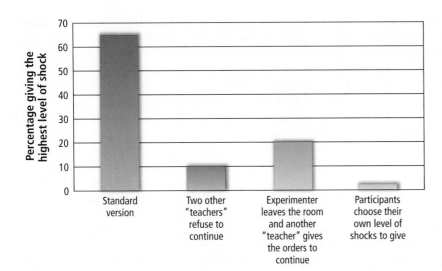

FIGURE 7.9

The results of different versions of the Milgram experiment

Obedience is highest in the standard version, where the participant is ordered to deliver increasing levels of shock to another person (*left bar*). Obedience drops when other participants model disobedience or when the authority figure is not present (*two middle bars*). Finally, when no orders are given to increase the shocks, almost no participants do so (*right bar*). The contrast in behaviour between the far-left and far-right bars indicates just how powerful the social norm of obedience is.

(Adapted from Milgram, 1974)

to tell the learner whether his response was correct. The real participant's job was to deliver the shocks, increasing their severity with each error, as in the original experiment. At 150 volts, when the learner gave his first vehement protest, the first confederate refused to continue despite the experimenter's command that he do so. At 210 volts, the second confederate refused to continue. The result? Seeing their peers disobey made it much easier for the actual participant to disobey as well. In this experiment, only 10 percent of the participants gave the maximum level of shock (see Figure 7.9). This result is similar to Asch's finding that people did not conform nearly as much when one accomplice bucked the majority and consistently gave the correct answer.

The Role of Informational Social Influence

Despite the power of the normative pressures in Milgram's original study, they are not the sole reason people complied. The experimenter was authoritative and insistent, but he did not point a gun at participants and tell them to "conform or else." The participants were free to get up and leave any time they wanted to. Why didn't they, especially when the experimenter was a stranger they had never met before and probably would never see again?

As we saw earlier, when people are in a confusing situation and unsure of what they should do, they use other people to reach a definition of the situation. Informational social influence is especially powerful when the situation is ambiguous, when it is a crisis, and when the other people in the situation have some expertise. The situation faced by Milgram's participants was clearly confusing, unfamiliar, and upsetting. It all seemed straightforward enough when the experimenter explained it to them, but then it turned into something else altogether. The learner cried out in pain, but the experimenter told the participant that while the shocks were painful, they did not cause any permanent tissue damage. The participant didn't want to hurt anyone, but he or she had agreed to be in the study and to follow directions. When in such a state of conflict, it was only natural for the participants to use an expert—the experimenter—to help them decide what they should do (Darley, 1995; Krakow & Blass, 1995; Meeus & Raaijmakers, 1995).

Another version of the experiment that Milgram performed supports the idea that informational influence was operative. This version was identical to the original one except for two critical changes. First, the experimenter never said which shock levels were to be given, leaving this decision up to the teacher (the real participant). Second, the situation was arranged so the experimenter was "unexpectedly" called away from the experiment. The participant was instructed to continue on, and another "teacher"—actually, a confederate, who was supposedly there to record how long it took the learner to respond—

said that he had just thought of a good system: How about if they increased the level of shock each time the learner made a mistake? He insisted that the real participant follow this procedure.

Note that in this situation the expertise of the person giving the commands has been removed. And in this situation, people were much less likely to use the non-expert as a source of information about how they should respond. As seen in Figure 7.9, in this version, compliance dropped from 65 percent giving the maximum amount of shock to only 20 percent. The fact that 20 percent still complied suggests that some people were so uncertain about what to do that they used even a non-expert as a guide. More recent research conducted at the University of British Columbia confirms that people are less likely to obey when they perceive that the authority figure is actually not an expert (Conway & Schaller, 2005). For example, in one study, participants were presented with a scenario in which they were employees having to choose between two computer network systems. Participants in the nonexpert condition were told that the boss did not know anything about computers; those in the expert condition were told that the boss had an advanced degree in computer networking. In both conditions, the boss issued a command to vote for one of the systems under consideration. Those who believed the boss did not have expertise were less likely to obey this order (even when told that the other employees all went along with it) than those who were told he had competence in this area.

An additional variation conducted by Milgram underscores the importance of authority figures as experts in eliciting obedience. In this variation, two experimenters gave the real participants their orders. At 150 volts, when the learner first cried out that he wanted to stop, the two experimenters began to disagree about whether they should continue the study. At this point, 100 percent of the participant teachers stopped responding.

Other Reasons Why We Obey

Both normative and informational social influences were very strong in Milgram's experiments. However, there are additional reasons that must be considered in order to explain fully why people acted so inhumanely.

Conforming to the Wrong Norm Sometimes we are on automatic pilot and don't realize that the social norm we are following is inappropriate or not applicable to the situation we are in. We don't mean to imply that Milgram's participants were completely mindless or unaware of what they were doing. All were terribly concerned about the plight of the victim. The problem was that they were caught in a web of conflicting norms, and it was difficult to determine which one to follow. At the beginning of the experiment, it was perfectly reasonable to obey the norm that says, "Obey expert, legitimate authority figures." The experimenter was confident and knowledgeable, and the study seemed a reasonable test of an interesting hypothesis. So, why not cooperate and do as they were told? But then gradually the rules of the game changed and this "obey authority" norm was no longer appropriate. The experimenter, who seemed so reasonable before, was asking people to inflict great pain on a fellow participant. But once people are following one norm, it can be difficult to switch midstream, realizing that this norm is no longer appropriate and that another norm—"Do not inflict needless harm on a fellow human being"—should be followed (Conway & Schaller, 2005; Modigliani & Rochat, 1995). We suspect that if, halfway through the experiment, Milgram's participants had been told to take a 15-minute break and go sit in a room by themselves, rather than continue with the fast-paced experiment, many more would have realized that they should no longer follow the norm to obey authority and would have refused to continue.

Self-Justification Second, it is important to remember that the experimenter asked people to increase the shocks in very small increments. The participants did not go from giving a small shock to giving a potentially lethal one. Instead, at any given point they were faced with the decision about whether to increase the amount of shock they had just given by 15 volts. As we saw in Chapter 6, every time a person makes an important or difficult decision, dissonance is produced, with resultant pressures to reduce it. An effective way of reducing dissonance produced by a difficult decision is to tell oneself that the decision was fully justified. However, because reducing dissonance provides a justification for the preceding action, in some situations, it makes a person vulnerable to pressures leading to an escalation of the chosen activity. Thus, in the Milgram study, once the participants agreed to administer the first shock, it created pressure on them to continue to obey. As the participants administered each successive level of shock, they had to justify it in their minds. Once a particular shock level was justified, it became very difficult for them to find a place where they could draw the line and stop. How could they say, in effect, "Okay, I gave him 200 volts, but not 215—never 215"? Each succeeding justification laid the groundwork for the next shock and would have been dissonant with quitting; 215 volts is not that different from 200, and 230 is not that different from 215. Those who did break off the series did so against enormous internal pressure to continue.

Mika Haritos-Fatouros (1988; see Staub, 1989) reports that this incremental approach was used by the Greek military dictatorship of the late 1960s to train torturers. In his interviews with former torturers, Haritos-Fatouros learned that their first contact with political prisoners was to bring them food and "occasionally" give them some blows. Next, they were put on guard while others conducted torture sessions. Then, they would take part in a few group floggings or beatings and the last step—being in charge of a torture session—"was announced suddenly to the [man] by the commander-in-chief without leaving him any time for reflection" (Haritos-Fatouros, 1988).

It's Not about Aggression   Before leaving our discussion of the Milgram studies, we should mention one other possible interpretation of his results. Did the participants act so inhumanely because there is an evil side to human nature, lurking just below the surface, ready to be expressed on the flimsiest excuse? After all, it was socially acceptable to inflict harm on another person in the Milgram experiment; in fact, participants were ordered to do so. Perhaps this factor allowed the expression of a universal aggressive urge.

To test this hypothesis, Milgram conducted another version of his study. Everything was the same except that the experimenter told the participants they could choose any level of shock they wished to give the learner when he made a mistake. Milgram gave people permission to use the highest levels, telling them there was a lot to be learned from all levels of shock. This instruction should have allowed any aggressive urges to be expressed unchecked. Instead, the participants chose to give very mild shocks (see Figure 7.9). Only 2.5 percent of the participants gave the maximum amount of shock. Thus, the Milgram studies do not show that people have an evil streak that seeps through when the surface is scratched. Rather, these studies demonstrate that social pressures can combine in insidious ways to make humane people act in an inhumane manner.

According to Philip Zimbardo (2007), a well-known social psychologist and former president of the American Psychological Association, the findings of Milgram's obedience studies provide insight into the horrific treatment and deaths of prisoners in Iraq's Abu Ghraib prison at the hands of U.S. soldiers. Zimbardo argues that many of the conditions that promoted the inflicting of pain on the learner in the Milgram experiments applied to the situation in Iraq in 2005. The American soldiers were in an unfamiliar, ambiguous situation in which the rules kept changing. The soldiers feared repercussions if they did not comply with orders from authority figures to torture and kill (Dittman, 2004; Hersh, 2004; Zimbardo, 2007). In most cases, the abuse began gradually and then escalated to more extreme forms. The soldiers did not feel personally responsible for their behaviour. In short, the conditions that were found to produce evil in the Milgram experiments, conducted more than 30 years ago, were reproduced in the Abu Ghraib prison. And in this real-world context, the results were even more dire. Sadly, the words of Stanley Milgram still apply to the kinds of atrocities, such as the treatment of the Iraqi prisoners, we are witnessing today:

> Even Eichmann was sickened when he toured the concentration camps, but in order to participate in mass murder he had only to sit at a desk and shuffle papers. At the same time the man in the camp who actually dropped Cyclon-B into the gas chambers is able to justify his behavior on the grounds that he is only following orders from above. Thus there is fragmentation of the total human act; no one man decides to carry out the evil act and is confronted with its consequences. The person who assumes full responsibility for the act has evaporated. Perhaps this is the most common characteristic of socially organized evil in modern society. (Milgram, 1976. pp. 183–84)

Epilogue: A Look at the Minority Who Disobeyed We have been focusing on the fact that nearly two-thirds of the participants in the Milgram study obeyed the experimenter and delivered the highest level of shock. However, this means that approximately one-third of the participants disobeyed. Can anything be learned from those who refused to continue giving the learner shocks? Recently, a Canadian researcher, Dominic Packer, conducted a meta analysis of Milgram's studies to find out (Packer, 2008). Specifically, Packer examined whether the learner's expression of pain, his request to be released from the experiment, or perhaps both had contributed to disobedience. It was found that in all of Milgram's studies, disobedience was most likely to occur at 150 volts. This was not the first time the learner expressed pain, but it was the first time he asked to be let out of the experiment (see Figure 7.8 on page 223). It is striking that the learner's expression of pain was not enough to invoke disobedience. According to Packer, these findings have implications for the humane treatment of prisoners. In his words:

> In response to global terrorism, the legal rights previously afforded to prisoners of war (e.g., Geneva conventions) have been reconsidered and, in part, replaced with assurances that interrogations will not cause undue pain. These assurances assume that agents of the law are as capable of appropriately responding to pain as they are of respecting well-specified legal rights. This reanalysis of Milgram's data suggests that this may not be the case. (Packer, 2008, p. 303)

SUMMARY

In this chapter, we focused on **conformity**, or how people change their behaviour as a result of the real (or imagined) influence of others. We found that there are two main reasons people conform: informational and normative social influences.

Informational social influence occurs when people do not know the correct (or best) thing to do or say. This reaction typically occurs in *ambiguous, confusing,* or *crisis* situations, where the definition of the situation is unclear. People look to the behaviour of others as an important source of information and use it to choose appropriate courses of action for themselves. *Experts* are powerful sources of influence, since they typically have the most information about appropriate responses.

Using others as a source of information can backfire, however, as when people panic because others are doing so. **Contagion** occurs when emotions and behaviours spread rapidly throughout a group. An example of extreme and misdirected informational social influence is **mass psychogenic illness**, the occurrence of similar physical symptoms in a group of people for which there is no known physical or medical cause. You can best resist the inappropriate use of others as a source of information by checking the information you are getting against your internal moral compass.

Normative social influence occurs for a different reason. We change our behaviour to match that of others not because they seem to know what is going on but because we want to remain a member of the group, continue to gain the advantages of group membership, and avoid the pain of ridicule and rejection. We conform to the group's **social norms**—implicit or explicit rules for acceptable behaviours, values, and attitudes. Normative social influence can occur even in unambiguous situations; people will conform to others for normative reasons even if they know that what they are doing is wrong. Whereas informational social influence usually results in **private acceptance**, whereby people genuinely believe in what other people are doing or saying, normative social influence usually results in **public compliance** but not private acceptance of other people's ideas and behaviours.

Social impact theory specifies when normative social influence is most likely to occur, by referring to the *strength, immediacy*, and *number* of the group members. We are more likely to conform when the group is one we care about, when the group members are unanimous in their thoughts or behaviours, and when the group size is three or more.

Failure to respond to normative social influence can be painful. We can resist inappropriate normative pressures by taking the time to stop and become aware of what social norms are operating, by finding an ally, and by gathering **idiosyncrasy credits** over time from a group whose membership we value.

Social influence operates on many levels in social life. It influences our eating habits, hobbies, fashion, and so on. Social influence is apparent in societal messages about the ideal body image for women and men, thereby contributing to feelings of dissatisfaction with one's body and to negative behaviours such as eating disorders and steroid use.

Minority influence, whereby a minority of group members influence the beliefs and behaviour of the majority, can occur under certain conditions. In order to influence a majority, minority group members must present their views consistently. Minorities influence majorities via informational, rather than normative, social influence.

Another form of social influence is **compliance**—conforming in response to requests from others. An effective compliance technique is the **door-in-the-face technique**, where a person starts out with a big request in order to get people to agree to a second, smaller request. This technique works because of the **reciprocity norm**; when the requester retreats from the larger to the smaller request, it puts pressure on people to reciprocate by agreeing to the smaller request. The **foot-in-the-door technique** is also effective; here the requester starts out with a very small request to get people to agree to a larger request. Another effective compliance technique is **lowballing**, in which a person makes a commitment to an attractive offer. The deal is then changed so that the offer is no longer as attractive. Nevertheless, the person tends to go along with this much less attractive deal.

One of the most insidious forms of social influence is **obedience**—conforming to the commands of an authority figure. In Milgram's classic studies of obedience, informational and normative pressures combined to cause chilling levels of obedience, to the point where a majority of participants administered what they thought were near-lethal shocks to a fellow human being. The participants were caught in a web of conflicting social norms and were asked to increase the level of shocks in small increments. After justifying to themselves that they had delivered one level of shock, it was very difficult for people to decide that a slightly higher level of shock was wrong. Unfortunately, the conditions that produced such extreme antisocial behaviour in Milgram's laboratory have been present in real-life tragedies, such as the Holocaust in World War II, the mass murders at My Lai in Vietnam, and more recently, the atrocities committed at the Abu Ghraib prison in Iraq.

PEARSON
mypsychlab

Along with a dynamic, electronic version of this text, MyPsychLab offers a wealth of resources to deepen your understanding and test your recall of the material in this chapter—including video and audio clips, simulations and activities, self-assessments, practice tests, and other study materials. The following specific resources are available for this chapter:

 Becoming a Detective of Social Influence: Robert Cialdini

 Car Salesman Example: Robert Cialdini

 Milgram Obedience Study Today

To access MyPsychLab, please visit www.mypsychlab.com (Student Access Code required—packaged with this book).

8

Group Processes:

Influence in Social Groups

I n 1998, Canadian military officials made a decision to vaccinate Canadian soldiers against anthrax, a deadly biological weapon, before deploying them to the Persian Gulf. One soldier who had served in the military for 26 years, Sergeant Michael Kipling, refused to be vaccinated. For his disobedience, Kipling was court martialled.

During the court martial, several facts came to light. One was that the anthrax vaccine was not licensed for use in Canada and, therefore, Health Canada had recommended that the military seek informed consent from soldiers before administering the drug. Another fact was that the military's legal advisers had made a similar recommendation. Canada's highest military commanders decided to ignore the advice of Health Canada and of their own lawyers, however, and imposed the vaccine on soldiers without their consent.

What were the consequences of making this decision? One consequence is the continuing debate over whether the medical symptoms experienced by half of the 4500 Canadians involved in the Gulf War are the result of the anthrax vaccine. Louise Richard, for example, was a healthy, athletic military nurse when she left for the Persian Gulf in 1991. Now she is too ill to work. She suffers from fatigue, depression, memory loss, gastrointestinal problems, and excessive bleeding. She has also lost all of her hair and has started to lose her teeth. Military officials blame the medical symptoms experienced by Gulf War veterans on stress and possible exposure to chemical warfare. Military personnel like Michael Kipling and Louise Richard believe that the anthrax vaccine is to blame.

Statistics Canada, with the cooperation of Canada's defence department, conducted a four-year study and concluded that Gulf War veterans do not suffer higher mortality and cancer rates than military personnel who were not deployed to Kuwait. These results, released on November 3, 2005, further angered Gulf War veterans, who accuse the government of biasing the research to avoid paying millions of dollars in disability benefits. Critics point out that the study focused only on cancer rates, rather than on the range of symptoms, such as those experienced by Louise Richard, that have come to be known as Gulf War syndrome (Blanchfield, 2005).

► Louise Richard before and after her tour of duty in the 1991 Persian Gulf War. She believes that the anthrax vaccine is responsible for her mysterious illnesses.

There was yet another, very serious, consequence of this decision. According to Canada's chief military judge, Colonel Guy Brais, who presided over Michael Kipling's court martial, the military's decision to impose the vaccine violated the human rights of soldiers such as Kipling. In his decision, Judge Brais agreed with the defence that the vaccine Kipling had been ordered to take could have been unsafe, and that his common law and Charter rights were therefore violated. In his words, "The government . . . could never be justified to impose inoculation of soldiers with unsafe and dangerous vaccines" (Edmonds, 2000).

Why would military officials ignore the advice of Health Canada and their own lawyers to impose a potentially unsafe vaccine on Canadian soldiers? Surely, Canada's top military commanders wouldn't be prepared to place Canadian soldiers at risk. And, surely, they wouldn't want to administer a possibly dangerous substance without obtaining informed consent from the soldiers. Or would they?

In this chapter, we will focus on how people interact in groups, and how groups can end up making decisions that have tragic consequences.

What Is a Group?

group

a collection of two or more people who interact with each other and are interdependent, in the sense that their needs and goals cause them to rely on each other

A **group** is defined as a collection of two or more people who interact with each other and are interdependent, in the sense that their needs and goals cause them to rely on one another (Cartwright & Zander, 1968; Lewin, 1948). Groups, then, are more than a bunch of people who happen to be occupying the same space. Rather, groups are people who have assembled together for a common purpose, such as citizens meeting to solve a community problem, or people who have gathered to blow off steam at a party. Stop for a moment to think of the number of groups to which you belong. Don't forget to include your family, campus groups, community groups (such as churches or synagogues), sports teams, and more temporary groups (such as your classmates in a small seminar). All of these count as groups because you interact with the other group members and you are interdependent, in the sense that you influence them and they influence you.

Why Do People Join Groups?

Why do people join groups? Forming relationships with other people fulfills a number of basic human needs. So basic, in fact, that there may be an innate need to belong to social groups. Roy Baumeister and Mark Leary (1995) argue that in our evolutionary past, there was a substantial survival advantage to establishing bonds with other people. People who bonded together were better able to hunt and grow food, find mates, and care for children. Consequently, the need to belong has become innate and is present in all societies. Consistent with this view, people in all cultures are motivated to form relationships with other people and to resist the dissolution of these relationships (Gardner, Pickett, & Brewer, 2000; Manstead, 1997). Not surprisingly, perhaps, groups become an important part of our identity, helping us to define who we are (Dion, 2000; Tropp & Wright, 2001).

Research by James Cameron (1999) suggests that the groups to which we belong even play an important role in defining who we expect to be in the future. He asked students at Mount Allison University how much they agreed with statements such as, "In a group of Mount Allison students, I really feel that I belong." Feeling a part of the university was associated with positive self-esteem and well being. Moreover, students who had a sense of belonging also believed that being a Mount Allison student would help them become the self they aspired to be in the future.

Group membership also plays an important role in motivating people to become involved in social change. For example, Patrick O'Neill (2000) examined collective action among a variety of groups, including board members of a transition house for battered women in Nova Scotia, peace activists in Vancouver, and members of a lower-class Montreal neighbourhood protesting the establishment of a toxic waste dump in their community. Across groups, O'Neill found that those who identified most strongly with their group were most likely to engage in social action. As we discuss next, groups also help establish social norms, the explicit or implicit rules defining what is acceptable behaviour.

◄ Groups have a number of benefits. Other people can be an important source of information. Groups are also an important part of our identity, helping us define who we are, and are a source of social norms, the explicit or implicit rules defining what is acceptable behaviour.

The Composition and Functions of Groups

The groups to which you belong probably vary in size from two or three members to several dozen members. Most social groups, however, range in size from two to six members (Desportes & Lemaine, 1998; Levine & Moreland, 1998). This is a result, in part, of our definition of social groups as involving interaction between members. If groups become too large, you cannot interact with all of the members. For example, the college or university you attend is not a social group, because you are unlikely to meet and interact with every student there.

Another important feature of groups is that the members tend to be alike in age, sex, beliefs, and opinions (George, 1990; Levine & Moreland, 1998; Magaro & Ashbrook, 1985). There are two reasons for the homogeneity of groups. First, many groups attract people who are already similar before they join (Feld, 1982). Second, groups operate in ways that encourage similarity in the members (Moreland, 1987). This can happen in a number of important ways, some of which we discussed in Chapter 7.

Social Norms As we saw in Chapter 7, *social norms* are a powerful determinant of our behaviour. If you belong to a political party, you can probably think of social norms present in your group, such as whether you participate in protest marches and how you are supposed to feel about rival political parties. These norms may not be shared by the members of other groups to which you belong, such as your mosque, church, or synagogue. Social norms are powerful determinants of human behaviour, as shown by what happens if people violate them too often: They are shunned by other group members and, in extreme cases, pressured to leave the group (Schachter, 1951; see Chapter 7).

social roles

shared expectations by group members about how particular people in the group are supposed to behave

Social Roles Most groups also have well-defined **social roles**—which are shared expectations about how particular people are supposed to behave (Hare, 2003). Whereas norms specify how all group members should behave, roles specify how people who occupy certain positions in the group should behave. A boss and an employee in a business occupy different roles and are expected to act in different ways in that setting. Like social norms, roles can be very helpful, because people know what to expect from each other. When members of a group follow a set of clearly defined roles, they tend to be satisfied and perform well (Barley & Bechky, 1994; Bettencourt & Sheldon, 2001).

There are, however, potential costs to social roles. One cost is that people can get so into a role that their personal identity and personality are lost. Suppose, for example, that you agreed to take part in a two-week psychology experiment in which you were randomly assigned to play the role of either a prison guard or a prisoner in a simulated prison. You might think that the role you were assigned to play would not be very important—after all, everyone knows it is only an experiment and that people are just pretending to be guards or prisoners. Philip Zimbardo and his colleagues, however, had a different hypothesis. They believed that social roles can be so powerful that they can take over our personal identities, and we become the role we are playing. To see if this is true, Zimbardo and colleagues conducted an unusual study. They converted rooms in the basement of the psychology department at Stanford University into a mock prison and paid students to play the role of either guard or prisoner (Haney, Banks, & Zimbardo, 1973). The role each student played was determined by the flip of a coin. The "guards" were outfitted with a uniform of khaki shirts and pants, a whistle, a police nightstick, and reflecting sunglasses; the "prisoners" were outfitted with a loose-fitting smock with an identification number stamped on it, rubber sandals, a cap made from a nylon stocking, and a locked chain attached to one ankle.

CHAPTER 8 Group Processes: Influence in Social Groups 235

◄ Philip Zimbardo and his colleagues randomly assigned students to play the role of prisoner or guard in a mock prison. The students assumed these roles all too well. Those playing the role of guard became quite aggressive, whereas those playing the role of prisoner became passive, helpless, and withdrawn. People got into their roles to the point where their personal identities and sense of decency somehow were lost.

The researchers planned to observe the students for two weeks to see whether they began to act like real prison guards and prisoners. As it turned out, the students quickly assumed these roles—so much so that the researchers had to end the experiment after only six days. Many of the guards became quite abusive, thinking of creative ways to verbally harass and humiliate the prisoners. The prisoners became passive, helpless, and withdrawn. Some prisoners, in fact, became so anxious and depressed that they had to be released from the study earlier than others. Remember, everyone knew that they were in a psychology experiment and that the "prison" was only make-believe. However, people got into their roles so much that their personal identities and sense of decency somehow were lost.

In Chapter 7, we referred to Philip Zimbardo's observation that many of the factors that contributed to the high levels of obedience in the classic Milgram study also were present in the recent abuse of Iraqi prisoners by American soldiers in Abu Ghraib prison. Zimbardo believes that the same psychological processes that operated in his mock prison, set up in a university basement more than 30 years ago, also were present in Abu Ghraib: the role of prison guard, the anonymity, and the dehumanization of the prisoners all contributed to the tragic loss of decency among the Americans in charge of the prison (Zimbardo, 2007). This is not to say that the American soldiers should be excused for their actions. The abuse came to light when one of the guards reported what was going on, and as in Zimbardo's study, there were some guards who treated the prisoners well. Thus, not everyone was caught in the web of their social roles, unable to resist. But as much as we would like to think that we would be one of these heroes, the lesson learned from the Zimbardo study—and from Milgram's obedience studies (discussed in Chapter 7)—is that most of us would be unable to resist the social influences in these powerful situations, and perhaps would perform acts we thought we were incapable of performing.

Another drawback of social roles is that there is a cost to acting inconsistently with the expectations associated with those roles. For example, part of the role of being a man in our society involves not wearing female attire or even carrying a purse. In an essay, "The Handbag," Alan Neal, host of the CBC Radio One show,

▶ Most groups have a number of well-defined social roles, which are shared expectations in a group about how particular people are supposed to behave. Roles can be very helpful, because people know what to expect from each other. However, people can get so far into a role that their personal identities and personalities get lost, sometimes with tragic consequences. Some people think that the abuse at the Abu Ghraib prison in Iraq was due to soldiers getting too far into their roles as prison guards.

The Other Story, confides how uncomfortable it is for a man to hold a woman's purse, even briefly:

> It doesn't matter that I think of myself as being an enlightened, egalitarian male. There is something about being handed a woman's handbag in a mall that completely destroys me. In all honesty, I would prefer to be handed a squirming ferret by the tail. Because there is no manly way to hold a purse. You hold it by the little hand straps and your wrist automatically bends. Trying to sling it off the shoulder conjures up images of bra straps or spaghetti straps. The only strap I've ever worn was not exactly for public viewing. (Neal, 2000)

Neal's obvious discomfort at deviating from the male role, though humorously described, derives from a very real intuition of what others will think of him if they see him carrying a purse in public. The accompanying Try It! describes a way that you can experience role violation for yourself.

Try it!

▶ What Happens When You Violate a Role?

Pick a behaviour that is part of gender roles in your culture and deliberately violate it. For example, if you are male, you might decide to put on makeup or carry a purse to your next class. If you are female, you might decide to dress like a male for a formal occasion, by wearing a jacket and tie. Keep a journal describing how others react to you. More than likely, you will encounter a good deal of social disapproval, such as people staring at you or questioning your behaviour. For this reason, you want to avoid role violations that are too extreme.

The social pressure that is brought to bear on people who do not conform explains why it can be so difficult to break out of the roles to which we are assigned, even when those roles are arbitrary. Of course, there is safety in numbers; when enough people violate role expectations, others do not act nearly so negatively, and as a result, the roles begin to change. For example, it is now much more acceptable for men to wear earrings than it was 25 years ago. To illustrate this safety in numbers, enlist the help of several same-sex friends and violate the same role expectation together. Again, note carefully how people react to you. Did you encounter more or less social disapproval in the group than you did as an individual?

Gender Roles   Role expectations are especially problematic when they are arbitrary or unfair, such as societal expectations based on people's gender. All societies have expectations about how people who occupy the roles of women and men should behave. In many cultures, women are expected to assume the role of wife and mother, with only limited opportunities to pursue other careers. Even in countries such as Canada, in which women can pursue careers, the options remain limited by gender-role stereotyping. For example, Lupaschuk and Yewchuk (1998) asked children in grades 4 to 12 residing in a rural community in Alberta what their lives would be like if they woke up the next day and discovered they were the other sex. The results showed that the occupational aspirations of boys and girls are influenced by traditional gender-role expectations. For example, a male junior high student remarked that if he were a girl, "people would expect me to do women's work like clean house or be a secretary." The researchers concluded that women are still constrained by expectations that they will pursue traditional occupations, and that child care and housework remain their responsibility.

This is not to say that role expectations haven't changed at all. In 1976, for example, 39 percent of women with children under the age of 16 were part of the paid workforce; by 2004, this number had risen to 73 percent (Canada, 2005f; www.statcan.gc.ca/ads-annonces/89-503-x/index-eng.htm). However, even in 2004, two-thirds of employed women were working in traditional female-dominated occupations (e.g., teaching, nursing, service and clerical)—a number that hasn't changed much over the past decade (Canada, 2005f). Moreover, women are often still expected to maintain the traditional role of childrearer and household manager. Conflict results, because women are expected to "do it all"—maintain a career, raise the children, clean the house, and attend to their husband's needs (Brislin, 1993; Eagly & Diekman, 2003). Not surprisingly, many women who work long days and have children at home report feeling time-stressed (Statistics Canada, 2006).

Women's growth in the workforce has necessitated a change in men's roles, as well. According to the Statistics Canada *Converging Family Roles* survey, in 1986, 54 percent of men reported carrying out household duties. By 2006, this number had risen to 69 percent. (In comparison, 90 percent of women reported steadily performing household duties over that period.) The number of hours per day that were spent on household tasks also increased, rising from 1.8 hours to 2.2 hours (Sanders, 2006). Women are benefiting from this change in men's roles. Research shows that the more husbands engage in household chores and errands, the better their wives' emotional health (Harris, 2008). Some reports even claim that when a husband does chores, the couple's sex life gets a boost! An Edmonton mother can vouch for the positive effects of a husband doing chores: "Just the fact that he would do something to ease the load is a huge turn-on," she says—far greater than the effects of receiving flowers or other gifts (Harris, 2008). Marketers have capitalized on the positive effects of "choreplay." A book and calendar series depicting fantasy images of men doing housework are enjoying brisk sales. The more serious bottom line is that the roles that people play, and the expectations that come with those roles, can have powerful effects on feelings and behaviour (Eagly & Steffen, 2000; Eagly & Diekman, 2003; Eagly, Diekman, & Johannesen-Schmidt, 2004).

Group Cohesiveness   Another important aspect of group composition is how tightly knit the group is. **Group cohesiveness** is defined as qualities of a group that bind members together and promote liking among them (Dion, 2000; Hogg, 1993; Holtz, 2004). If a group has formed primarily for social reasons, such as a group of friends who like to go to the movies together on weekends, then the more cohesive the group is, the better. This is pretty obvious; would you rather spend your free time with a bunch of people who don't care for each other or with a

group cohesiveness

qualities of a group that bind members together and promote liking among them tightly knit bunch of people who feel committed to each other? As might be expected, the more cohesive a group is, the more its members are likely to stay in the group, take part in group activities, and try to recruit like-minded members (Levine & Moreland, 1998; Pickett, Silver, & Brewer, 2002; Sprink & Carron, 1994). One drawback of group cohesiveness, however, is that the group members' concern with maintaining good relations can get in the way of finding good solutions to problems. We will return to this issue later in the chapter, when we discuss group decision making.

How Groups Influence the Behaviour of Individuals

Do you act differently when other people are around? Simply being in the presence of other people can have a variety of effects on your behaviour. We will begin by looking at how a group affects your performance on something with which you are very familiar: taking a test in a class.

Social Facilitation: When the Presence of Others Energizes Us

It is time for the final exam in your psychology class. You have spent countless hours studying the material, and you feel ready. When you arrive, you see that the exam is scheduled in a tiny, packed room. You squeeze into an empty desk, elbow to elbow with your classmates. The professor arrives and says that if any students are bothered by the close quarters, they can take the test by themselves in one of several smaller rooms down the hall. What should you do?

The question is whether the mere presence of others will affect your performance (Geen, 1989; Guerin, 1993; Kent, 1994; Sanna, 1992). The presence of other people can mean one of two things: (1) performing a task with others who are doing the same thing you are, or (2) performing a task in front of an audience that is not doing anything except observing you. The point is that, in either case, you are not interacting with these other people—they're just present in the same room, constituting a nonsocial group. Does their presence make a difference? If you take your exam in the crowded room, will you feel nervous and have trouble recalling the material? Or will the presence of classmates motivate you to do even better than if you took the test alone?

To answer this question, we need to talk about insects—cockroaches, in fact. Believe it or not, a classic study using cockroaches as research participants suggests an answer to the question of how you should take your psychology test. Robert Zajonc and colleagues built a contraption to see how cockroaches' behaviour was influenced by the presence of their peers (Zajonc, Heingartner, & Herman, 1969). The researchers placed a bright light (which cockroaches dislike) at the end of a runway and timed how long it took a roach to escape the light by running to the other end, where it could scurry into a darkened box (see the left side of Figure 8.1). The question was, did roaches perform this simple feat faster when they were by themselves or when they were in the presence of other cockroaches? You might be wondering how the researchers managed to persuade other cockroaches to be spectators. They did so by placing extra roaches in clear plastic boxes next to the runway. These roaches were in the bleachers, so to speak, observing the solitary cockroach do its thing (see Figure 8.1). It turned out that the individual cockroaches performed the task faster when they were in the presence of other roaches than when they were by themselves.

Simple maze — Goal, Audience boxes, Start, Floodlight

Complex maze — Goal, Audience boxes, Start, Floodlight

Now, we would not give advice on how you should take your psychology test based on one study that used cockroaches. But the story does not end here. There have been dozens of studies on the effects of the mere presence of others, involving human beings as well as other species such as ants and birds (e.g., Aiello & Douthitt, 2001; Rajecki, Kidd, & Ivins, 1976; Thomas, Skitka, Christen, & Jungena, 2002; Zajonc & Sales, 1966). There is a remarkable consistency to the findings of these studies. As long as the task is relatively simple and well learned—as escaping a light is for cockroaches—the mere presence of others improves performance. In one of the first social psychology experiments ever done, Norman Triplett (1898) asked children to wind up fishing line on a reel, either by themselves or in the presence of other children. They did so faster when in the presence of other children.

Mere social contact begets... a stimulation of the animal spirit that heightens the efficiency of each individual workman.
—Karl Marx, Das Kapital, 1867

Simple versus Difficult Tasks Before concluding that you should stay in the crowded classroom to take your exam, we need to consider another set of findings. Remember that we said the presence of others enhances performance on simple well-learned tasks. Escaping a light is old hat for a cockroach, and winding fishing line on a reel is not difficult, even for a child. What happens when the task is more difficult and done in the presence of others? To find out, Zajonc and

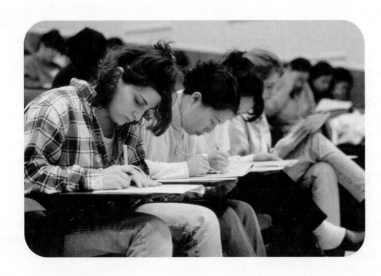

◄ Research on social facilitation finds that people do better on a well-learned task when in the presence of others than when they are alone. If students have studied hard and know the material well, they might be better off taking an exam in a room with many other people.

colleagues (1969) included another condition in the cockroach experiment. This time, the cockroaches had to solve a maze that had several runways, only one of which led to the darkened box (see the right side of Figure 8.1). When working on this more difficult task, the opposite pattern of results occurred. The roaches took longer to solve it when other roaches were present than when they were alone. Many other studies have also found that people and animals do worse in the presence of others when the task is difficult (e.g., Bond & Titus, 1983; Geen, 1989).

Arousal and the Dominant Response   In an influential article published in 1965, Robert Zajonc offered an elegant theoretical explanation for why the presence of others facilitates a well-learned or dominant response but inhibits a less practised or new response. His argument has two steps: First, the presence of others increases physiological arousal (i.e., our bodies become more energized). Second, when such arousal exists, it is easier to do something that is simple (called the *dominant response*) but harder to do something complex or learn something new. Consider, for example, something that is second nature to you, such as riding a bicycle or writing your name. Arousal, caused by the presence of other people watching you, should make it even easier to perform these well-learned behaviours. But let's say you have to do something more complex, such as learning a new sport or working on a difficult math problem. Now arousal will lead you to feel flustered and not do as well as if you were alone (Schmitt, Gilovich, Goore, & Joseph, 1986). This phenomenon is known as **social facilitation**—the tendency for people to do better on simple tasks, but worse on complex tasks, when they are in the presence of others and their individual performance can be evaluated.

Suppose, for example, that you decide to stop at a local pool hall and shoot a few racks. Will you perform better or worse if people are watching you wield your pool cue? As we have seen, it should depend on whether shooting pool is a simple or complex task for you. This is what James Michaels and colleagues (1982) found in a field study conducted in the pool hall of a university student union. A team of four students observed several different players from a distance, until they found ones who were experienced (defined as those who made at least two-thirds of their shots) or novices (defined as those who made no more than one-third of their shots). They then casually approached the table and watched people play.

Imagine that you are one of the players. There you are, shooting pool, when suddenly you notice four strangers standing around watching you. What will happen to your performance? The prediction made by social facilitation theory is clear. If you have played so much pool that you would feel comfortable challenging Minnesota Fats, the arousal caused by the presence of others should improve your game. If you are a novice and feel as if you are all thumbs, the arousal caused by the presence of others should make your game go to pieces. This is exactly what was found. The novices made significantly fewer of their shots when they were observed, whereas the experts made significantly more of their shots (Michaels, Blommel, Brocato, Linkous, & Rowe, 1982).

Why the Presence of Others Causes Arousal   Why does the presence of others lead to arousal? Researchers have developed three theories to explain the role of arousal in social facilitation:

1. Other people cause us to become particularly alert and vigilant.
2. They make us apprehensive about how we're being evaluated.
3. And they distract us from the task at hand.

The first explanation suggests that the presence of other people makes us more alert. When we are by ourselves reading a book, we don't have to pay attention to anything but the book; we don't have to worry that the lamp will ask us a

social facilitation

the tendency for people to do better on simple tasks, but worse on complex tasks, when they are in the presence of others and their individual performance can be evaluated question. When someone else is in the room, however, we have to be alert to the possibility that he or she will do something that requires us to respond. Because people are less predictable than lamps, we are in a state of greater alertness in their presence. This alertness, or vigilance, causes mild arousal. The beauty of this explanation—the one preferred by Robert Zajonc (1980)—is that it explains both the animal and the human studies. A solitary cockroach need not worry about what the cockroach in the next room is doing. However, it needs to be alert when in the presence of another member of its species—and the same goes for human beings.

The second explanation focuses on the fact that people are not cockroaches and are frequently concerned about how other people are evaluating them. When other people can see how you are doing, the stakes are raised. You feel as if the other people are evaluating you, and you will feel embarrassed if you do poorly and pleased if you do well. This concern about being judged, called *evaluation apprehension,* can cause mild arousal. According to this view, then, it is not the mere presence of others but the presence of others who are evaluating us that causes arousal and subsequent social facilitation (Blascovich, Mendes, Hunter, & Salomon, 1999; Bond, Atoum, & VanLeeuwen, 1996; Cottrell, 1968).

The third explanation centres on how distracting other people can be (Baron, 1986; Huguet et al., 1999; Muller, Atzeni, & Fabrizio, 2004). It is similar to Robert Zajonc's (1980) notion that we need to be alert when in the presence of others, except that it focuses on the idea that *any* source of distraction—be it the presence of other people or noise from the party going on in the apartment upstairs—will put us in a state of conflict, because it is difficult to concentrate on what we are doing. Trying to pay attention to two things at once produces arousal, as anyone knows who has ever tried to read the newspaper while a two-year-old clamours for attention. Consistent with this interpretation, there is evidence that nonsocial sources of distraction, such as a flashing light, cause the same kinds of social facilitation effects as does the presence of other people (Baron, 1986).

We have summarized research on social facilitation in the upper half of Figure 8.2. (We will discuss the lower half in a moment.) This figure illustrates that there is more than one reason that the presence of other people is arousing. The consequences of this arousal, however, are the same. When an individual is around other people, that individual does better on tasks that are simple and well learned, but worse on tasks that are complex and require them to learn something new.

We can now conclude that you should take your psychology exam in the presence of your classmates, assuming you know the material well, so that it is

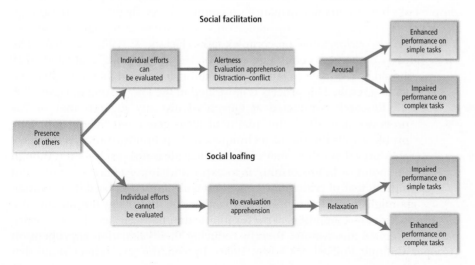

FIGURE 8.2

Social facilitation and social loafing

The presence of others can lead to social facilitation or social loafing. The important variables that distinguish the two are evaluation, arousal, and the complexity of the task.

(Adapted from Cottrell et al., 1968)

relatively simple for you to recall it. The arousal produced by being elbow to elbow with your classmates should improve your performance. We can also conclude, however, that when you study for an exam—that is, when you learn new material—you should do so by yourself and not in the presence of others. In this situation, the arousal caused by others will make it more difficult to concentrate on the new material.

Social Loafing: When the Presence of Others Relaxes Us

When you take your psychology exam, your individual efforts will be evaluated; that is, you will be graded on the test. This is typical of the research on social facilitation we have reviewed. People are working on something—either alone or in the presence of others—and their individual efforts are easily observed and evaluated. Often when you are in the presence of others, however, your efforts cannot be distinguished from those of the people around you. Such is the case when you clap after a concert (i.e., no one can tell how loudly you are clapping) or when you play an instrument in a band (i.e., your instrument blends in with all the others).

These situations are just the opposite of the kinds of social facilitation settings we have just considered. In social facilitation, the presence of others puts the spotlight on you, making you aroused. However, if being with other people means we can merge into a group, becoming less noticeable than when we are alone, we should become relaxed. Will this relaxation produced by becoming lost in the crowd lead to better or worse performance? Once again, the answer depends on whether we are working on a simple or a complex task.

Let's first consider simple tasks, such as trying to pull as hard as you can on a rope. The question of how working with others would influence performance on such a task was first studied in the 1880s by a French agricultural engineer, Max Ringelmann (1913). He found that when a group of men pulled on a rope, each individual exerted less effort than when he did it alone. A century later, social psychologists Bibb Latané, Kipling Williams, and Stephen Harkins (1979) called this **social loafing**, which is the tendency for people to do worse on simple tasks, but better on complex tasks, when they are in the presence of others and their individual performance cannot be evaluated. Social loafing in groups has since been found for a variety of simple tasks, such as clapping your hands, cheering loudly, and thinking of as many uses for an object as you can (Karau & Williams, 2001; Shepperd & Taylor, 1999).

But what about complex tasks? Recall that when our performance in a group cannot be identified, we become more relaxed. Recall also our earlier discussion of the effects of arousal on performance: Arousal enhances performance on simple tasks but impairs performance on complex tasks. By the same reasoning, becoming relaxed impairs performance on simple tasks—as we have just seen— but improves performance on complex tasks (Jackson & Williams, 1985). The idea is that when people are not worried about being evaluated, they should be less likely to tense up on a difficult task and therefore do it better as a result. This process is illustrated in the lower panel of Figure 8.2.

Research conducted at Queen's University suggests that similar processes may affect the quality of ideas generated by a group. One problem with the use of techniques such as brainstorming is that people worry that others may evaluate their ideas negatively—even though the point of brainstorming is to express whatever ideas come to mind without fear of criticism. Cooper and colleagues proposed that computers might provide an important vehicle for improving the quality of a group's ideas—computers allow for interaction between people, yet participants can remain anonymous, thereby reducing their evaluation apprehension (Cooper, Gallupe, Pollard, & Cadsby, 1998). Indeed, the researchers found that

social loafing

the tendency for people to do worse on simple tasks, but better on complex tasks, when they are in the presence of others and their individual performance cannot be evaluated

> *"Which of us...is to do the hard and dirty work for the rest—and for what pay?"*
>
> —John Ruskin (1819–1900)

participants in anonymous electronic groups found it easier to generate ideas and reported lower evaluation apprehension than did those in non-anonymous (i.e., electronic or in-person) discussion groups. Participants in anonymous electronic discussion groups also generated the greatest number of controversial ideas. This is supposed to be one of the benefits of brainstorming. However, there was an unexpected twist to these findings—it turned out that the kind of controversy generated under these conditions was not very desirable. In fact, some of the ideas generated by the anonymous electronic groups were highly offensive. For the discussion topic, "How to reduce the spread of AIDS," for example, participants generated ideas such as "Burn AIDS carriers at the stake like witches" and "Set a trap encouraging gays to come out of the closet and then eliminate them." The researchers observed that if one group member generated an inappropriate idea, it could set off a vicious cycle of group members attempting to outdo one another. Those who were offended by these responses simply stopped contributing ideas. Cooper and colleagues concluded that the use of computers can have benefits such as allowing for interaction while preserving anonymity—thereby lowering evaluation apprehension, but that safeguards may be necessary to ensure that the generation of controversial ideas does not spiral out of control.

Gender and Cultural Differences in Social Loafing: Who Slacks Off the Most?   Marie and Hans are working with several classmates on a class project, and no one can assess their individual contributions. Who is more likely to slack off and let the others do most of the work—Hans or Marie? If you said Hans, you are probably right. Karau and Williams (1993) reviewed more than 150 studies of social loafing and found that the tendency to loaf is stronger in men than in women. Why? As discussed in Chapter 5, women tend to be higher than men in *relational interdependence*, which is the tendency to focus on and care about personal relationships with others. Perhaps it is this focus that makes women less likely to engage in social loafing when in groups (Eagly, 1987; Wood, 1987).

Research also has found that the tendency to loaf is stronger in Western cultures than in Asian cultures, which may be due to the different self-definitions prevalent in these cultures (Karau & Williams, 1993). Asians are more likely to have an *interdependent view of the self*, which is a way of defining oneself in relation to other people (see Chapter 5). This self-definition may reduce the tendency toward social loafing when in groups. We should not, however, exaggerate these gender and cultural differences. Women and members of Asian cultures do engage in social loafing when in groups; they are just less likely to do so than men or members of Western cultures (Chang & Chen, 1995).

To summarize, you need to know two things to predict whether the presence of others will help or hinder your performance: whether your individual efforts can be evaluated and whether the task is simple or complex. If your performance can be evaluated, the presence of others will make you alert and aroused. This will lead to social facilitation effects, where people do better on simple tasks but worse on complex tasks (see upper half of Figure 8.2 on page 241). If your efforts cannot be evaluated (i.e., you are one cog in a machine), you are likely to become more relaxed. This leads to social loafing effects, where people do worse on simple tasks but better on complex tasks (see lower half of Figure 8.2).

These findings have numerous implications for the way in which groups should be organized. If you are a manager who wants your employees to work on a relatively simple problem, a little evaluation apprehension is not such a bad thing—it should improve performance. You shouldn't place your employees in groups where their individual performance cannot be observed, because social loafing (lowered performance on simple tasks) is likely to result. On the other hand, if you want your employees to work on a difficult, complex task, then lowering their evaluation apprehension—by placing them in groups in which their individual performance cannot be observed—is likely to result in better performance.

deindividuation

the loosening of normal constraints on behaviour when people are in a group, leading to an increase in impulsive and deviant acts

▲ When people lose their identity in a group, they are more likely to commit impulsive and deviant acts. Matti Baranovski, a Toronto teen, was brutally beaten to death in November 1999 by a group of youths wearing balaclavas, masks, goggles, and other disguises. Here, his grieving mother lays a wreath on the casket at his funeral.

Deindividuation: Getting Lost in the Crowd

So far, we have discussed the ways in which a group affects how hard people work and how successfully they learn new things. However, as was demonstrated by the Queen's University study on brainstorming in anonymous electronic discussion groups (Cooper et al., 1998), being in a group can also cause **deindividuation**, which is the loosening of normal constraints on behaviour, leading to an increase in impulsive and deviant acts (Lea, Spears, & de Groot, 2001). In other words, getting lost in a crowd—or hiding behind the anonymity of the internet—can lead to an unleashing of behaviours that individuals would never dream of doing otherwise (Lee, 2004).

Throughout history, there have been many examples of groups of people committing horrendous acts that no individual would do on his or her own. In Chapter 6, we discussed the chilling murder of a Somali teen by Canadian peacekeepers. In Chapter 7, we described the My Lai massacre during the Vietnam War, in which a group of American soldiers systematically murdered hundreds of defenceless women, children, and elderly men. We have also referred to the more recent abuse of Iraqi prisoners at the hands of American soldiers in Abu Ghraib prison. In Europe, mobs of soccer fans sometimes attack and bludgeon one another. Closer to home, male hockey fans report that the greater the number of male friends with whom they attend a game, the greater the probability that they will become involved in a fight, as shown by research conducted in Alberta (Russell & Arms, 1998). To give one last example, the United States has a shameful history of white people lynching African-American people. Brian Mullen (1986) analyzed newspaper accounts of 60 lynchings committed in the United States between 1899 and 1946, and discovered an interesting fact: The more people there were in the mob, the greater the savagery and viciousness with which they killed their victims.

Mullen (1986) also found that people who participated in these lynchings often did so cloaked in the anonymity of white robes and hooded masks. This combination of anonymity and being in a group can lead to deadly actions. Robert Watson (1973) studied 24 cultures and found that warriors who hid their identity before going into battle—by using face and body paint—were significantly more likely to kill, torture, or mutilate captive prisoners than were warriors who did not hide their identity. A chilling example of this phenomenon occurred on November 14, 1999, when 15-year-old Matti Baranovski and his friends were approached in a Toronto park by a group of youths looking for a fight. One of the youths wore ski goggles; another covered the lower half of his face with a blue bandana. Still others wore masks or balaclavas to disguise themselves. The youths approached Matti's friends, took their cigarettes, and searched their wallets for money. When Matti questioned what they were doing, they turned on him, viciously punching and kicking him in the head and body. The last kick in the face broke his neck. Matti died from these injuries. The trial for three of the accused finally ended in July 2003. Meir Mariani and William Cochrane were charged with manslaughter. Daniel Weitz, a Canadian-Israeli soldier, was acquitted. In trying to understand why such violence can occur, some analysts pointed to the fact that the attackers were in a group and that they were wearing disguises. As noted in one newspaper story, "Disguises tend to make those wearing them capable of far more terrible acts of violence than would normally occur" (Simmie, 1999).

Why Does Deindividuation Lead to Impulsive Acts? Exactly what is it about deindividuation that leads to impulsive—and often violent—acts? There are three factors. First, the presence of others, or the wearing of uniforms and disguises, makes people feel less accountable for their actions because it reduces the likelihood that any individual will be singled out and blamed (Diener, 1980; Prentice-Dunn & Rogers, 1989; Zimbardo, 1970). Second, the presence of others lowers self-awareness, thereby shifting people's attention away from their moral standards. As discussed in Chapter 5, it is difficult to focus inward on ourselves and outward on the world around us at the same time; consequently, at any given point, we vary as to how self-aware we are (Carver & Scheier, 1981; Duval & Wicklund, 1972). One consequence of focusing on ourselves is that we are reminded of our moral standards, making us less likely to behave in a deviant or antisocial manner (e.g., "I believe that hurting other people is wrong; I'm not going to throw a drink at this soccer fan—even if he is cheering for the 'wrong' team"). If we are focusing on our environment, however, self-awareness will be low and we will be more likely to forget our moral standards and act impulsively.

Finally, deindividuation also increases the extent to which people obey the group's norms, as shown in a meta analysis of more than 60 studies (Postmes & Spears 1998). When group members are together and deindividuated, they are more likely to act according to the group norms than other norms such as "It is wrong to hurt another human being." This latter explanation can account for why deindividuation does not always lead to aggressive or antisocial behaviour—it depends on what the norm of the group is. Imagine that you are at a raucous party at which everyone is dancing wildly to very loud music. To the extent that you feel deindividuated—it is dark, and you are dressed similarly to other people—you are more likely to join the group and let loose on the dance floor. If the group is angry and the norm is to act violently, then deindividuation will make people in the group act aggressively. Thus, it is the specific norm of the group that determines whether deindividuation will lead to positive or negative behaviours (Gergen, Gergen, & Barton, 1973; Johnson & Downing, 1979).

> *If you can keep your head when all about you are losing theirs. . . .*
>
> —Rudyard Kipling, "If," 1909

CONNECTIONS

Sports and Aggression: Does What You Wear Change Who You Are?

Most of us do not encounter lynch mobs, wars, and masked attackers on a day-to-day basis. It is not as uncommon, however, to be asked to wear uniforms that make us look like everyone else in the vicinity—a situation that might also make us feel less accountable for our actions and hence more aggressive. Does wearing a uniform, such as on a sports team, actually increase aggressiveness? A study by Rehm, Steinleitner, and Lilli (1987) indicates that it does. They randomly assigned fifth graders in German schools to various five-person teams, then watched the teams play handball against each other. All of the members of one team wore orange shirts and all of the members of the other team wore their normal street clothes. The children who wore the orange shirts, and who were therefore harder to tell apart, played the game significantly more aggressively than did the children who wore their everyday clothing—who were easier to identify.

Even the colour of a uniform can make a difference. Mark Frank and Thomas Gilovich (1988) noted that in virtually all cultures, the colour black is associated with evil and death. They examined penalty records and recorded the colour of uniforms worn by teams in the National Hockey League and the National Football League from 1970 to 1986. Interestingly, teams that wore black uniforms ranked near the top of their leagues in terms of penalties. Moreover, if a team switched to a non-black uniform, there was an immediate decrease in the number of penalties. These researchers also conducted an experiment in which participants played a game wearing either white or black uniforms. Those who wore black uniforms showed greater aggressiveness than did those who wore white uniforms.

In a hockey game in March 2004, Colorado Avalanche player Steve Moore suffered a broken neck and other injuries after being hit from behind by Todd Bertuzzi of the Vancouver Canucks. The National Hockey League fined the Canucks and suspended Bertuzzi; he was reinstated in August 2005, 17 months after the attack. He also pleaded guilty to assault in a Vancouver court and was given a sentence of one year's probation and community service. Moore has been unable to play again and has sued Bertuzzi and the Vancouver Canucks for $38 million in lost income and damages. In March 2008, Bertuzzi responded by filing a lawsuit against his former coach, Marc Crawford, claiming that Crawford told the players to make Moore "pay the price" for an earlier attack. The ill-fated game took place in Vancouver, which meant that Bertuzzi was wearing the dark-coloured uniform that Canucks players use during home games. Might Bertuzzi's assault have been less severe if the game had been played in Colorado, where he would have being wearing the "away" white uniform? Although we can't be sure, the research we have been discussing does raise the possibility that the colour of the uniform made part of the difference.

Thus, something as seemingly superficial as whether we are wearing a uniform while playing our favourite sport—as well as the colour of that uniform—can affect our level of aggressiveness.

Group Decisions: Are Two (or More) Heads Better than One?

We have just discussed that the presence of other people influences individual behaviour in a number of interesting ways. We turn now to one of the major functions of groups: to make decisions. In the Canadian judicial system, many verdicts are determined by groups of individuals (juries) rather than single individuals (see Social Psychology in Action 3: Social Psychology and the Law for a discussion of jury decision making). The Supreme Court of Canada is made up of nine justices—not a solitary sage member of the judiciary. Similarly, governmental and corporate decisions are frequently made by groups of people who meet to discuss the issues, and all Canadian prime ministers have a cabinet and the Privy Council to advise them.

Is it true that two (or more) heads are better than one? Most of us assume that the answer to this question is yes. A lone individual may be subject to all sorts of whims and biases, whereas several people together can exchange ideas, catch each other's errors, and reach better decisions. We have all taken part in group decisions in which we listened to someone else and thought to ourselves, "Hmm, that's a really good point—I would never have thought of that." In general, groups will do better than individuals if they rely on the person with the most expertise and if they combine their abilities and resources (Davis & Harless, 1996). In fact, in a recent study it was found that even the highest-performing individuals do better if they work in a group (Laughlin, Hatch, Silver & Boh, 2006). In this study, students working in groups (ranging in size from three to five people) were given math problems to solve. Groups of three or more solved the problem in about six equations. In comparison, when the very top students in each group worked alone, on average, they solved the problem in 6.5 equations.

Sometimes, though, two heads are not better than one (Kerr & Tindale, 2004). Several factors, as we will see, can cause groups to actually make worse decisions than individuals.

Process Loss: When Group Interactions Inhibit Good Problem Solving

One problem is that a group will do well only if the most talented member can convince the others that he or she is right—which is not always easy, given that many of us bear a strong resemblance to mules when it comes to admitting that we are wrong (Henry, 1995; Laughlin, 1980; Maier & Solem, 1952). You undoubtedly know what it's like to try to convince a group to follow your idea, be faced with opposition and disbelief, and then have to sit there and watch the group make the wrong decision. This is called **process loss**, which is defined as any aspect of group interaction that inhibits good problem solving (Steiner, 1972). Process loss can occur for a number of reasons. Groups might not try hard enough to find out who the most competent member is and instead rely on somebody who really doesn't know what he or she is talking about. The most competent member might find it difficult to disagree with everyone else in the group—recall our discussion of normative conformity pressures in Chapter 7. Other causes of process loss involve communication problems within the group— in some groups, people don't listen to each other; in others, one person is allowed to dominate the discussion while the others tune out (Sorkin, Hays, & West, 2001; Watson, Johnson, Kumar, & Critelli, 1998).

Failure to Share Unique Information Another interesting example of process loss is the tendency for groups to focus on what its members already know in common, failing to discuss information that some members have but others do not (Geitemeier & Schulz-Hardt, 2003; Stasser & Titus, 1985). Consider a medical team trying to decide on the course of treatment of a person with abdominal pain. All members share some knowledge, such as the fact that the patient is a male in his fifties with a history of digestive problems. Some members of the team, however, know things that the other members do not. The doctor who first examined the patient in the emergency room may be the only one who knows that the patient had mussels for dinner that night, whereas one of the attending physicians may be the only one to have seen the results of a blood test showing that the patient has an abnormally high white blood cell count. Obviously, to make the most informed decision, the group needs to pool all of the information and use it to decide on the best course of treatment.

As obvious as this is, there is a funny thing about groups: They tend to focus on the information they share and ignore unique information known only to one or a few members of the group. In one study, for example, participants met in groups of four to discuss which candidate for student body president was the most qualified (Stasser & Titus, 1985). In the shared information condition, each participant was given the same packet of information to read: data indicating that candidate A was the best choice for office. As seen in the upper row of Figure 8.3 on the next page, all participants in this condition knew that candidate A had eight positive qualities and four negative qualities, making him superior to the other candidates. Not surprisingly, when this group met to discuss the candidates, almost all of the members chose candidate A.

In the unshared information condition, each participant received a different packet of information. As seen in the lower row of Figure 8.3, each person knew that candidate A had two positive qualities and four negative qualities. However, the two positive qualities cited in each person's packet were unique, different from those listed in other participants' packets. Everyone learned that candidate a had the same four negative qualities; thus, if the participants shared the information in their packets, they would learn that candidate A had a total of eight positive qualities and four negative qualities—just as people in the shared information condition knew. Most of the groups in the unshared information condition never realized that candidate A had more good than bad qualities, because they focused on the information they shared rather than on the information they did not share. As a result, few of these groups chose candidate A.

Subsequent research has focused on ways to get groups to concentrate more on unshared information (Kelly & Karau, 1999; Postmes, Spears, & Cihangir, 2001; Stasser & Birchmeier, 2003). One way of accomplishing this is to make sure that group discussions last long enough to get beyond what everybody already knows. Unshared information is more likely to be brought up later in the discussion

process loss

any aspect of group interaction that inhibits good problem solving

> ❝ Nor is the people's judgement always true: The most may err as grossly as the few. ❞
>
> —*John Dryden*, Absalom and Achitophel, *1682*

FIGURE 8.3

When people are in groups, do they share information that only they know?

Participants in a study met to discuss candidates for an election. In the shared information condition (upper row of figure), each person was given the same positive and negative facts about the candidates. Candidate A was clearly the superior candidate, and most groups preferred him. In the unshared information condition (lower row of figure), each person was given the same four negative facts about candidate A, as well as two unique positive facts. In discussion, these people focused on the information they all shared and failed to mention the unique information; these groups no longer saw candidate A as superior.

(Adapted from Stasser & Titus, 1985.)

transactive memory

the combined memory of two people that is more efficient than the memory of either individual

groupthink

a kind of thinking in which maintaining group cohesiveness and solidarity is more important than considering the facts in a realistic manner

(Fraidin, 2004; Larson Christenson, Franz, & Abbott, 1998; Larson, Foster-Fishman, & Franz, 1998). Another approach is to assign different group members to specific areas of expertise so they know that they alone are responsible for certain types of information. If only one doctor's job is to monitor the blood tests, he or she is more likely to bring up this information and other members are more likely to pay attention to it (Stasser, Stewart, & Wittenbaum, 1995; Stewart & Stasser, 1995).

This last lesson has been learned by many couples, who know to rely on each other's memories for different kinds of information. One member of a couple might be responsible for remembering social engagements, while the other might be responsible for remembering when to pay the bills (Wegner, Erber & Raymond, 1991). The combined memory of two people that is more efficient than the memory of either individual is called **transactive memory** (Hollingshead, 2001; Wegner, 1995). By learning to specialize their memories and knowing what their partner is responsible for, couples often do quite well in remembering important information. The same can be true of groups of strangers, if they develop a system whereby different people are remembering different parts of a task (Liang, Moreland, & Argote, 1995; Moreland, 1999; Moreland, Argote, & Krishnan, 1996). In sum, the tendency for groups to fail to share important information known to only some of the members can be overcome if people learn who is responsible for what kinds of information and take the time to discuss these unshared data (Stasser, 2000).

Groupthink: Many Heads, One Mind A possible limitation of research on group problem solving is that most studies use people who have never met before and give them tasks that are unfamiliar and sometimes trivial. Would groups do better if their members were used to working with one another and if they were dealing with important, real-world problems? Our opening example of the Canadian military's decision to administer the anthrax vaccine suggests not. Let's see why.

Using real-world events, Irving Janis (1972, 1982) developed an influential theory of group decision making that he called **groupthink**—defined as a kind of thinking in which maintaining group cohesiveness and solidarity is more important than considering the facts in a realistic manner. According to Janis's theory,

Antecedents of groupthink	Symptoms of groupthink	Defective decision making
The group is highly cohesive: The group is valued and attractive, and people very much want to be members. **Group isolation:** The group is isolated, protected from hearing alternative viewpoints. **A directive leader:** The leader controls the discussion and makes his or her wishes known. **High stress:** The members perceive threats to the group. **Poor decision-making procedures:** No standard methods to consider alternative viewpoints.	**Illusion of invulnerability:** The group feels it is invincible and can do no wrong. **Belief in the moral correctness of the group:** "God is on our side." **Stereotyped views of out-group:** Opposing sides are viewed in a simplistic, stereotyped manner. **Self-censorship:** People decide themselves not to voice contrary opinions so as not to "rock the boat." **Direct pressure on dissenters to conform:** If people do voice contrary opinions, they are pressured by others to conform to the majority. **Illusion of unanimity:** An illusion is created that everyone agrees, for example, by not calling on people known to disagree. **Mindguards:** Group members protect the leader from contrary viewpoints.	**Incomplete survey of alternatives** **Failure to examine risks of the favoured alternative** **Poor information search** **Failure to develop contingency plans**

FIGURE 8.4

Groupthink: Antecedents, symptoms, and consequences

Under some conditions, maintaining group cohesiveness and solidarity is more important to a group than considering the facts in a realistic manner (see antecedents in first panel). When this happens, certain symptoms of groupthink occur, such as the illusion of invulnerability (see symptoms in middle panel). These symptoms lead to defective decision making (see final panel).

(Adapted from Janis, 1982)

groupthink is most likely to occur when certain preconditions are met, such as when the group is highly cohesive, isolated from contrary opinions, and ruled by a directive leader who makes his or her wishes known. When these preconditions of groupthink are met, several symptoms appear (outlined in Figure 8.4). The group begins to feel it is invulnerable and can do no wrong. Group members do not voice contrary views (self-censorship) because they are afraid of ruining the high morale or *esprit de corps* of the group, or because they are afraid of being criticized by others. If anyone does voice a contrary viewpoint, the rest of the group is quick to criticize that person, pressuring him or her to conform to the majority view. The perilous state of groupthink causes people to reach an inferior decision (see Figure 8.4). The group does not consider the full range of alternatives, does not develop contingency plans, and does not adequately consider the risks of its preferred choice.

Groupthink may well have been behind the decision of military leaders to go ahead with the anthrax vaccine despite the fact that Health Canada had not approved it and military lawyers had advised against it. Can you think of other major decisions that were plagued by groupthink? One example is of NASA launching the space shuttle *Challenger* in 1986, despite the objections of engineers who said that the freezing temperatures presented a severe danger to the rubber O-rings—the seals that eventually failed during the launch, causing the rocket to explode and kill all aboard. More recently, social psychologists and political pundits have analyzed whether then U.S. President George W. Bush's decision to invade Iraq in 2003 was a product of groupthink. Although a definitive answer has not been reached, it appears that many of the symptoms of groupthink were present (Aronson, Wilson, & Akert, 2007).

Closer to home, in October 2005, Canadian newspapers trumpeted the release of Peter C. Newman's scathing portrayal of former prime minister Brian Mulroney, including how he handled the Meech Lake Accord in 1990 (Newman, 2005). In June of that year, Brian Mulroney and the provincial premiers met behind closed doors for seven days to make a decision regarding constitutional reform. The conditions were ripe for groupthink. The politicians met in isolation—away from the media, their constituents, and their advisers. The meetings took place shortly before the accord would have to be ratified, leaving little time to discuss alternatives. Mulroney was a persuasive, directive leader who managed to convince the premiers that the Meech Lake Accord was the answer to Canada's unity problems, and that failure to sign the accord would place the

> "The only sin which we never forgive in each other is difference of opinion."
>
> —*Ralph Waldo Emerson,* Society and Solitude, *1870*

▲ The decision to launch the space shuttle *Challenger*, which exploded because of defective O-ring seals, appears to have been the result of groupthink on the part of NASA officials, who disregarded engineers' concerns about the quality of the seals.

country in political and economic peril. His goal in these discussions was to ensure that dissenters conformed. This was the context of his infamous quip that one simply needed to know when to roll the dice and the Meech Lake Accord would be a done deal. The final decision was reached when the most prominent dissenter, the premier of Quebec, was absent. Under these conditions, the group reached consensus—a consensus that unravelled as soon as the prime minister and the premiers emerged from their cloistered environment and returned to Ottawa and the provinces. The Meech Lake Accord faced a sudden death when several provinces refused to endorse it.

Since Janis first proposed his theory, it has been put to the test by a number of researchers (Adlag & Fuller, 1993; Ahlfinger & Esser, 2001; Hodson & Sorrentino, 1997; Hogg & Hains, 1998; Mohamed & Wiebe, 1996; Schafer & Crichlow, 1996; Tetlock et al., 1992). The upshot, according to a recent review, is that defective decision making may be more common that Janis originally assumed and it is triggered by fewer antecendent conditions than those shown in Figure 8.4 (Baron, 2005). If so, groups should be all the more careful to avoid making bad decisions.

Avoiding the Groupthink Trap A wise leader can take several steps to ensure that his or her group is immune to this style of decision making (Flowers, 1977; McCauley, 1989; Zimbardo & Andersen, 1993):

- **Remain impartial**. The leader should not take a directive role but should remain impartial.

- **Seek outside opinions**. The leader should invite outside opinions from people who are not members of the group and who are therefore less concerned with maintaining group cohesiveness.

- **Create subgroups**. The leader should divide the group into subgroups that first meet separately and then meet together to discuss their different recommendations.

- **Seek anonymous opinions**. The leader might also take a secret ballot or ask group members to write down their opinions anonymously; doing so would ensure that people give their true opinions, uncensored by a fear of recrimination from the group.

Group Polarization: Going to Extremes

Maybe you are willing to grant that groups sometimes make poor decisions. Surely, though, groups will usually make less-risky decisions than a lone individual will—one individual might be willing to bet the ranch on a risky proposition, but if others help make the decision, they will interject reason and moderation—or will they? The question of whether groups or individuals make more risky decisions has been examined in numerous studies. Participants are typically given the Choice Dilemmas Questionnaire, a series of stories that present a dilemma for the main character and ask the reader to choose how much probability of success there would have to be before the reader would recommend the risky alternative (Kogan & Wallach, 1964). People choose their answers alone and then meet in a group to discuss the options, arriving at a unanimous group decision for each dilemma.

Many of the initial studies found, surprisingly, that groups make riskier decisions than individuals do. An example of an item from a Choice Dilemmas Questionnaire about a chess player appears in the Try It! on page 252. When deciding alone, participants said the chess player should make the risky gambit only if there were at least a 30 percent chance of success. But after discussing the problem with others in a group, people said the chess player should go for it, even if there were only a 10 percent chance of success (Wallach, Kogan, & Bem, 1962). Findings such as these became known as the *risky shift*. But further research made it clear that such shifts were not the full story. It turns out that groups tend to make decisions that are more extreme in the same direction as the individual's initial predispositions, which, in the case of the chess problem, happened to be risky.

What would happen if people were initially inclined to be conservative? In such cases, groups tend to make even more conservative decisions than individuals do. Consider this problem: Domenic, a young married man with two children, has a secure but low-paying job and no savings. Someone gives him a tip about a stock that will triple in value if the company's new product is successful, but will plummet if the new product fails. Should Domenic sell his life insurance policy and invest in the company? Most people recommend a safe course of action here: Domenic should buy the stock only if the new product is certain to succeed. When they talk it over in a group, people become even more conservative, deciding that the new product would have to have a nearly 100 percent chance of success before they would recommend that Domenic buy stock in the company.

The finding that groups make more extreme decisions in the direction of the members' initial inclinations has become known as **group polarization**. The tendency is for groups to make decisions toward greater risk if the group members' initial tendency is to be risky and toward greater caution if the group members' initial tendency is to be cautious (Brown, 1965; Ohtsubo, Masuchi, & Nakanishi, 2002; Rodrigo & Ato, 2002; Teger & Pruitt, 1967).

Group polarization occurs for two main reasons. According to the *persuasive arguments* interpretation, all individuals bring to the group a set of arguments—some of which other individuals have not considered—to support their initial recommendation. For example, one person might stress that cashing in the life insurance policy is an unfair risk to Domenic's children, should he die prematurely. Another person might not have considered this possibility; upon hearing it, she becomes more conservative as well. The result is that group members end up with a greater number of arguments in support of their position than they initially started out with. A series of studies supports this interpretation of group polarization (Burnstein & Sentis, 1981; Burnstein & Vinokur, 1977).

According to the *social comparison* interpretation, when people discuss an issue in a group, they first check how everyone else feels. What does the group value—being risky or being cautious? In order to be liked, many people then take a position that is similar to everyone else's but a little more extreme. In this way, the individual supports the group's values and also presents himself or herself in a positive light—a person in the vanguard, an impressive thinker. This interpretation of group polarization has also received research support (Blaskovich, Ginsburg, & Veach, 1975; Brown, 1986; Isenberg, 1986; Zuber, Crott, & Werner, 1992).

Leadership in Groups

A critical question we have not considered yet is the role of the leader in group decision making. The question of what makes a great leader has long intrigued psychologists, historians, and political scientists (Bass, 1990, 1997; Chemers, 2000; Fiedler, 1967; Hogg, 2001; Hollander, 1985; Klenke, 1996; Simonton, 1987). One of the best-known answers to this question is the **great person theory**, which maintains that certain key personality traits make a person a good leader, regardless of the nature of the situation facing the leader. If the great person theory is true, we ought to be able to isolate the key aspects of personality that make someone a great leader. Is it a combination of intelligence, charisma, and courage? Is it better to be introverted or extroverted? Should we add a dollop of ruthlessness to the mix as well, as Niccolò Machiavelli suggested in 1513, in his famous treatise on leadership, *The Prince*? Or do highly moral people make the best leaders?

group polarization

the tendency for groups to make decisions that are more extreme than the initial inclinations of their members

great person theory

the theory that certain key personality traits make a person a good leader, regardless of the nature of the situation facing the leader

Try it!

▶ Choice Dilemmas Questionnaire

You will need four or five friends to complete this exercise. First, copy the questionnaire in the table below and give it to each of your friends to complete by themselves, without talking to each other. Do not tell anyone that he or she will be discussing the questionnaire with the others. Then bring everyone together and ask them to discuss the dilemma and arrive at a unanimous decision. They should try to reach consensus such that every member of the group agrees at least partially with the final decision. Finally, compare people's initial decisions (made alone) with the group decision. Who made the riskier decisions on average: people deciding by themselves or the group?

As discussed in the text, groups tend to make riskier decisions than individuals on problems such as these. Did you find the same thing? Why or why not? If the group did make a riskier decision, was it due more to the persuasive arguments interpretation discussed in the text, the social comparison interpretation, or both?

The Choice Dilemmas Questionnaire

A low-ranked participant in a national chess tournament, playing an early match against a highly favoured opponent, has the choice of attempting or not attempting a deceptive but risky manoeuvre that might lead to quick victory if it is successful, or to almost certain defeat if it fails. Please indicate the lowest probability of success that you would accept before recommending that the chess player play the risky move.

_____ 1 chance in 10 of succeeding

_____ 3 chances in 10 of succeeding

_____ 5 chances in 10 of succeeding

_____ 7 chances in 10 of succeeding

_____ 9 chances in 10 of succeeding

_____ I would not recommend taking the chance.

(Adapted from Wallach, Kogan, & Bem, 1962)

▲ There is a modest but positive relationship between intelligence and leadership effectiveness (Simonton, 1985; Stogdill, 1974). Supreme Court Chief Justice Beverley McLachlin, pictured here, graduated with a gold medal from the University of Alberta and is described as having an "unquenchable intellectual curiosity."

Leadership and Personality In the numerous studies that have been conducted, only weak relationships have been found between specific personal characteristics and leadership. Compared with nonleaders, leaders tend to be slightly more intelligent, more driven by the desire for power, more charismatic, more socially skilled, more adaptive and flexible, and more confident in their leadership abilities (Albright & Forziati, 1995; Chemers, Watson, & May, 2000; Judge, Bono, Ilies, & Gerhardt, 2002). What is most telling, however, is the absence of strong relationships. Moreover, surprisingly few personality characteristics correlate with leadership effectiveness. Bradley and colleagues (2002) followed Canadian Forces officer candidates over a five-year period and found little relation between personality variables and leadership ability—only one trait emerged as particularly useful in predicting who would make a good leader, and that was dominance. Why might that be? The researchers suggest that "military operations are not the place for insecure people" (Bradley, Nicol, Charbonneau, & Meyer, 2002).

University of British Columbia social psychologist Peter Suedfeld and his colleagues (Ballard & Suedfeld, 1988; Suedfeld, Conway III, & Eichorn, 2001) have identified another correlate of leadership effectiveness, namely *integrative complexity*—the ability to recognize more than one perspective on an issue and to be able to integrate these various perspectives. These researchers have found substantial correlations between integrative complexity and greatness among Canadian prime ministers and other prominent leaders.

Simonton (1987, 2001) gathered information on 100 personal attributes of all U.S. presidents, such as their family backgrounds, educational experiences, occupations, and personalities. Only three of these variables—height, family size, and the number of books a president published before taking office—correlated with how effective the presidents were in office, as rated by historians. Presidents who were tall, came from small families, and had published many books were more likely to be great leaders. The other 97 characteristics, including personality traits, were not related to leadership effectiveness at all.

We should point out that different ways of analyzing these markers of presidential greatness can produce different results. Stewart McCann (1992) at the University College of Cape Breton analyzed the same data Simonton did, using slightly different statistical techniques. His conclusion was that personological factors do predict greatness—more so than Simonton's analysis would suggest. The variables that emerged as important in McCann's analysis were IQ, height, attractiveness, tidiness, and achievement drive. Specifically, great presidents tend to be smart, tall, not good-looking, messy, and achievement-oriented. However, even this list is rather short.

Leadership: The Right Person in the Right Situation   As you know by now, one of the most important tenets of social psychology is that to understand social behaviour, it is not enough to consider personality traits alone—we must take the social situation into account as well. The inadequacy of the great person theory does not mean that personal characteristics are irrelevant to good leadership. Instead, being good social psychologists, we should consider both the nature of the leader and the situation in which the leading takes place. This view of leadership states that it is not enough to be a great person; you have to be the right person at the right time in the right situation. For example, in McCann's analysis of U.S. presidents, the spirit of the times was found to make a difference. A president was more likely to be considered great if the American public was in a phase of idealism and trying to improve society than if it was in a phase of materialism and self-centred gratification.

Similarly, the relationship between prime ministerial greatness and integrative complexity varies, depending on the situation. Generally, when people are under stress, their level of integrative complexity decreases—it is harder to see other points of view, integrate them, and come up with complex solutions when in crisis mode. Peter Suedfeld and his colleagues made the discovery that great leaders show just the opposite pattern—they increase in integrative complexity during a crisis and then return to their usual level of complexity afterward (Ballard & Suedfeld, 1988; Suedfeld, Conway III, & Eichorn, 2001). Although Pierre Trudeau had the highest integrative complexity among Canadian PMs, according to the work of Suedfeld and colleagues, consider the example of Lester B. Pearson, Canada's prime minister from 1963 to 1968. During the Suez invasion in 1956, when he was a minister in the federal government, he managed to negotiate an end to the fighting—an achievement that earned him the 1957 Nobel Peace Prize. Moreover, he came up with the idea of United Nations peacekeeping and was instrumental in bringing it to fruition. Interestingly, Pearson's integrative complexity—as coded from speeches he made during that time—increased during the Suez crisis and then returned to its usual (still high) level once the crisis had ended. Situational factors—in this case, a crisis situation—influenced how the qualities of a leader were manifest.

A comprehensive theory of leadership therefore needs to focus on characteristics of the leader, his or her followers, and the situation (Hollander, 1958; House, 1971; Sternberg & Vroom, 2002). The best-known theory of this type is Fred Fiedler's (1967, 1978) **contingency theory of leadership**. According to Fiedler, there are two kinds of leaders: those who are **task-oriented** and those who are **relationship-oriented**. The task-oriented leader is concerned more with getting the job done than with the feelings of and relationships among the workers. The relationship-oriented leader is concerned primarily with the feelings of and relationships among the workers. Task-oriented leaders do well in *high control* work situations—situations in which the leader has excellent

▲ The great charisma of Pierre Elliott Trudeau contributed to his rise as fifteenth prime minister of Canada in 1968. Trudeau was also the Canadian prime minister with the highest integrative complexity (Suedfeld, Conway III, & Eichorn, 2001). Overall, however, there is surprisingly little evidence that traits such as charisma, dominance, and self-confidence predict who will become an effective leader.

contingency theory of leadership

the theory that leadership effectiveness depends both on how task-oriented or relationship-oriented the leader is, and on the amount of control and influence the leader has over the group

task-oriented leader

a leader who is concerned more with getting the job done than with the feelings of and relationships among the workers

relationship-oriented leader

a leader who is concerned primarily with the feelings of and relationships among the workers

FIGURE 8.5

Fiedler's contingency theory of leadership

According to Fiedler, task-oriented leaders perform best when situational control is high or low, whereas relationship-oriented leaders perform best when situational control is moderate.

(Fiedler 1967, 1978)

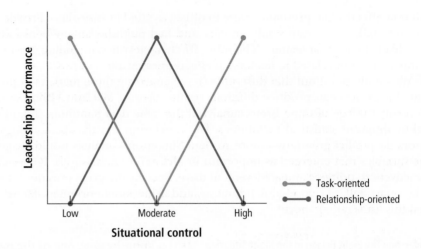

interpersonal relationships with subordinates, his or her position in the company is clearly perceived as powerful, and the work to be done by the group is structured and well defined. They also do well in *low control* work situations— situations in which the leader has poor relationships with subordinates and the work to be done is not clearly defined. When situational control is very high, people are happy, everything is running smoothly, and there is no need to worry about people's feelings and relationships. The leader who pays attention only to the task will get the most accomplished. When situational control is very low, the task-oriented leader is best at taking charge and imposing some order on a confusing, ill-defined work environment. Relationship-oriented leaders, however, are most effective in situations that are *moderate control* work situations.

Under these conditions, the wheels are turning fairly smoothly but some attention to the squeakiness caused by poor relationships and hurt feelings is needed. The leader who can soothe such feelings will be most successful (see Figure 8.5).

The contingency theory of leadership has been supported in studies of numerous types of leaders, including business managers, college administrators, military commanders, and postmasters (Chemers, 2000; Peters, Hartke, & Pohlmann, 1985; Schriesheim, Tepper, & Tetrault, 1994; Van Vugt & De Cremer, 1999).

> *Leadership cannot really be taught. It can only be learned.*
>
> —Harold Geneen, 1984

Gender and Leadership An old adage says that because of sex discrimination, a woman has to be "twice as good as a man" in order to advance. Unfortunately, there do seem to be differences in the ways that female and male leaders are evaluated (Biernat, Crandall, Young, Kobrynowicz, & Halpin, 1998). If a woman's style of leadership is stereotypically "masculine" (e.g., autocratic, "bossy," and task-oriented), she is evaluated more negatively than are men who have the same style (Eagly & Carli, 2003; Eagly, Makhijani, & Klonsky, 1992). This is especially true if men are doing the evaluating. In one study, for example, researchers instructed male and female accomplices to assume leadership roles in groups of students attempting to solve a business problem (Butler & Geis, 1990). Both the male and female leaders were assertive but cordial, taking charge of the group discussion. How did the other members of the group react to these assertive leaders? The results were discouraging. When a man took charge of the group and acted assertively, the group members reacted favourably. When a woman acted in the same fashion, the group members— especially the males—reacted much more negatively. It appears that many men are uncomfortable with women who use the leadership techniques that men typically use.

> *I wonder men dare trust themselves with men.*
>
> —William Shakespeare, Timon of Athens, 1600–1608

As more and more women enter the workforce, perhaps they are experiencing less bias. But stereotypes change slowly, and it is still the case that women are expected to be more *communal* (i.e., concerned with the welfare of others, warm, helpful, kind, affectionate) and men are expected to be more *agentic* (i.e., assertive, controlling, dominant, independent, self-confident). Do these gender roles influence how women are perceived in leadership roles? To find out, Alice Eagly and her colleagues have undertaken several reviews of the literature on gender and leadership (Carli & Eagly, 1999; Eagly & Karau, 2002; Eagly, Karau, & Makhijani, 1995; Eagly, Johannesen-Schmidt, & van Engen, 2003). The bad news is that there are two forms of prejudice against women. First, if women behave in the way they are "supposed" to behave according to societal norms—namely, in a communal fashion—they are often perceived as having less leadership potential. This is because people typically expect successful leaders to be more agentic than communal, especially in high-powered positions such as the head of a large corporation or the leader of a country. Second, once women become leaders, they are evaluated more negatively than men when they exhibit agentic leadership behaviour, again because these behaviours are contrary to how women are "supposed" to behave.

Thus, there is a double bind for women. If they conform to societal expectations about how they ought to behave, by being warm and communal, they are often perceived to have low leadership potential. If they succeed in attaining a leadership position and act in ways that leaders are expected to act—namely, in agentic, forceful ways, they are often perceived negatively for not acting as a woman "should." This double bind was vividly illustrated in the 2008 U.S. Democratic presidential race. Presidential candidate Hilary Clinton was frequently criticized for being cold and aloof. When she shed tears during a media interview in the midst of her gruelling campaign schedule, some commentators accused her of being too emotional and questioned whether she had what it took to be president of the United States. Others accused her of manufacturing the tears to combat her "ice queen" image. In commenting on this, Kim Campbell, who in 1993 served as Canada's only female prime minister, remarked that women in leadership are in a lose-lose situation: "Damned if you do, and damned if you don't." She went on to say, "It's a real risk for a woman to show emotion. . . . But if you don't, you'll be attacked for not caring enough" (Panetta, 2008). The conundrum that Campbell describes might help explain why there is a shortage of women in leadership roles in North America. In Canada, women make up 46.7 percent of the workforce (Canada, 2001) and 58 percent of all people who hold university degrees. (It may interest you to know that in psychology, 70 percent of the doctorates are awarded to women.) However, according to a survey conducted by the Canadian Association for University Teachers, women are still under-represented in academic positions, particularly at the senior level. For example, only 18 percent of full professors at Canadian universities are women (CAUT Bulletin, 2006). The percentage of women leaders is even lower when one examines non-academic occupations. In the United States, for example, fewer than 1 percent of the CEOs of *Fortune 500* companies are women, and only 4 percent of the top managers of these companies are women (Eagly & Karau, 2002).

The better news is that prejudice toward women leaders appears to be lessening. In a Gallup poll conducted in 1953, 63 percent of the people interviewed said that they preferred a man as a boss, 5 percent preferred a woman, and 25 percent had no preference. In a similar poll conducted in 2002, 32 percent preferred a man as a boss, 19 percent preferred a woman, and 49 percent stated that they had no preference (Eagly & Karau, 2002). Further, there is some evidence that people are becoming more accepting of women who act in stereotypical "male" ways (Twenge, 1997) and that there is a growing recognition that effective leaders must be able to act in stereotypical female (communal) ways as well as stereotypical male (agentic) ways (Eagly & Karau, 2002). Kim Campbell puts it this way: "Neither sex

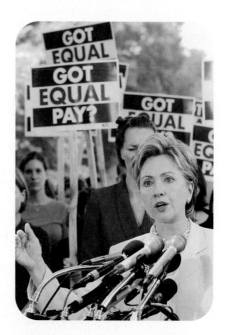

▲ Research shows that women seeking leadership roles can find themselves in a double-bind. If they conform to society's expectations about how they ought to behave, by being warm and communal, they are often perceived to have low leadership potential. If they become leaders and act in ways that leaders are expected to act, namely in agentic, forceful ways, they are often perceived negatively for not "acting like a woman should."

has a monopoly on these qualities. There are more differences within the sexes than between them. . . . You just have to let people do the job so that you begin to change your mind about . . . what a president of the United States looks like, and what a prime minister of Canada looks like" (Panetta, 2008).

Conflict and Cooperation

▲ Sometimes, people are able to resolve conflicts peacefully, such as a couple that has an amicable divorce. Other times conflicts escalate into rancour and violence. Social psychologists have performed experiments to test ways in which conflict resolution is most likely to occur.

We have just examined how people work together to make decisions; in these situations, group members have a common goal. Often, however, people have incompatible goals, placing them in conflict. This can be true of two individuals such as romantic partners who disagree about who should clean the kitchen, or two groups such as a labour union and company management who disagree over wages and working conditions. It can also be true of two nations, as in the case of the long-standing conflict between Israel and its Arab neighbours, or between peoples, as with the Shiites, Sunnis, and Kurds in Iraq. The opportunity for interpersonal conflict exists whenever two or more people interact. Sigmund Freud (1930) went so far as to argue that conflict is an inevitable by-product of civilization because the goals and needs of individuals often clash with the goals and needs of their fellow human beings. The nature of conflict and how it can be resolved has been the topic of a great deal of social psychological research (Deutsch, 1973; Levine & Thompson, 1996; Pruitt, 1998; Thibaut & Kelley, 1959).

Many conflicts are resolved peacefully, with little rancour. Couples can sometimes find a way to resolve their differences in a mutually acceptable manner, and labour disputes are sometimes settled with a friendly handshake. All too often, however, conflict erupts into open hostility. People may resort to violence to resolve their differences, as the murder rate in our country attests. Warfare between nations remains an all-too-common solution to international disputes. In fact, when wars over the past five centuries are examined, the twentieth century ranks first in the severity of wars—defined as the number of deaths per war—and ranks second in their frequency (Levy & Morgan, 1984). It is, therefore, of great importance to find ways to resolve conflicts peacefully.

Social Dilemmas

social dilemma

a conflict in which the most beneficial action for an individual, if chosen by most people, will have harmful effects on everyone

What is best for individuals is not always best for the group as a whole. Consider a recent publishing venture by the novelist Stephen King. He wrote two installments of a novel called *The Plant* and posted them on the internet, asking his readers to pay US$1 per installment. The deal he offered was simple: If at least 75 percent of the people who downloaded the installments paid the fee, he would keep writing and posting new installments. If fewer than 75 percent of the people paid up, he would stop writing, and no one would get the rest of the novel. King devised a classic **social dilemma**, a conflict in which the most beneficial action for an individual, if chosen by most people, will have harmful effects on everyone (Weber, Kopelman, & Messick, 2004). It was to any individual's financial advantage to download King's novel free of charge and let other people pay. If too many people took this approach, however, everyone would lose, because King said he would stop writing the novel. At first, people acted for the good of all; more than 75 percent paid for the first installment. As with many social dilemmas, however, people eventually acted in their own self-interest, to the detriment of all. The number of people who paid for their later installments dropped below 75 percent, and King stopped posting new ones, saying on his website that the book was "on hiatus."

One of the most common social dilemmas is illustrated by a game called the Prisoner's Dilemma. In this game, two people have to choose one of two options without knowing what the other person will choose. However, the number of points they win depends on the options chosen by both people. Suppose, for example, that you were playing the game with a friend. As shown in the accompanying Try It! you have to choose option X or option Y without knowing which option your friend will choose. Your payoff—the amount of money you win or lose—depends on the choices of both you and your friend. For instance, if both you and your friend choose option X, you both win $3. If, however, you choose option Y and your friend chooses option X, you win $6 and your friend loses $6. Which option would you choose? Many people begin by choosing Y. At worst, you will lose $1; at best, you will win the highest possible amount, $6. Choosing option X raises the possibility that both sides will win some money, but this is also a risky choice. If your partner chooses Y while you choose X, you stand to lose a great deal. Because people do not know how much they can trust their opponent, option Y frequently seems like the safest choice (Rapoport & Chammah, 1965). The rub is that both players will probably think this way, ensuring that both sides lose (see the lower right corner of the diagram in the Try It! box).

People's actions in these games seem to mirror many conflicts in everyday life. To find a solution that is desirable to both parties, people must trust each other. Often, they do not, and this lack of trust leads to an escalating series of competitive moves, so that in the end no one wins (Batson & Ahmad, 2001; Insko & Schopler, 1998; Kelley & Thibaut, 1978; Pruitt, 1998). Two countries locked in an arms race may feel that they cannot afford to disarm, out of fear that the other side will take advantage of their weakened position. The result is that both sides add furiously to their stockpile of weapons, neither side gaining superiority over the other and both spending money they could better use to solve domestic

Try it!

▶ The Prisoner's Dilemma

	Your Options	
Your Friend's Options	**Option X**	**Option Y**
Option X	You win $3 Your friend wins $3	You win $6 Your friend loses $6
Option Y	You lose $6 Your friend wins $6	You lose $1 Your friend loses $1

Instructions: Play this version of the Prisoner's Dilemma game with a friend. First, show the table above to your friend and explain how the game works. On each trial of the game, you and your friend can choose option X or option Y, without knowing what the other will choose. You should each write your choice on a folded piece of paper, both of which are then opened at the same time. The numbers in the table represent imaginary money that you and your friend win or lose on each trial. For example, if you choose option X on the first trial and your friend chooses option Y, you lose an imaginary $6 and your friend wins an imaginary $6. If both of you choose option Y, you both lose an imaginary $1. Play the game for 10 trials and keep track of how much "money" each of you wins or loses. Did you and your friend choose the cooperative option (option X) or the competitive option (option Y) more often? Why? Did a pattern of trust or mistrust develop over the course of the game?

problems (Deutsch, 1973). Such an escalation of conflict is also seen among couples who are divorcing. Sometimes, the goal seems to be to hurt the other person rather than to further one's own or the children's needs. In the end, both suffer because, metaphorically speaking, both partners choose option Y too often.

Increasing Cooperation in the Prisoner's Dilemma　Such escalating conflict, though common, is not inevitable. Many studies have found that when people play a Prisoner's Dilemma game they will under certain conditions adopt the more cooperative response (option X), ensuring that both sides end up with a positive outcome. Not surprisingly, if people are playing the game with a friend or if they expect to interact with their partner in the future, they are more likely to adopt a cooperative strategy that maximizes both their own profits and those of their partner (Pruitt & Kimmel, 1977). In addition, growing up in some societies, such as Asian cultures, seems to foster a more cooperative orientation than growing up in the West does (Bonta, 1997; Markus & Kitayama, 1991). In a recent study conducted with Chinese students in Hong Kong, it was found that showing symbols of Chinese culture before the game (e.g., a Chinese dragon) made people more cooperative, whereas showing them symbols of Western culture (e.g., an American flag) made them more competitive (Wong & Hong, 2005).

Even playing the game with a small, rather than a large, group increases the chances of cooperation, as demonstrated in a study by Gerard Seijts at the University of Manitoba and Gary Latham at the University of Toronto (Seijts & Latham, 2000). Participants in this study were told that they could invest money in either a personal account or a joint account. Any money placed in the joint account would be doubled and divided equally among the group members. This is a classic dilemma because you can make the most money if you put your money in a personal account and then benefit from the money others have put into the joint account. However, if everyone in the group adopts this strategy, it will not be very profitable. The greatest earnings result when the group adopts a cooperative strategy and everyone invests all of their money in the joint account. Seijts and Latham found that participants in three-person groups were more cooperative than participants in seven-person groups and, as a result, made more money. Members of seven-person groups were more likely to focus on maximizing their own gains rather than those of the group.

Finally, to increase cooperation, you can also try the **tit-for-tat strategy**—which is a way of encouraging cooperation by at first acting cooperatively but then always responding the way your opponent did (cooperatively or competitively) on the previous trial. This strategy communicates a willingness to cooperate as well as an unwillingness to sit back and be exploited if the partner does not cooperate. The tit-for-tat strategy is usually successful in getting the other person to respond with the cooperative trusting response (Axelrod, 1984; Messick & Liebrand, 1995; Parks & Rumble, 2001; Sheldon, 1999; Van Lange, Ouwerkerk, & Tazelaar, 2002). The analogy to the arms race would be to match not only any military buildup made by an unfriendly nation but also any conciliatory gesture, such as a ban on nuclear testing.

tit-for-tat strategy
a means of encouraging cooperation by at first acting cooperatively but then always responding the way your opponent did on the previous trial (i.e., cooperatively or competitively)

My own belief is that Russian and Chinese behavior is as much influenced by suspicion of our intentions as ours is by suspicion of theirs. This would mean that we have great influence over their behavior—that by treating them as hostile, we assure their hostility.

—J. William Fulbright (1905–1995)

Using Threats to Resolve Conflict

When caught in a conflict, many of us are tempted to use threats to get the other party to cave in to our wishes, believing that we should, in the words of Teddy Roosevelt, "speak softly and carry a big stick." Parents commonly use threats to get their children to behave, and teachers often threaten their students with demerits or a visit to the principal. Threats are often used on an international scale, as well, to further the interests of one nation over another (Turner & Horvitz, 2001).

The Deutsch and Krauss trucking game

FIGURE 8.6

The trucking game

Participants play the role as head of either Acme Trucking Company or Bolt Trucking Company. In order to earn money, they have to drive their trucks from the starting point to their destination as quickly as possible. The quickest route is the one-lane road, but both trucks cannot travel on this road at the same time. In some versions of the studies, participants were given gates that they used to block the other's progress on the one-lane road.

(Adapted from Deutsch & Krauss, 1960)

A classic series of studies by Morton Deutsch and Robert Krauss (1960, 1962) indicates that threats are not an effective means of reducing conflict. These researchers developed a game in which two participants imagined they were in charge of trucking companies, one named Acme and one named Bolt. The goal of each company was to transport merchandise as quickly as possible to a destination. The participants were paid 60 cents for each "trip" but had 1 cent subtracted for every second it took them to make the trip. The most direct route for each company was over a one-lane road, on which only one truck could travel at a time. This placed the two companies in direct conflict, as seen in Figure 8.6. If Acme and Bolt both tried to take the one-lane road, neither truck could pass and both would lose money. Each company could take an alternative route, but this was much longer, guaranteeing that they would lose at least 10 cents on each trial. The game lasted until each side had made 20 trips. How did the participants respond to this dilemma? After a while, most of them worked out a solution that allowed both trucks to make a modest amount of money. They took turns, one waiting until the other person crossed the one-lane road; then they would take that route as well.

In another version of the study, the researchers gave Acme a gate that could be lowered over the one-lane road, thereby blocking Bolt from using that route with a unilateral threat condition. You might think that using force—the gate—would increase Acme's profits, because all Acme had to do was threaten Bolt to "stay off the one-lane road or else." In fact, quite the opposite happened. When one side had the gate, both participants lost more than when neither side had the gate—as seen in the left panel of Figure 8.7 on the next page. This figure shows the total amount earned or lost by both sides. The Acme participants won slightly more than the Bolt participants when they had the gate but won substantially more when neither side had a gate. The Bolt participants did not like to be threatened and often retaliated by parking their truck on the one-lane road, blocking the other truck's progress. Meanwhile, the seconds ticked away and both sides lost money.

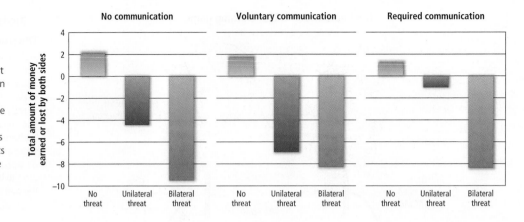

FIGURE 8.7

Results of the trucking game studies

The left panel shows the total amount of money the participants made when they could not communicate. When threats were introduced by giving one or both sides a gate, both sides lost more money. The middle panel shows the amount of money the participants made when they could communicate as little or as much as they wanted. Once again, giving them each a gate reduced the amount of money they made. The right panel shows the amount of money the participants made when they were required to communicate on every trial. Once again, giving them each a gate reduced their winnings.

(Adapted from Deutsch & Krauss, 1962)

What would happen if the situation were more equitable, with both sides having a gate? Surely, they would learn to cooperate very quickly, recognizing the stalemate that would ensue if both of them used their gate. To the contrary, both sides lost more money in the bilateral threat condition than in any of the other conditions (as you can see in the left panel of Figure 8.7). The owners of the trucking companies both threatened to use their gate and did so with great frequency. Once Acme used the gate to block Bolt, Bolt retaliated and blocked Acme the next time its truck came down the road—producing a stalemate that was not in either of their interests. Sound familiar? For several decades, the United States and the former Soviet Union were locked in an escalating nuclear arms race, each threatening the other with destruction. Sadly, similar conflicts exist in the world today, such as the arms race in India and Pakistan. Each country is stockpiling weapons (including nuclear warheads) to protect itself from the other.

Effects of Communication   There is a way in which the trucking game does not approximate real life—namely, that the two sides were not allowed to communicate with each other. Would the two adversaries work out their differences if they could talk them over? To find out, Deutsch and Krauss ran a version of their study in which the participants could communicate over an intercom. In one condition, the participants were allowed to speak as often or as little as they liked. As seen in Figure 8.7, this communication had very little effect (compare the middle panel with the left panel). Interestingly, people chose not to say much to each other in this condition, communicating on only about 5 of the 20 trials.

In another condition, the researchers decided to require the participants to communicate on every trial. Surely, if people were forced to talk to each other, they would cooperate more. But, again, no dramatic increase in profits occurred (see the right panel of Figure 8.7). Making people communicate reduced losses somewhat when Acme alone had the gate (the unilateral threat condition) but failed to increase cooperation in either of the two other conditions (no threat, bilateral threat). Overall, requiring people to communicate did not raise profits dramatically. Why not?

The problem with the communication in the trucking studies is that it did not foster trust. In fact, people used the intercom to convey threats. In a later version of their trucking study, Krauss and Deutsch specifically instructed people in how to communicate, telling them to work out a solution that was fair to both parties—one they would be willing to accept if they were in the other person's shoes. Under these conditions, verbal communication increased the amount of money both sides made, because it fostered trust instead of adding fuel to the competitive fires (Deutsch, 1973, 1990; Kerr & Kaufman-Gilliland, 1994; Krauss & Deutsch, 1966; Pruitt, 1998).

In the decades that have passed since the original trucking game studies were conducted, there has been a proliferation of electronic communication such as email, instant messaging, text messaging, and video-conferencing. Does the mode of communication affect the development of trust? According to a recent meta analysis, it does. Stuhlmacher and Citera (2005) found that negotiations conducted over electronic media were more hostile, and resulted in lower profits, than old-fashioned face-to-face negotiations. Electronic communication has many advantages, of course, but a down side is that it is harder to get to know people and learn to trust them.

Negotiation and Bargaining

In the laboratory games we have discussed so far, people's options are limited. They have to choose option X or Y in the Prisoner's Dilemma, and they have only a couple of ways of getting their truck to its destination in the trucking game. In everyday life, people often have a wide array of options. Consider two people haggling over the price of a car. Either the buyer or the seller can give in to all of the other's demands, to some of them, or to none of them; either party can walk away from the deal at any time. Given that there is considerable latitude in how people can resolve the conflict, communication between the parties is all the more important. By talking, bargaining, and negotiating, people can arrive at a satisfactory settlement. **Negotiation** is defined as a form of communication between opposing sides in a conflict, in which offers and counter-offers are made and a solution occurs only when both parties agree (DeDreu, Weingart, & Kwon, 2000; Galinsky, Mussweiler, & Medvec, 2002; Thompson, 2005). How successful are people at negotiating mutually beneficial solutions?

negotiation

a form of communication between opposing sides in a conflict, in which offers and counteroffers are made and a solution occurs only when both parties agree

One limit to successful negotiation is that people often assume they are locked in a conflict in which only one party can come out ahead. They don't realize that solutions favourable to both parties are available. A couple getting a divorce, for example, might lock horns and find it impossible to reach a financial settlement, until they realize that they have different priorities. Perhaps it is most important to one person to keep the furniture and the season tickets to the opera, whereas the other might want the china and the art collection. This type of compromise, called an **integrative solution**, is an outcome in which the parties in a conflict make trade-offs on issues according to their different interests; each side concedes the most on issues that are unimportant to it but important to the other side.

integrative solution

a solution to a conflict whereby the parties make trade-offs on issues according to their different interests; each side concedes the most on issues that are unimportant to it but important to the other side

It might seem that such integrative solutions would be relatively easy to achieve. After all, the two parties simply have to sit down and figure out which issues are most important to each. However, people often find it difficult to identify integrative solutions (Hoffman et al., 1999; Thompson, 1997). One barrier is a tendency for us to assume that what is important to us is obvious to everyone—including our opponent. However, this assumption is not necessarily warranted, as demonstrated in a study by Vorauer and Claude (1998). These researchers had students at the University of Manitoba participate in negotiation sessions; others observed the sessions. When later questioned, negotiators assumed that it was obvious what their goals had been during the interaction. This was especially true for negotiators who had been asked to reflect on their goals before entering the negotiation—probably a common occurrence in real-life negotiation situations. Importantly, even though negotiators believed that their goals were obvious, observers were no better than chance at identifying these goals.

If uninvolved outside observers are unable to tell what is important to us, chances are that those with whom we are engaged in conflict will be even less able to do so. Indeed, there is evidence that the more people have at stake in a negotiation, the more biased are their perceptions of their opponent. They will tend to distrust proposals made by the other side and to overlook interests they have in common (O'Connor & Carnevale, 1997; Ross & Ward, 1995, 1996). This

► Former prime minister Paul Martin, Canadian Assembly of First Nations chief Phil Fontaine, and other government and aboriginal leaders sign the Kelowna Accord in 2005. The accord designated funding to improve the employment, living conditions, and education of aboriginal peoples. The accord was heralded by aboriginal leaders because it involved a process of consultation and cooperation that brought federal government leaders, provincial ministers, territorial leaders, and aboriginal leaders to the table. (Paul Martin's Liberal Party subsequently lost the election. Prime Minister Stephen Harper's Conservative Party has not implemented the accord, despite calls from aboriginal leaders to do so.)

> *Yet there remains another wall. This wall constitutes a psychological barrier between us, . . . [a] barrier of distorted and eroded interpretation of every event and statement. . . . I ask, why don't we stretch our hands with faith and sincerity so that together we might destroy this barrier?*
>
> —Former Egyptian president Anwar al-Sadat, speaking before the Israeli Knesset, 1977

is one reason why people often use neutral mediators to solve labour disputes, legal battles, and divorce proceedings. Mediators are often in a better position to recognize that there are mutually agreeable solutions to a conflict (Carnevale, 1986; Kressel & Pruitt, 1989; Ross & La Croix, 1996).

As you might expect, culture plays a role in preferred conflict resolution strategies. For example, Gire (1997) conducted a study in which participants from a collectivist culture (Nigeria) and an individualist culture (Canada) read a scenario involving a dispute between neighbours. Nigerian participants expressed a greater preference for negotiation than did the Canadian participants.

The bottom line? When you are negotiating with someone, it is important to keep in mind that integrative solutions are often possible. Try to gain the other side's trust and communicate your own interests in an open manner. Remember that the way you construe the situation is not necessarily the same as the way the other party construes the situation. You may well discover that the other side communicates its interests more freely as a result, increasing the likelihood that you will find a solution beneficial to both parties.

SUMMARY

A **group** consists of two or more people who interact with each other and are interdependent, in the sense that their needs and goals cause them to influence each other. Groups have a number of benefits; in fact, there may be an innate need to belong that drives us to establish bonds with other people. Groups tend to consist of members who are similar to one another, in part

because groups have *social norms* that people are expected to obey. Groups have well-defined **social roles**—shared expectations about how people are supposed to behave. The roles that people assume in groups, and the expectations that come with those roles, are powerful determinants of people's feelings and behaviours in groups. **Group cohesiveness**, qualities of a group that bind members together and promote liking between members, is another important property of groups that influences the group's performance.

Simply being in the presence of other people has a number of interesting effects. When people's individual efforts on a task can be evaluated, the mere presence of others leads to **social facilitation**: Their performance is enhanced on simple tasks but impaired on complex tasks. When their individual efforts cannot be evaluated, the mere presence of others leads to **social loafing**: Performance is impaired on simple tasks but enhanced on complex tasks. Finally, the mere presence of others can lead to **deindividuation**, which is the loosening of normal constraints on behaviour when people are in groups, leading to an increase in impulsive and deviant acts.

One of the major functions of groups is to make decisions. Are groups better or worse than individuals at making decisions? It turns out that groups make better decisions than individuals if they are good at pooling ideas and listening to the expert members of the group. Often, however, **process loss** occurs, whereby the most expert individual is unable to sway the rest of the group. Further, groups often focus on the information they have in common and fail to share unique information. This latter problem can be avoided if the group knows that individual members have been assigned to specific areas of expertise. Many couples know that one member is responsible for remembering things the other is not responsible for. Consequently, they have an effective **transactive memory**, which is the combined memory of two people that is more efficient than the memory of either individual alone.

Tightly knit, cohesive groups are also prone to **groupthink**, a phenomenon in which maintaining group cohesiveness and solidarity is more important than considering the facts in a realistic manner. **Group polarization** indicates that groups are also prone to make more extreme decisions in the direction toward which its members were initially leaning; these group decisions can be more risky or more cautious, depending on the group members' initial inclinations.

Leaders usually play crucial roles in group decisions. There is little support for the **great person theory**, which argues that good leadership is purely a matter of having the right personality traits. Leadership effectiveness is a function of both the kind of person a leader is and the nature of the situation. Research on Fiedler's **contingency theory of leadership** has found that leadership performance depends on whether a group has a **task-oriented leader** or a **relationship-oriented leader** and on whether the work environment is high or low in situational control. There is a double bind for women leaders: If they conform to societal expectations about how they ought to behave—namely, being warm and communal—they are often perceived as having low leadership potential. If they succeed in attaining a leadership position and act in ways that leaders are expected to act—namely, in agentic, forceful ways—they are often perceived negatively for not acting as a woman "should."

Often people have incompatible goals, which places them in conflict with each other. A particularly interesting kind of conflict is a **social dilemma**, in which the most beneficial action for an individual, if chosen by most people, will have harmful effects on everyone. A commonly studied social dilemma is the Prisoner's Dilemma, in which two people must decide whether to look out for only their own interests or for their partner's interests as well. The **tit-for-tat strategy** is a useful way of dealing with conflict, allowing one to respond cooperatively or competitively, given the other person's response. Creating trust is crucial in solving this kind of conflict.

Finally, we examined the conditions under which hostilities are likely to increase or decrease, including how the use of threats and the inability to communicate can exacerbate a conflict. In **negotiation**, it is important to look for an **integrative solution**, whereby each side concedes the most on issues that are unimportant to it but important to its adversary.

PEARSON
mypsych lab

Along with a dynamic, electronic version of this text, MyPsychLab offers a wealth of resources to deepen your understanding and test your recall of the material in this chapter—including video and audio clips, simulations and activities, self-assessments, practice tests, and other study materials. The following specific resources are available for this chapter:

 Social Facilitation

 We versus They: Robert Cialdini

 The Stanford Prison Experiment

To access MyPsychLab, please visit www.mypsychlab.com (Student Access Code required—packaged with this book).

Interpersonal Attraction:
From First Impressions to Close Relationships

"Then I met Nina." These four little words changed a man's life. A few years ago, Bradley Bird, a Canadian newspaper writer in his early forties, was on a trip, covering a series of sad, dark events—the experiences of Chechen refugees and conflict in Kosovo and Kurdish Turkey. As he wearily boarded a bus in Georgia (in the Caucasus region near Russia), bracing himself for the 20-hour ride to northeast Turkey for one last story, a woman took the seat beside him. She was a tall, attractive, raven-haired woman in her thirties. As the bus headed into the night, the woman turned to him and asked his name. Bradley recalls, "I looked at her seriously for the first time and was pleased to see a face as lovely as I'd ever beheld, with dark mysterious eyes, a perfect nose, and full red lips" (Bird, 2001). The woman's name was Nina. To Bradley's surprise, he found himself asking her if there was a man in her life. She answered, "No." He surprised himself still more by saying, "You need me, and I need you." Because she said she spoke only a little English, he repeated it to make sure she understood. She smiled, and they gazed into each other's eyes. It was midnight and the driver turned off the interior lights. Her arm brushed against his in the darkness. "The sensation was incredible," Bradley exclaims, "electric, and I couldn't stop myself; I gave her arm a gentle squeeze." Nina reciprocated.

At first they tried to hide their feelings from the other passengers, but 12 hours into the ride, they were unable to contain their joy. Bradley informed the driver that his plans had changed and he would now stay on the bus an additional 13 hours so he could have more time with Nina. The driver and passengers began to celebrate with them. An older, heavy man brought out a bottle of vodka to mark the occasion. Bradley reports that by then, he and Nina were inseparable and began to make plans for her to come to Canada. He begged to accompany her to Sofia, Bulgaria, where she was going to visit her sister, but she refused. So he got off the bus in Istanbul. Instead of flying home as scheduled, he waited there for three weeks, hoping to catch Nina on her way back to Georgia. During that time, he tried to reach Nina at her sister's, but the phone number she had given him didn't work.

Reluctantly, he returned home and mailed her the documents she would need to get a visa. It was May.

Nina wrote back, assuring Bradley of her desire to be with him. She also told him that he would have to return to Turkey and plead her case to the Canadian embassy there. By this time, it was August, and Bradley had accepted a teaching position. What to do now? The answer was clear. Bradley promptly quit his job and spent the next few months trying to reach Nina to make arrangements for them to meet in Turkey. The phone lines were always busy or not working. In December, he decided he simply had to take action. He booked a flight to Turkey and two tickets to return to Canada. He managed to track down Nina's sister in Bulgaria and asked her to let Nina know that he was coming. "Oh, Bradley," she said, "Nina is back with her husband. Her daughter insisted on it." With those words, Bradley's dream of a life with Nina was shattered. But Bradley Bird isn't bitter. In his words, "I will always be grateful to Nina for giving me 33 of the happiest hours of my adult life" (Bird, 2001).

As Bradley Bird's experience illustrates, the need to love and be loved is one of the most fundamental human needs. Despite all of the warning signs—the fact that he had just met this woman and knew nothing about her, and had been given the wrong phone number for her sister in Bulgaria—Bradley just couldn't help himself. He fell in love with the mysterious Nina, and it changed his life. This man in his forties, who had experienced other relationships (he was once married), describes the bus ride with Nina as the happiest 33 hours of his adult life!

What, exactly, is love, and why are we so motivated to seek it? Or perhaps the question should be, why are we so motivated to seek it even when it comes at a high cost? Research conducted by Susan Boon and Karen Pasveer (1999) at the University of Calgary suggests that people are well aware of the risks associated with relationships. One of their research participants, a 26-year-old woman, wrote:

> Some of my friends who aren't in relationships are dying to get into one. I don't understand why because most of the time it's a more hurtful than it is an enjoyable experience. I told them, "Enjoy being single because it's more fun and I think it's a lot less hassle." Getting into a relationship . . . falling for somebody, and you're bound to set yourself up for a lot of hurt . . . and misery."

Despite the potential for hurt and misery, most people are highly motivated to find love. Why? This is one of the basic questions to be addressed in this chapter.

We will discuss the antecedents of attraction, from the initial liking of two people meeting for the first time to the love that develops in close relationships. We will also discuss how people maintain relationships once they have been formed, as well as the processes whereby relationships end. As we discuss this research, you may want to think about how you can put these social psychological findings to good use in your own life—although we can't guarantee that a thorough reading of this chapter will save you from completely rearranging your life because of a chance meeting with a gorgeous, mysterious stranger on a bus.

Major Antecedents of Attraction

When social psychologist Ellen Berscheid asked people of various ages what made them happy, at or near the top of their lists were making and maintaining friendships and having positive, warm relationships (Berscheid, 1985; Berscheid & Peplau, 1983; Berscheid & Reis, 1998). According to Arthur Aron and Elaine Aron, a central human motivation is self-expansion—the desire to overlap or blend with another person, so that you have access to that person's knowledge, insights, and experiences. By incorporating the other into yourself, you acquire new resources and deepen your own experience of life (Aron & Aron, 1986b; Aron, Mashek, & Aron, 2004; Aron, Fisher, Strong, Acevedo, Riela, & Tsapelas, 2008; Rempel & Burris, 2006). The absence of meaningful relationships with other people makes people feel lonely, worthless, hopeless, helpless, powerless, and alienated (Baumeister & Leary, 1995; Hartup & Stevens, 1997; Peplau & Perlman, 1982; Stroebe & Stroebe, 1996). We start this chapter with research on what attracts people to one another in the first place.

The Person Next Door: The Propinquity Effect

One of the simplest determinants of interpersonal attraction is proximity. The people who, by chance, you see and interact with most often are most likely to become your friends and lovers (Berscheid & Reis, 1998; Fehr, 1996; Moreland & Beach, 1992; Newcomb, 1961; Tsai, 2006). This includes people in your city, your neighbourhood, and on your street. Now, this might seem obvious. However, the striking thing about proximity and attraction, or the **propinquity effect** as social psychologists call it, is that it works on a micro level.

Consider a classic study conducted in a housing complex for married students at the Massachusetts Institute of Technology (MIT). Leon Festinger, Stanley Schachter, and Kurt Back (1950) tracked friendship formation among the couples in the various apartment buildings. For example, one section of the complex, Westgate West, consisted of 17 two-storey buildings, each having 10 apartments. The residents had been assigned to their apartments at random as vacancies opened up, and nearly all of them were strangers when they moved in. The researchers asked the residents to name their three closest friends in the housing project. Just as the propinquity effect would predict, 65 percent of the residents mentioned

> ❝ *Contrary to popular belief, I do not believe that friends are necessarily the people you like best; they are merely the people who got there first.* ❞
>
> —Sir Peter Ustinov, Dear Me, 1977

propinquity effect

the finding that the more we see and interact with people, the more likely they are to become our friends

FIGURE 9.1

The floor plan of a Westgate West building

All of the buildings in the MIT housing complex had the same floor plan.

(Adapted from Festinger, Schachter, & Back, 1950)

people who lived in the same building, even though the other buildings were not far away. Even more striking was the pattern of friendships within a building. Each Westgate West building was designed as shown in the drawing in Figure 9.1. The researchers found that 41 percent of the next-door neighbours indicated that they were close friends, 22 percent of those who lived two doors apart did so, and only 10 percent of those who lived on opposite ends of the hall did so.

Festinger and colleagues (1950) demonstrated that attraction and propinquity rely not only on actual physical distance but also on the more psychological, functional distance. *Functional distance* is defined as certain aspects of architectural design that make it likely that some people will come into contact with each other more often than with others. For example, consider the friendship choices of residents of apartments 1 and 5 in Figure 9.1. Couples living at the foot of the stairs, and in one case near the mailboxes, saw a great deal of upstairs residents. Sure enough, residents in apartments 1 and 5 throughout the complex had more friends upstairs than did dwellers in the other first-floor apartments. (You can map out propinquity effects in your life with the accompanying Try It! exercise.)

Try it!

▶ Mapping the Propinquity Effect in Your Life

In this exercise, you will examine the relationship between who your friends and acquaintances are and the place(s) where you spend time regularly. Does the propinquity effect explain who your friends are?

First, pick a physical space to focus on. You could choose your dormitory, apartment building, or the building in which you work. (We'll use a dormitory as an example.) Draw a rough floor plan of your dormitory. (You can decide whether you need to draw just your floor or more of the building.) Include the location of all dorm room doors, the stairs or elevator, and so on. Mark your room with a large X.

Second, think about who your close friends are on the floor; mark each of their rooms on your drawing with the number 1. Next, think about who your other friends are; mark each of their rooms with the number 2. Finally, think about your acquaintances, people you say hello to or chat with briefly now and then; mark each of their rooms with the number 3.

Now, examine the pattern of friendships on your drawing. Are your friends clustered near your room in physical space? Are the

rooms with numbers 1 and 2 among the closest to your room in physical space? Are they physically closer to your room than the ones with number 3? And what about the rooms that didn't get a number (meaning that you don't really know these people or interact with them)—are these rooms the farthest from yours?

Finally, examine your "propinquity map" for the presence of functional distance. Do aspects of the architectural design of your dorm or building make you more likely to cross paths with some residents than others? For example, the location of the bathroom, kitchen, living room, stairs or elevator, and mailboxes can play an important role in propinquity and friendship formation. These are all places you go to frequently; when walking to and from them, you pass some people's dorm rooms but not others'. Are the people who live along your path the ones you know best? If so, propinquity has played a big role in determining the people with whom you have formed relationships!

◄ Close friendships are often formed in university, in part because of propinquity.

The propinquity effect works because of familiarity, or the **mere exposure effect**—the more exposure we have to a stimulus, the more apt we are to like it. We see certain people a lot, and the more familiar they become, the more friendship blooms. Of course, if you feel negatively toward the person in question, then, not surprisingly, the more exposure you have to him or her, the greater your dislike (Swap, 1977). For example, during the 2005–06 federal election campaign, the Conservative Party ran a number of ads prominently featuring Stephen Harper. These ads seemed to backfire—more undecided voters said that the ads persuaded them to vote for the Liberals or NDP instead of for the Conservative Party. One newspaper dubbed this "The Harper Effect: The more we see him, the less we like him" (Panetta, 2005). Nevertheless, Stephen Harper managed to win the 2005–06 election and become the prime minister of Canada. However, the likeability issue surfaced again in the 2008 election. A newspaper article entitled, "Dion weak, but at least he's likeable" reported findings from a poll indicating that 55 percent of Canadians agreed with the statement, "There is something about Stephen Harper I just don't like" (Bryden, 2008). However, once again, Stephen Harper managed to override his likeability deficit and win the election. Thus, unless our feelings toward someone are negative, familiarity generally breeds attraction and liking (Bornstein, 1989; Bornstein & D'Agostino, 1992; Griffin & Sparks, 1990; Moreland & Zajonc, 1982; Zajonc, 1968).

A good example of propinquity and mere exposure effects is your classroom. All semester long, you see the same people. Does this increase your liking for them? Richard Moreland and Scott Beach (1992) tested this hypothesis by planting female research confederates in a large university classroom. The women did not interact with the professor or the other students; they simply walked in and sat quietly in the first row, where everyone could see them. The confederates differed in how many classes they attended, from 15 meetings down to the control condition of zero. At the end of the semester, the students in the class were shown slides of the women, whom they rated on several measures of liking and attraction. As you can see in Figure 9.2 on the next page, mere exposure had a definite effect on liking. Even though they had never interacted, the more often the students had seen the women in class, the more they liked them. These findings have been replicated in many other studies of university students' friendships, children's

mere exposure effect

the finding that the more exposure we have to a stimulus, the more we like it

FIGURE 9.2

The effect that mere exposure in the classroom has on attraction

The more often students saw a female confederate in their classroom, the more positively they rated her personality, even though they had never interacted with her.

(Adapted from Moreland & Beach, 1992)

friendships, and friendships among military and police trainees (Fehr, 2008; Foster, 2005; Gifford-Smith & Brownell, 2003; Segal, 1974; Sykes, 1983).

Before leaving this topic, we should note that familiarity can occur without physical exposure. These days, strangers can get to know each other through electronic mail and computer chat rooms. Computer-mediated communication offers a twist on the propinquity effect; the fact that someone is thousands of kilometres away no longer means you can't encounter him or her. Are online relationships the same as ones formed in everyday life? Do online relationships survive when they move from the computer screen to face-to-face interactions? Researchers are beginning to explore these questions (Lea & Spears, 1995; McKenna, 2008; McKenna & Bargh, 2000; Sprecher, Schwartz, Harvey, & Hatfield, 2008). The early results are encouraging.

For example, recent laboratory experiments have shown that people report being more comfortable revealing their "true" self to a partner over the internet compared with a face-to-face interaction (Bargh, McKenna, & Fitzsimons, 2002; McKenna, Green, & Gleason, 2002). Interestingly, McKenna and colleagues (2002) found that participants also tended to report more liking for an internet partner than a partner they met in person—even when, unbeknownst to them, it was actually the same person! Perhaps most importantly, research is showing that relationships formed over the internet resemble those developed face-to-face in terms of quality and depth (Bargh & McKenna, 2004). In addition, a recent two-year follow-up of romantic relationships originally formed over the internet found that breakup rates were similar to those generally reported for relationships formed in person (McKenna, Green, & Gleason, 2002). It is important to note that the research we have been discussing has focused on friendships and romantic relationships that form between people who are members of various online interest groups, news groups, and so on—in other words, the people interacting were not setting out with the intention of forming a relationship. The findings are quite different when the focus shifts to those who are actively seeking a romantic partner via online dating sites. In the latter case, people tend to be much more cautious about what they disclose, and relationships tend to develop more slowly—more like they would in the real world (McKenna, 2008; Sprecher, Wenzel, & Harvey, 2008). While there is still much to be learned about internet relationships, the data suggest that because of computers, propinquity may soon no longer be a prerequisite for the formation of relationships.

Similarity

Although propinquity does affect friendship choices, it is also the case that we don't become good friends with everyone who is near us in physical space. The "fuel" is **similarity**—the match between our interests, background, attitudes, and

similarity

attraction to people who are like us

values and those of the other person. Are we more attracted to people who are like us (the concept of similarity), or are we more attracted to people who are our opposites (the concept of **complementarity**)? Folk wisdom may suggest that "opposites attract," but research evidence proves that it is similarity, not complementarity, that draws people together (Berscheid & Reis, 1998).

Dozens of tightly controlled experiments have shown, for example, that if all you know about a person whom you've never met is his or her opinions on several issues, the more similar those opinions are to yours, the more you will like him or her (Byrne, 1997; Byrne & Nelson, 1965; McPherson, Smith-Lovin, & Cook, 2001). And what happens when you do meet? In a classic study, Theodore Newcomb (1961) randomly assigned male students at the University of Michigan to be roommates in a particular dormitory at the start of the school year. The critical question was, Would similarity predict friendship formation? The answer is yes. The men became friends with those who were demographically similar (e.g., shared a rural background) as well as with those who were similar in attitudes and values (e.g., were also engineering majors or also held liberal political views).

Since Newcomb conducted this research, dozens of studies have demonstrated that similarity in terms of attitudes and values is an important predictor of attraction in both friendships and romantic relationships (Fehr, 1996, 2008). Similarity in other domains matters as well. For example, we are more likely to be attracted to someone who enjoys the same kinds of leisure activities that we do (Werner & Parmelee, 1979). In fact, according to a study conducted at the University of Waterloo, for some people, similarity in terms of activity preferences is a stronger predictor of attraction than is similarity of attitudes (Jamieson, Lydon, & Zanna, 1987). We also are attracted to people who are similar to us in terms of interpersonal style and communication skills (Burleson & Samter, 1996).

Why is similarity so important in attraction? There are several possibilities. First, we tend to think that people who are similar to us will be inclined to like us. Given this reasonable assumption, we take the first steps and initiate a relationship (Berscheid, 1985; Condon & Crano, 1988). Second, people who are similar provide us with important social validation for our characteristics and beliefs—that is, they provide us with the feeling that we are right (Byrne & Clore, 1970). In contrast, when someone disagrees with us on important issues, we tend not to like the person (Rosenbaum, 1986). In addition to feeling validated, we are more likely

complementarity

attraction to people who are opposite to us

> " Life is to be fortified by many friendships. To love, and to be loved, is the greatest happiness of existence. "
>
> —Sydney Smith, 1771–1845

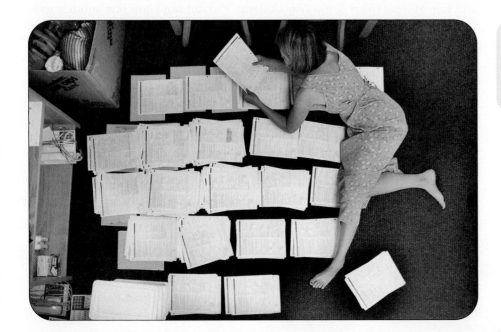

◀ An administrator in a college housing office sorts through roommate applications, placing them in piles according to their similar answers to questions about living habits and interests.

to feel understood by those who are similar to us. Murray, Holmes, Bellavia, Griffin, and Dolderman (2002) found that students in dating relationships and married couples living in the Kitchener-Waterloo area overestimated the degree of similarity between themselves and their partner. The greater the similarity they perceived, the more understood they felt by their partner. Feelings of understanding, in turn, predicted relationship satisfaction. Finally, the rewards-of-interaction explanation offers another reason why similarity leads to attraction (Berscheid & Walster (Hatfield), 1978; Burleson, 1994). According to this explanation, if a person feels the same way we do on important issues, we assume it would be enjoyable to spend time with him or her. Conversely, it is not very pleasant to interact with someone who disagrees with us on everything.

Thus, the desire to be liked, understood, and validated, as well as the desire to have enjoyable interactions, play a role in boosting the attractiveness of a like-minded person and diminishing the attractiveness of someone who is dissimilar (Byrne, Clore, & Smeaton, 1986; Cate & Lloyd, 1992; Dryer & Horowitz, 1997; Fehr, 1996; Holtz, 1997). Finally, we note that although we have been focusing on research showing that similarity leads to attraction, there is also evidence that attraction can lead to perceptions of similarity. In other words, the more attracted we are to someone, the more similar we assume that person is to us. According to a program of research conducted by Marian Morry at the University of Manitoba, this holds true for romantic relationships, same-sex friendships and cross-sex friendships (Morry, 2005a, 2007).

Reciprocal Liking

reciprocal liking

when you like someone and that person also likes you

Most of us like to be liked. Not surprisingly, **reciprocal liking**—liking someone who likes us in return—is one of the prime determinants of interpersonal attraction (Berscheid & Walster (Hatfield), 1978; Condon & Crano, 1988; Kenny, 1994; Kubitscheck & Hallinan, 1998; Secord & Backman, 1964). Liking is so powerful it can even make up for the absence of similarity. In one experiment, for example, when a young woman expressed interest in male research participants simply by maintaining eye contact, leaning toward them, and listening attentively, the men expressed great liking for her despite the fact that they knew she disagreed with them on important issues (Gold, Ryckman, & Mosley, 1984).

Interestingly, reciprocal liking can come about because of a self-fulfilling prophecy (see Chapter 3), as demonstrated in an experiment by Rebecca Curtis and Kim Miller (1986). University students who did not know one another took part in the study in pairs. The researchers led some students to believe that they were liked by the student with whom they would be paired. Other students were led to believe that they were disliked by their partner for the study. The pairs of students were then given an opportunity to have a conversation. Just as predicted, those individuals who thought they were liked behaved in more likeable ways with their partner; they disclosed more about themselves, disagreed less about the topic under discussion, and generally behaved in a warmer, more pleasant manner than did those individuals who thought they were disliked. As a result, their partners ended up liking them—more so than did the partners of students who believed they were disliked.

We should note that reciprocal liking effects can only occur if you like yourself in the first place. People with negative self-concepts tend to be skeptical about others actually liking them and therefore do not necessarily reciprocate liking (Swann, Stein-Seroussi, & McNulty, 1992).

The Effects of Physical Attractiveness on Liking

Propinquity, similarity, and reciprocal liking are not the only determinants of who we will come to like. We also are affected by people's looks—their physical attractiveness. How important is physical appearance to our first impressions of people? A classic study by Walster (Hatfield) and her colleagues revealed a surprising answer (Walster (Hatfield), Aronson, Abrahams, & Rottman, 1966). These researchers matched 752 incoming students at the University of Minnesota for a blind date at a dance during orientation week. The students had previously taken a battery of personality and aptitude tests; however, the researchers paired them up at random. On the night of the dance, the couples spent a few hours together dancing and chatting. They then evaluated their date and indicated whether they would like to date that person again. Of the many possible characteristics that could have determined whether they liked each other—such as their partner's intelligence, independence, sensitivity, or sincerity—the overriding determinant was physical attractiveness. What's more, there was no great difference between men and women on this score.

The powerful role that physical appearance plays in attraction is not limited to heterosexual relationships. When gay men participated in a "blind date" study like the one just described, they responded just as the heterosexual men and women had in the earlier study: The physical attractiveness of their dates was the strongest predictor of their liking for them (Sergios & Cody, 1985).

The findings of Walster (Hatfield) and colleagues' 1966 study, and subsequent replications, raise a perplexing issue. When people are asked about the qualities they desire in a dating partner or a mate, physical attractiveness is not at the top of the list (Buss & Barnes, 1986). Yet when it comes to people's actual behaviour—what people do, rather than what they say—appearance seems to be the only thing that matters, at least in situations where strangers are forming their first impressions of each other. Are people unaware of the importance they place on looks, or are they simply unwilling to admit that they so highly value such a superficial characteristic?

> *Oh, what vileness human beauty is, corroding, corrupting everything it touches.*
>
> —Orestes, 408 BC

To find out, Hadjistavropoulos and Genest (1994) designed a clever study. They presented female students at the University of Saskatchewan with photographs of men varying in physical attractiveness, along with descriptions of their (supposed) personality traits. The researchers found that attractive men were rated as more desirable to date than were unattractive men. Moreover, attractiveness was the strongest predictor of desirability—more so than personality information. So far, this sounds just like the other studies we have been describing. But here's the interesting twist: Some of the participants were connected to an impressive-looking apparatus that they were told was a highly accurate lie detector. The researchers reasoned that if people aren't aware of the emphasis they place on looks, lie detector participants should give the same responses as participants who are not connected to a lie detector. If, on the other hand, people are aware that they base their evaluations of people on looks but feel they shouldn't admit it, then those who are attached to a lie detector should be more likely to "confess" to this than those who are not. And that is exactly what happened. The findings suggest that we are aware of the value we place on looks—but as long as we can get away with it, we won't admit it.

> *Beauty is a greater recommendation than any letter of introduction.*
>
> —Aristotle, fourth century BC

Before leaving this topic we should note that although both sexes value attractiveness in a potential sexual partner (Graziano et al., 1993; Regan & Berscheid, 1995, 1997), there is a tendency for men, more so than for women, to place greater emphasis on looks particularly when choosing a long-term mate (Buss, 1989; Buss & Barnes, 1986; Feingold, 1990). Later, when we discuss evolutionary theories of love, we will consider some reasons for this gender difference.

What Is Attractive? Is physical attractiveness "in the eye of the beholder," or do we share some of the same notions of what is beautiful and handsome? From early childhood on, the media tell us what is beautiful. Moreover, this specific definition of beauty is associated with goodness. For example, illustrators of most traditional children's books, as well as the people who draw the characters in Disney movies, have taught us that the heroines—as well as the princes who woo and win them—all look alike. They all have regular features—small, pert noses; big eyes; shapely lips; blemish-free complexions—and slim, athletic bodies: pretty much like Barbie and Ken dolls.

Bombarded as we are with media depictions of attractiveness, it is not surprising to learn that we share a set of criteria for defining beauty (Fink & Penton-Voak, 2002; Tseëlon, 1995). Look at the photographs below of models and actors who are considered very attractive in Western cultures. Can you describe the facial characteristics that have earned them this label? Michael Cunningham (1986) designed a creative study to determine these standards of beauty. He asked male university students to rate the attractiveness of 50 photographs of women, taken from a college yearbook and from an international beauty pageant program. Cunningham then carefully measured the relative size of the facial features in each photograph. He found that high attractiveness ratings were given to faces with large eyes, a small nose, a small chin, prominent cheekbones and narrow cheeks, high eyebrows, large pupils, and a big smile. Cunningham and his colleagues also examined women's ratings of male beauty in the same manner. They found that higher attractiveness ratings of men were associated with large eyes, prominent cheekbones, a large chin, and a big smile (Cunningham, Barbee, & Pike, 1990).

There is some overlap in the men's and women's ratings. Both sexes admire large eyes in the opposite sex; these are considered to be a "baby face" feature, for newborn mammals have very large eyes for the size of their face. Baby face features are thought to be attractive because they elicit feelings of warmth and nurturance in perceivers—take, for example, our response to babies, kittens, and

▼ Research has found that we share some standards of beauty. In females, large eyes, prominent cheekbones and narrow cheeks, high eyebrows, and a small chin are associated with beauty; in males, large eyes, prominent cheekbones, and a large chin are rated as most beautiful. Today's popular models and actors—such as Natalie Portman, Jessica Alba, Ziyi Zhang, Benjamin Bratt, Patrick Dempsey, and Will Smith—fit these criteria.

puppies (e.g., Berry, 1995; McArthur & Berry, 1987; Zebrowitz, 1997; Zebrowitz & Montepare, 1992). Both sexes also admire prominent cheekbones in the opposite sex, an adult feature that is found only in the faces of those who are sexually mature. Note that the female face that is considered beautiful has more baby face features (small nose, small chin) than the handsome male face, suggesting that beauty in the female, more so than in the male, is associated with childlike qualities.

Cultural Standards of Beauty   Are people's perceptions of what is beautiful or handsome similar across cultures? According to a review of this literature by University of Toronto social psychologist Karen Dion (2002), the answer is a surprising yes (see also Cunningham et al., 1995; Jones & Hill, 1993; McArthur & Berry, 1987; Rhodes et al., 2001). Even though racial and ethnic groups do vary in specific facial features, people from a wide range of cultures agree on what is attractive in the human face. When researchers have asked participants from various countries, ethnicities, and racial groups to rate the physical attractiveness of photographed faces of people who also represent various countries, ethnicities, and racial groups, the participants' ratings agree to a remarkable extent. For example, one review of this literature found that correlations between participants' ratings ranged from 0.66 to 0.93 (Langlois & Roggman, 1990), which are very strong correlations (see Chapter 2). A meta analysis of many studies also found evidence for cross-cultural agreement in what constitutes a beautiful or handsome face (Langlois, Kalakanis, Rubenstein, Larson, Hallam, & Smoot, 2000). Although there is some variability from person to person, across large groups a consensus emerges: Perceivers think that some faces are just better looking than others, regardless of cultural background (Berscheid & Reis, 1998).

How can we explain these results? Judith Langlois and Lori Roggman have suggested that humans came to find certain dimensions as attractive during the course of our evolution (Langlois & Roggman, 1990; Langlois, Roggman, & Musselman, 1994). They hypothesized that attractive faces for both sexes are those whose features are the arithmetic mean—or average—for the species, not the extremes. To test this hypothesis, Langlois and her colleagues used computer technology to merge photographs of faces into a single face that is the exact mathematical average of the facial features of the original people's photographs. The photographs on the right show original photographs of two women and the result of merging the pictures. Interestingly, in studies conducted by Langlois and her colleagues, research participants judged the composite photograph (the arithmetic average of the faces) as more attractive than the individual photographs that made up the composite. This was the case for both male and female photographs. The facial composites produced what the researchers call a typical or "familiar" face. Individual variation in facial features is melted away in the composite; what is left is a good-looking human being, whose face has a familiar and highly pleasing aspect to it.

Do these results mean that "average" faces are the *most* attractive? Clearly not, as is evident by our response to movie stars and supermodels. It turns out that we like the "average" composite face because it has lost some of the atypical or unfamiliar variation that makes up individual faces. However, if a composite face is created with highly attractive faces, we find the composite more attractive than a composite made of faces that are average in attractiveness (Perrett, May, & Yoshikawa, 1994). Thus, the most attractive composite face is one that started out above average and then became even more attractive as variation was smoothed over.

The Power of Familiarity   The crucial variable that explains interpersonal attraction may actually be familiarity (Berscheid & Reis, 1998). We've seen that averaging the attractiveness of many faces together produces one face that looks typical,

▲ Physical attractiveness of composite faces. Langlois and Roggman (1990) created composites of faces using a computer. Pictured here is the first step in the process. The two women's photos (*top* and *middle*) are merged to create the "composite face" (*bottom*). This composite has facial features that are the mathematical average of the facial features of the two original women. The final step of the process occurs when up to 32 individuals' faces have been merged to create one face, the average of all of the prior faces. Perceivers rate the 32-photograph composite face as more physically attractive than any of the individual faces that create it. (From Langlois, Roggman, & Musselman, 1994)

familiar, and physically attractive (see also Halberstadt & Rhodes, 2000). Recent research has found evidence for an even more startling effect for familiarity: When research participants rated the attractiveness of faces, they preferred the faces that most resembled their own! The researchers then computer-morphed a picture of each participant's face—without the participant's knowledge—into that of a person of the opposite sex. When they presented this photo to participants, they gave the photo of their opposite-sex "clone" very high ratings of attractiveness (Little & Perrett, 2002).

Familiarity also underlies the other concepts we've been discussing: propinquity (people we see frequently become familiar through mere exposure), similarity (people who are similar to us will also seem familiar to us), and reciprocal liking (people who like each other get to know and become familiar with each other). All of these attraction variables may be expressions of our "underlying preference for the familiar and safe over the unfamiliar and potentially dangerous" (Berscheid & Reis, 1998, p. 210).

Assumptions about Attractive People   As you have probably observed, beauty "matters"— even when it shouldn't. We are attracted to that which is beautiful, and that can lead to unfair treatment. For example, in a study conducted with premature babies, it was found that neonatal nurses responded more positively to cuter babies and gave them better care. As a result, cuter babies gained weight more quickly and were discharged sooner than the less attractive babies (Badr & Abdallah, 2001).

Why might those who are physically attractive get preferential treatment? One answer lies in the assumption that we make about attractive individuals. Most people assume that physical attractiveness is highly correlated with other desirable traits. The results of many studies indicate that beauty constitutes a powerful stereotype—what Karen Dion, Ellen Berscheid, and Elaine Walster (Hatfield) (1972) have called the "what is beautiful is good" stereotype (Ashmore, Solomon, & Longo, 1996; Brigham, 1980; Hatfield & Sprecher, 1986a). Most research on this stereotype has been conducted with young people, usually university students. An exception is a study by Perlini, Bertolissi, and Lind (1999), who showed photographs of attractive and unattractive younger and older women to first-year university students and to senior citizens living in Sault Ste. Marie, Ontario. The researchers found that participants attributed more positive qualities to attractive women—regardless of their age. There was, however, one exception. Senior men attributed more positive qualities to attractive young women than to attractive older women. Thus, it appears that the "what is beautiful is good" stereotype applies across the lifespan, with one exception—older men seem to perceive that "what is beautiful *and younger* is good."

Luckily for those of us who do not look like supermodels, the stereotype is relatively narrow, affecting people's judgments about an individual only in specific areas. Meta analyses have revealed that physical attractiveness has the largest effect on both men's and women's attributions when they are making judgments about social competence. The beautiful are thought to be more sociable, extroverted, and popular than the less attractive. They are also seen as more sexual, more happy, and more assertive (Eagly, Ashmore, Makhijani, & Longo, 1991; Feingold 1992a).

Interestingly, the stereotype that the beautiful are particularly gifted in the area of social competence has some research support; highly attractive people do develop good social interaction skills and report having more satisfying interactions with others than do the less attractive (Berscheid & Reis, 1998; Feingold, 1992b; Reis, Nezlek, & Wheeler, 1980; Reis et al., 1982). An analysis of national survey data gathered by the Institute for Social Research at York University revealed that attractiveness and income also are positively correlated—at least for men (Roszell, Kennedy, & Grabb, 1989). Thus, there appears to be a kernel of truth in the "what is beautiful is good" stereotype. The reason is that beautiful people, from a young age, receive a great deal of social attention that helps them develop good social skills—which, in turn, may lead to other positive outcomes, such as interpersonal and occupational success. You probably recognize the self-fulfilling prophecy at work here, a concept we discussed in Chapter 3. The way we treat people affects how they behave and, ultimately, how they perceive themselves.

Can a "regular" person be made to act like a "beautiful" one through the self-fulfilling prophecy? Mark Snyder, Elizabeth Decker Tanke, and Ellen Berscheid (1977) decided to find out. They gave male university students a packet of information about another research participant, which included a photograph. The photograph was of either an attractive woman or an unattractive woman. The purpose of the photograph was to invoke the men's stereotype that "what is beautiful is good"—that the woman would be more warm, likeable, poised, and fun to talk to if she was physically attractive than if she was unattractive. The men then had a telephone conversation with a woman, whom they were told was the woman in the photograph; they actually spoke with a different woman. Did the men's beliefs create reality? Yes—the men who thought they were talking to an attractive woman responded to her in a warmer, more sociable manner than did the men who thought they were talking to an unattractive woman. Not only that, but the men's behaviour influenced how the women themselves responded. When observers later listened to a tape recording of the women's half of the conversation, they rated the women whose male partners thought they were physically attractive as more attractive, confident, animated, and warmer than the women whose male partners thought they were unattractive. In short, if a man thought he was talking to an attractive woman, he spoke to her in a way that brought out her best and most sparkling qualities.

This study was later replicated with the male and female roles switched. Andersen and Bem (1981) showed female participants a photograph of either an attractive or an unattractive man; the women then had a phone conversation with him. The men on the other end of the line were unaware of the women's belief about them. Just as in the Snyder, Tanke, and Berscheid (1977) study, the women acted on their stereotype of beauty, and the unknowing men responded accordingly.

Cultural Differences   Does the "what is beautiful is good" stereotype operate across cultures? The answer appears to be yes. Ladd Wheeler and Youngmee Kim (1997) asked students in Seoul, South Korea, to rate a number of yearbook photographs that varied in physical attractiveness. They found that the Korean male and female participants thought the more physically attractive people would be more socially skilled, friendly, and well adjusted—the same group of traits that North American participants thought went with physical attractiveness (see Table 9.1 on the next page).

But Korean and North American students differed in other traits they assigned to the beautiful, reflecting what is considered important and valuable in each culture (Markus, Kitayama, & Heiman, 1996; Triandis, 1995). For the North American students, who live in individualist cultures that value independence, individuality, and self-reliance, the "beautiful" stereotype included traits of personal strength (see Table 9.1). These traits were not part of the Korean "beautiful" stereotype. Instead, for the Korean students, who live in a collectivist culture that values harmonious group relations, the "beautiful" stereotype included traits that reflect integrity and concern for others—traits that were not part of the North American stereotype (see Table 9.1). In her review of this research on this topic, Karen Dion (2002) concluded that physical attractiveness stereotyping occurs cross-culturally, although more so in individualistic societies, where greater weight is placed on qualities of the individual, including his or her appearance.

▲In Western cultures, where independence is valued, the "beautiful" stereotype includes traits of personal strength. In more collectivistic Asian cultures, beautiful people are assumed to have traits that reflect integrity and concern for others.

TABLE 9.1

How culture affects the "what is beautiful is good" stereotype

The "what is beautiful is good" stereotype has been explored in two types of cultures: an "individualist" culture (North America) and a "collectivist" culture (Asia). Male and female research participants in the United States and Canada and in South Korea rated photographs of people with varying degrees of physical attractiveness. Their responses indicated that some of the traits that make up the stereotype are the same across cultures, while other traits that are associated with the stereotype are different in the two cultures. In both cultures, the physically attractive are seen as having more of the characteristics that are valued in that culture.

Traits that are shared in the Korean, American, and Canadian stereotype of "what is beautiful is good"

sociable	poised	well adjusted
likeable	extroverted	mature
popular	happy	sexually warm and responsive
friendly		

Additional traits that are present in the American and Canadian stereotype

strong	dominant	assertive

Additional traits that are present in the Korean stereotype

sensitive	trustworthy	empathic
honest	generous	

(Adapted from Eagly et al., 1991; Feingold, 1992a; Wheeler & Kim, 1997)

Attraction and the Misattribution of Arousal

Imagine that you go to see a scary movie with an extremely attractive date. As you are sitting there, you notice that your heart is thumping and you are a little short of breath. Is this because you are wildly attracted to your date, or because the movie is terrifying you? It is unlikely that you could say, "Fifty-seven percent of my arousal is due to the fact that my date is gorgeous, 32 percent is due to the scary movie, and 11 percent is due to indigestion from all the popcorn I ate." Because of this difficulty in pinpointing the precise causes of our arousal, we sometimes form mistaken emotions. You might think that most of your arousal is a sign of attraction to your date, when in fact a lot of it is due to the movie (or maybe even indigestion).

Many studies have demonstrated the occurrence of such **misattribution of arousal**, whereby people make mistaken inferences about what is causing them to feel the way they do (Ross & Olson, 1981; Schachter, Silversting, & Perlick, 1977; Storms & Nisbett, 1970; Valins, 1966; Zillman, 1978). Consider, for example, an intriguing field experiment by Donald Dutton and Arthur Aron (1974). Imagine you are one of the participants (all of whom were men). You are one of many people visiting the Capilano Canyon in scenic North Vancouver. Spanning the canyon is a narrow, 137-metre suspension bridge made of wooden planks attached to wire cables. You decide to walk across it. When you get a little way across, the bridge starts to sway from side to side. You feel as though you are about to tumble over the edge and you reach for the handrails, but they are so low that it feels even more likely that you will topple over. Then, you make the mistake of looking down. You see nothing but a sheer 70-metre drop to rocks and rapids below. You become more than a little aroused—your heart is thumping, you breathe rapidly, and you begin to perspire. At this point, an attractive young woman approaches you and asks whether you could fill out a questionnaire for her, as part of a psychology project on the effects of scenic attractions on people's creativity. You decide to help her out. After you complete the questionnaire, the woman thanks you and says she would be happy to explain her study in more detail. She tears off a corner of the questionnaire, writes down her name and phone number. How attracted do you think you would be to this woman? Would you phone her and ask her out?

misattribution of arousal

the process whereby people make mistaken inferences about what is causing them to feel the way they do

◀ When people are aroused, in this case due to crossing a scary bridge, they often misattribute this arousal to the wrong source—such as attraction to the person they are with.

Think about this for a moment, and now imagine that the same woman approaches you under different circumstances. You decide to take a leisurely stroll farther up the Capilano River. You notice a wide sturdy bridge made of heavy cedar planks. The bridge has high handrails, even though it is situated only 3 metres above a shallow rivulet that runs into the main river. You are peaceably admiring the scenery when the woman asks you to fill out her questionnaire. How attracted do you feel toward her now? Dutton and Aron's prediction is clear: If you are on the high, scary bridge, you will be considerably aroused and will mistakenly think some of this arousal is the result of attraction to the beautiful woman. This is exactly what happened in the actual experiment. Half of the men (50 percent) who were approached on the high suspension bridge telephoned the woman later, whereas relatively few of the men (12.5 percent) who were approached on the low, sturdy bridge called her. (As you probably have guessed, the woman was a confederate—someone hired by the researchers—and she approached only men who were not accompanied by a woman.) This type of misattribution of arousal has been found in subsequent studies with both women and men as participants (Meston & Frohlich, 2003; Zillman, 1978).

In summary, we have discussed four major determinants of attraction: propinquity, similarity, reciprocal liking, and physical attractiveness. After getting to this point in the chapter, you should be in a pretty good position to make a favourable first impression the next time you meet someone. Suppose you want Claudia to like you. You should hang around her (preferably on a high, scary bridge) so you become familiar, emphasize your similarity to her, and find ways of showing that you like her. It also wouldn't hurt to look your best. But what if you want to do more than make a good impression? What if you want to have a close friendship or a romantic relationship? Stay tuned.

Forming Close Relationships

Until recently, social psychologists have had little to say in answer to the question of how we form close relationships because research on interpersonal attraction focused almost exclusively on first impressions. Why? Primarily because long-term, close relationships are much more difficult to study scientifically than first impressions. As we explained in Chapter 2, random assignment to different conditions is the hallmark of an experiment. When studying first impressions, a researcher can randomly assign you to a get-acquainted session with someone who is similar or dissimilar to you. However, a researcher can't randomly assign you to the similar or dissimilar "lover" condition and make you have a relationship! In addition, psychologists face a daunting task when trying to measure such complex feelings as love and passion. However, as we will show, important strides have been made toward our understanding of close relationships.

Defining Love

In the opening of this chapter, we described Bradley Bird's falling-in-love experience. But what, exactly, is love? For centuries, philosophers, poets, and novelists have grappled with this question. More recently, social psychologists have attempted to provide a scientific answer. One of the first to attempt a scientific analysis of love was Zick Rubin (1970, 1973). He defined *love* as feelings of intimacy, attachment, and passion, and argued that love is a feeling distinct from liking. Subsequently, social psychologists attempted to dive deeper into the study of love and reached a conclusion that you may already have discovered. There probably isn't a single, simple definition of love because love comes in many forms.

> ❝ *Love is something so divine,*
> *Description would but make it less;*
> *'Tis what I feel,*
> *but can't define,*
> *'Tis what I know,*
> *but can't express.* ❞
>
> —*Beilby Porteus (1731–1808)*

> ❝ *Try to reason about love, and*
> *you will lose your reason.* ❞
>
> —*French proverb*

Companionate versus Passionate Love   If you have ever been in love, think back to how you felt about your sweetheart when you first got to know him or her. You probably felt a combination of giddiness, longing, joy, and anxiety—the kinds of feelings that Bradley Bird experienced when he met Nina. The ancient Greeks considered this strange, bewildering set of feelings to be a form of madness, causing all sorts of irrational and obsessional acts. Though times have changed, most people are familiar with the torment—and exhilaration—that comes with falling in love. Now think about how you feel toward your mother or your brother or a very close friend. You might also use the word *love* to describe how you feel about these important people in your life, but in this case the feelings are probably quite different from the feelings you have for your sweetheart.

Ellen Berscheid and Elaine Walster (Hatfield) (1974, 1978) attempted to capture this distinction when they proposed that there are two major kinds of love: companionate and passionate. **Companionate love** is defined as the feelings of intimacy and affection we feel toward someone with whom our lives are deeply intertwined. People can experience companionate love in nonsexual relationships, such as close friendships or familial relationships, or in sexual relationships,

companionate love

the feelings of intimacy and affection we feel for another person about whom we care deeply

▶ Actors Gwyneth Paltrow and Joseph Fiennes exemplify the early stages of passionate love in this scene from the film, *Shakespeare in Love*.

where they experience feelings of intimacy but not a great deal of heat and passion. **Passionate love** involves an intense longing for another person. When things are going well—the other person loves us, too—we feel great fulfillment and ecstasy. When things are not going well, we feel great sadness and despair. This kind of love is characterized by obsessive thoughts about the loved one, as well as heightened physiological arousal wherein we actually feel shortness of breath and a thumping heart when we are in our loved one's presence (Regan, 1998; Regan & Berscheid, 1999).

Elaine Hatfield and Susan Sprecher (1986b) developed a questionnaire to measure passionate love. Passionate love, as measured by this scale, consists of strong uncontrollable thoughts, intense feelings, and overt acts toward the target of one's affection. Find out if you are experiencing (or have experienced) passionate love, by filling out the questionnaire in the accompanying Try It!

passionate love

the feelings of intense longing, accompanied by physiological arousal, we feel for another person; when our love is reciprocated, we feel great fulfillment and ecstasy, but when it is not, we feel sadness and despair

Try it!

▶ The Passionate Love Scale

These items ask you to describe how you feel when you are passionately in love. Think of the person you love most passionately right now. (If you are not in love right now, think of the last person you loved passionately. If you have never been passionately in love, think of the person whom you came closest to caring for in that way.) Choose your answer by remembering how you felt at the time when your feelings were the most intense.

For each of the 15 items, choose the number between 1 and 9 that most accurately describes your feelings. The answer scale ranges from 1 "not at all true" to 9 "definitely true." Write the number you choose next to each item.

1	2	3	4	5	6	7	8	9
↑				↑				↑
Not at all true				Moderately true				Definitely true

1. I would feel deep despair if _____ left me.
2. Sometimes, I feel I can't control my thoughts; they are obsessively on _____.
3. I feel happy when I am doing something to make _____ happy.
4. I would rather be with _____ than anyone else.
5. I'd get jealous if I thought _____ were falling in love with someone else.
6. I yearn to know all about _____.
7. I want _____—physically, emotionally, and mentally.
8. I have an endless appetite for affection from _____.
9. For me, _____ is the perfect romantic partner.
10. I sense my body responding when _____ touches me.
11. _____ always seems to be on my mind.
12. I want _____ to know me—my thoughts, my fears, and my hopes.
13. I eagerly look for signs indicating _____'s desire for me.
14. I possess a powerful attraction for _____.
15. I get extremely depressed when things don't go right in my relationship with _____.

Scoring: Add up your scores for the 15 items. The total score can range from a minimum of 15 to a maximum of 135. The higher your score, the more your feelings for the person reflect passionate love; the items to which you gave a particularly high score reflect those components of passionate love that you experience most strongly.

(Adapted from Hatfield & Sprecher, 1986b)

"Ordinary" People's Definition of Love   So far we have been discussing social psychologists' answers to the question, What is love? Beverley Fehr (1988, 1994; Fehr & Russell, 1991) has been interested in how ordinary people define love. This is an important issue because the way in which people define love can determine how they act in their close relationships (e.g., deciding whether they are truly "in love," or whether they are experiencing the kind of love that leads to commitment). In an initial set of studies, Fehr (1988) asked students at the University of British Columbia to define love: Specifically, participants were asked to list the features or characteristics of the concept of love. The definitions of love that were generated included both companionate features (e.g., warmth, intimacy, caring) and passionate features (e.g., heart rate increases, sexual attraction, thinking about the other person all the time). In follow-up research, other participants were shown these features and asked to rate which were most important in defining love. As shown in Table 9.2, contrary to the stereotype that university students would view love only in passionate terms, Fehr found that companionate love was seen as capturing the meaning of love, more so than passionate love. Moreover, participants reported that they relied on the level of companionate love, rather than the level of passionate love, when deciding whether a relationship was progressing or deteriorating.

These studies have been replicated by researchers on the east coast of Canada (Button & Collier, 1991) and on the west coast of the United States (Aron & Westbay, 1996; Luby & Aron, 1990). Participants in these studies have shown remarkable agreement on the features of love. The companionate features of love are especially likely to be mentioned and also consistently receive the highest importance ratings. These findings suggest that, at least within North America, people tend to agree on the meaning of love (Fehr, 1993, 2001). Fehr and Russell (1991) examined ordinary people's conceptions of love from a slightly different angle by asking students at the University of British Columbia and at the University of Winnipeg to list different types of love. They found that the kinds of love listed could be grouped into companionate kinds of love (e.g., friendship love, familial love, maternal love) and passionate kinds of love (romantic love, passionate

TABLE 9.2

Ratings of features of love*

Highest Ratings		Lowest Ratings	
Trust	7.50	Think about the other all the time	4.45
Caring	7.28	Energy	4.28
Honesty	7.17	Heart rate increases	4.26
Friendship	7.08	Euphoria	4.12
Respect	7.01	Gazing at the other	4.10
Concern for the other's well-being	7.00	See only the other's good qualities	3.45
Loyalty	7.00	Butterflies in stomach	3.41
Commitment	6.91	Uncertainty	2.88
Accept other the way she/he is	6.82	Dependency	2.81
Supportiveness	6.78	Scary	2.28

*Ratings were made on a scale where 1 = extremely poor feature of love, and 8 = extremely good feature of love. The features of love to which students at the University of British Columbia assigned the highest ratings portray companionate love; the features that received the lowest ratings portray passionate love.

(Fehr, 1988)

love, infatuation, sexual love). Once again, the companionate kinds of love were regarded as capturing the true meaning of love. Thus, ordinary people's view of love fits nicely with Berscheid and Walster (Hatfield)'s companionate/passionate distinction (Fehr, 2001, 2006). Love is seen as including both companionate and passionate aspects, although the companionate aspect is considered to be the essence of love.

Gender and Love

Who is all mushy and romantic when it comes to love? Who is practical and solid? If you are like many people, you will answer "women" to the first question and "men" to the second. But think back to our opening story of Bradley Bird and you may come up with a different answer—one that is more consistent with the results of social psychological research. Indeed, when social psychologists began to conduct research on this question, they found that men fall in love more quickly than women and are more likely to endorse romantic beliefs such as "true love lasts forever." Men are also more likely than women to report having experienced love at first sight—as Bradley Bird can attest. In contrast, women hold a more practical, friendship-based orientation to love (essentially, a companionate view of love). One of the first studies that discovered these gender differences was conducted by Kenneth Dion and Karen Dion (1973) at the University of Toronto. These differences in how women and men view love continue to be found, even among culturally diverse participants (Dion & Dion, 1993; Hendrick & Hendrick, 1986, 1992; Hendrick, Hendrick, & Adler, 1988; Rubin, Peplau, & Hill, 1981; Sprecher & Metts, 1989). (We will discuss this research in greater detail in the following section, "Culture and Love.")

On the other hand, researchers are beginning to realize that there also are similarities in women's and men's definitions and experience of love (Hendrick & Hendrick, 1995). In studies conducted at the University of Winnipeg, Beverley Fehr and Ross Broughton (2001) obtained the classic finding—namely, that men gave higher ratings to romantic and passionate love than did women, and women's ratings of friendship love were higher than men's. However, some additional, interesting findings emerged. These researchers measured several kinds of companionate love (e.g., familial love, sisterly love, affection), rather than just friendship love, as is usually done. It turned out that men rated these other kinds of companionate love just as high as women did. Moreover even though men rated romantic, passionate kinds of love higher than did women, both sexes gave these kinds of love the lowest ratings and the companionate kinds of love the highest ratings. Fehr and Broughton concluded that women's and men's views of love are actually more similar than has been thought.

Culture and Love

Although love is certainly a universal emotion, how we experience it (and what we expect in relationships) is shaped by culture. For example, Japanese describe *amae* as an extremely positive emotional state in which one is a totally passive love object, indulged and taken care of by one's romantic partner, as in a mother–infant relationship. There is no equivalent word for *amae* in English or any other Western language; the closest in meaning is the word *dependency*, an emotional state that is considered by Western cultures to be unhealthy in adult relationships (Dion & Dion, 1993; Doi, 1988). The Chinese have an important relationship concept, *gan qing*, which differs from the Western view of romantic love. *Gan qing* is achieved by helping and working for another person; for example, a "romantic" act would be fixing someone's bicycle or helping them learn new

▶ While people all over the world experience love, how love is defined varies across cultures.

material (Gao, 1996). Another way of conceptualizing love is expressed by the Korean concept of *jung*. Much more than "love," *jung* is what ties two people together. Though couples in new relationships feel strong love for each other, they have not yet developed strong *jung*—that takes time and many mutual experiences. Interestingly, *jung* can develop in negative relationships, too—for example, between business rivals who dislike each other. *Jung* may unknowingly grow between them over time, with the result that they will feel that a strange connection exists (Lim & Choi, 1996). As you can see from these examples, how love is defined and experienced varies across cultures.

Throughout this book, we have noted that Western and Eastern cultures vary in important ways, with Western cultures emphasizing that the individual is autonomous, self-sufficient, and defined in terms of his or her personal qualities. Eastern cultures, in contrast, tend to be collectivistic, emphasizing the individual's loyalty to the group and defining him or her through membership in the group (Heine et al., 1999; Hofstede, 1984; Hui & Triandis, 1986; Markus, Kitayama, & Heiman, 1996; Triandis, 1995). According to Karen Dion and Kenneth Dion (1993, 1996, 2001), romantic love has less value in collectivist societies than in individualist societies. In individualist societies, romantic love is a heady, highly personal experience; one immerses oneself in the new partner and often virtually ignores friends and family for a while. The decision as to whom to become involved with or marry is for the most part a personal one. In comparison, in collectivist cultures, the individual in love must take into account the wishes of family and other group members; in fact, marriages are often by arrangement, with the respective families matching up the bride and groom (Adams, Anderson, & Adonu, 2004; Fiske, Kitayama, Markus, & Nisbett, 1998; Levine, Sato, Hashimoto, & Verma, 1995). For example, in West Africa, relationships with one's parents, siblings, and relatives are considered more important and influential than the more recent relationship one has formed with one's spouse. In many areas of West Africa, happily married couples do not live in the same house, nor do they expect to sleep together every night. In stark contrast to the pattern of intimate relationships in individualistic cultures, their connection and obligation to extended family takes precedence over that to their spouse. In individualistic cultures, the opposite is typically true (Adams, Garcia, Purdie-Vaughns, & Steele, 2004).

Consistent with these cultural differences, research has shown that people in individualistic cultures (e.g., the United States, Canada) value passionate love more than people from collectivist cultures (e.g., Asian countries) do, whereas people from collectivist cultures value companionate love more than people

TABLE 9.3

Cross-cultural evidence for passionate love based on anthropological research in 166 societies

Cultural Area	Passionate Love Present	Passionate Love Absent
Mediterranean	22 (95.7%)	1 (4.3%)
Sub-Saharan Africa	20 (76.9%)	6 (23.1%)
Eurasia	32 (97.0%)	1 (3.0%)
Insular Pacific	27 (93.1%)	2 (6.9%)
North America	24 (82.8%)	5 (17.2%)
South and Central America	22 (84.6%)	4 (15.4%)

(Data from Jankowiak & Fischer, 1992)

from individualistic cultures do (Dion & Dion, 1993; Gao, 1993; Jankowiak, 1995; Ting-Toomey & Chang, 1996). As Dion and Dion (1993) point out, companionate love is a "style of love that would not disrupt a complex network of existing family relationships" (p. 465). The results of a recent study are consistent with this interpretation (Uskul, Lalonde, & Cheng, 2007). In this study, participants were presented with a scenario in which Chinese parents who had moved to Canada were upset that their child was dating a European Canadian. Chinese-Canadian students were more likely to support the parents whereas European-Canadian students were more likely to support the dater. In another study, university students in 11 countries around the world were asked, "If a man [woman] had all the qualities you desired, would you marry this person if you were not in love with him [her]?" These researchers found that marrying for love was most important to participants in Western and Westernized countries (e.g., the United States, Brazil, England, and Australia) and of least importance to participants in less-developed Eastern countries (e.g., India, Pakistan, and Thailand) (Levine et al., 1995). This is not to say that passionate love is nonexistent in collectivist cultures. Reviewing the anthropological research on 166 societies, William Jankowiak and Edward Fischer (1992; Jankowiak, 1995) found evidence for passionate love in 147 of them, as you can see in Table 9.3. However, people in collectivist cultures are most likely to value and identify with companionate love.

The results of these studies indicate that the concept of romantic love is to some extent culturally specific (Dion & Dion, 1996; Gao & Gudykunst, 1995; Hatfield & Rapson, 1996, 2002; Hatfield & Sprecher, 1995; Sprecher, Aron, Hatfield, Cortese, Potapova, & Levitskaya, 1994). Love can vary in definition and behaviour in different societies. We all love, but we do not necessarily all love in the same way—or at least we don't describe it in the same way. Robert Moore noted, in summarizing his research in the People's Republic of China, "Young Chinese do fall deeply in love and experience the same joys and sorrows of romance as young Westerners do. But they do so according to standards that require . . . the individual [to] sacrifice personal interests for the sake of the family. . . . This means avoiding fleeting infatuations, casual sexual encounters, and a dating context [where] family concerns are forgotten" (Moore, 1998, p. 280).

Why Do We Love?

We began this chapter by asking, Why are people so highly motivated to seek loving relationships? If you were to ask a group of social psychologists this question, you would probably get a number of answers, depending on each psychologist's theoretical persuasion. Chances are that two of the answers would be, "It's all about survival" (evolutionary theories) and "It's all about your mother" (attachment theories). Probably each of these theories tells part of the story. As you read about them, you may wish to think about which theory seems to explain best your motivation for seeking love.

Evolutionary Explanations of Love

The basic tenet of evolutionary biology is that an animal's "fitness" is measured by its reproductive success—that is, its ability to pass on its genes to the next generation. Reproductive success is not just part of the game; it *is* the game. Has human behaviour evolved in specific ways to maximize reproductive success? Evolutionary psychologists say yes; they argue that males and females have very different agendas because of their differing roles in producing offspring. For women, reproduction is costly in terms of time, energy, and effort, and this means that they must consider carefully when and with whom to reproduce. In comparison, reproduction has few costs for males. The evolutionary approach argues that reproductive success for the two sexes translates into two very different behaviour patterns. Male animals would do best to pursue frequent pairings with many females, and female animals would do best to pair infrequently and only with a carefully chosen male (Berkow, 1989; Symons, 1979).

What does this have to do with falling in love? According to David Buss and colleagues (1985, 1988a, 1996a, 1996b; Buss & Schmitt, 1993), the **evolutionary approach** explains the different strategies of men and women in romantic relationships. Women, facing high reproductive costs, will look for a man who can supply the resources and support she needs to bear a child. Men will look for a woman who appears capable of reproducing successfully. More specifically, men will respond to the physical appearance of women, since age and health denote reproductive fitness; women will respond to the economic and career achievements of men, since these variables represent resources they and their offspring will need (Buss, 1988b). The Bradley Bird and Nina relationship described at the beginning of this chapter would seem to fit this profile. He was swept off his feet by her beauty; she may have been attracted to him because of the better life he could offer her.

Several studies have found support for these predictions. For example, Buss and colleagues (1989, 1990, 1996a, 1996b) asked more than 9000 adults in 37 countries, including various regions of Canada, how important and desirable various characteristics were in choosing a marriage partner. In general, the women valued ambition, industriousness, and good earning capacity in a potential mate more than the men did. The men valued physical attractiveness in a mate more than the women did—a finding echoed in other research discussed earlier (Buss & Barnes, 1986; Buss & Schmitt, 1993; Hatfield & Sprecher, 1995; Lundy, Tan, & Cunningham, 1998; Regan & Berscheid, 1997). Other survey studies have found that men prefer spouses who are younger than they are—youth indicating greater reproductive fitness, while women prefer spouses around their own age (Buss, 1989; Kenrick & Keefe, 1992). We should point out, however, that in these studies, the top characteristics on both women's and men's lists are the same, and they include honesty, trustworthiness, and a pleasant personality. In interpreting findings such as these, it is important to make a distinction between short-term and long-term mating goals. When it comes to having a short-term fling, both women and men focus on physical attractiveness, but when it comes to having a long-term relationship, both women and men focus less on looks and more on whether this person has desired qualities of a long-term mate (Little, Burriss, Jones, DeBruine, & Caldwell, 2008).

Buckle, Gallup, and Rodd (1996) used Statistics Canada information for 1978 to 1985 on patterns of marriage, divorce, and remarriage to test additional

> *Men seek to propagate widely, whereas women seek to propagate wisely.*
>
> —*Robert Hinde*, Animal Behaviour, 1984

evolutionary approach

an approach derived from evolutionary biology that states that men and women are attracted to different characteristics in each other—men are attracted by women's appearance; women are attracted by men's resources—because this maximizes their reproductive success hypotheses derived from evolutionary theory. They predicted, for example, that if marriage is driven by a reproductive agenda, women's prospects of marriage would decline with age. Indeed, they found that women are most likely to get married between the ages of 20 and 24 (prime reproductive years). Beyond this age, the chances of marriage decline quite dramatically. In contrast, getting older does not reduce a man's chances of marriage to the same extent. The researchers also predicted that women would be likely to terminate marriages in which the man does not appear to be a good prospect as a father/provider. Consistent with this prediction, they found that divorce is more likely to be initiated by women.

It may have occurred to you that the data we have been discussing could be explained in other ways. Indeed, the evolutionary approach to love has attracted its share of criticism and generated considerable controversy (Bradshaw, Bubier, & Sullivan, 1994; McKelvie & McLellan, 1993, 1994). Some social psychologists argue that the theory is untestable; we can't do an experiment to prove that evolutionary forces are the primary cause of current human behaviour (Sternberg & Beall, 1991). Others suggest that it is an oversimplification of extremely complex human behaviour (Travis & Yeager, 1991). It has also been argued that men value physical attractiveness and youth in a partner simply because they have been conditioned to do so by decades of advertising and media images (Hatfield & Rapson, 1993).

Still other researchers note that around the world women have less power, status, wealth, and other resources than men do. If women need to rely on men to achieve economic security, they must consider this characteristic when choosing a mate. In comparison, men are generally free to choose a woman using more frivolous criteria such as good looks (Rosenblatt, 1974). Interestingly, in an analysis of several countries, Gangestad (1993) found that the more economic power women had in a given culture, the more women were interested in a physically attractive man. A more recent study found that both women and men from wealthy families wanted a partner who was also wealthy. This study also found that both women and men who were good looking wanted to find their match: a beautiful or handsome mate (Buston & Emlen, 2003). So, as you can see, when discussing human mate preference, it is difficult to disentangle "nature" (inborn preferences) from "nurture" (cultural norms and gender roles). The evolutionary approach is an interesting, exciting, and controversial theory; further theorizing and research will reveal more about the role that biology plays in love.

Attachment Styles and Intimate Relationships

The evolutionary approach takes the long view—how people act today is based on behaviour patterns that evolved from our species' hominid past. Another theory of love also focuses on the past, but on the more recent past; **attachment theory** states that our behaviour in adult relationships is based on our experiences as infants with our parents or caregivers. This approach draws on the groundbreaking work of John Bowlby (1969, 1973, 1980) and Mary Ainsworth (Ainsworth, Blehar, Waters, & Wall, 1978) on how infants form bonds to their primary caregivers (usually their mother). The theory of **attachment styles** states that the kinds of bonds we form early in life influence the kinds of relationships we form as adults. Ainsworth and her colleagues (1978) identified three types of relationships between infants and their mothers.

- Infants with a **secure attachment style** typically have caregivers who are responsive to their needs and who show positive emotions when interacting with them. These infants trust their caregivers, are not worried about being abandoned, and come to view themselves as worthy and loved.

attachment theory

the theory that our behaviour in adult relationships is based on our experiences as infants with our parents or caregivers

attachment styles

the expectations people develop about relationships with others based on the relationship they had with their primary caregiver when they were infants

secure attachment style

an attachment style characterized by trust, a lack of concern with being abandoned, and the view that one is worthy and well liked

CONNECTIONS
Does Your Face Reveal Your "Intentions"?

Wouldn't life be easier if all you had to do was look at someone's face to know whether that person was interested in a short-term fling or a serious, long-term relationship? Recent research suggests that this may actually be the case! Lynda Boothroyd and colleagues (2008) administered a test to a group of British university students that assessed the extent to which they were open to short-term sexual relationships. They then took photos of those participants who scored very high on this scale and photos of those who scored low (i.e., those who were not open to casual sexual relationships). The photographs were then arranged in pairs, such that the photo of a person who was interested in casual sex would be paired with a photo of a person who was not open to casual sex. A new group of participants was shown these pairs and asked to "choose the individual that you feel is more open to short-term relationships, one-night stands, and the idea of sex without love." Were participants able to correctly identify who was open to casual sex and who wasn't? It turns out that women were good at making these kinds of judgments—and they were able to do this when looking at female and male faces. Men were somewhat less accurate (Boothroyd, Jones, Burt, DeBruine, & Perrett, 2008). In a follow-up study, it was found that women rated the men who were open to casual sex as less attractive for a long-term relationship than the men who were not open to casual sex. Keep in mind that these women didn't know these men's attitudes toward casual sex—all they had to go on was a photograph. These findings were obtained regardless of whether the researchers used actual photographs or composites (such as those shown below) in which they averaged faces of women and men who were open to casual sex and then averaged the faces of women and men who were not open to casual sex.

How should these findings be interpreted? Boothroyd and colleagues suggest that their findings are consistent with evolutionary theory. According to this theory, women and men have different "agendas" when they play the mating game. Men want to ensure successful reproduction (i.e., passing on their genes), whereas women want to find a partner who can be counted on to provide the resources required to raise offspring. From an evolutionary perspective, it would be advantageous for women to be able to detect which men are good long-term prospects. It would also be advantageous to be able to figure out sooner, rather than later, who is not a good long-term prospect, to avoid making a costly mistake. This may be why women need only to glance at a man's face in order to figure out his "intentions."

An interesting side note: Which person in the pairs of accompanying photographs do you find more attractive? In Boothroyd and colleagues' (2008) studies, both women and men rated the photographs of the women who were open to casual sex as more attractive than the photographs of the women who were not open to casual sex. This was not true for ratings of men's photographs. However, men who were open to casual sex were rated as more masculine looking by both women and men.

■ Infants with an **avoidant attachment style** typically have caregivers who are aloof and distant, rebuffing the infant's attempts to establish intimacy. These infants desire to be close to their caregiver but learn to suppress this need, as if they know that attempts to be intimate will be rejected. People with this style find it difficult to become close to other people.

■ Infants with an **anxious/ambivalent attachment style** typically have caregivers who are inconsistent and overbearing in their affection. These infants are unusually anxious, because they can never predict when and how their caregivers will respond to their needs. People with this style desperately seek closeness to others but experience mixed, conflicted feelings even when they are in a loving relationship.

avoidant attachment style

an attachment style characterized by a suppression of attachment needs, because attempts to be intimate have been rebuffed; people with this style find it difficult to develop intimate relationships

anxious/ambivalent attachment style

an attachment style characterized by a concern that others will not reciprocate one's desire for intimacy, resulting in higher-than-average levels of anxiety

The key assumption of attachment theory is that the particular attachment style we learn as infants and young children typically stays with us throughout life and generalizes to all of our relationships with other people (Fraley & Shaver, 2000; Hartup & Laursen, 1999; Mikulincer & Shaver, 2005, 2007). In a ground-breaking study, Cindy Hazan and Phillip Shaver (1987) asked adults to choose one of three descriptions designed to capture the three kinds of attachment styles described above, according to how they typically felt in romantic relationships. The researchers also asked people questions about their current and past relationships. The results of this study were consistent with an attachment theory perspective. Securely attached adults reported that they easily became close to other people, readily trusted others, and had satisfying romantic relationships. People with an avoidant style reported that they were uncomfortable becoming close to others, found it hard to trust others, and had less satisfying romantic relationships. People with an anxious/ambivalent style also tended to have less satisfying relationships but of a different type: They were likely to be obsessive and preoccupied with their relationships, fearing that their partners did not want to be as intimate or close as they desired.

These findings have been replicated in hundreds of studies (see Mikulincer & Shaver, 2007). For example, at the University of Toronto, Keelan, Dion, and Dion (1994) found that people who were securely attached maintained high levels of satisfaction, commitment, and trust in their romantic relationship over the four-month period of the study, whereas those who were insecurely attached (i.e., avoidant and anxious-ambivalent) showed decreases in satisfaction, commitment, and trust over time.

Not surprisingly, people's attachment style also affects how they handle conflict in their relationships. Lussier, Sabourin, and Turgeon (1997) examined the relation between attachment style and coping strategies among a sample of French-Canadian cohabiting and married couples. They found that when difficulties arose, secure participants reported using active task-centred coping strategies that were aimed at solving problems. These strategies were associated with marital well being. Anxious/ambivalent participants used passive, emotion-focused coping strategies—strategies that were associated with marital distress. As you might expect, avoidant participants tended to use passive, avoidant strategies. More recently, University of Western Ontario researcher Lorne Campbell and his colleagues had a large sample of dating couples participate in a two-week diary study in which they recorded the amount of conflict, social support, and quality that they perceived in their dating relationship. The researchers found that attachment anxiety was correlated with reports of high levels of conflict. In fact, anxiously attached participants reported more conflicts than their partners did. Moreover, in a follow-up laboratory session, when discussing an actual conflict, participants who were high in attachment anxiety reported greater distress during the interaction than participants who were low in attachment anxiety—even if their partner had responded in a positive manner (Campbell, Simpson, Boldry, & Kashy, 2005).

▲ Attachment theory predicts that the attachment style we learn as infants stays with us throughout life and generalizes to our relationships with other people.

❝ *In my very own self, I am part of my family.* ❞

—D. H. Lawrence (1885–1930)

Other research has shown that anxious people tend to worry that their partner will reject them. Sadly, research by Murray, Griffin, Rose, and Bellavia (2003) suggests that these beliefs may become a reality. In a study of married people, the researchers found that those with insecure attachment were more likely to internalize experiences of rejection from their partner, which led to decreases in self-esteem. This sensitivity to rejection predicted a decline in the partner's satisfaction over the course of a year (Murray et al., 2003).

Finally, we note that the fear of rejection that is typical of anxious/ambivalent people may impede their ability to form relationships in the first place. In a series of studies conducted at the University of Manitoba, Vorauer and colleagues (2003) found that people with anxious attachment are so afraid of rejection in a romantic relationship that they overestimate how much romantic interest they are communicating to a potential partner. The problem is that the target of their overtures may not even realize that an overture is being made (Vorauer, Cameron, Holmes, & Pearce, 2003).

In an important conceptual development pertaining to avoidant attachment, Simon Fraser University researcher Kim Bartholomew proposed that there are actually two kinds of avoidant attachment (Bartholomew, 1990; Bartholomew & Horowitz, 1991). People with a **fearful avoidant style** consciously desire intimate relationships but avoid them because they are afraid to trust others and worry that they will be hurt if they allow themselves to become too close to another person. People with a **dismissive avoidant style** claim that they do not need close relationships but, rather, prefer to be independent and self-sufficient. Bartholomew developed a scale to assess secure attachment, preoccupied attachment (similar to anxious/ambivalent attachment discussed earlier), and these two avoidant styles (Bartholomew & Horowitz, 1991; see Table 9.4). Research by Bartholomew and others has shown that people with a fearful avoidant style have a negative view of themselves and of other people, whereas people with a dismissive avoidant style have a positive view of themselves but a negative view of others (Bartholomew & Horowitz, 1991). People with a fearful style also report greater distress when a romantic relationship ends than do those with a dismissive style (Sprecher, Felmlee, Metts, Fehr, & Vanni, 1998).

fearful avoidant style
a type of avoidant attachment in which close relationships are avoided because of mistrust and fears of being hurt

dismissive avoidant style
a type of avoidant attachment in which the person is self-sufficient and claims not to need close relationships

TABLE 9.4

Measuring attachment styles

Secure Style	47%*	It is relatively easy for me to become emotionally close to others. I am comfortable depending on others and having others depend on me. I don't worry about being alone or having others not accept me.
Preoccupied (Anxious) Style	14%	I want to be completely emotionally intimate with others, but I often find that others are reluctant to get as close as I would like. I am uncomfortable being without close relationships, but I sometimes worry that others don't value me as much as I value them.
Dismissive Avoidant Style	18%	I am comfortable without close emotional relationships. It is very important for me to feel independent and self-sufficient, and I prefer not to depend on others or have them depend on me.
Fearful Avoidant Style	21%	I am somewhat uncomfortable getting close to others. I want emotionally close relationships, but I find it difficult to trust others completely, or to depend on them. I sometimes worry that I will be hurt if I allow myself to become too close to others.

*The percentages in each category are based on a sample of introductory psychology students.

(Adapted from Bartholomew & Horowitz, 1991)

A fundamental premise of attachment theory is that based on their interactions with their primary caregiver, people develop expectations about relationships—in particular, about whether others will be available and responsive to their needs. Do people with different attachment styles actually report having different expectations for relationships? To find out, Baldwin, Fehr, Keedian, Seidel, and Thomson (1993) conducted a study in which they presented students at the University of Winnipeg with sentence fragments such as, "If I trust my partner, my partner will. . . ." Participants with a secure attachment style showed faster reaction times when the fragment was completed with the word *care* than did those with an avoidant style. In contrast, the reaction times of avoidant participants were faster than those of securely attached participants when the sentence fragment was completed with the word *hurt*. Given these kinds of expectations for relationships, it is not surprising that securely attached individuals have the most satisfying, enduring relationships, whereas avoidant individuals are the most likely to report never having been in a loving romantic relationship.

Multiple Attachment Representations Please re-read the attachment descriptions in Table 9.4. For each description, try to think of a relationship—with a romantic partner, friend, or parent—in which you felt that way. When students at the University of Winnipeg were asked to do so, most of them were able to think of relationships that matched each style (Baldwin, Keelan, Fehr, Enns, & Koh-Rangarajoo, 1996). Indeed, it is now acknowledged that rather than possessing one single attachment style that applies to all of our relationships, we can have different kinds of attachment to different people in our lives (Fraley, 2002; Simpson, Rholes, Campbell, & Wilson, 2003). For example, Ross and Spinner (2001) asked students at the University of New Brunswick and adults from the adjacent community to fill out the Bartholomew and Horowitz (1991) scale for four specific relationships (e.g., mother, friend). The researchers found that relationship-specific attachment ratings are not necessarily the same as people's reports of their general attachment style— "Knowing, for example, that an individual is securely attached to his or her mother tells us relatively little about whether that individual is also securely attached in other relationships" (Ross & Spinner, 2001).

A similar conclusion was reached by McGill University researchers Tamarha Pierce and John Lydon (2001). In a series of studies, they found that people's overall attachment style is correlated with, but distinct from, their attachment in specific relationships (e.g., mother, father, best friend, and romantic partner). Interestingly, over time, attachment to specific partners changed in the direction of global overall attachment, rather than vice versa. In other words, if you are generally secure, your attachment in specific relationships will tend to become secure, whereas your attachment in any particular relationship is less likely to change your overall style.

Findings such as these have led researchers such as Mark Baldwin and Beverley Fehr (1995; Baldwin et al., 1996) to suggest that attachment styles might best be conceptualized as schemas, rather than as stable personality traits. (*Schemas* are mental structures that people use to organize information—in this case, relational information.) As we discussed in Chapter 3, schemas are resistant to change but not impossible to change. In the context of attachment theory, this is good news, because it implies that people can learn new and healthier ways of relating to others than they experienced in infancy (Kirkpatrick & Hazan, 1994; Kojetin, 1993). Indeed, there is mounting evidence that even if people had unhappy relationships with their parents, they are not doomed to a lifetime of unhappy relationships.

In summary, we began this section with the important question, Why do we love? According to evolutionary theories, we love in order to increase our chances of reproduction, thereby ensuring the survival of our species. According to attachment theory, we learned lessons about how worthy we are of love from our primary caregiver, and those lessons determine whether we seek loving relationships as well as the quality of those relationships.

Maintaining Close Relationships

So far we have been discussing theories and research on attraction. However, initial attraction is only the first chapter in the story of a relationship. Granted, some relationships read a lot like short stories—they may consist of only one chapter; other relationships, however, may evolve into novels, with many chapters. Social psychologists also have something to say about the process of maintaining a relationship once it has been formed.

Social Exchange Theories

Social exchange and equity theories are based on the simple notion that relationships operate on an economic model of costs and benefits, in much the way that the marketplace operates (Blau, 1964; Homans, 1961; Kelley & Thibaut, 1978; Thibaut & Kelley, 1959). **Social exchange theory** states that how people feel about their relationships will depend on their perception of the rewards they receive from the relationship and their perception of the costs they incur, as well as their perception of what kind of relationship they deserve and the probability that they could have a better relationship with someone else. In other words, we "buy" the best relationship we can get, one that gives us the most value for our emotional dollar. The basic concepts of social exchange theory are *reward, cost, outcome, comparison level,* and *comparison level for alternatives* (Thibaut & Kelley, 1959).

Rewards are the positive, gratifying aspects of the relationship that make it worthwhile and reinforcing. They include the positive personal characteristics and behaviour of your relationship partner (e.g., similarity, attractiveness, sense of humour) and your ability to acquire external resources by virtue of knowing this person (e.g., gaining access to money, status, activities, or other interesting people; Lott & Lott, 1974). Costs are, obviously, the other side of the coin; all friendships and romantic relationships have some costs attached to them (e.g., putting up with those annoying habits and characteristics of the other person). The outcome of the relationship is based on a calculation of the **reward/cost ratio**—you can think of it as a mathematical formula in which outcome equals rewards minus costs. (If you come up with a negative number, your relationship is not in good shape.)

How satisfied you are with your relationship depends on another variable—your **comparison level**, or your expectations about the levels of rewards and costs that you deserve in a relationship (Kelley & Thibaut, 1978; Thibaut & Kelley, 1959). Some people have a high comparison level, expecting to receive many rewards and incur few costs in their relationships. If a given relationship doesn't match this comparison level, they will be unhappy and unsatisfied. In contrast, people who have a low comparison level would be happy in the same relationship, because they expect relationships to be difficult and costly.

Finally, your satisfaction with a relationship also depends on your perception of the likelihood that you could replace it with a better one—or your **comparison level for alternatives**. There are a lot of people out there. Could a relationship with a different person—or even being alone—give you a better outcome, or greater rewards for fewer costs, than your current relationship does? People who have a high comparison level for alternatives—perhaps because they believe the world is full of fabulous people dying to meet them or because they are not afraid to be on their own—are more likely to get out of a relationship. People with a low comparison level for alternatives will be more likely to stay in a costly relationship because, to them, what they have is not great but they don't think they could find anything better out there.

Rewards, costs, and alternatives do not tell the whole story, however. As you may have observed, many people do not leave their partners,

social exchange theory

the theory that how people feel about a relationship depends on their perceptions of the rewards and costs of the relationship, the kind of relationship they deserve, and their chances of having a better relationship with someone else

reward/cost ratio

the notion that there is a balance between the rewards that come from a relationship and the personal cost of maintaining the relationship; if the ratio is not favourable, the result is dissatisfaction with the relationship

comparison level

people's expectations about the level of rewards and costs they deserve in a relationship

comparison level for alternatives

people's expectations about the level of rewards and punishments they would receive in an alternative relationship

> ❝ *What, after all, is our life but a great dance in which we are all trying to fix the best going rate of exchange?* ❞
>
> —*Malcolm Bradbury, 1992*

even when they are dissatisfied and their alternatives look bright. Caryl Rusbult and her colleagues would agree; they say that we need to consider at least one additional factor to understand close relationships: a person's level of investment in the relationship (Kelley, 1983; Rusbult, 1980, 1983, 1991; Rusbult, Martz, & Agnew, 1998). In her **investment model** of close relationships, Rusbult defines investments as anything that people have put into a relationship that will be lost if they leave it—tangible things, such as financial resources and possessions (e.g., a house), as well as intangible things, such as the emotional welfare of one's children, or time and emotional energy spent building the relationship. As seen in Figure 9.3, the greater the investment individuals have in a relationship, the less likely they are to leave, even if satisfaction is low and alternatives are available. In short, to predict whether people will stay in an intimate relationship, according to the investment model, we need to know (a) how satisfied they are with the relationship (i.e., the level of rewards minus costs); (b) whether they believe that attractive alternatives are available; and (c) the extent of their investment in the relationship.

To test this model, Rusbult (1983) asked students involved in heterosexual dating relationships to fill out questionnaires over a seven-month period. Every three weeks or so, people answered questions about each of the components of the model shown in Figure 9.3. Rusbult also kept track of whether the students stayed in the relationships or broke up with their partner. Consistent with the model, people's satisfaction, alternatives, and investments all predicted how committed they were to the relationship and whether it lasted. Subsequent studies have found similar results for married couples of diverse ages, for lesbian and gay couples, for close friends, and for residents of the United States, the Netherlands, and Taiwan (Lin & Rusbult, 1995; Rusbult, 1991; Rusbult & Buunk, 1993; Rusbult, Olson, Davis, & Hannon, 2001; see review by Rusbult & Van Lange, 2003).

Rusbult also has applied her investment model to the study of destructive relationships. She and John Martz (1995) interviewed women who had sought refuge at a shelter for battered women, asking them about their abusive romantic relationships and marriages. As the theory would predict, the researchers found that feelings of commitment to the abusive relationship were greater among women who had poorer economic alternatives to the relationship, who were more heavily invested in the relationship (e.g., were married, had children), and who were less dissatisfied with the relationship (e.g., reported receiving less severe forms of abuse). Thus, when it comes to long-term relationships, commitment is based on more than just the amount of rewards and punishments doled out (i.e., the level of satisfaction); it also depends on the quality of alternatives available and how heavily the individual has invested in the relationship.

investment model

the theory that people's commitment to a relationship depends on their satisfaction with the relationship in terms of rewards, costs, and comparison level; their comparison level for alternatives; and how much they have invested in the relationship that would be lost by leaving it

FIGURE 9.3

The investment model of commitment

People's commitment to a relationship depends on three variables: how satisfied they are (i.e., rewards minus costs), how much they feel they have invested in the relationship, and whether they have good alternatives to this relationship. These commitment variables in turn predict how stable the relationship will be. A woman who feels, for example, that the costs exceed the rewards in her relationship would have low satisfaction; if she also felt she had little invested in the relationship and a very attractive person was expressing interest in her, she would have a low level of commitment. The end result is low stability; most likely, she would break up with her current partner.

(Adapted from Rusbult, 1983)

Equity Theory

equity theory

the theory that people are happiest with relationships in which the rewards and costs that a person experiences, and the contributions that he or she makes to the relationship are roughly equal to the rewards, costs, and contributions of the other person

Some researchers have criticized social exchange theory for ignoring an essential variable in relationships—the notion of fairness. Proponents of **equity theory** argue that people are not just out to get the most rewards for the least cost; they are also concerned about equity in their relationships, wherein the rewards and costs they experience and the contributions they make to the relationship are comparable with the rewards, costs, and contributions of the other person (Homans, 1961; Walster (Hatfield), Walster, & Berscheid, 1978). These theorists describe equitable relationships as the most happy and stable type. In comparison, inequitable relationships result in one person feeling overbenefited (i.e., getting a lot of rewards, incurring few costs, devoting little time or energy to the relationship) or underbenefited (i.e., getting few rewards, incurring a lot of costs, devoting a lot of time and energy to the relationship).

According to equity theory, both underbenefited and overbenefited partners should feel uneasy about this state of affairs, and both should be motivated to restore equity to the relationship. This makes sense for the underbenefited person. Who wants to continue feeling miserable? But why should the overbenefited individual want to give up what social exchange theory indicates is a cushy deal—lots of rewards for little cost and little work? Hatfield and Walster (1978) argue that equity is all about fairness; people will eventually feel uncomfortable or even guilty if they get more than they deserve in a relationship. However, let's face facts—being overbenefited just doesn't feel as bad as being underbenefited, and research has, in fact, borne out that inequity is perceived as more of a problem by the underbenefited individual (Buunk & Prins, 1998; Clark & Chrisman, 1994; Hatfield, Greenberger, Traupmann, & Lambert, 1982; Sprecher, 1998; Sprecher & Schwartz, 1994; Traupmann et al., 1981; Van Yperen & Buunk, 1994).

Does equity theory operate in long-term relationships the same way it does in new or less intimate relationships? Not exactly. Elaine Hatfield and Richard Rapson (1993) note that in casual relationships we trade for inkind benefits—you lend someone your class notes, he buys you a beer. In intimate relationships, however, we trade very different resources, and it can be difficult to determine if equity has been achieved. As Hatfield and Rapson (1993) put it, does "dinner at an expensive restaurant on Monday balance out three nights of neglect due to a

▼ Close relationships can have either exchange or communal properties. Family relationships are typically communal; acquaintanceships are typically based on exchange, though they can become communal if they grow into friendships.

heavy workload"? In other words, long-term intimate relationships seem to be governed by a looser give-and-take notion of equity, rather than a rigid tit-for-tat strategy (Kollack, Blumstein, & Schwartz, 1994; Laursen & Hartup, 2002; Vaananen, Buunk, Kivimaki, Pentti, & Vahteva, 2005).

According to Margaret Clark and Judson Mills, interactions between new acquaintances or casual friends are governed by equity concerns and are called **exchange relationships**. In exchange relationships, people keep track of who is contributing what, and feel taken advantage of when they feel they are putting more into the relationship than they are getting out of it. On the other hand, interactions between close friends, family members, and romantic partners are governed less by an equity norm and more by a desire to help each other in times of need (Clark, 1984, 1986; Clark & Mills, 1979, 1993; Mills & Clark, 1982, 1994, 2001). In these **communal relationships**, people give in response to the other's needs, regardless of whether they are repaid. In fact, a critical feature of communal relationships is the perception that the other person will respond to one's needs with behaviours that communicate understanding and caring (Clark & Monin, 2006; Lemay, Clark, & Feeney, 2007; Reis, Clark & Holmes, 2004). These two kinds of relationships are summarized in Figure 9.4, below.

In a series of experiments, Margaret Clark and her colleagues varied whether people desired an exchange or a communal relationship with another person, and then observed the extent to which they were concerned with equity in the relationship. In these experiments, participants interacted with an interesting person and were told either that this person was new to the area and wanted to meet new people—thereby increasing their interest in establishing a communal relationship with the person—or that the other person was married and visiting the area for only a brief time—thereby making them more inclined to

exchange relationships

relationships governed by the need for equity (i.e., for a comparable ratio of rewards and costs)

communal relationships

relationships in which people's primary concern is being responsive to the other person's needs

> *The friendships which last are those wherein each friend respects the other's dignity to the point of not really wanting anything from him.*
>
> —Cyril Connolly (1903–1974)

FIGURE 9.4

Exchange versus communal relationships

Exchange Relationships are governed by

Equity Concerns:
(a) We like to be repaid immediately for our favours.
(b) We feel exploited when our favours are not returned.
(c) We keep track of who is contributing what to the relationship.
(d) Being able to help the person has no effect on our mood.

Communal Relationships are governed by

Responsiveness to the Other's Needs:
(a) We do not like to be repaid immediately for our favours.
(b) We do not feel exploited when our favours are not repaid.
(c) We do not keep track of who is contributing to the relationship.
(d) Being able to help the person puts us in a good mood.

favour an exchange relationship with the person (Clark, 1984; Clark & Mills, 1979; Clark & Waddell, 1985; Williamson & Clark, 1989, 1992). As predicted, people in the exchange condition operated according to the equity norm. People in the communal condition, thinking there was a chance for a long-term relationship, were relatively unconcerned with a tit-for-tat accounting of who was contributing what. These results are not limited to exchange and communal relationships created in the laboratory. Other studies show that ongoing friendships are more communal than relationships between strangers (Clark, Mills, & Corcoran, 1989).

Are people in communal relationships completely unconcerned with equity? No. As we saw earlier, people do feel distressed if they believe that their intimate relationships are inequitable (Canary & Stafford, 2001; Walster (Hatfield), Walster, & Berscheid, 1978). However, equity takes on a somewhat different form in communal relationships than it does in less intimate ones. In communal relationships, the partners are more relaxed about what constitutes equity at any given time; they believe that things will eventually balance out and a rough kind of equity will be achieved over time. If this is not the case—if they come to feel that there is a chronic imbalance—the relationship may end.

The Role of Commitment in Maintaining Relationships

Think about a time when you and a romantic partner or a friend went through a difficult period in your relationship. Did this strengthen your relationship, or did it cause the relationship to deteriorate? McGill University researcher John Lydon and his colleagues (Lydon, 1999; Lydon, Fitzsimons, & Naidoo, 2003; Lydon et al., 1999; Lydon & Zanna, 1990) would tell you that whether adversity has a positive or negative effect on a relationship depends on two factors: the level of adversity and the level of commitment to the relationship. According to Lydon's **commitment calibration hypothesis**, if the level of adversity is lower than the level of commitment, the relationship will not be threatened and therefore it will not be necessary to engage in efforts to maintain the relationship. Thus, a minor problem in a highly committed relationship is likely to have little effect on the relationship. What if, however, the level of adversity is greater than the level of commitment? This is another situation in which people will not engage in much relationship maintenance—but for a very different reason. Specifically, there is little incentive to "hang in there" if the difficulties you are experiencing surpass your level of commitment to the relationship.

So, when do people take steps to preserve their relationship? As you might have guessed by now, they do so when the level of adversity matches the level of commitment. To test this idea, Lydon and colleagues (1999) designed an ingenious experiment. Participants were graduate students and alumni of McGill University who were romantically involved (i.e., dating, cohabiting, or married). They were told that the purpose of the study was to test how well computers do at matching people for romantic relationships. In the first session, participants posed for a photograph and filled out a questionnaire about themselves that would be placed in their portfolio. They then returned for a second session, in which the researchers introduced either a moderate or high level of adversity. In other words, they tried to create a situation that would be either only moderately threatening (moderate adversity condition) or highly threatening (high adversity condition) to a relationship. How did they accomplish this?

Well, imagine that you are a participant in this study. In the first session, your portfolio is created—no big deal. When you arrive for your second session, a research assistant tells you that in this session you will be evaluating another person's portfolio. You are given a photograph of an extremely attractive opposite-sex person. The information in the person's portfolio indicates that this person is currently not romantically involved. Then the bombshell is dropped. The

commitment calibration hypothesis

the idea that the outcome of adversity on a relationship depends on the level of commitment: If the level of adversity is lower than the level of commitment, the relationship is not challenged, but if the level of adversity is higher than the level of commitment, the relationship ends; however, if the level of adversity is equal to the level of commitment, the relationship will be strengthened research assistant mentions that this person has seen the portfolios of participants in the previous session and, lo and behold, has chosen you as the best match for himself or herself! You are then asked how attracted you are to this person.

Based on the commitment calibration hypothesis, Lydon and colleagues expected that participants with only low or moderate commitment to their romantic relationship would not try to protect their relationship in this high-adversity situation. They would find the person in the portfolio very attractive and would say so. Participants who were highly committed to their relationships, however, were expected to engage in relationship maintenance efforts—in this case, by convincing themselves that they really were not all that attracted to this gorgeous, available person who wanted them. And that is exactly what was found.

And what about the moderate adversity condition? Participants in this condition also were shown the portfolio of an attractive opposite-sex person but were simply told that they would be evaluating this person. The researchers reasoned that this situation would be only moderately threatening to a relationship. As expected, in this condition, the participants who were moderately committed reported that they were not particularly attracted to the other person—less so than those who were high or low in commitment. In more recent research, Lydon and colleagues found that in moderate threat situations, people who are moderately committed also rate the attractive person as less good looking than do those who are low in commitment (Lydon, Fitzsimons, & Naidoo, 2003). In other words, we protect our relationship by convincing ourselves that we really aren't attracted to this person, who really isn't all that gorgeous, anyway!

In more recent research, Menzies-Tolman and Lydon (2005) have shown that the more committed people are to their relationships, the more "forgiving" they are of their partner's transgressions. More specifically, those who are high in commitment rate their partner's wrongdoings as less severe and are more likely to respond constructively compared with those who are less committed. Follow-up studies have shown that women are more likely than men to respond to relationship transgressions with constructive, accommodating responses, particularly in the face of a relationship threat, such as encountering an attractive, available opposite-sex partner (Lydon, Menzies-Tolman, Burton, & Bell, 2008). In other words, when temptation strikes, women react by shoring up their commitment to their current partner. Men are less likely to show this pattern. Interestingly, this gender difference disappears when men receive "coaching" on how to protect their relationships. Specifically, in one of their studies, men were asked to imagine being approached by an attractive alternative. Participants in the experimental group were asked to think about "When the guy/girl approaches, I will _____ to protect my relationship." In other words, these participants were being asked to come up with relationship-defending strategies. Participants in the control group were asked to think about strategies for staying focused while studying. Men who rehearsed relationship-defending strategies were later more likely to avoid the attractive alternative than those in the control condition. Put another way, the men who had been coached to defend their relationship responded in a relationship-enhancing way—just like women typically do (Lydon et al., 2008).

In conclusion, this program of research indicates that how committed we are to a relationship plays an important role in whether or not the relationship is maintained. When adversity strikes, people will take active steps to shore up a relationship only when the level of adversity is equal to their level of commitment. Thus, adversity can actually have a positive effect on relationship maintenance—but only if it comes in just the right amount. Finally, recent research shows that when people are committed to their relationships, they tend to perceive their partner's transgressions as less severe, react more constructively when their partner does something wrong, and take steps to protect their relationship when an attractive alternative comes on the scene.

The Role of Positive Illusions

Once a relationship has begun, there are inevitable conflicts and disappointments. During these times, we may experience doubts about our choice of partner and question whether ours really is a good relationship. Research conducted at the University of Waterloo suggests that under these circumstances we maintain our relationships by indulging in **positive illusions**—that is, fantasies in which we convince ourselves that we have the most wonderful partner and the most wonderful relationship in the world—regardless of the facts. This process of idealization has been explored in several studies by Sandra Murray, John Holmes, and their colleagues. (Sandra Murray received the prestigious American Psychological Association Award for Distinguished Early Career Contributions for this work.)

In one of their first studies, Murray and Holmes (1993) investigated whether people deal with doubts and uncertainties by weaving stories in which their partner's flaws are reinterpreted as virtues. In attempting to test this hypothesis, the researchers faced a challenge: How does one get people to have doubts about their partner? Here's how Murray and Holmes did it. Students in dating relationships were asked whether their partner tended to initiate conflicts. As expected, most participants reported that they did not have the kind of partner who starts fights. Those in the experimental group then read a fake *Psychology Today* article in which it was argued that engaging in conflict can be healthy for a relationship. This information was intended to threaten participants' views of their partner. Participants in the control group read an unrelated story.

Later, when asked again whether their partner initiated conflict, participants in the experimental group—but not those in the control group—changed their tune. They now reported that they, in fact, had partners who quite enjoyed a good fight! The researchers suggest that by taking this kind of poetic licence, these participants were able to maintain a positive view of their partner and their relationship.

In a subsequent study, Murray and Holmes (1999) identified another way in which we maintain our relationships—namely, by finding redeeming features in our partner's faults. Specifically, when they asked students at the University of Waterloo to write out their dating partner's faults, approximately half of their participants engaged in "yes, but" refutations. For example, one woman reported that her partner had a tendency to overreact to situations but added that she had come to realize he did so only to protect her.

The creative storytelling that people in these studies engaged in suggests that we are highly motivated to maintain positive perceptions of our partners and our relationships, regardless of the facts. Do we actually hold idealistic, rather than realistic, views of our partners? To find out, Murray, Holmes, and Griffin (1996a) asked dating and married couples to rate their own attributes, their partner's attributes, and attributes of an ideal partner. Take, for example, the case of Lucia and Mario. If Lucia's perception of Mario is accurate (i.e., based on reality), the way in which she rates him in terms of intelligence, humour, and consideration should be very similar to how Mario rates himself on these attributes. If, however, Lucia holds an idealistic view of Mario, she should rate him more positively than he rates himself. And that is exactly what these researchers found. In fact, participants' ratings of their partner closely resembled their ratings of an ideal partner. These findings have been confirmed in subsequent research (Murray et al., 2000; Murray et al., 2002; Murray, Holmes, & Griffin, 1996a).

The assumption in this research has been that people view their partner in highly positive ways as a means of maintaining their relationships. Is it actually beneficial to see our partners in idealistic ways? Wouldn't relationships be better

positive illusions

idealization of our romantic relationships and partners in order to maintain the relationship off if we perceived our partners as they really are? Apparently not. In fact, it would seem that the rosier the glasses through which we view our partners, the better. Murray and Holmes have consistently found that the more people idealize their partners and the more that their partner idealizes them, the greater their satisfaction with the relationship (Murray & Holmes, 1997, 1999; Murray et al, 2000; Murray, Holmes, & Griffin, 1996a). According to recent research conducted at the University of Manitoba, relationship satisfaction is particularly high when we idealize our partners in terms of traits that are important to relationships (e.g., caring, loving, affectionate) rather than in terms of less relationship-relevant traits (e.g., talkative, reserved) (Sciangula & Morry, in press).

Idealization also has survival value: relationships in which partners idealize one another are most likely to endure. For example, Murray, Holmes, and Griffin (1996b) conducted a longitudinal study in which they measured idealization and satisfaction among dating couples several times over a one-year period. The researchers found that couples who idealized each other at the outset experienced the greatest increases in satisfaction over the course of the year and the greatest decreases in conflicts and doubts. These couples also were more likely to be together a year later than were couples who did not idealize one another. Perhaps most astonishing was the finding that over time people began to live up to the idealized image their partner had of them. Stated differently, individuals who idealized their partners ultimately created the partners they wished for. Thus, in the world of close relationships, dreams can actually come true!

But you may be thinking, surely over time, idealization could lead to disappointment as people get to know who their partner "really" is. This important question was examined in a recent study in which married couples were studied over the first 13 years of their marriage. It was found that couples who had positive illusions about their spouse at the newlywed stage reported greater feelings of marital love than couples who started their marriage with less idealistic views of each other (Miller, Niehuis, & Huston, 2006). Thus, positive illusions appear to have lasting benefits.

Before leaving this topic, we should note that the effects we have been discussing tend to be stronger for women than for men. In a series of studies conducted at McGill University and Université de Moncton, it was found that men tend to engage in positive illusions only if they are highly committed to a relationship, whereas women are more likely to hold unrealistically positive perceptions of their partner regardless of their level of commitment (Gagné & Lydon, 2003).

Ending Close Relationships

As you may know first hand, some relationships resemble nightmares more than dreams come true. In Canada, just over one-third of marriages end in divorce (Canada, 2002). The dissolution of other kinds of relationships is not publicly recorded. However, in longitudinal studies of dating relationships, a typical finding is that half of the couples break up within a few years, with gay and lesbian relationships showing some of the highest rates of dissolution (Sprecher, 1994; Sprecher & Fehr, 1998). And even though people tend not to break up with friends formally, the loss of friendships is a common experience (Fehr, 1996). After several years of studying what love is and how it blooms, social psychologists have begun to explore the end of the story—how it dies.

Why Relationships End

As you might expect, the reasons that relationships end are complex and multifaceted. Moreover, different kinds of relationships end for different reasons. For example, common reasons given for the dissolution of marriage are financial difficulties, unemployment, alcoholism, sexual infidelity, low religiosity, and premarital pregnancy (Sprecher & Fehr, 1998; White, 1990). Not all of these reasons would apply to dating relationships or friendships. There are, however, some important commonalities across relationships.

One place to look for clues is among the predictors of attraction. If the factors that initially attracted you to someone are no longer present, the relationship is likely to be in trouble. For example, at the beginning of this chapter we identified similarity as an important predictor of attraction; as you might expect, if spouses, friends, or dating partners become dissimilar, the relationship is vulnerable to dissolution (Fehr, 1996; Sprecher & Fehr, 1998). Statements such as, "We grew apart" or "We seemed to be going in different directions" reflect the role of dissimilarity in the breakup of relationships. In a fascinating study, Diane Felmlee (1995) asked 300 university students to focus on a romantic relationship that had ended, and to list the qualities that had first attracted them to the person and the characteristics they ended up disliking most about the person. Felmlee found that 30 percent of these breakups could be classified as "fatal attractions." In other words, the qualities that were initially so attractive (e.g., "He's so unusual and different," "She's so exciting and unpredictable") became the very reasons why the relationship ended (e.g., "He and I have nothing in common," "I can never count on her"). "Fatal attractions" were most likely to occur for qualities on which the partners were dissimilar.

The theories of relationships discussed earlier also shed light on the issue of why relationships end. Social exchange theorists, for example, find that relationships are likely to end when rewards are low and costs are high (in other words, when the relationship is low in satisfaction), when attractive alternatives are available to one or both partners, or when the partners have invested little in the relationship (Rusbult, 1983; Rusbult, Martz, & Agnew, 1998). Equity also plays a role in the ending of relationships. People are likely to end relationships that they feel are inequitable—particularly if they are feeling underbenefited.

Finally, there is another reason that relationships end—a reason few of us are willing to admit: sheer boredom. According to Aron and Aron (1986a, 1996), as another person becomes familiar to us, there is less that is new and exciting for us to discover about him or her. The day-to-day routine of living together may lead people to feel that they are in a rut and are missing out on excitement and passion (Baumeister & Bratslavsky, 1999; Fincham & Bradbury, 1993). In a recent program of research conducted at the University of Manitoba and the

▶ Relationships can end for many reasons. In "fatal attractions," for example, the very qualities that once attracted you ("He's so mature and wise") can become the very reason you break up ("He's too old").

"Somehow I remember this one differently."

University of Winnipeg, Cheryl Harasymchuk has found that in both dating and marital relationships, boredom is associated with less enjoyment and excitement in relationships, and with lower relationship satisfaction (Harasymchuk, 2008; Harasymchuk & Fehr, 2007, 2008). This research also has shown that boredom is a unique challenge in relationships—reflecting the loss of something positive that was once present but now is missing, it is not the same as other negative processes such as conflict or hostility. According to University of Windsor researcher John La Gaipa (1982) boredom is also an issue in friendships. He maintains that friendships may dissolve because of boredom, but that boredom is not considered a socially acceptable basis for terminating a friendship. Thus, when asked why a friendship ended, people are likely to mention reasons such as disloyalty or betrayals of trust. We suspect that people who terminate a marriage would be especially likely to offer such reasons, even if the culprit was sheer boredom.

The Process of Breaking Up

Ending a relationship is one of life's more painful experiences. The pain is greatest for the person who is being rejected. If you have ever broken up with someone, however, you may be all too aware that it is no fun telling someone that you no longer wish to have a relationship. Consequently, it probably does not come as a surprise that people often use passive avoidance strategies when terminating a relationship. For example, Baxter (1982) asked people about the strategies they would use to end either a romantic relationship or a friendship. She identified four major strategies from these accounts: withdrawal/avoidance, positive tone (e.g., trying to prevent "hard feelings"), manipulative strategies (e.g., getting a third party to communicate the bad news), and open confrontation. For both types of relationships, people reported that they would be most likely to use positive tone strategies. They also said they would use withdrawal/avoidance strategies, especially for friendship terminations. Open confrontation was a more likely strategy for ending romantic relationships. Other research has shown that passive strategies such as withdrawal or avoidance are especially likely to be used in friendships, where people generally opt to let the relationship fade away (Fehr, 1996). In contrast, dating or marital relationships are less likely to simply wither on the vine—especially if one partner still wants the relationship to continue. Thus, more direct methods are generally necessary for these sorts of breakups (Baxter, 1985).

The Experience of Breaking Up

How do people feel when their relationship ends? One important factor is the role they played in the decision to end the relationship (Helgeson, 1994; Lloyd & Cate, 1985). For example, when Robin Akert (1998) asked 344 university students to focus on their most important former romantic relationship, she found that the single most powerful predictor of reactions to breakups was whether you were the one who did the breaking up or the one who was "dumped." Not surprisingly, if your partner broke up with you, you were miserable—participants in this situation reported high levels of loneliness, depression, unhappiness, and anger, and virtually all reported experiencing physical disorders (e.g., upset stomach, trouble sleeping) in the weeks after the breakup. In contrast, those who did the breaking up experienced the lowest levels of upset, pain, and stress, although they were not exempt from negative effects. In particular, they tended to experience guilt and unhappiness. Those who reported that the breakup was mutual fell in the middle of these two groups—they were not as upset or hurt as those who had been dumped, but they suffered more than those who did the breaking up. Thus, it appears that a mutual conclusion to a romantic relationship can be a more stressful experience than a unilateral decision to end it.

> *Love is like war; easy to begin but very hard to stop.*
>
> —H. L. Mencken

The degree of distress experienced after a breakup is influenced by other factors as well. For example, Sprecher and colleagues (1998) found that in addition to responsibility for the breakup, social exchange variables played a role (Sprecher, Felmlee, Metts, Fehr, & Vanni, 1998). As you might expect based on our earlier discussion of social exchange theory, people who reported high levels of relationship satisfaction and commitment were much more distressed when the relationship ended than those who were less satisfied and committed. Also consistent with social exchange theory, people experienced less distress if they were interested in an alternative relationship, but more distress if attractive alternatives were available to their former partner.

The good news is that the participants reported that they felt significantly less distressed currently than they had immediately after the breakup. Thus, if by some unfortunate circumstance your heart has been broken, take comfort in the fact that time really does heal wounds.

SUMMARY

In the first part of this chapter, we discussed the variables that cause initial attraction between two people. One such variable is physical proximity, or the **propinquity effect**. People you come into contact with the most are the most likely to become your friends and lovers. In general, exposure to any stimulus produces liking for it. This is known as the **mere exposure effect. Similarity** between people, whether in attitudes, demographic characteristics, values, or activity preferences, is another powerful cause of attraction and liking. (There is less evidence for **complementarity**—the idea that opposites attract.) How people behave toward us is also of importance. In general, we like others who like us. Thus, **reciprocal liking** is another determinant of attraction. What is common to these predictors of attraction is the sense of familiarity they provide. Though most people are reluctant to admit it, physical attractiveness also plays an important role. The "what is

beautiful is good" stereotype indicates that people assume that physical attractiveness is associated with other desirable traits. Finally, attraction can also occur due to **misattribution of arousal**—mistakenly assuming that feelings of physiological arousal from some other source are caused by the presence of an attractive person in our environment.

In the second part of this chapter, we examined love in close relationships. Social psychologists have offered several definitions of love. One important distinction is between **companionate love**—feelings of intimacy and affection for those with whom our lives are intertwined—and **passionate love**—feelings of intense longing and arousal. Ordinary people's definitions of love include both companionate and passionate love.

Although love is universal, there are gender and cultural differences in the definition and experience of love. Men hold a more romantic, passionate view of love than do women, although more recent research suggests that both women and men place the greatest emphasis on companionate love. People who live in individualist cultures are more likely to emphasize passionate love than are people who live in collectivist cultures, where companionate love is valued.

Numerous theories have been proposed to explain *why* human beings are so motivated to seek love. The **evolutionary approach to love** states that men and women are attracted to different characteristics in each other because this maximizes reproductive success. This view maintains that when choosing a long-term partner women care more about men's resources and men care more about women's appearance. **Attachment theory** points to people's past relationships, specifically with their primary caregiver, as a significant determinant of the quality of their close relationships as adults. Infants can be classified as having one of three types of **attachment style: secure, avoidant,** and **anxious/ambivalent.** The avoidant style can be further divided into **fearful avoidant** and **dismissive avoidant.** People who report having been securely attached as infants have the most intimate and satisfying relationships. Recent research suggests that people have different attachment patterns in different relationships, rather than an overall attachment style. Accordingly, it is suggested that attachment styles are best thought of as schemas, rather than as stable personality traits.

We also discussed how people maintain intimate relationships. **Social exchange theory** argues that how satisfied people feel in their relationships depends on their assessment of the **reward/cost ratio** in their relationship. In order to determine whether people will stay in a relationship, we also need to know their **comparison level:** the outcomes they have come to expect in relationships—and their **comparison level for alternatives:** their expectations about how happy they would be in other relationships or alone. According to the **investment model of close relationships,** to predict whether a relationship will last, we need to know each person's level of satisfaction, comparison level for alternatives, and how much has been invested in the relationship.

There are exceptions to the rules of social exchange. **Equity theory** states that we are happiest when relationships are fair—when what we contribute is comparable with what our partner contributes. Further, the notion of equity is different in long-term versus short-term relationships. Short-term relationships are usually **exchange relationships,** in which people are concerned about a fair distribution of rewards and costs. Long-term, intimate relationships are usually **communal relationships,** in which people are less concerned with an immediate accounting of who is contributing what and are more concerned with helping their partner when he or she is in need.

Commitment is important in maintaining relationships. According to the **commitment calibration hypothesis,** adversity can strengthen a relationship, but only if the level of adversity is equal to the level of commitment. **Positive illusions** also play a role in relationship maintenance. The more we idealize our partner, the greater our satisfaction with a relationship and the more likely that the relationship will endure.

Unfortunately, intimate relationships end. There are a number of reasons why, including dissimilarity between the partners. Relationships also end when costs are greater than rewards (i.e., when the relationship is no longer satisfying), when attractive alternatives are available, and when investments are low. If we believe that our reward/cost ratio is not comparable with our partner's, the relationship is inequitable and vulnerable to dissolution—especially if we believe that our partner is getting a better deal than we are (i.e., we feel underbenefited rather than overbenefited). People tend to use passive strategies when ending relationships, although these strategies may not be effective for ending romantic relationships. While the experience of breaking up is never pleasant, a powerful variable that predicts how a person will weather the breakup is the role he or she plays in the decision to terminate the relationship.

PEARSON
mypsychlab

Along with a dynamic, electronic version of this text, MyPsychLab offers a wealth of resources to deepen your understanding and test your recall of the material in this chapter—including video and audio clips, simulations and activities, self-assessments, practice tests, and other study materials. The following specific resources are available for this chapter:

Passionate Love Scale

Interpersonal Attraction

Men, Women, and Attraction: Michael Bailey

To access MyPsychLab, please visit www.mypsychlab.com (Student Access Code required—packaged with this book).

Prosocial Behaviour:
Why Do People Help?

In Chapter 2, we described how during the brutal stabbing death of Kitty Genovese, neighbours heard her screams for help. Many even watched the assault through their window. Yet, no one intervened. No one even called the police. This tragic event, which took place more than 30 years ago in New York City, may seem far removed today. But is it? Read on.

January 20, 2000. Montreal residents making their way to work passed a man lying on the sidewalk, arms outstretched, crying and begging for help. It was −41°C. The man was Gino LaPlante. He was 38 years old and suffered from psychiatric problems. Because he was lying in the middle of the sidewalk, people had to walk around him to avoid stepping on him. Anne Lavictoire was one of those people. However, unlike the others, she decided to see if she could help. She discovered that LaPlante's hands were already frozen. She called for an ambulance and tried to keep him warm. It took 15 or 20 minutes for an ambulance to arrive. By then, it was too late. Gino LaPlante had frozen to death on a sidewalk in Montreal on a cold Thursday morning.

June 3, 2006. The lead article in the *Winnipeg Free Press* begins with a question: "How could nearly a dozen Winnipegers turn their backs on a Good Samaritan who lay bleeding and unconscious on a Portage Avenue sidewalk?" (McIntyre, 2006). It all began when a panhandler started harrassing a woman standing at a bus stop. Murray Aklwenzie, a 60-year-old man, noticed and politely asked the panhandler to leave the woman alone. The panhandler then turned on Aklwenzie. The attack left Aklwenzie with a crushed skull and other near-fatal injuries. At least a dozen passersby witnessed the scene, but did nothing as Aklwenzie lay there, unconscious and bleeding. What about the woman who Aklwenzie had stepped in to help? She hopped on her bus when it arrived and never even notified the police.

December 6, 2002. Breann Voth, a teenager from Port Coquitlam, British Columbia, was on her way to catch the morning bus when she was murdered. Investigations into her death revealed that Voth's cries for help were heard in at least 15 households—yet, no one called the police. Her naked body was found later that morning on the banks of the Coquitlam River.

▲ Justice Peck is one of many people who exhibit prosocial behaviour. What makes some people help others even at considerable cost to themselves?

Based on these events, what is your view of human nature? Are human beings inclined to respond when they see another person in need? Can people be counted on to help? Now consider the following stories:

On July 22, 2005, Trent Fenwick, a 37-year-old man from Kelowna, British Columbia, travelled to Chicago, where he underwent surgery to remove one of his kidneys. Fenwick donated his kidney to a Chicago father with a 2-year-old son and a 3-month-old daughter, after reading about the man's need on the internet. Many people have wondered why Trent Fenwick would make this kind of sacrifice for a complete stranger. His answer? "Your heart's desire is to give, so you give in whatever way you are in peace about" (Gulli, 2005, p. A1).

In April 2008, a 14-year-old boy, Justice Peck, was about to go to bed in his Prince George, British Columbia, home when he thought he smelled smoke coming from his neighbour's duplex. He rushed over and opened the outside door to the duplex. The stairs were engulfed in fire. Peck jumped through the flames and alerted the occupants—a single mother with two young boys. They smashed a front window and climbed through it to safety. "If it wasn't for Justice," the mother said, "we would all be dead" (Peebles, 2008, p. A2).

Based on reading these stories, what is your view of human nature now? Are human beings inclined to respond when they see another person in need? Can people be counted on to help?

Why Do People Help?

Why is it that sometimes people perform acts of great self-sacrifice and heroism, whereas at other times they behave in uncaring, heartless ways, ignoring the desperate pleas of those in need? In this chapter, we will consider the major determinants of **prosocial behaviour**—which we define as any act performed with the goal of benefiting another person (Penner, Dovidio, Piliavin, Schroeder, 2005; Mikulincer & Shaver, in press). We will be particularly concerned with prosocial behaviour motivated by **altruism**—which is the desire to help another person, even if it involves a cost to the helper (Post, Underwood, Schloss, & Harlbut, 2002). Someone might act in a prosocial manner out of self-interest—hoping to get something in return. Altruism, on the other hand, is helping purely out of the desire to benefit someone else, with no benefit—but often a cost—to oneself. Murray Aklwenzie risked his life by intervening when a woman was being harassed at a bus stop. Trent Fenwick volunteered to have major surgery so that a stranger could live.

We will begin by considering the basic origins of prosocial behaviour and altruism. Why do people help others? Few questions have intrigued observers of the human condition as much as this one. Is the willingness to help a basic impulse with genetic roots? Is it something that must be taught and nurtured in

prosocial behaviour

any act performed with the goal of benefiting another person

altruism

the desire to help another person, even if it involves a cost to the helper childhood? Is there a pure motive for helping, such that people are willing to aid their fellow human beings even when they have nothing to gain? Or are people willing to help only when there is something in it for them? Let's see how psychologists have addressed these centuries-old questions.

Evolutionary Psychology: Instincts and Genes

According to Charles Darwin's (1859) theory of evolution, natural selection favours genes that promote the survival of the individual (see Chapter 9). Any gene that furthers our survival and increases the probability that we will produce offspring is likely to be passed on from generation to generation. Genes that lower our chances of survival, such as those that cause life-threatening diseases, reduce the chances that we will produce offspring and thus are less likely to be passed on. Several psychologists have pursued these ideas, spawning the field of evolutionary psychology, which is the attempt to explain social behaviour in terms of genetic factors that evolved over time according to the principles of natural selection (Buss, 2005; Ketelaar & Ellis, 2000; Pinker, 2002; Simpson & Kenrick, 1997).

Darwin realized early on that a potential problem exists with evolutionary theory. How can it explain altruism? If people's overriding goal is to ensure their own survival, why would they ever help others at a cost to themselves? It would seem that over the centuries, altruistic behaviour would disappear because people who acted that way would, by putting themselves at risk, produce fewer offspring than would people who acted selfishly. Genes promoting selfish behaviour would be more likely to be passed on—or would they?

Kin Selection One way that evolutionary psychologists attempt to resolve this dilemma is with the notion of **kin selection**, the idea that behaviours that help a genetic relative are favoured by natural selection (Hamilton, 1964; Meyer, 1999). People can increase the chances that their genes will be passed along not only by having their own children but also by ensuring that their genetic relatives have children. Because a person's blood relatives share some of his or her genes, the more that person ensures his or her survival, the greater the chance that that person's genes will flourish in future generations. Thus, natural selection should favour altruistic acts directed toward genetic relatives.

In one study that supports this view, people reported that they would be more likely to help genetic relatives than non-relatives in life-and-death situations, such

> *Altruism based on kin selection is the enemy of civilization. If human beings are to a large extent guided to favor their own relatives and tribe, only a limited amount of global harmony is possible.*
>
> —E. O. Wilson, "On Human Nature", 1978

kin selection

the idea that behaviour that helps a genetic relative is favoured by natural selection

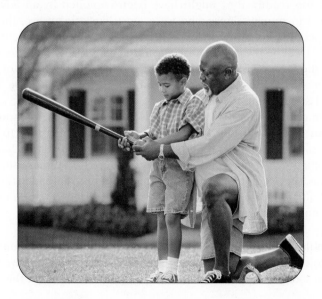

◀ According to evolutionary psychology, prosocial behaviour occurs in part because of kin selection.

as a house fire. People did not report that they would be more likely to help genetic relatives when the situation was non–life threatening. Interestingly, both men and women, as well as American and Japanese participants, followed this rule of kin selection in life-threatening situations (Burnstein, Crandall, & Kitayama, 1994). Of course, in this study, people only reported what they would do; this doesn't prove that in a real fire they would indeed be more likely to save their sibling than their friend. There is some anecdotal evidence from real emergencies, however, that is consistent with these results. Sime (1983) interviewed survivors of a fire at a vacation complex and found that when people became aware that there was a fire, they were much more likely to search for family members before exiting the building than they were to search for friends.

Evolutionary psychologists do not mean to imply that people consciously weigh the biological importance of their behaviour before deciding whether to help. It is not as if people crassly compute the likelihood that their genes will be passed on before deciding whether to help someone push his or her car out of a ditch. According to evolutionary theory, however, the genes of people who follow this "biological importance" rule are more likely to survive than the genes of people who do not. Thus, they argue that over the millennia, kin selection became ingrained in human behaviour.

A study by Korchmaros and Kenny (2006) has recently called this view into question. Participants were asked to list the names of immediate and extended family members and to report how close they felt to each of them. Next, they were presented with a variety of possible helping situations and were asked to report which family member they would be most likely to help. Contrary to the idea of kin selection, the degree of genetic relatedness did not predict willingness to help. Instead, the critical variable was the degree of closeness: Participants were most likely to help the family members to whom they had the closest emotional ties, rather than those to whom they were most closely related. The researchers suggest that evolution may actually have created the tendency to help those who are close to us, rather than the tendency to help those who are related to us. Clearly, additional research will be required to further disentangle this issue.

The Reciprocity Norm To explain altruism, evolutionary psychologists also point to the **norm of reciprocity**, which is the expectation that helping others will increase the likelihood that they will help us in the future. The idea is that as human beings were evolving, a group of completely selfish individuals, each living in his or her own cave, would have found it more difficult to survive than a group who had learned to cooperate with one another. Of course, if people cooperated too readily, they might have been exploited by an adversary who never helped in return. Those who were most likely to survive, the argument goes, were people who developed an understanding with their neighbours about reciprocity: "I will help you now, with the agreement that when I need help, you will return the favour." Because of its survival value, such a norm of reciprocity may have become genetically based (Cosmides & Tooby, 1992; De Waal, 1996; Shackelford & Buss, 1996; Trivers, 1971).

According to William Brown and Chris Moore (2000) at Dalhousie University, from an evolutionary perspective it would also be adaptive to be able to detect pure altruists from those who are cheaters (free riders who have no plans of reciprocating helpful acts in the future). In a series of studies using hypothetical scenarios, they demonstrated that people are remarkably adept at discerning true acts of altruism. The accompanying Try It! describes a way you can use the reciprocity norm to collect money for charity.

Learning Social Norms Nobel laureate Herbert Simon (1990) offered one more link between evolution and altruism. He argued that it is highly adaptive for individuals to learn social norms from other members of a society. Over the centuries, a

norm of reciprocity

the expectation that helping others will increase the likelihood that they will help us in the future

Try it!

▶ Does the Reciprocity Norm Work?

If you help people in some way, they will probably feel obligated to help you in the future. This exercise is designed to take advantage of the reciprocity norm to help you collect money for a good cause. Follow the procedures and see if it works for you.

1. Choose a charity or cause for which you would like to collect money.

2. Make a list of 10 to 15 friends and acquaintances you are willing to ask to give money to this charity.

3. To randomly assign conditions for this study, flip a coin for each name on the list. If the coin comes up tails, assign that person to the favour condition. If it comes up heads, assign that person to the no-favour condition.

4. Find a way to do a small favour for each person in the favour condition. For example, if you're going to the pop machine, offer to buy a drink for your friend. If you have a car, give him or her a ride somewhere. The exact favour doesn't matter and doesn't have to be the same for each person assigned to the favour condition. The key is that it be a little out of the ordinary, so your friend feels obligated to you.

5. After a day or two, ask everyone on your list if they can make a donation to your charity. Do not say anything about your earlier favours. Keep track of how much each person gives. Chances are, people in your favour condition will give more, on average, than people in your no-favour condition.

6. After you have done this exercise, discuss it with your friends and explain why you did what you did.

A word of warning: This technique can backfire if your friends perceive your favour as an attempt to manipulate them. That is why it is important to allow a day or so to pass between the time you help them and the time you ask them for a donation; if you ask them right after the favour, they are likely to feel that you helped only to get them to give money—and they may resent this intrusion.

culture learns such things as which foods are poisonous and how best to cooperate with one another, and the person who learns these rules is more likely to survive than the person who does not. Consequently, through natural selection, the ability to learn social norms has become part of our genetic makeup. One norm that people learn is the value of helping others; this is considered to be a valuable norm in virtually all societies. In short, people are genetically programmed to learn social norms, and one of these norms is altruism (Hoffman, 1981; Kameda, Takezawa, & Hastie, 2003).

In sum, evolutionary psychologists believe that people help others because of three factors that have become ingrained in our genes: kin selection, the norm of reciprocity, and the ability to learn and follow social norms. As we saw in Chapter 9, evolutionary psychology is a challenging and creative approach, but it does have its critics (Batson, 1998; Buller, 2005; Caporael & Brewer, 2000; Gould, 1997; Wood & Eagly, 2002). How, for example, can evolutionary theory explain why complete strangers help each other, even when there is no reason for them to assume that they share the same genes or that their favour will ever be returned? It seems absurd to say that 14-year-old Justice Peck somehow calculated how genetically similar the occupants of the burning house were to him before deciding to save their lives. And Trent Fenwick, who donated a kidney to a complete stranger, certainly did not expect that this man would return the favour. Clearly, other factors must be considered in order to explain why people help under such conditions. We turn to these factors next.

Social Exchange: The Costs and Rewards of Helping

Although some social psychologists disagree with evolutionary approaches to prosocial behaviour, they do agree that altruistic behaviour can be based on self-interest. In fact, social exchange theory (see Chapter 9) argues that much of

▶ Helping behaviour is common in virtually all species of animals. Sometimes, helping behaviour even crosses species lines. In August 1996, a three-year-old boy fell into a pit containing seven gorillas at the Brookfield, Illinois, zoo. Binti, a seven-year-old gorilla, immediately picked up the boy. After cradling him in her arms, she placed the boy near a door where zookeepers could get to him. Why did she help? Evolutionary psychologists would argue that prosocial behaviour is selected for and thus becomes part of the genetic makeup of members of many species. Social exchange theorists would argue that Binti had been rewarded for helping in the past. In fact, because she had been rejected by her mother, she had received training in parenting skills from zookeepers and had been rewarded for caring for a doll (Bils & Singer, 1996).

what we do stems from the desire to maximize our rewards and minimize our costs (Homans, 1961; Lawler & Thye, 1999; Thibaut & Kelley, 1959). What might be the rewards of helping? There are actually a number of them. First, as we saw with the norm of reciprocity, helping someone is an investment in the future, the social exchange being that someday someone will help you when you need it. Helping can also relieve the distress of the bystander. Considerable evidence indicates that people are aroused and disturbed when they see another person suffer, and that they help at least in part to relieve their own distress (Dovidio, 1984; Dovidio, Piliavin, Gaertner, Schroeder, & Clark, 1991; Piferi, Jobe, & Jones, 2006). Finally, by helping others, we can also gain such rewards as social approval from others and increased feelings of self-worth.

The other side of the coin, of course, is that helping can be costly. Helping decreases when the costs are high, as when it would put us in physical danger, result in pain or embarrassment, or take too much time (Dovidio et al., 1991; Piliavin, Piliavin, & Rodin, 1975), or, as in the case of Gino LaPlante, when people are rushing to work in −41°C weather. Not surprisingly, under such conditions, people are less likely to help. Thus, the basic assumption of social exchange theory is that people help only when the benefits outweigh the costs. True altruism, in which people help even when doing so is costly, does not exist, according to this theory.

If you are like many of our students, you may be experiencing discomfort over this view of helping behaviour, finding it to be a rather cynical portrayal of human nature. Is true altruism, motivated only by the desire to help someone else, really such a mythical act? Must we trace all prosocial behaviour to the self-interest of the helper? Well, a social exchange theorist might reply that there are many ways in which people can obtain gratification and we should be thankful that one way is by helping others. After all, wealthy people could decide to get pleasure only from lavish vacations, expensive cars, and gourmet meals at fancy restaurants. We should applaud their decision to give money to the disadvantaged, even if, ultimately, it is just another way for them to feel good about themselves. Prosocial acts are doubly rewarding in that they help both the giver and the recipient of the aid. Thus, it is to everyone's advantage to promote and praise such acts.

❝ *Let him who neglects to raise the fallen, fear lest, when he falls, no one will stretch out his hand to lift him up.* ❞

—*Saadi*, The Orchard, 1257

❝ *I once saw a man out of courtesy help a lame dog over a stile, and [the dog] for requital bit his fingers.* ❞

—*William Chillingworth (1602–1644)*

Calvin and Hobbes

by Bill Watterson

Still, many people are dissatisfied with the argument that all helping stems from self-interest. How can it explain why people go so far as to risk their lives for others, as Justice Peck did when he entered a burning house or Murray Aklwenzie did when he intervened when a woman was being harassed on the street? According to some social psychologists, people do have hearts of gold and sometimes help only for the sake of helping—as we shall see now.

Empathy and Altruism: The Pure Motive for Helping

C. Daniel Batson (1991) is the strongest proponent of the idea that people frequently help purely out of the goodness of their hearts. Batson acknowledges that people sometimes help others for selfish reasons; however, he argues that people's motives are sometimes purely altruistic, in that their only goal is to help the other person, even if doing so involves some cost. Pure altruism is likely to come into play, he maintains, when we feel empathy for the person in need of help. **Empathy** is defined as the ability to put ourselves in the shoes of another person, experiencing events and emotions the way that person experiences them. Suppose, for example, that you are at the grocery store and see a man holding a baby and a bag full of diapers, toys, and rattles. As the man reaches for a box of Cheerios, he loses his grip on the bag and all of its contents spill on the floor. Will you stop to help him pick up his things? According to Batson, it depends first on whether you feel empathy for him; if you do, you will help, regardless of what you have to gain. Your goal will be to relieve the man's distress, not to gain something for yourself. This is the crux of Batson's **empathy-altruism hypothesis**.

What if you do not feel empathy? If, for whatever reason, you do not share the other person's distress, then Batson says social exchange comes into play. What's in it for you? If there is something to be gained, such as obtaining approval from the man in the mall or from onlookers, you will help the man pick up his things. If you will not profit from helping, you will go on your way without stopping. (Batson's empathy-altruism hypothesis is summarized in Figure 10.1 on the next page.) Batson would, however, be the first to acknowledge that it can be very difficult to isolate the exact causes of complex social behaviours.

Consider a famous story about Abraham Lincoln. One day, while riding in a coach, Lincoln and a fellow passenger were debating the very question we are considering: Is helping ever truly altruistic? Lincoln argued that helping always stems from self-interest, whereas the other passenger took the view that true altruism exists. Suddenly, the men were interrupted by the screeching whine of a sow trying to save her piglets from drowning in a creek beside the coach track.

empathy

the ability to experience events and emotions (e.g., joy and sadness) the way another person experiences them

empathy-altruism hypothesis

the idea that when we feel empathy for a person, we will attempt to help him or her purely for altruistic reasons, regardless of what we have to gain

FIGURE 10.1
Batson's (1991) empathy-altruism theory

Lincoln promptly called out, "Driver, can't you stop for just a moment?" He jumped out of the coach, ran to the creek, and lifted the piglets to the safety of the bank. When he returned, his companion said, "Now, Abe, where does selfishness come in on this little episode?" "Why, bless your soul, Ed," Lincoln replied. "That was the very essence of selfishness. I should have had no peace of mind all day had I gone on and left that suffering old sow worrying over those pigs. I did it to get peace of mind, don't you see?" (Sharp, 1928). As this example shows, an act that seems truly altruistic is sometimes motivated by self-interest. How, then, can we tell which is which?

Batson and his colleagues have devised a series of clever experiments to unravel people's motives (Batson, Ahmad, & Stocks, 2004; Batson & Powell, 2003). Imagine you were one of the participants (Introductory Psychology students) in a study by Miho Toi and Daniel Batson (1982). You are asked to evaluate some tapes of new programs for your university's radio station. The one you hear is an interview with a student named Carol Marcy. She describes a bad automobile accident and explains that because she is still in a wheelchair, it has been very difficult to keep up with her course work. Carol mentions that she will have to drop her introductory psychology course unless she can find a student from whom she can borrow lecture notes. After you listen to the tape, the experimenter hands you an envelope marked "To the student listening to the Carol Marcy pilot tape" and says that it came from the professor supervising the research. The envelope contains a note from the professor, asking if the student who listened to this tape would be willing to meet with Carol and share his or her introductory psychology lecture notes.

As you have probably guessed, the point of the study was to look at the conditions under which people agreed to help Carol. Toi and Batson (1982) pitted two motives against each other: self-interest and empathy. First, they varied how much empathy people felt toward Carol: In the high-empathy condition, people were told to try to imagine how Carol felt about what had happened to her and how it had changed her life; in the low-empathy condition, they were told to try to be objective and to not be concerned with how Carol felt. As expected, participants in the high-empathy condition reported feeling more empathy with Carol than did those in the low-empathy condition.

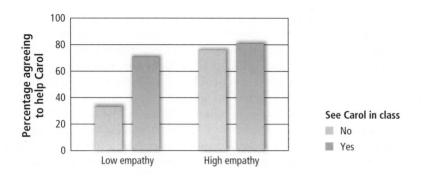

FIGURE 10.2

Altruism versus self-interest

Under what conditions did people agree to help Carol with the work she missed in her introductory psychology class? When empathy was high, people helped regardless of the costs and rewards (i.e., regardless of whether they would encounter her in class). When empathy was low, people were more concerned with the rewards and costs for them—they helped only if they would encounter Carol in class and thus feel guilty about not helping.

(Adapted from Toi & Batson, 1982)

Second, the researchers varied how costly it would be *not* to help Carol. In the high-cost condition, participants learned that Carol would start coming back to class the following week and happened to be in the same introductory psychology section as they were. Obviously, it would be unpleasant to refuse to help Carol and then run into her every week in class. In the low-cost condition, people learned that Carol would be studying at home and would not be coming to class; thus, they would never have to face her in her wheelchair and feel guilty about not helping her out.

When deciding whether to help Carol, did people take into account the costs involved? According to the empathy-altruism hypothesis, if empathy was high, people should have been motivated by genuine altruistic concern and should have helped regardless of the costs (see Figure 10.1). As you can see on the right side of Figure 10.2, this prediction was confirmed: in the high-empathy condition, about as many people agreed to help when they thought they would see Carol in class as when they thought they would not see her in class. This suggests that people had Carol's interests in mind, not their own. In the low-empathy condition, however, many more people agreed to help when they thought they would see Carol in class than when they thought they would not see her in class (see the left side of Figure 10.2). This suggests that when empathy was low, social exchange came into play, in that people based their decision to help on the costs and benefits to themselves. They helped when it was in their interests to do so (i.e., when they would see Carol in her wheelchair and feel guilty for not helping) but not otherwise (i.e., when they thought they would never see her again).

These sorts of findings are not limited to laboratory experiments. For example, Piferi and colleagues (2006) examined helping in the wake of the September 11, 2001, terrorist attacks in the United States. In this study, the researchers assessed a number of variables, including empathy, help given immediately after September 11, help given one year later, reasons for helping, and so on. The first finding of note was that participants who were high in empathy reported providing more help (e.g., donating money, giving blood) both immediately after 9/11 and one year later, compared with those who were low in empathy. Also consistent with Batson's empathy-altruism hypothesis, those whose primary motivation was to alleviate their distress were more likely to provide help immediately after the attacks but not one year later (when, presumably, their distress had lessened). In contrast, those who were motivated by altruistic motives were more likely to engage in sustained help provision—giving help both immediately after the attack and a year later (Piferi, Jobe, & Jones, 2006).

The important role of empathy also has been demonstrated in studies conducted with children. For example, a study conducted with children in British Columbia found that those who were able to put themselves in another person's shoes were more likely to behave in prosocial ways toward him or her (e.g., helping an experimenter who dropped a box of paper clips, letting a friend have a turn at an enjoyable game). In fact, empathy was related to helping among children as young as five years old (Roberts & Strayer, 1996). The research by Batson and colleagues suggests that sometimes people do behave in truly altruistic ways. In an interesting twist on this issue, researchers at the University of Waterloo hypothesized that people are most likely to help if the helpful act allows them to see themselves as altruistic—but not unconditionally so (Holmes, Miller, & Lerner, 2002). In other words, we will be helpful if we can disguise our altruism with a social exchange facade, making it look as though there was something in it for us. Why would we be motivated to do so? According to Holmes and colleagues, if we saw ourselves as pure altruists, we would feel compelled to help each and every time a need arose. Because none of us is able to offer unending help, we would be doomed to feelings of failure and despair. If we can instead construe helping situations in exchange terms, we can happily help in a given situation without feeling that we have now committed ourselves to helping forevermore.

To test this line of thinking, the researchers approached people on campus and asked them for either a straight-out charitable donation or to purchase candles in support of a charity. The charity was described as either high or low in need. In which condition did people donate the most money? As expected, they were most generous in the condition where they received something in exchange for helping (i.e., candles)—and when the need was high. This latter statement is important because it shows that people were not simply motivated by strict exchange ("I give you money; you give me a candle") but, rather, helped in response to a need. The way Holmes and colleagues put it, the candles didn't provide an incentive but an excuse for giving.

To sum up, we've identified three basic motives underlying prosocial behaviour:

1. Helping is an instinctive reaction to promote the welfare of those genetically similar to us (evolutionary psychology).

2. The rewards of helping often outweigh the costs, so helping is in our self-interest (social exchange theory).

► This touching story of early hominid prosocial behaviour is intriguing to think about in terms of different theories of prosocial behaviour. Evolutionary psychologists might argue that the caregivers helped the dwarf because he was a relative, and that people are programmed to help those who share their genes (i.e., kin selection). Social exchange theory would maintain that the dwarf's caregivers received sufficient rewards from their actions to outweigh the costs of caring for him. The empathy-altruism hypothesis would hold that the caregivers helped out of strong feelings of empathy and compassion for him—an interpretation supported by the article's final paragraph.

Study: Cavemen helped disabled

United Press International
NEW YORK—The skeleton of a dwarf who died about 12,000 years ago indicates that cave people cared for physically disabled members of their communities, a researcher said yesterday.

The skeleton of the 3-foot-high youth was initially discovered in 1963 in a cave in southern Italy but was lost to anthropologists until American researcher David W. Frayer reexamined the remains and reported his findings in the British journal Nature.

Frayer, a professor of anthropology at the University of Kansas at Lawrence, said in a telephone interview that the youth "couldn't have taken part in normal hunting of food or gathering activities so he was obviously cared for by others."

Archaeologists have found the remains of other handicapped individuals who lived during the same time period, but their disabilities occurred when they were adults, Frayer said.

"This is the first time we've found someone who was disabled since birth . . . .", Frayer said. He said there was no indication that the dwarf, who was about 17 at the time of his death, had suffered from malnutrition or neglect.

He was one of six individuals buried in the floor of a cave and was found in a dual grave in the arms of a woman, about 40 years old.

3. Under some conditions, powerful feelings of empathy and compassion for the victim prompt selfless giving (the empathy-altruism hypothesis).

Each of these approaches has its supporters and its critics.

Personal Determinants of Prosocial Behaviour: Why Do Some People Help More than Others?

If basic human motives were all there was to it, how could we explain the fact that some people are much more helpful than others? Clearly, we need to consider the personal determinants of prosocial behaviour that distinguish the helpful person from the selfish one.

Individual Differences: The Altruistic Personality

When you read the examples at the beginning of this chapter, did you think about the different personalities of the people involved? It is natural to assume that people such as Justice Peck, who saved a family when their house was on fire, and Greg Baytalan (introduced in Chapter 1), who gave up his vacation to assist in the gruesome task of transporting the bodies of tsunami victims to morgues, are cut from a different cloth—selfless, caring people who would never dream of ignoring someone's pleas for help. Psychologists have been quite interested in the nature of the **altruistic personality**—those aspects of a person's makeup that cause him or her to help others in a wide variety of situations (Eisenberg, Spinrad, Sadovsky, 2006; Mikulincer & Shaver, 2005, in press; Penner, 2002). Are some people more helpful "types" than others? As we have seen throughout this book, personality alone does not determine behaviour. Social psychologists argue that we also have to take the situation into account—in addition to an individual's personality.

Consider a classic study by Hugh Hartshorne and Mark May (1929). They observed how helpful 10 000 elementary and high school students were in a variety of situations, including the students' willingness to find stories and pictures

altruistic personality

aspects of a person's makeup that cause him or her to help others in a wide variety of situations

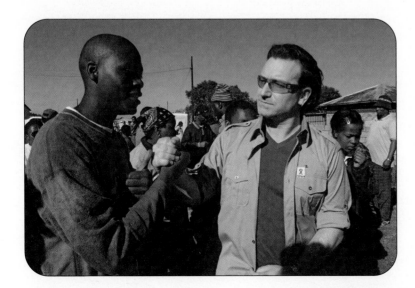

◄ Clearly, some people have more of an altruistic personality than others, causing them to engage in more prosocial behaviour. Personality, however, is not the whole story; the nature of the social situation also determines whether people help.

to give to hospitalized children, to donate money to charity, and to give small gifts to needy children. The researchers assumed that they were measuring the extent to which people had an altruistic personality.

Surprisingly, the extent to which the children were prosocial in one situation (e.g., finding many stories and pictures for the hospitalized children) was not highly related to how prosocial they were in another situation. The average correlation between helping in one situation and helping in another was only 0.23. This means that if you knew how helpful a child was in one situation, you could not predict with much confidence how helpful he or she would be in another. Moreover, researchers who have studied both children and adults have not found much evidence that people with high scores on personality tests of altruism are more likely to help than those with lower scores (Batson, 1998; Magoo & Khanna, 1991; Piliavin & Charng, 1990). Clearly, at least in many situations, personality is not a major determinant of whether people will help. We also need to take into account several other critical factors, such as the situational pressures that are affecting people, their gender, the culture in which they grew up, and even their current mood.

> *On reflecting at dinner that he had done nothing to help anybody all day, he uttered these memorable and praiseworthy words: 'Friends, I have lost a day.'*
>
> —*Suetonius,* Lives of the Twelve Caesars, second century AD

Gender Differences in Prosocial Behaviour

Consider two scenarios: (1) passing by a house, hearing the cries of young children, and smelling smoke, and entering the house to rescue the children; and (2) helping an elderly disabled neighbour with household chores. Are women or men most likely to help in each situation? As you've probably guessed, the answer is men in the first situation and women in the second situation (Eagly, 1987; Eagly & Crowley, 1986). In virtually all cultures, norms prescribe different traits and behaviours for males and females, learned as children are growing up. In Western cultures, the male sex role includes being chivalrous and heroic; females are expected to be nurturant and caring and to value close, long-term relationships.

> *Both men and women belie their nature when they are not kind.*
>
> —*Gamaliel Bailey (1807–1859)*

Indeed, the recipients of the Medal of Bravery bestowed by Canada's governor general for "acts of bravery in hazardous circumstances" tend to be men. For example, in 2007, 77 were awarded to men, compared with only 8 to women. Now consider the Governor General's Caring Canadian Award. This award honours Canadians who "have given extraordinary help or care to individuals, families, or groups, or supported community service or humanitarian causes." In 2007, 59 women

▶ Whereas men are more likely to perform chivalrous and heroic acts, women are more likely to be helpful in long-term relationships that involve greater commitment.

received this awared, compared to 35 men (see www.gg.ca/honours/awards/cca/index_e.asp).

Research confirms that helping that involves nurturance and commitment is more likely to be performed by women than by men (George, Carroll, Kersnick, & Calderon, 1998; Otten, Penner, & Waugh, 1988; Smith, Wheeler, & Diener, 1975). For example, a cross-cultural survey of adolescents found that in each of the seven countries studied, more girls than boys did volunteer work in their communities (Flanagan et al., 1998). Similarly, an analysis of volunteering among Canadians (aged 15 to 65 and over) found that women were more likely than men to engage in both formal and informal volunteering (Ekos Research Associates and Canadian Policy Research Networks, 1999). According to a Statistics Canada survey conducted in 2003, 35 percent of women aged 15 and over did unpaid work for a volunteer organization during that year (Canada, 2005f).

Cultural Differences in Prosocial Behaviour

In previous chapters, we noted that people who grow up in Western cultures tend to be individualist and have an independent view of the self, whereas people who grow up in Eastern cultures tend to be collectivist and have an interdependent view of the self. Does this cultural difference affect people's willingness to help others? Because people with an interdependent view of the self are more likely to define themselves in terms of their social relationships and have more of a sense of "connectedness" to others, we might predict that they'd be more likely to help a person in need.

However, it turns out that people in all cultures are more likely to help someone they define as a member of their **in-group**—the group with which an individual identifies. We are more likely to feel empathy for in-group members and this, in turn, leads to increased helping (Stürmer, Snyder, & Omoto, 2005). In contrast, people are less likely to help someone they perceive to be a member of an **out-group**—a group with which the individual does not identify (Brewer & Brown, 1998; see Chapter 12). Cultural factors come into play in determining how strongly people draw the line between in-groups and out-groups. In many interdependent cultures, the needs of in-group members are considered more important than those of out-group members. Consequently, members of these cultures are more likely to help in-group members than are members of individualist cultures (Leung & Bond, 1984; Miller, Bersoff, & Harwood, 1990; Moghaddam, Taylor, & Wright, 1993). However, because the line between "us" and "them" is more firmly drawn in interdependent cultures, people in these cultures are *less* likely to help members of out-groups than are people in individualist cultures (L'Armand & Pepitone, 1975; Leung & Bond, 1984; Triandis, 1994). McCrae and colleagues suggest this is the reason that Chinese people score lower than Canadians on scales that assess the altruistic personality type (McCrae, Yik, Trapnell, Bond, & Paulhus, 1998). Similarly, when Osamu Iwata (1992) compared the altruistic intentions of students in Canada and Japan by type of relationship, Canadian students expressed greater altruism toward "a person one happens to see occasionally but with whom he or she has no relation." However, Canadians and Japanese students did not differ when altruism was directed toward a person with whom one has "personal and close relations." Thus, to be helped by other people, it is important that they view you as a member of their in-group—as "one of them"—and this is especially true in interdependent cultures (Ting & Piliavin, 2000).

Before leaving this topic, we should point out that cultural norms about taking credit for helping others may also contribute to the perception that people from Asian cultures are less altruistic overall than are people from Western cultures. According to Lee, Cameron, Xu, Fu, and Board (1997), in Asian cultures,

in-group

the group with which an individual identifies, and of which he or she feels a member

out-group

a group with which the individual does not identify

children are taught to be modest and self-effacing—and this includes not seeking recognition for helpful acts. These researchers presented scenarios about helping to children (aged 7 to 11) in Canada and China. One of the scenarios described Kelly, who knew that her friend Anne had lost the money she needed for a class trip. Kelly secretly put some of her own money in Anne's pocket so that Anne could go on the trip. Later, a teacher asked Kelly if she knew who had given the money to Anne. Canadian children believed that Kelly should acknowledge this helpful act (thereby garnering the praise of the teacher); Chinese children believed that Kelly should not admit that she had done so because begging for praise would violate social norms of modesty. These researchers subsequently replicated this study with adults (university students, elementary school teachers, and parents) in Canada and China, and got exactly the same results (Fu, Lee, Cameron, & Xu, 2001).

The Effects of Mood on Prosocial Behaviour

Imagine you are at your local shopping mall. As you walk from one store to another, a fellow in front of you suddenly drops a manila folder, and papers flutter in all directions. He looks around in dismay, then bends down and starts to pick up the papers. Would you stop to help him? What do you think the average shopper would do? By now, you know that thinking about how many altruistic people there are in the world won't predict the answer. Other factors, including the mood people happen to be in at the time, can strongly affect behaviour—in this case, whether they will help.

Effects of Positive Moods: Feel Good, Do Good   Alice Isen and Paul Levin (1972) explored the effect of good moods on prosocial behaviour in shopping malls in San Francisco and Philadelphia. They boosted the mood of shoppers in a simple way—namely, by leaving a dime in the coin-return slot of a pay telephone at the mall and waiting for someone to find it. As the lucky shoppers left the phone with their newly found dime, an assistant of the researchers played the role of the man with the manila folder. He deliberately dropped the folder a few feet in front of the shopper, to see whether the shopper would stop to help him pick up his papers. It turned out that finding the dime had a dramatic effect on helping. Only 4 percent of the people who did not find a dime helped the man pick up his papers. In comparison, 84 percent of the people who found a dime helped.

Researchers have found this "feel good, do good" effect in diverse situations and have shown that it is not limited to the little boost we get when we find some money. People are more likely to help others when they are in a good mood for a number of reasons, including doing well on a test, receiving a gift, thinking happy thoughts, and listening to pleasant music (North, Tarrant, & Hargreaves, 2004). And when people are in a good mood, they are more helpful in many ways, including contributing money to charity, helping someone find a lost contact lens, tutoring another student, donating blood, and helping co-workers on the job (Carlson, Charlin, & Miller, 1988; Isen, 1999; Salovey, Mayer, & Rosenhan, 1991). See the accompanying Try It! for a way of doing your own test of the "feel good, do good" hypothesis.

What is it about being in a good mood that makes people more altruistic? Being in a good mood can increase helping for three reasons. First, a good mood makes us look on the bright side of life. If you saw the man drop his manila folder full of papers, you could view this incident in at least two ways. "What a klutz," you might think. "Let him clean up his own mess." Or you might have more sympathy for him, thinking, "Oh, that's too bad. The poor guy, he probably feels really frustrated." When we are in a good mood, we tend to see the good

Try it!

▶ Feel Good, Do Good?

Think back to the last time you smelled freshly baked chocolate chip cookies or other delicious aromas in a mall. Did it put you in a good mood? Robert Baron (1997) predicted that people would be in better moods when they are around pleasant fragrances, and that this improved mood would make them more helpful. Consistent with his prediction, shoppers were more likely to help a stranger (by giving change for a dollar, for example) when they were approached in locations with pleasant smells than when they were approached in locations with neutral smells. For pleasant smells, Baron used locations near a cookie store, a bakery, and a coffee shop. For areas with neutral smells, Baron picked locations that were similar in the volume of pedestrians, lighting, and proximity to mall exits, such as areas outside clothing stores.

See if you can replicate this effect. In a local mall, pick locations that have pleasant aromas and neutral aromas. At each location, approach an individual who is alone. Take out a loonie and ask the passerby for change. If the person stops and gives you change, count it as helping. If the person ignores you or says he or she does not have any change, count it as not helping. Baron (1997) found that 57 percent of people helped in the locations with pleasant aromas, whereas only 19 percent of people helped in the locations with neutral aromas. Did you replicate his results?

Warning: Before conducting this study you might want to seek the permission of the manager of the mall. The manager of the mall in which Baron (1997) conducted his study requested that the researchers only approach persons of the same gender as themselves, because of a concern that cross-gender requests for change would be perceived as pick-up attempts. You might want to follow this procedure as well.

side of other people, giving them the benefit of the doubt. A victim who might normally seem clumsy or annoying will, when we are feeling cheerful, seem like a decent, needy person who is worthy of our help (Carlson, Charlin, & Miller, 1988; Forgas & Bower, 1987).

Second, helping other people is an excellent way of prolonging our good mood. If we see someone in need of help, being a good Samaritan spawns even more good feelings, and we can walk away feeling terrific. In comparison, not helping when we know we should is a surefire downer, deflating our good mood (Clark & Isen, 1982; Isen, 1987; Lyubomirsky, Sheldon, & Schkade, 2005).

Finally, good moods increase self-awareness. As we noted in Chapter 5, at any given time, people vary in how much attention they pay to their feelings and values versus the world around them. Sometimes, we are particularly attuned to our internal worlds and, sometimes, we are not. Good moods increase the amount of attention we pay to ourselves, and this factor in turn makes us more likely to behave according to our values and ideals. Because most of us value altruism and because good moods increase our attention to this value, good moods increase helping behaviour (Berkowitz, 1987; Carlson, Charlin, & Miller, 1988; Salovey & Rodin, 1985).

> ❝ *If you want to be happy, practise compassion.* ❞
>
> —14th Dalai Lama (1935–)

Negative-State Relief: Feel Bad, Do Good What about when we are in a bad mood? Suppose that when you saw the fellow in the mall drop his folder, you were feeling down in the dumps—would this influence the likelihood that you would help the man? One kind of bad mood clearly leads to an increase in helping—feeling guilty (Baumeister, Stillwell, & Heatherton, 1994; Estrada-Hollenbeck & Heatherton, 1998). People often act on the idea that good deeds cancel out bad deeds. When they have done something that makes them feel guilty, helping another person balances things out, thereby reducing their guilty feelings.

For example, in one study, it was found that churchgoers were more likely to donate money to charities before attending confession than afterward, presumably because confessing to a priest reduced their guilt (Harris, Benson, & Hall, 1975). Thus, if you just realized you had forgotten your best friend's birthday, you would be more likely to help the fellow in the mall to repair your guilty feelings.

But suppose you just had a fight with a friend or just found out you did poorly on a test, and you are feeling sad. Given that feeling happy leads to greater helping, it might seem that feeling sad would decrease helping. Surprisingly, however, sadness can also lead to an increase in helping, at least under certain conditions (Carlson & Miller, 1987; Salovey, Mayer, & Rosenhan, 1991). When people are sad, they are motivated to engage in activities that make them feel better (Wegener & Petty, 1994). The idea that people help in order to alleviate their own sadness and distress is called the **negative-state relief hypothesis** (Cialdini, Darby, & Vincent, 1973; Cialdini & Fultz, 1990; Cialdini et al., 1987). It is an example of the social exchange theory approach to helping discussed earlier. People help someone else with the goal of helping themselves—namely, to relieve their own sadness and distress. In this way, if you are feeling down, you are more likely to donate money to a charity. The warm glow of helping the charity lifts us out of the doldrums (Cialdini, Darby, & Vincent, 1973). Similarly, following the terrorist attacks on September 11, 2001, many people dealt with their feelings of threat and terror by performing prosocial altruistic acts (Yum & Schenk-Hamlin, 2005). For example, one participant reported responding this way: "I gave money to firemen at a grocery store and comforted a friend with a missing relative. I gave blood to help the relief efforts" (Yum & Schenk-Hamlin, 2005, p. 275).

negative-state relief hypothesis

the idea that people help in order to alleviate their own sadness and distress

Situational Determinants of Prosocial Behaviour: When Will People Help?

Personality, gender, culture, and moods each contribute a piece to the puzzle of why people help others, but they are not the complete picture. To understand more fully why people help, we need to consider the social situation in which they find themselves.

Environment: Rural versus Urban

Suppose you are walking down the street one day when you see a man suddenly fall down and cry out in pain. He rolls up his pant leg, revealing a bandaged shin that is bleeding heavily. What would you do? When this event was staged in a small town, about half of the people who walked by stopped and offered to help. In large cities, only 15 percent of passersby stopped to help (Amato, 1983). Other studies have found that people in small towns are more likely to help when asked to help a lost child, give directions, or return a lost letter. The finding that help is more likely to be offered in small towns than in large cities has been reported in several countries, including Canada, the United States, Israel, Australia, Turkey, Great Britain, and Sudan (Hedge & Yousif, 1992; Steblay, 1987).

> " *Do not wait for extraordinary circumstances to do good action; try to use ordinary situations.* "
>
> —Jean Paul Richter (1763–1825)

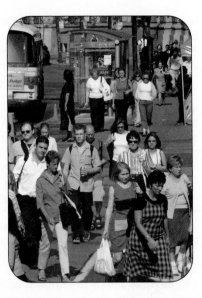

◀ People are less helpful in big cities than in small towns, not because of a difference in values but because the stress of urban life causes them to keep to themselves.

Why are people more likely to help in small towns? One possibility is that people who grow up in a small town are more likely to internalize altruistic values. If this were the case, people who grew up in small towns would be more likely to help, even if they were visiting a big city. Alternatively, the immediate surroundings, and not people's internalized values, might be the key. Stanley Milgram (1970) proposed an urban-overload hypothesis, which holds that people living in cities are constantly being bombarded with stimulation, and therefore they keep to themselves in order to avoid being overloaded by it. According to this **urban-overload hypothesis**, if you put urban dwellers in a calmer, less stimulating environment, they would be as likely as anyone else to reach out to others.

Interestingly, the evidence supports the urban-overload hypothesis more than it does the idea that living in cities makes people less altruistic by nature. A review of dozens of studies found that when an opportunity for helping arises, it matters more whether the incident occurs in a rural or urban area than which kind of person happens to be there (Steblay, 1987). Further, in field studies conducted in 36 cities in the United States, it was found that population density (the number of people per square kilometre) was more related to helping than was population size (Levine, Martinez, Brase, & Sorenson, 1994). The greater the density of people, the less likely people were to help. This makes sense, according to the urban-overload hypothesis: There should be more stimulation in an area packed with a lot of people than in an area where people are more spread out. The hustle and bustle in cities can be so overwhelming that even caring, altruistic people turn inward, responding less to those around them.

urban-overload hypothesis

the theory that because people living in cities are constantly being bombarded with stimulation, they keep to themselves in order to avoid being overloaded by it

CONNECTIONS

Does Belonging to a Community Make You More Helpful?

In many parts of the world, it is common for people to move far away from where they were raised (Hochstadt, 1999). In the year 2000, for example, nearly one in five Americans were living in a different state than they had been in 1995 (Migration and Geographic Mobility, 2003). As it turns out, people who have lived in one place for a long time are more likely to engage in prosocial acts that help the community. Living in one place for a long time leads to greater attachment to the community and more interdependence with one's neighbours, thereby increasing the likelihood that help and support will be reciprocated (Baumeister, 1986; Oishi, Rothman,

Snyder, Su, Zehm, Hertel, Gonzalez, & Sherman, 2007; Twenge, Baumeister, DeWall, Ciarocco, & Bartles, 2007). For example, Oishi and colleagues (2007) found that people who had lived in the Minneapolis–St. Paul area for a long time were more likely to purchase "critical habitat" licence plates compared with people who had recently moved to the area. (These licence plates cost an extra $30 per year and provide funds for the state to purchase and manage natural habitats.)

Perhaps it is not surprising that people who have lived in one place for a while feel more of a stake in their community. However, Oishi and colleagues (2007) found that helpfulness can increase quite quickly even in a one-time laboratory setting. Imagine you are in a study in which you are playing a trivia contest against four other students. The winner will receive a $10 gift certificate. The experimenter says that people in the group can help each other if they want, but that doing so might lower a person's chances of winning the prize. As the game progresses, one of your fellow group members keeps sighing and commenting that he doesn't know the answers to the questions. Would you offer him help or let him struggle on his own?

The answer, it turns out, depends on how long you have been in the group with the struggling student. In the actual study by Oishi and colleagues, there were four tasks in all (the trivia contest was the last one). Half of the participants remained together and worked on all of the tasks throughout the study, whereas the other half switched to a new group after each task. Thus, in the former condition, people had more of an opportunity to get to know each other and form a sense of community, whereas the experience of the latter group was more analogous to moving from one community to another. As the researchers predicted, people in the stable community condition were more likely to help the struggling student in their group than those in the more "transient" community condition. Another reason that people might be less helpful in big cities, then, is that residential mobility is higher in urban areas than in rural areas.

Finally, recent research shows that the converse is true as well—namely, that people who are not part of a community are less helpful. In a series of studies, Twenge and colleagues (2007) demonstrated that when people are excluded from social groups, they are less likely to engage in prosocial acts. For example, in one experiment, participants interacted in same-sex groups. Later, they were asked to name the two group members with whom they would most like to work. Participants in the acceptance condition were told that "everyone chose you," whereas those in the exclusion condition were told that they had been rejected by the group ("no one chose you"). Next, participants were told that the experiment was over and that they could leave, or, if they wished, stay and help out with some other experiments. The results were dramatic—90 percent of the participants who were accepted by the group agreed to help, whereas only 20 percent of those who were rejected by the group offered to do so (Twenge et al., 2007). In another experiment, the researchers found that socially excluded participants donated less money to a student emergency fund than those who were not excluded (Twenge et al., 2007). The bottom line? Prosocial behaviour is much more likely when people feel part of a group or a community.

Bystander Intervention: The Latané and Darley Model

Remember Kitty Genovese? We have just seen one reason why her neighbours may have turned a deaf ear to her cries for help. Her murder took place in New York City, one of the most densely populated areas in the world. Perhaps her neighbours were so overloaded with urban stimulation that they dismissed Genovese's cries as one small addition to the surrounding din. Although it is true that people help less in urban environments, this is not the only explanation for Genovese's neighbours' failure to help. Her desperate cries surely must have risen above the everyday noise of garbage trucks and car horns. Conversely, there have been cases in which people ignored the pleas of their neighbours in small towns (Hsu, 1995).

Bibb Latané and John Darley (1970) are two social psychologists who taught at universities in New York at the time of the Genovese murder. As we discussed in Chapter 2, they, too, were unconvinced that the only reason her neighbours failed to help were the stresses and stimulation of urban life. They focused on the fact that many people heard her cries. Paradoxically, they thought, it might be that the greater the number of bystanders who observe an emergency, the less likely it is that any one of them will help. As Bibb Latané (1987) put it, "We came up with the insight that perhaps what made the Genovese case so fascinating was itself what made it happen—namely, that not just one or two, but 38 people had watched and done nothing" (p. 78).

In a series of now-classic experiments, Latané and Darley (1970) found that in terms of receiving help, there is no safety in numbers. Think back to the seizure experiment we discussed in Chapter 2. In this study, a participant was taken to a cubicle, supposedly to take part in a group discussion of university life with students in other cubicles via an intercom system. One of the other students suddenly had a seizure, crying out for help, choking, and finally, falling silent. There was actually only one real participant in the study; the others, including the one who had the seizure, were prerecorded voices. The point of the study was to see whether the real participant tried to help the seizure victim, by trying to find him or by summoning the experimenter, or whether—like Kitty Genovese's neighbours—he or she simply sat there and did nothing. As Darley and Latané (1968) anticipated, the answer depended on how many people the participant thought witnessed the emergency. When people believed they were the only one listening to the student have the seizure, most of them (85 percent) helped within a minute. By 2.5 minutes, 100 percent of the people who thought they were the only bystander had offered assistance (see Figure 10.3). In comparison, when the research participants believed there was one other student listening, fewer people helped—only 62 percent in the first minute. As you can see in Figure 10.3, helping occurred more slowly when there were two bystanders, and never reached 100 percent, even after six minutes, at which point the experiment was terminated. Finally, when the participants believed there were four other students listening in addition to themselves, the percentage of people who helped dropped even more dramatically. Only 31 percent helped in the first minute, and after six minutes only 62 percent had offered help. Dozens of other studies, conducted both in the laboratory and in the field, have found the same thing. The greater the number of bystanders who witness an emergency, the less likely any one of them is to help the victim—a phenomenon called the **bystander effect**.

bystander effect

the finding that the greater the number of bystanders who witness an emergency, the less likely it is that any one of them will help

FIGURE 10.3

Bystander intervention: The presence of bystanders reduces helping

When people believed that they were the only one hearing a student having a seizure—when they were the lone bystander—most of them helped him immediately, and all did so within 2.5 minutes. When they believed that someone else was listening as well—that there were two bystanders—they were less likely to help and did so more slowly. And when they believed that four others were listening—that there were five bystanders—they were even less likely to help.

(Adapted from Darley & Latané, 1968)

Intervene and offer assistance

Notice the event (1)

Interpret the event as an emergency (2)

Assume responsibility (3)

Know appropriate form of assistance (4)

Implement decision (5)

Distracted; in a hurry (fail to notice)

Pluralistic ignorance (interpret the event as a nonemergency)

Diffusion of responsibility (fail to assume personal responsibility)

Lack of knowledge; lack of competence (can't offer appropriate help)

Danger to self; legal concerns; embarrassment (costs of helping too high)

EMERGENCY!

No intervention/no help is given

FIGURE 10.4

Bystander intervention decision tree: Five steps to helping in an emergency

According to Latané and Darley (1970), people go through five decision-making steps before they help someone in an emergency. If bystanders fail to take any one of the five steps, they will not help. Each step, as well as the possible reasons why people decide not to intervene, is outlined.

(Adapted from Latané & Darley, 1970)

Why is it that people are less likely to help when other bystanders are present? Latané and Darley (1970) developed a step-by-step description of how people decide whether to intervene in an emergency (see Figure 10.4). Part of this description, as we will see, is an explanation of how the number of bystanders can make a difference. But let's begin with the first step: whether people notice that someone needs help.

Noticing an Event Obviously, if people don't notice that an emergency has occurred, they will not intervene and offer to help. But what determines whether people notice an emergency? John Darley and Daniel Batson (1973) demonstrated that something as seemingly trivial as how much of a hurry people are in can make more of a difference than what kind of person they are. These researchers conducted a study that mirrored the parable of the good Samaritan, wherein many passersby failed to stop to help a man lying unconscious on the side of the road. The research participants were people we might think would be extremely altruistic—seminary students preparing to devote their lives to the ministry. The students were asked to walk to another building, where the researchers would record them making a brief speech. Some were told that they were late and should hurry to keep their appointment. Others were told that there was no rush, because the assistant in the other building was a few minutes behind schedule. As they walked to the other building, each of the students passed a man (an accomplice of the experimenters) who was slumped in a doorway. The man coughed and groaned as each student walked by. Did the seminary students stop to help him? If they were not in a hurry, most of them (63 percent) did. If they were hurrying to keep their appointment, however, only 10 percent stopped to help. Many of the students who were in a hurry did not even notice the man.

It is perhaps unsurprising that when people are in a rush, they pay less attention to what's going on around them, making them less likely to help someone in need. What is surprising is that such a seemingly trivial matter as how much of a hurry we are in can overpower the kind of people we are. Darley and

Batson (1973) tested the seminary students on a variety of personality measures that assessed how religious they were. They also varied the topic of the speech. Specifically, some students were asked to speak on the parable of the good Samaritan—surely, seminary students speaking on this topic would be especially likely to stop and help a man slumped in a doorway, given the similarity of this incident to the parable. However, if the students were in a hurry, they were unlikely to help, even if they were very religious individuals preparing to give a speech about the good Samaritan. We should note that Darley and Batson did find one variable that made a difference—namely, whether the students saw religion as a quest (an open-minded search for truth) versus a set of traditions. Those who viewed religion as a quest were no more likely to stop, but those who did stop were more responsive to the man's needs than those who viewed religion as a set of traditions.

Interpreting the Event as an Emergency   Even if people do notice someone slumped in a doorway, they might not stop and help. The next determinant of helping is whether the bystander interprets the event as an emergency—that is, as a situation where help is needed (see Figure 10.4). Is the person in the doorway drunk, or seriously ill? If we see white smoke coming out of a vent, is it something innocuous, such as mist from an air conditioner, or a sign that the building is on fire? Did that scream we just heard come from someone having a good time at a party, or is someone being attacked? If people assume that nothing is wrong when an emergency is taking place, obviously they will not help.

Interestingly, when other bystanders are present, people are more likely to assume that an emergency is something innocuous. To understand why, think back to our discussion of informational social influence in Chapter 7. This type of social influence occurs when we use other people to help us define reality. When we are uncertain about what's going on, such as whether or not the smoke we see is a sign of a fire, one of the first things we do is look around to see how other people are responding. If other people look up, shrug, and go about their business, we are likely to assume that there is nothing to worry about. If other people look panic-stricken and yell, "Fire!" we immediately assume that the building is, indeed, on fire. As we saw in Chapter 7, it's often a good strategy to use other people as a source of information when we are uncertain about what's going on. The danger in doing so, however, is that sometimes no one is sure what is happening. Since an emergency is frequently a sudden and confusing event, bystanders tend to freeze, watching and listening with blank expressions as they try to figure out what's taking place. When they glance at each other, they see an apparent lack of concern on the part of other bystanders. This results in a state of **pluralistic ignorance**. Bystanders assume that nothing is wrong in an emergency because no one else looks concerned.

Consider another classic experiment by Latané and Darley (1970). Imagine that you are participating in a study of people's attitudes toward the problems of urban life, and you arrive at the appointed time. A sign instructs you to fill out a questionnaire while you are waiting for the study to begin. You take a copy of the questionnaire, sit down, and work on it for a few minutes, when something odd happens. White smoke starts coming into the room through a small vent in the wall. Before long, the room is so filled with smoke you can barely see the questionnaire. What will you do? In fact, there was no real danger—the experimenters were pumping smoke into the room to see how people would respond to this potential emergency. Not surprisingly, when people were by themselves, most of them took action. Within two minutes, 50 percent of the participants left the room and found the experimenter down the hall, reporting that there was a potential fire in the building; by six minutes, 75 percent of the participants left the room to alert the experimenter.

pluralistic ignorance

the phenomenon whereby bystanders assume that nothing is wrong in an emergency because no one else looks concerned

But what would happen if people were not alone? Given that 75 percent of the participants who were by themselves reported the smoke, it would seem that the larger the group, the greater the likelihood that someone would report the smoke. In fact, this can be figured mathematically: If there is a 75 percent chance that any one person will report the smoke, there is a 98 percent chance that at least one person in a three-person group will do so. To find out whether more bystanders would increase the chances of helping, Latané and Darley (1970) included a condition in which everything was identical except that three people instead of one sat in the room as the smoke began to seep in. Surprisingly, in only 12 percent of the 3-person groups did someone report the smoke within 2 minutes, and in only 38 percent of the groups did someone report the smoke within 6 minutes. In the remaining groups, the participants sat there filling out questionnaires even when they had to wave away the smoke with their hands to see what they were writing. What went wrong?

Because it was not clear that the smoke constituted an emergency, the participants used each other as a source of information. If the people next to you glance at the smoke and then go on filling out their questionnaires, you will feel reassured that nothing is wrong—otherwise, why would they be acting so unconcerned? The problem is that they are probably looking at you out of the corner of their eyes, and seeing that you appear to be not overly concerned, they, too, are reassured that everything is okay. Group members gain false reassurance from each other whenever each person assumes that the others know more about what's going on than he or she does. And when the event is ambiguous—as when smoke is coming from a vent—people will convince each other that nothing is wrong (Clark & Word, 1972; Solomon, Solomon, & Stone, 1978).

Assuming Responsibility   Sometimes, it is obvious that an emergency is occurring, as when Kitty Genovese cried out, "Oh my God, he stabbed me! Please help me! Please help me!" (Rosenthal, 1964). Genovese's neighbours must have believed that something terrible was happening and that she desperately needed help. That they did nothing indicates that even if we interpret an event as an emergency, we have to decide that it is *our* responsibility—not someone else's—to do something about it. Here, again, the number of bystanders is a crucial variable. Think back to the Darley and Latané (1968) seizure experiment, in which participants believed they were the only one listening to the student while he had a seizure. The responsibility rested totally on their shoulders. If they didn't help, no one would, and the student might die. As a result, in this condition most people helped almost immediately, and all helped within a few minutes.

▶Emergency situations can be confusing. Does this man need help? Have the bystanders failed to notice him? Or has the behaviour of the others led each of them to interpret the situation as a nonemergency—an example of pluralistic ignorance?

◀ Kitty Genovese (*inset*) and the alley in which she was murdered. Ironically, she would probably be alive today had fewer people heard her desperate cries for help.

But what happens when there are many witnesses? A **diffusion of responsibility** occurs, whereby each bystander's sense of responsibility to help decreases as the number of witnesses increases. Because other people are present, no single bystander feels strong personal responsibility to take action. Recall from our earlier discussion that helping often entails costs; we can place ourselves in danger, and we can look foolish by overreacting or doing the wrong thing. Why should we risk these costs when many other people who can help are present? The problem is that everyone is likely to feel this way, making all of the bystanders less likely to help. This is particularly true if people cannot tell whether someone else has already intervened. When participants in the seizure experiment believed that other students were also hearing the crisis, they couldn't tell whether another student had already helped because the intercom system transmitted only the voice of the student having the seizure. Each student probably assumed that he or she did not have to help, because surely someone else had already done so. Similarly, Kitty Genovese's neighbours had no way of knowing whether someone else had called the police. Most likely, they assumed that someone else had already made the call. Tragically, everyone assumed it was somebody else's responsibility to take action, thereby leaving Genovese to fight her assailant alone. The sad irony of Genovese's murder is that she might have received help and survived the attack had *fewer* people heard her cries for help.

Knowing How to Help   Even if people have made it this far in the helping sequence—noticing an event has occurred, interpreting it as an emergency, and taking responsibility—an additional condition must still be met. The person must decide what form of help is appropriate (see Step 4 in Figure 10.4). Suppose, for example, that on a hot summer day you see a woman collapse in the street and you determine she is gravely ill. No one else seems to be helping, so you decide that it is up to you. But what should you do? Has the woman had a heart attack? Or is she suffering from heat stroke? Should you call an ambulance, administer CPR,

diffusion of responsibility

each bystander's sense of responsibility to help decreases as the number of witnesses to an emergency or crisis increases or try to get her out of the sun? If people don't know what form of assistance to give, obviously, they will be unable to help.

Deciding to Implement Help   Finally, even if you know exactly what kind of help is appropriate, there are still reasons why you might decide not to intervene. For one thing, you might not be qualified to deliver the right kind of help. Even if the woman on the street is complaining of chest pains, suggesting a heart attack, if you don't know how to administer CPR, you'll be unable to help her. Or you might be afraid of making a fool of yourself. It can be embarrassing to intervene, only to discover that a situation actually wasn't an emergency. And some forms of helping might be embarrassing in themselves. For example, Edwards (1975) conducted a study in South Africa, in which a female confederate "accidentally" dropped either her purse or a box of tampons while walking down a street. Nearly everyone (95 percent) who saw the woman drop her purse returned it. In comparison, 59 percent of bystanders returned the tampons. One potential helper was about to return the tampons but quickly dropped the box when he realized what it contained! This study was replicated in Canada by James McDonald and Stuart McKelvie (1992) at Bishop's University. In their study, a male confederate dropped either a mitten or a box of condoms while walking through a shopping mall. Nearly half (47 percent) of the people who saw him drop the mitten retrieved it. As for the condoms? Only 17 percent of bystanders returned them. One man "helped" by kicking the condoms along the floor of the mall until they caught up with the confederate! Thus, costs of helping such as embarrassment can be barriers to providing help.

Another cost of helping is fear of doing the wrong thing and making matters worse, or even of placing yourself in danger by trying to help. We began this chapter with the story of Murray Aklwenzie, a good Samaritan who stepped in to intervene when a panhandler was harassing a woman. The panhandler then turned on Aklwenzie and viciously attacked him. Aklwenzie had to relearn to walk and talk after the attack. Sadly, the injuries he sustained have left him permanently brain damaged. He is under constant care in a nursing home and does not even recognize his daughter or his grandchildren (McIntyre, 2006). In short, this single act of helping destroyed Murray's Aklwenzie's life.

In sum, five steps have to be taken before people will intervene in an emergency. They have to notice the event, interpret it as an emergency, decide it is their responsibility to help, know how to help, and decide to act. If people fail to take any one of these steps, they will not intervene. Given how difficult it can be to take all five steps, it is not surprising that incidents such as Kitty Genovese's murder can occur.

The Nature of the Relationship: Communal versus Exchange Relationships

A great deal of research on prosocial behaviour has looked at helping between strangers, such as Latané and Darley's research on bystander intervention. Although this research is very important, most helping in everyday life occurs between people who know each other well, such as family members and close friends. In Chapter 9, we distinguished between communal and exchange relationships. *Communal relationships* are those in which people's primary concern is the welfare of the other person (e.g., a child), whereas *exchange relationships* are those governed by concerns about equity—that what you put into the relationship equals what you get out of it. How does helping occur in communal relationships? It turns out that when the person in need of help is someone close to us, we are less concerned about the benefits that we may reap from helping and more concerned with simply responding to the needs of the other person (Clark & Monin, 2006; LeMay, Clark & Feeney, 2007). In support of this argument, Clark

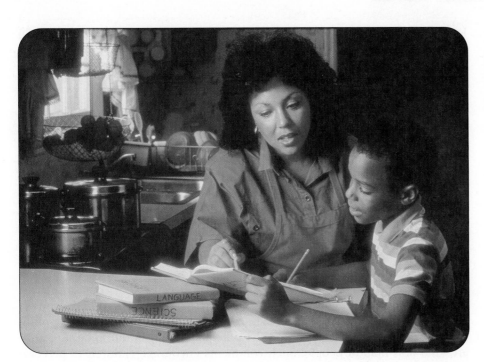

◄ In communal relationships, such as those between parents and their children, people are concerned less with who gets what and more with how much help the other person needs.

and colleagues have found that people in communal relationships pay less attention to who is getting what than do people in exchange relationships (Clark, 1984; Clark & Grote, 1998; Clark, Mills, & Corcoran, 1989).

How Can Helping Be Increased?

Most religions stress some version of Christianity's Golden Rule, urging us to do unto others as we would have others do unto us. There are many saintly people in the world who succeed in following this rule, devoting their lives to the welfare of others. We would all be better off, however, if prosocial behaviour were more common than it is. How can we get people, when faced with an emergency, to act more like Murray Aklwenzie and less like Kitty Genovese's neighbours?

Before addressing this question, we should point out that people do not always want to be helped. Imagine that you are sitting at a computer terminal in the library and are struggling to get access to a particular website. You can't figure out why the address you're trying doesn't seem to be working and are becoming increasingly frustrated as the computer responds with incomprehensible messages. A confident-looking guy strides into the room and peers over your shoulder for a few minutes. "You sure have a lot to learn," he says. "Step aside and let me show you how this works." How would you react? You might feel some gratitude, but probably you would also feel some resentment. His offer of help comes with a message: "You are too stupid to figure this out for yourself." Receiving help can make us feel inadequate and dependent. As a result, we do not always react positively when someone offers us aid. When we do not want to appear incompetent, we may suffer in silence—even if doing so lowers our chances of successfully completing a task (Brown, Nesse, & Vinokur, 2003; Nadler & Fisher, 1986; Schneider, Major, Luhtanen, & Crocker, 1996).

Nonetheless, the world would be a better place if more people helped their fellow human beings. How can we increase everyday acts of kindness, such as

> *When death, the great reconciler, has come, it is never our tenderness that we repent of, but our severity.*
>
> —George Eliot (Marian Evans), Adam Bede, 1859

looking out for an elderly neighbour or volunteering to read to kids at the local school? One answer is to cultivate helping behaviour early on. In addition, as we shall see, if we simply make people aware of the barriers to helping, they are more likely to engage in prosocial behaviours.

Instilling Helpfulness with Rewards and Models

Developmental psychologists have discovered that prosocial behaviour occurs early in life. Even children as young as 18 months frequently help others, such as assisting a parent with household tasks or trying to make a crying infant feel better (Volling, Kolak, & Kennedy, 2009). One powerful way to encourage prosocial behaviour is for parents and others to reward such acts with praise, smiles, and hugs. Several studies suggest that these kinds of rewards increase prosocial behaviour in children (Fischer, 1963; Grusec, 1991). Rewards should not, however, be emphasized too much. As you may recall from our discussion of the overjustification effect in Chapter 5, rewarding people too strongly for performing a behaviour can lower their intrinsic interest in it because they come to believe they are doing it only to get the reward. The trick is to encourage children to act prosocially but not to be too heavy-handed with rewards. One way of accomplishing this is to tell children, after they have helped, that they did so because they are kind and helpful people. Such comments encourage children to perceive themselves as altruistic people, so they will help in future situations even when no rewards are forthcoming (Grusec, Kuczynski, Rushton, & Simutis, 1979).

Another way for parents to increase prosocial behaviour in their children is to behave prosocially themselves. Children generally model behaviours they observe in others, including prosocial behaviours (Batson, 1998; Dodge, 1984; Mussen & Eisenberg-Berg, 1977). Children who observe their parents helping others (e.g., volunteering to help the homeless) learn that helping others is a valued act. Interviews with people who have gone to great lengths to help others—such as Christians who helped Jews escape from Nazi Germany during World War II—indicate that their parents were also dedicated helpers (London, 1970; Rosenhan, 1970).

Closer to home, S. Mark Pancer and Michael Pratt (1999) found that Canadian youths who spend time volunteering are likely to have parents who have instilled values of kindness and helping, and who model those behaviours. The

▶ An increasing number of schools and businesses are requiring people to perform community service. These programs can actually lower interest in volunteering if people feel they are doing so because of an external requirement. Encouraging people to volunteer while preserving the sense that they freely choose to do so is likely to increase people's intentions to volunteer again in the future.

response of one 17-year-old girl who participated in this research is illustrative. This girl's sister had been in an accident and, therefore, was temporarily unable to continue her after-school position working with a high-needs handicapped child. Here's her response:

> And so my mom and my sister convinced me to work [her] hours for her. . . . And this child, you really have to care for her to work with her. She's a really sad case. . . . You have to not lose patience with her. . . . My mom's a really caring person and she has a really strong bond with this little girl. She and my sister *should* be able to rely on me to help out on this.

The lesson for parents and other adults is clear: If you want children to be altruistic, act in altruistic ways yourself.

Increasing Awareness of the Barriers to Helping

Finally, there is evidence that simply being aware of the barriers to helping can increase people's chances of overcoming those barriers. Several years ago at Cornell University, some students intervened to prevent another student from committing suicide. As is often the case with emergencies, the situation was a very confusing one, and at first the bystanders were not sure what was happening or what they should do. The student who led the intervention said she was reminded of a lecture she had heard on bystander intervention in her introductory psychology class a few days earlier and had realized that if she didn't act, no one might (Savitsky, 1998). A similar incident took place at Vassar College, where some students looked outside their dormitory and saw a student being attacked by a mugger. Like Kitty Genovese's neighbours, most of them did nothing, probably because they assumed that someone else had already called the police. One of the students, however, immediately called the campus police because she was struck by how similar the situation was to the studies on bystander intervention she had read about in her social psychology course—even though she had taken the course more than a year earlier (Coats, 1998).

These are not controlled experiments, of course, and, therefore, we cannot be certain that the people who intervened were really spurred on by what they had learned in their psychology classes. Perhaps they were especially helpful people who would have helped anyway. Fortunately, this issue has been addressed experimentally. Beaman and colleagues (1978) randomly assigned students to listen to a lecture on Latané and Darley's (1970) bystander intervention research or to a lecture on an unrelated topic. Two weeks later, all of the students participated in what they thought was a completely unrelated sociology study, during which they encountered a student lying on the floor. Was he in need of help? Had he fallen and injured himself, or was he simply a student who had fallen asleep after pulling an all-nighter? As we have seen, when in an ambiguous situation such as this, people look to see how other people are reacting. Because an accomplice of the experimenter—posing as another participant—purposefully acted unconcerned, the natural thing for participants to do was assume that nothing was wrong. This is exactly what most participants did if they had not heard the lecture about bystander intervention research; in this condition, only 25 percent of them stopped to help the student. However, if participants had heard the lecture about bystander intervention, 43 percent stopped to help the student (Beaman, Barnes, Klentz, & McQuirk, 1978). Thus, knowing how we can unwittingly be influenced by others can by itself help us overcome this type of social influence. We can only hope that knowing about other barriers to prosocial behaviour will also make them easier to overcome.

If you want to learn more about the conditions under which people help others, try an experiment of your own design in the Try It! on the next page.

Try it!

▶ The Lost Letter Technique

Here is a way you can test many of the hypotheses about helping behaviour you have read about in this chapter—as well as hypotheses of your own.

An interesting way to study prosocial behaviour is to leave some stamped letters lying on the ground and see whether people pick them up and mail them. This procedure, called the *lost letter technique*, was invented by Stanley Milgram (1969). He found that people were more likely to mail letters addressed to organizations that they supported; for example, 72 percent of letters addressed to "Medical Research Associates" were mailed, whereas only 25 percent of letters addressed to "Friends of the Nazi Party" were mailed. (All were addressed to the same post office box so that Milgram could count how many were returned.)

Try the lost letter technique yourself. Put your address on the letters so that you can count how many are returned, but vary where you put the letters or to whom they are addressed. For example, drop some letters in a small town and some in an urban area to see whether people in small towns are more likely to mail them. Be sure to mark the envelopes in some way that will let you know where they were dropped; for example, put a small pencil mark on the back of the ones dropped in small towns. Studies by Bridges and Coady (1996) and Hansson and Slade (1977) found that people living in small towns were more likely to mail the letters. Or you might vary the ethnicity of the name of the person on the address, to see if people are more likely to help members of some ethnic groups than others. Be creative!

After deciding what you want to vary (e.g., the ethnicity or gender of the addressee), be careful to place envelopes of both types (e.g., those addressed to males and females) in similar locations. It is best to use a fairly large number of letters (e.g., a minimum of 15 to 20 in each condition) to get reliable results. Obviously, you should not leave more than one letter in the same location. You might want to team up with some classmates on this project, so that you can split the cost of the stamps.

SUMMARY

For centuries people have debated the determinants of **prosocial behaviour**—that is, an act performed with the goal of benefiting another person. People have been particularly intrigued with the causes of **altruism**, which is the desire to help another person even if it involves costs to the helper.

According to evolutionary theory, natural selection has produced prosocial behaviour in three ways:

1. People further the survival of their genes by helping genetic relatives (**kin selection**).

2. There is a survival advantage to following the **norm of reciprocity**, whereby people help strangers in the hope that they will receive help when they need it.

3. There is a survival advantage to the ability to learn and follow *social norms* of all kinds, including altruism.

Social exchange theory views helping behaviour as a weighing of rewards and costs; helping is motivated by self-interest—that is, people are more likely to help in situations where the rewards for helping are greater than the costs. Rewards include recognition, praise, and the relief of personal distress. Neither evolutionary psychology nor social exchange theory sees helping behaviour as a form of altruism; self-gain is always involved. In comparison, the **empathy-altruism hypothesis** suggests that people do sometimes behave in truly altruistic ways—namely, when they experience **empathy** for those in need.

Prosocial behaviour has multiple determinations, and both personal and situational factors can override or facilitate basic motives to help. Personal determinants of helping include the **altruistic personality**, the idea that some people are more helpful than others. Gender is another personal factor that comes into play. Although one sex is not more altruistic than the other, the ways in which men and women help often differ, with men more likely to help in heroic or chivalrous ways and women more likely to help in nurturant ways that involve a long-term commitment. People's cultural background also matters. Compared with members of individualist cultures, members of interdependent cultures are more likely to help people they view as members of their **in-group** but are less likely to help people they view as members of an **out-group**.

Mood also affects helping. Interestingly, being in either a good or a bad mood—compared with being in a neutral mood—can increase helping. Good moods increase helping for several reasons, including the fact that they allow us to see the good side of other people, making us more willing to help them. Bad moods can also increase helping. According to the **negative-state relief hypothesis**, helping someone makes us feel good, lifting us out of the doldrums.

Situational determinants of prosocial behaviour include rural versus urban environments, with helping behaviour more likely to occur in rural settings. One reason for this is the **urban-overload hypothesis**, which states that cities bombard people with so much stimulation that they keep to themselves to avoid being overloaded. The **bystander effect** specifies the impact of the number of bystanders on whether help is given: The fewer the bystanders, the better. The bystander decision model indicates that a potential helper must proceed through five steps before providing help: (1) notice the event, (2) interpret the event as an emergency (here, **pluralistic ignorance** can occur, whereby everyone assumes nothing is wrong, because no one else looks concerned), (3) assume personal responsibility (here, a **diffusion of responsibility** created by several bystanders may lead us to think it's not our responsibility to act), (4) know how to help, and (5) implement the help.

The nature of the relationship between the helper and the person in need is also an important determinant of helping. In exchange relationships, people are concerned with equity and they keep track of who is contributing what to the relationship. In communal relationships, people are concerned less with who gets what and more concerned with responding to the other person's needs.

How can helping be increased? One way is for parents to reward their children for helping. Rewards must be used carefully, however, or they will undermine the child's intrinsic interest in helping, causing an overjustification effect. Children also are more likely to be helpful when they observe adults engaging in helpful behaviours. Finally, research has indicated that teaching people about the determinants of prosocial behaviour makes them more aware of why they sometimes don't help, with the happy result that they help more in the future.

PEARSON mypsychlab

Along with a dynamic, electronic version of this text, MyPsychLab offers a wealth of resources to deepen your understanding and test your recall of the material in this chapter—including video and audio clips, simulations and activities, self-assessments, practice tests, and other study materials. The following specific resources are available for this chapter:

 Bystander Intervention

 Helping a Stranger

 Prosocial Behaviour

To access MyPsychLab, please visit www.mypsychlab.com (Student Access Code required—packaged with this book).

11

Aggression:
Why We Hurt Other People

October 28, 2006. Michael Levy, then 18 years old, was dancing with his girlfriend at a birthday party held at a hall in Surrey, British Columbia, when he was swarmed by a group of teens who viciously assaulted him. He had done nothing to provoke them. After punching him, smashing a bottle on his head, and spraying him with mace, one of the teens, Enrique Quintana, attacked him with an axe, severing his spine and leaving him numb below the chest. Quintana was given a 10-year jail term. Tuan Minh Nguyen, a teen who also participated in the attack, received a conditional sentence in the British Columbia courts in December 2007. There was outrage when television stations broadcast footage of him laughing with his friends in an elevator following his sentencing. In April 2008, the Crown appealed, asking for jail time. According to Crown prosecutor Joyce DeWitt-Van Oosten, "they [the attackers] robbed a young man not only of his physical well-being but his dream . . . anything less [than a jail sentence] must be appealed" (Lazaruk, 2008). Why would a group of teens brutally attack a young man who had done nothing to provoke them?.

In an article titled "Kids Who Kill," the *Winnipeg Free Press* documents a series of homicides in 2007 in which teens were charged with murder: Thirty-eight-year-old Thomas Roy Phillips was sitting in his vehicle when he was shot to death by teens. Twenty-two-year-old Ernestine Pascal was found in an abandoned building, the victim of blunt-force trauma inflicted by an 18-year-old woman and two teenage girls. She later died in a Winnipeg hospital. Twenty-one-year-old Kyle Boss, a father of two young children, was beaten to death on a Winnipeg street. Two boys, 14 and 16 years of age, were charged with second-degree murder (Owen, 2007).

▲ Michael Levy, a former weightlifter, is wheelchair bound as the result of a brutal attack by a group of teens.

Why is the rate of teen homicide rising at a time when the crime rate, in general, is declining? A newspaper writer asks, "Does violence in video games and the glorification of the gangster lifestyle in rap music have any influence on kids who kill?" (Owen, 2007, p. B4). Does social psychology have an answer to this disturbing question? Stay tuned.

In this chapter, we begin with the fundamental question, "What is aggression?" and then move on to another fundamental question, "What causes it?" Are human beings instinctively aggressive? Can situational factors cause "normal people" to commit violence? Can aggression be prevented or reduced? These are social psychological questions of the utmost importance. Needless to say, we don't have all the answers. By the time you reach the end of this chapter, however, we hope you will have gained some insight into the issues. But first, we explain what we mean by the term.

What Is Aggression?

> *Man's inhumanity to man*
> *Makes countless thousands mourn!*
> —Robert Burns, "Man Was Made to Mourn," 1784

For social psychologists, aggression is intentional behaviour aimed at causing either physical or psychological pain. It should not be confused with assertiveness—even though people often loosely refer to others as "aggressive" when they stand up for their rights, write letters to the editor complaining about real or imagined injustices, work extra hard, display a great deal of ambition, or are "go-getters." Similarly, in a sexist society, a woman who simply speaks her mind or makes the first move in a relationship might be called "aggressive" by some. Our definition is much more specific: **Aggression** is an intentional action aimed at doing harm or causing pain; as such, aggression might be physical or verbal. Whether it succeeds in its goal or not, it is still aggression. If someone throws a beer bottle at your head, and you duck so the bottle misses, the throwing was still an aggressive act. By the same token, if a drunk driver unintentionally runs you down while you're attempting to cross the street, that is not an act of aggression, even though the damage would be far greater than that caused by a flying beer bottle. The important thing is the intention.

It is also useful to distinguish between hostile and instrumental aggression (Berkowitz, 1993). **Hostile aggression** is an act of aggression stemming from feelings of anger and aimed at inflicting pain or injury. With **instrumental aggression**, there is an intention to hurt the other person, but the hurting takes place as a means to some goal other than causing pain. For example, in a professional football game, a defensive lineman will usually do whatever it takes to thwart his opponent (the blocker) and tackle the ball carrier. This typically includes intentionally inflicting pain on his opponent if doing so is useful in helping him get the blocker out of the way so he can get to the ball carrier. This is instrumental aggression. On the other hand, if he believes his opponent has been playing dirty, he might become angry and go out of his way to hurt the other player, even if doing so does not increase his opportunity to tackle the ball carrier. This is hostile aggression.

aggression

intentional behaviour aimed at causing either physical or psychological pain

hostile aggression

an act of aggression stemming from feelings of anger and aimed at inflicting pain

instrumental aggression

aggression as a means to some goal other than causing pain

Is Aggression Inborn or Learned?

For centuries, scientists, philosophers, and other serious thinkers have been arguing about the human capacity for aggressiveness. Some are convinced that aggression is an inborn, instinctive phenomenon. Others are just as certain that aggressive behaviour must be learned (Baron & Richardson, 1994; Berkowitz, 1993; Geen, 1998). The political philosopher Thomas Hobbes, in his classic work *Leviathan* (1651), took the view that we human beings, in our natural state, are brutes and that only by enforcing the law and order of society could we curb our natural instinct toward aggression. A century later, Jean-Jacques Rousseau argued just the opposite. Humans, he wrote in 1762, are "noble savages"—naturally gentle creatures born into a restrictive society that forces them to become hostile and aggressive.

Hobbes's more pessimistic view was elaborated on in the twentieth century by Sigmund Freud (1930), who theorized that human beings are born with an instinct toward life, which he called **Eros**, and an equally powerful death instinct, **Thanatos**, which leads to aggressive actions. Freud believed that aggressive energy must come out somehow, lest it continue to build up and produce illness. The analogy is one of water pressure building up in a container: unless energy is released, it will produce some sort of explosion. According to Freud, society performs an essential function in regulating this instinct and in helping people to *sublimate* it—that is, to turn the destructive energy into acceptable or useful behaviour.

> **Eros**
>
> the instinct toward life, posited by Freud

> **Thanatos**
>
> according to Freud, an instinctual drive toward death, leading to aggressive actions

Is Aggression Instinctual? Situational? Optional?

The Evolutionary Argument   In recent years evolutionary psychologists (Buss, 2004; Buss & Duntley, 2006) have entered into the discussion by arguing that aggression is genetically programmed into men because it enables them to perpetuate their genes. Males are theorized to aggress for two reasons: First, males behave aggressively to establish dominance over other males. The idea here is that the female will choose the male who is most likely to provide the best genes and the greatest protection and resources for offspring. Second, males aggress "jealously" to ensure that their mate(s) are not copulating with others. This ensures their paternity.

The evolutionary perspective receives tangential support from crime statistics, which show that males are most likely to engage in violence during their

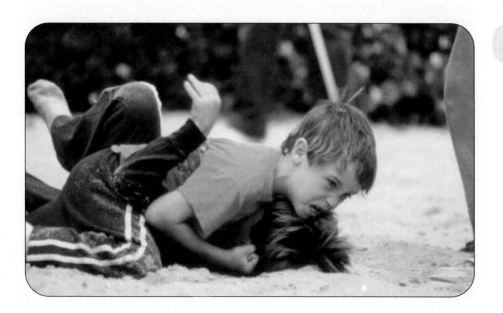

◀ Is this kind of aggression "only natural"?

Try it!

▶ Fighting and Its Attractiveness

Interview several of your male friends and ask them to reflect on their childhood and adolescent experiences with physical fighting or simply being challenged to fight. Ask them what they think was at stake in the fight. How difficult was it to back down? Ask them to elaborate on their answers.

Now, interview several of your female friends. Ask them the same questions you asked the men. Are their responses wildly different from those of the men? Why or why not? Now, ask the women to think about men they know in terms of possible relationships. Determine to what extent they consider physical aggressiveness to be attractive. Ask them to elaborate on their response. Do your findings support the evolutionary argument?

peak reproductive years—their teens and twenties (Canada, 2005e). Among young males, violence is typically initiated by issues related to "respect." For the males involved, the stakes seem high: They believe that they are fighting for their status in the group. Jealousy is another major reason why males aggress against each other and their mates (Wilson, Daly, & Weghorst, 1982; Schützwohl, 2004).

In most contemporary societies, social dominance and hence access to females is still largely (but certainly not entirely) based on status. But nowadays, status has taken on a different meaning. In most societies, the ability to physically intimidate other males in the group is no longer the primary attribute that attracts females. Rather, power is now based on attributes related to success such as high-status careers, wealth, and celebrity. These speculations from evolutionary social psychologists are interesting and provocative, but ultimately . . . well, speculative. (Conduct your own research following the steps in the accompanying Try It! box.)

Aggression among the Lower Animals As we have just discussed, the research supporting the evolutionary perspective is provocative but inconclusive because it is impossible to conduct a definitive experiment. Scientists have turned to experiments with non-human species to gain additional insight into the extent to which aggression may be hard-wired. Consider, for example, a common belief about cats and rats. Most people assume that cats will instinctively stalk and kill rats. Almost half a century ago, biologist Zing Yang Kuo (1961) attempted to demonstrate that this was a myth. He raised a kitten in the same cage with a rat. What did he find? Not only did the cat refrain from attacking the rat, but the two became close companions. Moreover, when given the opportunity, the cat refused either to chase or to kill other rats; thus, the benign behaviour was not confined to his buddy but was generalized to rats the cat had never encountered before.

Although this experiment is charming, it fails to prove that aggressive behaviour is not instinctive; it merely demonstrates that the aggressive instinct can be inhibited by early experience. What if an organism grows up without any experience with other organisms? Will it or won't it show aggressive tendencies? It turns out that rats raised in isolation (i.e., without any experience in fighting other rats) will attack a fellow rat when one is introduced into the cage. Moreover, the isolated rat uses the same pattern of threat and attack that experienced rats use (Eibl-Eibesfeldt, 1963). Thus, although aggressive behaviour can be modified by experience (as shown by Kuo's experiment), aggression apparently does not need to be learned.

◄When people say that aggression is "natural," they often point to our primate relatives. Chimpanzees (*left*) are indeed pretty belligerent and aggressive, but bonobos (*right*) are portrayed as apes who would rather make love than war.

We can gain still greater insight by observing the behaviour of those animals with which we have the most genetic similarity. Our closest relatives in the animal kingdom are two primates: the chimpanzees and the bonobos. Both species have 98 percent of their DNA in common with human beings. The chimpanzee is known for the aggressive behaviour of its male members (Watts, Muller, Amsler, Mbabazi, & Mitani, 2006; Watts & Mitani, 2001). In fact, chimps kill each other at about the same rate that humans in hunter-gatherer societies kill each other (Wrangham, Wilson, & Muller, 2006). Based on this research, we might conclude that humans, especially males, are genetically programmed for aggressive behaviour.

However, living across the river from chimpanzees (and out of their reach) are bonobos, our equally close genetic relative. Unlike the chimpanzee, the bonobo is known for its nonaggressive behaviour. In fact, bonobos are often referred to as the "make love, not war" ape (de Waal, 1995). For example, when the bonobos arrive at a feeding ground, they first engage in sexual play and then proceed to eat peacefully. In contrast, when chimps arrive at a feeding ground, they compete aggressively for the food. Also, unlike the chimps, bonobos form into female-dominated societies (Parish & de Waal, 2000). This image of the peaceful, love-making, "hippie" apes has widespread appeal. However, more recent research in which bonobos have been observed in their natural habitat (rather than in zoos) is casting doubt on this image. Apparently, all bonobos actually do hunt and kill other apes (Parker, 2007; Kahn, 2008), although perhaps not at the rate exhibited by chimps.

The near universality of aggression strongly suggests that aggressiveness has evolved and has been maintained because it has survival value (Lore & Schultz, 1993; Buss, 2004). At the same time, researchers underscore the point that nearly all organisms also seem to have evolved strong inhibitory mechanisms that enable them to suppress aggression when it is in their best interests to do so. Aggression is an optional strategy. Whether it is expressed is determined by the animal's previous social experiences as well as by the specific social context in which the animal finds itself.

Aggression and Culture

Social psychologists agree that aggression is an optional strategy. Moreover, where humans are concerned, because of the complexity and importance of our social interactions, the social situation takes on even greater importance than it does among the lower organisms (Bandura, 1973; Berkowitz, 1968, 1993; Lysak, Rule, & Dobbs, 1989). Indeed, there is a lot of support for the view that for humankind, innate patterns of behaviour are infinitely modifiable and flexible. Cross-cultural studies have found that human cultures vary widely in their degree of aggressiveness. European history, when condensed, consists of one major war after another; in contrast, certain so-called primitive peoples, such as the Lepcha of Sikkim, the Baka of central Africa, and the Arapesh of New Guinea, live in apparent peace and harmony, with acts of aggression being extremely rare (Baron & Richardson, 1994).

Changes in Aggression over Time   Within a given culture, changing social conditions frequently lead to striking changes in aggressive behaviour. For example, for hundreds of years, the Iroquois of North America lived peacefully as a hunting nation, without engaging in aggression against other tribes. But in the seventeenth century, barter with the newly arrived Europeans brought the Iroquois into direct competition with the neighbouring Huron over furs, which dramatically increased in value because they could then be traded for manufactured goods. A series of skirmishes with the Huron ensued, and within a short time, the Iroquois developed into ferocious warriors. It would be hard to argue that they were spectacular warriors because of uncontrollable aggressive instincts; rather, their aggressiveness almost certainly came about because a social change produced increases in competition (Hunt, 1940).

Aggression and a Culture of Honour   In more recent research, Vandello and Cohen (2003) have explored the idea that violence may be seen as more acceptable in *honour cultures*—that is, cultures that define male honour in terms of power, toughness, and the ability to protect one's property (e.g., Mediterranean; Middle Eastern and Arabic; Latin and South American cultures with Iberian roots; southern American states). Specifically, they found that participants from male honour cultures (e.g., Brazil, southern American states) were more likely than participants from non-honour cultures (e.g., northern American states) to believe that the infidelity of a female partner was damaging to the male partner's reputation and that his reputation could be restored through the use of violence against her. There was also the belief that the female partner should remain loyal, even if her male partner was violent.

Other research has shown that within the United States, homicide rates for white southern males are substantially higher than those for white northern males, especially in rural areas (Nisbett, 1993). Because of a "culture of honour" in the Deep South, southerners are more inclined to endorse violence for protection and in response to insults—a pattern that persists to this day. For example, in a recent analysis of pitcher aggression in baseball, it was found that pitchers often deliberately hit batters to restore justice, such as payback for having hit a home run earlier in the game or retaliation for a teammate having been hit. Interestingly, white pitchers who were born in the American South are 40 percent more likely to hit a batter than are non-southerners (Timmerman, 2007).

Closer to home, Wells, Graham, and West (1998) suggest that a code of male honour exists in a particular Canadian subculture, namely among security staff (bouncers) who work in bars. These researchers observed that bouncers (working in various bars in London, Ontario) were most likely to engage in excessive aggression against bar patrons when they perceived that their authority or masculinity was being threatened. More recent research by these investigators (Graham & Wells, 2001a, 2001b; Graham, West, & Wells, 2000) suggests that this code of male honour also applies to bar patrons. Trained observers recorded instances of aggression in various bars in London, Ontario, over a seven-month period. Analyses of these incidents revealed a "macho subculture" in which males bullied one another or made threatening comments in response to little or no provocation; in one incident, for example, a group of males gathered around two men embroiled in a confrontation. The situation deteriorated to the point where two of the onlookers started fighting with each other, while the others placed bets on who would win.

Taking these findings into account, we would conclude that while an instinctual component of aggression is almost certainly present in human beings, aggression is not caused entirely by instinct. There are clear examples of situational and social events that can produce aggressive behaviour.

Neural and Chemical Influences on Aggression

Aggressive behaviour in human beings, as well as in lower animals, is associated with an area in the core of the brain called the **amygdala**. When the amygdala is stimulated, docile organisms become violent; similarly, when neural activity in that area is blocked, violent organisms become docile (Moyer, 1976). But there is flexibility here also: The impact of neural mechanisms can be modified by social factors, even in subhumans. For example, if a male monkey is in the presence of other, less dominant monkeys, he will indeed attack the other monkeys when the amygdala is stimulated. But if the amygdala is stimulated while the monkey is in the presence of more dominant monkeys, he will not attack but instead will run away.

Certain chemicals have been shown to influence aggression as well. For example, **serotonin**, a chemical substance that occurs naturally in the midbrain, seems to have an inhibiting effect on impulsive aggression. In animals, when the flow of serotonin is disrupted, increases in aggressive behaviour frequently follow. Among humans, researchers have found that violent criminals have particularly low levels of naturally produced serotonin (Davidson, Putnam, & Larson, 2000). Moreover, in laboratory experiments on normal people, when the natural production of serotonin is interrupted, aggressive behaviour increases (Bjork, Dougherty, Moeller, Cherek, & Swann, 1999).

Too little serotonin can lead to increases in aggression, but so can too much **testosterone**, a male sex hormone. Laboratory animals injected with testosterone became more aggressive (Moyer, 1983). There is a parallel finding in humans; naturally occurring testosterone levels are significantly higher among prisoners convicted of violent crimes than among those convicted of nonviolent crimes. Also, once incarcerated, prisoners with higher testosterone levels violate more prison rules, especially those involving overt confrontation (Dabbs, Carr, Frady, & Riad, 1995; Dabbs et al., 1988). Similarly, juvenile delinquents have higher testosterone levels than do college students (Banks & Dabbs, 1996). Comparing fraternities at a U.S. college, those generally considered most rambunctious, less socially responsible, and "cruder" have the highest average testosterone levels (Dabbs, 2000; Dabbs, Hargrove, & Heusel, 1996).

In research conducted with non-criminal populations, the link between testosterone and aggression tends not to be as strong. For example, in a longitudinal program of research conducted with lower-class 12- and 13-year-old boys in Quebec, testosterone was not strongly related to physical aggression but was associated with social dominance (Tremblay, Schaal, Boulerice, Arseneault, Soussignan, Paquette, & Laurent, 1998). What are we to conclude? When researchers at Queen's University conducted a meta analysis of 45 studies, they found that overall a weak positive correlation exists between testosterone and aggression; the average correlation was 0.14 (Brook, Starzyk, & Quinsey, 2001). (Recall from Chapter 2 that correlations range from 0—no relation—to 1.00—a perfect correlation.) While testosterone may be a factor in some cases of aggression, there are many other causes.

amygdala

an area in the core of the brain that is associated with aggressive behaviour

serotonin

a chemical in the brain that may inhibit aggressive impulses

testosterone

a male sex hormone associated with aggression

Gender and Aggression

If testosterone levels affect aggressiveness—at least to some degree—does that mean that men are more aggressive than women? Apparently so; in a classic survey of research on children, Eleanor Maccoby and Carol Jacklin (1974) found that boys appear to be more aggressive than girls. For example, in one study, the investigators closely observed children at play in a variety of different cultures, including the United States, Switzerland, and Ethiopia. There was far more nonplayful pushing, shoving, and hitting among boys than among girls (Deaux & LaFrance, 1998).

But the research on gender differences is a bit more complicated than it might seem on the surface. Although research shows, for example, that young boys tend to be more overtly aggressive than young girls—in the sense that they lash out directly at the target person, girls tend to express their aggressive feelings more covertly—by gossiping, engaging in backbiting, and spreading false rumours about the target person (Coie, Cillessen, Dodge, Hubbard, Schwartz, Lemerise, & Bateman, 1999; Dodge & Schwartz, 1997; Pepler et al., 2004, 2005). Moreover, a meta analysis of 64 separate experiments found that while it is true that men are far more aggressive than women under ordinary circumstances, the gender difference becomes much smaller when men and women are actually provoked (Bettencourt & Miller, 1996). In fact, a study conducted at McGill University found that women were just as aggressive as men when subjected to strong provocation from a confederate (Hoaken & Pihl, 2000).

In other words, in everyday life situations, when nothing special is going on, men behave far more aggressively than women; but when people are subjected to frustration or insult, women will react almost as aggressively as men. It seems as though men are more likely than women to interpret ambiguous situations as provocative—and are therefore more likely to react aggressively in what we would consider everyday situations. A good example is road rage: Many men seem to regard being cut off in traffic as a personal insult and respond aggressively. Women are more likely to take such occurrences in stride.

This might help explain why the great majority of persons arrested for aggressive offences are men. When women are arrested, it is usually for property crimes (forgery, fraud, larceny), rather than for violent crimes (murder, aggravated assault). How can we explain these differences? Are males naturally predisposed to be more physically aggressive than females, or have they learned to behave that way? In short, does biology or social learning have the greater influence? We cannot be sure. In Canada, violent crime by female youths has increased over the past two decades (from 1986 to 2005; Canada, 2005e). The rate of serious violent crime among female adults nearly doubled over this period. In fact, the gap between women and men is narrowing—in 1986 there were nine men charged for every woman charged. By 2005, this ratio was 5:1 (Canada, 2005e). These statistics might indicate the influence of social learning (e.g., the loosening of restrictions on girls and women to behave in "feminine" ways). However, as indicated above, the rate of violent crime committed by men is still five times that of the female rate, which might suggest a biological difference (Canada, 2005e).

Does the Target Make a Difference? When examining the issue of gender differences, we must also consider another situational factor—namely, the target of aggression. Men's aggression is generally directed at other men—friends or strangers. Men's aggression is also more likely to take place in bars or other public places, more likely to involve alcohol consumption, and tends to have less of an emotional impact. Women's aggression, on the other hand, is much more likely to be directed at a romantic partner, is less likely to involve alcohol, and tends to have a highly negative emotional impact (Graham & Wells, 2001a, 2001b). For example,

TABLE 11.1

Percentage of Canadian university students who physically assaulted a dating partner in the last 12 months

City	Overall Assault Perpetration (%)			Severe Injury Perpetration (%)		
	Total	Male	Female	Total	Male	Female
London, ON	36.3	25.9	44.2	8.9	10.3	7.8
Montreal, QC	22.8	20.6	23.4	0.7	1.6	0.4
Winnipeg, MB	29.0	38.5	27.7	0.9	0.0	1.0
Hamilton, ON	23.0	13.5	24.5	3.0	5.4	2.6

(Based on Straus, 2004)

a meta analysis of well over 100 studies found that women are more likely than men to be physically aggressive toward their partners (Archer, 2000; for examples of Canadian studies that have found this gender difference, see also DeKeseredy & Kelly, 1993; Kwong, Bartholomew, & Dutton, 1999; Sharpe & Taylor, 1999). Recently, Straus (2004) examined rates of physical violence against dating partners among university students in 16 different countries, including Canada. There were a few exceptions, but overall women were more likely to report engaging in physical violence than were men (see left side of Table 11.1).

However, there are some important qualifiers. First, physical aggression is most likely to be reported among younger women in dating relationships. Women in longer-term marital relationships are more likely to be victims, rather than perpetrators, of violence (Canada, 2005a). Second, women's physical aggression does less damage than men's physical aggression; women are much more likely to suffer serious injuries at the hands of their male partner than the other way around. In the Straus (2004) study reported above, even though female university students generally were more likely to physically assault their dating partner than were men, the gender difference reversed when the analysis focused on perpetration of severe injuries—a greater percentage of male students had inflicted severe injury on their partner than did female students. In fact, Statistics Canada data show that women are at far greater risk of being murdered by their partners than are men. For example, in 2007, 82 percent of perpetrators of spousal homicide or attempted homicide were men (Canada, 2008). As one health official remarked, "Women worry when they go out; perhaps they should worry when they stay in" (quoted in Goode, 2000, p. F1). What is the risk of experiencing partner violence for women and men in Canada? See the Try It! on the next page to find out.

Does Culture Make a Difference?   Sex differences in aggressive behaviour tend to hold up across cultures. In one study, teenagers from 11 countries, mostly in Europe and Asia, were asked to read stories involving conflict among people and then write how the stories would end (Archer & McDaniel, 1995). In every one of the 11 countries, young men showed a greater tendency toward violent solutions to conflict than did young women. However, culture also played a major role; for example, women from Australia and New Zealand produced more violent responses than did men from Sweden and Korea. Overall, teenagers in New Zealand produced the most violent responses to these stories; Koreans generated the least violent responses. Young people from the United States ranked fourth and from Canada ranked seventh.

One final note before leaving this topic: Even if gender differences in aggression are at least partly attributable to biological factors, it does not excuse violent behaviour, nor does it mean that such behaviour cannot be altered by a social intervention—as we shall see.

Try it!

▶ The Incidence of Violence in Intimate Relationships

Violence in intimate relationships is usually assessed using the *conflict tactics scale* (or variations of it), in which people report whether their partner has used any of the following types of violence:

- threatened to hit
- threw something
- pushed, grabbed, or shoved
- slapped
- kicked, bit, or hit
- hit with something
- beat
- choked

- used, or threatened to use, a gun or knife
- sexually assaulted

To see how knowledgeable you are about the incidence of spousal violence (including common-law relationships) in Canada, answer the following questions:

1. Which of the above kinds of violence do you think is most common in marriages?
2. Which of the above kinds of violence is more likely to be experienced by women?
3. Which of the above kinds of violence is more likely to be experienced by men?

See page 369 for answers.

Alcohol and Aggression

As most socially active college and university students know, alcohol is a social lubricant that lowers people's inhibitions against committing behaviours frowned on by society, including acts of aggression (Desmond, 1987; Taylor & Leonard, 1983). The link between the consumption of alcoholic beverages and aggressive behaviour has been well established, and it appears even among people who have not been provoked and who do not usually behave aggressively when sober (Bailey & Taylor, 1991; Bushman & Cooper, 1990; White, 1997). This might explain why fistfights frequently break out in bars and nightclubs. For example, researchers at the Centre for Addiction and Mental Health in London, Ontario, recorded incidents of aggression—physical and nonphysical—in various bars in that city (Graham & Wells, 2001a, 2001b; Graham, West, & Wells, 2000). The role of alcohol was clear: The more people drank, the more likely they were to engage in aggression, especially severe forms of physical aggression (e.g., punching, kicking, brawling).

Unfortunately, these effects are not limited to the bar. Intoxication has been implicated as a factor in cases of air rage (Bronskill, 2007). And crime statistics reveal that more than half of the individuals who have committed violent crimes were drinking heavily at the time (Murdoch, Pihl, & Ross, 1990; Pihl & Peterson, 1995).

Finally, family violence also is often associated with alcohol use. Consider, for example, the following statistics: If a spouse drinks heavily, the rate of marital violence is six times higher than if a spouse drinks moderately or not at all (Canada, 2005a). Marital violence is between four and six times more likely if the husband is an alcoholic than if the husband is not an alcoholic (O'Farrell & Murphy, 1995). Not only is violence more likely to occur when alcohol is involved, but it also tends to be more severe (Dutton, 1995; Johnson, 2001; Wekerle & Wall, 2002; Wells, Graham, & West, 2000).

Sadly, it appears that the stage for alcohol-related aggression is set early on. York University psychologist Debra Pepler and her colleagues (2002) conducted a large-scale study of alcohol use and aggression in a sample of nearly 1000 youths in early adolescence. The vast majority were middle class and living in two-parent

"Oh, that wasn't me talking. It was the alcohol talking."

homes. The researchers discovered that by grade 6, approximately 10 percent of the boys and 4 percent of the girls reported alcohol use (e.g., getting drunk, buying or stealing beer or wine). By grade 8, these percentages had increased such that close to 35 percent of the boys and 25 percent of the girls reported alcohol use (Pepler, Craig, Connolly, & Henderson, 2002). When the researchers examined the relation between bullying and alcohol use, the results were shocking: "Both boys and girls who bullied others were almost five times more likely to report alcohol use than boys and girls who did not report bullying" (Pepler et al., 2002, p. 159). These researchers also examined the relation between alcohol and dating violence among those adolescents who had dating experience. The results mirrored those found for bullying: Dating aggression was up to five times more likely among adolescents who used alcohol compared with those who did not. Similar findings have been reported in other studies (Howard & Wang, 2003). These findings suggest that interventions aimed at reducing relationship violence and alcohol abuse must be introduced well before high school, given how early these detrimental patterns are established.

You may have noticed that the data we have been presenting are correlational, and as you well know by now, one cannot draw causal conclusions from correlational data. Is there any evidence that alcohol increases aggression in a direct manner? In other words, can we be sure that alcohol is a direct cause of aggression? Controlled laboratory experiments demonstrate that when individuals ingest enough alcohol to make them legally drunk, they tend to respond more violently to provocation than do those who have ingested little or no alcohol (Bushman, 1993; Lipsey et al., 1997; Taylor & Leonard, 1983). For example, research conducted at McGill University has found that intoxicated men who are provoked administer stronger shocks to a fictitious opponent than participants who are not intoxicated (Hoaken & Pihl, 2000; Pihl & Hoaken, 2002; Pihl, Young, Harden, Plotnick, Chamberlain, & Ervin, 1995).

The implications of these effects for close relationships were explored by MacDonald, Zanna, and Holmes (2000). In their study, male students at the University of Waterloo who were dating or married were asked to describe a conflict in their relationship. Participants in the alcohol condition then drank enough vodka to bring their blood alcohol level to Ontario's legal limit of 0.08. Participants in a placebo condition ingested a drink that smelled of alcohol but contained only a minuscule amount. Those in the control group did not receive drinks of any kind. The participants were then asked to evaluate the conflict they had previously described. The results were disturbing: Intoxicated participants reported more negative emotions when thinking about the conflict and had more negative perceptions of their partner's feelings than did participants in the other two conditions—who did not differ from one another. The researchers concluded that "alcohol can play a causal role in exacerbating relationship conflict" (MacDonald, Zanna, & Holmes, 2000, p. 190). In short, it appears that whenever people are intoxicated, the stage is set for aggression.

Pain, Discomfort, and Aggression

If an animal experiences pain and cannot flee the scene, it will almost invariably attack; this is true of rats, mice, hamsters, foxes, monkeys, crayfish, snakes, raccoons, alligators, and a host of other creatures (Azrin, 1967; Hutchinson, 1983). In these circumstances, animals will attack members of their own species, members of different species, or anything else in sight, including stuffed dolls and tennis balls. Do you think this is true of human beings as well? When Russell and Fehr (1994) asked students at the University of British Columbia to describe an experience of anger, physical pain was among the causes mentioned. Most of us probably can relate to the student who wrote that he experienced intense anger when he bashed his kneecap on the edge of a swimming pool. Most of us probably also know the feeling of wanting to lash out at the nearest available target in such situations.

Indeed, in a series of experiments, Leonard Berkowitz (1983, 1988) showed that students who underwent the pain of having their hand immersed in very cold water showed a sharp increase in their likelihood to aggress against other students.

By the same token, many theorists have postulated that other forms of bodily discomfort—such as heat, humidity, air pollution, and offensive odours—might act to lower the threshold for aggressive behaviour (Stoff & Cairns, 1997). Research conducted in the United States has found that the hotter it is on a given day, the greater the likelihood that riots and violent crimes will occur (Anderson & Anderson, 1984; Anderson, Bushman, & Groom, 1997; Bushman, Wang, & Anderson, 2005a, 2005b; Harries & Stadler, 1988). In the desert city of Phoenix, Arizona, drivers without air-conditioned cars are more likely to honk their horns in traffic jams than are drivers with air-conditioned cars (Kenrick & MacFarlane, 1986). And believe it or not, it has been shown that in major league baseball games, significantly more batters are hit by pitches when the temperature is above 32°C than when it is below that temperature (Reifman, Larrick, & Fein, 1988).

As you know by now, one has to be cautious about interpreting events that take place in natural settings. For example, the scientist in you might be tempted to ask whether increases in aggression are due to the temperature itself or merely due to the fact that more people are apt to be outside—getting in one another's way!—on hot days than on cool or rainy days. Fortunately, we can test this by conducting laboratory experiments. In one such experiment, students at the University of Alberta read ambiguous stories that could end with aggression or nonaggression. Here's an example of one of the stories:

> Todd was on his way home from work one evening when he had to brake quickly for a yellow light. The person in the car behind him . . . crashed into the back of Todd's car, causing a lot of damage to both vehicles. Fortunately, there were no injuries. Todd got out of his car and surveyed the damage. He then walked over to the other car.

The researchers found that participants who read these stories in an uncomfortably hot room (32°C) were more likely to complete the stories with aggression and frustration responses than were participants who performed the task at room temperature (21°C) (Rule, Taylor, & Dobbs, 1987). This study shows that people are more likely to have aggression on their minds when they are uncomfortably hot. Is there any evidence that they actually behave more aggressively?

To find out, Griffitt and Veitch (1971) had students take a test in either a room with normal temperature or a room where the temperature was allowed to soar to 32°C. The students in the hot room not only reported feeling more aggressive, but also expressed more hostility to a stranger. See the accompanying Try It! to conduct your own observational research on heat and aggression.

Try it!

▶ Heat, Humidity, and Aggression

The next time you find yourself caught in a traffic jam, try doing a simple, natural replication of the Kenrick and MacFarlane (1986) experiment. Consider the following hypothesis: The greater the heat and humidity, the greater the aggression.

- Take notes on how much aggression you observe (in the form of horn honking).

- Note the heat and humidity that day.
- The next two or three times you get caught in a traffic jam, do the same thing.

Can you discern a relationship between heat and humidity, and horn honking?

Situational Causes of Aggression

We've seen the effects of body chemistry, alcohol, and unpleasant physical experiences such as pain and heat on aggression. As we discussed, certain social situations are conducive to aggression—so conducive that even the most docile, laid-back person among us might resort to aggressive behaviour. What might some of these situations be?

Frustration as a Cause of Aggression

Imagine that your friend Alain is driving you to the airport so you can fly home for the holidays. Alain has picked you up a bit later than you feel comfortable with, but when you mention it, he accuses you of being overly anxious and assures you that he knows the route well and that you will arrive with time to spare. Halfway to the airport, you grind to a halt in bumper-to-bumper traffic. Once again, Alain assures you that there is plenty of time—but this time he sounds less confident. After a few minutes, your palms are sweating. You open the car door and survey the road ahead: There is nothing but gridlock as far as you can see. You get back in the car, slam the door, and glare at Alain. He smiles lamely and says, "How was I supposed to know there would be so much traffic?" Should he be prepared to duck?

As this all-too-familiar story suggests, frustration is a major cause of aggression. Frustration occurs when a person is thwarted on the way to an expected goal or gratification. All of us have experienced some degree of frustration from time to time; indeed, it's unlikely we can get through a week without experiencing it. According to **frustration-aggression theory**, people's perception that they are being prevented from obtaining a goal will increase the probability of an aggressive response (Dollard, Doob, Miller, Mowrer, & Sears, 1939). This does not mean that frustration always leads to aggression—but it frequently does, especially when frustration is a decidedly unpleasant experience. In a classic experiment by Barker, Dembo, and Lewin (1941), young children were shown a roomful of attractive toys that were kept out of reach by a wire screen. After a painfully long wait, the children were finally allowed to play with the toys. In a control condition, other children were allowed to play with the toys, without first being frustrated by a wait. These children played joyfully with the toys. However, when children in the frustrated group were finally given access to the toys, they were extremely destructive. Many smashed the toys, threw them against the wall, and stepped on them.

Several factors can increase frustration and accordingly will increase the probability that some form of aggression will occur. One such factor involves your closeness to the goal or the object of your desire. The closer the goal, the greater the expectation of pleasure that is thwarted; the greater the expectation, the more likely the aggression. This was demonstrated in a field experiment by Mary Harris (1974), who instructed confederates to cut in line in front of people who were waiting in a variety of places—for movie tickets, outside crowded restaurants, or at the checkout counter of a supermarket. On some occasions, the confederates cut in front of the second person in line; at other times, they cut in front of the twelfth person. The results were clear: The people standing behind the intruder were much more aggressive when the confederate cut in to the second place in line.

Aggression also increases when the frustration is unexpected. James Kulik and Roger Brown (1979) hired students to telephone strangers and ask for donations to a charity. The students were hired on a commission basis—that is, they received a small fraction of each dollar pledged. Some of the students were led to expect a high rate of contributions; others were led to expect far less success. The experiment was rigged so none of the potential donors agreed to make a contribution.

frustration-aggression theory

the theory that frustration—the perception that you are being prevented from obtaining a goal—will increase the probability of an aggressive response

▶ Road rage is often caused by frustration.

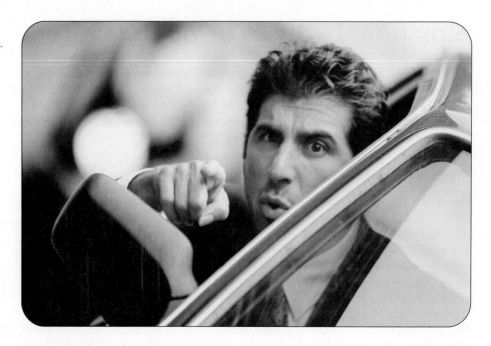

The experimenters found that the callers with high expectations directed more verbal aggression toward the non-donors, speaking more harshly and slamming down the phone with more force than the callers with low expectations.

As we've already said, frustration does not always produce aggression. Rather, it seems to produce anger or annoyance and a readiness to aggress if other things about the situation are conducive to aggressive behaviour (Berkowitz, 1978, 1988, 1989, 1993; Gustafson, 1989). What are those things? For one, the size and strength of the person responsible for your frustration—as well as that person's ability to retaliate—will influence whether you react with aggression. It is undoubtedly easier to slam the phone down on a reluctant donor who is miles away and has no idea who you are, than to take out your anger against your frustrator if he turns out to be a defensive lineman for the Edmonton Eskimos and is staring you in the face. Similarly, if the frustration is understandable, legitimate, and unintentional, the tendency to aggress will be reduced. In an experiment by Burnstein and Worchel (1962), for example, when a confederate "unwittingly" sabotaged the problem solving of his groupmates because his hearing aid stopped working, the resulting frustration did not lead to a measurable degree of aggression.

We should also point out that frustration is not the same as deprivation. For example, children who simply don't have toys do not aggress more than children who do have toys. In the toy experiment discussed earlier, frustration and aggression occurred because the children had every reason to expect to play with the toys, and their reasonable expectation was thwarted; this thwarting was what caused the children to behave destructively.

The Reverend Jesse Jackson (1981), with great insight, pointed out that the race riots that occurred in the United States in 1967 and 1968 took place in the middle of rising expectations and increased, though inadequate, social spending. In short, Jackson was suggesting that thwarted expectations were largely responsible for the frustration and aggression. A similar phenomenon occurred when the Berlin Wall came down and East Germans began to expect higher employment rates and wages. When these changes did not immediately materialize, high levels of anger and frustration ensued.

What causes aggression, then, is not deprivation but **relative deprivation**—the perception that you (or your group) have less than you deserve, less than what you have been led to expect, or less than what people similar to you have. For

relative deprivation

the perception that you have less than you deserve, less than what you have been led to expect, or less than what people similar to you have example, Tougas and her colleagues found that some Canadian policewomen experienced relative deprivation—they believed that they were excluded from opportunities and activities that were available to their male colleagues (Tougas, Rinfret, Beaton, De la Sablonnière, 2005). Researchers from universities in Canada and France recently tested whether South Africans who felt relative deprivation (e.g., in terms of their economic status relative to other South Africans) would report more negative attitudes toward immigrants to their country than those who felt less deprived. And that was exactly what they found (Dambrun, Taylor, McDonald, Crush, & Méot, 2006).

Feelings of relative deprivation have also been created in the laboratory (Wright, 1997; Wright, Taylor, & Moghaddam, 1990). For example, in one experiment, students at McGill University were told that everyone would begin as a member of a low-status group, but that there would be an opportunity to become a member of a high-status group depending on how they performed on a decision-making task. The many benefits of being in the high-status group were described—among them, the chance to win $100. After completing the decision-making task, some participants were told that the high-status group had decided to accept only those who scored at least 8.5, and that their mark was only 6. Other participants were told that they had just missed the cutoff with their mark of 8.2. All participants were then given various options for responding to the high-status group's decision not to accept them. Participants who almost made it into the high-status group responded differently from those who were told they were far from being accepted. Specifically, those who nearly made it were most likely to write a letter of protest demanding that the high-status group reverse its decision, even though they were told that the decision was final and that the high-status group disapproved of protest action. These participants also perceived greater injustice in the situation than did those who were far from being accepted. In contrast, those who were far from being accepted into the high-status group were more likely to passively resign themselves to remaining in the low-status group for the rest of the experiment (Wright, Taylor, & Moghaddam, 1990).

Direct Provocation and Reciprocation

Suppose that you are having lunch in the cafeteria, quietly minding your own business. While you're eating, you notice two guys whispering to each other and occasionally glancing in your direction. One of the guys picks up his lunch tray and walks toward you. He dumps his tray in the garbage next to you, dropping leftovers all over you. How would you respond?

This was one of the scenarios presented to male high school students in Nova Scotia in a study by Van Oostrum and Horvath (1997). The researchers found that the participants' response to situations such as this one depended on whether they perceived the other student's behaviour as intentional. Those who attributed hostile intentions (e.g., believed that the student spilled the tray "to be mean") reported that they would respond with aggression—more so than did students who interpreted the event as an accident or who believed that the other student's motives were ambiguous. Interestingly, the participants who reported the greatest use of aggression in their everyday lives were also the most likely to attribute hostile intent in the scenarios.

One cause of aggression, then, stems from the urge to reciprocate after being provoked by aggressive behaviour from another person. Although the Christian plea to "turn the other cheek" is wonderful advice, it does not appear to be the typical reaction of most human beings. This has been illustrated in countless experiments in and out of the laboratory. Typical of this line of research is an experiment by Robert Baron (1988), in which participants prepared an advertisement for a new product; their ad was then evaluated and criticized by an accomplice of the experimenter. In one condition, the criticism, while strong, was done in a gentle and considerate manner ("I think there's a lot of room for improvement"); in the other condition, the criticism was given in an insulting manner ("I don't think you could be original if you tried"). When provided with an opportunity to retaliate, subjects who were treated harshly were far more likely to do so than were those in the "gentle" condition.

It is important to point out that when provoked, people do not always recip- rocate. We ask ourselves: Was the provocation intentional or not? When con- vinced it was unintentional, most of us will not reciprocate (Kremer & Stephens, 1983). But to curtail an aggressive response, these mitigating circumstances must be known at the time of the provocation, as demon- strated in a study conducted at the University of Alberta. In this experi- ment, students were insulted by the experimenter's assistant. Half of the students were first told that the assistant was upset because he had just received an unfair grade on a chemistry exam; the other students received this information only after the insult was delivered. All partici- pants later had an opportunity to retaliate by choosing the level of unpleasant noise with which to zap the assistant. Those students who knew about the mitigat- ing circumstances before being insulted delivered less intense bursts of noise than did those who learned about the circumstances after they had been insulted (Johnson & Rule, 1986). Why the difference? At the time of the insult, the informed students simply did not take it personally and therefore had no strong need to retaliate. This interpretation is bolstered by evidence of their physiologi- cal arousal. At the time of the insult, the heartbeat of the insulted students did not increase as rapidly if they knew beforehand about their research partner's unhappy state of mind.

Social Exclusion

It is becoming an all-too-common theme: A high school or a university student shows up at school one day with a gun and goes on a killing rampage. Analyses of these tragedies paint a picture of the killers as socially isolated individuals who experienced rejection by their peers. They then deal with the pain of rejection by mounting a lethal attack on those whose acceptance they craved most. Is there validity to these kinds of analyses? Does social exclusion actually lead to aggressive behaviour? An extensive program of research suggests that it does (Baumeister, DeWall, Ciarocco, & Twenge, 2005; Twenge, Baumeister, Tice, & Stucke, 2001).

Imagine you were a participant in one of these studies. You arrive at a labo- ratory along with four or five other students. First, you spend 15 minutes chat- ting as part of a getting-acquainted exercise. Then, you are informed that the actual experiment involves working in groups on a task. You and the other students are asked to name the two people with whom you would most like to work. You eagerly write down the names of the two people you enjoyed most dur- ing the getting-acquainted discussion. The experimenter then collects the names and tells you she will be back shortly to announce the group assignments. To your horror, when she returns she says, "I hate to tell you this, but no one chose you as someone they wanted to work with." How would you react?

If you are like the actual participants in this study, you would react with aggression. The rest of the experiment was set up so participants were given an opportunity to deliver loud bursts of white noise to a confederate who insulted them. Those participants who had been rejected earlier were much more aggres- sive toward the confederate (i.e., gave longer and louder bursts of noise) than those who were told they had been accepted by the group. It is remarkable that the experience of being excluded from a group of strangers in a laboratory can provoke considerable levels of aggression. It is perhaps little wonder that those who experience the sting of rejection from classmates on a daily basis end up reacting with extreme aggression.

The good news is that social exclusion can also motivate us to form new social bonds. In a recent series of studies, it was found that when participants (university students) were socially excluded, they were more interested in forming new friendships with other students or becoming socially reconnected in other ways (Maner, DeWall, Baumeister, & Schaller, 2007). In one of the studies, a friendly interaction partner was rated as more sociable and positive by students who had just experienced social exclusion than by those in a control condition. The down side is that these effects only held when the excluded students felt that there would be opportunities for ongoing social interaction with the friendly person. Thus, after being socially excluded, we may be more interested in establishing social bonds with others, but only if there is a chance of continuing, future interactions.

Aggressive Objects as Aggressive Cues

Is it conceivable that the mere presence of an **aggressive stimulus**—an object associated with aggressive responses (e.g., a gun) might increase the probability of aggression? In a classic experiment by Leonard Berkowitz and Anthony LePage (1967), university students were made angry. Some of them were made angry in a room in which a gun was left lying around (ostensibly from a previous experiment), and others were made angry in a room in which a neutral object (a badminton racket) was substituted for the gun. Participants were then given the opportunity to administer electric shocks to a fellow student. Those individuals who had been made angry in the presence of the gun administered more intense electric shocks than did those made angry in the presence of the badminton racket (see Figure 11.1).

These basic findings have been borne out a great many times (Frodi, 1975; Turner & Leyens, 1992; Turner & Simons, 1974; Turner et al., 1977). The findings are provocative and point to a conclusion opposite to a familiar slogan often used by opponents of gun control: "Guns don't kill; people do." Guns do kill. Leonard Berkowitz (1981) put it this way, "An angry person can pull the trigger of his gun if he wants to commit violence; but the trigger can also pull the finger or otherwise elicit aggressive reactions from him, if he is ready to aggress and does not have strong inhibitions against such behaviour" (p. 12).

Consider Seattle, Washington, and Vancouver, British Columbia. They are virtually twin cities; they have similar climates, populations, economies, general crime rates, and rates of physical assault. They differ, however, in two respects: (a) Vancouver severely restricts handgun ownership, whereas Seattle does not, and (b) the murder rate in Seattle is more than twice as high as that in Vancouver (Sloan et al., 1988). Can the difference in murder rates be attributed to the

aggressive stimulus

an object that is associated with aggressive response (e.g., a gun) and whose mere presence can increase the probability of aggression

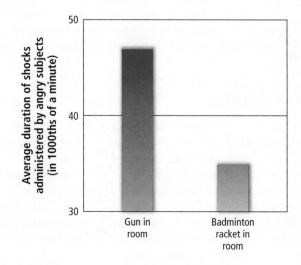

FIGURE 11.1

The trigger can pull the finger

Aggressive cues, such as weapons, tend to increase levels of aggression.

(Adapted from Berkowitz & LePage, 1967)

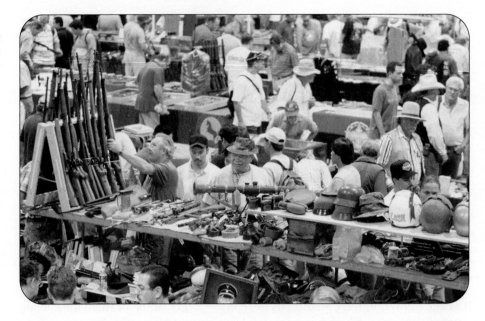

► Guns to the left of me, guns to the right of me ... Does the easy availability of guns in the United States contribute to the frequency and intensity of violence?

difference in restrictions on guns? We cannot be sure. But the laboratory experiments discussed above strongly suggest that the ubiquitous presence of that aggressive stimulus in the United States might be a factor. This speculation receives additional support from Dane Archer and Rosemary Gartner (1984), who, in a cross-national study of violence, found that the homicide rate in countries all over the world is highly correlated with the availability of handguns. Britain, for example, where handguns are banned, has one-quarter the population of the United States but just one-sixteenth as many homicides.

It is important to note that these effects only occur when we actually link an object with aggression. For example, in a recent series of studies, Bartholow and colleagues (2004) found that hunting guns were associated with aggression for non-hunters but not for hunters. On the other hand, assault guns were associated with aggression for both hunters and non-hunters alike (Bartholow, Anderson, Carnagey, & Benjamin, 2004). We should also point out that aggression can be cued by any aggressive stimulus—not just guns. For example, Josephson (1987) demonstrated that even neutral objects can come to be associated with aggression. In her study, some of the participants (young boys) were shown a violent television segment in which snipers communicated via walkie-talkies. Later, they played a game of floor hockey while observers recorded instances of aggression by speaking into either a walkie-talkie or a tape recorder. Participants showed greater aggression when the observers used walkie-talkies than when they used tape recorders. Thus, the walkie-talkie had become a violence-related cue, just from having been associated with violence in the television show the participants had seen earlier.

Imitation and Aggression

Children frequently learn to solve conflicts aggressively by imitating adults and their peers, especially when they see that the aggression is rewarded. For example, in many high-contact sports (e.g., football and hockey), the more aggressive players achieve the greatest fame and the highest salaries, and the more aggressive teams win more games. In these sports, it usually doesn't pay to be a gentle soul. Famed baseball manager Leo Durocher once said, "Nice guys finish last!" The data bear him out. For instance, the hockey players most frequently sent to the penalty box for overly aggressive play tend to be the ones who score the most goals (McCarthy & Kelly, 1978). What lessons are children learning from observing aggression among athletes and other adults?

In a classic series of experiments, Albert Bandura and his associates (1961, 1963) demonstrated the power of social learning. **Social learning theory** holds that we learn social behaviour (e.g., aggression) by observing others and imitating them. The basic procedure in the Bandura experiments was to have an adult knock around a plastic, air-filled "Bobo" doll (the kind that bounces back after it's been knocked down) while children observed. The adult would smack the doll around with the palm of his or her hand, strike it with a mallet, kick it, and yell aggressive things at it. The kids were then allowed to play with the doll. In these experiments, the children imitated the aggressive models and treated the doll in an abusive manner. Moreover, these children used identical actions and identical aggressive words to those of the adult. In addition, many went beyond mere imitation—they also engaged in novel forms of aggressive behaviour. In contrast, children in a control condition, who did not see the aggressive adult in action, almost never unleashed any aggression against the hapless doll.

Given findings such as these, it probably comes as no surprise that numerous studies have found that a large percentage of physically abusive people were themselves abused by their parents when they were kids (Dutton & Hart, 1992a, 1992b; Silver, Dublin, & Lourie, 1969; Straus & Gelles, 1980). When children experience aggressive treatment at the hands of their parents, they learn that violence is the way to respond to conflict or anger.

People may also imitate acts of violence performed by their peers. In April 1999, the shooting rampage of two students at Columbine High School in Littleton, Colorado, made news headlines around the world. Eric Harris and Dylan Klebold shot and killed 13 people at their high school before fatally shooting themselves. Later that month, a 14-year-old boy (who cannot be named because he was a minor) attending W. R. Meyers High School in Taber, Alberta, opened fire, killing one student and wounding another. Although it cannot be proven, it was widely speculated that the Taber tragedy was an imitation of the Columbine massacre. That was not an isolated case—similar threats increased dramatically throughout the country following the Taber shootings. According to Kevin Cameron, the social worker who led the crisis unit team sent to Taber, critical periods, such as the anniversary of the shootings, are associated with increased threats for at least three to five years afterward (Cameron, 2000). Indeed, on the one-year anniversary of the Columbine shootings, four students and one staff

social learning theory

the theory that we learn social behaviour (e.g., aggression) by observing others and imitating them

> 66 *Children have never been very good at listening to their elders, but they have never failed to imitate them.* 99
>
> —*James Baldwin,* Nobody Knows My Name, *1961*

◀ It is clear from the studies of Bandura and colleagues (1961, 1963) that children learn aggressive behaviour through imitation and modelling.

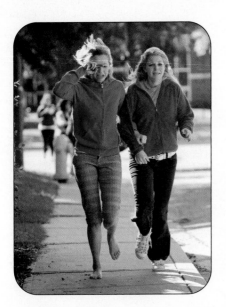

▲ Students from Luther College High School in Regina sob after an armed youth held approximately 300 of them hostage.

member at Cairine Wilson High School in Orleans, Ontario, were wounded when they were attacked by a knife-wielding student. Sadly, a decade later, the Columbine massacre continues to have an impact around the world. On April 16, 2007, 32 students and staff died in the Virginia Tech massacre, which was widely believed to be an anniversary shooting. And on September 24, 2008, Matti Saari, a student at a trade school in Finland opened fire on his fellow students and teachers. He killed 10 people before turning his gun on himself. This was the second school shooting in Finland in less than a year. In both cases, the gunmen had been fascinated by the Columbine shootings (Turula, 2008).

The Effects of Violence in the Media

If just watching people behave aggressively causes children to mistreat dolls, what does watching violence on television or in movies do to them—to all of us? And what about violent video games in which children participate in the destruction of cities, and the lopping off of heads and limbs of characters on their computer screens?

Most children in North America are immersed in TV violence. It has been estimated that by the time the average American child finishes elementary school, he or she will have seen 8000 murders and more than 100 000 other acts of violence (Eron, 2001). Analyses of the content of television shows have revealed that 58 percent of all television programs contain violence—and of those, 78 percent include no remorse, criticism, or penalty for the violence (Seppa, 1997). Indeed, some 40 percent of violent incidents seen on television are initiated by characters portrayed as heroes or other attractive role models for children (Cantor, 1994; Kunkel et al., 2001).

Exactly what do children learn from watching violence on television? In an impressive longitudinal program of research, Eron and Huesmann and their colleagues (Eron, 1982, 1987; Eron, Huesmann, Lefkowitz, & Walder, 1996) assessed television viewing habits of nearly 900 eight-year-old children. The children were asked to report which shows they watched on television and how frequently they watched them. (The shows were independently rated by judges as to how violent they were.) Then, the general aggressiveness of the children was rated by their teachers and classmates. The researchers found a significant correlation between the amount of violent TV watched and the children's aggressiveness. More striking was the finding that the impact of watching violent television accumulated over time—10 years later, when the original research participants were 18 years old, the correlation between television violence and aggression was stronger than it had been at age eight!

These sorts of findings have been obtained for adolescents and adults as well, as shown in a recent longitudinal study in which the behaviour of more than 700 families was monitored over a period of 17 years (Johnson, Cohen, Smailes, Kasen, & Brook, 2002). The findings were striking: There was a significant association between the amount of time spent watching television during adolescence and early adulthood and the likelihood of subsequent violent acts against others. This association was significant regardless of parental education, family income, and neighbourhood violence. Moreover, unlike most laboratory experiments on aggression, which understandably must use rather pallid measures of aggression (e.g., administering fake electric shocks or loud noises to the victim), this study—because it took place in the real world over a long period of time—was able to examine severe aggressive behaviour such as assault and armed robbery (Johnson et al., 2002).

Although these are powerful data, they do not definitively prove that watching a lot of violence on television causes children and adolescents to become

❝*Television has brought murder back into the home—where it belongs.*❞

—*Alfred Hitchcock, 1965*

❝*Death has been tidied up, cleansed of harmful ingredients, and repackaged in prime-time segments that pander to baser appetites but leave no unpleasant aftertaste. The Caesars of network television permit no mess on the living room floor.*❞

—*Donald Goddard, 1977*

violent adults. After all, it is at least conceivable that the aggressive kids were born with a tendency to enjoy violence and that this enjoyment manifested itself in both their aggressive behaviour and their liking for watching violence on television. Once again, we see the value of the controlled experiment in sorting out what causes what. To demonstrate conclusively that watching violence on television actually causes violent behaviour, the relationship must be shown experimentally.

Because this is an issue of great importance to society, it has been well researched. Although not all of the research is consistent, the overwhelming thrust of the experimental evidence is that watching violence does indeed increase the frequency of aggressive behaviour in children (see reviews of the literature by Cantor et al., 2001; Geen, 1998; Huesmann & Miller, 1994; Wood, Wong, & Chachere, 1991). For example, in an early experiment on this issue, Robert Liebert and Robert Baron (1972) exposed a group of children to an extremely violent television episode of a police drama. In a control condition, a similar group of children was exposed to an exciting but nonviolent television sporting event for the same length of time. Each child was then allowed to play in another room with a group of other children. Those who had watched the violent police drama showed far more aggression against their playmates than did those who had watched the sporting event.

To give another example, earlier, we referred to an experiment by Josephson (1987), who found that watching television violence has the greatest impact on youngsters who are somewhat prone to violence to begin with. In this experiment, nearly 400 boys from various Winnipeg schools were exposed to either a film depicting a great deal of police violence or an exciting, nonviolent film about bike racing. The boys then played a game of floor hockey. Exposure to the violent film had the effect of increasing the number of aggressive acts committed during the game—primarily by those boys who had previously been rated as highly aggressive by their teachers. These boys hit others with their sticks, threw elbows, and yelled aggressive things at their opponents to a much greater extent than was seen in either the boys rated as nonaggressive who had also watched the violent film or the boys rated as aggressive who had watched the nonviolent film. Thus, it may be that watching media violence in effect serves to give aggressive children "permission" to express their aggression. Josephson's experiment suggests that children who do not have aggressive tendencies to begin with do not necessarily act aggressively—at least, not on the basis of seeing only one violent film.

7/18/73

"AT LAST, A MOVIE WITHOUT ALL THOSE FILTHY SEX SCENES!"

OLIPHANT Copyright © 1973. Reprinted with permission of UNIVERSAL PRESS SYNDICATE. All Rights Reserved.

◄ Many people are unconcerned about the impact of watching violent entertainment; however, research shows that viewing violent content can have lasting ill effects.

▶ Media violence may serve to give kids already prone to aggression permission to be aggressive. It also may make children not prone to aggression more aggressive.

This last phrase is an important one, because it may be that even children who are not prone to aggression will become more aggressive if exposed to a steady diet of violent films over a long period. Indeed, that is exactly what was found in a set of field experiments performed in Belgium (Leyens, Camino, Parke, & Berkowitz, 1975; Parke et al., 1977).

Before leaving this topic, we should note that the kinds of effects we have been discussing extend to violence portrayed in the media more generally—not just in television programming. The Columbine High School killings raised the disturbing question of whether violent entertainment, such as violent video games, can contribute to aggression. Apparently Harris and Klebold enjoyed playing a bloody, extremely violent video game licensed by the U.S. military to train soldiers how to kill. For a class project, Harris and Klebold produced a videotape that was an eerie rendition of the killings they subsequently carried out. Their videotape, modelled after the video game, featured the two of them wearing trench coats, carrying guns, and killing school athletes.

Does playing violent video games actually produce aggressive behaviour? The answer is yes. Specifically, there is evidence that playing violent video games has the same kind of impact on children and adolescents that watching television does. In one study, violent video game playing was positively correlated with aggressive behaviour and delinquency in children (Anderson & Dill, 2000). This correlational study was followed by several laboratory experiments with university students. These experiments confirmed that exposure to violent video games does, in fact, increase aggressive thoughts and behaviours (Anderson & Dill, 2000; Bartholow & Anderson, 2002; Bushman & Anderson, 2002). (If this isn't enough to persuade you to curb time spent playing video games, we might note that Anderson and Dill also found that the more time the participants spent playing video games—violent or not—the lower their grades became!) More recently, these researchers have found that listening to songs with violent lyrics also increases aggressive thoughts and feelings of hostility among both male and female university students (Anderson, Carnagey, & Eubanks, 2003).

We end with a cautionary note: The data we have been discussing should not be construed as indicating that all people, or even a sizeable percentage of people, are motivated to commit violence through watching media violence or playing violent video games. However, the fact that some people are influenced—and that the results can be tragic—cannot be denied.

The Numbing Effect of Media Violence   Repeated exposure to difficult or unpleasant events tends to have a numbing effect on our sensitivity to those events. In one experiment, Victor Cline and his colleagues (1973) measured the physiological responses of several young men while they were watching a rather brutal and bloody boxing match. Those who watched a lot of television in their daily lives seemed relatively indifferent to the mayhem in the ring—that is, they showed little physiological evidence of excitement or anxiety. They treated the violence in a lackadaisical manner. On the other hand, those who typically watched relatively little television underwent major physiological arousal—the violence really bothered them (Cline, Croft, & Courrier, 1973).

Studies have also found that viewing television violence can subsequently numb people's reactions when they are faced with real-life aggression. In one study, participants watched either a violent police drama or an exciting but non-violent volleyball game (Thomas, Horton, Lippincott, & Drabman, 1977). After a short break, they observed a verbally and physically aggressive interaction between two preschoolers. Those who had watched the police show responded less emotionally—as measured by changes in galvanic skin response—than did those who had watched the volleyball game. It seems that viewing the initial violence served to desensitize them to further acts of violence; they were not upset by an incident that should have upset them. While such a reaction may psychologically protect us from upset, it may also have the unintended effect of increasing our indifference to victims of violence and perhaps rendering us more accepting of violence as a necessary aspect of modern life. In a follow-up experiment, Margaret Thomas (1982) took this reasoning a step further. She demonstrated that students exposed to a great deal of television violence not only showed physiological evidence of greater acceptance of violence but also, when subsequently given the opportunity to administer electric shocks to a fellow student, delivered more powerful electric shocks than did those in the control condition.

How Does Media Violence Affect Our View of the World?   If people are watching all of this murder and mayhem on the TV screen, wouldn't it be logical for them to conclude that it simply isn't safe to leave the house—especially after dark? This is precisely what many TV viewers do conclude (Gerbner, Gross, Morgan, Signorelli, & Shanahan, 2002). Adolescents and adults who are heavy TV viewers (who watch more than four hours per day) are more likely than light TV viewers (less than two hours per day) to have an exaggerated view of the degree of violence taking place outside of their home. Moreover, heavy TV viewers have a much greater fear of being personally assaulted.

Why Does Media Violence Affect Viewers' Aggression?   As we have suggested throughout this section, there are five distinct reasons that explain why exposure to violence via the media might increase aggression:

1. **"If they can do it, so can I."** When people watch characters on television, in films, or in video games expressing violence, it might simply weaken their previously learned inhibitions against violent behaviour.

2. **"Oh, so that's how you do it!"** When people watch characters on television, in films, or in video games expressing violence, it might trigger imitation, providing them with ideas as to how they might go about it.

3. **"I think it must be aggressive feelings that I'm experiencing."** Watching violence makes feelings of anger more easily available and makes an aggressive response more likely simply through priming, as we discussed in Chapter 3. Thus, exposing children to an endless supply of violence on television, in films, and in video games makes it more likely that aggression will come to their minds as a response to real-life situations.

4. **"Ho-hum, another brutal beating—what's on the other channel?"** Watching a lot of violence seems to reduce both our sense of horror about violence and our sympathy for the victims, thereby making it easier for us to live with violence and perhaps easier for us to act aggressively.

5. **"I'd better get him before he gets me!"** If watching a lot of TV makes you think the world is a dangerous place, you might be more apt to be hostile to a stranger who approaches you on the street.

Violent Pornography and Violence against Women

If viewing aggression in films and on television contributes to aggressiveness, doesn't it follow that exposure to pornographic material could increase the incidence of sexual aggression, such as rape? Many people think so. Lavoie, Robitaille, and Hébert (2000), for example, conducted discussion groups with youths who frequented a teen drop-in centre in Quebec City. Both males and females perceived pornography as a cause of sexual violence in relationships. Moreover, participants reported that it was not uncommon for them or their partners to imitate acts of sexual violence observed in pornographic movies or magazines. Similarly, Sommers and Check (1987) found that women living in shelters or attending counselling groups for battered women in the Toronto area reported much greater consumption of pornographic material by their partner than did a comparison group of women who were not battered. The battered women experienced higher levels of verbal aggression, physical aggression, and sexual aggression from their partners than did the control group. In addition, 39 percent of the battered women—versus 3 percent of the control group—answered yes to the question, "Has your partner ever upset you by trying to get you to do what he'd seen in pornographic pictures, movies, or books?"

Careful scientific research suggests an important distinction between simple pornography and violent pornography. By "violent pornography" we mean exactly what you might think: pornographic material that includes an element of violence against women. The findings from carefully controlled laboratory studies conducted over the past 25 years confirm that exposure to violent pornography is associated with greater acceptance of sexual violence toward women and is almost certainly a factor associated with actual aggressive behaviour toward women (Dean & Malamuth, 1997; Donnerstein & Berkowitz, 1981; Donnerstein & Linz, 1994; Malamuth & Brière, 1986; Malamuth et al., 1995). For example, Neil Malamuth and James Check (1981) asked students at the University of Manitoba to watch a movie shown at a campus theatre, supposedly as part of a study on the evaluation of movies. The participants saw either a movie that contained sexual violence against women or a nonviolent movie that portrayed a positive, caring relationship. Several days later, the students were asked to complete a sexual attitudes survey in their psychology class. The researchers found that male students who had viewed the movie containing sexual violence were more accepting of violence against women than were those who had seen the nonviolent movie.

Other studies have found that prolonged exposure to depictions of sexual violence against women ("slasher" or "snuff" films) makes viewers more accepting of this kind of violence and less sympathetic toward the victim (Linz, Donnerstein, & Penrod, 1984, 1988; Malamuth, 1981; Zillmann & Bryant, 1984). Thus, by now it is well-established that exposure to sexual violence is associated with greater acceptance of violence toward women and with more violent fantasies. But do laboratory studies show that men who view violent pornography actually behave aggressively toward women?

Sadly, the answer is yes. In one experiment (Donnerstein & Berkowitz, 1981), male participants were angered by a female accomplice. They were then shown one of three films—an aggressive erotic one involving rape, a purely erotic one without violence, or a film depicting non-erotic violence against women. After viewing one of these films, the men took part in a supposedly unrelated experiment that involved teaching the female accomplice by means of administering electric shocks to her whenever she gave incorrect answers. They were allowed to choose whatever level of shock they wished to use. (As with other experiments using this procedure, no shocks were actually received.) Only men who had previously seen the violent pornographic film subsequently administered intense shocks to the female accomplice.

There is also evidence showing that those who view violent pornographic films will administer more intense shocks to a female confederate than to a male confederate (Donnerstein, 1980). Unfortunately, these are not isolated findings. Researchers at the Canadian National Foundation for Family Research and Education conducted a meta analysis of 46 Canadian and U.S. studies on the effects of pornography and concluded that exposure to pornographic material (which, in their analysis, included violent pornography) has far-reaching negative consequences, such as an increased risk of developing sexually deviant tendencies, committing sexual offences, accepting the rape myth, and experiencing difficulties in one's intimate relationships (Paolucci-Oddone, Genius, & Violato, 2000).

How to Reduce Aggression

"Stop hitting your brother!" "Turn off the TV and go to your room!" Trying to curb the aggressive behaviour of their children, most parents use some form of punishment. Some deny privileges; others use force, believing in the old saying, "Spare the rod and spoil the child." How well does punishment work?

Does Punishing Aggression Reduce Aggressive Behaviour?

Punishment is a complex event, especially as it relates to aggression. On one hand, you might guess that punishing any behaviour, including aggression, would reduce its frequency. On the other hand, severe punishment itself usually takes the form of an aggressive act. The punishers are actually modelling aggressive behaviour for the person whose aggressive behaviour they are trying to stamp out, and their punishment might induce that person to imitate the action. This seems to be true—for children. As we mentioned earlier in this chapter, children who grow up with punitive, aggressive parents tend to be prone toward violence when they grow up (Vissing, Straus, Gelles, & Harrop, 1991).

Moreover, as we saw in Chapter 6, several experiments with preschoolers have demonstrated that the threat of relatively severe punishment for committing a transgression does not make the transgression less appealing to the child. However, the threat of mild punishment—of a degree just powerful enough to get the child to cease the undesired activity temporarily—can induce the child to try to justify his or her restraint and can make the behaviour less appealing (Aronson & Carlsmith, 1963; Freedman, 1965).

What about adults? The criminal justice system of most cultures administers harsh punishments as a means of retribution and to deter violent crimes. Does the threat of harsh punishments for violent crimes make such crimes less likely? Do people who are about to commit such crimes say to themselves, "I'd better think twice about this, because if I get caught, I'll be severely punished"? Here, the scientific evidence is mixed. Laboratory experiments indicate that punishment can act as a deterrent but only if two "ideal" conditions are met: (1) The punishment must be both prompt and certain, and (2) it must be unavoidable (Bower & Hilgard, 1981).

All punishment is mischief; all punishment itself is evil.

—Jeremy Bentham, Principles of Morals and Legislation, 1789

Needless to say, in the real world these ideal conditions are almost never met. In most North American cities, the probability that a person who has committed a violent crime will be apprehended, charged, tried, and convicted is not high. Moreover, promptness is rarely possible—punishment is typically delayed by months or even years. Consequently, in the complex world of the criminal justice system, severe punishment is unlikely to have the kind of deterrent effect it does in the laboratory.

Indeed, there is evidence that severe punishment does not seem to deter violent crimes. For example, the United States—where many states invoke the death penalty for murder—has a much higher rate of homicide than many other industrial countries, including Canada (Archer & Gartner, 1984). Moreover, the American states that have abolished the death penalty have not experienced the increase in capital crimes that some experts predicted (Archer & Gartner, 1984; Nathanson, 1987; Peterson & Bailey, 1988). A study by the National Academy of Sciences (see Berkowitz, 1993) demonstrated that consistency and certainty of punishment were far more effective deterrents of violent behaviour than was severe punishment.

Closer to home, in 1990, Manitoba instituted a family violence court to deal specifically with cases of family violence; in 1997, Ontario established similar courts. Other territories and provinces (Yukon, Saskatchewan, Alberta, and New Brunswick) have followed. These specialized courts are part of an overall response to family violence that includes a zero-tolerance policy for arrest, early intervention in domestic abuse situations, the use of Crown attorneys with expertise in family violence issues (e.g., sensitivity to victims' reluctance to testify, ensuring that the legal process does not revictimize victims of violence), and treatment programs for offenders and victims of family violence. The message being sent from these courts is that family violence is a serious crime with immediate, serious consequences.

The establishment of family violence courts has had several effects. The first has been a dramatic increase in the number of arrests and convictions. Importantly, the high rate of convictions has been coupled with an emphasis on rehabilitation; for example, most offenders are required to participate in treatment groups. It is too early to tell whether these initiatives will have long-term benefits or whether these courts have been effective in communicating that family violence is unacceptable. However, it is encouraging that there has been a steady decline in the rate of spousal assault since these courts were established (Canada, 2008).

Catharsis and Aggression

It is generally believed that one way to reduce feelings of aggression is to do something aggressive. "Get it out of your system" has been common advice for a great many years. So, if you are feeling angry, the belief goes, don't try to ignore it, but instead yell, scream, curse, throw a plate at the wall. Express the anger and it won't build up into something truly uncontrollable. This common belief is based on an oversimplification of the psychoanalytic notion of **catharsis** (Dollard, Doob, Miller, Mowrer, & Sears, 1939; Freud, 1933). As we noted earlier, Freud had a "hydraulic" idea of aggressive impulses: He believed that unless people were allowed to express their aggression in relatively harmless ways, the aggressive energy would be dammed up, pressure would build, and the energy would seek an outlet, either exploding into acts of extreme violence or manifesting itself as symptoms of mental illness.

Freud was a brilliant and complex thinker who invariably stopped short of giving simplistic advice. Unfortunately, his theory of catharsis has been boiled down to the dictum that people should "vent" their anger. The idea is that blowing off steam will not only make angry people feel better but will also serve to make them less likely to engage in subsequent acts of destructive violence. Does this square with the data?

catharsis

the notion that "blowing off steam"—by performing an aggressive act, watching others engage in aggressive behaviour, or engaging in a fantasy of aggression—relieves built-up aggressive energies and hence reduces the likelihood of further aggressive behaviour

The Effects of Aggression on Subsequent Acts of Aggression   Consider a study by Bushman, Baumeister, and Stack (1999). They asked university students to read an article, supposedly published in *Science*, titled, "Research Shows that Hitting Inanimate Objects Is an Effective Way to Vent Anger." In the article, a Harvard psychologist claimed that people who vent their anger by hitting a punching bag subsequently behave less aggressively toward others. Other participants read the same article, except that the word "Effective" in the title was changed to "Ineffective," and the article stated that venting one's anger did *not* reduce aggression. Later, all of the participants were insulted by a confederate. Some participants were given a chance to vent their anger by hitting a punching bag; other participants were not. Then, everyone was given an opportunity to deliver bursts of noise either to the person who insulted them or to a different person. It turned out that the most aggressive participants (i.e., those who delivered the longest and loudest blasts of noise) were those who had read the pro-catharsis message and had hit the punching bag. Moreover, they were equally aggressive, regardless of whether the target was the person who had angered them or an innocent person. Thus, it appears that venting anger actually increases anger rather than reduces it.

Similar findings have been obtained in studies examining whether participating in aggressive sports has a cathartic effect. For example, Patterson (1974) measured the hostility of high school football players, rating them both one week before and one week after the football season. If it were true that the intense competitiveness and aggressive behaviour that are part of playing football serve to reduce the tension caused by pent-up aggression, the players would be expected to exhibit a decline in hostility over the course of the season. Instead, the results showed a significant *increase* in feelings of hostility. This is not to say that people do not get pleasure from these games—they do. Engaging in these games, however, does not decrease participants' aggressive feelings; if anything, it increases them.

Some people believe in another variation of the catharsis hypothesis—namely, that watching competitive and aggressive games is a safe way to get rid of our aggressive impulses. Gordon Russell (1983), a sports psychologist at the University of Lethbridge, tested this proposition by measuring the hostility of spectators at an especially violent hockey game. As the game progressed, the spectators became increasingly belligerent; toward the end of the final period, their level of hostility was enormous and did not return to the pre-game level until several hours after the game was over. Similar results have been found among spectators at football games and wrestling matches (Arms, Russell, & Sandilands, 1979; Branscombe & Wann, 1992; Goldstein & Arms, 1971). As with participating in an aggressive sport, watching one serves to increase, rather than reduce, aggressive behaviour.

> " Something of vengeance I had tasted for the first time; an aromatic wine it seemed, on swallowing, warm and racy; its after-flavour, metallic and corroding, gave me a sensation as if I had been poisoned. "
>
> —*Charlotte Brontë, Jane Eyre, 1847*

◄ Fans watching aggressive sports do not become less aggressive—contrary to the idea of catharsis.

Blaming the Victim of Our Aggression   When somebody angers us, venting our hostility against that person does seem to relieve tension and make us feel better, at least temporarily—assuming that the person we vent on doesn't decide to vent back on us. But "feeling better" should not be confused with a reduction in hostility. Aggressing the first time can reduce your inhibitions against committing other such actions; in a sense, the aggression is legitimized, making it easier to carry out such assaults. Further, and more importantly, the main thrust of the research on this issue indicates that committing an overt act of aggression against a person changes one's feelings about that person—in a negative direction—thereby increasing the probability of future aggression against that person.

Does this material begin to sound familiar? It should. As we saw in Chapter 6, when one person does harm to another person, it sets in motion cognitive processes aimed at justifying the act of cruelty. Specifically, when you hurt another person, you experience cognitive dissonance. The cognition, "I have hurt Charlie" is dissonant with the cognition, "I am a decent, reasonable person." A good way for you to reduce dissonance is somehow to convince yourself that hurting Charlie was not an indecent, unreasonable, bad thing to do. You can accomplish this by convincing yourself that Charlie is a terrible human being who deserved to be hurt. This would especially hold if Charlie was an innocent victim of your aggression. In Chapter 6, we discussed experiments in which participants inflicted either psychological or physical harm on an innocent person who had done them no prior harm. The participants then proceeded to derogate their victims, convincing themselves that the victims were not nice people and therefore deserved what they got (Davis & Jones, 1960; Glass, 1964). This reduces dissonance, all right—but it also sets the stage for further aggression; once a person has succeeded in derogating someone, he or she finds it easier to do further harm to the victim in the future.

What happens if the victim isn't totally innocent? For example, what if the victim has done something that hurts or disturbs you and is, therefore, perhaps deserving of retaliation? Here, the situation becomes more complex. In a classic study (Kahn, 1966), a young man posing as a medical technician taking some physiological measurements from university students made derogatory remarks about them. In one condition, the participants were allowed to vent their hostility by expressing their feelings about the technician to his employer—an action that looked as though it would get the technician into serious trouble, perhaps even cost him his job. In another condition, the participants were not given the opportunity to express any aggression against the person who had aroused their anger. Those who were allowed to express their aggression subsequently felt greater dislike and hostility for the technician than did those who were inhibited from expressing their aggression. In other words, expressing aggression did not decrease the tendency to aggress; rather, it tended to *increase* it.

These results suggest that when people are angered, they frequently engage in overkill. In this case, costing the technician his job is much more devastating than the minor insult he delivered. The overkill produces dissonance in much the same way that hurting an innocent person produces dissonance. That is, if there is a major discrepancy between what the person did to you and the force of your retaliation, you must justify that discrepancy by derogating the object of your wrath.

If our reasoning is correct, it might help explain why it is that when two nations are at war, a relatively small percentage of the members of the victorious nation feel much sympathy for the innocent victims of their nation's actions. Near the end of World War II, when U.S. planes dropped atom bombs on Hiroshima and Nagasaki, more than 100 000 Japanese civilians—including many children—were killed, and countless thousands suffered severe injuries. Shortly thereafter, a poll of the American people indicated that less than 5 percent felt that those weapons should not have been used, whereas 23 percent felt that many more of them should have been used before giving Japan

> *In war, the state is sanctioning murder. Even when the war is over, this moral corruption is bound to linger for many years.*
> —Desiderius Erasmus, 1514

the opportunity to surrender. Why would so many U.S. citizens favour the wanton death and destruction of innocent victims? Our guess is that in the course of the war, a sizeable proportion of Americans adopted increasingly derogatory attitudes toward the Japanese, which made it easier to accept the fact that the U.S. military was causing them a great deal of misery. The more misery the Americans inflicted on them, the more the Americans derogated them—leading to an endless spiral of aggression and its justification, even to the point of favouring a delay in ending the war so that more destruction might be inflicted.

Does this sound like ancient history? Not too many years ago, Canada was involved in launching air attacks on Serbia. More than 5000 people were killed as a result of the bombings; most of them were civilians. Former prime minister Jean Chrétien proudly announced that Canada and its NATO allies had "carried the day" and congratulated the Canadian troops for their efforts. In a speech to the House of Commons on June 10, 1999, the day the bombings stopped, Chrétien repeatedly mentioned that it was a great day—a great day for the stability and security of Europe and a great day for Canada. Please note that we are not raising the question here of whether the war was just or necessary. The only question we are raising is this: How many Canadians do you suppose paused for a few moments to feel sadness or regret about the civilians killed in that war? Even more recently, what percentage of Canadians do you suppose have paused to feel sadness about the civilian lives lost as a result of Canada's involvement in Afghanistan? Considerable media attention has been placed on the tragic deaths of Canadian soldiers in Afghanistan: over 100 members of the Canadian Forces died between the first deployment in February 2002 and January 2009 (the time of writing). It is certainly appropriate to recognize and mourn these losses. What is not highlighted in the media, however, is the thousands of Afghani civilians who have lost their lives—and that number is likely to increase. Although it is difficult to get an exact count, it is estimated that each year, there have been approximately 1500 civilian casualties in Afghanistan. Organizations such as Human Rights Watch maintain that these estimates are conservative—the actual numbers are likely to be much higher. Polls conducted in the United States show that there is little sympathy for the innocent victims in such situations (see Aronson, Wilson, & Akert, 2007).

When a nation is at war, the impact of that situation extends even beyond feelings of hostility toward the enemy. Specifically, being at war makes the population—even the noncombatants—more prone to commit aggressive actions

▲ During World War II, Americans depicted the Japanese enemy as being vampires and other creatures.

◄During World War II, Americans tended to derogate Japanese by depicting them as less than human. This helped justify the destruction inflicted on them, as in the bombing of Nagasaki and Hiroshima.

against one another. Dane Archer and Rosemary Gartner (1976, 1984) compared the crime rates for 110 countries starting with the year 1900. They found that compared with similar nations that remained at peace, countries that fought wars exhibited substantial post-war increases in their homicide rates. This should not be surprising; it is consistent with everything we have been saying about the social causes of aggression. The fact that a nation is at war (1) weakens the population's inhibitions against aggression, (2) leads to imitation of aggression, (3) makes aggressive responses more available, and (4) numbs our senses to the horror of cruelty and destruction, making us less sympathetic toward the victims. In addition, being at war serves to legitimize to the population the use of violent solutions to address difficult problems. This phenomenon is likely to be more powerful now than ever before because, thanks to the magic of satellite transmission, we and our children can watch the war unfold in our living room as it happens, 24 hours a day.

> *To jaw-jaw is better than to war-war.*
>
> —Winston Churchill, 1954

What Are We Supposed to Do with Our Anger?

If violence leads to self-justification, which in turn breeds more violence, then what are we to do when we are feeling angry with someone? Stifling anger and sulking around the house, hoping that someone will read our mind, doesn't seem to be a good solution. Neither is brooding and ruminating by ourselves, which just prolongs and intensifies anger (Rusting & Nolen-Hoeksema, 1998). But if keeping our feelings bottled up and expressing them are both harmful, what are we supposed to do? This dilemma isn't as difficult as it might seem. First, it is possible to control our anger by actively enabling it to dissipate. "Actively enabling" means using such simple techniques as counting to 10 before shooting your mouth off (Tavris, 1989). Taking deep breaths or engaging in a distracting activity (working on a crossword puzzle, listening to soothing music, taking a bike ride, or even doing a good deed) are good ways of actively enabling the anger to fade away. But there is more to anger than simply controlling it, as we shall see.

Venting versus Self-Awareness Dissipating anger is not always best for you or for a relationship. If your close friend or romantic partner does something that makes you angry, you may want to express that anger in a way that helps you gain insight into yourself and the dynamics of the relationship. But for that to happen, the anger must be expressed in a nonviolent and nondemeaning way. You can do this (after counting to 10!) by making a clear, calm, and simple statement indicating that you are feeling angry and describing, nonjudgmentally, precisely what your friend or partner did to bring about those feelings. Such a statement in itself will probably relieve tension and make you feel better. At the same time, because you haven't actually harmed the target of your anger, such a response does not set in motion the cognitive processes that would lead you to justify your behaviour by ridiculing or derogating him or her. The person with whom you are angry also is more likely to react in a constructive manner. For example, in a study conducted at the University of Winnipeg, it was found that if participants were angry with their partner, they expected that their partner would react more positively if they, themselves, expressed their anger in positive, constructive ways (e.g., talking it over, expressing hurt feelings). On the other hand, participants expected that if they expressed anger in negative ways (e.g., with direct or indirect aggression), their partner would be likely to respond in kind (Fehr, Baldwin, Collins, Patterson, & Benditt, 1999).

> *I was angry with my friend; I told my wrath, my wrath did end.*
>
> —William Blake, "A Poison Tree," 1789–1794

When feelings of anger are expressed in a clear, open, nonpunitive manner, the result can be greater mutual understanding and a strengthening of the relationship. It almost seems too simple; yet, we have found such behaviour to be a reasonable option that will have more beneficial effects than, on one hand, shouting, name calling, and throwing dishes or, on the other hand, suffering in silence as you grin and bear it (Aronson, 2002).

While it is probably best to reveal your anger to the person who provoked it, at least if you are hoping to resolve the problem between you, sometimes it is helpful to write down your feelings in a journal. Just write your "deepest thoughts and feelings" about the event that has distressed you. Try to do this for 20 minutes a day for a few days and then reread what you have written. Can you see the situation differently? Do solutions offer themselves that you hadn't thought of? In experiments with people undergoing a wide range of traumatic events, those who were induced to write their "deepest thoughts and feelings" about the event felt healthier and suffered fewer physical illnesses 6 to 12 months later compared with people who were allowed to suffer in silence, who wrote about trivial topics, or who wrote about the details of the traumatic events but not their underlying feelings. The beneficial effects of "opening up" are due not simply to the venting of feelings but primarily to the insights and self-awareness that usually accompany such self-disclosure (Pennebaker, 1990).

Some additional corroboration for this suggestion comes from an experiment by Leonard Berkowitz and Bartholmeu Troccoli (1990). In their study, young women listened to another woman talk about herself as part of a job interview. Half of the listeners did so while extending their nondominant arm unsupported (thereby causing discomfort and mild pain); the others listened with their arms resting comfortably on the table. In each condition, half of the participants were asked to rate their feelings while they were listening to the job interview. This procedure provided a vehicle for the participants to understand their discomfort and gain insight into it. The results were striking. Those who experienced pain and discomfort during the interview, but were not given the opportunity to process it, experienced the most negative feelings toward the interviewee—and the more unpleasant the experience was for them, the more negatively they felt toward the interviewee. On the other hand, the participants who were given the opportunity to process their pain were able to avoid being unfairly harsh to the interviewee.

Defusing Anger through Apology   Earlier, we noted that when people had been frustrated by someone and then learned that the person simply couldn't do any better, frustration was less likely to bubble over into anger or aggression. This suggests that an effective way to reduce aggression in another person is to take some action aimed at diminishing the anger and annoyance that caused it.

Suppose you are scheduled to be at your friend's house at 7:30 p.m. in order to drive her to a concert scheduled to start at 8:00. She has been looking forward to the concert for months. You rush out of your house with just barely enough time to get there, but after driving for a few minutes you discover that you have a flat tire. By the time you change the tire and get to her house, you are already 20 minutes late for the concert. Imagine her response if you (a) casually walk in, grin at her, and say, "Oh well, it probably wouldn't have been such a good concert anyway. Lighten up; it's not a big deal," or (b) run in clearly upset, show her your dirty hands, explain what happened, apologize sincerely and profusely, and vow to find a way to make it up to her.

We would predict that your friend would be prone toward aggression in the first instance but not in the second, and a host of experiments supports our prediction (Baron, 1988, 1990; Ohbuchi & Sato, 1994; Weiner et al., 1987). Typically, any apology sincerely given and in which the perpetrator takes full responsibility is effective at reducing aggression.

With this in mind, one of the authors of this book (Elliot Aronson) has speculated about the great advantages that might be gained by equipping automobiles with "apology" signals. Picture the scene: You are at a stop sign and then proceed, but too late you realize that the right of way wasn't really yours. What happens? In most urban centres, the offended driver will honk his or her horn angrily at you, or open the window and give you that nearly universal one-fingered gesture of anger and contempt. Because nobody likes to be the recipient of such abuse, you might be tempted to honk back, thereby escalating the

▲ Mahatma Gandhi was effective in bringing about the independence of India from Britain, using and modelling nonviolent resistance. Being nonviolent in the face of violence is difficult but effective.

❝ *Man must evolve for all human conflict a method which rejects revenge, aggression, and retaliation.* ❞

—*Martin Luther King, Jr., Nobel Peace Prize acceptance speech, 1964*

anger and aggression. Such escalation might be avoided, though, if in addition to the horn (which throughout the world is most often used as an instrument of aggression), every car were equipped with an apology signal—perhaps at the push of a button, a little flag would pop up, saying, "Oops! Sorry!" In the foregoing scenario, had you pushed such a button as soon as you became aware of your transgression, doing so might well have defused the cycle of anger and retaliation that is all too frequently a part of the driving experience. One of our Eastern European readers wrote to tell us that in Poland and Hungary, people apologize by using their emergency flashing lights. If and when techniques such as these become widely used, road rage may become a thing of the past.

The Modelling of Nonaggressive Behaviour We've seen that children will be more aggressive—toward dolls as well as other children—if they witness others behaving aggressively in similar situations. What if we reverse things and expose children to nonaggressive models—to people who, when provoked, express themselves in a restrained, rational, pleasant manner? This has been tested in several experiments and found to work (Baron, 1972; Donnerstein & Donnerstein, 1976; Vidyasagar & Mishra, 1993). In these experiments, children first witnessed the behaviour of youngsters who behaved nonaggressively when provoked. When the children were subsequently placed in a situation in which they themselves were provoked, they showed a much lower frequency of aggressive responses than did children who were not exposed to the nonaggressive models.

Training in Communication and Problem-Solving Skills It is impossible to go through life—or sometimes to get through the day—without feeling frustrated, annoyed, or angry. Feeling anger is part of being human, but anger itself is not the problem. The problem is the *expression* of anger in violent or cruel ways. Yet, we are not born knowing how to express anger or annoyance constructively and nonviolently. Indeed, it seems almost natural to lash out when we are angry. In most societies, it is precisely the people who lack proper social skills who are most prone to violent solutions to interpersonal problems (Toch, 1980). One way to reduce violence, then, is to teach people how to communicate anger or criticism in constructive ways, how to negotiate and compromise when conflicts arise, and how to be more sensitive to the needs and desires of others.

There is some evidence that such formal training can be an effective means of reducing aggression (Studer, 1996). For example, in a classic experiment by Joel Davitz (1952), children were allowed to play in groups of four. Some of these groups were taught constructive ways to relate to each other, and they were rewarded for such behaviour; others were rewarded for aggressive or competitive behaviour. Next, the children were deliberately frustrated. They were told that they would be shown entertaining movies and be allowed to have fun. The experimenter began to show a movie and to hand out candy bars but, then, he abruptly terminated the movie at the point of highest interest and took the candy bars away. Now, the children were allowed to play freely, as the researchers watched for constructive or aggressive behaviours. The results? Children who had been trained for constructive behaviour displayed far more constructive activity and far less aggressive behaviour than did those who had been rewarded for aggression. Many elementary and secondary schools now train students to employ such nonaggressive strategies for resolving conflict (Eargle, Guerra, & Tolan, 1994; Educators for Social Responsibility, 2001).

Building Empathy Let's look at horn honking again. Picture the following scene: A long line of cars is stopped at a traffic light at a busy intersection; the light turns green; the lead car hesitates for 10 seconds. What happens? Almost inevitably, there will be an eruption of honking horns. In a controlled experiment, Robert Baron (1976) found that when the lead car failed to move after the light turned green, almost 90 percent of the drivers of the second car honked their horn in a relentless, aggressive manner. As part of the same experiment, a pedestrian crossed the street between the first and second cars while the light was still red and was out of the intersection by the time the light turned green. As you might imagine, this did not have an effect on the behaviour of the drivers of the next car in line—almost 90 percent honked their horn when the light turned green. In another condition the pedestrian was on crutches but managed to hobble across the street before the light turned green. Interestingly, in this condition the percentage of drivers who honked their horn dropped to 57 percent. Why? Apparently, seeing a person on crutches evoked feelings of empathy, which as you will recall from Chapter 10, is the ability to put oneself in the shoes of another person and vicariously experience some of the same feelings that person is experiencing. In this

CONNECTIONS

Teaching Empathy in School

"What would the world look like to you if you were as small as a cat?" "What birthday presents would make each member of your family happiest?" These questions form the basis of exercises designed by Norma Feshbach, who has pioneered the teaching of empathy in elementary schools. Thinking hard about the answers to such questions expands children's ability to put themselves in another's situation. This empathy-building program also involves having children listen to stories and then retell them from the point of view of each character. The children are then videotaped, playing the role of the different characters. Later, they view the tapes and analyze how people feel and look when they express different feelings.

Not only do children learn empathy, but this program also has several other positive effects. At the end of the program, children show higher self-esteem, greater generosity, more positive attitudes, and less aggressiveness compared with children who have not participated in it (Feshbach, 1989, 1997; Feshbach & Cohen, 1988).

At first glance, such a program may seem unrelated to academics. Yet, role playing and close analysis of stories is just what students do when putting on a play or analyzing a piece of literature. In reminiscing about his childhood, the Nobel Prize–winning physicist, Richard Feynman, reported that his father challenged his intellect by asking him to pretend he was a tiny creature who dwelled in their living room carpet. To deal with that challenge, Feynman needed, in effect, to crawl into the skin and persona of that creature and get a feel for what his life would be like in those circumstances. Such questions also encourage the kind of cognitive flexibility taught in corporate creativity programs. Thus, it should not surprise us that Norma Feshbach (1989, 1997) reports that students who have learned to develop greater empathic ability also tend to have higher academic achievement.

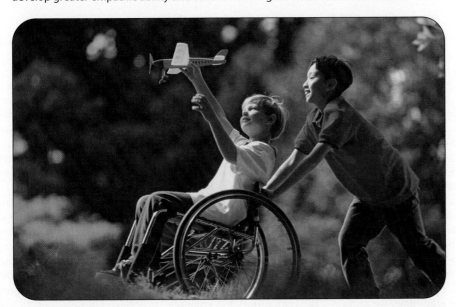

◄ Children who are taught to put themselves in others' shoes often have higher self-esteem, are more generous, and are less aggressive than children who lack skills of empathy.

instance, once evoked, the feeling of empathy infused the consciousness of the potential horn honkers and decreased their urge to be aggressive.

The important role of empathy is underscored in a series of studies conducted by Wohl and McGrath (2007) at Carleton University. This research focused on various kinds of transgressions (e.g., your friend offers to drop off a job application for you but fails to do so, and as a result, you lose out on a very attractive job). Participants in the close condition were made to focus on how recently the event occurred. Participants in the distant condition were induced to put the event "behind them" (by emphasizing that the event took place in the past). Those in the distant condition—who put the event behind them—reported more empathy for the aggressor than those in the close condition. And, importantly, the greater the empathy experienced, the lower the desire to seek revenge for the transgression.

Clearly, empathy is an important human phenomenon. As Feshbach (1989, 1997) observed, most people find it difficult to inflict pain on another human being unless they can find some way to dehumanize their victim. As we mentioned in Chapter 6, when Canadian soldiers were on a peacekeeping mission to Somalia, they referred to Somali people as "gimmes," "smufties," or "nignogs." We see this as a dehumanizing rationalization for acts of cruelty, such as the torture and killing of Shidane Arone; it's easier to commit violent acts against a "gimme" or a "nignog" than against a fellow human being. This kind of rationalization not only makes it possible for us to aggress against another person but also guarantees we will *continue* to aggress against him or her. Once we succeed in convincing ourselves that our enemy is not really a human being at all but just a "nignog," it lowers our inhibitions for committing all kinds of atrocities.

Understanding the process of dehumanization is the first step toward reversing it. Specifically, if it is true that most individuals must dehumanize their victims in order to commit an extreme act of aggression, then by building empathy among people, aggressive acts should become more difficult to commit. The research data lend strong support to this contention. In one study, students who had been trained to empathize—that is, to take the perspective of the other person—behaved less aggressively toward that person than students who had not received the training (Richardson, Hammock, Smith, & Gardner, 1994). In a similar study, Japanese students were told to shock another student as part of a learning experiment (Ohbuchi & Baba, 1988; Ohbuchi, Ohno, & Mukai, 1993). In one condition, the "victims" first disclosed something personal about themselves; in the other condition, they were not given this opportunity. Participants administered less severe shocks to the victim who had revealed personal information.

SUMMARY

Aggression is intentional behaviour aimed at doing harm or causing physical or psychological pain to another person. **Hostile aggression** involves having the goal of inflicting pain; **instrumental aggression** involves inflicting pain on the way to some other goal. Over the centuries, there has been a great deal of disagreement among scholars over whether aggressiveness is primarily instinctive or learned. Sigmund Freud theorized that human beings are born with an instinct toward life, called **Eros**, and a death instinct, **Thanatos**, which leads to aggressive actions. In Freud's view, aggressive energy must be released to avoid a building up that might result in an explosion.

Because aggressiveness has had survival value, most contemporary social psychologists accept the proposition that it is part of our evolutionary heritage. At the same time, we know

that human beings have developed exquisite mechanisms for controlling their aggressive impulses, and that human behaviour is flexible and adaptable to changes in the environment. Whether aggression is actually expressed depends on a complex interplay between our biological propensities and the social situation in which we find ourselves.

There are many causes of aggression, ranging from the neurological and chemical to the social. The area in the core of the brain called the **amygdala** is thought to control aggression. Recent evidence suggests that the chemical **serotonin** serves to inhibit aggressive behaviour; when the body's natural production of serotonin is disrupted, aggression increases. It is also clear that the hormone **testosterone** is correlated with aggressive behaviour; for example, prisoners convicted of violent crimes tend to have higher levels of testosterone than do those convicted of nonviolent crimes. This is consistent with the more general finding that men are more aggressive than women. At least one other chemical, alcohol, is associated with increases in aggression; alcohol acts as a general disinhibitor, lowering our inhibitions against violent behaviour. Pain and other physical discomforts (e.g., heat) will also increase aggressive behaviour.

Many causes of aggression are situational. The **frustration-aggression theory** states that the experience of frustration can increase the probability of an aggressive response. However, frustration alone does not automatically lead to aggression; it is more likely to produce aggression if one is thwarted on the way to a goal in a manner that is either illegitimate or unexpected. In addition, frustration is the result not simply of deprivation but of **relative deprivation**—the feeling that comes from knowing that you have less than what you deserve, less than what you have been led to expect, or less than what people similar to you have.

Aggression can also be produced by social provocation or the mere presence of an **aggressive stimulus**—or an object associated with aggressive responses, such as a gun. **Social learning theory** states that aggression can also be produced through the imitation of aggressive models, either in face-to-face situations or by viewing violence in films or on television. The possible effects of viewing violence in the media are of particular interest to social psychologists because of the pervasiveness of violent programming. Violence in the media has been shown not only to lead to greater aggressiveness in the viewer but also to create a numbing effect, making us more accepting of violence in society. The viewing of violent pornographic material promotes greater acceptance of sexual violence toward women and is associated with actual aggressive behaviour toward women.

Punishing aggressive behaviour in order to reduce it is tricky; punishment can be effective if it is not too severe and if it follows closely on the heels of the aggressive act. But severe or delayed punishment is not an effective way to reduce aggression. Similarly, there is no evidence to support the notion of **catharsis**—the idea that committing an aggressive action or watching others behave aggressively is a good way to get the impulse toward aggression out of one's system. It is much more likely that committing or witnessing aggression will trigger further acts of aggression. Once we have aggressed against someone, we tend to derogate the victim as a means of justifying our actions. This act of dehumanization makes it more likely that we will aggress again in the future.

Aggression can be reduced in a number of constructive ways. These include discussing the reasons for anger and hostility, modelling nonaggressive behaviour, training people in the use of nonviolent solutions to conflict and in communication and negotiation skills, and building people's empathy toward others. Building empathy is particularly useful as a means of thwarting the human tendency to dehumanize one's victim.

Scoring the Try It! Exercises
▶ **Page 344**

Note: The percentages we report below are based on Statistics Canada (2005a) information gathered on 24 000 Canadians. Respondents were asked whether violence with a current partner occurred in the past five years. In cases where a marriage had ended in the past five years, respondents reported on violence that had occurred with their former spouse. The rates of violence reported for these marriages that had ended were considerably higher than the rates of violence reported for marriages that were intact at the time of the survey.

1. The following were reported as the most prevalent kinds of spousal violence: pushed, shoved, or slapped (37%), kicked, bit, hit, hit with something (22%), followed by beat, choked, used or threatened to use a gun or knife (19%).

2. Women were more likely to report being pushed, shoved, or slapped (40% of women versus 34% of men). They were also much more likely than men to report the more severe forms of violence; for example, they were much more likely to report being beaten, choked, or threatened with a gun or knife, or actually had a gun or knife used on them (23% versus 15% of men), or having been sexually assaulted by their spouse (16% versus 0% of men).

3. Men were most likely to report being pushed, shoved, or slapped (34%) and being kicked, bit, hit, or hit with something (34% of men versus 10% of women).

PEARSON mypsychlab

Along with a dynamic, electronic version of this text, MyPsychLab offers a wealth of resources to deepen your understanding and test your recall of the material in this chapter—including video and audio clips, simulations and activities, self-assessments, practice tests, and other study materials. The following specific resources are available for this chapter:

 Media Violence

 Stanford Prison Experiment: Phil Zimbardo

 Students Discuss Columbine

To access MyPsychLab, please visit www.mypsychlab.com (Student Access Code required—packaged with this book).

Indian
Holocaust
1492 – ?

Printed in occupied Canada

Prejudice:
Causes and Cures

Meet Mary Young, director of the Aboriginal Student Services Centre at the University of Winnipeg. Mary grew up as a member of Bloodvein First Nation, an Anishinabe (Ojibway) community in northern Manitoba. When she was growing up, Mary understood that she was a Treaty Indian according to the federal Indian Act, but being Indian was not part of her identity. She thought of herself as Anishinabe, and she was comfortable with that identity. At the age of 14, she moved to Winnipeg with the dream of being the first person from Bloodvein to graduate from high school. With that move came the startling discovery that the other students thought of her as Indian. Moreover, Indian was not a neutral term—it was saturated with negative connotations. As a result, Mary was forced to adopt a new identity, and learned quickly that this new identity meant she was less acceptable, less deserving, and less worthy than the white students attending her high school.

In reflecting on these experiences, Mary comments, "When I left home at the age of fourteen . . . my goal was to finish high school. I never expected that I would have difficulty with my identity, my cultural background, nor did I think I was going to allow myself to feel ashamed of my family, including my own shame of being an 'Indian.'" To express her feelings about this life-shattering experience, Mary wrote the following poem.

▲ Mary Young felt the impact of racism in her life when she moved from her First Nations community to Winnipeg to attend high school.

AFRAID

I heard	Shame
"The Only Good Indian	I am afraid to open
Is a Dead Indian"	My mouth
I never heard that on	I know that I am not dead
The reserve	Does this mean
I was fine before I	I am no good?
Came to the city	I must be no good
What is wrong with me	Because I feel ugly
Now?	I hate being Indian
	Why was I born on the
I have no answer	Reserve anyway?
All I know is that	
I am afraid of making	There is nothing I can do
A mistake	To change that
I am afraid if I succeed	I can't change who I am
It will not make any	I'm afraid I am
Difference.	Not prepared to die
	Just yet
There was a time	So I have to try
Laughing at myself	Harder
Came easily	"To Be a Good Indian"
Now all I feel is	

Of all the social behaviours we discuss in this book, prejudice is perhaps the most widespread and certainly among the most dangerous. Prejudice touches nearly everyone's life. We are all victims or potential victims of stereotyping and discrimination, for no other reason than our membership in an identifiable group—whether it be related to ethnicity, religion, gender, national origin, sexual preference, obesity, skin colour, language, age, or disability. However, clearly some people are more victimized than others. People who are members of visible minorities report experiencing the greatest prejudice and discrimination, and if they are of a minority status in more than one way, they are especially likely to be discriminated against. Researchers at Wilfrid Laurier University (Foster, 2005) and at York University (Patterson, Cameron, & Lalonde, 1996) have found, for example, that women of colour feel that both gender and racial stereotypes are applied to them. Similarly, black-skinned immigrants to Canada experience more prejudice and discrimination than do white-skinned immigrants, and this experience is compounded for a black person who is Muslim or is female (Dion, 2001; Dion & Dion, 2001). Granted, many manifestations of prejudice are less frequent and less flagrant than they used to be. However, as the story of Mary Young illustrates, prejudice continues to exact a heavy toll on its targets. In this chapter, we will examine prejudice as a social psychological phenomenon. We will focus on two fundamental questions: What causes prejudice? And how can prejudice be reduced?

Prejudice: The Ubiquitous Social Phenomenon

The story of Mary Young illustrates that members of minority groups are often targets of prejudice at the hands of the dominant majority. Needless to say, this aspect of prejudice is extremely powerful and poignant. However, the truth is that prejudice is a two-way street; it flows from a minority group to the majority group, as well as from the majority to a minority. Any group can be a target of stereotyping and prejudice. However, as recent research conducted at the University of Victoria shows, stereotypes are most likely to be held for social groups (e.g., racial and ethnic groups rather than other groups such as jury members or the cast of a play; Spencer-Rodgers, Hamilton, & Sherman, 2007). Let us take one of the most superordinate social groups to which you belong—your nationality. Canadians are typically stereotyped as the nice, dull, boring "country cousins" of their more adventurous, exciting counterparts to the south. American television host Tucker Carlson put it this way: "Canada is a sweet country. It is like your retarded cousin. . . . You know he's nice but you don't take him seriously" (Gorham, 2005, p. A3). (Interestingly, research shows that Canadians and Americans actually have very similar personalities; Terracciano et al., 2005.) Even worse, some nations view Canada as hypocritical for calling other countries to task on unfair treatment of minority groups while allowing aboriginal peoples in Canada to live in poverty.

Your nationality is only one aspect of your identity that can cause you to be labelled and discriminated against. Racial and ethnic identity is a major focal point for prejudiced attitudes. Canada views itself as a country that embraces multiculturalism—a country that appreciates the diversity that different racial and ethnic groups contribute to its social fabric. However, all you have to do is ask a sample of Canadians about their attitudes toward aboriginals, Pakistanis, East Asians, and Sikhs and you quickly become aware that diversity is not always celebrated or even tolerated (Esses & Gardner, 1996; Pruegger & Rogers, 1993). In fact, people who belong to such groups are common targets of prejudice. (The Try It! on page 375 raises some interesting issues about the merits of multiculturalism.) Even particular subgroups of white Canadians are subjected to prejudice, as witnessed by the long-standing popularity of Newfie jokes, the tensions between anglophones and francophones in Quebec, and "centre of the universe" comments about Torontonians.

Other aspects of your identity also leave you vulnerable to prejudice: your gender, your sexual preference, your religion, and even your age. For example, researchers at Bishop's University found that people recommended harsher punishments for murder if the perpetrator was a 40-year-old man rather than a 20- or 60-year-old man (Bergeron & McKelvie, 2004). Even the labels used to refer to people can invoke prejudice (Donakowski & Esses, 1996). In a series of studies on the "Ms. stereotype," University of Toronto researchers found that women who preferred the title "Ms." were rated more negatively (i.e., perceived as less likeable) than women who preferred a traditional form of address (i.e., Miss or Mrs.; Dion, 1987; 1999; Dion & Schuller, 1991). Thirty years later, women who use "Ms." are still rated as more independent and competitive and less warm and nurturant than those who use the title Miss or Mrs., as shown by recent research conducted at the University of Winnipeg (Malcolmson & Sinclair, 2007).

Finally, even your profession or your hobbies can lead to you being stereotyped. We are all familiar with the "dumb jock" and "computer nerd" stereotypes. Some people have negative attitudes about blue-collar workers; others, about "MBA types." In fact, Kenneth Dion (1985) found that students at the University

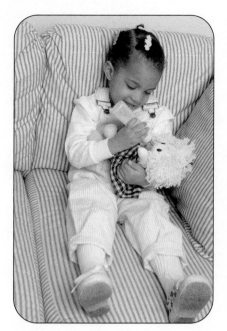

▲ If a child of colour believes that white dolls are more desirable than black dolls, what stereotypes has she internalized?

“ *A little black girl yearns for the blue eyes of a little white girl, and the horror at the heart of her yearning is exceeded only by the evil of fulfillment.* ”

—*Toni Morrison*, The Bluest Eye, *1993*

of Toronto reported greater prejudice toward people with low-status occupations than they did toward people of a different race or nationality. That is not to say that high-status occupations are exempt from stereotyping and prejudice, as witnessed by the popularity of lawyer jokes (Olson, Maio, & Hobden, 1999). The point is that none of us emerges completely unscathed from the effects of prejudice; it is a problem of and for all humankind.

In addition to being widespread, prejudice is dangerous. Simple dislike of a group can be relentless and can lead to extreme hatred, to thinking of its members as less than human, and to behaviour such as torture, murder, and genocide. But even when murder or genocide is not the culmination of prejudiced beliefs, the targets of prejudice will suffer in less dramatic ways. In a classic experiment conducted in the late 1940s, social psychologists Kenneth Clark and Mamie Clark (1947) demonstrated that African-American children—some of them only three years old—were already convinced that it was not particularly desirable to be black. In this experiment, the children were offered a choice between playing with a white doll or a black doll. The great majority of them rejected the black doll, feeling that the white doll was prettier and generally superior.

You may be thinking, "But that was more than 60 years ago and it took place in the United States. Surely these findings are no longer relevant, and surely they wouldn't apply to Canada!" As it turns out, all you have to do is substitute "aboriginal Canadian" for "African American." For example, Corenblum and Annis (1993; Corenblum, Annis, & Young, 1996) presented white and Native children attending schools in Brandon, Manitoba, with drawings of white and Native boys and girls. When asked which child they would like to play with, Native children were slightly more likely to choose a white child than a Native child. (White children overwhelmingly chose a white child.) Native children also attributed more positive qualities (e.g., friendliness) to a white child than to a Native child. Conversely, they attributed more negative qualities to a Native child (e.g., is bad, gets into fights) than to a white child.

We should note that significant changes have taken place over the past five or six decades. For example, African-American children have gradually become more content with black dolls than they were in 1947 (Gopaul-McNicol, 1987; Porter, 1971; Porter & Washington, 1979, 1989). And people are less prejudiced toward some stigmatized groups (e.g., gays and lesbians) than they used to be (Altemeyer, 2001). It would be a mistake, however, to conclude that prejudice has ceased to be a serious problem. As we shall see in this chapter, there are still many people who are blatantly prejudiced. There are also people who are prejudiced but do not openly admit it. We will also see that all of us are vulnerable to societal, situational, and psychological factors that lead us to favour our own group and denigrate members of other groups. There is no doubt that prejudice continues to exist, and it does so in countless subtle and not-so-subtle ways.

During the past half-century, social psychologists have contributed greatly to our understanding of the psychological processes underlying prejudice and have begun to identify and demonstrate some possible solutions. What is prejudice? How does it come about? How can it be reduced?

Prejudice, Stereotyping, and Discrimination Defined

Prejudice is an attitude. As we discussed in Chapter 6, attitudes are made up of three components: an affective or emotional component, representing the type of emotion linked with the attitude (e.g., anger, warmth); a cognitive component,

Try it!

▶ Multiculturalism: Is It Working?

In the United States, members of different nationalities or ethnic groups are expected to assimilate with the majority. In contrast, in Canada, cultural groups are encouraged to maintain their values and customs while participating in Canadian society. The American image is a "melting pot"; the Canadian image is a "cultural mosaic." Canada formally passed the Multiculturalism Act in 1987. Slogans such as "celebrating differences" reflect our country's multicultural orientation.

Does multiculturalism actually foster positive relationships between groups? Research conducted in the Netherlands, a country that also promotes multiculturalism, suggests that such policies can be beneficial. In a series of studies, it was found that members of the majority group (Dutch people) and a minority group (Turkish people living in the Netherlands) who favoured multiculturalism evaluated the minority group (Turks) more positively than those who advocated assimilation (Verkuyten, 2005). (Note that proponents of multiculturalism held the same stereotypes of these groups as did proponents of assimilation.)

There is another issue to consider when evaluating the merits of multiculturalism. As you may recall from Chapter 9, similarity is one of the best predictors of attraction and liking. This raises a disturbing question: Could it actually be counterproductive for intercultural relations to emphasize differences between groups? A study of English Canadians, French Canadians, Jews, and people from India, Algeria, and Greece living in Montreal found that the more similar the respondents perceived a group to be to their own group, the greater their willingness to associate with members of that group (Osbeck, Moghaddam, & Perreault, 1997). This research prompts some intriguing questions (which you may want to discuss with a friend):

1. What are the implications of these findings for Canada's policy of multiculturalism?

2. Is it actually possible to "celebrate differences"?

3. Are there ways in which basic similarities between groups could be highlighted, while allowing for an appreciation of differences?

involving the beliefs or thoughts (cognition) that make up the attitude; and a behavioural component, relating to one's actions—people don't simply hold attitudes; they usually act on them as well.

Prejudice: The Affective Component

Prejudice refers to the general attitude structure and its affective (emotional) component. Technically, prejudice can involve either positive or negative affect (Crandall & Schaller, 2005; Wright & Taylor, 2003). For example, you could be prejudiced against or in favour of Torontonians. In one case, your emotional reaction is negative: When a person is introduced to you as "Michael from Toronto," you will expect him to act in particular ways that you associate with "those snobbish Torontonians." Conversely, if your emotional reaction is positive, you will be delighted to meet another one of those "sophisticated, cosmopolitan Torontonians." While prejudice can involve either positive or negative affect, social psychologists—and people in general—use the word *prejudice* primarily when referring to negative attitudes about others. Consistent with general usage, we will define **prejudice** as a hostile or negative attitude toward people in a distinguishable group, based *solely* on their membership in that group. For example, when we say that an individual is prejudiced against aboriginal peoples, we mean that he or she feels hostility or disliking toward aboriginal peoples as a whole.

prejudice

a hostile or negative attitude toward a distinguishable group of people, based solely on their membership in that group

Stereotypes: The Cognitive Component

Close your eyes for a moment and imagine the appearance and characteristics of the following people: a high school cheerleader, a Sikh taxi driver, a Jewish

▲ Is this roughly the stereotypical image that came to mind when you were asked to imagine a Sikh taxi driver?

stereotype

a generalization about a group of people in which identical characteristics are assigned to virtually all members of the group, regardless of actual variation among the members

discrimination

unjustified negative or harmful action toward a member of a group, simply because of his or her membership in that group

❝ *Prejudices are the props of civilization.* ❞

—André Gide, 1939

doctor, a black musician. Our guess is that this task was not difficult. We all walk around with images of various "types" of people in our heads. The distinguished journalist Walter Lippmann (1922), who was the first to introduce the term *stereotype*, described the distinction between the world out there and stereotypes—"the little pictures we carry around inside our heads." Within a given culture, these pictures tend to be remarkably similar. For example, we would be surprised if your image of the cheerleader was anything but a person who is bouncy, full of pep, pretty, nonintellectual, and (of course!) female. We would also be surprised if the Jewish doctor or the Sikh taxi driver in your head were female—or if the black musician was playing classical music.

It goes without saying that there are male cheerleaders, female doctors, and black classical musicians. Deep down, we know that taxi drivers come in every size, shape, race, and gender. But we tend to categorize according to what we regard as normative within a culture. Stereotyping, however, goes a step beyond simple categorization. A **stereotype** is a generalization about a group of people in which identical characteristics are assigned to virtually all members of the group, regardless of actual variation among the members. Once formed, stereotypes are resistant to change on the basis of new information.

It is important to point out that stereotyping does not necessarily lead to negative or harmful behaviours. Often stereotyping is merely a way to simplify how we look at the world—and we all do it to some extent. Gordon Allport (1954), for example, described stereotyping as "the law of least effort." According to Allport, the world is just too complicated for us to have a highly differentiated attitude about everything. Instead, we maximize our cognitive time and energy by developing elegant, accurate attitudes about some topics, while relying on simple, sketchy beliefs for others. (This should remind you of the discussion of schemas in Chapter 3.) Given our limited information-processing capacity, it is reasonable for us to take shortcuts and adopt certain heuristics in our attempt to understand other people (Fiske, 1989b; Fiske & Depret, 1996; Taylor, 1981; Taylor & Falcone, 1982). On the other hand, if a stereotype blinds us to individual differences within a class of people, it is maladaptive and unfair, and can lead to discrimination. For one insight into where stereotypes come from, see the accompanying Try It! box.

Discrimination: The Behavioural Component

This brings us to the final component of prejudice—the action component. Stereotypic beliefs often result in unfair treatment. We call this **discrimination**—unjustified negative or harmful action toward the members of a group simply because of their membership in that group. If you are a grade 4 math teacher and you have the stereotypic belief that girls are hopeless at math, you might spend less time in the classroom coaching a girl than you would a boy. If you are a police officer and you have the stereotypic belief that black people are more violent than white people, this might affect your behaviour toward a specific black man you are trying to arrest.

Stewart Page examined discriminatory behaviour by landlords in two cities in Ontario (London and Windsor) and in Detroit, Michigan. In one study (Page, 1998), a caller inquiring about accommodation that had been advertised in a local paper identified himself or herself as gay/lesbian ("I guess it's only fair to tell you that I'm a gay person [or lesbian]"), or did not mention his or her sexual orientation. Landlords were most likely to claim that the accommodation was unavailable when they believed the caller was gay or lesbian. In a subsequent study, Page (1999) found that landlords were five times more likely to say that the accommodation was unavailable when the caller mentioned that she or he had AIDS.

Try it!

▶ Stereotype Content: Where Does It Come From?

Have you ever wondered where stereotypes come from? Who decides whether positive or negative characteristics apply to a given group? And who decides which particular positive or negative characteristics apply? These are questions that have been addressed in a program of research conducted at the University of British Columbia by Mark Schaller and his colleagues (Schaller & Conway, 1999, 2001, 2005; Schaller, Conway, & Tanchuk, 2002; Schaller & O'Brien, 1992). According to these researchers, the traits or characteristics of a group that other people are most likely to talk about are the traits that become part of the stereotype of that group. Moreover, the more these traits are talked about, the more likely it is they will remain part of that group's stereotype over time. In short, it is the traits that have the highest communicability, or "gossip" value, that will become part of the stereotype of a particular group. You may wish to test this hypothesis yourself or with a group of friends.

First, list the traits or characteristics you would be most likely to mention if you were talking about the following groups:

- White Canadians (more specifically, white Canadians living in Vancouver)
- Chinese
- East Indians
- First Nations

Now, check whether any of the traits you (or your friends) mentioned are part of the following stereotypes of these groups, as identified by a multicultural group of students at the University of British Columbia (Schaller, Conway, & Tanchuk, 2002):

- White Canadians: athletic, individualistic, pleasure loving, straightforward, sportsmanlike
- Chinese: ambitious, loyal to family ties, intelligent, efficient, conservative
- East Indians: very religious, tradition loving, aggressive, loyal to family ties, physically dirty
- First Nations: poor, physically dirty, lazy, tradition loving, superstitious

Schaller and colleagues' research suggests that you and your friends would be most likely to list the traits that are part of the stereotype of that group. These researchers also found that positive traits are more likely to become part of the stereotype of the largest groups in a society (in Vancouver, white Canadians, followed by Chinese people), whereas negative traits are more likely to become part of the stereotype of smaller groups (First Nations people). To make matters even worse, negative traits are more likely than positive traits to persist over time. In other words, once a negative trait becomes part of a stereotype of a group, it is very difficult to shed. Schaller and colleagues conclude that "in a sense, traits are like viruses: Those that are more highly communicable are more likely to infect the stereotypic beliefs of a population and are less likely to be gotten rid of" (Schaller, Conway, & Tanchuk, 2002).

More recent research suggests that gays and lesbians may also be vulnerable to job discrimination. In a field experiment, Hebl, Foster, Bigazzi, Mannix, and Dovidio (2002) had 16 confederates—8 male and 8 female students—apply for jobs at local stores. In some of their interviews, they were instructed to portray themselves as gay/lesbian; in others, they were not. In order to standardize the interactions, the applicants were all dressed similarly in jeans and pullover jackets. The researchers looked at two kinds of discrimination: formal and interpersonal.

To gauge formal discrimination, they examined whether there were differences in what the employer said about the availability of jobs, the employer's response to a request to use the bathroom, whether the employer allowed them to fill out a job application, and whether they received a callback. On these issues, the investigators found no significant differences; that is, in terms of formal discrimination, there was no evidence of discrimination against those portrayed as gay/lesbian. The employers could not be accused of treating gay and lesbian applicants unjustly.

On the other hand, there were strong indications of interpersonal discrimination against those portraying themselves as gay or lesbian. The employers were less verbally positive toward those presenting themselves as gay or lesbian, spent less time interviewing them, used fewer words while chatting with them, and made less eye contact with them than with the applicants who were not portrayed as gay or lesbian. In other words, it was clear from their behaviour that the potential employers were either uncomfortable or more distant with people they believed to be gay or lesbian. In summary, discrimination may not always be blatant but may operate in more subtle ways—an issue that we shall revisit later in this chapter.

What Causes Prejudice?

Prejudice might be built in, as part of our biological survival mechanism inducing us to favour our own family, tribe, or race, and to express hostility toward outsiders. On the other hand, it is conceivable that humans are naturally inclined to be friendly, open, and cooperative. If this were the case, then prejudice would not come naturally. Rather, the culture (parents, community, media) might, intentionally or unintentionally, instruct us to assign negative qualities and attributes to people who are different from us.

While social psychologists disagree on whether or not humans are naturally prejudiced, most would agree that the *specifics* of prejudice must be learned. How easy is it to learn prejudice? Sinclair and colleagues (2004) found that children in grades 4 and 5 shared their parents' racial attitudes, especially if they identified with their parents (Sinclair, Dunn, & Lowery, 2004). What about when children become adults? Do they still adopt their parents' prejudices? Researchers at the University of Waterloo took a close look at the folk wisdom that "the apple never falls far from the tree" by examining attitude and value similarity between parents and their adult children (Rohan & Zanna, 1996). They found that similarity was significantly stronger between children and parents when parents held egalitarian attitudes and values than when parents held prejudice-related attitudes and values. Why might this be? Our guess is that this discrepancy occurs because the culture as a whole is more egalitarian than the bigoted parents. Thus, when children of bigoted parents leave home (e.g., to go off to university), they are more likely to be exposed to competing views.

The Way We Think: Social Cognition

Our first explanation for what causes prejudice is that it is the inevitable by-product of the way we process and organize information—in other words, it is the dark side of human social cognition (see Chapter 3). Our tendency to categorize and group information together, to form schemas and to use these to interpret new or unusual information, to rely on potentially inaccurate heuristics (shortcuts in mental reasoning), and to depend on what are often faulty memory processes—all of these aspects of social cognition can lead us to form negative stereotypes and to apply them in a discriminatory way. Let's examine this dark side of social cognition more closely.

Social Categorization: Us versus Them   The first step in prejudice is the creation of groups—putting some people into one group based on certain characteristics and others into another group based on their different characteristics. This kind of categorization is the underlying theme of human social cognition (Brewer & Brown, 1998; Rosch & Lloyd, 1978; Taylor, 1981). For example, we make sense of the physical world by grouping animals and plants into taxonomies based on their physical characteristics; similarly, we make sense of our social world by grouping people according to characteristics such as their gender, nationality, ethnicity, and so on. When we encounter a person with certain characteristics (e.g., old, male), we rely on our perceptions of what people with similar characteristics have been like in the past to help us determine how to react to this person (Andersen & Klatzky, 1987). Thus, social categorization is both useful and necessary; however, this simple cognitive process has profound implications because the process of classifying people into groups is rarely a neutral one.

In-Group Bias It probably comes as no surprise that we evaluate in-group members more positively than out-group members. This is known as **in-group bias**. When researchers at Queen's University assessed the attitudes of more than 3000 Canadians toward 14 different ethnic groups, the results were clear— people assigned the most favourable ratings to their own ethnic group (Kalin & Berry, 1996). People even attribute more smiling and friendliness to the in-group, as demonstrated in a study by Beaupré and Hess (2003). These researchers had people of European, African, or Asian descent living in Quebec read scenarios such as "Marc/Anne is walking to the store in order to buy some milk." They were then shown a series of photographs of faces varying the degree of smiling, ranging from a neutral face to a big smile. Participants who were led to believe that the person in the story was of their own race (i.e., an in-group member) tended to choose a smiling face; those who were led to believe that the person in the story was of a different race (i.e., an out-group member) were more likely to choose a neutral face. Recent research by University of Western Ontario researcher Bertram Gawronski and his colleagues shows that when we encounter a friendly in-group member, there is a contrast effect, such that we now evaluate an out-group member especially negatively (Gawronski, Bodenhausen, & Banse, 2005).

> **in-group bias**
>
> the tendency to evaluate in-group members more positively than out-group members

Other research confirms that out-group members are often seen as possessing negative traits and are often disliked. Lalonde, Moghaddam, and Taylor (1987) found evidence of this among fans at home games of the McGill University hockey team. The fans rated the opposing teams higher in negative characteristics, such as arrogance and aggressiveness, than their own team. In fact, as the season progressed, the ratings of the two teams increasingly diverged.

This tendency to favour the in-group while denigrating the out-group is so pervasive that people show this bias even under the most minimal conditions. Such effects have been demonstrated by British social psychologist Henri Tajfel and his colleagues, who have created entities that they refer to as minimal groups (Tajfel, 1982a, 1982b; Tajfel & Billig, 1974; Tajfel & Turner, 1979). In these experiments, complete strangers are formed into groups using the most trivial criteria imaginable. For example, in one experiment, participants watched a coin toss that randomly assigned them to either group X or group W. In another experiment, participants were first asked to express their opinions about artists they had never heard of and were then randomly assigned to a group that appreciated either the "Klee style" or the "Kandinsky style," ostensibly by their picture preferences. The striking thing about the Tajfel research is that despite the fact that the participants were strangers prior to the experiment and didn't interact with one another during it, they behaved as if those who shared the same meaningless label were their dear friends or close kin. They liked the members of their own group better; they rated the members of their in-group as more likely than out-group members to have pleasant personalities and to have done better work. Most striking, the participants allocated more money and other rewards to those who shared their label, and did so in a rather hostile, cutthroat manner—that is, when given a clear choice, they preferred to give themselves only $2 if it meant giving an out-group person $1, rather than give themselves $3 if that meant the out-group member would receive $4.

"It's a cat calendar, so it may not be all that accurate."

These findings were subsequently replicated in a Canadian study. Amiot and Bourhis (2003) presented students at a college in Montreal with a description of a business merger between group K and group X. Participants were randomly assigned to one of these groups and asked to make a variety of decisions (e.g., allocating salary increases, number of work hours). As predicted, the students consistently favoured their own group when making these decisions and discriminated against the other group.

From these results, you can see that it doesn't take much to produce feelings of "us" and "them." In fact, researchers at the University of Alberta found that an in-group can be created simply by photographing people together (Burgess, Enzle, & Morry, 2000). In this study, pairs of strangers who were photographed together were more likely to use terms such as "we" and "us" and to report greater liking than pairs of strangers who sat next to each other but were not photographed together. (Note that taking a picture of each person separately did not produce this "we" feeling.)

Before leaving this topic, it is important to point out that the tendency to discriminate against the out-group is even stronger when people have chosen their group rather than been randomly assigned to it, as shown by research conducted with French-speaking Acadians in New Brunswick (Perreault & Bourhis, 1999). Thus, the effects we have been describing are likely to be even stronger in the real world than in the laboratory studies that we've been discussing.

Why Do We Show the In-Group Bias? Why do we show this tendency to favour the in-group and discriminate against the out-group, even when group membership is based on something as trivial as the toss of a coin or having a photo taken together? There is a two-part answer to this question. The first part is that belonging to a group gives us a social identity. The second part is that having a social identity contributes to feelings of self-esteem.

Social Identity Benefits If it is true that belonging to a group provides us with a social identity, we would expect that individuals who strongly identify with a group would be more likely to favour their group and discriminate against an out-group than individuals who only weakly identify with their group. Evidence of this was found in recent research conducted at the University of Waterloo (Sahdra & Ross, 2007). Canadian students were induced to feel either high or low identification with Canada. They were then asked to recall specific negative acts that Canadians have committed toward other groups (e.g., violence, hatred) as well as specific positive acts (e.g., kindness, bravery). Participants in the high-identification group were more likely to recall good deeds done by Canadians and less likely to recall bad deeds than those in the low-identification group.

There is also evidence that the more strongly one identifies with one's own group, the more likely one is to discriminate against an out-group. In a study by Gagnon and Bourhis (1996), French-Canadian university students were told that they were in group K or group W (based on a coin toss) and would be deciding how to allocate 5 percentage points to other participants' psychology grades. As predicted, those who identified most strongly with their group discriminated most against the other group when awarding grade points. Moreover, the more these participants discriminated, the more they liked being a member of their group.

In a real-world study, Serge Guimond (2000) assessed the attitudes of prospective Canadian military officers at the beginning and the end of a four-year officer training program. The more strongly the majority group (i.e., anglophones) identified with the military, the more negative they became in their attitudes toward out-groups (i.e., francophones, civilians, and immigrants to Canada). Why would identification with the military be associated with negative attitudes toward out-groups? Guimond suggests that the military reinforces dominant societal attitudes about the superiority of particular groups.

Findings such as these suggest that if a person's sense of social identity is threatened, he or she might be especially likely to discriminate against an out-group. This prediction was tested in a series of studies by Peter Grant (1992, 1993). Students at the University of Saskatchewan who cared about either a "women's issue" (e.g., women should be encouraged to apply for high-status jobs) or a "men's issue" (e.g., men's roles have become confusing and unclear) discussed these topics in same-sex groups. They were told that later they would also exchange ideas with an opposite-sex group. Before doing so, those in the high-threat condition were informed that the opposite-sex group couldn't care less about their issue and didn't see a need for change. Participants in the low-threat condition were told that the other group thought the issue was important and had come up with some strategies for change. As expected, participants whose identities were threatened (i.e., those who were told the other group didn't care about their issue) rated the other group more negatively than did those whose identities were not threatened.

Once again, these laboratory findings have been confirmed in real-world research. For example, Corenblum and Stephan (2001) found that the more Native people identified with their own group, the more likely they were to perceive white people as threatening their values and beliefs. These feelings of threat, in turn, predicted prejudice toward white people.

Self-Esteem Benefits Clearly, there is evidence that dividing the world into "us" and "them" gives us a sense of social identity. Why is this important? According to Tajfel (1982a, 1982b; Turner, Hogg, Oakes, Reicher, & Wetherell, 1987), it gives people a self-esteem boost if they believe that their group is superior and that other groups are inferior. Evidence of this was found in a study conducted by Louise Lemyre and Phillip Smith (1985). Participants were University of British Columbia students who were simply told that they were in the "red" group or the "blue" group. Some participants were then given an opportunity to discriminate against the out-group (by giving them fewer points), whereas others were not. Those who discriminated against the out-group showed higher self-esteem than did those who were not given the chance to discriminate. The researchers also included a condition in which participants were not assigned to any group but were allowed to discriminate against one of the groups. Interestingly, these participants did not show an increase in self-esteem. This result suggests that discriminating against others improves our self-esteem, but only when our social identity is involved.

As you might expect, when our self-esteem is threatened, we are especially likely to denigrate the out-group as a means of restoring feelings of self-worth. In a classic study, Meindl and Lerner (1984) threatened the self-esteem of some of their participants (English-speaking Canadians) by making them feel responsible for an accident in the laboratory. Other participants were not made to feel responsible for the accident. Feelings of group identification were manipulated by asking participants to rate various issues related to Quebec, either from the perspective of "a member of the English-speaking majority in Canada" or simply "as an individual." Participants who experienced a threat to their self-esteem rated French Canadians more negatively than those whose self-esteem had not been threatened, especially if their identity as an English-speaking Canadian had been made salient. Similar effects have been obtained in more recent research conducted at the University of Waterloo focusing on discrimination toward Native people (Jordan, Spencer, & Zanna, 2005). Thus, if we are feeling defensive and threatened, we are more likely to engage in discrimination than if our self-esteem is in good shape.

Out-Group Homogeneity Besides the in-group bias, another consequence of social categorization is the perception of **out-group homogeneity**—the belief that "they" are all alike (Linville, Fischer, & Salovey, 1989; Quattrone, 1986). George Quattrone and Edward E. Jones (1980) studied this phenomenon using rival universities: Princeton and Rutgers. The rivalry between these universities is based on athletics, academics, and even class-consciousness—Princeton is private and Rutgers is public. Male research participants at the two schools watched videotaped scenes in which a young man was asked to make a decision (e.g., in one videotape he was asked whether he wanted to listen to rock or classical music) while he participated in an experiment on auditory perception. The participants were told that the man was either a Princeton or a Rutgers student. Thus, the student in the videotape was portrayed as an in-group member for some of them; for others, he was an out-group member. Participants had to predict what the man in the videotape would choose. After they saw the man make his choice (e.g., rock or classical music), they were asked to predict what percentage of male students at that institution would make the same choice.

Did the predictions vary as a function of the in-group or out-group status of the target man? As you can see in Figure 12.1, the results support the out-group homogeneity hypothesis. When the target person was an out-group member, the participants believed his choice was more predictive of what his peers would choose than when he was an in-group member (a student at their own school). In other words, if you know something about one out-group member, it feels like you know something about all of them. Similar results have been found in a wide variety of experiments in the United States, Europe, and Australia (Duck, Hogg, & Terry, 1995; Hartstone & Augoustinos, 1995; Judd & Park, 1988; Ostrom & Sedikides, 1992). In Canada, Hilton, Potvin, and Sachdev (1989) assessed the perceptions that francophone landlords in Montreal held of French Quebecers, English Quebecers, Italians, Asians, and Haitians. And indeed, members of each out-group were perceived as more homogeneous than members of the in-group (i.e., French Quebecers).

Implications of Social Categorization for Reducing Prejudice We have seen that people gain social identity benefits from dividing the world into "us" and "them." Further,

---

out-group homogeneity

the perception that those in the out-group are more similar (homogeneous) to each other than they really are, as well as more similar than the members of the in-group are to each other

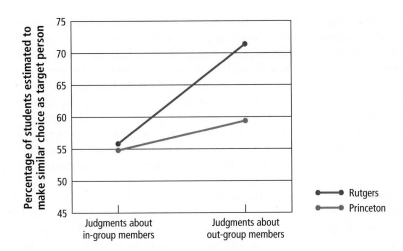

FIGURE 12.1

Judgments about in-group and out-group members

After watching the target person make a choice between two alternatives, participants were asked to estimate what percentage of students at their school (in-group) and their rival school (out-group) would make the same choice. An out-group homogeneity bias was found. Students' estimates for out-group members were higher (i.e., greater similarity) than for in-group members.

(Adapted from Quattrone & Jones, 1980)

people can boost their self-esteem by discriminating against "them." Is there a way to minimize such effects? Recent research provides some encouraging answers. One approach is to change people's perceptions of "us" and "them"—either by promoting a common identity or by emphasizing the superordinate groups to which both in-group and out-group members belong. Another approach is to provide people with an alternative route to self-esteem, so they won't have to step on others to be on top. Let's look at each of these in turn.

There is evidence that prejudice is diminished when groups share a common identity. In a series of studies with francophone and anglophone students at the University of Ottawa, Richard Clément and colleagues found that competence in the other group's language promoted feelings of identity with that group (Clément, Baker, & MacIntyre, 2003; Clément, Noels, & Deneault, 2001; Noels & Clément, 1996). The researchers suggest that at a very basic level, speaking the same language can help blur the distinction between "us" and "them." The down side of these findings was that anglophones still retained their own identity, even if they identified with francophones—presumably because they were the majority group. In contrast, for francophones (the minority group), increased identification with anglophones was associated with decreased identification with their own group. Thus, for those in a minority position, it may feel as though the only way to minimize the distinction between "us" and "them" is to become one of "them."

Recently, researchers have attempted to reduce prejudice by making salient the superordinate group to which members of both groups belong (Esses, Wagner, & Wolf, 2006; Levin, Prosser, Evans, & Reicher, 2005). For example, Wohl and Branscombe (2005) asked members of the Jewish Students' Association at two Canadian universities to answer questions about whether Germans should be forgiven for the Holocaust, how guilty contemporary Germans should feel, and so on. In the social identity condition, the Holocaust was described as "an event in which Germans behaved aggressively toward Jews." In the human identity condition, the Holocaust was described as "an event in which humans behaved aggressively toward other humans." As predicted, participants in the human identity condition were more willing to forgive and assigned less guilt to Germans today than those in the social identity condition. These effects were replicated with Native Canadian students attending the University of Alberta, who were asked to think about the treatment of Native peoples in Canadian history (Wohl & Branscombe, 2005).

In conceptually related research conducted at the University of Toronto, Van Bavel and Cunningham (2007) showed participants (who were non-black) photos of members of two mixed-race (black and white) sports teams. Participants in the experimental condition were told that they were a member of one of the teams; those in the control group were simply told to memorize the names of the team members. Participants who believed that they were part of a mixed-race team later showed less automatic racial bias (i.e., were not as likely to associate the words "black" and "bad" in an implicit association test) than those in the control group. The researchers concluded that people are less likely to automatically evaluate based on their race if other group memberships (in this case team membership) are made more salient or important.

We found these results encouraging. They suggest that prejudice and discrimination can be reduced when people's focus shifts from membership in their specific in-group to a broader group that includes members of the out-group.

Another avenue for minimizing discrimination against out-groups is to provide people with alternative routes to self-esteem. Based on self-affirmation theory (see Chapter 6), Fein and Spencer (1997) predicted that if people were affirmed in some way, they would be less likely to need to boost their self-esteem by derogating out-group members. To test this, participants in the self-affirmation condition were asked to write why certain values were important to them; other participants did not engage in this self-affirmation exercise. Next, all participants saw a video of a woman who was portrayed as Jewish, a group that was negatively stereotyped by the participants. Those who had not been affirmed rated the woman more negatively than those in the self-affirmation condition. More recent research confirms that if we can find some other domain in which to give our self-esteem a boost, we are less likely to derogate others in order to feel good about ourselves (Correll, Spencer, & Zanna, 2004; Fein, Hoshino-Browne, Davies, & Spencer, 2003; Sherman & Kim, 2005; Shira & Martin, 2005). The bottom line is that if you want to reduce prejudice against stigmatized groups, tell the people around you how great they are—this should reduce their need to put other people down.

What We Believe: Stereotypes

If we have a negative stereotype of a group, we will show prejudice toward members of that group. Right? While that is often the case, it's actually not that simple. It turns out that the relationship between stereotyping and prejudice is highly complex. One of the complexities is that our stereotypes are not activated in every situation. As you will see, whether our stereotypes are turned "on" or "off" has important implications for prejudice. It is also the case that our attitudes toward members of another group are determined not only by our stereotype of that group but also by our perception of that group's stereotype of "us."

The Activation of Stereotypes
Imagine this scenario. You are a member of a group engaged in judging another person's performance, and someone in your group makes an ugly, stereotypical comment about that individual. Will the comment affect your engaged in judgment of the performance? "No," you are probably thinking, "I'd disregard it completely." But would you be able to do so? Is it possible that the comment would trigger in your mind all the other negative stereotypes and beliefs about people in that group and affect your judgment about that particular individual—even if you neither believe the stereotype nor consider yourself prejudiced against that group?

In a classic study, Greenberg and Pyszczynski (1985) had participants watch a debate between an African American and a white person. When a confederate made a racist comment about the black debater, participants rated the black debater's performance lower than the white debater's performance. When no racist remark was made, the African-American and white debaters were rated as equally skilled. In other words, the derogatory comment activated other negative stereotypical beliefs about black people, so that the participants who heard it

CONNECTIONS

Can Social Categorization Affect Your Reaction to Terrorism?

For many people, September 11, 2001, marks the day that the threat of terrorism became a reality in their lives. The terrorist attacks that followed—such as the train bombings in Spain in 2004 and in India in 2005; the tourist bombings in Bali, Saudi Arabia, Egypt, and Jordan; and the subway bombings in England in 2005 have served to reinforce people's feelings of fear and vulnerability. Former Canadian prime minister Paul Martin warned, "This is a dangerous world and Canadians must not be complacent" (Robson, 2005, p. A3). He was implying that Canadians are not immune from the threat of terrorism. How afraid did the terrorist attacks on September 11 make you feel? Research suggests that your level of fear may depend on whether or not you include Americans in your in-group. Let's take a look at the details.

One week after the attacks on the World Trade Center in New York, European researchers conducted a series of studies in which they manipulated participants' sense of identity (Dumont, Yzerbyt, Wigboldus, & Gordijn, 2003). In one condition, participants were asked to focus on their identity as Europeans versus Americans. This condition was intended to make Americans the out-group. In the other condition, participants were asked to focus on their identity as Westerners versus Arabs. This condition was intended to make Americans part of the in-group. The researchers found that when Europeans included Americans in their in-group (i.e., their "Westerners" identity was made salient), greater fear was reported in response to the terrorist attacks than when Americans were portrayed as the out-group. Including Americans in the in-group also had some interesting behavioural implications: Participants were more willing to offer support and help to the victims, and were more likely to seek out information concerning how to prevent future attacks (e.g., lobbying NATO to intervene). Thus, reactions to terrorism were quite different, depending on whether participants were induced to regard Americans as part of the in-group or the out-group.

rated the same performance as less skilled than did those who had not heard the racist remark.

Henderson-King and Nisbett (1996) subsequently showed that all it took was one negative action by one African American (actually a confederate of the experimenters) to activate the negative stereotypes of African Americans and to discourage the participants from wanting to interact with different African Americans. These findings suggest that in most of us, stereotypes lurk just beneath the surface. It doesn't take much to activate a stereotype, and once activated, it can have dire consequences for how a particular member of that out-group is perceived and treated.

How does this activation process work? Patricia Devine differentiates between the automatic processing of information and the controlled processing of information (Devine, 1989a, 2003; Zuwerink, Montieth, Devine, & Cook, 1996). As discussed in Chapter 3, an automatic process is one over which we have no control. For example, even if you score very low on a prejudice scale, you are certainly familiar with certain stereotypes that exist in our culture, such as "Aboriginals are lazy," "Jews are money hungry," or "Homosexual men are effeminate." These stereotypes are automatically triggered under certain conditions—they just pop into one's mind. For people who are not deeply prejudiced, however, controlled processes can suppress or override these stereotypes. For example, such a person can say to himself or herself, "Hey, that stereotype isn't fair and it isn't right—Jews are no more money hungry than non-Jews. Ignore the stereotype about this person's ethnicity." What Devine's theory suggests, therefore, is a two-step model of cognitive processing: The automatic processing brings up information—in this case, stereotypes—but the controlled (or conscious) processing can refute or ignore it (see Figure 12.2).

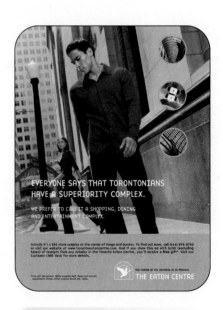

▲ According to Devine's theory, we exhibit both automatic and controlled processing of information. So, even though your automatic response to this ad might reflect prejudice, you could override the stereotypes behind that response by more controlled processing.

FIGURE 12.2

A two-step model of the cognitive processing of stereotypes

While the activation of stereotypes is a frequent occurrence, research suggests that there are some conditions under which we do not automatically do this (Clow & Esses, 2007; Devine, 2003; Fein, von Hippel, & Spencer, 2000; Kawakami, Dion, & Dovidio, 1998; Kunda, Davies, Adams, & Spencer, 2002; Quinn, Macrae, & Bodenhausen, 2003; Wittenbrink, Judd, & Park, 1997; see Blair, 2002, for a review). What are those conditions? Stay tuned.

The Motivation to Control Prejudice   One factor that influences whether stereotypes are automatically activated is the motivation to control prejudice—in other words, whether we want to be non-prejudiced. In a series of studies, Maddux and colleagues (2004) showed participants (white students) photographs of black or white faces presented on a computer screen. The researchers varied the background of each photograph to be either neutral (e.g., a church) or consistent with the negative stereotype of black people (e.g., a jail). When the background cued the stereotype (e.g., the jail), participants who were high in motivation to control prejudice were less likely to show automatic negative responses to black faces than did those who were low in motivation to control prejudice. Motivation to control prejudice did not affect responses when the context was neutral (e.g., the church). The researchers conclude that those of us who want to be non-prejudiced are less likely to activate negative stereotypes automatically when we encounter stereotype-relevant cues.

Researchers at the University of Ottawa have recently demonstrated that those who are motivated to control prejudice are less likely to show prejudice, both when measured at an explicit level and, importantly, when measured implicitly (using the IAT; Legault, Green-Demers, Grant, & Chung, 2007).

The Need to Feel Good about Ourselves   Another factor that determines whether we automatically activate stereotypes is whether we will get a self-esteem boost by doing so. Consider Michael, a university student who receives a negative evaluation on a term paper he wrote for a course taught by a black professor. Michael's stereotype of black people is that they are not very competent. How might Michael repair the damage to his self-esteem caused by receiving a low grade? Based on our discussion so far, you can probably answer this question. Michael can activate his stereotype of black people as incompetent. This allows him to dismiss the criticism of his work as stemming from an incompetent source, with the result that he will not feel as bad about his negative evaluation.

Now, consider Chris, a classmate of Michael's. He also subscribes to a stereotype of black people as incompetent. Unlike Michael, however, Chris received a very positive evaluation of his term paper. Chris is eager to accept the professor's praise and enjoy the boost in self-esteem that it produces. On the other hand, it is difficult to feel good about praise that comes from a person who has been stereotyped as incompetent. How can Chris resolve this dilemma? According to a groundbreaking program of research by Lisa Sinclair at the University of Winnipeg and Ziva Kunda at the University of Waterloo, Chris might inhibit—literally push out of his mind—his stereotype of black people. This would allow him to revel in the praise he received.

In a series of studies, Sinclair and Kunda (1999) have shown that we not only selectively activate stereotypes but can also inhibit, or push out of mind, stereotypes in the service of self-enhancement. In one of their studies, male students—none of whom was black—were asked to participate in research on managers' evaluations of employees' interpersonal skills. The participants first answered questions that supposedly assessed their interpersonal skills and then received an evaluation (via videotape) from either a white manager or a black manager (both confederates). Half of the participants received a positive evaluation (e.g., "I was very impressed with this person; I think he has really good interpersonal skills"), whereas the others received a negative evaluation (e.g., "I was not very impressed with this person").

Sinclair and Kunda predicted that participants who received negative feedback from the black manager would activate their (negative) stereotype of black people. In contrast, participants who were praised by the black manager were expected to inhibit the black stereotype. How could the researchers tell whether participants activated or inhibited their stereotype of black people? In the next phase of the experiment, the students participated in a supposedly unrelated study on word completions. The word fragments could be completed to form either racial or nonracial words. For example, _ _ACK could be completed as BLACK or as any number of nonracial words (e.g., SNACK); CR_ _ _ could be completed as CRIME or as a nonracial word (e.g., CREEK). The researchers reasoned that participants who activated their stereotype of black people would be most likely to use racial word completions, whereas those who inhibited their stereotype of black people would show the fewest racial word completions.

The results are shown in Figure 12.3 on the next page. In interpreting these findings, you may wish to think of the participants who were evaluated by a white manager as the control group. These participants give us a sense of how many racial word completions came to mind for participants who were not motivated to either activate or inhibit their stereotype of black people. As you can see, participants who received negative feedback from a black manager generated more racial words than did those who received negative feedback from a white manager. This is evidence of stereotype activation. In contrast, those who were praised by the black manager pushed the stereotype of black people out of their minds— they came up with even fewer racial word completions than did participants who were praised by a white manager. This is evidence of stereotype inhibition. Finally, as you might expect, participants who were criticized by the black manager rated his skill at evaluating them lower than did participants who were praised by a black manager. (White managers who gave negative feedback also were rated as less skilled than white managers who gave positive feedback, but this difference was not nearly so pronounced as it was for black managers.)

Number of racial completions as a function of feedback favourability and manager race

(Sinclair & Kunda, 1999)

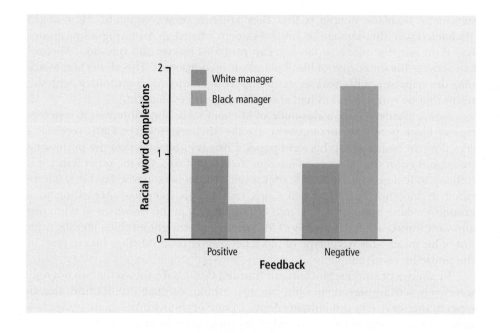

In subsequent research on stereotypes of women, Sinclair and Kunda (1999) found that students at the University of Waterloo rated their female professors as less competent than their male professors when they received a low grade in the course—but not when they received a high grade. As the researchers put it, "She's fine if she praised me but incompetent if she criticized me." In contrast, the ratings of male professors did not depend as much on the grades that students received from them.

In conceptually related research, Livingston and Sinclair (2008) examined reactions to aboriginal and white speakers who delivered a threatening message to University of Winnipeg students—namely, that the university was considering implementing an exit exam that students would have to pass in order to graduate. The speakers were portrayed as university administrators who presented arguments in favour of exit exams. The aboriginal speaker was rated more negatively (e.g., less competent, less professional), less persuasive, and as presenting lower-quality arguments than the white speaker (both speakers delivered the identical message). Students who were non-prejudiced were just as likely to show these effects as those who were high in prejudice toward aboriginals. The researchers conclude, "Regardless of their degree of prejudice, people may derogate stigmatized individuals and their messages when it suits their purposes" (Livingston & Sinclair, 2008, p. 10).

Before leaving this topic, we should point out that in everyday life, stereotype activation and inhibition can be quite a complex process. Most people belong to multiple groups, which means that a number of stereotypes can apply to the same person (Dunn & Spellman, 2003). Sinclair and Kunda (1999) suggest that we "pick and choose" which stereotypes to activate or inhibit—once again, depending on what will produce the greatest self-enhancement. For example, in one study, they focused on two stereotypes that have opposing implications for competence—the negative stereotype of black people and the positive stereotype of doctors. As in their earlier study, participants received either a positive or a negative evaluation, but this time it came from either a white doctor or a black doctor. The researchers predicted that when the black doctor delivered praise, the doctor stereotype would be activated (to bolster their desired positive impression of him) and the black stereotype would be inhibited (to prevent it from interfering with a positive impression of him). When he delivered criticism, just the opposite was expected—namely, that participants would bring the black stereotype to mind and push the doctor stereotype out of their minds. And that is exactly what happened.

In short, this research suggests that if we can salvage our self-esteem by activating negative stereotypes about a group, we will do so. However, if a negative stereotype will interfere with a self-esteem boost (e.g., when we are praised by a member of a stereotyped group), we simply push that stereotype out of our minds.

Meta-Stereotypes Research on stereotyping usually focuses on our perceptions of other groups. We are less likely to think about how members of other groups perceive *us*. However, Jacquie Vorauer and her colleagues (Vorauer, 2003; Vorauer, Hunter, Main, & Roy, 2000; Vorauer & Kumhyr, 2001; Vorauer, Main, & O'Connell, 1998) have raised the intriguing possibility that our level of prejudice depends not solely on our stereotype of a particular group but also on whether we think members of that group have a positive or negative stereotype of us. These researchers use the term **meta-stereotype** to refer to a person's beliefs regarding the stereotype that out-group members hold about their own group. For example, Vorauer and colleagues have found that white Canadians believe that Native Canadians perceive them as prejudiced, unfair, selfish, arrogant, wealthy, materialistic, phony, and so on (Vorauer, Main, & O'Connell, 1998).

What are the implications of this meta-stereotype? In one study, Vorauer and colleagues found that when white students expected to have an interaction with an aboriginal person, those who thought that they personally would be perceived in terms of the meta-stereotype (i.e., the stereotype that they believe that aboriginal people have of white people) anticipated that the interaction would be unpleasant. These participants also expressed the greatest amount of prejudice (Vorauer, Main, & O'Connell, 1998). Perhaps most striking, the participants' beliefs about whether an aboriginal person would stereotype them predicted their attitudes and reactions more strongly than did their own stereotypes of aboriginals. In other words, the way in which participants expected to be perceived by an out-group member was the most important determinant of their reactions—even more so than their own evaluation of that group.

We have seen that people report greater prejudice when they expect to be perceived in terms of the stereotype they believe others hold of their group. But does this actually happen? Do other people perceive us in terms of meta-stereotypes? To find out, Vorauer and Kumhyr (2001) had pairs of aboriginal and white Canadian students at the University of Manitoba engage in a getting-acquainted conversation. Afterward, each person rated their conversation partner and how they believed their conversation partner perceived them. The results were striking—white Canadians who were high in prejudice felt that they were stereotyped by their aboriginal partner when, in reality, they were not. Low-prejudice white participants did not feel as though they were stereotyped by their aboriginal conversation partner, and they were right. Interestingly, neither high- nor low-prejudice participants stereotyped their aboriginal partner, and indeed the aboriginal participants did not feel as though they had been the targets of prejudice. This story does not have a happy ending, however. It turned out that aboriginal participants who were paired with a high-prejudice white participant reported feeling self-critical, ashamed, and angry with themselves. In other words, the aboriginal participants attributed the negativity they experienced during the interaction to themselves, rather than to prejudice. Finally, recent reseearch shows that meta-stereotypes influence people's behaviour during interactions. Specifically, Goff and colleagues (2008) found that white participants who were reminded of the negative stereotype of whites as racist sat farther away from a black person than a white person during an interaction. The distance was even greater when they were told that the topic of discussion would be racial profiling (as opposed to a neutral topic). The researchers suggest

meta-stereotype

a person's beliefs regarding the stereotype that out-group members hold about their own group that the distancing was due to anxiety about confirming the meta-stereotype (Goff, Steele, & Davies, 2008).

Can Prejudice Be Reduced by Revising Stereotypical Beliefs?   It may seem obvious that if we want to reduce prejudice, we should simply change people's stereotypes. This makes a lot of sense, except for one problem—stereotypes are very resistant to change. After all, proof that they are accurate is always out there—when our beliefs guide us to see it. Moreover, we "hang on to" our stereotypes even in the face of contradictory evidence (Barbéra, 2003; Ickes, Patterson, Rajecki, & Tanford, 1982). This was demonstrated in a study by Taylor and Gardner (1969), who had anglophone students listen to a tape recording in which a French-Canadian speaker described himself in ways that were either consistent or inconsistent with English Canadians' stereotype of French Canadians as religious, emotional, talkative, sensitive, and proud. Even if the speaker completely contradicted the stereotype, he was still perceived in stereotypical terms (although less so than when he confirmed the stereotype).

Indeed, we seem to have a remarkable ability to explain away disconfirming evidence and thereby maintain our stereotypes, as illustrated by the 1951 cartoon in the margin of this page. While 10 Mexicans are seen in the background working hard, the cartoon focuses on the stereotypical image in the foreground. The cartoon's message is that the lazy individual is the true exemplar of his ethnic group. No matter how many others refute the stereotype, the cartoon is implying, it is still true. (Note that half a century ago, not only was this message considered acceptable but the cartoon was chosen as one of the best of the year.)

Sometimes the person we encounter may be so contrary to our stereotype that it is impossible to interpret the person's behaviour in stereotype-consistent terms. What do we do then? According to Ziva Kunda and Kathryn Oleson (1995, 1997), we may simply create a new "subtype" for this deviant member, particularly if we are able to come up with some justification for doing so. For example, in one study, the researchers presented University of Waterloo students with a description of a monogamous gay man—thereby contradicting the stereotype of gays as promiscuous. Some participants were given additional, neutral information—namely, that the man was an accountant. The researchers found that this irrelevant information was used as grounds for creating a new subtype, thereby leaving the original stereotype intact. In effect, these participants were saying "Gay men, in general, are promiscuous. The one exception is gay men who are accountants."

This tendency to create a new subcategory of exceptions to the rule can place the targets of stereotyping in a no-win situation. Consider, for example, the remarks of Sajjad, a participant in a study on discrimination experienced by Muslim students in Canadian schools (Zine, 2001). Sajjad moved to Canada from Guyana when he was seven years old. By junior high school he was all too aware that stereotypes are virtually impossible to overcome. In his words, "I'd given up a long time ago trying to impress other people, or trying to prove to other people that I'm a good black person, or I'm a good Indian person. . . . Even if I were to be a good person . . . they have a certain image of coloured people, so it's like, 'Well, all coloured people are bad, but he's a good one . . . he's an exception.'"

By now you may be feeling unconvinced that stereotypes actually can be changed. The good news is that when people are bombarded with many examples that are inconsistent with the stereotype, they do gradually modify their beliefs (Webber & Crocker, 1983). Thus, if you encounter someone who holds a stereotype that we find particularly annoying—namely, that professors are lazy—providing that person with information about many professors who contradict

Alain® 1951 The New Yorker: 25th Annual Album, Harper & Bros.

> *A fanatic is one who can't change his mind and won't change the subject.*
>
> —Winston Churchill, 1944

the stereotype (not just your social psychology professor) should lead that person to change his or her views.

The Way We Feel: Affect and Mood

So far, we have focused on the cognitive aspect of prejudice—namely, the stereotypes we hold of different groups. As we have seen, under certain conditions stereotyping is indeed related to prejudice. However, as Esses, Haddock, and Zanna (1993) point out, "there is more to prejudice than merely the attribution of stereotypes to groups." In their view, other factors must be considered, including emotion, symbolic beliefs, and behaviour. More specifically, Esses and colleagues suggest that the emotions elicited by a particular group are the most important determinant of our level of prejudice—even more important than our stereotype of that group (see also Cottrell & Neuberg, 2005; Cuddy, Fiske, & Glick, 2007; Fiske, Cuddy, Glick, & Xu, 2002). Prejudice is also a product of our symbolic beliefs—the perception that a particular group promotes or hinders values that we cherish. Finally, prejudice is also a product of our behaviour and our experiences with members of the group (Haddock, Zanna, & Esses, 1994; Maio, Esses, & Bell, 1994). Let's take a look at some of the evidence.

In one of their studies, Haddock, Zanna, and Esses (1993, 1994) assessed University of Waterloo students' attitudes toward four ethnic groups (English Canadians, French Canadians, Native Canadians, and Pakistanis) and toward gays and lesbians. To find out what best predicted attitudes, the researchers asked the participants to describe the emotions they experienced when thinking about members of each group, their stereotypic beliefs (i.e., "characteristics you would use to describe the group"), and their symbolic beliefs (i.e., "the values that you believe members of the group promote or hinder"). Behaviour was assessed by asking participants to describe the frequency of contact and quality of their most recent experiences with members of these groups.

It turns out that all of these variables were related to attitudes. However, overall, the strongest effects were found for emotion. There was some variability, though, depending on the group being rated. Specifically, emotion was the best predictor of attitudes for the groups toward which participants were least prejudiced (English Canadians and Native Canadians). For these groups, knowing how someone feels about members of the group would allow you to predict his or her level of prejudice with the greatest accuracy. Symbolic beliefs best predicted attitudes for the groups toward which participants were most prejudiced (Pakistanis and gays/lesbians). (Researchers at the University of Manitoba also have found that symbolic beliefs predict attitudes toward gay men and lesbian women; Mohipp & Morry, 2004.) For these groups, prejudice would be predicted most accurately by asking whether the group threatens people's important beliefs or values. Stereotypes did not strongly predict attitudes toward any of these groups when emotions, symbolic beliefs, and behaviour were taken into account.

Research by Corenblum and Stephan (2001) suggests that emotion is also a strong predictor of the prejudice that minority groups feel toward majority groups. In their study, white Canadians and Native Canadians were asked about their stereotypes, symbolic beliefs (i.e., agreement with statements such as "Natives and white Canadians have many incompatible values"), and emotions (specifically, anxiety about interacting with out-group members). All of these variables predicted the level of prejudice that white Canadians felt toward Native Canadians, but the strongest predictor was emotion. The same held true when predicting the level of prejudice that Native Canadians felt toward white Canadians. Thus, the more negative emotion people expect to feel while interacting

▲ Might a bigoted person approve of Canada's governor general? Only if she is perceived as an exception to the rule.

with members of another group, the greater their prejudice toward that group—regardless of whether their group is in a majority or minority position.

It is important to point out that even though we have been speaking of predictors of prejudice, the research we have been discussing does not actually tell us whether negative emotions *cause* people to be prejudiced toward certain groups. It may be the other way around—namely, that prejudice produces nasty feelings in people. How might we disentangle this? One way would be to change people's emotions and see if that has an effect on their attitudes. Esses and her colleagues did just that (Bell & Esses, 1997; Esses & Zanna, 1995). In a series of experiments conducted with students at various Ontario universities, they induced a positive, negative, or neutral mood (e.g., by having participants describe events in their lives that made them feel extremely happy, unhappy, or neutral). The findings were clear: Participants in a bad mood described various ethnic groups in more negative terms than did those who were in a good mood or a neutral mood.

We want to be clear on the point that these researchers are making. They are not saying that stereotyping never produces prejudice. Indeed, earlier in this chapter we presented evidence to the contrary. However, this research does suggest that an even stronger determinant of prejudice is how we feel about a group.

Reducing Prejudice by Changing People's Emotions These findings suggest that if we want to reduce prejudice, it might be best to design interventions that will speak to people's hearts rather than to their heads. Esses and Dovidio (2002) attempted to do just that. White participants were shown a videotape of a black man experiencing discrimination in several situations. Some participants were instructed to pay attention to their feelings; others were told to pay attention to their thoughts. Those who focused on their feelings subsequently expressed more willingness to engage in future contact with black people than did those who focused on their thoughts. Why? The researchers discovered that focusing on feelings about the discriminatory situations affected neither people's stereotypes of blacks nor their symbolic beliefs. However, it did affect their emotions: They now felt more positive toward blacks and therefore were more willing to interact with blacks in the future.

▶ Research has suggested that mood affects prejudice; people in a good mood feel more favourably toward other racial or ethnic groups.

The Way We Assign Meaning: Attributional Biases

The human tendency to make attributions for people's behaviour can also serve to perpetuate stereotyping and prejudice. As we discussed in Chapter 4, it is in our nature to make dispositional (internal) attributions—that is, to leap to the conclusion that a person's behaviour is due to his or her personality, and not the situation or the person's life circumstances. This is the familiar fundamental attribution error. Although attributing people's behaviour to their dispositions is often accurate, human behaviour is also shaped by situational factors. Thus, relying too heavily on dispositional attributions can lead us to make attributional mistakes. You can only imagine the problems and complications that arise when we overzealously act out the fundamental attribution error for a whole group of people. Thomas Pettigrew (1979) has called this the **ultimate attribution error** because we apply the fundamental attribution error to entire groups of people.

To use gender stereotypes as an example, Janet Swim and Lawrence Sanna (1996) carefully studied some 58 separate experiments done over the previous 20 years. They found that if a man was successful on a task, observers attributed his success to ability; if a woman was successful at that same task, observers attributed her success to hard work (see also Deaux & Emsweiler, 1974; Feldman-Summers & Kiesler, 1974).

As you might expect, such effects are not limited to gender stereotypes. Corenblum, Annis, and Young (1996) showed white and Native children attending elementary schools in Brandon, Manitoba, videos in which a white child and a Native child performed a task. When a white child performed well, both Native and white participants made dispositional attributions for the child's performance (e.g., being smart); when a white child performed poorly, both Native and white participants made external attributions (e.g., bad luck). Exactly the opposite pattern was observed when making attributions for the performance of a Native child—good performance was attributed to external factors (e.g., luck, an easy task) by both Native and white children; poor performance was attributed to internal factors (e.g., not being smart).

These findings suggest that when people conform to our stereotype, we tend to blind ourselves to clues about why they might have behaved as they did. Instead, we assume that their behaviour is due to something about their character or disposition, and not their situation. In other words, we explain the behaviour of out-group members in a way that perpetuates our stereotypes of them, thereby fostering prejudice.

Prejudice and Economic Competition: Realistic Conflict Theory

One of the most obvious sources of conflict and prejudice is competition—for scarce resources, for political power, and for social status. Indeed, it can be said that whatever problems result from the simple in-group versus out-group phenomenon, they will be magnified by real economic, political, or status competition. **Realistic conflict theory** holds that limited resources lead to conflict among groups and result in prejudice and discrimination (Cottrell & Neuberg, 2005; Jackson, 1993; Sherif, 1966; White, 1977). More specifically, conflict and prejudice are most likely to result when we perceive that our group may miss out on a limited resource and when we perceive that another group (an out-group) is competing with us for that resource (Esses, Dovidio, Danso, Jackson, & Semenya, 2005). Thus, prejudiced attitudes tend to increase when times are tense and conflict exists between groups over mutually exclusive goals.

Economic and Political Competition Whenever people compete for any scarce resource, the stage is set for prejudice. In his classic study of prejudice in a small

> *" The cause is hidden, but the result is known. "*
> —Ovid, first century AD

ultimate attribution error

our tendency to make dispositional attributions about an entire group of people

realistic conflict theory

the theory that limited resources lead to conflict between groups and result in increased prejudice and discrimination

▶ Conflict over valuable land has fuelled racial tension between non-Native residents of Caledonia, Ontario, and Native protestors who claim that the land belongs to them.

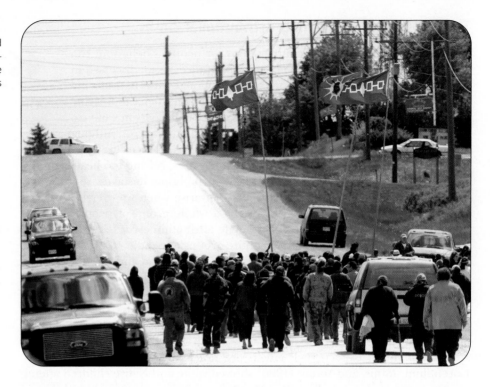

U.S. industrial town, John Dollard (1938) was among the first to document the relation between discrimination and economic competition. While initially there was no discernible prejudice against new German immigrants to the town, as jobs grew scarce, prejudice flourished. Similarly, in the nineteenth century, when Chinese immigrants in the United States joined the gold rush in California, in direct competition with white miners of Anglo-Saxon origin, they were described as "depraved and vicious . . . gross gluttons, . . . bloodthirsty and inhuman" (Jacobs & Landau, 1971). However, only a few years later, when they were willing to accept back-breaking work as labourers on the Transcontinental Railroad—work that few white Americans were willing to do—they were regarded as sober, industrious, and law abiding. With the end of the Civil War came an influx of former soldiers into an already tight job market. This was immediately followed by a dramatic increase in negative attitudes toward the Chinese. The stereotype changed to one characterizing them as criminal, conniving, crafty, and stupid (Jacobs & Landau, 1971).

Closer to home, prejudice toward Native peoples has increased in Caledonia, Ontario, as a result of a dispute over a land claim. Six Nations aboriginals claim that a housing development in the town sits on land that was stolen from them more than 200 years ago. Aboriginal protesters began to occupy the land in 2006, resulting in violent confrontations between town residents and the protesters. David Boyter, a Caledonia resident, comments, "When we moved into Caledonia nobody ever thought of who was native or who was white. Now there's a terrific rift, and the rift will be there for generations to come" (Caledonia Land Conflict, 2007).

These real-world examples suggest that when times are tough and resources are scarce, in-group members feel more threatened by members of the out-group, with the result that incidents of prejudice, discrimination, and violence toward out-group members increase. How might this hypothesis be tested? We might look for increases in violent acts directed at minority group members during times of economic hardship. Carl Hovland and Robert Sears (1940) did just that, by correlating two sets of very different data: (a) the price of cotton in the southern United States from 1882 to 1930, and (b) the number of lynchings of southern African Americans during that same period. During this period, cotton was by far the most important crop in the South; as cotton went, so went the economy. Hovland and Sears found that as the price of cotton dropped, the number of lynchings increased. In short, as members of the in-group experienced the hardships of an economic depression, they became more hostile toward out-group members, whom they almost certainly perceived as a threat to their liveli-hood. Other studies conducted in the United States also have found that prejudice is most pronounced when white people and African Americans are in close com-petition for jobs (Simpson & Yinger, 1958; Vanneman & Pettigrew, 1972).

In Canada, Douglas Palmer documented that attitudes toward immigra-tion mirror unemployment rates. Between 1975 and 1995, the unemployment rate increased and so did negative attitudes about immigration (Palmer, 1996). Between 1996 and 1998, the unemployment rate dropped and—you guessed it—so did opposition toward immigration (Palmer, 2000). In conceptually similar research, Tougas and colleagues (2003) examined the attitudes of franco-phones living in Quebec toward immigrants. Participants who believed that the percentage of immigrants was increasing also tended to agree with state-ments such as "In comparison with immigrants, the Québécois are disadvan-taged in terms of job opportunities." These feelings of threat, in turn, predicted negative attitudes toward immigrants (Tougas, De la Sablonnière, Legace, & Kocum, 2003).

The astute reader will have noticed that the research we have been describing is correlational; experimental research designs allow us to make cause-and-effect statements with far more confidence than we can on the basis of correlational research (see Chapter 2). How might we study the relationship between compe-tition and prejudice experimentally?

In what has become a classic experiment, Muzafer Sherif and his colleagues (1961) tested realistic conflict theory using the natural environment of a Boy Scout camp. The participants in the camp were normal, well-adjusted, 12-year-old boys who were randomly assigned to one of two groups, the Eagles or the Rattlers. Each group stayed in its own cabin, and the cabins were located quite a distance apart. The boys were placed in situations designed to increase the cohe-siveness of their own group by arranging enjoyable activities, such as hiking and swimming, and by having them work on various building projects, prepar-ing group meals, and so on. After feelings of cohesiveness developed within each group, the researchers set up a series of competitive activities in which the two groups were pitted against each other—for example, in games such as football, baseball, and tug-of-war—where prizes were awarded to the winning team. These competitive games aroused feelings of conflict and tension between the two groups. In addition, the investigators created other situations to further intensify the conflict. For example, a camp party was arranged, but each group was told it started at a different time, thereby ensuring that the Eagles would arrive well before the Rattlers. Half of the food at the party was fresh, appealing, and appe-tizing; the other half was squashed, ugly, and unappetizing. As you'd expect, the early-arriving Eagles ate well, and the late-coming Rattlers were not happy with what they found. They began to call the exploitive group some rather uncompli-mentary names. Because the Eagles believed that they deserved what they got (first come, first served), they resented the name calling and responded in kind. Name calling escalated into food throwing, and within a short time the boys were throwing punches and a full-scale riot ensued. In short, competition led to high levels of dislike and hostility.

Closer to home, Esses, Jackson, and Armstrong (1998; Esses, Dovidio, Jackson, & Armstrong, 2001) conducted a series of experiments to see whether perceived competition for resources causes unfavourable attitudes toward immigrants.

Participants in these experiments read one of two editorials on immigration to Canada. In the competition condition, the editorial focused on the scarcity of jobs in Canada and the high rate of participation of skilled immigrants in the job market; in the no-competition condition, the job market was not mentioned. Next, participants were told that because of a natural disaster in the country of Sandir (a fictitious country), a new group of immigrants, the Sandirians, would be arriving in Canada. The researchers described the Sandirians in positive terms: ambitious, hard-working, smart, family-oriented, spiritual, and religious. Participants in the competition condition later construed the traits of the Sandirians more negatively than did those in the no-competition condition (e.g., "Since they are family-oriented, they are probably not too accepting of others outside the family"). These participants also expressed more negative attitudes toward the idea of Sandirian immigration to Canada and toward immigrants in general than did participants in the no-competition condition.

Reducing Prejudice by Fostering Common Goals   We just described a classic experiment in which Sherif and colleagues (1961) created prejudice by setting up competition between two groups of boys at a summer camp. How did Sherif and colleagues reduce hostility between the groups? Their first step was to eliminate competitive games and promote a great deal of nonconflictual social contact. Once hostility had been aroused, however, simply eliminating the competition did not eliminate the hostility. Indeed, hostility continued to escalate, even when the two groups were engaged in such benign activities as watching movies together. But these researchers eventually did succeed. How? By having the boys experience **mutual interdependence**—a situation where two or more groups need each other and must depend on each other in order to accomplish a goal that is important to each group. For example, the investigators set up an emergency situation by damaging the water supply system. The only way the system could be repaired was for all of the Rattlers and Eagles to cooperate immediately. On another occasion, the camp truck broke down while the boys were on a camping trip. To get the truck going again, it was necessary to pull it up a steep hill. This could be accomplished only if all of the boys pulled together, regardless of whether they were Eagles or Rattlers. Eventually, these sorts of situations brought about a diminution of hostile feelings and negative stereotyping among the campers. In fact, after these cooperative situations were introduced, the number of boys who said their closest friend was in the other group increased dramatically (see Figure 12.4).

mutual interdependence

a situation in which two or more groups need each other and must depend on each other in order to accomplish a goal that is important to each group

---

FIGURE 12.4

Intergroup relations

Intergroup tensions were eased only after members engaged in cooperative activities.

(Adapted from Sherif et al., 1961)

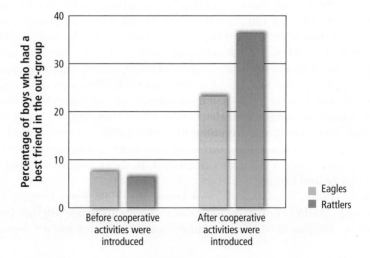

The Way We Conform: Normative Rules

We've seen that prejudice is created and maintained by many forces in the social world. Some operate within the individual, such as the way we process information and assign meaning to events; some operate on whole groups of people, such as the effects of competition, conflict, and frustration. Our final explanation for what causes prejudice also occurs at the group level—conformity to normative standards or rules in the society. As Thomas Pettigrew (1958, 1985, 1991) has noted, many people hold prejudiced attitudes and engage in discriminatory behaviour in order to conform to, or fit in with, the prevailing majority view of their culture. It's as if people say, "Hey, everybody else thinks X's are inferior; if I treat X's with respect, people might not like me. I think I'll just go along with everybody else." Pettigrew argues convincingly that although economic competition, frustration, and social cognition processes do account for some prejudice, by far the greatest determinant of prejudice is slavish conformity to social norms.

Recent programs of research underscore the important role that social norms play in perpetuating prejudice (Sechrist, Stangor, & Killen, 2005). For example, in a series of studies, Stangor and colleagues (2001) assessed European-American students' stereotypes of African Americans. They also were asked to estimate the beliefs that other students at their university held about African Americans. Later, participants received (false) feedback that their estimate of the other students' beliefs was actually incorrect. Some participants were told that the other students actually held more positive beliefs about African Americans than the participant had thought. Other participants were told that the students at their university actually had more negative beliefs about African Americans than the participant had thought. What was the effect of learning these social norms? Those who discovered that other students were actually more positive in their views of African Americans expressed more positive attitudes toward African Americans than before they learned about this social norm. Sadly, the opposite was true as well—those who learned that the other students felt negatively toward African Americans subsequently became more negative as well (Stangor, Sechrist, & Jost, 2001).

In another program of research, Christian Crandall and colleagues (2002) asked participants to rate a large number of social groups in terms of how acceptable it is to have negative feelings toward each group. Other participants rated how positively or negatively they personally felt toward each of these groups. The correlation between the two sets of ratings was astonishingly high: 0.96. (Recall that a perfect correlation is 1.00.) In other words, "to ask people about the norms regarding prejudice is, in practical terms, the same as asking people how they personally feel" (Crandall, Eshleman, & O'Brien, 2002). The researchers note that although we may start out being hesitant to accept the norms of any given group, over time, as we begin to identify with the group, we internalize its norms and make them our own. Other research has shown that we are particularly likely to rely on social norms (i.e., what other people think) when developing attitudes toward groups with which we have little familiarity (Sechrist et al., 2005).

From a social norms perspective, the most effective way to combat prejudice is to try to change the attitudes of entire groups of people (e.g., creating a culture of fair treatment in the workplace). Obviously, it's not always possible to intervene and change a group's norms. When group change isn't possible, social norm information can be used at least to change the attitudes of individuals, as demonstrated by Stangor and colleagues' (2001) research described above.

Modern Prejudice As you are no doubt aware, prejudice toward racial or ethnic minorities has become socially unacceptable (Crandall et al., 2002). As a result, many people have become more careful—outwardly acting unprejudiced, but

modern prejudice

outwardly acting unprejudiced while inwardly maintaining prejudiced attitudes

" We all decry prejudice, yet all are prejudiced. "

—Herbert Spencer, biologist
and philosopher, 1873

inwardly maintaining their prejudiced views. This phenomenon is known as **modern prejudice** (Dovidio & Gaertner, 1996; Gaertner & Dovidio, 1986; McConahay, 1986). In other words, people have learned to hide their prejudice in order to avoid being labelled racist or sexist, but when the situation is "safe," their prejudice will be revealed. For example, Evans, Garcia, Garcia, and Baron (2003) found that participants rated various ethnic groups much more positively when an experimenter was in the room than they did when alone in the room or completing the same scale over the internet. In fact, when an experimenter was present, participants rated various out-groups even more positively than their own group—presumably to show just how unprejudiced they were. In another study, Allen Hart and Marian Morry (1997) showed white students a videotape of a black person and a white person making speeches. When the speakers performed well, participants bent over backward to show that they were not prejudiced and rated the black speaker even more positively than the white speaker. However, when the performance was poor, participants attributed more negative characteristics to the black speaker than to the white speaker.

Modern prejudice has some disturbing real-world implications. For example, research conducted in the United States (Hill & Pfeifer, 1992; Pfeifer & Ogloff, 1991) and Canada (Pfeifer & Ogloff, 2003) has found that jurors will assign greater guilt and recommend more severe punishment for offenders who are of a different race than the jurors are—but only when the situation is ambiguous enough that their behaviour cannot be labelled racist. If jurors are given highly explicit instructions about how to assign guilt, they are much less likely to make discriminatory recommendations.

Given the properties of modern prejudice, social psychologists conducting research on prejudice face a rather formidable challenge. The kinds of attitudes they are most interested in studying are the kinds of attitudes people may be least willing to admit. Thus, it has been necessary to develop subtle or unobtrusive measures. As we mentioned earlier in this chapter (see also Chapter 6), researchers are now beginning to measure attitudes, including prejudice, using the Implicit Association Test (IAT). The task for participants is to respond to words or pictures presented on a computer screen, allowing the researcher to see whether, for example, a participant responds more quickly to unpleasant words when a black face has been shown on the computer than when a white face is shown. (To try out the Implicit Association Test, or IAT, see https://implicit.harvard.edu/implicit.)

There also has been an effort to construct attitude questionnaires in a way that assesses prejudice in a more unobtrusive manner. For example, the Modern Racism Scale is a subtle, indirect measure of racial prejudice (McConahay, 1986). It turns out that people who are reluctant to express blatant prejudice nevertheless are quite willing to agree with statements such as "Minorities are getting too demanding in their push for special rights." Research conducted in Canada, the United States, and Britain has shown that those who score high on modern prejudice scales are more likely to be prejudiced against black people than those who score low (Kawakami, Dion, & Dovidio, 1998; Lepore & Brown, 1997; Tougas, Desruisseaux, Desrochers, St-Pierre, Perrino, & De la Sablonnière, 2004; Wittenbrink, Judd, & Park, 1997).

At the University of Ottawa, Francine Tougas and her colleagues have developed a scale—the Neosexism Scale—to assess sexist attitudes in a more subtle manner (Tougas, Brown, Beaton, & Joly, 1995). Parallel to the issue of racism, these researchers reasoned that people who are opposed to equality for women may be reluctant to say so directly but might find it acceptable to express disagreement with social policies aimed at increasing the status of women. Accordingly, the Neosexism Scale asks respondents to indicate how much they agree with statements such as "Women will make more progress by being patient and not pushing too hard for change." In a study of male managers working in a Canadian federal agency, Beaton, Tougas, and Joly (1996) found that those who scored high on neosexism were more likely to show a pro-male bias when evaluating women's and men's competence (e.g., they believed that male managers were more competent in general than female managers), and reported less willingness to support women in the workplace than did managers who scored low. These researchers also found that secretaries who scored high on neosexism were opposed to affirmative action programs for women and, like the male managers in the previous study, showed a pro-male bias when evaluating women's and men's competence (Tougas, Brown, Beaton, & St-Pierre, 1999). Finally, a study conducted with students at the University of Windsor found that neosexism was associated with negative attitudes toward the feminist movement and toward lesbians and gay men (Campbell, Schellenberg, & Senn, 1997).

Individual Differences in Prejudice

As we have mentioned repeatedly throughout this chapter, no one is immune from prejudice. The simple act of classifying people into groups tends to bring with it value judgments about which groups are better than others. However, as you probably have observed, some people do seem to hold more prejudiced attitudes than others. Indeed, research confirms that certain kinds of people are especially likely to hold negative attitudes toward members of out-groups. More specifically, those who are high in right-wing authoritarianism, religious fundamentalism, and social dominance orientation are more likely to be more prejudiced than those who are low in these dimensions.

Right-Wing Authoritarianism

Bob Altemeyer (1981, 1988, 1996) has identified an individual difference variable—right-wing authoritarianism—that is strongly associated with prejudice. *Right-wing authoritarianism* is defined in terms of three clusters of attitudes:

- authoritarian submission—a high degree of submission to authority figures in society
- authoritarian aggression—aggression directed toward groups that are seen as legitimate targets by authority figures, and
- conventionalism—a high degree of conformity to the rules and conventions that are established by authority figures

Right-wing authoritarianism is associated with statements such as, "Once our government leaders give us the 'go ahead,' it will be the duty of every patriotic citizen to help stomp out the rot that is poisoning our country from within" (Altemeyer, 1998).

In research conducted at the University of Manitoba over the past three decades, Altemeyer (1981, 1996, 1998) has found strong positive correlations between right-wing authoritarianism and racial prejudice. Similarly, at the University of Waterloo, Haddock, Zanna, and Esses (1993) found that participants who are high in right-wing authoritarianism express more negative attitudes than low right-wing authoritarians toward French Canadians, Natives, and Pakistanis. In addition, those who are high in right-wing authoritarianism hold traditional, nonegalitarian attitudes toward women (e.g., believing that women should be subservient to men; Altemeyer, 1996, 1998; Perrott, Miller, & Delaney, 1997) and have negative attitudes toward feminists (Haddock & Zanna, 1994). Finally, those who are high in right-wing authoritarianism show especially high levels of prejudice toward gays and lesbians (Altemeyer, 1996, 1998; Altemeyer & Hunsberger, 1992; Haddock, Zanna, & Esses, 1993; Hunsberger, 1996; Whitley, 1999).

Reducing Prejudice among Right-Wing Authoritarians   Can the attitudes of right-wing authoritarians be changed? This is a tall order, indeed. Given that right-wing authoritarians are especially prejudiced toward gays and lesbians, Altemeyer (1988, 2001) has focused on ways of changing attitudes toward this group. One strategy that has proven effective is to create awareness that attitudes generally have become more positive toward the gay and lesbian community (Altemeyer, 2001). When right-wing authoritarians are shown that their attitudes are much more negative than other people's, they tend to change them because conforming to social norms is important to them.

Another strategy for reducing prejudice is to encourage interaction with members of out-groups. (The benefits of contact are discussed more fully at the end of this chapter.) Altemeyer decided to find out if right-wing authoritarians would change their attitudes if they personally knew a gay or lesbian person. He did so by telling one of his psychology classes that he was gay and was actively involved in the gay rights movement. (Altemeyer actually is not gay, although a newspaper article describing this demonstration reported that he was, which apparently came as quite a surprise to his in-laws!) What effect did this revelation have on the right-wing authoritarians in his class? They subsequently became more positive in their attitudes toward gays as a group (see Altemeyer, 2001). Thus, there is reason to be optimistic that prejudice can be reduced, even among right-wing authoritarians.

Religious Fundamentalism

Research conducted at Wilfrid Laurier University by Bruce Hunsberger (1995, 1996) and at the University of Manitoba (Altemeyer & Hunsberger, 1992, 1993) suggests that religious fundamentalism is another individual difference variable that is related to prejudice. *Religious fundamentalism* is defined as a belief in the absolute and literal truth of one's religious beliefs. People who are high in fundamentalism also believe that their religion is the "right" one and that forces of evil are constantly threatening to undermine its truth. (Note that the term *fundamentalism* does not refer to a specific religion but, rather, to any religious beliefs that are seen as portraying the ultimate truth.)

Studies conducted with university students and community samples have shown that religious fundamentalism is correlated with racial prejudice as well as with negative attitudes toward single mothers and gays and lesbians (the behaviour of these latter groups is seen as immoral; Altemeyer & Hunsberger, 1992, 1993; Jackson & Esses, 1997). Hunsberger (1996), for example, assessed religious fundamentalism and attitudes toward gays and lesbians among Muslims, Jews, and Hindus living in Toronto. Within each group, the greater the fundamentalism, the greater the hostility toward the gay and lesbian community.

It may have crossed your mind that there are similarities between religious fundamentalism and right-wing authoritarianism. Indeed, Altemeyer and Hunsberger (1993) have reached the conclusion that fundamentalism is a religious manifestation of right-wing authoritarianism.

Finally, we want to emphasize that these researchers are not saying that religion *per se* is associated with prejudice but, rather, that there is a relation between prejudice and the way in which certain people hold their religious beliefs. Those who regard their beliefs as the absolute truth that must be zealously followed are likely to be prejudiced. This is not the case for those who have a flexible, open, and questioning orientation to religion (known as religious quest). In fact, religious quest tends to be negatively correlated with prejudice (Altemeyer & Hunsberger, 1992, 1993).

Social Dominance Orientation

Another individual difference variable that is related to prejudice is *social dominance orientation* (Pratto, Sidanius, Stallworth, & Malle, 1994; Sidanius, Levin, & Pratto, 1996). Individuals who are high in social dominance orientation believe that groups of people are inherently unequal and that it is acceptable for some groups in society to benefit more than others. They prefer to be in the advantaged group, even if it means treating other groups badly. For example, people high in social dominance orientation agree with statements such as "To get ahead in life, it is sometimes necessary to step on others."

Research conducted in Canada, China, Israel, Mexico, New Zealand, Taiwan, and the United States has shown that social dominance orientation is associated with racial prejudice, sexism, and negative attitudes toward gays and lesbians (Altemeyer, 1998; Pratto et al., 1994, 2000; Sidanius, Levin, & Pratto, 1996; Whitley, 1999). People who are high in social dominance orientation also hold negative attitudes toward immigration. They oppose offering assistance to immigrant groups because they believe that any gains made by immigrants occur at their expense (Esses, Jackson, & Armstrong, 1998; Esses, Dovidio, Jackson, & Armstrong, 2001). More recently, Esses and researchers at other Ontario universities have shown that people who are high in social dominance orientation also tend to dehumanize refugees—seeing them as immoral and as trying to unjustly sneak into Canada (Esses, Veenvliet, Hodson, & Mihic, 2008).

Social dominance orientation does not only affect attitudes toward outgroups. According to a recent series of experiments conducted at Guelph University and the University of Waterloo, organizational leaders who are high in social dominance orientation are more likely to make unethical decisions (e.g., exploiting the labour pool of poor countries) than those who are low in this trait (Son Hing, Bobocel, Zanna, & McBride, 2007). Further, the combination of a high social dominance orientation leader with a right-wing authoritarian follower is especially likely to result in unethical decision making on a variety of issues.

Finally, it may interest you to know that research conducted with French-Canadian university students found that law students score higher on social dominance orientation (and prejudice) than do psychology students. Moreover, upper-year law students score higher on social dominance orientation than first-year law students, whereas the opposite is true for psychology students (Guimond, Dambrun, Michinov, & Durarte, 2003).

Reducing Prejudice among People High in Social Dominance Orientation   How do you reduce prejudice among people who do not see the need for change? Esses and colleagues (2001) reasoned that perhaps those who are high in social dominance orientation would be less prejudiced if they could be persuaded that they do not necessarily lose out when others get ahead. To find out, they had participants read an editorial making claims such as "It is not the case that when immigrants make gains in employment, it is at the expense of Canadians living here." Did this message have any impact on those who were high in social dominance orientation? Sadly, no. In fact, these sorts of arguments seemed to backfire, such that those who were high in social dominance orientation became even more negative toward immigrants than did participants in a control condition. It appears that a challenge to their worldview only caused them to bolster their beliefs.

Does this leave any hope that the attitudes of people high in social dominance orientation can be changed? In a second attempt to reduce prejudice among those high in social dominance orientation, Esses and colleagues (2001) constructed editorials that were intended to create a sense of shared identity between the participants and immigrant groups. For example, it was pointed out that most Canadians immigrated to this country and that the participants themselves could probably trace their own ethnic roots. This more indirect approach met with success—those who were high in social dominance orientation later expressed more positive attitudes toward immigrants than those who read a neutral editorial. (Note that those who were low in social dominance orientation were unaffected by the editorials because they weren't as prejudiced to begin with.)

Unfortunately, in subsequent research conducted in Canada and Germany, Esses, Wagner and Wolf (2006) found that focusing on a common identity is not always effective. For example, in Germany, where people are less willing to include immigrants as part of their identity, creating feelings of a common identity backfired, such that participants high in social dominance orientation reported even more negative attitudes toward immigrants than those who were asked to focus on their national identity as Germans.

Reducing prejudice among those high in social dominance orientation will continue to be a challenge, given that people with this trait believe that prejudice cannot be changed. More disturbingly, they do not see a need for prejudice to be reduced (Hodson, & Esses, 2005).

Effects of Stereotyping, Prejudice, and Discrimination

Stereotyping, prejudice and discrimination can have insidious effects, such as poverty, war, torture, and genocide. Even when prejudice doesn't cost an individual's life, he or she can still pay a very high price in terms of the psychological consequences of prejudice and discrimination. For example, when a member of a majority group mistreats a member of a disadvantaged group, the disadvantaged person is unlikely to perform well, thereby confirming the majority group member's negative stereotype and, in turn, perpetuating the discrimination. You probably recognize this as our old friend the *self-fulfilling prophecy* once again rearing its head. Moreover, fears that one will confirm the negative stereotype of one's group also can impede performance, as we shall see shortly. Perhaps most tragic of all, even when the poor performance of disadvantaged groups is clearly the result of discrimination, they may nevertheless blame themselves rather than place the blame where it deserves to be placed—on the shoulders of those who are engaging in the discriminatory behaviour.

Self-Fulfilling Prophecies

All other things being equal, if you believe that Amy is stupid and treat her accordingly, chances are that she will not say a lot of clever things in your presence. This is the well-known self-fulfilling prophecy, discussed in Chapter 3. How does this come about? If you believe that Amy is stupid, you probably will not ask her interesting questions and you will not listen intently while she is talking; indeed, you might even look out the window or yawn. You behave this way because of a simple expectation: Why waste energy paying attention to Amy if she is unlikely to say anything smart or interesting? This is bound to have an important impact on Amy's behaviour, for if you aren't paying attention when she is talking to you, she will feel uneasy and will probably clam up, and not come out with the poetry and wisdom within her. This in turn serves to confirm the belief you had about her in the first place. The circle is closed; the self-fulfilling prophecy is complete.

The relevance of this phenomenon to stereotyping and discrimination was demonstrated in an elegant experiment by Carl Word, Mark Zanna, and Joel Cooper (1974). They asked white university undergraduates to interview several job applicants; some of the applicants were white and others were African Americans. Unwittingly, the students displayed discomfort and lack of interest when interviewing African-American applicants; for example, they sat farther away, they tended to stammer when talking, and they terminated the interview far sooner than when they were interviewing white applicants. Can you guess how this behaviour might have affected the African-American applicants? To find out, the researchers, in a second experiment, systematically varied the behaviour of the interviewers (actually confederates) so it coincided with the way the real interviewers had treated the African-American or white interviewees in the first experiment. But in the second experiment, all of the interviewees were white. The researchers videotaped the proceedings and had the applicants rated by independent judges. They found that those applicants who were interviewed the way African Americans had been interviewed in the first experiment were judged to be far more nervous and far less effective than those who were interviewed the way white applicants had been interviewed in the first experiment. In sum, these experiments clearly demonstrated that when African Americans are interviewed by whites, they are unintentionally placed at a disadvantage and are not likely to perform as well as their white counterparts (see Figure 12.5).

In a recent series of studies conducted by University of Toronto researcher Glenn Adams and colleagues (2006), it was found that the mere suggestion of sexism (a female confederate casually mentioning that the male experimenter seemed sexist) caused women to perform more poorly on a logic test compared with women who did not hear the sexism remark (Adams, Garcia, Purdie-Vaughns, & Steele, 2006).

On a societal level, the insidiousness of the self-fulfilling prophecy goes even farther. Suppose there is a general belief that a particular group is irredeemably stupid, uneducable, and fit only for menial jobs. Why waste educational resources on them? Hence, they are given inadequate schooling. What do you find 30 years later? An entire group that, with few exceptions, is fit only for menial jobs. "See? I was right all the time," says the bigot. "How fortunate that we didn't waste our precious educational resources on such people!" The self-fulfilling prophecy strikes again.

FIGURE 12.5

An experiment demonstrating self-fulfilling prophecies

Stereotype Threat

It is well established that academic test performance varies among different cultural groups. For example, in the United States, it has been found that although there is considerable overlap, Asian Americans perform slightly better than European Americans, who in turn perform better than African Americans. Why does this occur? There may be any number of explanations—economic, cultural, historical, or political. Claude Steele and Joshua Aronson have come up with another factor having to do with the anxiety that is produced by negative stereotypes—specifically, the fear that one's behaviour will conform to the stereotype of one's group (Aronson, Quinn, & Spencer, 1998; Steele, 1997; Steele & Aronson, 1995a, 1995b; Steele, Spencer, & Aronson, 2002). This phenomenon is referred to as **stereotype threat**. When African-American students, for example, find themselves in highly evaluative educational situations, most tend to experience apprehension about confirming the existing negative cultural stereotype of intellectual inferiority. In effect, an African-American student is saying, "If I perform poorly on this test, it will reflect poorly on me and on my race." This extra burden of apprehension in turn interferes with the student's ability to perform well in these situations.

stereotype threat

the apprehension experienced by members of a minority group that they might behave in a manner that confirms an existing cultural stereotype

> ❝I will look at any additional evidence to confirm the opinion to which I have already come.❞
>
> —Lord Hugh Molson, British politician (1950s–1960s)

In one of their experiments, Steele and Aronson (1995a) administered a difficult verbal test, the GRE, individually to African-American and white students at Stanford University. Half of the students of each race were led to believe that the investigator was interested in measuring their intellectual ability; the other half were led to believe that the investigator was merely trying to develop the test itself—and because the test was not yet valid or reliable, they were assured that their performance would mean nothing in terms of their actual ability. The results confirmed the researchers' speculations: White students performed equally well regardless of whether they believed the test was being used as a diagnostic tool. African-American students who believed the test was non-diagnostic of their abilities performed as well as white students. But the African-American students who thought that the test was measuring their abilities did not perform as well as white students or as well as the African-American students in the other group. In subsequent experiments in the same series, Steele and Aronson also found that if race is made more salient, the decrement in performance among African-American students is even more pronounced.

Stereotype threat applies to gender as well. As you know, a common stereotype is that men are better at math than women are. Spencer, Steele, and Quinn (1999) showed that when women are led to believe that men generally performed better on a particular test, they do not perform as well as men. However, when women are told that the test does not generally show gender differences, they perform just as well as men. These effects have been replicated by many other researchers in the United States (e.g., Brown & Pinel, 2003) and in Germany (Keller & Dauenheimer, 2003). In a Canadian study (Walsh, Hickey, & Duffy, 1999), male and female university students in Newfoundland were told that they would be taking a math test. The researchers mentioned that on Part A of the test, men typically scored higher than women and that the purpose of Part B was to compare the performance of Canadian students with American students. (These instructions were reversed for other students, such that they were told that Part A was a comparison with American students, and that on Part B, men usually outperformed women.) Women scored lower than men only on the part of the test where they expected to be outperformed by men. They did as well as men on the part they believed was a comparison of the performance of Canadian and American university students.

Sadly, stereotype threat has widespread effects (Davies, Spencer, & Claude, 2005; Davies, Spencer, & Steele, 2005; von Hippel, von Hippel, Conway, Preacher, Schooler, & Radvansky, 2005). In a recent series of studies, Jennifer Steele, at York

University, and Nalini Ambady (2006) found that simply reminding women of their gender (e.g., by subliminally presenting female stereotype words) results in more negative attitudes toward math (women in the other conditions were exposed to either male stereotype words or neutral words). And it's not just attitudes that are affected. Davies and colleagues (2002) found that stereotype threat can lead women—even women who are good at math—to avoid taking math tests and to shy away from math-related careers (Davies, Spencer, Quinn, & Gerhardstein, 2002).

Here's an interesting twist: What if you happen to be an Asian woman and you also are aware of the stereotype that Asians are good at math? Might you perform differently depending on which stereotype about you is activated? Shih, Pittinsky, and Ambady (1999) raised the intriguing possibility that performance might differ, depending on which of an individual's identities was activated: her identity as an Asian or as a woman. The researchers conducted a fascinating study in which they administered the Canadian Math Competition test to a group of female Asian-American university students. Some of the women were reminded of their ethnicity before they took the test; others were reminded of their gender (a control group was not reminded of any identity before taking the test). Remarkably, the participants who had been reminded that they were Asian had the highest performance on the test, whereas those who had been reminded that they were women had the lowest performance (the control group scored in between these two groups).

These findings suggest that although stereotype threat usually has negative effects, being reminded of a positive stereotype associated with one's identity (e.g., Asians are good at math) can lead to improved performance. But even positive stereotypes can have negative effects. For example, there is evidence that people sometimes choke under the pressure of having to live up to the high expectations that others have of their group (Cheryan & Bodenhausen, 2000; Shih, Ambady, Richeson, Fujita, & Gray, 2002).

Before leaving this topic, we should note that the effects we have been discussing are not limited to women. In a series of studies, Joshua Aronson and colleagues (1999) demonstrated that white men do not perform as well on math exams when competing with Asian men (Aronson, Lustina, Good, Keough, Steele, & Brown, 1999).

©1992 Gary Hallgren

Can the effects of stereotype threat be overcome? Research aimed at reducing the effects of stereotype threat has tended to focus on test-taking performance. This research shows that the effects of stereotype threat are diminished if students are made aware that it is normal for members of stereotyped groups to experience test anxiety (Aronson & Williams, 2006; Johns, Schmader, & Martens, 2005), if they are exposed to successful role models from the stereotyped group (Marx & Roman, 2002; McIntyre, Paulson, & Lord, 2003), or if they are given a reminder that they are good students just before taking a test (Good, Aronson, & Harder, 2008; McGlone & Aronson, 2006). For women, stereotype threat is reduced if they are told that there are no gender differences in the performance domain, as demonstrated by research conducted at the University of Waterloo (Davies et al., 2005), or if they are told that gender differences in math performance are the result of differences in experience, rather than genetics, as shown in recent research conducted at the University of British Columbia (Dar-Nimrod & Heine, 2006). Another effective strategy is to have people engage in self-affirmation before they begin an evaluative task. For example, at the University of Alberta, Schimel and colleagues (2004) found that female students who were given a self-affirmation exercise before taking a math test performed better than those in a control condition.

Disengagement and Disidentification

Individuals who are the targets of negative stereotypes, prejudice, and discrimination may cope by psychologically disengaging their self-esteem in stereotype-relevant domains. In other words, these individuals learn to detach their self-esteem from their performance, such that whether they succeed or fail has little effect on their overall self-worth. For example, Major and colleagues (1998) gave success or failure feedback on a bogus intelligence test to African-American and European-American students. European-American students showed higher self-esteem after success than after failure; African-American students had similar levels of self-esteem regardless of the feedback they received (Major, Spencer, Schmader, Wolfe, & Crocker, 1998). What are the consequences of disengagement from tasks such as academic tests? According to Claude Steele (1997, Nussbaum & Steele, 2007), when people are vulnerable to negative stereotypes in a domain that is important to them (e.g., academic performance), they may eventually redefine their self-concept, such that the performance domain is no longer part of their self-identity. This process is referred to as **disidentification**. In other words, members of stigmatized groups may convince themselves that performing well in a particular domain isn't a central part of who they are. The problem is that when people convince themselves that they don't actually care, or that it isn't important to perform well in a given domain, it undermines their motivation and, not surprisingly, their performance suffers. As you might expect, research is showing that disengagement and disidentification have the most negative effects when they become a chronic, habitual response to prejudice and discrimination (Major et al., 1998; Nussbaum & Steele, 2007).

Self-Blaming Attributions for Discrimination

Can you explain the following paradox? Numerous studies have found that members of disadvantaged groups often report that their group is discriminated against but that they, personally, have not been the target of discrimination (Carvallo & Pelham, 2006; Dion & Kawakami, 1996; Taylor, Ruggiero, & Louis, 1996; Taylor, Wright, Moghaddam, & Lalonde, 1990). For example, in research conducted at Carleton University (Foster & Matheson, 1999; Gill & Matheson, 2006) and at the University of Western Ontario (Quinn, Roese, Pennington, & Olson, 1999), women reported greater group than personal discrimination in terms of

---

disidentification

the process by which targets of negative stereotypes redefine their self-concept, such that the performance domain is no longer a part of their identity pay equity, career opportunities, and sexual harassment. Similarly, members of the East Indian community in Ottawa (Clément, Noels, & Deneault, 2001) and members of aboriginal and other visible minority groups in Prince George, British Columbia (Michalos & Zumbo, 2001), claim that there is greater discrimination against their group than against them personally. To give one final example, in Toronto, the Housing New Canadians Project examined experiences of discrimination among three immigrant groups—Jamaicans, Poles, and Somalis—and found that the personal-group discrimination discrepancy was most evident among the two most visible minority groups (because they are black; Dion, 2001). In other words, members of these groups maintained that their group, overall, had encountered greater housing discrimination than they, personally, had experienced.

How can we explain these findings? There are several possible answers. One explanation is that members of negatively stereotyped groups distance themselves from the group in order to avoid having the group's negative characteristics attributed to them. For example, in one study, female students at the University of Western Ontario were given feedback that their experiences were either highly similar or highly dissimilar to that of other women. Participants who were made to feel similar to their group (i.e., women) subsequently felt more vulnerable to group-based discrimination than those who were made to feel dissimilar to other women (Hodson & Esses, 2002). Thus, claiming that my group gets discriminated against—but not me, personally—is one way of saying that I don't have the negative qualities that are attributed to my group.

Recent research has shown that people who have a high need to belong are especially likely to claim they experience less personal discrimination than their group as a whole. Because personal discrimination carries with it the sting of personal rejection, it feels less threatening to believe that although your group is a target of discrimination, you, personally, are not (Carvallo & Pelham, 2006). Interestingly, in a study of gender discrimination, the researchers found that if participants were made to feel accepted (e.g., did a word search task with words such as "welcomed," "adored," "included"), the personal-group discrimination effect was reversed—these participants now reported higher levels of personal discrimination in their lives and lower levels of group discrimination.

Another explanation for the personal-group discrimination discrepancy has to do with the attributions that people make for their performance. In a series of studies conducted at McGill University, Karen Ruggiero and Donald Taylor (1995, 1997; Taylor, Ruggiero, & Louis, 1996) found that when given failure feedback, members of stigmatized groups (e.g., women, members of racial minority groups) tended to blame themselves for their poor performance—even when told that their evaluators were known to discriminate against their group. Remarkably, participants who were told that there was a 75 percent chance they had been discriminated against blamed themselves as much as those who were told there was a 25 percent chance of discrimination.

Why would participants blame themselves—rather than discrimination—for their poor performance even when told that there was a 75 percent chance that they had been discriminated against? The researchers found that doing so cost the participants performance self-esteem (feeling good about one's achievements), but allowed them to salvage feelings of social self-esteem (feeling socially accepted) and perceived control.

Other research has shown that people may blame themselves when discriminated against because they don't want to be perceived as complainers (Hodson & Esses, 2002; Sechrist, Swim, & Stangor, 2004). Whatever the reason, self-blaming has damaging effects. For example, research conducted at Wilfrid Laurier University has shown that blaming oneself for low performance—even when it is clear that one's low scores are due to discrimination—extracts a cost in terms of well being (Foster & Tsarfati, 2005). Self-blaming also can set up a vicious cycle:

If minority group members blame themselves for negative outcomes, majority group members are able to justify their ongoing discrimination (Ruggiero & Taylor, 1997).

Before leaving this topic, we should note that members of disadvantaged groups do not always minimize the discrimination they experience. Sometimes, they are actually hypervigilant for such signs (Major, Quinton, & McCoy, 2002; Wright & Taylor, 2003). Why? According to Brenda Major and her colleagues (Crocker & Major, 1989; Major, Kaiser, & McCoy, 2003), under some conditions, it can actually be less damaging to our sense of self-esteem if we blame negative outcomes, such as a poor mark on a test, on discrimination rather than on our own shortcomings. For example, if the group isn't very important to you, then you can salvage your self-esteem by deciding that the negative outcome you experienced was due to discrimination, rather than your lack of ability (McCoy & Major, 2003).

Interventions for Reducing Prejudice and Discrimination

> It is never too late to give up our prejudices.
> —Henry David Thoreau, Walden, 1854

Sometimes subtle, sometimes brutally overt, prejudice is indeed ubiquitous. Does this mean that prejudice is an essential aspect of human social interaction and will therefore always be with us? We social psychologists do not take such a pessimistic view. People can change. But how? We have offered several clues throughout this chapter. We have shown that getting people to focus on positive aspects of themselves (self-affirmation) reduces the need to denigrate others in order to get a boost in self-esteem. We have also seen that blurring the distinction between "us" and "them" can improve attitudes toward out-groups. We have discussed how promoting common goals—mutual interdependence—fosters cooperation and liking between groups. We will now focus on a few more general strategies for eliminating, or at least reducing, this noxious aspect of human social behaviour.

Learning Not to Hate

> The world is full of pots jeering at kettles.
> —François de la Rochefoucauld, Maxims, 1665

It is obvious that parents and teachers play a crucial role in educating children to treat others in a nondiscriminatory manner. The important role that teachers can play was illustrated by the life-altering lesson in prejudice that Jane Elliott (1977), a teacher in Riceville, Iowa, taught her grade 3 class. Elliott was concerned that her young students were leading too sheltered a life. The children all lived in rural Iowa, they were all white, and they were all Christian. Elliott felt it was important to give them some direct experience about what stereotyping and discrimination felt like, from both sides. To achieve this end, Elliott divided her class by eye colour. She told her students that blue-eyed people were superior to brown-eyed people—smarter, nicer, more trustworthy, and so on. The brown-eyed youngsters were required to wear special collars around their necks so they would be instantly recognizable as a member of the inferior group. She gave special privileges to the blue-eyed youngsters; for example, they got to play longer at recess, could have second helpings at the cafeteria, and received extra praise in the classroom. How did the children respond?

In a matter of hours, Elliott succeeded in creating a microcosm of a prejudiced society in her classroom. Just a few hours before the experiment began, the children had been a cooperative, cohesive group; once the seeds of divisiveness were planted, there was trouble. The "superior" blue-eyed kids made fun of the brown-eyed kids, refused to play with them, tattled on them to the teacher, thought up new restrictions and punishments for them, and even started a fistfight in the schoolyard. The "inferior" brown-eyed kids became self-conscious, depressed, and demoralized. They performed poorly on classroom tests that day.

The next day, Elliott switched the stereotypes about eye colour. She said she'd made a dreadful mistake—that brown-eyed people were really the superior ones. She told the brown-eyed kids to put their collars on the blue-eyed kids. They gleefully did so. The tables had turned—and the brown-eyed kids exacted their revenge.

On the morning of the third day, Elliott explained to her students that they had been learning about prejudice and discrimination, and how it feels to be a person of colour. The children discussed the two-day experience and clearly understood its message. In a follow-up, Elliott met with these students at a class reunion when they were in their mid-twenties. Their memories of the exercise were startlingly clear—they reported that the experience had a powerful and lasting impact on their lives. They felt that they were less prejudiced and more aware of discrimination against others because of this childhood experience.

Jane Elliott's eye colour exercise has been used widely in classrooms in many countries, including Canada, and in other settings (e.g., with prison staff) with the hope that experiencing discrimination first hand will make people less likely to behave in discriminatory ways.

Although adults obviously play an important role in socializing children not to be prejudiced, an intriguing study by Aboud and Doyle (1996) suggests that children also may be effective at teaching one another. Participants in this research were white students in grades 3 and 4 attending various schools in Quebec. First, their attitudes toward whites, blacks, and Chinese Canadians were assessed. Then, the researchers paired a high-prejudice child with a low-prejudice child and asked them to discuss their perceptions of different racial groups. Low-prejudice children were more likely than high-prejudice children to point out negative characteristics of whites and similarities across racial groups. For example, if a prejudiced child mentioned that a black classmate or a Chinese classmate had been mean, a low-prejudice child would point out white classmates who had been mean as well. Importantly, these discussions had the effect of reducing prejudice among the high-prejudice children. Happily, the opposite did not occur—high-prejudice children did not create prejudice among low-prejudice children. These findings are encouraging and suggest that peers also may play an important role in teaching one another not to hate.

The Contact Hypothesis

As you have perhaps experienced in your own life, repeated contact with members of an out-group can have a positive effect on stereotypes and prejudice. People often feel anxious, however, about interacting with out-group members (Mendes, Gray, Mendoza-Denton, Major, & Epel, 2007). One worry is that out-groups might be hostile and unfriendly toward us (Plant & Devine, 2003). Another worry is that we might say or do something that makes us look prejudiced—even if we're not. According to Vorauer and Turpie (2004), people may choke under the pressure of trying to appear unprejudiced to the point where they actually show less warmth and responsiveness than they otherwise would. These researchers had white students at the University of Manitoba engage in an interaction (via videotape) with an aboriginal person. Ironically, it was the participants who were least prejudiced who were most likely to show these "choking" effects.

There is yet another complicating factor: Jacquie Vorauer and colleagues have found that when interacting with out-group members, we believe that it is

CONNECTIONS

Can Playing Video Games Make You Less Prejudiced?

Is there a way to overcome people's reluctance to interact with members of out-groups? A recent, intriguing study offers promise. At York University, Kawakami and colleagues (2007) had non-black participants play a video game in which they were trained with a joystick to either approach photos of white faces and avoid photos of black faces, or to do the opposite (i.e., approach blacks and avoid whites). Participants in a control group simply moved the joystick to the left or right. Those who were in the "approach blacks" condition later showed lower levels of implicit prejudice toward blacks compared with those in the "avoid blacks" and control groups. In a subsequent study, the researchers found that participants who approached photographs of black faces in the video game sat closer to a black confederate during an interaction after the game compared with participants in the other groups. Thus, approaching blacks in a video game actually translated into more positive behaviours in a real-life contact situation (Kawakami, Phills, Steele, & Dovidio, 2007).

obvious that we are showing interest and friendliness—when it actually may not be all that obvious to our interaction partner. This perception sets up a vicious cycle—the other person doesn't seem to be reciprocating our friendly overtures, and, therefore, we aren't very keen on forming a friendship with him or her. These effects have been demonstrated in interactions between white Canadians and Native Canadians (Vorauer, 2005) and between white Canadians and Chinese participants (Vorauer & Sakamoto, 2006). Low-prejudice people are most likely to overestimate the friendliness they've shown, leading to the counterintuitive result that their interactions with out-group members are actually more negative than those of high-prejudice people.

Thus, although it may seem obvious that the first step toward reducing prejudice would be to bring members of different groups into contact with one another, it isn't as easy as it may seem. In his strikingly prescient masterwork, *The Nature of Prejudice*, Gordon Allport stated the contact hypothesis in this way:

> Prejudice may be reduced by equal status contact between majority and minority groups in the pursuit of common goals. The effect is greatly enhanced if this contact is sanctioned by institutional supports (i.e., by law, custom or local atmosphere), and provided it is of a sort that leads to the perception of common interests and common humanity between members of the two groups. (Allport, 1954)

In other words, Allport is not talking about mere contact; he is clear that contact must be between people who are of equal status and in pursuit of common goals. Four decades of research have substantiated Allport's early claim that these conditions must be met before contact will lead to a decrease in prejudice between groups (Cook, 1985). Let's now turn to a discussion of these conditions.

Two of the key factors in the success of contact are *mutual interdependence* and a *common goal* (Amir, 1969, 1976). We have already seen the importance of these factors when discussing Sherif and colleagues' (1961) classic study of cooperation between hostile groups of Boy Scouts at a summer camp.

The third condition is *equal status*. At the boys' camp (Sherif et al., 1961), the group members were very much the same in terms of status and power. When status is unequal, however, interactions can easily follow stereotypical patterns: The bosses will act like stereotypical bosses, the employees will act like stereotypical subordinates—and no one will learn new, disconfirming information about the other group (Pettigrew, 1969; Wilder, 1984). The whole point of contact is to allow people to learn that their stereotypes are inaccurate; contact and interaction should lead to disconfirmation of negative stereotyped beliefs.

Fourth, contact must occur in a *friendly, informal setting*, where in-group members can interact with out-group members on a one-to-one basis (Brewer & Miller, 1984; Cook, 1984; Wilder, 1986). Simply placing two groups in contact in a room where they can remain segregated will do little to promote their understanding or knowledge of one another.

Fifth, through friendly, informal interactions *with multiple members* of the out-group, an individual will learn that his or her beliefs about the out-group are wrong. It is crucial for the individual to believe that the out-group members he or she comes to know are typical of their group; otherwise, the stereotype can be maintained by labelling one out-group member as the exception (Wilder, 1984).

Sixth and last, contact is most likely to lead to reduced prejudice when *social norms that promote and support equality* among groups are operating in the situation (Amir, 1969; Wilder, 1984). We know the power of social norms; here, they can be harnessed to motivate people to reach out to members of the out-group. If the boss in a work setting, or the professor in a classroom, creates and reinforces a norm of acceptance and tolerance, group members will modify their own behaviour to fit the norm.

To sum up, suspicious or even hostile groups will reduce their stereotyping, prejudice, and discriminatory behaviour when these six conditions of contact are met: mutual interdependence; a common goal; equal status; informal, interpersonal contact; multiple contacts; and social norms of equality (Aronson & Bridgeman, 1979; Cook, 1984; Riordan, 1978).

> *We must recognize that beneath the superficial classification of sex and race the same potentialities exist, recurring generation after generation only to perish because society has no place for them.*
>
> —Margaret Mead, Male and Female, 1943

Cooperation and Interdependence: The Jigsaw Classroom

Let's paint a scenario. Imagine a grade 6 student of Mexican origin, whom we will call Carlos. Carlos has been attending schools in an underprivileged neighbourhood for his entire life. Because the schools in his neighbourhood were not well equipped or well staffed, his first five years of education were somewhat deficient. Suddenly, without much warning or preparation, he is bused to a school in a predominantly white, middle-class neighbourhood. Carlos must now compete against white, middle-class students ho have had better preparation than he has had, and who have been reared to hold white, middle-class values, which include working hard in pursuit of good grades, raising one's hand enthusiastically whenever the teacher asks a question, and so on. In effect, Carlos has been thrust into a highly competitive situation for which he is unprepared and in which payoffs are made for abilities he has not yet developed. The white kids might quickly conclude that Carlos is stupid, unmotivated, and sullen—just as they had suspected (Wilder & Shapiro, 1989). Moreover, Carlos might conclude that the white kids are arrogant showoffs. This is an example of the self-fulfilling prophecy we discussed earlier.

Is it possible to get white students and minority students to have equal status, be mutually dependent, and pursue common goals? One of the authors of this textbook (Elliot Aronson) got to find out. In 1971, the school system of Austin, Texas, was desegregated. Within a few weeks, the schools were in turmoil. African-American, white, and Mexican-American children were in open conflict; fistfights broke out between the various racial groups in the corridors and schoolyards. The school superintendent invited Elliot Aronson, who was then a professor at the University of Texas, to enter the system with the mandate to

jigsaw classroom

a classroom setting designed to reduce prejudice between children by placing them in small, desegregated groups and making each child dependent on the other children in the group to learn the course material and do well in the class

> ❝ Two are better than one because they have a good reward for their toil. For if they fail, one will lift up his fellow, but woe to him who is alone when he falls and has not another to lift him up. Again, if two lie together, they are warm; but how can one be warm alone? ❞
>
> —*Ecclesiastes 4:9–12*

do anything within reason to create a more harmonious environment. After spending a few days observing the dynamics of several classrooms, Aronson and his graduate students were strongly reminded of the situation that existed in Sherif and colleagues' (1961) camp experiment. With the findings of that study in mind, they developed a technique that created an interdependent classroom atmosphere, designed to encourage the students of various racial and ethnic groups to pursue common goals. They called it the **jigsaw classroom**, because it resembled the assembling of a jigsaw puzzle (Aronson, 1992; Aronson & Bridgeman, 1979; Aronson & Gonzalez, 1988; Aronson & Patnoe, 1997; Aronson, Stephan, Sikes, Blaney, & Snapp, 1978).

How the Jigsaw Classroom Works Students are placed in diverse six-person learning groups. The day's lesson is divided into six paragraphs, so that each student has one segment of the written material. For example, if the students are to learn about the life of Mother Teresa, her biography is arranged in six parts; each student has possession of a unique and vital part of the information, which, like the pieces of a jigsaw puzzle, must be put together before anyone can learn the whole picture. The individual must learn his or her own section and teach it to the other members of the group who do not have any other access to that material. So, if Debbie wants to do well on the ensuing exam about the life of Mother Teresa, she must pay close attention to Carlos (who is reciting on Mother Teresa's childhood), to Natalie (who is reciting on Mother Teresa's humanitarian actions), and so on. Through the jigsaw process, the children begin to pay more attention to each other and to show respect for each other. As you might expect, a child like Carlos would respond to this treatment by simultaneously becoming more relaxed and more engaged; this would inevitably produce an improvement in his ability to communicate. And the other students would begin to realize that Carlos is a lot smarter than they thought he was. They begin to like him. Carlos begins to enjoy school more; his academic performance begins to improve and so does his self-esteem. The vicious circle has been broken.

The formal data that Aronson and his colleagues gathered from the jigsaw experiments were clear and striking. Compared with students in traditional classrooms, students in jigsaw groups showed a decrease in prejudice and stereotyping, as well as an increase in their liking for their group mates, both within and across ethnic boundaries. In addition, children in the jigsaw classrooms performed better on objective exams, liked school more, and showed a significantly greater increase in self-esteem than did children in traditional classrooms. Moreover, children in schools where the jigsaw technique was practised developed a greater ability to empathize with others and showed substantial evidence of true integration—that is, in the schoolyard there was far more intermingling among the various races and ethnic groups than in the yards of schools using more traditional classroom techniques (Aronson & Bridgeman, 1979).

The jigsaw approach was first tested in 1971; since then, several similar cooperative techniques have been developed (Cook, 1985; Johnson & Johnson, 1987, 1989; Meier, 1995; Sharan, 1980; Slavin, 1980, 1996). The striking results described above have been successfully replicated in thousands of classrooms in all regions of the United States, and in other countries as well (Jürgen-Lohmann, Borsch, & Giesen, 2001). What began as a simple experiment in one school setting is slowly becoming an important force in the field of public education. Unfortunately, the operative word is *slowly*. The educational system, like all bureaucracies, tends to resist change. As the tragedies of the all-too-frequent school shootings illustrate, this slowness can have devastating consequences (Aronson, 2000).

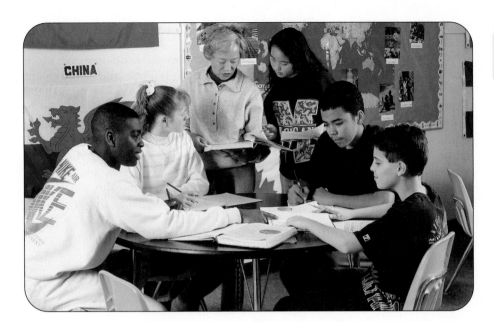

◀When the classroom is structured so students of various ethnic groups work together cooperatively, prejudice decreases.

The Extended Contact Hypothesis

We have seen that contact between groups can be highly effective in reducing prejudice. It isn't always possible, however, to have members of different groups interact, particularly under the "right" conditions—that is, where both groups meet the requirements of the contact hypothesis (mutual interdependence; a common goal; equal status; informal, interpersonal contact; multiple contacts; and social norms of equality). Fortunately, research on the **extended contact hypothesis** conducted by Simon Fraser University researcher Stephen Wright and his colleagues suggests that prejudice can be reduced simply by informing people that a member of their own group has a close relationship with an out-group member (e.g., Brody, Wright, Aron, McLaughlin-Volpe, 2009; Wright, Brody, & Aron, 2005; Wright, Aron, McLaughlin, & Ropp, 1997). Take a moment to think about a racial or ethnic group to which you do not belong. Then ask yourself how many people in your racial or ethnic group are friends with members of that group. Wright and colleagues have found that the greater the number of people in our group who have friendships with out-group members, the less prejudiced we are toward that group. These effects hold for both majority and minority groups.

These findings imply that prejudice between groups could be reduced by creating cross-group friendships and making members of each group aware of these friendships. Is that possible? Wright and colleagues (1997) decided to find out. In a fascinating study, they recreated Sherif and colleagues' (1961) summer camp study in which conflict was created between two groups of boys, except they did so in their laboratory. Here's how it worked. At the beginning of the four-day study, university students were assigned to either the blue group or the green group. Over the next few days, the groups engaged in activities that were designed to create conflict and hostility between them. Then, one member of each group was selected to participate in a supposedly unrelated experiment, which was actually a friendship-building exercise. Later, these participants were asked to describe the experience to their group. Remarkably, the discovery that one of the group members was now friends with the "enemy" caused the remaining group members to adopt more positive attitudes toward the out-group as a

extended contact hypothesis

the mere knowledge that a member of one's own group has a close relationship with a member of another group can reduce one's prejudice toward that group whole. They also became more generous to the out-group when allocating monetary rewards (Wright et al., 1997).

Other research by Wright, Aron, and colleagues confirms that the more friends you have in a particular out-group, the more positive your attitudes are toward their group as a whole. Moreover, the closer you are to these friends, the more you like the entire group (Brody et al., 2009; McLaughlin-Volpe, Aron, Wright, & Reis, 2000; Wright & van der Zande, 1999). These results are highly encouraging. The take-home message is that if you make the effort to become friends with a member of an out-group, it can have rather far-reaching effects. You are likely to feel more positively about the out-group as a whole. Moreover, as members of the groups to which you belong learn about this friendship, they will become less prejudiced toward that group. Thus, you alone truly can make a difference.

SUMMARY

Prejudice is a widespread phenomenon, present in all walks of life. Social psychologists define **prejudice** as a hostile or negative attitude toward a distinguishable group of people based solely on their group membership. A **stereotype** is the cognitive component of prejudice; it is defined as a generalization about a group whereby identical characteristics are assigned to virtually all members, regardless of actual variation among the members. **Discrimination**, the behavioural component of prejudice, is defined as unjustified negative or harmful action toward members of a group based on their membership in that group. As a broad-based and powerful attitude, prejudice has many causes. We discussed five aspects of social life that bring about prejudice: the way people think, the way people feel, the way people assign meaning or make attributions, the way people allocate resources, and the way people conform to social rules.

Social cognition processes (i.e., the way we think) are an important element in the creation and maintenance of stereotypes and prejudice. Categorization of people into groups leads to the formation of *in-groups* and *out-groups*. The **in-group bias** means that we treat members of our own group more positively than members of the out-group, as demonstrated by the research on minimal groups. The perception of **out-group homogeneity** is another consequence of categorization: In-group members perceive out-group members as being more similar to one another than the in-group members are to one another.

Stereotypes are widely known; even if you do not believe them, they can affect your cognitive processing of information about an out-group member. Recent research has shown that stereotypes can be selectively activated or inhibited, depending on motivational factors, most notably self-enhancement. The stereotypes that we believe out-groups hold of us, known as **meta-stereotypes**, also play a role in prejudice—we expect more negative interactions with, and show more prejudice toward, members of groups who we believe hold negative stereotypes of us.

Our emotions or moods also determine how prejudiced we are. When we are in a good mood, we are likely to evaluate members of out-groups more favourably than when we are in a

bad mood. In addition, the attributions we make can serve to perpetuate prejudice. We tend to attribute the negative behaviours of out-group members to internal, dispositional factors, rather than taking situational factors into account. This attributional tendency is known as the **ultimate attribution error**.

Realistic conflict theory states that prejudice is the inevitable by-product of real conflict between groups for limited resources, whether involving economics, power, or status. Competition for resources leads to derogation of and discrimination against the competing out-group.

Finally, we learn the appropriate norms of our culture, including stereotypes and prejudices. The desire to be accepted and fit in leads us to go along with stereotyped beliefs rather than to challenge them. People who are high in **modern prejudice** tend to be prejudiced but aren't willing to admit it because current social norms suggest that these kinds of prejudice are no longer acceptable.

Several individual difference variables are associated with prejudice. Those who are high in right-wing authoritarianism, religious fundamentalism, and social dominance are more likely to be prejudiced against out-groups than are those who are low in these traits.

Prejudice, stereotyping, and discrimination can have devastating effects on their targets. Research on *self-fulfilling prophecies* suggests that we may unknowingly create stereotypical behaviour in out-group members through our treatment of them. Members of an out-group also may experience **stereotype threat**—a fear that they will behave in a manner that confirms an existing stereotype about their group. Individuals who are targets of prejudice also may disengage their self-esteem from their performance feedback, such that receiving positive or negative feedback has no effect on their self-esteem. This process of disengagement can ultimately lead to **disidentification**, the process by which targets of negative stereotypes redefine their self-concept so that the performance domain is no longer central to their identity. There is also evidence that targets of discrimination may blame themselves for their poor performance as a means of preserving social self-esteem or the perception of control, or to avoid being labelled as "complainers."

Finally, on a societal level, the most important question to be asked is: How can prejudice be reduced? One approach is to nip it in the bud by teaching children not to be prejudiced. Another effective way of reducing prejudice is through contact— bringing in-group and out-group members together; mere contact, however, is not enough and can even exacerbate the existing negative attitudes. Instead, according to the *contact hypothesis*, contact situations must include the following conditions: **mutual** **interdependence**; a common goal; equal status; informal, interpersonal contact; multiple contacts; and social norms of equality. The **jigsaw classroom**, a learning atmosphere in which children must depend on each other and work together to learn and to reach a common goal, has been found to be a powerful way to reduce stereotyping and prejudice among children of different ethnicities. Finally, research on the **extended contact hypothesis** has shown that the mere knowledge that a member of an in-group is friends with an out-group member can reduce prejudice toward that group.

PEARSON
mypsychlab

Along with a dynamic, electronic version of this text, MyPsychLab offers a wealth of resources to deepen your understanding and test your recall of the material in this chapter—including video and audio clips, simulations and activities, self-assessments, practice tests, and other study materials. The following specific resources are available for this chapter:

 Unconscious Stereotyping

 Prejudice

 We versus They: Robert Cialdini

To access MyPsychLab, please visit www.mypsychlab.com (Student Access Code required—packaged with this book).

Social Psychology
in Action 1

Social Psychology and the Environment

The news is full of stories about countries wreaking havoc on the environment. The destruction of the rainforests in Brazil, industrial pollution in China—the list goes on and on. Which region do you think is considered "one of the world's top environmental hot zones" by the United Nations? It may surprise you to learn that the answer is Alberta's tar sands. This region of northern Alberta has become a hotbed of energy production, mining bitumen, an oil product, from the tar sands that span a vast area along the Athabasca River. In fact, the tar sands project is considered to be the largest energy project in the world. One of the resources that is being expended in order to produce bitumen is natural gas, which accounts for 60 percent of the operating costs of the tar sands projects. Andrew Nikiforuk, author of *Tar Sands: Dirty Oil and the Future of a Continent*, reports that "using natural gas to melt a resource as dirty as bitumen, is, as one executive said, like 'burning a Picasso for heat'" (Nikiforuk, 2008, p. 15). Wasted natural gas is not the only cost. The production of each barrel of bitumen requires three barrels of fresh water from the Athabasca River. Ninety percent of that water ends up in what is known as the tailing ponds—one of the world's largest collections of toxic waste. The death of ducks on the tailing ponds, located along the Athabaska River, is one of the consequences, but the effects are more widespread. According to a report released by the University of Toronto's Munk Centre in October 2008, the environmental impact of Alberta's tar sands will not be limited to Western Canada, but will extend all the way to the Great Lakes, threatening water and air quality around the world's largest body of fresh water (Mittelstaedt, 2008). Toxins from the tailing ponds are seeping into groundwater that serves nearby communities. Over the last 10 years, rare cancers have been documented among residents of Fort Chipewyan, a community downstream from the tailing ponds. Dr. John O'Connor, a family physician in the area, was concerned that these cancers were the result of toxins in the environment, and in December 2006, he issued a health warning. Government officials from Health Canada responded by filing a complaint with the Alberta College of Physicians and Surgeons, accusing the doctor of raising "undue alarm."

O'Connor was then called before the registrar of the College of Physicians and Surgeons to defend himself against these charges. He never anticipated that speaking out about his concerns would result in a career-threatening struggle that could cost him his medical licence.

A series of government studies has concluded that there is no need to be alarmed about the health effects of the tar sands project. However, quite a different conclusion was drawn by an Alberta ecologist and statistician, Kevin Timoney, who released an independent report in November 2007. According to Timoney, "The findings of my study indicate that there is cause for concern in that there are contaminants in the food supply that are associated with . . . types of cancer observed in the community. Certainly, these contaminants come from tar sands" (as quoted in De Souza, 2007).

Imagine living in an area described as Canada's worst toxic waste site and hearing that people who live where you do show particularly high rates of cancer. How would this affect you? Sadly, the residents of Fort Chepewyan are not the only Canadians in this type of circumstance. Residents of Nova Scotia living near the Sydney tar ponds have faced such a situation for years. For nearly a century, emissions and waste products from Sydney's Sysco steel plant have been dumped there. There are high levels of carcinogenic materials in this hazardous toxic site. To find out how people are affected by living in such an environment, researchers at the University College of Cape Breton interviewed junior high school students attending a school near the tar ponds (O'Leary & Covell, 2002). These adolescents reported worrying about environmental issues and about their own health and that of their families—more so than students attending a school 40 kilometres away. Worse still, the adolescents who worried most about health showed the highest level of depression. (Overall, depression levels were higher than the national average among both groups of adolescents. The researchers suggest that even the students who lived 40 kilometres away may have felt affected by this environmental hazard.)

Clearly, even among 12- to 14-year-olds, living in a toxic environment creates stress. A study conducted with two communities in Ontario found that even nonhazardous landfill sites create stress and reduce well-being among residents (Wakefield & Elliott, 2000). These researchers found that decision-making processes (e.g., whether or not the government allowed public input, divisions in the community over the effects of the site) often created as much stress as the final outcome.

In short, it is clear that Canada's physical environment is being harmed in multiple ways, and it is taking a toll on the planet's inhabitants. However, as long as people continue to consume massive amounts of energy, projects such as Alberta's tar sands will go on. Changes in attitudes and behaviour are urgently needed to avoid environmental catastrophe. Social psychologists have studied a number of techniques involving social influence and social interaction that encourage people to behave in more environmentally sound ways (Geller, 2002; Oskamp, 1995; Sundstrom, Bell, Busby, & Asmus, 1996; Vining & Ebreo, 2002). We turn to these now.

Applied Research in Social Psychology

Since its inception, the field of social psychology has been interested in applying what it knows to solve practical problems. Kurt Lewin (1946), generally recognized as the founder of empirical social psychology, made three key points:

- Social psychological questions are best tested with the experimental method.
- These studies can be used to understand basic psychological processes and to develop theories about social influence.
- Social psychological theories and methods can be used to address pressing social problems.

If you've read the first 12 chapters of this book, you know a lot about these points—especially the first two. In Chapter 2 you read about the importance of using the experimental method to test causal hypotheses, and in subsequent chapters you read about numerous social psychological experiments and how they have increased our understanding of important theoretical questions, such as how people think about themselves and the social world, respond to social influence, change their attitudes, and help and hurt their fellow humans.

These topics dealt directly with important applied issues, such as bullying, racism, bystander intervention, and decision making. To many of us in the field, the beauty of social psychology is that by its very nature it addresses both basic and applied questions about human behaviour. Research on stereotyping and prejudice, for example, investigates basic theoretical questions about the ways in which people form impressions of each other, as well as applied questions about how stereotyping and prejudice might be reduced.

As we discussed in Chapter 2, though, a distinction can still be made between *basic research*, which is concerned primarily with theoretical issues, and *applied research*, which is concerned primarily with addressing specific real-world problems. Although much of the research we have discussed so far has touched on practical problems, it falls squarely in the category of basic research. As Kurt Lewin (1951) said, "There is nothing so practical as a good theory," by which he meant that to solve difficult social problems, we must first understand the underlying psychological dynamics of human nature and social influence. Increasingly, though, social psychologists are conducting studies designed specifically to address practical problems. In fact, social psychologists are better equipped than many other disciplines to study applied problems, for reasons we now discuss.

Capitalizing on the Experimental Method

One of the most important lessons of social psychology is the value of conducting experiments to answer questions about social influence. Nowhere is this more important than in finding ways to solve applied questions, such as getting people to reduce energy consumption. Only by conducting experiments (as opposed to observational or correlational studies; see Chapter 2) can we hope to discover which solutions will work the best.

Most people seem to understand this lesson in other domains, such as research on medical treatments. Suppose that a chemist found a new compound that seems to be an effective pain killer—the initial studies with rats look very promising, but studies on humans have not yet been conducted. Should we allow a drug company to go ahead and market the drug to people? Not so fast, most of us would think. Who knows how safe the drug is for humans? It might turn out to have dangerous side effects, as seems to have been the case with Vioxx. There should be extensive clinical trials in humans, in which people are randomly assigned to receive the new drug or a placebo, to see whether it really does reduce pain, and whether it has any serious side effects. Indeed, federal law requires extensive testing and approval before drugs become available to the public.

We have laxer standards when it comes to testing psychological and social "treatments." If someone wants to try a new energy conservation technique, a new educational initiative, or a program to reduce prejudice, they can usually do so without a lot of rigorous testing of the intervention. A company might try a new program to reduce energy usage or institute a mandatory diversity training program, for example, before such techniques have been tested experimentally.

Well, you might think, what's the harm? Trying a new energy conservation program hardly puts people at risk, and we certainly don't want to inhibit innovation by subjecting people to cumbersome testing guidelines. And can't we find out whether these interventions work by interviewing people afterward or seeing whether their behaviour changes (e.g., do they use less energy after the conservation program)? Unfortunately, the solution not so simple. It is difficult to test the effectiveness of an intervention in the absence of a randomly assigned control group, and failing to conduct such tests can have serious consequences.

Consider interventions such as Critical Incident Stress Debriefing, a therapeutic procedure in which therapists are brought in immediately following natural disasters, terrorist attacks, plane crashes, or other traumas. For example, following the September 11, 2001, terrorist attacks, 9000 counsellors were rushed to New York City to carry out critical incident debriefing. This intervention involves encouraging survivors of traumatic events to open up and talk about the trauma. The idea is that by intervening immediately, counsellors decrease the likelihood that survivors will experience post-traumatic stress disorder. Makes sense, doesn't it? Indeed, people who have undergone critical incident debriefing claim that it helped them. So why bother doing research on the effectiveness of this intervention? Well, it turns out that when controlled experiments have been conducted (in which some people are randomly assigned to undergo critical incident debriefing and others are not), the results are not so encouraging. According to a recent review of the literature by Harvard psychologist Richard McNally and his colleagues (2003), there is "no convincing evidence" that psychological debriefing techniques prevent post-traumatic stress disorder (McNally, Bryant, & Ehlers, 2003, p. 72). Moreover, these researchers found that in some studies, having people focus on the trauma and talk about it right after it happened actually made things worse. Based on findings such as these, McNally and colleagues concluded that critical incident debriefing may actually "impede natural recovery" (p. 72) and went on to recommend that "for scientific and ethical reasons, professionals should cease compulsory debriefing of trauma-exposed people (p. 72). Thus, quite a different picture emerges when carefully controlled experiments on the effectiveness of critical incident debriefing are conducted.

▲ Following the September 11, 2001, terrorist attacks, more than 9000 counsellors rushed to New York City to help survivors deal with the trauma and stress and prevent post-traumatic stress disorder.

Social Psychology to the Rescue

Social psychologists are in a unique position to find solutions to applied problems, such as whether the widespread practice of critical incident debriefing is effective or possibly even harmful. First, the field of social psychology is a rich source of theories about human behaviour that people can draw on to devise solutions to social problems. Second, of equal importance, social psychologists know how to perform rigorous experimental tests of these solutions to see if they work (Wilson, 2005).

We return now to the issue with which we began this chapter—namely, how to get people to act in environmentally responsible ways.

Using Social Psychology to Achieve a Sustainable Future

Social psychologists have adopted a variety of approaches to try to get people to behave in more environmentally responsible ways. What these approaches have in common is that they are inspired by social psychological theories and they use the experimental method to evaluate whether the approach is effective (Abrahmse, Steg, & Vlek, 2005; Geller, 2002; Oskamp, 1995, 2000).

Resolving Social Dilemmas

Be honest: When you think about the topic of energy conservation, how do you feel? If you are like us, you know that you should conserve energy and reduce CO_2 emissions, but the prospect of changing habits doesn't seem very appealing. It involves personal sacrifice, such as using our cars less, turning down the thermostat in winter and the air conditioner in summer, and buying fewer consumer

"Help!"

goods. "Why should I be the one to do these things," you might think, "when I see plenty of other people driving SUVs, heating and cooling their houses with abandon, and buying stuff they don't really need?"

Good question. What we have here is a classic **social dilemma**. As we discussed in Chapter 8, a social dilemma is a conflict in which the most beneficial action for an individual will, if chosen by most people, have a harmful effect on everyone. It is in everyone's self-interest to use as much energy as he or she wants; after all, one person's contribution to global warming is minuscule. But if we all adopt that attitude, we will all suffer the consequences.

Of particular relevance to energy conservation is a type of social dilemma called the *commons dilemma*, a situation in which everyone takes from a common pool of goods that will replenish itself if used in moderation but will disappear if overused. Examples include the use of limited resources such as water and energy. Individuals benefit by using as much as they need, but if everyone does so, shortages result (Dawes, 1980; Kortenkamp & Moore, 2001; Levine & Moreland, 1998; Pruitt, 1998; Sibley & Liu, 2003; Weber, Kopelman, & Messick, 2004).

To give an example, Canada's National Parks face the dilemma of development for tourism, which potentially could destroy the very beauty that tourists are coming to see. Edgar Jackson (1987) found that people's views on preservation of land versus development of land for recreational purposes depended on the kinds of recreational activities they engaged in. In a survey conducted with residents of Calgary and Edmonton, he found that people who performed mechanized (e.g., snowmobiling) and consumptive (e.g., fishing) recreational activities more strongly favoured development. Those who preferred activities such as canoeing or hiking more strongly favoured preservation of the environment.

How can we resolve social dilemmas and persuade people to act for the greater good of everyone, rather than purely out of self-interest? Social psychologists have devised some fascinating laboratory games to try to answer this question. Imagine you arrive for a study and discover that there are six other participants you have never met. The experimenter gives you and the other participants $6 and says that each of you can keep the money. There is, however, another option. Each person can donate his or her money to the rest of the group, to be divided equally among the six other members. If anyone does so, the experimenter will double

social dilemma

a conflict in which the most beneficial action for an individual will, if chosen by most people, have a harmful effect on everyone

> ❝ The earth we abuse and the living things we kill, in the end, take their revenge; for in exploiting their presences we are diminishing our future. ❞
>
> —Marya Mannes, 1958

TABLE SPA1.1

Amount of money you stand to win in the Orbell, van de Kragt, and Dawes (1988) experiment

You can either keep your $6 or donate it to the six other group members. If you donate it, the money will be doubled, so that each group member will receive $2. Most people who play this game want to keep their money to maximize their own gains. The more people who keep their money, however, the more everyone loses.

Other People's Decisions:	6 Keep, 0 Give	5 Keep, 1 Gives	4 Keep, 2 Give	3 Keep, 3 Give	2 Keep, 4 Give	1 Keeps, 5 Give	0 Keep 6 Give
Your Decision							
Keep your $6	$6	$8	$10	$12	$14	$16	$18
Give your $6	$0	$2	$4	$6	$8	$10	$12

(Adapted from Orbell, van de Kragt, & Dawes, 1988)

the contribution. For example, if you donate your money, it will be doubled to $12 and divided evenly among the six other participants. If other group members donate their money to the pot, it will be doubled and you will get a share.

Think about the dilemma you face. If everyone (including you) cooperates by donating his or her money to the group, once it is doubled and divided up, your share will be $12—double what you started with. Donating your money is risky, however; if you are the only one who does so, you will end up with nothing, while having increased everyone else's winnings (see Table SPA1.1). Clearly, the most selfish—and safest—course of action is to keep your money, hoping that everyone else donates theirs. That way, you would make up to $18—your $6 plus your share of the money everyone else threw into the pot. Of course, if everyone thinks this way, you'll make only $6, because no one will donate any money to the group.

If you are like most of the participants in the actual study, you would keep your six bucks (Orbell, van de Kragt, & Dawes, 1988). After all, as you can see in Table SPA1.1, you will always earn more money by keeping what you have than by giving it away (i.e., the winnings in the top row of Table SPA1.1 are always higher than the winnings in the bottom row). The only problem with this strategy is that because most people adopt it, everyone suffers. That is, the total pool of money to be divided remains low, because few people donate to the group, which would allow the experimenter to double the money. As with many social dilemmas, most people look out for themselves, and as a result, everyone loses.

How can people be persuaded to trust their fellow group members, cooperating in such a way that everyone benefits? It is notoriously difficult to resolve social dilemmas, as indicated by the effort required to get people to conserve water when there are droughts, recycle their waste goods, clean up a common area in a dormitory or apartment, or reduce the use of pesticides and thereby lower the production level and visual appeal of produce. In another condition of the experiment discussed, the researchers discovered an intriguing result: Simply allowing the group to talk together for 10 minutes dramatically increased the number of members who donated money to the group—from 38 percent to 79 percent (Orbell et al., 1988).

Communication works in two ways. First, when people make a public commitment to help, they are more likely to follow through. If people can take the selfish route privately, undiscovered by their peers, they will often do so. However, if their actions are public, the kinds of normative pressures we discussed in Chapter 7 come into play, making people's behaviour more consistent with group norms. For example, Scott (1999) found that residents of the Greater Toronto Area recycled a higher number of products when they felt social pressure to do so. As one respondent remarked, "[people] feel they have to because

▶ When people can communicate with each other, they are more likely to act for the social good rather than selfishly. Communication works in two ways. First, when people make a public commitment to help, it is harder to back down. Second, when people communicate, they are more likely to establish a sense of group identity and solidarity, which makes them more likely to act for the good of the group.

their neighbours put out a blue box." There is another way in which communication works: When people communicate, they are more likely to establish a sense of group identity or solidarity, which makes them more likely to act for the good of the group (Weber, Kopelman, & Messick, 2004).

The finding that communication works is encouraging, but it may be limited to small groups that are able to communicate face to face. What happens when an entire community is caught in a social dilemma? When large groups are involved, alternative approaches are needed.

Conveying and Changing Social Norms

One approach is to remind people of social norms: the rules a group has for the acceptable behaviours, values, and beliefs of its members (see Chapter 7). People follow two kinds of social norms: **injunctive norms**, which are people's perceptions of the behaviour that is approved or disapproved of by others, and **descriptive norms**, which are people's perceptions of how others actually behave (Cialdini, 2003).

Robert Cialdini and his colleagues have illustrated the power of social norms in persuading people to stop engaging in behaviours that harm the environment, such as littering, stealing wood from national park forests, and laundering towels after a single use (Cialdini, Kallgren, & Reno, 1991; Cialdini, Reno, & Kallgren, 1990; Griskevicius, Cialdini, & Goldstein, 2008; Kallgren, Reno, & Cialdini, 2000). Compared with other environmental problems, littering may not seem all that serious a matter. Many people think that it isn't a big deal to toss their paper cup on the side of the road instead of putting it in a garbage can (or even better, a recycling bin!). Unfortunately, those paper cups add up. For example, in the state of California, each year $41 million is spent cleaning up litter ("Litter Bugs," 2005). The stuff we discard is polluting North American water systems, endangering wildlife, and costing millions of dollars.

How can people be persuaded not to litter? Reno, Cialdini, and Kallgren (1993) conducted a field experiment to investigate the power of injunctive norms. As people left a local library and approached their cars in the parking lot, a confederate walked by them, picked up a fast-food bag that had been discarded on the ground, and put the bag in the trash. In a control condition, no bag was on the ground, and the confederate

injunctive norms

people's perceptions of the behaviour that is approved or disapproved of by others

descriptive norms

people's perceptions of how other people actually behave in a given situation, regardless of whether the behaviour is approved or disapproved of by others

❝ *We live in an environment whose principal product is garbage.* ❞

—*Russell Baker, 1968*

Try it!

▶ Reducing Littering Using Injunctive Norms

See if you can get people to pick up litter by invoking injunctive norms, using the techniques discovered by Reno, Cialdini, and Kallgren (1993). This exercise is easier to do with a friend who can unobtrusively observe if people litter. Here's how it works:

Find an environment in which people are likely to litter. In the psychology building at one of our universities, for example, the place where people pick up the student newspaper would be appropriate. The paper often comes with an advertising insert, and when people pick up the paper, they often discard the insert on the floor.

Next, plant a conspicuous piece of litter in this environment. Reno and colleagues (1993) used a fast-food bag stuffed with litter. Place it in a location where people are sure to see it, such as near a doorway.

In one condition, wait until an individual enters the environment and is in full view of the piece of trash you have planted. Then, pick up the trash, throw it away, and go on your way. It is critical that the person realizes it wasn't your bag but that you decided to pick it up and throw it away anyway. In a second condition, walk by the trash, glance at it, and continue on your way without picking it up.

The observer should watch to see whether people litter; for example, whether they throw the paper's advertising insert on the floor or put it in a garbage can or recycling bin.

Reno, Cialdini, and Kallgren (1993) found that when people saw someone pick up another person's litter, they were much less likely to litter themselves. Did you replicate this effect? Why or why not?

simply walked by the library patrons. When the patrons got to their car, they found a pamphlet on their windshield. The question was how many of these people would litter by throwing the pamphlet on the ground. Reno and colleagues hypothesized that seeing the confederate pick up the fast-food bag would be a vivid reminder of the injunctive norm—littering is bad, and other people disapprove of it—and hence would reduce the participant's own inclination to litter. They were right. In this condition, only 7 percent of the people tossed the pamphlet on the ground, compared with 37 percent in the control condition. If you would like to try to replicate this effect in an experiment of your own, see the accompanying Try It! box.

What is the best way to communicate *descriptive norms* against littering? The most straightforward way, it would seem, would be to clean up all of the litter in an environment to illustrate that "no one litters here." In general, this is true. The less litter an environment has, the less likely people are to litter (Huffman, Grossnickle, Cope & Huffman, 1995; Reiter & Samuel, 1980). There is, however, an interesting exception to this finding. Cialdini and colleagues (1990) figured that seeing one conspicuous piece of litter on the ground, spoiling an otherwise clean environment, would be a better reminder of descriptive norms than seeing a completely clean environment. The single piece of trash sticks out like a sore thumb, reminding people that no one has littered here—except for one thoughtless person. In comparison, if there is no litter on the ground, people might not even think about the descriptive norm. Ironically, then, littering may be more likely to occur in a totally clean environment than in one containing a single piece of litter.

To test this hypothesis, the researchers stuffed students' mailboxes with brochures and then observed, from a hidden vantage point, how many of the students dropped them on the floor (Cialdini, Reno, & Kallgren, 1990). In one condition, the researchers cleaned up the mailroom so there were no other pieces of litter to be seen. In another condition, they placed one very noticeable piece of litter on the floor—a hollowed-out piece of watermelon. In a third condition, they not only put the watermelon rind on the floor but also spread out dozens of discarded brochures. As predicted, the lowest rate of littering occurred in the

▶ Besides being unsightly, litter can cost millions of dollars to clean up. Social psychologists have found that emphasizing various kinds of social norms against littering is an effective way to prevent it.

condition where there was a single piece of litter on the floor (see Figure SPA1.1). The single violation of a descriptive norm highlighted the fact that no one had littered except the one idiot who had dropped the watermelon rind. Now that people's attention was focused on the descriptive norm against littering, virtually none of the students littered. The highest percentage of littering occurred when the floor was littered with many brochures; here, it was clear that there was a descriptive norm in favour of littering, and many of the students followed suit.

In more recent research, Cialdini and colleagues have tested whether descriptive norms can be used to encourage hotel patrons to re-use their towels (Goldstein, Cialdini, & Griskevicius, 2008). This behaviour not only saves water but also reduces energy consumption and the use of toxic chemicals (e.g., detergents, bleaches). Specifically, the researchers posted signs in hotel rooms urging guests to re-use their towels. In addition, the signs focused on the benefits to the environment ("Help save the environment") or invoked a descriptive norm ("Almost 75% of guests who are asked to participate in our new resource savings program do help by using towels more than once"). It turned out that the use of a descriptive norm was the most effective—a significantly greater number of guests re-used their towels in this condition than in the "save the environment" condition. Thus, something as simple as telling people that others are performing pro-environment behaviours can promote positive social change.

FIGURE SPA1.1

Descriptive norms and littering

Who littered the least—people who saw that no one else had littered, people who saw one piece of litter on the floor, or people who saw several pieces of litter? As shown in the figure, it was people who saw one piece of litter. Seeing the single piece of litter was most likely to draw people's attention to the fact that most people had not littered, making participants less likely to litter themselves.

(Adapted from Cialdini, Reno, & Kallgren, 1990)

What happens when there are no norms for acting in environmentally responsible ways, or are even norms for behaving in the opposite manner? In this situation, the first step is to change the norm. This isn't always easy, of course, but sometimes people underestimate what they can do to change injunctive norms, particularly if they are high status members of a group. Suppose, for example, that you are a member of a fraternity or sorority in which many people drive gas-guzzling SUVs. Perhaps that is the vehicle of choice for you and your peers; maybe it's even a sign of status and prestige. No one likes to "break the rules," and though you might have been thinking about trading in your Jeep Grand Cherokee for a car with a hybrid engine like the Toyota Prius, you worry about what your friends will say.

Often, though, people overestimate the strength of an injunctive norm—for example, how much our friends would really care if we traded in our SUV. Several studies have shown that university students tend to overestimate other injunctive norms, such as what their friends think about drinking alcohol. Many college students believe that their peers are more in favour of drinking than they actually are (Borsari & Carey, 2005). The same might be true about cars—other people in your social group might be thinking about getting more fuel-efficient cars, but are reluctant to say so.

Even if your friends would look disparagingly at your purchase of a Toyota Prius, someone has to be the first to change an injunctive norm. As we saw in Chapter 7, it is easier to buck the tide if we can get just one other person to go along with us, so you might first try to convince a friend who is looking to buy a car to consider a hybrid. If this doesn't work, just go for it. You might be surprised by how much you alone can change a norm, especially if you keep reminding people how much you are saving on gas, and that SUVs are not nearly as safe as people think they are (Gladwell, 2004).

Making It Easy to Keep Track of Energy Consumption

A problem with some environmental social dilemmas is that it is not easy for people to keep track of how much of a resource they are using, such as water or electricity. During a drought, for example, people may be asked to conserve water, but it is not easy for them to monitor how many litres a day they are using. One pair of researchers reasoned that making it easy for people to keep track of their water use would make it easier for them to act on their concern for the greater good (Van Vugt & Samuelson, 1999). They compared two communities in the Hampshire region of England during a severe drought in the summer of 1995. The houses in one community had been equipped with water meters that allowed residents to monitor how much water they were consuming. The houses in the other community did not have meters. As expected, when people felt that the water shortage was severe, those in the metered houses consumed less water than those in the unmetered houses. Further, there was evidence that they did so not purely out of self-interest (i.e., using less water would save money) but also out of concern for the collective good. Similar results have been found in studies that make it easier for people to keep track of how much electricity they are using (Abrahamse, Steg, Vlek, & Rothengatter, 2005). Thus, one simple way to resolve an environmental social dilemma is to make it easier for people to monitor their consumption, which in turn makes it easier for them to act on their good intentions (Van Vugt, 2001). Nowadays, some cars display on the dashboard the current gas mileage the car is getting; we suspect that this alone will make people try to achieve better mileage or even drive their cars less.

Making Energy Loss Vivid

Historically, we have felt perfectly content using as much energy as we needed, assuming that the planet had an infinite supply of wood, oil, natural gas, and electrical power. Indeed, according to research conducted with geography students at the University of Alberta, people favour the continued exploitation of such resources, with less support for the idea of energy conservation, development of solar power, and other alternatives (Jackson, 1985). To this day, Alberta continues to be one of the provinces most strongly opposed to the energy-conservation measures proposed in the Kyoto Accord. Regardless of one's views on this particular agreement, one thing is clear: There is not an unlimited supply of resources.

Can people be motivated to engage in energy conservation? Let's take private homes as an example. Through simple measures such as increasing ceiling, wall, and floor insulation; plugging air leaks; using more efficient light bulbs; and properly maintaining furnaces, the typical energy consumer could reduce the amount of energy used to heat, light, and cool his or her home by 30 percent to 75 percent (Williams & Ross, 1980). The technology needed to increase energy efficiency currently exists and is well within the financial means of most homeowners. This technology would not only save energy but also save the individual homeowner a great deal of money. Indeed, when McKenzie-Mohr, Nemiroff, Beers, and Desmarais (1995) interviewed residents of British Columbia, they found that both environmental concerns and cost-saving concerns predicted the use of energy-saving devices such as compact fluorescent bulbs and programmable thermostats. However, despite the fact that the societal and financial advantages of conservation have been well publicized, the vast majority of homeowners have not taken action. How come? Why have North Americans been slow to act in a manner that is in their economic self-interest? This lack of compliance has perplexed economists and policy makers, because they have failed to see that the issue is partly a social psychological one.

In Chapter 4, we noted that people's attention is typically directed to the aspects of their environment that are conspicuous and vivid. Elliot Aronson and his colleagues (Aronson, 1990; Aronson & Yates, 1985; Coltrane, Archer, & Aronson, 1986) reasoned that energy conservation in the home is not a particularly vivid problem, so people do not spend much time thinking about it. The bill for natural gas and electricity comes only once a month and is spread out over dozens of appliances; thus, the homeowner has no clear idea of which of the many appliances is using the most energy. It is as if you were buying food in a grocery store where the prices of individual items weren't marked and you were billed a lump sum at the end of the month. How would you know what to do to save money on your purchases? Perhaps if the sources of energy consumption were made more vivid, people would take action.

To test this hypothesis, Aronson and his colleagues (Aronson & Gonzales, 1990; Gonzales, Aronson, & Costanzo, 1988) worked with several energy auditors in California. As in many U.S. states, California utility companies offer a free service wherein an auditor will come to people's homes and give them a customized assessment of what needs to be done to make their homes more energy-efficient. What a deal! The problem was that fewer than 20 percent of the individuals requesting audits actually followed the auditors' recommendations.

To increase compliance, the Aronson research team trained the auditors to present their findings in a more vivid manner. For example, let's consider weather stripping. For most people, a small crack under the door didn't seem like a huge drain of energy, so when an auditor told them they should put in some weather stripping, they thought, "Yeah, big deal." Aronson and his colleagues told the auditors to make this statement more vivid:

> If you were to add up all the cracks around and under the doors of your home, you'd have the equivalent of a hole the size of a football in your living room wall. Think for a moment about all the heat that would escape from a hole that size. That's precisely why I'm recommending that you install weather stripping. (Gonzales et al., 1988, p. 1052)

Similar attempts were made to make other problems more vivid; for example, referring to an attic that lacks insulation as a "naked attic that is like facing winter not just without an overcoat, but without any clothing at all" (p. 1052).

The results were striking. The percentage of homeowners who followed the vivid recommendations jumped to 61 percent. This study demonstrates that people will, in fact, act in a manner that is sensible in terms of environmental goals and their own economic self-interest, but if old habits are involved, the communication must be one that is vivid enough to break through those established habits.

Introducing a Little Competitiveness

Other researchers have demonstrated that a little competitiveness helps people conserve energy (Staats, Harland, & Wilke, 2004). For example, in a study by Siero and colleagues (1996), employees at one unit of a factory in the Netherlands were urged to engage in energy-saving behaviour. Announcements were placed in the company magazine asking people to perform behaviours such as closing windows during cold weather and turning off lights when leaving a room. In addition, the employees received weekly feedback on their behaviour; graphs were posted that showed how much they had improved their energy-saving behaviour. This intervention resulted in modest improvement. By the end of the program, the number of times people left the lights on, for example, decreased by 27 percent (Siero, Bakker, Dekker, & van den Burg, 1996).

Another unit of the factory took part in an identical program, with one difference. In addition to receiving weekly feedback on their own energy-saving actions, they received feedback about how the other unit was doing. The researchers hypothesized that this social comparison information would motivate people to do better than their colleagues in the other unit. As seen in Figure SPA1.2, they were right: By the end of the program, the number of times people left the lights on had decreased by 61 percent. Clearly, engaging people's competitive spirit can have a significant impact on their behaviour.

Inducing Hypocrisy

In many areas of the world, water is becoming an increasingly scarce resource. One cause is population growth in areas that have limited water supplies. Another is droughts, which are becoming more frequent as the temperature of the earth rises. Thirty years ago, 10 percent to 15 percent of the earth was drought-stricken; today that figure is closer to 30 percent ("Drought's Growing Reach," 2005).

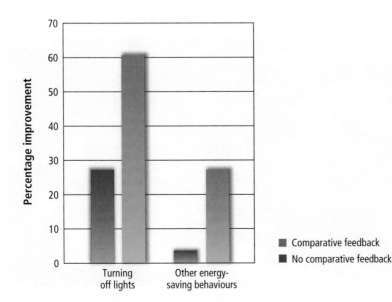

FIGURE SPA1.2

Effects of comparative feedback on energy-saving behaviour

Two units of a factory were urged to conserve energy, and then received feedback about how their unit was doing. Only one of the units, however, received comparative feedback about how they were doing relative to the other unit. As seen in the graph, workers in this second unit improved their behaviour the most, especially by turning off the lights more often.

(Adapted from Siero et al., 1996)

Several years ago, when California was experiencing severe water shortages, the administrators at one campus of the University of California realized that an enormous amount of water was being wasted by students using the university athletic facilities. The administrators posted signs in the shower rooms of the gymnasiums, exhorting students to conserve water by taking briefer, more efficient showers. The signs appealed to the students' conscience by urging them to take brief showers and to turn off the water while soaping up. The administrators were confident that the signs would be effective because the vast majority of students at this campus were ecology-minded and believed in preserving natural resources. However, systematic observation revealed that fewer than 15 percent of the students complied with the conservation message on the posted signs.

The administrators were puzzled—perhaps the majority of the students hadn't paid attention to the sign? After all, a sign on the wall is easy to ignore. So, administrators made each sign more obtrusive, putting it on a tripod at the entrance to the showers so the students needed to walk around the sign in order to get into the shower room. While this increased compliance slightly (19 percent turned off the shower while soaping up), it apparently made a great many students angry. The sign was continually being knocked over and kicked around, and a large percentage of students took inordinately *long* showers, apparently as a reaction against being told what to do. The sign was doing more harm than good, which puzzled the administrators even more. Time to call in the social psychologists.

Elliot Aronson and his students (Dickerson, Thibodeau, Aronson, & Miller, 1992) decided to apply the hypocrisy technique used successfully in an earlier study to increase condom purchases (see Chapter 6). The procedure involved intercepting female students who were on their way from the swimming pool to the women's shower room, introducing the experimental manipulations, and then having a research assistant casually follow them into the shower room, where the assistant unobtrusively timed their showers. Research participants in one condition were asked to respond to a brief questionnaire about their water use, a task designed to make them mindful of how they sometimes wasted water while showering. In another condition, research participants made a public commitment, exhorting others to take steps to conserve water. Specifically, these participants were asked to sign their names to a public poster that read, "Take Shorter Showers. Turn Shower Off While Soaping Up. If I Can Do It, So Can YOU!" In the crucial condition—the "hypocrisy" condition—the participants did both; that is, they were made mindful of their own wasteful behaviour and indicated publicly (on the poster) that they were practising water conservation. In short, they were made aware that they were preaching behaviour they themselves

▶ In a study by Dickerson, Thibodeau, Aronson, and Miller (1992), university students who were made aware that they were advocating conservation behaviour they themselves were not practising changed their behaviour by taking shorter showers.

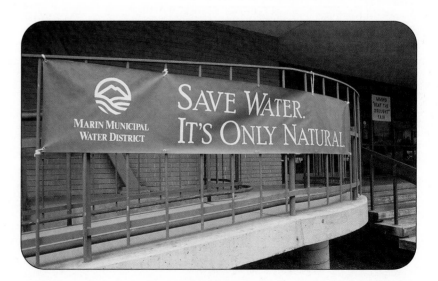

were not practising. Just as in the condom study (Chapter 6), participants who were made to feel like hypocrites changed their behaviour so they could feel good about themselves. In this case, they took very brief showers. Indeed, the procedure was so effective that the average time students in this condition spent showering was reduced to 3.5 minutes. The hypocrisy procedure has also been found to increase other environmentally sound practices, such as recycling (Fried & Aronson, 1995).

Removing Small Barriers to Achieve Big Changes

Sometimes the best way to change people's behaviour is simply to make it easy for them to do so. To reduce the amount of garbage that ends up in landfills, many cities are encouraging people to recycle materials such as glass, paper, and aluminum. However, as you know, it can be inconvenient to do so; in some areas, you have to load your car with boxes of cans and bottles and drop them off at a recycling centre, which might be several kilometres from your house. Other cities have curbside recycling, whereby a truck picks up recycling materials that you put out on the curb on a designated day. Even then, though, you have to remember to separate your cans, bottles, and newspapers, and find a place to store them until pick-up day. We therefore have another social dilemma—a behaviour (recycling) that, while good for us all, is effortful and unpleasant for individuals. As you might imagine, several social psychologists have turned their attention to ways of getting people to recycle more.

There have been two general approaches to this problem. First, some psychologists have focused on ways of changing people's attitudes and values in a pro-environment direction, with the assumption that behaviour will follow. This assumption is consistent with social psychological research on attitudes, which has found that under certain conditions people's attitudes are good predictors of their behaviour (see Chapter 6). Indeed, several studies have found that people's attitudes toward recycling are good predictors of their recycling behaviour, suggesting that a mass media campaign that targets people's attitudes is a good way to go (Cheung, Chan, & Wong, 1999; Ewing, 2001; Knussen, Yule, & MacKenzie, 2004; Oskamp, Burkhardt, Schultz, Hurin, & Zelezny, 1998; Valle, Rebelo, & Reis, 2005).

Sometimes, though, we might fail to act consistently with our attitudes, despite our best intentions. Perhaps the recycling centre is too far away, or we just can't find the time to sort our trash, even though we know we should. For example, research conducted with residents of Cornwall, Ontario, found that a major reason why people failed to engage in pro-environmental actions was, "I just can't

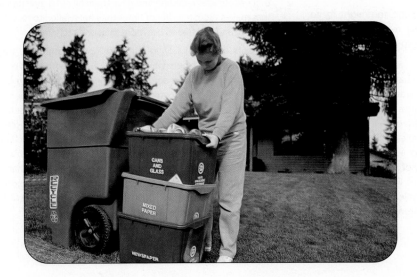

◄ Social psychologists have identified several ways of increasing the likelihood that people will recycle materials such as bottles, cans, and newspapers. One way is to make it as convenient as possible—for example, by offering curbside pickup, as shown in this photo of the recycling service in Toronto.

seem to make the effort to change my habits" (Pelletier, Dion, Tuson, & Green-Demers, 1999). Kurt Lewin (1947), one of the founders of social psychology, made the observation that big social changes can sometimes occur by removing small barriers from people's environments (Ross & Nisbett, 1991). When it comes to behaviours such as recycling, it might be better to simply make it hassle-free, such as by instituting curbside recycling, than to try to change people's attitudes toward the environment. Indeed, the results of studies on recycling conducted with residents of Edmonton (Wall, 1995) and four communities in the Greater Toronto Area (Scott, 1999), as well as a 1991 Statistics Canada survey on the environment (Berger, 1997), all converge on the same conclusion—namely, that "people will take pro-environmental actions if they have access to a convenient way of doing so" (Berger, 1997). Increasing the number of recycling bins in a community, instituting curbside recycling, and allowing residents to mix materials instead of having to sort them have all been found to increase people's recycling behaviour (Domina & Koch, 2002; Ludwig, Gray, & Rowell, 1998; Schultz, Oskamp, & Mainieri, 1995).

The moral? There are two ways to get people to act in more environmentally sound ways. One method is to try to change people's attitudes in a pro-environmental direction; this will motivate them to act in environmentally friendly ways, even if there are barriers that make it hard to do so, such as having to find a box for their bottles and cans and then take it to a recycling centre. It is often easier, however, simply to remove the barriers, such as by instituting curbside recycling and giving people containers. When it is easy to comply, many people will, even if they do not have strong pro-environmental attitudes. Now that you have read about several ways of changing people's behaviour in ways that help the environment, you are in a position to try them out yourself. See the accompanying Try It! exercise.

Try it!

▶ Changing Environmentally Damaging Behaviour

Use the techniques discussed in this chapter to change people's behaviour in ways that help the environment. Here's how to proceed:

1. Choose the behaviour you want to change. You might try to increase the amount that you and your roommates recycle, reduce the amount of energy wasted in your dorm, or increase water conservation.

2. Choose the technique you will use to change the behaviour. You might, for example, use the comparative feedback technique used by Frans Siero and colleagues (1996) to increase energy conservation. Encourage two areas of your dormitory to reduce energy use or to recycle, and give each feedback about how they are doing relative to the other area. (To do this, you will have to have an easy, objective way of measuring people's behaviour, such as the number of times lights are left on at night or the number of cans that are recycled.) Or you might try the hypocrisy technique used by Elliot Aronson and colleagues

(Aronson et al., 1991; Dickerson et al., 1992) to increase water conservation, whereby you ask people to sign a public poster that encourages recycling and have them fill out a questionnaire that makes them mindful of times they have failed to recycle. Be creative and feel free to use more than one technique.

3. Measure the success of your intervention. Find an easy way to measure people's behaviour, such as the amount they recycle. Assess their behaviour before and after your intervention. If possible, include a control group of people who do not receive your intervention (randomly assigned, of course). In the absence of such a control group, it will be difficult to gauge the success of your intervention; for example, if people's behaviour changes over time, you won't be able to tell if it is because of your intervention or some other factor (e.g., an article on recycling that happened to appear in the newspaper). By comparing the changes in behaviour in your target group to the control group, you will have a better estimate of the success of your intervention.

SUMMARY

By its very nature, social psychology addresses both basic and applied questions about human behaviour. Social psychologists have conducted a good deal of applied research on important social and psychological issues, such as how people can adopt a more sustainable lifestyle. One of the most important lessons of social psychology is the value of conducting experiments to answer questions about social influence. This lesson is important when testing the effectiveness of interventions designed to solve an applied problem. Some interventions have backfired and had negative effects because they were not adequately tested. Social psychologists are in a unique position to find solutions to applied problems. First, the field of social psychology is a rich source of theories about human behaviour that people can draw upon to devise solutions to problems. Second, social psychologists know how to perform rigorous experimental tests of these solutions to see if they work.

Social psychologists are increasingly conducting applied research to address the issue of how to achieve a sustainable future. People are harming the environment in many ways, as illustrated by the tar sands project in Alberta, which is introducing deadly toxins into the environment. Social psychologists have devised a number of approaches to encourage people to adopt a more sustainable lifestyle. One approach has been to focus on resolving **social dilemmas.** Energy conservation is a type of social dilemma called a *commons dilemma*, a situation in which everyone takes from a common pool of goods that will replenish itself if used in moderation but will disappear if overused. It is in any individual's interest to consume as much as possible, but if everyone acts that way everyone loses—there are

no resources left. Social psychologists have studied the conditions under which people are most likely to act for the common good, such as when people are encouraged to communicate with each other.

Another approach is to target social norms. Research shows that it is effective to remind people of both **injunctive** and **descriptive norms** against environmentally damaging acts, such as littering and washing towels after only one use. People can also attempt to change norms by acting as a personal example and role model.

One simple technique to get people to use less energy is to make it easier for them to know how much energy they are using—for example, by providing them with water meters that display consumption. It also helps to give people information in which energy loss is conveyed in a vivid manner. Another successful approach is to introduce a little competitiveness. Units in a company that were competing with each other to conserve energy were more successful than units that were encouraged to save but did not compete.

It works to arouse dissonance in people by making them feel that they are not practising what they are preaching—for example, that even though they believe in water conservation, they are taking long showers. People who are reminded of their hypocrisy are more likely to engage in pro-environmental behaviours such as water conservation. Finally, research has shown that big changes can be achieved by removing small barriers. Removing barriers that make pro-environmental behaviours difficult, such as instituting curbside recycling and providing people with recycling bins, has been shown to be effective.

PEARSON mypsychlab

Along with a dynamic, electronic version of this text, MyPsychLab offers a wealth of resources to deepen your understanding and test your recall of the material in this chapter—including video and audio clips, simulations and activities, self-assessments, practice tests, and other study materials. The following specific resources are available for this chapter:

 Psychologists at Work

 A Message from the 2002 APA President: Phil Zimbardo

 9/11 Post-Traumatic Stress Disorder

To access MyPsychLab, please visit www.mypsychlab.com (Student Access Code required—packaged with this book).

Social Psychology
in Action 2

Social Psychology and Health

Meet Elvira Toews, a dynamic, vivacious, 73-year-old woman. At social gatherings, Elvira's infectious, joyous laugh can be heard above the sounds of the crowd. Indeed, Elvira's trademark qualities are enthusiasm, humour, and joie de vivre. You might think that someone with such a sparkling personality and hearty laugh has had an easy life. Not at all. Elvira has experienced some of life's most traumatic and difficult stressors. Her husband suffered from manic depression all of his adult life. Their 42-year marriage ended tragically when he committed suicide. Two years after this devastating loss, in 2000, Elvira was faced with other major stressors, including heart surgery. Although the surgery was helpful, her ability to engage in physical activity, such as walking, has remained limited. In more recent years, Elvira has had to cope with painful arthritis in her back, which further restricts how much she can get around.

Many people would crumble under the stress that Elvira has experienced. But she is determined to make the most of life. One of her most valued resources is the knowledge that she and her husband loved each other and that he wanted her to be happy. She also draws strength from her close relationship with her two daughters. In addition to these assets, Elvira possesses a large measure of resilience and extraordinary determination. When it became apparent that her physical mobility was not likely to improve, Elvira decided that she would rely on her cognitive abilities to keep her active and give her life meaning. Given her love of words, she pursued competitive Scrabble playing and has achieved an advanced ranking. Although travel is difficult and challenging, Elvira manages to make her way to Scrabble competitions in various cities across North America. She can even be found giving her opponents a run for their money on Scrabble cruises!

People who know Elvira are struck by the fact that her feisty spirit, her pleasant smile, and the sparkle in her eyes have not diminished, despite the life-shattering stressors she has experienced. In her words, "I can honestly say I am happy." How does Elvira Toews manage to live such a rewarding life? Is it her positive outlook or is she simply blessed with good genes? As

▲ Elvira Toews manages to live a joyful, upbeat life despite having experienced personal tragedies.

you will see, it may be more than a coincidence that Elvira is so upbeat and in control of her life, despite the painful events she has had to endure in the past and the chronic health problems she copes with on a daily basis.

In this module, we're concerned with the application of social psychology to physical and mental health, which is a flourishing area of research (Bailis & Segall, 2004; Cohen & Herbert, 1996; Salovey, Rothman, & Rodin, 1998; Taylor, 1995). We will focus on topics related to the interface of social psychology and health: how people cope with stress in their lives, the relationship between their coping styles and their physical and mental health, and how we can get people to behave in healthier ways.

Stress and Human Health

There is more to health than germs and disease—we also need to consider the amount of stress in our lives and how we deal with that stress (Inglehart, 1991). A great deal of anecdotal evidence indicates that stress can affect the body in dramatic ways. Consider the following examples, reported by the psychologist W. B. Cannon (1942):

- A New Zealand woman eats a piece of fruit and then learns that it came from a forbidden supply reserved for the chief. She is horrified and her health deteriorates. The next day she dies—even though it was a perfectly fine piece of fruit.

- A man in Africa has breakfast with a friend, eats heartily, and goes on his way. A year later, he learns that his friend made the breakfast from a wild hen, a food strictly forbidden in the man's culture. The man immediately begins to tremble and is dead within 24 hours.

- An Australian man's health deteriorates after a witch doctor casts a spell on him. He recovers only when the witch doctor removes the spell.

These examples probably sound pretty bizarre. But if we fast-forward to the beginning of the twenty-first century, we find many similar cases of sudden death following a psychological trauma. When people undergo a major upheaval in their lives, such as losing a spouse, declaring bankruptcy, or being forced to resettle in a new culture, their chance of dying increases (Morse, Martin, & Moshonov, 1991). Or consider the plight of an older person who is institutionalized in a long-term healthcare facility. In many such institutions in Canada, the residents have little responsibility for or control over their own lives: They cannot choose what to eat, what to wear, or even when to go to the bathroom. Residents in such institutions often become passive and withdrawn, and fade into death as if they have simply given up. Quite a contrast from the zest shown by Elvira Toews as she proceeds through her seventies!

Stress also takes a toll on its victims in other ways. According to research conducted at McGill University, Holocaust survivors—particularly those who were adolescents or young adults at the end of World War II—continue to experience negative psychological effects, such as paranoia and depression, more than 40 years after they were persecuted (Sigal & Weinfeld, 2001). Similarly, the cruelty and abuse some First Nations children suffered in residential schools during the twentieth century continue to have traumatic effects on the survivors (Hanson & Hampton, 2000). And many people experienced psychological and physical problems after the terrorist attacks on September 11, 2001, in the United States (Lampert, Baron, McPherson, & Lee, 2002; Schlenger et al., 2002; Silver, Holman, McIntosh, Poulin, & Gil-Rivas, 2002). Finally, as you know all too well, university life is fraught with stress. A large-scale study of university students across Canada found that psychological distress (e.g., anxiety, depression) was significantly higher among students than in Canada's general population (Adlaf, Gliksman, Demers, & Newton-Taylor, 2001). The good news was that distress declined with each successive year in university. So rest reassured—things will get better as you go along!

As these examples suggest, our physical and psychological health is closely tied to the amount of stress in our lives. As we will see, we need to consider not only the amount of stress in our lives but also how we deal with that stress.

Effects of Negative Life Events

Among the pioneers in research on stress was Hans Selye (1956, 1976), who defined *stress* as the body's physiological response to threatening events. Selye focused on how the human body adapts to threats from the environment, regardless of the source of a threat, be it a psychological or physiological trauma. Later researchers have examined what it is about a life event that makes it threatening. Holmes and Rahe (1967), for example, suggested that stress is the degree to which people have to change and readjust their lives in response to an external event. The more change required, the more stress occurs. Thus, if a spouse or partner dies, just about every aspect of a person's life is disrupted, leading to a great deal of stress. This definition of stress applies to happy events in one's life as well, if the event causes a person to change his or her daily routine. Graduating from university is a happy occasion, but it can be stressful because of the major changes it sets in motion in one's life. Similarly, many people look forward to retirement, failing to anticipate the extent of life change that occurs as a result of this transition. A study of Bell Canada retirees, for example, found that for many people, retirement caused considerable instability and stress (Marshall, Clarke, & Ballantyne, 2001).

To assess such life changes, Holmes and Rahe (1967) developed a measure called the Social Readjustment Rating Scale. Here's how the scale works: Respondents get a list of life events such as "divorce" and "trouble with boss," each of which has been assigned a certain number of points, depending on how stressful it is (e.g., "divorce" gets 73 points, whereas "trouble with boss" gets 23). People check all events that have occurred in their lives over the past year. The points assigned to each event are added up to get an overall "life change" score. Several studies have found that the higher people's score, the worse their physical and mental health (Seta, Seta, & Wang, 1990; Tesser & Beach, 1998).

The original scale is a bit dated and did not include events that many college or university students find stressful, such as taking final exams. The Try It! exercise on the next page contains a version that has been developed specifically for students. Go ahead and take it and figure out your score. How did you do? When the researchers who developed the scale gave it to a sample of undergraduates, the average score was 1247 (Renner & Mackin, 1998).

It seems pretty obvious that people who are experiencing a lot of change and upheaval in their lives are more likely to feel anxious and get sick. But a closer look reveals that these findings aren't all that straightforward. One problem, as

The College Life Stress Inventory

Copy the stress rating number into the last column for any event that has occurred in your life in the past year; then add your scores.

Event	Stress Rating	Your Score
Being raped	100	_____
Finding out that you are HIV-positive	100	_____
Being accused of rape	98	_____
Death of a close friend	97	_____
Death of a close family member	96	_____
Contracting a sexually transmitted disease (other than AIDS)	94	_____
Concerns about being pregnant	91	_____
Finals week	90	_____
Concerns about your partner being pregnant	90	_____
Oversleeping for an exam	89	_____
Flunking a class	89	_____
Having a boyfriend or girlfriend cheat on you	85	_____
Ending a steady dating relationship	85	_____
Serious illness in a close friend or family member	85	_____
Financial difficulties	84	_____
Writing a major term paper	83	_____
Being caught cheating on a test	83	_____
Drunk driving	82	_____
Sense of overload in school or work	82	_____
Two exams in one day	80	_____
Cheating on your boyfriend or girlfriend	77	_____
Getting married	76	_____
Negative consequences of drinking or drug use	75	_____
Depression or crisis in your best friend	73	_____
Difficulties with parents	73	_____
Talking in front of a class	72	_____
Lack of sleep	69	_____
Change in housing situation (hassles, moves)	69	_____
Competing or performing in public	69	_____
Getting in a physical fight	66	_____
Difficulties with a roommate	66	_____
Job changes (applying, new job, work hassles)	65	_____
Declaring a major or concerns about future plans	65	_____
A class you hate	62	_____
Drinking or use of drugs	61	_____
Confrontations with professors	60	_____
Starting a new semester	58	_____
Going on a first date	57	_____
Registration	55	_____
Maintaining a steady dating relationship	55	_____
Commuting to campus or work, or both	54	_____
Peer pressures	53	_____
Being away from home for the first time	53	_____
Getting sick	52	_____
Concerns about your appearance	52	_____
Getting straight A's	51	_____
A difficult class that you love	48	_____
Making new friends; getting along with friends	47	_____
Fraternity or sorority rush	47	_____
Falling asleep in class	40	_____
Attending an athletic event (e.g., football game)	20	_____
Sum of Your Scores		_____

you may have recognized, is that most studies in this area use correlational designs rather than experimental designs. Just because life changes are correlated with health problems, this does not mean that the life changes *caused* the health problems. (See our discussion in Chapter 2 of correlation and causality.) Some researchers have argued persuasively that it is not life changes that cause health problems; rather, people with certain personality traits, such as the tendency to experience negative moods, are more likely to experience life difficulties and to have health problems (Schroeder & Costa, 1984; Watson & Pennebaker, 1989).

Another problem with inventories such as Holmes and Rahe's original scale is that it focuses on stressors experienced by the middle class and under-represents stressors experienced by the poor and members of minority communities. Variables such as poverty and racism are potent causes of stress (Clark, Anderson, Clark, & Williams, 1999; Gibbons, Gerrard, & Cleveland, 2004; Jackson, Brown, Williams, Torres, Sellers, & Brown, 1996). To understand the relationship between stress and health, we need to understand better such community-level and cultural-level variables as poverty and racism.

Perceived Stress and Health

Simply adding up the number of negative life events that people experience—such as divorcing or losing one's job—violates a basic principle of social psychology: Subjective situations have more of an impact on people than objective situations (Griffin & Ross, 1991). Of course, some situations are objectively bad for our health, regardless of how we interpret them (Jackson & Inglehart, 1995; Taylor, Repetti, & Seeman, 1997). Still, there are events that seem to have negative effects only on the people who construe them in negative ways. For some students, writing a term paper is a major hassle; for others, it's a minor inconvenience (or even an enjoyable experience). Some people view a major life change such as getting divorced as a liberating escape from an abusive relationship, whereas others

◀ Some of these events are happy; yet, they cause stress. Which of these situations might cause you to experience stress?

stress

the negative feelings and beliefs that occur whenever people feel unable to cope with demands from their environment

view it as a devastating personal failure. As recognized by Richard Lazarus (1966, 2000) in his pioneering work on stress, it is subjective, not objective, stress that causes problems. An event is stressful for people only if they interpret it as stressful; thus, we can define **stress** as the negative feelings and beliefs that occur whenever people feel unable to cope with demands from their environment (Lazarus & Folkman, 1984).

Studies using this subjective definition of stress confirm the idea that it is the life experiences that we perceive as negative that are bad for our health. For example, when Lefrançois and colleagues (2000) administered a French version of the Holmes and Rahe (1967) Social Readjustment Rating Scale (modified to focus on the life changes associated with aging) to elderly people in Quebec, it was the life changes regarded as negative that were associated with the greatest psychological distress (Lefrançois, Leclerc, Hamel, & Gaulin, 2000).

Stress caused by negative interpretations of events can even affect our immune systems, making us more susceptible to disease. Consider the common cold. When people are exposed to the virus that causes a cold, 20 percent to 60 percent of them become sick. Is it possible that stress is a determinant of who will become ill? To find out, Cohen, Tyrrell, and Smith (1991, 1993) asked volunteers to spend a week at a research institute in southern England. As a measure of stress, the participants listed recent events that had had a negative impact on their lives. (Consistent with our definition of stress, the participants listed only events that they perceived to be negative.) The researchers then gave participants nasal drops that contained either the virus that causes the common cold or saline (saltwater). The participants were subsequently quarantined for several days so that they had no contact with other people.

The results? The people who were experiencing a great deal of stress in their lives were more likely to catch a cold from the virus (see Figure SPA2.1). Among people who reported the least amount of stress, about 27 percent came down with a cold. This rate increased steadily in relation to the amount of stress people reported, topping out at a rate of nearly 50 percent in the group that was experiencing the most stress. This effect of stress was found even when several other factors that influence catching a cold were taken into account, such as the time of year and the participant's age, weight, and sex. This study, along with others like it, shows that the more stress people experience, the lower their immunity to diseases (Doyle, Gentile, & Cohen, 2006; O'Leary, 1990; Stone, Bovbjerg, Neale, Napoli, Valdimarsdottir, Cox, Hayden, & Gwaltney, 1992).

The results from Cohen and colleagues' correlational study have been confirmed in research using experimental designs. For example, there are studies in which people's immune responses are measured before and after undergoing

FIGURE SPA2.1

Stress and the likelihood of catching a cold

People were first exposed to the virus that causes the common cold, then isolated. The greater the amount of stress they were experiencing, the greater the likelihood that they caught a cold from this virus.

(Adapted from Cohen, Tyrell, & Smith, 1991)

mildly stressful tasks in the laboratory, such as solving mental arithmetic problems continuously for six minutes or giving speeches on short notice. It turns out that even relatively mild stressors such as these can lead to a suppression of the immune system (Cacioppo, 1998; Cacioppo et al., 1998).

The finding that stress has negative effects on people's health raises an important question: What exactly is it that makes people perceive a situation as stressful? One important determinant, as we will now see, is the amount of control that they believe they have over the event.

Feeling in Charge: The Importance of Perceived Control

How much control do you have over your own life? Are you able to decide what to do with each day? When and what to eat? When to study? When to go out with friends? Research in social psychology suggests that the feeling that we don't have control is detrimental to our psychological and physical health. Shelley Taylor and her colleagues (1984), for example, interviewed women with breast cancer and found that many of them believed that they could control whether their cancer returned. Here is how one man described his wife: "She got books, she got pamphlets, she studied, she talked to cancer patients. She found out everything that was happening to her and she fought it. She went to war with it. She calls it 'taking in her covered wagons and surrounding it'" (quoted in Taylor, 1989; Taylor, Lichtman, & Wood, 1984). The researchers found that women who believed that their cancer was controllable were better adjusted psychologically (see also Folkman & Moskowitz, 2000).

Subsequent studies have found that a high sense of **perceived control**, defined as the belief that we can influence our environment in ways that determine whether we experience positive or negative outcomes, is associated with good mental and physical health (Burger, 1992; Skinner, 1995, 1996; Thompson, 1999). For example, Helgeson and Fritz (1999) interviewed patients who had undergone a coronary angioplasty because of diseased arteries. The people who had a high sense of control over their futures were less likely to experience subsequent heart problems than those with a low sense of control (Helgeson, 2003; Helgeson & Fritz, 1999).

perceived control

the belief that we can influence our environment in ways that determine whether we experience positive or negative outcomes

The benefits of perceived control have been demonstrated in a variety of other domains. A study conducted with clients at sexual assault centres in southern Ontario found that rape victims who believed that they generally had control over outcomes in their lives experienced less depression and showed fewer symptoms of post-traumatic stress six months or more after the event than rape victims who felt that they had little control (Regehr, Cadell, & Jansen, 1999). In a very different vein, longitudinal research conducted by the Canadian Aging Research Network with elderly residents of Manitoba found that those who perceived that they had control over housework and outdoor work were more likely to see themselves as having good health—more so than elderly people who perceived less control. Importantly, those who perceived control actually were in better health (Chipperfield, Perry, & Menec, 1999) and tended to live longer (Menec & Chipperfield, 1997). Finally, in other research conducted at the University of Manitoba it was found that first-year students who felt that they had control over their academic performance reported less anxiety and boredom and actually received better grades than those who perceived less control (Perry, 2003; Perry, Hladkyj, Pekrun, & Pelletier, 2001).

Of course, studies such as these are using correlational, rather than experimental, designs. Researchers measure the amount of control people are experiencing and correlate this with their psychological and physical adjustment. Such studies cannot prove that feelings of control *cause* good physical or emotional health; for example, it is possible that good physical or emotional health causes one to feel more in control. Indeed, Menec, Chipperfield, and Perry (1999) found that elderly people who believed that they were in good health were also more likely to perceive control over their lives and engage in control-enhancing strategies. It is also possible that some third variable contributes to both good health and feelings of control (Johnson & Krueger, 2005). To address the question of whether feelings of control have beneficial causal effects, we need to conduct experimental studies in which people are randomly assigned to conditions of "high" versus "low" perceived control. Fortunately, a number of such experimental studies have been conducted (Heckhausen & Schulz, 1995; Ratelle, Baldwin, & Vallerand, 2005; Rodin, 1986).

One of the most famous series of studies on the importance of perceived control was conducted by David Glass and Jerome Singer (1972). In a typical experiment, participants were given several problems to solve, such as complex addition problems, and a proofreading task. While they worked on these problems, they heard loud bursts of noise coming from various sources—a mimeograph machine, a typewriter, or two people speaking in Spanish. The noise was played at 108 decibels—about what you would hear if you were operating a riveting machine or were standing near the runway when a large commercial jet took off.

In one condition, the bursts of noise occurred at unpredictable lengths and at unpredictable intervals over the course of the 25-minute session. In a second condition, people heard the same sequence of noises but were given a sense of control over them. The experimenter told participants that they could stop the noise at any point by pressing a button. "Whether or not you press the button is up to you," explained the experimenter. "We'd prefer that you do not, but that's entirely up to you" (Glass & Singer, 1972). A key fact to remember is that *no one* actually pressed the button. People in this condition heard the same amount of noise as people in the uncontrollable noise condition; the only difference was that they believed they could stop the noise whenever they wanted to. Finally, a third condition was included wherein people worked on the problem in peace and quiet. After the 25-minute session was over, people in all conditions worked on new problems without any noise present.

Interestingly, the noise had little effect on people during the initial 25-minute session. As long as a task was not too complex, people could bear down and ignore unpleasant noises, doing just as well on the problems as people who worked on them in quiet surroundings. A different picture emerged, however, when people worked on problems in the next session, in which everyone could work in peace and quiet. As you can see in Figure SPA2.2, those who had endured the uncontrollable noises made significantly more errors during this session than did people who had not heard noises during the first session. In contrast, the people who

FIGURE SPA2.2

Noise and Perceived Control

People who believed they could control the noxious noise did about as well on a subsequent task as people who heard no noise at all.

(Adapted from Glass & Singer, 1972)

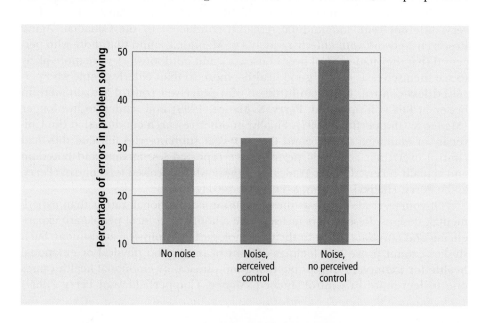

heard the noises but believed they could control them did almost as well on the subsequent problems as those who heard no noise at all (see Figure SPA2.2). When people knew they could turn off the noise at any point, the noise was much easier to tolerate and did not impair later performance—even though these people had never actually turned it off.

In a conceptually similar study by Drury Sherrod (1974), high school students worked on problems in a room that was jam-packed with other people. Some students were told that they had the option of leaving, although the researchers would prefer that they stay. Others were not given this choice. Students in a control condition worked on the problems in uncrowded conditions. Later, all participants worked on a series of difficult puzzles in an uncrowded room. As with the Glass and Singer (1972) study on the effects of noise, the students who were crowded—whether or not they had a sense of control—initially solved as many problems as those who had worked in uncrowded conditions. However, for the students who did not have the option of leaving in the first part of the study, the lack of control eventually took its toll—they ended up attempting to solve fewer of the difficult puzzles than students in the other two conditions. In fact, the students who had perceived control attempted almost as many difficult puzzles as the students who had not been crowded at all.

Subsequent research conducted at the University of Manitoba underscores the importance of perceived control. Cramer, Nickels, and Gural (1997) found that participants who were told that there was nothing they could do to escape bursts of loud noise (78 decibels) resembling sirens of emergency vehicles felt more helpless than did those who were told they had some control. Interestingly, among those who were told that they had some control, helplessness was reduced to the same extent, regardless of whether they were told that they had 25 percent, 50 percent, or 75 percent control. As the researchers put it, "A little control may go far to shield a person from feelings of helplessness, and additional control provides little extra protection" (Cramer et al., 1997).

Increasing Perceived Control in Nursing Homes Some of the most dramatic effects of perceived control have been found in studies of older people in nursing homes. Many people who live in nursing homes and hospitals feel that they have lost control of their lives (Raps, Peterson, Jonas, & Seligman, 1982). People are often placed in long-term care facilities against their wishes, and once there, have little say in what they do, whom they see, or what they eat. For example, an observational study of residents at a nursing home in Alberta found that patients tended to sit passively and to rely on nursing staff to initiate contact (Intrieri & Morse, 1997).

Ellen Langer and Judith Rodin (1976) believed that it would be beneficial for residents of a nursing home if their feelings of control were increased. They asked the director of a nursing home in Connecticut to convey to the residents that contrary to what they might think, they had a lot of responsibility for their own lives. Here is an excerpt of his speech:

> Take a minute to think of the decisions you can and should be making. For example, you have the responsibility of caring for yourselves, of deciding whether or not you want to make this a home you can be proud of and happy in. You should be deciding how you want your rooms to be arranged—whether you want it to be as it is or whether you want the staff to help you rearrange the furniture. You should be deciding how you want to spend your time. . . . If you are unsatisfied with anything here, you have the influence to change it. . . . These are just a few of the things you could and should be deciding and thinking about now and from time to time every day. (Langer & Rodin, 1976)

The director went on to say that a movie would be shown on two nights the following week and that the residents should decide on which night they wanted to attend. Finally, he gave each resident a gift of a houseplant, emphasizing that it was up to the resident to take care of it.

The director also gave a speech to residents assigned to a comparison group. This speech was different in one crucial way—all references to making decisions and residents being responsible for themselves were deleted. The director emphasized that he wanted the residents to be happy, but he did not say anything about the control they had over their lives. He said that a movie would be shown on two nights the next week and that the residents would be assigned to see it on one night or the other. He gave plants to these residents as well, but said that the nurses would take care of the plants.

The director's speech might not seem like a major change in the lives of the residents. The people in the induced control group heard one speech about the responsibility they had for their lives and were given one plant to water. That doesn't seem like very strong stuff, does it? But to an institutionalized person who feels helpless and constrained, even a small boost in control can have a dramatic effect. Indeed, residents in the induced control group became happier and more active than did residents in the comparison group (Langer & Rodin, 1976). Most dramatic of all, the induced control intervention affected the residents' health and mortality. One and a half years after the director's speech, 30 percent of residents in the comparison condition had died, compared with only 15 percent of residents in the induced control group (Rodin & Langer, 1977; see left side of Figure SPA2.3).

Richard Schulz (1976) increased feelings of control in residents of nursing homes in a different way. Schulz started a program in a North Carolina nursing home in which undergraduates visited the residents once a week for two months. In the induced control condition, the residents decided when the visits would occur and how long they would last. In a randomly assigned comparison condition, it was the students, not the residents, who decided when the visits would occur and how long they would last. While residents received visits in both conditions, in only one could they control the visits' frequency and duration. This may seem like a minor difference but, again, giving the residents some semblance of control over their lives had dramatic effects. After two months, those in the induced control condition were happier, healthier, more active, and were taking fewer medications than those in the comparison group. Schulz returned to the nursing home several months later to assess the long-term effects of his intervention, including its effect on mortality rates. Based on the results of the Langer and Rodin (1976) study, we might expect that those residents who could control

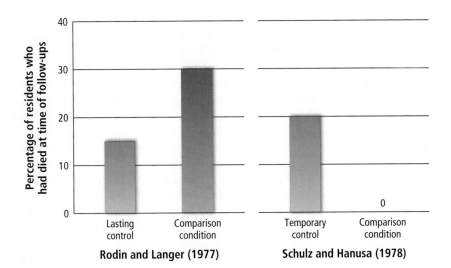

FIGURE SPA2.3
Perceived control and mortality

In two studies, elderly residents in nursing homes were made to feel more in control of their lives. In one (Rodin & Langer, 1977), the intervention endured over time so that people continued to feel in control. As seen in the left side of the figure, this intervention had positive effects on mortality rates. Those who received it were more likely to be alive 18 months later than those who did not. In the other study (Schulz & Hanusa, 1978), the intervention was temporary. Being given control and then having it taken away had negative effects on mortality rates, as seen in the right side of the figure.

(Adapted from Rodin & Langer, 1977, and Schulz & Hanusa, 1978)

the students' visits would be healthier and more likely to still be alive than residents who could not. However, there is a crucial difference between the two studies; the residents in the Langer and Rodin study were given an enduring sense of control, whereas the residents in the Schulz study experienced control and then lost it when the students' visits ceased. Langer and Rodin's participants could continue to choose which days to participate in different activities, to take care of their plant, and to feel they could make a difference in what happened to them—even after the study ended. By contrast, when Schulz's study was over and the students stopped visiting, the residents who could control the visits suddenly had that control removed.

Unfortunately, Schulz's intervention had an unintended effect. Once the program ended, the people in the induced control group did worse (Schulz & Hanusa, 1978). Compared with people in the comparison group, they were more likely to have experienced deteriorating health and zest for life, and they were more likely to have died (see the right side of Figure SPA2.3). This study has sobering implications for the many programs in which volunteers visit residents of nursing homes, prisons, and mental hospitals. These programs might be beneficial in the short run but do more harm than good after they end.

Disease, Control, and Well-Being   We end this discussion with some words of caution. First, the link between perceived control and distress is stronger in Western cultures than in Asian cultures. Sastry and Ross (1998) found that Asians reported that perceived control was less important to them than did Westerners and that there was less of a relationship between perceived control and psychological distress among Asians. The researchers argue that in Western cultures, where individualism and personal achievement are prized, people are more likely to feel distressed when they cannot control their destinies. A sense of control is less of an issue in Asian cultures because Asians tend to place greater value on collectivism and putting the social group ahead of individual goals.

Second, even in Western societies, there is a danger in exaggerating the relationship between perceived control and physical health. The social critic Susan Sontag (1978, 1988) perceptively observed that when a society is plagued by a deadly but poorly understood disease, such as tuberculosis in the nineteenth century and AIDS today, the illness is often blamed on some kind of human frailty, such as lack of faith, moral weakness, or a broken heart. As a result, people sometimes blame themselves for their illnesses, even to the point where they do not seek effective treatment. Even though it is beneficial for people to feel that they are in control of their illnesses, the downside of this strategy is that if they do not get better, they may blame themselves for failing to recover. Tragically, diseases such as cancer can be fatal no matter how much control a person feels. Take, for example, Lance Armstrong's well-publicized battle with cancer. One of the doctors who treated the world-famous cyclist put it this way, "I've seen wonderful, positive people not make it in the end . . . and some of the most miserable, ornery people survive to resume their ornery lives" (Armstrong, 2000, p. 127). It only adds to the tragedy if people with serious diseases feel a sense of moral failure, blaming themselves for a disease that was unavoidable.

For people living with serious illness, maintaining some form of control when their health is failing has important benefits. Researchers have found that even when people who are seriously ill with cancer or AIDS feel no control over the disease, many of them believe that they can still control the *consequences* of the disease (e.g., their emotional reactions and some of the physical symptoms, such as how tired they feel; Thompson, Nanni, & Levine, 1994). And the more people feel they can control the consequences of their illness, the better adjusted they are, even if they know they cannot control the eventual course of the disease. In short, it is important to feel in control of something—even if it is not the disease itself (Heckhausen & Schulz, 1995; Thompson, 2002).

Knowing You Can Do It: Self-Efficacy

Believing we have control over our lives is one thing; believing that we can actually execute the specific behaviours that will get us what we want is another. Sam might have a general sense that he is in control of his life, but will this mean that he will find it easy to stop smoking? According to Albert Bandura, a highly influential social psychologist (who was born in Alberta and studied at the University of British Columbia), we have to examine his **self-efficacy**, which is the belief in one's ability to carry out specific actions that produce desired outcomes (Bandura, 1997; Bandura & Locke, 2003; Benight & Bandura, 2004). If Sam believes that he can perform the behaviours that will enable him to quit smoking—throwing away his cigarettes, avoiding situations in which he is most tempted to smoke, distracting himself when he craves a cigarette—then chances are he will succeed. If he has low self-efficacy in this domain, believing that he can't perform the behaviour necessary to quit, then he is likely to fail.

self-efficacy

the belief in one's ability to carry out specific actions that produce desired outcomes

© Vahan Shirvanian/www.CartoonStock.com

"Maybe we shouldn't have kicked all our bad habits."

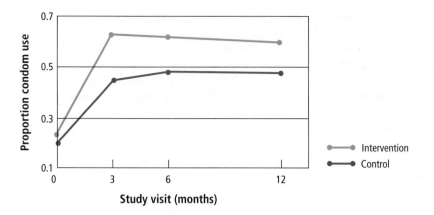

FIGURE SPA2.4

Effects of an intervention on the proportion of times people reported using condoms during sex

People visiting clinics that treat sexually transmitted diseases were randomly assigned either to an intervention condition (that tried to increase their self-efficacy about using condoms, their knowledge about condom use, and their motivation to use condoms) or to a control condition. People in the intervention condition showed a significant increase in the proportion of times they reported using condoms, even 12 months after the study began.

(From NIMH Multisite *HIV* Prevention Trial Group [1998, June 19]. The NIMH Multisite HIV Prevention Trial: Reducing HIV sexual risk behavior. *Science*, 280, 1889–1894)

In the 1990s, the National Institute of Mental Health sponsored an intervention to get people to engage in safer sex that targeted people's self-efficacy in the domain of condom use—namely, their beliefs that they could bring up the topic in a conversation with a potential sexual partner and convince their partner that they should use condoms (NIMH Multisite HIV Prevention Trial Group, 1998). The intervention also taught people how to use condoms and attempted to increase their motivation to do so. Specifically, participants were recruited from waiting rooms of clinics that treated sexually transmitted diseases in seven cities in the United States, and were randomly assigned to an intervention or control condition. Participants in the intervention condition attended seven sessions over a two-week period, in which they watched videotapes, listened to presentations, and engaged in role-playing exercises, all with the goal of increasing their sense of self-efficacy about condom use, their motivation to use condoms, and their knowledge about how to use them. Participants in the control condition attended a one-hour AIDS education session. All participants completed a battery of measures at intervals of 3, 6, and 12 months, including the percentage of times they reported using condoms during sex.

People's level of self-efficacy has been found to predict a number of other important health behaviours, such as the likelihood that they will quit smoking, lose weight, lower their cholesterol, and exercise regularly (Bandura, 1997; Salovey, Rothman, Detweiler, & Steward, 2000). For example, a study of more than 1000 high school students in Toronto found that those who were high in self-efficacy in the area of exercise were more likely to engage in vigorous physical exercise than those who had low self-efficacy in this area (Allison, Dwyer, & Makin, 1999).

As seen in Figure SPA2.4, people in both conditions reported an increase in condom use, but the increase was significantly larger in the intervention condition. And there was evidence that the intervention worked by improving people's sense of self-efficacy (NIMH Multisite HIV Prevention Trial Group, 2001). A review of the more than 350 interventions designed to promote safer sex confirms that it works to increase people's self-efficacy about condom use (Albarracín, Durantini, & Earl, 2006; Albarracín, Gillette, Earl, Glasman, Durantini, & Ho, 2005).

Again, it is not a general sense of control that predicts engaging in healthier behaviour, but the confidence that one can perform the specific behaviour in question. A person might have high self-efficacy in one domain, such as high confidence that he or she can lose weight, but low self-efficacy in another domain, such as low confidence that he or she can quit smoking.

Self-efficacy increases the likelihood that people will engage in the desired behaviour in two ways. First, it influences people's persistence and effort at a task. People with low self-efficacy tend to give up easily, whereas people high in self-efficacy set higher goals, try harder, and persist more in the face of failure—thereby increasing the likelihood that they will succeed (Cervone & Peake, 1986;

Litt, 1988). Second, self-efficacy influences the way our bodies react while we are working toward our goals. For example, people with high self-efficacy experience less anxiety while working on a difficult task, and their immune system functions more optimally (Bandura, Cioffi, Taylor, & Brouillard, 1988; Wiedenfield, O'Leary, Bandura, Brown, Levine, & Raska, 1990). In short, self-efficacy operates as a kind of self-fulfilling prophecy. The more you believe that you can accomplish something, such as quitting smoking, the greater the likelihood that you will.

How can self-efficacy be increased? A study by Blittner, Goldberg, and Merbaum (1978) on smoking cessation suggests one way. Adult smokers who wanted to quit smoking were randomly assigned to one of three conditions. In the self-efficacy condition, participants were told that they had been chosen for the study because they "showed that they had strong willpower and great potential to control and conquer their desires and behaviour." These participants then underwent a 14-week smoking cessation program. Participants in the treatment-alone condition underwent the same program as people in the self-efficacy condition, with one important difference: instead of being told that they had been selected because of their high potential for quitting, they were told that they had been chosen at random for the treatment program. Finally, participants in the no-treatment control condition neither received self-efficacy instructions nor took part in the treatment program; they were told that they would be contacted for the study at a later time.

As seen in Figure SPA2.5, the self-efficacy instructions were quite effective. By the end of the treatment period, 67 percent of people in the self-efficacy condition had quit smoking, compared with only 28 percent in the treatment-alone group and 6 percent in the no-treatment control group (Blittner et al., 1978). Remember that the only way in which these conditions differed was that in the self-efficacy condition, participants were led to believe that they had high potential for quitting smoking.

Researchers at York University and Wilfrid Laurier University have recently shown that another way to increase self-efficacy is to visualize or picture success (Vasquez & Buehler, 2007). In a series of studies, university students were asked about an important academic task such as a test or essay that they would be writing in the next few weeks. Participants who were asked to imagine that they were an observer, seeing themselves carrying out the task successfully, subsequently reported higher achievement motivation (e.g., "I plan to put a lot of time and energy into this task") than participants who did not engage in this kind of visualization.

FIGURE SPA2.5

The role of self-efficacy in smoking cessation

Adult smokers were randomly assigned to one of three conditions. In the self-efficacy condition, people were told that they were selected for the study because they had great potential to quit. They then underwent a 14-week smoking cessation program. People in the treatment-alone condition participated in the same program, but were told that they had been randomly selected for it. People in the no-treatment control condition did not take part in the program. At the end of the 14-week period, substantially more people in the self-efficacy condition had quit smoking. Believing that we have the ability to carry out beneficial behaviour—having high self-efficacy—is an important determinant of whether we succeed.

(Adapted from Blittner, Goldberg, & Merbaum, 1978)

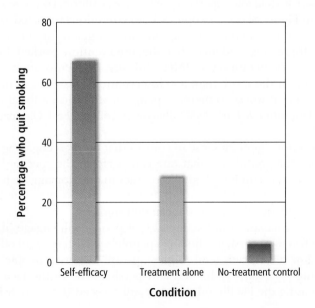

Finally, recent research by Koestner and colleagues (2006) suggests yet another way in which self-efficacy can be increased. These researchers had students at McGill University come to the laboratory early in January and report one of their New Year's resolutions. (Most resolutions pertained to academic or social goals.) Participants in the self-efficacy condition were asked to think about past instances of mastering a similar goal, to think of someone who could provide support to them while pursuing their goal, and to think of a person similar to themselves who had mastered a similar goal. Other participants were asked to write out an implementation plan—the specific steps they were going to take to achieve their goals. Participants in a third condition received the self-efficacy intervention and were asked to write out their implementation plan. Five months later, the participants were contacted again to asses whether their New Year's resolutions had been achieved. The greatest success was found among those who had received the self-efficacy intervention and who had spelled out their plan for achieving their goal (Koestner, Horberg, Gaudreau, Powers, Di Dio, & Bryan et al., 2006).

The bottom line is this: Believing that we can do something is a powerful determinant of whether we actually succeed.

Explaining Negative Events: Learned Helplessness

What happens when we experience a setback? Despite our belief in ourselves, perhaps we failed to quit smoking or did poorly on a midterm. Another important determinant of our physical and mental health is how we explain to ourselves why a negative event occurred. Consider two university students who both get poor grades on their first calculus test. Student A says to herself, "I'll bet the professor deliberately made the test difficult, to motivate us to do better. I'll just have to study harder. If I really buckle down for the next test, I'll do better." Student B says to himself, "Wow, I guess I can't really cut it. I was worried that I wasn't smart enough to make it in university and, boy, was I ever right." Which student do you think will do better on the next test? Clearly the first one, because she has explained her poor performance in a way that is more flattering to herself and makes her feel more in control. In contrast, the second student is expressing **learned helplessness**—pessimism that results from attributing a negative event to stable, internal, and global factors (Abramson, Seligman, & Teasdale, 1978; Overmier, 2002; Seligman, 1975; Wise & Rosqrist, 2006).

If we think that a negative event has a stable cause, we've made a **stable attribution**—we believe that the event was caused by things that will not change over time (e.g., our intelligence) as opposed to factors that can change over time (e.g., the amount of effort we put into a task). Explaining this negative event as stemming from an internal cause—that is, making an **internal attribution**—means we believe that something about us caused the event (e.g., our own ability or effort) as opposed to factors that are external to us (e.g., the difficulty of a test). Finally, explaining an event as the result of a global or widespread cause—that is, making a **global attribution**—is the belief that the event is caused by factors that apply in a large number of situations (e.g., our general intelligence, which will influence our performance in many areas) rather than factors that are specific and apply in only a limited number of situations (e.g., how good we are at math, which will affect our performance in math courses but not in other courses). According to learned helplessness theory, making stable, internal, and global attributions for negative events leads to hopelessness, depression, reduced effort, and difficulty in learning (see Figure SPA2.6 on the next page).

Student B, for example, believes that the cause of his poor grade is stable (being unintelligent will last forever), internal (something about him is to blame), and global (being unintelligent will affect him in many situations other than calculus classes). This kind of explanation will lead to learned helplessness,

learned helplessness

the state of pessimism that results from explaining a negative event as stemming from stable, internal, and global factors

stable attribution

the belief that the cause of an event is a result of factors that will not change over time, as opposed to unstable factors that will change over time

internal attribution

the belief that the cause of an event is factors inherent in you, as opposed to factors that are external to you (e.g., the difficulty of a test)

global attribution

the belief that the cause of an event is a result of factors that apply in a large number of situations, as opposed to the belief that the cause is specific and applies in only a limited number of situations

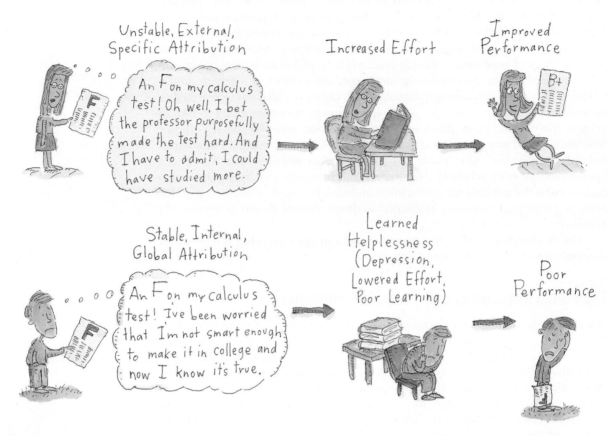

THE THEORY OF LEARNED HELPLESSNESS

Unstable, External, Specific Attribution

An F on my calculus test! Oh well, I bet the professor purposefully made the test hard. And I have to admit, I could have studied more.

Increased Effort

Improved Performance

B+

Stable, Internal, Global Attribution

An F on my calculus test! I've been worried that I'm not smart enough to make it in college and now I know it's true.

Learned Helplessness (Depression, Lowered Effort, Poor Learning)

Poor Performance

FIGURE SPA2.6

The theory of learned helplessness

Explaining a negative event in a pessimistic manner leads to learned helplessness (i.e., depression, lowered effort, poor learning).

thereby producing depression, reduced effort, and the inability to learn new things. Student A, in contrast, believes that the cause of her poor grade is unstable (the professor will make the tests easier, and she can study harder next time), external (the professor intentionally made the test hard), and specific (the things that caused her poor calculus grade are unlikely to affect anything else, such as her grade in English). People who explain bad events in this more optimistic way are less likely to be depressed and in better health, and do better in school and in their careers (Dweck, 1999; Joiner & Wagner, 1995; Perry, 2003; Peterson & Seligman, 1984; Seligman & Schulman, 1986; Snyder, Irving, & Anderson, 1991; Sweeney, Anderson, & Bailey, 1986).

Research by Rempel, Ross, and Holmes (2001) suggests that those who make optimistic attributions for negative events also do better in their close relationships. Married couples living in the Waterloo area were asked to discuss a problem in their relationship. The researchers then examined whether couples who were high in trust made different attributions for problems in their relationship than couples who were low in trust. Indeed, high-trust couples were found to make positive global attributions for their partner's behaviour. Even when discussing a conflict, these couples were optimistic; they focused on the enduring, positive aspects of their partner and the relationship. In contrast, low-trust couples showed a pattern of negative, pessimistic attributions; in other words, for these couples, learned helplessness had set in.

Returning to the example of Student A and Student B, note that we do not know the real reason our hypothetical students did poorly on their calculus test. Instead, learned helplessness theory states that it is more important to consider people's perceptions of these causes. The real causes, of course, are not irrelevant.

Students who truly lack ability in calculus are likely to do poorly on future calculus tests. Often in life, however, what actually causes our behaviour is not so clearcut or fixed. In such situations, people's attributions about the causes of their problems can be very important.

Consider, for example, cyclist Lance Armstrong's comeback after he had recovered from cancer. In his first races, he did fairly well, finishing fourteenth in a five-day race through Spain and nineteenth in an eight-day race from Nice to Paris. He was used to winning, however, and initially explained his failure to do so in this way: "Well, I've just been through too much. I've been through three surgeries, three months of chemo, and a year of hell, and that's the reason I'm not riding well. My body is just never going to be the same" (Armstrong, 2000, p. 188). Note that he attributed his poor performance to a cause that was internal (his lowered physical abilities), stable (a condition that would not change), and global (a condition that would influence many aspects of his life, not just one race). Had he persisted in explaining his performance in this way, surely he would not have gone on to win the Tour de France. Instead, he had the insight to recognize that every cyclist has ups and downs and that no one wins every race. "What I really should have been saying," Armstrong realized, "was, 'Hey, it's just a bad day'"—an attribution to a cause that was external (the particular circumstances, not something about him), unstable (something likely to change), and specific (something limited to that one situation).

Can learned helplessness be overcome? To find out, Tim Wilson and Patricia Linville (1982, 1985) conducted a study with first-year university students. They assumed that many first-year students experience academic difficulties because of a damaging pattern of attributions. Because of the difficulty of adjusting to a new academic and social environment, the first year of university has its rough spots for nearly everyone. The problem is that many first-year students do not realize how common such adjustment problems are and assume that their problems come from personal predicaments that are unlikely to change—just the kind of attribution that leads to learned helplessness. Wilson and Linville tried to combat this pessimism by convincing first-year students that the causes of poor performance are often temporary. In the treatment condition, the students watched videotaped interviews of four senior students, each of whom mentioned that his or her grades had been poor or mediocre during the first year of study but had improved significantly since then. The students were also given statistics indicating that academic performance is often poor in the first year of university but improves thereafter. The researchers hypothesized that this simple message

◄ Students who realize that poor academic performance in the first year of university is common and that they are likely to improve will probably do better than students who believe that poor performance is a result of personal shortcomings that are unlikely to change.

would help prevent learned helplessness, increasing the students' motivation to try harder and removing needless worries about their abilities. Judging by the students' subsequent performance, this is just what happened. Compared with students in a control group who participated in the study but did not watch the videotaped interviews or see the statistics, students in the treatment condition improved their grades more in the following year and were less likely to drop out. Similar results have been found in studies in other countries, including Canada and Belgium (Menec, Perry, Struthers, Schonwetter, Hechter, & Eichholz, 1994; Van Overwalle & De Metsenaere, 1990; Wilson, Damiani, & Shelton, 2002). Because people's attributions were not directly measured in the Wilson and Linville (1982) study, we can only infer that the students improved their academic performance because of a beneficial change in their attributions. But the results are encouraging. In summary, we have seen that our feelings of control and self-efficacy, and the kinds of attributions we make for our performance, are important determinants of our psychological and physical health. The power of our minds over our bodies is, of course, limited. But research shows that perceived control, self-efficacy, and optimistic attributions are beneficial, making it easier for us to cope with the hardships life deals us.

Coping with Stress

No one always feels in control, of course, and sometimes it is difficult to avoid being pessimistic after something bad happens. The death of a loved one, an acrimonious divorce, and the loss of a job are extremely stressful events. Considerable research indicates that people exhibit various reactions, or **coping styles**, in the face of potentially stressful events (e.g., Aspinwall & Taylor, 1997; Lazarus & Folkman, 1984; Lehman, Davies, DeLongis, & Wortman, 1993; Salovey, Rothman, Detweiler, & Steward, 2000; Somerfield & McCrae, 2000). What are these styles and how successful are they? We examine a few coping styles here, beginning with research on differences in the way that men and women cope with stress.

Gender Differences in Coping with Stress

If you have ever been to a dog park, you know that dogs respond in one of two ways when they are attacked: Sometimes they respond in kind and a dogfight ensues. Other times, the dog that is attacked will take off as fast as he or she can, tail between its legs. Walter Cannon (1932) termed this the **fight-or-flight response**, defined as responding to stress by either attacking the source of the stress or fleeing from it. The fight-or-flight response has been viewed as the way in which all mammals respond to stress. When under threat, mammals are energized by the release of hormones such as norepinephrine and epinephrine, and like the dogs in the park, they either go on the attack or retreat as quickly as they can.

That, at least, has been the accepted story for many years. Shelley Taylor and her colleagues (2000) pointed out a little-known fact about research on the fight-or-flight syndrome: Most of it has been done on males, particularly male rats. Taylor and her colleagues argue that the fight-or-flight response does not work well for females because they typically play a greater role in caring for children. Fighting is not a good option for a pregnant female or one tending offspring. Consequently, Taylor and her colleagues argue, a different way of responding to stress has evolved in females, the **tend-and-befriend response**. Instead of fighting

coping styles

the ways in which people react to stressful events

fight-or-flight response

responding to stress by either attacking the source of the stress or fleeing from it

tend-and-befriend response

responding to stress with nurturant activities designed to protect oneself and one's offspring (tending) and creating social networks that provide protection from threats (befriending) or fleeing, women respond to stress with nurturant activities designed to protect themselves and their offspring (tending) and creating social networks that provide protection from threats (befriending). Tending has a number of benefits for both the mother and the child. For example, a quiet child is less likely to be noticed by predators, and nurturing behaviour leads to lower stress and improved immune functioning. Befriending involves the creation of close ties with other members of the species, which also confers a number of advantages. A close-knit group can exchange resources, watch out for predators, and share child care. As we saw in Chapter 5, women are more likely than men to develop intimate friendships, cooperate with others, and focus their attention on social relationships (Fehr, 1996). This is especially so when they are under stress. Research conducted in the United States (Matud, 2004; Tamres, Janicki, & Helgeson, 2002) and in the Canadian Maritimes (Day & Livingstone, 2003) confirms that when stressed, women are more likely to seek out others, particularly other women.

It is easy to oversimplify gender differences such as these. While gender differences in coping do exist, the magnitude of these differences is not very large (Tamres, Janicki, & Helgeson, 2002). Further, seeking social support can benefit both women and men, as we'll see next.

Social Support: Getting Help from Others

One of the striking things about cyclist Lance Armstrong's recovery from cancer was the amount of support he received from his family and friends. His mother, to whom he was very close, took an active role in his treatment and recovery. She stayed by his side as much as possible and organized his schedule, prescription medicines, and diet. A close circle of friends stayed with him as well, many travelling great distances to visit him in the hospital and support him during his treatments. For example, 24 hours after his brain surgery, a group of friends took him to dinner at a restaurant across the street from the hospital. Armstrong also developed close friendships with many of the doctors and nurses who treated him.

Social support, defined as the perception that others are responsive and receptive to one's needs, is very helpful when dealing with stress (Helgeson & Cohen, 1996; Ryff & Singer, 2001; Sarason, Sarason, & Pierce, 1990; Stroebe & Stroebe, 1996; Uchino, Uno, & Holt-Lunstad, 1999). In one study, for example,

social support

the perception that others are responsive and receptive to one's needs

◄ Women are somewhat more likely than men to develop intimate friendships, cooperate with others, and focus their attention on social relationships, particularly when under stress. Shelley Taylor and her colleagues (2000) have referred to this as a tend-and-befriend strategy, responding to stress with nurturant activities designed to protect oneself and one's offspring (tending) and creating social networks that provide protection from threats (befriending).

the effects of social support were evaluated among a group of Canadian women who had been widowed in the previous two years (Stewart, Craig, MacPherson, & Alexander, 2001). The women met weekly in small groups led by a peer—a woman who also was widowed—and a mental health professional. At the end of the 20-week program, the participants showed a number of improvements, including increased positive affect and increased hope and confidence. To give another example, following the terrorist attacks on September 11, 2001, a number of people reported dealing with the sense of threat by spending time talking to others (Yum & Schenck-Hamlin, 2005).

Social support also plays an important role in the workplace, particularly for those in high-stress occupations. In a study of more than 800 Canadian and American firefighters, it was found that those who received social support at work and from their families were less likely to suffer from post-traumatic stress disorder (Corneil, Beaton, Murphy, Johnson, & Pike, 1999). Similarly, in a study of physicians, nurses, and technicians employed at cancer clinics in southern Ontario, it was found that stress was less likely to impair job performance for those healthcare professionals who perceived that social support was available in their workplace (Stewart & Barling, 1996). Clearly, when we believe that we have someone to lean on, we can deal better with life's stresses.

Research also shows that social support plays an important role in cases of life-threatening illnesses. In one study, David Spiegel and his colleagues (1989) randomly assigned women with advanced breast cancer to a social support condition or a control condition. Women in the social support condition met weekly with doctors and other patients to discuss their problems and fears, whereas people in the control group did not have access to this support system. Social support not only improved women's moods and reduced their fears but also lengthened their lives by an average of 18 months. These are certainly dramatic findings!

Finally, evidence for the importance of social support also comes from cross-cultural studies. People who live in cultures that stress interdependence and collectivism suffer less from stress-related diseases, possibly because it is easier for people in these cultures to obtain social support (Bond, 1991; Brislin, 1993; Cross & Vick, 2001). People who live in cultures that emphasize individualism are more likely to "go it alone"—and their health pays the price. For example, a study of elderly women and men living in Quebec found that those who were lacking in social support experienced greater psychological distress (e.g., depression, anxiety) than those with adequate social support (Lefrançois et al., 2000). According to recent research conducted with parents of children with a disability (recruited from the Society for Manitobans with Disabilities), feeling a lack of support from one's spouse while trying to cope with the many stresses of having a disabled child is associated with greater psychological distress (Marin, Holtzman, DeLongis, & Robinson, 2007). Perhaps more dramatically, the availability of social support has even been found to affect longevity. In a study using a large sample of American men and women in the years 1967 to 1969, it was found that men with a low level of social support were 2 to 3 times more likely to die over the next 12 years than were men with a high level of social support; women with a low level of social support were 1.5 to 2 times more likely to die (House, Robbins, & Metzner, 1982). Interestingly, it is not just receiving social support that is beneficial: A recent study of people aged 65 and over found that those who *gave* support to others, such as helping family members with childcare or doing errands for a neighbour, lived longer than people who did not (Brown, Nesse, & Vinokur, 2003).

It is important to point out that people do not always need or want comfort and advice from others. According to the **buffering hypothesis**, we are in greatest need of social support when we are under stress (Cohen & Wills, 1985; Koopman,

buffering hypothesis

the hypothesis that we need social support only when we are under stress, because it protects us against the detrimental effects of this stress

Hermanson, Diamond, Angell & Spiegel, 1998; Pierce, Frone, Russell, & Cooper, 1996). When times are tough—you've just broken up with your girlfriend or boyfriend, or your parents have gone off the deep end again—social support helps in two ways. First, it can help you interpret an event as less stressful than you otherwise would. Suppose you've just found out that you have midterms in your psychology and calculus classes on the same day. If you have several friends in these classes who can commiserate with you and help you study, you are likely to find the tests less of a big deal than if you had to cope with them on your own. Second, even if we do interpret an event as stressful, social support can help us cope. Suppose you've just done poorly on a midterm and feel bad about it. It's best to have close friends to help you deal with this and figure out how to do better on the next test (Stroebe & Stroebe, 1996). To get an idea of the amount of social support you feel is available in your life, complete the accompanying Try It! quiz.

Try it!

▶ Social Support

This scale is made up of a list of statements, each of which may or may not be true about you. For each statement, choose T (for probably true) if the statement is true about you, or F (for probably false) if the statement is not true about you.

You may find that many of the statements are neither clearly true nor clearly false. If so, try to decide quickly whether probably true or probably false is more descriptive of you. Although some questions will be difficult to answer, it is important that you pick one alternative or the other. Remember to circle only one of the alternatives for each statement.

Read each item quickly but carefully before responding. Remember that this is not a test and there are no right or wrong answers.

1.	There is at least one person I know whose advice I really trust.	T	F
2.	There is really no one I can trust to give me good financial advice.	T	F
3.	There is really no one who can give me objective feedback about how I'm handling my problems.	T	F
4.	When I need suggestions for how to deal with a personal problem, I know there is someone I can turn to.	T	F
5.	There is someone whom I feel comfortable going to for advice about sexual problems.	T	F
6.	There is someone I can turn to for advice about handling hassles over household responsibilities.	T	F
7.	I feel that there is no one with whom I can share my most private worries and fears.	T	F
8.	If a family crisis arose, few of my friends would be able to give me good advice about how to handle it.	T	F
9.	There are very few people I trust to help solve my problems.	T	F
10.	There is someone I could turn to for advice about changing my job or finding a new one.	T	F

Scoring: You get one point each time you answered true (T) to questions 1, 4, 5, 6, and 10 and one point for each time you answered false (F) to questions 2, 3, 7, 8, and 9.

This scale was developed to measure what the researchers call appraisal social support, or "the perceived availability of someone to talk to about one's problems" (Cohen, Mermelstein, Kamarach, & Hoberman, 1985, pp. 75–76). One of their findings was that when people were not under stress, those low in social support had no more physical symptoms than those high in social support. However, when people were under stress, those low in social support had more physical symptoms than those high in social support. This is support for the buffering hypothesis. We need social support the most when times are tough. Another finding was that women scored reliably higher on the social support scale than men did. If you scored lower than you would like, you might want to consider reaching out to others more when you are under stress.

(Adapted from Cohen et al., 1985)

Personality and Coping Styles

Some people, of course, are more likely to seek help from others or, more generally, to react in adaptive ways when under stress. Others seem to react badly when the going gets tough. As seen earlier in our discussion of learned helplessness, part of this comes from the way people explain the causes of a particular setback; explaining the setback in an optimistic way leads to better coping than explaining events in a pessimistic way. Other researchers have looked at this from the vantage point of individual differences, the aspects of people's personalities that make them different from other people.

Optimism Some people are by nature optimistic, generally expecting the best out of life, whereas others always see the dark underside. As you might have guessed, there is evidence that optimistic people react better to stress and are generally healthier than pessimists (Carver & Scheier, 2003; Salovey et al., 2000; Segerstrom, 2005). To get an idea of how optimistic you tend to be, complete the accompanying Try It! exercise.

The good news is that most people have been found to have an optimistic outlook on life. In fact, there is evidence that most people are *unrealistically* optimistic about their lives (Armor & Taylor, 1998; Taylor & Brown, 1988, 1994). As you may recall, in Chapter 4, we discussed research on unrealistic optimism

Try it!

▶ The Life Orientation Test

Indicate the extent of your agreement or disagreement with each of the following 10 statements, using the scale below. Be as accurate and honest as you can on each item, and try not to let your answer to one question influence your answer to other questions. There are no right or wrong answers.

0	1	2	3	4
strongly disagree	disagree	neutral	agree	strongly agree

1. In uncertain times, I usually expect the best. _____
2. It's easy for me to relax. _____
3. If something can go wrong for me, it will. _____
4. I'm always optimistic about my future. _____
5. I enjoy my friends a lot. _____
6. It's important for me to keep busy. _____
7. I hardly ever expect things to go my way. _____
8. I don't get upset too easily. _____
9. I rarely count on good things happening to me. _____
10. Overall, I expect more good things to happen to me than bad. _____

Scoring: First, reverse your answers to questions 3, 7, and 9. That is, for these questions, change 0 to 4, 1 to 3, 3 to 1, and 4 to 0. Then, total these reversed scores and the scores you gave to questions 1, 4, and 10. (Ignore questions 2, 5, 6, and 8, because they were filler items.)

This is a measure of dispositional optimism created by Scheier, Carver, and Bridges (1994). According to these researchers, the higher your score, the more optimistic your approach to life. The average score for university students in their study was 14.3, with no significant differences between women and men. Several studies have found that optimistic people cope better with stress and are healthier than their pessimistic counterparts.

showing that we tend to expect that good events are more likely to happen to us than to our peers, and that negative events are less likely to happen to us than to our peers.

This kind of unrealistic optimism would be a problem if it caused people to make serious mistakes about their prospects in life. Obviously, it would not be a good idea to convince ourselves that we will never get lung disease and therefore we're free to smoke as much as we want. Fortunately, most people have a healthy balance of optimism and reality monitoring. We manage to put a positive spin on many aspects of our lives, which leads to increased feelings of control and self-efficacy. At the same time, most people are able to keep their optimistic biases in check when they are faced with a real threat and need to take steps to deal with that threat (Armor & Taylor, 1998). Consider again cyclist Lance Armstrong's battle with cancer. In one sense, he was quite realistic, finding out all he could about the disease and the latest treatments and seeking the advice of many experts. He even learned to read X-rays as well as the doctors. Despite the severity of his disease, however, and the very real possibility that it might kill him, he was able to maintain a sense of optimism: "What is stronger, fear or hope? . . . Initially, I was very fearful and without much hope, but, as I sat there and absorbed the full extent of my illness, I refused to let the fear completely blot out my optimism" (Armstrong, 2000, p. 99).

> ❝ *Between the optimist and the pessimist the difference is droll; The optimist sees the doughnut, The pessimist the hole.* ❞
>
> —McLandburgh Wilson, 1915

Type A versus Type B Personality Another personality variable that has received a great deal of attention is the **Type A versus Type B personality**, which is a personality typology based on how people typically confront challenges in their lives (Rosenman, 1993). The Type A individual is typically competitive, impatient, hostile, aggressive, and control-oriented, whereas the Type B person is typically patient, relaxed, and noncompetitive. We are all familiar with the Type A personality—this is the person who honks and yells at other drivers when they don't drive to his or her satisfaction. People with this personality type appear to deal with stress efficiently and aggressively. Their hard-driving, competitive approach to life pays off in some respects; Type A individuals tend to get good grades in university and to be successful in their careers (Kliewer, Lepore, & Evans, 1990; Ovcharchyn, Johnson, & Petzel, 1981). However, this success comes

Type A versus Type B personality

a personality typology based on how people typically confront challenges in their lives; the Type A person is typically competitive, impatient, hostile, and control-oriented, whereas the Type B person is typically patient, relaxed, and noncompetitive

◄ People with Type A personality—those who are impatient, competitive, and hostile—are more likely to develop coronary disease than people with a Type B personality—those who are relaxed, patient, and nonhostile. Recent research suggests that it is hostility in particular that is most related to coronary disease.

with some costs. According to research conducted at York University, Type A individuals spend relatively little time on nonwork activities (Burke & Greenglass, 1990) and have more difficulty balancing their work and family lives. For example, Esther Greenglass (1991) found that among female professors, those who were Type A had high career aspirations and reported conflict between professional and familial roles. Type A women with children were particularly hard-driven; they spent an average of 86 hours per week working on job-related and household tasks.

Numerous studies show that Type A individuals are more prone to coronary heart disease than are Type B individuals (Matthews, 1988). What is it about the Type A personality that links it to heart disease? The most likely culprit is hostility (Farber & Burge-Callaway, 1998; Krantz & McCeney, 2002; Smith, 2003; Williams, 2002). Competitiveness and a fast-paced life might not be so bad by themselves, but people who are also chronically hostile are more at risk for coronary disease. Given this risk, it would seem especially important for Type A people to maintain an exercise program. The tricky part is that Type A people turn almost every situation—even exercise—into a competitive one, with the result that exercise can actually have counterproductive effects. For example, in a recent study, Masters, Lacaille, and Shearer (2003) had Type A university students pedal an exercise bike. Those in the competitive condition were told that the researchers would record their distance to see which participant was best. Participants in the noncompetitive condition were simply told that their distance would be recorded. Type A participants in the competitive condition later exhibited greater hostility and other negative emotions than those in the noncompetitive condition. Thus, an activity that should have been beneficial ended up putting Type A participants at even greater risk of coronary problems.

Type A personality may be one explanation for why Stewart McCann (2001, 2003) at the University College of Cape Breton found that people who peak early in their careers have shorter lives. He documented this tendency to "die young if you peak early" among American and French presidents, American state governors, Canadian prime ministers, Nova Scotia premiers, and distinguished psychologists, to name a few. McCann suggests that Type A personality may play a role in the higher mortality rate among such high achievers.

A number of factors determine whether you are Type A or Type B. You are more likely to be a Type A if you are male, your parents are Type A, and you live in an urban rather than a rural area (Rosenman, 1993). The culture in which you grow up may also play a part. There is a higher rate of coronary disease in many Western cultures than in many Asian countries, such as Japan. Why? In Western cultures, where individualism and competitiveness are prized, personality types more like Type A might be encouraged (Triandis, 1995). Second, people who live in cultures that stress collectivism might have more support from other people when they experience stress and, as we have seen, such social support is a valuable way of making stress more manageable (Triandis, 1995).

Hardiness   There are other personality traits that are related to stress and coping. Kenneth Dion has examined the personality variable of hardiness in relation to a particular kind of stress—namely, the stress of being a victim of prejudice and discrimination (Dion, 2002, 2003). **Hardiness** is a combination of self-esteem and a sense of control that helps people interpret and deal with stressful events in a positive, effective manner. In one study, Dion and his colleagues assessed hardiness, stress symptoms, and perceptions of discrimination among members of Toronto's Chinese community (Dion, Dion, & Pak, 1992). They found that discrimination was correlated with psychological stress—but only for those who were low in hardiness. People with hardy personalities reported just as much discrimination—but much less stress.

hardiness

a personality trait defined as a combination of self-esteem and a sense of control

Why might this be? Foster and Dion (2001) wondered whether people make different attributions for negative events, depending on their level of hardiness. To find out, they conducted a study on gender discrimination and found that hardy women tended to attribute discrimination to specific, unstable factors rather than to global, stable factors. In other words, the hardy participants, unlike their less hardy counterparts, treated the discrimination they experienced as an isolated event, and not as an ongoing issue that pervaded all aspects of their lives.

Resilience   Recently, researchers have turned their attention to yet another personality trait—namely, **resilience**, defined as the ability to bounce back from negative experiences and adapt to the demands of life. In one study, the researchers measured resilience among University of Michigan students in the spring of 2001. Those who were high in resilience showed higher life satisfaction, greater optimism, more positive emotions, and less depression than those who were low in resilience (Frederickson, Tugade, Waugh, & Larkin, 2003). As you well know, later in that year, on September 11, 2001, terrorists hijacked and crashed four passenger airplanes in the United States, resulting in more civilian casualties in one day than any other event in American history. Frederickson and colleagues (2003) explored whether the students' reactions to this event would differ, depending on their level of resilience. They found that people experienced negative emotions in the wake of this event, regardless of how resilient they were (i.e., as measured the previous spring). Those who were high in resilience, however, experienced more positive emotions (such as gratitude and love) and less depression than those who were low in resilience. Additional analyses revealed that it was these positive emotions that were the active ingredient in protecting these participants from depression. The researchers concluded that the experience of positive emotions accounts for why resilient people cope better with negative life events and experience greater life satisfaction in general (Fredrickson et al., 2003).

Other research has shown that people are able to "bounce back" fairly quickly from traumatic events, such as terrorist attacks (Bonanno, 2004, 2005; Tucker, Pfefferbaum, Doughty, Jones, Jordan, & Nixon, 2002). In fact, resilience may be the norm rather than the exception. Studies of bereaved spouses, for example, typically find that fewer than half show signs of significant, long-term distress. The others show no signs of depression and are able to experience positive emotions (Bonanno, Moskowitz, Papa, & Folkman, 2005).

Investigations such as these fall largely in the domain of personality psychology, in that they focus on traits that set people apart. What is it about one person that makes him or her more resistant to health problems than another person? The social psychologist takes a different tack, asking instead, Can we identify ways of coping with stress that everyone can adopt to make it easier to deal with the challenges of life?

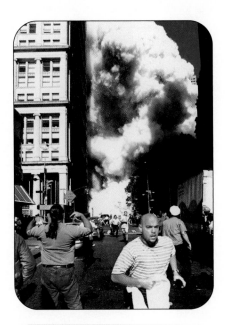

▲ People are surprisingly resilient in the face of stressful events. Studies of reactions to the 9/11 terrorist attacks, for example, have found that relatively few people showed long-term signs of depression or other mental health problems.

resilience

the ability to recover from negative experiences and adapt to the demands of life

Opening Up: Making Sense of Traumatic Events

When something traumatic happens to you, is it best to try to bury it as deeply as you can and never talk about it, or to spend time thinking about the event and discussing it with others? Although folk wisdom has long held that it is best to open up, only recently has this assumption been put to the test. James Pennebaker and his colleagues (Niederhoffer & Pennebaker, 2002; Pennebaker 1990, 1997, 2004; Sloan & Marx, 2004) have conducted a number of interesting experiments on the value of opening up about traumatic events. Pennebaker and Beale (1986), for example, asked university students to write for 15 minutes on each of four consecutive nights about a traumatic event that they experienced.

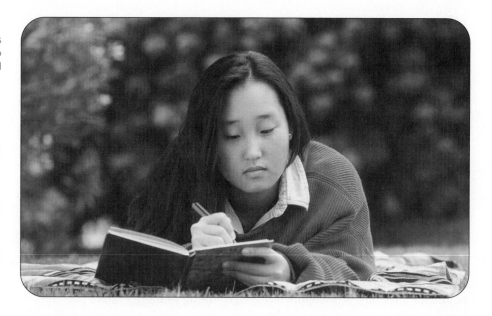

▶ Research by Pennebaker (1990) shows that there are long-term health benefits to writing or talking about one's personal traumas.

The traumas they chose to write about were highly personal and in many cases quite tragic, including such events as rape and the death of a sibling. Students in a control condition wrote for the same amount of time about a trivial event.

Writing about these events certainly was upsetting in the short term: Students who wrote about traumatic events reported more negative moods and showed greater increases in blood pressure. But there were dramatic long-term benefits: These same students were less likely to visit the student health centre during the next six months, and they reported having fewer illnesses. Similarly, in other research, first-year university students who wrote about the problems of entering university (Pennebaker, Colder, & Sharp, 1990) and survivors of the Holocaust who disclosed the most about their World War II experiences improved their health over the next several months (Pennebaker, Barger, & Tiebout, 1989; Pennebaker, Colder, & Sharp, 1990). Other research confirms the importance of opening up about traumatic events. For example, a study of more than 2000 Ontario nurses found that those who reported having a friend to confide in experienced fewer stress-related health problems, although this relation was more likely to hold for women than for men (Walters, Lenton, French, Eyles, Mayr, & Newbold, 1996).

What is it about opening up that leads to better health? Pennebaker (1997) argues that people who write or talk about negative events construct a more meaningful narrative or story that explains the events. He has analyzed hundreds of pages of writing from his participants and finds that the people who improve the most are those who began with rather incoherent, disorganized descriptions of their problem and ended with coherent, organized stories that explained the event and gave it meaning. Once people are able to gain insight into an experience and feel they understand it, they are better able to put it behind them (Hemenover, 2003; Kelly, Klusas, von Weiss, & Kenny, 2001). Further, people might be less inclined to suppress thoughts about a traumatic event if they have written about it. Trying to suppress thoughts can lead to a preoccupation with those very thoughts, because the act of not trying to think about them can actually make us think about them more (Wegner, 1994). Thus, writing about or confiding in others about a traumatic event can help us gain a better understanding of the event and move forward with life.

Prevention: Using Social Psychological Interventions to Promote Healthier Behaviour

In addition to helping people reduce stress, social psychologists can offer some insight into how to get people to change their health habits more directly: to stop smoking, to lose weight, to eat a healthier diet, and to stop abusing alcohol or other drugs. In fact, this is an area in which social psychology can be especially helpful.

North Americans are doing a pretty good job of improving some of their health habits; for instance, the percentage of the Canadian population aged 15 and over who are smokers has been declining slowly and steadily. Currently, this figure is down to 20 percent (Canada, 2005b). People today are also more likely to avoid high-cholesterol and fatty foods than they were a few years ago, and more women are getting Pap smears to detect cervical cancer. In addition, a recent survey found an increase in seat belt usage, an increase in mammography exams for women aged 40 and over, and an increase in flu shots for people over the age of 65 (Nelson, Bland, Powell-Griner, Klein, Wells, Hogelin, & Marks, 2002). There is definitely room for improvement, however. The number of obese Canadian adults and children has increased substantially over the last 25 years. In 1978–1979, the adult obesity rate in Canada was 14 percent; by 2004, this number had risen to 23 percent (Canada, 2005c). The largest increase in obesity has occurred for adults between the ages of 25 and 34—in this age group, obesity has nearly tripled, increasing from 9 percent to 21 percent over the last 25 years. There is also widespread concern about the increase in obesity among children. According to a House of Commons Health Committee Report, in 1978, 15 percent of Canadian children were overweight or obese. By 2004, this number had risen to 26 percent (O'Neill, 2007). Rob Merrifield, who chaired the House of Commons report, made the shocking statement that "For the first time in recorded history, our younger generations are expected to live shorter lives than their parents due to obesity" (quoted in O'Neill, 2007).

In addition, binge drinking on university campuses is occurring at an alarmingly high rate (Wechsler, Lee, Kuo, Siebring, Nelson, & Lee, 2002). A study conducted at York University found that students who drink alcohol tend to do so two to three times per week, and on each occasion generally consume five or six standard drinks (e.g., five or six bottles of beer). For male students, this results in an average of 16 drinks per week; for female students, the weekly average is 13 drinks. According to the researchers, this level of alcohol consumption qualifies as "heavy social drinking" (Wall, Hinson, & McKee, 1998). Binge drinkers are more likely to have a number of health problems, including high blood pressure, heart disease, meningitis, and sexually transmitted diseases. They are also more likely to be in car accidents, die by drowning, and experience domestic violence (Naimi, Brewer, Mokdad, Serdula, Denny, & Marks, 2003).

Finally, as we discussed in Chapter 6, people who are at risk for getting AIDS are not taking as many precautions as they should. For example, a study conducted in Ontario found that only 29 percent of young adults who had engaged in casual sex over the past year had always used a condom (Herold & Mewhinney, 1993). A more recent Canada-wide health survey reported similar findings—namely, that 30 percent of young people reported not having used a condom the last time they had sex. This percentage was even higher (nearly 44 percent) among adults aged 20 to 24 (Canada, 2005d).

We realize that we have just maligned what many people consider to be the chief pleasures of life: sex, eating, drinking, and smoking. Health problems resulting from these behaviours are prevalent precisely because they are so pleasurable—in some cases (e.g., smoking), addictive. It is thus a challenge to find ways to change people's attitudes and behaviours in ways that lead to better health habits. How might we do so?

Let's rewind and think back to Chapter 6, in which we discussed social psychological research on attitude change. In that chapter, we focused on a number of ways in which people's attitudes can be changed. For example, we discussed the use of fear-arousing communications to persuade people to change their attitudes and behaviours. As we mentioned in that chapter, the Canadian government has placed graphic photographs of people suffering from lung cancer and other smoking-related diseases on cigarette packages, with the intent of frightening them into quitting, or not starting, smoking. Many public service advertisements take this approach, trying to scare people into applying sunscreen, using condoms, and wearing seat belts or helmets. These approaches can be effective as long as the level of fear is not so threatening that people tune out the message. It is also important to provide people with specific recommendations for how they can avoid the feared event.

We also discussed the use of cognitive dissonance to promote attitude change. One program of research relevant to health issues is Aronson and colleagues' (Aronson et al., 1991; Stone et al., 1994) use of hypocrisy to induce cognitive dissonance. As you may recall from Chapter 6, in this research, participants in the hypocrisy condition were reminded of their own failures to use condoms and were asked to make a videotape advocating the use of condoms that would be shown to high school students. The researchers hypothesized that these students would reduce the resultant dissonance by subsequently purchasing more condoms than participants in the other conditions (for whom dissonance was not created). And that is exactly what was found.

Message Framing: Stressing Gains versus Losses

Attitude change also depends on the way in which persuasive messages are framed. Suppose, for example, that you were devising a public service ad to lower fatalities from skin cancer. Your goal is to get people to examine their skin regularly for cancer and to use sunscreen when they are exposed to the sun. You could frame your message in terms of what people have to lose by not performing these behaviours; for example, you might emphasize that most skin cancers are fatal if not detected at an early stage. Or you could frame your message in a more positive way by emphasizing what people have to gain; for example, you could say that skin cancers are curable if detected early and that people can decrease their chances of getting skin cancer by using sunscreen.

It might seem that these different messages would have the same effect; after all, they convey the same information—it is a good idea to examine your skin regularly and use sunscreen. It turns out, though, that framing messages in terms of losses versus gains can make a big difference (Jones, Sinclair, & Courneya, 2003; Rothman & Salovey, 1997). When trying to get people to engage in behaviour that will *prevent* disease, it is best to use a "gain frame," emphasizing what they have to gain by engaging in this behaviour (e.g., using sunscreen; Linville, Fischer, & Fischhoff, 1993; Rothman, Martino, Bedell,

Detweiler, & Salovey, 1999). When trying to get people to *detect* the presence of a disease, it is best to use a "loss frame," emphasizing what they have to lose by avoiding this behaviour (e.g., the costs of not examining one's skin for cancer; Meyerowitz & Chaiken, 1987; Rothman, 2000). To give an example, Rothman and colleagues (1993) presented women with information trying to get them to avoid skin cancer. Some participants received a message that focused on the positive benefits of being concerned about skin cancer (e.g., "If they are detected early, most of these cancers are curable"). Other participants received a message framed in terms of the negative consequences of not being concerned about skin cancer (e.g., "Unless they are detected and treated early, most of these cancers are not curable"). It turned out that the gain-framed message worked best with prevention behaviour (i.e., requesting a sample of sunscreen). The loss-framed message worked best on detection behaviour (i.e., the women's intention to perform exams of their skin; Rothman, Salovey, Antone, Keough, & Martin, 1993). So, before designing your public health ad, decide which kind of behaviour you are going to target—a prevention or detection behaviour—and design your ad accordingly.

Now that you have read about several of the factors that influence health behaviour, see if you can improve your habits by taking the advice in the accompanying Try It! exercise.

Try it!

▶ Changing Your Health Habits

Pick a health habit of yours and try to improve it, using the principles we have discussed in this chapter. For example, you might try to lose a few kilograms, exercise more, or cut down on your smoking. This is not easy, of course—if it were, we would all be svelte, physically fit nonsmokers! We suggest that you start small with a limited goal; try to lose 2 kilograms, for example, or increase your exercise by one or two hours a week. Here are some specific suggestions as to how to change your behaviour:

■ Increase your feelings of control over your behaviour, particularly your self-efficacy in this domain. One way to do this is to start small. If you are trying to lose weight, for example, begin slowly with some easy-to-control behaviour. You might start by eliminating one food or beverage from your diet that you do not like all that much but that is pretty fattening. Suppose, for example, that you drink a 200-calorie fruit juice five times a week. Replacing the juice with water will save 52 000 calories a year, which is equivalent to 6 kilograms! The idea is to gain mastery over your

behaviour slowly, improving your feelings of self-efficacy. When you've mastered one behaviour, try another. You can do it!

■ If you experience a setback, such as eating two pieces of cake at a birthday party, avoid a damaging pattern of attributions. Do not assume that the setback was a result of internal, stable, global causes—this will cause learned helplessness. Remember that almost everyone fails the first time they try to diet or quit smoking. It often takes people several attempts; therefore, a setback or two is not because of something unchangeable about you. Keep trying.

■ It can be stressful to change a well-ingrained habit, and it is at times of stress that social support is most important. Talk with your friends and family about your attempts to change your behaviour. Seek their advice and support. Even better, convince several friends to try these techniques with you. Make it a group project, in which you and your friends support each other's efforts to alter your behaviour.

SUMMARY

Stress, defined as the negative feelings that occur when people feel that they cannot cope with their environment, has been found to have a number of negative effects, such as impairment of the immune system. One key determinant of stress is how much **perceived control** people have over their environment. The less control people believe they have, the more likely it is that the event will cause them physical and psychological problems. For example, the loss of control experienced by many older people in nursing homes can have negative effects on their health and mortality. It is also important for people to have high **self-efficacy** in a particular domain, which is the belief in one's ability to carry out specific actions that produce desired outcomes. In addition, the way in which people explain the causes of negative events is critical to how stressful those events will be. When bad things happen, **learned helplessness** results if people make **stable**, **internal**, and **global attributions** for those events. Learned helplessness leads to depression, reduced effort, and difficulty in learning new material.

Coping styles refer to the ways in which people react to stressful events. Men are more likely to react to stress with a **fight-or-flight response**, reacting to stress by either attacking the source of the stress or fleeing from it. Women are more likely to react to stress with a **tend-and-befriend response**, reacting to stress with nurturant activities designed to protect oneself and one's offspring (tending) and creating social networks that provide protection from threats (befriending). **Social support**—the perception that other people are responsive to one's needs—is beneficial for men and women. According to the **buffering hypothesis**, social support is especially helpful in times of stress by making people less likely to interpret an event as stressful and helping them cope with stressful events.

Research on personality traits, such as optimism, the **Type A versus Type B personality**, **hardiness**, and **resilience** focuses on how different types of people deal with stress and how these different styles are related to their physical health. Optimistic, hardy, and resilient people tend to react better to stress and to be healthier. Type A individuals—particularly those with high levels of hostility—are more at risk for coronary disease.

Other researchers focus on ways of coping with stress that everyone can adopt. Several studies show that opening up, which involves writing or talking about one's problems, has long-term health benefits.

It is also important to explore strategies for getting people to act in healthier ways. One strategy is to present people with persuasive communications urging them to adopt better health habits. For example, fear messages can persuade people to change their attitudes and behaviour. Techniques that arouse cognitive dissonance, such as making people feel hypocritical about their failures to use condoms, are effective as well because people will change their health habits in order to reduce the unpleasantness of dissonance. It is also important to tailor persuasive messages to the kinds of behaviour you want people to adopt. To get people to perform detection behaviour, such as examining their skin for cancer, it is best to use messages framed in terms of losses (the negative consequences of failing to act). To get people to perform preventive behaviour, such as using sunscreen, it is best to use messages framed in terms of gains (the positive consequences of performing the behaviour).

Along with a dynamic, electronic version of this text, MyPsychLab offers a wealth of resources to deepen your understanding and test your recall of the material in this chapter—including video and audio clips, simulations and activities, self-assessments, practice tests, and other study materials. The following specific resources are available for this chapter:

 Coping Strategies and Their Effects

 Stress and Health

 Optimism and Resilience

To access MyPsychLab, please visit www.mypsychlab.com (Student Access Code required—packaged with this book).

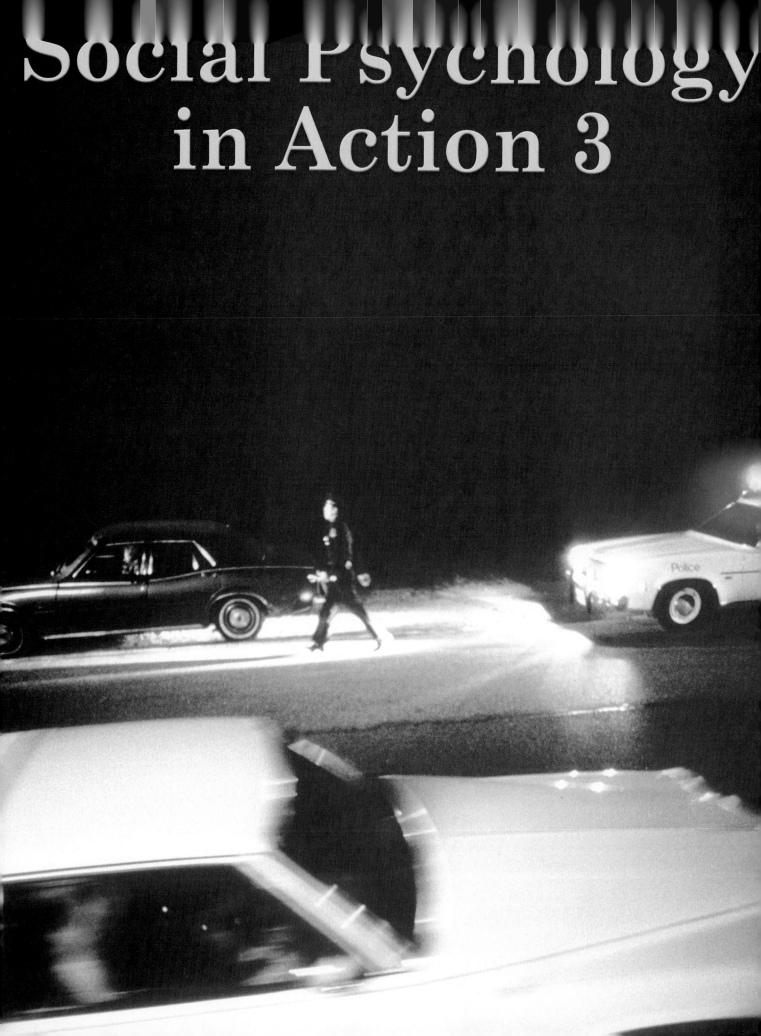

Social Psychology
in Action 3

Social Psychology and the Law

Two days before Christmas in 1981, 16-year-old Barbara Stoppel was found strangled in the Winnipeg doughnut shop where she worked. Several people reported that they had seen a tall, lanky man wearing a cowboy hat near the doughnut shop around the time she was killed. Police artists composed a sketch of the suspect based on the descriptions offered by these eyewitnesses. The police sketch looked a lot like Thomas Sophonow, a tall, lanky hotel doorman from Vancouver who was in Winnipeg at the time. Moreover, several witnesses testified that they had seen him leaving the doughnut shop around the time that Stoppel was strangled.

On the basis of this evidence, Sophonow was charged with murder. His trial in 1982 resulted in a hung jury (jury members were unable to reach a verdict). He was tried a second time in 1983; that jury found him guilty of second-degree murder after only four hours of deliberation. Sophonow appealed the conviction and was tried a third time in 1985. This time, after five days of deliberation (a record in Canada), a "problematic" juror was removed, after which the remaining jurors rendered their verdict: guilty of second-degree murder. Sophonow again appealed. At this point, he had spent four years in prison for a murder he claimed he did not commit. In December 1985, after conducting an extensive examination of this case, the Manitoba Court of Appeal argued that he should not face a fourth trial and set him free—but did not declare him innocent. Many people, including Winnipeg's chief of police, continued to believe that Sophonow was Stoppel's killer.

In 1998, Winnipeg police reopened the case because Sophonow lobbied for DNA testing of gloves that had been found at the scene of the crime. (DNA testing was not available at the time of his trials.) It is unclear whether this turned out to be useful evidence because many people, including Sophonow and a Crown attorney, had tried on the gloves in court. However, police did finally reach the conclusion that Sophonow was not Stoppel's killer and announced that they had a new suspect. On June 8, 2000, after more than 18 years of agony, a sobbing Sophonow accepted apologies from the Winnipeg police and the Crown for sending him to prison for a crime he had not committed.

▶ Thomas Sophonow (*left*) endured three trials and spent four years in jail for a murder he did not commit. His wrongful conviction was due in part to his resemblance to the police sketch circulated at the time. Terry Samuel Arnold (*right*), who became the prime suspect in the Barbara Stoppel case, bore a striking resemblance to Sophonow. Although we will probably never know whether he was Stoppel's killer, Arnold had a long history of violent crime. He committed suicide on March 29, 2005, before his case went to trial.

Life did not return to normal for Sophonow, however. The following year, he had to relive the trauma of his arrest, wrongful conviction, and imprisonment during an inquiry into what went wrong. The judge presiding over the inquiry awarded Sophonow $2.6 million in compensation. However, collecting the compensation turned out to be an uphill battle. More than a year after the inquiry, the city of Winnipeg and the province of Manitoba were still embroiled in a controversy over whose responsibility it was to pay up. A cheque was eventually issued to Mr. Sophonow on February 22, 2003. He decided to accept the settlement so that he could begin to get on with his life.

The case of Thomas Sophonow raises a number of important questions. If he was innocent, why did eyewitnesses say that he was the person leaving the scene of the crime? And why did two juries believe them? How common are such miscarriages of justice? In this module, we will discuss the answers to these and other questions, focusing on the role that social psychological processes play in the legal system.

The Canadian Justice System

Let's begin with a brief review of the Canadian justice system, which consists of criminal and civil law. In civil cases, one party (the plaintiff) brings a complaint against another (the defendant) for violating the former's rights in some way. In this module, we are mostly interested in criminal law. When someone commits a crime and the police arrest a suspect, the Crown attorney's office usually decides whether there is enough evidence to press formal charges. (Sometimes at a preliminary hearing, a judge decides whether there will be a trial.) If there is adequate evidence to press charges, lawyers for the defence and the prosecution gather additional evidence and negotiate with each other. As a result of these negotiations, the defendant may plead guilty to a lesser charge. About a quarter of cases go to trial, during which a jury or a judge decides the defendant's fate.

All of these steps in the legal process are intensely social psychological. In criminal cases, first impressions of the accused and of witnesses have a powerful effect on police investigators and jurors. Attributions about what caused the criminal behaviour are made by police, lawyers, jurors, and the judge; prejudiced beliefs and stereotypical ways of thinking affect those attributions. Attitude change and persuasion techniques abound in the courtroom, as lawyers for each side (i.e., the public and the accused) argue their case and as jurors later debate with one another; and the processes of social cognition affect the jurors' decision making when deciding guilt or innocence. Social psychologists have studied the legal system a great deal in recent years, both because it offers an excellent applied setting in which to examine basic psychological processes and because of its immense importance in daily life. If you, through no fault of your own, are accused of a crime—as Thomas Sophonow was—what do you need to know to convince the system of your innocence?

As we progress through this module, we will from time to time refer to the Thomas Sophonow case, which vividly illustrates many of the points we want to make. We will begin our discussion with the most troubling aspect of the Sophonow case: eyewitness testimony. How accurate are people at identifying someone who has committed a crime?

Eyewitness Testimony

In countries such as Canada, the legal system assigns a great deal of significance to eyewitness testimony. If you are fingered by an eyewitness as the culprit, you are quite likely to be convicted, even if considerable circumstantial evidence indicates you are innocent. Thomas Sophonow was convicted largely because of the testimony of eyewitnesses who claimed that they had seen him near the doughnut shop at about the time of the murder. There were, however, reasons to be suspicious of this testimony. Some witnesses admitted that they had come forward because of the rewards being offered for information on the case. One witness told a dramatic tale of having chased Sophonow after the murder, finally catching him on a bridge, where a fight ensued. This story was never corroborated. Numerous witnesses claimed that, with each trial, their initially sketchy memories had become sharper and more accurate. There also should have been skepticism about the clarity with which witnesses could have seen Sophonow, given that the murder occurred between 8:15 and 8:45 p.m. on a winter evening. Moreover, witnesses offered conflicting reports of the direction in which he had headed. Despite the lack of physical evidence linking Sophonow to the scene of the crime, the eyewitness testimony that he had been in the vicinity of the doughnut shop was enough to convict him—twice.

Systematic experiments have confirmed that jurors rely heavily on eyewitness testimony when they are deciding whether someone is guilty. Unfortunately, jurors also tend to overestimate the accuracy of eyewitnesses (Ellsworth & Mauro, 1998; Loftus, 1979; Potter & Brewer, 1999; Wells & Olson, 2003). Rod Lindsay and his colleagues (1981) conducted a clever experiment that illustrates both of these points. The researchers staged the theft of a calculator in front of unsuspecting University of Alberta students, and then tested how accurately the students could pick out the "thief" from a set of six photographs. In one condition, it was difficult to identify the thief because he had worn a knit cap pulled over his ears and was in the room for only 12 seconds. In the second condition, the thief

The accuracy of eyewitness identification

The accuracy of eyewitness identification depends on the viewing conditions at the time the crime was committed. As in this study, however, most jurors believe that witnesses can correctly identify the criminal even when viewing conditions are poor.

(Adapted from Lindsay, Wells, & Rumpel, 1981)

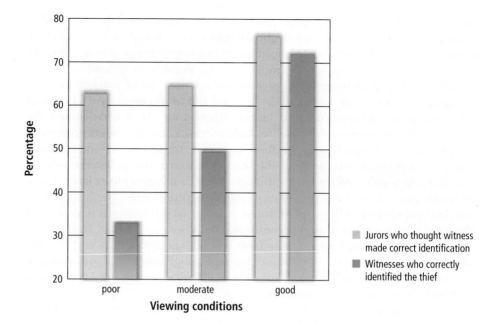

■ Jurors who thought witness made correct identification

■ Witnesses who correctly identified the thief

had worn the knit cap higher on his head, revealing some of his hair, so it was easier to identify him. In the third condition, the thief had worn no hat and had stayed in the room for 20 seconds, making it easiest to identify him. The first set of results was as we'd expect: The more visual information available about the thief, the higher the percentage of students who correctly identified him in the photo lineup (see Figure SPA3.1).

In the next stage of the experiment, a researcher playing the role of lawyer questioned the students about their eyewitness identifications, just as a real lawyer would cross-examine witnesses in a trial. These question-and-answer sessions were videotaped. A new group of participants, playing the role of jurors, watched the videotapes of these cross-examinations and rated the extent to which they believed the witnesses had correctly identified the thief. As shown in Figure SPA3.1, the jurors overestimated the accuracy of the witnesses, especially in the condition where the thief was difficult to identify (Lindsay, Wells, & Rempel, 1981).

Researchers have documented many cases of wrongful arrest, and in a remarkably high proportion of these cases, the wrong person was convicted because an eyewitness mistakenly identified him or her as the criminal (Penrod & Cutler, 1999; Sporer, Koehnken, & Malpass, 1996; Wells, Wright, & Bradfield, 1999; Yarmey, 2001a; for a review of this literature in the context of Canadian law, see Read, Connolly, & Turtle, 2001). Gary Wells and his colleagues (1998), for example, examined 40 cases in which DNA evidence—obtained after the conviction of a suspect—indicated that the suspect was innocent. In 36 of these cases, an eyewitness had falsely identified the suspect as the criminal; five of these falsely accused people were on death row when they were exonerated. According to University of Guelph psychologist A. Daniel Yarmey, "Mistaken eyewitness identification is responsible for more wrongful convictions than all other causes combined" (Yarmey, 2001a).

Why Are Eyewitnesses Often Wrong?

The problem is that our minds are not like video cameras, which can record an event, store it over time, and play it back later with perfect accuracy. Think back to our discussion of social perception in Chapter 4, the study of how we form impressions of, and make inferences about, other people. We saw that a number of distortions can occur. Because eyewitness identification is a form of social perception, it is subject to similar problems, particularly those involving memory.

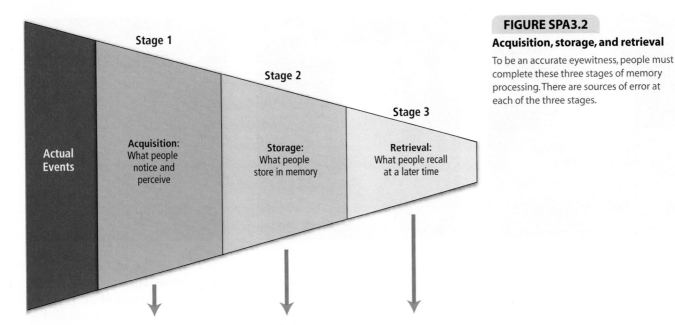

FIGURE SPA3.2

Acquisition, storage, and retrieval

To be an accurate eyewitness, people must complete these three stages of memory processing. There are sources of error at each of the three stages.

To be an accurate witness, a person must successfully complete three stages of memory processing: acquisition, storage, and retrieval of the events witnessed. **Acquisition** refers to the process whereby people notice and pay attention to information in the environment. Because people cannot perceive everything that is happening around them, they acquire only a subset of the information available in the environment. **Storage** refers to the process by which people store in memory information they have acquired from the environment. **Retrieval** refers to the process by which people recall information stored in their memory (see Figure SPA3.2). Eyewitnesses can be inaccurate because of problems at any of these three stages.

Acquisition There are a number of factors that limit the amount of information about a crime that people take in, such as how much time they have to watch an event and the nature of the viewing conditions. As obvious as this may sound, people sometimes forget how these factors limit eyewitness reports of crimes (Read, Connolly, & Turtle, 2001; Yarmey, Jacob, & Porter, 2002). Crimes usually occur under the very conditions that make acquisition difficult: quickly, unexpectedly, and under poor viewing conditions, such as at night. As we have already mentioned, Barbara Stoppel's murder took place after dark on a winter evening. Presumably, it would have been quite difficult for eyewitnesses to get a good look at the murderer making his getaway.

Consider a more recent case that took place in the United States: In October of 1997, four young men in Fairbanks, Alaska, went on a rampage, attacking passersby at random. By the end of the night, they had killed a teenage boy and severely wounded an older man, Franklin Dayton. Eventually, four suspects were arrested and convicted of the crimes, largely on the basis of eyewitness testimony of Fairbanks resident Arlo Olson. Olson testified that he had seen the defendants attack Dayton from "a couple of blocks away"—a distance that was later determined to be 137 metres, one and a half lengths of a football field.

acquisition

the process by which people notice and pay attention to information in the environment; people cannot perceive everything that is happening around them, so they acquire only a subset of the information available in the environment

storage

the process by which people store in memory information they have acquired from the environment

retrieval

the process by which people recall information stored in their memory

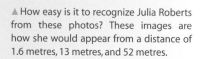

▲ How easy is it to recognize Julia Roberts from these photos? These images are how she would appear from a distance of 1.6 metres, 13 metres, and 52 metres.

How much should we trust Olson's testimony? To answer this question, Geoffrey Loftus and Erin Harley (2005) calculated the amount of detail that is lost in the perception of a face as distance increases. As an illustration, look at the photographs of Julia Roberts above. The one on the left is how Roberts's face would appear if she were standing 1.6 metres away from you. No problem recognizing her here; perhaps you would ask Roberts for her autograph. The middle picture is how her face would appear if she were standing 13 metres away from you. In this case, you might think, "Hmm, that woman looks kind of like Julia Roberts; maybe I'll get a closer look." The picture on the right is how Roberts would appear if she were standing 52 metres away. Here, it would probably never dawn on you that a famous celebrity was in the vicinity.

When Loftus and Harley (2005) showed photographs like these to research participants, they found that accuracy in identifying the celebrities began to drop when the simulated distance exceeded 7.5 metres. At 10 metres only 75 percent of the participants recognized the face, and at 23 metres, only 25 percent of the participants did so. It thus seems unlikely that Arlo Olson could have identified the suspects in the Fairbanks murder case from a distance of 137 metres.

Patricia Tollestrup, John Turtle, and John Yuille (1994) found similar eyewitness errors in their analysis of Canadian criminal cases. They examined records of robbery and fraud cases handled by the RCMP in Vancouver in which a suspect was caught and confessed to the crime. The researchers compared the descriptions of the criminals given by eyewitnesses and victims with the criminals' actual physical characteristics (e.g., were witnesses correct that a criminal had blond hair and a moustache?). Eyewitnesses weren't too bad at remembering some details—100 percent of bystanders correctly remembered whether the criminal had facial hair (although crime victims correctly remembered this only 60 percent of the time). However, only 48 percent of the bystanders and 38 percent of the victims correctly remembered the suspect's hair colour. Most important, neither bystanders nor victims did a very good job of picking the criminal out of a lineup; they correctly identified the criminal only 48 percent of the time.

We should also remember that eyewitnesses who are victims of a crime will be terribly afraid, and this alone can make it difficult to take in everything that is happening. The more stress people are under, the worse their memory for people involved in and the details of a crime (Deffenbacher, Bornstein, & Penrod, 2004). Another reason why victims of crimes have poor memory for a suspect is that they tend to focus their attention on any weapon they see and less on the suspect's features (Christianson, 1992; Loftus, Miller, & Burns, 1978; Pickel, 1998; Shaw & Skolnick, 1999). If someone points a gun at you and demands your money, your attention is likely to be on the gun rather than on whether the robber has blue or brown eyes. (Note that this is also true for people who witness crimes. Tollestrup, Turtle, and Yuille (1994) found that 73 percent of eyewitnesses correctly identified a police suspect when no weapon was present during a crime; this figure dropped to 31 percent when a weapon was present.)

Finally, the information people notice and pay attention to is also influenced by what they expect to see. Consider our friend Alan, a social psychologist who is an expert on social perception. One Sunday, Alan was worried because his neighbour, a frail woman in her eighties, did not appear for church. After knocking on her door repeatedly and receiving no response, Alan jimmied open a window and searched her house. Soon his worst fears were realized: The woman was lying dead on the floor of her bedroom. Shaken, Alan returned to his house and telephoned the police. After spending a great deal of time in the woman's house, a detective came over and asked Alan some pointed questions, such as whether he had noticed any suspicious activity in the past day or two. Alan was confused by this line of questioning and finally burst out, "Why are you asking me these questions? Isn't it obvious that she died of old age? Shouldn't we be notifying her family?" Now it was the detective's turn to look puzzled. "Aren't you the one who discovered the body?" he asked. Alan said he was. "Well," said the detective, "didn't you notice that her bedroom had been ransacked, that there was broken glass everywhere, and that there was a belt tied around her neck?"

It turned out that Alan's neighbour had been strangled by a man who had come to spray her house for insects. There had been a fierce struggle, and the fact that the woman was murdered could not have been more obvious. But Alan saw none of the signs. He was worried that his elderly neighbour had passed away. When he discovered that she had in fact died, he was quite upset, and the furthest thing from his mind was that she had been murdered. As a result, he saw what he expected to see and failed to see the unexpected. When the police later showed him photographs of the crime scene, he felt as though he had never been there. He recognized almost nothing.

Research confirms that people are poor at noticing the unexpected. In one study, participants watched a videotape of two teams passing a basketball back and forth and counted the number of times one team passed the ball to the other. Thirty-five seconds into the film, something weird happened: A woman in a gorilla suit walked into the middle of the basketball game, turned toward the camera, thumped her chest, and then walked away. Meanwhile, the basketball players continued with their passing game. Although it seems like everyone would notice such a bizarre interruption, only half did. The other half simply

> *When an actual perceptual fact is in conflict with expectation, expectation may prove a stronger determinant of perception and memory than the situation itself.*
> —Gordon Allport and Leo Postman, The Psychology of Rumor, 1947

◄ Suppose you were watching a video of two groups of people passing a basketball back and forth and counting the number of passes one team threw to the other. Would you notice the fact that a person dressed in a gorilla suit entered the scene, faced the camera, and thumped her chest? Only 50 percent of the participants noticed the gorilla in a study by Simons & Chabris (1999). People often fail to notice changes in their environments that are unexpected, especially if they are concentrating on something else (e.g., counting the passes). (From Simons & Chabris, 1999)

didn't see the gorilla at all (Simons & Chabris, 1999). Given that crimes are almost always highly unexpected events, it is no surprise that people often fail to notice key details in the crime scene (Rensink, 2002; Simons & Ambinder, 2005).

Unfamiliar events or people are also more difficult to remember than familiar events or people. For example, people are better at recognizing faces within their own race, a phenomenon known as **own-race bias**. White people are better at recognizing white faces than black or Asian faces, black people are better at recognizing black than white faces, and Asians are better at recognizing Asian than white faces (Johnson & Fredrickson, 2005; Levin, 2000; Meissner & Brigham, 2001b). Own-race bias occurs because people have more contact with members of their own race, allowing them to better learn how to distinguish one individual from another (Meissner & Brigham, 2001b). These effects are evident at an early age. For example, Corenblum and Meissner (2006) showed Euro-Canadian children (in grades 2 to 8) and university students in Brandon, Manitoba, photos of African-American faces, Native-Canadian faces, and Euro-Canadian faces. Later, they were given a large set of photographs and asked to identify which ones they had seen earlier (some of the photographs had, in fact, been presented earlier; others were new). Participants were most accurate at identifying own-race faces (i.e., Euro-Canadian faces), followed by Native-Canadian faces, and then African-American faces. The authors point out that accuracy rates reflected the amount of contact these students had with each of these racial groups. Overall, younger children (in grades 2 to 6) were not as accurate as those in grades 7 and 8 and the university students. However, even the youngest children still showed own-race bias.

Another study looked at how three different groups could recognize white and Asian faces: white residents of France, Koreans who grew up in Korea, and Koreans who had been adopted by white French families when they were children. As expected, the first two groups showed own-race bias: The whites had better recall for white faces, and the Koreans had better recall for Asian faces. What about the Koreans who grew up in white families? They had better memory for white faces, which is consistent with the idea that we are best remembering faces that are of the race with which we have the most contact (Sangrigoli, Pallier, Argenti, Ventureyra, & Schonen, 2005).

There is evidence that when people examine same-race faces, they pay close attention to individuating features that distinguish that face from others, such as the height of the cheekbones or the contour of the forehead. When people see the face of a person of another race, they tend to classify the face in terms of race and stop at that. Daniel Levin (2000), a researcher who has investigated this hypothesis, observes that "When a White person looks at another White person's nose, they're likely to think to themselves, 'That's John's nose.' When they look at a Black person's nose, they're likely to think, 'That's a Black nose'" (as quoted in Carpenter, 2000, p. 44). In a series of studies, Levin demonstrated that when people are required to move beyond their initial snap judgments and pay attention to individuating information, they are actually quite capable of discriminating between cross-race faces.

Storage Many people think that memory is like a collection of photographs. We record a picture of an event, such as the face of a robber, and place it in our memory "album." In reality, few of us have a photographic memory. Further, memories, like real photographs, fade with age. However, it is tempting to believe that the picture, once stored, cannot be altered or retouched, and that details cannot be added to or subtracted from the image. If the robber we saw was clean-shaven, surely we will not pencil in a moustache at some later time.

Unfortunately, our memories are far from indelible. People can become confused about where they heard or saw something; memories in one "album" get confused with memories in another. As a result, people can have quite inaccurate recall about what they saw. In the case of Thomas Sophonow, the police—who

---

own-race bias

the finding that people are better at recognizing faces of their own race than those of other races were under extreme pressure to make an arrest—arranged for a key witness to meet Sophonow "accidentally" at the remand centre where he was being held. Is it possible that actually seeing Sophonow altered the witness's memory of the appearance of the "tall, lanky man with a cowboy hat" he allegedly had seen the night of the murder? The answer to this question is yes.

This answer is based on years of research on **reconstructive memory**, the distortion of memories of an event by information encountered after the event has occurred (Lindsay & Read, 2006; Loftus, 1979, 2005; McDonald & Hirt, 1997; Weingardt, Toland, & Loftus, 1994). According to this research, information that we obtain after witnessing an event can change our memory of the event. In a classic study, Elizabeth Loftus and colleagues (Loftus, Miller, & Burns, 1978) showed students 30 slides depicting different stages of an automobile accident. The content of one slide varied; some students saw a car stopped at a stop sign, whereas others saw the same car stopped at a yield sign (see the photos below). After the slide show, the students were asked several questions about the car accident they had "witnessed." The key question varied how the traffic sign was described. In one version, the question was, "Did another car pass the red Datsun while it was stopped at the stop sign?" In another version, the question was, "Did another car pass the red Datsun while it was stopped at the yield sign?" Thus, for half of the participants, the question described the traffic sign as they had in fact seen it. But for the other half, the wording of the question subtly introduced new information—for example, if they had seen a stop sign, the question described it as a yield sign. Would this small change—akin to what might occur when witnesses are being questioned by police investigators or attorneys—influence people's memories of the actual event?

All of the participants were shown the two pictures reproduced below and were asked which one they had originally seen. Most people (75 percent) who

◄ Research participants saw one of these pictures and then tried to remember whether they had seen a stop sign or a yield sign. Many of those who heard leading questions about the street sign made mistaken reports about which sign they had seen.
(From Loftus, Miller, & Burns, 1978)

were asked about the sign they had actually seen chose the correct picture; that is, if they had seen a stop sign and were asked about a stop sign, most of them correctly identified the stop sign photograph. (Note that 25 percent made a crucial mistake on what would seem to be an easy question.) However, of those who had received the misleading question, only 41 percent chose the correct photograph (Loftus et al., 1978). In subsequent experiments, Loftus (1979) found that misleading questions can change people's minds about how fast a car was going, whether broken glass was at the scene of an accident, whether a traffic light was green or red, or whether a robber had a moustache.

In subsequent research along the same lines, Jennifer Tomes and Albert Katz (1997) showed students at the University of Western Ontario crime episodes from various films. For example, one episode from *Talons of the Eagle* showed a woman at an airport, putting her luggage in a red convertible car. A man in a truck drove up and stole her luggage and coat. The woman screamed at him and he drove away. Later, when questioned about the incident, some participants received incorrect information. For example, one question made reference to the assailant's blue truck, when in fact the truck was rust-coloured; in another question it was mentioned that the woman dropped her purse—even though she had not carried one. When participants were again questioned about the crimes, those who had been exposed to misinformation were more likely to have incorporated it into their memory of the event compared with a control group that had not been exposed to misinformation.

Researchers at Dalhousie University have found that people are especially likely to incorporate misinformation into their memories when the event they have witnessed produces negative emotion—which is likely to be the case whenever people witness crimes (Porter, Spencer, & Birt, 2003).

Studies such as these show that the way in which the police and lawyers question witnesses can change the witnesses' reports about what they saw. But we might ask, Do misleading questions alter what is stored in eyewitnesses' memories, or do the questions change only what these people are willing to report, without retouching their memories? Although there is controversy over the answer to this question (Koriat, Goldsmith, & Pansky, 2000; Loftus & Hoffman, 1989; McCloskey & Zaragoza, 1985; Smith & Ellsworth, 1987), most researchers endorse the following position: Misleading questions cause a problem with **source monitoring**, the process by which people try to identify the source of their memories (Johnson, Hashtroudi, & Lindsay, 1993; Lyle & Johnson, 2006; Mitchell & Johnson, 2000; Mitchell, Johnson & Mather, 2003).

In research conducted at Bishop's University, for example, when participants received information about a crime via a radio broadcast and in written form, there was a tendency to confuse the source of these statements. Most frequently, this took the form of thinking they'd heard something on the radio that they had actually read about (Eberman & McKelvie, 2002). Similarly, in the Tomes and Katz (1997) study we discussed earlier, people who saw a rust-coloured truck but received the misleading question about a blue truck now had two pieces of information in memory: the rust-coloured truck and the blue truck. This is all well and good, as long as they could remember where these memories came from: the rust-coloured truck from the crime they saw earlier, and the blue truck from the question they were asked later. The problem is that people often become mixed up about where they heard or saw something—in this case, mistakenly believing that the truck in the crime scene was blue. In short, when information is stored in memory, it is not always well tagged as to where it came from.

The implications for legal testimony are sobering. Eyewitnesses who are asked misleading questions often report seeing things that were not really there. In addition, eyewitnesses might be confused as to why a suspect looks familiar.

> *Give us a dozen healthy memories, well-formed, and . . . we'll guarantee to take any one at random and train it to become any type of memory we might select—hammer, screwdriver, wrench, stop sign, yield sign, Indian chief—regardless of its origin or the brain that holds it.*
>
> —Elizabeth Loftus and Hunter Hoffman (1989)

source monitoring

the process whereby people try to identify the source of their memories

"Take your time, Mrs. Scradler, and tell us which of these men you saw looking in your second-story window."

Thomas Sophonow might have looked familiar to eyewitnesses because he happened to resemble the police sketch or because they had seen him in the earlier trials or, as in the case of one witness, because he had seen Sophonow at the remand centre.

Retrieval Suppose the police have arrested a suspect and want to see if you, the eyewitness, can identify the person. Typically, the police arrange a lineup of suspects at the police station, where you will be asked whether one of several people is the perpetrator. Sometimes you will be asked to look through a one-way mirror at an actual lineup of the suspect and some foils (people known not to have committed the crime). Other times you will be asked to examine videotapes of a lineup or photographs of the suspect and the foils. In each case, if a witness identifies a suspect as the culprit, the suspect is likely to be charged and convicted of the crime. After all, the argument goes, if an eyewitness saw the suspect commit the crime and then picked the suspect out of a lineup later, that's pretty good evidence the suspect is the guilty party.

Do lineups result in correct identifications? Research conducted with people living in southern Ontario suggests that lineups have a higher success rate than the alternative of showing eyewitnesses only one person (Yarmey, Yarmey, & Yarmey, 1996). More specifically, Yarmey and colleagues found that if only one person was shown and that person was innocent, a mistaken identification was four times more likely than when the same person appeared in a six-person lineup. Errors were especially likely if the innocent person wore clothing similar to that worn by the person who committed the crime. Thus, the use of lineups appears to be better than the alternative of presenting only one person and asking eyewitnesses whether that person committed the crime.

This is not to say, however, that lineups are without problems. Just as there are problems with acquisition and storage of information, so too can there be problems with how people retrieve information from their memory (Ellsworth & Mauro, 1998; Wells & Olson, 2003). A number of things other than the image of a person that is stored in memory can influence whether eyewitnesses will pick someone out of a lineup. Witnesses often choose the person in a lineup who most resembles the criminal, even if the resemblance is not strong.

Suppose, for example, that a 19-year-old woman commits a robbery and the police mistakenly arrest you, a 19-year-old woman, for the crime. They put you in a lineup and ask witnesses to pick out the criminal. Which do you think would be more fair: if the other people in the lineup were a 20-year-old man, a 3-year-old child, and an 80-year-old woman; or if the other people were all 19-year-old women? In the former case, the witnesses might pick you only because you are the one who most resembles the actual criminal (Buckhout, 1974). In the latter case, it is much less likely that the witnesses will mistake you for the criminal, because everyone in the lineup is the same age and sex as the culprit (Wells, 1993; Wells & Luus, 1990).

In the Thomas Sophonow case, apparently witnesses were asked by police to identify the man with the cowboy hat they had seen outside the doughnut shop from a photographic lineup. Nine of the photographs had been taken indoors and none of the people wore hats. The tenth photo—the photo of Thomas Sophonow—was larger than the others, was taken outdoors, and showed him wearing a cowboy hat. Police later admitted that the photo gallery was biased and presented a less biased lineup to the witnesses. According to Elizabeth Loftus, who testified at the inquiry into Sophonow's wrongful conviction, it is highly unlikely that the new, fairer lineup would have reversed the damage done by the first one. In her words, "That's like trying to squeeze toothpaste back in the tube" (Loftus, quoted in Janzen, 2001).

To avoid this "best guess" problem, wherein witnesses pick the person who looks most like the suspect, as well as other problems with lineup identifications, social psychologists recommend that police follow these steps:

- *Ensure that everyone in the lineup resembles the witness's description of the suspect.* Doing so will minimize the possibility that the witness will simply choose the person who looks most like the culprit (Wells et al., 1998).

- *Tell the witnesses that the person suspected of the crime may or may not be in the lineup.* If witnesses believe that the culprit is present, they are much more likely to choose the person who looks most like the culprit, rather than saying that they aren't sure or that the culprit is not present. In short, false identifications are more likely to occur when people believe that the culprit is in the lineup (Clark, 2005; Malpass & Devine, 1981; Wells et al., 1998, 2000).

- *Do not always include the suspect in an initial lineup.* If a witness picks out someone as the culprit from a lineup that includes only foils (i.e., a blank lineup), you will know the witness is not reliable. In a study conducted at the University of Alberta, for example, 61 percent of the research participants who made an identification from a blank lineup failed to identify the correct person later when he was actually present in a photo lineup. In contrast, of participants who correctly indicated that the suspect was not in the blank lineup, only 31 percent later made a mistaken identification when shown a lineup containing the suspect (Wells, 1984).

- *Make sure that the person conducting the lineup does not know which person in the lineup is the suspect.* This avoids the possibility that the person will unintentionally communicate to the witness who the suspect is (Wells et al., 1998).

- *Present pictures of people sequentially instead of simultaneously.* Doing so makes it more difficult for witnesses to compare all of the pictures, choosing the one that most resembles the criminal, even when the criminal is not actually in the lineup (Meissner, Tredoux, & Parker, 2005; Sporer, 1994; Steblay, Dysart, Fulero, & Lindsay, 2001). For example, in a study conducted at Queen's University, 35 percent of research participants exposed to a simultaneous lineup mistakenly identified an innocent person as the perpetrator, whereas only 18 percent of those exposed to a sequential lineup made a mistaken identification (Lindsay & Wells, 1985).

- *Present witnesses with photographs of people and sound recordings of their voices.* Witnesses who both see and hear members of a lineup are much more likely to identify the person they saw commit a crime than are people who only see pictures or only hear voice recordings (Melara, DeWitt-Rickards, & O'Brien, 1989). In fact, Yarmey and colleagues (2001) found that people are really quite inaccurate when identifying voices—much less accurate than they think they are. For example, if a voice was unfamiliar to the participants, the false identification rate was 45 percent (Yarmey, Yarmey, Yarmey, & Parliament, 2001).

- *Composite face programs should perhaps be avoided.* Sometimes witnesses are asked to reconstruct the face of a suspect, using computer programs that are designed for this purpose. Typically, the faces that witnesses generate with these programs do not look much like the actual suspect. Further, a recent study found that people who generated faces with these programs actually had a worse memory for the suspect than people who did not (Wells, Charman, & Olson, 2005).

- *Try to minimize the time between the crime and the identification of suspects.* Studies based on staged crimes (Yarmey, Yarmey, & Yarmey, 1996) and actual crimes reported in RCMP records (Tollestrup, Turtle, & Yuille, 1994) have found that the longer the time that elapses between seeing a suspect and being asked to identify the person from a lineup, the greater the likelihood of error (Read, Connolly, & Turtle, 2001).

Judging Whether Eyewitnesses Are Mistaken

Suppose you are a police detective or a member of a jury who is listening to a witness describe a suspect. How can you tell whether the witness's memory is accurate or whether he or she is making one of the many mistakes in memory we have just documented? It might seem that the answer to this question is pretty straightforward: Pay careful attention to how confident the witness is. Suppose the witness stands up in the courtroom, points her finger at the defendant, and says, "That's the man I saw commit the crime. There's absolutely no doubt in my mind—I'd recognize him anywhere." Sounds pretty convincing, doesn't it? Compare this testimony with a witness who says, "Well, gee, I'm really not sure, because it all happened so quickly. If I had to guess, I'd say it was the defendant, but I could be wrong." Which witness would you be more likely to believe? The eyewitness who was more confident, of course. And you would not be alone—there is evidence that confident witnesses are more likely to be believed by police investigators, judges, and jurors (Read, Connolly, & Turtle, 2001).

In the Thomas Sophonow case, Sophonow testified that on the evening of Barbara Stoppel's murder, he had stopped at a store to buy some food. While he was there, he decided to purchase stockings filled with treats to distribute to children who would have to spend Christmas in a hospital. At the second trial, the court heard testimony from a ward clerk at a Winnipeg hospital, who testified that a man fitting Sophonow's description had arrived at her desk between 8:10 and 8:30 p.m. on December 23 with Christmas stockings for sick children. The clerk had told him that her hospital didn't have a children's ward, but she gave him directions to three hospitals that did. Employees of those hospitals verified that a tall, slim man had arrived with Christmas stockings; however, none of them was certain that the man had been Sophonow, nor was any clerk certain of the exact date that the stockings had been delivered. In contrast, the eyewitnesses who identified him as the man near the doughnut shop became more confident of their descriptions with each trial. Who did the jurors believe? The witnesses who presented their testimony with greater confidence, apparently.

Does Certainty Mean Accuracy? The only problem—and it is a big one—is that numerous studies have shown that a witness's confidence is not strongly related to his or her accuracy (Brewer & Wells, 2006; Olsson, 2000; Read, Connolly, & Turtle, 2001; Smith, Kassin, & Ellsworth, 1989; Wells, Olson, & Charman, 2002; Yarmey, Jacob, & Porter, 2002). It is dangerous to assume that because a witness is very confident, he or she must therefore be correct. For example, in the calculator theft experiment we discussed earlier, witnesses who saw the crime under poor viewing conditions—in which the "thief" wore the cap over his ears—had as much confidence in their identifications as did witnesses who saw the crime under moderate or good viewing conditions, even though the former were considerably less accurate (Lindsay et al., 1981; see Figure SPA3.1 on page 470).

Similar results were obtained at the University of Alberta when Wells, Lindsay, and Ferguson (1978) conducted another version of the calculator theft study described earlier (Lindsay et al., 1981). Participants in this study were asked to identify the calculator "thief" from a photo lineup as well as to indicate how certain they were that they had identified the correct person. The correlation between participants' confidence that they had made a correct identification and the accuracy of their identifications was only 0.29 (recall that a perfect correlation is 1.00). Participants also were asked questions about the event, as if under cross-examination in a trial. Other research participants, serving as jurors, observed the cross-examinations. It turned out that jurors were more likely to believe confident, rather than unconfident, witnesses—a disturbing finding, given the weak relation between accuracy and confidence. Moreover, it's not only jurors who are prone to equating certainty with accuracy. Wise and Safer (2004) distributed a survey to 160 U.S. judges in which various statements about eyewitness testimony were presented. Only 32 percent of the judges disagreed with the statement "At trial, an eyewitness's confidence is a good predictor of his or her accuracy in identifying the defendant as the perpetrator of the crime."

> *No subjective feeling of certainty can be an objective criterion for the desired truth.*
>
> —Hugo Münsterberg, On the Witness Stand, 1908

Signs of Accurate Testimony How, then, can we tell whether a witness's testimony is correct? It is by no means easy, but research by David Dunning and Lisa Beth Stern (1994; Stern & Dunning, 1994) suggests some answers. They showed participants a film in which a man stole some money from a woman's wallet, asked participants to pick the man out of a photo lineup, and then asked participants to describe how they had made up their minds. Accurate witnesses tended to say that they didn't really know how they recognized the man, that his face just "popped out" at them. Inaccurate witnesses tended to say that they used a process of elimination whereby they deliberately compared one face with another. Ironically, taking more time and thinking more carefully about the pictures was associated with making more mistakes. We should, therefore, be more willing to believe a witness who says, "I knew it was the defendant as soon as I saw him in the lineup" than one who says, "I compared everyone in the lineup, thought about it, and decided it was the defendant." Subsequent research has shown that people are most accurate when they make their judgment quickly—in 10 seconds or less (Dunning & Perretta, 2002; Weber, Brewer, & Wells, 2004).

The Problem with Verbalization It would seem that another way to improve accuracy of eyewitness identification would be to tell people to write down a description of the suspect as soon as they can, to help them remember what they saw. Studies by Jonathan Schooler and Tonya Engstler-Schooler (1990), however, show that trying to put an image of a face into words can make people's memory worse. They showed students a film of a bank robbery. Participants in the verbalization condition were asked to write a detailed description of the robber's face. Those in the no-verbalization condition spent the same amount of time completing an unrelated task. All students then tried to identify the robber from a photo lineup of eight faces. It might seem that writing a description of the robber would be a good memory aid and make people's identifications more accurate. In fact, the opposite was true: Only 38 percent of the people in the verbalization condition correctly identified the robber, compared with 64 percent of the people in the no-verbalization condition.

Schooler and Engstler-Schooler (1990; see also Meissner & Brigham, 2001b; Schooler, Fiore, & Brandimonte, 1997; Wickham & Swift, 2006) suggest that trying to put a face into words is difficult and impairs memory for that face. Using the word *squinty* to describe a robber's eyes, for example, might be a general description of what his eyes looked like but probably does not capture the subtle contours of his eyes, eyelids, eyelashes, eyebrows, and upper cheeks. When you see the photo lineup, if you look for eyes that are squinty, doing so interferes with your attention to the finer details of the faces. If you ever witness a crime, then, you should not try to put into words what the criminal looked like. And if you hear someone say she or he wrote down a description of the criminal and then deliberated long and hard before deciding whether the person was present at a lineup, you might doubt the accuracy of the witness's identification.

To sum up, several factors make eyewitness testimony inaccurate, leading to all too many false identifications. Perhaps the criminal law system in Canada should rely less on eyewitness testimony than it now does. This might mean that some guilty people go free, but it would avoid many false convictions. To see how accurate you and your friends are at eyewitness testimony, and to illustrate some of the pitfalls we have discussed, tackle the accompanying Try It! exercise.

Try it!

▶ The Accuracy of Eyewitness Testimony

Try this demonstration with a group of friends who you know will be gathered in one place, such as a dorm room or an apartment. The idea is to stage an incident in which someone comes into the room suddenly, acts in a strange manner, and then leaves. Your friends will then be asked to recall as much as they can about this person, to see if they are good eyewitnesses. Here are some specific instructions about how you might do this:

1. Take one friend, whom we will call the actor, into your confidence before you do this exercise. Ideally, the actor should be a stranger to the people who will be the eyewitnesses. The actor should suddenly rush into the room where you and your other friends are gathered and act in a strange (but nonthreatening) manner. For example, the actor could hand someone a flower and say, "The flower man cometh!" Or, he or she could go up to each person and say something unexpected, such as, "Meet me in Moscow at New Year's." Ask the actor to hold something in his or her hand during this episode, such as a pencil, a shoelace, or a banana. Keep track of how long the episode takes. Remember: The actor should not act in a violent or threatening way, or make the eyewitnesses uncomfortable. The goal is to act in unexpected and surprising ways, not to frighten people.

2. After a few minutes, the actor should leave the room. Inform your friends that you staged this event as a demonstration of eyewitness testimony and that if they are willing, they should try to remember, in as much detail as possible, what occurred. Ask them to write down answers to these questions:

   a. What did the actor look like? Write down a detailed description.
   b. What did the actor say? Write down his or her words as best as you can remember.
   c. How much time passed between the moment the actor entered the room and the point at which he or she left?
   d. Did the actor touch anyone? If so, whom did he or she touch?
   e. What was the actor holding in his or her hand?

3. After everyone has answered these questions, ask them to read their answers out loud. How much did they agree? How accurate were people's answers? Discuss with your friends why they were correct or incorrect in their descriptions.

Note: This demonstration will work best if you have access to a video camera and can record the actor's actions. That way, you can play the video to assess the accuracy of the eyewitnesses' descriptions. If you cannot record it, you can ask the actor to repeat his or her actions.

Judging Whether Eyewitnesses Are Lying

There is yet another reason eyewitness testimony can be inaccurate: Even if witnesses have very accurate memories for what they saw, they might deliberately lie when on the witness stand. In the Thomas Sophonow case, some witnesses admitted that they testified because they wanted a reward. It also turned out that the man who told the wild tale of chasing and catching Sophonow on a bridge was lying. To make matters worse, the Crown relied on jailhouse informants who claimed that Sophonow had confessed to them that he was Barbara Stoppel's killer. Deals had been struck with these informants in exchange for their testimony. Why couldn't two different sets of jurors see through these stories?

Sadly, the Sophonow case is not unique in this regard. In other cases of wrongful conviction, such as those of David Milgaard and Donald Marshall, police and jury members believed the false stories of the acquaintances who testified against them. Sometimes, the truth is never established.

How can we tell whether witnesses are lying or telling the truth? Several studies have tested people's ability to detect deception (Bond & Atoum, 2000; DePaulo & Friedman, 1998; Ekman, 2002; Gordon & Miller, 2000). In a typical study, participants watch a video or listen to an audiotape of people who are lying half of the time and telling the truth half of the time. The participants' task is to distinguish the lies from the truths. In a review of over 250 such studies, Bond and DePaulo (2006) found that whereas people are better than chance at telling lies from truths, their level of accuracy is not impressive: On average, people were correct only 54 percent of the time (where 50 percent would be guessing at chance levels). And as with eyewitness testimony, confidence that you have correctly identified the lies and truths is not strongly correlated with accuracy, as demonstrated by researchers at Dalhousie University (Porter, Woodworth, & Birt, 2000).

Interestingly, people with a lot of experience dealing with liars (e.g., U.S. customs officers, detectives, judges) are no more accurate at detecting deception than are university students (e.g., DePaulo & Pfeiffer, 1986). Porter and colleagues (2000) obtained similar findings when comparing Canadian federal parole officers with Dalhousie University students—both groups performed at, or below, chance levels. These researchers found that if people—in this case, parole officers and university students—are given extensive training, their accuracy at detecting deception can improve— but their performance remains far from perfect (Porter et al., 2000).

Are Polygraph Machines Accurate at Detecting Lies? If people are poor lie detectors, perhaps machines can do better. You've probably heard of a **polygraph** or "lie detector"—a machine that measures people's physiological responses, such as their heart rate and breathing rate. Polygraph operators attempt to tell if someone is lying by observing how that person responds physiologically while answering questions. The assumption is that when people lie they become anxious, and this anxiety can be detected by increases in heart rate, breathing rate, and so on.

Polygraphs have both strong supporters (e.g., Raskin, Honts, & Kircher, 1997) and steadfast critics (e.g., Lykken, 1998). How well do these tests actually work? First, polygraph results are only as good as the person operating and interpreting the test. With several responses being measured, it is not always easy to tell whether a person has had more of a physiological response to one question than to another. One disturbing finding is that operators often disagree with one another, suggesting that the test is by no means infallible (Ellsworth & Mauro, 1998). Research conducted at the University of New Brunswick has shown that even the order in which questions are asked can influence the results (Cullen & Bradley, 2004).

> " *A man's most valuable trait is a judicious sense of what not to believe.* "
>
> —Euripides (c. 480–406 BC)

polygraph

a machine that measures people's physiological responses (e.g., heart rate); polygraph operators attempt to tell if someone is lying by observing how that person responds physiologically while answering questions

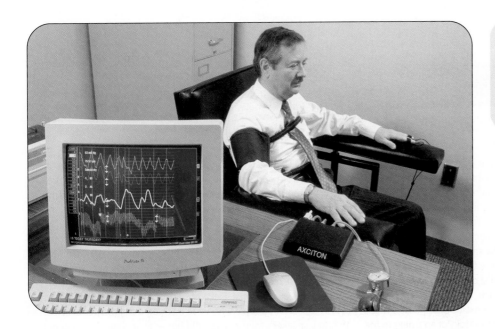

Granted, when the test is administered under optimal conditions by an experienced examiner, it does reveal whether someone is lying or telling the truth at levels better than chance. But even then it is not perfect (Ben-Shakhar & Elaad, 2003; Ellsworth & Mauro, 1998; Iacono & Patrick, 1999; Saxe, 1994). The error rates vary somewhat, depending on the technique used to administer the test. Some studies have found that false negatives—in which liars are found to be telling the truth—are the most common kind of error (Honts, 1994). In contrast, research conducted with inmates in a B.C. prison found that there was a tendency for the test to mistakenly classify as liars those who were actually telling the truth (Patrick & Iacono, 1989). One review concluded that averaging across all the different techniques, the polygraph typically misidentifies between 10 percent and 15 percent of liars as truth tellers (false negatives) and between 10 percent and 15 percent of truth tellers as liars (false positives; Ekman, 2002). Because of the rate of error, Canada does not allow the results of polygraph tests to be used in court. In Thomas Sophonow's third trial, his defence lawyer attempted to have him take a lie detector test in court, but the judge refused. We might note that after Sophonow was acquitted, he took a lie detector test when he was interviewed on the television program *W5* in 1986 and passed with flying colours.

If falsehood, like truth, had only one face, we would be in better shape. For we would take as certain the opposite of what the liar said. But the reverse of truth has a hundred thousand shapes.

—Montaigne, Essays, 1575

Researchers continue to try to develop better lie detectors, using measures such as patterns of brain waves, involuntary eye movements, and blood flow in the face using high-definition thermal imaging technology (Knight, 2004; Pavlidis, Eberhardt, & Levine, 2002). So far, however, none of these measures has proved to be any better than the polygraph (National Research Council, 2003). A concern with all physiological measures of deception is whether guilty people can learn to beat the tests. There is some evidence that people can deliberately act in ways that reduce the validity of the results of polygraph tests, such as biting their tongue and doing mental arithmetic. The search continues, but there is still no perfect lie detection machine that can always differentiate lies from the truth (Iacono, 2000; Kleiner, 2002).

To see how well you and your friends can tell whether someone is lying, do the Try It! on the next page. How did you do? It would be nice if there were a foolproof method of telling whether someone is lying. If so, people such as David Milgaard, Stephen Truscott, Donald Marshall, and Thomas Sophonow—to name a few— would not have had to spend years in prison for crimes they did not commit.

Try it!

▶ Lie Detection

The purpose of this exercise, which should be done with a group of friends, is to see how well people can tell if someone is lying. Ask for a volunteer to be the speaker and the others to be the audience. The speaker's job will be to lie about how much he or she likes five acquaintances from high school, and to tell the truth about how much he or she likes five other acquaintances from high school. The audience's job is to try to guess when the speaker is telling the truth and when he or she is lying. Here are some specific instructions:

Instructions for the speaker: Make a list of 10 people you knew in high school and think about how much you liked each person. Randomly choose 5 people and put a T next to their names. These are the people about whom you will be truthful. Put an L next to the other names. These are the people about whom you will lie. Take a few minutes to think about what you will say. When you are ready, describe your feelings toward each person (truthfully or not) to the audience. Give a few sentences about each person.

Instructions for the audience: The speaker will be describing his or her feelings about 10 acquaintances from high school. He or she will be telling the truth about half of the people and lying about the

other half. Listen carefully and try to guess when the speaker is telling the truth and when he or she is lying. You may use any cues you want to make your decision. Write down the numbers 1 to 10, and put "Truth" or "Lie" next to the number of each person the speaker describes.

Variation: Here is an interesting variation you can try. Have half of the audience sit with their backs to the speaker so they can hear but not see him or her. The other half of the audience should sit facing the speaker. Which group was better at detecting when the speaker was lying? Bella DePaulo, Dan Lassiter, and Julie Stone (1983) found that people who were instructed to pay special attention to a speaker's tone of voice did better at lie detection than did people instructed to pay attention to how the speaker looked. When people can see a speaker, they tend to focus on facial cues that they think are good indications of lying but which, in fact, are not. Therefore, the group of people who cannot see the speaker might rely more on tone of voice and may, as a result, be more accurate.

See page 500 for scoring instructions.

Can Eyewitness Testimony Be Improved?

We have seen a number of ways in which eyewitness testimony can go wrong. Given the importance of such testimony in criminal trials, are there ways to improve it? Two general approaches have been tried but, unfortunately, neither has proven to be very successful.

The first involves hypnosis. You may have seen movies in which a witness to a terrible crime has no memory of what occurred—until he or she is put under hypnosis. Then, while in a trance-like state, the person is able to describe the murderer in great detail. Unfortunately, this is one area in which the movies do not reflect real life. University of Toronto psychologist Marilyn Smith (1983) conducted a review of the literature and concluded that there is no hard evidence that people's memories improve when they are hypnotized. Subsequent research supports this conclusion (Ellsworth & Mauro, 1998; Erdelyi, 1994; Kebbell & Wagstaff, 1998; see review by Read, Connolly, & Turtle, 2001). In fact, there is some evidence that when people are under hypnosis they are more susceptible to suggestion, coming to believe they saw things that they did not (Lynn, Lock, Loftus, Krackow, & Lilienfeld, 2003; Scoboria, Mazzoni, Kirsch, & Milling, 2002). Even worse, people tend to become more confident in their memories after they have been hypnotized, even if they are no more accurate (Spiegel & Spiegel, 1987). This is dangerous because, as we saw earlier, juries often interpret a witness's confidence as a gauge of his or her accuracy, even though confidence is not strongly related to accuracy.

The second way people have tried to increase eyewitness accuracy is with the use of the **cognitive interview** (Geiselman & Fischer, 1989). With this technique, a trained interviewer tries to improve an eyewitness's memory by focusing the

cognitive interview
a technique whereby a trained interviewer tries to improve eyewitnesses' memories by focusing their attention on the details and context of the event

individual's attention on the details and context of the event. This is done chiefly by asking the person to recall the event several times from different starting points (e.g., from the beginning of the event and from the middle of the event) and by asking the person to create a mental image of the scene. Unfortunately, this technique has not proved to be any better than hypnosis. In fact, it may increase errors and confabulations of memory, especially when used with children (Finger & Pezdek, 1999; Fisher, Brennan, & McCauley, 2001; Whitehouse, Orne, Dinges, Bates, Nadon, & Orne 2005). One reason for this is that repeatedly imagining an event has been found to increase source monitoring errors, whereby people become confused about whether they actually witnessed an event or simply imagined it later (Johnson, Raye, Wang, & Taylor, 1979).

So far, then, researchers have not found a tried-and-true way to improve eyewitnesses' memories. However, what can be done is to take steps to avoid the pitfalls we have discussed. According to a leading expert in this area, Gary Wells, the most effective approach for reducing the rate of false convictions in the legal system is to improve how police conduct eyewitness interviews and identification procedures. Wells has assisted in developing a National Institute of Justice guide for law enforcement on eyewitness evidence, which outlines procedures for obtaining more accurate information from eyewitnesses. Recommendations include avoiding leading or suggestive questions when interviewing witnesses, telling witnesses that the suspect may or may not be in a lineup, and so on. The hope is that these procedures will prevent witness bias from occurring in the first place (Cynkar, 2007).

The Recovered Memory Debate   Another form of eyewitness memory has received a great deal of attention: the case in which a person recalls having been the victim of a crime, typically sexual abuse, after many years of being consciously unaware of that fact. Not surprisingly, the accuracy of such **recovered memories** has been hotly debated (McNally, 2003; Pezdek & Banks, 1996; Schooler & Eich, 2000). This debate received extensive media attention in Canada in 1992, when John Popowich, a Saskatoon police officer, was charged with sexually assaulting children at a daycare centre. The children claimed that he and other adults had forced them to drink blood, perform sexual acts, and watch people having their eyes plucked out. These charges came at a time when *false memory syndrome* was receiving a lot of attention in the media and the courts; as a result, the children's testimony was believed. After a 10-year fight that took a tremendous toll on his personal and professional life, Popowich managed to establish his innocence. In the summer of 2002, Saskatchewan's justice minister issued an apology to Popowich for his wrongful conviction and agreed to pay $1.3 million in compensation (Millin, 2002).

The question of the accuracy of recovered memories is highly controversial. On one side are writers such as Ellen Bass and Laura Davis (1994), who claim that it is not uncommon for women who were sexually abused to repress these traumas so that they have absolutely no memory of them. The abuse and its subsequent repression, according to this view, are responsible for many psychological problems, such as depression and eating disorders. Later in life, often with the help of a psychotherapist, these events can be "recovered" and brought back into memory. On the other side of the controversy are academic psychologists who argue that the accuracy of recovered memories cannot be accepted on faith (e.g., Loftus, 2003; Schacter, 1996; Schooler, 1999). These psychologists acknowledge that sexual abuse and other childhood traumas are a terrible problem and more common than we would like to think. They further agree that claims of sexual abuse should be taken very seriously and fully investigated, and that when sufficient evidence of guilt exists, the person responsible for the abuse should be prosecuted.

But here's the problem: What is "sufficient evidence"? Is it enough that someone remembers, years later, that he or she has been abused, in the absence

recovered memories
recollections of an event, such as sexual abuse, that have been forgotten or repressed

false memory syndrome

remembering a past traumatic experience
that is objectively false but nevertheless
accepted as true

of any other evidence of abuse? According to many researchers, the answer is no, because of **false memory syndrome**: People can recall a past traumatic experience that is objectively false but that they believe is true (Kihlstrom, 1996). There is evidence that people can acquire vivid memories of events that never occurred, especially if another person—such as a psychotherapist—suggests that the events occurred (Johnson & Raye, 1981; Loftus, 1993; Schooler & Eich, 2000). According to recent research conducted by Kealy and colleagues (2006), people are especially likely to start believing false events if they are asked to describe the events in great detail. In this research, students were asked to think of two real events that happened to them before age 12 and to come up with two events that didn't actually happen. They were then asked to describe one of the events in great detail (e.g., the location of the event, the time it occurred, the visual scene). Events that were elaborated on (i.e., described in vivid detail) later were rated as more truthful than those that were not elaborated on. This effect occurred for both real and made-up events (Kealy, Kuiper, & Klein, 2006). The results suggest that if people are asked to provide elaborate details of an event, they may come to believe their story, even if the event never occurred.

In addition to numerous laboratory demonstrations of false memories, evidence from everyday life also indicates that memories of abuse or other traumas can be false. Often, these memories are contradicted by objective evidence (e.g., no evidence of satanic murders can be found); sometimes, people who suddenly acquire such memories decide later that the events never occurred; and, sometimes, the memories are so bizarre (e.g., that people were abducted by aliens) as to strain credulity. Unfortunately, some psychotherapists do not sufficiently consider that by suggesting past abuse, they may be planting false memories rather than helping clients remember real events.

This is not to say, however, that all recovered memories are inaccurate. While scientific evidence for repression and recovery—the idea that something can be forgotten for years and then recalled with great accuracy—is sparse, there may be instances in which people do suddenly remember traumatic events that really did occur (Schooler, 1999). Thus, any claim of abuse should be taken with the utmost seriousness. Unfortunately, however, it is very difficult to distinguish the accurate memories from the false ones in the absence of any corroborating evidence.

Recently, researchers at Dalhousie University and at Grant MacEwan College have taken a first step in trying to disentangle truthful versus fabricated reports of traumatic experiences (Porter, Peace, & Emmett, 2007). In this research, participants were asked to describe an actual traumatic experience and to also make up a traumatic experience. They then answered a number of questions, such as how stressful each experience was, how intense its impact, what their emotional reaction was, and so on. It turned out that descriptions of fabricated traumatic events contained fewer specific details about time and place than did descriptions of actual traumas and were rated as less believable by coders (who didn't know which accounts were real and which were fabricated). When asked about their reactions to these events, participants reported stronger emotional reactions to the fabricated traumas than to the actual traumas—even though when describing these events, fabricated accounts actually were less emotional than accounts of actual traumas. This tendency to "go over the top" when reporting on reactions to fabricated traumas was also reflected in participants' reports of how much they thought about the event, their level of traumatic stress, and their experience of post-traumatic stress disorder symptoms—all of these reactions were reported more strongly when describing a fake, rather than a real, traumatic event. Thus, when attempting to determine whether an accusation is true or false, investigators might do well to rely on the signs of fabrication identified in this work.

Are there other kinds of evidence that can be used by the legal system that might be less susceptible to the kinds of inaccuracies that plague eyewitness testimony? We turn to this issue next.

Other Kinds of Evidence

There are a number of other kinds of evidence that police investigators, judges, and juries can rely on in reaching decisions about the guilt or innocence of people accused of crimes. They can turn to experts for information (e.g., about an accused person's mental state). They also can rely on physical evidence such as fingerprints or DNA tests conducted on hair samples or blood. Legal professionals and juries also can base their verdicts on statistical evidence—the probability that the accused committed the crime. As we shall see, juries find some of these kinds of evidence more persuasive than others.

Expert Testimony

A number of thorny issues surround the use of expert testimony in court (Pfeifer, 1997). Research conducted at York University suggests that jurors may not always understand judges' instructions about the kinds of evidence that are permissible from an expert witness and the kinds of evidence that should be disregarded (Schuller & Paglia, 1999; see Schuller & Yarmey, 2001, for a review). It is important that jurors know how to properly evaluate expert testimony, because research has shown that jurors are influenced by such information.

In one study, for example, students at York University and visitors to the Ontario Science Centre were presented with a transcript of a homicide case based on an actual case, in which an abused woman shot and killed her husband (Schuller & Hastings, 1996). Participants in the expert testimony condition read that a psychologist had testified that the woman's behaviour should be understood in terms of battered wife syndrome. The psychologist explained that battered wife syndrome resembles post-traumatic stress disorder in terms of its emotional and psychological consequences. Participants in the control condition were not exposed to any expert testimony. Did expert testimony have an effect on the mock jurors' verdicts? The answer is yes. Participants who received expert testimony were more likely to conclude that the woman acted out of self-defence than were participants who did not hear expert testimony. Importantly, those who received expert testimony also rendered a more lenient verdict.

In Canada, the courts have shown a tendency to move away from expert testimony (Peters, 2001; Yarmey, 2001b; but see Saunders, 2001, for a different opinion). Why is this the case? According to Martin Peters, a Toronto criminal lawyer, some judges believe that much of what experts—in particular, psychological experts—have to offer is common sense. In other words, jury members are assumed to already know whatever a psychologist might have to offer. Other judges are concerned that jury members will rely too heavily on what the experts say, rather than critically evaluate information themselves (Peters, 2001). Not surprisingly, psychologists argue that they do have something to offer the legal system. As A. Daniel Yarmey (2001b) points out, research on the accuracy of eyewitness testimony and on identification of suspects from lineups has revealed important information that is not part of common sense knowledge. Given that wrongful convictions are generally a result of mistaken eyewitness identification, experts can provide the kind of information that would enable jurors to properly evaluate such evidence. Fortunately, some judges agree. According to the Honourable Mr. Justice Jamie W. S. Saunders of the Nova Scotia Court of Appeal, expert testimony does have a place in Canadian courts, provided that certain guidelines are followed (e.g., experts must be independent and objective).

It is not only jurors who would benefit from being informed about research on errors and biases in eyewitness testimony. Earlier, we mentioned Wise and Safer's (2004) finding that only 32 percent of the U.S. judges who responded to their survey were aware that eyewitness confidence is not strongly correlated with accuracy. Overall, they found that judges were correct on only 55 percent of the questions asked about eyewitness testimony and its unreliability. Psychologists with expertise in eyewitness testimony are now being used to educate judges in the U.S. legal system on the various inaccuracies in eyewitness testimony. The intent is for judges to pass on this information when instructing jury members on how to evaluate eyewitness testimony. Gary Wells, one of the experts who has given lectures to groups of judges, points out that this approach holds considerable promise (Cynkar, 2007). One advantage is that judges can disseminate information on the pitfalls of eyewitness testimony each time they preside over a case, rather than having an expert brought in for each trial to instruct jury members (who would use this information on a one-time basis).

Physical Evidence

When crimes occur, forensic experts scrutinize the scene for footprints, fingerprints, and samples of hair or fibres. In addition, in recent years, DNA testing has become much more accurate, and courts increasingly rely on this kind of evidence. When Larry Fisher was tried for the murder of Gail Miller—the murder for which David Milgaard had been wrongfully convicted—DNA testing proved that he had raped Miller. The jury then used this information to infer that he had killed her as well. The same kind of evidence that was used to convict Larry Fisher was also used to exonerate Guy Paul Morin. Morin was wrongfully convicted of sexually assaulting and killing his neighbour's nine-year-old daughter in 1986. In 1995, he was exonerated on the basis of DNA evidence. To give a final example, in 1990, James Driskoll was charged with the first-degree murder of Perry Dean Harder. DNA evidence played an important role in securing his release after he had spent 13 years in prison. In September 2008, the city of Winnipeg and the province of Manitoba agreed to a $4 million settlement as compensation for his wrongful conviction.

What about other kinds of physical evidence that might not be as conclusive as DNA testing? Research conducted by Elizabeth Loftus (1974, 1983) suggests that other kinds of physical evidence tend not to be very persuasive. In one study, for example, Loftus (1974) presented research participants with a description of a robbery of a grocery store and the murder of its owner. Participants in the

▶ A vial of melted snow containing semen samples found at the scene where Gail Miller was murdered in 1969 was the source of DNA evidence used to exonerate David Milgaard and to convict Larry Fisher. In 2005–06, the government held a public inquiry into Milgaard's wrongful conviction and imprisonment.

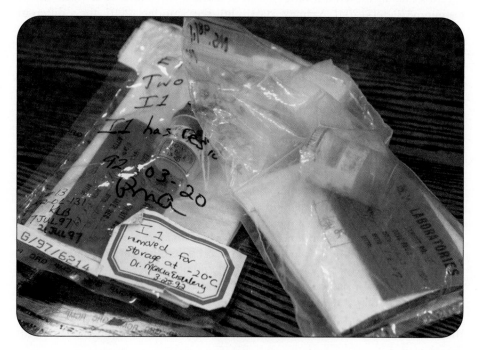

physical evidence condition read that the defendant had been found with large sums of cash and that traces of the cleaning solution used on the store's floor had been found on his shoes. Those in the eyewitness testimony condition read that a store clerk had identified the defendant as the killer. Participants in a third condition received both physical and eyewitness evidence, but the eyewitness testimony was discredited; specifically, participants were told that the eyewitness had poor vision. It turned out that physical evidence alone was not very convincing to these mock jurors—only 18 percent of them rendered a guilty verdict. In sharp contrast, 72 percent of participants who received eyewitness testimony believed that the defendant was guilty. Perhaps most disturbing, 68 percent of participants who received eyewitness testimony that was later discredited nevertheless considered the defendant to be guilty.

In the Thomas Sophonow case, physical evidence was presented at the third trial that made it unlikely that he could have been at the doughnut shop at the time of Barbara Stoppel's murder. Sophonow testified that he had telephoned his mother in Vancouver before delivering the Christmas stockings to hospitals. Telephone records confirmed that he had placed the call at 7:56 p.m. from a location that would have made it difficult to reach the doughnut shop by the time the murder took place (between 8:15 and 8:45 p.m.). Consistent with Loftus's research, jurors obviously did not find this evidence very convincing, choosing instead to believe the reports of people who claimed to have seen Sophonow at the scene of the crime.

Statistical Evidence

Consider a hypothetical case that legal scholars have frequently debated. A bus hits and kills a dog. Although it is not known to which company the bus belongs, 80 percent of the buses on the route where the dog was killed are owned by the Blue Bus company. The key question is whether the Blue Bus company should be held liable for this accident based on this statistical information alone. According to civil law—which applies to cases such as this—the Blue Bus company should be held responsible if it is "more likely than not" that a Blue Bus killed the dog.

Gary Wells (1992) presented this case to students at the University of Alberta. He found that participants who were told that 80 percent of the buses on the route were owned by the Blue Bus company were extremely reluctant to assign guilt to the Blue Bus company on this basis; only 8 percent of them held the Blue Bus company liable. In another condition, participants were told that a weigh station attendant had seen a Blue Bus on that road earlier that day but that his reports tended to be only 80 percent accurate; remarkably, in this case, 67 percent of participants assigned responsibility for the accident to the Blue Bus company. Even though the probabilities were the same in each condition (80 percent), participants were much more swayed by eyewitness testimony than by statistical evidence (i.e., 67 percent versus 8 percent convictions). Interestingly, when Wells presented the Blue Bus case to experienced judges, he found that they were no more likely than university students to assign guilt based on statistical evidence alone.

Might there be conditions under which people would be willing to place more weight on statistical evidence? Edward Wright and colleagues (1996) designed a study to answer this question. They presented the Blue Bus case to students at St. Francis Xavier University, varying the amount of time participants had before presenting their verdict, to determine whether having a lot of time to think about this kind of evidence might cause people to rely on it more. Some participants were also given the opportunity to discuss the evidence with others, to see if group discussion might increase reliance on statistical evidence. However, neither extended decision-making time nor group discussion made participants more likely to assign guilt to the Blue Bus company (Wright, MacEachern, Stoffer, & MacDonald, 1996).

Based on these findings, it appears that when considering different kinds of evidence, juries and judges tend to be persuaded by the kind of evidence that is most likely to be unreliable—the reports of other people. If eyewitnesses claim that they saw the person (or bus) in question, juries are likely to render a guilty verdict based on that testimony. Physical evidence and especially statistical evidence apparently are not very persuasive at all. In short, it seems that what is most likely to convince us of something is hearing another person say that it is so.

Juries: Group Processes in Action

Juries are of particular interest to social psychologists because the way they reach verdicts is directly relevant to social psychological research on group processes and social interaction. The right to be tried by a jury of one's peers has a long tradition in Canadian law. Trial by jury was an established institution in England at the beginning of the seventeenth century, and this tradition was adopted by Canada in 1867. Despite this tradition, the jury system has often come under attack. We have already discussed several cases in which juries in Canada have reached the wrong decision and convicted innocent people.

The jury system also has been criticized on grounds that jurors may lack the ability to understand complex evidence and reach a dispassionate verdict (Arkes & Mellers, 2002; Devine, Clayton, Dunford, Seying, & Pryce, 2001). According to research conducted at Simon Fraser University, jury members' comprehension of the instructions given to them by judges is remarkably low. In one of the studies in this research program, participants acting as mock jurors understood just over 60 percent of what they had been told (Rose & Ogloff, 2001). A former dean of the Harvard Law School put it this way: "Why should anyone think that 12 persons brought in from the street, selected in various ways for their lack of general ability, should have any special capacity for deciding controversies between persons?" (Kalven & Zeisel, 1966).

The jury system has its staunch supporters, of course, and few people argue that it should be abolished altogether. The point is that it is not a perfect system and that based on research in social psychology, there are ways we might expect it to go wrong (Levett, Danielsen, Kovera, & Cutler, 2005). Problems can arise at all phases of a jury trial, including the way in which jurors process information during the trial and the way in which they deliberate in the jury room after all of the evidence has been presented.

> ❝ 'Tis with our judgments as our watches,
> None go just alike, yet each believes his own. ❞
>
> —*Alexander Pope,* Essay on Criticism, *1711*

How Jurors Process Information during the Trial

How do individual jurors think about the evidence they hear during a trial? As we saw in Chapter 3, people often construct theories and schemas to interpret the world around them, and the same is true of jurors. Some psychologists suggest that jurors decide on one story that best explains all of the evidence; they then try to fit this story to the possible verdicts they are allowed to render. If one of those verdicts fits well with their preferred story, they are likely to vote to convict on that charge (Hastie & Pennington, 2000; Pennington & Hastie, 1992). This finding has important implications for how lawyers present their cases. Lawyers typically present the evidence in one of two ways: In the first, called *story order*, they present the evidence in the sequence in which events occurred, corresponding as closely as possible to the story they want the jurors to believe. In the second, called *witness order*, they present witnesses in the sequence they think will have the greatest impact, even if this means that events are described out of order. A lawyer might save his or her best witness for last, for example, so that the

"Your Honor, we're going to go with the prosecution's spin."

trial ends on a dramatic and memorable note, even if this witness describes events that occurred early in the alleged crime.

If you were a lawyer, in which order would you present the evidence? You probably can guess which order Pennington and Hastie hypothesized would be most successful. If jurors are ultimately swayed by the story or schema they think best explains the sequence of events, the best strategy should be to present the evidence in story order and not in witness order. To test this hypothesis, Pennington and Hastie (1988) asked mock jurors to listen to a simulated murder trial. The researchers varied the order in which the defence attorney and the prosecuting attorney presented their cases. In one condition, both used the story order, whereas in another condition, both used the witness order. In other conditions, one attorney used the story order, whereas the other used the witness order.

The results provided clear and dramatic support for the story order strategy. As seen in Table SPA3.1, when the prosecutor used the story order and the defence used the witness order, the jurors were most likely to believe the prosecutor—78 percent voted to convict the defendant. When the prosecutor used the witness order and the defence used the story order, the tables were turned—only 31 percent voted to convict. One reason the conviction rate in felony trials is so high (approximately 80 percent in the United States) is that in real trials, prosecutors usually present evidence in story order, whereas defence attorneys usually use witness order. To those of our readers who are budding lawyers, remember this when you are preparing for your first trial!

TABLE SPA3.1

How should lawyers present their cases?

Lawyers can present their cases in a variety of ways. This study found that story order, in which lawyers present the evidence in the order that corresponds most closely to the story they want the jurors to believe, works best.

Percentage of People Voting to Convict the Defendant

Prosecution Evidence	Defence Evidence	
	Story Order	Witness Order
Story order	59	78
Witness order	31	63

(Adapted from Pennington & Hastie, 1988)

Confessions: Are They Always What They Seem?

Imagine that you are a member of a jury at a murder trial. The prosecution presents what seems to be some pretty damning evidence—namely, a video of the defendant confessing to the crime. "OK, I admit it," you hear the defendant say, "I was the one who pulled the trigger." More than likely you would vote to convict. Why would the defendant admit to the crime if he or she was innocent? Many cases never even go to trial, because the defendant pleads guilty after confessing to the crime.

Confessions, however, are not always what they seem. Consider the case of a woman who was raped and brutally beaten while jogging in New York City's Central Park in 1989. The woman was in a coma for several days and when she awoke she had no memory of the attack. Soon, however, the police arrested five African-American and Hispanic teenagers who had been in the park that night. The boys confessed to the crime and provided lurid details of what happened. Four of the confessions were videotaped and played at the trial, and largely on this basis, all of the teenagers were convicted and given long prison sentences.

The only problem is that it is now clear that the boys were innocent. Thirteen years later Matias Reyes, in prison for three rapes and a murder, confessed to the crime, claiming he had acted alone. His DNA matched semen recovered from the victim (none of the teenagers' DNA matched), and he gave details of the crime scene that were known only to the police. In 2002, a judge vacated the convictions of all five boys.

If the boys were innocent, why did they confess to the crime? Research by Saul Kassin (2005) and others has shown that the interrogation process can go wrong in ways that elicit false confessions, even to the point where innocent suspects come to believe that they actually did commit the crime. One problem is that police investigators are often convinced that the suspect is guilty, and this belief biases how they conduct the interrogation. They ask leading questions, isolate suspects and put them under considerable stress, claim that an eyewitness has identified the suspect, and sometimes make false promises. The suspects in the Central Park jogger case, for example, were questioned for up to 30 hours, and the police detectives implied that they could go home if they would sign a confession (Kassin, 2005). This is all well and good if the suspect really is guilty, and if the techniques succeed in making him confess. As we saw earlier, however, people—even trained investigators—are not very good at detecting whether someone is lying, which means that innocent people are sometimes subjected to these techniques.

Surely, you might think, such a case is an aberration; innocent people normally do not confess to something they didn't do. Imagine, though, that you were in an experiment conducted by Kassin and Kiechel (1996). You arrive for the session and learn that your job is to type some letters into a computer that are to be read by another participant. Before you begin, the experimenter cautions you not to press the ALT key next to the space bar because doing so would cause the program to crash and the session would be ruined. With this warning in mind, you begin typing. Everything goes smoothly at first, but after a minute the program freezes. The experimenter, clearly upset, says you must have hit the ALT key—which you clearly did not because, in fact, the computer crashing incident was staged and happened to everyone. No participant in fact hit the ALT key—the point was to see whether the experimenter could convince people that they had, and elicit a false confession from them.

The researchers varied two things about this situation that were designed to make false confessions more likely. First, they varied the speed at which people typed. In one condition, people were instructed to type 43 words per minute, which most people could do at a relaxed pace. In another, they were instructed to type 67 words per minute, a very fast rate that made errors more likely—and

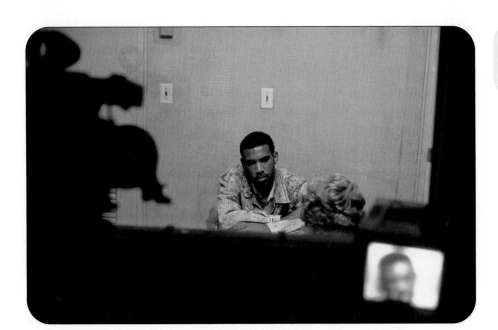

made it less clear to people whether their finger had accidentally hit the ALT key. In addition, the experimenter asked the other participant (who was actually an accomplice) what she had seen. In one condition, she reluctantly admitted that she had seen you press the ALT key, whereas in another she replied that she hadn't seen anything.

Imagine you were in the condition in which you had to type at the frenzied pace and the other participant says she saw you press the ALT key. You don't *remember* doing it, but the program did crash, and why would the other person lie? In this condition, most people came to believe (falsely) that they had, in fact, hit the dreaded ALT key. Everyone agreed to sign a statement saying they had done it, and 65 percent of the participants admitted they had when asked privately by another accomplice posing as the next participant. In contrast, when people typed at a slow pace, and the other participant said she didn't see anything, few people came to believe that they had pressed the ALT key.

It's one thing to be talked into believing that you pressed the wrong computer key, but quite another to be convinced that you committed a brutal murder. However, investigators often use similar tactics to elicit confessions, such as telling people that an eyewitness had seen them commit the crime (Kassin, 2005). After many hours of prolonged interrogation innocent people can become so psychologically fatigued that they don't know what to think, and may even come to believe that they are guilty. In fact, in a large number of cases in which DNA evidence exonerated defendants who had been falsely convicted of a crime, the defendant had confessed ("False Confessions," 2006).

One way to eradicate coerced confessions is to require that interrogations be put on video, so a jury can view the recording and judge for themselves whether the defendant was coerced into admitting things he or she didn't do. In 2003, Illinois passed a law requiring that all police interrogations of suspects in homicide cases be electronically recorded. Although this is a step forward, it raises another potential problem. Almost all videos of interrogations focus on the suspect rather than on the interrogator asking the questions. Well, of course they do, you might think; the whole point is to judge how the suspect is responding to the questioning, so it is no surprise that the camera focuses on him or her. The dedicated student of social psychology, however, will recognize this as a problem. As we discussed in Chapter 4, people's judgments about the causes of another person's behaviour are influenced by what is visually salient to them.

When we focus our attention on one person in a group, we tend to think that he or she is having a disproportionately large influence on the conversation.

Research by Dan Lassiter (2004) has shown that the same thing is true when people watch video recordings of confessions. He showed people a video of the same confession from different camera angles and asked them to judge how voluntary or coerced the confession was. People thought that the confession was most voluntary (i.e., the least coerced) when the camera focused on the suspect; here, people had the sense that the suspect was in charge of what was happening. When the camera showed both the suspect and the interrogator, people thought the confession was less voluntary. And when the camera focused only on the interrogator, people thought the confession was the least voluntary (the most coerced). Remember, everyone heard the same confession; all that differed was their visual perspective. In part because of this research, at least one American state (Wisconsin) now requires that both the suspect and the questioner be shown in video interviews.

Deliberations in the Jury Room

As any lawyer can tell you, a crucial part of the jury process occurs out of sight, when jurors deliberate before deciding on the verdict. Even if most jurors are inclined to vote to convict, there might be a persuasive minority that changes their fellow jurors' minds. Sometimes, this can be a minority of one, as in the classic movie *12 Angry Men*. When this film begins, a jury has just finished listening to the evidence in a murder case and all of the jurors except one vote to convict the defendant. Over the next 90 minutes, however, the lone holdout, played by Henry Fonda, convinces his peers that there is reason to doubt that the young Hispanic defendant is guilty. At first, the other jurors pressure Fonda to change his mind using techniques of normative and informational conformity (as discussed in Chapter 7), but in the end, reason triumphs and the other jurors come to see that the Fonda character is right.

As entertaining as this movie is, research indicates that it does not reflect the reality of most jury deliberations (Devine, Clayton, Dunford, Seying, & Pryce, 2001; Ellsworth & Mauro, 1998). In a study of more than 200 juries in actual criminal trials, the researchers found that in 97 percent of cases, the jury's final decision was the same as the one favoured by a majority of the jurors on the initial vote

▶ In the classic movie *12 Angry Men*, Henry Fonda persuades the rest of his fellow jurors to change their minds about a defendant's guilt. In real life, however, such cases of a minority in a jury persuading the majority to change the verdict are rare.

(Kalven & Zeisel, 1966). Just as we saw in Chapter 7 on conformity, majority opinion usually carries the day, bringing dissenting jurors into line. And what happens if a dissenting juror does not succumb to pressure to go along with the majority opinion? In Chapter 7, we found that dissenters may eventually be ejected from the group. This may have been the case in the third Sophonow trial, where jurors were unable to reach a unanimous verdict after five long days of deliberation—apparently because one juror refused to go along with the rest of the group. In a startling move, the judge dismissed this juror because she supposedly had claimed to possess "psychic powers and special gifts." The juror who was removed maintains that she said no such thing. Once the problematic juror was removed, the remaining 11 members swiftly rendered their guilty verdict.

> *A court is no better than each . . . of you sitting before me on this jury. A court is only as sound as its jury, and a jury is only as sound as the [people] who make it up.*
>
> —Harper Lee, To Kill a Mockingbird, 1960

If jury deliberation is stacked toward the initial majority opinion, why not just abandon the deliberation process, letting the jury's initial vote determine a defendant's guilt or innocence? This would not be a good idea for two reasons: First, forcing juries to reach a unanimous verdict makes them consider the evidence more carefully, rather than simply assuming that their initial impressions of the case were correct (Hastie, Penrod, & Pennington, 1983). Second, even if minorities seldom succeed in persuading the majority to change their minds about guilt or innocence, minorities often do change people's minds about *how* guilty a person is. In criminal trials, juries usually have some discretion about the type of guilty verdict they can reach. In a murder trial, for example, they can often decide whether to convict the defendant of first-degree murder, second-degree murder, or manslaughter. Pennington and Hastie (1990) found that people on a jury who have a minority point of view often convince the majority to change their minds about the specific verdict to render. Thus, although a minority of jurors is unlikely to convince a majority to change its verdict from first-degree murder to not guilty, they may well persuade the majority to change the verdict to second-degree murder.

Why Do People Obey the Law?

Ultimately, the success of the legal system depends on keeping people out of it. We should, of course, find ways to improve the accuracy of eyewitness testimony and help juries make better decisions. Even more important, though, is finding ways to prevent people from committing crimes in the first place. We therefore close with a discussion of how to get people to obey the law.

Do Severe Penalties Deter Crime?

Crime rates have been dropping. According to Statistics Canada (Canada, 2005e), the crime rate in 2004 was 12 percent lower than a decade earlier. And a recent Statistics Canada report on homicide documented a 10 percent decrease in the national homicide rate in 2006, compared with the year before (Owen, 2007). Analysts have attributed the decrease in crime to the aging of the population (most violent crimes are committed by adolescents and young adults), Canada's economy, and new approaches to preventing and solving crimes. Similar reasons have been given for the decline in violent crime that has been observed in the United States; however, in 1997, the U.S. attorney general at the time believed that stiffer penalties for crimes were at least partly responsible ("Juveniles Committing Fewer Violent Crimes," 1997). It seems to make perfect sense that the harsher the penalty for a crime, the less likely people would be to commit it. As we have seen many times in this book, however, common sense is not always correct, and in the case of crime and prison sentences, the story is not as straightforward as it might seem.

deterrence theory

the theory that people refrain from criminal activity because of the threat of legal punishment, as long as the punishment is perceived as relatively severe, certain, and swift

Let's begin with a theory that stiff penalties do prevent crimes. According to **deterrence theory**, people refrain from criminal activity because of the threat of legal punishment, as long as the punishment is perceived as severe, certain, and swift (Carlsmith, Darley, & Robinson, 2002; Gibbs, 1985; Williams & Hawkins, 1986). Undoubtedly, this theory is correct under some circumstances. As we mentioned in Chapter 11, several Canadian provinces have set up special family violence courts to ensure that penalties for domestic violence are relatively severe, certain, and swift. There are promising signs that these courts are effective in reducing family violence. Note that because these courts combine certain, swift punishment with rehabilitation, it is difficult to determine whether reductions in violence are attributable to punishment or to rehabilitation, or to both.

Consider another example. Imagine you are heading to downtown Edmonton for an important interview one day and become ensnarled in a traffic jam. At last the traffic clears, but unless you hurry, you will be late. "Maybe I'll speed up just a little," you think, as the speedometer creeps up to 125 kilometres per hour. Your decision to exceed the speed limit was probably based on a consideration of the fact that you are unlikely to get caught, and if you are, the penalty won't be too severe. However, suppose you knew that the Yellowhead Trail is always patrolled by the Edmonton Police Service and that the penalty for speeding is a five-year prison sentence. Chances are you would not dare to press too hard on the accelerator.

In this example, we have made a couple of important assumptions. First, we assumed that you know the penalties for speeding. Second, we assumed that you have control over your behaviour and that whether you speed is a rational decision that you make after reflecting on the consequences. For many crimes, however, these assumptions do not hold. Surveys have found that many people are ignorant of the penalties for different crimes; if they do not know what the penalties are, the penalties cannot act as a deterrent. (To see how well you know the penalties for various federal crimes, complete the accompanying Try It! quiz.) Further, other types of crimes are not based on a rational decision-making process. Many murders, for example, are impulsive crimes of passion committed by people in highly

> *American legislators suffer from a monumental illusion in their belief that long prison sentences will reduce the crime rate.*
>
> —Jack Gibbs, 1985

Try it!

▶ Are You Aware of the Penalties for Crimes?

Deterrence theory holds that legal penalties will prevent crimes if they are perceived to be severe, certain, and swift. If people are unaware that a crime has a severe penalty, however, those penalties cannot act as a deterrent. Are you aware of the penalties specified in the Criminal Code of Canada for the crimes listed below? Take the following quiz to find out.

What Are the Penalties for These Crimes?

1. First-degree murder (deliberate, planned murder). Note that first-degree murder charges also apply if someone dies as a result of another crime being committed (e.g., a bank teller or store clerk is killed during a robbery).

2. Second-degree murder (deliberate, but unplanned, murder)

3. Manslaughter (causing the death of another person accidentally or through carelessness)

4. Communication for prostitution

5. Break and enter

6. Drug trafficking

7. Impaired driving (or having a blood-alcohol content of more than 0.08)

8. False pretence (e.g., forging a cheque)

9. Assisting suicide

10. Sexual assault

See page 500 for the answers.

emotional states, not by people who carefully weigh the pros and cons. In general, severe penalties will only work as a deterrent when people know what the penalties are, believe that they are relatively certain to be caught, and weigh the consequences before deciding whether to commit a crime.

To illustrate these points, let's consider two different kinds of crimes: drunk driving and murder. The decision about whether to drink and drive is one that most of us can control; when we go to a party or a bar and know that we will be driving home afterward, we can decide how much we will drink. Given that this decision is a fairly rational one—at least, under most circumstances—we would expect that certain, severe penalties would act as a deterrent. Researchers in the United States have found some support for this conclusion by comparing states with different drunk-driving laws. (Such research cannot be conducted in Canada because drunk driving falls under the federal Criminal Code, and, therefore, penalties are the same from province to province.) These U.S. studies have found that increasing the severity of penalties for drunk driving is not related, by itself, to a lower rate of alcohol-related, motor vehicle fatalities. Consistent with deterrence theory, however, increasing the certainty of being caught for drunk driving—by checking the blood alcohol level of all motorists stopped at sobriety checkpoints—is associated with a lower rate of alcohol-related accidents (Evans, Neville, & Graham, 1991; Stuster & Blowers, 1995; Voas, Holder, & Gruenewald, 1999). These results suggest that severity of the penalty itself does not act as a deterrent but that an increase in the certainty of being caught does.

Now, consider a very different crime and a very different penalty—murder and capital punishment. Canadians who favour capital punishment tend to believe that it has a deterrent effect (Haddock & Zanna, 1998; Vidmar, 1974), even though capital punishment has been abolished in Canada. A majority of U.S. citizens support the death penalty for murder, in part because they believe that it acts as a deterrent. Of course, there is no more severe penalty than death, and if the death penalty prevents even a few murders, it might be worth it—or so the argument goes. To see if this argument is valid, several studies have compared the murder rates in states that have the death penalty with those that do not; the murder rates in states before and after they adopted the death penalty; and the murder rates in other countries before and after they adopted the death penalty. The results are clear: There is no evidence that the death penalty prevents murders (Archer & Gartner, 1984; Bedau, 1997; Ellsworth & Mauro, 1998; Sorenson, Wrinkle, Brewer, & Marquart, 1999).

Opponents of the death penalty point out, as we mentioned earlier, that most murders are crimes of passion that are not preceded by a rational consideration

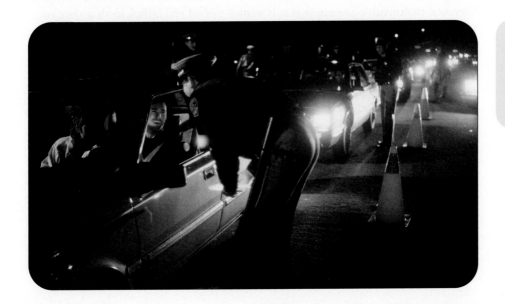

◀ Increasing the certainty of being caught for drunk driving—by checking the blood alcohol level of every motorist stopped at a sobriety checkpoint like this one—is associated with a lower rate of alcohol-related accidents.

of the consequences. Because people are not considering the consequences of their actions, the death penalty does not act as a deterrent. Further, the mistakes made whereby innocent people have been sentenced to death add up to an astonishing number.

Proponents of the death penalty say that severity of the crime is not enough; as argued by deterrence theory, severe penalties must be applied with certainty and speed. The last of these conditions is almost never met. In the United States, the time between a conviction for murder and the execution of the convicted murderer is often many years, because of the slowness of the judicial system and the many avenues of appeal open to prisoners on death row. Were the process sped up, this argument goes, the death penalty *could* act as a deterrent.

Although this is an empirical question, there is reason to doubt that the death penalty would act as a deterrent, even if it were applied swiftly. We refer to a few studies that have found that executions are followed not by a decrease but by an *increase* in murders (Archer & Gartner, 1984; Bailey & Peterson, 1997). This might seem like a bizarre finding; why would the execution of a convicted murderer *increase* the likelihood that someone else would commit a murder? If you recall our discussion on aggression in Chapter 11, the finding makes sense. As we saw, observing someone else commit a violent act weakens people's inhibitions against aggression, leads to imitation of aggression, and numbs their sense of horror over violence. Could it be that observing the government put someone to death lowers other people's inhibitions, making them more likely to commit murders? While the data are not conclusive, this argument makes eminent social psychological sense—and there is some evidence to support it (Bailey & Peterson, 1997).

Procedural Justice: People's Sense of Fairness

We have just seen that one reason people obey the law is their fear of being caught and punished. An even more important reason, however, is their moral values about what constitutes good behaviour. People will obey a law if they think that it is just, even if they are unlikely to be caught breaking it. For example, many people are honest on their tax returns because they think that cheating is wrong, not because they fear being caught for cheating. Thus, if you were a lawmaker, you could try to prevent crime in one of two ways: You could increase the penalties for breaking the law and the probability that people will be caught, or you could try to convince people that the law is just and fair. As we have seen, the former approach is difficult and sometimes ineffective. If we wanted to prevent people from driving through red lights, we could increase the penalties for doing so and station a police officer at every intersection; it would be far simpler, however, to convince people that it is wrong to run red lights, so that they comply with the law even when no police officers are around.

procedural justice

people's judgments about the fairness of the procedures used to determine outcomes, such as whether they are innocent or guilty of a crime

What determines whether people think a law is just? One important factor is their perception of the fairness of legal proceedings. **Procedural justice** is defined as people's judgments about the fairness of the procedures used to determine outcomes, such as whether they are innocent or guilty of a crime (Blader & Tyler, 2003; Heuer, Penrod, Hafer, & Cohn, 2002; Kelley & Thibaut, 1978; Miller & Ratner, 1996; Skarlicki, Ellard, & Kelln, 1998; Tyler et al., 1997; Wenzel, 2000). People who feel that they have been treated fairly are more likely to comply with the law than are people who feel that they have been treated unfairly (Tyler, 1990). Consider, for example, what happens when the police are called because of a domestic assault. What determines whether the person accused of assault will repeat this crime in the future? It turns out that one factor is whether suspects feel that they were treated fairly by the police ("Misconceptions about why people obey laws," 1997).

As another example, imagine that you receive a traffic ticket for failing to stop at a stop sign. You believe that the ticket is unfair because your view of the stop sign was obstructed by branches from a large tree that should have been trimmed by the city. You decide to go to court to protest the ticket. You take photographs of the tree, make careful diagrams of the intersection, and spend hours practising your testimony before your friends. Finally, your day in court arrives. Now, imagine that one of two things occurs. In the first scenario, your ticket is dismissed without a hearing because the officer who gave you the ticket could not appear in court that day. In the second scenario, you get to present your case. The judge listens carefully, asks you a number of questions, and compliments you on your photographs and diagrams. After carefully considering all the facts, however, she rules against you, arguing that the stop sign, while obstructed, was still visible. Which outcome would you prefer—the first or the second? Surely, the first one, you might think, because there you receive a positive outcome: no fine, no points on your driving record, no increase in your insurance rates. Research by Tom Tyler (1990), however, suggests that people prefer the second scenario. There, even though the outcome was negative, people have a greater sense of procedural justice—they had their day in court and were treated with fairness and respect. It is often more important to people to maintain a sense of procedural justice than to receive positive outcomes.

In summary, social psychological research indicates that the Canadian legal system can go wrong in a number of ways. Juries rely heavily on eyewitness testimony, when in fact such testimony is often in error. Determining when witnesses are telling the truth is difficult, even with the use of polygraphs. And because juries are groups of people who try to reach consensus by discussing, arguing, and bargaining, the kinds of conformity pressures and group processes we discussed in Chapter 7 can lead to faulty decisions. By illuminating these problems in their research, however, social psychologists can help initiate change in the legal system—change that will lead to greater fairness and equity and to a greater sense of procedural justice. Most important of all, heeding psychological research on these questions might reduce the number of cases in which people like Thomas Sophonow languish in prison for crimes they did not commit.

SUMMARY

Many social psychological principles predict how people will respond in the legal arena. Because of the limitations of memory, eyewitness testimony is often inaccurate. Several factors bias the **acquisition**, **storage**, and **retrieval** of what people observe, sometimes leading to the false identification of criminals. For example, research on the **own-race bias** shows that people find it more difficult to recognize members of other races than members of their own race. Research on **reconstructive memory** indicates that errors in **source monitoring** can occur, whereby people become confused about where they saw or heard something. Jurors often place a great deal of faith in eyewitness testimony, even though memories can be unreliable or influenced by later suggestions, and jurors are not very good at determining when someone is lying. The **polygraph** is also an imperfect measure of lie detection. As a result, false testimony by eyewitnesses and others sometimes goes undetected. Researchers have tried to develop ways of improving eyewitness testimony, but neither hypnosis nor the **cognitive interview** has been very successful at improving eyewitness accuracy.

There is a great deal of controversy over another form of eyewitness testimony, namely the accuracy of people's memories about their own past traumatic experiences. How valid are **recovered memories**—the sudden recollection of events, such as sexual abuse, that had been forgotten or repressed? Though recovered memories may be true in some instances, they can also be the result of **false memory syndrome**, whereby people come to believe the memory is true when actually it is not. False memories are especially likely to occur when an authoritative person suggests to us that an event occurred. Recent research suggests that people report more extreme reactions to fabricated traumas than to actual traumas, and that there are differences in how actual and fake traumatic events are described. For example, fabricated accounts contain fewer details about the time and place of the event.

Other kinds of evidence are admitted in court as well, including expert testimony, physical evidence, and statistical evidence (i.e., information on the probability that the accused committed the crime). People generally do not find physical or statistical evidence convincing, preferring instead to rely on eye-witness testimony, despite its inaccuracies.

Juries are of particular interest to social psychologists because the way they reach verdicts is directly relevant to social psychological research on group processes and social interaction. Jurors are susceptible to the same kinds of biases and social pressures we documented in earlier chapters. During a trial, they attempt to make sense of the testimony and often decide on one story that explains all of the evidence. Juries are, thus, most swayed by lawyers who present the evidence in a way that tells a consistent story. During deliberations, jurors with minority views are often pressured into conforming with the view of the majority; as a result, verdicts usually correspond to the initial feelings of the majority of jurors.

Recent research has examined whether confessions to crimes are necessarily true. The interrogation techniques used by the police can sometimes produce false confessions. The video

recording of interrogation is a safeguard against this, although focusing the camera solely on the suspect increases the likelihood that viewers will think that the person voluntarily confessed.

It is also important to examine people's perceptions of the legal system, because these perceptions have a lot to do with how likely people are to obey the law. **Deterrence theory** holds that people refrain from criminal activity if they view penalties as severe, certain, and swift. Deterrence theory may be correct about crimes that are the result of rational thought about the consequences, but it is unlikely to apply to crimes of passion that are not rational, such as many murders. There is no evidence that the death penalty deters murder, and there is even some evidence that it leads to an increase in the murder rate. Finally, people are more likely to obey the law if their sense of **procedural justice** is high—that is, if they believe that the procedures used to determine guilt or innocence are fair.

Scoring for the Try It! Exercises

▶ **Page 484**

The speaker, when done, should reveal when he or she was telling the truth versus lying. The audience members should tally how often they were right. People should be correct half of the time just by guessing; scores that are substantially above 50 percent may indicate that a person is good at detecting deception (or that the speaker is poor at lying!). Trade notes about what kinds of cues people paid attention to in the speaker. What did the speaker do that made you think he or she was telling a lie?

▶ **Page 496**

According to the Criminal Code of Canada, the following are the maximum and minimum penalties for the crimes listed. (Note that if a minimum penalty is not specified, there is no minimum penalty for that crime.)

1. First-degree murder. Maximum sentence: life imprisonment; minimum sentence: 25 years' imprisonment without parole

2. Second-degree murder. Maximum sentence: life imprisonment; minimum sentence: 10 years' imprisonment without parole

3. Manslaughter. Maximum sentence: life imprisonment

4. Communication for prostitution. You may be surprised to learn that prostitution itself is not illegal in Canada, but communicating about it either verbally or nonverbally is illegal. The person offering sexual services or the person seeking sexual services can be charged. Maximum sentence: 6 months' imprisonment and $2000 fine

5. Break and enter. Of a home, the maximum sentence is life imprisonment; of another kind of building, the maximum sentence is 10 years' imprisonment.

6. Drug trafficking. Sentences vary depending on the drug being sold. For cocaine, the maximum sentence is life imprisonment. For steroids, the maximum sentence is 3 years' imprisonment.

7. Impaired driving. The maximum penalty is 5 years' imprisonment. If it is a first offence, the minimum penalty is a $300 fine. If it is a second offence, the minimum penalty is 14 days' imprisonment.

8. False pretence. Maximum sentence: 10 years' imprisonment

9. Assisting suicide. Maximum sentence: 14 years' imprisonment

10. Sexual assault. The maximum penalty is 10 years' imprisonment; minimum penalty: 4 years' imprisonment. If a firearm is used, the maximum penalty is 14 years' imprisonment.

Along with a dynamic, electronic version of this text, MyPsychLab offers a wealth of resources to deepen your understanding and test your recall of the material in this chapter—including video and audio clips, simulations and activities, self-assessments, practice tests, and other study materials. The following specific resources are available for this chapter:

 Psychologists at Work

 Stanford Prison Experiment: Phil Zimbardo

To access MyPsychLab, please visit www.mypsychlab.com (Student Access Code required—packaged with this book).

Glossary

accessibility   the extent to which schemas and concepts are at the forefront of people's minds and are therefore likely to be used when making judgments about the social world

acquisition   the process by which people notice and pay attention to information in the environment; people cannot perceive everything that is happening around them, so they acquire only a subset of the information available in the environment

actor/observer difference   the tendency to see other people's behaviour as dispositionally caused, while focusing more on the role of situational factors when explaining one's own behaviour

affect blend   a facial expression in which one part of the face is registering one emotion and another part of the face is registering a different emotion

affectively based attitude   an attitude based primarily on people's emotions and feelings about the attitude object

aggression   intentional behaviour aimed at causing either physical or psychological pain

aggressive stimulus   an object that is associated with aggressive response (e.g., a gun) and whose mere presence can increase the probability of aggression

altruism   the desire to help another person, even if it involves a cost to the helper

altruistic personality   aspects of a person's makeup that cause him or her to help others in a wide variety of situations

amygdala   an area in the core of the brain that is associated with aggressive behaviour

anxious/ambivalent attachment style   an attachment style characterized by a concern that others will not reciprocate one's desire for intimacy, resulting in higher-than-average levels of anxiety

applied research   studies designed specifically to solve a particular social problem; building a theory of behaviour is usually secondary to solving the specific problem

archival analysis   a form of the observational method, whereby the researcher examines the accumulated documents, or archives, of a culture (e.g., diaries, novels, magazines, and newspapers)

attachment styles   the expectations people develop about relationships with others based on the relationship they had with their primary caregiver when they were infants

attachment theory   the theory that our behaviour in adult relationships is based on our experiences as infants with our parents or caregivers

attitude inoculation   the process of making people immune to attempts to change their attitudes by initially exposing them to small doses of the arguments against their position

attitude   an evaluation of a person, object, or idea

attribution theory   a description of the way in which people explain the causes of their own and other people's behaviour

automatic thinking   thinking that is nonconscious, unintentional, involuntary, and effortless

availability heuristic   a mental shortcut whereby people base a judgment on the ease with which they can bring something to mind

avoidant attachment style   an attachment style characterized by a suppression of attachment needs, because attempts to be intimate have been rebuffed; people with this style find it difficult to develop intimate relationships

base rate information   information about the frequency of members of different categories in the population

basic research   studies that are designed to find the best answer as to why people behave the way they do and that are conducted purely for reasons of intellectual curiosity

behaviourally based attitude   an attitude based primarily on observations of how one behaves toward an attitude object

behaviourism   a school of psychology maintaining that to understand human behaviour one need only consider the reinforcing properties of the environment—that is, how positive and negative events in the environment are associated with specific behaviours

belief in a just world   a form of defensive attribution wherein people assume that bad things happen to bad people and that good things happen to good people

buffering hypothesis   the hypothesis that we need social support only when we are under stress, because it protects us against the detrimental effects of this stress

bystander effect   the finding that the greater the number of bystanders who witness an emergency, the less likely it is that any one of them will help

catharsis   the notion that "blowing off steam"—by performing an aggressive act, watching others engage in aggressive behaviour, or engaging in a fantasy of aggression—relieves built-up aggressive energies and hence reduces the likelihood of further aggressive behaviour

causal theories   theories about the causes of one's own feelings and behaviours; typically, we learn such theories from our culture (e.g., "absence makes the heart grow fonder")

cognitive dissonance   a feeling of discomfort caused by the realization that one's behaviour is inconsistent with one's attitudes or that one holds two conflicting attitudes

cognitive interview   a technique whereby a trained interviewer tries to improve eyewitnesses' memories by focusing their attention on the details and context of the event

cognitively based attitude   an attitude based primarily on a person's beliefs about the properties of an attitude object

commitment calibration hypothesis   the idea that the outcome of adversity on a relationship depends on the level of commitment: If the level of adversity is lower than the level of commitment, the relationship is not challenged, but if the level of adversity is higher than the level of commitment, the relationship ends; however, if the level of adversity is equal to the level of commitment, the relationship will be strengthened

communal relationships   relationships in which people's primary concern is being responsive to the other person's needs

companionate love the feelings of intimacy and affection we feel for another person about whom we care deeply

comparison level people's expectations about the level of rewards and costs they deserve in a relationship

comparison level for alternatives people's expectations about the level of rewards and punishments they would receive in an alternative relationship

complementarity attraction to people who are opposite to us

compliance a change in behaviour in response to a direct request from another person

conformity a change in behaviour as a result of the real or imagined influence of other people

consensus information information about the extent to which other people behave the same way as the actor does toward the same stimulus

consistency information information about the extent to which the behaviour between one actor and one stimulus is the same across time and circumstances

construal the way in which people perceive, comprehend, and interpret the social world

contagion the rapid transmission of emotions or behaviour through a crowd

contingency theory of leadership the theory that leadership effectiveness depends both on how task-oriented or relationship-oriented the leader is, and on the amount of control and influence the leader has over the group

controlled thinking thinking that is conscious, intentional, voluntary, and effortful

coping styles the ways in which people react to stressful events

correlation coefficient a statistical technique that assesses how well you can predict one variable based on another (e.g., how well you can predict people's weight from their height)

correlational method the technique whereby researchers systematically measure two or more variables and assess the relation between them (i.e., how much one can be predicted from the other)

correspondence bias the tendency to infer that people's behaviour corresponds to or matches their disposition (personality)

counter-attitudinal advocacy the process that occurs when a person states an opinion or attitude that runs counter to his or her private belief or attitude

counterfactual thinking mentally changing some aspect of the past as a way of imagining what might have been

covariation model a theory stating that in order to form an attribution about what caused a person's behaviour, we systematically note the pattern between the presence (or absence) of possible causal factors and whether or not the behaviour occurs

cover story a description of the purpose of a study given to participants that is different from its true purpose; cover stories are used to maintain psychological realism

cross-cultural research research conducted with members of different cultures, to see whether the psychological processes of interest are present in both cultures or whether they are specific to the culture in which people were raised

debriefing the process of explaining to the participants, at the end of the experiment, the purpose of the study and exactly what transpired

deception the procedure whereby participants are misled about the true purpose of a study or the events that will actually transpire

decode to interpret the meaning of the nonverbal behaviour other people express, such as deciding that a pat on the back was an expression of condescension and not kindness

defensive attributions explanations for behaviour that avoid feelings of vulnerability and mortality

deindividuation the loosening of normal constraints on behaviour when people are in a group, leading to an increase in impulsive and deviant acts

dependent variable the variable a researcher measures to see if it is influenced by the independent variable; the researcher hypothesizes that the dependent variable will depend on the level of the independent variable

descriptive norms people's perceptions of how other people actually behave in a given situation, regardless of whether the behaviour is approved or disapproved of by others

deterrence theory the theory that people refrain from criminal activity because of the threat of legal punishment, as long as the punishment is perceived as relatively severe, certain, and swift

diffusion of responsibility each bystander's sense of responsibility to help decreases as the number of witnesses to an emergency or crisis increases

discrimination unjustified negative or harmful action toward a member of a group, simply because of his or her membership in that group

disidentification the process by which targets of negative stereotypes redefine their self-concept, such that the performance domain is no longer a part of their identity

dismissive avoidant style a type of avoidant attachment in which the person is self-sufficient and claims not to need close relationships

display rules culturally determined rules about which nonverbal behaviours are appropriate to display

distinctiveness information information about the extent to which one particular actor behaves in the same way to different stimuli

door-in-the-face technique a technique to get people to comply with a request, whereby people are presented first with a large request, which they are expected to refuse, and then with a smaller, more reasonable request, to which it is hoped they will acquiesce

downward social comparison the process whereby we compare ourselves with people who are worse than we are on a particular trait or ability

elaboration likelihood model the theory that there are two ways in which persuasive communications can cause attitude change: the central route occurs when people are motivated and have the ability to pay attention to the arguments in the communication, and the peripheral route occurs when people do not pay attention to the arguments but are instead swayed by surface characteristics (e.g., who gave the speech)

emblems nonverbal gestures that have well-understood definitions within a given culture; they usually have direct verbal translations, such as the "okay" sign

empathy-altruism hypothesis the idea that when we feel empathy for a person, we will attempt to help him or her purely for altruistic reasons, regardless of what we have to gain

empathy the ability to experience events and emotions (e.g., joy and sadness) the way another person experiences them

encode to express or emit nonverbal behaviour, such as smiling or patting someone on the back

equity theory the theory that people are happiest with relationships in which the rewards and costs that a person experiences, and the contributions that he or she makes to the relationship are roughly equal to the rewards, costs, and contributions of the other person

Eros the instinct toward life, posited by Freud

ethnography the method by which researchers attempt to understand a group or culture by observing it from the inside without imposing any preconceived notions they might have

evolutionary approach an approach derived from evolutionary biology that states that men and women are attracted to different characteristics in each other—men are attracted by women's appearance; women are attracted by men's resources—because this maximizes their reproductive success

evolutionary psychology the attempt to explain social behaviour in terms of genetic factors that evolved over time according to the principles of natural selection

exchange relationships relationships governed by the need for equity (i.e., for a comparable ratio of rewards and costs)

experimental method the method in which the researcher randomly assigns participants to different conditions and ensures that these conditions are identical except for the independent variable (the one thought to have a causal effect on people's responses)

explicit attitudes attitudes that we consciously endorse and can easily report

extended contact hypothesis the mere knowledge that a member of one's own group has a close relationship with a member of another group can reduce one's prejudice toward that group

external attribution the inference that a person is behaving a certain way because of something about the situation he or she is in; the assumption is that most people would respond the same way in that situation

external justification a person's reason or explanation for dissonant behaviour that resides outside the individual (e.g., in order to receive a large reward or avoid a severe punishment)

external validity the extent to which the results of a study can be generalized to other situations and to other people

extrinsic motivation the desire to engage in an activity because of external rewards or pressures, not because we enjoy the task or find it interesting

false memory syndrome remembering a past traumatic experience that is objectively false but nevertheless accepted as true

fear-arousing communication a persuasive message that attempts to change people's attitudes by arousing their fears

fearful avoidant style a type of avoidant attachment in which close relationships are avoided because of mistrust and fears of being hurt

field experiments experiments conducted in natural settings, rather than in the laboratory

fight-or-flight response responding to stress by either attacking the source of the stress or fleeing from it

foot-in-the-door technique a technique to get people to comply with a request, whereby people are presented first with a small request, to which they are expected to acquiesce, followed by a larger request, to which it is hoped they will also acquiesce

frustration-aggression theory the theory that frustration—the perception that you are being prevented from obtaining a goal—will increase the probability of an aggressive response

fundamental attribution error the tendency to overestimate the extent to which people's behaviour is attributable to internal, dispositional factors, and to underestimate the role of situational factors

fundamental attribution error the tendency to overestimate the extent to which people's behaviour stems from internal, dispositional factors and to underestimate the role of situational factors

Gestalt psychology a school of psychology stressing the importance of studying the subjective way in which an object appears in people's minds, rather than the objective physical attributes of the object

global attribution the belief that the cause of an event is a result of factors that apply in a large number of situations, as opposed to the belief that the cause is specific and applies in only a limited number of situations

great person theory the theory that certain key personality traits make a person a good leader, regardless of the nature of the situation facing the leader

group cohesiveness qualities of a group that bind members together and promote liking among them

group polarization the tendency for groups to make decisions that are more extreme than the initial inclinations of their members

group a collection of two or more people who interact with each other and are interdependent, in the sense that their needs and goals cause them to rely on each other

groupthink a kind of thinking in which maintaining group cohesiveness and solidarity is more important than considering the facts in a realistic manner

hardiness a personality trait defined as a combination of self-esteem and a sense of control

heuristic-systematic model of persuasion the theory that there are two ways in which persuasive communications can cause attitude change: people either process the merits of the arguments (known as systematic processing) or are swayed by factors that are peripheral to the message itself, such as "Experts are always right" (known as heuristic processing)

hostile aggression an act of aggression stemming from feelings of anger and aimed at inflicting pain

hypothesis a testable statement or idea about the relationship between two or more variables

idiosyncrasy credits the credits a person earns, over time, by conforming to a group's norms; if enough idiosyncrasy credits are earned, the person can, on occasion, behave deviantly without retribution from the group

implicit attitudes attitudes that are involuntary, uncontrollable, and at times unconscious

implicit personality theory a type of schema people use to group various kinds of personality traits together; for example, many people believe that if someone is kind, he or she is generous as well

in-group bias the tendency to evaluate in-group members more positively than out-group members

in-group the group with which an individual identifies, and of which he or she feels a member

independent variable the variable a researcher changes or varies to see if it has an effect on some other variable

independent view of the self defining oneself in terms of one's own internal thoughts, feelings, and actions, and not in terms of the thoughts, feelings, and actions of other people

individual differences the aspects of people's personalities that make them different from other people

informational social influence conforming because we believe that others' interpretation of an ambiguous situation is more correct than ours and will help us choose an appropriate course of action

informed consent the procedure whereby researchers explain the nature of the experiment to participants before it begins, and obtain their consent to participate

injunctive norms people's perceptions of what behaviour is approved or disapproved of by others

instrumental aggression aggression as a means to some goal other than causing pain

insufficient punishment the dissonance aroused when individuals lack sufficient external justification for having resisted a desired activity or object, usually resulting in individuals devaluing the forbidden activity or object

integrative solution a solution to a conflict whereby the parties make trade-offs on issues according to their different interests; each side concedes the most on issues that are unimportant to it but important to the other side

interdependent view of the self defining oneself in terms of one's relationships to other people; recognizing that one's behaviour is often determined by the thoughts, feelings, and actions of others

interjudge reliability the level of agreement between two or more people who independently observe and code a set of data; by showing that two or more judges independently come up with the same observations, researchers ensure that the observations are not the subjective impressions of one individual

internal attribution the belief that the cause of an event is factors inherent in you, as opposed to factors that are external to you (e.g., the difficulty of a test)

internal justification the reduction of dissonance by changing something about oneself (e.g., one's attitude or behaviour)

internal validity ensuring that nothing other than the independent variable can affect the dependent variable; this is accomplished by controlling all extraneous variables and by randomly assigning people to different experimental conditions

intrinsic motivation the desire to engage in an activity because we enjoy it or find it interesting, not because of external rewards or pressures

introspection the process whereby people look inward and examine their own thoughts, feelings, and motives

investment model the theory that people's commitment to a relationship depends on their satisfaction with the relationship in terms of rewards, costs, and comparison level; their comparison level for alternatives; and how much they have invested in the relationship that would be lost by leaving it

jigsaw classroom a classroom setting designed to reduce prejudice between children by placing them in small, desegregated groups and making each child dependent on the other children in the group to learn the course material and do well in the class

judgmental heuristics mental shortcuts people use to make judgments quickly and efficiently

justification of effort the tendency for individuals to increase their liking for something they have worked hard to attain

kin selection the idea that behaviour that helps a genetic relative is favoured by natural selection

learned helplessness the state of pessimism that results from explaining a negative event as stemming from stable, internal, and global factors

looking-glass self the idea that we see ourselves through the eyes of other people and incorporate their views into our self-concept

lowballing an unscrupulous strategy whereby a salesperson induces a customer to agree to purchase a product at a very low cost, then subsequently raises the price; frequently, the customer will still make the purchase at the inflated price

mass psychogenic illness the occurrence of similar physical symptoms in a group of people for which there is no known physical or medical cause

mere exposure effect the finding that the more exposure we have to a stimulus, the more apt we are to like it

meta-stereotype a person's beliefs regarding the stereotype that out-group members hold about their own group

meta analysis a statistical technique that averages the results of two or more studies to see if the effect of an independent variable is reliable

minority influence the case where a minority of group members influences the behaviour or beliefs of the majority

misattribution of arousal the process whereby people make mistaken inferences about what is causing them to feel the way they do

modern prejudice outwardly acting unprejudiced while inwardly maintaining prejudiced attitudes

mundane realism the extent to which an experiment is similar to real-life situations

mutual interdependence a situation in which two or more groups need each other and must depend on each other in order to accomplish a goal that is important to each group

negative-state relief hypothesis the idea that people help in order to alleviate their own sadness and distress

negotiation a form of communication between opposing sides in a conflict, in which offers and counteroffers are made and a solution occurs only when both parties agree

nonverbal communication the way in which people communicate, intentionally or unintentionally, without words; nonverbal cues include facial expressions, tone of voice, gestures, body position and movement, the use of touch, and eye gaze

norm of reciprocity the expectation that helping others will increase the likelihood that they will help us in the future

normative social influence the influence of other people that leads us to conform in order to be liked and accepted by them; this type of conformity results in public compliance with but not necessarily with private acceptance of the group's beliefs and behaviours

obedience conformity in response to the commands of an authority figure

observational method the technique whereby a researcher observes people and systematically records measurements of their behaviour

operational definition the precise specification of how variables are measured or manipulated

out-group homogeneity the perception that those in the out-group are more similar (homogeneous) to each other than they really are, as well as more similar than the members of the in-group are to each other

out-group a group with which the individual does not identify

overconfidence barrier the barrier that results when people have too much confidence in the accuracy of their judgments; people's judgments are usually not as correct as they think they are

overjustification effect the case whereby people view their behaviour as caused by compelling extrinsic reasons, making them underestimate the extent to which their behaviour was caused by intrinsic reasons

own-race bias the finding that people are better at recognizing faces of their own race than those of other races

passionate love the feelings of intense longing, accompanied by physiological arousal, we feel for another person; when our love is reciprocated, we feel great fulfillment and ecstasy, but when it is not, we feel sadness and despair

perceived control the belief that we can influence our environment in ways that determine whether we experience positive or negative outcomes

perceptual salience information that is the focus of people's attention; people tend to overestimate the causal role of perceptually salient information

performance-contingent rewards rewards that are based on how well we perform a task

perseverance effect the finding that people's beliefs about themselves and the social world persist even after the evidence supporting these beliefs is discredited

persuasive communication communication (e.g., a speech or television advertisement) advocating a particular side of an issue

pluralistic ignorance the phenomenon whereby bystanders assume that nothing is wrong in an emergency because no one else looks concerned

polygraph a machine that measures people's physiological responses (e.g., heart rate); polygraph operators attempt to tell if someone is lying by observing how that person responds physiologically while answering questions

positive illusions idealization of our romantic relationships and partners in order to maintain the relationship

postdecision dissonance dissonance that is inevitably aroused after a person makes a decision; such dissonance is typically reduced by enhancing the attractiveness of the chosen alternative and devaluing the rejected alternatives

prejudice a hostile or negative attitude toward a distinguishable group of people, based solely on their membership in that group

priming the process by which recent experiences increase the accessibility of a schema, trait, or concept

private acceptance conforming to other people's behaviour out of a genuine belief that what they are doing or saying is right

probability level (p-value) a number, calculated with statistical techniques, that tells researchers how likely it is that the results of their experiment occurred by chance and not because of the independent variable(s); the convention in science, including social psychology, is to consider results significant if the probability level is less than 5 in 100 that the results might be attributable to chance factors and not the independent variables studied

procedural justice people's judgments about the fairness of the procedures used to determine outcomes, such as whether they are innocent or guilty of a crime

process loss any aspect of group interaction that inhibits good problem solving

product placement strategically placed products in movies and television shows that are intended to persuade us

propinquity effect the finding that the more we see and interact with people, the more likely they are to become our friends

prosocial behaviour any act performed with the goal of benefiting another person

psychological realism the extent to which the psychological processes triggered in an experiment are similar to psychological processes that occur in everyday life; psychological realism can be high in an experiment, even if mundane realism is low

public compliance conforming to other people's behaviour publicly, without necessarily believing in what they are doing or saying

random assignment to condition the process whereby all participants have an equal chance of taking part in any condition of an experiment; through random assignment, researchers can be relatively certain that differences in the participants' personalities or backgrounds are distributed evenly across conditions

random selection a way of ensuring that a sample of people is representative of a population, by giving everyone in the population an equal chance of being selected for the sample

rationalization trap the potential for dissonance reduction to produce a succession of self-justifications that ultimately result in a chain of stupid or immoral actions

realistic conflict theory the theory that limited resources lead to conflict between groups and result in increased prejudice and discrimination

reciprocal liking when you like someone and that person also likes you

reciprocity norm a social norm by which the receipt of something positive from another person requires you to reciprocate, or behave similarly, in response

reconstructive memory the process whereby memories for an event become distorted by information encountered after the event has occurred

recovered memories recollections of an event, such as sexual abuse, that have been forgotten or repressed

relationship-oriented leader a leader who is concerned primarily with the feelings of and relationships among the workers

relative deprivation the perception that you have less than you deserve, less than what you have been led to expect, or less than what people similar to you have

replication repeating a study, generally with different subject populations, or in different settings, or using different methods

representativeness heuristic a mental shortcut whereby people classify something according to how similar it is to a typical case

resilience the ability to recover from negative experiences and adapt to the demands of life

retrieval the process by which people recall information stored in their memory

reward/cost ratio the notion that there is a balance between the rewards that come from a relationship and the personal cost of maintaining the relationship; if the ratio is not favourable, the result is dissatisfaction with the relationship

schemas mental structures people use to organize their knowledge about the social world around themes or subjects and that influence the information people notice, think about, and remember

secure attachment style an attachment style characterized by trust, a lack of concern with being abandoned, and the view that one is worthy and well liked

self-affirmation theory a theory suggesting that people will reduce the impact of a dissonance-arousing threat to their self-concept by focusing on and affirming their competence on some dimension unrelated to the threat

self-awareness the act of thinking about ourselves

self-awareness theory the idea that when people focus their attention on themselves, they evaluate and compare their behaviour with their internal standards and values

self-concept the contents of the self; that is, our knowledge about who we are

self-discrepancy theory the theory that we become distressed when our sense of who we truly are—our actual self—is discrepant from our personal standards or desired self-conceptions

self-efficacy the belief in one's ability to carry out specific actions that produce desired outcomes

self-enhancement an unrealistically positive view of oneself

self-esteem people's evaluations of their own self-worth—that is, the extent to which they view themselves as good, competent, and decent

self-fulfilling prophecy the case whereby people (a) have an expectation about what another person is like, which (b) influences how they act toward that person, which (c) causes that person to behave consistently with their original expectations

self-perception theory the theory that when our attitudes and feelings are uncertain or ambiguous, we infer these states by observing our behaviour and the situation in which it occurs

self-reference effect the tendency for people to remember information better if they relate it to themselves

self-schemas mental structures that people use to organize their knowledge about themselves and that influence what they notice, think about, and remember about themselves

self-serving attributions explanations for one's successes that credit internal, dispositional factors and explanations for one's failures that blame external, situational factors

self-verification theory   a theory suggesting that people have a need to seek confirmation of their self-concept, whether the self-concept is positive or negative; in some circumstances, this tendency can conflict with the desire to uphold a favourable view of oneself

serotonin   a chemical in the brain that may inhibit aggressive impulses

similarity   attraction to people who are like us

social cognition   how people think about themselves and the social world; more specifically, how people select, interpret, remember, and use social information

social comparison theory   the idea that we learn about our own abilities and attitudes by comparing ourselves with other people

social dilemma   a conflict in which the most beneficial action for an individual, if chosen by most people, will have harmful effects on everyone

social exchange theory   the theory that how people feel about a relationship depends on their perceptions of the rewards and costs of the relationship, the kind of relationship they deserve, and their chances of having a better relationship with someone else

social facilitation   the tendency for people to do better on simple tasks, but worse on complex tasks, when they are in the presence of others and their individual performance can be evaluated

social impact theory   the theory that conforming to social influence depends on the strength of the group, its immediacy, and the number of other people in the group

social learning theory   the theory that we learn social behaviour (e.g., aggression) by observing others and imitating them

social loafing   the tendency for people to do worse on simple tasks, but better on complex tasks, when they are in the presence of others and their individual performance cannot be evaluated

social norms   the implicit or explicit rules a group has for the acceptable behaviours, values, and beliefs of its members

social perception   the study of how we form impressions of and make inferences about other people

social psychology   the scientific study of the way in which people's thoughts, feelings, and behaviours are influenced by the real or imagined presence of other people

social role theory   the theory that sex differences in social behaviour derive from society's division of labour between the sexes; this division leads to differences in gender-role expectations and sex-typed skills, both of which are responsible for differences in men's and women's social behaviour

social roles   shared expectations by group members about how particular people in the group are supposed to behave

social support   the perception that others are responsive and receptive to one's needs

source monitoring   the process whereby people try to identify the source of their memories

stable attribution   the belief that the cause of an event is a result of factors that will not change over time, as opposed to unstable factors that will change over time

stereotype threat   the apprehension experienced by members of a minority group that they might behave in a manner that confirms an existing cultural stereotype

stereotype   a generalization about a group of people in which identical characteristics are assigned to virtually all members of the group, regardless of actual variation among the members

storage   the process by which people store in memory information they have acquired from the environment

stress   the negative feelings and beliefs that occur whenever people feel unable to cope with demands from their environment

subliminal messages   words or pictures that are not consciously perceived but that supposedly influence people's judgments, attitudes, and behaviours

surveys   research in which a representative sample of people are asked questions about their attitudes or behaviour

task-contingent rewards   rewards that are given for performing a task, regardless of how well the task is done

task-oriented leader   a leader who is concerned more with getting the job done than with the feelings of and relationships among the workers

tend-and-befriend response   responding to stress with nurturant activities designed to protect oneself and one's offspring (tending) and creating social networks that provide protection from threats (befriending)

terror management theory   the realization that we are going to die produces fear, and people will go to great lengths to reduce this feeling

testosterone   a male sex hormone associated with aggression

Thanatos   according to Freud, an instinctual drive toward death, leading to aggressive actions

theory   an organized set of principles that can be used to explain observed phenomena

theory of planned behaviour   a theory that the best predictors of a person's planned, deliberate behaviours are the person's attitudes toward specific behaviours, subjective norms, and perceived behavioural control

thought suppression   the attempt to avoid thinking about something a person would prefer to forget

tit-for-tat strategy   a means of encouraging cooperation by at first acting cooperatively but then always responding the way your opponent did on the previous trial (i.e., cooperatively or competitively)

transactive memory   the combined memory of two people that is more efficient than the memory of either individual

two-step process   analyzing another person's behaviour first by making an automatic internal attribution and only then thinking about possible situational reasons for the behaviour, after which one may adjust the original internal attribution

Type A versus Type B personality   a personality typology based on how people typically confront challenges in their lives; the Type A person is typically competitive, impatient, hostile, and control-oriented, whereas the Type B person is typically patient, relaxed, and noncompetitive

ultimate attribution error   our tendency to make dispositional attributions about an entire group of people

unrealistic optimism   a form of defensive attribution wherein people think that good things are more likely to happen to them than to their peers and that bad things are less likely to happen to them than to their peers

upward social comparison   the process whereby we compare ourselves with people who are better than we are on a particular trait or ability

urban-overload hypothesis   the theory that because people living in cities are constantly being bombarded with stimulation, they keep to themselves in order to avoid being overloaded by it

Yale Attitude Change Approach   the study of the conditions under which people are most likely to change their attitudes in response to persuasive messages; researchers in this tradition focus on "who said what to whom"—that is, on the source of the communication, the nature of the communication, and the nature of the audience

References

Abela, J. R. Z., Webb, C. A., Wagner, C., Ho, M-H. R, & Adams, P. (2006). The role of self-criticism, dependency, and hassles in the course of depressive illness: A multiwave longitudinal study. *Personality and Social Psychology Bulletin, 32,* 328–338.

Abelson, R. P., Kinder, D. R., Peters, M. D., & Fiske, S. T. (1982). Affective and semantic components in political person perception. *Journal of Personality and Social Psychology, 42,* 619–630.

Aboud, F. E., & Doyle, A.B. (1996). Does talk of race foster prejudice or tolerance in children? *Canadian Journal of Behavioural Science, 28,* 161–170.

Abrahamse, W., Steg, L., & Vlek, C. (2005). A review of intervention studies aimed at household energy conservation. *Journal of Environmental Psychology, 25,* 273–291.

Abrahamse, W., Steg, L., Vlek, C., & Rothengatter, T. (2005). A review of intervention studies aimed at household energy conservation. *Journal of Environmental Psychology, 25,* 273–291.

Abrams, D., Marques, J. M., Bown, N., & Henson, M. (2000). Pro-norm and anti-norm deviance within and between groups. *Journal of Personality and Social Psychology, 78,* 906–912.

Abrams, D., Wetherell, M., Cochrane, S., Hogg, M. A., & Turner, J. C. (1990). Knowing what to think by knowing who you are: Self-categorization and the nature of norm formation, conformity, and group polarization. *British Journal of Social Psychology, 29,* 97–119.

Abramson, L. Y., Seligman, M. E. P., & Teasdale, J. D. (1978). Learned helplessness in humans: Critique and reformulation. *Journal of Abnormal Psychology, 87,* 49–74.

Adams, G., Anderson, S. L., & Adonu, J. K. (2004). The cultural grounding of closeness and intimacy. In D. J. Mashek & A. Aron (Eds.), *Handbook of Closeness and Intimacy.* (pp. 321–342). Mahwah, NJ: Lawrence Erlbaum Associates.

Adams, G., Garcia, D. M., Purdie-Vaughns, V., & Steele, C. M. (2006). The detrimental effects of a suggestion of sexism in an instruction situation. *Journal of Experimental Social Psychology, 42,* 602–615.

Adlaf, E. M., Demers, A., & Gliksman, L. (Eds.) (2005). Canadian Campus Survey 2004. CAMH. Toronto, ON: Centre for Addiction and Mental Health.

Adlaf, E. M., Gliksman, L., Demers, A., & Newton-Taylor, B. (2001). The prevalence of elevated psychological distress among Canadian undergraduates: Findings from the 1998 Canadian Campus Survey. *Journal of American College Health, 50,* 67–72.

Adlag, R. J., & Fuller, S. R. (1993). Beyond fiasco: A reappraisal of the groupthink phenomenon and a new model of group decision processes. *Psychological Bulletin, 113,* 533–552.

Agrell, S. (2008, April 19). The perils of legislating a healthy aesthetic. *Globe and Mail.* www.theglobeandmail.com/servlet/story/RTGAM.20080419.wthinNEW0419_2/BNStory/specialScienceandHealth/home.

Ahlfinger, N. R., & Esser, J. K. (2001). Testing the groupthink model: Effects of promotional leadership and conformity predisposition. *Social Behavior and Personality, 29,* 31–41.

Aiello, J. R., & Douthitt, E. A. (2001). Social facilitation from Triplett to electronic performance monitoring. *Group Dynamics: Theory, Research, and Practice, 5,* 163–80.

Ainsworth, M. D. S., Blehar, M. C., Waters, E., & Wall, S. (1978). *Patterns of attachment: A psychological study of the strange situation.* Hillsdale, NJ: Erlbaum.

Ajzen, I. (1985). From intentions to actions: A theory of planned behavior. In J. Kuhl & J. Beckmann (Eds.), *Action-control: From cognition to behavior.* (pp. 11–39.) Heidelberg, Germany: Springer.

Ajzen, I. (2001). Nature and operation of attitudes. *Annual Review of Psychology, 52,* 27–58.

Ajzen, I., & Fishbein, M. (1980). *Understanding attitudes and predicting social behavior.* Englewood Cliffs, NJ: Prentice Hall.

Ajzen, I., & Fishbein, M. (2005). The influence of attitudes on behavior. In D. Albarracín, B. T. Johnson, & M. P. Zanna (Eds.), *The handbook of attitudes.* (pp. 173–221.) Mahwah, NJ: Erlbaum.

Ajzen, I., & Sexton, J. (1999). Depth of processing, belief congruence, and attitude-behavior correspondence. In S. Chaiken & Y. Trope (Eds.), *Dual-process theories in social psychology.* (pp. 117–138.) New York: Guilford Press.

Akert, R. M. (1998). Terminating romantic relationships: The role of personal responsibility and gender. Unpublished manuscript, Wellesley College.

Albarracín, D., Durantini, M. R., & Earl, A. N. (2006). Empirical and theoretical conclusions of an analysis of outcomes of HIV-prevention interventions. *Current Directions in Psychological Science, 15,* 73–78.

Albarracín, D., Gillette, J. C., Earl, A. N., Glasman, L. R., Durantini, M. R., & Ho, M. (2005). A test of major assumptions about behavior change: A comprehensive look at the effects of passive and active HIV-prevention interventions since the beginning of the epidemic. *Psychological Bulletin, 131,* 856–897.

Albright, L., & Forziati, C. (1995). Cross-situational consistency and perceptual accuracy in leadership. *Personality and Social Psychology Bulletin, 21,* 1269–1276.

Allen, V. L., & Levine, J. M. (1969). Consensus and conformity. *Journal of Personality and Social Psychology, 5,* 389–399.

Allison, K. R., Dwyer, J. M., & Makin, S. (1999). Self-efficacy and participation in vigorous physical activity by high school students. *Health Education and Behavior, 26,* 12–24.

Allison, P. D. (1992). The cultural evolution of beneficent norms. *Social Forces, 71,* 279–301.

Allport, G. (1954). *The nature of prejudice.* Reading, MA: Addison-Wesley.

Allport, G. W. (1985). The historical background of social psychology. In G. Lindzey & E. Aronson (Eds.), *The handbook of social psychology.* (Vol. 1, pp. 1–46.) Reading, MA: Addison-Wesley.

Altemeyer, B. (1981). *Right-wing authoritarianism.* Winnipeg, MB: The University of Manitoba Press.

Altemeyer, B. (1988). *Enemies of freedom: Understanding right-wing authoritarianism.* San Francisco, CA: Jossey-Bass Publishers.

Altemeyer, B. (1996). *The authoritarian specter.* Cambridge, MA: Harvard University Press.

Altemeyer, B. (1998). The other "authoritarian personality." In M. P. Zanna (Ed.), *Advances in experimental social psychology.* (Vol. 30.) San Diego, CA: Academic Press Limited.

Altemeyer, B. (2001). Changes in attitudes toward homosexuals. *Journal of Homosexuality, 42,* 63–75.

Altemeyer, B., & Hunsberger, B. (1992). Authoritarianism, religious fundamentalism, quest, and prejudice. *The International Journal for the Psychology of Religion, 2*, 113–133.

Altemeyer, B., & Hunsberger, B. (1993). Reply to Gorsuch. *International Journal for the Psychology of Religion, 3*, 33–37.

Amato, P. R. (1983). Helping behavior in urban and rural environments: Field studies based on a taxonomic organization of helping episodes. *Journal of Personality and Social Psychology, 45*, 571–586.

Ambady, N., Bernieri, F. J., & Richeson, J. A. (2000). Toward a histology of social behavior: Judgmental accuracy from thin slices of the behavioral stream. In M. P. Zanna (Ed.), *Advances in experimental social psychology.* (Vol. 32, pp. 201–271.) San Diego, CA: Academic Press.

Ambady, N., & Rosenthal, R. (1992). Thin slices of expressive behavior as predictors of interpersonal consequences: A meta-analysis. *Psychological Bulletin, 111*, 256–274.

Ambady, N., & Rosenthal, R. (1993). Half a minute: Predicting teacher evaluations from thin slices of nonverbal behavior and physical attractiveness. *Journal of Personality and Social Psychology, 64*, 431–441.

Amiot, C. E., & Bourhis, R. Y. (2003). Discrimination and the positive-negative asymmetry effects: Ideological and normative process. *Personality and Social Psychology Bulletin, 29.*5, 597–608.

Amiot, C. E., Vallerand, R. J., & Blanchard, C. M. (2006). Passion and psychological adjustment: A test of the person-environment fit hypothesis. *Personality and Social Psychology Bulletin, 32*, 220–229.

Amir, I. (1969). Contact hypothesis in ethnic relations. *Psychological Bulletin, 71*, 319–342.

Amir, Y. (1976). The role of intergroup contact in change of prejudice and ethnic relations. In P. Katz (Ed.), *Towards the elimination of racism.* New York: Pergamon Press.

Andersen, S. M. (1984). Self-knowledge and social inference: II. The diagnosticity of cognitive/affective and behavioral data. *Journal of Personality and Social Psychology, 46*, 294–307.

Andersen, S. M., & Bem, S. L. (1981). Sex typing and androgyny in dyadic interaction: Individual differences in responsiveness to physical attractiveness. *Journal of Personality and Social Psychology, 41*, 74–86.

Andersen, S. M., & Klatzky, R. L. (1987). Traits and social stereotypes: Levels of categorization in person perception. *Journal of Personality and Social Psychology, 53*, 235–246.

Andersen, S. M., & Ross, L. D. (1984). Self-knowledge and social inference: I. The impact of cognitive/affective and behavioral data. *Journal of Personality and Social Psychology, 46*, 280–293.

Anderson, C. A. (1995). Implicit personality theories and empirical data: Biased assimilation, belief perseverance and change, and covariation detection sensitivity. *Social Cognition, 13*, 25–48.

Anderson, C. A. (1999). Attributional style, depression, and loneliness: A cross-cultural comparison of American and Chinese students. *Personality and Social Psychology Bulletin, 25*, 482–499.

Anderson, C. A., & Anderson, D. C. (1984). Ambient temperature and violent crime: Tests of the linear and curvilinear hypotheses. *Journal of Personality and Social Psychology, 46*, 91–97.

Anderson, C. A., Bushman, B. J., & Groom, R. W. (1997). Hot years and serious and deadly assault: Empirical tests of the heat hypothesis. *Journal of Personality and Social Psychology, 73*, 1213–1223.

Anderson, C. A., Carnagey, N. L., & Eubanks, J. (2003). Exposure to violent media: The effects of songs with violent lyrics of aggressive thoughts and feelings. *Journal of Personality and Social Psychology, 84*, 960–971.

Anderson, C. A., & Dill, K. E. (2000). Video games and aggressive thoughts, feelings, and behavior in the laboratory and in life. *Journal of Personality and Social Psychology, 78*, 772–790.

Anderson, C. A., Lepper, M. R., & Ross, L. (1980). The perseverance of social theories: The role of explanation in the persistence of discredited information. *Journal of Personality and Social Psychology, 39*, 1037–1049.

Anderson, C. A., & Lindsay, J. J. (1998). The development, perseverance, and change of naive theories. *Social Cognition, 16*, 8–30.

Anderson, J. L., Crawford, C. B., Nadeau, J., & Lindberg, T. (1992). Was the Duchess of Windsor right? A cross-cultural review of the socioecology of ideals of female body shape. *Ethology and Sociobiology, 13*, 197–227.

Anthony, D. B., Holmes, J. G., & Wood, J. V. (2007). Social acceptance and self-esteem: Tuning the sociometer to interpersonal value. *Journal of Personality and Social Psychology, 92*, 1024–1039.

Aquino, K., Reed, A., II, Thau, S., & Freeman, D. (2007). A grotesque and dark beauty: How moral identity and mechanisms of moral disengagement influence cognitive and emotional reactions to war. *Journal of Experimental Social Psychology, 43*, 385–392.

Archer, D. (1997). Unspoken diversity: Cultural differences in gestures. *Qualitative Sociology, 20*, 79–105.

Archer, D., & Akert, R. M. (1980). The encoding of meaning: A test of three theories of social interaction. *Sociological Inquiry, 50*(3–4), 393–419.

Archer, D., & Akert, R. M. (1984). Problems of context and criterion in nonverbal communication: A new look at the accuracy issue. In M. Cook (Ed.), *Issues in person perception.* (pp. 114–144.) London and New York: Methuen.

Archer, D., & Gartner, R. (1976). Violent acts and violent times: A comparative approach to postwar homicide rates. *American Sociological Review, 41*, 937–963.

Archer, D., & Gartner, R. (1984). *Violence and crime in cross-national perspective.* New Haven, CT: Yale University Press.

Archer, D., & McDaniel, P. (1995). Violence and gender: Differences and similarities across societies. In R. B. Ruback & N. A. Weiner (Eds.), *Interpersonal violent behaviors: social and cultural aspects.* (pp. 63–88.) New York: Springer Publishing.

Archer, J. (2000). Sex differences in aggression between heterosexual partners: A meta-analytic review. *Psychological Bulletin, 126*, 651–680.

Arendt, H. (1965). *Eichmann in Jerusalem: A report on the banality of evil.* New York: Viking.

Arkes, H. R., & Mellers, B. A. (2002). Do juries meet our expectations? *Law and Human Behavior, 26*, 625–639.

Armor, D. A., & Taylor, S. E. (1998). Situated optimism: Specific outcome expectancies and self-regulation. In M. P. Zanna (Ed.), *Advances in experimental social psychology.* (Vol. 30, pp. 309–379.) San Diego, CA: Academic Press.

Arms, R. L., Russell, G. W., & Sandilands, M. L. (1979). Effects on the hostility of spectators of viewing aggressive sports. *Social Psychology Quarterly, 42*, 275–279.

Armstrong, L. (2000). *It's not about the bike: My journey back to life.* New York: Putnam.

Arnett, J. (1995). The young and the reckless: Adolescent reckless behavior. Current Directions in *Psychological Science, 4*: June, 67–71.

Aron, A., & Aron, E. N. (1986a). Falling in love: Prospective studies of self-concept change. *Journal of Personality and Social Psychology, 69*, 1102–1112.

Aron, A., & Aron, E. N. (1986b). *Love and the expansion of the self.* New York: Hemisphere.

Aron, A., & Aron, E. N. (1996). Self and self-expansion in relationships. In G. J. O. Fletcher & J. Fitness (Eds.), *Knowledge structures in close relationships: A social psychological approach.* (pp. 325–344.) Mahwah, NJ: Erlbaum.

Aron, A., Fisher, H. E., Strong, G., Acevedo, B., Riela, S., & Tsapelas, I. (2008). Falling in love. In S. Sprecher, A. Wenzel, & J. Harvey (Eds.). *Handbook of relationship initiation.* (pp. 315–336). New York: Taylor & Francis.

Aron, A., Mashek, D., & Aron, E. N. (2004). Closeness, intimacy, and including the other in the self. In D. Mashek & A. Aron (Eds.), *Handbook of closeness and intimacy.* (pp. 27–41.) Mahwah, NJ: Lawrence Erlbaum.

Aron, A., & Westbay, L. (1996). Dimensions of the prototype of love. *Journal of Personality and Social Psychology, 70*, 535–551.

Aronson, E. (1968). Dissonance theory: Progress and problems. In R. P. Abelson, E. Aronson, W. J. McGuire, T. M. Newcomb, M. J. Rosenberg, and P. H. Tannenbaum (Eds.), *Theories of cognitive consistency: A sourcebook.* (pp. 5–27.) Chicago, IL: Rand McNally.

Aronson, E. (1969). The theory of cognitive dissonance: A current perspective. In L. Berkowitz (Ed.), *Advances in experimental social psychology.* (Vol. 4, pp. 1–34.) New York: Academic Press.

Aronson, E. (1990). Applying social psychology to prejudice reduction and energy conservation. *Personality and Social Psychology Bulletin, 16*, 118–132.

Aronson, E. (1992). Stateways can change folkways. In R. Baird & S. Rosenbaum (Eds.), *Bigotry, prejudice and hatred: Definitions, causes and solutions.* Buffalo, NY: Prometheus Books.

Aronson, E. (1997a). The giving away of psychology—and condoms. *APS Observer, 10*, 17–35.

Aronson, E. (1997b). The theory of cognitive dissonance: The evolution and vicissitudes of an idea. In C. McGarty & S. Alexander Haslam (Eds.), *The message of social psychology: Perspectives on mind in society.* (pp. 20–35.) Oxford, UK: Blackwell.

Aronson, E. (1998). Dissonance, hypocrisy, and the self-concept. In E. Harmon-Jones & J. S. Mills (Eds.), *Cognitive dissonance theory: Revival with revisions and controversies.* Washington, DC: American Psychological Association.

Aronson, E. (2000). *Nobody left to hate: Teaching compassion after Columbine.* New York: Worth/Freeman.

Aronson, E. (2002). Drifting my own way: Following my nose and my heart. In R. Sternberg (Ed.), *Psychologists defying the crowd: Stories of those who battled the establishment and won.* (pp. 3–31.) Washington, DC: American Psychological Association.

Aronson, E., & Bridgeman, D. (1979). Jigsaw groups and the desegregated classroom: In pursuit of common goals. *Personality and Social Psychology Bulletin, 5*, 438–446.

Aronson, E., & Carlsmith, J. M. (1963). Effect of severity of threat in the devaluation of forbidden behavior. *Journal of Abnormal and Social Psychology, 66*, 584–588.

Aronson, E., & Carlsmith, J. M. (1968). Experimentation in social psychology. In G. Lindzey & E. Aronson (Eds.), *The handbook of social psychology.* (Vol. 2, pp. 1–79.) Reading, MA: Addison-Wesley.

Aronson, E., Chase, T., Helmreich, R., & Ruhnke, R. (1974). A two-factor theory of dissonance reduction: The effect of feeling stupid or feeling awful on opinion change. *International Journal for Research and Communication, 3*, 59–74.

Aronson, E., Ellsworth, P. C., Carlsmith, J. M., & Gonzalez, M. H. (1990). Methods of research in social psychology. (2nd ed.) New York: McGraw-Hill.

Aronson, E., Fried, C., & Stone, J. (1991). Overcoming denial and increasing the intention to use condoms through the induction of hypocrisy. *American Journal of Public Health, 81*, 1636–1638.

Aronson, E., & Gonzales, M. (1990). The social psychology of energy conservation. In J. Edwards (Ed.), *Social influence processes and prevention.* New York: Plenum.

Aronson, E., & Gonzalez, A. (1988). Desegregation, jigsaw, and the Mexican-American experience. In P. A. Katz & D. Taylor (Eds.), *Towards the elimination of racism: Profiles in controversy.* (pp. 310–30.) New York: Plenum.

Aronson, E., & Mettee, D. (1968). Dishonest behavior as a function of differential levels of induced self-esteem. *Journal of Personality and Social Psychology, 9*, 121–127.

Aronson, E., & Mills, J. (1959). The effect of severity of initiation on liking for a group. *Journal of Abnormal and Social Psychology, 59*, 177–181.

Aronson, E., & Patnoe, S. (1997). *Cooperation in the classroom: The jigsaw method.* New York: Longman.

Aronson, E., Stephan, C., Sikes, J., Blaney, N., & Snapp, M. (1978). *The jigsaw classroom.* Beverly Hills, CA: Sage.

Aronson, E., Wilson, T. D., & Akert, R. M. (2007). *Social psychology.* Upper Saddle River, NJ: Pearson/Prentice Hall.

Aronson, E., Wilson, T. D., & Brewer, M. (1998). Experimental methods. In D. Gilbert, S. Fiske, & G. Lindzey (Eds.), *The handbook of social psychology.* (4th ed., Vol. 1, pp. 99–142.) New York: Random House.

Aronson, E., & Yates, S. (1985). Social psychological aspects of energy conservation. In D. Hafemeister, H. Kelly, & B. Levi (Eds.), *Energy sources: Conservation and renewables.* (pp. 81–91.) New York: American Institute of Physics Press.

Aronson, J., & Williams, J. (2004). *Stereotype threat: Forewarned is forearmed.* New York: New York University.

Aronson, J. M., Cohen, J., & Nail, P. (1998). Self-affirmation theory: An update and appraisal. In E. Harmon-Jones & J. S. Mills (Eds.), *Cognitive dissonance theory: Revival with revisions and controversies.* Washington, DC: American Psychological Association.

Aronson, J. M., Lustina, M. J., Good, C., Keough, K., Steele, C. M., & Brown, J. (1999). When white men can't do math: Necessary and sufficient factors in stereotype threat. *Journal of Experimental Social Psychology, 35*, 29–46.

Aronson, J. M., Quinn, D., & Spencer, S. (1998). Stereotype threat and the academic underperformance of women and minorities. In J. K. Swim & C. Stangor (Eds.), *Stigma: The target's perspective.* (pp. 83–103.) San Diego, CA: Academic Press.

Arthur, B. (2008, August 12). Humidity wears down Dancevic. *National Post*, p. B3.

Asch, S. E. (1946). Forming impressions of personality. *Journal of Abnormal and Social Psychology, 41*, 258–290.

Asch, S. E. (1951). Effects of group pressure upon the modification and distortion of judgment. In H. Guetzkow (Ed.), *Groups, leadership, and men.* Pittsburgh, PA: Carnegie Press.

Asch, S. E. (1955). Opinions and social pressure. *Scientific American, 193*, 31–35.

Asch, S. E. (1956). Studies of independence and conformity: A minority of one against a unanimous majority. *Psychological Monographs, 70*, 9 (Whole No. 416).

Asch, S. E. (1957). An experimental investigation of group influence. In *Symposium on preventive and social psychiatry.* (pp. 15–17.) Walter Reed Army Institute of Research. Washington, DC: U.S. Government Printing Office.

Ashmore, R. D., Solomon, M. R., & Longo, L. C. (1996). Thinking about fashion models' looks: A multidimensional approach to the structure of perceived physical attractiveness. *Personality and Social Psychology Bulletin, 22*, 1083–1104.

Aspinwall, L. G., & Taylor, S. E. (1993). Effects of social comparison direction, threat, and self-esteem on affect, evaluation, and expected success. *Journal of Personality and Social Psychology, 64*, 708–722.

Aspinwall, L. G., & Taylor, S. E. (1997). A stitch in time: Selfregulation and proactive coping. *Psychological Bulletin, 121*, 417–436.

Associated Press. (2000, April 3). Parents led kids to death: Childhood seen as sinful by cult.

Atlas, R. S., & Pepler, D. J. (1998). Observations of bullying in the classroom. *Journal of Educational Research, 92*, 86–99.

Aune, K. S. & Aune, R. K. (1996). Cultural differences in the self-reported experience and expression of emotions in relationships. *Journal of Cross-Cultural Psychology, 27*, 67–81.

Aviezer, H., Hassin, R. R., Ryan, J., Grady, C., Susskind, J., Anderson, A., Moscovitch, M., & Bentin, S. (2008). Angry, disgusted, or afraid? Studies on the malleability of emotion perception. *Psychological Science, 19*, 724–732.

Axelrod, R. (1984). *The evolution of cooperation.* New York: Basic Books.

Azrin, N. H. (1967, May). Pain and aggression. *Psychology Today*, pp. 27–33.

Babad, E. (1993). Pygmalion—25 years after interpersonal expectations in the classroom. In P. D. Blank (Ed.), *Interpersonal expectations: Theory, research, and applications.* (pp. 125–153.) New York: Cambridge University Press.

Badr, L. K., & Abdallah, B. (2001). Physical attractiveness of premature infants affects outcome at discharge from the NICU. *Infant Behavior and Development, 24,* 129–133.

Bailey, D. S., & Taylor, S. P. (1991). Effects of alcohol and aggressive disposition on human physical aggression. *Journal of Research in Personality, 25,* 334–342.

Bailey, W. C., & Peterson, R. D. (1997). Murder, capital punishment, and deterrence: A review of the literature. In H. A. Bedau (Ed.), *The death penalty in America: Current controversies.* (pp. 135–161.) New York: Oxford University Press.

Bailis, D. S., & Segall, A. (2004). Self-determination and social comparison in a health-promotion setting. *Basic and Applied Social Psychology, 26,* 25–33.

Baldwin, M. W. (1992). Relational schemas and the processing of social information. *Psychological Bulletin, 112,* 461–484.

Baldwin, M. W., Carrell, S. E., & Lopez, D. F. (1990). Priming relationship schemas: My advisor and the pope are watching me from the back of my mind. *Journal of Experimental Social Psychology, 26,* 435–454.

Baldwin, M. W., & Fehr, B. (1995). On the instability of attachment style ratings. *Personal Relationships, 2,* 247–261.

Baldwin, M. W., Fehr, B., Keedian, E., Seidel, M., & Thomson, D. W. (1993). An exploration of the relational schemata underlying attachment styles: Self-report and lexical decision approaches. *Personality and Social Psychology Bulletin, 19,* 746–754.

Baldwin, M. W., Granzberg, A., Pippus, L., & Pritchard, E. T. (2003). Cued activation of relational schemas: Self-evaluation and gender effects. *Canadian Journal of Behavioural Science, 35,* 153–163.

Baldwin, M. W., & Holmes, J. O. (1987). Salient private audiences and awareness of the self. *Journal of Personality and Social Psychology, 52,* 1087–1098.

Baldwin, M. W., Keelan, J. P. R., Fehr, B., Enns, V., & Koh-Rangarajoo, E. (1996). Social-cognitive conceptualizations of attachment working models: Availability and accessibility effects. *Journal of Personality and Social Psychology, 71,* 94–109.

Baldwin, M. W., & Meunier, J. (1999). The cued activation of attachment relational schemas. *Social Cognition, 17,* 209–227.

Baldwin, M. W., & Sinclair, L. (1996). Self-esteem and "if . . . then" contingencies of interpersonal acceptance. *Journal of Personality and Social Psychology, 71,* 1130–1141.

Ballard, E. J., & Suedfeld, P. (1988). Performance ratings of Canadian prime ministers: Individual and situational factors. *Political Psychology, 9,* 291–302.

Bandura, A. (1973). *Aggression: A social learning analysis.* Englewood Cliffs, NJ: Prentice Hall.

Bandura, A. (1997). *Self-efficacy: The exercise of control.* New York: Freeman.

Bandura, A., Cioffi, D., Taylor, C. B., & Brouillard, M. E. (1988). Perceived self-efficacy in coping with cognitive stressors and opioid activation. *Journal of Personality and Social Psychology, 55,* 479–488.

Bandura, A., & Locke, E. A. (2003). Negative self-efficacy and goal effects revisited. *Journal of Applied Psychology, 88,* 87–99.

Bandura, A., Ross, D., & Ross, S. (1961). Transmission of aggression through imitation of aggressive models. *Journal of Abnormal and Social Psychology, 63,* 575–582.

Bandura, A., Ross, D., & Ross, S. (1963). Imitation of film-mediated aggressive models. *Journal of Abnormal and Social Psychology, 66,* 3–11.

Banks, T., & Dabbs, J. M., Jr. (1996). Salivary testosterone and cortisol in delinquent and violent urban subculture. *Journal of Social Psychology, 136,* 49–56.

Barbéra, E. (2003). Gender schemas: Configuration and activation process. *Canadian Journal of Behavioural Science, 35,* 176–184.

Bargh, J. A. (1994). The four horseman of automaticity: Awareness, intention, efficiency, and control in social cognition. In R. S. Wyer Jr., & T. K. Srull (Eds.), *Handbook of Social Cognition.* (Vol. 1, pp. 1–40.) Hillsdale, NJ: Erlbaum.

Bargh, J. A. (1996). Automaticity in social psychology. In E. T. Higgins & A. W. Kruglanski (Eds.), *Social psychology: Handbook of basic principles.* (pp. 169–183.) New York: Guilford.

Bargh, J. A. (Ed.) (2007). *Social psychology and the unconscious: The automaticity of higher mental processes.* Philadelphia, PA: Psychology Press.

Bargh, J. A., & Chartrand, T. L. (1999). The unbearable automaticity of being. *American Psychologist, 54,* 462–479.

Bargh, J. A., & Ferguson, M. J. (2000). Beyond behaviorism: On the automaticity of higher mental processes. *Psychological Bulletin, 126,* 925–945.

Bargh, J. A., Gollwitzer, P. M., Lee-Chai, A., Barndollar, K., & Trötschel, R. (2001). The automated will: Nonconscious activation and pursuit of behavioral goals. *Journal of Personality and Social Psychology, 81,* 1014–1027.

Bargh, J. A., & McKenna, K. Y. A. (2004). The internet and social life. *Annual Review of Psychology, 55,* 573–590.

Bargh, J. A., & McKenna, K. Y. A., & Fitzsimons, G. M. (2002). Can you see the real me? Activation and expression of the "true self" on the Internet. *Journal of Social Issues, 58,* 33–48.

Bargh, J. A., & Pietromonaco, P. (1982). Automatic information processing and social perception: The influence of trait information presented outside of conscious awareness on impression formation. *Journal of Personality and Social Psychology, 43,* 437–49.

Barker, R., Dembo, T., & Lewin, K. (1941). Frustration and aggression: An experiment with young children. *University of Iowa Studies in Child Welfare, 18,* 1–314.

Barley, S. R., & Bechky, B. A. (1994). In the backrooms of science: The work of technicians in science labs. *Work and Occupations, 21,* 85–126.

Baron, R. A. (1972). Reducing the influence of an aggressive model: The restraining effects of peer censure. *Journal of Experimental Social Psychology, 8,* 266–275.

Baron, R. A. (1976). The reduction of human aggression: A field study on the influence of incompatible responses. *Journal of Applied Social Psychology, 6,* 95–104.

Baron, R. A. (1988). Negative effects of destructive criticism: Impact on conflict, self-efficacy, and task performance. *Journal of Applied Psychology, 73,* 199–207.

Baron, R. A. (1990). Countering the effects of destructive criticism: The relative efficacy of four interventions. *Journal of Applied Psychology, 75,* 235–245.

Baron, R. A. (1997). The sweet smell of . . . helping: Effects of pleasant ambient fragrance on prosocial behavior in shopping malls. *Personality and Social Psychology Bulletin, 23,* 498–503.

Baron, R. A., & Richardson, D. R. (1994). *Human aggression.* (2nd ed.) New York: Plenum.

Baron, R. S. (1986). Distraction/conflict theory: Progress and problems. In L. Berkowitz (Ed.), *Advances in experimental social psychology.* (Vol. 19, pp. 1–40.) Orlando, FL: Academic Press.

Baron, R. S. (2005). So right it's wrong: Groupthink and the ubiquitous nature of polarized group decision making. In M. P. Zanna (Ed.), *Advances in experimental social psychology.* (Vol. 37, pp. 219–253.) San Diego, CA: Academic Press.

Baron, R. S., Vandello, J. A., & Brunsman, B. (1996). The forgotten variable in conformity research: Impact of task importance on social influence. *Journal of Personality and Social Psychology, 71,* 915–927.

Barrett, L. F., Lane, R. D., Sechrest, L., & Schwartz, G. E. (2000). Sex differences in emotional awareness. *Personality and Social Psychology Bulletin, 26,* 1027–1035.

Bartholomew, K. (1990). Avoidance of intimacy: An attachment perspective. *Journal of Social and Personal Relationships, 7,* 147–178.

Bartholomew, K., & Horowitz, L. M. (1991). Attachment styles among young adults: A test of a four-category model. *Journal of Personality and Social Psychology, 61,* 226–244.

Bartholomew, R., & Wessely, S. (2007). Canada's "toxic bus": The new challenge for law enforcement in the post-9/11 world/Mass psychogenic illness. *Canadian Journal of Criminology and Criminal Justice, 49,* 657–671.

Bartholomew, R. E., & Wessely, S. (2002). Protean nature of mass sociogenic illness: From possessed nuns to chemical and biological terrorism. *British Journal of Psychiatry, 180,* 300–306.

Bartholow, B. D., & Anderson, C. A. (2002). Effects of violent video games on aggressive behavior: Potential sex differences. *Journal of Experimental Social Psychology, 38,* 283–290.

Bartholow, B. D., Anderson, C. A., Carnagey, N. L., & Benjamin, Jr., A. J. (2004). Interactive effects of life experience and situational cues on aggression: The weapons priming effect in hunters and nonhunters. *Journal of Experimental Social Psychology, 41,* 48–60.

Bartlett, D. C. (1932). *Remembering.* Cambridge: Cambridge University Press.

Bartz, J. A., & Lydon, J. E. (2006). Navigating the interdependence dilemma: Attachment goals and the use of communal norms with potential close others. *Journal of Personality and Social Psychology, 91,* 77–96.

Bass, B. M. (1990). *Bass and Stogdill's handbook of leadership: Theory, research, and managerial applications.* (3rd ed.) New York: Free Press.

Bass, B. M. (1997). Does the transactional-transformational leadership paradigm transcend organizational and national boundaries? *American Psychologist, 52,* 130–139.

Bass, E., & Davis, L. (1994). *The courage to heal: A guide for women survivors of child sexual abuse.* (3rd ed.) New York: HarperCollins.

Bassili, J. N. (2003). The minority slowness effect: Subtle inhibitions in the expression of views not shared by others. *Journal of Personality and Social Psychology, 84,* 261–276.

Bassili, J. N., & Brown, R. D. (2005). Implicit and explicit attitudes: Research, challenges, and theory. In D. Albarracín, B. T. Johnson, & M. P. Zanna (Eds.), *The handbook of attitudes.* (pp. 543–574.) Mahwah, NJ: Erlbaum.

Batson, C. D. (1991). *The altruism question: Toward a social-psychological answer.* Hillsdale, NJ: Erlbaum.

Batson, C. D. (1998). Altruism and prosocial behavior. In D. Gilbert, S. Fiske, & G. Lindzey (Eds.), *The handbook of social psychology.* (4th ed., Vol. 2, pp. 282–316.) New York: McGraw-Hill.

Batson, C. D., & Ahmad, N. (2001). Empathy-induced altruism in a prisoner's dilemma II: What if the target of empathy has defected? *European Journal of Social Psychology, 31,* 25–36.

Batson, C. D., Ahmad, N., & Stocks, E. L. (2004). Benefits and liabilities of empathy-induced altruism. In A. G. Miller (Ed.), *The social psychology of good and evil.* (pp. 359–385.) New York: Guilford.

Batson, C. D., & Powell, A. A. (2003). Altruism and prosocial behavior. In T. Millon & M. J. Lerner (Eds.), *Handbook of psychology: Personality and social psychology.* (Vol. 5, pp. 463–484.) New York: Wiley.

Baumeister, R. F. (1986). *Identity: Cultural change and the struggle for self.* New York: Oxford University Press.

Baumeister, R. (Ed.) (1993). *Self-esteem: The puzzle of low self-regard.* New York: Plenum.

Baumeister, R. F. (1991). *Escaping the self: Alcoholism, spirituality, masochism, and other flights from the burden of selfhood.* New York: Basic Books.

Baumeister, R. F. (1998). The self. In D. T. Gilbert, S. T. Fiske, & G. Lindzey (Eds.), *The handbook of social psychology.* (4th ed., Vol. 1, pp. 680–740.) New York: McGraw-Hill.

Baumeister, R. F., & Bratslavsky, E. (1999). Passion, intimacy, and time: Passionate love as a function of change in intimacy. *Personality and Social Psychology Review, 3,* 49–67.

Baumeister, R. F., DeWall, C. N., Ciarocco, N. J., & Twenge, J. M. (2005). Social exclusion impairs self-regulation. *Journal of Personality and Social Psychology, 88*(4), 589–604.

Baumeister, R. F., & Hetherington, T. F. (1996). Self-regulation failure: An overview. *Psychological Inquiry, 7,* 1–15.

Baumeister, R. F., & Leary, M. R. (1995). The need to belong: Desire for interpersonal attachment as a fundamental human motivation. *Psychological Bulletin, 117,* 497–529.

Baumeister, R. F., Muraven, M., & Tice, D. M. (2000). Ego depletion: A resource model of volition, self-regulation, and controlled processing. *Social Cognition, 18,* 130–150.

Baumeister, R. F., & Vohs, K. D. (2003). Self-regulation and the executive function of the self. In M. R. Leary & J. P. Tangney (Eds.), *Handbook of self and identity.* (pp. 197–217.) New York: Guilford Press.

Baumeister, R. F., & Sommer, K. L. (1997). What do men want? Gender differences and two spheres of belongingness: Comment on Cross and Madson (1997). *Psychological Bulletin, 122,* 38–44.

Baumeister, R. F., Stillwell, A. M., & Heatherton, T. F. (1994). Guilt: An interpersonal approach. *Psychological Bulletin, 115,* 243–267.

Baxter, L. A. (1982). Strategies for ending relationships: Two studies. *Western Journal of Speech Communication, 47,* 85–98.

Baxter, L. A. (1985). Accomplishing relationship disengagement. In S. Duck & D. Perlman (Eds.), *Understanding personal relationships.* (pp. 243–265.) London, UK: Sage.

Beaman, A. L., Barnes, P. J., Klentz, B., & McQuirk, B. (1978). Increasing helping rates through informational dissemination: Teaching pays. *Personality and Social Psychology Bulletin, 4,* 406–411.

Beaman, A. L., Klentz, B., Diener, E., & Svanum, S. (1979). Objective self-awareness and transgression in children: A field study. *Journal of Personality and Social Psychology, 37,* 1835–1846.

Beaton, A. M., Tougas, F., & Joly, S.(1996). Neosexism among male managers: Is it really a matter of numbers? *Journal of Applied Social Psychology, 26,* 2189–2203.

Beaupré, M. G., & Hess, U. (2003). In my mind we all smile: A case of in-group favoritism. *Journal of Experimental Social Psychology, 39,* 371–377.

Beaupré, M. G., & Hess, U. (2006). An ingroup advantage for confidence in emotion recognition judgments: The moderating effect of familiarity with the expressions of outgroup members. *Personality and Social Psychology Bulletin, 32,* 16–26.

Becker, M. H., & Josephs, J. G. (1988). AIDS and behavioral change to reduce risk: A review. *American Journal of Public Health, 78,* 394–410.

Bedau, H. A. (Ed.) (1997). *The death penalty in America: Current controversies.* New York: Oxford University Press.

Behrmann, M., Winocur, G., & Moscovitch, M. (1992). Dissociation between mental imagery and object recognition in a brain-damaged patient. *Nature, 359,* 636–637.

Bell, D. W., & Esses, V. (1997). Ambivalence and response amplification toward Native peoples. *Journal of American Social Psychology, 27,* 1063–1084.

Bell, D. W., & Esses, V. M. (2002). Ambivalence and response amplification: A motivational perspective. *Personality and Social Psychology Bulletin, 28,* 1143–1152.

Bell, S. T., Kuriloff, P. J., & Lottes, I. (1994). Understanding attributions of blame in stranger rape and date rape situations: An examination of gender, race, identification, and students' social perceptions of rape victims. *Journal of Applied Social Psychology, 24,* 1719–1734.

Bem, D. J. (1972). Self-perception theory. In L. Berkowitz (Ed.), *Advances in experimental social psychology.* (Vol. 6, pp. 1–62.) New York: Academic Press.

Benham, G., Woody, E. Z., Wilson, K. S., & Nash, M. R. (2006). Expect the unexpected: Ability, attitude, and responsiveness to hypnosis. *Journal of Personality and Social Psychology, 91,* 342–350.

Benight, C. C., & Bandura, A. (2004). Social cognitive theory of posttraumatic recovery: The role of perceived self-efficacy. *Behaviour Research and Therapy, 42,* 1129–1148.

Ben-Shakhar, G., & Elaad, E. (2003). The validity of psychophysiological detection of information with the guilty knowledge test: A meta-analytic review. *Journal of Applied Psychology, 88,* 131–151.

Berger, I. E. (1997). The demographics of recycling and the structure of environmental behavior. *Environment and Behavior, 29*, 515–531.

Bergeron, C. E., & McKelvie, S. J. (2004). Effects of defendant age on severity of punishment for different crimes. *Journal of Social Psychology, 144*, 75–90.

Berkow, J. H. (1989). *Darwin, sex, and status: Biological approaches to mind and culture.* Toronto, ON: University of Toronto Press.

Berkowitz, L. (1968, September). Impulse, aggression, and the gun. *Psychology Today,* pp. 18–22.

Berkowitz, L. (1978). Whatever happened to the frustration-aggression hypothesis? *American Behavioral Scientist, 21*, 691–708.

Berkowitz, L. (1981, June). How guns control us. *Psychology Today,* pp. 11–12.

Berkowitz, L. (1983). Aversively simulated aggression. *American Psychologist, 38*, 1135–1144.

Berkowitz, L. (1987). Mood, self-awareness, and willingness to help. *Journal of Personality and Social Psychology, 52*, 721–729.

Berkowitz, L. (1988). Frustrations, appraisals, and aversively stimulated aggression. *Aggressive Behavior, 14*, 3–11.

Berkowitz, L. (1989). Frustration-aggression hypothesis: Examination and reformulation. *Psychological Bulletin, 106*, 59–73.

Berkowitz, L. (1993). *Aggression: Its causes, consequences, and control.* New York: McGraw-Hill.

Berkowitz, L., & LePage, A. (1967). Weapons as aggression-eliciting stimuli. *Journal of Personality and Social Psychology, 7*, 202–207.

Berkowitz, L., & Troccoli, B., (1990). Feelings, direction of attention, and expressed evaluations of others. *Cognition and Emotion, 4*, 305–325.

Bernard, M. M., Maio, G. R., & Olson, J. M. (2003). The vulnerability of values to attack: Inoculation of values and value-relevant attitudes. *Personality and Social Psychology Bulletin, 29*, 63–75.

Berns, G. S., Chappelow, J., Zink, C. F., Pagnoni, G., Martin-Skurski, M. E., & Richards, J. (2005). Neurobiological correlates of social conformity and independence during mental rotation. *Biological Psychiatry, 58*, 245–253.

Berry, D. S. (1995). Beyond beauty and after affect: An event perception approach to perceiving faces. In R. A. Eder (Ed.), *Craniofacial anomalies: Psychological perspectives.* (pp. 48–75.) New York: Springer-Verlag.

Berry, J. W. (1967). Independence and conformity in subsistence-level societies. Journal of *Personality and Social Psychology, 7*, 415–418.

Berscheid, E. (1985). Interpersonal attraction. In G. Lindzey & E. Aronson (Eds.), *The handbook of social psychology.* (pp. 413–484.) New York: McGraw-Hill.

Berscheid, E., & Peplau, L. A. (1983). The emerging science of relationships. In H. H. Kelley, E. Berscheid, A. Christensen, J. H. Harvey, T. L. Huston, G. Levinger, E. McClintock, L. A. Peplau, & D. R. Peterson (Eds.), *Close relationships.* (pp. 1–19.) New York: Freeman.

Berscheid, E., & Reis, H. T. (1998). Attraction and close relationships. In D. Gilbert, S. Fiske, & G. Lindzey (Eds.), The handbook of social psychology (4th ed., Vol. 2, pp. 193–281). New York: McGraw-Hill.

Berscheid, E., & Walster (Hatfield), E. (1974). A little bit about love. In T. L. Huston (Ed.), *Foundations of interpersonal attraction.* (pp. 355–381.) New York: Academic Press.

Berscheid, E., & Walster (Hatfield), E. (1978). *Interpersonal attraction.* Reading, MA: Addison-Wesley.

Bettencourt, B. A., & Miller, N. (1996). Gender differences in aggression as a function of provocation: A meta-analysis. *Psychological Bulletin, 119*, 422–447.

Bettencourt, B. A., & Sheldon, K. (2001). Social roles as mechanism for psychological need satisfaction within social groups. *Journal of Personality and Social Psychology, 81*, 1131–1143.

Bickman, L. (1974). The social power of a uniform. *Journal of Applied Social Psychology, 4*, 47–61.

Biehl, M., Matsumoto, D., Ekman, P., Hearn, V., Heider, K., Kudoh, T., & Ton, V. (1997). Matsumoto and Ekman's Japanese and Caucasian facial expressions of emotion (JACFEE): Reliability and cross-national differences. *Journal of Nonverbal Behavior, 21*, 3–21.

Biernat, M., Crandall, C. S., Young, L. V., Kobrynowicz, D., & Halpin, S. M. (1998). All that you can be: Stereotyping of self and others in a military context. *Journal of Personality and Social Psychology, 75*, 301–317.

Biesanz, J. C., West, S. G., & Millevoi, A. (2007). What do you learn about someone over time? The relationship between length of acquaintance and consensus and self-other agreement in judgments of personality. *Journal of Personality and Social Psychology, 92*, 119–135.

Bils, J., & Singer, S. (1996, August 16). Gorilla saves tot in Brookfield ape pit. *Chicago Tribune*, p. 1.

Bird, B. (2001, January 28). Love as fleeting as a bus ride. *Winnipeg Free Press*, p. B5.

Bjork, J. M., Dougherty, D. M., Moeller, F. G., Cherek, D. R., & Swann, A. C. (1999). The effects of tryptophan depletion and loading on laboratory aggression in men: Time course and a food-restricted control. *Psychopharmacology, 142*, 24–30.

Blader, S. L., & Tyler, T. R. (2003). A four-component model of procedural justice: Defining the meaning of a "fair" process. *Personality and Social Psychology Bulletin, 6*, 747–758.

Blair, I. V. (2002). The malleability of automatic stereotypes and prejudice. *Personality and Social Psychology Review, 6*, 242–261.

Blais, M. R., Sabourin, S., Boucher, C., & Vallerand, R. (1990). Toward a motivational model of couple happiness. *Journal of Personality and Social Psychology, 59*, 1021–1031.

Blanchfield, M. (2000, June 21). I will never be able to trust my leaders again. *Ottawa Citizen* Online. www.ottawacitizen.com/national/000227/3666380.html.

Blanchfield, M. (2005, November 4). Study ignores Gulf War syndrome symptoms. *Winnipeg Free Press*, p. A17.

Blank, P. D. (Ed.) (1993). *Interpersonal expectations: Theory, research, and applications.* New York: Cambridge University Press.

Blanton, H., Pelham, B. W., De Hart, T., & Carvallo, M. (2001). Overconfidence as dissonance reduction. *Journal of Experimental Social Psychology, 37*, 373–385.

Blascovich, J., Mendes, W. B., Hunter, S. B., & Salomon, K. (1999). Social "facilitation" as challenge and threat. *Journal of Personality and Social Psychology, 77*, 68–77.

Blaskovich, J., Ginsburg, G. P., & Veach, T. L. (1975). A pluralistic explanation of choice shifts on the risk dimension. *Journal of Personality and Social Psychology, 31*, 422–429.

Blass, T. (2000). *Obedience to authority: Current perspectives on the Milgram paradigm.* Mahwah, NJ: Erlbaum.

Blass, T. (1999). The Milgram paradigm after 31 years: Some things we now know about obedience to authority. *Journal of Applied Social Psychology, 29*(5), 955–978.

Blass, T. (2004). *The man who shocked the world: The life and legacy of Stanley Milgram.* New York: Basic Books.

Blau, P. M. (1964). *Exchange and power in social life.* New York: Wiley.

Bless, H., Strack, F., & Walther, E. (2001). Memory as a target of social influence? Memory distortions as a function of social influence and metacognitive knowledge. In J. P. Forgas & W. D. Kipling (Eds.), *Social influence: Direct and indirect processes.* (pp. 167–183.) Philadelphia: Psychology Press.

Blittner, M., Goldberg, J., & Merbaum, M. (1978). Cognitive self-control factors in the reduction of smoking behavior. *Behavior Therapy, 9*, 553–561.

Boadle, A. (1994, November 8). Pictures of Somali beaten to death shock Canadians [Reuters]. http://burn.ucsd.edu/archives/riot-l/1994.Nov/0012.html.

Bochner, S. (1994). Cross-cultural differences in the self-concept: A test of Hofstede's individualism/collectivism distinction. *Journal of Cross-Cultural Psychology, 25*, 273–283.

Bonanno, G. (2005). Resilience in the face of potential trauma. *Current Directions in Psychological Science, 14,* 135–138.

Bonanno, G. A. (2004). Loss, trauma, and human resilience: Have we underestimated the human capacity to thrive after extremely aversive events? *American Psychologist, 59,* 20–28.

Bonanno, G. A., Moskowitz, J.T., Papa, A., & Folkman, S. (2005). Resilience to loss in bereaved spouses, bereaved parents, and bereaved gay men. *Journal of Personality and Social Psychology, 88,* 827–843.

Bonanno, G. A., Rennicke, C., & Dekel, S. (2005). Self-enhancement among high-exposure survivors of the September 11th terrorist attack: Resilience or social maladjustment? *Journal of Personality and Social Psychology, 88,* 984–998.

Bond, C. F., Atoum, A. O., & VanLeeuwen, M. D. (1996). Social impairment of complex learning in the wake of public embarrassment. *Basic and Applied Social Psychology, 18,* 31–44.

Bond, C. F. Jr., & DePaulo, B. M. (2006). Accuracy of deception judgments. *Personality and Social Psychology Review, 10,* 214–234.

Bond, C. F., & Titus, L. J. (1983). Social facilitation: A meta-analysis of 241 studies. *Psychological Bulletin, 94,* 264–292.

Bond, Jr., C. F., & Atoum, A. O. (2000). International deception. *Personality and Social Psychology Bulletin, 26,* 385–395.

Bond, M. H. (Ed.) (1988). *The cross-cultural challenge to social psychology.* Newbury Park, CA: Sage.

Bond, M. H. (1991). Chinese values and health: A culture-level examination. *Psychology and Health, 5,* 137–152.

Bond, M. H. (1996). Chinese values. In M. H. Bond (Ed.), *The handbook of Chinese psychology.* (pp. 208–226.) Hong Kong: Oxford University Press.

Bond, R., & Smith, P. B. (1996). Culture and conformity: A meta-analysis of studies using Asch's (1952b, 1956) Line Judgment task. *Psychological Bulletin, 119,* 111–137.

Bonta, B. D. (1997). Cooperation and competition in peaceful societies. *Psychological Bulletin, 121,* 299–320.

Boon, S. D., & Pasveer, K. A. (1999). Charting the topography of risky relationship experiences. *Personal Relationships, 6,* 317–336.

Boothroyd, L. G., Jones, B. C., Burt, D. M., DeBruine, L. M., & Perrett, D. I. (2008). Facial correlates of sociosexuality. *Evolution and Human Behavior, 29,* 211–219.

Bornstein, R. F. (1989). Exposure and affect: Overview and meta-analysis of research, 1968–1987. *Psychological Bulletin, 106,* 265–289.

Bornstein, R. F., & D'Agostino, P. R. (1992). Stimulus recognition and the mere exposure effect. *Journal of Personality and Social Psychology, 63,* 545–552.

Bornstein, R. F., & Pittman, T. S. (Eds.) (1992). *Perception without awareness: Cognitive, clinical, and social perspectives.* New York: Guilford.

Borsari, B., & Carey, K. B. (2005). Descriptive and injunctive norms in college drinking: A meta-analytic integration. *Journal of Studies on Alcohol, 64,* 331–341.

Bourgeois, M. J., & Bowen, A. (2001). Self-organization of alcohol-related attitudes and beliefs in a campus housing complex: An initial investigation. *Health Psychology, 20,* 434–437.

Bourgeois, P., & Hess, U. (2008). The impact of social context on mimicry. *Biological Psychology, 77,* 434–352.

Bowker, A. (2006). The relationship between sports participation and self-esteem during early adolescence. *Canadian Journal of Behavioural Science, 38,* 214–229.

Bower, G. H., & Hilgard, E. R. (1981). *Theories of learning.* (15th ed.) Englewood Cliffs, NJ: Prentice Hall.

Bowlby, J. (1969). *Attachment and loss*: Vol. 1. Attachment. New York: Basic Books.

Bowlby, J. (1973). *Attachment and loss*: Vol. 2. Separation: Anxiety and anger. New York: Basic Books.

Bowlby, J. (1980). *Attachment and loss*: Vol. 3. Loss. New York: Basic Books.

Bradfield, A., & Wells, G. L. (2005). Not the same old hindsight bias: Outcome information distorts a broad range of retrospective judgments. *Memory & Cognition, 33,* 120–130.

Bradley, J. P., Nicol, A. A. M., Charbonneau, D., & Meyer, J. P. (2002). Personality correlates of leadership development in Canadian Forces officer candidates. *Canadian Journal of Behavioural Science, 34,* 92–103.

Bradshaw, R. H., Bubier, N. E., & Sullivan, M. (1994). The effects of age and gender on perceived facial attractiveness: A reply to McLellan and McKelvie. *Canadian Journal of Behavioural Science, 26,* 199–204.

Branscombe, N. R., Owen, S., Garstka, T. A., & Coleman, J. (1996). Rape and accident counterfactuals: Who might have done otherwise and would it have changed the outcome? *Journal of Applied Social Psychology, 26,* 1042–1067.

Branscombe, N. R., & Wann, D. L. (1992). Role of identification with a group, arousal, categorization processes, and self-esteem in sports spectator aggression. *Human Relations, 45,* 1013–1033.

Branswell, B. (1998, June 1). Pain and pride. *Maclean's, 111*(22), 21.

Breckler, S. J., & Wiggins, E. C. (1989). On defining attitude and attitude theory: Once more with feeling. In A. R. Pratkanis, S. J. Breckler, & A. G. Greenwald (Eds.), *Attitude structure and function.* (pp. 407–427.) Hillsdale, NJ: Erlbaum.

Brehm, J. W. (1956). Postdecision changes in the desirability of alternatives. *Journal of Abnormal and Social Psychology, 52,* 384–389.

Brewer, M. B., & Brown, R. J. (1998). Intergroup relations. In D. Gilbert, S. Fiske, & G. Lindzey (Eds.), *The handbook of social psychology.* (4th ed., Vol. 2, pp. 554–594.) New York: McGraw-Hill.

Brewer, M. B., & Gardner, W. L. (1996). Who is this "we"? Levels of collective identity and self representations. *Journal of Personality and Social Psychology, 71,* 83–93.

Brewer, M. B., & Miller, N. (1984). Beyond the contact hypothesis: Theoretical perspectives on desegregation. In N. Miller & M. B. Brewer (Eds.), *Groups in contact: The psychology of desegregation.* (pp. 281–302.) New York: Academic Press.

Brewer, N., & Wells, G. L. (2006). The confidence-accuracy relationship in eyewitness identification: Effects of lineup instructions, foil similarity, and target-absent base rates. *Journal of Experimental Psychology: Applied, 12,* 11–30.

Bridges, F. S., & Coady, N. P. (1996). Affiliation, urban size, urgency, and cost of responses to lost letters. *Psychological Reports, 79,* 775–780.

Brigham, J. C. (1980). Limiting conditions of the "physical attractiveness stereotype": Attributions about divorce. *Journal of Research in Personality, 14,* 365–375.

Brislin, R. (1993). *Understanding culture's influence on behavior.* Fort Worth, TX: Harcourt Brace.

Brody, S., Wright, S. C., Aron, A., & McLaughlin-Volpe, T. (2009). Compassionate love for individuals in other social groups. In B. Fehr, S. Sprecher, & L. Underwood, L. (Eds.). *The science of compassionate love: Theory, research, and applications.* (pp. 283–308.) Malden, MA: Blackwell Publishers.

Bronskill, J. (2007, May 19). Feds have plan to help airlines combat "air rage." *Winnipeg Free Press,* p. A9.

Brook, A. S., Starzyk, K. B., & Quinsey, V. L. (2001). The relationship between testosterone and aggression: a meta-analysis. *Aggression and Violent Behavior, 6,* 579–599.

Brophy, J. E. (1983). Research on the self-fulfilling prophecy and teacher expectations. *Journal of Educational Psychology, 75,* 631–661.

Brown, J. D. (1990). Evaluating one's abilities: Shortcuts and stumbling blocks on the road to self-knowledge. *Journal of Experimental Social Psychology, 26,* 149–167.

Brown, R. (1965). Social psychology. New York: Free Press.

Brown, R. (1986). Social psychology: The second edition. New York: Free Press.

Brown, R. P., & Pinel, E. C. (2003). Stigma on my mind: Individual differences in the experience of stereotype threat. *Journal of Experimental Social Psychology, 39,* 626–33.

Brown, S. L., Nesse, R. M., & Vinokur, A D. (2003). Providing social support may be more beneficial than receiving it: Results from a prospective study of mortality. *Psychological Science, 14,* 320–327.

Brown, T. C., & Latham, G. P. (2006). The effect of training in verbal self-guidance on performance effectiveness in an MBA program. *Canadian Journal of Behavioural Science, 38,* 1–11.

Brown, W. M., & Moore, C. (2000). Is prospective altruist-detection an evolved solution to the adaptive problem of subtle cheating in cooperative ventures? Supportive evidence using the Wason selection task. *Evolution and Human Behavior, 21,* 25–37.

Bryden, J. (2008, May 9). Dion weak, but at least he's likable. *Winnipeg Free Press,* p. A13.

Buckle, L., Gallup, G. G., & Rodd, Z. A. (1996). Marriage as a reproductive contract: Patterns of marriage, divorce and remarriage. *Ethology and Sociobiology, 17,* 363–377.

Buehler, R., & Griffin, D. (1994). Change-of-meaning effects in conformity and dissent: Observing construal processes over time. *Journal of Personality and Social Psychology, 67,* 984–996.

Buehler, R., Griffin, D. W., & Ross, M. (2002). Inside the planning fallacy: The causes and consequences of optimistic time preferences. In T. Gilovich, D. W. Griffin, & D. Kahneman (Eds.), *Heuristics and biases: The psychology of intuitive judgment* (pp. 250–270.) New York: Cambridge University Press.

Buller, D. J. (2005). *Adapting minds: Evolutionary psychology and the persistent quest for human nature.* Cambridge, MA: MIT Press.

Burger, J. M. (1981). Motivational biases in the attribution of responsibility for an accident: A meta-analysis of the defensive-attribution hypothesis. *Psychological Bulletin, 90,* 496–512.

Burger, J. M. (1986). Increasing compliance by improving the deal: The that's-not-all technique. *Journal of Personality and Social Psychology, 51,* 277–283.

Burger, J. M. (1992). Desire for control: Personality, social, and clinical perspectives. New York: Plenum.

Burger, J. M. (1999). The foot-in-the-door compliance procedure: A multiple-process analysis and review. *Personality and Social Psychology Review, 3,* 303–325.

Burger, J. M. (in press). Replicating Milgram: Would people still obey? *American Psychologist.*

Burgess, M., Enzle, M. E., & Morry, M. (2000). The social psychological power of photography: Can the image-freezing machine make something out of nothing? *European Journal of Social Psychology, 30,* 595–612.

Burke, R.J., & Greenglass, E. R. (1990). Type A Behavior and non-work activities. *Personality and Individual Differences, 11,* 945–952.

Burleson, B. R. (1994). Friendship and similarities in social-cognitive and communicative abilities: Social skill bases of interpersonal attraction in childhood. *Personal Relationships, 1,* 371–389.

Burleson, B. R., & Samter, W. (1996). Similarity in the communication skills of young adults: Foundations of attraction, friendship, and relationship satisfaction. *Communication Reports, 9,* 127–139.

Burnstein, E., Crandall, C., & Kitayama, S. (1994). Some neo-Darwinian decision rules for altruism: Weighing cues for inclusive fitness as a function of the biological importance of the decision. *Journal of Personality and Social Psychology, 67,* 773–789.

Burnstein, E., & Sentis, K. (1981). Attitude polarization in groups. In R. E. Petty, T. M. Ostrom, & T. C. Brock (Eds.), *Cognitive responses in persuasion.* (pp. 197–216.) Hillsdale, NJ: Erlbaum.

Burnstein, E., & Vinokur, A. (1977). Persuasive argumentation and social comparison as determinants of attitude polarization. *Journal of Experimental Social Psychology, 13,* 315–332.

Burnstein, E., & Worchel, P. (1962). Arbitrariness of frustration and its consequences for aggression in a social situation. *Journal of Personality, 30,* 528–540.

Burt, M. R. (1980). Cultural myths and supports for rape. *Journal of Personality and Social Psychology, 38,* 217–230.

Burton, K. D., Lydon, J. E., D'Alessandro, D. U., & Koestner, R. (2006). The differential effects of intrinsic and identified motivation on well-being and performance: Prospective, experimental, and implicit approaches to self-determination theory. *Journal of Personality and Social Psychology, 91,* 750–762.

Bushman, B. J. (1993). Human aggression while under the influence of alcohol and other drugs: An integrative research review. *Current Directions in Psychological Science, 2,* 148–152.

Bushman, B. J., Baumeister, R. F., & Stack, A. D. (1999). Catharsis, aggression, and persuasive influence: Self fulfilling or self-defeating prophecies? *Journal of Personality and Social Psychology, 76,* 367–376.

Bushman, B. J., & Cooper, H. M. (1990). Alcohol and human aggression: An integrative research review. *Psychological Bulletin, 107,* 341–354.

Bushman, B. J., Wang, M. C., & Anderson, C. A. (2005a). Is the curve relating temperature to aggression linear or curvilinear? Assaults and temperature in Minneapolis re-examined. *Journal of Personality and Social Psychology, 89,* 62–66.

Bushman, B. J., Wang, M. C., & Anderson, C. A. (2005b). Is the curve relating temperature to aggression linear or curvilinear? A response to Bell (2005) and to Cohn and Rotton (2005). *Journal of Personality and Social Psychology, 89,* 74–77.

Buss, D. M. (1985). Human mate selection. *American Scientist, 73,* 47–51.

Buss, D. M. (1988a). The evolution of human intrasexual competition. *Journal of Personality and Social Psychology, 54,* 616–628.

Buss, D. M. (1988b). Love acts: The evolutionary biology of love. In R. J. Sternberg & M. L. Barnes (Eds.), *The psychology of love.* (pp. 110–118.) New Haven, CT: Yale University Press.

Buss, D. M. (1989). Sex differences in human mate preferences: Evolutionary hypotheses tested in 37 cultures. *Behavioral and Brain Sciences, 12,* 1–49.

Buss, D. M. (1994). *The evolution of desire.* New York: Basic Books.

Buss, D. M. (1996a). The evolutionary psychology of human social strategies. In E. T. Higgins & A. W. Kruglanski (Eds.), *Social psychology: Handbook of basic principles.* (pp. 3–38.) New York: Guilford.

Buss, D. M. (1996b). Sexual conflict: Evolutionary insights into feminism and the "battle of the sexes." In D. Buss & N. Malamuth (Eds.), *Sex, power, conflict: Evolutionary and feminist perspectives.* (pp. 296–318.) New York: Oxford University Press.

Buss, D. M. (1999). *Evolutionary psychology: The new science of the mind.* Needham Heights, MA: Allyn & Bacon.

Buss, D. M. (2004). *Evolutionary psychology: The new science of the mind.* (2nd ed. Boston: Allyn & Bacon.

Buss, D. M. (Ed.) (2005). *The handbook of evolutionary psychology.* Hoboken, NJ: Wiley.

Buss, D. M., Abbott, M., Angleitner, A., Biaggio, A., Blanco-Villasenor, A., Bruchon-Schweitzer, M., Ch'u, H., Czapinski, J., Deraad, B., Ekehammar, B., El Lohamy, N., Fioravanti, M., Georgas, J., Gjerde, P., Guttman, R., Hazan, F., Iwawaki, S., Janakiramaiah, N., Khosroshani, F., Kreitler, S., Lachenicht, L., Lee, M., Liik, K., Little, B., Mika, S., Moadel-Shahid, M., Moane, G., Montero, M., Mundy-Castle, A. C., Niit, T., Nsenduluka, E., Pienkowski, R., Pirttila-Backman, A., Ponce de Leon, J., Rousseau, J., Runco, M., Safir, M. P., Samuels, C., Sanitioso, R., Serpell, R., Smid, N., Spencer, C., Tadinac, M., Todorova, E. N., Troland, K., Van Den Brande, L., Van Heck, G., Van Langenhove, L., & Yang, K. (1990). International preferences in selecting mates: A study of 37 cultures. *Journal of Cross-Cultural Psychology, 21,* 5–47.

Buss, D. M., & Barnes, M. (1986). Preferences in human mate selection. *Journal of Personality and Social Psychology, 50,* 559–570.

Buss, D. M., & Duntley, J. D. (2006). The evolution of aggression. In M. Schaller, J. A. Simpson, & D. T. Kenrick (Eds.), *Evolution and social psychology.* (pp. 263–285.) Madison, CT: Psychosocial Press.

Buss, D. M., & Kenrick, D. T. (1998). Evolutionary social psychology. In D. Gilbert, S. Fiske, & G. Lindzey (Eds.), *The handbook of social psychology* (4th ed., Vol. 2, pp. 982–1026.) New York: Random House.

Buss, D. M., & Schmitt, D. P. (1993). Sexual strategies theory: An evolutionary perspective on human mating. *Psychological Bulletin, 100,* 204–232.

Buston, P. M., & Emlem, S. T. (2003). Cognitive processes underlying human mate choice: The relationship between self-perception and mate preference in Western society. *Proceedings of the National Academy of Sciences, 100,* 8805–8810.

Butler, D., & Geis, F. L. (1990). Nonverbal affect responses to male and female leaders: Implications for leadership evaluations. *Journal of Personality and Social Psychology, 58,* 48–59.

Butler, E. A., Egloff, B., Wilhelm, F. H., Smith, N. C., Erickson, E. A., & Gross, J. J. (2003). The social consequences of expressive suppression. *Emotion, 3,* 48–67.

Button, C. M., & Collier, D. R. (1991, June). A comparison of people's concepts of love and romantic love. Paper presented at the Canadian Psychological Association Conference, Calgary, Alberta.

Buunk, B. P., Oldersma, F. L., & de Dreu, C. K. W. (2001). Enhancing satisfaction through downward comparison: The role of relational discontent and individual differences in social comparison orientation. *Journal of Experimental Social Psychology, 37,* 452–467.

Buunk, B. P., & Prins, K. S. (1998). Loneliness, exchange orientation, and reciprocity in friendships. *Personal Relationships, 5,* 1–14.

Byrne, D. (1997). An overview (and underview) of research and theory within the attraction paradigm. *Journal of Social and Personal Relationships, 14,* 417–431.

Byrne, D., & Clore, G. L. (1970). A reinforcement model of evaluative processes. *Personality: An International Journal, 1,* 103–128.

Byrne, D., Clore, G. L., & Smeaton, G. (1986). The attraction hypothesis: Do similar attitudes affect anything? *Journal of Personality and Social Psychology, 51,* 1167–1170.

Byrne, D., & Nelson, D. (1965). Attraction as a linear function of positive reinforcement. *Journal of Personality and Social Psychology, 1,* 659–663.

Cacioppo, J. T. (1998). Somatic responses to psychological stress: The reactivity hypothesis. *Advances in Psychological Science, 2,* 87–112.

Cacioppo, J. T., Berntson, G. G., Malarkey, W. B., Kiecolt-Glaser, J. K., Sheridan, J. F., Poehlmann, K. M., Burleson, M. H., Ernst, J. M., Hawkley, L. C., & Glaser, R. (1998). Autonomic, neuroendocrine, and immune responses to psychological stress: The reactivity hypothesis. *Annals of the New York Academy of Sciences, 840,* 664–673.

Cafri, G., & Thompson, J. K. (2004). Measuring male body image: A review of the current methodology. *Psychology of Men and Masculinity, 5,* 18–29.

Cafri, G., Thompson, J. K., Ricciardelli, L., McCabe, M., Smolak, L., & Yesalis, C. (2005). Pursuit of the muscular ideal: Physical and psychological consequences and putative risk factors. *Clinical Psychology Review, 25,* 215–239.

Caledonia land conflict convoy comes to Queen's Park. (2007, May 2). www.citynews.ca/news/news_10544. Accessed November 2008.

Calder, B. J., & Staw, B. M. (1975). Self-perception of intrinsic and extrinsic motivation. *Journal of Personality and Social Psychology, 31,* 599–605.

Callan, M. J., Ellard, J. H., & Nicol, J. E. (2006). The belief in a just world and immanent justice reasoning in adults. *Personality and Social Psychology Bulletin, 32,* 1646–1658.

Cameron, J. E. (1999). Social identity and the pursuit of possible selves: Implications for the psychological well-being of university students. *Group Dynamics: Theory, Research and Practice, 3,* 179–189.

Cameron, J. J., Ross, M., & Holmes, J. G. (2002). Loving the one you hurt: Positive effects of recounting a transgression against an intimate partner. *Journal of Experimental Social Psychology, 38,* 307–314.

Cameron, K. (2000). Student threats in the aftermath of the Taber and Littleton school shootings: How seriously do we take them? *Psynopsis, Fall,* 13.

CAMH (2003). The 2003 Ontario student drug use drug report: Executive summary. The Centre for Addiction and Mental Health. www. camh.net/pdf/osdus2003-execsummary.pdr. Accessed April 2005.

Campbell, B., Schellenberg, E. G., & Senn, C. Y. (1997). Evaluating measures of contemporary sexism. *Psychology of Women Quarterly, 21,* 89–102.

Campbell, D. T., & Stanley, J. C. (1967). Experimental and quasi-experimental designs for research. Chicago, IL: Rand McNally.

Campbell, J. D. (1986). Similarity and uniqueness: The effects of attribute type, relevance, and individual differences in self-esteem and depression. *Journal of Personality and Social Psychology, 50,* 281–294.

Campbell, J. D. (1990). Self-esteem and clarity of the self-concept. *Journal of Personality and Social Psychology, 59,* 538–549.

Campbell, J. D., Assanand, S., & DiPaula, A. (2000). Structural features of the self-concept and adjustment. In A. Tesser, R. B. Felson, & J. M. Suls (Eds.), *Psychological perspectives on self and identity.* (pp. 67–87.) Washington, DC: American Psychological Association.

Campbell, J. D., & Fairey, P. J. (1989). Informational and normative routes to conformity: The effect of faction size as a function of norm extremity and attention to the stimulus. *Journal of Personality and Social Psychology, 57,* 457–468.

Campbell, J. D., & Fehr, B. (1990). Self-esteem and perceptions of conveyed impressions: Is negative affectivity associated with greater realism? *Journal of Personality and Social Psychology, 58,* 122–133.

Campbell, J. D., Trapnell, P. D., Heine, S. J., Katz, I. M., Lavallee, L. F., & Lehman, D. R. (1996). Self-concept clarity: Measurement, personality correlates, and cultural boundaries: Correction. *Journal of Personality and Social Psychology, 70,* 141–156.

Campbell, L., Lackenbauer, S. D., & Muise, A. (2006). When is being known or adored by romantic partners most beneficial? Self-perceptions, relationship length, and responses to partner's verifying and enhancing appraisals. *Personality and Social Psychology Bulletin, 32,* 1283–1294.

Campbell, L., Simpson, J. A., Boldry, J., & Kashy, D. A. (2005). Perceptions of conflict and support in romantic relationships: The role of attachment anxiety. *Journal of Personality and Social Psychology, 88,* 510–531.

Canada (1997). Report of the Somalia Commission of Inquiry. Ottawa, ON: Department of National Defence. Available at www.dnd.ca/somalia/somaliae.htm/Canada. Accessed July 1999.

Canada (2001). Shaping the nation's workforce: Immigrants, demand for skills, and an aging population. *2001 Census.* Statistics Canada. www12.statcan.ca/english/census01/products/analytic/companion/paid/canada.cfm#3. Accessed September 2005.

Canada (2002, May 4). Divorces, 2001, 2002. Statistics Canada. *The Daily.* www.statcan.ca/Daily/English/040504/d04050a.htm. Accessed September 2005.

Canada (2005a, July 14). Family violence in Canada: A statistical profile. Statistics Canada. *The Daily.* www.statcan.ca/Daily/English/050714/d050714a.htm. Accessed August 2005.

Canada (2005b, August 11). Canadian tobacco use monitoring survey, February–December 2004. Statistics Canada. *The Daily.* www.statcan.ca/Daily/English/050811/d050811c.htm. Accessed October 2005.

Canada (2005c, July 6). Canadian community health survey, 2004: Obesity among children and adults. Statistics Canada. *The Daily.* www.statcan.ca/Daily/English/050706/d050706a.htm. Accessed October 2005.

Canada (2005d, May 3). Canadian community health survey, 2003: Early sexual intercourse, condom use, and sexually transmitted diseases, 1998/99 to 2000/01 and 2003. Statistics Canada. *The Daily*. www.statcan.ca/Daily/English/050503/d050503a.htm. Accessed October 2005.

Canada. (2005e, July 21). Crime statistics. *The Daily*. www.statcan.ca/Daily/English/050721/d050721a.htm. Accessed November 2005.

Canada. (2005f). Women in Canada: A guide to understanding the changing roles of women and men in Canada. www.statcan.gc.ca/ads-annonces/89-503-x/index-eng.htm. Accessed November 2005.

Canada (2007). Deaths, by selected grouped causes and sex, Canada, provinces and territories. Statistics Canada, Table 102-0552. http://cansim2.statcan.ca/cgi-win/cnsmcgi.exe?Lang=E&RootDir=CII/&ResultTemplate=CII/CII___&Array_Pick=1&ArrayId=1020552. Accessed December 2008.

Canada (2008). Family violence in Canada: A statistical profile. Statistics Canada, Catalogue No. 85-224-X. www.statcan.gc.ca/pub/85-224-x/85-224-x2008000-eng.pdf. Accessed October 2008.

Canary, D. J., & Stafford, L. (2001). Equity in the preservation of personal relationships. In J. Harvey & A. Wenzel (Eds.), *Close romantic relationships: Maintenance and enhancement.* (pp. 133–151.) Mahwah, NJ: Erlbaum.

Cannon, W. B. (1932). *The wisdom of the body.* New York: Norton.

Cannon, W. B. (1942). "Voodoo" death. *American Anthropologist, 44,* 169–181.

Cantor, J. (1994). Confronting children's fright responses to mass media. In D. Zillmann, J. Bryant, & Aletha C. Huston (Eds.), *Media, children, and the family: Social scientific, psychodynamic, and clinical perspectives.* (pp. 139–150.) Hillsdale, NJ: Erlbaum.

Cantor, J., Bushman, B. J., Huesmann, L. R., Groebel, J., Malamuth, N. M., Impett, E. A., Donnerstein, E., & Smith, S. (2001). Some hazards of television viewing: Fears, aggression, and sexual attitudes. In D. G. Singer & J. L. Singer (Eds.), *Handbook of children and the media.* (pp. 207–307.) Thousand Oaks, CA: Sage.

Cantril, H. (1940). *The invasion from Mars: A study in the psychology of panic.* New York: Harper & Row.

Caporael, L. R., & Brewer, M. B. (2000). Metatheories, evolution, and psychology: Once more with feeling. *Psychological Inquiry, 11,* 23–26.

Carli, L. L. (1999). Cognitive reconstruction, hindsight, and reactions to victims and perpetrators. *Personality and Social Psychology Bulletin, 25,* 966–979.

Carli, L. L., & Eagly, A. H. (1999). Gender effects on social influence and emergent leadership. In G. N. Powell (Ed.), *Handbook of gender and work.* (pp. 203–222.) Thousand Oaks, CA: Sage.

Carlsmith, K. M., Darley, J. M., & Robinson, P. H. (2002). Why do we punish? Deterrence and just deserts as motives for punishment. *Journal of Personality and Social Psychology, 83,* 284–299.

Carlson, M., Charlin, V., & Miller, N. (1988). Positive mood and helping behavior: A test of six hypotheses. *Journal of Personality and Social Psychology, 55,* 211–229.

Carlson, M., & Miller, N. (1987). Explanation of the relationship between negative mood and helping. *Psychological Bulletin, 102,* 91–108.

Carlston, D. E., & Skowronski, J. J. (1994). Savings in the relearning of trait information as evidence of spontaneous inference generation. *Journal of Personality and Social Psychology, 66,* 840–856.

Carnevale, P. J. (1986). Strategic choice in mediation. *Negotiation Journal, 2,* 41–56.

Carpenter, S. (2000, December). Why do "they all look alike"? *Monitor on Psychology,* 44–45.

Carroll, J. M., & Russell, J. A. (1996). Do facial expressions signal specific emotions? Judging emotion from the face in context. *Journal of Personality and Social Psychology, 70,* 205–218.

Cartwright, D., & Zander, A. (Eds.) (1968). *Group dynamics: Research and theory* (3rd ed.) New York: Harper & Row.

Carvallo, M., & Pelham, B. W. (2006). When fiends become friends: The need to belong and perceptions of personal and group discrimination. *Journal of Personality and Social Psychology, 90,* 94–108.

Carver, C. S. (2003). Self-awareness. In M. R. Leary & J. P. Tangney (Eds.), *Handbook of self and identity.* (pp. 179–196.) New York: Guilford Press.

Carver, C. S., & Scheier, M. F. (1981). *Attention and self-regulation: A control-theory approach to human behavior.* New York: Springer-Verlag.

Carver, C. S., & Scheier, M. F. (1998). *On the self-regulation of behavior.* New York: Cambridge University Press.

Cate, R. M., & Lloyd, S. A. (1992). *Courtship.* Newbury Park, CA: Sage.

CAUT survey shows PSE gender inequity widespread. (2006, April). *CAUT Bulletin,* p. A9.

Cervone, D., & Peake, P. (1986). Anchoring, efficacy, and action: The influence of judgmental heuristics on self-efficacy judgments and behavior. *Journal of Personality and Social Psychology, 50,* 492–501.

Chaiken, S. (1980). Heuristic versus systematic information processing and the use of source versus message cues in persuasion. *Journal of Personality and Social Psychology, 39,* 752–766.

Chaiken, S. (1987). The heuristic model of persuasion. In M. P. Zanna, J. M. Olson, & C. P. Herman (Eds.), *Social influence: The Ontario Symposium.* (Vol. 5, pp. 3–39.) Hillsdale, NJ: Erlbaum.

Chaiken, S., & Baldwin, M. W. (1981). Affective–cognitive consistency and the effect of salient behavioral information on the self perception of attitudes. *Journal of Personality and Social Psychology, 41,* 1–12.

Chaiken, S., Liberman, A., & Eagly, A. H. (1989). Heuristic and systematic information processing within and beyond the persuasion context. In J. S. Uleman & J. A. Bargh (Eds.), *Unintended thought.* (pp. 212–252.) New York: Guilford Press.

Chaiken, S., Wood, W., & Eagly, A. H. (1996). Principles of persuasion. In E. T. Higgins & A. W. Kruglanski (Eds.), *Social psychology: Handbook of basic principles.* (pp. 702–742.) New York: Guilford.

Chang, C., & Chen, J. (1995). Effects of different motivation strategies on reducing social loafing. *Chinese Journal of Psychology, 37,* 71–81.

Chassin, L., Presson, C. G., & Sherman, S. J. (1990). Social psychological contributions to the understanding and prevention of adolescent cigarette smoking. *Personality and Social Psychology Bulletin, 16,* 133–151.

Cheadle, B. (2005, January 17). Volunteers recall grim work for Martin. *Winnipeg Free Press,* www.winnipegfreepress.com. Accessed February 2005.

Chemers, M. M. (2000). Leadership research and theory: A functional integration. *Group Dynamics: Theory, Research, and Practice, 4,* 27–43.

Chemers, M. M., Watson, C. B., & May, S. T. (2000). Dispositional affect and leadership effectiveness: A comparison of self-esteem, optimism, and efficacy. *Personality and Social Psychology Bulletin, 26,* 267–277.

Chen, M., & Bargh, J. A. (1997). Nonconscious behavioral confirmation processes: The self-fulfilling consequences of automatic stereotype activation. *Journal of Experimental Social Psychology, 33,* 541–560.

Chen, S., & Andersen, S. M. (1999). Relationships from the past in the present: Significant-other representations and transference in interpersonal life. In M. P. Zanna (Ed.), *Advances in experimental social psychology.* (Vol. 31, pp. 123–190.) San Diego, CA: Academic Press.

Chen, S., & Chaiken, S. (1999). The heuristic-systematic model in its broader context. In S. Chaiken & Y. Trope (Eds.), *Dual-process theories in social psychology.* (pp. 73–96.) New York: Guilford Press.

Cheryan, S. & Bodenhausen, G. V. (2000). When positive stereotypes threaten intellectual performance: The psychological hazards of "model minority" status. *Psychological Science, 11*:5, 399–402.

Cheung, S. F., Chan, D. K., & Wong, Z. S. (1999). Reexamining the theory of planned behavior in understanding wastepaper recycling. *Environment and Behavior, 31*, 587–612.

Chia, A., & Costigan, C. L. (2006). Understanding the multidimensionality of acculturation among Chinese Canadians. *Canadian Journal of Behavioural Science, 38*, 311–324.

Chipperfield, J. G., Perry, R. P., & Menec, V. H. (1999). Primary and secondary control-enhancing strategies: Implications for health in later life. *Journal of Aging and Health, 11*, 517–539.

Chiu, C., Morris, M. W., Hong, Y., & Menon, T. (2000). Motivated cultural cognition: The impact of implicit cultural theories on dispositional attribution varies as a function of need for closure. *Journal of Personality and Social Psychology, 78*, 247–259.

Choi, I., & Nisbett, R. E. (1998). Situational salience and cultural differences in the correspondence bias and in the actor-observer bias. *Personality and Social Psychology Bulletin, 24*, 949–960.

Christensen, L. (1988). Deception in psychological research: When is its use justified? *Personality and Social Psychology Bulletin, 14*, 664–675.

Christianson, S. (1992). Emotional stress and eyewitness memory: A critical review. *Psychological Bulletin, 112*, 284–309.

Church, A. H. (1993). Estimating the effects of incentives on mail survey response rates: A meta-analysis. *Public Opinion Quarterly, 57*, 62–79.

Cialdini, R. B. (1993). *Influence: Science and practice.* (3rd ed.) New York: HarperCollins.

Cialdini, R. B. (2000). *Influence: Science and practice.* (4th ed.) Boston: Allyn & Bacon.

Cialdini, R. B. (2003). *Crafting normative messages to protect the environment. Current Directions in Psychological Science, 12*, 105–109.

Cialdini, R. B., Caciopppo, J., Basset, R., & Miller, J. (1978). Low-ball procedure for producing compliance: Commitment then cost. *Journal of Personality and Social Psychology, 36*, 463–476.

Cialdini, R. B., Darby, B. L., & Vincent, J. E. (1973). Transgression and altruism: A case for hedonism. *Journal of Experimental Social Psychology, 9*, 502–516.

Cialdini, R. B., & Fultz, J. (1990). Interpreting the negative mood-helping literature via "mega"-analysis: A contrary view. *Psychological Bulletin, 107*, 210–214.

Cialdini, R. B., & Goldstein, N. J. (2004). Social influence: Compliance and conformity. *Annual Review of Psychology, 55*, 591–621.

Cialdini, R. B., Green, B. L., & Rusch, A. J. (1992). When tactical pronouncements of change become real change: The case of reciprocal persuasion. *Journal of Personality and Social Psychology, 63*, 30–40.

Cialdini, R. B., Kallgren, C. A., & Reno, R. R. (1991). A focus theory of normative conduct: A theoretical refinement and reevaluation of the role of norms in human behavior. In M. P. Zanna (Ed.), *Advances in experimental social psychology.* (Vol. 24, pp. 201–234.) San Diego, CA: Academic Press.

Cialdini, R. B., Reno, R. R., & Kallgren, C. A. (1990). A focus theory of normative conduct: Recycling the concept of norms to reduce littering in public places. *Journal of Personality and Social Psychology, 58*, 1015–1026.

Cialdini, R. B., Schaller, M., Houlihan, D., Arps, K., Fultz, J., & Beaman, A. L. (1987). Empathy-based helping: Is it selflessly or selfishly motivated? *Journal of Personality and Social Psychology, 52*, 749–758.

Cialdini, R. B., & Trost, M. R. (1998). Social influence: Social norms, conformity, and compliance. In D. Gilbert, S. Fiske, & G. Lindzey (Eds.), *The handbook of social psychology.* (4th ed., Vol. 2, pp. 151–192.) New York: McGraw-Hill.

Cialdini, R. B., Trost, M. R., & Newsom, J. T. (1995). Preference for consistency: The development of a valid measure and the discovery of surprising behavioral implications. *Journal of Personality and Social Psychology, 69*, 318–328.

Cialdini, R. B., Vincent, J. E., Lewis, S. K., Catalan, J., Wheeler, D., & Darby, B. L. (1975). Reciprocal concessions procedure for inducing compliance: The door-in-the-face technique. *Journal of Personality and Social Psychology, 31*, 206–215.

Clark, K., & Clark, M. (1947). Racial identification and preference in Negro children. In T. M. Newcomb & E. L. Hartley (Eds.), *Readings in social psychology.* (pp. 169–178.) New York: Holt.

Clark, M. S. (1984). Record keeping in two types of relationships. *Journal of Personality and Social Psychology, 47*, 549–577.

Clark, M. S., & Chrisman, K. (1994). Resource allocation in intimate relationships: Trying to make sense of a confusing literature. In M. J. Lerner & G. Mikula (Eds.), *Entitlement and the affectional bond: Justice in close relationships.* (pp. 65–88.) New York: Plenum.

Clark, M. S., & Grote, N. K. (1998). Why aren't indices of relationship costs always negatively related to indices of relationship quality? *Personality and Social Psychology Review, 2*, 2–17.

Clark, M. S., & Isen, A. M. (1982). Toward understanding the relationship between feeling states and social behavior. In A. H. Hastorf & A. M. Isen (Eds.), *Cognitive social psychology.* (pp. 73–108.) New York: Elsevier.

Clark, M. S., & Mills, J. (1979). Interpersonal attraction in exchange and communal relationships. *Journal of Personality and Social Psychology, 37*, 12–24.

Clark, M. S., & Mills, J. (1993). The difference between communal and exchange relationships: What it is and is not. *Personality and Social Psychology Bulletin, 19*, 684–691.

Clark, M. S., Mills, J., & Corcoran, D. M. (1989). Keeping track of needs and inputs of friends and strangers. *Personality and Social Psychology Bulletin, 15*, 533–542.

Clark, M. S., & Monin, J. K. (2006). Giving and receiving communal responsiveness as love. In R. J. Sternberg & K. Weis (Eds.), *The new psychology of love.* (pp. 200–221.) New Haven, CT: Yale University Press.

Clark, M. S., & Waddell, B. (1985). Perception of exploitation in communal and exchange relationships. *Journal of Social and Personal Relationships, 2*, 403–413.

Clark, R., Anderson, N. B., Clark, V. R., & Williams, D. R. (1999). Racism as a stressor for African Americans. *American Psychologist, 54*, 805–816.

Clark III, R. D., & Word, L. E. (1972). Why don't bystanders help? Because of ambiguity? *Journal of Personality and Social Psychology, 24*, 392–400.

Clarke, V. A., Lovegrove, H., Williams, A., & Macpherson, M. (2000). Unrealistic optimism and the Health Belief Model. *Journal of Behavioral Medicine, 23*, 367–376.

Clément, R. Baker, S. C., & MacIntyre, P. D. (2003). Willingness to communicate in a second language: The effects of context, norms, and vitality. *Journal of Language and Social Psychology, 22*, 190–209.

Clément, R., Noels, K. A., & Deneault, B. (2001). Interethnic contact, identity, and psychological adjustment: The mediating and moderating roles of communication. *Sex Roles, 57*, 559–577.

Cline, V. B., Croft, R. G., & Courrier, S. (1973). Desensitization of children to television violence. *Journal of Personality and Social Psychology, 27*, 360–365.

Clow, K. A., & Esses, V. M. (2007). Expectancy effects in social stereotyping: Automatic and controlled processing in the neely paradigm. *Canadian Journal of Behavioural Science, 39*, 161–173.

Coates, L. (1997). Causal attributions in sexual assault trial judgments. *Journal of Language and Social Psychology, 16*, 278–296.

Coats, E. (1998). Bystander intervention (E-mail response to G. Mumford, Tobacco update 3/20/98). www.stolaf.edu/cgi-bin/mailarchivesearch.pl?directory=/home/www/people/huff/SPSP&listname=archive98&location=683178. Accessed December 2006.

Cohen, S., & Herbert, T. B. (1996). Health psychology: Psychological factors and physical disease from the perspective of human psychoneuroimmunology. *Annual Review of Psychology, 47*, 113–142.

Cohen, S., Mermelstein, R., Kamarack, T., & Hoberman, H. (1985). Measuring the functional components of social support. In I. G. Sarason & B. R. Sarason (Eds.), *Social support: Theory, research, and applications.* (pp. 73–94.) The Hague, Netherlands: Martines Nijhoff.

Cohen, S., Tyrrell, D. A. J., & Smith, A. P. (1991). Psychological stress in humans and susceptibility to the common cold. *New England Journal of Medicine, 325,* 606–612.

Cohen, S., Tyrrell, D. A. J., & Smith, A. P. (1993). Negative life events, perceived stress, negative affect, and susceptibility to the common cold. *Journal of Personality and Social Psychology, 64,* 131–140.

Cohen, S., & Wills, T. A. (1985). Stress, social support, and buffering. *Psychological Bulletin, 98,* 310–357.

Cohn, L. D. & Adler, N. E. (1992). Female and male perceptions of ideal body shapes. *Psychology of Women Quarterly, 16,* 69–79.

Coie, J. D., Cillessen, A. H. N., Dodge, K. A., Hubbard, J. A., Schwartz, D., Lemerise, E. D., & Bateman, H. (1999). It takes two to fight: A test of relational factors and a method for assessing aggressive dyads. *Developmental Psychology, 35,* 1179–1188.

Colligan, M. J., Pennebaker, J. W., & Murphy, L. R. (Eds.) (1982). *Mass psychogenic illness: A social psychological analysis.* Hillsdale, NJ: Erlbaum.

Collins, R. L. (1996). For better or worse: The impact of upward social comparison on self-evaluations. *Psychological Bulletin, 119,* 51–69.

Coltrane, S., Archer, D., & Aronson, E. (1986). The social-psychological foundations of successful energy conservation programs. *Energy Policy, 14,* 133–148.

Combating childhood obesity. (2007, Fall/Winter). *True Azure,* p. 14–16.

Condon, J. W., & Crano, W. D. (1988). Inferred evaluation and the relation between attitude similarity and interpersonal attraction. *Journal of Personality and Social Psychology, 54,* 789–797.

Correll, J., Park, B., Judd, C. M., & Wittenbrink, B. (2002). The police officer's dilemma: Using ethnicity to disambiguate potentially threatening individuals. *Journal of Personality and Social Psychology, 83,* 1314–1329.

Conway III, L. G., & Schaller, M. (2005). When authorities' commands backfire: Attributions about consensus and effects on deviant decision making. *Journal of Personality and Social Psychology, 89,* 311–326.

Conway, M., & Dubé, L. (2002). Humor in persuasion on threatening topics: Effectiveness is a function of audience sex role orientation. *Personality and Social Psychology Bulletin, 28,* 863–873.

Cook, S. W. (1984). Cooperative interaction in multiethnic contexts. In N. Miller & M. Brewer (Eds.), *Groups in contact: The psychology of desegregation.* New York: Academic Press.

Cook, S. W. (1985). Experimenting on social issues: The case of school desegregation. *American Psychologist, 40,* 452–460.

Cooley, C. H. (1902). *Human nature and social order.* New York: Scribner's.

Cooper, W. H., Gallupe, R. B., Pollard, S., & Cadsby, J. (1998). Some liberating effects of anonymous electronic brainstorming. *Small Group Research, 29,* 147–178.

Corenblum, B. (2003). What children remember about ingroup and outgroup peers: Effects of stereotypes on children's processing of information about group members. *Journal of Experimental Child Psychology, 86,* 32–66.

Corenblum, B., & Annis, R. (1993). Development of racial identity in minority and majority children: An affect discrepancy model. *Canadian Journal of Behavioural Science, 25,* 499–521.

Corenblum, B., Annis, R., & Young, S. (1996). Effects of own group success or failure on judgments of task performance by children of different ethnicities. *European Journal of Social Psychology, 26,* 777–798.

Corenblum, B., & Meissner, C. A. (2006). Recognition of faces of ingroup and outgroup children and adults. *Journal of Experimental Child Psychology, 93,* 187–206.

Corenblum, B., & Stephan, W. G. (2001). White fears and Native apprehensions: An integrated threat theory approach to intergroup attitudes. *Canadian Journal of Behavioural Science, 33,* 251–268.

Corneil, W., Beaton, R., Murphy, S., Johnson, C., & Pike, K. (1999). Exposure to traumatic incidents and prevalence of post-traumatic stress symptomatology in urban firefighters in two countries. *Journal of Occupational Health Psychology, 4,* 131–141.

Correll, J., Park, B., Judd, C. M., & Wittenbrink, B. (2002). The police officer's dilemma: Using ethnicity to disambiguate potentially threatening individuals. *Journal of Personality and Social Psychology, 83,* 1314–1329.

Correll, J., Spencer, S. J., & Zanna, M. P. (2004). An affirmed sense and an open mind: Self-affirmation and sensitivity to argument strength. *Journal of Experimental Social Psychology, 40,* 350–356.

Cosmides, L., & Tooby, J. (1992). Cognitive adaptations for social exchange. In J. H. Barkow, L. Cosmides, & J. Tooby (Eds.), *The adapted mind: Evolutionary psychology and the generation of culture.* (pp. 163–228.) New York: Oxford University Press.

Cottrell, C. A., & Neuberg, S. L. (2005). Different emotional reactions to different groups: A sociofunctional threat-biased approach to "prejudice." *Journal of Personality and Social Psychology, 88,* 770–789.

Cottrell, N. B. (1968). Performance in the presence of other human beings: Mere presence, audience, and affiliation effects. In E. C. Simmel, R. A. Hoppe, & G. A. Milton (Eds.), *Social facilitation and imitative behavior.* (pp. 91–110.) Boston, MA: Allyn & Bacon.

Cottrell, N. B., Wack, K. L., Sekerak, G. J., & Rittle, R. (1968). Social facilitation in dominant responses by the presence of an audience and the mere presence of others. *Journal of Personality and Social Psychology, 9,* 245–250.

Courage, M. L., Edison, S. C., & Howe, M. L. (2004). Variability in the early development of visual self-recognition. *Infant Behavior and Development, 27,* 509–532.

Courneya, K. S., & Friedenreich, C. M. (1997). Determinants of exercise during colorectal cancer treatment: An application of the theory of planned behavior. *Oncology Nursing Forum, 24,* 1715–1723.

Courneya, K. S., & Friedenreich, C. M. (1999). Utility of the theory of planned behavior for understanding exercise during breast cancer treatment. *Psycho-Oncology, 8,* 112–122.

Craig, W. M., & Pepler, D. J. (1997). Observations of bullying and victimization in the school yard. *Canadian Journal of School Psychology, 13,* 41–60.

Cramer, K. M., Nickels, J. B., & Gural, D. M. (1997). Uncertainty of outcomes, prediction of failure, and lack of control as factors explaining perceived helplessness. *Journal of Social Behavior and Personality, 12,* 611–630.

Crandall, C. S., D'Anello, S., Sakalli, N., Lazarus, E., Wieczorkowska, G., & Feather, N. T. (2001). An attribution-value model of prejudice: Anti-fat attitudes in six nations. *Personality and Social Psychology Bulletin, 27,* 30–37.

Crandall, C. S., Eshelman, A., & O'Brien, L. (2002). Social norms and the expression and suppression of prejudice: The struggle for internalization. *Journal of Personality and Social Psychology, 82,* 359–378.

Crandall, C. S. & Schaller, M. (Eds.) (2005). *Social psychology of prejudice: Historical and contemporary issues.* Lawrence, KS: Lewinian Press.

Crawford, C., & Krebs, D. L. (1998). *Handbook of evolutionary psychology.* Mahwah, NJ: Erlbaum.

Crawford, T. (2004, June 25). Dangerous chemical discovered as probable cause of toxic bus mystery. *The Canadian Press.*

Crites, S. L., Jr., Fabrigar, L. R., & Petty, R. E. (1994). Measuring the affective and cognitive properties of attitudes: Conceptual and methodological issues. *Personality and Social Psychology Bulletin, 20,* 619–634.

Crocker, J., & Major, B. (1989). Social stigma and self-esteem: The self-protective properties of stigma. *Psychological Review, 96,* 608–630.

Cross, S. E., Bacon, P. L., & Morris, M. L. (2000). The relational-interdependent self-construal and relationships. *Journal of Personality and Social Psychology, 78,* 791–808.

Cross, S. E., & Madson, L. (1997). Elaboration of models of the self: Reply to Baumeister and Sommer (1997) and Martin and Rubble (1997). *Psychological Bulletin, 122,* 51–55.

Cross, S. E., & Vick, N. V. (2001). The interdependent self-construal and social support: The case of persistence in engineering. *Personality and Social Psychology Bulletin, 27,* 820–832.

Crowley, A. E., & Hoyer, W. D. (1994). An integrative framework for understanding two-sided persuasion. *Journal of Consumer Research, 20,* 561–574.

Croyle, R. T., & Jemmott III, J. B. (1990). Psychological reactions to risk factor testing. In J. A. Skelton & R. T. Croyle (Eds.), *The mental representation of health and illness.* (pp. 121–157.) New York: Springer-Verlag.

Crutchfield, R. A. (1955). Conformity and character. *American Psychologist, 10,* 191–198.

Csikszentmihalyi, M., & Figurski, T. J. (1982). Self-awareness and aversive experience in everyday life. *Journal of Personality, 50,* 15–28.

Cuddy, A. J. C., Fiske, S. T., & Glick, P. (2007). The BIAS map: Behaviors from intergroup affect and stereotypes. *Journal of Personality and Social Psychology, 92,* 631–648.

Cullen, M. C., & Bradley, M. T. (2004). Positions of truthfully answered controls on control question test with the polygraph. *Canadian Journal of Behavioural Science, 36,* 167–176.

Cunningham, M. R. (1986). Measuring the physical in physical attractiveness: Quasi-experiments on the sociobiology of female facial beauty. *Journal of Personality and Social Psychology, 50,* 925–935.

Cunningham, M. R., Barbee, A. R., & Pike, C. L. (1990). What do women want? Facialmetric assessment of multiple motives in the perception of male facial physical attractiveness. *Journal of Personality and Social Psychology, 59,* 61–72.

Cunningham, M. R., Roberts, A. R., Barbee, A. P., Druen, P. B., & Wu, C. (1995). "Their ideas of beauty are, on the whole, the same as ours": Consistency and variability in the cross-cultural perception of female physical attractiveness. *Journal of Personality and Social Psychology, 68,* 261–279.

Curtis, R. C., & Miller, K. (1986). Believing another likes or dislikes you: Behaviors making the beliefs come true. *Journal of Personality and Social Psychology, 51,* 284–290.

Cusumano, D. L., & Thompson, J. K. (1997). Body image and body shape ideals in magazines: Exposure, awareness, and internalization. *Sex Roles, 37,* 701–721.

Cynkar, A. (June, 2007). Order in the court. *Monitor on Psychology,* pp. 48–49.

Dabbs, Jr., J. M. (2000). *Heroes, rogues, and lovers.* New York: McGraw-Hill.

Dabbs, Jr., J. M., Carr, T. S., Frady, R. L., & Riad, J. K. (1995). Testosterone, crime, and misbehavior among 692 male prison inmates. *Personality and Individual Differences, 18,* 627–633.

Dabbs, Jr., J. M., Hargrove, M. F., & Heusel, C. (1996). Testosterone differences among college fraternities: Well-behaved vs. rambunctious. *Personality and Individual Differences, 20,* 157–161.

Dabbs, Jr., J. M., Ruback, R. B., Frady, R. L., Hopper, C. H., & Sgoutas, D. S. (1988). Saliva testosterone and criminal violence among women. *Personality and Individual Differences, 7,* 269–275.

Dahl, D. W., Gorn, G. J., & Weinberg, C. B. (1998). Condom carrying behavior among college students. *Canadian Journal of Public Health, 89,* 368–370.

Dambrun, M., Taylor, D. M., McDonald, D. A., Crush, J., & Méot, A. (2006). The relative deprivation-gratification continuum and the attitudes of South Africans toward immigrants: A test of the V-curve hypothesis. *Journal of Personality and Social Psychology, 91,* 1032–1044.

D'Angelo, A. M. (2000, February 14). No charges in bridge fall. *North Shore News.* www.nsnews.com/issues00/w021400/02110001.html.

Daniel, M., & Nelson, K. (2004, August 20). In search of rush teens risk lives surfing on cars. *Boston Globe,* pp. B1, B4.

Darke, P. R., & Chaiken, S. (2005). The pursuit of self-interest: Self-interest bias in attitude judgment and persuasion. *Journal of Personality and Social Psychology, 89,* 864–883.

Darley, J. M. (1995). Constructive and destructive obedience: A taxonomy of principal-agent relationships. *Journal of Social Issues, 51,* 125–154.

Darley, J. M., & Akert, R. M. (1993). *Biographical interpretation: The influence of later events in life on the meaning of and memory for earlier events.* Unpublished manuscript, Princeton University.

Darley, J. M., & Batson, C. D. (1973). From Jerusalem to Jericho: A study of situational and dispositional variables in helping behavior. *Journal of Personality and Social Psychology, 27,* 100–108.

Darley, J. M., & Latané, B. (1968). Bystander intervention in emergencies: Diffusion of responsibility. *Journal of Personality and Social Psychology, 8,* 377–383.

Dar-Nimrod, I., & Heine, S. J. (2006). Exposure to scientific theories affects women's math performance. *Science, 314,* 435.

Darwin, C. (1872). The expression of emotions in man and animals. London, UK: John Murray.

Darwin, C. R. (1859). *The origin of species.* London, UK: John Murray.

Das, E. H. J., de Wit, J. B. F., & Stroebe, W. (2003). Fear appeals motivate acceptance of action recommendations: Evidence for a positive bias in the processing of persuasive messages. *Personality and Social Psychology Bulletin, 29,* 650–664.

Davidson, A. R., & Jaccard, J. J. (1979). Variables that moderate the attitude behavior relation: Results of a longitudinal survey. *Journal of Personality and Social Psychology, 37,* 1364–1376.

Davidson, R., Putnam, K., & Larson, C. (2000). Dysfunction in the neural circuitry of emotion regulation: A possible prelude to violence. *Science, 289,* 591–594.

Davies, M. F. (1997). Belief persistence after evidential discrediting: The impact of generated versus provided explanations on the likelihood of discredited outcomes. *Journal of Experimental Social Psychology, 33,* 561–578.

Davies, P. G., Spencer, S. J., & Claude, M. (2005). Clearing the air: Identity safety moderates the effects of stereotype threat on women's leadership aspirations. *Journal of Personality and Social Psychology, 88,* 276–287.

Davies, P. G., Spencer, S. J., Quinn, D. M., & Gerhardsteine, R. (2002). Consuming images: How television commercials that elicit stereotype threat can restrain women academically and professionally. *Personality and Social Psychology Bulletin, 28,* 1615–1628.

Davies, P. G., Spencer, S. J., & Steele, C. M. (2005). Clearing the air: Identity safety moderates the effects of stereotype threat on women's leadership aspirations. *Journal of Personality and Social Psychology, 88,* 276–287.

Davies, R. (1991). Murther and walking spirits. Toronto, ON: McClelland and Stewart.

Davis, C., Lehman, D., Cohen Silver, R., Wortman, C., & Ellard, J. (1996). Self-blame following a traumatic event: The role of perceived avoidability. *Personality and Social Psychology Bulletin, 22,* 557–567.

Davis, C. G., & Lehman, D. R. (1995). Counterfactual thinking and coping with traumatic life events. In N. J. Roese & J. M. Olson (Eds.), *What might have been: The social psychology of counterfactual thinking.* (pp. 353–374.) Mahwah, NJ: Erlbaum.

Davis, C. G., Lehman, D. R., Wortman, C. B., Silver, R. C., & Thompson, S. C. (1995). The undoing of traumatic life events. *Personality and Social Psychology Bulletin, 21,* 109–124.

Davis, D. D., & Harless, D. W. (1996). Group versus individual performance in a price-searching experiment. *Organizational Behavior and Human Decision Processes, 66,* 215–227.

Davis, K. E., & Jones, E. E. (1960). Changes in interpersonal perception as a means of reducing cognitive dissonance. *Journal of Abnormal and Social Psychology, 61,* 402–410.

Davison, K. P., Pennebaker, J. W., & Dickerson, S. S. (2000). Who talks? The social psychology of illness support groups. *American Psychologist, 55,* 205–217.

Davitz, J. (1952). The effects of previous training on post-frustration behavior. *Journal of Abnormal and Social Psychology, 47,* 309–315.

Dawes, R. M. (1980). Social dilemmas. *Annual Review of Psychology, 31,* 169–193.

Day, A. L., & Livingstone, H. A. (2003). Gender differences in perceptions of stressors and utilization of social support among university students. *Canadian Journal of Behavioural Science, 35,* 73–83.

Dean, K. E., & Malamuth N. M. (1997). Characteristics of men who aggress sexually and of men who imagine aggressing: Risk and moderating variables. *Journal of Personality and Social Psychology, 72,* 499–455.

Deaux, K., & Emsweiler, T. (1974). Explanations of successful performance of sex-linked tasks: What is skill for male is luck for the female. *Journal of Personality and Social Psychology, 29,* 80–85.

Deaux, K., & LaFrance, M. (1998). Gender. In D. T. Gilbert, S. T. Fiske, & G. Lindzey (Eds.), *The handbook of social psychology.* (4th ed., Vol. 1, pp. 788–828.) New York: McGraw-Hill.

Deaux, K., & Major, B. (1987). Putting gender into context: An interactive model of gender-related behavior. *Psychological Review, 94,* 369–389.

DeBono, K. G., & Snyder, M. (1995). Acting on one's attitudes: The role of a history of choosing situations. *Personality and Social Psychology Bulletin, 21,* 629–636.

Deci, E. L., Koestner, R., & Ryan, R. M. (1999a). A meta-analytic review of experiments examining the effects of extrinsic rewards. *Psychological Bulletin, 125,* 627–668.

Deci, E. L., Koestner, R., & Ryan, R. M. (1999b). The undermining effect is a reality after all—extrinsic rewards, task interest, and self-determination: Reply to Eisenberger, Pierce, and Cameron (1999) and Lepper, Henderlong, and Gingras (1999). *Psychological Bulletin, 125,* 692–700.

Deci, E. L., & Ryan, R. M. (1985). *Intrinsic motivation and self-determination in human behavior.* New York: Plenum.

Deci, E. L., & Ryan, R. M. (Eds.) (2002). *Handbook of self-determination research.* Rochester, NY: University of Rochester Press.

De Dreu, C. K. W., & De Vries, N. K. (Eds.) (2001). *Group consensus and minority influence: Implications for innovation.* Oxford, UK: Blackwell Publishers.

De Dreu, C. K. W., Weingart, L. R., & Kwon, S. (2000). Influence of social motives on integrative negotiation: A meta-analytic review and test of two theories. *Journal of Personality and Social Psychology, 78,* 889–905.

Deffenbacher, K. A., Bornstein, B. H., & Penrod, S. D. (2004). A meta-analytic review of the effects of high stress on eyewitness memory. *Law and Human Behavior, 28,* 687–706.

De Hoog, N., Stroebe, W., & de Wit, J. B. (2005). The impact of fear appeals on processing and acceptance of action recommendations. *Personality and Social Psychology Bulletin, 31,* 24–33.

DeJong, W., & Winsten, J. A. (1989). *Recommendations for future mass media campaigns to prevent preteen and adolescent substance abuse.* Unpublished manuscript, Center for Health Communication, Harvard School of Public Health.

DeKeseredy, W. S., & Kelly, K. (1993). Woman abuse in university and college dating relationships: The contribution of the ideology of familial patriarchy. *Journal of Human Justice, 4,* 25–52.

Depape, A. R., Hakim-Larson, J., Voelker, S., Page, S., & Jackson, D. L. (2006). Self-talk and emotional intelligence in university students. *Canadian Journal of Behavioural Science, 38,* 250–260.

DePaulo, B. M., Epstein, J. A., & Wyer, M. M. (1993). Sex differences in lying: How women and men deal with the dilemma of deceit. In M. Lewis & C. Saarni (Eds.), *Lying and deception in everyday life.* (pp. 126–147.) New York: Guilford Press.

DePaulo, B. M., & Friedman, H. S. (1998). Nonverbal communication. In D. Gilbert, S. Fiske, & G. Lindzey (Eds.), *The handbook of social psychology.* (4th ed., Vol. 2, pp. 3–40.) New York: McGraw Hill.

DePaulo, B. M., Kenny, D. A., Hoover, C. W., Webb, W., & Oliver, P. (1987). Accuracy of person perception: Do people know what kinds of impressions they convey? *Journal of Personality and Social Psychology, 52,* 303–315.

DePaulo, B. M., Lassiter, G. D., & Stone, J. I. (1983). Attentional determinants of success at detecting deception and truth. Personality and Social Psychology Bulletin, *8,* 273–279.

DePaulo, B. M., & Pfeiffer, R. L. (1986). On-the-job experience and skill at detecting deception. *Journal of Applied Social Psychology, 16,* 249–267.

Desmond, E. W. (1987, November 30). Out in the open. *Time,* pp. 80–90.

De Souza, M. (2007, November 12). Doctor alleges oilsands coverup. CanWest News Service. www.canada.com/calgaryherald/news/story.html?id=8c9ccc7f-9ea7-4564-a8b3-d7f2dfc099e9. *Calgary Herald.* Accessed November 2008.

Desportes, J. P., & Lemaine, J. M. (1998). The sizes of human groups: An analysis of their distributions. In D. Canter, J. C. Jesuino, L. Soczka, & G. M. Stephenson (Eds.), *Environmental social psychology.* (pp. 57–65.) Dordrecht, Netherlands: Kluwer.

Deutsch, M. (1973). *The resolution of conflict: Constructive and destructive processes.* New Haven, CT: Yale University Press.

Deutsch, M. (1990). Cooperation, conflict, and justice. In S. A. Wheelan, E. A. Pepitone, & V. Abt (Eds.), *Advances in field theory.* (pp. 149–164.) Newbury Park, CA: Sage.

Deutsch, M., & Gerard, H. G. (1955). A study of normative and informational social influence upon individual judgment. *Journal of Abnormal and Social Psychology, 51,* 629–636.

Deutsch, M., & Krauss, R. M. (1960). The effect of threat upon interpersonal bargaining. *Journal of Abnormal and Social Psychology, 61,* 181–189.

Deutsch, M., & Krauss, R. M. (1962). Studies of interpersonal bargaining. *Journal of Conflict Resolution, 6,* 52–76.

Devine, D. J., Clayton, L. D., Dunford, B. B., Seying, R., & Pryce, J. (2001). Jury decision making: 45 years of empirical research on deliberating groups. *Psychology, Public Policy, and Law, 7,* 622–727.

Devine, P. G. (1989a). Automatic and controlled processes in prejudice: The roles of stereotypes and personal beliefs. In A. R. Pratkanis, S. J. Breckler, & A. G. Greenwald (Eds.), *Attitude structure and function.* (pp. 181–212.) Hillsdale, NJ: Erlbaum.

Devine, P. G. (1989b). Stereotypes and prejudice: Their automatic and controlled components. *Journal of Personality and Social Psychology, 56,* 5–18.

Devine, P. G. (2003). A modern perspective on the classic American dilemma. *Psychological Inquiry, 14*(3), 244–250.

Devine, P. G., & Monteith, M. J. (1999). Automaticity and control in stereotyping. In S. Chaiken & Y. Trope (Eds.), *Dual-process theories in social psychology.* (pp. 339–360.) New York: Guilford Press.

de Waal, F. B. M. (1995, March). Bonobo sex and society: The behavior of a close relative challenges assumptions about male supremacy in human evolution. *Scientific American,* 82–88.

de Waal, F. (1996). *Good natured: The origins of right and wrong in humans and other animals.* Cambridge, MA: Harvard University Press.

Dickerson, C., Thibodeau, R., Aronson, E., & Miller, D. (1992). Using cognitive dissonance to encourage water conservation. *Journal of Applied Social Psychology, 22,* 841–854.

Diener, E. (1980). Deindividuation: The absence of self-awareness and self-regulation in group members. In P. B. Paulus (Ed.), *Psychology of group influence.* (pp. 209–242.) Hillsdale, NJ: Erlbaum.

Diener, E., & Wallbom, M. (1976). Effects of self-awareness on antinormative behavior. *Journal of Research in Personality, 10,* 107–111.

Dijksterhuis, A. (2004). Think different: The merits of unconscious thought in preference development and decision making. *Journal of Personality and Social Psychology, 87,* 586–598.

Dijksterhuis, A., & Aarts, H. (2002). *The power of the subliminal: On subliminal persuasion and other potential applications.* Unpublished manuscript.

Dijksterhuis, A., Aarts, H., & Smith, P. K. (2005). The power of the subliminal: On subliminal persuasion and other potential applications. In R. R. Hassin, J. S. Uleman, & J. A. Bargh (Eds.), *The new unconscious.* (pp. 77–106.) New York: Oxford University Press.

Dijksterhuis, A., & Nordgren, L. F. (2006). A theory of unconscious thought. *Perspectives on Psychological Science, 1*(2), 95–109.

Dijksterhuis, A., Preston, J., Wegner, D. M., & Aarts, H. (2008). Effects of subliminal priming of self and god on self-attribution of authorship for events. *Journal of Experimental Social Psychology, 44,* 2–9.

Dijksterhuis, A., & van Knippenberg, A. (1996). The knife that cuts both ways: Facilitated and inhibited access to traits as a result of stereotype activation. *Journal of Experimental Social Psychology, 32,* 271–288.

Dillard, J. P. (1991). The current status of research on sequential-request compliance techniques. *Personality and Social Psychology Bulletin, 17,* 283–288.

Dillard, J. P., Plotnick, C. A., Godbold, L. C., Freimuth, V. S. & Edgar, T. (1996). The multiple affective outcomes of AIDS PSAs: Fear appeals do more than scare people. *Communication Research, 23,* 44–72.

Dion, Karen K. (2002). Cultural perspectives on facial attractiveness. In G. Rhodes (Ed.), *Facial attractiveness: Evolutionary, cognitive, and social perspectives.* (pp. 239–259.) Westport, CT: Ablex Publishing.

Dion, K. K., Berscheid, E., & Walster (Hatfield), E. (1972). What is beautiful is good. *Journal of Personality and Social Psychology, 24,* 285–290.

Dion, K. K., & Dion, K. L. (1996). Cultural perspectives on romantic love. *Personal Relationships, 3,* 5–17.

Dion, K. K., & Dion, K. L. (2001). Gender and cultural adaptation in immigrant families. *Journal of Social Issues, 57,* 511–521.

Dion, Kenneth L. (1985). Social distance norms in Canada: Effects of stimulus characteristics and dogmatism. *International Journal of Psychology, 20,* 743–749.

Dion, K. L. (1987). What's in a title? The Ms. stereotype and images of women's titles of address. *Psychology of Women Quarterly, 11*(1), 21–36.

Dion, K. L. (1999). Ms. as a title of address. In H. Tierney (Ed.), *Women's studies encyclopedia: Revised and expanded edition.* (Vol. 2, G–P, pp. 954–957.) Westport, CT: Greenwood Press.

Dion, K. L. (2000). Canada. In A. E. Kazdin (Ed.), *Encyclopedia of psychology.* (Vol. 2, pp. 5–12.) Washington, DC/New York: American Psychological Association & Oxford University Press.

Dion, K. L. (2001). Immigrants' perceptions of discrimination in Toronto, ON: The Housing New Canadians project. *Journal of Social Issues, 57,* 523–539.

Dion, K. L. (2002). The social psychology of perceived prejudice and discrimination. *Canadian Psychology, 43,* 1–10.

Dion, K. L. (2003). Prejudice, racism, and discrimination. In T. Millon & M. J. Lerner (Eds.), *Handbook of psychology: Personality and social psychology.* (Vol. 5, pp. 507–536.) Hoboken, NJ: John Wiley & Sons.

Dion, K. L., & Dion, K. K. (1973). Correlates of romantic love. *Journal of Consulting and Clinical Psychology, 41,* 51–56.

Dion, K. L., & Dion, K. K. (1987). Belief in a just world and physical attractiveness stereotyping. *Journal of Personality and Social Psychology, 52,* 775–780.

Dion, K. L., & Dion, K. K. (1993). Gender and ethnocultural comparisons in styles of love. *Psychology of Women Quarterly, 17,* 463–473.

Dion, K. L., Dion, K. K., & Pak, A. W. (1992). Personality-based hardiness as a buffer for discrimination-related stress in members of Toronto's Chinese community. *Canadian Journal of Behavioural Science, 24,* 517–536.

Dion, K. L., & Kawakami, K. (1996). Ethnicity and perceived discrimination in Toronto, ON: Another look at the personal/group discrimination discrepancy. *Canadian Journal of Behavioural Science, 28,* 203–213.

Dion, K. L., Pak, A., & Dion, K. K. (1990). Stereotyping physical attractiveness. *Journal of Cross Cultural Psychology, 21,* 158–179.

Dion, K. L., & Schuller, R. A. (1991). The Ms. stereotype: Its generality and its relation to managerial and marital status stereotypes. *Canadian Journal of Behavioural Science, 23,* 25–40.

Dittman, M. (2004, October). What makes good people do bad things? *Monitor on Psychology,* p. 68–69.

Dix, T. (1993). Attributing dispositions to children: An interactional analysis of attribution in socialization. *Personality and Social Psychology Bulletin, 19,* 633–643.

Dodge, K. A., & Schwartz, D. (1997). Social information processing mechanisms in aggressive behavior. In D. M. Stoff & J. Breiling (Eds.), *Handbook of antisocial behavior.* (pp. 171–180.) New York: Wiley.

Dodge, M. K. (1984). Learning to care: Developing prosocial behavior among one- and two-year-olds in group settings. *Journal of Research and Development in Education, 17,* 26–30.

Doi, T. (1988). An experimental investigation of the validity of the characteristic space theory and the measurement of social motivation. *Japanese Journal of Experimental Social Psychology, 27,* 139–148.

Dolin, D. J., & Booth-Butterfield, S. (1995). Foot-in-the-door and cancer prevention. *Health Communication, 7,* 55–66.

Dollard, J. (1938). Hostility and fear in social life. *Social Forces, 17,* 15–26.

Dollard, J., Doob, L., Miller, N., Mowrer, O. H., & Sears, R. R. (1939). *Frustration and aggression.* New Haven, CT: Yale University Press.

Domina, T., & Koch, K. (2002). Convenience and frequency of recycling: Implications for including textiles in curbside recycling programs. *Environment and Behavior, 34,* 216–238.

Donakowski, D. W., & Esses, V. M. (1996). "Native Canadians," "First Nations," and "Aboriginals": The effect of labels on attitudes toward Native peoples. *Canadian Journal of Behavioural Science, 28,* 86–91.

Donnerstein, E. (1980). Aggressive erotica and violence against women. *Journal of Personality and Social Psychology, 39,* 269–272.

Donnerstein, E., & Berkowitz, L. (1981). Victim reactions in aggressive erotic films as a factor in violence against women. *Journal of Personality and Social Psychology, 41,* 710–724.

Donnerstein, E., & Donnerstein, M. (1976). Research in the control of interracial aggression. In R. G. Green & E. C. O'Neal (Eds.), *Perspectives on aggression.* (pp. 133–168.) New York: Academic Press.

Donnerstein, E., & Linz, D. (1994). Sexual violence in the mass media. In M. Costanzo, S. Oskamp et al. (Eds.), *Violence and the law: Claremont symposium on applied social psychology.* (Vol. 7, pp. 9–36.) Thousand Oaks, CA: Sage.

Double deception. (2000, April 1). *Winnipeg Free Press.* [Letter to editor.]

Don't stand by . . . stand up! (2006, October). *Our Schools,* p. 4.

Dovidio, J. F. (1984). Helping behavior and altruism: An empirical and conceptual overview. In L. Berkowitz (Ed.), *Advances in experimental social psychology.* (Vol. 17, pp. 361–427.) New York: Academic Press.

Dovidio, J. F., & Gaertner, S. L. (1996). Affirmative action, unintentional racial biases, and intergroup relations. *Journal of Social Issues, 52,* 51–75.

Dovidio, J. F., Kawakami, K., & Gaertner, S. L. (2002). Implicit and explicit prejudice and interracial interaction. *Journal of Personality and Social Psychology, 82,* 62–68.

Dovidio, J. F., Piliavin, J. A., Gaertner, S. L., Schroeder, D. A., & Clark III, R. D. (1991). The arousal cost-reward model and the process of intervention. In M. S. Clark (Ed.), *Review of personality and social psychology.* (Vol. 12, pp. 86–118.) Newbury Park, CA: Sage.

Doyle, W. J., Gentile, D. A., & Cohen, S. (2006). Emotional style, nasal cytokines, and illness expression after experimental rhinovirus exposure. *Brain, Behavior and Immunity, 20,* 175–181.

Dryer, D. C., & Horowitz, L. M. (1997). When do opposites attract? Interpersonal complementarity versus similarity. *Journal of Personality and Social Psychology, 72,* 592–603.

Duck, J., Hogg, M., & Terry, D. (1995). Me, us and them: Political identification and the third-person effect in the 1993 Australian federal election. *European Journal of Social Psychology, 25,* 195–215.

Dugas, D. (2005, January 14). Canadians opened wallets in record numbers: polls. *Winnipeg Free Press,* p. A14.

Dumont, M., Yzerbyt, V., Wigboldus, D., & Gordijn, E. (2003). Social categorization and fear reactions to the September 11th terrorist Attacks. *Personality and Social Psychology Bulletin, 29,* 1509–1520.

Dunn, E. W., Biesanz, J. C., Human, L. J., & Finn, S. (2007). Misunderstanding the affective consequences of everyday social interactions: The hidden benefits of putting one's best face forward. *Journal of Personality and Social Psychology, 92,* 990–1005.

Dunn, E. W., Brackett, M. A., Ashton-James, C., Schneiderman, E., & Salovey, P. (2007). On emotionally intelligent time travel: Individual differences in affective forecasting ability. *Personality and Social Psychology Bulletin, 33,* 85–93.

Dunn, E. W., & Spellman, B. A. (2003). Forgetting by remembering: Stereotype inhibition through rehearsal of alternative aspects of identity. *Journal of Experimental Social Psychology, 39,* 420–433.

Dunning, D. & Perretta, S. (2002). Automaticity and eyewitness accuracy: A 10- to 12-second rule for distinguishing accurate from inaccurate positive identifications. *Journal of Applied Psychology, 87,* 951–962.

Dunning, D., & Stern, L. B. (1994). Distinguishing accurate from inaccurate eyewitness identifications via inquiries about decision processes. *Journal of Personality and Social Psychology, 67,* 818–835.

Dutton, D. G. (1995). *The domestic assault of women: Psychological and criminal justice perspectives.* Vancouver, BC: UBC Press.

Dutton, D. G., & Aron, A. P. (1974). Some evidence for heightened sexual attraction under conditions of high anxiety. *Journal of Personality and Social Psychology, 30,* 510–517.

Dutton, D. G., & Hart, S. D. (1992a). Evidence for long-term, specific effects of childhood abuse and neglect on criminal behavior in men. *International Journal of Offender Therapy and Comparative Criminology, 36,* 129–137.

Dutton, D. G., & Hart, S. D. (1992b). Risk markers for family violence in a federally incarcerated population. *International Journal of Law and Psychiatry, 15,* 101–112.

Duval, S., & Wicklund, R. A. (1972). *A theory of objective self-awareness.* New York: Academic Press.

Duval, T. S., & Silvia, P. J. (2002). Self-awareness, probability of improvement, and the self-serving bias. *Journal of Personality and Social Psychology, 82,* 49–61.

Dweck, C. S. (1999). *Self-theories: Their role in motivation, personality, and development.* Bristol, PA: Taylor & Francis.

Eagly, A. H. (1987). *Sex differences in social behavior: A social-role interpretation.* Hillsdale, NJ: Erlbaum.

Eagly, A. H., Ashmore, R. D., Makhijani, M. G., & Longo, L. C. (1991). What is beautiful is good, but . . . : A meta-analytic review of research on the physical attractiveness stereotype. *Psychological Bulletin, 110,* 109–128.

Eagly, A. H., & Carli, L. L. (1981). Sex of researchers and sex-typed communications as determinants of sex differences in influenceability: A meta-analysis of social influence studies. *Psychological Bulletin, 90,* 1–20.

Eagly, A. H., & Carli, L. L. (2003). The female leadership advantage: An evaluation of the evidence. *Leadership Quarterly, 14,* 807–834.

Eagly, A. H., & Chaiken, S. (1975). An attribution analysis of communicator characteristics on opinion change: The case of communicator attractiveness. Journal of *Personality and Social Psychology, 32,* 136–244.

Eagly, A. H., & Chaiken, S. (1998). Attitude structure and function. In D. T. Gilbert, S. T. Fiske, & G. Lindzey (Eds.), *The handbook of social psychology.* (4th ed., Vol. 1, pp. 269–322.) New York: McGraw-Hill.

Eagly, A. H., & Crowley, M. (1986). Gender and helping behavior: A meta-analytic review of the social psychological literature. *Psychological Bulletin, 100,* 283–308.

Eagly, A. H., & Diekman, A. B. (2003). The malleability of sex differences in response to changing social roles. In L. G. Aspinwall, & U. M. Staudinger (Eds.), *A psychology of human strengths: Fundamental questions and future directions for a positive psychology.* (pp. 103–115.) Washington, D.C.: American Psychological Association.

Eagly, A. H., Diekman, A. B., Johannesen-Schmidt, M. C., & Koenig, A. M. (2004). Gender gaps in sociopolitical attitudes: A social psychological analysis. *Journal of Personality and Social Psychology, 87,* 796–798.

Eagly, A. H., Johannesen-Schmidt, M. C., & van Engen, M. L. (2003). Transformational, transactional, and laissez-faire leadership styles: A meta-analysis comparing women and men. *Psychological Bulletin, 129,* 569–591.

Eagly, A. H., & Karau, S. J. (2002). Role congruity theory of prejudice toward female leaders. *Psychological Review, 109,* 573–598.

Eagly, A. H., Karau, S. J., & Makhijani, M. G. (1995). Gender and the effectiveness of leaders: A meta-analysis. *Psychological Bulletin, 117,* 125–145.

Eagly, A. H., Makhijani, M. G., & Klonsky, B. G. (1992). Gender and the evaluation of leaders: A meta-analysis. *Psychological Bulletin, 111,* 3–22.

Eagly, A. H., & Steffen, V. J. (2000). Gender stereotypes stem from the distribution of women and men into social roles. In C. Stangor (Ed.), *Stereotypes and prejudice: Essential readings.* (pp. 142–160.) Philadelphia: Psychology Press.

Eargle, A., Guerra, N., & Tolan, P. (1994). Preventing aggression in inner-city children: Small group training to change cognitions, social skills, and behavior. *Journal of Child and Adolescent Group Therapy, 4,* 229–242.

Eberhardt, J. L., Goff, P. A., Purdie, V. J., & Davies, P. G. (2004). Seeing Black: Race, crime, and visual processing. *Journal of Personality and Social Psychology, 87*:6, 876–893.

Eberman, C., & McKelvie, S. J. (2002). Vividness of visual memory and source memory for audio and text. *Applied Cognitive Psychology, 16,* 87–95.

Edmonds, S. (2000, May 5). Judge agrees anthrax vaccine unsafe. The Canadian Press. www.canoe.ca/Health0005/05_anthrax. html. Accessed July 2000.

Educators for Social Responsibility (2001). *About the Resolving Conflict Creatively Program.* www.esrnational. org/about-rccp.html. Accessed March 2004.

Edwards, D. J. A. (1975). Returning a dropped object: Effect of response cost and number of potential helpers. *Journal of Social Psychology, 97,* 169–171.

Edwards, K. (1990). The interplay of affect and cognition in attitude formation and change. *Journal of Personality and Social Psychology, 59,* 202–216.

Edwards, K., & von Hippel, W. (1995). Hearts and minds: The priority of affective versus cognitive factors in person perception. *Personality and Social Psychology Bulletin, 21,* 996–1011.

Eibl-Eibesfeldt, I. (1963). Aggressive behavior and ritualized fighting in animals. In J. H. Masserman (Ed.), *Science and psychoanalysis.* (Vol. 6. Violence and war.) New York: Grune & Stratton.

Eisenberg, N., Spinrad, T. L., & Sadovsky, A. (2006). Empathy-related responding in children. In M. Killen & J. G. Smetana (Eds.), *Handbook of moral development.* (pp. 517–549.) Mahwah, NJ: Erlbaum.

Eiser, J. R., & Ford, N. (1995). Sexual relationships on holidays: A case of situational disinhibition. *Journal of Social and Personal Relationships, 12,* 323–339.

Ekman, P. (1965). Communication through nonverbal behavior: A source of information about an interpersonal relationship. In S. S. Tomkins & C. E. (Eds.), *Affect, cognition, and personality.* (pp. 390–442.) New York: Springer-Verlag.

Ekman, P. (1993). Facial expression and emotion. *American Psychologist, 48,* 384–392.

Ekman, P. (1994). Strong evidence for universals in facial expressions: A reply to Russell's mistaken critique. *Psychological Bulletin, 115,* 268–287.

Ekman, P. (2002). *Telling lies: Clues to deceit in the marketplace, politics, and marriage.* New York: Norton.

Ekman, P., & Davidson, R. J. (Eds.) (1994). *The nature of emotion: Fundamental questions.* New York: Oxford University Press.

Ekman, P., & Friesen, W. V. (1969). The repertoire of nonverbal behavior: Categories, origins, usage, and coding. *Semiotica, 1,* 49–98.

Ekman, P., & Friesen, W. V. (1971). Constants across cultures in the face and emotion. *Journal of Personality and Social Psychology, 17,* 124–129.

Ekman, P., & Friesen, W. V. (1975). *Unmasking the face.* Englewood Cliffs, NJ: Prentice Hall.

Ekman, P., & Friesen, W. V. (1986). A new pan-cultural facial expression of emotion. *Motivation and Emotion, 10,* 159–168.

Ekman, P., Friesen, W. V., O'Sullivan, M., Chan, A., Diacoyanni-Tarlatzis, I., Heider, K., Krause, R., LeCompre, W. A., Pitcairn, T., Ricci-Bitti, P. E., Scherer, K., Tomita, M., & Tzavras, A. (1987). Universals and cultural differences in the judgments of facial expressions of emotions. *Journal of Personality and Social Psychology, 53,* 712–717.

Ekman, P., & O'Sullivan, M. (1988). The role of context in interpreting facial expression: Comment on Russell & Fehr (1987). *Journal of Experimental Psychology: General, 117,* 86–88.

Ekman, P., O'Sullivan, M., & Matsumoto, D. (1991). Confusions about content in the judgment of facial expression: A reply to "Contempt and the relativity thesis." *Motivation and Emotion, 15,* 169–176.

Ekos Research Associates and Canadian Policy Research Networks. (1999, April). *Analysis of Volunteering: Results from the 1997 National Survey of Giving, volunteering and Participating.* Ottawa, ON: Applied Research Branch: Strategic Policy, Human Resources Canada.

Elfenbein, H. A., & Ambady, N. (2002). On the universality and cultural specificity of emotion recognition: A meta-analysis. *Psychological Bulletin, 128,* 203–235.

Elliott, J. (1977). The power and pathology of prejudice. In P. Zimbardo & F. Ruch (Eds.), *Psychology and life.* (9th ed., diamond printing.) Glenview, IL: Scott Foresman.

Ellsworth, P. C., & Mauro, R. (1998). Psychology and law. In D. Gilbert, S. Fiske, & G. Lindzey (Eds.), *The handbook of social psychology.* (4th ed., Vol. 2, pp. 684–732.) New York: McGraw Hill.

Emery, N. J, & Clayton, N. S. (2005). Animal cognition. In. J. J. Bolhuis (Ed.), *Behavior of animals: Mechanisms, function, and evolution.* (pp. 170–196.) Malden, MA: Blackwell.

Endo, Y., Heine, S. J., & Lehman, D. R. (2000). Culture and positive illusions in close relationships: How my relationships are better than yours. *Personality and Social Psychology Bulletin, 26,* 1571–1586.

Eraker, S. A., & Politser, P. (1988). How decisions are reached: Physicians and the patient. In J. Dowie & A. S. Elstein (Eds.), *Professional judgment: A reader in clinical decision making.* (pp. 379–394.) Cambridge, UK: Cambridge University Press.

Erdelyi, M. H. (1994). Hypnotic hypermnesia: The empty set of hypermnesia. *International Journal of Clinical and Experimental Hypnosis, 42,* 379–390.

Eron, L. D. (1982). Parent–child interaction, television violence, and aggression of children. *American Psychologist, 37,* 197–211.

Eron, L. D. (1987). The development of aggressive behavior from the perspective of a developing behaviorism. *American Psychologist, 42,* 425–442.

Eron, L. D. (2001) Seeing is believing: How viewing violence alters attitudes and aggressive behavior. In A. C. Bohart & D. J. Stipek (Eds.), *Constructive and destructive behavior: Implications for family, school, and society.* (pp. 49–60.) Washington, DC: American Psychological Association.

Eron, L. D., Huesmann, L. R., Lefkowitz, M. M., & Walder, L. O. (1996). Does television violence cause aggression? In D. F. Greenberg (Ed.), Criminal careers. *The international library of criminology, criminal justice, and penology.* (Vol. 2, pp. 311–321.) Aldershot, UK: Dartmouth Publishing Company Limited.

Esses, V., Jackson, L., & Armstrong, T. (1998). Intergroup competition and attitudes toward immigrants and immigration: An instrumental model of group conflict. *Journal of Social Issues, 54,* 699–724.

Esses, V. M., & Dovidio, J. F. (2002). The role of emotions in determining willingness to engage in intergroup contact. *Personality and Social Psychology Bulletin, 28,* 1202–1214.

Esses, V. M., Dovidio, J. F., Danso, H. A., Jackson, L. M., & Semenya, A. (2005). Historical and modern perspectives on group competition. In C. S. Crandall & M. Schaller (Eds.). *Social psychology of prejudice: Historical and contemporary issues.* (pp. 94–112.) Lawrence, KS: Lewinian Press.

Esses, V. M., Dovidio, J. F., Jackson, L., & Armstrong, T. L. (2001). The immigration dilemma: The role of perceived group competition, ethnic prejudice, and national identity. *Journal of Social Issues, 57,* 389–412.

Esses, V. M., & Gardner, R. C. (1996). Multiculturalism in Canada: Context and current status. *Canadian Journal of Behavioural Science, 28,* 145–152.

Esses, V. M., Haddock, G., & Zanna, M. P. (1993). Values, stereotypes, and emotions as determinants of intergroup attitudes. In D. M. Mackie & D. L. Hamilton (Eds.), *Affect, cognition, and stereotyping: Interactive processes in group perception.* San Diego, CA: Academic Press, Inc.

Esses, V. M., Veenvliet, S., Hodson, G., & Mihic, L. (2008). Justice, morality, and the dehumanization of refugees. *Social Justice Research, 21,* 4–25.

Esses, V. M., Wagner, U., & Wolf, C. (2006). Perceptions of national identity and attitudes toward immigrants and immigration in Canada and Germany. *International Journal of Intercultural Relations, 30,* 653–669.

Esses, V. M., & Zanna, M. P. (1995). Mood and the expression of ethnic stereotypes. *Journal of Personality and Social Psychology, 69,* 1052–1068.

Estabrooks, P., & Carron, A. V. (1999). The influence of the group with elderly exercisers. *Small Group Research, 30,* 438–452.

Estrada-Hollenbeck, M., & Heatherton, T. F. (1998). Avoiding and alleviating guilt through prosocial behavior. In J. Bybee (Ed.), *Guilt and children.* (pp. 215–231.) San Diego, CA: Academic Press.

Evans, D. C., Garcia, D. J., Garcia, D. M., & Baron, R. S. (2003). In the privacy of their own homes: Using the Internet to assess racial bias. *Personality and Social Psychology Bulletin, 29:2,* 273–284.

Evans, W. N., Neville, D., & Graham, J. D. (1991). General deterrence of drunk driving: Evaluation of American policies. *Risk Analysis, 11,* 279–289.

Ewing, G. (2001). Altruistic, egoistic, and normative effects on curbside recycling. *Environment and Behavior, 33,* 733–764.

Fabrigar, L. R., & Petty, R. E. (1999). The role of affective and cognitive bases of attitudes in susceptibility to affectively and cognitively based persuasion. *Personality and Social Psychology Bulletin, 25,* 363–381.

Fabrigar, L. R., Petty, R. E., Smith, S. M., & Crites, S. L. J. (2006). Understanding knowledge effects on attitude-behavior consistency: The role of relevance, complexity, and amount of knowledge. *Journal of Personality and Social Psychology, 90,* 556–577.

Faiola, A. (2004, August 31). Japanese women live, and like it, on their own. *Washington Post,* p. A01.

Falck, R., & Craig, R. (1988). Classroom-oriented, primary prevention programming for drug abuse. *Journal of Psychoactive Drugs, 20,* 403–408.

False Confessions (2006). Innocence Project. www.innocenceproject.org/understand/False-Confessions.php. Accessed December 2008.

Farber, E. W., & Burge-Callaway, K. (1998). Differences in anger, hostility, and interpersonal aggression in Type A and Type B adolescents. *Journal of Clinical Psychology, 54,* 945–952.

Fazio, R. H. (1990). Multiple processes by which attitudes guide behavior: The MODE model as an integrative framework. In M. P. Zanna (Ed.), *Advances in experimental social psychology.* (Vol. 23, pp. 75–109.) San Diego: Academic Press.

Fazio, R. H. (2000). Accessible attitudes as tools for object appraisal: Their costs and benefits. In G. Maio & J. Olson (Eds.), *Why we evaluate: Functions of attitudes.* (pp. 1–36.) Mahwah, NJ: Erlbaum.

Fazio, R. H., & Olson, M. A. (2003). Implicit measures in social cognition research: Their meaning and uses. *Annual Review of Psychology,54,* 297–327.

Fehr, B. (1988). Prototype analysis of the concepts of love and commitment. *Journal of Personality and Social Psychology, 55,* 557–579.

Fehr, B. (1993). How do I love thee? Let me consult my prototype. In S. Duck (Ed.), *Individuals in relationships.* (pp. 87–120.) Newbury Park, CA: Sage.

Fehr, B. (1994). Prototype-based assessment of laypeople's views of love. *Personal Relationships, 1,* 309–331.

Fehr, B. (1996). *Friendship processes.* Thousand Oaks, CA: Sage Publications.

Fehr, B. (2001). The status of theory and research on love and commitment. In G. Fletcher and M. Clark (Eds.), *The Blackwell handbook of social psychology: Interpersonal processes.* Oxford, UK: Blackwell Publishers.

Fehr, B. (2006). A prototype approach to studying love. In R. J. Sternberg & K. Weis (Eds.). *The new psychology of love.* (pp. 225–246.) New Haven, CT: Yale University Press.

Fehr, B. (2008). Friendship formation. In S. Sprecher, A. Wenzel, & J. Harvey (Eds.). *Handbook of relationship initiation,* (pp. 29–54.) New York: Taylor & Francis.

Fehr, B., & Baldwin, M. (1996). Prototype and script analyses of laypeople's knowledge of anger. In G. J. O. Fletcher, and J. Fitness (Eds.), *Knowledge structures in close relationships: A social psychological approach.* Mahwah, NJ: Erlbaum.

Fehr, B., Baldwin, M., Collins, L., Patterson, S., & Benditt, R. (1999). Anger in close relationships: An interpersonal script analysis. *Personality and Social Psychology Bulletin, 25,* 299–312.

Fehr, B., & Broughton, R. (2001). Gender and personality differences in conceptions of love: An interpersonal theory analysis. *Personal Relationships, 8,* 115–136.

Fehr, B., & Russell, J. A. (1991). The concept of love viewed from a prototype perspective. *Journal of Personality and Social Psychology, 60,* 425–438.

Fein, S., Hoshino-Browne, E., Davies, P. G., & Spencer, S. J. (2003). Self-image maintenance goals and sociocultural norms in motivated social perception. In S. Spencer & S. Fein (Eds.) *Motivated social perception: The Ontario symposium.* (Vol. 99, pp. 21–44.) Mahwah, NJ: Erlbaum.

Fein, S., & Spencer, S. J. (1997). Prejudice as self-image maintenance: Affirming the self through derogating others. *Journal of Personality and Social Psychology, 73,* 31–44.

Fein, S., von Hippel, W., & Spencer, S. J. (2000). To stereotype or not to stereotype: Motivation and stereotype activation, application, and inhibition. *Psychological Inquiry, 10,* 49–54.

Feingold, A. (1990). Gender differences in effects of physical attractiveness on romantic attraction: A comparison across five research paradigms. *Journal of Personality and Social Psychology, 59,* 981–993.

Feingold, A. (1992a). Gender differences in mate selection preferences: A test of the parental investment model. *Psychological Bulletin, 112,* 125–139.

Feingold, A. (1992b). Good-looking people are not what we think. *Psychological Bulletin, 111,* 304–341.

Feld, S. L. (1982). Social structural determinants of similarity among associates. *American Sociological Review, 47,* 797–801.

Feldman-Summers, S., & Kiesler, S. B. (1974). Those who are number two try harder: The effect of sex on attributions of causality. *Journal of Personality and Social Psychology, 38,* 846–855.

Felmlee, D. H. (1995). Fatal attractions: Affection and dissatisfaction in intimate relationships. *Journal of Social and Personal Relationships, 12,* 295–311.

Feshbach, N. D. (1989). Empathy training and prosocial behavior. In J. Groebel & R. A. Hinde (Eds.), *Aggression and war: Their biological and social bases.* (pp. 101–111.) New York: Cambridge University Press.

Feshbach, N. D. (1997). Empathy: The formative years—implications for clinical practice. In A. C. Bohart & L. S. Greenberg (Eds.), *Empathy reconsidered: New directions in psychotherapy.* (pp. 33–59.) Washington, DC: American Psychological Association.

Feshbach, N. D., & Cohen, S. (1988). Training affect comprehension in young children: An experimental evaluation. *Journal of Applied Developmental Psychology, 9,* 201–210.

Festinger, L. (1954). A theory of social comparison processes. *Human Relations, 7,* 117–140.

Festinger, L. (1957). *A theory of cognitive dissonance.* Stanford, CA: Stanford University Press.

Festinger, L., & Carlsmith, J. M. (1959). Cognitive consequences of forced compliance. *Journal of Abnormal and Social Psychology, 58,* 203–211.

Festinger, L., & Maccoby, N. (1964). On resistance to persuasive communications. *Journal of Abnormal and Social Psychology, 68,* 359–366.

Festinger, L., Riecken, H. W., & Schachter, S. (1956). *When prophecy fails.* Minneapolis, MN: University of Minnesota Press.

Festinger, L., Schachter, S., & Back, K. (1950). *Social pressures in informal groups: A study of human factors in housing.* New York: Harper & Bros.

Festinger, L., & Thibaut, J. (1951). Interpersonal communication in small groups. *Journal of Abnormal and Social Psychology, 46,* 92–99.

Fiedler, F. (1967). *A theory of leadership effectiveness.* New York: McGraw-Hill.

Fiedler, F. (1978). The contingency model and the dynamics of the leadership process. In L. Berkowitz (Ed.), *Advances in experimental social psychology.* (Vol. 11, pp. 59–112.) Orlando, FL: Academic Press.

Fiedler, K., Walther, E., & Nickel, S. (1999). Covariation-based attribution: On the ability to assess multiple covariations of an effect. *Personality and Social Psychology Bulletin, 25,* 607–622.

Fincham, F. D., & Bradbury, T. N. (1993). Marital satisfaction, depression, and attributions: A longitudinal analysis. *Journal of Personality and Social Psychology, 64,* 442–452.

Fine, G. A., & Elsbach, K. D. (2000). Ethnography and experiment in social psychological theory building: Tactics for integrating qualitative field data with quantitative lab data. *Journal of Experimental Social Psychology, 36,* 51–76.

Finger, K., & Pezdek, K. (1999). The effect of cognitive interview on face identification accuracy: Release from verbal overshadowing. *Journal of Applied Social Psychology, 84,* 340–348.

Fink, B., & Penton-Voak, I. (2002). Evolutionary psychology of facial attractiveness. *Current Directions in Psychological Science, 11,* 154–158.

Finney, P. D. (1987). When consent information refers to risk and deception: Implications for social research. *Journal of Social Behavior and Personality, 2,* 37–48.

Fischer, W. F. (1963). Sharing in preschool children as a function of amount and type of reinforcement. *Genetic Psychology Monographs, 68,* 215–245.

Fischhoff, B., Gonzalez, R., Lerner, J. S., & Small, D. A. (2005). Evolving judgments of terror risks: Foresight, hindsight, and emotion. *Journal of Experimental Psychology: Applied, 11,* 124–139.

Fishbein, M., & Ajzen, I. (1975). *Belief, attitude, intention, and behavior: An introduction to theory and research.* Reading, MA: Addison-Wesley.

Fishbein, M., Chan, D., O'Reilly, K., Schnell, D., Wood, R., Beeker, C., & Cohn, C. (1993). Factors influencing gay men's attitudes, subjective norms, and intentions with respect to performing sexual behaviors. *Journal of Applied Social Psychology, 23,* 417–438.

Fisher, R. P., Brennan, K. H., & McCauley, M. R. (2001). The cognitive interview method to enhance eyewitness recall. In M. L. Eisen (Ed.), *Memory and suggestibility in the forensic interview.* (pp. 265–286.) Mahwah, NJ: Erlbaum.

Fiske, A. P., Kitayama, S., Markus, H. R., & Nisbett, R. E. (1998). The cultural matrix of social psychology. In D. Gilbert, S. Fiske, & G. Lindzey (Eds.), *The handbook of social psychology.* (4th ed., Vol. 2, pp. 915–981.) New York: McGraw Hill.

Fiske, S. T. (1989a). Examining the role of intent: Toward understanding its role in stereotyping and prejudice. In J. S. Uleman & J. A. Bargh (Eds.), *Unintended thought.* (pp. 253–283.) New York: Guilford.

Fiske, S. T. (1989b). *Interdependence and stereotyping: From the laboratory to the Supreme Court (and back).* Invited address, American Psychological Association, New Orleans.

Fiske, S. T., Cuddy, A. J. C., Glick, P., & Xu, J. (2002). A model of (often mixed) stereotype content: Competence and warmth respectively follow from perceived status competition. *Journal of Personality and Social Psychology, 82,* 878–902.

Fiske, S. T., & Depret, E. (1996). Control, interdependence, and power: Understanding social cognition in its social context. In W. Stroebe & M. Hewstone (Eds.), *European Review of Social Psychology, 7,* 31–61. New York: Wiley.

Fiske, S. T., & Taylor, S. E. (1991). *Social cognition* (2nd ed.) New York: McGraw-Hill.

Flanagan, C. A., Bowes, J. M., Jonsson, B., Csapo, B., & Sheblanova, E. (1998). Ties that bind: Correlates of adolescents' civic commitments in seven countries. *Journal of Social Issues, 54,* 457–475.

Fletcher, G. J. O., & Ward, C. (1988). Attribution theory and processes: A cross-cultural perspective. In M. H. Bond (Ed.), *The cross-cultural challenge to social psychology.* Newbury Park, CA: Sage.

Flowers, M. L. (1977). A lab test of some implications of Janis' groupthink hypothesis. *Journal of Personality and Social Psychology, 35,* 888–897.

Folkman, S., & Moskowitz, J. T. (2000). The context matters. *Personality and Social Psychology Bulletin, 26,* 150–151.

Fong, G. T., Krantz, D. H., & Nisbett, R. E. (1986). The effects of statistical training on thinking about everyday problems. *Cognitive Psychology, 18,* 253–292.

Foot, R. (2007, May 30). Believers plan new journey to centre of the Earth. *Winnipeg Free Press,* p. A2.

Forgas, J. P., & Bower, G. H. (1987). Mood effects on person-perception judgments. Journal of Personality and Social Psychology, 53, 53–60.

Forster, J., Liberman, N., & Higgins, E. T. (2005). Accessibility from active and fulfilled goals. *Journal of Experimental Social Psychology, 41,* 220–239.

Foster, G. (2005). Making friends: A nonexperimental analysis of social pair formation. *Human Relations, 58,* 1443–1465.

Foster, M. (2005, June). Double jeopardy in coping with discrimination: Differences between white and visible minority women. Paper presented at the Canadian Psychological Association Conference, Montreal, Quebec.

Foster, M., & Dion, K. L. (2001, June). Hardiness and responses to perceived discrimination: Buffer or denial? In K. L. Dion (Chair). *Social psychology of prejudice: Cognitive perspectives.* Symposium conducted at the American Psychological Association Convention, Toronto, Ontario.

Foster, M., & Matheson, K. (1999). Perceiving and responding to the personal/group discrimination discrepancy. *Personality and Social Psychology Bulletin, 25,* 1319–1329.

Foster, M. D., & Tsarfati, E. M. (2005). The effects of meritocracy beliefs on women's well-being after first-time gender discrimination. *Personality and Social Psychology Bulletin, 31,* 1730–1738.

Fouts, G., & Burggraf, K. (1999). Television situation comedies: Female body images and verbal reinforcements. *Sex Roles, 40,* 473–479.

Fox, J. (1980). Making decisions under the influence of memory. *Psychological Review, 87,* 190–211.

Frager, R. (1970). Conformity and anticonformity in Japan. *Journal of Personality and Social Psychology, 15,* 203–210.

Fraidin, S. N. (2004). When is one head better than two? Interdependent information in group decision making. *Organizational Behavior and Human Decision Processes, 93,* 102–113.

Fraley, R. C. (2002). Attachment stability from infancy to adulthood: Meta-analysis and dynamic modeling of developmental mechanisms. *Personality and Social Psychology Review, 6,* 123–151.

Fraley, R. C., & Shaver, P. R. (2000). Adult romantic attachment: Theoretical developments, emerging controversies, and unanswered questions. *Review of General Psychology, 4,* 132–154.

Frank, M. G., & Gilovich, T. (1988). The dark side of self and social perceptions: Black uniforms and aggression in professional sports. *Journal of Personality and Social Psychology, 54,* 74–85.

Frankel, Glenn. (2005, 24 July). London Police Had Expressed "Deep Regret" for Bystander Shooting. www.washingtonpost.comRetrieved August 3, 2005.

Fredrickson, B. L., Roberts, T., Noll, S. M., Quinn, D. M., & Twenge, J. M. (1998). That swimsuit becomes you: Sex differences in self-objectification, restrained eating, and math performance. *Journal of Personality and Social Psychology, 75,* 269–284.

Fredrickson, B. L., Tugade, M., Waugh, C., & Larkin, G. (2003). What good are positive emotions in crises? A prospective study of resilience and emotions following the terrorist attacks on the United States on September 11th, 2001. *Journal of Personality and Social Psychology, 84,* 365–376.

Freedman, D., Pisani, R., Purves, R., & Adhikari, A. (1991). *Statistics.* (2nd ed.) New York: Norton.

Freedman, J. L. (1965). Long-term behavioral effects of cognitive dissonance. *Journal of Experimental and Social Psychology, 1,* 145–155.

Freedman, J. L., & Fraser, S. C. (1966). Compliance without pressure: The foot-in-the-door technique. *Journal of Personality and Social Psychology, 4,* 195–202.

Freud, S. (1930). *Civilization and its discontents.* Joan Rivière (Trans.) London, UK: Hogarth Press.

Freud, S. (1933). *New introductory lectures on psycho-analysis.* New York: Norton.

Fried, C., & Aronson, E. (1995). Hypocrisy, misattribution, and dissonance reduction: A demonstration of dissonance in the absence of aversive consequences. *Personality and Social Psychology Bulletin, 21,* 925–933.

Frodi, A. (1975). The effect of exposure to weapons on aggressive behavior from a cross-cultural perspective. *International Journal of Psychology, 10,* 283–292.

Fu, G., Lee, K., Cameron, C. A., & Xu, F. (2001). Chinese and Canadian adults' categorization and evaluation of lie- and truth-telling about prosocial and antisocial behaviors. *Journal of Cross-Cultural Psychology, 32,* 720–727.

Funder, D. C., & Colvin, C. R. (1988). Friends and strangers: Acquaintanceship, agreement, and the accuracy of personality judgment. *Journal of Personality and Social Psychology, 55,* 149–158.

Gabriel, S., & Gardner, W. L. (1999). Are there "his" and "hers" types of interdependence? The implications of gender differences in collective versus relational interdependence for affect, behavior, and cognition. *Journal of Personality and Social Psychology, 77,* 642–655.

Gabriel, S., & Gardner, W. L. (2004). Are there "his" and "hers" types of interdependence? The implications of gender differences in collective versus relational interdependence for affect, behavior, and cognition. In H. T. Reis & C. E. Rusbult (Eds.), *Close relationships: Key readings.* (pp. 405–420.) Philadelphia, PA: Taylor & Francis.

Gackle, P. (2008, August 9). McLean funeral picketers fear backlash. *Winnipeg Free Press*, p. A5.

Gaertner, S. L., & Dovidio, J. F. (1986). The aversive form of racism. In J. F. Dovidio & S. L. Gaertner (Eds.), *Prejudice, discrimination, and racism: Theory and research.* (pp. 61–89.) New York: Academic Press.

Gagné, F. M., & Lydon, J. E. (2001). Mind-set and close relationships: When bias leads to (in)accurate predictions. *Journal of Personality and Social Psychology, 81,* 85–96.

Gagné, F. M., & Lydon, J. E. (2003). Identification and the commitment shift: Accounting for gender differences in relationship illusions. *Personality and Social Psychology Bulletin, 29:7,* 907–919.

Gagné, F., Lydon, J. E., & Bartz, J. (2003). Effects of mindset on the predictive validify of relationship constructs. *Journal Personality and Social Psychology, 35,* 292–304.

Gagnon, A., & Bourhis, R. Y. (1996). Discrimination in the minimal group paradigm: Social identity or self-interest? *Personality and Social Psychology Bulletin, 22,* 1289–1301.

Galinsky, A. D., Mussweiler, T., & Medvec, V. H. (2002). Disconnecting outcomes and evaluations: The role of negotiator focus. *Journal of Personality and Social Psychology, 83,* 1131–1140.

Gallese, V., Fadiga, L., Fogassi, L., & Rizzolatti, G. (1996). Action recognition in the premotor cortex. *Brain, 119(2),* 593–609.

Gallup, G. G. (1977). Self-recognition in primates: A comparative approach to the bidirectional properties of consciousness. *American Psychologist, 32,* 329–338.

Gallup, G. G. Jr., Anderson, J. R., & Shillito, D. J. (2002). The mirror test. In M. Bekoff & C. Allen (Eds.), *Cognitive animal: Empirical and theoretical perspectives on animal cognition.* (pp. 325–333.) Cambridge, MA: MIT Press.

Gallup, G. G., & Suarez, S. D. (1986). Self-awareness and the emergence of mind in humans and other primates. In J. Suls & A. G. Greenwald (Eds.), *Psychological perspectives on the self.* (Vol. 3, pp. 3–26.) Hillsdale, NJ: Erlbaum.

Gangestad, S. W. (1993). Sexual selection and physical attractiveness: Implications for mating dynamics. *Human Nature, 4,* 205–235.

Gao, G. (1993, May). An investigation of love and intimacy in romantic relationships in China and the United States. Paper presented at the annual conference of the International Communication Association, Washington, DC.

Gao, G. (1996). Self and other: A Chinese perspective on interpersonal relationships. In W. B. Gudykunst, S. Ting-Toomey, & T. Nishida (Eds.), *Communication in personal relationships across cultures.* (pp. 81–101.) Thousand Oaks, CA: Sage.

Gao, G., & Gudykunst, W. B. (1995). Attributional confidence, perceived similarity, and network involvement in Chinese and European American romantic relationships. *Communication Quarterly, 43,* 431–445.

Gardner, R. C., MacIntyre, P. D., & Lalonde, R. N. (1995). The effects of multiple social categories on stereotyping. *Canadian Journal of Behavioural Science, 27,* 466–483.

Gardner, W. L., Pickett, C. L., & Brewer, M. B. (2000). Social exclusion and selective memory: How the need to belong influences memory for social events. *Personality and Social Psychology Bulletin, 26,* 486–496.

Garfinkle, H. (1967). *Studies in ethnomethodology.* Englewood Cliffs, NJ: Prentice Hall.

Gauthier, I., Behrmann, M., & Tarr, M. J. (1999). Can face recognition really be disassociated from object recognition? *Journal of Cognitive Neuroscience, 11,* 249–370.

Gawronski, B., & Bodenhausen, G. V. (2005). Accessibility effects on implicit social cognition: The role of knowledge activation and retrieval experiences. *Journal of Personality and Social Psychology, 89,* 672–685.

Gawronski, B., Bodenhausen, G. V., & Banse, R. (2005). We are, therefore they aren't: Ingroup construal as a standard of comparison for outgroup judgments. *Journal of Experimental Social Psychology, 41,* 515–526.

Gawronski, B., Bodenhausen, G. V., & Becker, A. P. (2007). I like it, because I like myself: Associative self-anchoring and post-decisional change of implicit evaluations. *Journal of Experimental Social Psychology, 43,* 221–232.

Geddes, J. (2008, March 10). The Chuck Cadman affair—from someone who was there. Macleans.ca. www.macleans.ca/article.jsp?content=20080310_093557_2860. Accessed October 2008.

Geen, R. (1998). Aggression and anti-social behavior. In D. Gilbert, S. Fiske, & G. Lindzey (Eds.), *The handbook of social psychology.* (4th ed., Vol. 2, pp. 317–356.) New York: McGraw Hill.

Geen, R. G. (1989). Alternative conceptions of social facilitation. In P. B. Paulus (Ed.), *Psychology of group influence.* (2nd ed., pp. 15–51.) Hillsdale, NJ: Erlbaum.

Geiselman, R. E., & Fischer, R. P. (1989). The cognitive interview technique for victims and witnesses of crime. In D. C. Raskin (Ed.), *Psychological methods in criminal investigation and evidence.* (pp. 191–215.) New York: Springer.

Geller, E. S. (2002). The challenge of increasing proenvironmental behavior. In R. B. Bechtel & A. Churchman (Eds.), *Handbook of environmental psychology.* (pp. 525–540.) New York: Wiley.

George, D. M., Carroll, P., Kersnick, R., & Calderon, K. (1998). Gender-related patterns of helping among friends. *Psychology of Women Quarterly, 22,* 685–704.

George, J. M. (1990). Personality, affect, and behavior in groups. *Journal of Applied Psychology, 75,* 107–116.

Gerard, H. B. (1953). The effect of different dimensions of disagreement on the communication process in small groups. *Human Relations, 6,* 249–271.

Gerard, H. B., & Mathewson, G. C. (1966). The effects of severity of initiation on liking for a group: A replication. *Journal of Experimental Social Psychology, 2,* 278–287.

Gerard, H. B., Wilhelmy, R. A., & Conolley, E. S. (1968). Conformity and group size. *Journal of Personality and Social Psychology, 8,* 79–82.

Gerbner, G., Gross, L., Morgan, M., Signorielli, N., & Shanahan, J. (2002). Growing up with television: Cultivation processes. In J. Bryant & D. Zillmann (Eds.), *Media effects: Advances in theory and research.* (pp. 43–67.) Mahwah, NJ: Erlbaum.

Gerdes, E. P. (1979). College students' reactions to social psychological experiments involving deception. *Journal of Social Psychology, 107,* 99–110.

Gergen, K. J., Gergen, M. M., & Barton, W. H. (1973, July). Deviance in the dark. *Psychology Today,* pp. 129–130.

Gibbons, F. X. (1978). Sexual standards and reactions to pornography: Enhancing behavioral consistency through self-focused attention. *Journal of Personality and Social Psychology, 36,* 976–987.

Gibbons, F. X., Gerrard, M., & Cleveland, M. J. (2004). Perceived discrimination and substance use in African American parents and their children: A panel study. *Journal of Personality and Social Psychology, 86,* 517–529.

Gibbs, J. P. (1985). Deterrence theory and research. *Nebraska Symposium on Motivation, 33,* 87–130.

Giesler, R., Josephs, R., & Swann, W. (1996). Self-verification in clinical depression: The desire for negative evaluation. *Journal of Abnormal Psychology, 105,* 358–368.

Gifford, R. (1991). Mapping nonverbal behavior on the interpersonal circle. *Journal of Personality and Social Psychology, 61,* 279–288.

Gifford, R. (1994). A lens-mapping framework for understanding the endcoding and decoding of interpersonal dispositions in nonverbal behavior. *Journal of Personality and Social Psychology, 66,* 398–412.

Gifford-Smith, M. E., & Brownell, C. A. (2003). Childhood peer relationships: Social acceptance, friendships, and peer networks. *Journal of School Psychology, 41,* 235–284.

Gigerenzer, G. (2000). *Adaptive thinking: Rationality in the real world.* Oxford, UK: Oxford University Press.

Gilbert, D. T. (1989). Thinking lightly about others: Automatic components of the social inference process. In J. S. Uleman & J. A. Bargh (Eds.), *Unintended thought.* (pp. 189–211.) New York: Guilford Press.

Gilbert, D. T. (1991). How mental systems believe. *American Psychologist, 46,* 107–119.

Gilbert, D. T. (1993). The assent of man: Mental representation and the control of belief. In D. M. Wegner & J. W. Pennebaker, (Eds.), *The handbook of mental control.* (pp. 57–87.) Englewood Cliffs, NJ: Prentice Hall.

Gilbert, D. T. (1998a). Ordinary personology. In D. T. Gilbert, S. T. Fiske, & G. Lindzey (Eds.), *The handbook of social psychology.* (4th ed., Vol. 2, pp. 89–150.) New York: McGraw-Hill.

Gilbert, D. T. (1998b). Speeding with Ned: A personal view of the correspondence bias. In J. M. Darley & J. Cooper (Eds.), *Attribution and social interaction.* (pp. 5–36.) Washington, DC: American Psychological Association.

Gilbert, D. T. (2006). *Stumbling on happiness.* New York: Knopf.

Gilbert, D. T., & Ebert, J. E. J. (2002). Decisions and revisions: The affective forecasting of changeable outcomes. *Journal of Personality and Social Psychology, 82,* 503–514.

Gilbert, D. T., & Hixon, J. G. (1991). The trouble of thinking: Activation and applications of stereotypical beliefs. *Journal of Personality and Social Psychology, 60,* 509–517.

Gilbert, D. T., & Malone, P. S. (1995). The correspondence bias. *Psychological Bulletin, 117,* 21–38.

Gilbert, D. T., & Osborne, R. E. (1989). Thinking backward: Some curable and incurable consequences of cognitive busyness. *Journal of Personality and Social Psychology, 57,* 940–949.

Gilbert, D. T., Pelham, B. W., & Krull, D. S. (1988). On cognitive busyness: When person perceivers meet persons perceived. *Journal of Personality and Social Psychology, 54,* 733–740.

Gill, R., & Matheson, K. (2006). Responses to discrimination: The role of emotion and expectations for emotional regulation. *Personality and Social Psychology Bulletin, 32,* 149–161.

Gilovich, T. (1991). *How we know what isn't so: The fallibility of human reasoning in everyday life.* New York: Free Press.

Gilovich, T., & Griffin, D. W. (2002). Introduction: Heuristics and biases, now and then. In T. Gilovich, D. W. Griffin, & D. Kahneman (Eds.), *Heuristics and biases: The psychology of intuitive judgment.* (pp. 1–18.) New York: Cambridge University Press.

Gilovich, T., & Medvec, V. H. (1995). The experience of regret: What, when, and why. *Psychological Review, 102,* 379–395.

Gilovich, T., Medvec, V. H., & Chen, S. (1995). Commission, omission, and dissonance reduction: Coping with regret in the "Monty Hall" problem. *Personality and Social Psychology Bulletin, 21,* 182–190.

Gilovich, T., & Savitsky, K. (2002). Like goes with like: The role of representativeness in erroneous and pseudoscientific beliefs. In T. Gilovich, D. W. Griffin, & D. Kahneman (Eds.), *Heuristics and biases: The psychology of intuitive judgment.* (pp. 617–624.) New York: Cambridge University Press.

Gimlin, D. (1994). The anorexic as overconformist: Toward a reinterpretation of eating disorders. In K. A. Callaghan (Ed.), *Ideals of feminine beauty: Philosophical, social, and cultural dimensions.* (pp. 99–111.) Westport, CN: Greenwood.

Gire, J. T. (1997). The varying effect of individualism-collectivism on preference for methods of conflict resolution. *Canadian Journal of Behavioural Science, 29,* 38–43.

Gladwell, M. (2004). Big and bad. *New Yorker, 79,* 28–33.

Glass, D. C. (1964). Changes in liking as a means of reducing cognitive discrepancies between self-esteem and aggression. *Journal of Personality, 32,* 531–549.

Glass, D. C., & Singer, J. E. (1972). *Urban stress: Experiments on noise and social stressors.* New York: Academic Press.

Godin, G., Maticka-Tyndale, E., Adrien, A., Manson-Singer, S., Willams, D., & Cappon, P. (1996). Cross-cultural testing of three social cognitive theories: An application to condom use. *Journal of Applied Social Psychology, 26,* 1556–1586.

Goethals, G. R., & Darley, J. M. (1977). Social comparison theory: An attributional approach. In J. M. Suls & R. L. Miller (Eds.), *Social comparison processes: Theoretical and empirical perspectives.* (pp. 259–278.) Washington, DC: Hemisphere/Halsted.

Goff, P. A., Steele, C. M., & Davies, P. G. (2008). The space between us: Stereotype threat and distance in interracial contexts. *Journal of Personality and Social Psychology, 94,* 91–107.

Gold, J. A., Ryckman, R. M., & Mosley, N. R. (1984). Romantic mood induction and attraction to a dissimilar other: Is love blind? *Personality and Social Psychology Bulletin, 10,* 358–368.

Goldstein, J. H., & Arms, R. L. (1971). Effect of observing athletic contests on hostility. *Sociometry, 34,* 83–90.

Goldstein, N., Cialdini, R. B., & Griskevicius, V. (2008). A room with a viewpoint: Using social norms to motivate environmental conservation in hotels. *Journal of Consumer Research, 35.*

Goleman, D. (1982, January). Make-or-break resolutions. *Psychology Today,* p. 19.

Gonzales, M. H., Aronson, E., & Costanzo, M. (1988). Using social cognition and persuasion to promote energy conservation: A quasi-experiment. *Journal of Applied Social Psychology, 18,* 1049–1066.

Good, C. Aronson, J., & Harder, J. (2008). Problems in the pipeline: Stereotype threat and women's achievement in high-level math courses. *Journal of Applied Developmental Psychology, 29*(1), 17–28.

Goode, E. (2000, February 15). When women find love is fatal. *New York Times,* pp. F1*ff.*

Gopaul-McNicol, S.-A. A. (1987). A cross-cultural study of the effects of modeling, reinforcement, and color meaning word association on doll color preference of Black preschool children and White preschool children in New York and Trinidad. *Dissertation Abstracts International, 48,* 340–341.

Gorassini, D. R., & Olson, J. M. (1995). Does self-perception change explain the foot-in-the-door effect? *Journal of Personality and Social Psychology, 69,* 91–105.

Gordon, A. K., & Miller, A. G. (2000). Perspective differences in the construal of lies: Is deception in the eye of the beholder? *Personality and Social Psychology Bulletin, 26,* 46–55.

Gorham, B. (2005, December 20). We're slow and "stalking" America, says TV pundit. *Winnipeg Free Press,* p. A3.

Gould, S. J. (1997, June 26). Evolution: The pleasures of pluralism. *The New York Review,* pp. 47–52.

Graham, K., & Wells, S. (2001a). The two worlds of aggression for men and men. *Sex Roles, 45,* 595–622.

Graham, K., & Wells, S. (2001b). Aggression among young adults in the social context of the bar. *Addiction Research & Theory, 9,* 193–219.

Graham, K., West, P., & Wells, S. (2000). Evaluating theories of alcohol-related aggression using observations of young adults in bars. *Addiction, 95,* 847–863.

Granberg, D., & Brown, T. (1989). On affect and cognition in politics. *Social Psychology Quarterly, 52,* 171–182.

Grant, M. J., Button, C. M., Hannah, T. E., & Ross, A. S. (2003). The role of ideological consistency in attitude inferences. *Current Research in Social Psychology, 9*:3, 32–49.

Grant, P. R. (1992). Ethnocentrism between groups of unequal power in response to perceived threat to social identity and valued resources. *Canadian Journal of Behavioural Science, 24,* 348–370.

Grant, P. R. (1993). Reactions to intergroup similarity: Examination of the similarity-differentiation and the similarity-attraction hypothesis. *Canadian Journal of Behavioural Science, 25,* 28–44.

Graziano, W. G., Jensen-Campbell, L. A., & Finch, J. F. (1997). The self as a mediator between personality and adjustment. *Journal of Personality and Social Psychology, 73,* 392–404.

Graziano, W. G., Jensen-Campbell, L. A., Shebilske, L. J., & Lundgren, S. R. (1993). Social influence, sex differences, and judgments of beauty: Putting the interpersonal back in interpersonal attraction. *Journal of Personality and Social Psychology, 65,* 522–531.

Greenberg, J., & Musham, C. (1981). Avoiding and seeking self-focused attention. *Journal of Research in Personality, 15*, 191–200.

Greenberg, J., & Pyszczynski, T. (1985). The effect of an overheard slur on evaluations of the target: How to spread a social disease. *Journal of Experimental Social Psychology, 21*, 61–72.

Greenberg, J., Pyszczynski, T., & Solomon, S. (1986). The causes and consequences of the need for self-esteem: A terror management theory. In R. F. Baumeister (Ed.), *Public self and private self.* (pp. 189–212.) New York: Springer-Verlag.

Greenberg, J., Solomon, S., & Pyszczynski, T. (1997). Terror management theory of self-esteem and cultural worldviews: Empirical assessments and conceptual refinements. In M. P. Zanna (Eds.), *Advances in experimental social psychology.* (Vol. 29, pp. 61–139.) San Diego, CA: Academic Press.

Green-Demers, I., Pelletier, L. G., Stewart, D. G., & Gushue, N. R. (1998). Coping with the less interesting aspects of training. Toward a model of interest and motivation enhancement in individual sports. *Basic and Applied Social Psychology, 20*, 251–261.

Greenglass, E. R. (1991). Type A behavior, career aspirations, and role conflict in professional women. In M. J. Strube (Ed.), *Type A Behavior.* Newbury Park, CA: Sage.

Greenwald, A. G., & Banaji, M. R. (1989). The self as a memory system: Powerful, but ordinary. *Journal of Personality and Social Psychology, 57*, 41–54.

Greenwald, A. G., & Banaji, M. R. (1995). Implicit social cognition: Attitudes, self-esteem, and stereotypes. *Psychological Review, 102*, 4–27.

Greenwald, A. G., McGhee, D. E., & Schwartz, J. L. K. (1998). Measuring individual differences in implicit cognition: The Implicit Association Test. *Journal of Personality and Social Psychology, 74*, 1464–1480.

Greenwald, A. G., & Nosek, B. A. (2001). Health of the Implicit Association Test at age 3. *Zeitschrift für Experimentelle Psychologie, 48*, 85–93.

Greenwald, A. G., Spangenberg, E. R., Pratkanis, A. R., & Eskenazi, J. (1991). Double-blind tests of subliminal self-help audiotapes. *Psychological Science, 2*, 119–122.

Griffin, D., & Buehler, R. (1993). Role of construal processes in conformity and dissent. *Journal of Personality and Social Psychology, 65*, 657–669.

Griffin, D., & Buehler, R. (1999). Frequency, probability, and prediction: Easy solutions to cognitive illusions. *Cognitive Psychology, 38*, 48–78.

Griffin, D., & Kahneman, D. (2003). Judgmental heuristics: Human strengths or human weaknesses? In L. G. Aspinwall, & U. M. Staudinger (Eds.), *A psychology of human strengths: Fundamental questions and future directions for a positive psychology.* (pp. 165–178.) Washington, DC: American Psychological Association.

Griffin, D. W., & Ross, L. (1991). Subjective construal, social inference, and human misunderstanding. In L. Berkowitz (Ed.), *Advances in experimental social psychology.* (Vol. 24, pp. 319–359.) San Diego, CA: Academic Press.

Griffin, E., & Sparks, G. G. (1990). Friends forever: A longitudinal exploration of intimacy in same-sex pairs and platonic pairs. *Journal of Social and Personal Relationships, 7*, 29–46.

Griffitt, W., & Veitch, R. (1971). Hot and crowded: Influences of population density and temperature on interpersonal affective behavior. *Journal of Personality and Social Psychology, 17*, 92–98.

Griskevicius, V., Cialdini, R. B., & Goldstein, N. J. (2008). Applying (and resisting) peer influence. *MIT Sloan Management Review, 49*, 83–88.

Groopman, J. (2007, January 29). What's the trouble? *New Yorker,* pp. 36–41.

Gross, J. J. (1998). Antecedent- and response-focused emotion regulation: Divergent consequences for experience, expression, and physiology. *Journal of Personality and Social Psychology, 74*, 224–237.

Gross, J. J., & Levenson, R. W. (1993). Emotional suppression: Physiology, self-report, and expressive behavior. *Journal of Personality and Social Psychology, 64*, 970–986.

Gross, J. J., & Levenson, R. W. (1997). Hiding feelings: The acute effects of suppressing negative and positive emotion. *Journal of Abnormal Psychology, 106*, 95–103.

Grouzet, F. M. E., Kasser, T., Ahuvia, A., Dols, J. M. F., Kim, Y., Lau, S. et al. (2005). The structure of goal contents across 15 cultures. *Journal of Personality and Social Psychology, 89*, 800–816.

Grusec, J. E. (1991). The socialization of altruism. In M. S. Clark (Ed.), Review of personality and social psychology (Vol. 12, pp. 9–33). Newbury Park, CA: Sage.

Grusec, J. E., Kuczynski, L., Rushton, J. P., & Simutis, Z. M. (1979). Modeling, direct instruction, and attributions: Effects on altruism. *Developmental Psychology, 14*, 51–57.

Guay, F., Mageau, G. A., & Vallerand, R. J. (2003). On the hierarchical structure of self-determined motivation: A test of top-down, bottom-up, reciprocal, and horizontal effects. *Personality and Social Psychology Bulletin, 29.*8, 992–1004.

Gudykunst, W. B., Ting-Toomey, S., & Nishida, T. (1996). *Communication in personal relationships across cultures.* Thousand Oaks, CA: Sage Publications.

Guerin, B. (1993). Social facilitation. Cambridge, UK: Cambridge University Press.

Guilbault, R. L., Bryant, F. B., Brockway, J. H., & Posavac, E. J. (2004). A meta-analysis of research on hindsight bias. *Basic and Applied Social Psychology, 26*, 103–117.

Guimond, S. (1999). Attitude change during college: Normative or informational social influence? *Social Psychology of Education, 2*, 237–261.

Guimond, S. (2000). Group socialization and prejudice: the social transmission of intergroup attitudes and beliefs. *European Journal of Social Psychology, 30*, 335–354.

Guimond, S., Chatard, A., Martinot, D., Crisp, R. J., & Redersdorff, S. (2006). Social comparison, self-stereotyping, and gender differences in self-construals. *Journal of Personality and Social Psychology, 90*, 221–242.

Guimond, S., Dambrun, M., Michinov, N., & Durarte, S. (2003). Does social dominance generate prejudice? Integrating individual and contextual determinants of intergroup cognitions. *Journal of Personality and Social Psychology, 84*(4), 697–721.

Guimond, S., & Dubé, L. (1989). La representation des causes de l'inferiorité economique des québecois francophones. *Canadian Journal of Behavioural Science, 21*, 28–39.

Guimond, S., & Palmer, D. L. (1996). The political socialization of commerce and social science students: Epistemic authority and attitude change. *Journal of Applied Social Psychology, 26*, 1985–2013.

Guisinger, S., & Blatt, S. J. (1994). Individuality and relatedness: Evolution of a fundamental dialect. *American Psychologist, 49*, 104–111.

Gulli, C. (2005, September 17). Why I gave a stranger a kidney. *National Post,* p. A1.

Gustafson, R. (1989). Frustration and successful vs. unsuccessful aggression: A test of Berkowitz' completion hypothesis. *Aggressive Behavior, 15*, 5–12.

Guthrie, M. (2005, January 11). "Housewives" drives home ad. *New York Daily News.* www.nydailynews.com/entertainment/ent_radio/story/269947p-231207c.html. Accessed January 2006.

Haddock, G., & Zanna, M. P. (1994). Preferring "housewives" to "feminists": Categorization and the favorability of attitudes toward women. *Psychology of Women Quarterly, 18*, 25–52.

Haddock, G., & Zanna, M. P. (1998). Assessing the impact of affective and cognitive information in predicting attitudes toward capital punishment. *Law and Human Behavior, 22*, 325–339.

Haddock, G., Zanna, M. P., & Esses, V. M. (1993). Assessing the structure of prejudicial attitudes: The case of attitudes toward homosexuals. *Journal of Personality and Social Psychology, 65*, 1105–1118.

Haddock, G., Zanna, M. P., & Esses, V. M. (1994). The (limited) role of trait-laden stereotypes in predicting attitudes toward Native peoples. *British Journal of Social Psychology, 33*, 83–106.

Hadjistavropoulos, T., & Genest, M. (1994). The understanding of the role of physical attractiveness in dating preferences: Ignorance or taboo? *Canadian Journal of Behavioural Science, 26*, 298–318.

Hafer, C. L. (2000a). Do innocent victims threaten the belief in a just world? Evidence from a modified Stroop task. *Journal of Personality and Social Psychology, 79*, 165–173.

Hafer, C. L. (2000b). Investment in long-term goals and commitment to just means drive the need to believe in a just world. *Personality and Social Psychology Bulletin, 26*, 1059–1073.

Hafer, C. L. (2002). Why we reject innocent victims. In M. Ross & D. T. Miller (Eds.) *The justice motive in everyday life.* (pp. 109–126.) New York: Cambridge University Press.

Hafer, C. L., & Bègue, L. (2005). Experimental research on just-world theory: Problems, developments, and future challenges. *Psychological Bulletin, 131*, 128–167.

Hafer, C. L., Reynolds, K. L., Obertynski, M. A. (1996). Message comprehensibility and persuasion: Effects of complex language in counter attitudinal appeals to laypeople. *Social Cognition, 14*, 317–337.

Haidt, J., & Keltner, D. (1999). Culture and facial expression: Open-ended methods find more faces and a gradient of recognition. *Cognition and Emotion, 13*, 225–266.

Halberstadt, J. B., & Rhodes, G. (2000). The attractiveness of nonface averages: Implications for an evolutionary explanation of the attractiveness of average faces. *Psychological Science, 11*, 285–289.

Hall, E. T. (1969). *The hidden dimension.* Garden City, NY: Doubleday.

Hall, J. A. (1979). *A cross-national study of gender differences in nonverbal sensitivity.* Unpublished manuscript, Northeastern University.

Hall, J. A. (1984). *Nonverbal sex differences: Communication accuracy and expressive style.* Baltimore, MD: Johns Hopkins University Press.

Hall, V. (2008, August 12). Out of ammo. *National Post*, p. B1.

Hamamura, T., Heine, S. J., & Paulhus, D. L. (2007). Cultural differences in response styles: The role of dialectical thinking. *Personality and Individual Differences, 44*, 932–942.

Hamamura, T., Heine, S. J., & Takemoto, T. R. S. (in press). Why the better-than-average effects is a worse-than-average measure of self-enhancement: An investigation of conflicting findings from studies of East Asian self-evaluations. *Motivation and Emotion.*

Hamilton, V. L., Sanders, J., & McKearney, S. J. (1995). Orientations toward authority in an authoritarian state: Moscow in 1990. *Personality and Social Psychology Bulletin, 21*, 356–365.

Hamilton, W. D. (1964). The genetical evolution of social behavior. *Journal of Theoretical Biology, 7*, 1–52.

Hammond, D., Fong, G. T., Borland, R., Cummings, M., McNeill, A., & Driezen, P. (2007). Text and graphic warnings on cigarette packages: Findings from the International Tobacco Control Country study. *American Journal of Preventive Medicine, 32*, 202–209.

Han, S., & Shavitt, S. (1994). Persuasion and culture: Advertising appeals in individualistic and collectivistic societies. *Journal of Experimental Social Psychology, 30*, 326–350.

Haney, C., Banks, C., & Zimbardo, P. (1973). Interpersonal dynamics in a simulated prison. *International Journal of Criminology and Penology, 1*, 69–97.

Hankin, B. L., Fraley, R. C., & Abela, J. R. Z. (2005). Daily depression and cognitions about stress: Evidence for a traitlike depressogenic cognitive style and the prediction of depressive symptoms in a prospective daily diary study. *Journal of Personality and Social Psychology, 88*, 673–685.

Hansen, C. H., & Hansen, R. D. (1988). Finding the face in the crowd: An anger superiority effect. *Journal of Personality and Social Psychology, 17*, 917–924.

Hansen, E. M., Kimble, C. E., & Biers, D. W. (2001). Actors and observers: Divergent attributions of constrained unfriendly behavior. *Social Behavior and Personality, 29*, 87–104.

Hanson, I., & Hampton, M. R. (2000). Being Indian: Strengths sustaining First Nations Peoples in Saskatchewan residential schools. *Canadian Journal of Community Mental Health, 19*, 127–142.

Hansson, R. O., & Slade, K. M. (1977). Altruism toward a deviant in a city and small town. *Journal of Applied Social Psychology, 7*, 272–279.

Harackiewicz, J. M. (1979). The effects of reward contingency and performance feedback on intrinsic motivation. *Journal of Personality and Social Psychology, 37*, 1352–1363.

Harackiewicz, J. M. (1989). Performance evaluation and intrinsic motivation processes: The effects of achievement orientation and rewards. In D. M. Buss & N. Cantor (Eds.), *Personality psychology: Recent trends and emerging directions.* (pp. 128–137.) New York: Springer-Verlag.

Harackiewicz, J. M., Durik, A. M., & Barron, K. E. (Eds.) (2005). *Multiple goals, optimal motivation, and the development of interest.* New York: Cambridge University Press.

Harackiewicz, J. M., & Elliot, A. J. (1993). Achievement goals and intrinsic motivation. *Journal of Personality and Social Psychology, 65*, 904–915.

Harackiewicz, J. M., & Elliot, A. J. (1998). The joint effects of target and purpose goals on intrinsic motivation: A mediational analysis. *Personality and Social Psychology Bulletin, 24:7*, 675–689.

Harackiewicz, J. M., Manderlink, G., & Sansone, C. (1984). Rewarding pinball wizardry: Effects of evaluation and cue value on intrinsic interest. *Journal of Personality and Social Psychology, 47*, 287–300.

Harasymchuk, C. (2008, February). Relational boredom and its correlates: Validation of a scale using individual and couple level analyses. Paper presented at the Society for Personality and Social Psychology conference, Albuquerque, New Mexico.

Harasymchuk, C., & Fehr, B. (2008, July). Relational boredom: Correlates and unique contribution to satisfaction. In C. Harasymchuk and G. Strong (Chairs). *Routine, rituals, and boredom in relationships.* Symposium conducted at the International Association for Relationship Research, Providence, Rhode Island.

Hare, B., & Tomasello, M. (2005). Human-like social skills in dogs? *Trends in Cognitive Sciences, 9*(9), 439–444.

Haritos-Fatouros, M. (1988). The official torturer: A learning model for obedience to the authority of violence. *Journal of Applied Social Psychology, 18*, 1107–1120.

Harmon-Jones, E., & Mills, J. S. (1998). *Cognitive dissonance theory: Revival with revisions and controversies.* Washington, DC: American Psychological Association.

Harries, K. D., & Stadler, S. J. (1988). Heat and violence: New findings from Dallas field data, 1980–1981. *Journal of Applied Social Psychology, 18*, 129–138.

Harrigan, J. A., & O'Connell, D. M. (1996). How do you feel when feeling anxious? Facial displays of anxiety. *Personality and Individual Differences, 21*, 205–212.

Harris, C. R., & Pashler, H. (2004). Attention and the processing of emotional words and names: Not so special after all. *Psychological Science, 15*, 171–178.

Harris, M. (1974). Mediators between frustration and aggression in a field experiment. *Journal of Experimental and Social Psychology, 10*, 561–571.

Harris, M. (1986). Helping the person with an altered self-image. *Geriatric Nursing, 7*, 90–92.

Harris, M. (2008). How do I love thee? Let me do the chores. *Winnipeg Free Press*, p. A16.

Harris, M. B., Benson, S. M., & Hall, C. (1975). The effects of confession on altruism. *Journal of Social Psychology, 96*, 187–192.

Harris, P. (1996). Sufficient grounds for optimism? The relationship between perceived controllability and optimistic bias. *Journal of Social and Clinical Psychology, 15*, 9–52.

Harrison, J. A., & Wells, R. B. (1991). Bystander effects on male helping behavior: Social comparison and diffusion of responsibility. *Representative Research in Social Psychology, 19*, 53–63.

Harrison, L. A., & Abrishami, G. (2004). Dating violence attributions: Do they differ for in-group and out-group members who have a history of dating violence? *Sex Roles, 51*, 543–550.

Hart, A. J., & Morry, M. M. (1997). Trait inferences based on racial and behavioral cues. *Basic & Applied Social Psychology, 19,* 33–48.

Hart, D., & Damon, W. (1986). Developmental trends in self-understanding. *Social Cognition, 4,* 388–407.

Hartshorne, H., & May, M. A. (1929). *Studies in the nature of character: Studies in service and self-control.* (Vol. 2.) New York: Macmillan.

Hartstone, M., & Augoustinos, M. (1995). The minimal group paradigm: Categorization into two versus three groups. *European Journal of Social Psychology, 25,* 179–193.

Hartup, W. W., & Laursen, B. (1999). Relationships as developmental contexts: Retrospective themes and contemporary issues. In W. A. Collins & B. Laursen (Eds.), *Relationships as developmental contexts: Minnesota Symposia on Child Psychology.* (Vol. 30, pp. 13–35.) Mahwah, NJ: Erlbaum.

Hartup, W. W., & Stevens, N. (1997). Friendships and adaptation in the life course. *Psychological Bulletin, 121,* 355–370.

Hassin, R. R., Uleman, J. S., & Bargh, J. A. (Eds.) (2005). *The new unconscious.* New York: Oxford University Press.

Hastie, R., & Pennington, N. (2000). Explanation-based decision making. In T. Connolly & H. R. Arkes (Eds.), *Judgment and decision making: An interdisciplinary reader.* (2nd ed., pp. 212–228.) New York: Cambridge University Press.

Hastie, R., Penrod, S. D., & Pennington, N. (1983). *Inside the jury.* Cambridge, MA: Harvard University Press.

Hatfield, E., Greenberger, E., Traupmann, J., & Lambert, P. (1982). Equity and sexual satisfaction in recently married couples. *Journal of Sex Research, 18,* 18–32.

Hatfield, E., & Rapson, R. L. (1993). *Love, sex, and intimacy: Their psychology, biology, and history.* New York: HarperCollins.

Hatfield, E., & Rapson, R. L. (1996). *Love and sex: Cross-cultural perspectives.* Needham Heights, MA: Allyn & Bacon.

Hatfield, E., & Rapson, R. L. (2002). Passionate love and sexual desire: Cultural and historical perspectives. In A. L. Vangelisti, H. T. Reis, & M. A. Fitzpatrick (Eds.), *Stability and change in relationships.* (pp. 306–324.) New York: Cambridge University Press.

Hatfield, E., & Sprecher, S. (1986a). *Mirror, mirror: The importance of looks in everyday life.* Albany, NY: State University of New York Press.

Hatfield, E., & Sprecher, S. (1986b). Measuring passionate love in intimate relationships. *Journal of Adolescence, 9,* 383–410.

Hatfield, E., & Sprecher, S. (1995). Men's and women's preferences in marital partners in the United States, Russia, and Japan. *Journal of Cross-Cultural Psychology, 26,* 728–750.

Hatfield, E., & Walster, G. W. (1978). *A new look at love.* Reading, MA: Addison-Wesley.

Haugtvedt, C. P., & Wegener, D. T. (1994). Message order effects in persuasion: An attitude strength perspective. *Journal of Consumer Research, 21,* 205–218.

Hawa, R., Munro, B. E., & Doherty-Poirier, M. (1998). Information, motivation and behaviour as predictors of AIDS risk reduction among Canadian first-year university students. *Canadian Journal of Human Sexuality, 7,* 9–18.

Hazan, C., & Shaver, P. (1987). Romantic love conceptualized as an attachment process. *Journal of Personality and Social Psychology, 52,* 511–524.

Hébert, Y., Bernard, J., deMan, A. F., & Farrar, D. (1989). Factors related to the use of condoms among French-Canadian university students. *Journal of Social Psychology, 129,* 707–709.

Hebl, M., Foster, J., Bigazzi, J., Mannix, L., & Dovidio, J. (2002). Formal and interpersonal discrimination: A field study of bias toward homosexual applicants. *Personality and Social Psychology Bulletin, 28,* 815–825.

Heckhausen, J., & Schulz, R. (1995). A life-span theory of control. *Psychological Review, 102,* 284–304.

Hedge, A., & Yousif, Y. H. (1992). Effects of urban size, urgency, and cost on helpfulness. *Journal of Cross-Cultural Psychology, 23,* 107–115.

Heider, F. (1958). The psychology of interpersonal relations. New York: Wiley.

Heine, S. J. (2001). Self as cultural product: An examination of East Asian and North American selves. *Journal of Personality, 69,* 881–906.

Heine, S. J. (2003). Making sense of East Asian self-enhancement. *Journal of Cross-Cultural Psychology, 34,* 596–602.

Heine, S. J. (2005). Where is the evidence for pancultural self-enhancement? A reply to Sedikides, Gaertner, and Toguchi (2003). *Journal of Personality and Social Psychology, 89,* 531–538.

Heine, S. J. (2008). *Cultural Psychology.* New York: Norton.

Heine, S. J., Buchtel, E. E. (in press). Personality: The universal and the culturally specific. *Annual Review of Psychology.*

Heine, S. J., Buchtel, E. E., & Norenzayan, A. (2008). What do cross-national comparisons of personality tell us? *Psychological Science, 19,* 309–313.

Heine, S. J., & Hamamura, T. (2007). In search of East Asian self-enhancement. *Personality and Social Psychology Review, 11,* 1–24.

Heine, S. J., Kitayama, S., & Lehman, D. R. (2001). Cultural differences in self-evaluation: Japanese readily accept negative self-relevant information. *Journal of Cross-Cultural Psychology, 32,* 434–443.

Heine, S. J., & Lehman, D. R. (1995). Cultural variation in unrealistic optimism: Does the West feel more vulnerable than the East? *Journal of Personality and Social Psychology, 68,* 595–607.

Heine, S. J., & Lehman, D. R. (1997a). Culture, dissonance, and self-affirmation. *Personality and Social Psychology Bulletin, 23,* 389–400.

Heine, S. J., & Lehman, D. R. (1997b). The cultural construction of self-enhancement: An examination of group serving biases. *Journal of Personality and Social Psychology, 72,* 1268–1283.

Heine, S. J., & Lehman, D. R. (1999). Culture, self-discrepancies, and self-satisfaction. *Personality and Social Psychology Bulletin, 25,* 915–925.

Heine, S. J., Lehman, D. R., Markus, H. R., & Kitayama, S. (1999). Is there a universal need for positive self-regard? *Psychological Review, 106,* 766–794.

Heine, S. J., Lehman, D. R., Peng, K., & Greenholtz, J. (2002). What's wrong with cross-cultural comparisons of subjective Likert scales? The reference-group effect. *Journal of Personality and Social Psychology, 82,* 903–918.

Heine, S. J., Proulx, T., & Vohs, K. D. (2006). The meaning maintenance model: On the coherence of social motivations. *Personality and Social Psychology Review, 10,* 88–110.

Heine, S. J., & Raineri, A. (in press). Self-improving motivations and collectivism: The case of Chileans. *Journal of Cross-Cultural Psychology.*

Heine, S. J., & Renshaw, K. (2002). Interjudge agreement, self-enhancement, and liking: Cross-cultural perspectives. *Personality and Social Psychology Bulletin, 28,* 578–587.

Heine, S. J., Takata, T., & Lehman, D. R. (2000). Beyond self-presentation: Evidence for self-criticism among Japanese. *Personality and Social Psychology Bulletin, 26,* 71–78.

Hejmadi, A., Davidson, R. J., & Rozin, P. (2000). Exploring Hindu Indian emotion expressions: Evidence for accurate recognition by Americans and Indians. *Psychological Science, 11,* 183–187.

Helgeson, V. S. (1994). The effects of self-beliefs and relationship beliefs on adjustment to a relationship stressor. *Personal Relationships, 1,* 241–258.

Helgeson, V. S. (2003). Cognitive adaptation, psychological adjustment, and disease progression among angioplasty patents: 4 years later. *Health Psychology, 22,* 30–38.

Helgeson, V. S., & Cohen, S. (1996). Social support and adjustment to cancer: Reconciling descriptive, correlational, and intervention research. *Health Psychology, 15,* 135–148.

Helgeson, V. S., & Fritz, H. L. (1999). Cognitive adaptation as a predictor of new coronary events after percutaneous transluminal coronary angioplasty. *Psychosomatic Medicine, 61,* 488–495.

Hemenover, S. H. (2003). The good, the bad, and the healthy: Impacts of emotional disclosure of trauma on resilient self-concept and psychological distress. *Personality and Social Psychology Bulletin, 29*:10, 1236–1244.

Henderson-King, E., & Nisbett, R. E. (1996). Anti-black prejudice as a function of exposure to the negative behavior of a single black person. *Journal of Personality and Social Psychology, 71*, 654–664.

Hendrick, S. S., & Hendrick, C. (1986). A theory and method of love. *Journal of Personality and Social Psychology, 50*, 392–402.

Hendrick, S. S., & Hendrick, C. (1995). Gender differences and similarities in sex and love. *Personal Relationships, 4*, 281–297.

Hendrick, S. S, Hendrick, C., & Adler, N. L. (1988). Romantic relationships: Love, satisfaction, and staying together. *Journal of Personality and Social Psychology, 54*, 980–988.

Henley, N. M. (1977). *Body politics: Power, sex, and nonverbal communication.* Englewood Cliffs, NJ: Prentice Hall.

Henry, R. A. (1995). Using relative confidence judgments to evaluate group effectiveness. *Basic and Applied Social Psychology, 16*, 333–350.

Herold, E. S., & Mewhinney, D. (1993). Gender differences in casual sex and AIDS prevention: A survey of dating bars. *Journal of Sex Research, 30*, 36–42.

Hersh, S. M. (1970). *My Lai 4: A report on the massacre and its aftermath.* New York: Vintage Books.

Hersh, S. M. (2004, April 30). Annals of National Security: Torture at Abu Ghraib, *The New Yorker.* www.newyorker.com/fact/content/?040510fa_fact. Accessed October 2005.

Hess, U., & Blairy, S. (2001). Facial mimicry and emotional contagion to dynamic emotional facial expressions and their influence on decoding accuracy. *International Journal of Psychophysiology, 40*, 129–141.

Hess, U., Philippot, P., & Blairy, S. (1998). Facial reactions to emotional facial expressions: Affect or cognition? *Cognition and Emotion, 12*, 509–531.

Heuer, L., Penrod, S., Hafer, C. L., & Cohn, I. (2002). The role of resource and relational concerns for procedural justice. *Personality and Social Psychology Bulletin, 28*(11), 1468–1482.

Heunemann, R. L., Shapiro, L. R., Hampton, M. C., & Mitchell, B. W. (1966). A longitudinal study of gross body composition and body conformation and their association with food and activity in the teenage population. *American Journal of Clinical Nutrition, 18*, 325–338.

Hewstone, M., & Jaspars, J. (1987). Covariation and causal attribution: A logical model of the intuitive analysis of variance. *Journal of Personality and Social Psychology, 53*, 663–672.

Higgins, E. T. (1987). Self-discrepancy: A theory relating self and affect. *Psychological Review, 94*, 319–340.

Higgins, E. T. (1989). Self-discrepancy theory: What patterns of self-beliefs cause people to suffer? In L. Berkowitz (Ed.), *Advances in experimental social psychology.* (Vol. 22, pp. 93–136.) New York: Academic Press.

Higgins, E. T. (1996). Knowledge application: Accessibility, applicability, and salience. In E. T. Higgins and A. R. Kruglanski (Eds.), *Social psychology: Handbook of basic principles.* (pp. 133–168.) New York: Guilford.

Higgins, E. T. (1997). Beyond pleasure and pain. *American Psychologist, 52*, 1280–1300.

Higgins, E. T. (1998). Promotion and prevention: Regulatory focus as a motivational principle. In M. P. Zanna (Ed.), *Advances in experimental social psychology.* (Vol. 30, pp. 1–46.) San Diego, CA: Academic Press.

Higgins, E. T. (1999). Self-discrepancy: A theory relating self and affect. In R. F. Baumeister (Ed.), *The self in social psychology.* (pp. 150–181.) Philadelphia: Psychology Press.

Higgins, E. T. (2005). Value from regulatory fit. *Current Directions in Psychological Science, 14*, 209–213.

Higgins, E. T., & Bargh, J. A. (1987). Social cognition and social perception. *Annual Review of Psychology, 38*, 369–425.

Higgins, E. T., Bond, R. N., Klein, R., & Strauman, T. (1986). Self-discrepancies and emotional vulnerability: How magnitude, accessibility, and type of discrepancy influence affect. *Journal of Personality and Social Psychology, 51*, 5–15.

Higgins, E. T., & Brendl, C. M. (1995). Accessibility and applicability: Some "activation rules" influencing judgment. *Journal of Experimental Social Psychology, 31*, 218–243.

Higgins, E. T., Klein, R., & Strauman, T. (1987). Self-discrepancies: Distinguishing among self-states, self-state conflicts, and emotional vulnerabilities. In K. M. Yardley & T. M. Honess (Eds.), *Self and identity: Psychosocial perspectives.* (pp. 173–186.) New York: Wiley.

Higgins, E. T., Rholes, W. S., & Jones, C. R. (1977). Category accessibility and impression formation. *Journal of Experimental Social Psychology, 13*, 141–154.

Hill, A. J., Boudreau, F., Amyot, E., Dery, D., & Godin, G. (1997). Predicting the stages of smoking acquisition according to the theory of planned behavior. *Journal of Adolescent Health, 21*, 107–115.

Hill, A. J., Oliver, S., & Rogers, P. J. (1992). Eating in the adult world: The rise of dieting in childhood and adolescence. *British Journal of Clinical Psychology, 31*, 95–105.

Hill, E., & Pfeifer, J. E. (1992). Nullification instructions and juror guilt ratings: An examination of modern racism. *Contemporary Social Psychology, 16*, 6–10.

Hilton, A., Potvin, L., & Sachdev, I. (1989). Ethnic relations in rental housing: A social psychological approach. *Canadian Journal of Behavioural Science, 21*, 121–131.

Hirt, E. R., Kardes, F. R., & Markman, K. D. (2004). Activating a mental simulation mind-set through generation of alternatives: Implications for debiasing in related and unrelated domains. *Journal of Experimental Social Psychology, 40*(3), 374–383.

Hoaken, P. N. S., & Pihl, R. O. (2000). The effects of alcohol intoxication on aggressive responses in men and women. *Alcohol and Alcoholism, 35*, 471–477.

Hobbes, T. (1986 [1651]). *Leviathan.* Harmondsworth, UK: Penguin Press.

Hobden, K. L., & Olson, J. M. (1994). From jest to antipathy: Disparagement humor as a source of dissonance-motivated attitude change. *Basic and Applied Social Psychology, 15*, 239–249.

Hochstadt, S. (1999). *Mobility and modernity: Migration in Germany, 1820–1989.* Ann Arbor, MI: University of Michigan Press.

Hodges, B. H., & Geyer, A. L. (2006). A nonconformist account of the Asch experiments: Values, pragmatics, and moral dilemmas. *Personality and Social Psychology Review, 10*, 2–19.

Hodson, G., & Esses, V. M. (2002). Distancing oneself from negative attributes and the personal/group discrimination discrepancy. *Journal of Experimental Social Psychology, 38*, 500–507.

Hodson, G., & Esses, V. M. (2005). Lay perceptions of ethnic prejudice: Causes, solutions, and individual differences. *European Journal of Social Psychology, 35*, 329–344.

Hodson, G., & Olson, J. M. (2005). Testing the generality of the name letter effect: Name initials and everyday attitudes. *Personality and Social Psychology Bulletin, 31*, 1099–1111.

Hodson, G., & Sorrentino, R. M. (1997). Groupthink and uncertainty orientation: Personality differences in reactivity to the group situation. *Group Dynamics, 1*, 144–155.

Hodson, R. (2004). A meta-analysis of workplace ethnographies: Race, gender, and employee attitudes and behavior. *Journal of Contemporary Ethnography, 33*, 4–38.

Hoffman, A. J., Gillespie, J. J., Moore, D. A., Wade-Benzoni, K. A., Thompson, L. L., & Bazerman, M. H. (1999). A mixed-motive perspective on the economics versus environmental debate. *American Behavioral Scientist, 42*, 1254–1276.

Hoffman, C., Lau, I., & Johnson, D. R. (1986). The linguistic relativity of person cognition: An English-Chinese comparison. *Journal of Personality and Social Psychology, 51*, 1097–1105.

Hoffman, H. G., Granhag, P. A., See, S. T. K., & Loftus, E. F. (2001). Social influences on reality-monitoring decisions. *Memory and Cognition, 29*, 394–404.

Hoffman, M. L. (1981). Is altruism a part of human nature? *Journal of Personality and Social Psychology, 40,* 121–137.

Hofmann, W., Gawronski, B., Gschwendner, T., Le, H., & Schmitt, M. (2005). A meta-analysis on the correlation between the Implicit Association Test and explicit self-report measures. *Personality and Social Psychology Bulletin, 31,* 1369–1385.

Hofstede, G. (1984). *Culture's consequences: International differences in work-related values.* Newbury Park, CA: Sage.

Hofstede, G. (1986). Cultural differences in teaching and learning. *International Journal of Intercultural Relations, 10,* 301–320.

Hogg, M. A. (1992). *The social psychology of group cohesiveness: From attraction to social identity.* London, UK: Harvester-Wheatsheaf.

Hogg, M. A. (1993). Group cohesiveness: A critical review and some new directions. In W. Stroebe & M. Hewstone (Eds.), *European review of social psychology.* (Vol. 4, pp. 85–111.) Chichester, UK: Wiley.

Hogg, M. A. (2001). A social identity theory of leadership. *Personality and Social Psychology Review, 5,* 184–200.

Hogg, M. A., & Hains, S. C. (1998). Friendship and group identification: A new look at the role of cohesiveness in groupthink. *European Journal of Social Psychology, 28,* 323–341.

Hollander, E. P. (1958). Conformity, status, and idiosyncrasy credit. *Psychological Review, 65,* 117–127.

Hollander, E. P. (1960). Competence and conformity in the acceptance of influence. *Journal of Abnormal and Social Psychology, 61,* 361–365.

Hollander, E. P. (1985). Leadership and power. In G. Lindzey & E. Aronson (Eds.), *Handbook of social psychology.* (3rd ed., Vol. 2, pp. 485–537.) New York: McGraw-Hill.

Hollingshead, A. B. (2001). Cognitive interdependence and convergent expectations in transactive memory. *Journal of Personality and Social Psychology, 81,* 1080–1089.

Holmberg, D., & MacKenzie, S. (2002). So far so good: Scripts for romantic relationship development as predictors of relational well-being. *Journal of Social and Personal Relationships, 19,* 777–796.

Holmes, J. G., Miller, D. T., & Lerner, M. J. (2002). Committing altruism under the cloak of self-interest: The exchange fiction. *Journal of Experimental Social Psychology, 38,* 144–151.

Holmes, T. H., & Rahe, R. H. (1967). The social readjustment rating scale. *Journal of Psychosomatic Research, 11,* 213–218.

Holtz, R. (1997). Length of group membership, assumed similarity, and opinion certainty: The dividend for veteran members. *Journal of Applied Social Psychology, 27,* 539–555.

Holtz, R. (2004). Group cohesion, attitude projection, and opinion certainty: Beyond interaction. *Group Dynamics: Theory, Research, and Practice, 8,* 112–125.

Homans, G. C. (1961). *Social behavior: Its elementary forms.* New York: Harcourt Brace & World.

Honts, C. R. (1994). Psychophysiological detection of deception. *Current Directions in Psychological Science, 3,* 77–82.

Hornsey, M. J., & Jetten, J. (2004). The individual within the group: Balancing the need to belong with the need to be different. *Personality and Social Psychology Review, 8,* 248–264.

Hornsey, M. J., & Jetten, J. (2005). Loyalty without conformity: Tailoring self-perception as a means of balancing belonging and differentiation. *Self and Identity, 4,* 81–95.

Hornsey, M. J., Jetten, J., McAuliffe, B. J., & Hogg, M. A. (2006). The impact of individualist and collectivist group norms on evaluations of dissenting group members. *Journal of Experimental Social Psychology, 42,* 57–68.

Hoshino-Browne, E., Zanna, A. S., Spencer, S. J., Zanna, M. P., Kitayama, S., & Lackenbauer, S. (2005). On the cultural guises of cognitive dissonance: The case of easterners and westerners. *Journal of Personality and Social Psychology, 89,* 294–310.

House, J. S., Robbins, C., & Metzner, H. L. (1982). The association of social relationships and activities with mortality: Prospective evidence from the Tecumseh Community Health Study. *American Journal of Epidemiology, 116,* 123–140.

House, R. J. (1971). A path-goal theory of leadership effectiveness. *Administrative Science Quarterly, 16,* 321–338.

Hovland, C. I., Janis, I. L., & Kelley, H. H. (1953). *Communication and persuasion: Psychological studies of opinion change.* New Haven, CT: Yale University Press.

Hovland, C. I., & Sears, R. R. (1940). Minor studies in aggression: 6. Correlation of lynchings with economic indices. *Journal of Psychology, 9,* 301–310.

Hovland, C. I., & Weiss, W. (1951). The influence of source credibility on communication effectiveness. *Public Opinion Quarterly, 15,* 635–650.

Howard, D. E., & Wang, M. Q. (2003). Risk profiles of adolescent girls who were victims of dating violence. *Adolescence, 38,* 1–14.

Hsu, S. S. (1995, April 8). Fredericksburg searches its soul after clerk is beaten as 6 watch. *Washington Post,* pp. A1, A13.

Huesmann, L. R., & Miller, L. S. (1994). Long-term effects of repeated exposure to media violence in childhood. In L. R. Huesmann (Ed.), *Aggressive behavior: Current perspectives.* (pp. 153–186.) New York: Plenum.

Huffman, K. T., Grossnickle, W. F., Cope, J. G., & Huffman, K. P. (1995). Litter reduction: A review and integration of the literature. *Environment and Behavior, 27,* 153–183.

Huguet, P., Galvaing, M. P., Monteil, J. M., & Dumas, F. (1999). Social presence effects in the Stroop task: Further evidence for an attentional view of social facilitation. *Journal of Personality and Social Psychology, 77,* 1011–1025.

Hui, C. H., & Triandis, H. C. (1986). Individualism-collectivism: A study of cross-cultural researchers. *Journal of Cross-Cultural Psychology, 17,* 225–248.

Hull, J. G. (1981). A self-awareness model of the causes and effects of alcohol consumption. *Journal of Personality and Social Psychology, 90,* 586–600.

Hull, J. G., & Young, R. D. (1983). Self-consciousness, self-esteem, and success-failure as determinants of alcohol consumption in male social drinkers. *Journal of Personality and Social Psychology, 44,* 1097–1109.

Hull, J. G., Young, R. D., & Jouriles, E. (1986). Applications of the self-awareness model of alcohol consumption: Predicting patterns of use and abuse. *Journal of Personality and Social Psychology, 51,* 790–796.

Hunsberger, B. (1995). Religion and prejudice: The role of religious fundamentalism, quest, and right-wing authoritarianism. *Journal of Social Issues, 51,* 113–129.

Hunsberger, B. (1996). Religious fundamentalism, right-wing authoritarianism and hostility toward homosexuals in non-Christian religious groups. *International Journal for the Psychology of Religion, 6,* 39–49.

Hunt, G. T. (1940). *The wars of the Iroquois.* Madison, WI: University of Wisconsin Press.

Hurley, D., & Allen, B. P. (1974). The effect of the number of people present in a nonemergency situation. *Journal of Social Psychology, 92,* 27–29.

Hutchinson, R. R. (1983). The pain-aggression relationship and its expression in naturalistic settings. *Aggressive Behavior, 9,* 229–242.

Hynie, M., & Lydon, J. E. (1995). Women's perceptions of female contraceptive behavior: Experimental evidence of the sexual double standard. *Psychology of Women Quarterly, 19,* 563–581.

Hynie, M., & Lydon, J. E. (1996). Sexual attitudes and contraceptive behavior revisited: Can there be too much of a good thing? *Journal of Sex Research, 33,* 127–134.

Hynie, M., Lydon, J. E., Cote, S., & Wiener, S. (1998). Relational sexual scripts and women's condom use: The importance of internalized norms. *Journal of Sex Research, 35,* 370–380.

Hynie, M., MacDonald, T. K., & Marques, S. (2006). Self-conscious emotions and self-regulation in the promotion of condom use. *Personality and Social Psychology Bulletin, 32,* 1072–1084.

Iacono, W. G. (2000). The detection of deception. In J. T. Cacioppo & L. G. Tassinary (Eds.), *Handbook of psychophysiology.* (2nd ed., pp. 772–793.) New York: Cambridge University Press.

Iacono, W. G., & Patrick, C. J. (1999). Polygraph ("lie detector") testing: The state of the art. In A. K. Hess & I. B. Weiner (Eds.), *The handbook of forensic psychology*. (2nd ed., pp. 440–473.) New York: Wiley.

Igou, E. R., & Bless, H. (2003). Inferring the importance of arguments: Order effects and conversational rules. *Journal of Experimental Social Psychology, 39*, 91–99.

Ickes, W., Patterson, M. L., Rajecki, D. W., & Tanford, S. (1982). Behavioral and cognitive consequences of reciprocal versus compensatory responses to preinteraction expectancies. *Social Cognition, 1*, 160–190.

Inglehart, M. R. (1991). *Reactions to critical life events: A social psychological analysis*. New York: Praeger.

Insko, C. A., & Schopler, J. (1998). Differential trust of groups and individuals. In C. Sedikides & J. Schopler (Eds.), *Intergroup cognition and intergroup behavior*. (pp. 75–107.) Mahwah, NJ: Erlbaum.

Intrieri, R. C., & Morse, J. M. (1997). A sequential analysis of verbal and nonverbal interaction of two long-term care residents. *Journal of Applied Gerontology, 16*, 477–494.

Inzlicht, M., Aronson, J., Good, C., & McKay, L. (2006). A particular resiliency to threatening environments. *Journal of Experimental Social Psychology, 42*(3), 323–336.

Isen, A. M. (1987). Positive affect, cognitive processes, and social behavior. In L. Berkowitz (Ed.), *Advances in experimental social psychology*. (Vol. 20, pp. 203–253.) San Diego, CA: Academic Press.

Isen, A. M. (1999). Positive affect. In T. Dalgleish & M. J. Power (Eds.), *Handbook of cognition and emotion*. (pp. 521–539.) Chichester, UK: Wiley.

Isen, A. M., & Levin, P. A. (1972). Effect of feeling good on helping: Cookies and kindness. *Journal of Personality and Social Psychology, 21*, 384–388.

Isenberg, D. J. (1986). Group polarization: A critical review and meta-analysis. *Journal of Personality and Social Psychology, 50*, 1141–1151.

Iwata, O. (1992). A comparative study of person perception and friendly altruistic behavior intentions between Canadian and Japanese undergraduates. In S. Iwawaki, Y. Kashima, & K. Leving (Eds.), *Innovations in cross cultural psychology*. Amsterdam, Netherlands: Swets & Zeitlinger.

Izard, C. E. (1994). Innate and universal facial expressions: Evidence from developmental and cross-cultural research. *Psychological Bulletin, 115*, 288–299.

Jackson, E. L. (1985). Environmental attitudes and preferences for energy resource options. *Journal of Environmental Education, 17*, 23–30.

Jackson, E. L. (1987). Outdoor recreation participation and views on resource development and preservation. *Leisure Sciences, 9*, 235–250.

Jackson, J. (1981, July 19). Syndicated newspaper column.

Jackson, J. M., & Williams, K. D. (1985). Social loafing on difficult tasks: Working collectively can improve performance. *Journal of Personality and Social Psychology, 49*, 937–942.

Jackson, J. S., Brown, T. N., Williams, D. R., Torres, M., Sellers, S. L., & Brown, K. (1996). Racism and the physical and mental health status of African Americans: A thirteen-year national panel study. *Ethnicity and Disease, 6*, 132–147.

Jackson, J. S., & Inglehart, M. R. (1995). Reverberation theory: Stress and racism in hierarchically structured communities. In S. E. Hobfoll & M. W. de Vries (Eds.), *Extreme stress and communities: Impact and intervention*. (pp. 353–373.) Dordrecht, Netherlands: Kluwer Academic Publishers.

Jackson, J. W. (1993). Realistic group conflict theory: A review and evaluation of the theoretical and empirical literature. *Psychological Record, 43*, 395–413.

Jackson, L. A. (1992). *Physical appearance and gender: Socio-biological and sociocultural perspectives*. Albany, NY: State University of New York Press.

Jackson, L. A., Hunter, J. E., & Hodge, C. N. (1995). Physical attractiveness and intellectual competence: A meta-analytic review. *Social Psychology Quarterly, 58*, 108–122.

Jackson, L. M., & Esses, V. M. (1997). Of scripture and ascription: The relation between religious fundamentalism and intergroup helping. *Personality and Social Psychology Bulletin, 23*, 893–906.

Jacobs, P., & Landau, S. (1971). *To serve the devil*. (Vol. 2, p. 71.) New York: Vintage Books.

Jain, S. P., & Posavac, S. S. (2001). Prepurchase attribute verifiability, source credibility, and persuasion. *Journal of Consumer Psychology, 11*(3), 169–180.

James, J. M., & Bolstein, R. (1992). Large monetary incentives and their effect on mail survey response rates. *Public Opinion Quarterly, 56*, 442–453.

James, W. (1890). *The principles of psychology*. New York: Holt.

Jamieson, D. W., Lydon, J. E., & Zanna, M. P. (1987). Attitude and activity preference similarity: Differential bases of interpersonal attraction for low and high self-monitors. *Journal of Personality and Social Psychology, 53*, 1052–1060.

Janes, L. M., & Olson, J. M. (2000). Jeer pressure: The behavioral effects of observing ridicule of others. *Personality and Social Psychology Bulletin, 26*, 474–485.

Janicik, G. A., & Larrick, R. P. (2005). Social network schemas and the learning of incomplete networks. *Journal of Personality and Social Psychology, 88*, 348–364.

Janis, I. L. (1972). *Victims of groupthink*. Boston, MA: Houghton Mifflin.

Janis, I. L. (1982). *Groupthink*. (2nd ed.) Boston, MA: Houghton Mifflin.

Janis, I. L., & Feshbach, S. (1953). Effects of fear-arousing communications. *Journal of Abnormal and Social Psychology, 49*, 78–92.

Jankowiak, W. (1995). Introduction. In W. Jankowiak (Ed.), *Romantic passion: A universal experience?* (pp. 1–19.) New York: Columbia University Press.

Jankowiak, W. R., & Fischer, E. F. (1992). A cross-cultural perspective on romantic love. *Ethnology, 31*, 149–155.

Janzen, L. (2001, May 13). Police photos, lineups faulted in Sophonow case. *Winnipeg Free Press*, p. A3.

Jecker, J., & Landy, D. (1969). Liking a person as a function of doing him a favor. *Human Relations, 22*, 371–378.

Jepson, C., & Chaiken, S. (1990). Chronic issue-specific fear inhibits systematic processing of persuasive communications. *Journal of Social Behavior and Personality, 5*, 61–84.

Job, R. F. S. (1988). Effective and ineffective use of fear in health promotion campaigns. *American Journal of Public Health, 78*, 163–167.

Johns, M., Schmader, T., & Martens, A. (2005). Knowing is half the battle: Teaching stereotype threat as a means of improving women's math performance. *Psychological Science, 16*, 175–179.

Johnson, D. W., & Johnson, R. T. (1987). *Learning together and alone: Cooperative, competitive, and individualistic learning*. (2nd ed.) Englewood Cliffs, NJ: Prentice Hall.

Johnson, D. W., & Johnson, R. T. (1989). *A meta-analysis of cooperative, competitive, and individualistic goal structures*. Hillsdale, NJ: Erlbaum.

Johnson, H. (2001). Contrasting views of the role of alcohol in cases of wife assault. *Journal of Interpersonal Violence, 16*, 54–72.

Johnson, J. G., Cohen, P., Smailes, E. M., Kasen, S., & Brook, J. (2002). Television viewing and aggressive behavior during adolescence and adulthood. *Science, 295*, 2468–2471.

Johnson, K. J., & Fredrickson, B. L. (2005). We all look the same to me: Positive emotions eliminate the own-race bias in face recognition. *Psychological Science, 16*, 875–881.

Johnson, M. K., Hashtroudi, S., & Lindsay, D. S. (1993). Source monitoring. *Psychological Bulletin, 114*, 3–28.

Johnson, M. K., & Raye, C. L. (1981). Reality monitoring. *Psychological Review, 88*, 67–85.

Johnson, M. K., Raye, C. L., Wang, A. Y., & Taylor, T. H. (1979). Fact and fantasy: The roles of accuracy and variability in confusing imaginations with perceptual experiences. *Journal of Experimental Psychology: Human Learning and Memory, 5*, 229–240.

Johnson, R. D., & Downing, R. L. (1979). Deindividuation and valence of cues: Effects of prosocial and antisocial behavior. *Journal of Personality and Social Psychology, 37,* 1532–1538.

Johnson, T. E., & Rule, B. G. (1986). Mitigating circumstance information, censure, and aggression. *Journal of Personality and Social Psychology, 50,* 537–542.

Joiner, Jr., T. E., & Wagner, K. D. (1995). Attributional style and depression in children and adolescents: A meta-analytic review. *Clinical Psychology Review, 15,* 777–798.

Johnson, W., & Krueger, R. F. (2005). Higher perceived life control decreases genetic variance in physical health: Evidence from a national twin study. *Journal of Personality and Social Psychology, 88,* 165–173.

Jonas, E., Schimel, J., Greenberg, J., & Pyszczynski, T. (2002). The scrooge effect: Evidence that mortality salience increases prosocial attitudes and behavior. *Personality and Social Psychology Bulletin, 28*(10), 1342–1353.

Jones, D., & Hill, K. (1993). Criteria of facial attractiveness in five populations. *Human Nature, 4,* 271–296.

Jones, E. E. (1979). The rocky road from acts to dispositions. *American Scientist, 34,* 107–117.

Jones, E. E. (1990). *Interpersonal perception.* New York: Freeman.

Jones, E. E., & Davis, K. E. (1965). From acts to dispositions: The attribution process in social psychology. In L. Berkowitz (Ed.), *Advances in experimental social psychology.* (Vol. 2, pp. 219–266.) New York: Academic Press.

Jones, E. E., & Harris, V. A. (1967). The attribution of attitudes. *Journal of Experimental Social Psychology, 3,* 1–24.

Jones, E. E., & Nisbett, R. E. (1972). The actor and the observer: Divergent perceptions of the causes of behavior. In E. E. Jones, D. E. Kanouse, H. H. Kelley, R. E. Nisbett, S. Valins, & B. Weiner (Eds.), *Attribution: Perceiving the causes of behavior.* (pp. 79–94.) Morristown, NJ: General Learning Press.

Jones, L. W., Sinclair, R. W., & Courneya, K. S. (2003). The effects of source credibility and message framing on exercise intentions, behavior and attitudes: An integration of the elaboration likelihood model and prospect theory. *Journal of Applied Social Psychology, 33,* 179–196.

Jordan, C. H., Spencer, S. J., & Zanna, M. P. (2005). Types of high self-esteem and prejudice: How implicit self-esteem relates to ethnic discrimination among high explicit self-esteem individuals. *Personality and Social Psychology Bulletin, 31,* 693–702.

Jordan, C. H., Whitfield, M., & Zeigler-Hill, V. (2007). Intuition and the correspondence between implicit and explicit self-esteem. *Journal of Personality and Social Psychology, 93,* 1067–1079.

Josephson, W. (1987). Television violence and children's aggression: Testing the priming, social script, and disinhibition prediction. *Journal of Personality and Social Psychology, 53,* 882–890.

Judd, C. M., & Park, B. (1988). Out-group homogeneity: Judgments of variability at the individual and group levels. *Journal of Personality and Social Psychology, 54,* 778–788.

Judge rules ACLU discrimination suit against Continental Airlines can go forward (2002). www.aclu.org/RacialEquality/RacialEquality.cfm?ID=10994&c=133.

Jürgen-Lohmann, J., Borsch, F., & Giesen, H. (2001). Kooperatives Lernen an der Hochschule: Evaluation des Gruppenpuzzles in Seminaren der Pädagogischen Psychologie. *Zeitschrift für Pädagogische Psychologie, 15,* 74–84.

Jussim, L. (1986). Self-fulfilling prophecies: A theoretical and integrative review. *Psychological Review, 93,* 429–445.

Juveniles committing fewer violent crimes (1997, Oct. 3). *Charlottesville Daily Progress,* pp. A1, A9.

Kahn, M. (1966). The physiology of catharsis. *Journal of Personality and Social Psychology, 3,* 278–298.

Kahn, M. (2008, October 15). "Hippie" apes not all peace and love. *Globe and Mail.* www.theglobeandmail.com/servlet/story/RTGAM.20081015.wbonobo1015/BNStory/Science/home. Accessed October 2008.

Kahneman, D., & Frederick, S. (2002). Representativeness revisited: Attribute substitution in intuitive judgment. In T. Gilovich, D. W. Griffin, & D. Kahneman (Eds). *Heuristics and biases: The psychology of intuitive judgment.* (pp. 49–81.) New York: Cambridge University Press.

Kahneman, D., & Miller, D. T. (1986). Norm theory: Comparing reality to its alternatives. *Psychological Review, 93,* 136–153.

Kahneman, D., & Tversky, A. (1973). On the psychology of prediction. *Psychological Review, 80,* 237–251.

Kahneman, D., & Tversky, A. (1982). The simulation heuristic. In D. Kahneman, P. Slovic, & A. Tversky (Eds.), *Judgment under uncertainty: Heuristics and biases.* (pp. 201–208.) New York: Cambridge University Press.

Kalin, R., & Berry, J. W. (1996). Interethnic attitudes in Canada: Ethnocentrism, consensual hierarchy and reciprocity. *Canadian Journal of Behavioural Sciences, 28,* 253–261.

Kallgren, C. A., Reno, R. R., & Cialdini, R. B. (2000). A focus theory of normative conduct: When norms do and do not affect behavior. *Personality and Social Psychology Bulletin, 26,* 1002–1012.

Kalven, Jr., H., & Zeisel, H. (1966). *The American jury.* Boston, MA: Little, Brown.

Kameda, T., Takezawa, M., & Hastie, R. (2003). The logic of social sharing: An evolutionary game analysis of adaptive norm development. *Personality and Social Psychology Review, 7,* 2–19.

Kammrath, L. K., & Dweck, C. (2006). Voicing conflict: Preferred conflict strategies among incremental and entity theorists. *Personality and Social Psychology Bulletin, 32,* 1497–1508.

Kappas, A. (1997). The fascination with faces: Are they windows to our soul? *Journal of Nonverbal Behavior, 21,* 157–162.

Karau, S. J., & Williams, K. D. (1993). Social loafing: A meta-analytic review and theoretical integration. *Journal of Personality and Social Psychology, 65,* 681–706.

Karau, S. J., & Williams, K. D. (2001). Understanding individual motivation in groups: The collective effort model. In M. E. Turner (Ed.), *Groups at work—theory and research: Applied social research.* (pp. 113–141.) Mahwah, NJ: Erlbaum.

Kassarjian, H., & Cohen, J. (1965). Cognitive dissonance and consumer behavior. *California Management Review, 8,* 55–64.

Kassin, S. M. (2005). On the psychology of confessions: Does innocence put innocents at risk? *American Psychologist, 60,* 215–228.

Kassin, S. M., & Kiechel, K. L. (1996). The social psychology of false confessions: Compliance, internalization, and confabulation. *Psychological Science, Vol 7*(3), May 1996. pp. 125–128.

Katz, D. (1960). The functional approach to the study of attitudes. *Public Opinion Quarterly, 24,* 163–204.

Katz, J., & Joiner, T. E. (2002). Being known, intimate, and valued: Global self-verification and dyadic adjustment in couples and roommates. *Journal of Personality, 70,* 33–58.

Kawakami, K., Dion, K. L., & Dovidio, J. F. (1998). Racial prejudice and stereotype activation. *Personality and Social Psychology Bulletin, 24,* 407–416.

Kawakami, K., Phills, C. E., Steele, J. R., & Dovidio, J. F. (2007). (Close) distance makes the heart grow fonder: Improving implicit racial attitudes and interracial interactions through approach behaviors. *Journal of Personality and Social Psychology, 92,* 957–971.

Kealy, K. L. K., Kuiper, N. A., & Klein, D. N. (2006). Characteristics associated with real and made-up events: The effects of event valence, event elaboration, and individual differences. *Canadian Journal of Behavioural Science, 38,* 158–175.

Kebbell, M. R., & Wagstaff, G. F. (1998). Hypnotic interviewing: The best way to interview eyewitnesses? *Behavioral Sciences and the Law, 16,* 115–129.

Keelan, J. P. R., Dion, K. L., & Dion, K. K. (1994). Attachment style and heterosexual relationships among young adults: A short-term panel study. *Journal of Social and Personal Relationships, 11,* 201–214.

Keenan, J. P., Gallup, G. G.., & Falk, D. (2003). *The face in the mirror: The search for the origins of consciousness.* New York: HarperCollins.

Keller, J., & Dauenheimer, D. (2003). Stereotype threat in the classroom: Dejection mediates the disrupting threat effect on women's math performance. *Personality and Social Psychology Bulletin, 29,* 371–381.

Kelley, H. H. (1950). The warm-cold variable in first impressions of persons. *Journal of Personality, 18,* 431–439.

Kelley, H. H. (1955). The two functions of reference groups. In G. E. Swanson, T. M. Newcomb, & E. L. Hartley (Eds.), *Readings in social psychology.* (2nd ed., pp. 410–414.) New York: Holt.

Kelley, H. H. (1967). Attribution theory in social psychology. In D. Levine (Ed.), *Nebraska Symposium on Motivation.* (Vol. 15, pp. 192–238.) Lincoln, NE: University of Nebraska Press.

Kelley, H. H. (1972). Attribution in social interaction. In E. E. Jones, D. E. Kanouse, H. H. Kelley, R. E. Nisbett, S. Valins, & B. Weiner (Eds.), *Attribution: Perceiving the causes of behavior.* (pp. 1–26.) Morristown, NJ: General Learning Press.

Kelley, H. H. (1973). The process of causal attribution. *American Psychologist, 28,* 107–128.

Kelley, H. H. (1983). Love and commitment. In H. H. Kelley, E. Berscheid, A. Christensen, J. H. Harvey, T. L. Huston, G. Levinger, E. McClintock, L. A. Peplau, & D. R. Peterson (Eds.), *Close relationships.* (pp. 265–314.) New York: Freeman.

Kelley, H. H., & Thibaut, J. (1978). *Interpersonal relations: A theory of interdependence.* New York: Wiley.

Kelly, A. E., Klusas, J. A., von Weiss, R. T., & Kenny, C. (2001). What is it about revealing secrets that is beneficial? *Personality and Social Psychology Bulletin, 27,* 651–665.

Kelly, J. R., & Karau, S. J. (1999). Group decision making: The effects of initial preferences and time pressure. *Personality and Social Psychology Bulletin, 25,* 1342–1354.

Kelman, H. C. (1997). Group processes in the resolution of international conflicts: Experiences from the Israeli–Palestinian case. *American Psychologist, 52,* 212–220.

Keltner, D., & Shiota, M. N. (2003). New displays and new emotions: A commentary on Rozin and Cohen. *Emotion, 3,* 86–91.

Kerr, N. L., & Tindale, R. S. (2004). Groups performance and decision making. *Annual Review of Psychology, 55,* 623–655.

Kenny, D. A. (1994). Using the social relations model to understand relationships. In R. Erber & R. Gilmour (Eds.), *Theoretical Frameworks for Personal Relationships.* (pp. 111–127.) Hillsdale, NJ: Erlbaum.

Kenrick, D. T., & Keefe, R. C. (1992). Age preferences in mates reflect sex differences in human reproductive strategies. *Behavioral and Brain Sciences, 15,* 75–133.

Kenrick, D. T., & MacFarlane, S. W. (1986). Ambient temperature and horn honking: A field study of the heat/aggression relationship. *Environment and Behavior, 18,* 179–191.

Kent, M. V. (1994). The presence of others. In A. P. Hare, H. H. Blumberg, M. F. Davies, & M. V. Kent (Eds.), *Small group research: A handbook.* (pp. 81–105.) Norwood, NJ: Ablex.

Kerr, N. L., & Kaufman-Gilliland, C. M. (1994). Communication, commitment, and cooperation in social dilemmas. *Journal of Personality and Social Psychology, 66,* 513–529.

Kerr, N. L., & Tindale, R. S. (2004). Groups performance and decision making. *Annual Review of Psychology, 55,* 623–655.

Ketelaar, T., & Ellis, B. J. (2000). Are evolutionary explanations unfalsifiable? Evolutionary psychology and the Lakatosian philosophy of science. *Psychological Inquiry, 11,* 1–21.

Key, W. B. (1973). *Subliminal seduction.* Englewood Cliffs, NJ: Signet.

Key, W. B. (1989). *Age of manipulation: The con in confidence and the sin in sincere.* New York: Holt.

Kiesler, C. A., & Kiesler, S. B. (1969). *Conformity.* Reading, MA: Addison-Wesley.

Kihlstrom, J. F. (1987). The cognitive unconscious. *Science, 237,* 1445–1452.

Kihlstrom, J. F. (1996). The trauma-memory argument and recovered memory therapy. In K. Pezdek & W. P. Banks (Eds.), *The recovered memory/false memory debate.* (pp. 297–311.) San Diego, CA: Academic Press.

Kihlstrom, J. F., Beer, J. S., & Klein, S. B. (2003). Self and identity as memory. In M. R. Leary & J. P. Tangney (Eds.), *Handbook of self and identity.* (pp. 68–90.) New York: Guilford Press.

Killen, J. D. (1985). Prevention of adolescent tobacco smoking: The social pressure resistance training approach. *Journal of Child Psychology and Psychiatry, 26,* 7–15.

Kim, M. P., & Rosenberg, S. (1980). Comparison of two structural models of implicit personality theory. *Journal of Personality and Social Psychology, 38,* 375–389.

Kim, U., & Berry, J. W. (1993). *Indigenous psychologies: Research and experience in cultural context.* Newbury Park, CA: Sage.

Kim, U., Triandis, H. C., Kagitcibasi, C., Choi, S. C., & Yoon, G. (Eds.) (1994). *Individualism and collectivism: Theory, method and applications.* Thousand Oaks, CA: Sage.

Kirkpatrick, L. A., & Hazan, C. (1994). Attachment styles and close relationships: A four-year prospective study. *Personal Relationships, 1,* 123–142.

Kitayama, S., & Markus, H. R. (1994). Culture and the self: How cultures influence the way we view ourselves. In D. Matsumoto (Ed.), *People: Psychology from a cultural perspective.* (pp. 17–37.) Pacific Grove, CA: Brooks/Cole.

Kitayama, S., & Uchida, Y. (2005). Interdependent agency: An alternative system for action. In R. M. Sorrentino & D. Cohen (Eds.), *Cultural and social behavior: The Ontario Symposium.* (Vol. 10, pp. 137–164.) Mahwah, NJ: Erlbaum.

Klein, W. M. (1996). Maintaining self-serving social comparisons: Attenuating the perceived significance of risk-increasing behaviors. *Journal of Social and Clinical Psychology, 15,* 120–142.

Kleiner, M. (Ed.) (2002). *Handbook of polygraph testing.* San Diego, CA: Academic Press.

Klenke, K. (1996). *Women and leadership: A contextual perspective.* New York: Springer.

Kliewer, W., Lepore, S. J., & Evans, G. W. (1990). The costs of Type B behavior: Females at risk in achievement situations. *Journal of Applied Social Psychology, 20,* 1369–1382.

Knapp, M. & Hall, J. A. (2006). *Nonverbal communication in human interaction.* Belmont, CA: Thomson Wadsworth.

Knäuper, B., Kornik, R., Atkinson, K., Guberman, C., & Aydin, C. (2005). Motivation influences the underestimation of cumulative risk. *Personality and Social Psychology Bulletin, 31,* 1511–1523.

Knee, C. R., Lonsbary, C., Canevello, A., Patrick, H. (2005). Self-determination and conflict in romantic relationships. *Journal of Personality and Social Psychology, 89,* 997–1009.

Knox, R. E., & Inkster, J. A. (1968). Postdecision dissonance at post time. *Journal of Personality and Social Psychology, 8,* 319–323.

Knussen, C., Yule, F., & MacKenzie, J. (2004). An analysis of intentions to recycle household waste: The roles of past behaviour, perceived habit, and perceived lack of facilities. *Journal of Environmental Psychology, 24,* 237–246.

Koehler, D. J., & Poon, C. S. K. (2006). Self-predictions overweight strength of current intentions. *Journal of Experimental Social Psychology, 42,* 517–524.

Koestner, R., Horberg, E. J., Gaudreau, P., Powers, T., Di Dio, P., Bryan, C., Jochum, R., & Salter, N. (2006). Bolstering implementation plans for the long haul: The benefits of simultaneously boosting self-concordance or self-efficacy. *Personality and Social Psychology Bulletin, 32,* 1547–1558.

Koestner, R., & Losier, G. F. (2002). Distinguishing three ways of being internally motivated: A closer look at introjection, identification, and intrinsic motivation. In E. L. Deci & R. M. Ryan (Eds.), *Handbook of self-determination research.* (pp. 101–121.) Rochester, NY: University of Rochester Press.

Kogan, N., & Wallach, M. A. (1964). *Risk-taking: A study in cognition and personality.* New York: Holt.

Kojetin, B. A. (1993). *Adult attachment styles with romantic partners, friends, and parents.* Unpublished doctoral dissertation, University of Minnesota, Minneapolis.

Kollack, P., Blumstein, P. & Schwartz, P., (1994). The judgment of equity in intimate relationships. *Social Psychology Quarterly, 57,* 340–351.

Koopman, C., Hermanson, K., Diamond, S., Angell, K., & Spiegel, D. (1998). Social support, life stress, pain and emotional adjustment to advanced breast cancer. *Psycho-Oncology, 7,* 101–111.

Korchmaros, J. D., & Kenny, D. A. (2006). An evolutionary and close-relationship model of helping. *Journal of Social and Personal Relationships, 23,* 21–43.

Koriat, A., Goldsmith, M., & Pansky, A. (2000). Toward a psychology of memory accuracy. *Annual Review of Psychology, 51,* 481–537.

Kortenkamp, K. V., & Moore, C. F. (2001). Ecocentrism and antropocentrism: Moral reasoning about ecological commons dilemmas. *Journal of Environmental Psychology, 21,* 261–272.

Krajick, K. (1990, July 30). Sound too good to be true? Behind the boom in subliminal tapes. Newsweek, 116, 60–61.

Krakow, A., & Blass, T. (1995). When nurses obey or defy inappropriate physician orders: Attributional differences. *Journal of Social Behavior and Personality, 10,* 585–594.

Krantz, D. S, & McCeney, M. K. (2002). Effects of psychological and social factors on organic disease: A critical assessment of research on coronary heart disease. *Annual Review of Psychology, 53,* 341–369.

Krauss, R. M., & Deutsch, M. (1966). Communication in interpersonal bargaining. *Journal of Personality and Social Psychology, 4,* 572–577.

Kremer, J. F., & Stephens, L. (1983). Attributions and arousal as mediators of mitigation's effects on retaliation. *Journal of Personality and Social Psychology, 45,* 335–343.

Kressel, K., & Pruitt, D. G. (1989). A research perspective on the mediation of social conflict. In K. Kressel & D. G. Pruitt (Eds.), *Mediation research: The process and effectiveness of third party intervention.* (pp. 394–435.) San Francisco, CA: Jossey-Bass.

Kristiansen, C. M., & Giulietti, R. (1990). Perceptions of wife abuse: Effects of gender, attitudes toward women, and just-world beliefs among college students. *Psychology of Women Quarterly, 14,* 177–189.

Krosnick, J. A., & Alwin, D. F. (1989). Aging and susceptibility to attitude change. *Journal of Personality and Social Psychology, 57,* 416–425.

Krueger, J., Ham, J. J., & Linford, K. (1996). Perceptions of behavioral consistency: Are people aware of the actor-observer effect? *Psychological Science, 7,* 259–264.

Kruger, K., Epley, N., Packer, J., & Ng, Z. (2005). Egocentricism over e-mail: Can we communicate as well as we think? *Journal of Personality and Social Psychology, 89*(6), 925–936.

Kruglanski, A. W., & Mayseless, O. (1990). Classic and current social comparison research: Expanding the perspective. *Psychological Bulletin, 108,* 195–208.

Kruglanski, A. W., & Webster, D. M. (1991). Group members' reactions to opinion deviates and conformists at varying degrees of proximity to decision deadline and of environmental noise. *Journal of Personality and Social Psychology, 61,* 212–225.

Krull, D. S. (1993). Does the grist change the mill? The effect of the perceiver's inferential goal on the process of social inference. *Personality and Social Psychology Bulletin, 19,* 340–348.

Kubitschek, W. N., & Hallinan, M. T. (1998). Tracking and students' friendships. *Social Psychology Quarterly, 61,* 1–15.

Kuhl, J. (1983). Emotion, cognition, and motivation: I. Towards a systems-oriented theory of the development of emotions. English abstract of German article Emotion, kognition und motivation: I. auf dem wege zu einer systemtheoretischen betrachtung der emotionsgenese. *Sprache & Kognition, 2,* 1–27.

Kulik, J., & Brown, R. (1979). Frustration, attribution of blame, and aggression. *Journal of Experimental Social Psychology, 15,* 183–194.

Kunda, Z. (1990). The case for motivated reasoning. Psychological Bulletin, 108, 480–498.

Kunda, Z. (1999). *Social cognition: Making sense of people.* Cambridge, MA,: MIT Press.

Kunda, Z., Davies, P. G., Adams, B. D., & Spencer, S. J. (2002). The dynamic time course of stereotype activation: Activation, dissipation, and resurrection. *Journal of Personality and Social Psychology, 82,* 283–299.

Kunda, Z., Fong, G. T., Sanitioso, R., & Reber, E. (1993). Directional questions about self-conceptions. *Journal of Experimental Social Psychology, 29,* 63–86.

Kunda, Z., & Oleson, K. C. (1995). Maintaining stereotypes in the face of disconfirmation: Constructing grounds for subtyping deviance. *Journal of Personality and Social Psychology, 68,* 565–579.

Kunda, Z., & Oleson, K. C. (1997). When exceptions prove the rule: How extremity of deviance determines the impact of deviant examples on stereotypes. *Journal of Personality and Social Psychology, 72,* 965–979.

Kunda, Z., Sinclair, L., & Griffin, D. (1997). Equal ratings but separate meanings: Stereotypes and the construal of traits. *Journal of Personality and Social Psychology, 72,* 720–734.

Kunkel, D., Wilcox, B., Hill-Scott, K., Greenberg, B. S., Rampoldi-Hnilo, L., Montgomery, K. C., Jordan, A. B., Hogan, M. J., Brown, J. A., & Trotta, L. (2001). Part III: Policy issues and advocacy. In D. G. Singer, & J. L. Singer (Eds.), *Handbook of children and the media.* (pp. 587–719.) Thousand Oaks, CA: Sage Publications.

Kunz, P. R., & Woolcott, M. (1976). Season's greetings: From my status to yours. *Social Science Research, 5,* 269–278.

Kuo, Z. Y. (1961). Genesis of the cat's response to the rat. In *Instinct.* (p. 24.) Princeton, NJ: Van Nostrand.

Kwong, M. J., Bartholomew, K., & Dutton, D. G. (1999). Gender differences in patterns of relationship violence in Alberta. *Canadian Journal of Behavioural Science, 31,* 150–160.

La France, M., Hecht, M. A., & Paluck, E. L. (2003). The contingent smile: A meta-analysis of sex differences in smiling. *Psychological Bulletin, 129,* 305–334.

La Gaipa, J. J. (1982). Rules and rituals in disengaging from relationships. In S. Duck (Ed.), *Personal relationships.* (Vol. 4 Dissolving personal relationships, pp. 189–210.) London, UK: Academic Press.

Lalancette, M. F., & Standing, L. (1990). Asch fails again. *Social Behavior and Personality, 18,* 7–12.

Lalonde, R. N., Moghaddam, F. M., & Taylor, D. M. (1987). The process of group differentiation in a dynamic intergroup setting. *Journal of Social Psychology, 127,* 273–287.

Lam, K. C. H., Buehler, R., McFarland, C., Ross, M., & Cheung, I. (2005). Cultural differences in affective forecasting: The role of focalism. *Personality and Social Psychology Bulletin, 31,* 1296–1309.

Lamb, C. S., Jackson, L. A., Cassiday, P. B., & Priest, D. J. (1993). Body figure preferences of men and women: A comparison of two generations. *Sex Roles, 28,* 345–358.

Lambert, A. J., & Raichle, K. (2000). The role of political ideology in mediating judgments of blame in rape victims and their assailants: A test of the just world, personal responsibility, and legitimization hypotheses. *Personality and Social Psychology Bulletin, 26,* 853–863.

Lampert, R., Baron, S. J., McPherson, C. A., & Lee, F. A. (2002). Heart rate variability during the week of September 11, 2001. *Journal of the American Medical Association, 288,* 575.

Langer, E. J., & Rodin, J. (1976). The effects of choice and enhanced personal responsibility for the aged: A field experiment. *Journal of Personality and Social Psychology, 34,* 191–198.

Langlois, J. H., Kalakanis, L., Rubenstein, A. J., Larson, A., Hallam, M., & Smoot, M. (2000). Maxims or myths of beauty? A meta-analytic and theoretical review. *Psychological Bulletin, 126,* 390–423.

Langlois, J. H., & Roggman, L. A. (1990). Attractive faces are only average. *Psychological Science, 1,* 115–121.

Langlois, J. H., Roggman, L. A., & Musselman, L. (1994). What is average and what is not average about attractive faces? *Psychological Science, 5,* 214–220.

LaPiere, R. T. (1934). Attitudes vs. actions. *Social Forces, 13,* 230–237.

L'Armand, K., & Pepitone, A. (1975). Helping to reward another person: A cross-cultural analysis. *Journal of Personality and Social Psychology, 31,* 189–198.

Larson, J. R., Jr., Christensen, C., Franz, T. M., & Abbott, A. S. (1998). Diagnosing groups: The pooling, management, and impact of shared and unshared case information in team-based medical decision making. *Journal of Personality and Social Psychology, 75,* 93–108.

Larson, J. R., Jr., Foster-Fishman, P. G., & Franz, T. M. (1998). Leadership style and the discussion of shared and unshared information in decision-making groups. *Personality and Social Psychology Bulletin, 24,* 482–495.

Lassiter, G. D. (2004). *Interrogations, confessions, and entrapment.* New York: Kluwer Academic/Plenum.

Latané, B. (1981). The psychology of social impact. *American Psychologist, 36,* 343–356.

Latané, B. (1987). From student to colleague: Retracing a decade. In N. E. Grunberg, R. E. Nisbett, J. Rodin, & J. E. Singer (Eds.), *A distinctive approach to psychological research: The influence of Stanley Schachter.* (pp. 66–86.) Hillsdale, NJ: Erlbaum.

Latané, B., & Bourgeois, M. J. (2001). Successfully simulating dynamic social impact: Three levels of prediction. In J. P. Forgas & K. D. Williams (Eds.), *Social influence: Direct and indirect processes.* (pp. 61–76.) Philadelphia, PA: Psychology Press.

Latané, B., & Dabbs, J. M. (1975). Sex, group size, and helping in three cities. *Sociometry, 38,* 108–194.

Latané, B., & Darley, J. M. (1968). Group inhibition of bystander intervention. *Journal of Personality and Social Psychology, 10,* 215–221.

Latané, B., & Darley, J. M. (1970). *The unresponsive bystander: Why doesn't he help?* Englewood Cliffs, NJ: Prentice Hall.

Latané, B., & L'Herrou, T. (1996). Spatial clustering in the conformity game: Dynamic social impact in electronic games. *Journal of Personality and Social Psychology, 70,* 1218–1230.

Latané, B., & Nida, S. (1981). Ten years of research on group size and helping. *Psychological Bulletin, 89,* 308–324.

Latané, B., Williams, K., & Harkins, S. (1979). Many hands make light work: The causes and consequences of social loafing. *Journal of Personality and Social Psychology, 37,* 822–832.

Lau, R. R., & Russell, D. (1980). Attributions in the sports pages: A field test of some current hypotheses about attribution research. *Journal of Personality and Social Psychology, 39,* 29–38.

Laughlin, P. R. (1980). Social combination processes of cooperative problem-solving groups as verbal intellective tasks. In M. Fishbein (Ed.), *Progress in social psychology.* (Vol. 1, pp. 127–155.) Hillsdale, NJ: Erlbaum.

Laughlin, P. R., Hatch, E. C., Silver, J. S., & Boh, L. (2006). Groups perform better than the best individuals on letters-to-numbers problems: Effects of group size. *Journal of Personality and Social Psychology, 90,* 644–651.

Laursen, B., & Hartup, W. W. (2002). The origins of reciprocity and social exchange in friendships. In L. Brett & W. G. Graziano (Eds.), *Social exchange in development: New directions for child and adolescent development.* (pp. 27–40.) San Francisco, CA: Jossey-Bass/Pfeiffer.

Laver, R. (1994, October 17). Apocolypse now. *Maclean's,* p. 14.

Lavine, H., Sweeney, D., & Wagner, S. H. (1999). Depicting women as sex objects in television advertising: Effects on body dissatisfaction. *Personality and Social Psychology Bulletin, 25,* 1049–1058.

Lavoie, F., Robitaille, L., & Hébert, M. (2000). Teen dating relationships and aggression. *Violence Against Women, 6,* 6–36.

Lawler, E. J., & Thye, S. R. (1999). Bringing emotions into social exchange theory. *Annual Review of Sociology, 25,* 217–244.

Lawson, K. L. (2003). Perceptions of deservedness of social aid as a function of prenatal diagnostic testing. *Journal of Applied Social Psychology, 33*(1), 76–90.

Lazaruk, S. (2008, April 13). Crown appeals sentence. *The Province.* www.canada.com/theprovince/news/story.html?id=cd87b3e8-3b2e-4ddd-9981-ec9a4e3ca27b. Accessed December 2008.

Lazarus, R. S. (1966). *Psychological stress and the coping process.* New York: McGraw-Hill.

Lazarus, R. S. (2000). Toward better research on stress and coping. *American Psychologist, 55,* 665–673.

Lazarus, R. S., & Folkman, S. (1984). *Stress, appraisal, and coping.* New York: Springer-Verlag.

Lea, M., & Spears, R. (1995). Love at first byte: Building personal relationships over computer networks. In J. T. Wood & S. W. Duck (Eds.), *Understudied relationships: Off the beaten track.* (pp. 197–233.) Thousand Oaks, CA: Sage.

Lea, M., Spears, R., & de Groot, D. (2001). Knowing me, knowing you: Anonymity effects on social identity processes within groups. *Personality and Social Psychology Bulletin, 27,* 526–537.

Leary, M. R. (2004). The self we know and the self we show: Self-esteem, self-presentation, and the maintenance of interpersonal relationships. In M. B. Brewer & M. Hewstone (Eds.), *Emotion and motivation.* (pp. 204–224.) Malden, MA: Blackwell.

Leary, M. R., & Tangney, J. P. (2003). The self as an organizing construct in the behavioral and social sciences. In M. R. Leary & J. P. Tangney (Eds.), *Handbook of self and identity.* (pp. 3–14.) New York: Guilford Press.

Leathers, D. G. (1997). *Successful nonverbal communication: Principles and applications.* Boston, MA: Allyn & Bacon.

Lee, E. (2004). Effects of visual representation on social influence in computer-mediated communication: Experimental tests of the social identity model of deindividuation effects. *Human Communication Research, 30,* 234–259.

Lee, F., Hallahan, M., & Herzog, T. (1996). Explaining real-life events: How culture and domain shape attributions. *Personality and Social Psychology Bulletin, 22,* 732–741.

Lee, K., Cameron, C. A., Xu, F., Fu, G., & Board, J. (1997). Chinese and Canadian children's evaluations of lying and truth telling: Similarities and differences in the context of pro- and antisocial behaviors. *Child Development, 68,* 924–934.

Lee, Y., & Seligman, M. E. P. (1997). Are Americans more optimistic than the Chinese? *Personality and Social Psychology Bulletin, 23,* 32–40.

Lefrançois, R., Leclerc, G., Hamel, S., & Gaulin, P. (2000). Stressful life events and psychological distress of the very old: Does social support have a moderating effect? *Archives of Gerontology and Geriatrics, 31,* 243–255.

Legault, L., Green-Demers, I., Grant, P., & Chung, J. (2007). On the self-regulation of implicit and explicit prejudice: A self-determination theory perspective. *Personality and Social Psychology Bulletin, 33,* 732–749.

Lehman, D. R., Davies, C. G., DeLongis, A., & Wortman, C. B. (1993). Positive and negative life changes following bereavement and their relkations to adjustment. *Journal of Social and Clinical Psychology, 12,* 90–112.

Leippe, M., & Eisenstadt, D. (1998). A self-accountability model of dissonance reduction: Multiple modes on a continuum of elaboration. In E. Harmon-Jones & J. S. Mills (Eds.), *Cognitive dissonance theory: Revival with revisions and controversies.* Washington, DC: American Psychological Association.

Leippe, M. R., & Eisenstadt, D. (1994). Generalization of dissonance reduction: Decreasing prejudice through induced compliance. *Journal of Personality and Social Psychology, 67,* 395–413.

Leishman, K. (1988, February). Heterosexuals and AIDS. *Atlantic Monthly.*

Lemay, E. P., Clark, M. S., & Feeney, B. C. (2007). Projection of responsiveness to needs and the construction of satisfying communal relationships. *Journal of Personality and Social Psychology, 92,* 834–853.

Lemyre, L., & Smith, P. M. (1985). Intergroup discrimination and self-esteem in the minimal group paradigm. *Journal of Personality and Social Psychology, 49,* 660–670.

Lenton, A. P., & Bryan, A. (2005). An affair to remember: The role of sexual scripts in perceptions of sexual intent. *Personal Relationships, 12,* 483–498.

Lepore, L., & Brown, R. (1997). Category and stereotype activation: Is prejudice inevitable? *Journal of Personality and Social Psychology, 72,* 275–287.

Lepper, M. (1995). Theory by numbers? Some concerns about meta-analysis as a theoretical tool. *Applied Cognitive Psychology, 9,* 411–422.

Lepper, M. (1996). Intrinsic motivation and extrinsic rewards: A commentary on Cameron and Pierce's meta-analysis. *Review of Educational Research, 66,* 5–32.

Lepper, M. R., Corpus, J. H., & Iyengar, S. S. (2005). Intrinsic and extrinsic motivational orientations in the classroom: Age differences and academic correlates. *Journal of Educational Psychology, 97,* 184–196.

Lepper, M. R., Greene, D., & Nisbett, R. E. (1973). Undermining children's intrinsic interest with extrinsic reward: A test of the over-justification hypothesis. *Journal of Personality and Social Psychology, 28,* 129–137.

Lepper, M. R., Keavney, M., & Drake, M. (1996). Intrinsic motivation and extrinsic rewards: A commentary on Cameron and Pierce's meta analysis. *Review of Educational Research, 66,* 5–32.

Lerner, M. J. (1980). *The belief in a just world: A fundamental decision.* New York: Plenum.

Lerner, M. J., & Miller, D. T. (1978). Just world research and the attribution process: Looking back and ahead. *Psychological Bulletin, 85,* 1030–1051.

Lerner, M. J., & Simmons, C. H. (1966). Observer's reaction to the "innocent victim": Compassion or rejection? *Journal of Personality and Social Psychology, 4,* 203–210.

Leung, K. (1996). Beliefs in Chinese culture. In M. H. Bond (Ed.), *The handbook of Chinese psychology.* (pp. 247–262.) Hong Kong: Oxford University Press.

Leung, K., & Bond, M. H. (1984). The impact of cultural collectivism on reward allocation. *Journal of Personality and Social Psychology, 47,* 793–804.

Leventhal, H., Watts, J. C., & Pagano, F. (1967). Effects of fear and instructions on how to cope with danger. *Journal of Personality and Social Psychology, 6,* 313–321.

Levett, L. M., Danielsen, E. M., Kovera, M. B., & Cutler, B. L. (2005). The psychology of jury and juror decision making. In N. Brewer, K. D. Williams (Eds.), *Psychology and law: An empirical perspective.* (pp. 365–406.) New York, NY US: Guilford Press.

Levin, D. T. (2000). Race as a visual feature: Using visual search and perceptual discrimination tasks to understand face categories and the cross-race recognition deficit. *Journal of Experimental Psychology: General, 129,* 559–574.

Levin, M., Prosser, A., Evans, D., & Reicher, S. (2005). Identity and emergency intervention: How social group membership and inclusiveness of group boundaries shape helping behavior. *Journal of Personality and Social Psychology Bulletin, 31*:4, 443–453.

Levine, J. M. (1989). Reaction to opinion deviance in small groups. In P. B. Paulus (Ed.), *Psychology of group influence.* (2nd ed., pp. 187–231.) Hillsdale, NJ: Erlbaum.

Levine, J. M. (1999). Solomon Asch's legacy for group research. *Personality and Social Psychology Review, 3,* 358–364.

Levine, J. M., Higgins, E. T., & Choi, H.-S. (2000). Development of strategic norms in groups. *Organizational Behavior and Human Decision Processes, 82,* 88–101.

Levine, J. M., & Moreland, R. L. (1998). Small groups. In D. Gilbert, S. Fiske, & G. Lindzey (Eds.), *The handbook of social psychology.* (4th ed., Vol. 2, pp. 415–469.) New York: McGraw Hill.

Levine, J. M., Moreland, R. L., & Choi, S. (2001). Group socialization and newcomer innovation. In M. Hogg & S. Tindale (Eds.), *Blackwell Handbook of Social Psychology: Group Processes.* (pp. 86–106.) Oxford, UK: Blackwell Publishers.

Levine, J. M., & Thompson, L. (1996). Conflict in groups. In E. T. Higgins & A. W. Kruglanski (Eds.), *Social psychology: Handbook of basic principles.* (pp. 745–776.) New York: Guilford.

Levine, M. P., & Smolak, L. (1996). Media as a context for the development of disordered eating. In L. Smolak, M. P. Levine, &

R. Striegel-Moore (Eds.), *Developmental psychopathology of eating disorders: Implications for research, prevention, and treatment.* (pp. 235–257.) Mahwah, NJ: Erlbaum.

Levine, R., Sato, S., Hashimoto, T., & Verma, J. (1995). Love and marriage in eleven cultures. *Journal of Cross Cultural Psychology, 26,* 554–571.

Levine, R. V., Martinez, T. S., Brase, G., & Sorenson, K. (1994). Helping in 36 U.S. cities. *Journal of Personality and Social Psychology, 67,* 69–82.

Levy, J. S., & Morgan, T. C. (1984). The frequency and seriousness of war: An inverse relationship? *Journal of Conflict Resolution, 28,* 731–749.

Lewin, K. (1943). Defining the "field at a given time." *Psychological Review, 50,* 292–310.

Lewin, K. (1946). Action research and minority problems. *Journal of Social Issues, 2,* 34–46.

Lewin, K. (1947). Frontiers in group dynamics. *Human Relations, 1,* 5–41.

Lewin, K. (1948). *Resolving social conflicts: Selected papers in group dynamics.* New York: Harper.

Lewin, K. (1951). Problems of research in social psychology. In D. Cartwright (Ed.), *Field theory in social science.* (pp. 155–169.) New York: Harper & Row.

Lewis, M., & Ramsay, D. (2004). Development of self-recognition, personal pronoun use, and pretend play during the 2nd year. *Child Development, 75,* 1821–1831.

Leyens, J. P., Camino, L., Parke, R. D., & Berkowitz, L. (1975). Effects of movie violence on aggression in a field setting as a function of group dominance and cohesion. *Journal of Personality and Social Psychology, 32,* 346–360.

L'Heureux-Dubé, C. (2001). Beyond the myths: Equality, impartiality, and justice. *Journal of Social Distress and the Homeless, 10,* 87–104.

Liang, D. W., Moreland, R., & Argote, L. (1995). Group versus individual training and group performance: The mediating role of transactive memory. *Personality and Social Psychology Bulletin, 21,* 384–393.

Liberman, A., & Chaiken, S. (1992). Defensive processing of personally relevant health messages. *Personality and Social Psychology Bulletin, 18,* 669–679.

Liebert, R. M., & Baron, R. A. (1972). Some immediate effects of televised violence on children's behavior. *Developmental Psychology, 6,* 469–475.

Lim, T.-S., & Choi, S.-H. (1996). Interpersonal relationships in Korea. In W. B. Gudykunst, S. Ting-Toomey, & T. Nishida (Eds.), *Communication in personal relationships across cultures.* (pp. 122–136.) Thousand Oaks, CA: Sage.

Lindsay, D. S., & Read, J. D. (2006). Adults' memories of long-past events. In L. Nilsson & N. Ohta (Eds.), *Memory and society: Psychological perspectives.* (pp. 51–72.) New York: Psychology Press.

Lindsay, R. C. L., & Wells, G. L. (1985). Improving eyewitness identifications from lineups: Simultaneous versus sequential lineup presentation. *Journal of Applied Psychology, 70,* 556–564.

Lindsay, R. C. L., Wells, G. L., & Rumpel, C. M. (1981). Can people detect eyewitness-identification accuracy within and across situations? *Journal of Applied Psychology, 66,* 79–89.

Linville, P. W., Fischer, G. W., & Fischhoff, B. (1993). AIDS risk perceptions and decision biases. In J. B. Pryor & G. D. Reeder (Eds.), The social psychology of HIV infection. (pp. 5–38.) Hillsdale, NJ: Erlbaum.

Linville, P. W., Fischer, G. W., & Salovey, P. (1989). Perceived distributions of characteristics of in-group and out-group members: Empirical evidence and a computer simulation. *Journal of Personality and Social Psychology, 57,* 165–188.

Linz, D. G., Donnerstein, E., & Penrod, S. (1984). The effects of multiple exposures to filmed violence against women. *Journal of Communication, 34,* 130–147.

Linz, D. G., Donnerstein, E., & Penrod, S. D. (1988). Effects of long-term exposure to violent and sexually degrading depictions of women. *Journal of Personality and Social Psychology, 55,* 758–768.

Lippmann, W. (1922). *Public opinion.* New York: Free Press.

Lipsey, M. W., Wilson, D. B., Cohen, M. A., & Derzon, J. H. (1997). Is there a causal relationship between alcohol use and violence? A synthesis of evidence. In M. Galanter (Ed.), *Recent developments in alcoholism* (Vol. 13 Alcohol and violence: Epidemiology, neurobiology, psychology, and family issues, pp. 245–282.) New York: Plenum.

Litt, M. D. (1988). Self-efficacy and perceived control: Cognitive mediators of pain tolerance. *Journal of Personality and Social Psychology, 54,* 149–160.

Little, A. C., Burriss, R. P., Jones, B. C., DeBruine, L. M., & Caldwell, C. A. (2008). Social influence in human face preference: Men and women are influenced more for long-term than short-term attractiveness decisions. *Evolution and Human Behavior, 29,* 140–146.

Little, A. C., & Perrett, D. I. (2002). Putting beauty back in the eye of the beholder. *Psychologist, 15,* 28–32.

Livingston, S. D., & Sinclair, L. (2008). Taking the watchdog off its leash: Personal prejudices and situational motivations jointly predict derogation of a stigmatized source. *Personality and Social Psychology Bulletin, 34,* 210–223.

Lloyd, S. A., & Cate, R. M. (1985). The developmental course of conflict in dissolution of premarital relationships. *Journal of Social and Personal Relationships, 2,* 179–194.

Lockwood, P. (2002). Could it happen to you? Predicting the impact of downward social comparison on the self. *Journal of Personality and Social Psychology, 82,* 343–358.

Lockwood, P., & Kunda, Z. (1997). Superstars and me: Predicting the impact of role models on the self. *Journal of Personality and Social Psychology, 73,* 91–103.

Lockwood, P., & Kunda, Z. (1999). Increasing salience of one's best selves can undermine inspiration by outstanding role models. *Journal of Personality and Social Psychology, 76,* 214–228.

Lockwood, P. & Kunda, Z. (2000). Outstanding role models: Do they inspire or demoralize us? In A. Tesser, R. B. Felson, & J. M. Suls (Eds.), *Psychological perspectives on self and identity.* (pp. 147–170.) Washington, DC: American Psychological Association.

Lockwood, P., Marshall, T. C., & Sadler, P. (2005). Promoting success or preventing failure: Cultural differences in motivation by positive and negative role models. *Personality and Social Psychology Bulletin, 31*:3, 379–392.

Lockwood, P., Sadler, P., Fyman, K., & Tuck, S. (2004). To do or not to do: Using positive and negative role models to harness motivation. *Social Cognition, 22*(4), 422–450.

Lodish, L. M., Abraham, M., Kalmenson, S., Lievelsberger, J., Lubetkin, B., Richardson, B., & Stevens, M. E. (1995). How TV advertising works: A meta-analysis of 389 real-world split-cable TV advertising experiments. *Journal of Marketing Research, 32,* 125–139.

Loftus, E. F. (1974). Reconstructing memory. The incredible eyewitness. *Psychology Today, 8,* 116–119.

Loftus, E. F. (1979). *Eyewitness testimony.* Cambridge, MA: Harvard University Press.

Loftus, E. F. (1983). Silence is not golden. *American Psychologist, 38,* 564–572.

Loftus, E. F. (1993). The reality of repressed memories. *American Psychologist, 48,* 518–537.

Loftus, E. F. (2003). The dangers of memory. In R. J. Sternberg (Ed). *Psychologists defying the crowd: Stories of those who battled the establishment and won.* (pp. 105–117.) Washington, DC: American Psychological Association.

Loftus, E. F. (2005). Planting misinformation in the human mind: A 30-year investigation of the malleability of memory. *Learning and Memory, 12,* 361–366.

Loftus, E. F., & Hoffman, H. G. (1989). Misinformation and memory: The creation of new memories. *Journal of Experimental Psychology: General, 118,* 100–104.

Loftus, E. F., Miller, D. G., & Burns, H. J. (1978). Semantic integration of verbal information into a visual memory. *Journal of Experimental Psychology: Human Learning and Memory, 4,* 19–31.

Loftus, G. R., & Harley, E. M. (2005). Why is it easier to identify someone close than far away? *Psychonomic Bulletin and Review, 12,* 43–65.

London, P. (1970). The rescuers: Motivational hypotheses about Christians who saved Jews from the Nazis. In J. R. Macaulay & L. Berkowitz (Eds.), *Altruism and helping behavior.* (pp. 241–250.) New York: Academic Press.

Lonner, W., & Berry, J. (Eds.) (1986). *Field methods in cross-cultural research.* Beverly Hills, CA: Sage.

Lord, C. G., Lepper, M. R., & Preston, E. (1984). Considering the opposite: A corrective strategy for social judgment. *Journal of Personality and Social Psychology, 47,* 1231–1243.

Lord, C. G., Scott, K. O., Pugh, M. A., & Desforges, D. M. (1997). Leakage beliefs and the correspondence bias. *Personality and Social Psychology Bulletin, 23,* 824–836.

Lore, R. K., & Schultz, L. A. (1993). Control of human aggression. *American Psychologist, 48,* 16–25.

Losier, G. F., & Koestner, R. (1999). Intrinsic versus identified regulation in distinct political campaigns: The consequences of following politics for pleasure versus personal meaningfulness. *Personality and Social Psychology Bulletin, 25,* 287–298.

Lott, A. J., & Lott, B. E. (1974). The role of reward in the formation of positive interpersonal attitudes. In T. Huston (Ed.), *Foundations of interpersonal attraction.* New York: Academic Press.

Luby, V., & Aron, A. (1990, July). A prototype structuring of love, like, and being in love. Paper presented at the Fifth International Conference on Personal Relationships, Oxford, UK.

Ludwig, T. D., Gray, T. W., & Rowell, A. (1998). Increasing recycling in academic buildings: A systematic replication. *Journal of Applied Behavior Analysis, 31,* 683–686.

Lumsdaine, A. A., & Janis, I. L. (1953). Resistance to "counterpropaganda"; produced by one-sided and two-sided "propaganda" presentations. *Public Opinion Quarterly, 17,* 311–318.

Lundy, D. E., Tan, J., & Cunningham, M. R. (1998). Heterosexual romantic preferences: The importance of humor and physical attractiveness for different types of relationships. *Personal Relationships, 5,* 311–325.

Lupaschuk, D., & Yewchuk, C. (1998). Student perceptions of gender roles: Implications for counsellors. *International Journal for the Advancement of Counseling, 20,* 301–318.

Lussier, Y., Sabourin, S., & Turgeon, C. (1997). Coping strategies as moderators of the relationship between attachment and marital adjustment. *Journal of Social and Personal Relationships, 14,* 777–791.

Lydon, J. E. (1999). Commitment and adversity: A reciprocal relation. In A. Jeffrey & J. Warren (Eds.), *Handbook of interpersonal commitment and relationship stability.* New York: Plenum Publishers.

Lydon, J. E., Fitzsimons, G. M., & Naidoo, L. (2003). Devaluation versus enhancement of attractive alternatives: A critical test using the calibration paradigm. *Personality and Social Psychology Bulletin, 29,* 349–359.

Lydon, J. E., Meana, M., Sepinwall, D., Richards, N., & Mayman, S. (1999). The commitment calibration hypothesis: When do people devalue attractive partners? *Personality and Social Psychology Bulletin, 25,* 152–161.

Lydon, J. E., Menzies-Tolman, D., Burton, K., & Bell, C. (2008). If-then contingencies and the differential effects of availability of an attractive alternative on relationship maintenance for men and women. *Journal of Personality and Social Psychology, 95,* 50–65.

Lydon, J. E., & Zanna, M. P. (1990). Commitment in the face of adversity: A value-affirmation approach. *Journal of Personality and Social Psychology, 58,* 1040–1047.

Lykken, D. T. (1998). *A tremor in the blood: Uses and abuses of the lie detector.* New York: Plenum.

Lyle, K. B., & Johnson, M. K. (2006). Importing perceived features into false memories. *Memory, 14,* 197–213.

Lynn, S. J., Lock, T., Loftus, E., Krackow, E., & Lilienfeld, S. O. (2003). The remembrance of things past: Problematic memory recovery techniques in psychotherapy. In S. O. Lilienfeld & S. J. Lynn (Eds.), *Science and pseudoscience in clinical psychology.* (pp. 205–239.) New York: Guilford Press.

Lysak, H., Rule, B. G., & Dobbs, A. R. (1989). Conceptions of aggression: Prototype or defining features? *Personality and Social Psychology Bulletin, 15,* 233–243.

Lyubomirsky, S., Caldwell, N. D., & Nolen-Hoeksema, S. (1993). Effects of ruminative and distracting responses to depressed mood on retrieval of autobiographical memories. *Journal of Personality and Social Psychology, 75,* 166–177.

Lyubomirsky, S., Sheldon, K. M., Schkade, D. (2005). Pursuing happiness: The architecture of sustainable change. *Review of General Psychology, 9,* 111–131.

Maddon, S., Guyll, M., Spoth, R., & Willard, J. (2004). The synergistic accumulative effect of parents' beliefs on childrens' drinking behavior. *Psychological Science, 15,* 837–845.

Maddux, W. W., Barden, J., Brewer, M. B., Petty, R. E. (2004). Saying no to negativity: The effects of context and motivation to control prejudice on automatic evaluative responses. *Journal of Experimental Social Psychology, 41,* 19–35.

Magaro, P. A., & Ashbrook, R. M. (1985). The personality of societal groups. *Journal of Personality and Social Psychology, 48,* 1479–1489.

Magoo, G., & Khanna, R. (1991). Altruism and willingness to donate blood. *Journal of Personality and Clinical Studies, 7,* 21–24.

Maier, N. R. F., & Solem, A. R. (1952). The contribution of a discussion leader to the quality of group thinking: The effective use of minority opinions. *Human Relations, 5,* 277–288.

Maio, G. R., Bell, D. W., & Esses, V. M. (1996). Ambivalence in persuasion: The processing of messages about immigrant groups. *Journal of Experimental Social Psychology, 32,* 513–536.

Maio, G. R., Esses, V. M., & Bell, D. W. (1994). The formation of attitudes toward new immigrant groups. *Journal of Applied Social Psychology, 24,* 1762–1776.

Maio, G. R., & Olson, J. M. (1995). Relations between values, attitudes, and behavioral intentions: The moderating role of attitude function. *Journal of Experimental Social Psychology, 31,* 266–285.

Maio, G. R., Olson, J. M., & Bush, J. E. (1997). Telling jokes that disparage groups: Effects on the joke teller's stereotypes. *Journal of Applied Social Psychology, 27,* 1986–2000.

Major, B., & Gramzow, R. H. (1999). Abortion as stigma: Cognitive and emotional implications of concealment. *Journal of Personality and Social Psychology, 77,* 735–745.

Major, B., Quinton, W. J., & McCoy, S. K. (2002). Antecedents and consequences of attributions to discrimination: Theoretical and empirical advances. In M. P. Zanna (Ed.), *Advances in Experimental Social Psychology.* (Vol. 34, pp. 251–330.) San Diego, CA: Academic Press.

Major, B., Kaiser, C. R., & McCoy, S. K. (2003). It's not my fault: When and why attributions to prejudice protect self-esteem. *Personality and Social Psychology Bulletin, 29.*6, 772–781.

Major, B., Spencer, S., Schmader, T., Wolfe, C., & Crocker, J. (1998). Coping with negative stereotypes about intellectual performance: The role of psychological disengagement. *Personality and Social Psychology Bulletin, 24,* 34–50.

Malamuth, N. (1983). Human sexuality. In D. Perlman & P. C. Cozby (Eds.), *Social psychology.* New York: Holt, Rinehart & Winston.

Malamuth, N. M. (1981). Rape fantasies as a function of exposure to violent sexual stimuli. *Archives of Sexual Behavior, 10,* 33–47.

Malamuth, N. M., & Brière, J. (1986). Sexual violence in the media: Indirect effects on aggression against women. *Journal of Social Issues, 42,* 75–92.

Malamuth, N. M., & Check, J. U. (1981). The effects of mass media exposure on acceptance of violence against women: A field experiment. *Journal of Sex Research, 15,* 436–446.

Malamuth, N. M., Linz, D., Heavey, C. L., Barnes, G., & Acker, M. (1995). Using the confluence model of sexual aggression to predict men's conflict with women: A 10-year follow-up study. *Journal of Personality and Social Psychology, 69,* 353–369.

Malcolmson, K. A., & Sinclair, L. (2007). The Ms. stereotype revisited: Implicit and explicit facets. *Psychology of Women Quarterly, 31,* 305–310.

Malle, B. F., & Knobe, J. (1997). Which behaviors do people explain? A basic actor-observer asymmetry. *Journal of Personality and Social Psychology, 72,* 288–304.

Malloy, T. E. (2001). Difference to inference: Teaching logical and statistical reasoning through on-line interactivity. *Behavior Research Methods, Instruments, and Computers, 33,* 270–273.

Malpass, R. S., & Devine, P. G. (1981). Eyewitness identification: Lineup instructions and the absence of the offender. *Journal of Applied Psychology, 66*(4), 482–489.

Mandal, M. K., Bryden, M. P., & Bulman-Fleming, M. B. (1996). Similarities and variations in facial expressions of emotions: Cross-cultural evidence. *International Journal of Psychology, 31,* 49–58.

Mandel, D. R., & Dhami, M. K. (2005). "What I did" versus "what I might have done": Effect of factual versus counterfactual thinking on blame, guilt, and shame in prisoners. *Journal of Experimental Social Psychology, 41,* 627–635.

Mandel, D. R., & Lehman, D. R. (1996). Counterfactual thinking and ascriptions of cause and preventability. *Journal of Personality and Social Psychology, 71,* 450–463.

Mandler, G. (1975). *Mind and emotion.* New York: Wiley.

Maner, J. K., DeWall, C. N., Baumeister, R. F., & Schaller, M. (2007). Does social exclusion motivate interpersonal reconnection? Resolving the "porcupine problem." *Journal of Personality and Social Psychology, 92,* 42–55.

Manstead, A. S. R. (1997). Situations, belongingness, attitudes, and culture: Four lessons learned from social psychology. In G. McGarty & H. S. Haslam (Eds.), *The message of social psychology: Perspectives on mind and society.* (pp. 238–251.) Oxford: Blackwell.

Mantler, J., Schellenberg, E. G., & Page, J. S. (2003). Attributions for serious illness: Are controllability, responsibility, and blame different constructs. *Canadian Journal of Behavioural Science, 35*(2), 142–152.

Maracek, J., & Mettee, D. R. (1972). Avoidance of continued success as a function of self-esteem, level of esteem certainty, and responsibility for success. *Journal of Personality and Social Psychology, 22,* 90–107.

Marigold, D. C., Holmes, J. G., & Ross, M. (2007). More than words: Reframing compliments from romantic partners fosters security in low self-esteem individuals. *Journal of Personality and Social Psychology, 92,* 232–248.

Marin, T. J., Holtzman, S., DeLongis, A., & Robinson, L. (2007). Coping and the response of others. *Journal of Social and Personal Relationships, 24,* 951–969.

Marion, R. (1995, August). The girl who mewed. *Discover,* pp. 38–40.

Markman, K. D., Gavanski, I., Sherman, S. J., & McMullen, M. N. (1995). The impact of perceived control on the imagination of better and worse possible worlds. *Personality and Social Psychology Bulletin, 21,* 588–595.

Markus, H. (1977). Self-schemata and processing information about the self. *Journal of Personality and Social Psychology, 35,* 63–78.

Markus, H., & Kitayama, S. (1991). Culture and the self: Implications for cognition, emotion, and motivation. *Psychological Review, 98,* 224–253.

Markus, H. R., & Kitayama, S. (2001). The cultural construction of self and emotion: Implications for social behavior. In W. G. Parrott (Ed.), *Emotions in social psychology: Essential readings.* (pp. 119–137.) Philadelphia: Psychology Press.

Markus, H. R., Kitayama, S., & Heiman, R. J. (1996). Culture and "basic" psychological principles. In E. T. Higgins & A. W. Kruglanski (Eds.), *Social psychology: Handbook of basic principles.* (pp. 857–913.) New York: Guilford.

Markus, H. R., & Zajonc, R. B. (1985). The cognitive perspective in social psychology. In G. Lindzey & E. Aronson (Eds.), *Handbook of social psychology.* (3rd ed., Vol. 1, pp. 137–230.) New York: McGraw-Hill.

Marshall, V. W., Clarke, P. J., & Ballantyne, P. J. (2001). Instability in the retirement transition. *Research on Aging, 23*, 379–409.

Martin, A. J., Berenson, K. R., Griffing, S., Sage, R. E., Madry, L., Bingham, L. E., & Primm, B. J. (2000). The process of leaving an abusive relationship: The role of risk assessments and decision certainty. *Journal of Family Violence, 15*, 109–122.

Martin, L. L., & Tesser, A. (1996). Some ruminative thoughts. In R. S. Wyer, Jr. (Ed.), *Advances in social cognition.* (Vol. 9, pp. 1–47.) Hillsdale, NJ: Erlbaum.

Martin, R., Hewstone, M., & Martin, P. Y. (2003). Resistance to persuasive messages as a function of majority and minority source status. *Journal of Experimental Social Psychology, 39*(6), 585–593.

Marx, D. M. & Roman, J. S. (2002). Female role models: Protecting women's math test performance. *Personality and Social Psychology Bulletin, 28*, 1183–1193.

Masters, K. S., Lacaille, R. A., & Shearer, D. S. (2003). The acute affective response of type A behaviour pattern individuals to competitive and noncompetitive exercise. *Canadian Journal of Behavioural Science, 35*, 25–34.

Masuda, T., Ellsworth, P. C., Mesquita, B., Leu, J., Tanida, S., & Van de Veerdonk, E. (2008). Placing the face in context: Cultural differences in the perception of facial emotion. *Journal of Personality and Social Psychology, 94*, 365–381.

Maticka-Tyndale, E. (1992). Social construction of HIV transmission and prevention among heterosexual young adults. *Social Problems, 39*, 238–252.

Maticka-Tyndale, E., Herold, E. S., & Mewhinney, D. (1998). Casual sex on spring break: Intentions and behaviors of Canadian students. *Journal of Sex Research, 35*, 254–264.

Maticka-Tyndale, E., Herold, E. S., & Mewhinney, D. (2001). Casual sex on spring break: Intentions and behaviors of Canadian students. In R. F. Baumeister (Ed.), *Social psychology and human sexuality: Key readings in social psychology.* (pp. 173–186.) Philadelphia, PA: Psychology Press.

Matsumoto, D., & Ekman, P. (2004). The relationship among expressions, labels, and descriptions of contempt. *Journal of Personality and Social Psychology, 87*(4), 529–540.

Matthews, K. A. (1988). Coronary heart disease and Type A behaviors: Update on and alternative to the Booth-Kewley and Friedman (1987) quantitative review. *Psychological Bulletin, 104*, 373–380.

Matud, M. P. (2004). Gender differences in stress and coping styles. *Personality and Individual Differences, 37*, 1401–1415.

Maupin, H. E., & Fisher, R. J. (1989). The effects of superior female performance and sex-role orientation on gender conformity. *Canadian Journal of Behavioural Science, 21*, 55–69.

McAlister, A., Perry, C., Killen, J., Slinkard, L. A., & Maccoby, N. (1980). Pilot study of smoking, alcohol, and drug abuse prevention. *American Journal of Public Health, 70*, 719–721.

McAllister, H. A. (1996). Self-serving bias in the classroom: Who shows it? Who knows it? *Journal of Educational Psychology, 88*, 123–131.

McArthur, L. (1972). The how and what of why: Some determinants and consequences of causal attribution. *Journal of Personality and Social Psychology, 22*, 171–193.

McArthur, L. Z., & Baron, R. M. (1983). Toward an ecological theory of social perception. *Psychological Review, 90*, 215–238.

McArthur, L. Z., & Berry, D. S. (1987). Cross cultural agreement in perceptions of babyfaced adults. *Journal of Cross-Cultural Psychology, 18*, 165–192.

McCabe, M. P., & Ricciardelli, L. A. (2003a). Sociocultural influences on body image and body changes among adolescent boys and girls. *Journal of Social Psychology, 143*, 5–26.

McCabe, M. P., & Ricciardelli, L. A. (2003b). A longitudinal study of body change strategies among adolescent males. *Journal of Youth and Adolescence, 32*, 105–113.

McCann, S. J. (1992). Alternative formulas to predict the greatness of U.S. presidents: Personological, situational, and zeitgeist factors. *Journal of Personality and Social Psychology, 62*, 469–479.

McCann, S. J. H. (2001). The precocity-longevity hypothesis: Earlier peaks in career achievement predict shorter lives. *Personality and Social Psychology Bulletin, 27*, 1429–1439.

McCann, S. J. H. (2003). Younger achievement age predicts shorter life for governors: Testing the precocity-longevity with artifact controls. *Personality and Social Psychology Bulletin, 29*, 164–169.

McCarthy, J. F., & Kelly, B. R. (1978). Aggressive behavior and its effect on performance over time in ice hockey athletes: An archival study. *International Journal of Sport Psychology, 9*, 90–96.

McCauley, C. (1989). The nature of social influence in groupthink: Compliance and internalization. *Journal of Personality and Social Psychology, 57*, 250–260.

McCloskey, M., & Zaragoza, M. (1985). Misleading postevent information and memory for events: Arguments and evidence against memory impairment hypotheses. *Journal of Experimental Psychology: General, 114*, 1–16.

Maccoby, E. E., & Jacklin, C. N. (1974). *The psychology of sex differences.* Stanford, CA: Stanford University Press.

McConahay, J. B. (1986). Modern racism, ambivalence, and the Modern Racism Scale. In J. F. Dovidio & S. L. Gaertner (Eds.), *Prejudice, discrimination, and racism: Theory and research.* (pp. 91–125.) New York: Academic Press.

McCoy, S. K., & Major, B. (2003). Group identification moderates emotional responses to perceived prejudice. *Personality and Social Psychology Bulletin, 29*(8), 1005–1017.

McCrae, R. R., Yik, M. S. M., Trapnell, P. D., Bond, M. H., & Paulhus, D. L. (1998). Interpreting personality profiles across cultures: Bilingual, acculturation, and peer rating studies of Chinese undergraduates. *Journal of Personality and Social Psychology, 74*, 1041–1055.

MacDonald, G., Zanna, M. P., & Holmes, J. G. (2000). An experimental test of the role of alcohol in relationship conflict. *Journal of Experimental Social Psychology, 36*, 182–193.

McDonald, H. E., & Hirt, E. R. (1997). When expectancy meets desire: Motivational effects in reconstructive memory. *Journal of Personality and Social Psychology, 72*, 5–23.

McDonald, J., & McKelvie, S. J. (1992). Playing safe: Helping rates for a dropped mitten and a box of condoms. *Psychological Reports, 71*, 113–114.

MacDonald, T. K., Fong, G. T., Zanna, M. P., & Martineau A. M. (2000). Alcohol myopia and condom use: Can alcohol intoxication be associated with more prudent behaviour? *Journal of Personality and Social Psychology, 78*, 605–619.

MacDonald, T. K., & Martineau, A. M. (2002). Self-esteem, mood, and intentions to use condoms: When does low self-esteem lead to risky health behaviors? *Journal of Experimental Social Psychology, 38*, 299–306.

MacDonald, T. K., & Ross, M. (1999). Assessing the accuracy of predictions about dating relationships. How and why do lovers' predictions differ from those made by observers? *Personality and Social Psychology Bulletin, 25*, 1417–1429.

MacDonald, T. K., & Zanna, M. P. (1998). Cross-dimension ambivalence toward social groups: Can ambivalence affect intentions to hire feminists? *Personality and Social Psychology Bulletin, 24*, 427–441.

MacDonald, T. K., Zanna, M., & Fong, G. (1996). Why common sense goes out the window: Effects of alcohol on intentions to use condoms. *Personality and Social Psychology Bulletin, 22*, 763–775.

McElwain, A. K., Korabik, K., & Rosin, H. M. (2005). An examination of gender differences in work-family conflict. *Canadian Journal of Behavioural Science, 37*, 283–298.

McFarland, C., Beuhler, R., von Rûti, R., Nguyen, L., & Alvaro, C. (2007). The impact of negative moods on self-enhancing cognitions: The role of reflective versus ruminative mood orientations. *Journal of Personality and Social Psychology, 93*, 728–750.

McFarland, C., & Miller, D. (1990). Judgments of self-other similarity. *Personality and Social Psychology Bulletin, 16*, 475–484.

McFarland, C., & Miller, D. T. (1994). The framing of relative performance feedback: Seeing the glass as half empty or half full. *Journal of Personality and Social Psychology, 66*, 1061–1073.

McFarlane, J., Martin, C. L., & Williams, T. M. (1988). Mood fluctuations: Women versus men and menstrual versus other cycles. *Psychology of Women Quarterly, 12*, 201–233.

McGlone, M., & Aronson, J. (2006). Stereotype threat, identity salience, and spatial reasoning. *Journal of Applied Developmental Psychology, 27*(5), 486–493.

McGraw, A. P., Mellers, B. A., & Tetlock, P. E. (2005). Expectations and emotions of Olympic athletes. *Journal of Experimental Social Psychology, 41*, 438–446.

McGregor, C., Darke, S., Ali, R., & Christie, P. (1998). Experience of non-fatal overdose among heroin users in Adelaide, Australia: Circumstances and risk perceptions. *Addiction, 93*, 701–711.

McGregor, I., Gailliot, M. T., Vasquez, N. A., & Nash, K. A. (2007). Ideological and personal zeal reactions to threat among people with high self-esteem: Motivated promotion focus. *Personality and Social Psychology Bulletin, 33*, 1587–1599.

McGregor, I., Nail, P. R., Marigold, D. C., & Kang, S. (2005). Defensive pride and consensus: Strength in imaginary numbers. *Journal of Personality and Social Psychology, 89*, 978–996.

McGuire, W. J. (1964). Inducing resistance to persuasion. In L. Berkowitz (Ed.), *Advances in experimental social psychology*. (Vol. 1, pp. 192–229.) New York: Academic Press.

McGuire, W. J. (1968). Personality and susceptibility to social influence. In E. F. Borgatta & W. W. Lambert (Eds.), *Handbook of personality theory and research*. (pp. 1130–1187.) Chicago, IL: Rand McNally.

McHugo, G. J., & Smith, C. A. (1996). The power of faces: A review of John T. Lanzetta's research on facial expression and emotion. *Motivation and Emotion, 21*, 85–120.

McIntrye, M. (2006, June 3). Could no one have helped samaritan? *Winnipeg Free Press*, p. A3.

McIntyre, R. B, Paulson, R. M., & Lord, C. G. (2003). Alleviating women's mathematics stereotype threat through salience of group achievements. *Journal of Experimental Social Psychology, 39*(1), 83–90.

McKelvie, S. J. (1995). Biases in the estimated frequency of names. *Perceptual and Motor Skills, 81*, 1331–1338.

McKelvie, S. J. (1997). The availability heuristic: Effects of fame and gender on the estimated frequency of male and female names. *Journal of Social Psychology, 137*, 63–78.

McKelvie, S. J., & McLellan, B. (1993). "Effects of age and gender on perceived facial attractiveness." Reply. *Canadian Journal of Behavioural Science, 26*, 205–209.

McKelvie, S. J., & McLellan, B. (1994). Effects of age and gender on perceived facial attractiveness: Reply. *Canadian Journal of Behavioural Science, 26*, 205–209.

McKenna, K. Y. A. (2008). MySpace or your place: Relationship initiation and development in the wired and wireless world. In S. Sprecher, A. Wenzel, & J. Harvey (Eds.), *Handbook of relationship initiation*. (pp. 235–247.) New York: Taylor & Francis.

McKenna, K. Y. A., & Bargh, J. A. (2000). Plan 9 from cyberspace: The implications of the Internet for personality and social psychology. *Personality and Social Psychology Review, 4*, 57–75.

McKenna, K. Y. A., Green, A. S., & Gleason, M. J. (2002). Relationship formation on the Internet: What's the big attraction? *Journal of Social Issues, 58*, 9–31.

McKenzie-Mohr, D., Nemiroff, L. S., Beers, L., & Desmarais, S. (1995). Determinants of responsible environmental behavior. *Journal of Social Issues, 51*, 139–156.

Mackie, D. M. (1987). Systematic and nonsystematic processing of majority and minority persuasive communications. *Journal of Personality and Social Psychology, 53*, 41–52.

McLaughlin-Volpe, T., Aron, A., Wright, S. C., & Reis, H. T. (2000). *Intergroup social interactions and intergroup prejudice: Quantity versus quality*. Unpublished manuscript. As cited in Brody et al. (2009).

McNally, R. J. (2003). *Remembering trauma*. Cambridge, MA: Harvard University Press.

McNally, R. J., Bryant, R. A., & Ehlers, A. (2003). Does early psychological intervention promote recovery from posttraumatic stress? *Psychological Science in the Public Interest, 4*, 45–79.

McPherson, M., Smith-Lovin, L., & Cook, J. M. (2001). Birds of a feather: Homophily in social networks. *Annual Review of Sociology, 27*, 415–444.

Mead, G. H. (1934). *Mind, self, and society*. Chicago, IL: University of Chicago Press.

Medvec, V. H., Madey, S. F., & Gilovich, T. (1995). When less is more: Counterfactual thinking and satisfaction among Olympic medalists. *Journal of Personality and Social Psychology, 69*, 603–610.

Medvec, V. H., Madey, S. F., & Gilovich, T. (2002). When less is more: Counterfactual thinking and satisfaction among Olympic medalists. In T. Gilovich, D. Griffin, & D. Kahneman (Eds.), *Heuristics and biases: The psychology of intuitive judgment*. (pp. 625–635.) Cambridge, UK: Cambridge University Press.

Meeus, W. H. J., & Raaijmakers, Q. A. W. (1995). Obedience in modern society: The Utrecht Studies. *Journal of Social Issues, 51*, 155–175.

Meier, D. (1995). *The power of their ideas*. New York: Beacon.

Meindl, J. R., & Lerner, M. J. (1984). Exacerbation of extreme response to an out-group. *Journal of Personality and Social Psychology, 47*, 71–83.

Meissner, C. A., & Brigham, J. C. (2001) A meta-analysis of the verbal overshadowing effect in face identification. *Applied Cognitive Psychology, 15*, 603–616.

Meissner, C. A., Tredoux, C. G., & Parker, J. F. (2005). Eyewitness decisions in simultaneous and sequential lineups: A dual-process signal detection theory analysis. *Memory and Cognition, 33*, 783–792.

Melara, R. D., DeWitt-Rickards, T. S., & O'Brien, T. P. (1989). Enhancing lineup identification accuracy: Two codes are better than one. *Journal of Applied Psychology, 74*, 706–713.

Mendes, W. B., Gray, H. M., Mendoza-Denton, R., Major, B., & Epel, E. S. (2007). Why egalitarianism might be good for your health: Physiological thriving during stressful intergroup encounters. *Psychological Science, 18*(11), 991–998.

Menec, V. H., & Chipperfield, J. G. (1997). The interactive effect of perceived control and functional status on health and mortality among young-old and old-old adults. *Journal of Gerontology: Psychological Sciences, 52B*, 118–126.

Menec, V. H., Chipperfield, J. G., & Perry, R. P. (1999). Self-perceptions of health: A prospective analysis of mortality, control, and health. *Journal of Gerontology: Psychological Sciences, 54B*, 85–93.

Menec, V. H., & Perry, R. P. (1998). Reactions to stigmas among Canadian students: Testing attribution-affect-help judgment model. *Journal of Social Psychology, 138*, 443–453.

Menec, V. H., Perry, R. P., Struthers, C. W., Schonwetter, D. J., Hechter, F. J., & Eichholz, B. L. (1994). Assisting at-risk college students with attributional retraining and effective teaching. *Journal of Applied Social Psychology, 24*, 675–701.

Menzies-Toman, D. A., & Lydon, J. E. (2005). Commitment-motivated benign appraisals of partner transgressions: Do they facilitate accommodation? *Journal of Social and Personal Relationships, 22*, 111–128.

Merikle, P. M. (1988). Subliminal auditory messages: An evaluation. *Psychology and Marketing, 5*, 355–372.

Merton, R. K. (1948). The self-fulfilling prophecy. *Antioch Review, 8*, 193–210.

Messick, D., & Liebrand, W. B. G. (1995). Individual heuristics and the dynamics of cooperation in large groups. *Psychological Review, 102*, 131–145.

Meston, C. M., & Frohlich, P. F. (2003). Love at first fright: Partner salience moderates roller-coaster-induced excitation transfer. *Archives of Sexual Behavior, 32*(6), 537–544.

Metcalfe, J. (1998). Cognitive optimism: Self-deception or memory-based processing heuristics? *Personality and Social Psychology Review, 2,* 100–110.

Mewhinney, D. M., Herold, E. S., & Maticka-Tyndale, E. (1995). Sexual scripts and risk taking of Canadian university students on spring break in Daytona Beach, Florida. *Canadian Journal of Human Sexuality, 4,* 273–288.

Meyer, P. (1999). The sociobiology of human cooperation: The interplay of ultimate and proximate causes. In J. M. G. van der Dennen & D. Smillie (Eds.), *The Darwinian heritage and sociobiology: Human evolution, behavior, and intelligence.* (pp. 49–65.) Westport, CT: Praeger.

Meyerowitz, B. E., & Chaiken, S. (1987). The effect of message framing on breast self-examination attitudes, intentions, and behavior. *Journal of Personality and Social Psychology, 52,* 500–510.

Michalos, A. C., & Zumbo, B. D. (2001). Ethnicity, modern prejudice, and the quality of life. *Social Indicators Research, 53,* 189–222.

Michaels, J. W., Blommel, J. M., Brocato, R. M., Linkous, R. A., & Rowe, J. S. (1982). Social facilitation and inhibition in a natural setting. *Replications in Social Psychology, 2,* 21–24.

Middleton, W., Harris, P., & Surman, M. (1996). Give 'em enough rope: Perception of health and safety risks in bungee jumpers. *Journal of Social and Clinical Psychology, 15,* 68–79.

Migration and geographic mobility in metropolitan and nonmetropolitan America, 1995–2000 (2003). United States Census Bureau. www.census.gov/prod/2003pubs/censr-9.pdf. Accessed April 2006.

Mikulincer, M., & Shaver, P. R. (2005). Attachment theory and emotions in close relationships: Exploring the attachment-anxiety dynamics of emotional reactions to relational events. *Personal Relationships, 12,* 149–168.

Mikulincer, M. & Shaver, P. R. (2007). *Attachment in adulthood: Structure, dynamics, and change.* New York: Guilford Press.

Mikulincer, M. & Shaver, P. R. (in press). *Handbook of prosocial emotion.* Washington, DC: APA Press.

Milgram, S. (1963). Behavioral study of obedience. *Journal of Abnormal and Social Psychology, 67,* 371–378.

Milgram, S. (1969, March). The lost letter technique. *Psychology Today,* pp. 30–33, 67–68.

Milgram, S. (1970). The experience of living in cities. *Science, 167,* 1461–1468.

Milgram, S. (1974). *Obedience to authority: An experimental view.* New York: Harper & Row.

Milgram, S. (1976). Obedience to criminal orders: The compulsion to do evil. In T. Blass (Ed.), *Contemporary social psychology: Representative readings.* (pp. 175–184.) Itasca, IL: F. E. Peacock.

Milgram, S., & Sabini, J. (1978). On maintaining urban norms: A field experiment in the subway. In A. Baum, J. E. Singer, & S. Valins (Eds.), *Advances in environmental psychology.* (Vol. 1, pp. 9–40.) Hillsdale, NJ: Erlbaum.

Mill, D., Gray, T., & Mandel, D. R. (1994). Influence of research methods and statistics courses on everyday reasoning, critical abilities, and belief in unsubstantiated phenomena. *Canadian Journal of Behavioural Science, 26,* 246–258.

Miller, A. F. (1995). Constructions of the obedience experiments: A focus upon domains of relevance. *Journal of Social Issues, 51,* 33–53.

Miller, A. G. (1986). *The obedience experiments: A case study of controversy in social science.* New York: Praeger.

Miller, A. G., Ashton, W., & Mishal, M. (1990). Beliefs concerning the features of constrained behavior: A basis for the fundamental attribution error. *Journal of Personality and Social Psychology, 59,* 635–650.

Miller, C. E., & Anderson, P. D. (1979). Group decision rules and the rejection of deviates. *Social Psychology Quarterly, 42,* 354–363.

Miller, C. T. (1982). The role of performance-related similarity in social comparison of abilities: A test of the related attributes hypothesis. *Journal of Experimental Social Psychology, 18,* 513–523.

Miller, D. T., & McFarland, C. (1986). Counterfactual thinking and victim compensation: A test of norm theory. *Personality and Social Psychology Bulletin, 12,* 513–519.

Miller, D. T., & McFarland, C. (1987). Pluralistic ignorance: When similarity is interpreted as dissimilarity. *Journal of Personality and Social Psychology, 53,* 298–305.

Miller, D. T., & Ratner, R. K. (1996). The power of the myth of self-interest. In L. Montada & M. Lerner (Eds.), *Current societal concerns about justice.* (pp. 25–48.) New York: Plenum.

Miller, D. T., & Ross, M. (1975). Self-serving biases in the attribution of causality: Fact or fiction? *Psychological Bulletin, 82,* 213–225.

Miller, D. T., & Taylor, B. R. (2002). Counterfactual thought, regret, and superstition: How to avoid kicking yourself. In T. Gilovich, D. Griffin, & D. Kahneman (Eds.), *Heuristics and biases: The psychology of intuitive judgment.* (pp. 367–378.) Cambridge, UK: Cambridge University Press.

Miller, D. T., Turnbull, W., & McFarland, C. (1990). Counterfactual thinking and social perception: Thinking about what might have been. In M. P. Zanna (Ed.), *Advances in experimental social psychology.* (Vol. 23, pp. 305–331.) San Diego, CA: Academic Press.

Miller, J. G. (1984). Culture and the development of everyday social explanation. *Journal of Personality and Social Psychology, 46,* 961–978.

Miller, J. G., Bersoff, D. M., & Harwood, R. L. (1990). Perceptions of social responsibilities in India and the United States: Moral imperatives or personal decisions? *Journal of Personality and Social Psychology, 58,* 33–47.

Miller, N., & Campbell, D. T. (1959). Recency and primacy in persuasion as a function of the timing of speeches and measurements. *Journal of Abnormal and Social Psychology, 59,* 1–9.

Miller, P. J. E., Niehuis, & Huston, T. L. (2006). Positive illusions in marital relationships: A 13-year longitudinal study. *Personality and Social Psychology Bulletin, 32,* 1579–1594.

Millin, L. (2002, August 7). Just forget recovered memory. *Winnipeg Free Press,* p. A12.

Mills, J. (1958). Changes in moral attitudes following temptation. *Journal of Personality, 26,* 517–531.

Mills, J., & Clark, M. S. (1982). Communal and exchange relationships. In L. Wheeler (Ed.), *Review of personality and social psychology.* (Vol. 2, pp. 121–144.) Beverly Hills, CA: Sage.

Mills, J., & Clark, M. S. (1994). Communal and exchange relationships: Controversies and research. In R. Erber & R. Gilmour (Eds.), *Theoretical frameworks for personal relationships.* (pp. 29–42.) Hillsdale, NJ: Erlbaum.

Mills, J., & Clark, M. S. (2001). Viewing close romantic relationships as communal relationships: Implications for maintenance and enhancement. In J. Harvey & A. Wenzel (Eds.), *Close romantic relationships: Maintenance and enhancement.* (pp. 13–25.) Mahwah, NJ: Erlbaum.

Mills, J. S., Polivy, J., Herman, C. P., & Tiggemann, M. (2002). Effects of exposure to thin media images: Evidence of self-enhancement among restrained eaters. *Personality and Social Psychology Bulletin, 28,* 1687–1699.

Misconceptions about why people obey laws and accept judicial decisions (1997, September). *American Psychological Society Observer, 5,* 12–13, 46.

Mitchell, K. J., & Johnson, M. K. (2000). Source monitoring: Attributing mental experiences. In E. Tulving & F. I. Craik (Eds.), *Oxford handbook of memory.* (pp. 179–195.) New York: Oxford University Press.

Mitchell, K. J., Johnson, M. K., & Mather, M. (2003). Source monitoring and suggestibility to misinformation: Adult age-related differences. *Applied Cognitive Psychology, 17,* 107–119.

Mittelstaedt, M. (2008, October 8). Oil sands will pollute Great Lakes, report warns. *Globe and Mail.* www.theglobeandmail.com/servlet/story/RTGAM.20081008.wlakes08/BNStory/National/home. Accessed October 2008.

Modigliani, A., & Rochat, F. (1995). The role of interaction sequences and the timing of resistance in shaping obedience and defiance to authority. *Journal of Social Issues, 51,* 107–123.

Moghaddam, F. M., Taylor, D. M., & Wright, S. C. (1993). *Social psychology in cross-cultural perspective.* New York: Freeman.

Mohamed, A. A., & Wiebe, F. A. (1996). Toward a process theory of groupthink. *Small Group Research, 27,* 416–430.

Mohipp, C., & Morry, M. M. (2004). The relationship of symbolic beliefs and prior contact to heterosexuals' attitudes toward gay men and lesbian women. *Canadian Journal of Behavioural Science, 36,* 36–44.

Montemayor, R., & Eisen, M. (1977). The development of self-conceptions from childhood to adolescence. *Developmental Psychology, 13,* 314–319.

Moore, R. L. (1998). Love and limerance with Chinese characteristics: Student romance in the PRC. In V. C. de Munck (Ed.), *Romantic love and sexual behavior.* (pp. 251–283.) Westport, CT: Praeger.

Moore, T. E. (1995). Subliminal self-help tapes: An empirical test of perceptual consequences. *Canadian Journal of Behavioural Science, 27,* 9–20.

Moray, N. (1959). Attention in dichotic listening: Affective cues and the influence of instructions. *Quarterly Journal of Experimental Psychology, 11,* 56–60.

Moreland, R. L. (1987). The formation of small groups. In C. Hendrick (Ed.), *Review of personality and social psychology.* (Vol. 8, pp. 80–110.) Newbury Park, CA: Sage.

Moreland, R. L. (1999). Transactive memory: Learning who knows what in work groups and organizations. In L. L. Thompson & J. M. Levine (Eds.), *Shared cognition in organizations: The management of knowledge.* (pp. 3–31.) Mahwah, NJ: Erlbaum.

Moreland, R. L., Argote, L., & Krishnan, R. (1996). Socially shared cognition at work: Transactive memory and group performance. In J. L. Nye & A. M. Brower (Eds.), *What's social about social cognition?* (pp. 57–84.) Thousand Oaks, CA: Sage.

Moreland, R. L., & Beach, R. (1992). Exposure effects in the classroom: The development of affinity among students. *Journal of Experimental Social Psychology, 28,* 255–276.

Moreland, R. L., & Zajonc, R. B. (1982). Exposure effects in person perception: Familiarity, similarity, and attraction. *Journal of Experimental Social Psychology, 18,* 395–415.

Morris, M. W., & Peng, K. (1994). Culture and cause: American and Chinese attributions for social and physical events. *Journal of Personality and Social Psychology, 67,* 949–971.

Morris, W. N., & Miller, R. S. (1975). The effects of consensus-breaking and consensus-preempting partners on reduction of conformity. *Journal of Experimental Social Psychology, 11,* 215–223.

Morry, M. M. (2005a). Relationship satisfaction as a predictor of similarity ratings: A test of the attraction-similarity hypothesis. *Journal of Social and Personal Relationships, 22,* 561–584.

Morry, M. M. (2005b). Allocentrism and friendship satisfaction: The mediating roles of disclosure and closeness. *Canadian Journal of Behavioural Science, 37(3),* 211–222.

Morry, M. M. (2007). The attraction-similarity hypothesis among cross-sex friends: Relationship satisfaction, perceived similarities, and self-serving perceptions. *Journal of Social and Personal Relationships, 24,* 117–138.

Morry, M. M., & Harasymchuk, C. (2005). Perceptions of locus of control and satisfaction in friendships: The impact of problem-solving strategies. *Journal of Social and Personal Relationships, 22,* 183–206.

Morry, M. M., & Kito, M. (in press). Relational-interdependent self-construal as a predictor of relationship quality: The mediating roles of one's own behaviors and perceptions of the fulfillment of friendship functions. *Journal of Social Psychology.*

Morry, M. M., & Staska, S. L. (2001). Magazine exposure: Internalization, self-objectification, eating attitudes, and body satisfaction in male and female university students. *Canadian Journal of Behavioural Science, 33,* 269–279.

Morry, M. M., & Winkler, E. (2001). Student acceptance and expectation of sexual assault. *Canadian Journal of Behavioural Science, 33,* 188–192.

Morse, D. R., Martin, J., & Moshonov, J. (1991). Psychosomatically induced death: Relative to stress, hypnosis, mind control, and voodoo: Review and possible mechanisms. *Stress Medicine, 7,* 213–232.

Moscovici, S. (1985). Social influence and conformity. In G. Lindzey & E. Aronson (Eds.), *Handbook of social psychology.* (Vol. 2, pp. 347–412.) New York: McGraw-Hill.

Moscovici, S. (1994). Three concepts: Minority, conflict, and behavioral style. In S. Moscovici, A. Mucchi-Faina, & A. Maass (Eds.), *Minority Influence.* (pp. 233–251.) Chicago, IL: Nelson-Hall.

Moscovici, S., & Nemeth, C. (1974). Minority influence. In C. Nemeth (Ed.), *Social psychology: Classic and contemporary integrations.* (pp. 217–249.) Chicago, IL: Rand McNally.

Moscovitch, M., Winocur, G., & Behrmann, M. (1997). What is special about face recognition? Nineteen experiments on a person with visual object agnosia and dyslexia but normal face recognition. *Journal of Cognitive Neuroscience, 9,* 555–604.

Moskalenko, S., & Heine, S. (2003). Watching your troubles away: Television viewing as a stimulus for subjective self-awareness. *Personality and Social Psychology Bulletin, 29,* 76–85.

Moyer, K. E. (1983). The physiology of motivation: Aggression as a model. In C. J. Scheier & A. M. Rogers (Eds.), *G. Stanley Hall Lecture Series.* (Vol. 3.) Washington, DC: American Psychological Association.

Mukai, T. (1996). Mothers, peers, and perceived pressure to diet among Japanese adolescent girls. *Journal of Research in Adolescence, 6,* 309–324.

Mukai, T., Kambara, A., & Sasaki, Y. (1998). Body dissatisfaction, need for social approval, and eating disturbances among Japanese and American college women. *Sex Roles, 39,* 751–771.

Mullen, B. (1986). Atrocity as a function of lynch mob composition: A self-attention perspective. *Personality and Social Psychology Bulletin, 12,* 187–197.

Mullen, B., Rozell, D., & Johnson, C. (2001). Ethnophaulisms for ethnic immigrant groups: The contributions of group size and familiarity. *European Journal of Social Psychology, 31,* 231–246.

Muller, D., Atzeni, T., & Fabrizio, B. (2004). Coaction and upward social comparison reduce the illusory conjunction effect: Support for distraction-conflict theory. *Journal of Experimental Social Psychology, 40,* 659–665.

Mummery, W. K., & Wankel, L. M. (1999). Training adherence in adolescent competitive swimmers: An application of the theory of planned behavior. *Journal of Sport and Exercise Psychology, 21,* 313–328.

Muraven, M., Tice, D. M., & Baumeister, R. F. (1998). Self-control as limited resource: Regulatory depletion patterns. *Journal of Personality and Social Psychology, 74,* 774–789.

Murdoch, D., Pihl, R. O., & Ross, D. (1990). Alcohol and crimes of violence: Present issues. *International Journal of Addictions, 25,* 1065–1081.

Murray, S. L., Bellavia, G., Feeney, B., Holmes, J. G., & Rose, P. (2001). The contingencies of interpersonal acceptance: When romantic relationships function as a self-affirmational resource. *Motivation and Emotion, 25,* 163–189.

Murray, S. L., Griffin, D. W., Rose, P., & Bellavia, G. M. (2003). Calibrating the sociometer: The relational contingencies of self-esteem. *Journal of Personality and Social Psychology, 85(1),* 63–84.

Murray, S. L., Haddock, G., and Zanna, M. P. (1996). On creating value-expressive attitudes: An experimental approach. In Seligman, Olson, & Zanna (Eds.), *The psychology of values: The Ontario symposium.* (Vol. 8.) Mahwah, NJ: Erlbaum.

Murray, S. L., & Holmes, J. G. (1993). Seeing virtues in faults: Negativity and the transformation of interpersonal narratives in close relationships. *Journal of Personality and Social Psychology, 65,* 707–722.

Murray, S. L., & Holmes, J. G. (1997). A leap of faith? Positive illusions in romantic relationships. *Personality and Social Psychology Bulletin, 23*, 586–604.

Murray, S. L., & Holmes, J. G. (1999). The (mental) ties that bind: Cognitive structures that predict relationship resilience. *Journal of Personality and Social Psychology, 77*, 1228–1244.

Murray, S. L., Holmes, J. G., Bellavia, G., Griffin, D. W., & Dolderman, D. (2002). Kindred spirits? The benefits of egocentrism in close relationships. *Journal of Personality and Social Psychology, 82*, 563–581.

Murray, S. L., Holmes, J. G., Dolderman, D., & Griffin, D. W. (2000). What the motivated mind sees: Comparing friends' perspectives to married partners' views of each other. *Journal of Experimental Social Psychology, 36*, 600–620.

Murray, S. L., Holmes, J. G., & Griffin, D. W. (1996a). The benefits of positive illusions: Idealization and the construction of satisfaction in close relationships. *Journal of Personality and Social Psychology, 70*, 79–98.

Murray, S. L., Holmes, J. G., & Griffin, D. W. (1996b). The self-fulfilling nature of positive illusions in romantic relationships: Love is not blind, but prescient. *Journal of Personality and Social Psychology, 71*, 1155–1180.

Murray, S. L., Holmes, J. G., MacDonald, G., & Ellsworth, P. C. (1998). Through the looking glass darkly? When self-doubts turn into relationship insecurities. *Journal of Personality and Social Psychology, 75*, 1459–1480.

Murray, S. L., Rose, P., Holmes, J. G., Derrick, J., Podchaski, E. J., Bellavia, G., et al. (2005). Putting the partner within reach: A dyadic perspective on felt security in close relationships. *Journal of Personality and Social Psychology, 88*, 327–347.

Mussen, P., & Eisenberg-Berg, N. (1977). *Roots of caring, sharing, and helping: The development of prosocial behavior in children.* San Francisco, CA: Freeman.

Mussweiler, T., Strack, F., & Pfeiffer, T. (2000). Overcoming the inevitable anchoring effect: Considering the opposite compensates for selective accessibility. *Personality and Social Psychology Bulletin, 26*, 1142–1150.

Nadler, A., & Fisher, J. D. (1986). The role of threat to self-esteem and perceived control in recipient reactions to help: Theory development and empirical validation. In L. Berkowitz (Ed.), *Advances in experimental social psychology.* (Vol. 19, pp. 81–123.) New York: Academic Press.

Nail, P. R., McDonald, G., & Levy, D. A. (2000). Proposal of a four-dimensional model of social response. *Psychological Bulletin, 126*, 454–470.

Naimi, T., Brewer, B., Mokdad, A., Serdula, M., Denny, C., & Marks, J. (2003). Binge drinking among U.S. adults. *Journal of the American Medical Association, 289*, 70–75.

Nasco, S. A., & Marsh, K. L. (1999). Gaining control through counterfactual thinking. *Personality and Social Psychology Bulletin, 25*, 556–568.

Nathanson, S. (1987). *An eye for an eye? The morality of punishing by death.* Totowa, NJ: Roman & Littlefield.

Neal, A. (2000, July 7). The handbag. *The other story.* [Radio broadcast.] Canadian Broadcasting Corporation. www.ottawa.cbc.ca/theotherstory/handbag.html. Broadcast November 14, 2000.

Neisser, U. (1976). *Cognition and reality: Principles and implications of cognitive psychology.* San Francisco, CA: Freeman.

Nelson, D. E., Bland, S., Powell-Griner, E., Klein, R., Wells, H. E., Hogelin, G., & Marks, J. S. (2002). State trends in health risk factors and receipt of clinical preventive services among US adults during the 1990s. *Journal of the American Medical Association, 287*, 2659–2667.

Nemeroff, C. J., Stein, R. I., Diehl, N. S., & Smilack, K. M. (1995). From the Cleavers to the Clintons: Role choices and body orientation as reflected in magazine article content. *International Journal of Eating Disorders, 16*, 167–176.

Nemeth, C. J., & Chiles, C. (1988). Modeling courage: The role of dissent in fostering independence. *European Journal of Social Psychology, 18*, 275–280.

Newby-Clark, I. R., McGregor, I., & Zanna, M. P. (2002). Thinking and caring about cognitive inconsistency: When and for whom does attitudinal ambivalence feel uncomfortable? *Journal of Personality and Social Psychology, 82*, 157–166.

Newcomb, T. M. (1961). The acquaintance process. New York: Holt, Rinehart & Winston.

Newman, L. S. (1991). Why are traits inferred spontaneously? A developmental approach. *Social Cognition, 9*, 221–253.

Newman, L. S. (1996). Trait impressions as heuristics for predicting future behavior. *Personality and Social Psychology Bulletin, 22*, 395–411.

Newman, P. C. (2005). *The secret Mulroney tapes: Confessions of a prime minister.* Toronto, ON: Random House.

Nguyen, M., Beland, F., Otis, J., & Potvin, L. (1996). Diet and exercise profiles of 30- to 60-year-old male smokers: Implications for community heart health programs. *Journal of Adolescent Health, 21*, 107–115.

Niederhoffer, K. G., & Pennebaker, J. W. (2002). Sharing one's story: On the benefits of writing or talking about emotional experience. In C. R. Snyder & S. J. Lopez (Eds.), *Handbook of positive psychology.* (pp. 573–583.) London, UK: Oxford University Press.

Nikiforuk, A. (2008). *Tar sands: Dirty oil and the future of the continent.* Vancouver, BC: Greystone Books.

NIMH Multisite HIV Prevention Trial Group (1998, June 19). The NIMH Multisite HIV Prevention Trial: Reducing sexual HIV risk behavior. *Science, 280*, 1889–1894.

NIMH Multisite HIV Prevention Trial Group (2001). Social-cognitive theory mediators of behavior change in the National Institute of Mental Health Multisite HIV Prevention Trial. *Health Psychology, 20*, 369–376.

Nisbett, R. E. (1993). Violence and U.S. regional culture. *American Psychologist, 48*, 441–449.

Nisbett, R. E. (2003). *The geography of thought: How Asians and Westerners think differently . . . and why.* New York: Free Press.

Nisbett, R. E., Fong, G. T., Lehman, D. R., & Cheng, P. W. (1987). Teaching reasoning. *Science, 238*, 625–631.

Nisbett, R. E., Krantz, D. H., Jepson, C., & Kunda, Z. (1983). The use of statistical heuristics in everyday inductive reasoning. *Psychological Review, 90*, 339–363.

Nisbett, R. E., & Ross, L. (1980). *Human inference: Strategies and shortcomings of human judgment.* Englewood Cliffs, NJ: Prentice Hall.

Nisbett, R. E., & Wilson, T. D. (1977a). Telling more than we can know: Verbal reports on mental processes. *Psychological Review, 84*, 231–259.

Nisbett, R. E., & Wilson, T. D. (1977b). The halo effect: Evidence for unconscious alteration of judgments. *Journal of Personality and Social Psychology, 35*, 250–256.

Noels, K. A., & Clément, R. (1996). Communicating across cultures: Social determinants and acculturative consequences. *Canadian Journal of Behavioural Science, 28*, 214–228.

Noels, K. A., Clément, R., Pelletier, L. G. (1999). Perceptions of teachers' communicative style and students' intrinsic and extrinsic motivation. *Modern Language Journal, 83*, 23–34.

Norenzayan, A., Choi, I., & Nisbett, R. E. (1999). Eastern and Western perceptions of causality for social behavior: Lay theories about personalities and situations. In D. A. Prentice & D. T. Miller (Eds.), *Cultural divides: Understanding and overcoming group conflict.* (pp. 239–272.) New York: Russell Sage Foundation.

Norenzayan, A., & Hansen, I. G. (2006). Belief in supernatural agents in the face of death. *Personality and Social Psychology Bulletin, 32*, 174–187.

Norenzayan, A., & Heine, S. J. (2005). Psychological universals: What are they and how can we know? *Psychological Bulletin, 131*, 763–784.

North, A. C., Tarrant, M., & Hargreaves, D. J. (2004). The effects of music on helping behavior: A field study. *Environment and Behavior, 36,* 266–275.

Nosek, B. A., Banaji, M. R., & Greenwald, A. G. (2002). Math = male, me = female, therefore math fi me. *Journal of Personality and Social Psychology, 83,* 44–59.

Nowak, A., Szamrej, J., & Latané, B. (1990). From private attitude to public opinion: A dynamic theory of social impact. *Psychological Review, 97,* 362–376.

Nowatzki, J., & Morry, M. M. (in press). Women's intentions regarding, and acceptance of, self-sexualizing behaviour. *Psychology of Women Quarterly.*

Nussbaum, A. D., & Steele, C. M. (2007). Situational disengagement and persistence in the face of adversity. *Journal of Experimental Social Psychology, 43,* 831–844.

O'Connor, K. M., & Carnevale, P. J. (1997). A nasty but effective negotiation strategy: Misrepresentation of a common-value issue. *Personality and Social Psychology Bulletin, 23,* 504–515.

O'Farrell, T. J., & Murphy, C. M. (1995). Marital violence before and after alcoholism treatment. *Journal of Consulting and Clinical Psychology, 63,* 256–262.

O'Hara, J. (2000, March 6). The hell of hazing. *Maclean's,* pp. 50–52.

Ohbuchi, K., & Baba, R. (1988). Selection of influence strategies in interpersonal conflicts: Effects of sex, interpersonal relations, and goals. *Tohoku Psychologica Folia, 47,* 63–73.

Ohbuchi, K., Ohno, T., & Mukai, H. (1993). Empathy and aggression: Effects of self-disclosure and fearful appeal. *Journal of Social Psychology, 133,* 243–253.

Ohbuchi, K., & Sato, K. (1994). Children's reactions to mitigating accounts: Apologies, excuses, and intentionality of harm. *Journal of Social Psychology, 134,* 5–17.

Ohtsubo, Y., Masuchi, A., & Nakanishi, D. (2002). Majority influence process in group judgment: Test of the social judgment scheme model in a group polarization context. *Group Processes and Intergroup Relations, 5,* 249–261.

Oishi, S., Rothman, A. J., Snyder, M., Su, J., Zehm, K., Hertel, A. W., Gonzalez, M. H., & Sherman, G. D. (2007). The socioecological model of procommunity action: The benefits of residential stability. *Journal of Personality and Social Psychology, 93,* 831–844.

Oishi, S., Schimmack, U., & Colcombe, S. J. (2003). The contextual and systematic nature of life satisfaction judgments. *Journal of Experimental Social Psychology, 39,* 232–247.

Oishi, S., Wyer, R. S., & Colcombe, S. J. (2000). Cultural variation in the use of current life satisfaction to predict the future. *Journal of Personality and Social Psychology, 78,* 434–445.

O'Leary, J., & Covell, K. (2002). The tar ponds kids: Toxic environments and adolescent well-being. *Canadian Journal of Behavioural Science, 34,* 34–43.

Olson, J. M., Goffin, R. D., & Haynes, G. A. (2007). Relative versus absolute measures of explicit attitudes: Implications for predicting diverse attitude-relevant criteria. *Journal of Personality and Social Psychology, 93,* 907–926.

Olson, J. M., Maio, G. R., & Hobden, K. L. (1999). The (null) effects of exposure to disparagement humor on stereotypes and attitudes. *Humor: International Journal of Humor Research, 12,* 195–219.

Olson, J. M., & Zanna, M. P. (1993). Attitudes and attitude change. *Annual Review of Psychology, 44,* 117–154.

Olsson, N. (2000). A comparison of correlation, calibration, and diagnosticity as measures of the confidence-accuracy relationship. *Journal of Applied Psychology, 85,* 504–511.

Olweus, D. (1996). Bullying at school: Knowledge base and an effective intervention program. In C. Ferris & T. Grisso (Eds.), *Understanding aggressive behavior in children.* (New York Academy of Sciences, Annals of the New York Academy of Sciences. Vol. 794. pp. 265–276.) New York: Academy of Sciences.

Olweus, D. (1997). Tackling peer victimization with a school-based intervention program. In D. Fry & K. Bjorkqvist (Eds.), *Cultural variation in conflict resolution: Alternatives to violence.* (pp. 215–231.) Mahwah, NJ: Erlbaum.

Olweus, D. (2004). The Olewus Bullying Prevention Programme: Design implementation issues and a new national initiative in Norway. In P. K. Smith, D. Pepler, & K. Rigby (Eds.), *Bullying in schools: How successful can interventions be?* (pp. 13–36.) Cambridge, UK: Cambridge University Press.

O'Neill, J. (2007, March 28). Obesity expected to shorten kids' lives. *Winnipeg Free Press,* p. A12.

O'Neill, P. (2000). Cognition in social context. In J. Rappaport & E. Seidman (Eds.) *Handbook of community psychology.* (pp. 115–132.) New York: Springer Publishing.

Onishi, N. (2004, August 7). A princess's distress pierces Japan's veil of secrecy. *New York Times.* http://query.nytimes.com/gst/fullpage.html?res=9B01EEDD103CF934A3575BC0A9629C8B63&sec=health&spon=&pagewanted=all. Accessed December 2008.

Oppenheimer, D. M. (2004). Spontaneous discounting of availability in frequency judgment tasks. *Psychological Science, 15,* 100–105.

Opposition MPs grill PM again about Cadman affair (2008, March 5). *CBC News/cbc.ca.* www.cbc.ca/canada/story/2008/03/05/harper-cadman.html. Accessed October 2008.

Orbell, J. M., van de Kragt, A. J. C., & Dawes, R. M. (1988). Explaining discussion-induced comparison. *Journal of Personality and Social Psychology, 54,* 811–819.

Osbeck, L. M., Moghaddam, F. M., & Perrault. (1997). Similarity and attraction among majority and minority groups in a multicultural context. *International Journal of Intercultural Relations, 21,* 113–123.

Oskamp, S. (1995). Applying social psychology to avoid ecological disaster. *Journal of Social Issues, 51,* 217–238.

Oskamp, S. (2000). A sustainable future for humanity? How can psychology help? *American Psychologist, 55,* 496–508.

Oskamp, S., Burkhardt, R. I., Schultz, P. W., Hurin, S., & Zelezny, L. (1998). Predicting three dimensions of residential curbside recycling: An observational study. *Journal of Environmental Education, 29,* 37–42.

Osofsky, M. J., Bandura, A., & Zimbardo, P. G. (2005). The role of moral disengagement in the execution process. *Law and Human Behavior, 29,* 371–393.

Ostrom, T., & Sedikides, C. (1992). Out-group homogeneity effects in natural and minimal groups. *Psychological Bulletin, 112,* 536–552.

Otten, C. A., Penner, L. A., & Waugh, G. (1988). That's what friends are for: The determinants of psychological helping. *Journal of Social and Clinical Psychology, 7,* 34–41.

Ovcharchyn, C. A., Johnson, H. H., & Petzel, T. P. (1981). Type A behavior, academic aspirations, and academic success. *Journal of Personality, 49,* 248–256.

Overmier, J. B. (2002). On learned helplessness. *Integrative Physiological and Behavioral Science, 37,* 4–8.

Owen, B. (2007, October, 14). Kids who kill. *Winnipeg Free Press,* pp. B1, B4.

Owen, K. I., Wright, S. C., & Brody, S. M. (2001). Bicultural friends: When group membership salience matters. Paper presented at the Western Psychological Association Conference, Maui, Hawaii.

Oyserman, D., Kemmelmeier, M., Fryberg, S., Brosh, H., & Hart-Johnson, T. (2003). Racial-ethnic self-schemas. *Social Psychology Quarterly, 66,* 333–347.

Packer, D. J. (2008). Identifying systematic disobedience in Milgram's obedience experiments. *Psychological Science, 3,* 301–304.

Page, S. (1998). Accepting the gay person: Rental accommodation in the community. *Journal of Homosexuality, 36,* 31–39.

Page, S. (1999). Accommodating persons with AIDS: Acceptance and rejection in rental situations. *Journal of Applied Social Psychology, 29,* 261–270.

Palmer, D. L. (1996). Determinants of Canadian attitudes toward immigration: More than just racism? *Canadian Journal of Behavioural Science, 28*, 180–192.

Palmer, D. L. (2000). *Canadian attitudes in the wake of the boats from China.* Submitted to Citizenship and Immigration Canada.

Pancer, S. M., & Pratt, M. W. (1999). Social and family determinants of community service involvement in Canadian youth. In M. Yates & J. Youniss (Eds.), *Roots of civic identity: International perspectives on community service and activism in youth.* Cambridge, UK: Cambridge University Press.

Panetta, A. (2005, December 14). The Harper effect: The more we see him, the more we dislike him, poll suggests. *Winnipeg Free Press,* pp. A1, A11.

Panetta, A. (2008, January 10). Canada's first female PM springs to defence of Hillary Clinton. Canadian Press. http://cnews.canoe.ca/CNEWS/Canada/2008/01/10/4766419-cp.html. Accessed September 2008.

Paolucci-Oddone, E., Genius, M., & Violato, C. (2000). A meta-analysis of the published research on the effects of pornography. In C. Violato (Ed.), *The changing family and child development.* (pp. 48–59.) Burlington, VT: Ashgate Publishing.

Parish, A. R., & De Waal, F. B. M. (2000). The other "closest living relative": How bonobos (pan paniscus) challenge traditional assumptions about females, dominance, intra- and intersexual interactions, and hominid evolution. In D. LeCroy & P. Moller (Eds.), *Evolutionary perspectives on human reproductive behavior.* (pp. 97–113.) New York: New York Academy of Sciences.

Parke, R. D., Berkowitz, L., Leyens, J. P., West, S. G., & Sebastian, R. J. (1977). Some effects of violent and nonviolent movies on the behavior of juvenile delinquents. In L. Berkowitz (Ed.), *Advances in experimental social psychology.* (Vol. 10, pp. 135–172.) New York: Academic Press.

Parker, I. (2007, July 30). Swingers: Bonobos are celebrated as peace-loving, matriarchal, and sexually liberated. Are they? *New Yorker.* www.newyorker.com/reporting/2007/07/30/070730fa_fact_parker?printable=true. Accessed October 2008.

Parks, C. D., & Rumble, A. C. (2001). Elements of reciprocity and social value orientation. *Personality and Social Psychology Bulletin, 27*, 1301–1309.

Patch, M. E., Hoang, V. R., & Stahelski, A. J. (1997). The use of meta-communication in compliance: Door-in-the-face and single-request strategies. *Journal of Social Psychology, 137*, 88–94.

Patrick, C. J., & Iacono, W. G. (1989). Psychopathy, threat, and polygraph test accuracy. *Journal of Applied Psychology, 74*, 347–355.

Patterson, A. (1974, September). Hostility catharsis: A naturalistic quasi-experiment. Paper presented at the meeting of the American Psychological Association, New Orleans.

Patterson, L. A., Cameron, J. E., & Lalonde, R. N. (1996). The intersection of race and gender: Examining the politics of identity in women's studies. *Canadian Journal of Behavioural Science, 28*, 229–239.

Patton, E., & Johns, G. (2007). Women's absenteeism in the popular press: Evidence for a gender-specific absence culture. *Human Relations, 60*, 1579–1612.

Paulhus, D. L. (1998). Interpersonal and intrapsychic adaptiveness of trait self-enhancement: A mixed blessing? *Journal of Personality and Social Psychology, 74*, 1197–1208.

Paulhus, D. L., & Bruce, M. N. (1992). The effect of acquaintanceship on the validity of personality impressions: A longitudinal study. *Journal of Personality and Social Psychology, 63*, 816–824.

Paulhus, D. L., & Morgan, K. L. (1997). Perceptions of intelligence in leadership groups: The dynamic effects of shyness and acquaintance. *Journal of Personality and Social Psychology, 72*, 581–591.

Paulhus, D. L., & Reynolds, S. (1995). Enhancing target variance in personality impressions: Highlighting the person in person perception. *Journal of Personality and Social Psychology, 69*, 1233–1242.

Pavlidis, I., Eberhardt, N. L., & Levine, J. A. (2002). Seeing through the face of deception: Thermal imaging offers a promising hands-off approach to mass security screening. *Nature, 415*, 35.

Payne, B. K. (2001). Prejudice and Perception: The role of automatic and controlled processes in misperceiving a weapon. *Journal of Personality and Social Psychology, 81*, 1–12.

Payne, B. K., Shimizu, Y., & Jacoby, L. L. (2005). Mental control and visual illusions: Toward explaining race-biased weapon misidentifications. *Journal of Experimental Social Psychology, 41*, 36–47.

Peebles, F. (2008, April 10). Teen saves family from fire. *Prince George Citizen.* www.princegeorgecitizen.com/20080410126500/local/news/teen-saves-family-from-fire.html. Accessed November 2008.

Pelletier, L. G. (2002). A motivational analysis of self-determination for pro-environmental behaviors. In E. L. Deci & R. M. Ryan (Eds.), *Handbook of self-determination research.* (pp. 205–232.) Rochester, NY: University of Rochester Press.

Pelletier, L. G., Dion, S., Tuson, K., & Green-Demers, I. (1999). Why do people fail to adopt environmental protective behaviors? Toward a taxonomy of environmental amotivation. *Journal of Applied Social Psychology, 29*, 2481–2504.

Pelletier, L. G., Fortier, M. S., Vallerand, R. J., & Briere, N. M. (1996). *Perceived autonomy support, motivation, and persistence in physical activity: A longitudinal investigation.* Unpublished manuscript, University of Ottawa.

Pennebaker, J. W. (1990). *Opening up: The healing powers of confiding in others.* New York: William Morrow.

Pennebaker, J. W. (1997). Writing about emotional experiences as a therapeutic process. *Psychological Science, 8*, 162–166.

Pennebaker, J. W. (2004). Theories, therapies, and taxpayers: On the complexities of the expressive writing paradigm. *Clinical Psychology: Science and Practice, 11*, 138–142.

Pennebaker, J. W., Barger, S. D., & Tiebout, J. (1989). Disclosure of traumas and health among Holocaust survivors. *Psychosomatic Medicine, 51*, 577–589.

Pennebaker, J. W., & Beale, S. K. (1986). Confronting a traumatic event: Toward an understanding of inhibition and disease. *Journal of Abnormal Psychology, 95*, 274–281.

Pennebaker, J. W., Colder, M., & Sharp, L. K. (1990). Accelerating the coping process. *Journal of Personality and Social Psychology, 58*, 528–537.

Penner, L. A. (2002). Dispositional and organizational influences on sustained volunteerism: An interactionist perspective. *Journal of Social Issues, 58*, 447–467.

Penner, L. A., Dovidio, J. F., Piliavin, J. A., & Schroeder, D. A. (2005). Prosocial behavior: Multilevel perspectives. *Annual Review of Psychology, 56*, 365–392.

Pennington, N., & Hastie, R. (1988). Explanation-based decision making: Effects of memory structure on judgment. *Journal of Experimental Psychology: Learning, Memory, and Cognition, 14*, 521–533.

Pennington, N., & Hastie, R. (1990). Practical implications of psychological research on juror and jury decision making. *Personality and Social Psychology Bulletin, 16*, 90–105.

Pennington, N., & Hastie, R. (1992). Explaining the evidence: Tests of the story model for juror decision making. *Journal of Personality and Social Psychology, 62*, 189–206.

Pennington, N., & Hastie, R. (1993). Reasoning in explanation-based decision making. *Cognition, 49*, 123–163.

Peplau, L. A., & Perlman, D. (1982). Perspectives on loneliness. In L. A. Peplau & D. Perlman (Eds.), *Loneliness: A sourcebook of current theory, research, and therapy.* (pp. 1–18.) New York: Wiley.

Pepler, D., Craig, W. M., O'Connell, P., Atlas, R., & Charach, A. (2004). Making a difference in bullying: Evaluation of a systemic school-based programme in Canada. In P. K. Smith, D. Pepler, & K. Rigby (Eds.), *Bullying in schools: How successful can interventions be?* (pp. 125–140.) Cambridge, UK: Cambridge University Press.

Pepler, D., Smith, P. K., & Rigby, K. (2004). Looking back and looking forward: Implications for making interventions work effectively. In P. K. Smith, D. Pepler, & K. Rigby (Eds.), *Bullying in schools: How successful can interventions be?* (pp. 307–324.) Cambridge, UK: Cambridge University Press.

Pepler, D. J., & Craig, W. M. (1995). A peek behind the fence: Naturalistic observations of aggressive children with remote audiovisual recording. *Developmental Psychology, 31,* 548–553.

Pepler, D. J., Craig, W. M., Connolly, J., & Henderson, K. (2002). Bullying, sexual harassment, dating violence, and substance abuse among adolescents. In C. Wekerle, & A. Wall (Eds.), *The violence and addiction equation.* (pp. 153–168.) New York: Taylor & Francis.

Pepler, D. J., Craig, W. M., Ziegler, S., & Charach, A. (1994). An evaluation of anti-bullying intervention in Toronto schools. *Canadian Journal of Community Mental Health, 13,* 95–110.

Perlini, A. H., Bertolissi, S., & Lind, D. L. (1999). The effect of women's age and physical appearance on evaluations of attractiveness and social desirability. *Journal of Social Psychology, 139,* 343–351.

Perlini, A. H., & Ward, C. (2000). HIV prevention intentions: The effects of role-play and behavioural commitment on knowledge and attitudes. *Canadian Journal of Behavioural Science, 32,* 133–143.

Perreault, S. & Bourhis, R. Y. (1999). Ethnocentrism, social identification, and discrimination. *Personality and Social Psychology Bulletin, 25,* 92–103.

Perrett, D. I., May, K. A., & Yoshikawa, S. (1994). Facial shape and judgments of female attractivenesss. *Nature, 368,* 239–242.

Perrott, S. B., Miller, Y. M., & Delaney, M. E. (1997). Attitudes toward the mandatory arrest response to domestic battering: Gender and institutional differences from a traditional and a women's university. *Legal and Criminological Psychology, 2,* 35–49.

Perry, R. P. (2003). Perceived (academic) control and causal thinking in achievement settings. *Canadian Psychology, 44*(4), 312–331.

Perry, R. P., Hladkyj, S., Pekrun, R. H., & Pelletier, S. T. (2001). Academic control and action control in the achievement of college students: A longitudinal field study. *Journal of Educational Psychology, 93,* 776–789.

Peters, L. H., Hartke, D. D., & Pohlmann, J. T. (1985). Fiedler's contingency theory of leadership: An application of the meta-analysis procedures of Schmidt and Hunter. *Psychological Bulletin, 97,* 274–285.

Peters, M. (2001). Forensic psychological testimony: Is the courtroom door now locked and barred? *Canadian Psychology, 42,* 101–108.

Peterson, C., & Seligman, M. E. P. (1984). Causal explanations as a risk factor for depression: Theory and evidence. *Psychological Review, 91,* 347–374.

Peterson, R. D., & Bailey, W. C. (1988). Murder and capital punishment in the evolving context of the post–Furman era. *Social Forces, 66,* 774–807.

Petrie, K. J., Booth, R. J., & Pennebaker, J. W. (1998). The immunological effects of thought suppression. *Journal of Personality and Social Psychology, 75,* 1264–1272.

Petrie, T. A., Austin, L. J., Crowley, B. J., Helmcamp, A., Johnson, C. E., Lester, R., Rogers, R., Turner, J., & Walbrick, K. (1996). Sociocultural expectations for attractiveness for males. *Sex Roles, 35,* 581–602.

Pettigrew, T. F. (1958). Personality and sociocultural factors and intergroup attitudes: A cross-national comparison. *Journal of Conflict Resolution, 2,* 29–42.

Pettigrew, T. F. (1969). Racially separate or together? *Journal of Social Issues, 25,* 43–69.

Pettigrew, T. F. (1979). The ultimate attribution error: Extending Allport's cognitive analysis of prejudice. *Personality and Social Psychology Bulletin, 5,* 461–476.

Pettigrew, T. F. (1985). New black-white patterns: How best to conceptualize them? *Annual Review of Sociology, 11,* 329–346.

Pettigrew, T. F. (1991). Normative theory in intergroup relations: Explaining both harmony and conflict. Special Issue: Conflict and harmony in pluralistic societies. *Psychology and Developing Societies, 3,* 3–16.

Pettijohn II, T. F., & Jungeberg, B. J. (2004). Playboy playmate curves: Changes in facial and body feature preferences across social and economic conditions. *Personality and Social Psychology Bulletin, 30*:9, 1186–1197.

Petty, R. E., Cacioppo, J. T., Strathman, A. J., & Priester, J. R. (2005). To think or not to think: Exploring two routes to persuasion. In T. C. Brock & M. C. Green (Eds.), *Persuasion: Psychological insights and perspectives.* (pp. 81–116.) Thousand Oaks, CA: Sage Publications, Inc.

Petty, R. E. (1995). Attitude change. In A. Tesser (Ed.), *Advanced social psychology.* (pp. 195–255.) New York: McGraw-Hill.

Petty, R. E., & Cacioppo, J. T. (1986). *Communication and persuasion: Central and peripheral routes to attitude change.* New York: Springer-Verlag.

Petty, R. E., Haugtvedt, C. P., & Smith, S. M. (1995). Elaboration as a determinant of attitude strength. In R. E. Petty & J. A. Krosnick (Eds.), *Attitude strength: Antecedents and consequences.* (pp. 93–130.) Mahwah, NJ: Erlbaum.

Petty, R. E., & Wegener, D. T. (1999). The elaboration likelihood model: Current status and controversies. In S. Chaiken & Y. Trope (Eds.), *Dual-process theories in social psychology.* (pp. 41–72.) New York: Guilford Press.

Petty, R. E., Wegener, D. T., & Fabrigar, L. R. (1997). Attitudes and attitude change. *Annual Review of Psychology, 48,* 609–647.

Pezdek, K., & Banks, W. P. (Eds.) (1996). *The recovered memory/false memory debate.* San Diego, CA: Academic Press.

Pfeifer, J. E. (1997). Social psychology in the courtroom. In S. W. Sadava & D. R. McCreary (Eds.), *Applied social psychology.* Upper Saddle River, New Jersey: Prentice-Hall.

Pfeifer, J. E., & Ogloff, J. R. P. (1991). Ambiguity and guilt determinations: A modern racism perspective. *Journal of Applied Social Psychology, 21,* 1713–1725.

Pfeifer, J. E., & Ogloff, J. R. P. (2003). Mock juror ratings of guilt in Canada: Modern racism and ethnic heritage. *Social Behavior and Personality, 31*(3), 301–312.

Phillips, A. G., & Silvia, P. J. (2005). Self-awareness and the emotional consequences of self-discrepancies. *Personality and Social Psychology Bulletin, 31,* 703–713.

Pickel, K. L. (1998). Unusualness and threat as possible causes of "weapons focus." *Memory, 6,* 277–295.

Pickett, C. L., Silver, M. D., & Brewer, M. B. (2002). The impact of assimilation and differentiation needs on perceived group importance and judgments of ingroup size. *Personality and Social Psychology Bulletin, 28,* 546–558.

Pierce, R. S., Frone, M. R., Russell, M., & Cooper, M. L. (1996). Financial stress, social support, and alcohol involvement: A longitudinal test of the buffering hypothesis in a general population survey. *Health Psychology, 15,* 38–47.

Pierce, T., & Lydon, J. E. (2001). Global and specific relational models in the experience of social interactions. *Journal of Personality and Social Psychology, 80,* 613–631.

Piferi, R. L., Jobe, R. L., & Jones, W. H. (2006). Giving to others during national tragedy: The effects of altruistic and egoistic motivations on long-term giving. *Journal of Social and Personal Relationships, 23,* 171–184.

Pihl, R. O., & Hoaken, P. N. S. (2002). Biological bases of addiction and aggression in close relationships. In C. Wekerle, & A. Wall (Eds.), *The violence and addiction equation.* (pp. 25–43.) New York: Taylor & Francis.

Pihl, R. O., & Peterson, J. (1995). Drugs and aggression: Correlations, crime and human manipulative studies and some proposed mechanisms. *Journal of Psychiatric Neuroscience, 20,* 141–149.

Pihl, R. O., Young, S. N., Harden, P., Plotnick, S., Chamberlain, B., & Ervin, F. R. (1995). Acute effect of altered tryptophan levels and alcohol on aggression in normal human males. *Psychopharmacology, 119,* 353–360.

Piliavin, I. M., Piliavin, J. A., & Rodin, J. (1975). Costs, diffusion, and the stigmatized victim. *Journal of Personality and Social Psychology, 32,* 429–438.

Piliavin, J. A., & Charng, H. (1990). Altruism: A review of recent theory and research. *Annual Review of Sociology, 16,* 27–65.

Piliavin, J. A., Dovidio, J. F., Gaertner, S., & Clark III, R. D. (1981). *Emergency intervention.* New York: Academic Press.

Piliavin, J. A., & Piliavin, I. M. (1972). The effect of blood on reactions to a victim. *Journal of Personality and Social Psychology, 23,* 253–261.

Pincus, W. (2006, February 10). Ex-cia official faults use of data on Iraq. *Washington Post,* p. A1.

Pinker, S. (2002). *The blank slate: The modern denial of human nature.* New York: Viking.

Pinkus, R. T., Lockwood, P., Schimmack, U., & Fournier, M. A. (2008). For better and worse: Everyday social comparisons between romantic partners. *Journal of Personality and Social Psychology, 95,* 1180–1201.

Plaks, J. E., & Stecher, K. (2007). Unexpected improvement, decline, and stasis: A prediction confidence perspective on achievement success and failure. *Journal of Personality and Social Psychology, 93,* 667–684.

Plant, E. A., & Devine, P. G. (2003). The antecedents and implication of interracial anxiety. *Personality and Social Psychology Bulletin, 29*(6), 790–801.

Pope, H. G., Jr., Olivardia, R., Gruber, A. J., & Borowiecki, J. (1999). Evolving ideals of male body image as seen through action toys. *International Journal of Eating Disorders, 26,* 65–72.

Pope, H. G., Jr., Phillips, K. A., & Olivardia, R. (2000). *The Adonis complex: The secret crisis of male body obsession.* New York: Freeman.

Porter, J. R. (1971). *Black child, white child: The development of racial attitudes.* Cambridge, MA: Harvard University Press.

Porter, J. R., & Washington, R. E. (1979). Black identity and self-esteem, 1968–1978. *Annual Review of Sociology.* Stanford, CA: Annual Reviews.

Porter, J. R., & Washington, R. E. (1989). Developments in research on black identity and self-esteem, 1979–1988. *Revue Internationale de Psychologie Sociale, 2,* 339–353.

Porter, S., Peace, K. A., & Emmett, K. A. (2007). You protest too much, methinks: Investigating the features of truthful and fabricated reports of traumatic experiences. *Canadian Journal of Behavioural Science, 39,* 79–91.

Porter, S., Spencer, L., & Birt, A. R. (2003). Blinded by emotion? Effect of the emotionality of a scene on susceptibility to false memories. *Canadian Journal of Behavioural Science 35,* 165–175.

Porter, S., Woodworth, M., & Birt, A. (2000). Truth, lies, and videotape: An investigation of the ability of federal parole officers to detect deception. *Law and Human Behavior, 24,* 643–658.

Post, S. G., Underwood, L.G., Schloss, J. P., & Hurlbut, W. B. (Eds.) (2002). *Altruism & altruistic love: Science, philosophy, and religion in dialogue.* New York: Oxford University Press.

Postmes, T., & Spears, R. (1998). Deindividuation and antinormative behavior: A meta-analysis. *Psychological Bulletin, 123,* 238–259.

Postmes, T., Spears, R., & Cihangir, S. (2001). Quality of decision making and group norms. *Journal of Personality and Social Psychology, 80,* 918–930.

Potter, R., & Brewer, N. (1999). Perceptions of witness behavior-accuracy relationships held by police, lawyers, and mock-jurors. *Psychiatry, Psychology, and Law, 6,* 97–103.

Pratkanis, A. R. (1992). The cargo-cult science of subliminal persuasion. *Skeptical Inquirer, 16,* 260–272.

Pratkanis, A. R., & Aronson, E. (1991). Subliminal sorcery: Who is seducing whom? *USA Today, 120,* 64–66.

Pratto, F., Sidanius, J., Stallworth, L. M. & Malle, B. F. (1994). Social dominance orientation: A personality variable predicting social and political attitudes. *Journal of Personality and Social Psychology, 67,* 741–763.

Pratto, F., Sidanius, J., Stallworth, L. M., & Malle, B. F. (2000). Social dominance orientation: A personality variable predicting social and political attitudes. In C. Stangor, & C. Stangor (Eds.), *Stereotypes and prejudice: Essential readings.* (pp. 259–288.) New York: Psychology Press.

Prentice-Dunn, S., & Rogers, R. W. (1989). Deindividuation and the self-regulation of behavior. In P. B. Paulus (Ed.), *Psychology of group influence.* (2nd ed., pp. 87–109.) Hillsdale, NJ: Erlbaum.

Proctor, J. (2007, June 21). Talk of the devil. CBC Radio, The Current.

Pronin, E., Lin, D. Y., & Ross, L. (2002). The bias blind spot: Perceptions of bias in self versus others. *Personality and Social Psychology Bulletin, 28,* 369–381.

Pruegger, V. J., & Rogers, T. B. (1993). Development of a scale to measure cross-cultural sensitivity in the Canadian context. *Canadian Journal of Behavioural Science, 25,* 615–621.

Pruitt, D. G. (1998). Social conflict. In D. Gilbert, S. Fiske, & G. Lindzey (Eds.), *The handbook of social psychology.* (4th ed., Vol. 2, pp. 470–503.) New York: McGraw Hill.

Pruitt, D. G., & Kimmel, M. J. (1977). Twenty years of experimental gaming: Critique, synthesis, and suggestions for the future. *Annual Review of Psychology, 28,* 363–392.

Quattrone, G. A. (1982). Behavioral consequences of attributional bias. *Social Cognition, 1,* 358–378.

Quattrone, G. A. (1986). On the perception of a group's variability. In S. Worchel & W. G. Austin (Eds.), *Psychology of intergroup relations.* (2nd ed.) Chicago, IL: Nelson-Hall.

Quattrone, G. A., & Jones, E. E. (1980). The perception of variability within ingroups and outgroups: Implications for the law of small numbers. *Journal of Personality and Social Psychology, 38,* 141–152.

Quinn, K. A., Macrae, C. N., & Bodenhausen, G. V. (2003). Stereotyping and impression formation: How categorical thinking shapes person perception. In M. A. Hogg & J. Cooper (Eds.), *Sage handbook of social psychology.* (pp. 87–109.) Thousand Oaks, CA: Sage.

Quinn, K. A., Roese, N. J., Pennington, G. L., & Olson, J. M. (1999). The personal/group discrimination discrepancy: The role of informational complexity. *Personality and Social Psychology Bulletin, 25,* 1430–1440.

R. v. Ewanchuk (1998). Alberta Court of Appeal, 52. Available at www.albertacourts.ab.ca/webpage/jdb/current_judgments-ca.htm.

Rajecki, D. W., Kidd, R. F., & Ivins, B. (1976). Social facilitation in chickens: A different level of analysis. *Journal of Experimental Social Psychology, 12,* 233–246.

Ramsey, S. J. (1981). The kinesics of femininity in Japanese women. *Language Sciences, 3,* 104–123.

Rapoport, A., & Chammah, A. M. (1965). *Prisoner's Dilemma: A study in conflict and cooperation.* Ann Arbor, MI: University of Michigan Press.

Raps, C. S., Peterson, C., Jonas, M., & Seligman, M. E. P. (1982). Patient behavior in hospitals: Helplessness, reactance, or both? *Journal of Personality and Social Psychology, 42,* 1036–1041.

Raskin, D. C., Honts, C. R., & Kircher, J. C. (1997). The scientific status of research on polygraph techniques: The case for polygraph tests. In D. L. Faigman, D. H. Kaye, M. J. Saks, & J. Sanders (Eds.), *Modern scientific evidence: The law and science of expert testimony.* (pp. 565–582.) St. Paul, MN: West.

Ratelle, C. F., Baldwin, M. W., & Vallerand, R. J. (2005). On the cued activation of situational motivation. *Journal of Experimental Social Psychology, 41*, 482–487.

Read, J. D., Connolly, D., & Turtle, J. W. (2001). Memory in legal contexts: Remembering events, circumstances, and people. In R. A. Schuller, & J. R. P. Ogloff (Eds.) (2001). *Introduction to psychology and law: Canadian perspectives.* (pp. 95–125.) Toronto, ON: University of Toronto Press.

Redersdorff, S., & Guimond, S. (2006). Comparing oneself over time: the temporal dimension of social comparison. In S. Guimond (Ed.). *Social comparison and social psychology* (pp. 76–96). New York: Cambridge University Press.

Reeves, R. A., Baker, G. A., Boyd, J. G., & Cialdini, R. B. (1991). The door-in-the-face technique: Reciprocal concessions vs. self-presentational explanations. *Journal of Social Behavior and Personality, 6*, 545–558.

Regan, P. C. (1998). Of lust and love: Beliefs about the role of sexual desire in romantic relationships. *Personal Relationships, 5*, 139–157.

Regan, P. C., & Berscheid, E. (1995). Gender differences in beliefs about the causes of male and female sexual desire. *Personal Relationships, 2*, 345–358.

Regan, P. C., & Berscheid, E. (1997). Gender differences in characteristics desired in a potential sexual and marriage partner. *Journal of Psychology and Human Sexuality, 9*, 25–37.

Regan, P. C., & Berscheid, E. (1999). *Lust: What we know about human sexual desire.* Thousand Oaks, CA: Sage.

Regan, P. C., Snyder, M., & Kassin, S. M. (1995). Unrealistic optimism: Self-enhancement or person positivity? *Personality and Social Psychology Bulletin, 21*, 1073–1082.

Regehr, C., Cadell, S., & Jansen, K. (1999). Perceptions of control and long-term recovery from rape. *American Journal of Orthopsychiatry, 69*, 110–115.

Rehm, J., Steinleitner, M., & Lilli, W. (1987). Wearing uniforms and aggression: A field experiment. *European Journal of Social Psychology, 17*, 357–360.

Reifman, A. S., Larrick, R., & Fein, S. (1988). The heat-aggression relationship in major-league baseball. Paper presented at the meeting of the American Psychological Association, San Francisco.

Reis, H. T., Clark, M. S., & Holmes, J. G. (2004). Perceived partner responsiveness as an organizing construct in the study of intimacy and closeness. In D. J. Mashek & A. Aron (Eds.), *Handbook of closeness and intimacy.* (pp. 201–225.) New York: Oxford University Press.

Reis, H. T., & Judd, C.M. (Eds.) (2000). *Handbook of research methods in social and personality psychology.* New York, NY: Cambridge University Press.

Reis, H. T., Nezlek, J., & Wheeler, L. (1980). Physical attractiveness in social interaction. *Journal of Personality and Social Psychology, 38*, 604–617.

Reis, H. T., Wheeler, L., Speigel, N., Kernis, M. H., Nezlek, J., & Perri, M. (1982). Physical attractiveness in social interaction 2: Why does appearance affect social experience? *Journal of Personality and Social Psychology, 43*, 979–996.

Reiss, D., & Marino, L. (2001). Mirror self-recognition in the bottlenose dophin: A case of cognitive convergence. *Proceedings of the National Academy of Sciences, 98*, 5937–5942.

Reiter, S. M., & Samuel, W. (1980). Littering as a function of prior litter and the presence or absence of prohibitive signs. *Journal of Applied Social Psychology, 10*, 45–55.

Rempel, J. K., & Burris, C. T. (2006). Push-you-pull-you: The boundaried self in close relationships. *Personality and Social Psychology Bulletin, 32*, 256–269.

Rempel, J. K., Ross, M., & Holmes, J. G. (2001). Trust and communicated attributions in close relationships. *Journal of Personality and Social Psychology, 81*, 57–64.

Renaud, J. M., & McConnell, A. R. (2002). Organization of the self-concept and the suppression of self-relevant thoughts. *Journal of Experimental Social Psychology, 38*, 79–86.

Renner, M. J., & Mackin, R. S. (1998). A life stress instrument for classroom use. *Teaching of Psychology, 25*, 46–48.

Reno, R. R., Cialdini, R. B., & Kallgren, C. A. (1993). The transsituational influence of social norms. *Journal of Personality and Social Psychology, 64*, 104–112.

Rensink, R. A. (2002). Change detection. *Annual Review of Psychology, 53*, 245–277.

Rentfrow, P. J., & Gosling, S. D. (2006). Message in a ballad: The role of music preferences in interpersonal perception. *Psychological Science, 17*, 236–242.

Reynolds, L. (2000, March 22). Some folks call Tillie "a miracle worker." *Winnipeg Free Press*, p. D3.

Rhodes, G., Yoshikawa, S., Clark, A., Lee, K., McKay, R., & Akamatsu, S. (2001). Attractiveness of facial averageness and symmetry in non-Western cultures: In search of biologically based standards of beauty. *Perception, 30*, 611–625.

Rhodes, N., & Wood, W. (1992). Self-esteem and intelligence affect influenceability: The mediating role of message reception. *Psychological Bulletin, 111*, 156–171.

Rholes, W. S., Newman, L. S., & Ruble, D. N. (1990). Understanding self and other: Developmental and motivational aspects of perceiving persons in terms of invariant dispositions. In E. T. Higgins & R. M. Sorrentino (Eds.), *Handbook of motivation and cognition: Foundations of social behavior.* (Vol. 2.) New York: Guilford.

Ricciardelli, L. A., & McCabe, M. P. (2003). A longitudinal analysis of the role of psychosocial factors in predicting body change strategies among adolescent boys. *Sex Roles, 48*, 349–360.

Richards, J. M., & Gross, J. J. (1999). Composure at any cost? The cognitive consequences of emotion suppression. *Personality and Social Psychology Bulletin, 25*, 1033–1044.

Richardson, D., Hammock, G., Smith, S., & Gardner, W. (1994). Empathy as a cognitive inhibitor of interpersonal aggression. *Aggressive Behavior, 20*, 275–289.

Richardson, H. R. L., Beazley, R. P., Delaney, M. E., & Langille, D. E. (1997). Factors influencing condom use among students attending high school in Nova Scotia. *Canadian Journal of Human Sexuality, 6*, 185–196.

Rigby, K., & Johnson, B. (2006–2007). Playground heroes. *Greater Good, 3*(2), 14–17.

Rigby, K., Smith, P. K., & Pepler, D. (2004). Working to prevent school bullying: Key issues. In P. K. Smith, D. Pepler, & K. Rigby (Eds.), *Bullying in schools: How successful can interventions be?* (pp. 1–12.) Cambridge, UK: Cambridge University Press.

Riggs, J. M., & Gumbrecht, L. B. (2005). Correspondence bias and American sentiment in the wake of September 11, 2001. *Journal of Applied Social Psychology, 35*, 15–28.

Ringelmann, M. (1913). Recherches sur les moteurs animés: Travail de l'homme. *Annales de l'Institut National Argonomique, 12*, 2e srie, 1–40.

Riordan, C. A. (1978). Equal-status interracial contact: A review and revision of a concept. *International Journal of Intercultural Relations, 2*, 161–185.

Roberts, M. (2008, July 22). Polygamist leader charged with sexual assault. Associated Press. *Globe and Mail.*

Roberts, M. (2008, August 5). Texas child welfare officials want 8 children from sect back in state care. Associated Press. *Globe and Mail.*

Roberts, W., & Strayer, J. (1996). Empathy, emotional expressiveness, and prosocial behavior. *Child Development, 67*, 449–470.

Robins, R. W., & Beer, J. S. (2001). Positive illusions about the self: Short-term benefits and long-term costs. *Journal of Personality and Social Psychology, 80*, 340–352.

Robins, R. W., Spranca, M. D., & Mendelsohn, G. A. (1996). The actor-observer effect revisited: Effects of individual differences and repeated social interactions on actor and observer attributions. *Journal of Personality and Social Psychology, 71*, 375–389.

Robson, M. (2005, July 30). We must fight terror: PM. *Winnipeg Free Press*, p. A3.

Rodin, J. (1986). Aging and health: Effects of the sense of control. *Science, 233,* 1271–1276.

Rodin, J., & Langer, E. J. (1977). Long-term effects of a control-relevant intervention with the institutional aged. *Journal of Personality and Social Psychology, 35,* 897–902.

Rodrigo, M. F., & Ato, M. (2002). Testing the group polarization hypothesis by using logit models. *European Journal of Social Psychology, 32,* 3–18.

Roesch, S. C., & Amirkhan, J. H. (1997). Boundary conditions for self-serving attributions: Another look at the sports pages. *Journal of Applied Social Psychology, 27,* 245–261.

Roese, N. J. (1994). The functional basis of counterfactual thinking. *Journal of Personality and Social Psychology, 66,* 805–818.

Roese, N. J. (1997). Counterfactual thinking. *Psychological Bulletin, 121,* 133–148.

Roese, N. J., & Olson, J. M. (1993). Self-esteem and counterfactual thinking. *Journal of Personality and Social Psychology, 65,* 199–206.

Roese, N. J., & Olson, J. M. (1995). Outcome controllability and counterfactual thinking. *Personality and Social Psychology Bulletin, 21,* 620–628.

Roese, N. J., & Olson, J. M. (1996). Counterfactuals, causal attributions, and the hindsight bias: A conceptual integration. *Journal of Experimental Social Psychology, 32,* 197–227.

Roese, N. J., & Olson, J. M. (1997). Counterfactual thinking: The intersection of affect and function. In M. Zanna (Ed.), *Advances in experimental social psychology.* (Vol. 29.) San Diego, CA: Academic Press.

Rogers, P. (1998). The cognitive psychology of lottery gambling: A theoretical review. *Journal of Gambling Studies, 14,* 111–134.

Rogers, R. (1983). Cognitive and physiological processes in fear appeals and attitude change: A revised theory of protection motivation. In J. T. Cacioppo & R. E. Petty (Eds.), *Social psychophysiology: A sourcebook.* (pp. 153–176.) New York: Guilford Press.

Rohan, M., & Zanna, M. (1996). Value transmission in families. In C. Seligman, J. Olson, & M. Zanna (Eds.), *The psychology of values: The Ontario symposium on personality and social psychology.* (Vol. 8, pp. 253–276.) Mahwah, NJ: Erlbaum.

Rollason, K. (2008, June 21). Dumas' death likened to J. J. Harper's. *Winnipeg Free Press,* p. A5.

Rosch, E., & Lloyd, B. (Eds.) (1978). *Cognition and categorization.* Hillsdale, NJ: Erlbaum.

Rose, V. G., & Ogloff, J. R. P. (2001). Evaluating the comprehensibility of jury instructions: A method and an example. *Law and Human Behavior, 25,* 409–431.

Rosenbaum, M. E. (1986). The repulsion hypothesis: On the non-development of relationships. *Journal of Personality and Social Psychology, 51,* 1156–1166.

Rosenberg, L. A. (1961). Group size, prior experience, and conformity. *Journal of Abnormal and Social Psychology, 63,* 436–437.

Rosenberg, M. J., Davidson, A. J., Chen, J., Judson, F. N., & Douglas, J. M. (1992). Barrier contraceptives and sexually transmitted diseases in women: A comparison of female-dependent methods and condoms. *American Journal of Public Health, 82,* 669–674.

Rosenblatt, P. C. (1974). Cross-cultural perspectives on attraction. In T. L. Huston (Ed.), *Foundations of interpersonal attraction.* (pp. 79–99.) New York: Academic Press.

Rosenhan, D. L. (1970). The natural socialization of altruistic autonomy. In J. R. Macaulay & L. Berkowitz (Eds.), *Altruism and helping behavior.* (pp. 251–268.) New York: Academic Press.

Rosenman, R. H. (1993). Relationship of the Type A behavior pattern with coronary heart disease. In L. Goldberger & S. Breznitz (Eds.), *Handbook of stress: Theoretical and clinical aspects.* (2nd ed., pp. 449–476) New York: Free Press.

Rosenthal, A. M. (1964). *Thirty-eight witnesses.* New York: McGraw-Hill.

Rosenthal, R. (1994). Interpersonal expectancy effects: A 30-year perspective. *Current Directions in Psychological Science, 3,* 176–179.

Rosenthal, R. (1995). Critiquing Pygmalion: A 25-year perspective. *Current Directions in Psychological Science, 4,* 171–172.

Rosenthal, R., & De Paulo, B. M. (1979). Sex differences in accommodation in nonverbal communication. In R. Rosenthal (Ed.), *Skill in nonverbal communication: Individual differences.* (pp. 68–103.) Cambridge, MA: Oelgeschlager, Gunn & Hain.

Rosenthal, R., & Jacobson, L. (1968). *Pygmalion in the classroom: Teacher expectation and student intellectual development.* New York: Holt, Rinehart & Winston.

Ross, L. (1977). The intuitive psychologist and his shortcomings: Distortions in the attribution process. In L. Berkowitz (Ed.), *Advances in experimental social psychology.* (Vol. 10, pp. 173–220.) Orlando, FL: Academic Press.

Ross, L. (1998). Comment on Gilbert. In J. M. Darley & J. Cooper (Eds.), *Attribution and social interaction.* (pp. 53–66.) Washington, DC: American Psychological Association.

Ross, L., Amabile, T. M., & Steinmetz, J. L. (1977). Social roles, social control, and biases in social perception. *Journal of Personality and Social Psychology, 35,* 485–494.

Ross, L., Lepper, M. R., & Hubbard, M. (1975). Perseverance in self perception and social perception: Biased attributional processes in the debriefing paradigm. *Journal of Personality and Social Psychology, 32,* 880–892.

Ross, L., & Nisbett, R. E. (1991). *The person and the situation: Perspectives of social psychology.* New York: McGraw-Hill.

Ross, L., & Samuels, S. M. (1993). *The predictive power of personal reputation versus labels and construal in the Prisoner's Dilemma game.* Unpublished manuscript, Stanford University.

Ross, L., & Ward, A. (1995). Psychological barriers to dispute resolution. In M. P. Zanna (Ed.), *Advances in experimental social psychology.* (Vol. 27, pp. 255–304.) San Diego, CA: Academic Press.

Ross, L., & Ward, A. (1996). Naive realism: Implications for social conflict and misunderstanding. In T. Brown, E. Reed, & E. Turiel (Eds.), *Values and knowledge.* Hillsdale, NJ: Erlbaum.

Ross, L. R., & Spinner, B. (2001). General and specific attachment representations in adulthood: Is there a relationship? *Journal of Social and Personal Relationships, 18,* 747–766.

Ross, M., Heine, S. J., Wilson, A. E., & Sugimori, S. (2005). Cross-cultural discrepancies in self-appraisals. *Personality and Social Psychology Bulletin, 31,* 1175–1188.

Ross, M., McFarland, C., Conway, M., & Zanna, M. P. (1983). Reciprocal relation between attitudes and behavior recall: Committing people to newly formed attitudes. *Journal of Personality and Social Psychology, 45,* 257–267.

Ross, M., & Olson, J. M. (1981). An expectancy-attribution model of the effects of placebos. *Psychological Review, 88,* 408–437.

Ross, M., & Sicoly, F. (1979). Egocentric biases in availability and attribution. *Journal of Personality and Social Psychology, 45,* 257–267.

Ross, M., & Wilson, A. E. (2002). It feels like yesterday: Self-esteem, valence of personal past experiences, and judgments of subjective distance. *Journal of Personality and Social Psychology, 82,* 792–803.

Ross, M., Xun, W. Q. E., & Wilson, A. E. (2002). Language and the bicultural self. *Personality and Social Psychology Bulletin, 28,* 1040–1050.

Ross, W., & La Croix, J. (1996). Multiple meanings of trust in negotiation theory and research: A literature review and integrative model. *International Journal of Conflict Management, 7,* 314–360.

Roszell, P., Kennedy, D., & Grabb, E. (1989). Physical attractiveness and income attainment among Canadians. *Journal of Psychology, 123,* 547–559.

Rotenberg, K. J. (1998). Stigmatizations of transitions in loneliness. *Journal of Social and Personal Relationships, 15,* 565–576.

Rothman, A. J. (2000). Toward a theory-based analysis of behavioral maintenance. *Health Psychology, 19,* 64–69.

Rothman, A. J., & Hardin, C. D. (1997). Differential use of the availability heuristic in social judgment. *Personality and Social Psychology Bulletin, 23,* 123–138.

Rothman, A. J., Martino, S. C., Bedell, B. T., Detweiler, J. B., & Salovey, P. (1999). The systematic influence of gain- and loss-framed messages on interest in and use of different types of health behavior. *Personality and Social Psychology Bulletin, 25,* 1355–1369.

Rothman, A. J., & Salovey, P. (1997). Shaping perceptions to motivate healthy behavior: The role of message framing. *Psychological Bulletin, 121,* 3–19.

Rothman, A. J., Salovey, P., Antone, C., Keough, K., & Martin, C. D. (1993). The influence of message framing on intentions to perform health behaviors. *Journal of Experimental Social Psychology, 29,* 408–432.

Rubenfeld, S., Sinclair, L., & Clément, R. (2007). Second language learning and acculturation: The role of motivation and goal congruence. *Canadian Journal of Applied Linguistics, 10,* 309–324.

Rubin, Z. (1970). Measurement of romantic love. *Journal of Personality and Social Psychology, 16,* 265–273.

Rubin, Z. (1973). *Liking and loving: An invitation to social psychology.* New York: Holt, Rinehart & Winston.

Rubin, Z., Peplau, L. A., & Hill, C. T. (1981). Loving and leaving: Sex differences in romantic attachments. *Sex Roles, 7,* 821–835.

Rudman, L. A. (2004). Sources of implicit attitudes. *Current Directions in Psychological Science, 13,* 79–82.

Rudman, L. A., & Borgida, E. (1995). The afterglow of construct accessibility: The behavioral consequences of priming men to view women as sexual objects. *Journal of Experimental Social Psychology, 31,* 493–517.

Ruggiero, K. M., & Taylor, D. M. (1995). Coping with discrimination: How disadvantaged group members perceive the discrimination that confronts them. *Journal of Personality and Social Psychology, 68,* 826–838.

Ruggiero, K. M., & Taylor, D. M. (1997). Why minority group members perceive or do not perceive the discrimination that confronts them: The role of self-esteem and perceived control. *Journal of Personality and Social Psychology, 72,* 373–389.

Rule, B. G., Taylor, B. R., & Dobbs, A. R. (1987). Priming affects of heat on aggressive thoughts. *Social Cognition, 5,* 131–143.

Rusbult, C. E. (1980). Commitment and satisfaction in romantic associations: A test of the investment model. *Journal of Experimental Social Psychology, 16,* 172–186.

Rusbult, C. E. (1983). A longitudinal test of the investment model: The development (and deterioration) of satisfaction and commitment in heterosexual involvements. *Journal of Personality and Social Psychology, 45,* 101–117.

Rusbult, C. E. (1991). Commitment processes in close relationships: The investment model. Paper presented at the meeting of the American Psychological Association, San Francisco.

Rusbult, C. E., & Buunk, A. P. (1993). Commitment processes in close relationships: An interdependence analysis. *Journal of Social and Personal Relationships, 10,* 175–204.

Rusbult, C. E., & Martz, J. M. (1995). Remaining in an abusive relationship: An investment model analysis of nonvoluntary dependence. *Personality and Social Psychology Bulletin, 21,* 558–571.

Rusbult, C. E., Martz, J. M., & Agnew, C. R. (1998). The investment model scale: Measuring commitment level, satisfaction level, quality of alternatives, and investment size. *Personal Relationships, 5,* 357–391.

Rusbult, C. E., Olsen, N., Davis, N. L., & Hannon, P. (2001). Commitment and relationship maintenance mechanisms. In J. H. Harvey & A. Wenzel (Eds.), *Close romantic relationships: Maintenance and enhancement.* (pp. 87–113.) Mahwah, NJ: Lawrence Erlbaum Associates.

Rusbult, C. E., & Van Lange, P. A. M. (2003). Interdependence, interaction and relationships. *Annual Review of Psychology, 54,* 351–375.

Russell, F. (2008, March 12). Reckless, mean-spirited partisan without limit. *Winnipeg Free Press,* p. A13.

Russell, G. W. (1983). Psychological issues in sports aggression. In J. H. Goldstein (Ed.), *Sports violence.* New York: Springer-Verlag.

Russell, G. W., & Arms, R. L. (1998). Toward a social psychological profile of would-be rioters. *Aggressive Behavior, 24,* 219–226.

Russell, J. A. (1994). Is there universal recognition of emotion from facial expressions? A review of the cross-cultural studies. *Psychological Bulletin, 115,* 102–141.

Russell, J. A., & Fehr, B. (1987). Relativity in the perception of emotion in facial expressions. *Journal of Experimental Psychology: General, 116,* 223–237.

Russell, J. A., & Fehr, B. (1988). The role of context in interpreting facial expression: Reply to Ekman and O'Sullivan. *Journal of Experimental Psychology: General, 117,* 89–90.

Russell, J. A., & Fehr, B. (1994). Fuzzy concepts in a fuzzy hierarchy: Varieties of anger. *Journal of Personality and Social Psychology, 67,* 186–205.

Russell, J. A., Suzuki, N., & Ishida, N. (1993). Canadian, Greek, and Japanese freely produced emotion labels for facial expressions. *Motivation and Emotion, 17,* 337–351.

Rusting, C. L., & Nolen-Hoeksema, S. (1998). Regulating responses of anger: Effects of rumination and distraction on angry mood. *Journal of Personality and Social Psychology, 74,* 790–803.

Rutter, D. R., Quine, L., & Albery, I. P. (1998). Perceptions of risk in motorcyclists: Unrealistic optimism, relative realism, and predictions of behaviour. *British Journal of Psychology, 89,* 681–696.

Ryan, B., Jr. (1991). *It works! How investment spending in advertising pays off.* New York: American Association of Advertising Agencies.

Ryan, R. M., & Deci, E. L. (1996). When paradigms clash: Comments on Cameron and Pierce's claim that rewards do not undermine intrinsic motivation. *Review of Educational Research, 66,* 33–38.

Ryan, R. M., & Deci, E. L. (2000). Intrinsic and extrinsic rewards: Classic definitions and new directions. *Current Educational Psychology, 25,* 54–67.

Ryff, C. D., & B. H. Singer (Eds.) (2001). *Emotion, social relationships, and health.* New York: Oxford University Press.

Sacks, O. (1987). *The man who mistook his wife for a hat and other clinical tales.* New York: Harper & Row.

Sagarin, B. J., Cialdini, R. B., Rice, W. E., & Serna, S. B. (2002). Dispelling the illusion of invulnerability: The motivations and mechanisms of resistance to persuasion. *Journal of Personality and Social Psychology, 83,* 526–541.

Sahdra, B., & Ross, M. (2007). Group identification and historical memory. *Personality and Social Psychology Bulletin, 33,* 384–395.

Sakellaropoulo, M., & Baldwin, M. W. (2007). The hidden sides of self-esteem: Two dimensions of implicit self-esteem and their relation to narcissistic reactions. *Journal of Experimental Social Psychology, 43,* 995–1001.

Salganik, M. J., Dodds, P. S., & Watts, D. J. (2006). Experimental study of inequality and unpredictability in an artificial cultural market. *Science, 311,* 854–856.

Salovey, P., Mayer, J. D., & Rosenhan, D. L. (1991). Mood and helping: Mood as a motivator of helping and helping as a regulator of mood. In M. S. Clark (Ed.), *Prosocial behavior: Review of personality and social psychology.* (Vol. 12, pp. 215–237.) Newbury Park, CA: Sage.

Salovey, P., & Rodin, J. (1985). Cognitions about the self: Connecting feeling states and social behavior. In P. Shaver (Ed.), *Self, situations, and social behavior: Review of personality and social psychology.* (Vol. 6, pp. 143–166.) Beverly Hills, CA: Sage.

Salovey, P., Rothman, A. J., Detweiler, J. B., & Steward, W. T. (2000). Emotional states and physical health. *American Psychologist, 55,* 110–121.

Salovey, P., Rothman, A. J., & Rodin, J. (1998). Social psychology and health behavior. In D. Gilbert, S. Fiske, & G. Lindzey (Eds.), *The handbook of social psychology.* (4th ed., Vol. 2, pp. 633–683.) New York: McGraw-Hill.

Sande, G., Goethals, G., Ferrari, L., & Worth, L. (1989). Value guided attributions: Maintaining the moral self-image and the diabolical enemy-image. *Journal of Social Issues, 45,* 91–118.

Sande, G. H., Goethals, G. R., & Radloff, C. E. (1988). Perceiving one's own traits and others': The multifaceted self. *Journal of Personality and Social Psychology, 54,* 13–20.

Sande, G. N., Ellard, J. H. & Ross, M. (1986). Effect of arbitrarily assigned status labels on self-perceptions and social perceptions: The mere position effect. *Journal of Psychology and Social Psychology, 50,* 684–689.

Sanders, C. (2006, July 20). Canadian fathers stepping up. *Winnipeg Free Press,* p. A5.

Sanger, D. E. (1993, May 30). The career and the kimono. *New York Times Magazine,* pp. 18–19.

Sangrigoli, S., Pallier, C., Argenti, A. M., Ventureyra, V. A. G., & de Schonen, S. (2005). Reversibility of the other-race effect in face recognition during childhood. *Psychological Science, 16,* 440–444.

Sanitioso, R., Kunda, Z., & Fong, G. T. (1990). Motivated recruitment of autobiographical memories. *Journal of Personality and Social Psychology, 59,* 229–241.

Sanna, L. J. (1992). Self-efficacy theory: Implications for social facilitation and social loafing. *Journal of Personality and Social Psychology, 62,* 774–786.

Sanna, L. J., Carter, S. E., & Small, E. M. (2006). The road not taken: Counterfactual thinking over time. In L. J. Sanna & E. C. Chang (Eds.), *Judgments over time: The interplay of thoughts, feelings, and behaviors.* (pp. 163–181.) New York: Oxford University Press.

Sanna, L. J., & Schwarz, N. (2004). Integrating temporal biases: The interplay of focal thoughts and accessibility experiences. *Psychological Science, 15,* 474–481.

Sansone, C., & Harackiewicz, J. M. (1996). "I don't feel like it": The function of interest in self-regulation. In L. L. Martin & A. Tesser (Eds.), *Striving and feeling: Interactions among goals, affect, and self-regulation.* (pp. 203–228.) Mahwah, NJ: Erlbaum.

Sarason, I. G., Sarason, B. R., & Pierce, G. R. (Eds.) (1990). *Social support: An interactional view.* New York: Wiley.

Sargent, J. D., Dalton, M. A., Beach, M. L., Mott, L. A., Tickle, J. J., Ahrens, M. B., & Heatherton, T. F. (2002). Viewing tobacco use in movies: Does it shape attitudes that mediate adolescent smoking? *American Journal of Preventive Medicine, 22,* 137–145.

Sastry, J., & Ross, C. E. (1998). Asian ethnicity and the sense of personal control. *Social Psychology Quarterly, 61,* 101–120.

Sato, T., & Cameron, J. E. (1999). The relationship between collective self-esteem and self construal in Japan and Canada. *Journal of Social Psychology, 139,* 426–435.

Saunders, J. W. S. (2001). Experts in court: A view from the bench. *Canadian Psychology, 42,* 109–118.

Savitsky, K. (1998). Embarrassment study [e-mails]. Society for Personal and Social Psychology e-mail list archive. www.stolaf.edu/cgi-bin/mailarchivesearch.pl?directory=/home/www/people/huff/SPSP&listname=archive98. Accessed June 2006.

Saxe, L. (1994). Detection of deception: Polygraph and integrity tests. *Current Directions in Psychological Science, 3,* 69–73.

Schachter, S. (1951). Deviation, rejection, and communication. *Journal of Abnormal and Social Psychology, 46,* 190–207.

Schachter, S., Silverstein, B., & Perlick, D. (1977). Studies of the interaction of psychological and pharmacological determinants of smoking: V. psychological and pharmacological explanations of smoking under stress. *Journal of Experimental Psychology: General, 106*(1), 31–40.

Schacter, D. L. (1996). *Searching for memory: The brain, the mind, and the past.* New York: Basic Books.

Schafer, M., & Crichlow, S. (1996). Antecedents of groupthink: A quantitative study. *Journal of Conflict Resolution, 40,* 415–435.

Schaller, M., Asp, C. H., Rosell, M. C., & Heim, S. J. (1996). Training in statistical reasoning inhibits formation of erroneous group stereotypes. *Personality and Social Psychology Bulletin, 22,* 829–844.

Schaller, M., & Conway III, L. G. (1999). Influence of impression-management goals on the emerging contents of group stereotypes: Support for social-evolutionary process. *Personality and Social Psychology Bulletin, 25,* 819–833.

Schaller, M., & Conway III, L. G. (2001). From cognition to culture: The origins of stereotypes that really matter. In G. B. Moskowitz (Ed.), *Cognitive social psychology: The Princeton symposium on the legacy and future of social cognition.* (pp. 163–176.) Mahwah, NJ: Erlbaum.

Schaller, M., & Conway III, L. G., (2005). The substance of prejudice: Biological- and social- evolutionary perspectives on cognition, culture, and the contents of stereotypical beliefs. In C. S. Crandall & M. Schaller (Eds.), *Social psychology of prejudice: Historical and contemporary issues.* (pp. 145–160.) Lawrence, KS: Lewinian Press.

Schaller, M., & Conway III, L. G., & Tanchuk, T. L. (2002). Selective pressures on the once and future contents of ethnic stereotypes: Effects of the communicability of traits. *Journal of Personality and Social Psychology, 82,* 861–877.

Schaller, M., & O'Brien, M. (1992). "Intuitive analysis of covariance" and group stereotype formation. *Personality and Social Psychology Bulletin, 18,* 776–785.

Schaller, M., Park, J. H., & Mueller, A. (2003). Fear of the dark: Interactive effects of beliefs about danger and ambient darkness on ethnic stereotypes. *Personality and Social Psychology Bulletin, 29*(5), 637–649.

Scheier, M. F., Carver, C. S., & Bridges, M. W. (1994). Distinguishing optimism from neuroticism (and trait anxiety, self-mastery, and self-esteem): A revision of the Life Orientation Test. *Journal of Personality and Social Psychology, 67,* 1063–1078.

Schimel, J., Arndt, J., Banko, K. M., & Cook, A. (2004). Not all self-affirmations were created equal: The cognitive and social benefit of affirming the intrinsic (vs. extrinsic) self. *Social Cognition, 22*(1), 75–99.

Schimel, J., Hayes, J., Williams, T., & Jahrig, J. (2007). Is death really the worm at the core? Converging evidence that worldview threat increases death-thought accessibility. *Journal of Personality and Social Psychology, 92,* 789–803.

Schimmack, U., & Oishi, S. (2005). The influence of chronically and temporarily accessible information on life satisfaction judgements. *Journal of Personality and Social Psychology, 89,* 395–406.

Schlenger, W. E., Caddell, J. M., Ebert, L., Jordan, B. K., Rourke, K. M., Wilson, D., Thalji, L., Dennis, M., Fairbank, J. A., & Kulka, R. A. (2002). Psychological reactions to terrorist attacks: Findings from the National Study of Americans' Reactions to September 11. *Journal of the American Medical Association, 288,* 581–588.

Schmeichel, B. J., & Baumeister, R. F. (2004). Self-regulatory strength. In R. F. Baumeister, & K. D. Vohs (Eds.), *Handbook of self-regulation: Research, theory, and applications.* (pp. 84–98.) New York: Guilford.

Schmitt, B. H., Gilovich, T., Goore, N., & Joseph, L. (1986). Mere presence and social facilitation: One more time. *Journal of Experimental Social Psychology, 22,* 228–241.

Schneider, D. J. (1973). Implicit personality theory: A review. *Psychological Bulletin, 79,* 294–309.

Schneider, M. E., Major, B., Luhtanen, R., & Crocker, J. (1996). Social stigma and the potential costs of assumptive help. *Personality and Social Psychology Bulletin, 22,* 201–209.

Schoeneman, T. J., & Rubanowitz, D. E. (1985). Attributions in the advice columns: Actors and observers, causes and reasons. *Personality and Social Psychology Bulletin, 11,* 315–325.

Schooler, J. W. (1999). Seeking the core: The issues and evidence surrounding recovered accounts of sexual trauma. In L. M. Williams & V. L. Banyard (Eds.), *Trauma and memory.* (pp. 203–216.) Thousand Oaks, CA: Sage.

Schooler, J. W., & Eich, E. (2000). Memory for emotional events. In E. Tulving & F. I. M. Craik (Eds.), *The Oxford handbook of memory*. (pp. 379–392.) Oxford, UK: Oxford University Press.

Schooler, J. W., & Engstler-Schooler, T. Y. (1990). Verbal overshadowing of visual memories: Some things are better left unsaid. *Cognitive Psychology, 22,* 36–71.

Schooler, J. W., Fiore, S. M., & Brandimonte, M. A. (1997). At a loss from words: Verbal overshadowing of perceptual memories. *Psychology of Learning and Motivation, 37,* 291–340.

Schriesheim, C. A., Tepper, B. J., & Tetrault, L. A. (1994). Least preferred co-worker score, situational control, and leadership effectiveness: A meta-analysis of contingency model performance predictions. *Journal of Applied Psychology, 79,* 561–573.

Schroeder, D. H., & Costa, Jr., P. T. (1984). Influence of life event stress on physical illness: Substantive effects or methodological flaws? *Journal of Personality and Social Psychology, 46,* 853–863.

Schuller, R. A., & Hastings, P. A. (1996). Trials of battered women who kill: The impact of alternative forms of expert evidence. *Law and Human Behavior, 20,* 167–187.

Schuller, R. A., & Paglia, A. (1999). An empirical study: Juror sensitivity to variations in hearsay conveyed via expert evidence. *Law and Psychology Review, 23,* 131–152.

Schuller, R. A., & Yarmey, M. (2001). The jury: Deciding guilt and innocence. In R. A. Schuller, & J. R. P. Ogloff (Eds.) (2001). *Introduction to psychology and law: Canadian perspectives.* (pp. 157–187.) Toronto, ON: University of Toronto Press.

Schultz, P. W., Oskamp, S., & Mainieri, T. (1995). Who recycles and when? A review of personal and situational factors. *Journal of Environmental Psychology, 15,* 105–121.

Schulz, R. (1976). Effects of control and predictability on the physical and psychological well-being of the institutionalized aged. *Journal of Personality and Social Psychology, 33,* 563–573.

Schulz, R., & Hanusa, B. H. (1978). Long-term effects of control and predictability-enhancing interventions: Findings and ethical issues. *Journal of Personality and Social Psychology, 36,* 1202–1212.

Schuman, H., & Kalton, G. (1985). Survey methods. In G. Lindzey & E. Aronson (Eds.), *Handbook of social psychology.* (3rd ed., Vol. 1, pp. 635–697.) New York: McGraw-Hill.

Schützwohl, A. (2004). Which infidelity type makes you more jealous? Decision strategies in a forced-choice between sexual and emotional infidelity. *Evolutionary Psychology, 2,* 121–128.

Schwartz, S. H. (1992). Universals in the content and structure of values: Theoretical advances and empirical tests in 20 countries. In M. P. Zanna (Ed.), *Advances in experimental social psychology.* (Vol. 25, pp. 1–65.) San Diego, CA: Academic Press.

Schwartz, S. H., & Gottlieb, A. (1976). Bystander reactions to a violent theft: Crime in Jerusalem. *Journal of Personality and Social Psychology, 34,* 1188–1199.

Schwarz, N. (1999). Self-reports: How the questions shape the answers. *American Psychologist, 54,* 93–105.

Schwarz, N., Bless, H., Strack, F., Klumpp, G., Rittenauer-Schatka, H., & Simmons, A. (1991). Ease of retrieval as information: Another look at the availability heuristic. *Journal of Personality and Social Psychology, 61,* 195–202.

Schwarz, N., Groves, R. M., & Schuman, H. (1998). Survey methods. In D. Gilbert, S. Fiske, & G. Lindzey (Eds.), *The handbook of social psychology.* (4th ed., Vol. 1, pp. 143–179.) New York: Random House.

Schwarz, N., Hippler, H. J., Deutsch, B., & Strack, F. (1985). Response scales: Effects of category range on reported behavior and comparative judgments. *Public Opinion Quarterly, 49,* 388–395.

Schwarz, N., & Sudman, S. (Eds.) (1996). *Answering questions.* San Fransisco, CA: Jossey-Bass Publishers.

Schwarz, N., & Vaughn, L. A. (2002). The availability heuristic revisited: Ease of recall and content of recall as distinct sources of information. In T. Gilovich, D. W. Griffin, & D. Kahneman (Eds.), *Heuristics and biases: The psychology of intuitive judgment.* (pp. 103–119.) New York: Cambridge University Press.

Sciangula, A. M., & Morry, M. M. (in press). Self-esteem and perceived regard: How I see myself affects my relationship satisfaction. *Journal of Social Psychology.*

Scoboria, A., Mazzoni, G., Kirsch, I., & Milling, L. S. (2002). Immediate and persisting effects of misleading questions and hypnosis on memory reports. *Journal of Experimental Psychology: Applied, 8,* 26–32.

Scott, D. (1999). Equal opportunity, unequal results: Determinants of household recycling intensity. *Environment and Behavior, 31,* 267–290.

Scott, S. (2002, October). The man who reads faces. *Elm Street,* pp. 78–91.

Sears, D. O. (1981). Life stage effects on attitude change, especially among the elderly. In S. B. Kiesler, J. N. Morgan, & V. K. Oppenheimer (Eds.), *Aging: Social change.* (pp. 183–204.) New York: Academic Press.

Sechrist, G. B., Stangor, C., & Killen, M. (2005). Prejudice as social norms. In C. S. Crandall & M. Schaller (Eds.), *Social psychology of prejudice: Historical and contemporary issues.* (pp. 163–183.) Lawrence, KS: Lewinian Press.

Sechrist, G. B., Swim, J. K., Stangor, C. (2004). When do the stigmatized make attributions to discrimination occurring to the self and others? The roles of self-presentation and need for control. *Journal of Personality and Social Psychology, 87:1,* 111–122.

Secord, P. F., & Backman, C. W. (1964). *Social psychology.* New York: McGraw-Hill.

Sedikides, C., & Anderson, C. A. (1994). Causal perceptions of intertrait relations: The glue that holds person types together. *Personality and Social Psychology Bulletin, 21,* 294–302.

Segal, M. W (1974). Alphabet and attraction: An unobtrusive measure of the effect of propinquity in a field setting. *Journal of Personality and Social Psychology, 30,* 654–657.

Segerstrom, S. C. (2005). Optimism and immunity: Do positive thoughts always lead to positive effects? *Brain, Behavior, and Immunity, 19*(3), 195–200.

Séguin, C., Pelletier, L. G., & Hunsley, J. (1999). Predicting environmental behaviors: The influence of self-determined motivation and information about perceived environmental health risks. *Journal of Applied Social Psychology, 29,* 1582–1604.

Seijts, G. H., & Latham, G. P. (2000). The effects of goal setting and group size on performance in a social dilemma. *Canadian Journal of Behavioural Science, 32,* 104–116.

Seligman, M. E. P. (1975). *Helplessness: On depression, development, and death.* San Francisco, CA: W. H. Freeman.

Seligman, M. E. P., & Schulman, P. (1986). Explanatory style as a predictor of productivity and quitting among life insurance agents. *Journal of Personality and Social Psychology, 50,* 832–838.

Selye, H. (1956). *The stress of life.* New York: McGraw-Hill.

Selye, H. (1976). *Stress in health and disease.* Woburn, MA: Butterworth.

Semin, G. R., Higgins, E. T., de Montes, L. G., Estourget, Y., & Valencia, J. F. (2005). Linguistic signatures of regulatory focus: How abstraction fits promotion more than prevention. *Journal of Personality and Social Psychology, 89,* 36–45.

Seppa, N. (1997). Children's TV remains steeped in violence. *APA Monitor, 28,* p. 36.

Sergios, P. A., & Cody, J. (1985). Physical attractiveness and social assertiveness skills in male homosexual dating behavior and partner selection. *Journal of Social Psychology, 125,* 505–514.

Seta, J. J., Seta, C. E., & Wang, M. A. (1990). Feelings of negativity and stress: An averaging-summation analysis of impressions of negative life experiences. *Personality and Social Psychology Bulletin, 17,* 376–384.

Shackelford, T. K., & Buss, D. M. (1996). Betrayal in mateships, friendships, and coalitions. *Personality and Social Psychology Bulletin, 22,* 1151–1164.

Shadel, W. G., Cervone, D., Niaura, R., & Abrams, D. B. (2004). Developing an integrative social-cognitive strategy for personality assessment at the level of the individual: An illustration with regular cigarette smokers. *Journal of Research in Personality, 38,* 394–419.

Sharan, S. (1980). Cooperative learning in small groups. *Review of Educational Research, 50,* 241–271.

Sharpe, D., Adair, J. G., & Roese, N. J. (1992). Twenty years of deception research: A decline in subjects' trust? *Personality and Social Psychology Bulletin, 18,* 585–590.

Sharpe, D., & Taylor, J. K. (1999). An examination of variables from a social-developmental model to explain physical and psychological dating violence. *Canadian Journal of Behavioural Science, 31,* 165–175.

Sharp, F. C. (1928). *Ethics.* New York: Century.

Shavitt, S. (1989). Operationalizing functional theories of attitude. In A. R. Pratkanis, S. J. Breckler, & A. G. Greenwald (Eds.), *Attitude structure and function.* (pp. 311–337.) Hillsdale, NJ: Erlbaum.

Shavitt, S. (1990). The role of attitude objects in attitude function. *Journal of Experimental Social Psychology, 26,* 124–148.

Shaw, J. I., & Skolnick, P. (1999). Weapon focus and gender differences in eyewitness accuracy: Arousal versus salience. *Journal of Applied Social Psychology, 29,* 2328–2341.

Sheldon, K. M. (1999). Learning the lessons of tit-for-tat: Even competitors can get the massage. *Journal of Personality and Social Psychology, 77,* 1245–1253.

Shepperd, J. A., & Taylor, K. M. (1999). Social loafing and expectancy-value theory. *Personality and Social Psychology Bulletin, 25,* 1147–1158.

Sherif, M. (1936). *The psychology of social norms.* New York: Harper.

Sherif, M. (1966). *In common predicament: Social psychology of intergroup conflict and cooperation.* Boston, MA: Houghton Mifflin.

Sherif, M., Harvey, O. J., White, J., Hood, W., & Sherif, C. (1961). *Intergroup conflict and cooperation: The robber's cave experiment.* Norman: University of Oklahoma, Institute of Intergroup Relations.

Sherman, D. K., & Kim, H. S. (2002). Affective perseverance: The resistance of affect to cognitive invalidation. *Personality and Social Psychology Bulletin, 28,* 224–237.

Sherman, D. K., & Kim, H. S. (2005). Is there an "I" in "Team"? The role of the self in group-serving judgments. *Journal of Personality and Social Psychology, 88,* 108–120.

Sherman, J. W., & Klein, S. B. (1994). Development and representation of personality impressions. *Journal of Personality and Social Psychology, 67,* 972–983.

Sherrod, D. R. (1974). Crowding, perceived control, and behavioral aftereffects. *Journal of Applied Social Psychology, 4,* 171–186.

Shestowsky, D., Wegener, D. T., & Fabrigar, L. R. (1998). Need for cognition and interpersonal influence: Individual differences in impact on dyadic decisions. *Journal of Personality and Social Psychology, 74,* 1317–1328.

Shih, M., Ambady, N., Richeson, J. A., Fujita, K., & Gray, H. M. (2002). Stereotype performance boosts: The impact of self-relevance and that manner of stereotype activation. *Journal of Personality and Social Psychology, 83,* 638–647.

Shih, M., Pittinsky, T. L., & Ambady, N. (1999). Stereotype susceptibility: Identity salience and shifts in quantitative performance. *Psychological Science, 10,* 80–83.

Shira, I., & Martin, L. L. (2005). Stereotyping, self-affirmation, and the cerebral hemispheres. *Personality and Social Psychology Bulletin, 31,* 846–856.

Shotland, R. L., & Straw, M. K. (1976). Bystander response to an assault: When a man attacks a woman. *Journal of Personality and Social Psychology, 34,* 990–999.

Showers, C., & Zeigler-Hill, V. (2003). Organization of self-knowledge: Features, functions, and flexibility. In M. R. Leary & J. P. Tangney (Eds.), *Handbook of self and identity.* (pp. 47–67.) New York: Guilford Press.

Shultz, T. R., Léveillé, E., & Lepper, M. R. (1999). Free choice and cognitive dissonance revisited: Choosing "lesser evils" versus "greater goods." *Personality and Social Psychology Bulletin, 25,* 40–48.

Sibley, C. G., & Liu, J. H. (2003). Differentiating active and passive littering: A two-stage process model of littering behavior in public spaces. *Environment and Behavior, 35,* 415–433.

Sidanius, J., Levin, S., & Pratto, F. (1996). Consensual social dominance orientation and its correlates within the hierarchical structure of American society. *International Journal of Intercultural Relations, 20,* 385–408.

Siero, F. W., Bakker, A. B., Dekker, G. B., & van den Burg, M. T. C. (1996). Changing organizational energy consumption behavior through comparative feedback. *Journal of Environmental Psychology, 16,* 235–246.

Sigal, J. J., & Weinfeld, M. (2001). Do children cope better than adults with potentially traumatic stress? A 40-year follow-up of Holocaust survivors. *Psychiatry, 64,* 69–80.

Silver, L. B., Dublin, C. C., & Lourie, R. S. (1969). Does violence breed violence? Contributions from a study of the child abuse syndrome. *American Journal of Psychiatry, 126,* 404–407.

Silver, R., Holman, E., A., McIntosh, D. N., Poulin, M., & Gil-Rivas, V. (2002). Nationwide longitudinal study of psychological responses to September 11. *Journal of the American Medical Association, 2882,* 1235–1244.

Silverstein, B., Perdue, L., Peterson, B., & Kelly, E. (1986). The role of the mass media in promoting a thin standard of bodily attractiveness for women. *Sex Roles, 14,* 519–532.

Silvia, P. J., & Abele, A. E. (2002). Can positive affect induce self-focused attention? Methodological and measurement issues. *Cognition and Emotion, 16,* 845–853.

Sime, J. D. (1983). Affiliative behavior during escape to building exits. *Journal of Environmental Psychology, 3,* 21–41.

Simmie, S. (1999, November 20). Pumping up the "level of cruelty." *Toronto Star,* p. A3.

Simon, H. A. (1990). A mechanism for social selection and successful altruism. *Science, 250,* 1665–1668.

Simons, D. J., & Ambinder, M. S. (2005). Change blindness: Theory and consequences. *Current Directions in Psychological Science, 14,* 44–48.

Simons, D. J., & Chabris, C. F. (1999). Gorillas in our midst: Sustained inattentional blindness for dynamic events. *Perception, 1999, 28,* 1059–1074.

Simonton, D. K. (1985). Intelligence and personal influence in groups: Four nonlinear models. *Psychological Review, 92,* 532–547.

Simonton, D. K. (1987). *Why presidents succeed: A political psychology of leadership.* New Haven, CT: Yale University Press.

Simonton, D. K. (1999). Significant samples: The psychological study of eminent individuals. *Psychological Methods, 4,* 425–451.

Simonton, D. K. (2001). Predicting presidential performance in the United States: Equation replication on recent survey results. *Journal of Social Psychology, 141,* 293–307.

Simpson, G. E., & Yinger, J. M. (1958). *Racial and cultural minorities: An analysis of prejudice and discrimination.* New York: Harper.

Simpson, J. A., & Kenrick, D. T. (Eds.) (1997). *Evolutionary social psychology.* Mahwah, NJ: Erlbaum.

Simpson, J. A., Rholes, W. S., Campbell, L., & Wilson, C. L. (2003). Changes in attachment orientations across the transition to parenthood. *Journal of Experimental Social Psychology, 39,* 317–331.

Sinclair, L., & Kunda, Z. (1999). Reactions to a black professional: Motivated inhibition and activation of conflicting stereotypes. *Journal of Personality and Social Psychology, 77,* 885–904.

Sinclair, L., & Kunda, Z. (2000). Motivated Stereotyping of Women: She's Fine if She Praised Me but Incompetent if She Criticized Me. *Personality and Social Psychology Bulletin, 26,* 1329–1342.

Sinclair, S., Dunn, E., & Lowery, B. S. (2004). The relationship between parental racial attitudes and children's implicit prejudice. *Journal of Experimental Social Psychology, 41,* 283–289.

Sirois, F. (1982). Perspectives on epidemic hysteria. In M. J. Colligan, J. W. Pennebaker, & L. R. Murphy (Eds.), *Mass psychogenic illness: A social psychological analysis.* (pp. 217–236.) Hillsdale, NJ: Erlbaum.

Sistrunk, F., & McDavid, J. W. (1971). Sex variable in conforming behavior. Journal of *Personality and Social Psychology, 17,* 200–207.

Skarlicki, D. P., Ellard, J. H., & Kelln, B. R. C. (1998). Third-party perceptions of a layoff: Procedural, derogation, and retributive aspects of justice. *Journal of Applied Psychology, 83,* 119–127.

Skerritt, J. (2007, July 10). Manitoba teens are out-puffing their peers. *Winnipeg Free Press,* p. A3.

Skinner, B. F. (1938). *The behavior of organisms.* New York: Appleton-Century-Crofts.

Skinner, E. A. (1995). *Perceived control, motivation, and coping.* Thousand Oaks, CA: Sage.

Skinner, E. A. (1996). A guide to constructs of control. *Journal of Personality and Social Psychology, 71,* 549–570.

Slavin, R. E. (1980). Cooperative learning and desegregation. Paper presented at the meeting of the American Psychological Association.

Slavin, R. E. (1996). Cooperative learning in middle and secondary schools. *Clearing House, 69, Young adolescents at risk* (special ed.), 200–205.

Sloan, D. M., & Marx, B. P. (2004). Taking pen to hand: Evaluating theories underlying the written disclosure paradigm. *Clinical Psychology: Science and Practice, 11,* 121–137.

Sloan, J. H., Kellerman, A. L., Reay, D. T., Ferris, J. A., Koepsell, T., Rivara, F. P., Rice, C., Gray, L., & LoGerfo, J. (1988). Handgun regulations, crime, assaults, and homicide: A tale of two cities. *New England Journal of Medicine, 319,* 1256–1261.

Slovic, P., & Lichtenstein, S. (1971). Comparison of Bayesian and regression approaches to the study of information processing in judgment. *Organizational Behavior and Human Performance, 6,* 649–744.

Slusher, M. P., & Anderson, C. A. (1989). Belief perseverance and self-defeating behavior. In R. Curtis (Ed.), *Self-defeating behaviors: Experimental research, clinical impressions, and practical implications.* (pp. 11–40.) New York: Plenum.

Smith, A. E., Jussim, L., & Eccles, J. (1999). Do self-fulfilling prophecies accumulate, dissipate, or remain stable over time? *Journal of Personality and Social Psychology, 77,* 548–565.

Smith, M. B., Bruner, J., & White, R. W. (1956). *Opinions and personality.* New York: Wiley.

Smith, M. C. (1983). Hypnotic memory enhancement of witnesses: Does it work? *Psychological Bulletin, 94,* 387–407.

Smith, P. B., & Bond, M. H. (1999). *Social psychology across cultures* (2nd ed.). Needham Heights, MA: Allyn & Bacon.

Smith, P. K., Pepler, D., Rigby, K. (Eds.). (2004). *Bullying in schools: How successful can interventions be?* Cambridge, UK: Cambridge University Press.

Smith, R. E., Wheeler, G., & Diener, E. (1975). Faith without works: Jesus people, resistance to temptation, and altruism. *Journal of Applied Psychology, 5,* 320–330.

Smith, S. M., Fabrigar, L. R., Powell, D. M., & Estrada, M. (2007). The role of information-processing capacity and goals in attitude-congruent selective exposure effects. *Personality and Social Psychology Bulletin, 33,* 948–960.

Smith, S. S., & Richardson, D. (1983). Amelioration of deception and harm in psychological research: The important role of debriefing. *Journal of Personality and Social Psychology, 44,* 1075–1082.

Smith, T. W. (2003). Hostility and health: Current status of a psychosomatic hypothesis. In P. Salovey & A. J. Rothman (Eds.), *Social psychology of health.* (pp. 325–341.) New York: Psychology Press.

Smith, V. L., & Ellsworth, P. C. (1987). The social psychology of eyewitness accuracy: Misleading questions and communicator expertise. *Journal of Applied Psychology, 72,* 294–300.

Smith, V. L., Kassin, S. M., & Ellsworth, P. C. (1989). Eyewitness accuracy and confidence: Within- versus between-subjects correlations. *Journal of Applied Psychology, 74,* 356–359.

Snyder, C. R., Irving, L. M., & Anderson, J. R. (1991). Hope and health. In C. R. Snyder & D. R. Forsyth (Eds.), *Handbook of clinical and social psychology.* (pp. 285–305.) New York: Pergamon.

Snyder, M. (1984). When belief creates reality. In L. Berkowitz (Ed.), *Advances in experimental social psychology.* (Vol. 18, pp. 247–305.) Orlando, FL: Academic Press.

Snyder, M., & DeBono, K. G. (1989). Understanding the functions of attitudes: Lessons for personality and social behavior. In A. R. Pratkanis, S. J. Breckler, & A. G. Greenwald (Eds.), *Attitude structure and function.* (pp. 339–359.) Hillsdale, NJ: Erlbaum.

Snyder, M., Tanke, E. D., & Berscheid, E. (1977). Social perception and interpersonal behavior: On the self-fulfilling nature of social stereotypes. *Journal of Personality and Social Psychology, 35,* 656–666.

Soames, R. F. (1988). Effective and ineffective use of fear in health promotion campaigns. *American Journal of Public Health, 78,* 163–167.

Solomon, L. Z., Solomon, H., & Stone, R. (1978). Helping as a function of number of bystanders and ambiguity of emergency. *Personality and Social Psychology Bulletin, 4,* 318–321.

Solomon, S., Greenberg, J., & Pyszczynski, T. (1991). Terror management theory of self-esteem. In C. R. Snyder, D. R. Forsyth (Eds.), *Handbook of social and clinical psychology: The health perspective.* (pp. 21–40.) Elmsford, NY: Pergamon Press.

Sommers, E. K., & Check, J. V. (1987). An empirical investigation of the role of pornography in the verbal and physical abuse of women. *Violence and Victims, 2,* 189–209.

Son Hing, L. S., Bobocel, D. R., Zanna, M. P., & McBride, M. V. (2007). Authoritarian dynamics and unethical decision making: High social dominance orientation leaders and high right-wing authoritarianism followers. *Journal of Personality and Social Psychology, 92,* 67–81.

Sontag, S. (1978). *Illness as metaphor.* New York: Farrar, Straus & Giroux.

Sontag, S. (1988). *AIDS and its metaphors.* New York: Farrar, Straus & Giroux.

Sorensen, J., Wrinkle, R. Brewer, V., & Marquart, J. (1999). Capital punishment and deterrence: Examining the effect of executions on murder in Texas. *Crime and Delinquency, 45,* 481–493.

Sorkin, A. R. (2003, June 5). Despite shuffle, Stewart still in charge. *New York Times,* p. C1, C5.

Sorkin, R. D., Hays, C. J., & West, R. (2001). Signal-detection analysis of group decision making. *Psychological Review, 108,* 183–203.

Sorrels, J. P., & Kelley, J. (1984). Conformity by omission. *Personality and Social Psychology Bulletin, 10,* 302–305.

Spencer, S., Steele, C. M., & Quinn, D. (1997). *Under suspicion of inability: Stereotype threat and women's math performance.* Unpublished manuscript, Stanford University.

Spencer, S. J., Josephs, R. A., & Steele, C. M. (1993). Low self-esteem: The uphill battle for self-integrity. In R. F. Baumeister (Ed.), *Self-esteem and the puzzle of low self-regard.* (pp. 21–36.) New York: Wiley.

Spencer, S. J., Steele, C. M., & Quinn, D. M. (1999). Stereotype threat and women's math performance. *Journal of Experimental Social Psychology, 35,* 4–28.

Spencer-Rodgers, J., & Collins, N. L. (2006). Risk and resilience: Dual effects of perceptions of group disadvantage among Latinos. *Journal of Experimental Social Psychology, 42,* 729–737.

Spencer-Rodgers, J., Hamilton, D. L., & Sherman, S. J. (2007). The central role of entitativity in stereotypes of social categories and task groups. *Journal of Personality and Social Psychology, 92,* 369–388.

Spencer-Rodgers, J., Williams, M. J., Hamilton, D. L., Peng, K., & Wang, L. (2007). Culture and group perception: Dispositional and stereotypic inferences about novel and national groups. *Journal of Personality and Social Psychology, 93,* 525–543.

Spiegel, D., Bloom, J. R., Kraemer, H. C., & Gottheil, E. (1989). Psychological support for cancer patients. *Lancet, 2,* 1447.

Spiegel, H., & Spiegel, D. (1987 [1978]). *Trance and treatment: Clinical uses of hypnosis.* Washington, DC: American Psychiatric Press.

Spitzberg, B. H., & Rhea, J. (1999). Obsessive relational intrusion and sexual coercion victimization. *Journal of Interpersonal Violence, 14,* 3–20.

Spitzer, B. L., Henderson, K. A., & Zivian, M. T. (1999). Gender differences in population versus media body sizes: A comparison over four decades. *Sex Roles, 40,* 545–565.

Sporer, S. L. (1994). Decision times and eyewitness identification accuracy in simultaneous and sequential lineups. In D. F. Ross, J. D. Read, & M. P. Toglia (Eds.), *Adult eyewitness testimony: Current trends and developments.* (pp. 300–327.) New York: Cambridge University Press.

Sporer, S. L., Koehnken, G., & Malpass, R. S. (1996). Introduction: 200 years of mistaken identification. In S. L. Sporer, R. S. Malpass, & G. Koehnken (Eds.), *Psychological issues in eyewitness identification.* (pp. 1–6.) Mahwah, NJ: Erlbaum.

Sprecher, S. (1994). Two sides to the breakup of dating relationships. *Personal Relationships, 1,* 199–222.

Sprecher, S. (1998). The effect of exchange orientation on close relationships. *Social Psychology Quarterly, 61,* 230–231.

Sprecher, S., Aron, A., Hatfield, E., Cortese, A., Potapova, E., & Levitskaya, A. (1994). Love: American style, Russian style, and Japanese style. *Personal Relationships, 1,* 349–369.

Sprecher, S., & Fehr, B. (1998). The dissolution of close relationships. In J. H. Harvey (Ed.), Perspectives on loss: A sourcebook. (pp. 99–112.) Philadelphia, PA: Taylor & Francis.

Sprecher, S., Felmlee, D., Metts, S., Fehr, B., & Vanni, D. (1998). Factors associated with distress following the breakup of a close relationship. *Journal of Social and Personal Relationships, 15,* 791–809.

Sprecher, S., & Metts, S. (1989). Development of the "Romantic Beliefs Scale" and examination of the effects of gender and gender-role orientation. *Journal of Social and Personal Relationships, 6,* 387–411.

Sprecher, S., & Schwartz, P. (1994). Equity and balance in the exchange of contributions in close relationships. In M. J. Lerner & G. Mikula (Eds.), *Entitlement and the affectional bond: Justice in close relationships.* (pp. 11–42.) New York: Plenum.

Sprecher, S., Schwartz, P., Harvey, J., & Hatfield, E. (2008). TheBusinessofLove.com: Relationship initiation at Internet matchmaking services. In S. Sprecher, A. Wenzel, & J. Harvey (Eds.), *Handbook of relationship initiation.* (pp. 249–265.) New York: Taylor & Francis.

Sprecher, S., Wenzel, A., & Harvey, J. (Eds.) (2008). *Handbook of relationship initiation.* New York: Taylor & Francis.

Sprink, K. S., & Carron, A. V. (1994). Group cohesion effects in exercise classes. *Small Group Research, 25,* 26–42.

Staats, H., Harland, P., & Wilke, H. A. M. (2004). Effecting durable change: A team approach to improve environmental behavior in the household. *Environment and Behavior, 36,* 341–367.

Stangor, C., Sechrist, G. B., & Jost, J. T. (2001). Changing racial beliefs by providing consensus information. *Personality and Social Psychology Bulletin, 27,* 484–494.

Stapel, D. A., & Koomen, W. (2000). How far do we go beyond the information given? The impact of knowledge activation on interpretation and inference. *Journal of Personality and Social Psychology, 78,* 19–37.

Starzyk, K. B., Holden, R. R., Fabrigar, L. R., & MacDonald, T. K. (2006). The personal acquaintance measure: A tool for appraising one's acquaintance with any person. *Journal of Personality and Social Psychology, 90,* 833–847.

Stasser, G. (2000). Information distribution, participation, and group decision: Explorations with the DISCUSS and SPEAK models. In D. R. Ilgen & C. L. Hulin (Eds.), *Computational modeling of behavior in organizations: The third scientific discipline.* (pp. 135–161.) Washington, DC: American Psychological Association.

Stasser, G., & Birchmeier, Z. (2003). Group creativity and collective choice. In P. B. Paulus, & B. A. Nijstad (Eds.), *Group creativity: Innovation through collaboration.* (pp. 85–109.) New York: Oxford University Press.

Stasser, G., Stewart, D. D., & Wittenbaum, G. M. (1995). Expert roles and information exchange during discussion: The importance of knowing who knows what. *Journal of Experimental and Social Psychology, 31,* 244–265.

Stasser, G., & Titus, W. (1985). Pooling of unshared information in group decision making: Biased information sampling during discussion. *Journal of Personality and Social Psychology, 48,* 1467–1478.

Staub, E. (1974). Helping a distressed person: Social, personality, and stimulus determinants. In L. Berkowitz (Ed.), *Advances in experimental social psychology.* (Vol. 7, pp. 293–341.) New York: Academic Press.

Staub, E. (1989). *The roots of evil: The origins of genocide and other group violence.* Cambridge, UK: Cambridge University Press.

Steblay, N. M. (1987). Helping behavior in rural and urban environments: A meta-analysis. *Psychological Bulletin, 102,* 346–356.

Steblay, N. M., Dysart, J., Fulero, S. M., & Lindsay, R. C. L. (2001). Eyewitness accuracy rates in sequential and simultaneous lineup presentations: A meta-analytic comparison. *Law and Human Behavior, 25,* 459–473.

Steele, C. M. (1988). The psychology of self-affirmation: Sustaining the integrity of the self. In L. Berkowitz (Ed.), *Advances in experimental social psychology.* (Vol. 21, pp. 261–302.) New York: Academic Press.

Steele, C. M. (1997). A threat in the air: How stereotypes shape intellectual identity and performance. *American Psychologist, 52,* 613–629.

Steele, C. M., & Aronson, J. M. (1995a). Stereotype threat and the intellectual test performance of African-Americans. *Journal of Personality and Social Psychology, 69,* 797–811.

Steele, C. M, & Aronson, J. (1995b). Stereotype vulnerability and intellectual performance. In E. Aronson, (Ed.), *Readings about the social animal.* (7th ed.) New York: Freeman.

Steele, C. M., Spencer, S. J., & Aronson, J. M. (2002). Contending with group image: The psychology of stereotype and social identity threat. In M. P. Zanna (Ed.), *Advances in experimental social psychology.* (Vol. 34, pp. 379–440.) San Diego, CA: Academic Press.

Steele, C. M., Spencer, S. J., & Josephs, R. (1992). *Seeking self-relevant information: The effects of self-esteem and stability of the information.* Unpublished manuscript, University of Michigan.

Steele, C. M., Spencer, S. J., & Lynch, M. (1993). Self-image resilience and dissonance: The role of affirmational resources. *Journal of Personality and Social Psychology, 64,* 885–896.

Steele, J. R., & Ambady, N. (2006). "Math is hard!" The effect of gender priming on women's attitudes. *Journal of Experimental Social Psychology, 42,* 428–436.

Steiner, I. D. (1972). *Group process and productivity.* New York: Academic Press.

Stern, L. B., & Dunning, D. (1994). Distinguishing accurate from inaccurate eyewitness identifications: A reality monitoring approach. In D. F. Ross, J. D. Read, & M. P. Toglia (Eds.), *Adult eyewitness testimony: Current trends and developments.* (pp. 273–299.) New York: Cambridge University Press.

Sternberg, R. J., & Beall, A. E. (1991). How can we know what love is? An epistemological analysis. In G. J. O. Fletcher & F. D. Fincham (Eds.), *Cognition in close relationships.* (pp. 257–278.) Hillsdale, NJ: Erlbaum.

Sternberg, R. J., & Vroom, V. (2002). The person versus the situation in leadership. *Leadership Quarterly, 13,* 301–323.

Stewart, D. D., & Stasser, G. (1995). Expert role assignment and information sampling during collective recall and decision making. *Journal of Personality and Social Psychology, 69,* 619–628.

Stewart, M., Craig, D., MacPherson, K., & Alexander, S. (2001). Promoting positive affect and diminishing loneliness of widowed seniors through a support intervention. *Public Health Nursing, 18,* 54–63.

Stewart, W., & Barling, J. (1996). Daily work stress, mood, and interpersonal job performance: A mediational model. *Work and Stress, 10*, 336–351.

Stoff, D. M., & Cairns, R. B. (Eds.) (1997). *Aggression and violence: Genetic, neurobiological, and biosocial perspectives.* Mahwah, NJ: Erlbaum.

Stogdill, R. M. (1974). *Handbook of leadership.* New York: Free Press.

Stone, A. A., Bovbjerg, D. H., Neale, J. M., Napoli, A., Valdimarsdottir, H., Cox, D., Hayden, F. G., & Gwaltney, J. M. (1992). Development of common cold symptoms following experimental rhinovirus infection is related to prior stressful life events. *Behavioral Medicine, 18*(3), 115–120.

Stone, J., Aronson, E., Crain, A. L., Winslow, M. P., & Fried, C. (1994). Inducing hypocrisy as a means of encouraging young adults to use condoms. *Personality and Social Psychology Bulletin, 20*, 116–128.

Stormo, K. J., Lang, A. R., & Stritzke, W. G. K. (1997). Attributions about acquaintance rape: The role of alcohol and individual differences. *Journal of Applied Social Psychology, 27*, 279–305.

Storms, M. D., & Nisbett, R. E. (1970). Insomnia and the attribution process. *Journal of Personality and Social Psychology, 16*, 319–328.

Strahan, E. J., Spencer, S. J., & Zanna, M. P. (2002). Subliminal priming and persuasion: Striking while the iron is hot. *Journal of Experimental Social Psychology, 38*, 556–568.

Straus, M. A. (2004). Prevalence of violence against dating partners by male and female university students worldwide. *Violence Against Women, 10*, 790–811.

Strauss, M. A., & Gelles, R. J. (1980). *Behind closed doors: Violence in the American family.* New York: Anchor/Doubleday.

Stroebe, W., & Stroebe, M. (1996). The social psychology of social support. In E. T. Higgins & A. W. Kruglanski (Eds.), *Social psychology: Handbook of basic principles.* (pp. 597–621.) New York: Guilford.

Struthers, C. W., Dupuis, R., & Eaton, J. (2005). Promoting forgiveness among co-workers following a workplace transgression: The effects of social motivation training. *Canadian Journal of Behavioural Science, 37*, 299–308.

Studer, J. (1996). Understanding and preventing aggressive responses in youth. *Elementary School Guidance and Counseling, 30*, 194–203.

Stuhlmacher, A. F., & Citera, M. (2005). Hostile behavior and profit in virtual negotiation: A meta-analysis. *Journal of Business and Psychology, 20*, 69–93.

Stürmer, S., Snyder, M., & Omoto, A. (2005). Prosocial emotions and helping: The moderating role of group membership. *Journal of Personality and Social Psychology, 88*:3, 532–546.

Stuster, J. W., & Blowers, M. A. (1995). *Experimental evaluation of sobriety checkpoint programs.* Report No. DTNH22-91-C-07204. Washington, DC: National Highway Safety Administration.

Sudman, S., Bradburn, N., & Schwarz, N. (1996). *Thinking about answers: The application of cognitive processes to survey methodology.* San Fransisco, CA: Jossey-Bass Publishers.

Suedfeld, P. (2003). Specific and general attributional patterns of holocaust survivors. *Canadian Journal of Behavioural Science, 35*(2), 133–141.

Suedfeld, P., Conway III, L. G., & Eichorn, D. (2001). Studying Canadian leaders at a distance. In O. Feldman & L. O. Valenty (Eds.), *Profiling political leaders: Cross-cultural studies of personality and behavior.* (pp. 3–19.) Westport, CT: Praeger Publishers/ Greenwood Publishing Group.

Suls, J., & Fletcher, B. (1983). Social comparison in the social and physical sciences: An archival study. *Journal of Personality and Social Psychology, 44*, 575–580.

Suls, J. M., Martin, R., & Wheeler, L. (2000). Three kinds of opinion comparison: The triadic model. *Personality and Social Psychology Review, 4*, 219–237.

Suls, J. M., & Miller, R. L. (Eds.) (1977). *Social comparison processes: Theoretical and empirical perspectives.* Washington, DC: Hemisphere/Halstead.

Summers, G., & Feldman, N. S. (1984). Blaming the victim versus blaming the perpetrator: An attributional analysis of spouse abuse. *Journal of Social and Clinical Psychology, 2*, 339–347.

Sundstrom, E., Bell, P. A., Busby, P. L., & Asmus, C. (1996). Environmental psychology. *Annual Review of Psychology, 47*, 485–512.

Swann Jr., W. B. (1990). To be adored or to be known? The interplay of self-enhancement and self-verification. In R. M. Sorrentino & E. T. Higgins (Eds.), *Motivation and cognition.* (pp. 404–448.) New York: Guilford Press.

Swann, Jr., W. B. (1996). *Self-traps: The elusive quest for higher self-esteem.* New York: W. H. Freeman.

Swann, Jr., W. B., Bosson, J. K., & Pelham, B. W. (2002). Different partners, different selves: Strategic self-verification of circumscribed identities. *Personality and Social Psychology Bulletin, 28*, 1215–1228.

Swann, Jr., W. B., & Ely, Jr., R. J. (1984). A battle of wills: Self-verification versus behavioral confirmation. *Journal of Personality and Social Psychology, 46*, 1287–1302.

Swann, Jr., W. B., & Hill, C. A. (1982). When our identities are mistaken: Reaffirming self-conceptions through social interaction. *Journal of Personality and Social Psychology, 43*, 59–66.

Swann, Jr., W. B., & Pelham, B. W. (1988). *The social construction of identity: Self-verification through friend and intimate selection.* Unpublished manuscript, University of Texas-Austin.

Swann, Jr., W. B., & Schroeder, D. B. (1995). The search for beauty and truth: A framework for understanding reactions to evaluations. *Personality and Social Psychology Bulletin, 21*, 1307–1318.

Swann, Jr., W. B., Stein-Seroussi, A., & McNulty, S. E. (1992). Outcasts in a white-lie society: The enigmatic worlds of people with negative self-concepts. *Journal of Personality and Social Psychology, 62*, 618–624.

Swap, W. C. (1977). Interpersonal attraction and repeated exposure to rewarders and punishers. *Personality and Social Psychology Bulletin, 3*, 248–251.

Sweeney, P. D., Anderson, K., & Bailey, S. (1986). Attributional style in depression: A meta-analytic review. *Journal of Personality and Social Psychology, 50*, 974–991.

Swim, J., & Sanna, L. (1996). He's skilled, she's lucky: A meta-analysis of observers' attributions for women's and men's successes and failures. *Personality and Social Psychology Bulletin, 22*, 507–519.

Sykes, R. E. (1983). Initial interaction between strangers and acquaintances: A multivariate analysis of factors affecting choice of communication partners. *Human Communication Research, 10*, 27–63.

Symons, C. S., & Johnson, B. T. (1997). The self-reference effect in memory: A meta-analysis. *Psychological Bulletin, 121*, 371–394.

Symons, D. (1979). *The evolution of human sexuality.* New York: Oxford University Press.

Tafarodi, R. W., Kang, S., & Milne, A. B. (2002). When different becomes similar: Compensatory conformity in bicultural visible minorities. *Personality and Social Psychology Bulletin, 28*, 1131–1142.

Tajfel, H. (1982a). *Social identity and intergroup relations.* Cambridge, UK: Cambridge University Press.

Tajfel, H. (1982b). Social psychology of intergroup relations. *Annual Review of Psychology, 33*, 1–39.

Tajfel, H., & Billig, M. (1974). Familiarity and categorization in intergroup behavior. *Journal of Experimental Social Psychology, 10*, 159–170.

Tajfel, H., & Turner, J. C. (1979). An integrative theory of social contact. In W. Austin & S. Worchel (Eds.), *The social psychology of intergroup relations.* Monterey, CA: Brooks/Cole.

Tamres, L. K., Janicki, D., & Helgeson, V. S. (2002). Sex differences in coping behavior: A meta-analytic review. *Personality and Social Psychology Review, 6*, 2–30.

Tanford, S., & Penrod, S. (1984). Social influence model: A formal integration of research on majority and minority influence processes. *Psychological Bulletin, 95*, 189–225.

Tang, K. (2000). Cultural stereotypes and the justice system: The Canadian case of *R. v. Ewanchuk. International Journal of Offender Therapy and Comparative Criminology, 44*, 681–691.

Tang, S., & Hall, V. C. (1995). The overjustification effect: A meta-analysis. *Applied Cognitive Psychology, 9*, 365–404.

Tavris, C. (1984). On the wisdom of counting to ten: Personal and social dangers of anger expression. *Review of Personality and Social Psychology, 5*, 170–191.

Tavris, C. (1989). *Anger: The misunderstood emotion* (Rev. Ed.). New York: Touchstone Books/Simon & Schuster.

Tavris, C., & Aronson, E. (2007). *Mistakes were made (but not by me).* New York: Harcourt.

Taylor, D. M., & Gardner, R. C. (1969). Ethnic stereotypes: There effects on the perception of communicators of varying credibility. *Canadian Journal of Psychology, 23*, 161–173.

Taylor, D. M., Ruggiero, K. M., & Louis, W. R. (1996). Personal/group discrimination discrepancy: Towards a two-factor explanation. *Canadian Journal of Behavioural Science, 28*, 193–202.

Taylor, D. M., Wright, S. C., Moghaddam, F. M, & Lalonde, R. M. (1990). The personal/group discrimination discrepancy: Perceiving my group, but not myself, to be a target fro discrimination. *Personality and Social Psychology Bulletin, 16*, 254–262.

Taylor, S. E. (1981). A categorization approach to stereotyping. In D. L. Hamilton (Ed.), *Cognitive processes in stereotyping and intergroup relations.* (pp. 418–429.) Hillsdale, NJ: Erlbaum.

Taylor, S. E. (1989). *Positive illusions: Creative self-deception and the healthy mind.* New York: Basic Books.

Taylor, S. E. (1995). *Health psychology.* (3rd ed.) New York: McGraw-Hill.

Taylor, S. E., & Brown, J. (1988). Illusion and well-being: A social psychological perspective on mental health. *Psychological Bulletin, 103*, 193–210.

Taylor, S. E., & Brown, J. D. (1994). Positive illusions and well-being revisited: Separating fact from fiction. *Psychological Bulletin, 116*, 21–27.

Taylor, S. E., & Falcone, H. (1982). Cognitive bases of stereotyping: The relationship between categorization and prejudice. *Personality and Social Psychology Bulletin, 8*, 426–432.

Taylor, S. E., & Fiske, S. T. (1975). Point of view and perceptions of causality. *Journal of Personality and Social Psychology, 32*, 439–445.

Taylor, S. E., Klein, L. C., Lewis, B. P., Gruenewald, T. L., Gurung, R. A. R., & Updegraff, J. A. (2000). Biobehavioral responses to stress in females: Tend-and-befriend, not fight-or-flight. *Psychological Review, 107*, 411–429.

Taylor, S. E., Lichtman, R. R., & Wood, J. V. (1984). Attributions, beliefs about control, and adjustment to breast cancer. *Journal of Personality and Social Psychology, 46*, 489–502.

Taylor, S. E., Repetti, R. L., & Seeman, T. (1997). Health psychology: What is an unhealthy environment and how does it get under the skin? *Annual Review of Psychology, 48*, 411–447.

Taylor, S. P., & Leonard, K. E. (1983). Alcohol and human physical aggression. In R. Geen & E. Donnerstein (Eds.), *Aggression: Theoretical and empirical reviews.* New York: Academic Press.

Teger, A. L., & Pruitt, D. G. (1967). Components of group risk taking. *Journal of Experimental Social Psychology, 3*, 189–205.

Terracciano, A., Abdel-Khalek, A. M., Ádám, N., Adamovová, L., Ahn, C.-k., Ahn, H.-n., Alansari, B. M., Alcalay, L., Allik, J., Angleitner, A., Avia, M. D., Ayearst, L. E., Barbaranelli, C., Beer, A., Borg-Cunen, M. A., Bratko, D., Brunner-Sciarra, M., Budzinski, L., Camart, N., Dahourou, D., De Fruyt, F., de Lima, M. P., del Pilar, G. E. H., Diener, E., Falzon, R., Fernando, K., Ficková, E., Fischer, R., Flores-Mendoza, C., Ghayur, M. A., Gülgöz, S., Hagberg, B., Halberstadt, J., Halim, M. S., Horebíocková, M., Humrichouse, J., Jensen, H. H., Jocic, D. D., Jónsson, F. H., Khoury, B., Klinkosz, W., Kneozeviec, G., Lauri, M. A., Leibovich, N., Martin, T. A., Marusic, I., Mastor, K. A., Matsumoto, D., McRorie, M., Meshcheriakov, B., Mortensen, E. L., Munyae, M., Nagy, J., Nakazato, K., Nansubuga, F., Oishi, S., Ojedokun, A. O., Ostendorf, F., Paulhus, D. L., Pelevin, S., Petot, J.-M., Podobnik, N., Porrata, J. L., Pramila, V. S., Prentice, G., Realo, A., Reátegui, N., Rolland, J.-P., Rossier, J., Ruch, W., Rus, V. S., Sánchez-Bernardos, M. L., Schmidt, V., Sciculna-Calleja, S., Sekowski, A., Shakespeare-Finch, J., Shimonaka, Y., Simonetti, F., Sineshaw, T., Siuta, J., Smith, P. B., Trapnell, P. D., K. K. Trobst, K. K., Wang, L., Yik, M., Zupanocioc, A., & McCrae, R. R. (2005). National character does not reflect mean personality trait levels in 49 cultures. *Science, 310*, 96–100.

Tesser, A., & Beach, S. R. H. (1998). Life events, relationship quality, and depression: An investigation of judgment discontinuity in vivo. *Journal of Personality and Social Psychology, 74*, 36–52.

Tesser, A., Campbell, J., & Mickler, S. (1983). The role of social pressure, attention to the stimulus, and self-doubt in conformity. *European Journal of Social Psychology, 13*, 217–233.

Tetlock, P. E., Peterson, R. S., McGuire, C., Chang, S., & Field, P. (1992). Assessing political group dynamics: A test of the group-think model. *Journal of Personality and Social Psychology, 63*, 403–425.

Thibault, P., Bourgeois, P., & Hess, U. (2006). The effect of group-identification on emotion recognition: The case of cats and basketball players. *Journal of Experimental Social Psychology, 42*, 676–683.

Thibaut, J. W., & Kelley, H. H. (1959). *The social psychology of groups.* New York: Wiley.

Thibodeau, R., & Aronson, E. (1992). Taking a closer look: Reasserting the role of the self-concept in dissonance theory. *Personality and Social Psychology Bulletin, 18*, 591–602.

Thomas, M. (1982). Physiological arousal, exposure to a relatively lengthy aggressive film, and aggressive behavior. *Journal of Research in Personality, 16*, 72–81.

Thomas, M. H., Horton, R., Lippincott, E., & Drabman, R. (1977). Desensitization to portrayals of real-life aggression as a function of exposure to television violence. *Journal of Personality and Social Psychology, 35*, 450–458.

Thomas, S. L., Skitka, L. J., Christen, S., & Jurgena, M. (2002). Social facilitation and impression formation. *Basic and Applied Social Psychology, 242*, 67–70.

Thomas, W. I. (1928). *The child in America.* New York: Alfred A. Knopf.

Thompson, J. K., & Heinberg, L. J. (1999). The media's influence on body image disturbance and eating disorders: We've reviled them, now can we rehabilitate them? *Journal of Social Issues, 55*, 339–353.

Thompson, L. (1997). *The mind and heart of the negotiator.* Englewood Cliffs, NJ: Prentice-Hall.

Thompson, L. L. (2005). *The heart and mind of the negotiator* (3rd ed.). Upper Saddle River, NJ: Prentice-Hall.

Thompson, S. C. (1999). Illusions of control: How we overestimate our personal influence. *Current Directions in Psychological Science, 8*, 187–190.

Thompson, S. C. (2002). The role of personal control in adaptive functioning. In C. R. Snyder & S. J. Lopez (Eds.), *Handbook of positive psychology.* (pp. 202–213.) London, UK: Oxford University Press.

Thompson, S. C., Nanni, C., & Levine, A. (1994). Primary versus secondary and central versus consequence-related control in HIV-positive men. *Journal of Personality and Social Psychology, 67*, 540–547.

Tihanyi, E. (1999). Who I am because of who she was. In G. Valle (Ed.) *Our grandmothers, ourselves: Reflections of Canadian women.* (pp. 102–108.) Vancouver, BC: Raincoast Books.

Timmerman, T. A. (2007). "It was a thought pitch": Personal, situational, and target influences on hit-by-pitch events across time. *Journal of Applied Psychology, 92*, 876–884.

Ting, J., & Piliavin, J. A. (2000). Altruism in comparative international perspective. In J. Phillips, B. Chapman, & D. Stevens (Eds.), *Between state and market: Essays on charities law and policy in Canada.* (pp. 51–105.) Montreal, QC, and Kingston, ON: McGill-Queens University Press.

Ting-Toomey, S., & Chang, L. (1996). Cross cultural interpersonal communication: Theoretical trends and research directions. In W. B. Gudykunst, S. Ting-Toomey, & T. Nishada (Eds.), *Communication in personal relationships across cultures.* Thousand Oaks, CA: Sage.

Toch, H. (1980). *Violent men.* (rev. ed.) Cambridge, MA: Schenkman.

Toi, M., & Batson, C. D. (1982). More evidence that empathy is a source of altruistic motivation. *Journal of Personality and Social Psychology, 43,* 281–292.

Tollestrup, P., Turtle, J., & Yuille, J. (1994). Actual victims and witnesses to robbery and fraud: An archival analysis. In D. F. Ross, J. D. Read, & M. P. Toglia (Eds.), *Adult eyewitness testimony: Current trends and developments.* New York: Cambridge University Press.

Tomes, J. L., & Katz, A. N. (1997). Habitual susceptibility to misinformation and individual differences in eyewitness memory. *Applied Cognitive Psychology, 11,* 233–251.

Tormala, Z. L., & Petty, R. E. (2002). What doesn't kill me makes me stronger: The effect of resisting persuasion on attitude certainty. *Journal of Personality and Social Psychology, 83*:6, 1298–1313.

Toronto (2000). *Research group on drug use.* Toronto, ON: Department of Public Health.

Tougas, F., Brown, R., Beaton, A. M., & Joly, S. (1995). Neosexism: *Plus ça change, plus c'est pareil. Personality and Social Psychology Bulletin, 21,* 842–849.

Tougas, F., Brown, R., Beaton, A., & St-Pierre, L. (1999). Neosexism among women: The role of personally experienced social mobility attempts. *Personality and Social Psychology Bulletin, 25,* 1487–1497.

Tougas, F., De La Sablonnière, R., Lagacé, M., & Kocum, L. (2003). Intrusiveness of minorities: Growing pains for the majority group? *Journal of Applied Social Psychology, 33*(2), 283–298.

Tougas, F., Desruisseaux, J.-C., Desrochers, A., St-Pierre, L., Perrino, A., & De la Sablonnière, R. (2004). Two forms of racism and their related outcomes: The bad and the ugly. *Canadian Journal of Behavioural Science, 36*:3, 177–189.

Tougas, F., Rinfret, N., Beaton, A. M., De la Sablonnière, R. (2005). Policewomen acting in self-defense: Can psychological disengagement protect self-esteem from the negative outcomes of relative deprivation? *Journal of Personality and Social Psychology, 88*(5), 790–800.

Tracy, J. L., & Robins, R. W. (2006). Appraisal antecedents of shame and guilt: Support for a theoretical model. *Personality and Social Psychology Bulletin, 32,* 1339–1351.

Tracy, J. L., & Robins, R. W. (2007). The psychological structure of pride: A tale of two facets. *Journal of Personality and Social Psychology, 92,* 506–525.

Trampe, D., Stapel, D. A., & Siero, F. W. (2007). On models and vases: Body dissatisfaction and proneness to social comparison effects. *Journal of Personality and Social Psychology, 92,* 106–118.

Trappey, C. (1996). A meta-analysis of consumer choice and subliminal advertising. *Psychology and Marketing, 13,* 517–530.

Traupmann, J., Petersen, R., Utne, M., & Hatfield, E. (1981). Measuring equity in intimate relations. *Applied Psychology Measurement, 5,* 467–480.

Travis, C. B., Phillippi, R. H., & Tonn, B. E. (1989). Judgment heuristics and medical decisions. *Patient Education and Counseling, 13,* 211–220.

Travis, C. B., & Yeager, C. P. (1991). Sexual selection, parental investment, and sexism. *Journal of Social Issues, 47,* 117–129.

Tremblay, R. E., Schaal, B., Boulerice, B., Arseneault, L., Soussignan, R. G., Paquette, D., & Laurent, D. (1998). Testosterone, physical aggression, dominance, and physical development in early adolescence. *International Journal of Behavioral Development, 22,* 753–777.

Triandis, H. C. (1989). The self and social behavior in differing cultural contexts. *Psychological Review, 96,* 506–520.

Triandis, H. C. (1990). Cross-cultural studies of individualism and collectivism. In J. J. Berman (Ed.), *Nebraska Symposium on Motivation, 1989.* (pp. 41–133.) Lincoln, NE: University of Nebraska Press.

Triandis, H. C. (1994). *Culture and social behavior.* New York: McGraw-Hill.

Triandis, H. C. (1995). *Individualism and collectivism.* Boulder, CO: Westview Press.

Triplett, N. (1898). The dynamogenic factors in pace making and competition. *American Journal of Psychology, 9,* 507–533.

Trivers, R. L. (1971). The evolution of reciprocal altruism. *Quarterly Review of Biology, 46,* 35–57.

Tropp, L. R., & Wright, S. C. (2001). Ingroup identification as the inclusion of ingroup in the self. *Personality and Social Psychology Bulletin, 27,* 585–600.

Tsai, M. (2006). Sociable resources and close relationships: Intimate relatives and friends in Taiwan. *Journal of Social and Personal Relationships, 23,* 151–169.

Tseëlon, E. (1995). *The presentation of woman in everyday life.* Thousand Oaks, CA: Sage.

Tucker, P., Pfefferbaum, B., Doughty, D. B., Jones, D. E., Jordan, F. B., & Nixon, S. J. (2002). Body handlers after terrorism in Oklahoma City: Predictors of posttraumatic stress and other symptoms. *American Journal of Orthopsychiatry, 72,* 469–475.

Turner, C., & Leyens, J. (1992). The weapons effect revisited: The effects of firearms on aggressive behavior. In P. Suedfeld & P. Tetlock (Eds.), *Psychology and social policy.* (pp. 201–221.) New York: Hemispheres.

Turner, C., & Simons, L. (1974). Effects of subject sophistication and evaluation apprehension on aggressive responses to weapons. *Journal of Personality and Social Psychology, 30,* 341–348.

Turner, C., Simons, L., Berkowitz, L., & Frodi, A. (1977). The stimulating and inhibiting effects of weapons on aggressive behavior. *Aggressive Behavior, 3,* 355–378.

Turner, J. C., Hogg, M. A., Oakes, P. J., Reicher, S. D., & Wetherell, M. S. (1987). *Rediscovering the social group: A self-categorization theory.* Oxford, UK: Blackwell Publishers.

Turner, M. E., & Horvitz, T. (2001). The dilemma of threat: Group effectiveness and ineffectiveness under adversity. In M. E. Turner (Ed.), *Groups at work: Theory and research.* (pp. 445–470.) Mahwah, NJ: Erlbaum.

Turula, M. (2007, August 11). Eight shot dead at Finnish school. *Winnipeg Free Press.* www.winnipegfreepress.com/historic/ 32558084.html. Accessed November 2008.

Turula, M. (2008, November 8). 8 shot dead at Finnish school. *Winnipeg Free Press,* p. A3.

Tversky, A., & Kahneman, D. (1973). Availability: A heuristic for judging frequency and probability. *Cognitive Psychology, 5,* 207–232.

Tversky, A., & Kahneman, D. (1974). Judgment under uncertainty: Heuristics and biases. *Science, 185,* 1124–1131.

Twenge, J. M., Baumeister, R. F., DeWall, C., Ciarocco, N. J., & Bartles, J. M. (2007). Social exclusion decreases prosocial behaviour. *Journal of Personality and Social Psychology, 92,* 56–66.

Twenge, J. M., Baumeister, R. F., Tice, D. M., & Stucke, T. S. (2001). If you can't join them, beat them: Effects of social exclusion on aggressive behavior. *Journal of Personality and Social Psychology, 81,* 1058–1069.

Tyler, T. R. (1990). *Why people obey the law.* New Haven, CT: Yale University Press.

Uchino, B. N., Uno, D., & Holt-Lunstad, J. (1999). Social support, physiological processes, and health. *Current Directions in Psychological Science, 8,* 145–148.

Uehara, E. S. (1995). Reciprocity reconsidered: Gouldner's "moral norm of reciprocity" and social support. *Journal of Social and Personal Relationships, 12,* 483–502.

Uskul, A. K., Lalonde, R. N., & Cheng, L. (2007). Views on interracial dating among Chinese and European Canadians: The roles of culture, gender, and mainstream cultural identity. *Journal of Social and Personal Relationships, 24,* 891–911.

Uzzell, D. (2000). Ethnographic and action research. In G. M. Breakwell, S. Hammond, & C. Fife-Schaw (Eds.), *Research methods in psychology.* (2nd ed., pp. 326–337.) Thousand Oaks, CA: Sage.

Vaananen, A., Buunk, B. P., Kivimaki, M., Pentti, J., & Vahteva, J. (2005). When is it better to give than to receive? Long-term health effects of perceived reciprocity in support exchange. *Journal of Personality and Social Psychology, 89,* 176–193.

Valins, S. (1966). Cognitive effects of false heart-rate feedback. *Journal of Personality and Social Psychology, 4,* 400–408.

Valle, P. O. D., Rebelo, E., & Reis, E. (2005). Combining behavioral theories to predict recycling involvement. *Environment and Behavior, 37,* 364–396.

Van Vugt, M., & De Cremer, D. C. (1999). Leadership in social dilemmas: The effects of group identification on collective actions to provide public goods. *Journal of Personality and Social Psychology, 76,* 587–599.

Vallerand, R. J. (1997). Toward a hierarchical model of intrinsic and extrinsic motivation. *Advances in Experimental Social Psychology, 29,* 271–360.

Vallerand, R. J., Fortier, M. S., & Guay, F. (1997). Self-determination and persistence in real-life setting: Toward a motivational model of high school dropout. *Journal of Personality and Social Psychology, 72,* 1161–1176.

Vallerand, R. J., & Ratelle, C. F. (2002). Intrinsic and extrinsic motivation: A hierarchical model. In E. L. Deci & R. M. Ryan (Eds.), *Handbook of self-determination research.* (pp. 37–63.) Rochester, NY: University of Rochester Press.

Vallone, R. P., Griffin, D. W., Lin, S., & Ross, L. (1990). The overconfident prediction of future actions and outcomes by self and others. *Journal of Personality and Social Psychology, 58,* 582–592.

Van Bavel, J. J., & Cunningham, W. A. (2007, June). Shifting intergroup evaluations using arbitrary coalitions. Paper presented at the Canadian Psychological Association Conference, Ottawa, Ontario.

Van Boven, L., White, K., Kamanda, A., & Gilovich, T. (2003). Intuitions about situational correction in self and others. *Journal of Personality and Social Psychology, 85*(2), 249–258.

Vandello, J. A., & Cohen, D. (2003) Male honor and female fidelity: Implicit cultural scripts that perpetuate domestic violence. *Journal of Personality and Social Psychology, 84,* 997–1010.

van de Vijver, F., & Leung, K. (1997). *Methods and data analyses for cross-cultural research.* Thousand Oaks, CA: Sage.

Van Lange, P. A. M., Ouwerkerk, J. W., & Tazelaar, M. J. A. (2002). How to overcome the detrimental effects of noise in social interaction: The benefits of generosity. *Journal of Personality and Social Psychology, 82,* 768–780.

Vanneman, R. D., & Pettigrew, T. (1972). Race and relative deprivation in the urban United States. *Race, 13,* 461–486.

VanOostrum, N., & Horvath, P. (1997). The effects of hostile attribution on adolescents' aggressive responses to social situations. *Canadian Journal of School Psychology, 13,* 729–738.

Van Overwalle, F., & De Metsenaere, M. (1990). The effects of attribution-based intervention and study strategy training on academic achievement in college freshmen. *British Journal of Educational Psychology, 60,* 299–311.

Van Vugt, M. (2001). Community identification moderating the impact of financial incentives in a natural social dilemma: Water conservation. *Personality and Social Psychology Bulletin, 27,* 1440–1449.

Van Vugt, M., & Samuelson, C. (1999). The impact of personal metering in the management of a natural resource crisis: A social dilemma analysis. *Personality and Social Psychology Bulletin, 25,* 731–745.

Van Yperen, N. W., & Buunk, B. P. (1994). Social comparison and social exchange in marital relationships. In M. J. Lerner & G. Mikula (Eds.), *Entitlement and the affectional bond: Justice in close relationships.* (pp. 89–116.) New York: Plenum.

Vasquez, N. A., & Buehler, R. (2007). Seeing future success: Does imagery perspective influence achievement motivation? *Personality and Social Psychology Bulletin, 33,* 1392–1405.

Verkuyten, M. (2005). Ethnic group identification and group evaluation among minority and majority groups: Testing the multiculturalism hypothesis. *Journal of Personality and Social Psychology, 88,* 121–138.

Vidmar, N. (1974). Retributive and ulitarian motives and other correlates of Canadian attitudes toward the death penalty. *Canadian Psychologist, 15,* 337–356.

Vidyasgar, P., & Mishra, H. (1993). Effect of modelling on aggression. *Indian Journal of Clinical Psychology, 20,* 50–52.

Vining, J., & Ebreo, A. (2002). Emerging theoretical and methodological perspectives on conservation behavior. In R. B. Bechtel & A. Churchman (Eds.), *Handbook of environmental psychology.* (pp. 541–558.) New York: Wiley.

Vissing, Y., Straus, M., Gelles, R., & Harrop, J. (1991).Verbal aggression by parents and psychosocial problems of children. *Child Abuse and Neglect, 15,* 223–238.

Voas, R. B., Holder, H. D., & Gruenewald, P. J. (1999). The effect of drinking and driving interventions on alcohol-related traffic crashes within a comprehensive community trial. *Addiction, 92,* S221–S236.

Voelpel, S. C., Eckhoff, R. A., & Forster, J. (2008). David against Goliath? Group size and bystander effects in virtual knowledge sharing. *Human Relations, 61,* 271–295.

Vohs, K. D., Baumeister, R. F., & Ciarocco, N. J. (2005). Self-regulation and self-presentation: Regulatory resource depletion impairs impression management and effortful self-presentation depletes regulatory resources. *Journal of Personality and Social Psychology, 88,* 632–657.

Volling, B. L., Kolak, A. M., & Kennedy, D. E. (2009). Empathy and compassionate love in early childhood: Development and family influence. In B. Fehr, S. Sprecher, & L. Underwood, L. (Eds.), *The science of compassionate love: Theory, research, and applications.* (pp. 161–200.) Malden, MA: Blackwell Publishers.

von Hippel, W., Hawkins, C., & Schooler, J. W. (2001). Stereotype distinctiveness: How counterstereotypic behavior shapes the self-concept. *Journal of Personality and Social Psychology, 81,* 193–205.

von Hippel, W., von Hippel, C., Conway, L., Preacher, K. J., Schooler, J. W., & Radvansky, G. A. (2005). Coping with stereotype threat: Denial as an impression management strategy. *Journal of Personality and Social Psychology, 89,* 22–35.

Vorauer, J. D. (2001). The other side of the story: Transparency estimation in social interaction. In G. B. Moskowitz (Ed.), *Cognitive social psychology: The Princeton symposium on the legacy and future of social cognition.* (pp. 261–276.) Mahwah, NJ: Erlbaum.

Vorauer, J. D. (2003). Dominant group members in intergroup interaction: Safety or vulnerability in numbers? *Personality and Social Psychology Bulletin, 29,* 498–511.

Vorauer, J. D. (2005). Miscommunications surrounding efforts to reach out across group boundaries. *Personality and Social Psychology Bulletin, 31,* 1653–1664.

Vorauer, J. (2008). Unprejudiced and self-focused: When intergroup contact is experienced as being about the ingroup rather than the outgroup. *Journal of Experimental Social Psychology, 44,* 912–919.

Vorauer, J. D., & Cameron, J. J. (2002). So close, and yet so far: Does collectivism foster transparency overestimation? *Journal of Personality and Social Psychology, 83,* 1344–1352.

Vorauer, J. D., Cameron, J. J., Holmes, J. G., & Pearce, D.G. (2003). Invisible overtures: Fears of rejection and the signal amplification bias. *Journal of Personality and Social Psychology, 84*(4), 793–812.

Vorauer, J. D., & Claude, S. D. (1998). Perceived versus actual transparency of goals in negotiation. *Personality and Social Psychology Bulletin, 24,* 371–385.

Vorauer, J. D., Hunter, A. J., Main, K., & Roy, S. (2000). Meta-stereotype activation: Evidence from indirect measures for specific evaluative concerns experienced by members of dominant groups in intergroup interaction. *Journal of Personality and Social Psychology, 78,* 690–707.

Vorauer, J. D., & Kumhyr, S. M. (2001). Is this about you or me? Self-versus other-directed judgments and feelings in response to intergroup interaction. *Personality and Social Psychology Bulletin, 27,* 706–719.

Vorauer, J. D., Main, K., & O'Connell, G. B. (1998). How do individuals expect to be viewed by members of lower status groups? Content and implications of meta stereotypes. *Journal of Personality and Social Psychology, 75,* 917–937.

Vorauer, J. D., & Miller, D. T. (1997). Failure to recognize the effect of implicit social influence on the presentation of self. *Journal of Personality and Social Psychology, 73,* 281–295.

Voraurer, J. D., & Ross, M. (1999). Self-awareness and feeling transparent: Failing to suppress one's self. *Journal of Experimental Social Psychology, 35,* 415–440.

Vorauer, J. D., Sakamoto, Y. (2006). I thought we could be friends, but . . . : Systematic Miscommunication and defensive distancing as obstacles to cross-group friendship formation. *Psychological Science, 17,* 326–331.

Vorauer, J. D., & Turpie, C. A. (2004). Disruptive effects of vigilance on dominant group members' treatment of outgroup members: Choking versus shining under pressure. *Journal of Personality and Social Psychology, 87*:3, 384–399.

Wakefield, S., & Elliott, S. J. (2000). Environmental risk perception and well-being: effects of the landfill siting process in two southern Ontario communities. *Social Science & Medicine, 50,* 1139–1154.

Wakefield, M., Flay, B., & Nichter, M. (2003). Role of the media in influencing trajectories of youth smoking. *Addiction, 98*(Suppl1), Special issue: Contexts and adolescent tobacco use trajectories, 79–103.

Walker, L. J., & Frimer, J. A. (2007). Moral personality of brave and caring exemplars. *Journal of Personality and Social Psychology, 93,* 845–860.

Wall, A., Hinson, R. E., & McKee, S. A. (1998). Alcohol outcome expectancies, attitude toward drinking and the theory of planned behavior. *Journal of Studies on Alcohol, 59,* 409–419.

Wall, G. (1995). Barriers to individual environmental action: The influence of attitudes and social experiences. *Canadian Review of Sociology and Anthropology, 32,* 465–489.

Wallach, M. A., Kogan, N., & Bem, D. J. (1962). Group influences on individual risk taking. *Journal of Abnormal and Social Psychology, 65,* 75–86.

Walsh, M., Hickey, C., & Duffy, J. (1999). Influence of item content and stereotype situation on gender differences in mathematical problem solving. *Sex Roles, 41,* 219–240.

Walster, E. (1966). Assignment of responsibility for an accident. *Journal of Personality and Social Psychology, 3,* 73–79.

Walster, E., Aronson, V., Abrahams, D., & Rottman, L. (1966). Importance of physical attractiveness in dating behavior. *Journal of Personality and Social Psychology, 5,* 508–516.

Walster, E., & Festinger, L. (1962). The effectiveness of "overheard" persuasive communication. *Journal of Abnormal and Social Psychology, 65,* 395–402.

Walster (Hatfield), E., Aronson, V., Abrahams, D., & Rottman, L. (1966). Importance of physical attractiveness in dating behavior. *Journal of Personality and Social Psychology, 5,* 508–516.

Walster (Hatfield), E., Walster, G. W., & Berscheid, E. (1978). *Equity: Theory and research.* Needham Heights, MA: Allyn & Bacon.

Walters, V., Lenton, R., French, S., Eyles, J., Mayr, J., & Newbold, B. (1996). Paid work, unpaid work and social support: A study of the health of male and female nurses. *Social Science Medical, 43,* 1627–1636.

Walther, E., Bless, H., Strack, F., Rackstraw, P., Wagner, D., & Werth, L. (2002). Conformity effects in memory as a function of group size, dissenters and uncertainty. *Applied Cognitive Psychology, 16,* 793–810.

Wang, H., Masuda, T., & Ishii, K. (2008, February). Comparing patterns of attention between Canadians and East Asian international students. Paper presented at the Society for Social Psychology and Personality Conference, Albuquerque, New Mexico.

Wang, T., Brownstein, R., & Katzev, R. (1989). Promoting charitable behavior with compliance techniques. *Applied Psychology: An International Review, 38,* 165–184.

Wasswa, H. (2002, March 16). Uganda cult deaths remain a mystery. Associated Press. www.rickross.com/reference/tencommandments/tencommandments117.html. (October 22, 2002).

Watkins, D., Adair, J., Akande, A., Gerong, A., McInerney, D., Sunar, D., Watson, S., Wen, Q., & Wondimu, H. (1998). Individualism-collectivism, gender and the self-concept: A nine-culture investigation. *Psychologia: An International Journal of Psychology in the Orient, 41,* 259–271.

Watkins, D., Akande, A., Fleming, J., Ismail, M., Lefner, K., Regmi, M., Watson, S., Yu, J., Adair, J., Cheng, C., Gerong, A., McInerney, D., Mpofu, E., Singh–Sengupta, S., & Wondimu, H. (1998). Cultural dimensions, gender, and the nature of self-concept: A fourteen-country study. *International Journal of Psychology, 33,* 17–31.

Watson, D., & Pennebaker, J. W. (1989). Health complaints, stress, and distress: Exploring the central role of negative affectivity. *Psychological Review, 96,* 234–254.

Watson, J. (1924). *Behaviorism.* Chicago, IL: University of Chicago Press.

Watson, R. I. (1973). Investigation into deindividuation using a cross-cultural survey technique. *Journal of Personality and Social Psychology, 25,* 342–345.

Watson, W. E., Johnson, L., Kumar, K., & Critelli, J. (1998). Process gain and process loss: Comparing interpersonal processes and performance of culturally diverse and non-diverse teams across time. *International Journal of Intercultural Relations, 22,* 409–430.

Watts, D. P., Muller, M., Amsler, S. J., Mbabazi, G., and Mitani, J. C. (2006, February). Lethal intergroup aggression by chimpanzees in Kibale National Park, Uganda. *American Journal of Primatology, 68*(2), 161–180.

Wayment, H. A. (2006). Attachment style, empathy, and helping following a collective loss: Evidence from the September 11 terrorist attacks. *Attachment and Human Development, 8,* 1–9.

Webber, R., & Crocker, J. (1983). Cognitive processes in the revision of stereotypic beliefs. *Journal of Personality and Social Psychology, 45,* 961–977.

Weber, J. M., Kopelman, S., & Messick, D. M. (2004). A conceptual review of decision making in social dilemmas: Applying a logic of appropriateness. *Personality and Social Psychology Review, 8,* 281–307.

Weber, E. U., Bockenholt, U., Hilton, D. J., & Wallace, B. (1993). Determinants of diagnostic hypothesis generation: Effects of information, base rates, and experience. *Journal of Experimental Psychology: Learning, Memory, and Cognition, 19,* 1151–1164.

Webster, D. M. (1993). Motivated augmentation and reduction of the overattributional bias. *Journal of Personality and Social Psychology, 65,* 261–271.

Wechsler, H., Lee, J. E., Kuo, M., Siebring, M., Nelson, T. F., & Lee, H. (2002). Trends in college binge drinking during a period of increased prevention efforts: Findings from 4 Harvard School of Public Health college alcohol study surveys, 1993–2001. *Journal of American College Health, 50,* 203–217.

Weeden, J., & Sabini, J. (2005). Physical attractiveness and health in Western societies: A review. *Psychological Bulletin, 131,* 635–653.

Wegener, D. T., & Petty, R. E. (1994). Mood management across affective states: The hedonic contingency hypothesis. *Journal of Personality and Social Psychology, 66,* 1034–1048.

Wegener, D. T., & Petty, R. E. (1995). Flexible correction processes in social judgment: The role of naive theories in corrections for perceived bias. *Journal of Personality and Social Psychology, 68,* 36–51.

Wegner, D. M. (1992). You can't always think what you want: Problems in the suppression of unwanted thoughts. In M. P. Zanna (Ed.), *Advances in experimental social psychology.* (pp. 193–225.) San Diego, CA: Academic Press.

Wegner, D. M. (1994). Ironic processes of mental control. *Psychological Review, 101,* 34–52.

Wegner, D. M. (1995). A computer network model of human transactive memory. *Social Cognition, 13,* 319–339.

Wegner, D. M. (2002). *The illusion of conscious will.* Cambridge, MA: MIT Press.

Wegner, D. M. (2004). Precis of "The illusion of conscious will." *Behavioral & Brain Sciences, 27,* 649–659.

Wegner, D. M., & Bargh, J. A. (1998). Control and automaticity in social life. In D. Gilbert, S. Fiske, & G. Lindzey (Eds.), *The handbook of social psychology.* (4th ed., Vol. 1, pp. 446–498.) New York: McGraw Hill.

Wegner, D. M., Erber, R., & Raymond, P. (1991). Transactive memory in close relationships. *Journal of Personality and Social Psychology, 61,* 923–929.

Wegner, D. M., Wenzlaff, R. M., & Kozak, M. (2004). Dream rebound: The return of suppressed thoughts in dreams. *Psychological Science, 15,* 232–236.

Wehrle, T., Kaiser, S., Schmidt, S., & Scherer, K. R. (2000). Studying the dynamics of emotional expression using synthesized facial muscle movements. *Journal of Personality and Social Psychology, 78,* 105–119.

Weiner, B., Amirkhan, J., Folkes, V. S., & Verette, J. A. (1987). An attributional analysis of excuse giving: Studies of a naive theory of emotion. *Journal of Personality and Social Psychology, 52,* 316–324.

Weingardt, K. R., Toland, H. K., & Loftus, E. F. (1994). Reports of suggested memories: Do people truly believe them? In D. F. Ross, J. D. Read, & M. P. Toglia (Eds.), *Adult eyewitness testimony: Current trends and developments.* (pp. 3–26.) New York: Cambridge University Press.

Weinstein, N. D. (1980). Unrealistic optimism about future life events. *Journal of Personality and Social Psychology, 39,* 806–820.

Weinstein, N. D., & Klein, W. M. (1996). Unrealistic optimism: Present and future. *Journal of Social and Clinical Psychology, 15,* 1–8.

Weir, W. (1984, October 15). Another look at subliminal "facts." *Advertising Age,* p. 46.

Wekerle, C., & Wall, A. (2002). Introduction: The overlap between relationship violence and substance abuse. In C. Wekerle, & A. Wall (Eds.), *The violence and addiction equation.* (pp. 1–21.) New York: Taylor & Francis.

Wells, G. L. (1984). The psychology of lineup identifications. *Journal of Applied Social Psychology, 14,* 89–103.

Wells, G. L. (1992). Naked statistical evidence of liability: Is subjective probability enough? *Journal of Personality and Social Psychology, 62,* 739–752.

Wells, G. L. (1993). What do we know about eyewitness identification? *American Psychologist, 48,* 553–571.

Wells, G. L., Charman, S. D., & Olson, E. A. (2005). Building face composites can harm lineup identification performance. *Journal of Experimental Psychology: Applied, 11,* 147–156.

Wells, G. L., Lindsay, R. C. L., & Ferguson, T. (1978). Accuracy, confidence, and juror perceptions in eyewitness identification. *Journal of Applied Psychology, 64,* 440–448.

Wells, G. L., & Luus, C. A. E. (1990). Police lineups as experiments: Social methodology as a framework for properly conducted lineups. *Personality and Social Psychology Bulletin, 16,* 106–117.

Wells, G. L., Malpass, R. S., Lindsay, R. C. L., Fisher, R. P., Turtle, J. W., & Fulero, S. M. (2000). From the lab to the police station. *American Psychologist, 55,* 581–598.

Wells, G. L., & Olson, E. A. (2003). Eyewitness testimony. *Annual Review of Psychology, 54,* 277–295.

Wells, G. L., Olson, E. A., & Charman, S. D. (2002). The confidence of eyewitnesses in their identifications from lineups. *Current Directions in Psychological Science, 11,* 151–154.

Wells, G. L., Small, M., Penrod, S. D., Malpass, R. S., Fulero, S. M., & Brimacombe, C. A. E. (1998). Eyewitness identification procedures: Recommendations for lineups and photospreads. *Law and Human Behavior, 22,* 603–645.

Wells, G. L., Wright, E. F., & Bradfield, A. L. (1999) Witnesses to crime: Social and cognitive factors governing the validity of people's reports. In R. Roesch, S. D. Hart, & J. R. P. Ogloff (Eds.), *Psychology and law: The state of the discipline.* (pp. 53–88.) New York: Kluwer.

Wells, S., Graham, K., & West, P. (1998). "The good, the bad, and the ugly": Responses by security staff to aggressive incidents in public drinking settings. *Journal of Drug Issues, 28,* 817–836.

Wells, S., Graham, K., & West, P. (2000). Alcohol-related aggression in the general population. *Journal of Studies on Alcohol, 61,* 626–632.

Wells, W. D. (Ed.) (1997). *Measuring advertising effectiveness.* Mahwah, NJ: Erlbaum.

Wenzlaff, R. M., & Bates, D. E. (2000). The relative efficacy of concentration and suppression strategies of mental control. *Personality and Social Psychology Bulletin, 26,* 1200–1212.

Werner, C., & Parmelee, P. (1979). Similarity of activity preferences among friends: Those who play together stay together. *Social Psychology Quarterly, 42,* 62–66.

Werth, L., & Foerster, J. (2002). Implicit person theories influence memory judgments: The circumstances under which metacognitive knowledge is used. *European Journal of Social Psychology, 32,* 353–362.

Weyant, J. M. (1996). Application of compliance techniques to direct-mail requests for charitable donations. *Psychology and Marketing, 13,* 157–170.

Whatley, M. A., Webster, J. M., Smith, R. H., & Rhodes, A. (1999). The effect of a favor on public and private compliance: How internalized is the norm of reciprocity? *Basic and Applied Social Psychology, 21,* 251–259.

Wheeler, L., & Kim, Y. (1997). What is beautiful is culturally good: The physical attractiveness stereotype has different content in collectivistic cultures. *Personality and Social Psychology Bulletin, 23,* 795–800.

Wheeler, L., Koestner, R., & Driver, R. (1982). Related attributes in the choice of comparison others: It's there, but it isn't all there is. *Journal of Experimental Social Psychology, 18,* 489–500.

White, H. (1997). Longitudinal perspective on alcohol and aggression during adolescence. In M. Galanter (Ed.), *Recent developments in alcoholism: Vol. 13. Alcohol and violence: Epidemiology, neurobiology, psychology, and family issues.* (pp. 81–103.) New York: Plenum.

White, K., & Lehman, D. R. (2005a). Culture and social comparison seeking: The role of self-motives. *Personality and Social Psychology Bulletin, 31,* 232–242.

White, K., & Lehman, D. R. (2005b). Looking on the bright side: Downward counterfactual thinking in response to negative life events. *Personality and Social Psychology Bulletin, 31,* 1413–1424.

White, K., Lehman, D. R., & Cohen, D. (2006). Culture, self-construal, and affective reactions to successful and unsuccessful others. *Journal of Experimental Social Psychology, 42,* 582–592.

White, L. K. (1990). Determinants of divorce: A review of research in the eighties. *Journal of Marriage and the Family, 52,* 904–912.

White, P. A. (2002). Causal attribution from covariation information: The evidential evaluation model. *European Journal of Social Psychology, 32,* 667–684.

White, R. K. (1977). Misperception in the Arab–Israeli conflict. *Journal of Social Issues, 33,* 190–221.

Whitehouse, W. G., Orne, E. C., Dinges, D. F., Bates, B. L., Nadon, R., & Orne, M. T. (2005). The cognitive interview: Does it successfully avoid the dangers of forensic hypnosis? *American Journal of Psychology, 118*(2), 213–234.

Whitley, Jr., B. E. (1999). Right-wing authoritarianism, social dominance orientation, and prejudice. *Journal of Personality and Social Psychology, 77*, 126–134.

Whorf, B. L. (1956). *Language, thought, and reality*. New York: Wiley.

Wicker, A. W. (1969). Attitudes versus actions: The relationship between verbal and overt behavioral responses to attitude objects. *Journal of Social Issues, 25*, 41–78.

Wicker, B., Keysers, C., Plailly, J., Royet, J. P., Gallese, V., & Rizzolatti, G. (2003). Both us disgusted in my insula: The common neural basis of seeing and feeling disgust. *Neuron, 40*(3), 655–664.

Wickham, L. H. V., & Swift, H. (2006). Articulatory suppression attenuates the verbal overshadowing effect: A role for verbal encoding in face identification. *Applied Cognitive Psychology, 20*(2), 157–169.

Wiedenfeld, S. A., O'Leary, A., Bandura, A., Brown, S., Levine, S., & Raska, K. (1990). Impact of perceived self-efficacy in coping with stressors on components of the immune system. *Journal of Personality and Social Psychology, 59*, 1082–1094.

Wilder, D. A. (1984). Intergroup contact: The typical member and the exception to the rule. *Journal of Experimental Psychology, 20*, 177–194.

Wilder, D. A. (1986). Social categorization: Implications for creation and reduction of intergroup bias. In L. Berkowitz (Ed.), *Advances in experimental social psychology*. (Vol. 19, pp. 291–355.) New York: Academic Press.

Wilder, D. A., & Shapiro, P. N. (1989). Role of competition-induced anxiety in limiting the beneficial impact of positive behavior by an outgroup member. *Journal of Personality and Social Psychology, 56*, 60–69.

Williams, K. R., & Hawkins, R. (1986). Perceptual research on general deterrence: A critical review. *Law and Society Review, 20*, 545–572.

Williams, R. B. (2002). Hostility, neuroendocrine changes, and health outcomes. In H. G. Koenig & H. J. Cohen (Eds.), *The link between religion and health: Psychoneuroimmunology and the faith factor*. (pp. 160–173.) London, UK: Oxford University Press.

Williams, R. H., & Ross, M. H. (1980, March–April). Drilling for oil and gas in our houses. *Technology Review*, pp. 24–36.

Williams, S. S., Kimble, D. L., Covell, N. H., Weiss, L. H., Newton, K. J., Fisher, J. D., & Fisher, W. A. (1992). College students use implicit personality theory instead of safer sex. *Journal of Applied Social Psychology, 22*, 921–933.

Williams, T. P., & Sogon, S. (1984). Group composition and conforming behavior in Japanese students. *Japanese Psychological Research, 26*, 231–234.

Williamson, G. M., & Clark, M. S. (1989). Providing help and desired relationship type as determinants of changes in moods and self-evaluations. *Journal of Personality and Social Psychology, 56*, 722–734.

Williamson, G. M., & Clark, M. S. (1992). Impact of desired relationship type on affective reactions to choosing and being required to help. *Personality and Social Psychology Bulletin, 18*, 10–18.

Wilson, A. E., & Ross, M. (2000). The frequency of temporal-self and social comparisons in people's personal appraisals. *Journal of Personality and Social Psychology, 78*, 928–942.

Wilson, A. E., & Ross, M. (2001). From chump to champ: People's appraisals of their earlier and current selves. *Journal of Personality and Social Psychology, 80*, 572–584.

Wilson, M., Daly, M., & Weghorst, S. J. (1982). Male sexual jealousy. *Ethology and Sociobiology, 3*, 11–27.

Wilson, T. D. (1985). Strangers to ourselves: The origins and accuracy of beliefs about one's own mental states. In J. H. Harvey & G. Weary (Eds.), *Attribution in contemporary psychology*. (pp. 9–36.) New York: Academic Press.

Wilson, T. D. (1994). The proper protocol: Validity and completeness of verbal reports. *Psychological Science, 5*, 249–252.

Wilson, T. D. (2002). *Strangers to ourselves: Self-insight and the adaptive unconscious*. Cambridge, MA: Harvard University Press.

Wilson, T. D. (2005). The message is the method: Celebrating and exporting the experimental approach. *Psychological Inquiry, 16*, 185–193.

Wilson, T. D., & Brekke, N. C. (1994). Mental contamination and mental correction: Unwanted influences on judgments and evaluations. *Psychological Bulletin, 116*, 117–142.

Wilson, T. D., Centerbar, D. B., & Brekke, N. (2002). Mental contamination and the debiasing problem. In T. Gilovich, D. W. Griffin, & D. Kahneman (Eds.), *Heuristics and biases: The psychology of intuitive judgment*. (pp. 185–200.) New York: Cambridge University Press.

Wilson, T. D., Damiani, M., & Shelton, N. (2002). Improving the academic performance of college students with brief attributional interventions. In J. Aronson (Eds.), *Improving academic achievement: Impact of psychological factors on education*. (pp. 88–108.) San Diego, CA: Academic Press.

Wilson, T. D., Gilbert, D. T., & Wheatley, T. (1998). Protecting our minds: The role of lay beliefs. In V. Yzerbyt, G. Lories, & B. Dardenne (Eds.), *Metacognition: Cognitive and social dimensions*. (pp. 171–201.) Thousand Oaks, CA: Sage.

Wilson, T. D., Houston, C. E., & Meyers, J. M. (1998). Choose your poison: Effects of lay beliefs about mental processes on attitude change. *Social Cognition, 16*:1, 114–132.

Wilson, T. D., Laser, P. S., & Stone, J. I. (1982). Judging the predictors of one's own mood: Accuracy and the use of shared theories. *Journal of Experimental Social Psychology, 18*, 537–556.

Wilson, T. D., Lindsey, S., & Schooler, T. Y. (2000). A model of dual attitudes. *Psychological Review, 107*, 101–126.

Wilson, T. D., & Linville, P. W. (1982). Improving the academic performance of college freshmen: Attribution therapy revisited. *Journal of Personality and Social Psychology, 42*, 367–376.

Wilson, T. D., & Linville, P. W. (1985). Improving the performance of college freshmen using attributional techniques. *Journal of Personality and Social Psychology, 49*, 287–293.

Wilson, T. D., Lisle, D., Schooler, J., Hodges, S. D., Klaaren, K. J., & LaFleur, S. J. (1993). Introspecting about reasons can reduce post-choice satisfaction. *Personality and Social Psychology Bulletin, 19*, 331–339.

Wilson, T. D., & Stone, J. I. (1985). Limitations of self-knowledge: More on telling more than we can know. In P. Shaver (Ed.), *Review of personality and social psychology*. (Vol. 6, pp. 167–183.) Beverly Hills, CA: Sage.

Winerman, L. (2005). The mind's mirror. *Monitor on Psychology, 36*(9), 48–50.

Winslow, R. W., Franzini, L. R., & Hwang, J. (1992). Perceived peer norms, casual sex, and AIDS risk prevention. *Journal of Applied Social Psychology, 22*, 1809–1827.

Wintre, M. G., & Bowers, C. D. (2007). Predictors of persistence to graduation: Extending a model and data on the transition to university model. *Canadian Journal of Behavioural Science, 39*, 220–234.

Wise, D., & Rosqvist, J. (2006). Explanatory style and well-being. In J. C. Thomas, D. L. Segal, & M. Hersen (Eds.), *Comprehensive handbook of personality and psychopathology, Vol. 1: Personality and everyday functioning*. (pp. 285–305.) Hoboken, NJ: Wiley.

Wise, R. A. & Safer, M. A. (2004). What US judges know and believe about eyewitness testimony. *Journal of Applied Cognitive Psychology, 18*, 427–443.

Wisman, A., & Goldenberg, J. L. (2005). From the grave to the cradle: Evidence that mortality salience engenders a desire for offspring. *Journal of Personality and Social Psychology, 89*, 46–61.

Wittenbrink, B., Judd, C. M., & Park, B. (1997). Evidence for racial prejudice at the implicit level and its relationship with questionnaire measures. *Journal of Personality and Social Psychology, 72*, 262–274.

Wohl, M. J. A., & Branscombe, N. R. (2005). Forgiveness and collective guilt assignment to historical perpetrator groups depend on level of social category inclusiveness. *Journal of Personality and Social Psychology, 88*(2), 288–303.

Wohl, M. J. A., & McGrath, A. L. (2007). The perception of time heals all wounds: Temporal distance affects willingness to forgive following an interpersonal transgression. *Personality and Social Psychology Bulletin, 33,* 1023–1035.

Wolfgang, A., & Wolofsky, Z. (1991). The ability of new Canadians to decode gestures generated by Canadians of Anglo-Celtic backgrounds. *International Journal of Intercultural Relations, 15,* 47–64.

Wong, R. Y., & Hong, Y. (2005). Dynamic influences of culture on cooperation in a Prisoner's Dilemma game. *Psychological Science, 16,* 429–434.

Wood, J. V. (1996). What is social comparison and how should we study it? *Personality and Social Psychology Bulletin, 22,* 520–537.

Wood, J. V., Heimpel, S. A., Newby-Clark, I. R., & Ross, M. (2005). Snatching defeat from the jaws of victory: Self-esteem differences in the experience and anticipation of success. *Journal of Personality and Social Psychology, 89,* 764–780.

Wood, J. V., Michela, J. L., & Giordano, C. (2000). Downward comparison in everyday life: Reconciling self-enhancement models with the mood-cognition priming model. *Journal of Personality and Social Psychology, 79,* 563–579.

Wood, J. V., Taylor, S. E., & Lichtman, R. R. (1985). Social comparison in adjustment to breast cancer. *Journal of Personality and Social Psychology, 49,* 1169–1183.

Wood, W. (1987). Meta-analytic review of sex differences in group performance. *Psychological Bulletin, 102,* 53–71.

Wood, W., & Eagly, A. H. (2002). A cross-cultural analysis of the behavior of women and men: Implications for the origins of sex differences. *Psychological Bulletin, 128,* 699–727.

Wood, W., Lundgren, S., Ouellette, J. A., Busceme, S., & Blackstone, J. (1994). Minority influence: A meta-analytic review of social influence processes. *Psychological Bulletin, 115,* 323–345.

Wood, W., Pool, G. J., Leck, K., & Purvis, D. (1996). Self-definition, defensive processing, and influence: The normative impact of majority and minority groups. *Journal of Personality and Social Psychology, 71,* 1181–1193.

Wood, W., & Quinn, J. M. (2003). Forewarned and forearmed? Two meta-analytic syntheses of forewarnings of influence appeals. *Psychological Bulletin, 129,* 119–138.

Wood, W., Wong, F. Y., & Chachere, G. (1991). Effects of media violence on viewers' aggression in unconstrained social interaction. *Psychological Bulletin, 109,* 371–383.

Word, C. O., Zanna, M. P., & Cooper, J. (1974). The nonverbal mediation of self-fulfilling prophecies in interracial interaction. *Journal of Experimental Social Psychology, 10,* 109–120.

Wrangham, R. W., Wilson, M. L., & Muller, M. N. (2006, January). Comparative rates of violence in chimpanzees and humans. *Primates* 47(1), 14–26.

Wright, E. F., Luus, C. A. E., & Christie, S. D. (1990). Does group discussion facilitate the use of consensus information in making causal attributions? *Journal of Personality and Social Psychology, 59,* 261–269.

Wright, E. F., MacEachern, L., Stoffer, E., & MacDonald, N. (1996). Factors affecting the use of naked statistical evidence of liability. *Journal of Social Psychology, 136,* 677–688.

Wright, E. F., Rule, B., Ferguson, T., McGuire, G., & Wells, G. (1992). Misattribution of dissonance and behaviour-consistent attitude change. *Canadian Journal of Behavioural Science, 24,* 456–464.

Wright, R. (1994). *The moral animal: Why we are the way we are: The new science of evolutionary psychology.* New York: Random House.

Wright, S. C. (1997). Ambiguity, social influence, and collective action: Generating collective protest in response to tokenism. *Personality and Social Psychology Bulletin, 23,* 1277–1290.

Wright, S. C., Aron, A., McLaughlin, T., & Ropp, S. A. (1997). The extended contact effect: Knowledge of cross-group friendships and prejudice. *Journal of Personality and Social Psychology, 73,* 73–90.

Wright, S. C., Brody, S. M., & Aron, A. (2005). Intergroup contact: Still our best hope for improving intergroup relations. In C. S. Crandall & M. Schaller (Eds.), *Social psychology of prejudice: Historical and contemporary issues.* (pp. 115–142.) Lawrence, KS: Lewinian Press.

Wright, S. C. & Taylor, D. M. (2003). The social psychology of cultural diversity: Social stereotyping, prejudice, and discrimination. In M. A. Hogg & J. Cooper (Eds.), *Sage Handbook of Social Psychology.* (pp. 432–457) London, UK: Sage.

Wright, S. C., Taylor, D., Moghaddam, F. (1990). Responding to membership in a disadvantaged group: From acceptance to collective protest. *Journal of Social and Personality Psychology, 58,* 994–1003.

Wright, S. C., & van der Zande, C. C. (1999, October). Bicultural friends: When cross-group friendships cause improved intergroup attitudes. Paper presented at the Society for Experimental Social Psychology Conference, St. Louis, MO.

Wrosch, C., Miller, G. E., Scheier, M. F., & de Pontet, S. B. (2007). Giving up on unattainable goals: Benefits for health? *Personality and Social Psychology Bulletin, 33,* 251–265.

Wyer, R. S., & Srull, T. K. (1989). *Memory and cognition in its social context.* Hillsdale, NJ: Erlbaum.

Yarmey, A. D. (2001a). Expert testimony: Does eyewitness memory research have probative value for the courts? *Canadian Psychology, 42,* 92–100.

Yarmey, A. D. (2001b). Police investigations. In R. A. Schuller, & J. R. P. Ogloff (Eds.) (2001). *Introduction to psychology and law: Canadian perspectives.* (pp. 59–94.) Toronto, ON: University of Toronto Press.

Yarmey, A, D. Jacob, J., & Porter, A. (2002). Person recall in field settings. *Journal of Applied Social Psychology, 32*:11, 2354–2367.

Yarmey, A. D., Yarmey, A. L., Yarmey, M. J., & Parliament, L. (2001). Commonsense beliefs and the identification of familiar voices. *Applied Cognitive Psychology, 15,* 283–299.

Yarmey, A. D., Yarmey, M. J., & Yarmey, A. L. (1996). Accuracy of eyewitness identifications in showups and lineups. *Law and Human Behavior, 20,* 459–477.

Yik, M. S., Bond, M. H., & Paulhus, D. L. (1998). Do Chinese self-enhance or self-efface? It's a matter of domain. *Personality and Social Psychology Bulletin, 24,* 399–406.

Yik, M. S. M., Meng, Z., & Russell, J. A. (1998). Adults' freely produced emotion labels for babies' spontaneous facial expressions. *Cognition and Emotion, 12,* 723–730.

Yik, M. S. M., & Russell, J. A. (1999). Interpretation of faces: A cross-cultural study of a prediction from Fridlund's theory. *Cognition and Emotion, 13,* 93–104.

York, A. (2001, April 26). The product placement monster that E.T. spawned. *Salon.* http://archive.salon.com/tech/feature/2001/04/26/product_placement/print.html. Accessed September 2006.

Zillmann, D. (1978). Attribution and misattribution of excitatory reactions. In J. H. Harvey, W. J. Ickes, & R. F. Kidd (Eds.), *New directions in attribution research.* (Vol. 2, pp. 335–370.) Hillsdale, NJ: Erlbaum.

Yum, Y., & Schenck-Hamlin, W. (2005). Reactions to 9/11 as a function of terror management and perspective taking. *Journal of Social Psychology, 145,* 265–286.

Zajonc, R. B. (1965). Social facilitation. *Science, 149,* 269–274.

Zajonc, R. B. (1968). Attitudinal effects of mere exposure. *Journal of Personality and Social Psychology, 9,* Monograph Suppl. 2, Pt. 2.

Zajonc, R. B. (1980). Compresence. In P. B. Paulus (Ed.), *Psychology of group influence.* (pp. 35–60.) Hillsdale, NJ: Erlbaum.

Zajonc, R. B., Heingartner, A., & Herman, E. M. (1969). Social enhancement and impairment of performance in the cockroach. *Journal of Personality and Social Psychology, 13,* 83–92.

Zajonc, R. B., & Sales, S. M. (1966). Social facilitation of dominant and subordinate responses. *Journal of Experimental Social Psychology, 2,* 160–168.

Zanna, M., & Cooper, J. (1974). Dissonance and the pill: An attribution approach to studying the arousal properties of dissonance. *Journal of Personality and Social Psychology, 29,* 703–709.

Zanna, M., Goethals, G. R., & Hill, J. (1975). Evaluating a sex-related ability: Social comparison with similar others and standard setters. *Journal of Experimental Social Psychology, 11,* 86–93.

Zanna, M., & Rempel, J. K. (1988). Attitudes: A new look at an old concept. In D. Bar-Tal & A. W. Kruglanski (Eds.), *The social psychology of attitudes.* (pp. 315–334.) New York: Cambridge University Press.

Zanna, M. P., & Fazio, R. H. (1982). The attitude-behavior relation: Moving toward a third generation of research. In M. P. Zanna, E. T. Higgins, & C. P. Herman (Eds.), *Consistency in social behavior: The Ontario Symposium.* (Vol. 2, pp. 283–301.) Hillsdale, NJ: Erlbaum.

Zanna, M. P., & Sande, G. N. (1987). The effects of collective actions on the attitudes of individual group members: A dissonance analysis. In M. P. Zanna, J. M. Olson, C. P. Herman's (Eds.), *Consistency in social behavior: The Ontario Symposium.* (Vol. 5, Social Influence.) Hillsdale, NJ: Erlbaum.

Zanot, E. J., Pincus, J. D., & Lamp, E. J. (1983). Public perceptions of subliminal advertising. *Journal of Advertising, 12,* 39–45.

Zebrowitz, L. A. (1997). *Reading faces: Window to the soul?* Boulder, CO: Westview Press.

Zebrowitz, L. A., & Montepare, J. M. (1992). Impressions of babyfaced individuals across the life-span. *Developmental Psychology, 28,* 1143–1152.

Zebrowitz-McArthur, L. (1988). Person perception in cross-cultural perspective. In M. H. Bond (Ed.), *The cross-cultural challenge to social psychology.* (pp. 245–265). Newbury Park, CA: Sage.

Zillman, D., & Bryant, J. (1984). Effects of massive exposure to pornography. In N. M. Malamuth & E. Donnerstein (Eds.), *Pornography and sexual aggression.* (pp. 115–138.) Orlando, FL: Academic Press.

Zimbardo, P. (2007). *The Lucifer effect: Understanding how good people turn evil.* New York: Random House.

Zimbardo, P. G. (1970). The human choice: Individuation, reason, and order versus deindividuation, impulse, and chaos. In W. J. Arnold & D. Levine (Eds.), *Nebraska Symposium on Motivation: 1969.* (Vol. 17, pp. 237–307.) Lincoln, NE: University of Nebraska Press.

Zimbardo, P. G., & Andersen, S. (1993). Understanding mind control: Exotic and mundane mental manipulations. In M. D. Langone (Ed.), *Recovery from cults.* (pp. 104–125.) New York: Norton.

Zine, J. (2001). Muslim youth in Canadian schools: Education and the politics of religious identity. *Anthropology & Education Quarterly, 32,* 399–423.

Zuber, J. A., Crott, H. W., & Werner, J. (1992). Choice shift and group polarization: An analysis of the status of arguments and social decision schemes. *Journal of Personality and Social Psychology, 62,* 50–61.

Zuwerink, J., Monteith, M., Devine, P., & Cook, D. (1996). Prejudice toward Blacks: With and without compunction? *Basic and Applied Social Psychology, 18,* 131–150.

Credits

Common Art: Corbis Royalty Free; Suza Scalora/Photodisc/Getty Images

Chapter 1

Text and Art: p. 14: (Figure 1.1) Adapted from L. Ross and S.M. Samuels. *The predictive power of personal reputation versus labels and construal in the Prisoner's Dilemma Game.* Unpublished manuscript. Stanford University. Copyright © 1993. Reprinted by permission of Dr. Lee Ross.

Photos and Cartoons: p. 2: JL de Zorzi/© JL de Zorzi/CORBIS All Rights Reserved; p. 5: Courtesy of the University of Vermont; p. 7: Jeff McIntosh/ CP Photo Archive; p. 8 AP Photo/Laura Rauch; p. 14: © B. Setiz/Photo Researchers, Inc.; p. 16: (top) Getty Images, Inc.—Hulton Archive Photos; p. 16: (bottom) Archives of the History of American Psychology, The University of Akron; p. 17: (top) Archives of the History of American Psychology, The University of Akron; p. 17: (bottom) Photograph courtesy of Trudy Festinger. Reprinted by permission; p. 19: AP Wide World Photos; p. 24: (top left) Bob Daemmrich/The Image Works; p. 24: (bottom left) Kathy Sloane/Photo Researchers; p. 24: (right) Canadian Public Health Association.

Chapter 2

Text and Art: p. 52 (Figure 2.2) From "Canadian code of ethics for psychologists," Canadian Psychological Association, 1991, and "Ethical principles of psychologists and code of conduct," *American Psychologist*, Vol. 47, pp. 1597–1611. Copyright 1992 by the American Psychological Association. Adapted with permission.

Photos and Cartoons: p. 26: Henry Groskinsky/Time & Life Pictures/Getty Images/Time Life Pictures; p. 33: Henry Groskinsky/Time & Life Pictures/ Getty Images/Time Life Pictures; p. 35: (left) The Advertising Archives; p. 35: (right) Michael Newman/PhotoEdit Inc.; p. 38 Courtesy of the Library of Congress; p. 39: Joe Byrska/Winnipeg Free Press; p. 45: Lewis J. Merrim/Photo Researchers, Inc.; p. 48: (left) REUTERS/Reuters TV/Corbis/Bettmann; p. 48: (right) David Austen/Stock Boston; p. 53: Gary Larson/The Far Side by Gary Larson © 1993 FarWorks, Inc. All Rights Reserved. Used with permission.

Chapter 3

Text and Art: p. 61: (Figure 3.1) Adapted from Correll, Joshua; Park, Bernadette; Judd, Charles M; Wittenbrink, Bernd. The police officer's dilemma: Using ethnicity to disambiguate potentially threatening individuals. *Journal of Personality & Social Psychology*. Vol. 83 (6) Dec 2002, pp. 1314–1329. Copyright © 2002 by the American Psychological Association; p. 67: (Figure 3.3) Higgins et. al., "Category accessibility and impressing formation," *Journal of Experimental Psychology*, Vol. 13, pp. 141–154, 1977, American Psychological Association, reprinted with permission; p. 68: (Figure 3.4) L. Ross, M.R. Lepper and M. Hubbard, "Perseverance in self-perception and social perception: Biased attributional processes in the debriefing paradigm," *Journal of Personality and Social Psychology*, Vol. 32, pp. 880–892, 1975, American Psychological Association, adapted with permission of the APA and the author; p. 76: (Figure 3.7) N. Schwartz et al., "Ease of retrieval as information: Another look at the availability heuristic," *Journal of Personality and Social Psychology*, Vol. 61, pp. 195–202, 1991, American Psychological Association, adapted with permission of the APA and the author; p. 79: (Figure 3.8) A. Dijksterhuis, "Think different: The merits of unconscious thought in preference development and decision making," *Journal of Personality and Social Psychology*, Vol. 87, pp. 586–598, 2004, American Psychological Association, adapted with permission of the APA and the author.

Photos and Cartoons: p. 56: brianchina/Alamy; p. 58: Photograph by KC Armstrong; p. 59: Gala/SuperStock, Inc.; p. 61: Joshua Correll/Joshua Correll/Courtesy Charles Judd, University of Colorado; p. 63: National Archives and Records Administration; p. 65: Mark Lyons/AP Wide World Photos; p. 70: Mary Kate Denny/Photo Edit; p. 72: Irven De Vore/Anthro-Photo File; p. 75: Jose Luis Pelaez/© Jose Luis Pelaez/CORBIS All Rights Reserved; p. 80: Frank Fernandes/Maxpp/Landov LLC; p. 82: (left): The Canadian Press/Larry MacDougal; p. 82: (right): Reuters/David Gray.

Chapter 4

Text and Art: p. 97: (Figure 4.1) Based on Archer, 1991, 1997a, 1997b; Gudykunst, Ting-Toomey, & Nishida, 1996; Hewitt & Alquahtani, 2003; Knapp & Hall, 1997; Richmond & McCroskey, 1995; p. 98: (excerpt) Malamuth, N. (1983). Human sexuality. In D. Perlman & P. C. Cozby (Eds.), *Social Psychology*. New York: Holt, Rinehart & Winston. Reprinted by permission. p. 100: Kruger, Epley, Parker and Ng, "Egocentrism over e-mail: Can we communicate as well as we think?" from *Journal of Personality and Social Psychology*, Vol. 89, No. 6, p. 930, 2005, American Psychological Association, reprinted with permission of the APA and the author; p. 103: (Figure 4.3) C. Hoffman, I. Lau and D.R. Johnson, "The linguistic relativity of person cognition" An English-Chinese comparison," *Journal of Personality and Social Psychology*, Vol. 51, pp. 1097–1105, 1986, American Psychological Association, reprinted with permission of the APA and the author; p. 108: (Figure 4.5) From "The attribution of attitudes," by E.E. Jones and V.V. Harris in *Journal of Experimental Social Psychology*, Vol. 28, pp. 255–276. Copyright © 1992. Reprinted with permission from Elsevier; p. 109: (Figure 4.6) Adapted from S.E. Taylor and S.T. Fiske, "Point of view and perceptions of causality." *Journal of Personality and Social Psychology*, Vol. 32, pp. 439–445. Copyright © 1975 by the American Psychological Association. Reprinted by permission of the APA and the author; (Figure 4.7) adapted from S.E. Taylor and S.T. Fiske, "Point of view and perceptions of causality." *Journal of Personality and Social Psychology*, Vol. 32, pp. 439–445. Copyright © 1975 by the American Psychological Association. p. 112: (Figure 4.9) Adapted from Morris, M. W., & Peng, K. (1994). "Culture and cause: American and Chinese attributions for social and physical events." *Journal of Personality and Social Psychology*, Vol. 67, pp. 949–971. Copyright © by the 1994 American Psychological Association. p. 121: Reprinted by permission of Rhona Raskin, Clinical Counsellor/Advice Columnist.

Photos and Cartoons: p. 88: Fox Broadcasting/Photofest; p. 93: (top left) Toby Maudsley/Toby Maudsley/Getty Images, Inc.; (top middle) Alan Weiner/Getty Images, Inc.—Liaison; (top right) Lynn McLaren/Index Stock Imagery, Inc.; (bottom left) Guido Alberto Rossi/© Guido Alberto Rossi/TIPS Images; (bottom middle) Richard Pan/Stock Photos, Inc.; (bottom right) Costa Manos/Magnum Photos, Inc.; p. 94: Courtesy of San Francisco State University; p. 96: Dr. Paul Ekman/Human Interaction Laboratory; p. 97: (top left) Michel Setboun/© SETBOUN/CORBIS; (bottom left) Carol Beckwith & Angela Fisher/© Carol Beckwith & Angela Fisher/HAGA/The Image Works; (bottom middle) Bill Bachmann/Photo Researchers, Inc.; (top middle) Sundberg, Dag/Getty Images Inc.—Image Bank; (right) Sisse Brimberg/National Geographic Image Collection; p. 102: (left) Chris Scwarz/Ponopresse; p. 102: (right) John Slater/John Slater/Getty Images, Inc.; p. 104: Hartmut Schwarzbach/Peter Arnold, Inc.; p. 115: The Canadian Press/Ryan Remiorz.

Chapter 5

Text and Art: p. 128: (Try It! Box) Adapted from Campbell, J. D., Trapnell, P. D., Heine, S. J., Katz, I. M., Lavallee, L. F., & Lehman, Dr. R. (1996). Self-concept clarity: Measurement, personality correlates, and cultural boundaries. *Journal of Personality and Social Psychology*, Vol. 70, p. 145. Copyright © 1996 by the

Chapter 10

Text and Art: p. 312: (Figure 10.1) Batson, *The Altruism Question: Toward a Social Psychological Answer.* 1991 Lawrence Erlbaum Associates. p. 313: (Figure 10.2) Adapted from M. Toi and C.D. Batson, "More evidence that empathy is a source of altruistic motivation." *Journal of Personality and Social Psychology*, Vol. 43, pp. 281–292. Copyright © 1982 by the American Psychological Association; p. 323: (Figure 10.3) Darley et al., "Bystander Intervention in emergencies: Diffusion and responsibility," *Journal of Personality and Social Psychology*, Vol. 8, p. 380, 1968, American Psychological Association, adapted with permission of the APA and the author. p. 324: (Figure 10.4) Adapted from Latané & Darley, *The Unresponsive Bystander: Why Doesn't He Help?* Copyright 1970. Reprinted by permission of Simon & Schuster.

Photos and Cartoons: p. 304: © Patrick Robert/Sygma/CORBIS; p. 305: Prince George Citizen/Brent Braaten; p. 342: Suzanne Plunket/P Wide World Photos; p. 307: Ariel Skelley/© Ariel Skelley/CORBIS All Rights Reserved; p. 310: Robert Allison/Contact Press Images Inc.; p. 311: CALVIN AND HOBBES © 1995 Watterson. Reprinted with permission of UNIVERSAL PRESS SYNDICATE. All Rights Reserved; p. 315: Themba Hadebe/AP Wide World Photos; p. 350: UPI/Corbis/Bettmann. p. 316: Corbis Royalty Free; p. 321: (left) Bob Sacha/© Bob Sacha/CORBIS All Rights Reserved; p. 321: (right) © Dick Hemingway; p. 326: Steve McCurry/Magnum Photos, Inc.; p. 327: New York Times Pictures; p. 329: Charles Gupton/Stock Boston; p. 330: Myrleen Ferguson/PhotoEdit Inc.

Chapter 11

Text and Art: p. 351: Adapted from L. Berkowitz and A. LePage, "Weapons as aggression—eliciting stimuli." *Journal of Personality and Social Psychology*, Vol. 7, pp. 202–207. Copyright © 1967 by the American Psychological Association.

Photos and Cartoons: p. 334: Robert Trippett/© Robert Trippett/SIPA Press; p. 335: Jason Payne/Province; p. 337: Catherine Ursillo/Photo Researchers, Inc.; p. 339: (left and right) Karl Ammann/Nature Picture Library; p. 344: © The New Yorker Collection 1975 Dana Fradon from cartoonbank.com. All Rights Reserved; p. 348: Yellow Dog Productions/Getty Images Inc.—Image Bank; p. 352: Chris Martinez/Getty Images, Inc.—Liaison; p. 353: Albert Bandura, Stanford University; D. Ross & S.A. Ross, "Imitation of film-mediated aggressive models." *Journal of Abnormal and Social Psychology*, 1963, Vol. 66, p. 8; p. 355: OLIPHANT © 1973. Reprinted with permission of UNIVERSAL PRESS SYNDICATE. All Rights Reserved; p. 356: The Canadian Press/Troy Fleece; p. 357: Miramax Films/Picture Desk, Inc./Kobal Collection; p. 361: Photo Researchers, Inc.; p. 363: (top) U. S. Army Photograph; p. 363: (bottom) © Bettmann/CORBIS All Rights Reserved; p. 366: CP Photo Archive; p. 367: Michael Pole/© Michael Pole/CORBIS All Rights Reserved.

Chapter 12

Text and Art: p. 372: (poem) © Mary Young; p. 383: (Figure 12.1) G.A. Quattrone and E.E. Jones, "The perception of variability within ingroups and outgroups: Implications for the law of small numbers," *Journal of Personality and Social Psychology*, Vol. 38, pp. 141–152, 1980, American Psychological Association, adapted with permission; p. 388: (Figure 12.3) Sinclair, L. & Kunda, Z. (1999). Reactions to a black professional: Motivated inhibition and activation of conflicting stereotypes. *Journal of Personality and Social Psychology*, Vol. 77, pp. 885–904. Copyright © 1999 by the American Psychological Association.

Photos and Cartoons: p. 370: REUTERS/Andy Clark; p. 371: © Mary Young; p. 374: Laura Dwight/PhotoEdit Inc.; p. 376: Copyright © Larry Fisher, Quad City Times/The Boston Globe; p. 380: © The New Yorker Collection 1995 Jack Ziegler from cartoonbank.com. All Rights Reserved; p. 385: Photograph courtesy of Ron Baxter Smith; p. 390: © The New Yorker Collection 1940 Alain from cartoonbank.com. All Rights Reserved; p. 391: REUTERS/Chris Wattie/Landov; p. 392: Michael Newman/PhotoEdit; p. 394: The Canadian Press/Nathan Denette; p. 405: Jack Delano/Courtesy of the Library of Congress; p. 413: Tom Watson/ Merrill Education.

Social Psychology in Action 1

Text and Art: p. 426: (Figure SPA1.2) R.B. Cialdini, R.R. Reno and C.A. Kallgren, "A focus theory of normative conduct: Recycling the concept of norms to reduce littering in public places," *Journal of Personality and Social Psychology*, Vol. 58, pp. 1015–1026, 1990, American Psychological Association, adapted with permission of the APA and the author.

Photos and Cartoons: p. 416 Chico Batata/© Chico Batata/CORBIS All Rights Reserved; p. 418: The Canadian Press/Larry MacDougal; p. 421: Thomas Nilsson/Getty Images, Inc.; p. 460: (top) Diana Haecker/Courtesy of Nome Nugget, Nome, Alaska; p. 422: © The New Yorker Collection 1991 Mike Stevens from cartoonbank.com. All Rights Reserved; p. 423 Robert E. Daemmrich/Getty Images Inc.—Stone Allstock; p. 426: Pearson Education/PH College; p. 431: Philip James Corwin/© Philip James Corwin/CORBIS. All Rights Reserved.

Social Psychology in Action 2

Text and Art: p. 440: (Figure SPA2.1) S. Cohen, D.Tyrrell and A.P. Smith, "Psychological Stress and Susceptibility to the Common Cold," *The New England Journal of Medicine*, Vol. 325, pp. 606–612, Aug. 29, No. 9, Copyright © 1991 Massachusetts Medical Society. All Rights Reserved. Adapted with permission; p. 442: (Figure SPA2.2) Glass, D.C. and Singer, J. E., *Urban Stress: Experiments on Noise and Social Stressors.* Copyright 1972 by Academic Press. Reprinted by permission; p. 445: (Figure SPA2.3) Langer et al. "The effects of choice and enhanced personal responsibility for the aged: A field experiment." *Journal of Personality and Social Psychology*, 34. Copyright © 1976 by the American Psychological Association. Reprinted by permission of the APA and Ellen Langer (Professor of Psychology at Harvard University); p. 447: (Figure SPA2.4) From: NIMH Multisite HIV Prevention Trial Group. (1998, June 19). "The NIMH Multisite HIV Prevention Trial: Reducing HIV sexual risk behavior." *Science*, 280, pp. 1889–1894.

Photos and Cartoons: p. 434: Landov LLC; p. 436: photograph courtesy of Elvira Toews; p. 439: (top left) Robert Brenner/PhotoEdit Inc.; (top right) Ryan McVay/Getty Images, Inc.—Photodisc; (bottom left) Thomas Hoepker/Magnum Photos, Inc.; (bottom right) Elena Rooraid/PhotoEdit Inc.; p. 444: Telegraph Colour Library/Getty Images, Inc.; p. 446: © Vahan Shirvanian/www.CartoonStock.com; p. 451: John Giustina/John Giustina/Getty Images, Inc.; p. 453: SuperStock, Inc.; p. 457: Richard Wolowicz/Getty Images; p. 459: Doug Kanter/SIPA Press; p. 460: David Young-Wolff/PhotoEdit Inc.; p. 462: Sexuality Education Resource Centre, Winnipeg; p. 508: Markus Matzel/Das Fotoarchiv./Peter Arnold, Inc. p. 503: Bob Daemmrich/Stock Boston.

Social Psychology in Action 3

Text and Art: p. 470: C.L. Lindsay, G.L. Wells and C.M. Rumpel, "Can people detect eyewitness-identification accuracy within and across situations?" *Journal of Applied Psychology*, Vol. 66, pp. 79–89, 1981, American Psychological Association, reprinted with permission of the APA and the author.

Photos and Cartoons: p. 466: Miramax/Photofest; p. 468: (left) Ken Gigliotti/CP Photo Archive; p. 468: (right) CP Photo Archive/Winnipeg Free Press; p. 472: (three photos) Arnold Magnani/Arnold Magnani/Getty Images, Inc.; p. 473: From: Simons, D.J. & Chabris, C.F., "Gorillas in Our Midst: Sustained inattentional blindness for dynamic events". Perception 1999, 28, p. 1070. Figure provided by Daniel Simons; p. 520: (top and bottom) Loftus, E. F., Miller, D. G., Burns, H. J., (1978). "Semantic integration of verbal information into a visual memory." *Journal of Experimental Psychology, Human Learning and Memory*, Vol. 4, pp. 19–31; p. 477: CLOSE TO HOME © 2002 John McPherson. Reprinted with permission of UNIVERSAL PRESS SYNDICATE. All Rights Reserved; p. 483: Mark C. Burnett/Photo Researchers, Inc.; p. 491: The New Yorker Collection 1997, Mike Twohy from cartoonbank.com. All rights reserved; p. 493: Getty Images, Inc.—Liaison; p. 494: Photofest; p. 497: Spencer Grant/ PhotoEdit Inc.

Name Index

Subject Index